A Practical Guide to Red Hat®Linux®

SECOND EDITION

A Practical Guide to Red Hat® Linux®

SECOND EDITION

Fedora™ Core and
Red Hat Enterprise Linux

Mark G. Sobell

PRENTICE
HALL
PTR

Prentice Hall Professional Technical Reference
Upper Saddle River, New Jersey 07458
www.phptr.com

Library of Congress Cataloging-in-Publication Data

Sobell, Mark G.
    A practical guide to Red Hat Linux : Fedora Core and Red Hat Enterprise Linux / Mark
G. Sobell.—2nd ed.
      p. cm.
    ISBN 0-13-147024-8 (pbk. : alk. paper)
    Includes bibliographical references and index.
    1. Linux.   2. Operating systems (Computers). I. Title.
QA76.76.O63S59485 2005
005.26'8—dc22

                  2004013326

Production Manager: Tyrrell Albaugh
Composition: Mark G. Sobell
Publishing Partner: Mark Taub
Editorial Assistant: Noreen Regina
Cover Design: Chuti Prasertsith
Marketing Manager: Robin O'Brien

Pearson Education Ltd.
Pearson Education Australia Pty., Limited
Pearson Education South Asia Pte. Ltd.
Pearson Education Asia Ltd.
Pearson Education Canada, Ltd.
Pearson Educación de Mexico, S.A. de C.V.
Pearson Education—Japan
Pearson Malaysia S.D.N. B.H.D.

for my guys,
Sam, Zach, and Max

Brief Contents

Contents

PART I Installing Red Hat Linux   21

2 Installation Overview   23

3 Step-by-Step Installation   43

PART II Getting Started with Red Hat Linux   73

4 Introduction to Red Hat Linux   75

5 The Linux Utilities   117

PART III Digging Into Red Hat Linux   215

8 Linux GUIs: X, GNOME, and KDE   217

9 The Shell II: The Bourne Again Shell   251

10 Networking and the Internet   323

PART IV System Administration   367

11 System Administration: Core Concepts   369

14 Printing with CUPS   485

15 Rebuilding the Linux Kernel   507

16 Administration Tasks   521

17 Configuring a LAN   551

PART V   Using Clients and Setting Up Servers   561

18   OpenSSH: Secure Network Communication   563

19   FTP: Transferring Files Across a Network   583

20   sendmail: Setting Up Mail Clients, Servers, and More   609

21 NIS: Network Information Service   637

22 NFS: Sharing Filesystems   655

23 Samba: Integrating Linux and Windows   675

24 DNS/BIND: Tracking Domain Names and Addresses   699

25 iptables: Setting Up a Firewall 737

26 Apache (httpd): Setting Up a Web Server 759

PART VI Programming   803

27 Programming Tools   805

28 Programming the Bourne Again Shell   851

PART VII Appendixes 901

A Regular Expressions 903

B Help 913

C Security 921

D The Free Software Definition   943

E The Linux 2.6 Kernel   947

Preface

The book   Whether you are an end user, a system administrator, or a little of each, this book explains, with step-by-step examples, how to get the most out of your Fedora Core or Red Hat Enterprise Linux system. In 28 chapters, this book takes you from installing a Fedora Core or Red Hat Enterprise Linux system through understanding its inner workings, to setting up secure servers.

The audience   This book is designed for a wide range of readers; it does not require programming experience, but some experience using a general-purpose computer is helpful. This book is appropriate for

- **Students** taking a class in which they use Linux
- **Home users** who want to set up and/or run Linux
- **Professionals** who use Linux at work
- **System administrators** who need an understanding of Linux and the tools that are available to them
- **Computer science students** studying the Linux operating system
- **Programmers** who need to understand the Linux programming environment
- **Technical executives** who want to get a grounding in Linux

Benefits   *A Practical Guide to Red Hat® Linux®, Second Edition: Fedora Core™ and Red Hat Enterprise Linux* gives you a broad understanding of many facets of Linux, from installing Red Hat linux through using and customizing it. Regardless of your background, this book gives you the knowledge you need to get on with your work: You will come away from this book understanding how to use Linux, and this book will remain a valuable reference for years to come.

This Book Includes the Full Fedora Core 2 on Four CDs

> **tip ||**   **The CDs in This Book Hold the *Full Release* of Fedora Core 2**
>
> This book includes the full Fedora Core version 2 CDs, not the truncated publisher's edition CDs. These four CDs include the complete release of Red Hat's Fedora Core 2. See fedora.redhat.com for details.

A Practical Guide to Red Hat® Linux®, Second Edition, includes CDs that you can use to install or upgrade to Fedora Core 2. Chapter 2 helps you get ready to install, and Chapter 3 provides step-by-step instructions on installing, Fedora Core from these CDs. This book guides you through learning about, using, and administrating Fedora Core or Red Hat Enterprise Linux.

This book covers Fedora Core 2 and Red Hat Enterprise Linux version 3.

Features of This Book

This book is designed and organized so you can get the most out of it in the shortest amount of time. You do not have to read this book in page order. Once you are comfortable using Linux, you can use this book as a reference: Look up a topic of interest in the table of contents or index and read about it. Or think of this book as a catalog of Linux topics: Flip through the pages until a topic catches your eye. This book has many pointers to Web sites where you can get additional information: Consider the Web an extension of this book.

A Practical Guide to Red Hat® Linux®, Second Edition, is structured with the following features:

- In this book, the term **Red Hat Linux** refers to both **Fedora Core** and **Red Hat Enterprise Linux**. Features that apply to one operating system or the other only are marked as such using these markers: FEDORA or RHEL.

- **Optional sections** mean you can read the book at different levels, returning to more difficult material when you are ready.

- **Caution boxes** highlight procedures that can easily go wrong, giving you guidance before you run into trouble.

- **Tip boxes** highlight places in the text where you can save time by doing something differently or when it may be useful or just interesting to have additional information.

- **Security boxes** point out places where you can make your system more secure. The **security appendix** gives you a quick background in system security issues.

- Concepts are illustrated by **practical examples** throughout the book.

- **Chapter summaries** provide a review of the important points covered in each chapter.

- **Review exercises** are included at the end of each chapter for readers who want to hone their skills. Answers to even-numbered exercises are at www.sobell.com.

- This book provides resources for **finding, downloading, and installing software**: Web sites, Apt, yum, BitTorrent, and Red Hat Network (RHN).

- Important **GNU tools**, including gcc, gdb, GNU Configure and Build System, make, gzip, and many others are described in detail.

- Pointers throughout provide help in obtaining **online documentation** from many sources including the local system, the Red Hat Web site, and other locations on the Internet.

- Many useful URLs (Internet addresses) point to sites where you can obtain software, security programs and information, and more.

Key Topics This Book Covers

This book contains a lot of information. This section distills and summarizes what is in the book. You may also want to review the table of contents for more detail. This book

Installation

- Describes how to download from the Internet and burn Fedora Core Installation CDs.

- Helps you plan your hard disk layout and use Disk Druid or fdisk to partition disks.

- Explains the use of the Logical Volume Manager (LVM) to grow and migrate partitions without interrupting users.

- Describes in detail how to install Red Hat Linux from CDs, a hard disk, or over a network using FTP, NFS, or HTTP. Covers responses to the **boot:** prompt and how to work with **Anaconda**, Red Hat's graphical installer.

- Covers the details of installing and customizing the X Window System, including XFree86 (*RHEL*) and the new X.org (*FEDORA*) version of X.

Working with
Red Hat Linux

- Introduces the graphical desktop and explains how to use desktop tools including the Panel, Panel menu, Main menu, Window Operations menu, Desktop menu, Desktop switcher, and terminal emulator.

- Presents the KDE desktop and covers using Konqueror to manage files, start programs, and browse the Web.

- Covers the GNOME desktop and the Nautilus file manager.

- Explains how to customize your desktop.

- Covers the Borne Again Shell (bash) in three chapters, including a full chapter on shell programming that includes many sample scripts.

- Explains the command line interface and covers 30+ command line utilities.

- Presents a tutorial on the vim (vi work-alike) editor.

- Covers networks and network protocols.

- Explains hostnames, IP addresses, subnets, and how to look up domain names and IP addresses on the Internet.

- Covers distributed computing and the client/server model.

System administration

- Explains how to use the Red Hat system-config-* tools to configure the display, DNS, Apache, a network interface, and more. You can also use the tools to add users and manage local and remote printers. See page 393 for a list.

- Describes how to use the following tools to download software and keep a system current:

  - yum   Downloads software from the Internet, keeping a system up-to-date and resolving dependencies as it goes.

  - **Apt**   An alternative to yum. You can also use synaptic, a graphical interface to Apt.

  - **BitTorrent**   Good for distributing large amounts of data such as the Fedora installation CDs.

  - up2date   Red Hat's tool for keeping system software current.

- Covers graphical system administration tools, including the Main menu, GNOME and KDE menu systems, KDE Control Center, and KDE Control Panel.

- Explains system operation, including the boot process, init scripts, emergency mode, single- and multiuser mode, and what to do if the system crashes.

- Describes files, directories, and filesystems, including types of files and filesystems, **fstab**, automatically mounted filesystems, filesystem integrity checks, filesystem utilities, and how to tune filesystems.

- Covers backup utilities, including tar, cpio, dump, and restore.

- Explains how to rebuild the kernel.

Security
- Helps you manage basic system security issues using ssh (secure shell), **vs-ftpd** (secure FTP server), Apache (Web server), iptables (firewall), and more.
- Describes how to set up a chroot jail to protect a server.
- Explains how to use TCP wrappers to control who can access a server.
- Covers controlling servers using the **xinetd** super server.

Clients and Servers
- Explains how to set up and use the most popular Linux servers, providing a chapter on each: Apache, Samba, OpenSSH, **sendmail**, DNS, NFS, FTP, iptables, and NIS, all included with Red Hat Linux.
- Covers setting up a CUPS print server.
- Describes how to set up and use a DHCP server.

Programming
- Covers programming tools including the GNU gcc compiler, make, and CVS for managing source code.
- Explains how to debug a C program.
- Describes how to work with shared libraries.
- Provides a complete chapter on shell programming using bash, including many examples.

Details

Part I   Part I, "Installing Red Hat Linux," discusses how to install either version of Red Hat Linux. **Chapter 2** presents an overview of installing Red Hat Linux, including hardware requirements, downloading and burning CD-ROMs, and planning the layout of the hard disk. **Chapter 3** is a step-by-step guide to installing either version of Red Hat Linux and covers installing from CDs, from a local hard disk, and over the network using FTP, NFS, or HTTP, as well as how to set up the X Window System for a customized graphical user interface (GUI).

Part II   Part II, "Getting Started with Red Hat Linux," familiarizes you with Red Hat Linux, covering logging in, the graphical user interface, utilities, the filesystem, and the shell. **Chapter 4** introduces desktop features, including the panel and the Main menu, explains how to use Konqueror to manage files, run programs, and browse the Web, and covers finding documentation, login problems, and using the window manager. **Chapter 5** introduces the shell command line interface, describes over 30 useful utilities, and presents a tutorial on the vim (vi) text editor. **Chapter 6** discusses the Linux hierarchical filesystem, covering files, filenames, pathnames, working with directories, access permissions, and hard and symbolic links. **Chapter 7** introduces the Borne Again Shell (bash) and discusses command line arguments and options, how to redirect input to and output from commands, running programs in the background, and using the shell to generate and expand filenames.

> **tip ||**　　　　　　　　　　　　**Experienced Users May Want to Skim Part II**
>
> If you have used a UNIX/Linux system before, you may want to skim over or skip some or all of the chapters in Part II. All readers should take a look at "Conventions Used in This Book" (page 16), which explains the typographic and layout conventions that this book uses, and "Getting the Facts: Where to Find Documentation" (page 94) which points you toward both local and remote sources of Linux and Red Hat documentation.

Part III　Part III, "Digging Into Red Hat Linux," goes into more detail about working with Red Hat Linux. **Chapter 8** discusses the graphical user interface and includes a section on how to run a graphical program on a remote system and have the display appear locally. The section on GNOME talks about GNOME utilities and explains how to use the Nautilus file manager, including its new spatial view, while the section on KDE explains more about Konqueror and the KDE utilities. **Chapter 9** extends the bash shell coverage from Chapter 7, explaining how to redirect errors, avoid overwriting files, and how to work with job control, processes, startup files, important shell builtin commands, parameters, shell variables, and aliases. **Chapter 10** explains networks, network security, and the Internet and discusses types of networks, subnets, protocols, addresses, hostnames, and various network utilities. The section on distributed computing describes the client/server model and some of the servers you can use on a network. Details of setting up and using clients and servers is reserved for Part V.

Part IV　In seven chapters, Part IV covers system administration. **Chapter 11** discusses core concepts such as Superuser, SELinux (Security Enhanced Linux), system operation, general information about how to set up a server, DHCP, and PAM. **Chapter 12** explains the Linux filesystem, going into detail about types of files, including special and device files, how to use fsck to verify filesystems, and using tune2fs to change filesystem parameters. **Chapter 13** explains how to keep a system up-to-date by downloading software from the Internet and installing it, including examples of using Red Hat's up2date utility, yum, Apt, and BitTorrent. **Chapter 14** explains how to set up the CUPS printing system so you can print on the local system and on remote systems. **Chapter 15** details rebuilding the Linux kernel. **Chapter 16** covers additional administration tasks, including setting up user accounts, backing up files, scheduling automated tasks, tracking disk usage, and general problem solving. **Chapter 17** explains how to set up a local area network (LAN), covering hardware (including wireless) and software setup.

Part V　Part V goes into detail about setting up servers and connecting to them with clients. With one chapter apiece, this part of the book covers the following clients/servers:

- **OpenSSH**　Set up an OpenSSH server and use sh, scp, and sftp to communicate securely over the Internet.

- **FTP**　Set up a **vsftpd** secure FTP server and use any of several FTP clients to exchange files.

- **Mail**   Configure **sendmail** and use Webmail, POP3, or IMAP to retrieve email; use SpamAssassin to combat spam.

- **NIS**   Set up NIS to make system administration of a LAN easier.

- **NFS**   Share filesystems between systems on a network.

- **Samba**   Share filesystems and printers between Windows and Linux systems.

- **DNS/BIND**   Set up a domain name server to let other systems on the Internet know the names and IP addresses of your systems they may need to contact.

- **iptables**   Set up a firewall to protect local systems.

- **Apache**   Set up an HTTP server that serves Web pages that browsers can view.

Part VI Part VI covers programming. **Chapter 27** discusses programming tools and environments available under Red Hat Linux, including the C programming language and debugger, make, shared libraries, and source code management using CVS. **Chapter 28** goes into depth about shell programming using bash, with extensive examples.

Part VII Part VII includes appendixes on regular expressions, where to find help on the Web, system security, and free software. This part also includes an extensive glossary with over 500 entries and a comprehensive index.

Supplements

My home page (www.sobell.com) contains downloadable listings of the longer programs from the book as well as pointers to many interesting and useful Linux sites on the World Wide Web, a list of corrections to the book, answers to even-numbered exercises, and a solicitation for corrections, comments, and suggestions.

Thanks

First and foremost I want to thank my editor at Prentice Hall PTR, Mark L. Taub, who encouraged and prodded me (carrot and stick approach) and kept me on track. Mark is unique in my experience: An editor who works with the tools I am writing about. Because Mark runs Linux on his home computer, we could share experiences as I wrote. His comments and direction were invaluable. Thank you, Mark T.

A big "Thank You" to the folks who read through the drafts of the book and made comments that caused me to refocus parts of the book where things were not clear or were left out altogether.

First, I want to thank David Chisnall who helped with all parts of the book. David's broad knowledge of computers and operating systems gives this edition a unique perspective that helps bring tough concepts into focus.

Thank you to Carsten Pfeiffer, Software Engineer and KDE Developer; Aaron Weber, Ximian; Matthew Miller, Boston University; Cristof Falk, Software Developer at CritterDesign; Scott Mann, IBM, Systems Managment and Integration Professional; Steve Elgersma, Computer Science Department, Princeton University; Scott Dier, University of Minnesota; and Robert Haskins, Computer Net Works.

Thanks also to the folks at Prentice Hall PTR who helped bring this book to life, especially Tyrrell Albaugh, production manager, who gave me guidance and much latitude in producing the book; Heather Fox, publicist; Greg Yurchuk, college marketing manager; Dan DePasquale, marketing manager; Robin O'Brien, executive marketing manager; Noreen Regina, editorial assistant; and everyone else who worked behind the scenes to make this book happen.

I am also indebted to Denis Howe, the editor of *The Free On-line Dictionary of Computing* (FOLDOC). Dennis has graciously permitted me to use entries from his compilation. Be sure to look at the dictionary (www.foldoc.org).

Thanks also to the following people who helped with the first edition of this book: Dustin Puryear, Puryear Information Technology; Gabor Liptak, Independent Consultant; Bart Schaefer, Chief Technical Officer, iPost; Michael J. Jordan, Web Developer, Linux Online Inc.; Steven Gibson, owner of SuperAnt.com; John Viega, Founder and Chief Scientist, Secure Software, Inc.; K. Rachael Treu, Internet Security Analyst, Global Crossing; Kara Pritchard, K & S Pritchard Enterprises, Inc; Glen Wiley, Capitol One Finances; Karel Baloun, Senior Software Engineer, Looksmart, Ltd.; Matthew Whitworth; Dameon D. Welch-Abernathy, Nokia Systems; Josh Simon, Consultant; Stan Isaacs; and Dr. Eric H. Herrin, II, Vice President, Herrin Software Development, Inc. And thanks to Doug Hughes, long-time system designer and administrator, who gave me a big hand with the sections on system administration, networks, the Internet, and programming.

Thanks to Lorraine Callahan and Steve Wampler, who researched, wrote, analyzed reviews, and coordinated all the efforts that went into the first Linux book. Thanks for help on my first Linux book also goes to Ronald Hiller, Graburn Technology, Inc.; Charles A. Plater, Wayne State University; Bob Palowoda, Tom Bialaski, Sun Microsystems; Roger Hartmuller, TIS Labs at Network Associates; Kaowen Liu, Andy Spitzer, Rik Schneider, Jesse St. Laurent, Steve Bellenot, Ray W. Hiltbrand, Jennifer Witham, Gert-Jan Hagenaars, and Casper Dik.

A Practical Guide to Red Hat® Linux®, Second Edition, is based in part on two of my previous UNIX books: *UNIX System V: A Practical Guide* and *A Practical*

Guide to the UNIX System. Many people helped me with those books, and thanks here go to Pat Parseghian, Dr. Kathleen Hemenway, and Brian LaRose; Byron A. Jeff, Clark Atlanta University; Charles Stross; Jeff Gitlin, Lucent Technologies; Kurt Hockenbury; Maury Bach, Intel Israel Ltd.; Peter H. Salus; Rahul Dave, University of Pennsylvania; Sean Walton, Intelligent Algorithmic Solutions; Tim Segall, Computer Sciences Corporation; Behrouz Forouzan, DeAnza College; Mike Keenan, Virginia Polytechnic Institute and State University; Mike Johnson, Oregon State University; Jandelyn Plane, University of Maryland; Arnold Robbins and Sathis Menon, Georgia Institute of Technology; Cliff Shaffer, Virginia Polytechnic Institute and State University; and Steven Stepanek, California State University, Northridge, for reviewing the book.

I also continue to be grateful to the many people who helped with the early editions of my UNIX books. Special thanks to Roger Sippl, Laura King, and Roy Harrington for introducing me to the UNIX system. My mother, Dr. Helen Sobell, provided invaluable comments on the original manuscript at several junctures. Also thanks to Isaac Rabinovitch, Professor Raphael Finkel, Professor Randolph Bentson, Bob Greenberg, Professor Udo Pooch, Judy Ross, Dr. Robert Veroff, Dr. Mike Denny, Joe DiMartino, Dr. John Mashey, Diane Schulz, Robert Jung, Charles Whitaker, Don Cragun, Brian Dougherty, Dr. Robert Fish, Guy Harris, Ping Liao, Gary Lindgren, Dr. Jarrett Rosenberg, Dr. Peter Smith, Bill Weber, Mike Bianchi, Scooter Morris, Clarke Echols, Oliver Grillmeyer, Dr. David Korn, Dr. Scott Weikart, and Dr. Richard Curtis.

Dr. Brian Kernighan and Rob Pike graciously allowed me to reprint the **bundle** script from their book *The UNIX Programming Environment* (Prentice Hall, 1984).

I take responsibility for errors and omissions. If you find one or just have a comment, let me know (mgs@sobell.com) and I'll fix it in the next printing. My home page (www.sobell.com) contains a list of errors and those who found them, as well as copies of the longer scripts from the book and pointers to many interesting Linux pages.

Mark G. Sobell
San Francisco, California

Welcome to Linux

The Linux *kernel* was developed by Finnish undergraduate student Linus Torvalds, who used the Internet to make the source code immediately available to others for free. Torvalds released Linux version 0.01 in September 1991.

The new operating system came together with a lot of hard work. Programmers throughout the world were quick to extend the kernel and develop other tools, adding functionality to match that already found in both BSD UNIX and System V UNIX (SVR4) and adding new functionality as well.

The Linux operating system, developed through the cooperation of many, many people around the world, is a *product of the Internet* and is a *FREE* operating system: All the source code is free. You are free to study it, redistribute it, and modify it. As a result, the code is available free of cost—no charge for the software, source, documentation, or support (via newsgroups, mailing lists, and other Internet resources). As the GNU Free Software Definition (reproduced in Appendix D, also at www.gnu.org/philosophy/free-sw.html) puts it:

> "Free software" is a matter of liberty, not price. To understand the concept, you should think of "free" as in "free speech," not as in "free beer."

The GNU-Linux Connection

An operating system is the low-level software that schedules tasks, allocates storage, and handles the interfaces to peripheral hardware, such as printers, disk drives, the

1

screen, keyboard, and mouse. An operating system has two main parts: the *kernel* and the *system programs*. The kernel allocates machine resources, including memory, disk space, and *CPU* (page 965) cycles, to all other programs that run on the computer. The system programs perform higher-level housekeeping tasks, often acting as servers in a client/server relationship. *Linux* is the name of the kernel that Linus Torvalds presented to the world in 1991 and that many others have worked on to enhance, stabilize, expand, and make more secure.

Fade to 1983

Richard Stallman (www.stallman.org) announces[1] the GNU Project for creating an operating system, both kernel and system programs, and presents the GNU Manifesto,[2] which begins as follows:

> GNU, which stands for Gnu's Not UNIX, is the name for the complete UNIX-compatible software system which I am writing so that I can give it away free to everyone who can use it.

Some years later, Stallman added a footnote to the preceding sentence when he realized that it was creating confusion:

> The wording here was careless. The intention was that nobody would have to pay for *permission* to use the GNU system. But the words don't make this clear, and people often interpret them as saying that copies of GNU should always be distributed at little or no charge. That was never the intent; later on, the manifesto mentions the possibility of companies providing the service of distribution for a profit. Subsequently I have learned to distinguish carefully between "free" in the sense of freedom and "free" in the sense of price. Free software is software that users have the freedom to distribute and change. Some users may obtain copies at no charge, while others pay to obtain copies—and if the funds help support improving the software, so much the better. The important thing is that everyone who has a copy has the freedom to cooperate with others in using it.

In the manifesto, after explaining a little about the project and what has been accomplished so far, Mr. Stallman continues:

> **Why I Must Write GNU**
> I consider that the golden rule requires that if I like a program I must share it with other people who like it. Software sellers want

---

1. www.gnu.org/gnu/initial-announcement.html

2. www.gnu.org/gnu/manifesto.html

to divide the users and conquer them, making each user agree not to share with others. I refuse to break solidarity with other users in this way. I cannot in good conscience sign a nondisclosure agreement or a software license agreement. For years I worked within the Artificial Intelligence Lab to resist such tendencies and other inhospitalities, but eventually they had gone too far: I could not remain in an institution where such things are done for me against my will.

So that I can continue to use computers without dishonor, I have decided to put together a sufficient body of free software so that I will be able to get along without any software that is not free. I have resigned from the AI Lab to deny MIT any legal excuse to prevent me from giving GNU away.

Next Scene, 1991

The GNU Project has moved well along toward its goal. Much of the GNU Operating System, except for the kernel, is complete. Richard Stallman later writes:

> By the early '90s we had put together the whole system aside from the kernel (and we were also working on a kernel, the GNU Hurd,[3] which runs on top of Mach[4]). Developing this kernel has been a lot harder than we expected, and we are still working on finishing it.[5]
>
> ...[M]any believe that once Linus Torvalds finished writing the kernel, his friends looked around for other free software, and for no particular reason most everything necessary to make a UNIX-like system was already available.
>
> What they found was no accident—it was the GNU system. The available free software[6] added up to a complete system because the GNU Project had been working since 1984 to make one. The GNU Manifesto had set forth the goal of developing a free UNIX-like system, called GNU. The Initial Announcement of the GNU Project also outlines some of the original plans for the GNU system. By the time Linux was written, the [GNU] system was almost finished.[7]

3. www.gnu.org/software/hurd/hurd.html

4. www.gnu.org/software/hurd/gnumach.html

5. www.gnu.org/software/hurd/hurd-and-linux.html

6. See Appendix D or www.gnu.org/philosophy/free-sw.html.

7. www.gnu.org/GNU/Linux-and-gnu.html

The Code Is Free

Part of the tradition of free software dates back to the days when UNIX was released to universities at nominal cost, which contributed to its success and portability. This tradition died as UNIX was commercialized and manufacturers regarded the source code as proprietary, making it effectively unavailable. Another problem with the commercial versions of UNIX was complexity. As each manufacturer tuned UNIX for a specific architecture, it became less portable and too unwieldy for teaching and experimentation. Two professors created their own stripped-down UNIX look-alikes for educational purposes: Doug Comer created XINU[8] and Andrew Tanenbaum created MINIX.[9] It was Linus Torvalds's experience with MINIX that led him on the path to creating his own UNIX-like operating system.

You can obtain Linux at no cost over the Internet (page 35). You can also obtain the GNU code via the United States mail at a modest cost for materials and shipping. You can support the Free Software Foundation by buying the same (GNU) code in higher-priced packages, and you can buy commercial packaged releases of Linux (called *distributions*), such as Red Hat, that include installation instructions, software, and support.

GPL Linux and GNU software are distributed under the terms of the GNU General Public License (GPL, www.gnu.org/licenses/licenses.html). The GPL says you have the right to copy, modify, and redistribute the code covered by the agreement, but when you redistribute the code, you must also distribute the same license with the code, making the code and the license inseparable. If you get the source code off the Internet for an accounting program that is under the GPL and modify the code and redistribute an executable version of the program, you must also distribute the modified source code and the GPL agreement with it. Because this is the reverse of the way a normal copyright works (it gives rights instead of limiting them), it has been termed a *copyleft*. (This paragraph is not a legal interpretation of the GPL; it is here only to give you an idea of how it works. Refer to the GPL itself when you want to make use of it.)

Have Fun!

Two key words for Linux are, "Have Fun!" These words pop up in prompts and documentation. The UNIX—now the Linux—culture is steeped in humor that can be seen throughout the system. For example, less is more—GNU has replaced the UNIX paging utility named more with an improved utility named less. The utility to view PostScript documents is named ghostscript, and one of several replacements for the vi editor is named elvis. While machines with Intel processors have "Intel Inside"

---

8. www.cs.purdue.edu/research/xinu.html

9. www.cs.vu.nl/~ast/minix.html

logos on their outside, some Linux machines sport "Linux Inside" logos. And Torvalds himself has been seen wearing a T-shirt bearing a "Linus Inside" logo.

The Linux 2.6 Kernel

The Linux 2.6 kernel was released on December 17, 2003. This new kernel offers many features that offer increased security and speed. Some of these features benefit end users directly while others help developers produce better code and find problems more quickly. Which kernel you are using does not affect most of the utilities and programs covered in this book. Exceptions are noted.

FEDORA Fedora Core 2 and above include the 2.6 kernel.

RHEL Red Hat maintains its own fork (version) of the 2.4 kernel for Red Hat Enterprise Linux. Red Hat's version of the kernel includes some features from the 2.6 kernel.

See Appendix E for a description of the new features in the Linux 2.6 kernel.

The Heritage of Linux: UNIX

The UNIX system was developed by researchers who needed a set of modern computing tools to help them with their projects. The system allowed a group of people working together on a project to share selected data and programs while keeping other information private.

Universities and colleges played a major role in furthering the popularity of the UNIX operating system through the "four-year effect." When the UNIX operating system became widely available in 1975, Bell Labs offered it to educational institutions at nominal cost. The schools, in turn, used it in their computer science programs, ensuring that computer science students became familiar with it. Because UNIX was such an advanced development system, the students became acclimated to a sophisticated programming environment. As these students graduated and went into industry, they expected to work in a similarly advanced environment. As more of these students worked their way up in the commercial world, the UNIX operating system found its way into industry.

In addition to introducing students to the UNIX operating system, the Computer Systems Research Group (CSRG) at the University of California at Berkeley made significant additions and changes to it. They made so many popular changes that one of the versions of the system is called the Berkeley Software Distribution (BSD) of the UNIX system (or just Berkeley UNIX). The other major version is UNIX System V, which descended from versions developed and maintained by AT&T and UNIX System Laboratories.

What Is So Good About Linux?

In recent years Linux has emerged as a powerful and innovative UNIX work-alike. Its popularity is surpassing that of its UNIX predecessors. Although it mimics UNIX in many ways, the Linux operating system departs from UNIX in several significant ways: The Linux kernel is implemented independently of both BSD and System V, the continuing development of Linux is taking place through the combined efforts of many capable individuals throughout the world, and Linux puts the power of UNIX within easy reach of business and personal computer users. Today, over the Internet, skilled programmers submit additions and improvements to the operating system to Linus Torvalds, GNU, or one of the other authors of Linux.

Applications A rich selection of applications is available for Linux—both free and commercial—as well as a wide variety of tools: graphical, word processing, networking, security, administration, Web server, and many others. Large software companies have recently seen the benefit in supporting Linux and have on-staff programmers whose job it is to design and code the Linux kernel, GNU, KDE, or other software that runs on Linux. Linux conforms more and more closely to POSIX standards, and some distributions and parts of others meet this standard. See "Standards" on page 8 for more information. These facts mean that Linux is becoming more and more mainstream and is respected as an attractive alternative to other popular operating systems.

Peripherals Another aspect of Linux that appeals to users is the amazing breadth of peripherals that is supported and the speed with which new peripherals are supported. Frequently, Linux supports a peripheral or interface card before any company does.

Software Also important to users is the amount of software that is available—not just source code (which needs to be compiled) but also prebuilt binaries that are easy to install and ready to run. These include more than free software—Netscape has been available for Linux from the start and included Java support before it was available from many commercial vendors. Now its sibling, Mozilla, is also a viable browser, mail client, and newsreader, performing many other functions as well.

Platforms Linux is not just for Intel-based platforms but has been ported to and runs on the Power PC—including Apples (ppclinux), the Compaq (nee DEC) Alpha-based machines, MIPS-based machines, Motorola 68K-based machines, and IBM S/390. Nor is Linux just for single-processor machines: As of version 2.0, it runs on multiple processor machines (SMPs). As of version 2.5.2, Linux includes an O(1) scheduler, which dramatically increases scalability on SMP systems.

Emulators Finally, Linux supports programs, called *emulators*, that run code intended for other operating systems. By using emulators you can run some DOS, Windows, and MacIntosh programs under Linux. QEMU is a CPU-only emulator; it executes x86 Linux binaries on non-x86 Linux systems.

Why Linux Is Popular with Hardware Companies and Developers

Two trends in the computer industry set the stage for the popularity of UNIX and Linux. First, advances in hardware technology created the need for an operating system that could take advantage of available hardware power. In the mid-1970s, minicomputers began challenging the large mainframe computers because, in many applications, minicomputers could perform the same functions less expensively. More recently, powerful 64-bit processor chips, plentiful and inexpensive memory, and lower-priced hard-disk storage have allowed hardware companies to install multiuser operating systems on desktop computers.

Proprietary operating systems Second, with the cost of hardware continually dropping, hardware manufacturers can no longer afford to develop and support proprietary operating systems. A *proprietary* operating system used to be written and owned by the manufacturer of the hardware (for example, DEC/Compaq owns VMS). Manufacturers need a generic operating system that they can easily adapt to their machines. A *generic* operating system is written outside of the company manufacturing the hardware and is sold (UNIX, Windows) or given (Linux) to the manufacturer. Linux is a generic operating system because it runs on different types of hardware produced by different manufacturers. Of course, if a manufacturer can pay only for development and avoid per unit costs (as they have to pay to Microsoft for each copy of Windows they sell), developers are much better off. In turn, software developers need to keep the prices of their products down; they cannot afford to convert their products to run under many different proprietary operating systems. Like hardware manufacturers, software developers need a generic operating system.

Although the UNIX system once met the needs of hardware companies and researchers for a generic operating system, over time it has become more proprietary as each manufacturer adds support for specialized features and introduces new software libraries and utilities.

Linux has emerged to serve both needs. It is a generic operating system that takes advantage of available hardware power.

Linux Is Portable

A *portable* operating system is one that can run on many different machines. More than 95 percent of the Linux operating system is written in the C programming language, and C is portable because it is written in a higher-level, machine-independent language. (The C compiler is written in C.)

Because Linux is portable, it can be adapted (ported) to different machines and can meet special requirements. For example, Linux is used in embedded computers, such as the ones found in cell phones, PDAs, and the cable boxes on top of many TVs. The file structure takes full advantage of large, fast hard disks. Equally important, Linux was originally designed as a multiuser operating system—it was not modified to serve several users as an afterthought. Sharing the computer's power among many users and giving them the ability to share data and programs are central features of the system.

Because it is adaptable and takes advantage of available hardware, Linux now runs on many different microprocessor-based systems as well as mainframes. The popularity of the microprocessor-based hardware drives Linux; these microcomputers are getting faster all the time, at about the same price point. Linux on a fast microcomputer has become good enough to displace workstations on many desktops. And the microcomputer/workstation marketplace is totally different from the mainframe marketplace. Linux also benefits both the users, who do not like having to learn a new operating system for each vendor's hardware, and the system administrators, who like having a consistent software environment.

The advent of a standard operating system has aided the development of the software industry. Now software manufacturers can afford to make one version of a product available on machines from different manufacturers.

Standards

Individuals from companies throughout the computer industry have joined together to develop a standard named POSIX (Portable Operating System Interface for computer Environments), which is based largely on the UNIX System V Interface Definition (SVID) and other earlier standardization efforts. These efforts have been spurred by the United States government, which needs a standard computing environment to minimize training and procurement costs. Now that these standards are gaining acceptance, software developers are able to develop applications that run on all conforming versions of UNIX, Linux, and other operating systems.

The C Programming Language

More than 95 percent of the Linux operating system is written in C. Ken Thompson wrote the UNIX operating system in 1969 in PDP-7 assembly language. Assembly language is machine dependent: Programs written in assembly language work on only one machine or, at best, one family of machines. Therefore, the original UNIX operating system could not easily be transported to run on other machines (it was not portable).

To make UNIX portable, Thompson developed the B programming language, a machine-independent language, from the BCPL language. Dennis Ritchie developed the C programming language by modifying B and, with Thompson, rewrote UNIX in C in 1973. After this rewrite, the operating system could be transported more easily to run on other machines.

That was the start of C. You can see in its roots some of the reasons why it is such a powerful tool. C can be used to write machine-independent programs. A programmer who designs a program to be portable can easily move it to any computer that has a C compiler. C is also designed to compile into very efficient code. With the advent of C, a programmer no longer had to resort to assembly language to get code that would run well (that is, quickly, although an assembler will always generate more efficient code than a high-level language).

C is a good systems language. You can write a compiler or an operating system in C. It is highly structured, but it is not necessarily a high-level language. C allows a programmer to manipulate bits and bytes, as is necessary when writing an operating system. But it also has high-level constructs that allow efficient, modular programming.

In the late 1980s, the American National Standards Institute (ANSI) defined a standard version of the C language, commonly referred to as *ANSI C* or *C89* (for the year the standard was published). Ten years later, the C99 standard was published; C99 is supported by the GNU Project's C compiler (named gcc). The original version of the language is often referred to as *Kernighan & Ritchie* (or *K&R*) C, named for the authors of the book that first described the C language.

Another researcher at Bell Labs, Bjarne Stroustrup, created an object-oriented programming language named *C++*, which is built on the foundation of C. Because object-oriented programming is desired by many employers today, C++ is preferred over C in many environments. The GNU Project's C compiler and its C++ compiler (g++) are integral parts of the Linux operating system.

Overview of Linux

The Linux operating system has many unique and powerful features. Like other operating systems, Linux is a control program for computers. But like UNIX, it is also a well-thought-out family of utility programs (Figure 1-1) and a set of tools allowing users to connect and use these utilities to build systems and applications.

Linux Has a Kernel Programming Interface

The Linux kernel, the heart of the Linux operating system, is responsible for allocating the computer's resources and scheduling user jobs so that each one gets its fair share of system resources, including access to the CPU; peripheral devices, such as disk and CD-ROM storage; printers; and tape drives. Programs interact with the kernel through *system calls*, special functions with well-known names. A programmer can use a single system call to interact with many kinds of devices. For example, there is one **write** system call, not many device-specific ones. When a program issues a **write** request, the kernel interprets the context and passes the request to the appropriate device. This flexibility allows old utilities to work with devices that did

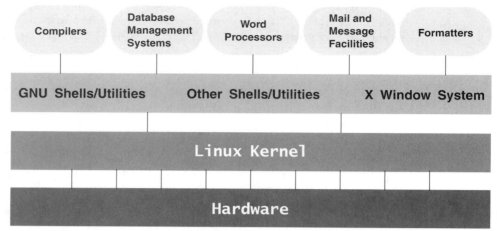

Figure 1-1 A layered view of the Linux operating system

not exist when the utilities were originally written, and it makes it possible to move programs to new versions of the operating system without rewriting them (provided that the new version recognizes the same system calls). See page 947 for information on the Linux 2.6 kernel.

Linux Can Support Many Users

Depending on the hardware and what types of tasks the computer performs, a Linux system can support from 1 to more than 1000 users, each concurrently running a different set of programs. The cost of a computer that can be used by many people at the same time is less per user than that of a computer that can be used by only a single person at a time. The cost is less because one person cannot generally use all the resources a computer has to offer. No one can keep the printers going constantly, keep all the system memory in use, keep the disks busy reading and writing, keep the modems in use, and keep the terminals busy. A multiuser operating system allows many people to use all the system resources almost simultaneously. The use of costly resources can be maximized, and the cost per user can be minimized. These are the primary objectives of a multiuser operating system.

Linux Can Run Many Tasks

Linux is a fully protected multitasking operating system, allowing each user to run more than one job at a time. Although processes can communicate with one another, they are also fully protected from one another, just as the kernel is protected from all processes. You can run several jobs in the background while giving all your attention to the job being displayed on your screen, and you can switch back and

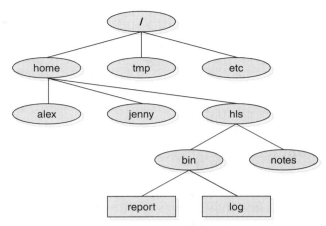

Figure 1-2   The Linux filesystem structure

forth between jobs. If you are running the X Window System (page 14), you can run different programs in different windows on the same screen and watch all of them. With this capability, users can be more productive.

Linux Provides a Secure Hierarchical Filesystem

A *file* is a collection of information, such as text for a memo or report, an accumulation of sales figures, an image, a song, or an executable program created by a compiler. Each file is stored under a unique identifier on a storage device, such as a hard disk. The Linux filesystem provides a structure whereby files are arranged under *directories,* which are like folders or boxes. Each directory has a name and can hold other files and directories. Directories, in turn, are arranged under other directories, and so forth, in a treelike organization. This structure helps users keep track of large numbers of files by grouping related files into directories. Each user has one primary directory and as many subdirectories as required (Figure 1-2).

With the idea of making it easier for system administrators and software developers, a group got together over the Internet and developed the Linux Filesystem Standard (FSSTND), which has evolved into the Linux Filesystem Hierarchy Standard (FHS). Before this standard was adopted, key programs were located in different places in different Linux distributions. Today, you can sit down at a Linux system and know where to expect to find any given standard program (page 167).

Another mechanism, *linking,* allows a given file to be accessed by means of two or more different names. The alternative names can be located in the same directory as the original file or in another directory. Links can be used to make the same file appear in several users' directories, enabling them to share the file easily. Windows uses the term *shortcut* in place of *link*.

As with most multiuser operating systems, Linux allows users to protect their data from access by other users. Linux also allows users to share selected data and programs with certain other users by means of a simple but effective protection scheme. This level of security is provided by file access permissions, which limit which users can read from, write to, or execute a file. Access Control Lists (ACLs) have recently been added to the Linux kernel and are available in Fedora Core 2. ACLs give users and administrators finer-grained control over file access permissions.

The Shell: Command Interpreter and Programming Language

In a textual environment, the shell, a command interpreter, acts as an interface between you and the operating system. When you enter a command at a terminal, the shell interprets the command and calls the program you want. A number of shells are available for Linux; the three most popular ones are

- The Bourne Again Shell (bash), an enhanced version of the Bourne Shell, one of the original UNIX shells
- The TC Shell (tcsh), an enhanced version of the C Shell, developed as part of BSD UNIX
- The Z Shell (zsh), incorporates features from a number of shells, including the Korn Shell

Because users often prefer different shells, multiuser systems can have a number of different shells in use at any given time. The choice of shells demonstrates one of the powers of the Linux operating system: the ability to provide a customized user interface.

Besides its function of interpreting commands from a terminal or workstation keyboard and sending them to the operating system, the shell is a high-level programming language. Shell commands can be arranged in a file for later execution (DOS and Windows call this a *batch* file). This flexibility allows users to perform complex operations with relative ease, often with rather short commands, or to build with surprisingly little effort elaborate programs that perform highly complex operations.

Filename Generation

When you are typing commands to be processed by the shell, you can construct patterns using characters that have special meanings to the shell. These patterns are a kind of shorthand: Rather than typing in complete filenames, users can type in patterns, and the shell expands them into matching filenames. A pattern can save you the effort of typing in a long filename or a long series of similar filenames. Patterns can also be useful when you know only part of a filename or cannot remember the exact spelling.

Device-Independent Input and Output

Devices (such as a printer or terminal) and disk files all appear as files to Linux programs. When you give the Linux operating system a command, you can instruct it to send the output to any one of several devices or files. This diversion is called output *redirection*.

In a similar manner, a program's input that normally comes from a keyboard can be redirected so that it comes from a disk file instead. Input and output are *device independent*; they can be redirected to or from any appropriate device.

As an example, the cat utility normally displays the contents of a file on the terminal screen. When you run a cat command, you can easily cause its output to go to a disk file instead of the terminal.

Shell Functions

One of the most important features of the shell is that users can use it as a programming language. Because the shell is an interpreter, it does not compile programs written for it but interprets them each time they are loaded from the disk. Loading and interpreting programs can be time-consuming.

Many shells, including bash and zsh, include shell functions that the shell holds in memory so it does not have to read them from the disk each time you want to execute them. The shell also keeps functions in an internal format so it does not have to spend as much time interpreting them.

Job Control

Job control is a shell feature that allows users to work on several jobs at once, switching back and forth between them as desired. When you start a job, it is frequently in the foreground, so it is connected to your terminal. Using job control, you can move the job you are working with into the background and continue running it there while working on or observing another job in the foreground. If a background job needs your attention, you can move it into the foreground so it is once again attached to your terminal. The concept of job control originated with BSD UNIX, where it appeared in the C Shell.

A Large Collection of Useful Utilities

Linux includes a family of several hundred utility programs, often referred to as *commands*. These utilities perform functions that are universally required by users. An example is sort. The sort utility puts lists (or groups of lists) in alphabetical or numerical order and can be used to sort by part number, last name, city, zip code, telephone number, age, size, cost, and so forth. The sort utility is an important programming tool and is part of the standard Linux system. Other utilities allow users to create, display, print, copy, search, and delete files, as well as to edit, format, and typeset text. The man (for manual) and info utilities provide online documentation of Linux itself.

Interprocess Communication

Linux allows users to establish both pipes and filters on the command line. A *pipe* sends the output of one program to another program as input. A *filter* is a special form of a pipe that processes a stream of input data to yield a stream of output data. A filter processes another program's output, altering it. The filter's output then becomes input to another program.

Pipes and filters frequently join utilities to perform a specific task. For example, you can use a pipe to send the output of the cat utility to sort, a filter, and then use another pipe to send the output of sort to a third utility, lpr, that sends the data to a printer. Thus, in one command line, you can use three utilities together to sort and print a file.

System Administration

The system administrator, who on a Linux system is frequently the owner and only user of the system, has many responsibilities. The first responsibility may be to set up the system and install the software.

Once the system is up and running, the system administrator is responsible for downloading and installing software (including upgrading the operating system), backing up and restoring files, and managing such system facilities as printers, terminals, servers, and a local network. The system administrator is also responsible for setting up accounts for new users on a multiuser system, bringing the system up and down as needed, and taking care of any problems that arise.

Additional Features of Linux

The Linux developers included features from BSD, System V, Sun Microsystems' Solaris, as well as new features, in Linux. Also, although most of the tools found on UNIX exist for Linux, in many cases, these tools have been replaced by more modern counterparts. The following sections describe many of the popular tools and features available under Linux.

GUI: Graphical User Interfaces

The X Window System, also called X, was developed in part by researchers at the Massachusetts Institute of Technology and provides the foundation for the GUIs available with Linux. Given a terminal or workstation screen that supports X, a

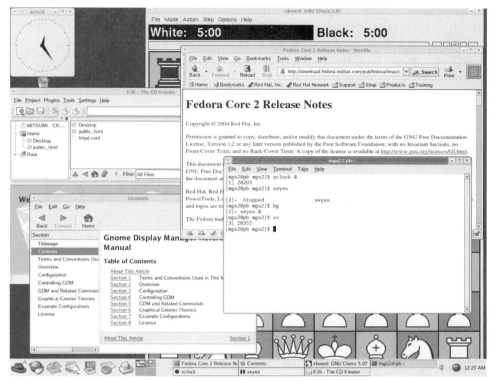

Figure 1-3   A GNOME workspace

user can interact with the computer through multiple windows on the screen, display graphical information, or use special-purpose applications to draw pictures, monitor processes, or preview formatted output. X is an across-the-network protocol that allows a user to open a window on a workstation or computer system that is remote from the CPU generating the window.

Usually, two layers run under X: a desktop manager and a window manager. A *desktop manager* is a picture-oriented user interface that enables you to interact with system programs by manipulating icons instead of typing the corresponding commands to a shell. Red Hat includes GNOME (Figure 1-3) and KDE.

A *window manager* is a program that runs under the desktop manager and allows you to open and close windows, start programs running, and set up a mouse so it does various things, depending on how and where you click. It is the window manager that gives your screen its personality. Microsoft Windows allows you to change the color of key elements in a window, but a window manager under X allows you to change the overall look and feel of your screen: change the way a window looks and works (you can give a window different borders, buttons, and scrollbars), set up virtual desktops, create menus, and more.

Several popular window managers run under X and Linux. Red Hat provides Metacity (default under GNOME) and kwin (default under KDE); other window managers, such as Sawfish and WindowMaker, are available. Chapters 4 and 8 have more information on GUIs.

(Inter)networking Utilities

Linux network support includes many valuable utilities that enable you to access remote systems over a variety of networks. Besides giving you the ability to send email to users on other machines, you can access files on disks mounted on other computers as if they were located on your machine, make your files available to other computers in a similar manner, copy files back and forth, run programs on remote machines while displaying the results on your local machine, and perform many other operations across local area networks (LANs) and wide area networks (WANs), including the Internet.

Layered on top of this network access is a wide range of application programs that extend the computer's resources around the globe. You can carry on conversations with people throughout the world, gather information on a wide variety of subjects, and download new software over the Internet quickly and reliably. Chapter 10 discusses networks, the Internet, and the Linux network facilities.

Software Development

One of the strengths of Linux is its rich software development environment. You can find compilers and interpreters for many computer languages. Besides C and C++, other languages available for Linux are Ada, Fortran, Java, Lisp, Pascal, Perl, Python, and many others. The bison utility generates parsing code that makes it easier to write programs to build compilers (tools that parse files containing structured information), whereas flex generates scanners, code that recognizes lexical patterns in text. The make utility and GNU's automatic configuration utility (configure) make it easy to manage complex development projects; source code management systems, such as CVS, simplify version control. Several debuggers, including ups and gdb, help in tracking down and repairing software defects. The GNU C compiler (gcc) works with the gprof profiling utility to let programmers determine where potential bottlenecks are in a program's performance. The C compiler includes options to perform extensive checking of C code that can make the code more portable and reduce debugging time. These and other software development tools are discussed in Chapter 27.

Conventions Used in This Book

This book uses conventions to make its explanations shorter and clearer. The following paragraphs describe these conventions.

Red Hat Linux

In this book, the term *Red Hat Linux* refers to both Fedora Core and Red Hat Enterprise Linux. Features that apply to one operating system or the other only are marked as such, using these markers: FEDORA or RHEL.

Examples

The text is set in this type, whereas examples are shown in a `monospaced font` (also called a *fixed-width* font) as follows:

```
$ cat practice
This is a small file I created
with a text editor.
```

See the next section for a discussion of why part of the first line is in boldface.

Items You Enter

Everything you enter at the keyboard is printed in boldface: Within the text, **this bold typeface** is used; within examples and screens, `this one` is used. See the previous section for an example: In the first line, the dollar sign ($) is a prompt that Linux displays, so it is not bold; the remainder of the first line is entered by a user, so it is in boldface.

Utility Names

Names of utilities are printed in this bold sans serif typeface. This book references the emacs editor, the ls utility or ls command (or just ls), but instructs you to enter ls –a on the command line. The text distinguishes between utilities, which are programs, and the instructions you give on the command line to invoke the utilities.

Filenames

Filenames appear in the text font but in **bold**. Examples are **memo5, letter.1283,** and **reports**. Filenames may include upper- and lowercase letters; however, Linux is *case sensitive* (page 961), so **memo5, MEMO5,** and **Memo5** name three different files.

Characters and Character Strings

Within the text, characters and character strings are marked by putting them in a **bold font**. This convention avoids the need for quotation marks or other delimiters to surround a string. An example is the following string, which is displayed by the passwd utility: **Sorry, passwords do not match.**

Buttons and Labels

In the sections of the book that describe a GUI (graphical user interface), you will see words in a **bold** typeface. This font indicates that you can click a mouse button when the mouse pointer is over these words on the screen or over a button with this name.

Keys and Characters

This book uses SMALL CAPS for three kinds of items:

- Important keyboard keys, such as the SPACE bar and the RETURN,[10] ESCAPE, and TAB keys.

- The characters that keys generate, such as the SPACEs generated by the SPACE bar.

- Keyboard keys that you press with the CONTROL key, such as CONTROL-D. (Even though D is shown as an uppercase letter, you do not have to press the SHIFT key; enter CONTROL-D by holding the CONTROL key down and pressing **d**.)

Prompts and RETURNs

Most textual examples include the *shell prompt*—the signal that Linux is waiting for a command—as a dollar sign ($) or sometimes a percent sign (%). The prompt is not in boldface, because you do not enter it. Do not enter the prompt on the keyboard when you are experimenting with examples from this book. If you do, the examples will not work.

Examples *omit* the RETURN keystroke that you must use to execute them. An example of a command line is

```
$ vi memo.1204
```

To use this example as a model for running the vi editor, give the command **vi memo.1204** and press the RETURN key. (Press ESCAPE **ZZ** to exit from vi; see page 145 for more on vi.) This method of entering commands makes the examples in the book correspond to what appears on your screen.

Menu Selection Path

The menu selection path is the name of the menu or where the menu is located, followed by a colon, a SPACE, and the menu selection(s) separated by ⇨s. The whole

---

10. Different keyboards use different keys to move the *cursor* (page 966) to the beginning of the next line. This book always refers to the key that ends a line as the RETURN key. Your keyboard may have a RET, NEWLINE, Enter, RETURN, or other key. Some keyboards have a key with a bent arrow on it. (The key with the bent arrow is not an arrow key. Arrow keys have straight shafts.) Use the corresponding key on your keyboard each time this book asks you to press RETURN.

menu selection path is in **bold** type. You can read **Konqueror menubar: Tools⇨Find** as "From the Konqueror menubar, select **Tools** and from **Tools**, select **Find**."

Definitions

All entries marked with ꜰᴏʟᴅᴏᴄ are courtesy of Denis Howe, editor, the Free Online Dictionary of Computing (www.foldoc.org) and are used with permission. This site is an ongoing work containing not just definitions but also anecdotes and trivia.

optional ‖

> ### Optional Information
>
> Passages marked as optional are not central to the concepts presented in the chapter but often involve more challenging concepts. A good strategy when reading a chapter is to skip the optional sections and then return to them after you are comfortable with the main ideas presented in the chapter. This is an optional paragraph.

URLs (Web Addresses)

Web addresses, or URLs, have an implicit **http://** prefix, unless **ftp://** or **https://** is shown. You do not normally need to specify a prefix when the prefix is **http://**, but you must use a prefix from a browser when you specify an FTP or secure HTTP site. The result is that you can specify a URL in a browser exactly as shown in this book.

Tip, Caution, and Security Boxes

The following boxes highlight information that may be helpful while you are using or administrating a Linux system.

tip ‖   **This Is a Tip Box**

A tip box may help keep you from repeating a common mistake or may point toward additional information.

caution ‖   **This Box Warns You About Something**

A caution box warns you about a potential pitfall ahead.

security ‖   **This Box Marks a Security Note**

A security box marks a potential security issue. These notes are usually for system administrators, but some apply to all users.

Chapter Summary

The Linux operating system grew out of the UNIX heritage to become a popular alternative to traditional systems (that is, Windows) available for microcomputer (PC) hardware. UNIX users will find a familiar environment in Linux. Distributions of Linux contain the expected complement of UNIX utilities, contributed by programmers around the world, including the set of tools developed as part of the GNU Project. The Linux community is committed to the continued development of the system. Support for new microcomputer devices and features is added soon after the hardware becomes available, and the tools available on Linux continue to be refined. With many commercial software packages available to run on Linux platforms and many hardware manufacturers offering it on their systems, it is clear that the system has evolved well beyond its origin as an undergraduate project to become an operating system of choice for academic, commercial, professional, and personal use.

Exercises

1. What is *free software?* List three characteristics of free software.
2. Why is Linux popular? Why is it popular in academia?
3. What are multiuser systems? Why are they successful?
4. What is the Free Software Foundation/GNU? Linux? Which parts of the Linux operating system did each provide? Who else has helped build and refine this operating system?
5. In what language is Linux written? What does the language have to do with the success of Linux?
6. What is a utility program?
7. What is a shell? How does it work with the kernel? With the user?
8. How can you use utility programs and a shell to create your own applications?
9. Why is the Linux filesystem referred to as *hierarchical?*
10. What is the difference between a multiprocessor and a multiprocessing system?
11. Give an example of when you would want to use a multiprocessing system.
12. Approximately how many people wrote Linux? Why is this unique?
13. What are the key terms of the GNU General Public License?

PART I
Installing Red Hat Linux

Installation Overview

Installing Red Hat Linux is the process of copying operating system files from media to the local system and setting up configuration files so that Linux runs properly on the local hardware. You can install Linux from many types of media, including CDs or a hard disk and files on other systems that you access over a network. There are also different types of installations including fresh installations, upgrades from older versions of Red Hat Linux, and dual-boot installations. You can perform the installation manually or set up Kickstart to install Red Hat Linux automatically.

This chapter discusses the installation: planning, how to divide the hard disk into partitions, obtaining the files for the installation, burning CDs if necessary, and collecting information about the system you will need when you install the system. Chapter 3 (page 43) covers the actual installation.

Red Hat developed Anaconda, an installation tool that performs an interactive installation using a GUI, to automate and make friendlier the process of installing Linux. If you have standard hardware, you can typically insert the first installation CD and boot a system, press RETURN a few times, change CDs a few times, and Linux is installed. However, you may want to customize your system and/or have nonstandard hardware: Anaconda gives you many choices as the installation process unfolds. Refer to "Booting the System: The boot: Prompt" (page 44) and "The Anaconda Installer" (page 46) for information about customizing Red Hat Linux installation.

More Information

Web SELinux FAQ   people.redhat.com/kwade/fedora-docs/selinux-faq-en
X.org release notes   freedesktop.org/~xorg/X11R6.7.0/doc/RELNOTES.html
Memtest   www.memtest86.com
Hardware compatibility   hardware.redhat.com
LVM   www.sistina.com/products_lvm.htm
BitTorrent   bitconjurer.org/BitTorrent

Downloads *FEDORA*   Red Hat's site; includes server, mirrors, and BitTorrent
fedora.redhat.com/download
FEDORA   download.fedora.redhat.com/pub/fedora/linux/core
FEDORA   mirrors   fedora.redhat.com/download/mirrors.html
FEDORA   BitTorrent tracker and software   torrent.dulug.duke.edu
RHEL   ftp://ftp.redhat.com/pub/redhat/linux/enterprise
RHEL mirrors   www.redhat.com/download/mirror.html

Planning the Installation

The biggest parts of planning an installation are determining how to divide the hard
disk into partitions or, in the case of a dual-boot system, where to put the Linux
partition, and deciding which software packages to install. In addition to these topics, this section discusses hardware requirements for Red Hat Linux, Fedora Core
versus Red Hat Enterprise Linux, fresh installations versus upgrading, and classes
of installations (server, workstation, and so on).

Considerations

SELinux If you are going to want to use SELinux, turn it on when you install Linux
(page 44). Because SELinux sets extended attributes on files, it is an involved process to turn on SELinux after you install Linux.

GUI On most installations except servers, you probably want to install a graphical interface. The X Window System is required for any graphical interface. In addition, select GNOME, KDE, or both.

Chapter 4, "Introduction to Red Hat Linux," uses examples from KDE to introduce the graphical desktop. Install KDE if you want to follow these examples. You
can remove KDE later if you like.

On a server, you normally dedicate as many resources to the server and as few to
anything not required by the server. For this reason, servers do not usually include a
graphical interface.

Installation Requirements

Hardware Red Hat Linux can run on many different types of hardware. This section details installation on Intel and compatible platforms such as AMD, Cyrix, and VIA. Within these platforms, Red Hat Linux runs on much of the available hardware. You can view Red Hat's hardware list, from certified to unsupported, at hardware.redhat.com. There are many Internet sites that discuss Linux hardware; use Google to search on **linux hardware** or **linux** and the specific hardware you want more information on (for example, **linux sata** or **linux nf7s**). There are many HOWTOs that cover specific hardware and a Linux Hardware Compatibility HOWTO, although it becomes dated rather quickly. Red Hat Linux usually runs on systems that Windows runs on, unless you have a very new or unusual component in the system.

Memory (RAM) You need a minimum of 64 megabytes of RAM for a system that runs in text mode (no GUI) and 192-256 megabytes for graphical system. Because Linux makes good use of extra memory, the more memory your system has, the faster it will run. Additional memory is one of the most cost-effective ways you can speed up a Linux system.

CPU Red Hat Linux requires a minimum of a 200 megahertz Pentium-class processor or the equivalent AMD or other processor for text mode and at least a 400 megahertz Pentium II processor or the equivalent for graphical mode.

Disk space The amount of disk space you need depends on which version of Red Hat Linux you install, which packages you install, how many languages you install, and how much space you need for user data (your files). Table 2-1 shows the *minimum* amount of disk space required.

table 2-1 ‖	Minimum Required Disk Space
Class of Installation	**Minimum Disk Space Required**
Personal Desktop	2.3 gigabytes
Workstation	3.0 gigabytes
Server	1.1–1.5 gigabytes (no graphical environment) 6.9 gigabytes (everything including graphical environment)
Custom	0.62–6.9 gigabytes

BIOS setup Modern computers can be set to boot from a CD, floppy diskette, or hard disk. The BIOS determines the order in which the system tries to boot from each device. You may need to change this order: Make sure the BIOS is set up to try booting from the CD before it tries to boot from the hard drive. See "CMOS," next.

CMOS CMOS is the persistent memory that stores system configuration information. To change the BIOS setup, you need to edit the information stored in CMOS. When the system boots, it displays a brief message about how to enter **System Setup** or **CMOS Setup** mode. Usually, you need to press Del or F2 while the system is booting. Press the

key that is called for, and move the cursor to the screen and line that deal with booting the system. Generally, there is a list of three or four devices that the system tries
to boot from; failing the first, the system tries the second and so on. Manipulate the
list so the CD is the first choice, save your choices, and reboot. Refer to the hard-
ware/BIOS manual for more information.

What Are You Installing: Fedora Core or Red Hat Enterprise Linux?

This book describes two products: Fedora Core and Red Hat Enterprise Linux. This
section briefly explains the differences between these products.

FEDORA The Fedora Project is sponsored by Red Hat and supported by the open-source
community. With releases, called Fedora Core, coming out about every six months,
it is a Linux distribution that tests cutting edge code; it is not a supported Red Hat
product and is not recommended for production environments where stability is important. Fedora aims at staying similar to the upstream projects it incorporates, including the kernel, while Red Hat Enterprise Linux includes many changes
introduced by Red Hat.

RHEL Red Hat Enterprise Linux is sold by annual subscription that includes Red Hat Network (page 467) and technical support. It is more stable but less cutting edge than
Fedora Core Linux.

Red Hat Enterprise Linux AS and Red Hat Enterprise Linux ES function identically
and are designed to run servers. ES is licensed for x86 compatible systems with one
or two CPUs and up to 8 gigabytes of memory. AS is licensed for servers of any size
and architecture.

Red Hat Enterprise Linux WS (workstation) supports x86, Itanium, and AMD64
architectures on the desktop/client side, running office productivity and software
development applications. WS does not include all the server applications that come
with AS and ES and is not designed for a server environment.

Installing a Fresh Copy or Upgrading an Existing Red Hat System?

An *upgrade* replaces the Linux kernel and utilities on an already installed version of
Red Hat Linux with newer versions. During an upgrade, the installation program
attempts to preserve both system and user data files. An upgrade brings utilities that
are present in the old version up-to-date but does not install new utilities (you can
install them later if you like). Existing configuration files are preserved by renaming
with a **.rpmsave** extension. A log of the upgrade is kept in **/root/upgrade.log**. Before
upgrading a system, back up all files on the system.

caution ‖   **A Fresh Installation Yields a More Stable System Than an Upgrade**

For better system stability, Red Hat recommends that you back up your data and perform a fresh
install rather than upgrade.

An *installation* writes all fresh data to a disk. The installation program overwrites all system programs and data as well as the kernel. You can preserve some user data during an installation depending on where it is located and how you format/partition the disk.

Types of Installations (*FEDORA*)

With Fedora, there are four classes of Red Hat Linux you can install. The class you select determines which software packages are installed. You can modify this list of packages during the installation. Under Red Hat Enterprise Linux, you determine the "class" of installation by selecting the packages you want to install.

Personal Desktop   Good if you are new to Linux. This installation gives you a GUI and installs many of the programs you are likely to need.

Workstation   For software developers and system administrators. This installation gives you a GUI and installs many software development and system administration tools.

Server   For administrators who want to deploy a Linux-based server without doing heavy customization. This installation has more services and fewer end-user programs. Although you do not normally bring up a GUI on a server, GNOME and KDE are available.

Custom   Presents you with all the programs and services that Red Hat supports and lets you decide which you want to install. This installation gives you full control over which packages you install. Recommended for experienced users only.

Regardless of the type of installation you choose, you can always add or remove programs once the system is up and running. For more information, refer to "system-config-packages: Adds and Removes Software Packages" on page 453.

Graphical or Textual Installation?

There are several ways to install Red Hat Linux. You can choose a graphical installation, which displays graphics on the screen and allows you to use the mouse, window buttons, and scroll lists to choose how you want to configure the system. The Anaconda utility controls a graphical installation. If you have a smaller system with less memory or a system with an unsupported graphics board, you can use the text-mode installation. This mode performs the same functions as the graphical mode, but it uses plain text to prompt you with questions about how you want to configure the system.

Setting Up the Hard Disk

Formatting and free space   Hard disks must be prepared in several ways so an operating system can write to and read from them. Formatting is the first step in preparing a disk for use. Normally, you will not need to format a hard disk as this is done at the factory. The next step in preparing a disk for use is to divide it into partitions. The area of the disk that is not occupied by partitions is called *free space*. A new disk has no partitions: It is all free space. Under DOS/Windows, the term *formatting* means writing a filesystem on a partition; see "Filesystems," following.

Partitions   A *partition,* or *slice,* is a section of a hard disk that has a name, such as **/dev/hda1**, so you can address it separately from other sections. During installation you can use Disk Druid (page 53) to create partitions on the hard disk. After installation you can use fdisk (page 58) to manipulate partitions.

Filesystems   Before most programs can write to a partition, a *data structure* (page 966), called a *filesystem,* needs to be written on a partition. The mkfs (make filesystem) utility, similar to the DOS/Windows format utility, writes a filesystem on a partition. There are many types of filesystems. Red Hat Linux typically creates **ext3** filesystems for data, while Windows uses FAT and NTFS filesystems. Apple uses HFS (Hierarchical Filesystem) and HFS+. OS X uses either HFS+ or UFS. Under DOS/Windows, filesystems are labeled **C:**, **D:**, and so on (sometimes a whole disk is a single partition). Under Linux, typical filesystem names are **/boot**, **/var**, and **/usr**. You can have different types of partitions on the same drive, including both Windows and Linux partitions. Under Linux, the fsck (filesystem check) utility (page 447) checks the integrity of filesystem data structures.

Filesystem independence   The state of one filesystem does not affect other filesystems: One filesystem on a drive may be corrupt and unreadable while other filesystems function normally. One filesystem may be full so you cannot write to it while others have plenty of room for more data.

Primary and Extended Partitions

Partitioning allows you to divide a disk into a maximum of eight separate *partitions,* or subdisks. You can use each partition independently for swap devices, filesystems, databases, other functions, and even other operating systems.

Unfortunately, disk partitions follow the template established for DOS machines a long time ago. There are two types of partitions: primary and extended. At most, a disk can hold four primary and extended partitions in any combination. Extended partitions can each be subdivided into additional partitions; primary partitions cannot. If you want more than four partitions on a drive, and you usually do, at least one of the four partitions must be an extended partition.

One way to set up a disk is to divide it into three primary partitions and one extended partition. The three primary partitions are the sizes you want the final partitions to be. The extended partition occupies the rest of the disk. Once you establish the extended partition, you can subdivide it into additional partitions that are each the size you want.

Partitioning a Disk

During installation, Anaconda calls Disk Druid to set up disk partitions. This section discusses how to plan partition sizes. For more information, refer to "Using Disk Druid to Partition the Disk" on page 53.

refer to "Using Disk Druid to Partition the Disk" on page 53.

---

tip || **Under Red Hat, Druid Means Wizard**

Red Hat uses the term *druid* at the ends of names of programs that guide you through a task-driven chain of steps. Other operating systems call these types of programs *wizards*.

Planning Partitions

It can be difficult to plan partition sizes appropriately if you are new to Linux. For this reason many people choose to have only two partitions. Partition 1 is reserved for the swap partition, which can be any size from 0 to many hundreds of megabytes or, rarely, gigabytes. Partition 0 is designated as root (/) and contains the remainder of the disk space. This setup makes managing space quite easy. But if a program runs amok, or your system receives a *DoS attack* (page 968), the entire disk can fill up, and system accounting and logging information (which may contain data that can tell you what went wrong) may be lost.

When Disk Druid sets up partitions automatically, it sets up the two partitions described earlier and a **/boot** partition that holds a copy of the operating system and other information the system needs at boot time.

Older disks used a constant number of sectors per track. This made positioning the disk head easier but resulted in a lot of wasted space on the outer tracks. Newer disks use an encoding named ZBR (zone-bit recording): The sector size of the disk stays constant, which means that the outer cylinders have more sectors. Consequently, more information passes under the disk head per disk revolution, and data access is faster on these sectors. These outer cylinders correspond to the lower cylinder numbers (cylinders starting at zero). Put your speed-critical data on the lower-numbered cylinders.

Partition Suggestions

The following paragraphs discuss additional partitions you may want to create. Consider setting up LVM (page 32) *before* you create partitions; LVM allows you to change partition sizes easily after the system is installed.

(swap) Linux temporarily stores programs and data on this part of the disk when it does not have enough RAM to hold all the information it is processing (page 435). Although it is not required, most systems perform better with a swap partition.

/boot This partition holds the kernel and other data the system needs when it boots. Red Hat recommends that the **/boot** partition be 100 megabytes. Although you can omit the **/boot** partition, it is useful in many cases. Some older BIOSs require the **/boot** partition (or the root [**/**] partition if there is no **/boot** partition) to be near the start of the disk.

/var   The name *var* is short for *variable:* The data in this partition changes frequently. Because it holds the bulk of system logs, package information, and accounting data, making **/var** a separate partition is a good idea. If a user runs a job that uses up all the disk space, the logs will not be affected. A good size for the **/var** partition is anything from about 500 megabytes up to several gigabytes for extremely active systems with many verbose daemons and a lot of printer activity (files in the print queue are stored on **/var**). Systems serving as license servers for licensed software often fall into the category of extremely active systems.

/home   It is a common strategy to put user home directories in their own disk or partition. If you do not have a separate disk for the home directories, put them in their own partition. Common partition names are **/home** and **/usr/home**.

---

tip ‖   **Set Up Partitions to Aid in Making Backups**

Plan your partitions around what data you want to back up and how often you want to back it up. One very large partition can be more difficult to back up than several smaller ones.

/ (root)   Some administrators choose to separate the root (**/**), **/boot**, and **/usr** partitions. By itself, the root partition usually consumes less than 30 megabytes of disk space. On occasion, you may install a special program that has many kernel drivers that consume a lot of space in the root partition. If you expect to run into this situation, you need to adjust the space allotted to the root partition accordingly.

/usr   Separating the **/usr** partition can be useful if you want to export **/usr** to another machine and want the security that a separate partition can give. The size of **/usr** depends largely on the number of packages you install.

---

tip ‖   **Where to Put the /boot Partition**

On older systems, the **/boot** partition must reside *completely below cylinder 1,023* of the disk. When you have more than one hard drive, the **/boot** partition must also reside on a drive on

- Multiple IDE or EIDE drives: the primary controller
- Multiple SCSI drives: ID 0 or ID 1
- Multiple IDE and SCSI drives: the primary IDE controller or SCSI ID 0

/usr/local   Finally, **/usr/local** and **/opt** are other candidates for separation. If you plan to install
and /opt   many packages in addition to Red Hat Linux, you may want to keep them on a separate partition. If you install the additional software in the same partition as the users' home directories, for example, it may start to encroach on the users' disk space. Many sites keep all the **/usr/local** or **/opt** software on one server and export it to

others. If you choose to create a **/usr/local** or **/opt** partition, its size should be appropriate to the software you plan to install.

Table 2-2 gives guidelines for minimum sizes for partitions used by Linux. Size other partitions, such as **/home, /opt,** and **/usr/local,** according to need and the size of the drive. If you are not sure how you are going to use additional disk space, you can create extra partitions using whatever names you like (for example, **/b01, /b02,** and so on).

table 2-2 ‖	Example Partition Sizes
/boot	100 megabytes
/ (root)	500 megabytes
(swap)	Two times the amount of RAM (memory) in the system with a minimum of 500 megabytes
/home	As large as necessary; depends on the number of users and the type of work they do
/tmp	Minimum of 500 megabytes
/usr	Minimum of 1.7–5.5 gigabytes, depending on which Red Hat Linux programs you install. These figures assume **/usr/local** is a separate partition. Refer to "Disk space" on page 25 for more information on the size of Red Hat Linux.
/var	Minimum of 500 megabytes

RAID

RAID (Redundant Array of Inexpensive/Independent Disks) employs two or more hard disk drives or partitions in combination to improve fault tolerance and/or performance. Applications and utilities see the multiple drives/partitions as a single logical device. RAID, which can be implemented in hardware (faster) or software (Red Hat gives you this option), spreads data across multiple disks. Depending on which level you choose, RAID can provide data redundancy to protect data in the case of hardware failure. Although it can also improve disk performance by increasing read/write speed and throughput, RAID uses quite a bit of CPU time, which may be a consideration in some situations.

caution ‖	Do Not Replace Backups with RAID

Do not use RAID as a replacement for regular backups. If your system undergoes a catastrophic failure, RAID will be useless. Earthquake, fire, theft, and so on may leave your entire system inaccessible (if your hard drives are destroyed or missing). RAID does not take care of something as simple as replacing a file when you delete it by accident. In these cases, a backup on removable media (that has been removed) is the only way you will be able to restore a filesystem.

Disk Druid gives you the choice of implementing RAID level 0, 1, or 5:

- **RAID Level 0 (striping)**   Improves performance but offers no redundancy. The storage capacity of the RAID device is equal to that of the member partitions or disks.

- **RAID Level 1 (mirroring)**   Provides simple redundancy, improving data reliability, and can improve the performance of read-intensive applications. The storage capacity of the RAID device is equal to one of the member partitions or disks.

- **RAID Level 5 (disk striping with parity)**   Provides redundancy and improves (most notably, read) performance. The storage capacity of the RAID device is equal to that of the member partitions or disks, minus one of the partitions or disks (assuming they are all the same size).

LVM (Logical Volume Manager)

The Logical Volume Manager (LVM) allows you to change the size of logical volumes (LV, the LVM equivalent of partitions) on the fly: Using LVM, if you find you made a mistake in setting up logical volumes or your needs change, you can make LVs smaller or larger easily without affecting user data. You must choose to use LVM at the time you install the system or add a hard disk; you cannot retroactively apply it to a disk full of information. LVM supports IDE and SCSI drives as well as multiple devices such as those found in RAID partitions.

LVM groups disk components (hard disks or storage device arrays), called *physical volumes* (PVs), into a storage pool, or virtual disk, called a *volume group* (VG). See Figure 2-1. You allocate a portion of a VG to create a *logical volume* (LV).

An LV is similar in function to a traditional disk partition in that you can create a filesystem on an LV. It is much easier, however, to change and move LVs than partitions: When you run out of space on a filesystem on an LV, you can grow (expand) the LV and its filesystem, into empty or new disk space, or you can move the filesystem to a larger LV. LVM's disk space manipulation is transparent to users; service is not interrupted.

LVM also eases the burdens of storage migration. When you outgrow or need to upgrade PVs, LVM can move data to new PVs, again without interrupting users.

For specifics, refer to www.sistina.com/products_lvm.htm, the *LVM HOWTO*, the **lvm** man page, and the "See also" man pages listed at the bottom of the **lvm** man page.

How the Installation Works

The following steps outline the process of installing Red Hat Linux from CDs using Anaconda. Installation from other media follows similar steps. See Chapter 3 for the specifics of how to perform the installation.

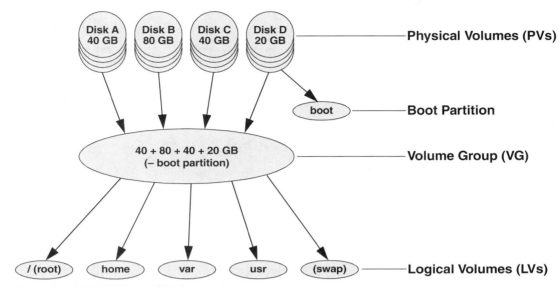

Figure 2-1   LVM: Logical Volume Manager

1. Insert the first installation CD in the computer and turn on or reset the computer.

2. After going through computer-specific hardware diagnostics, the computer displays the initial install screen with the **boot:** prompt at the bottom (page 44).

3. You can enter commands and press RETURN following the **boot:** prompt, press RETURN without entering commands, or wait for a minute without entering anything; the computer boots Red Hat Linux from the installation CD.

4. As part of the boot process, Red Hat Linux creates multiple *RAM disks* (page 991) that it uses in place of a hard disk used for a normal boot operation. Tools used during the installation are copied to the RAM disks. The use of RAM disks allows the installation process to run through the specification and design phases without writing to the hard disk and enables you to opt out of the installation at any point before the system warns you it is about to write to the hard disk. If you opt out before this point, the system is left in its original state. For more information, refer to "About to Install" on page 52.

5. You can check the installation media at this point.

6. Anaconda starts, usually probing the hardware before starting the X Window System for a graphical installation.

7. Anaconda collects information about how you want to install Red Hat Linux.

8. When Anaconda is finished collecting information, it warns you that it is **About to Install** and writes the operating system files to the hard disk.

9. When you reboot the system, installation scripts ask you some questions to complete the installation (page 52).

10. The Red Hat Linux system is ready to use.

The Medium: Where Is the Source Data?

When you install Red Hat Linux, you copy operating system files from a source, frequently a CD, to the target computer's hard disk. There are two formats and many possible sources for the files.

Formats

Red Hat Linux operating system files can be stored as directory hierarchies on CDs or a hard disk or as CD images on a hard disk (called *ISO images* after ISO9660, the standard defining the CD filesystem). Although the format is different, the content is the same. You can install Red Hat Linux or burn a CD from either format, although most people use the ISO images to burn CDs as it is more convenient.

Sources

This chapter details installing Red Hat Linux from CDs and ISO image files. It does not cover installing from directory hierarchies; you use exactly the same techniques to install from a directory hierarchy as from an ISO image. Directory hierarchies are more cumbersome to work with than ISO images because they contain many files; each ISO image is a single file.

You can automate the installation using Kickstart (page 57).

Following is a list of possible locations for the source files for an installation:

CD

You can purchase or burn CDs for installing Fedora Core. Or, you can use the CDs included with this book.

RHEL Red Hat Enterprise Linux CDs are sold by Red Hat and its distributors.

Although Red Hat does not provide ISO images for Red Hat Enterprise Linux, it does provide source RPM files (SRPMS), a different set for each of the architectures Red Hat supports. Go to **ftp.redhat.com** and cd to **/pub/redhat/linux/enterprise/*rel*/en/*arch*/SRPMS**, where *rel* is the release number and *arch* is the architecture you want to download files for (AMD64, i386, ia64, and so on), to download the SRPMS files. Or you can look at www.redhat.com/download/mirror.html for a list of sites that provide these files. Because Red Hat does not provide ISO images for Red Hat Enterprise Linux, this book does not discuss how to install Red Hat Enterprise Linux from downloaded files. It does cover how to install Red Hat Enterprise Linux from the CDs you buy from Red Hat.

FEDORA This book includes the CDs necessary for installing Fedora Core. Alternatively, Fedora CDs can be purchased from third-party vendors or you can download the Fedora ISO images and install from the images or burn your own CDs (next section).

Hard Disk

FEDORA You can store ISO image files on the target system's hard disk if it is already running Linux. You need to burn only the first installation CD or the rescue CD (page 39) for a hard disk installation.

Network

FEDORA You can use ISO image files from a server system that the target system can connect to over a network during installation. Network installations can be done using FTP, NFS, or HTTP. Unless you have a fast Internet connection, it is not advisable to perform an installation over the Internet as it can take a very long time; downloading ISO files is a more reliable and possibly less frustrating option. You need to burn only the first installation CD or the rescue CD (page 39) for a network installation.

Downloading, Burning, and Installing a CD Set (*FEDORA*)

You can download and burn Fedora Core CDs. Although you will not get the customer support that comes with Red Hat Enterprise Linux, you will not pay Red Hat for the software. One of the beauties of free software (Appendix D) is that it is always available for free. Red Hat makes it easy to obtain and use Fedora Core by providing ISO images of its CDs online. These files are large, over 600 megabytes each, and there are four of them, so they take days to download using a 56K modem and hours using a broadband connection.

This section tells you how to find the files you need, download them using a couple of different techniques, check that they downloaded correctly, and burn them to CDs.

caution ‖	**You Can Download and Burn the CDs on Any Operating System**

You can download and burn the CDs on any computer that is connected to the Internet, has a browser, has enough space on the hard disk to hold the ISO files (about 2.5 gigabytes), and can burn a CD.

If you do not have enough space on the hard disk for all four CDs, you can download and burn them one at a time (each takes just over 600 megabytes). You can use ftp in place of a browser to download the files. For more information, refer to "JumpStart: Downloading Files Using ftp" on page 585.

Finding a Site to Download From

The Fedora Web site maintains the ISO images you need. Other (mirror) sites also maintain these packages. You can use a Browser or ftp to download the files from one of these sites. Alternatively, you can use BitTorrent to download the ISO images, see page 38.

To conserve network bandwidth, try to download from a mirror site that is close to you. Failing that, you can download from the Red Hat site.

Mirror sites   Locate a mirror site by pointing a browser at the following URL:

    fedora.redhat.com/download/mirrors.html

Scroll through the list of mirror sites to find a site near you and click that site's URL. The display will be similar to that shown in Figure 2-2. (FTP and HTTP sites look a little different from each other.)

Figure 2-2   The top-level Fedora download directory at redhat.com

The Red Hat site   To download files from the Red Hat Fedora site, point a browser at the following URL, which locates the Red Hat Web page at the top of the directory hierarchy that holds the Fedora Core files (Figure 2-2):

    download.fedora.redhat.com/pub/fedora/linux/core/

When you have located a site to download from, continue with the next section.

Finding the Right Files and Downloading Them

The pathname of the Fedora Core files differs from site to site; see the following examples:

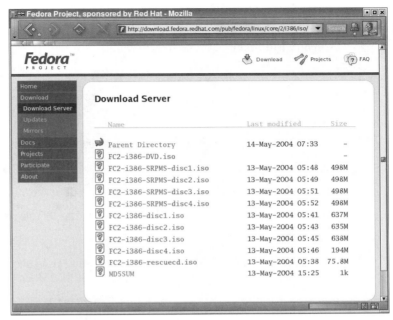

Figure 2-3   The **iso** directory for Fedora Core 2 at redhat.com

```
/pub/linux/fedora/core/2/i386/iso
/fedora/core/2/i386/iso
/fedora/linux/core/2/i386/iso
```

All sites share a common path following the **core** directory (bold in the preceding list). Table 2-3 shows the hierarchy below the **core/2** directory, the directory hierarchy that holds the Fedora Core 2 release. If you are downloading other than Fedora Core 2, go to the directory hierarchy below the appropriately numbered directory (**3**, **4**, and so on). These hierarchies will parallel the Fedora Core 2 directory.

Click (open) directories until you get to the **iso** directory for the release you want to download (Figure 2-3). Click on the five files listed following, one at a time, to download them. Replace **FC2** with the name of the release you are downloading.

```
FC2-i386-disc1.iso
FC2-i386-disc2.iso
FC2-i386-disc3.iso
FC2-i386-disc4.iso
MD5SUM
```

The four large *✳*.iso files hold the ISO images of the Fedora Core CDs. The short **MD5SUM** file holds the MD5 checksums that you can use to make sure the downloaded files are correct (page 38). You may want to download the rescue CD image (**FC2-i386-rescuecd.iso**) as well (page 39). The **FC2-i386-SRPMS-disc✳.iso** files hold the source code for Fedora Core; you do not normally need these files to install Fedora.

table 2-3 ‖	Relative Locations of Fedora Core Files (Fedora Core 2 Shown)
Location in the ❊/fedora/linux Directory Hierarchy	**Contains**
core/2	Fedora Core Linux version 2 directory hierarchy.
core/2/SRPMS	Fedora source RPM files.
core/2/i386	Fedora files for the x86 architecture.
core/2/i386/debug	Fedora debugging programs.
core/2/i386/iso/disc[1–4].iso	Fedora installation CDs 1 through 4 (compiled).
core/2/i386/iso/rescuecd.iso	Fedora rescue CD (page 39).
core/2/i386/iso/MD5SUM	MD5 sums for the ISO files in the same directory.
core/2/i386/os	Individual Fedora rpm packages.
core/2/i386/os/RELEASE-NOTES-en	Fedora release notes in English. (Also RELEASE-NOTES-en.html)
core/2/x86_64	Fedora files for the AMD64 architecture. This directory hierarchy is almost the same as the i386 hierarchy.

Depending on the speed of the Internet connection and how busy the site you are downloading from is, it may be better to wait until one download finishes before starting the next. (Using ftp [page 585], you can queue the downloads so they proceed sequentially without intervention.)

Once you have downloaded the four installation ISO files, the MD5 checksum file, and optionally the rescue CD ISO file, the next step is to check that the files are correct. See "Checking the Files," following the next section.

Using BitTorrent to Download the ISO Image Files

You can use BitTorrent (page 478) to obtain the ISO images; BitTorrent is available for Windows and Mac OS X (bitconjurer.org/BitTorrent) so you can download and burn the Fedora CDs on a Windows machine or a Mac. See "BitTorrent" on page 478 for information on using BitTorrent from Linux. You can obtain BitTorrent for Fedora and the tracker for the ISO files from torrent.dulug.duke.edu.

Checking the Files

The **MD5SUM** file contains the *MD5* (page 982) sums for each of the ISO files. When you process a file using the md5sum utility, md5sum generates a number based on the file. If that number matches the corresponding number in the MD5SUM file, the downloaded file is correct:

```
$ grep i386-disc1 MD5SUM; md5sum FC2-i386-disc1.iso
c366d585853768283dac6cdcefcd3a2d  FC2-i386-disc1.iso
c366d585853768283dac6cdcefcd3a2d  FC2-i386-disc1.iso
```

Check each of the ISO images you downloaded in the same manner. Computing an MD5 sum for a large file takes a while. The two long strings that the preceding command displays must be identical: If they are not, you must download the file again.

---

tip || **Test the ISO Files and Test the CDs**

It is a good idea to test the ISO image files when they are downloaded and the burned CDs before you use them to install Red Hat Linux. A bad file on a CD may not show up until you have finished installing Red Hat Linux and have it running. At that point, it may be difficult and time-consuming to figure out where the problem is. Testing the files and CDs takes a few minutes, but can save you hours if something is not right. If you want to do only one test, test the CD.

Burning the CDs

An ISO image file is an exact image of what needs to be on the CD. Putting that image on a CD involves a different process than copying files to a CD. The CD burning software you use has a special selection for burning an ISO image. It will be labeled something similar to **Record CD from CD Image** or **Burn CD Image**. Refer to the instructions for the software you are using for information on how to burn an ISO image file to a CD.

---

tip || **You Need Only to Burn the Rescue CD for a Hard Disk or Network Installation**

If you are installing Linux from files on a hard disk on the target system or from files on another system on a network using FTP, NFS, or HTTP, you need a way to boot the system to begin the installation. The rescue CD (following) or the first installation CD can serve that purpose. Once the system is booted, you have no need for the CDs.

---

tip || **Make Sure the Software Is Set Up to Burn an ISO Image**

Burning an ISO image is not the same as copying files to a CD. As discussed in the text, you must make sure the CD burning software is set up to burn an ISO image. If you simply copy the ISO file to the CD, it will not work to install Fedora.

Rescue CD

The rescue CD cannot do anything the first installation CD cannot do. However, it holds less information so you can download and burn it more quickly than the first installation CD.

Rescue mode You can use the rescue CD to bring a system up in rescue mode. Bringing a system up and working in rescue mode are discussed on page 377.

Hard disk or network installation You can use the rescue CD the same way you use the first installation CD to boot the system to begin a hard disk or network installation: After booting from either CD, give the command **linux askmethod** in response to the **boot:** prompt. See page 45 for more information.

Collecting Information About the System

It is not difficult to install and bring up a Linux system, but the more you know about the process before you start, the easier it is. The installation software collects information about the system and can help you make decisions. However, the system will work better when you know how you want your disk partitioned rather than letting the installation program partition it without your input. The screen will be easier to use if you know what resolution you want. There are many details, and the more details you take control of, the happier you will be with the finished product. Finding the information that this section asks for will help ensure that you end up with a system you understand and know how to change when you need to.

Some of the information is trivial to obtain: When the installation program asks what kind of mouse you have, you can look at it and perhaps turn it over to read the label. More and more, the installation software probes the hardware and figures out what you have. Newer equipment is more likely to report on itself than older equipment is.

It is critical to have certain pieces of information before you start. When you are upgrading Linux from an earlier version, you need to have a list of the disk partitions and where each is mounted so you do not overwrite existing data. One thing Linux can never figure out is all the relevant names and IP addresses (unless you are running DHCP, in which case most of the addresses are set up for you).

Following is a list of items you may need information about. Get as much information on each item as you can: manufacturer, model number, size (megabytes, gigabytes, and so forth), number of buttons, chipset (for boards), and so on. Some items, such as the network interface card (NIC), may be built into the motherboard.

- Hard disks
- CD
- Memory (you don't need it for installation, but it is good to know)
- SCSI interface card

- Network interface card (NIC)
- Video interface card (including the amount of video RAM/memory)
- Sound card and compatibility with standards, such as SoundBlaster
- Mouse (PS/2, USB, AT, and number of buttons)
- Monitor (size, maximum resolution)
- IP addresses and names, unless you are using DHCP (page 408), in which case the IP addresses for the system are dynamically assigned. Most of this information comes from the system administrator or ISP.

  - System hostname (anything you like)

  - System address

  - Network mask (netmask)

  - Gateway address (the connecting point to the network/Internet) or a phone number when you use a dial-up connection

  - Addresses for your nameservers, also called DNS addresses

  - Domain name (not required)

Chapter Summary

When you install Red Hat Linux, you copy operating system files from media to the local system and set up configuration files so that Linux runs properly on the local hardware. You can install Linux from many types of media, including CDs or hard disks, and files on other systems that you access over a network. Operating system files can be stored as directory hierarchies on CDs or a hard disk or as CD (ISO) images on a hard disk. You can use a browser, ftp, or BitTorrent to obtain the ISO images. It is a good idea to test the ISO image files when they are downloaded and the burned CDs before you use them to install Red Hat Linux.

The biggest parts of planning an installation are determining how to divide the hard disk into partitions and deciding which software packages to install. If you are going to want to use SELinux, turn it on when you install Linux (page 44). Because SELinux sets extended attributes on files, it is an involved process to turn on SELinux after you install Linux.

The Fedora Project is sponsored by Red Hat and supported by the open-source community. Fedora Core is a Linux release that tests cutting-edge code; it is not recommended for production environments. Red Hat Enterprise Linux is more stable than Fedora Core.

Exercises

1. Briefly, what does the process of installing an operating system such as Red Hat Linux involve?

2. What is Anaconda?

3. Would you set up a GUI on a server system? Why or why not?

4. A system boots from the hard disk. In order to install Linux, you need it to boot from a CD. How can you get the system to boot from a CD?

5. What is free space on a hard disk? What is a filesystem?

6. What is an ISO image? How do you burn an ISO image to a CD?

Advanced Exercises

7. List two reasons why you should not use RAID in place of backups.

8. What are RAM disks and how are they used during installation?

9. What is MD5? How does it work to ensure that an ISO image file you download is correct?

Step-by-Step Installation

3

Chapter 2 covered planning the installation: requirements, an upgrade versus a clean installation, classes of installations, planning the layout of the hard disk, how to obtain the files you need for the installation including how to download and burn ISO (CD) images, and collecting the information about the system you will need during installation. This chapter steps through the process of installing either Red Hat Enterprise Linux or Fedora Core. Frequently, the installation is quite simple, especially if you have done a good job of planning. Sometimes you may run into a problem or have a special circumstance; this chapter gives you the tools to use in these cases.

Installing Red Hat Linux

To begin most installations, insert the first installation CD into the CD drive and turn on or reset the system. For hard disk and network-based installations, you can use the rescue CD (page 39) in place of the first installation CD.

The system boots from the CD and displays a screen of instructions with a **boot:** prompt at the bottom. Refer to "BIOS setup" on page 25 if the system does not boot from the CD.

You cannot boot from a floppy diskette Because most kernels have grown too large to fit on a floppy diskette, you cannot boot from a floppy. You cannot fit a standard Fedora Core 2 (and later) kernel on a floppy diskette. You may be able to fit some Red Hat Enterprise Linux kernels on a diskette. Fedora gives you the option of booting from a USB pen drive using the **diskboot.img** file.

> **tip ‖**   **Disable SATA Adapters If You Are Not Using SATA**
>
> Many newer motherboards come with SATA (Serial ATA) adapters ready for use. If you do not have
> SATA devices, the presence of these adapters can dramatically lengthen the time it takes the sys-
> tem to boot. Before starting the installation, disable SATA adapters in the BIOS. For more informa-
> tion, refer to "CMOS" on page 25.

Booting the System: The boot: Prompt

Normal installation   You can give many different commands at a **boot:** prompt. If you are installing from
CDs, you can generally press RETURN without entering a command to start installing
Red Hat Linux. Or you can just wait; if you do not type anything for a minute, the
installation proceeds as though you pressed RETURN.

Display problems   If you have problems with the display during installation, give the following command, which turns off video memory, in response to the **boot:** prompt:

```
boot: linux nofb
```

SELinux   By default, Fedora is installed with SELinux (page 379) turned off. Unless you need
a very secure system, you do not need to turn this feature on. Give the following
command to install Fedora with SELinux turned on:

```
boot: linux selinux
```

When you give this command to install Fedora, the Firewall screen allows you to set
up SELinux (Figure 3-5, page 51).

Non-CD installations   If you are installing from other than CDs, that is, if you are installing from files on
the local hard disk or from files on another system using FTP, NFS, or HTTP, give
the following command in response to the **boot:** prompt:

```
boot: linux askmethod
```

Booting   As the system boots, text scrolls on the monitor, pausing occasionally. After a while
(up to a few minutes, depending on the speed of the system), the installer displays a
graphical or pseudographical display, depending on the system you are installing
and the commands you gave at the **boot:** prompt.

The balance of this section covers the commands you can give in response to the
boot: prompt. Unless you are having problems with the installation or have special
requirements, you can skip to the next section, "The Anaconda Installer" on
page 46.

Boot Commands

All the commands (except for **memtest86**) you can give in response to the **boot:**
prompt consist of the word **linux** followed by an argument that is passed to the
Anaconda installer. Many of the commands can be combined. For example, to install Linux in text mode using a terminal running at 115,200 baud, no parity, 8
bits, connected to the first serial device, give the following command (the
,115200n8 is optional):

```
boot: linux text console=ttyS0,115200n8
```

The next command installs Red Hat Linux in graphical mode (by default) on a monitor with a resolution of 1024x768, without probing for any devices. The installation program asks you to specify the source of the installation data (CD, FTP site, or other).

```
boot: linux resolution=1024x768 noprobe askmethod
```

Following are some of the commands you can give at the **boot:** prompt. Each command must be terminated with RETURN.

RETURN   Without entering a command, press RETURN in response to the **boot:** prompt to perform a graphical installation from CDs. This installation probes the computer to determine as much as possible about the hardware.

memtest86   *FEDORA*   Calls memtest86 when you boot from a CD only. The GPL-licensed memtest86 utility is a standalone memory test for x86-based computers. Press **C** to configure the test, ESCAPE to exit. See www.memtest86.com for more information.

linux askmethod   Gives you a choice of installation sources: local CD or hard drive or over a network using NFS, FTP, or HTTP.

- **Local CD**   Displays the CD Found screen, which allows you to test the installation media (the same as if you had just pressed RETURN).

- **Hard drive**   Prompts for the partition and directory that contains the ISO images of the installation CDs.

- **NFS, FTP,** or **HTTP**   Displays the Configure TCP/IP screen from which you can select DHCP or enter the system's IP address, netmask, default gateway (IP), and primary nameserver.

linux lowres   Runs the installation program at a resolution of 640x480. See also **linux resolution**.

linux mem=*xxx*M   Overrides the detected memory size. Replace *xxx* with the number of megabytes of RAM in the computer.

linux mediacheck   Tests one or more installation CDs using an MD5 sum. This option works with the CD, DVD, hard drive ISO, and NFS ISO installation methods. For more information, refer to "Check the CDs" on page 47.

FEDORA   This test is performed automatically during a normal CD installation.

linux nofb   **no framebuffer**   Turns off the framebuffer (video memory). Useful when problems occur when the graphical phase of the installation starts. Particularly useful for systems with LCD displays.

linux noprobe   Disables hardware probing for all devices, including network cards (NICs), graphics cards, and the monitor. Forces you to select devices from a list. You must know exactly which cards or chips the system uses when you use this command. Use when probing causes the installation to hang or otherwise fail. This command allows you to give arguments for each device driver you specify.

Linux rescue   Puts the system in rescue mode; see page 377 for details.

linux resolution=*WxH*   Specifies the resolution of the monitor you are using for a graphical installation. For example, **resolution=1024x768** specifies a monitor with a resolution of 1024 by 768 pixels.

linux selinux   *FEDORA*   Enables SELinux (page 379) on the system you are installing. When you give this command to install Fedora, the Firewall screen allows you to set up SELinux (Figure 3-5, page 51).

linux skipddc   Allows you to configure the monitor manually; see **linux noprobe** for more information.

linux text   Installs Linux using pseudographical mode. Although the images on the screen appear to be graphical, they are composed entirely of text characters.

linux vnc   *FEDORA*   Installs over a VNC (Virtual Network Computing) remote desktop session. After providing an IP address, you can control the installation remotely using a VNC client from a remote computer. You can download the VNC client, which runs on several platforms, from www.realvnc.com.

The Anaconda Installer

Anaconda, the program that installs Red Hat Linux, is written in Python and C, identifies the hardware, builds the filesystems, and installs or upgrades the Red Hat Linux operating system. Anaconda can run in textual or graphical (default) interactive mode or in batch mode (see "Using the Kickstart Configurator" on page 57).

tip ||

Anaconda Does Not Write to the Hard Disk Until It Displays the About to Install Screen

While you are installing Red Hat Linux, until Anaconda displays the About to Install screen, you can press CONTROL-ALT-DEL to abort the installation process and reboot without making any changes to the hard disk.

Exactly which screens Anaconda displays depends on whether you are installing Fedora or Red Hat Enterprise Linux and which command(s) you specified following the **boot:** prompt (preceding). With some exceptions, notably if you are running a text-mode installation, Anaconda starts by probing the video card, monitor, and mouse and by starting a native X server with a log in **/tmp/X.log**. (This log is not preserved unless you complete the installation.)

While it is running, Anaconda opens the virtual consoles (page 103) shown in Table 3-1. You can display a virtual console by pressing CONTROL-ALT-F*x* where F*x* is the function key that corresponds to the virtual console number.

At any time during the installation, you can go virtual console 2 (CONTROL-ALT-F2) and give commands to see what is going on. Do not give any commands that change any part of the installation procedure.

table 3-1 ‖	Virtual Console Assignments During Installation
1	Installation dialog
2	Shell
3	Installation log
4	System messages
5	Miscellaneous messages
7	GUI interactive installation

Using Anaconda

Anaconda provides a NEXT button at the lower-right of each of the installation screens and a BACK button next to it on most screens. When you have completed the entries on an installation screen, click **NEXT**, or, from a text install, press the TAB key until the NEXT button is highlighted and then press RETURN. Select **BACK** to return to the previous screen.

Initially, each of the graphical installation screens is divided into two columns: a narrow help column on the left and information and prompts about the installation on the right. Select the **Hide Help** button (lower-left) to remove the help column. Select **Release Notes** (next to Hide Help) to display the release notes for the version of Red Hat Linux you are installing.

caution ‖	Check the CDs

FEDORA   Because Red Hat does not manufacture Fedora disks, during a CD-based Fedora installation, Anaconda displays the pseudographical CD Found screen before starting the installation. From this screen, you can verify that the installation CDs do not have any errors. Checking the CDs takes a few minutes and can save you hours of aggravation if the installation fails due to bad media.

RHEL+FEDORA   You can force the display of the CD Found screen by giving the command **linux mediacheck** in response to the **boot:** prompt (page 45).

Anaconda Screens

Following is a list of screens that Anaconda displays during a default installation. It may display different screens depending on what commands you give and choices you make.

CD Found   *FEDORA*   Allows you to check as many installation CDs as you like, in any order. Choose **OK** to test the media, **Skip** to bypass the test. See the preceding TIP. This screen is displayed in pseudotext mode and does not appear in two columns. Use the TAB key to move between choices; press RETURN to select the highlighted choice.

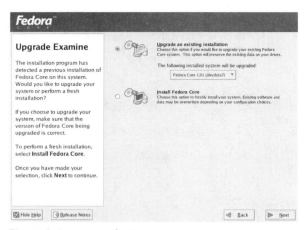

Figure 3-1   Upgrade Examine screen

During a graphical installation, when you leave the CD Found screen, Anaconda displays messages telling you it is probing for the devices it will use during installation. After probing, it starts the X server.

Welcome   Displayed after Anaconda obtains enough information to start the X Window System. There is nothing for you to do on this screen except hide the help panel and display the release notes. Select **NEXT**.

Language Selection   Select the language you want to use for the installation. This language is not necessarily the same language that the installed system displays.

Keyboard Configuration   Select the type of keyboard attached to the system.

Mouse   Displayed only if the type of mouse cannot be determined. Select the type of mouse attached to the system. Mark the **Emulate 3 buttons** box if you have a two-button mouse and want the system to respond as though you had pressed the middle button when you press the two mouse buttons at the same time.

Monitor   *FEDORA*   Displayed only if the monitor cannot be probed successfully. Select the brand and model of the monitor attached to the system. Select a generic LCD or CRT display if the monitor is not listed. You can specify the Sync frequencies in place of the monitor brand and model, but be careful: Specifying the wrong values can ruin some older hardware.

Upgrade Examine   If it detects a version of Red Hat Linux on the hard disk that it can upgrade, Anaconda gives you the choice of upgrading the existing installation or overwriting the existing installation with a new one (Figure 3-1). Refer to "Installing a Fresh Copy or Upgrading an Existing Red Hat System?" on page 26 for help in making this selection.

Installation Type   *FEDORA*   Select the type of installation you want (Figure 3-2): Personal Desktop, Workstation, Server, or Custom. Refer to "Types of Installations (**FEDORA**)" on page 27 for help in answering this question.

Figure 3-2   Installation Type screen

Disk Partitioning Setup   Select Automatically partition or Manually partition with Disk Druid. The automatic selection gives you the option of reviewing and changing the partitions Anaconda sets up. For more information, refer to "Using Disk Druid to Partition the Disk" on page 53.

Boot Loader Configuration   By default, Anaconda installs the grub boot loader (page 514). If you do not want to install a boot loader, click **Change boot loader** and select **Do not install a boot loader.** When you install Red Hat Linux on a machine that already runs another operating system, Anaconda frequently recognizes the other operating system and sets up grub so you can boot from either operating system. Refer to "Setting Up a Dual-Boot System" on page 61. You can manually add other operating systems to grub's list of bootable systems by clicking **Add** and specifying a label and device to boot from. For a more secure system, specify a boot loader password.

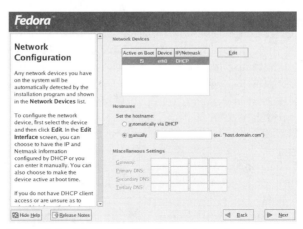

Figure 3-3   Network Configuration window

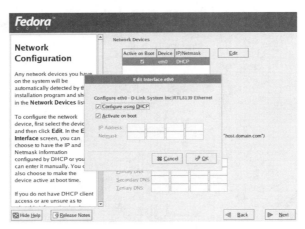

Figure 3-4   Network Configuration: Edit Interface window

Network Configuration   Specify network configuration information (Figure 3-3). This screen has three frames: Network Devices, Hostname, and Miscellaneous Settings. If you are using DHCP to set up the network interface, you do not need to change anything.

The Network Devices frame lists the network devices the installer knows about. Normally, you want network devices to become active when the system boots; remove the mark from the check box at the left of a device if you do *not* want it to become active when the system boots.

To configure a network device manually (not using DHCP), highlight the device and click **Edit** to the right of the list of devices. Anaconda displays the Edit Interface window (Figure 3-4). Remove the mark from the Configure using DHCP check box and enter the IP address and netmask in the appropriate boxes before clicking **OK**.

If you are not using DHCP, click **manually** under Set the hostname and enter the name of the system. When you turn off DHCP configuration in Network Devices, Anaconda allows you to specify a gateway address, and one or more DNS (nameserver) addresses. You do not have to specify more than one DNS address, although it can be useful to have two in case one nameserver stops working. Click **Next**.

Firewall   Set up a firewall (Figure 3-5). First, select **No firewall** or **Enable firewall**. If you select Enable firewall, select the services that you want the firewall to allow to pass through to the system. Selecting WWW (HTTP) does not allow HTTPS (secure HTTP), which is used for secure browser connections to financial institutions and when giving credit card information, through the firewall. Specify **https:tcp** in **Other ports** to allow secure HTTP to pass. If you have multiple network devices (one of which may be a dial-up line), you may want to consider one of them to be trusted. Never trust a device connected to the Internet. Put a mark in the check box next to any trusted devices in the box labeled **If you would like to allow all traffic from a device, select it below.** If Anaconda displays the SELinux combo box shown

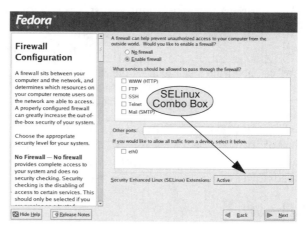

Figure 3-5 Firewall Configuration screen showing SELinux combo box

in Figure 3-5, select the state you want SELinux (page 379) to be in when you start the system. The chapter on iptables (page 737) has information on how to build a more complete and functional firewall.

Additional Language Support — Select languages that the installed system will support. The default language is the language the system will boot up in. Select as many other languages as you like from the list.

Time Zone — Specify the time zone the system is located in. Click on a location on the map or scroll through the list and highlight the appropriate selection. Put a mark in the check box if your system clock is set to *UTC* (page 1004).

Root Password — Specify the **root** password.

After you specify the **root** password, Anaconda pauses to read the software package information.

Package Installation Defaults — In this screen, Anaconda lists the packages it will install by default. Choose **Install default software packages** to install this list of packages or **Customize software packages to be installed** to modify the list. Regardless of your selection, you can change which packages are installed on a system at any time; refer to "system-config-packages: Adds and Removes Software Packages" on page 453.

caution || **Install KDE to Follow the Examples in Chapter 4**

Chapter 4, "Introduction to Red Hat Linux," uses examples from KDE to introduce the graphical desktop. Install KDE if you want to follow these examples. You can remove KDE later if you like.

Package Group Selection — If you choose to accept the default list of software packages (previous screen), Anaconda skips this screen. Select the groups and packages you want to install. For more information, refer to "system-config-packages: Adds and Removes Software Packages" on page 453.

About to Install   Anaconda displays the About to Install screen just before it starts installing Red Hat Linux on the hard disk.

caution ‖   **This Is When Anaconda Writes to the Hard Disk**

You can abort the installation by pressing CONTROL-ALT-DEL at any point up to and including this screen without making any changes to the system. Once you press **NEXT** in the About to Install screen, Anaconda writes to the hard disk.

Installing   After you press **NEXT**, Anaconda installs Red Hat Linux. Depending on the number of software packages you are installing, this process can take quite a while. Anaconda keeps you informed of its progress and requests CDs (if you are installing from CDs) as it needs them.

When You Reboot

When Anaconda instructs you to do so, remove the installation CD if present and reboot the system. The system boots Red Hat Linux and asks a few questions before allowing you to log in.

License Agreement   First, Anaconda displays the Welcome screen, followed by the License Agreement screen. Select **Yes I agree to the License Agreement** if you agree with the terms of the licence agreement.

Date and time   The next screen allows you to set the date and time. Running the Network Time Protocol (NTP) causes the system clock to reset itself periodically from a clock on the Internet. If the system is connected to the Internet, you may want to select **Enable Network Time Protocol** and choose a server from the combo box.

Display   Next, Anaconda displays the Display screen, which allows you to specify the resolution and color depth of the monitor.

User Account   The next screen allows you to set up user accounts. You can set up user accounts now or once the system is fully operational. For more information, refer to "Configuring User and Group Accounts" on page 521.

Sound Card   The Sound Card window identifies the sound card and has a button that can play a test sound. There is nothing that you can configure from the Sound Card window.

Additional CDs   Next, the system asks if you have additional CDs for installing more software packages.

Finish Setup   Finally, from the Finish Setup screen, click **NEXT** to complete the setup and display the login screen.

When you leave the Finish Setup screen, you are done with the installation. You can use the system and set it up as you desire. You may want to customize the desktop as explained in Chapters 4 and 8 or set up servers as discussed in Part V of this book.

Initializing Databases

After booting the system, log in as, or su to, **root** and update the **whatis** database so that whatis (page 137) and apropos (page 137) work properly. Then update the slocate database so that slocate works properly. (The slocate [secure locate] utility allows you to index and search for files on your system quickly and securely.) Instead of updating these databases when you install the system, you can wait for cron to run them overnight, but whatis, apropos, and slocate will not work until the next day. The best way to update these databases is to run the cron scripts that run them daily. Working as **root**, give the following commands:

```
# /etc/cron.daily/makewhatis.cron
# /etc/cron.daily/slocate.cron
```

These utilities run for up to several minutes and may complain about not being able to find a file or two. When you get the prompt back, your **whatis** and **slocate** databases are up-to-date.

Installation Tasks

This section details some common tasks you may need to perform during or after installation. It covers using Disk Druid to partition the disk during installation, using fdisk to modify partitions after installation, using Kickstart to automate installation, and setting up a system that will boot either Windows or Linux (a dual boot system).

Using Disk Druid to Partition the Disk

Disk Druid, a graphical disk-partitioning program that can add, delete, and modify partitions on a hard drive, is part of the Red Hat installation system. You can use Disk Druid only while you are installing a system: It cannot be run on its own. You can use fdisk (page 58) to manipulate partitions after you install Red Hat Linux. As explained earlier, if you want a basic set of partitions, you can allow Disk Druid to partition the hard drive automatically.

Clone and RAID Disk Druid includes Clone, a tool that copies the partitioning scheme from a single drive to as many other drives as needed. The Clone option is useful for making multiple copies of a RAID partition/drive when you are creating a large RAID array of identical partitions or identically partitioned drives. Click the **RAID** button to access the Clone tool, which is active only when at least one unallocated RAID partition exists.

Disk Partitioning Setup During installation, the Disk Partitioning Setup screen gives you the choice between automatically and manually partitioning the hard disk. Choose automatic partitioning if you do not want to make any decisions about how to split up the hard disk.

Automatic Partitioning The Automatic Partitioning screen gives you the following choices:

- **Remove all Linux partitions**   Removes all Linux partitions, deleting the data on those partitions and creating one or more chunks of *free space* (page 972) on the disk. You can create new partitions using the free space.

If there is only a Linux system on the disk, this choice is the same as the next one.

- **Remove all partitions**   Deletes all the data on the disk and gives you a free space the size of the disk to work with, as though you were working with a new drive.

- **Keep all partitions and use existing free space**   Forces you to install Red Hat Linux in the free space on the disk. Does not work if there is not enough, free space.

tip ‖   **The Disk Is Not Partitioned Until Later**

Disk Druid does not write to the hard disk; it creates a table that specifies how you want the hard disk partitioned. The disk is partitioned and formatted when you click **Next** from the About to Install screen.

Choosing automatic partitioning causes anaconda to split the free space, if possible, into three partitions: **/boot** (about 100 megabytes), swap (up to a few thousand megabytes), and **/** (root), which gets the bulk of the disk space.

The Automatic Partitioning screen has a frame that allows you to choose the hard disk you want to install Red Hat Linux on. This frame has meaning only if you have more than one hard disk. At the bottom of the screen is a check box, **Review (and modify if needed) the partitions created.** Put a check mark in this box to display the initial Disk Druid window (Figure 3-6) when you click **Next.**

Disk Setup   When you choose to partition the hard disk manually, Anaconda displays the Disk Setup screen, which is the Disk Druid main screen, shown in Figure 3-6 with the Help column hidden. This screen has three sections, from the top: a graphical representation of the disk drive(s) showing how each is partitioned, a row of command buttons, and a graphical table listing one partition per line. If you are starting with a new disk, no partitions are listed on the screen.

The row of command buttons has the following buttons:

- **New**   Adds a new partition to the disk (page 55).
- **Edit**   Edits the highlighted partition (page 56).
- **Delete**   Deletes the highlighted partition.
- **Reset**   Cancels the changes you have made and causes the Disk Druid table to revert so it matches the layout of the disk.
- **RAID**   Enables you to create software RAID partitions and to join two or more RAID partitions into a RAID device (page 31).
- **LVM**   Enables you to create LVM physical volumes, which you can then use to create LVM logical volumes (page 32).

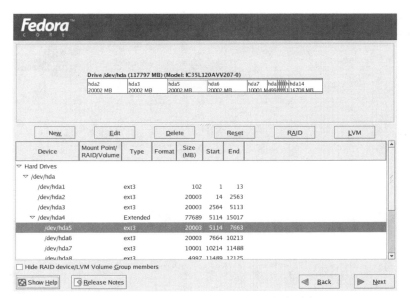

Figure 3-6   Disk Druid: Main screen with Help hidden

The Disk Druid table has the following columns:

- **Device**   The name of the device in the **/dev** directory (for example, **/dev/hda1**).

- **Mount Point/RAID/Volume**   Specified where the partition will be mounted when the system is brought up (for example, **/usr**). Also used to specify the RAID device or LVM volume the partition is part of.

- **Type**   The type of partition, such as ext3, swap, or LVM.

- **Format**   A check mark in this column indicates the partition will be formatted as part of the installation procedure. All data on the partition will be lost.

- **Size**   The size of the partition in megabytes.

- **Start**   The number of the block the partition starts on.

- **End**   The number of the block the partition ends on.

At the bottom of the screen is a check box that allows you to hide RAID device and LVM volume group members. Do not check this box if you want to see all the information about the disk drives.

Add a new partition   In order to add a new partition to a hard drive, there must be enough free space on the hard drive to accommodate the partition. Click the **New** button to add a partition; Disk Druid displays the Add Partition window (Figure 3-7). Specify the mount

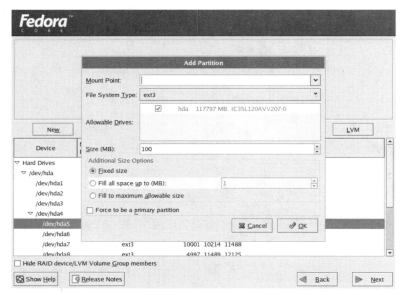

Figure 3-7 Disk Druid: Add Partition window

point (the name of the directory that the partition will be mounted over [page 442]) and the filesystem type; use the arrow buttons at the right end of these text boxes to display drop-down menus of choices. If there is more than one drive, mark the check box next to the drive you want the partition to be created on in the Allowable Drives frame. Specify the desired size of the partition and, in the Additional Size Options frame, mark **Fixed size** to create the partition close to the size you specify. Because of block-size constraints, partitions are not usually exactly the size you specify. Mark **Fill all space up to** (**MB**) and fill in the maximum size you want the partition to be to create a partition that takes up the existing free space, up to the maximum size you specify. In other words, Disk Druid does not complain if it cannot create the partition as large as you would like. Mark the third choice, **Fill to maximum allowable size**, to cause the partition to occupy all the remaining free space on the disk, regardless of size. Mark the **Force to be a primary partition** check box to create a primary partition. Click **OK**, and Disk Druid adds the partition to its table (but does not write to the hard disk).

Edit an existing partition

To modify an existing partition, highlight the partition in the Disk Druid table or the graphical representation of the disk drive and click the **Edit** button; Disk Druid displays the Edit Partition window (Figure 3-8). From this window, you can change the mount point of a partition or format the partition as another type (ext3, vfat, swap, and so on). You cannot change the size of a partition from this window; instead, you must delete the partition and create a new partition of the desired size.

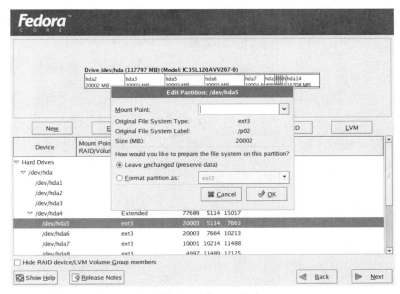

Figure 3-8   Disk Druid: Edit Partition window

Using the Kickstart Configurator

Kickstart is Red Hat's program that completely or partially automates the same installation and postinstallation configuration on one or more machines. You create a single file that answers all the questions that are normally asked during an installation. Then the installation script refers to this file instead of asking you the questions. Using Kickstart, you can automate language selection, network configuration, keyboard selection, boot loader installation, disk partitioning, mouse selection, X Window System configuration, and more.

The system-config-kickstart (*FEDORA*) and redhat-config-kickstart (*RHEL*) utilities run the Kickstart Configurator (Figure 3-9), which creates a Kickstart installation script.

Figure 3-9 shows the first window the Kickstart Configurator displays. The first text box, Language, is the language that will be used for installation. The Language Support box, toward the bottom of the window, is the language that the new system will use after installation.

To generate a Kickstart file (**ks.cfg** by default), go through each section of this window (along the left side) and fill in the answers and mark the appropriate boxes. Click the **Help** button for instructions on completing these tasks. When you are finished and click **Save File**, the Kickstart Configurator gives you a chance to review the generated script before it saves the file.

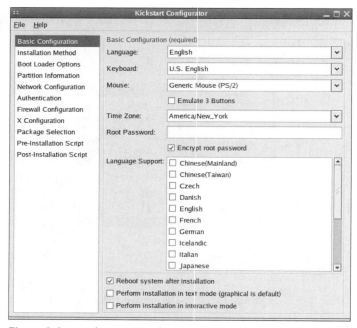

Figure 3-9   Kickstart Configurator

fdisk: **Reports On and Partitions a Hard Disk**

The fdisk utility reports on and manipulates hard disk partitions. You can display the size (in 1024-byte blocks) of a hard disk by using the fdisk with the –s option followed by the device name of the hard drive:

```
# fdisk -s /dev/hda
12714912
```

Run fdisk with the –l option to display information about partitions on the drives you specify:

```
# /sbin/fdisk -l /dev/hda

Disk /dev/hda: 123.5 GB, 123522416640 bytes
255 heads, 63 sectors/track, 15017 cylinders
Units = cylinders of 16065 * 512 = 8225280 bytes

    Device Boot    Start       End    Blocks   Id  System
/dev/hda1    *        1        13    104391   83  Linux
/dev/hda2            14      2563  20482875   83  Linux
/dev/hda3          2564      5113  20482875   83  Linux
/dev/hda4          5114     15017  79553880    f  Win95 Ext'd (LBA)
/dev/hda5          5114      7663  20482843+  83  Linux
/dev/hda6          7664     10213  20482843+  83  Linux
/dev/hda7         10214     11488  10241406   83  Linux
```

```
/dev/hda8      11489    12125    5116671    83  Linux
/dev/hda9      12126    12252    1020096    83  Linux
/dev/hda10     12253    12379    1020096    83  Linux
/dev/hda11     12380    12506    1020096    83  Linux
/dev/hda12     12507    12633    1020096    83  Linux
/dev/hda13     12634    12887    2040223+   82  Linux swap
/dev/hda14     12888    15017   17109193+   8e  Linux LVM
```

In the preceding output, **/dev/hda4** is an extended partition (page 28), **/dev/hda13** is a swap partition (page 435), and **/dev/hda14** specifies a part of the disk that is managed by LVM (page 32).

In addition to reporting on the layout and size of a disk drive, you can use fdisk interactively to modify the layout. Be *extremely* careful when using fdisk in this manner, and always back up the system before starting. Changing the partition information (the *partition table*) on a disk destroys the information on the disk. Read the fdisk man page and the *Linux Partition mini-HOWTO* before modifying a partition table.

caution ‖   fdisk **Can Destroy Everything**

Be as careful with fdisk as you would be with a utility that formats a hard drive. Changes you make with fdisk can easily result in the loss of large amounts of data. If you are using fdisk and have any question about what you are doing, back out with **q** (quit without saving changes)—your changes do not take effect until you exit from fdisk.

To partition a disk, start fdisk without any options and give an **m** command, which displays the following help message. You can safely ignore a warning message about the number of cylinders being too large.

```
# /sbin/fdisk /dev/hda

Command (m for help): m
Command action
    a    toggle a bootable flag
    b    edit bsd disklabel
    c    toggle the dos compatibility flag
    d    delete a partition
    l    list known partition types
    m    print this menu
    n    add a new partition
    o    create a new empty DOS partition table
    p    print the partition table
    q    quit without saving changes
    s    create a new empty Sun disklabel
    t    change a partition's system id
    u    change display/entry units
    v    verify the partition table
    w    write table to disk and exit
    x    extra functionality (experts only)
```

When you choose **p** (print), fdisk displays the current partitions on the disk:

```
Command (m for help): p
Disk /dev/hda: 123.5 GB, 123522416640 bytes
255 heads, 63 sectors/track, 15017 cylinders
Units = cylinders of 16065 * 512 = 8225280 bytes
   Device Boot    Start      End     Blocks   Id  System
/dev/hda1    *        1       13     104391   83  Linux
/dev/hda2            14     2563   20482875   83  Linux
/dev/hda3          2564     5113   20482875   83  Linux
/dev/hda4          5114    15017   79553880    f  Win95 Ext'd (LBA)
/dev/hda5          5114     7663  20482843+   83  Linux
/dev/hda6          7664    10213  20482843+   83  Linux
/dev/hda7         10214    11488   10241406   83  Linux
/dev/hda8         11489    12125    5116671   83  Linux
/dev/hda9         12126    12252    1020096   83  Linux
/dev/hda10        12253    12379    1020096   83  Linux
/dev/hda11        12380    12506    1020096   83  Linux
/dev/hda12        12507    12633    1020096   83  Linux
/dev/hda13        12634    12887   2040223+   82  Linux swap
/dev/hda14        12888    15017  17109193+   8e  Linux LVM
```

Each disk entry includes the filename within the **/dev** directory, the cylinders the partition starts and ends on (use **u** to change the units to sectors), the number of 1024 (1 kilobyte) blocks, the ID number of the partition type (l [ell] lists the partition types), and the name of the partition type.

In the preceding example partition 4 defines an extended partition that includes almost the entire disk. You cannot make changes to this partition without affecting all the partitions within it. Following are guidelines to remember when defining a partition table for a disk. For more information, refer to "Partitioning a Disk" on page 29.

- Do not modify the partition that defines the entire disk. This partition is called the **backup**, or **overlap**, partition.

- Do not overlap partitions that contain data. If the first partition ends at cylinder 187, the second partition should begin at cylinder 188. If you overlap partitions, the filesystem will become corrupt as data for overlapping files is written to the disk. Because the overlap partition contains no data or filesystem, it is safe to have other partitions overlap it.

- Never put a raw partition on cylinder 0. A few sectors on cylinder 0 are reserved for such things as the disk label, bad blocks, and partition tables. A filesystem will preserve this information, but when you use cylinder 0 as part of a raw partition, this information is deleted, and the disk may become unusable. An example of a raw partition is a swap partition (page 435) or raw database partition, as used for a Sybase or Oracle database. Start all raw partitions at cylinder 1 or greater.

- It is a good idea to put **/boot** at the beginning of the drive (partition 1) so that there is no issue of Linux having to boot from a partition too far into the drive. When you can afford the disk space, it is desirable to put each major filesystem on a separate partition. Many people choose to combine root, **/var**, and **/usr** into a single partition, which generally results in less wasted space but can, on rare occasions, cause problems. You can also put the contents of the **boot** directory in the root filesystem.

- When using megabytes to specify the size of a partition, remember to check how many cylinders have been allocated so you know where to begin the next partition.
- Use tune2fs (page 447) to make all partitions, except swap and **/boot,** type ext3, unless you have a reason to do otherwise.

The following sequence of commands defines a 300 megabyte, bootable, Linux partition as partition 1 on a clean disk:

```
# /sbin/fdisk /dev/hda

Command (m for help): n            (create new partition)
Command action
   l    logical (5 or over)
   p    primary partition (1-4)
p                                  (select primary partition)
Partition number (1-4): 1          (select partition number 1)
First cylinder (1-1582, default 1):    (allow first cylinder to default to 1)
Using default value 1
Last cylinder or +size or +sizeM or +sizeK (1-2, default 2): +300M  (300 MB partition)
Command (m for help): t            (set partition type)
Partition number (1-12): 1         (specify which partition)
Hex code (type L to list codes): 83    (83 is Linux, 82 is Linux swap, press L for a list)
Changed system type of partition 1 to 83

Command (m for help): a            (specify a bootable partition)
Partition number (1-12): 1         (specify partition 1 as bootable)
```

After defining a partition using **k** or **m** to specify kilobytes or megabytes, run **p** to check for the ending cylinder. Do this before defining the next contiguous partition so that you do not waste space or have any overlap. After setting up all the partitions and exiting from fdisk with a **w** command, make a filesystem (mkfs, page 397) on each partition that is to hold a filesystem (not swap). Use mkswap (page 435) to create a swap partition. You can use e2label (page 396) to label partitions.

Setting Up a Dual-Boot System

caution || **Windows and Dual Boot**

Installing Fedora Core 2 in dual boot configurations with Windows XP or 2K can result in the Windows partition becoming inaccessible. The problem is caused when Anaconda modifies the partition table in the master boot record (MBR). THIS PROBLEM CAN OCCUR EVEN WHEN YOU DO NOT MODIFY THE PARTITION TABLE.

Please check the Fedora site (fedora.redhat.com) and the author's Web page (www.sobell.com) for the latest information.

A dual-boot system is one that can boot one of two operating systems. Dual-boot in this section refers to a system that can boot Windows or Linux. The biggest problem in setting up a dual-boot system, assuming you want to add Linux to a Windows system, is finding disk space for Linux. The Linux+WindowsNT mini-HOWTO covers installing Linux first and Windows NT second or the other way around. The next section discusses several ways to create the needed space.

Creating Free Space on a Windows System

Typically, you install Red Hat Linux in free space on a hard disk. In order to add Red Hat Linux to a Windows system, you must provide enough free space (refer to "Disk space" on page 25) on a hard disk that already contains Windows. There are several ways to provide/create free space. Following are some ways, from easiest to most difficult:

Use existing free space If there is sufficient free space on the Windows disk, you can install Linux there. This technique is best, but there is rarely enough free space on an installed hard disk.

Add a new disk drive Add another disk drive to the system and install Linux on the new disk, which contains only free space. This technique is very easy and clean but requires a new disk drive.

Remove a Windows partition If you can delete a big enough Windows partition, you can install Linux in its place. In order to delete a Windows partition, you must have multiple partitions under Windows and be willing to lose any data in the partition you delete. In many cases, you can move the data from the partition you delete to another Windows partition.

Once you are sure a partition contains no useful information, you can use Disk Druid to delete it when you install Linux: From the Disk Partition screen (page 49), choose to partition the disk with Disk Druid manually, highlight the partition you want to delete, and click the **Delete** button. After deleting the partition, you can install Red Hat Linux in the free space left by the partition you removed.

Installing Red Hat Linux as the Second Operating System

After creating enough free space on a Windows system (previous section), start installing Red Hat Linux. When you get to the Disk Partitioning Setup screen (page 49), you must choose manual partitioning if you need to delete a Windows partition. You can choose either automatic or manual partitioning if you already have free space to install Red Hat Linux in. If you partition the disk automatically, choose to keep all partitions and install Red Hat Linux in free space (page 27). If you partition the disk manually, use Disk Druid (page 53) to delete the appropriate Windows partition if necessary and create the Red Hat Linux partitions in the free space. When you boot, you will be able to choose which operating system you want to run.

The X Window System

With the introduction of Fedora Core 2, Red Hat replaced the XFree86 X Window System with the X.org Foundation X11R6.7.0 X Window System (X.org and freedesktop.org). The X.org X server is functionally equivalent to the one distributed by XFree86 because most of the code is the same. See "XFree86 and X.org" on page 218 for more information on the transition. For more information on the X.org release of X, go to freedesktop.org/~xorg/X11R6.7.0/doc/RELNOTES.html. Red Hat Enterprise Linux and Fedora Core 1 use XFree86.

---

tip ‖   **The XF86Config and xorg.conf Files**

The X Window System configuration files are kept in the **/etc/X11** directory. Under XFree86 (Fedora Core 1 and Red Hat Enterprise Linux), the primary configuration file is named **XF86Config**; under X.org (Fedora Core 2 and later), the file is named **xorg.conf**. They are basically the same file with two names. If X.org does not find **xorg.conf**, it uses **XF86Config**.

If you have an **XF86Config** file you want to move to Fedora Core 2, copy it and rename it **xorg.conf**.

If you specified any kind of graphical desktop, such as GNOME or KDE, you installed X.org or XFree86 when you installed Linux. X.org and XFree86 each comprise almost twenty rpm packages; the easiest way to install X.org or XFree86 on an already installed Linux system is to use [system|redhat]-config-packages (page 453).

Most of the X software is installed under the **/usr/X11R6** directory. The **/usr/X11R6/bin** directory contains the utilities that are part of X and makes interesting browsing. This directory contains most of the utilities whose names begin with **x**, such as xterm, xmag, and xeyes. The configuration files are kept in **/etc/X11**; the file used to guide the initial setup is **/etc/X11/xorg.conf** (FEDORA) or **/etc/X11/XF86Config** (RHEL).

system-config-display: Configuring the Display

The easiest way to configure X.org or XFree86 is to run system-config-display (FEDORA) or redhat-config-xfree86 (RHEL), both of which display the Display settings window. The two utilities display different windows, with redhat-config-xfree86 offering a subset of the options offered by system-config-display. This section explains how to use system-config-display. The redhat-config-xfree86 Display and Advanced tabs display the same information as the system-config-display Settings and Hardware tabs respectively.

Figure 3-10 shows the Settings tab of the Display settings window where you can specify the resolution and color depth for the monitor. Normally, the system probes the monitor and fills in these values. If not, check the specifications for the monitor and select the appropriate values from these combo boxes. It is all right to specify a lower resolution than a monitor is capable of, but you can damage an older monitor by specifying a resolution higher than the monitor is capable of. A color depth of 8 bits equates to 256 colors, 16 bits to thousands of colors, and 24 or 32 bits to millions of colors.

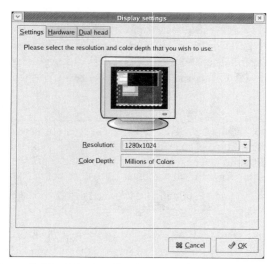

Figure 3-10   Display Settings window, Settings tab

Next, click the Hardware tab. Again, the system normally probes for the monitor type and brand and model of video card; these values appear next to the words **Monitor Type** and **Video Card**. You can manually select a monitor or video card. Figure 3-11 shows the Monitor selection window superimposed on the Hardware tab of the Display settings window.

Specify a monitor   To specify a monitor, click **Configure** across from the words **Monitor Type**; system-config-display displays the Monitor window. Scroll down until you see the manufacturer of monitor you are using and click the triangle to the left of the name of the manufacturer; system-config-display opens a list of models made by that manufacturer. Scroll through the list of models. Click to highlight the model you are using; click **OK**. If an appropriate model is not listed, scroll to the top of the list and click the triangle next to Generic CRT Display or Generic LCD Display, depending on the type of display you are setting up. From one of these lists, select the maximum resolution your monitor is capable of. Click **OK**.

Specify a video card   To specify a video card, click **Configure** adjacent to the words **Video Card**; system-config-display displays the Video Card window. Scroll down until you see the manufacturer and model of the video card in your system. Click **OK**.

Specify two monitors   The Dual head tab allows you to specify a second video card that can drive a second monitor. Specify the monitor type, video card, resolution, and color depth as you did earlier. You can choose to have each monitor display a desktop or to have the two monitors display a single desktop (spanning desktops). Click **OK** to close the Display settings window.

The system-config-display utility generates an **xorg.conf** (*FEDORA*) or **XF86Config** (*RHEL*) file (next section) with the information you entered.

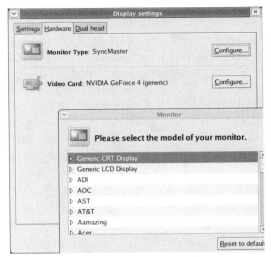

Figure 3-11   Display Settings window, Hardware tab

The xorg.conf and XF86Config Files

The **xorg.conf** (*FEDORA*) and **XF86Config** (*RHEL*) files comprise sections that can appear in any order. The format of a section is

> *Section "name"*
>   *entry*
>   *...*
> *EndSection*

where ***name*** is the name of the section. A typical ***entry*** occupies multiple physical lines but is actually one logical line, consisting of a keyword followed by zero or more integer, real, or string arguments. Keywords in these files are not case sensitive and underscores (_) within keywords are ignored. Most strings are not case sensitive and SPACEs and underscores in most strings are ignored. All strings must appear within double quotation marks.

The Option keyword provides free-form data to server components and is followed by the name of the option and optionally a value. All Option values must be enclosed within double quotation marks.

Boolean Options take a value of **TRUE** (**1, on, true, yes**) or **FALSE** (**0, off, false, no**); no value is the same as **TRUE**. You can prepend **No** to the name of a Boolean Option to reverse the sense of the Option.

The sections that can appear in an **xorg.conf** or **XF86Config** file are

ServerFlags	Global Options (optional)
ServerLayout	Binds Screen(s) and InputDevice(s)

Files	Locations of configuration files
Module	Modules to be loaded (optional)
InputDevice	Keyboard(s) and pointer(s)
Monitor	Monitor(s)
Device	Video card(s)
Screen	Binds device(s) and monitor(s)
VideoAdaptor	Configures the Xv extension (optional)
Modes	Video modes (optional)
DRI	Direct Rendering Infrastructure (optional)
Vendor	Vendor-specific information (optional)

This chapter covers the sections you most likely need to work with: ServerLayout, InputDevice, Monitor, Device, and Screen. The excerpts from the **xorg.conf** file used in this chapter come from a file generated by system-config-display.

ServerLayout

The ServerLayout section appears first in some **xorg.conf** and **XF86Config** files because it summarizes the other sections that are used to specify the server. The following ServerLayout section names the server **single head configuration** and specifies that the server comprises the sections named Screen0, Mouse0, Keyboard0, and DevInputMice.

The term *core* in this file means *primary;* there must be exactly one CoreKeyboard and one CorePointer. The AlwaysCore argument indicates that the device reports core events and is used here to allow a non-USB and a USB mouse to work at the same time. The result is that you can use either type of mouse interchangeably without modifying the **xorg.conf** or **XF86Config** file:

```
Section "ServerLayout"
        Identifier  "single head configuration"
        Screen    0  "Screen0" 0 0
        InputDevice "Mouse0" "CorePointer"
        InputDevice "Keyboard0" "CoreKeyboard"
        InputDevice "DevInputMice" "AlwaysCore"
EndSection
```

Refer to the following sections for explanations of the sections specified in Server-Layout.

InputDevice

There must be at least two InputDevice sections: one specifying the keyboard and one specifying the pointer (usually a mouse). The format of an InputDevice section is

Section "InputDevice"
    *Identifier "**id_name**"*
    *Driver "**drv_name**"*
    options

    ...
EndSection

where **id_name** is a unique name for the device and **drv_name** is the driver to use for the device, typically **keyboard** or **mouse**. The system-config-display and redhat-config-xfree86 utilities typically create three InputDevice sections. The following section defines a keyboard device named Keyboard0 that uses the **keyboard** driver. The keyboard model is a 105-key PC keyboard. You can change **pc105** to **microsoft** if you are using a US Microsoft Natural keyboard, although the differences are minimal. See www.xfree86.org/current/XKB-Config.html for a complete list of keyboard (XKB) options.

```
Section "InputDevice"
        Identifier  "Keyboard0"
        Driver      "keyboard"
        Option      "XkbModel" "pc105"
        Option      "XkbLayout" "us"
EndSection
```

To change the language the keyboard supports, change the argument to the XkbLayout Option to, for example, **fr** for French.

The next InputDevice section defines a mouse named Mouse0 that uses the **mouse** driver. The Device Option specifies a PS2 device. The ZAxisMapping Option maps the Z axis, the mouse wheel, to virtual mouse buttons 4 and 5 that are used to scroll a window. For more information, refer to "Remapping Mouse Buttons" on page 223. When set to YES, the Emulate3Buttons Option enables the user of a two-button mouse to emulate a 3-button mouse by pressing the two buttons simultaneously. See www.xfree86.org/current/mouse.html for a complete list of mouse options.

```
Section "InputDevice"
        Identifier  "Mouse0"
        Driver      "mouse"
        Option      "Protocol" "IMPS/2"
        Option      "Device" "/dev/psaux"
        Option      "ZAxisMapping" "4 5"
        Option      "Emulate3Buttons" "no"
EndSection
```

The next InputDevice section is similar to the previous one except the Device Option specifies a USB mouse. See "ServerLayout" on page 66 for a discussion.

```
Section "InputDevice"

# If the normal CorePointer mouse is not a USB mouse then
```

```
# this input device can be used in AlwaysCore mode to let you
# also use USB mice at the same time.
        Identifier  "DevInputMice"
        Driver      "mouse"
        Option      "Protocol" "IMPS/2"
        Option      "Device" "/dev/input/mice"
        Option      "ZAxisMapping" "4 5"
        Option      "Emulate3Buttons" "no"
EndSection
```

Monitor

The **xorg.conf** and **XF86Config** files must have at least one Monitor section. The easiest way to set up this section is to use the system-config-display or redhat-config-xfree86 utility, which either determines the type of monitor automatically by probing or allows you to select from a list of monitors.

caution ‖	**Do Not Guess at Values for HorizSync or VertRefresh**

If you configure the Monitor section manually, do not guess at the scan rates (HorizSync and Vert-Refresh); on older monitors, you can destroy the hardware by choosing scan rates that are too high.

The following section defines a monitor named Monitor0. The VendorName and ModelName are for reference only and do not affect the way the system works. The optional DisplaySize specifies the height and width of the screen in millimeters, allowing X to calculate the DPI of the monitor. HorizSync and VertRefresh specify ranges of vertical refresh frequencies and horizontal sync frequencies for the monitor. These values are available from the manufacturer. The dpms Option specifies the monitor is *DPMS* (page 969) compliant (has built-in energy saving features).

```
Section "Monitor"
        Identifier   "Monitor0"
        VendorName   "Monitor Vendor"
        ModelName    "Dell D1028L"
        DisplaySize  360 290
        HorizSync    31.0 - 70.0
        VertRefresh  50.0 - 120.0
        Option       "dpms"
EndSection
```

Your Monitor section may mention DDC (Display Data Channel); DDC can be used by a monitor to inform a video card about its properties.

Device

The **xorg.conf** and **XF86Config** files must have at least one Device section to specify the type of video card in the system. The VendorName and BoardName are for reference only and do not affect the way the system works. The easiest way to set up this section is to use the system-config-display or redhat-config-xfree86 utility, both of which usually determine the type of video card by probing. The following Device section specifies that Videocard0 uses the **tdfx** driver:

```
Section "Device"
        Identifier  "Videocard0"
        Driver      "tdfx"
        VendorName  "Videocard vendor"
        BoardName   "Voodoo3 (generic)"
EndSection
```

Screen

The **xorg.conf** and **XF86Config** files must have at least one Screen section. This section binds a video card specified in the Device section with a display specified in the Monitor section. The following Screen section specifies that Screen0 comprises Videocard0 and Monitor0, both defined elsewhere in the file. The DefaultDepth entry specifies the default *color depth* (page 963), which can be overridden in the Display subsection (next).

Each Screen section must have at least one Display subsection. The following subsection specifies a color Depth and three Modes. The modes specify screen resolutions in dots-per-inch (DPI). The first mode is the default; you can switch between modes while X is running by pressing CONTROL-ALT-KEYPAD+ or CONTROL-ALT-KEYPAD–. You must use the plus or minus on the numeric keypad when giving these commands. X ignores invalid modes.

```
Section "Screen"
        Identifier  "Screen0"
        Device      "Videocard0"
        Monitor     "Monitor0"
        DefaultDepth    24
        SubSection  "Display"
         Depth      24
         Modes          "1024x768" "800x600" "640x480"
        EndSubSection
EndSection
```

Multiple Monitors

X has supported multiple screens for a long time. X.org and XFree86 support multimonitor configurations using either two graphics cards or a dual-head card. Both of these setups are usually configured the same way because the drivers for dual-head cards provide a secondary virtual device.

Traditionally, each screen in X is treated as a single entity. Each window must be on one screen or another. More recently, the Xinerama extension allows windows to be split across two or more displays. This extension is supported by X.org and XFree86 and works with most video drivers. When using Xinerama, you must set all screens to the same color depth.

For each screen, you must define a Device, Monitor, and Screen section in the **xorg.conf** or **XF86Config** file. These sections are exactly the same as for a single screen configuration; each screen must have a unique identifier. If you are using a dual-head card, the Device section for the second head is likely to require a BusID value to enable the driver to determine that you are not referring to the primary display. The following section identifies the two heads on an ATi Radeon 8500 card. For other dual-head cards, consult the documentation provided with the driver (for example, give the command **man mga** to display information on the **mga** driver):

```
Section "Device"
        Identifier    "Videocard0"
        Driver        "radeon"
        VendorName    "ATi"
        BoardName     "Radeon 8500"
EndSection
Section "Device"
        Identifier    "Videocard1"
        Driver        "radeon"
        VendorName    "ATi"
        BoardName     "Radeon 8500"
        BusID         "PCI:1:5:0"
EndSection
```

Once you have defined the screens, use the ServerLayout section to tell X where they are in relation to each other. Each screen is defined in the following form:

Screen ScreenNumber "Identifier" Position

The *ScreenNumber* is optional. If omitted, X numbers screens in the order they are specified, starting with 0. The *Identifier* is the same Identifier used in the Screen sections. The *Position* can be either absolute or relative. The easiest way to define screen positions is to give one screen an absolute position, usually with the coordinates of the origin, and then use the LeftOf, RightOf, Above, and Below keywords to indicate the positions of the other screens:

```
Section "ServerLayout"
        Identifier      "Multihead layout"
        Screen      0   "Screen0" LeftOf "Screen1"
        Screen      1   "Screen1" 0 0
        InputDevice     "Mouse0" "CorePointer"
        InputDevice     "Keyboard0" "CoreKeyboard"
        InputDevice     "DevInputMice" "AlwaysCore"
        Option          "Xinerama" "on"
        Option          "Clone" "off"
EndSection
```

Two options can control the behavior of a multimonitor layout: Xinerama causes the screens to act as if they were a single screen and Clone causes each of the screens to display the same thing.

gdm: Displays a Graphical Login

Traditionally, users were expected to log in on a text-based terminal and then start the X server. Today, most desktop systems and workstations provide a graphical login. Red Hat Linux uses the GNOME display manager (gdm) to provide this functionality, even if you are bringing up a KDE desktop.

Configuring gdm

The gdmsetup utility configures the login presented by gdm by editing the heavily commented **/etc/X11/gdm/gdm.conf** file. By default, **root** can log in both locally and remotely. It is usually a good idea to disable remote **root** logins because, when a user logs in remotely using gdm, the password is sent in cleartext across the network.

Using kdm

The kdm utility is the KDE equivalent of gdm. There is no benefit in using kdm in place of gdm: Both perform the same function. Using gdm does not force you to use GNOME.

The configuration file for kdm, **/etc/X11/xdm/kdmrc**, is heavily commented. You can edit the kdm configuration using the KDE control panel, but doing so removes the comments from the file.

More Information

Web XFree86   xfree86.org, xfree86.org/current has README files on many topics.
DRI   www.xfree86.org/current/DRI.html
Mouse Configuration   www.xfree86.org/current/mouse.html
Keyboard Configuration   www.xfree86.org/current/XKB-Config.html
X.org   X.org, freedesktop.org
X.org release notes   freedesktop.org/~xorg/X11R6.7.0/doc/RELNOTES.html

Chapter Summary

Most installations of Red Hat Linux begin by booting from the first installation CD. When the system boots from the CD, it displays a **boot:** prompt. You can respond to this prompt with different commands, by pressing RETURN without entering a command, or not at all. In all cases, the system boots Red Hat Linux from the CD. If you are installing from files on the local hard disk or over a network, give the command **linux askmethod** in response to the **boot:** prompt:

The program that installs Red Hat Linux is named Anaconda. Anaconda identifies the hardware, builds the filesystems, and installs or upgrades the Red Hat Linux operating system. Anaconda can run in textual or graphical (default) interactive mode or in batch mode (Kickstart). Anaconda does not write to the hard disk until it displays the About to Install screen. Until you see this screen, you can press CONTROL-ALT-DEL to abort the installation without making any changes to the hard disk.

The Disk Druid graphical disk-partitioning program can add, delete, and modify partitions on a hard drive during installation. The fdisk utility reports on and manipulates hard disk partitions before or after installation.

A dual-boot system is one that can boot one of two operating systems, frequently Windows and Linux. The biggest problem in setting up a dual-boot system, assuming you want to add Linux to a Windows system, is finding disk space for Linux.

With the introduction of Fedora Core 2, Red Hat replaced XFree86 with X.org Foundation's X11R6.7.0 X Window System. The X.org X server is functionally equivalent to the one distributed by XFree86 because most of the code is the same. Under X.org, the primary configuration file is named **/etc/X11/xorg.conf**.

Red Hat Linux uses the GNOME display manager (gdm) to provide a graphical login, even if you are using a KDE desktop. The gdmsetup utility configures the login presented by gdm by editing the **/etc/X11/gdm/gdm.conf** file.

Exercises

1. What is the difference between Xinerama and traditional multimonitor X11?

2. What command would you give in response to the **boot:** prompt to begin an FTP installation?

3. Describe the Anaconda installer.

4. Where on the disk should you put your **/boot** partition or the root (**/**) partition if you do not use a **/boot** partition?

5. If the graphical installer does not work, what three things should you try?

6. When should you specify an ext2 filesystem in place of ext3?

7. Describe Disk Druid.

8. When does a Red Hat Linux system start X by default?

Advanced Exercises

9. If you do not install GRUB on the master boot record of the hard disk, how can you boot Linux?

10. Why would you place **/var** at the start of the disk?

11. Assume you have four screens, screen0 through screen3, configured. How would you instruct X.org that your screen layout was a T shape with the first screen at the bottom and the others in a row above it?

PART II
Getting Started with Red Hat Linux

Introduction to Red Hat Linux

4

One way or another you are sitting in front of a computer that is running Red Hat Linux. This chapter takes you on a tour of the system to give you some ideas about what you can do with it. The tour does not go into depth about choices, options, menus, and so on; that is left for you to experiment with and there is more coverage in later chapters. Instead, this chapter presents a cook's tour of the Linux kitchen; as you read it, you will have a chance to sample the dishes that you will enjoy more fully as you read the rest of the book.

Following the tour are sections on where to find Linux documentation (page 94), more about logging in on the system, including information about passwords (page 101), and more about working with windows (page 110).

On the next page, read the tip about the dangers of misusing the powers of Superuser. Heeding that warning, feel free to experiment with your system: Click icons, choose items from menus, and have fun.

Curbing Your Power: Superuser/root/Administrator Access

While you are logged in as the user named **root**, you are referred to as *Superuser* or *administrator* and have extraordinary privileges. You can read from or write to any file on the system, execute programs that ordinary users cannot, and more. On a multiuser system you may not be permitted to know the **root** password, but someone, usually the *system administrator*, knows the **root** password and maintains the system. When you are running Linux on your own computer, you will assign a password to **root** when you install Linux. Refer to "System Administrator and Superuser" on page 371 for more information.

caution ‖   **Do Not Experiment as Superuser**

Feel free to experiment when you are logged in as yourself. When you log in as Superuser, also called **root** or administrator, or anytime you give the Superuser/**root**/administrator password, do only what you have to do and make sure you know exactly what you are doing. When you have completed the task at hand, revert to working as yourself. Working as Superuser/**root**/administrator, you can damage the Linux system to the extent that you will need to reinstall Red Hat Linux to get it working again.

See "System Administration" on page 92 for tasks you may want to perform working as administrator.

A Tour of the Red Hat Linux Desktop

GNOME (www.gnome.org), a product of the GNU project (page 4), is the user-friendly default desktop manager under Red Hat Linux. KDE (www.kde.org), the K Desktop Environment, is a powerful desktop manager and complete set of tools you can use in place of GNOME. This tour presents KDE, a full-featured, mature desktop environment that has a rich assortment of configurable tools and features. After you log in, this section discusses several important features of the desktop, including the Main panel and the Main menu, and how to use some of the unique features of windows under KDE. Along the way, you will see how to roll up a window so only its title bar remains on the desktop, move easily from one desktop or window to another, and configure the desktop to please your senses. As the tour continues, you learn to work with files and browse the Web using Konqueror, one of the primary KDE tools. The tour concludes with coverage of the KDE Control Center, the key to customizing your desktop, and a discussion of how to use the Panel menu to modify the panel to suit your needs.

As Red Hat is installed, when you log in, you use GNOME. Because the examples in this chapter are based on KDE, you must tell the system that you want to run KDE before you log in. The following section explains how to log in to a KDE environment.

Logging In on the System

Figure 4-1 shows the Login screen with the **Choose a session** dialog box. The word/icon buttons at the bottom of the screen allow you to work in a different language, specify a desktop manager, reboot the system, and turn it off. Click the word **Session** and the system displays the **Choose a session** dialog box that allows you to choose whether you want to run GNOME, KDE, or another desktop manager. To follow the examples in this chapter, click the radio button next to **KDE**; then click

OK to close the dialog box. If the KDE radio button is not there, KDE is probably not installed; refer to "Installing KDE" on page 78.

refer to "Installing KDE" on page 78.

---

tip ‖   **Choose a session Does Not Change Your Default Desktop**

As installed, Red Hat Linux logs you into the GNOME desktop environment by default. Using **Choose a session** affects only the next login; it does not change your default desktop manager. As the system noted when you logged in, you must run switchdesk if you want to log in on KDE as a matter of course. For more information, refer to "switchdesk: Changing Your Default Desktop" on page 106.

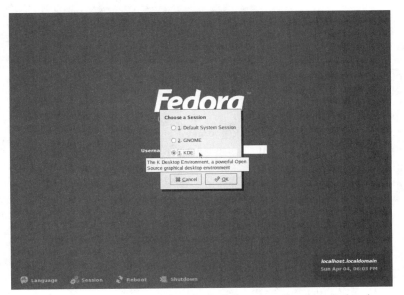

Figure 4-1   The login screen with the **Choose a Session** dialog box

---

caution ‖   **Click and Right Click**

This book uses the term **click** when you need to click the left mouse button and **right click** when you need to click the right mouse button.

Enter your username in the text box in the middle of the screen labeled **Username** and press RETURN. The label changes to **Password**. Enter your password and press RETURN. The system displays a workspace with a panel along the bottom, some icons at the upper-left, and the word **Fedora** at the upper-right (Figure 4-2). If you get an error message, try entering your username and password again. Make sure the CAPS LOCK key is not on; the system is sensitive to the case of your entries. See page 103 for help with login problems and page 104 if you want to change your password.

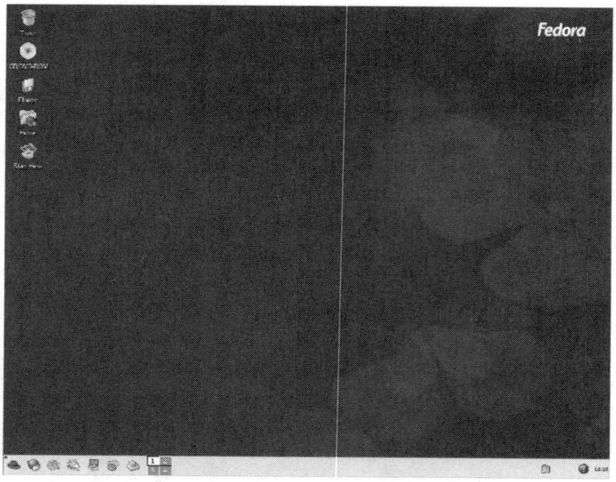

Figure 4-2   The initial screen

tip || **Installing KDE**

You should have the KDE desktop environment installed on the system to follow the examples in this chapter. You can use the GNOME desktop environment, but some of the examples will not work the same way. To install KDE, log in on the system as described earlier, omitting the step that has you click **Session** (do not click the KDE radio button).

Once you are logged in, click the red hat at the lower-left of the screen. Slide the mouse pointer until it is over **System Settings** on the pop-up menu. Click **Add/Remove Applications** from the pop-up submenu. Supply the **root** password when the system asks for it. After a pause, the system displays the Package Management window.

Under the Desktops bar, click the box next to KDE Desktop Environment so that a mark appears in the box. Click **Update**. The system will ask you for the CD it needs to install KDE. Follow the instructions and the system will install KDE.

Getting the Most from the Desktop

When you are working in a complex environment and using many windows to run a variety of programs simultaneously, it is convenient to divide your desktop into several areas, each *appearing* as a desktop unto itself and occupying the entire display screen. These areas are virtual desktops. The *workspace* is what is on the screen: buttons/icons, toolbars/panels, windows, and the *root window* (the unoccupied space on the workspace, page 84). Typically, GNOME and KDE are set up with a desktop with four workspaces.

Desktop theme   In a GUI, a *theme* is a recurring pattern and overall look that (ideally) pleases the eye and is easy to interpret and use. To view a wide variety of themes, go to themes.freshmeat.net or www.kde-look.org. Using themes, you can control the appearance of KDE, GNOME, and most other desktop environments.

tip ||

Is It a Desktop, a Workspace, or What?

Confusion reigns over naming the subcomponents, or divisions, of a desktop. This book, in conformance with GNOME documentation, refers to everything that usually occupies your display monitor, or screen, as a *workspace; desktop* refers to the sum of your workspaces. Or, put another way, the desktop is divided into workspaces.

KDE documentation and screens use the term *desktop* in place of *workspace* as just defined.

The Power of the Desktop: Using the Main Panel

When you log in, KDE displays a workspace that includes the KDE Main panel, the key to getting your work done easily and efficiently. The Main panel is the strip with icons that act as buttons (Figure 4-3) along the bottom of the workspace. A panel does not allow you to do anything you could not do otherwise; it simply collects things in one place and makes your work with the system easier. Because the Main panel is easy to configure, you can set it up to hold the tools you use frequently, arranged the way you want: application launchers to start, for example, email and word processing programs, menus (including the Main menu, represented by the red hat), *applets* (applications that are small enough to be executed within a panel), and special objects (such as a Logout button). You can create additional panels, called *extensions,* or *extension panels,* to hold different groups of tools. This book uses the term *panel* to refer to both the Main and extension panels.

Figure 4-3   The KDE Main panel

Tooltips   Tooltips (Figure 4-4), available from both GNOME and KDE, is a minicontext help system that you activate by moving your mouse pointer over a button, icon, window border, or applet (such as those on a panel) and leaving it there for a moment (called *hovering*). When you do this, GNOME and KDE display a brief explanation of the object your mouse pointer is hovering over.

Figure 4-4   A tooltip

Icons/buttons   The icons/buttons on the panel display menus, launch programs, and display information. The Web browser button starts Mozilla. The email button (the stamp and letter) starts Evolution, an email and calendaring application (www.ximian.com/products/evolution). The writing button (the pen and paper) brings up OpenOffice.org Writer, a word processor. You can start almost anything on the system using a button on a panel.

Panel Icon menu   The Panel Icon menu allows you to remove the icon from the panel, move the icon within the panel, and view and change the icon's properties. It also contains the Panel menu (page 92) as a submenu. Some icons have additional context-based selections whereas some applets have a different menu. Right click an icon on the panel to display the Panel Icon menu.

Pager   Each rectangle in the *pager,* the group of rectangles labeled 1-4 on the panel, represents a workspace (Figure 4-5). Click a rectangle to display the corresponding workspace. To see how this works, click the rectangle labeled **2**. This rectangle becomes light to indicate that you are viewing workspace 2. While you are working with workspace 2, click the Mozilla icon on the panel (the picture of the earth with a mouse wrapped around it). Mozilla opens a window and a tiny window appears in rectangle number 2 in the pager. Now, click the rectangle labeled **3** and open OpenOffice.org Writer by clicking the panel icon with a pen and paper on it. With Writer in workspace 3 and Mozilla in workspace 2, you can click the rectangles in the pager to switch back and forth between the workspaces. GNOME calls this tool the *Workspace Switcher.*

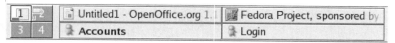

Figure 4-5   The pager (left) and the taskbar (right)

Taskbar   To the right of the pager is the *taskbar,* a group of skinny, horizontal rectangles with an icon and the name of a program in each one. You can use the taskbar to change to a specific window regardless of which workspace it appears on. Click one of the rectangles and the corresponding program/window appears on the screen; KDE switches to a different workspace if necessary. If the window running the program you clicked on is not visible because it is buried under other windows, clicking a rectangle on the taskbar pops the window to the top of the stack of windows. GNOME calls this tool the *Window List.* If you have a lot of applications running on various workspaces, you can configure the taskbar to show only the applications on the current workspace.

Launching Applications from the Main Menu

The red hat icon at the left end of the panel has a function similar to that of the Start button on a Windows system: Click it to display the Main menu. From the Main menu and its submenus, you can launch many of the applications that are present on the system. As distributed by Red Hat, this menu is very similar under GNOME and KDE.

KNotes   You can use the Main menu to launch KNotes, a reminder system that looks like Post-it® notes. After you click the red hat to display the Main menu, without pressing a mouse button, move the mouse to slide the mouse pointer over the Main menu until it is over **Accessories**. The system displays the Accessories submenu. Again, without pressing a mouse button, move the mouse pointer until it is over **KNotes**.

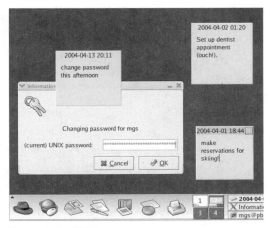

Figure 4-6   KNotes

(Under *RHEL*, **KNotes** is located on the More Accessories submenu of the Accessories submenu.) Click **KNotes** to display a small, yellow window that you can type in (Figure 4-6).

You can use these windows to leave yourself reminders. Although KNotes may seem trivial, it offers many things to experiment with. Click and drag the titlebar at the top of a KNote to move it. Right click the titlebar to display the KNotes menu. When you start KNotes, it puts an icon toward the right end of the panel. Right and left click this icon and see what happens.

Copy icons to a panel To copy a selection from the Main menu to a panel, left drag the item from the Main menu to a panel. To remove an icon from a panel, right click the icon and choose **Remove** from the pop-up menu.

Logging off At the bottom of the Main menu is **Logout**. Click this selection to log off the system.

Feel free to experiment Try selecting different items from the Main menu and see what you discover. Many of the submenus have submenus with even more selections. For example, the **Preferences** submenu has a **More Preferences** selection that displays a submenu with more selections. Following are some applications you may want to try working with:

- OpenOffice.org's word processor, Writer, is a full-featured Word processor that can import and export Word documents. Click on the panel icon that depicts a couple of sheets of paper and a pen or, from the Main menu, select **Office⇨OpenOffice.org Writer**.

- Mozilla is a powerful, full-featured Web browser that can send and receive email, work with newsgroups, and maintain an address book in addition to navigating the Web. Click the panel icon of the world with a mouse wrapped around it to start Mozilla. You can also select various Mozilla functions from **Main menu: Internet**.

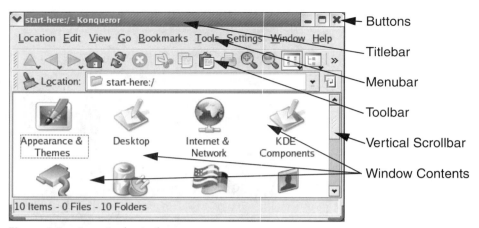

Figure 4-7   A typical window

- The gaim Instant Messenger (IM) client allows you to chat on the Internet with other people who are using IM clients such as AOL, MSN, Yahoo, and others. To start gaim, select **Main menu: Internet⇨Messaging Client**.

  The first time you start gaim, it opens the Accounts window. Click **Add** and enter information about your IM account. Put marks in the check boxes next to **Remember password** and **Auto-login** if you want gaim to log you in automatically when you start it. Click **Save**. In the main gaim window, click **Sign on**. Go to gaim.sourceforge.net for more information, including gaim documentation and plugins that add features to gaim.

Controlling Windows I

On a display screen, a *window* is a region that runs, or is controlled by, a particular program (Figure 4-7). Because you can control the look and feel of windows, even the buttons they display, your windows may not look like the ones in this book. (Select **Main menu: Preferences⇨More Preferences⇨Control Center⇨Appearance & Themes⇨Window Decorations** to customize windows in your account.)

Titlebar   A titlebar (Figures 4-7 and 4-8) appears at the top of most windows and in many ways controls the window it is attached to. You can change the appearance and function of a titlebar, but you will usually have at least the functionality of the buttons shown in Figure 4-8.

The minimize button collapses the window to its rectangle in the taskbar on the panel; click the rectangle on the taskbar to restore the window. Clicking the maximize button expands the window so it occupies the whole workspace; click the same button on the titlebar, which now appears with a double-window icon, to restore the window to its former size. Clicking the maximize button with the middle or right mouse button expands the window vertically or horizontally. Use the same or a different mouse button to click the maximize button again and see what hap-

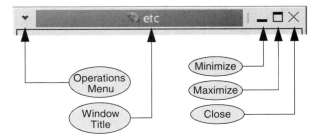

Figure 4-8   A titlebar

pens. Clicking the close button closes the window and terminates the program that was running in the window. Click the Operations menu button to see a menu of window operations. Right click the titlebar and drag the window to reposition it.

Toolbar   A toolbar (Figure 4-7) appears usually at the top of a window and contains icons, text, applets, menus, and more that you can work with. There are many kinds of toolbars. The titlebar is not a toolbar; it is part of the window decoration placed there by the window manager (page 111).

Window Operations menu   The Window Operations menu (Figure 4-8) contains most of the common operations that you need to perform on any window. You can access this menu by clicking the Window Operations menu button or by right clicking the titlebar.

Context menu   A context menu is one that applies specifically to the window you click. Frequently, a right click brings up a context menu. Try right clicking on each of the icons on the desktop. Depending on what the icon represents, you get a different menu. For example, the context (icon) menu is different for the Trash, CD/DVD, and Home icons. Try right clicking with the mouse pointer in different places; you will find some interesting menus.

Changing the Input Focus (Window Cycling)

In addition to using the taskbar (page 80), you can change which window has the input focus by using the keyboard; this process is called *window cycling*. When you press ALT-TAB, the input focus moves to the window that was active just before the currently active window, making it easy to switch back and forth between two windows. When you hold ALT and press TAB multiple times, the focus moves from window to window, and you see in the center of the workspace a box that displays the titlebar information from the window that currently has the input focus. Under KDE, you can hold ALT and SHIFT and repeatedly press TAB to cycle in the other direction.

Under KDE, you can cycle workspaces using CONTROL-TAB.

Shading a Window

When you double-click a KDE titlebar (Figure 4-8), the window rolls up like a window shade, leaving only the titlebar visible. Double-click the titlebar again to restore the window.

KDE offers shade-hover mode, which keeps shaded any windows that you have shaded unless the mouse pointer is over that window. In this mode, few windows clutter your workspace; there are just shaded windows. When the mouse pointer hovers over the titlebar of a shaded window for a short time, the window unshades. When you move the mouse pointer off the window, it immediately shades again. In order to put a window in shade-hover mode, you must shade it once manually. After that, shading and unshading are automatic.

Cutting and Pasting Objects Using the Clipboard

There are two, similar ways to cut/copy and paste objects on the desktop. You can use the clipboard, technically called the *copy buffer,* to copy or move objects: You explicitly copy an object to the buffer and then paste it somewhere else. Applications that follow the user interface guidelines use CONTROL-X to cut, CONTROL-C to copy, and CONTROL-V to paste.

Less familiar is the *selection* or *primary* buffer, which always contains the last object you selected. The middle mouse button pastes the contents of the selection buffer at the location of the mouse pointer (if you are using a two-button mouse, click both buttons at the same time to simulate clicking the middle button).

For both of these techniques, you start by selecting the object (text, figure, and so on) by left dragging over the object(s) you want to select. You can also double-click to select a word or triple-click to select a line.

Next, to use the clipboard, explicitly copy (CONTROL-C) or move (CONTROL-X) the object.[1] If you want to use the selection buffer, skip this step.

Finally, paste the selected object by positioning the mouse pointer where you want to put the object and pressing CONTROL-V or CONTROL-SHIFT-Insert (clipboard method) or by pressing the middle mouse button (selection buffer method).

Using the clipboard, you can give as many commands as you like between the CONTROL-C or CONTROL-X and CONTROL-V, as long as you do not use another CONTROL-C or CONTROL-X.

Using the selection buffer, you can give other commands after selecting the object and before you paste it, as long as you do not deselect the object.

You can use klipper, the KDE clipboard utility, to paste previously selected objects. See page 246 for information on klipper.

Controlling the Desktop Using the Root Window

The *root window* is any part of the desktop that is not occupied by a window, panel, icon, or other object; it is the part of the desktop where you can see the background.

---

1. CONTROL-C does not copy text in a terminal emulator window because the shell running in the window intercepts the control character before the terminal emulator can receive it. You must either use the selection buffer in this environment or use copy/paste from the **Edit** selection on the Menubar.

Desktop icons Icons on the root window respond appropriately to a double-click: A program starts running, a data file (such as a letter, calendar, or URL) runs the program that created it (with the data file loaded or, in the case of a URL, with the browser displaying the appropriate Web page), and a directory brings up the Konqueror File Manager (page 87). Within Konqueror, you can move/copy/link a file or directory by dragging and dropping it and selecting **Move/Copy/Link** from the resulting pop-up menu and you can run or edit a file by double-clicking it. Right click an icon that is not in a panel to display the Generic Icon menu (following).

Generic Icon menus Display a Generic Icon menu by right clicking an icon that is not on a panel. The Generic Icon menu is the only way to perform some operations with icons on the root window. Figure 4-9 shows the Trash icon's Generic Icon menu.

Figure 4-9   The Trash icon's Generic Icon menu

The Desktop menu Display the Desktop menu by right clicking on the root window. You can open a window or perform another task by making a selection from the Desktop menu. Both KDE and GNOME have desktop menus, although each presents a different set of choices.

Configure Desktop The Configure Desktop selection on the Desktop menu opens the Configure Desktop window (Figure 4-10), which gives you a lot of choices to experiment with. Each icon in the vertical panel on the left of this window displays a different set of choices on the right. Some icons, such as Behavior, display multiple tabs to the right, each tab displaying a different set of choices.

Desktop background Click **Background** on the left panel of the Configure Desktop window to change the desktop background settings (Figure 4-10). At the top of the right side of this window is a box labeled **Setting for Desktop**. Initially, the box says **All Desktops,** meaning that whatever changes you make to the desktop using the rest of this window apply to all (four) workspaces. You can click **All Desktops** and choose to have the settings apply to a single workspace. Using this technique you can make each of your workspaces look different.

Click the radio button next to **Picture** and choose a file with an image to use as wallpaper. Or you can click **No Picture** and choose a pattern and color(s) for the desktop background. Choose a pattern from the combo box adjacent to **Colors** and click one of the two color bars under the combo box. KDE displays the Select Color window. This window gives you several ways of selecting a color. Try clicking the palette and moving the resulting crosshairs cursor over a color you like anywhere on the screen, and clicking again to select the color. Refer to "**kcolorchooser**: Selects a Color" on page 244 for more information on the Select Color window.

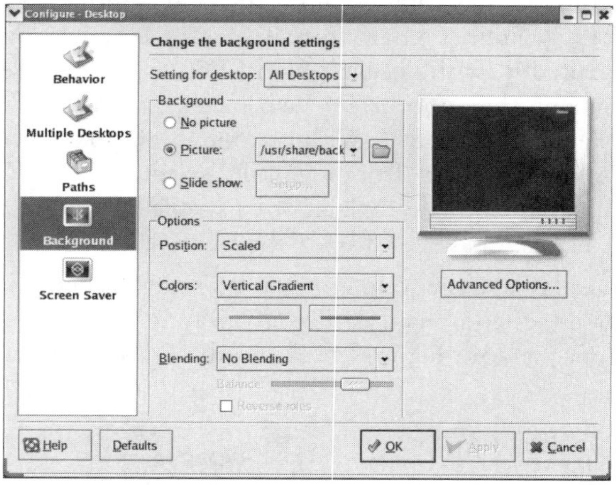

Figure 4-10   The Configure Desktop window

Experiment with the choices in the Background and Options frames to create a desktop background that pleases you. Click **Defaults** and then **Apply** to return the background to its initial state.

GNOME and KDE   The Configure Desktop window gives you many, many choices of how you want things to look and work. The abundance of choices demonstrates a major difference between KDE and GNOME, the two major Linux desktop managers. While GNOME has moved toward simple sophistication, giving the user a standard interface with fewer choices, KDE has moved toward configurability. If you try to configure the GNOME desktop manager, you will have fewer choices but find that each choice is well thought out and powerful. Some users prefer one approach; others prefer the other.

Running Commands from the Terminal Emulator/Shell

A *terminal emulator* is a window that functions as a character-based terminal and is displayed in a graphical environment. To open a terminal emulator window under KDE or GNOME, click the red hat at the lower-left of the screen to display the Main menu and select **System Tools▷Terminal**. Because you are already logged in and are creating a subshell in a desktop environment, you do not need to log in again. Once you have opened a terminal, try giving the command **man man** to read about the man utility (page 94) that displays Linux man(ual) pages. Chapter 5 describes utilities that you can run from a terminal emulator.

You can run character-based programs that would normally run on a terminal in a terminal emulator window. You can also start graphical programs, such as xeyes, from it. A graphical program opens its own window. When you run a program from GNOME or KDE, you may be asked whether you want to run the program in a terminal. When you say YES, the program runs in a terminal emulator window (Figure 4-11).

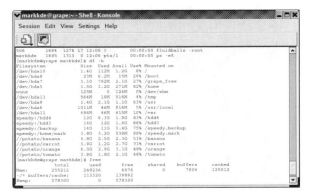

Figure 4-11   A konsole terminal emulator window

When you are typing in a terminal emulator window, several characters, including *, $, [, and], have special meanings. Avoid using these characters until you have read "Special Characters" on page 118.

The shell   Once you open a terminal emulator window, you are communicating with the command interpreter known as the *shell*. The shell plays an important part in much of your communication with Linux. When you enter a command at the keyboard in response to the shell prompt on the screen, the shell interprets the command and initiates the appropriate action. This action may be executing your program, calling a compiler or a Linux utility or another standard program, or giving you an error message telling you that you entered a command incorrectly. When you are working on a GUI, you bypass the shell and execute a program by clicking an icon or name. Refer to Chapter 7 (page 189) for more information on the shell.

Using Konqueror to Manage Files, Run Programs, and Browse the Web

Konqueror is the desktop tool you will probably use most often. It is similar to, but more powerful than, Windows (Internet) Explorer and easily morphs among a file manager, browser, and executor of many programs, both within and outside the borders of its window. Even though Konqueror is much more than a Web browser, its name takes its place in the evolution of browsers: Navigator, Explorer, and now Konqueror, spelled with a K because it is part of KDE (Figure 4-12). As an aside, Apple chose to use KHTML, Konqueror's HTML rendering engine, to create its browser and continued the tradition, naming the browser "Safari."

Konqueror provides network transparent access, which means that it is as easy to work with files on remote systems as it is to work with local files, and you can copy files from/to a remote system, using the same techniques you use for copying files locally.

Because it opens an application within itself, Konqueror makes the process of clicking and viewing almost any type of file transparent. Click a **pdf** (Acrobat) file/icon

Figure 4-12   Konqueror the Web browser

within Konqueror, and it opens the file within the Konqueror window, using KG-hostview. You see the file that you clicked open within the Konqueror window.

The most important feature of the Web browser, the file manager, and the other faces of Konqueror is that each of these separate tools is seamlessly integrated into the same window and shares appearance, tools (such as bookmarks), menu system, icons, and functional characteristics. You can browse from a Web site to an FTP site, copy a file from the FTP site to your local filesystem or desktop as though you were copying it locally, and run, edit, or display the file within a Konqueror view or in another window.

Getting started   You can bring up Konqueror as a browser or a file manager, and you can switch from one to the other while you are working with it. Double-click the **Home** icon on the workspace to open Konqueror the file manager. Once Konqueror is open, enter a URL, such as fedora.redhat.com, in the location bar and press RETURN to switch Konqueror to browser mode. You can toggle the Navigation Panel (the narrow sub-window on the left) on/off by pressing F9 or selecting **Konqueror menubar: Window⇨Show Navigation Panel**.

Because you can change the appearance and functionality of Konqueror very easily, what your system displays may not match what is shown and described in this book.

Konqueror works with different kinds of targets: plain files (including executable, sound, graphical, and so on), directory files, and URLs, including HTTP and FTP addresses. You specify the target by clicking the target's icon within a Konqueror *view* (subwindow) or entering its pathname/address in the location bar. Konqueror takes action based on the kind of target you specify:

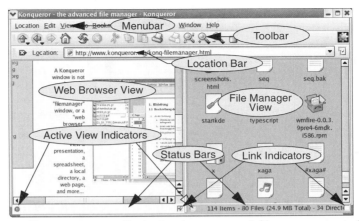

Figure 4-13   Konqueror displaying browser and file manager windows

- **Plain file** (local or remote): If the file is executable, Konqueror runs it (see "Executing files," next). If it is not executable, Konqueror tries to find the appropriate utility or application to open it.
- **Directory file:** Displays the contents of the directory in a Konqueror File Manager view.
- **HTTP address:** Opens the URL in the HTML viewer, which has been loaded and embedded within the Konqueror window.
- **FTP address:** Treats a file obtained by ftp just as it would treat a local plain or directory file.

MIME/executing files   MIME (Multipurpose Internet Mail Extension) types were originally used to describe how specific types of files that were attached to email were to be handled. Today, MIME types describe how many types of files are to be handled, based on their contents or filename extensions. Both GNOME and KDE use MIME types to figure out which program to use to open a file. An example of a MIME *type* is **audio/x-mp3**. The MIME *group* is **audio** and the MIME *subtype* is **x-mp3**. This MIME type is associated with the KDE Media Player. (There are many MIME groups; some are application, audio, image, inode, message, text, and video.)

When you click a file whose name is **bigtime.mp3**, KDE examines the file's *magic number* (page 982) to determine its MIME type. If that technique fails, KDE looks at the file's filename extension, in this case **mp3**. When KDE determines the file's MIME type is **audio/x-mp3**, it calls the KDE Media Player to open the file.

Running a program   In the Konqueror location bar, enter **/usr/X11R6/bin/xclock** RETURN, an executable file that runs a graphical program. After checking that you really want to run it, Konqueror runs xclock. When you want to run a character-based (text mode) program, use **Konqueror menubar: Tools⇨Run Command** or press ALT-F2 to open the Run Command window. After entering the name of the program you want to run, click **Options** and put a check mark next to **Run in terminal window**. For more information, refer to "Run Command" on page 245.

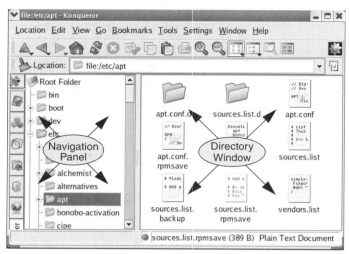

Figure 4-14   The Konqueror file manager displaying icons

Views   Choose **Konqueror menubar: Window** to add and remove views (subwindows) from the Konqueror display. The choices in this menu always work on the *active view,* the one with a green dot at the lower-left (or the only view). See Figure 4-13. For more information refer to "Views II" on page 241.

Toolbar   The Konqueror toolbar (the toolbar with the icons in Figure 4-14) is straightforward. A right arrow at the right end of the toolbar indicates that not all the icons would fit in the width of the window. Click the arrow to display (and choose from) the remaining icons.

File Manager   The Konqueror File Manager view allows you to work with the filesystem graphically. The Navigation panel (press F9 to display it) helps navigate the filesystem; first, click either the root or home folder icon on the vertical stack of icons in the Navigation panel; then click a directory in the Navigation panel to display its contents in the Directory window. Click a file in the Directory window to execute it, display its contents, and so on, depending on the contents of the file.

Customizing Your Desktop with the Control Center

The KDE Control Center and the GNOME start-here window present information on, and allow you to control, many aspects of the desktop environment. Each tool works differently; this section discusses the KDE Control Center. Bring up the GNOME start-here window by clicking the Start Here icon on the desktop; display the KDE Control Center by choosing **Main menu: Preferences⇨More Preferences⇨Control Center**. As shown in Figure 4-15, the left column of the Control Center has three tabs at the top.

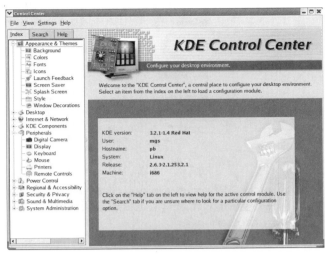

Figure 4-15   The KDE Control Center

The column at the left of the Control Center window displays a list of categories such as **Appearance & Themes** and **Power Control**. You may have to click the tab marked **Index** at the top of the column to display this list. Each of the categories has a box to its left with a plus (**+**) or a minus (**–**) in it. Click a plus to expand the category and display topics within the category; click a minus to hide the topics.

When you click a topic, the Control Center displays information about the topic on the right side of the window. Frequently, there are tabs at the top of this information. Click the tabs, make the changes you want, and click **Apply** at the lower-right of the Control Center window to make your changes take effect.

Left-handed mouse   For example, you can change the setup of the mouse buttons so they are suitable for a left-handed person by clicking the plus in the box next to **Peripherals** to expand this category and then clicking the topic labeled **Mouse** (Figure 4-16). On the right side of the window, click the tab marked **General** and under Button Mapping, click the radio button next to **Left handed**. Finally, click the **Apply** button at the lower-right of the window. Now the functions of the right and left mouse buttons are reversed.

Help   Highlight a topic and click the Help tab at the top of the left column to display information about the selected topic.

Administrator mode   Some topics, such as those in the System Administration category, control system functions and require Administrator mode (Superuser) access to the system: Click **Administrator Mode** at the bottom of the window and enter the Superuser (**root**) password to display and work with these topics.

The following section briefly describes some of the categories and topics in the KDE Control Center.

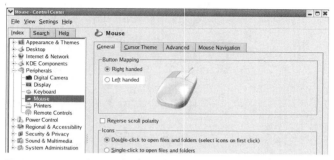

Figure 4-16   The KDE Control Center mouse topic

Appearance & Themes   Appearance & Themes topics control how information is presented to the user, including desktop elements (background, colors, fonts, and icons), screen saver, and window decorations.

Desktop   The Desktop topics control how the desktop, including panels and windows, works.

Internet & Network   The Internet & Network topics control email, file sharing, and desktop sharing. This category includes a subcategory for setting up Web browsing with Konqueror (page 88). This subcategory controls the use of cache, cookies, plugins, stylesheets, browser identification, and other Konqueror-specific settings.

Peripherals   The Peripherals topics control the system monitor (display), the system keyboard and mouse, system printers, and an optional digital camera.

Power Control   The Power Control topics control battery operation and monitoring for battery-powered computers and energy conservation settings for the monitor (display).

Regional & Accessibility   The Regional & Accessibility topics control accessibility for disabled users, country and language specific settings, hot keys, and keyboard layout and shortcuts.

Security & Privacy   The Security & Privacy topics control how passwords are displayed and remembered, privacy settings, and cryptographic settings, including configuring SSL and managing certificates.

Sound & Multimedia   The Sound & Multimedia topics control the sound system, playing audio CDs, the sound mixer, the system bell, and system notifications.

System Administration   Many of the topics in the System Administration category require you to click **Administrator Mode** and enter the Superuser (**root**) password. Working as yourself, you can modify your password and perform other tasks. Working as Superuser, you can change the system date and time, install fonts, and change the way users log in on the system.

Customizing the Main Panel Using the Panel Menu

Adding icons   The Panel menu provides tools to customize the panel. Right click an icon on the panel and select **Panel Menu** or click an empty space on the panel to display the Panel menu (Figure 4-17). The **Add** selection displays a submenu that in turn displays submenus of applets, application buttons, and special buttons you can add to

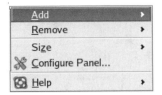

Figure 4-17   The Panel menu

the panel. The **Extension** selection adds other panels to the desktop. Experiment, adding icons to the panel; you cannot do any harm. You can an add an entire application menu by clicking **Add This Menu** at the top of an Application Button menu. Remove an icon from the panel by right clicking the icon and selecting **Remove**.

Moving icons   You can move panel icons by dragging them using the middle mouse button. To shove bordering icons, hold the SHIFT button while dragging.

Configuring the panel   The **Configure Panel** selection on the Panel menu displays the Configure Panel window which determines the location, appearance, and functionality of the panel (Figure 4-18). When you have more than one panel, the icons in the left column allow you to select which panel you want to work with. One icon selects the taskbar (page 80) for modification. The tabs near the top of the window present different aspects of the panel for you to modify. Try changing the appearance or arrangement of the panel. Click **Apply** to make changes take effect. Click **Defaults** and then **Apply** to return things to the way they were when you started.

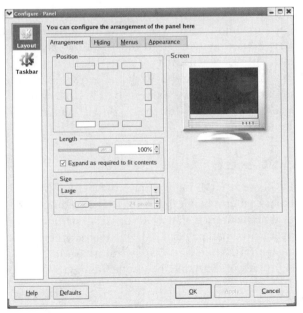

Figure 4-18   The Configure Panel window

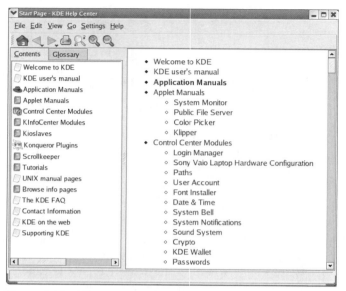

Figure 4-19   The KDE Help Center

Getting the Facts: Where to Find Documentation

Distributions of Linux, including Red Hat, typically come without hardcopy reference manuals. However, online documentation has always been one of Linux's strengths. The manual (or man) and info pages have been available via the man and info utilities since early releases. Both the GNOME and KDE desktops provide graphical help centers. With the growth of Linux and the Internet, the sources of documentation have expanded. The following sections discuss some of the places you can look for information on various aspects of Linux in general and Red Hat Linux in particular.

The KDE Help Center

Display the KDE Help Center by clicking **Main menu: Help**. Figure 4-19 shows the Help Center when it first opens. The column on the left gives you a choice of the type of documentation you want to view, including the KDE FAQ, the KDE User's Manual, Linux man pages, GNU info pages, Control Center information, and more. Click an item on the left to display information about the item on the right and a list of subtopics, if available, below the item. GNOME provides a similar help center.

man: Displaying the System Manual

The character-based man (manual) utility displays pages, known as man pages, from the system documentation. This documentation is useful when you know what util-

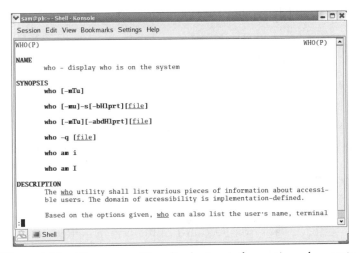

Figure 4-20   The man utility displaying information about who

ity you want to use but have forgotten exactly how to use it. You can also refer to the man pages to get more information about specific topics or to determine what features are available with Linux. Because the descriptions in the system documentation are often terse, they are most helpful if you already understand basically what a utility does.

Because man is a character-based utility, you need to open a terminal emulator window (page 86) to run it. (You can also log in on a virtual terminal [page 103] and run it from there.)

To find out more about a utility, including the man utility itself, give the command **man**, followed by the name of the utility. For example, Figure 4-20 shows the command **man who** displaying information about the who utility.

The command **man man** displays information on man. The man utility automatically sends the output through a *pager*, usually less (page 120), which allows you to view a file one screen at a time. When you display a manual page in this way, less displays a prompt (:) at the bottom of the screen after each screen of text and waits for you to request another screen by pressing the SPACE bar. Pressing **h** (help) displays a list of the less commands that you can use. Pressing **q** (quit) stops man and gives you a shell prompt. You can search for topics covered by man pages by using the apropos utility (page 137, or give the command **man apropos**).

Based on the FHS (Filesystem Hierarchy Standard, page 167), the Linux system manual and the man pages are divided into ten sections. Each section describes related tools:

1. User Commands
2. System Calls
3. Subroutines
4. Devices

5. File Formats
6. Games
7. Miscellaneous
8. System Administration
9. Local
10. New

This layout closely mimics the way the set of UNIX manuals has always been divided. Unless you specify a manual section, man displays the earliest occurrence in the manual of the word you specify on the command line. Most users find the information they need in sections 1, 6, and 7; programmers and system administrators frequently need to consult the other sections.

In some cases, there are manual entries for different tools with the same name. For example, the following command displays the manual page for the write utility (page 141) from section 1 of the system manual:

```
$ man write
```

To see the manual page for the **write** system call from section 2, enter

```
$ man 2 write
```

This command instructs man to look only in section 2 for the manual page. Use the **–a** option[2] to view all the man pages for a given subject (press **q** to move to the next section); use **man –a write** to view all the man pages for write.

---

tip ‖   **You Can Use Konqueror to View** man **and** info **Pages**

You can view man and info pages by entering, for example, **man:cat** or **info:cat** in Konqueror's location bar (Figure 4-13, page 89) or the Run Command box (page 89). Also, the KDE Helpcenter offers direct access to these pages.

---

tip ‖   man **and** info **Display Different Information**

The info utility (page 97) displays more complete and up-to-date information on GNU utilities than does man. When a man page displays abbreviated information on a utility that is covered by info, the man page refers you to info. The man utility frequently displays the only information on non-GNU utilities; when info displays information on non-GNU utilities, it is frequently a copy of the man page.

---

2. An option modifies the way a utility or command works. Options are specified as one or more letters that are preceded by one or two hyphens (there are exceptions). The option appears following the name of the utility you are calling and a SPACE. Any other *arguments* (page 957) to the command follow the option and a SPACE. For more information, refer to "Options" on page 190.

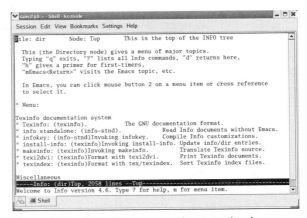

Figure 4-21   The first screen that info displays

info: **Displaying Information About Utilities**

The character-based info utility is a menu-based hypertext system developed by the GNU project and distributed with Red Hat Linux. As with man, you must run info from a terminal emulator window (page 86). The info utility includes a tutorial on itself (give the command **info info** or go to www.gnu.org/software/texinfo/manual/info) and documentation on many Linux shells, utilities, and programs developed by the GNU project (page 1). Figure 4-21 shows the screen that info displays when you give the command **info**. Because the information on this screen is drawn from an editable file, your display may differ. When you see the initial info screen, you can press

- **h** to go through an interactive tutorial on info
- **?** to list info commands
- SPACE to scroll through the menu of items you can get information on
- **m**, followed by the name of the menu item you want to go to
- **q** to quit

The notation info uses to describe keyboard keys may not be familiar to you. The notation **C-h** is the same as CONTROL-H." Similarly, **M-x** means hold down the META or ALT key and press **x**. (On some systems, you need to press ESCAPE and then x to duplicate the function of META-x.)

After giving the command **info**, press the SPACE bar a few times to scroll the display. Figure 4-22 shows the entry for sleep. The asterisk at the left end of the line means that this entry is the beginning of a menu item. Following the asterisk is the name of the menu item, followed by a colon, the name of the package (in parentheses) that

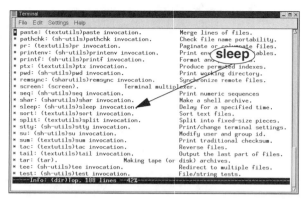

Figure 4-22   The screen that info displays after you press SPACE a few times

the menu item belongs to, other information, and, on the right, a description of the item. In most cases the package name corresponds to the name of the rpm package (page 455) that contains the file.

The name of the menu item is what you type in a menu command to view information on that item. To get information on sleep, give the command **m sleep**, followed by a RETURN. When you type **m** (for *menu*), the cursor moves to the bottom line of the window or screen and displays **Menu item:**. Typing **sleep** displays **sleep** on that line, and pressing RETURN takes you to the menu item you have chosen.

Figure 4-23 shows the *top node* of information on sleep. A node is one group of information that you can scroll through with the SPACE bar. To get to the next node, press **n**. Press **p** to get to the previous node. You can always press **d** to get to the initial menu, shown in Figure 4-21.

As you read this book and learn about new utilities, you can use man or info to find out more about the utilities. If you can print PostScript documents, you can print a manual page with the man utility using the **–t** option (for example, **man –t cat | lpr** prints information about the cat utility). Better yet, use a browser to look at the documentation at www.redhat.com, fedora.redhat.com, or www.tldp.org and print the information from the browser.

HOWTOs: Finding Out How Things Work

A HOWTO document explains in detail how to do something related to Linux, from setting up a specialized piece of hardware to performing system administration to setting up specific networking software. Mini-HOWTOs offer shorter explanations. As with Linux software, one person or a few people generally are responsible for a HOWTO document, yet many people contribute to it.

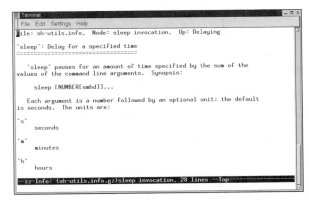

Figure 4-23   The info page on the sleep utility

The Linux Documentation Project (LDP, page 101) site houses most HOWTO and mini-HOWTO documents. Use a browser to go to www.tldp.org, click **HOWTOs**, and pick the index you want to use to find a HOWTO or mini-HOWTO. Or use the LDP search feature on its home page to find HOWTOs and more.

Getting Help with Your System

KDE and GNOME provide similar help facilities. Each provides tooltips (page 79), a context-sensitive help system, and Menubar Help selections. You can also click the red hat at the lower-left of the screen to display the Main menu and select **Help** to display a system help window; GNOME and KDE display different information.

Finding Help Locally

The **/usr/src/linux✳/Documentation** (present only if you installed the kernel source code) and **/usr/share/doc** directories often contain more detailed and different information about a utility than does man or info. Frequently, this information is meant for people who will be compiling and modifying the utility, not just using it. These directories hold thousands of files, each containing information on a separate topic.

Using the Internet to Get Help

The Internet provides many helpful sites. Aside from sites that carry various forms of documentation, you can enter an error message that you are having a problem with in a search engine such as Google (www.google.com). Enclose the error mes-

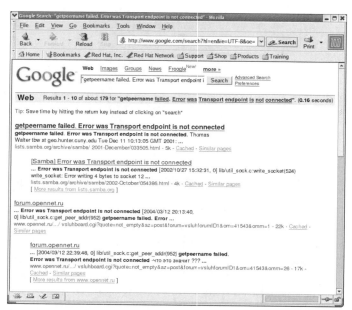

Figure 4-24   Google reporting on an error message

sage within double quotation marks to improve the quality of your results. You will likely find a post concerning your problem and how to solve it. See Figure 4-24.

The Red Hat Web site   The Red Hat and Fedora Web sites are rich sources of information. Following is a list of some locations that may be of interest:

- **Manuals** for Red Hat Linux through Red Hat Linux 9 and *RHEL* are available at www.redhat.com/docs.

- You can find Red Hat **Tips, FAQS,** and **HOWTOs** at www.redhat.com/support/resources/howto.

- You can query the **Red Hat Knowledgebase** (requires free registration) at kbase.redhat.com.

- *FEDORA* **documentation** is available at fedora.redhat.com/docs. (See fedora.redhat.com/docs/about for more information.)

- *RHEL+FEDORA* The **home pages** (www.redhat.com and fedora.redhat.com) have a wealth of information.

- *RHEL+FEDORA* **support forums** are online discussions about any Red Hat-related issues that people want to raise. One forum is dedicated to new users; others to Apache, the X Window System, and so on. Go to www.redhat.com/mailman/listinfo to browse the lists.

- **Hardware help** is available from the Red Hat hardware compatibility list (HCL) at hardware.redhat.com.

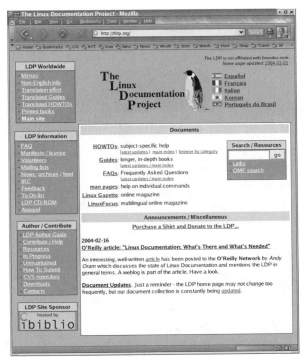

Figure 4-25   The Linux Documentation Project home page

GNU GNU makes many of its manuals available at www.gnu.org/manual. In addition, go to the GNU home page (www.gnu.org) for more documentation and other GNU resources. Many of the GNU pages and resources are available in a wide variety of languages.

The Linux The Linux Documentation Project (www.tldp.org), which has been around for al-
Documentation Project most as long as Linux, houses a complete collection of guides, HOWTOs, FAQs, man pages, and Linux magazines. The home page supports English, Brazilian, Spanish, and French and is easy to use, supporting local text search. It also has a complete set of links (Figure 4-25) that can help you find almost anything you want that is related to Linux (click **Links/Resources** in the Search box or go to www.tldp.org/links). The links page has sections on general information, events, getting started, user groups, mailing lists, and newsgroups, each containing many subsections.

More About Logging In

Refer to "Logging In on the System" on page 76 for information about logging in on the system and "**switchdesk**: Changing Your Default Desktop" on page 106 if you want to change the desktop environment (KDE or GNOME) you log in on as a matter of course.

Unless you are the only user of your system, your system is not connected to any other systems, the Internet, or a modem, and you are the only one with physical access to your system, it is a bad idea to allow any user to log in without a password.

The Login Screen

There are four icon/word pairs at the bottom of the login screen (Figure 4-1, page 77). Click these icons to change aspects of the session you are about to log in to.

- **Language**   When you want to change the language of the window titles, prompts, error messages, and so on, select the language you want from the list that appears when you click this icon/word.

  Just after you log in, the system asks whether you want to make this change in languages permanent or if it is a one-time change. The language changes affect GNOME and KDE and may affect applications.

- **Session**   Displays the **Choose a session** dialog box (Figure 4-1, page 77), which gives you four choices concerning the session you are about to start. It does not change your default desktop; use switchdesk (page 106) for this purpose. Choose one of the following, click **OK**, and continue logging in:

  - **GNOME**   Brings up GNOME, the default desktop environment.

  - **Default System Session**   Brings up your default desktop environment.

  - **KDE**   Brings up the KDE Desktop Environment.

  - **Failsafe Terminal**   Brings up an xterm terminal emulator window without a desktop manager. This setup allows you to log in on a minimal desktop, in case your standard login does not work well enough to allow you to log in to fix a login problem.

- **Reboot**   Shuts down and reboots the system.

- **Shutdown**   Shuts down the system and turns off the power.

As you are logging in, after you enter your username and press RETURN, the system displays information about the last login on this account, showing when it took place and where it originated. You can use this information to see whether anyone else may have accessed this account since you last used it. If someone has, perhaps an unauthorized user has learned your password and has logged on as you. In the interest of security, advise the system administrator of the circumstances that made you suspicious and change your password (page 104).

What to Do If You Cannot Log In

When you enter your username or password incorrectly, the system displays **Incorrect username or password. Letters must be typed in the correct case.** after you finish entering both your username *and* password.

This message tells you that you have entered either the login name *or* password incorrectly or that they are not valid. The message does not differentiate between an unacceptable login name and an unacceptable password in order to discourage unauthorized people from guessing names and passwords to gain access to the system. Some common reasons logins fail are listed following:

- **Log In on the Right Machine**
  One reason the login/password combination may not be valid is because you are trying to log in on the wrong machine. On a larger, networked system, you may have to specify the machine that you want to connect to before you can log in.

- **Login Name and Password Are Case Sensitive**
  Make sure the CAPS LOCK key is off and that you enter your name and password exactly as specified or as you set them up.

- **Make Sure Your Login Name Is Valid**
  Another reason the login/password combination may not be valid is that you have not been set up as a user. If you are administrating the system, refer to "Configuring User and Group Accounts" on page 521. Otherwise, check with the system administrator.

Refer to "Changing Your Password" on page 104 when you want to change your password.

Logging Out

To log out, click the red hat at the lower-left of the display and Choose **Logout** from the window that pops up. From a character-based interface, press CONTROL-D or give the command **exit** in response to the shell prompt.

Using Virtual Consoles

When running Linux on a personal computer, you frequently work with the display and keyboard attached to the computer. Using this physical console, you can access up to 63 *virtual consoles* (also called *virtual terminals*). Some are set up to allow logins, whereas others act as graphical displays. You switch between virtual consoles by holding down the CONTROL and ALT keys and pressing a function key corresponding to the console you want to view. For example, CONTROL-ALT-F5 displays the fifth virtual console. This book refers to the console that you see when you first boot your computer (or press CONTROL-ALT-F1) as the *system console,* or *console.*

By default, six virtual consoles are active and have text login sessions running. When you want to use both a character-based interface and a GUI, you can set up a character-based session on one virtual console and a graphical session on another. Whichever virtual console you start a graphical session from, the graphical session finds the first unused virtual console (number seven by default).

Logging In Remotely: Terminal Emulation and telnet

When you are not using a console, terminal, or other device connected directly to the Linux system you are logging in on, you are probably connected to the Linux system using terminal emulation software on another system. Running on your local computer, this software connects to the Linux system via a network (Ethernet, asynchronous phone line, PPP, or other type) and allows you to log in on the Linux machine.

caution ‖	Make Sure **TERM** Is Set Correctly

No matter how you connect, make sure you have the **TERM** variable set to the type of terminal your emulator is emulating. For more help, see "Specifying a Terminal" on page 920.

When you log in via a dial-up line, the connection is straightforward: You instruct the emulator program to contact the computer, it dials the phone, and you get a login prompt from the remote system. When you log in via a directly connected network, you use telnet (not secure) or ssh (page 570) to connect to the computer. The telnet program has been implemented on many machines, not just on Linux systems. Most user interfaces to TELNET include a terminal emulator. From your Apple, PC, or UNIX machine, give the command **telnet**, followed by the name or IP address (refer to "Host Address" on page 334) of the machine you want to log in on. For examples and more detail, refer to "Running Commands from the Terminal Emulator/Shell" on page 86 and "**telnet**: Logs in on a Remote System" on page 344. For more information about logging in from a terminal emulator, see "Logging In from a Terminal" on page 106.

Changing Your Password

If someone else assigned you a password, it is a good idea to give yourself a new one. A good password is seven or eight characters long and contains a combination of numbers, upper- and lowercase letters, and punctuation characters. Avoid using control characters (such as CONTROL-H) because they may have a special meaning to the system, making it impossible for you to log in. Do not use names, words from English or other languages, or other familiar words that someone can easily guess.

For security reasons none of the passwords you enter is ever displayed by any utility.

security || **Protect Your Password**

Do not allow someone to find out your password: *Do not* put your password in a file that is not encrypted, allow someone to watch you type your password, give it to someone you do not know (a system administrator never needs to know your password), or write it down.

security || **Choose a Password That Is Difficult to Guess**

Do not use phone numbers, names of pets or kids, birthdays, words from a dictionary (not even a foreign language), and so forth. Do not use permutations of these items.

security || **Differentiate Between Important and Less Important Passwords**

It is important to differentiate between important and less important passwords. For example, Web site passwords for blogs or download-access are not very important; it is not bad if you choose the same password for these types of sites. However, your login, mailserver, and bank account Web site passwords are critical: Never use these passwords for an unimportant Web site.

To change your password, click the red hat at the left end of the panel to display the Main menu and select **Preferences⇨Password**. Or you can give the command **passwd** from a terminal emulator or other command line.

The first item the system asks you for is your *old* password. This password is verified to ensure that an unauthorized user is not trying to alter your password. Next, the system requests the new password.

Your password should meet the following criteria to be relatively secure. Only the first item is mandatory.

- It must be at least six characters long (or longer if the system administrator sets it up that way).

- It should not be a word in a dictionary of any language, no matter how seemingly obscure.

- It should not be the name of a person, place, pet, or other thing that might be discovered easily.

- It should contain at least two letters and one digit.

- It should not be your login name, the reverse of your login name, or your login name shifted by one or more characters.

- If you are changing your password, the new password should differ from the old one by at least three characters. Changing the case of a character does not make it count as a different character.

Refer to "Keeping the System Secure" on page 540 for more information about choosing a password.

After you enter your new password, the system asks you to retype it to make sure you did not make a mistake when you entered it the first time. If the new password is the same both times you enter it, your password is changed. If the passwords differ, it means that you made an error in one of them, and the system displays an error message:

```
Sorry, passwords do not match
```

If your password is not long enough, the system displays the following message:

```
BAD PASSWORD: it is too short
```

When it is too simple, the system displays this message:

```
BAD PASSWORD: it is too simplistic/systematic
```

When it is formed from words, the system displays this message:

```
BAD PASSWORD: it is based on a dictionary word
```

Enter a longer or more complex password in response to the **New password:** prompt.

When you successfully change your password, you change the way you log in. If you forget your password, Superuser can change it and tell you your new password.

switchdesk: **Changing Your Default Desktop**

The switchdesk utility tells the system which desktop you want to log in to by default: KDE or GNOME. Initially, your account is set up to log in to GNOME by default. This section explains how to use switchdesk to change your default desktop to KDE.

The switchdesk utility will be dropped from Fedora Core 3; when you select a different desktop when you log in, you will be asked if you want to make the new desktop your permanent desktop.

An easy way to run switchdesk is to open a terminal emulator (click the red hat at the lower-left of the screen to display the Main menu and select **System Tools ⇨ Terminal**, page 86) and give the command **switchdesk kde**, followed by a RE-TURN. Figure 4-26 shows what this command and the system response look like in a konsole terminal emulator window. Once you give this command, you will log in to KDE without needing to click **Session** on the login screen.

You can give the command **switchdesk gnome** to change the default desktop manager back to GNOME.

Logging In from a Terminal

To log in on a terminal, terminal emulator, or other text-based device, enter your username and password in response to the system prompts. If you are using a *terminal* (page 1001) and your screen does not display the word **login:**, check whether the terminal is plugged in and turned on, and then press the RETURN key a few times.

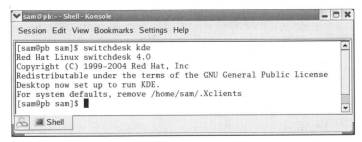

Figure 4-26   Running switchdesk from a terminal emulator

If **login:** still does not appear, try pressing CONTROL-Q. If you are using a *workstation* (page 1006), make sure it is running. Run ssh (page 570), telnet (page 344), or whatever communications/emulation software you have to log in on the system. Try logging in, making sure that you enter your login name as it was specified when your account was set up; the routine that verifies the login name and password is case sensitive.

Next, the *shell prompt* (or just *prompt*) appears, indicating that you have successfully logged in; it indicates that the system is ready for you to give it a command. The shell prompt line may be preceded by one or two short messages called the *message of the day*, or **motd** (page 430), and *issue*. These messages generally identify the version of Red Hat Linux that is running, along with any local messages placed in either the **/etc/motd** or the **/etc/issue** file. The usual prompt is a dollar sign ($). Red Hat establishes a prompt of *[user@host directory]$*, where *user* is your login name, *host* is the name of the local system, and *directory* is the name of the directory you are working in. For information on how to change your prompt, refer to page 284.

Bringing a GUI Up from a Character-Based Display

Once you have logged in on a virtual console, you can start a graphical display by giving the following command to bring up your default desktop manager:

```
$ startx
```

If startx does not work, run switchdesk (page 106) to select GNOME or KDE, depending on which is installed on the system.

Correcting Mistakes

This section explains how to correct typos and other errors you may make while you are logged in on a character-based display. Because the shell and most other utilities do not interpret the command line or other text until after you press RETURN, you can correct typing mistakes before you press RETURN.

You can correct typing mistakes in several ways: erase one character at a time, back up a word at a time, or back up to the beginning of the command line in one step.

After you press RETURN, it is too late to correct a mistake; you can either wait for the command to run to completion or abort execution of the program (page 108).

Erasing a Character

While entering characters from the keyboard, you can back up and erase a mistake by pressing the *erase key* once for each character you want to delete. The erase key backs over as many characters as you wish. It does not, in general, back up past the beginning of the line.

---

tip || CONTROL-Z **Suspends a Program**

Although not a way of correcting a mistake, you may press the suspend key (typically CONTROL-Z) by mistake and wonder what happened (you will see a message containing the word **Stopped**). You have just stopped your job, using job control (page 262). Give the command fg to continue your job in the foreground, and you should be back to where you were before you pressed the suspend key. For more information, refer to "bg: Sends a Job to the Background" on page 264.

The default erase key is BACKSPACE. If this key does not work, try DELETE or CONTROL-H. If these keys do not work, give the following stty[3] command to set the erase and line kill (see "Deleting a Line" second section following) keys to their defaults

```
$ stty ek
```

Deleting a Word

You can delete a word you entered by pressing CONTROL-W. A *word* is any sequence of characters that does not contain a SPACE or TAB. When you press CONTROL-W, the cursor moves left to the beginning of the current word (as you are entering a word) or the previous word (when you have just entered a SPACE or TAB), removing the word.

Deleting a Line

Any time before you press RETURN, you can delete a line you are entering by pressing the *line kill* key, or *kill key*. When you press this key, the cursor moves to the left, erasing characters as it goes, back to the beginning of the line. The default line kill key is CONTROL-U. If this key does not work, try CONTROL-X. If these keys do not work, give the following command to set the erase and line kill keys to their defaults:

```
$ stty ek
```

Aborting Execution

Sometimes you may want to terminate a running program. A Linux program may be performing a lengthy task such as displaying the contents of a file that is several hundred pages or copying a file that is not the one you meant to copy.

---

3. The command stty is an abbreviation for *set teletypewriter*, the first terminal that UNIX was run on. Today stty is commonly thought of as *set terminal*.

To terminate a program from a character-based display, press the *interrupt key* (CONTROL-C or sometimes DELETE or DEL). When you press this key, the Linux operating system sends a terminal interrupt signal to the program you are running and to the shell. Exactly what effect this signal has depends on the program. Some programs stop execution immediately, whereas others ignore the signal. Some programs take other actions. When it receives a terminal interrupt signal, the shell displays a prompt and waits for another command.

If these methods do not terminate the program, try stopping the program with the suspend key (typically CONTROL-Z), giving the **jobs** command to verify the job number of the program, and using kill to abort the program. The job number is the number within the brackets at the left end of the line that **jobs** displays ([1]). The **kill** command uses –TERM to send a termination signal[4] to the job specified by the job number, which is preceded by a percent sign (**%1**):

```
$ bigjob
^Z
[1]+  Stopped                 bigjob
$ jobs
[1]+  Stopped                 bigjob
$ kill -TERM %1

[1]+  Stopped                 bigjob
$ RETURN
[1]+  Killed                  bigjob
```

The **kill** command returns a prompt; press RETURN again to see the confirmation message. For more information on job control, refer to "Running a Program in the Background" on page 204.

Killing a job that is running under a GUI is straightforward. At the upper-right corner of most windows is a button with an **X** on it. Move the mouse pointer so that its tip is over the **X**. If you leave the mouse stationary for a moment, instructions on how to kill the window appear. With the mouse pointer still over the **X**, kill the window by clicking the left mouse button. You may need to click several times.

Repeating/Editing Command Lines

To repeat a previous command, press the UP ARROW key. Each time you press it, you see an earlier command line. To reexecute the displayed command line, press RETURN. Press DOWN ARROW to browse through the command lines in the other direction.

The RIGHT and LEFT ARROW keys move you back and forth along the displayed command line. At any point along the command line, you add characters by typing them. Use the erase key to remove characters from the command line.

For more complex command line editing, see page 295.

---

4. When the terminal interrupt signal does not work, use the kill (–KILL) signal. A running program cannot ignore kill; it is sure to abort the program (page 375).

Controlling Windows II

Refer to "Controlling Windows I" on page 82 for an introduction to using windows under Red Hat Linux. This section discusses changing the way you change the input focus on the desktop, changing the resolution of the display, and understanding the window and session managers.

Changing the Input Focus

When you type on the keyboard, the window manager (page 111) directs the characters you are typing somewhere, usually to a window. The *active window* (the window accepting input from the keyboard) is said to have the *input focus*. Depending on how you set up your account, you can use the mouse in one of three ways to change the input focus. (You can also use the keyboard; see page 83.)

- **click-to-focus** (*explicit focus*)   Gives the input focus to a window when you click the window; that window continues to accept input from your keyboard regardless of the position of the mouse pointer. The window loses the focus when you click another window. Although clicking the middle or the right mouse button also activates a window, use only the left mouse button for this purpose; other buttons may have unexpected effects when you use them to activate a window.

- **focus-follows-mouse** (*sloppy focus, point to give focus,* or *enter-only*)   Gives the input focus to a window when you move the mouse pointer onto the window. That window maintains the input focus until you move the mouse pointer onto another window, at which point the new window gets the focus. Specifically, when you move the mouse pointer off a window and onto the root window, the window that had the focus does not lose it.

- **focus-under-mouse**   Same as focus-follows-mouse (KDE).

- **focus-strictly-under-mouse** (*enter-exit*)   Gives the input focus to a window when you move the mouse pointer onto the window. That window maintains the input focus until you move the mouse pointer off the window with the focus, at which point no window has the focus. Specifically, when you move the mouse pointer off a window and onto the root window, the window that had the focus loses it, and input from the keyboard is lost.

GNOME   Under GNOME, use **Main menu: Preferences⇨Windows** to change the focus policy: Put a mark in the check box next to **Select windows when the mouse moves over them** to select focus-follows-mouse policy. When there is no mark in this check box, click-to-focus is in effect. Click **Close**.

KDE   Under KDE, use the Control Center to change focus policy: Select **Main menu: Preferences**⇨**More Preferences**⇨**Control Center**; from the Control Center select **Desktop**⇨**Window Behavior** and choose the focus policy you want. Click **Apply**.

To determine which window has the input focus, compare the window borders; the border color of the active window is different from the others or, on a monochrome display, is darker. Another indication that a window is active is that the keyboard cursor is a solid rectangle; in windows that are not active, it is an outline of a rectangle.

Which keyboard focus method are you using? If you position the mouse pointer in a window and that window does not get the input focus, your window manager is configured to use the click-to-focus method. If the border of the window changes, you are using the focus-follows-mouse/focus-under-mouse or focus-strictly-under-mouse method. To determine which of these methods you are using, start typing something, with the mouse pointer on a window. Then move the mouse pointer over the root window and continue typing. If characters continue to appear within the window, you are using focus-follows-mouse/focus-under-mouse. Otherwise, you are using focus-strictly-under-mouse.

Changing the Resolution of the Display

The X server (the basis for the Linux graphical interface, page 217) starts at a specific display resolution and color depth. Although you can change the color depth only when you start an X server, you can switch a running X server between different resolutions. The number of resolutions available depends both on your display hardware and on how X has been configured on your system (see page 63 for details). Many users prefer to do most of their work at a higher resolution but might want to switch to a lower resolution for some tasks, such as playing games. You can move between different display resolutions by pressing either CONTROL-ALT-KEYPAD-+ or CONTROL-ALT-KEYPAD--, using the + and - on the keyboard's numeric keypad.

Changing to a lower resolution has the effect of zooming in on your display, so you may no longer be able to view the entire workspace at once. If you are using a scrollbar and it is moved off the screen by lowering the resolution, you will not be able to scroll the display until you change back to a higher resolution.

Understanding the Window Manager

A *window manager*, the program that controls the look and feel of the basic GUI, runs on top of a desktop manager (typically KDE or GNOME) and controls all aspects of the windows in the X Window System environment. The window manager defines the appearance of the windows on your desktop, as well as how you operate and position them: open, close, move, resize, iconify, and so on. The window manager may also handle some session management functions, such as how to pause, resume, restart, or end a windowing session (page 113).

A window manager controls *window decorations:* the titlebar and border of a window. Aside from the aesthetic aspects of changing window decoration, you can alter the functionality by modifying the number and placement of buttons on the titlebar.

The window manager takes care of window manipulation so that the client programs do not need to. This setup is very different from that of many other operating systems, and the way that GNOME and KDE deal with window managers is different from other desktop environments. Window managers do more than manage windows by providing a useful, good-looking, graphical shell to work from. Their open design allows users to define their own policy down to the fine details.

Theoretically, GNOME and KDE are not dependent on any particular window manager and can work with any of several window managers. Because of their flexibility, you would not see major parts of the desktop environment change if you were to switch from one window manager to another. These desktop managers work with a window manager to make your work environment intuitive and easy to use. The desktop manager does not control window placement but does get information from the window manager about window placement.

Red Hat Window Managers

Metacity, the default window manager for GNOME, provides window management and starts many components through GNOME panel commands. It also communicates with and facilitates access to other components in the environment. The kwin window manager is the default window manager for KDE.

Using the standard X libraries, individual programmers have created such window managers as vtwm (Virtual Tab Window Manager), gwm (GNU Window Manager), afterstep (a NeXTStep clone), and fvwm2 (originally Feeble Virtual Window Manager). These window managers are readily available and are free of charge.

optional ||

Using a Window Manager Without a Desktop Manager

It is interesting to see exactly where the line between a window manager and a desktop manager falls. Toward this end, you can run the Failsafe Terminal from the Login screen: Specify **Session⇨Failsafe Terminal** and log in. You should see a clean screen with an undecorated window running xterm. You can give commands from this window to open other windows. Try xeyes, xterm, and xclock. Give the command **exit** to return to the Login screen.

Session Management

A session starts when you log in and ends when you log out or reset the session. With a fully compliant GNOME or KDE application, these desktop managers can *session manage* your data. When you run a managed session, the desktop looks pretty much the same when you log in as it did when you logged out the previous time. The data in this case includes not only the data that the application manipulates but also all the information about the state of the application when you end your session: what windows were open and where they were located, what each of the applications was doing, and so forth.

Chapter Summary

As with many operating systems, your access to the system is authorized when you log in. You enter your username on the Login screen, followed by a password. You can change your password at any time. Choose a password that is difficult to guess and that conforms to the criteria imposed by the utility that changes your password.

As implemented by Red Hat, the KDE desktop appears very similar to the GNOME desktop. Underneath the veneer are two desktop managers that perform many of the same functions, yet work very differently.

The system administrator is responsible for maintaining the system. On a single-user system, you are the system administrator. On a small, multiuser system, you or another user is the system administrator, or this job may be shared. On a large, multiuser system or network of systems, there is frequently a full-time system administrator. When extra privileges are required to perform certain system tasks, the system administrator logs in as the **root** user by entering the user name **root** and the **root** password. While logged in in this manner, this user is called Superuser or administrator. On a multiuser system, several trusted users may be given the **root** password. Do not work as Superuser as a matter of course. When you have to do something that requires Superuser privileges, work as Superuser for only as long as you need to; revert to working as yourself as soon as possible.

Understanding the desktop and its components is key to getting the most out of the system. The Main panel offers a convenient way to launch applications, either directly by clicking icons or by using the Main menu. The Main menu is a multilevel menu that you can use to maintain the system and to start many of the most common applications on the system. A window is the graphical manifestation of an application. You can control the size, location, and appearance of a window by clicking buttons on its titlebar. A terminal emulator allows you to use the Linux command line interface from a graphical environment. You can use a terminal emulator to launch both textual and graphical programs.

Konqueror is a multipurpose tool, one of the most important on the desktop. You can use it to run programs, browse the Web, and manage files. Konqueror is transparent to the network: You can work with local or remote files and not know the difference. Konqueror's power comes from the seamless integration of its functions.

The Control Center provides a way of setting/changing many characteristics of KDE and kwin, the KDE window manager. Using the Control Center, you can control Web and file browsing with Konqueror, the look and feel of your desktop, the sound component of the system, network aspects of the desktop, and personalization of the desktop, including options that make it easier for people with special needs to use. For Superuser, the Control Center contains a module on system administration.

The man utility provides online documentation on system utilities. This utility is helpful to new Linux users, as well as to experienced users who must often delve into the system documentation for information on the fine points of a utility's behavior. The info utility helps the beginner and expert alike. This utility includes a tutorial on its use and documentation on many Linux utilities.

Exercises

1. The following error message is displayed when you attempt to log in with an incorrect username *or* an incorrect password:

   ```
   Incorrect username or password. Letters must be typed in the correct
   case.
   ```

   This message does not indicate whether your username, your password, or both are invalid. Why does it not tell you?

2. Give three examples of poor password choices. What is wrong with each? Include one that is too short. Give the error message the system displays.

3. Is **fido** an acceptable password? Give several reasons why or why not?

4. What is a context menu? How does a context menu differ from other menus?

5. What happens when you right click the root window? How can you use this?

6. Where is the Main menu button, and what does it look like? Why is it an important tool?

7. What is the primary function of the Main menu?

8. What is input focus? When no window has the input focus, what happens to the letters you type on the keyboard? Which type of input focus do you think you would like to work with? Why?

9. What are the functions of a Window Operations menu? How do you display this menu?

10. What is the Main panel? What does your Main panel show you, and what can you do with it? Discuss the Pager and Taskbar applets.

11. What are tooltips? How are they useful?

Advanced Exercises

12. What happens when you ALT + right drag within a window? What difference does it make where the mouse pointer is within the window (top, side, and so on) when you start to drag?

13. Try the experiment described in "Using a Window Manager Without a Desktop Manager" on page 112. What is missing from the screen? Based only on what you see, describe what a window manager provides. How does a desktop manager make it easier to work with a GUI?

14. When the characters you type do not appear on the screen, what might be wrong? How can you fix it?

15. What happens when you run vim from the Run Command window without specifying that it be run in a terminal? Where does the output go?

16. You saw that man pages for write appear in sections 1 and 2 of the system manual. Explain how you can use man to determine what sections of the system manual contain a manual page with a given name.

17. How many man pages are in the **Devices** subsection of the system manual? (*Hint*: **Devices** is a subsection of **Special Files**.)

The Linux Utilities

5

When Linus Torvalds introduced Linux, and for a long time thereafter, Linux did not have a graphical interface: It ran on character-based terminals only. All the tools ran from a command line. Today, the Linux GUI is important, but many people, especially system administrators, run many command line programs. In a lot of cases, command line utilities are faster, more powerful, or more complete than their GUI counterparts. Sometimes, there is no GUI counterpart to a text-based utility, and some people just prefer the hands-on feeling of the command line.

tip || **Run These Utilities from a Command Line**

This chapter describes command line, or text-based, utilities. You can experiment with these utilities from a terminal emulator within a GUI (page 86) or from a virtual console (page 103).

When you work with a command line interface, you are working with the shell (Chapters 7, 9, and 28). Before you start working with the shell, it is important to understand something about the characters that are special to the shell, so this chapter starts with a discussion of special characters. The chapter then describes five basic utilities you can use to create and manipulate files: ls, cat, less, more, and rm. It continues by describing several other file manipulation utilities, as well as utilities that find out who is logged in; that communicate with other users; that print, compress, and decompress files; and that unpack archived files. The chapter concludes with a tutorial on how to create and edit files using the vim editor.

Special Characters

Special characters, which have a special meaning to the shell, are discussed in "File-name Generation/Pathname Expansion" on page 207. These characters are mentioned here so that you can avoid accidentally using them as regular characters until you understand how the shell interprets them. For example, avoid using any of these characters in a filename (even though emacs and some other programs do) until you learn how to quote them (next). The standard special characters are

    & ; | * ? ' " ` [ ] ( ) $ < > { } ^ # / \ % ! ~ +

Although not considered special characters, RETURN, SPACE, and TAB also have special meanings to the shell. RETURN usually ends a command line and initiates execution of a command. The SPACE and TAB characters separate elements on the command line and are collectively known as *whitespace,* or *blanks.*

If you need to use as a regular character one of the characters that has a special meaning to the shell, you can *quote* (or *escape*) it. When you quote a special character, you keep the shell from giving it special meaning. The shell treats a quoted special character as a regular character.[1]

To quote a character, precede it with a backslash (\). When you have two or more special characters together, you must precede each with a backslash (for example, enter ** as **). You can quote a backslash just as you would quote any other special character—by preceding it with a backslash (\\).

Another way of quoting special characters is to enclose them between single quotation marks, as in ' ** '. You can quote many special and regular characters between a pair of single quotation marks, as in ' **This is a special character: >** ' . The regular characters remain regular, and the shell also interprets the special characters as regular characters.

The only way to quote the erase character (CONTROL-H), the line kill character (CONTROL-U), and other control characters (try CONTROL-M) is by preceding any one with a CONTROL-V. Single quotation marks and backslashes do not work. Try the following:

```
$ echo 'xxxxxx CONTROL-U'
$ echo 'xxxxxx CONTROL-V CONTROL-U'
```

Basic Utilities

One of the important advantages of Linux is that it comes with thousands of utilities that perform myriad functions. You will use utilities whenever you use Linux, whether you use them directly by name from the command line or indirectly from a

---

1. A backslash (/), however, is always a separator in a pathname, even when you quote it.

```
$ ls
practice
$ cat practice
This is a small file that I created
with a text editor.
$ rm practice
$ ls
$ cat practice
cat: practice: No such file or directory
$
```

Figure 5-1   Using ls, cat, and rm on the file named **practice**

menu or icon. The following sections discuss some of the most basic and important utilities; these utilities are available from a character-based interface. Some of the more important utilities are also available from a GUI, and some are available only from a GUI.

The term *directory* is used extensively in the next sections. A directory is a resource that can hold files. On other operating systems, including Windows, and frequently under the Linux GUI, a directory is referred to as a folder, which is a good analogy: A directory is a folder that can hold files.

caution || **In This Chapter You Work In Your Home Directory**

When you log in on the system, you are working in a directory that is called your *home directory*. In this chapter that is the only directory you use: All the files you create in this chapter are in your home directory.

ls: Lists the Names of Files

Using the editor of your choice (a GUI editor is fine), create a small file named **practice** in your directory. After exiting from the editor, you can use the ls (list) utility to display a list of the names of the files in the directory. The first command in Figure 5-1 shows ls listing the name of the **practice** file. (You may also see files the system or a program created automatically.) Subsequent commands in Figure 5-1 display the contents of the file and remove the file. These commands are described next.

cat: Displays a Text File

The cat utility displays the contents of a text file. The name of the command is derived from *catenate*, which means to join together, one after the other. (Figure 7-8 on page 198 shows how to use cat to string together the contents of three files.)

A convenient way to display the contents of a file to the screen is by giving the command **cat**, followed by a SPACE and the name of a file. Figure 5-1 shows cat displaying the contents of **practice**. This figure shows the difference between the ls and cat utilities. The ls utility displays the *name* of a file, whereas cat displays the *contents* of a file.

rm: Deletes a File

The rm (remove) utility deletes a file. Figure 5-1 shows rm deleting the file named **practice**. After rm deletes the file, ls and cat show that **practice** is no longer in the directory. The ls utility does not list its filename, and cat says that it cannot open the file. Use rm carefully.

---

tip ‖   **Safer Way of Removing Files**

You can use the interactive form of rm to make sure that you delete only the file(s) you intend to delete. When you follow rm with the **−i** option (see footnote 2 on page 96) and the name of the file you want to delete, rm displays the name of the file and asks you to respond with **y** (yes) or **n** (no) before it deletes the file. The **−i** option is set up by default for the **root** user on Red Hat Linux:

```
$ rm -i toollist
rm: remove 'toollist'? y
```

Optional: You can create an alias (page 305) and put it in your startup file (page 164) so that rm always runs in interactive mode.

---

less Is more: Displaying a Text File One Screen at a Time

When you want to view a file that is longer than one screen, you can use either the less or the more utility. Each of these utilities pauses after displaying a screen of text. Because these files show one page at a time, they are called *pagers*. Although they are very similar, they have subtle differences. At the end of the file, for example, less displays an **EOF** (end of file) message and waits for you to press **q** before returning you to the shell, whereas more returns you directly to the shell. In both utilities, you can press **h** to display a help screen that lists commands you can use while paging through a file. Give the commands **less practice** and **more practice** in place of the **cat** command in Figure 5-1 to see how these commands work. Use the command **less /etc/termcap** instead if you want to experiment with a longer file. Refer to the less man page for more information.

---

tip ‖   **Filename Completion**

After you enter one or more letters of a filename on a command line, press TAB, and the shell completes as much of the filename as it can. When only one filename starts with the characters you entered, the shell completes the filename and places a SPACE after it. You can keep typing, or you can press RETURN to execute the command at this point. When the characters you entered do not uniquely identify a filename, the shell completes what it can and waits for more input. When pressing TAB does not change the display, press TAB again to display a list of possible completions. Refer to "Completion" on page 302.

---

hostname: Displays Your Machine Name

The hostname command displays the name of the machine you are working on. Use this command if you are not sure that you are logged in on the right machine.

```
$ hostname
bravo
```

Working with Files

The following sections describe utilities that copy, move, and print files.

cp: Copies a File

The cp (copy) utility (Figure 5-2) makes a copy of a file. This utility can copy any file, including text and executable program (binary) files. You can use cp to make a backup copy of a file or a copy to experiment with.

A cp command line uses the following syntax to specify source and destination files:

cp source-file destination-file

The *source-file* is the name of the file that cp is going to copy. The *destination-file* is the name that cp assigns to the resulting—new—copy of the file.

tip ‖   **cp Can Destroy a File**

If the *destination-file* exists *before* you give a cp command, cp overwrites it. Because cp overwrites (and destroys the contents of) an existing *destination-file* without warning, you must take care not to cause cp to overwrite a file that you need. You can use the cp interactive (**−i**) option; it checks with you before it overwrites a file. Options are discussed on page 190. The following example assumes that the file named **orange.2** exists before you give the cp command. The user answers **y** to overwrite the file:

```
$ cp -i orange orange.2
cp: overwrite 'orange.2'? y
$
```

The command line shown in Figure 5-2 copies the file named **memo** to **memo.copy**. The period is part of the filename—just another character. The initial ls command shows that **memo** is the only file in the directory. After the cp command, the second ls shows both files, **memo** and **memo.copy**, in the directory.

Sometimes it is useful to incorporate the date in the name of a copy of a file. The following exampleincludes the date January 30 (0130):

```
$ ls
memo
$ cp memo memo.copy
$ ls
memo memo.copy
```

Figure 5-2   cp copies a file

```
$ cp memo memo.0130
```

Although it has no significance to Linux, the date can help you find a version of a file that you created on a certain date. The date can also help you avoid overwriting existing files by providing a unique filename each day. Refer to "Filenames" on page 159.

Use scp (page 572) or ftp (page 583) when you need to copy a file from one system to another on a common network.

mv: Changes the Name of a File

The mv (move) utility can rename a file without making a duplicate, or copy, of it. The mv command line specifies an existing file and a new filename using the same syntax as cp:

mv existing-filename new-filename

The command line in Figure 5-3 changes the name of the file **memo** to **memo.0130**. The initial ls command shows that **memo** is the only file in the directory. After you give the mv command, **memo.0130** is the only file in the directory. Compare this to the earlier cp example.

The mv utility can be used for more than changing the name of a file. Refer to "mv, cp: Moves or Copies a File" on page 171.

```
$ ls
memo
$ mv memo memo.0130
$ ls
memo.0130
```

Figure 5-3   mv renames a file

lpr: Prints a File

The lpr (line printer) utility places one or more files in a print queue for printing. Linux provides print queues so that only one job gets printed on a given printer at a time. A queue allows several people or jobs to send output simultaneously to a single printer with the expected results. On machines with access to more than one printer, you can use the –P option to instruct lpr to place the file in the queue for a specific printer, including one that is connected to another machine on the network. The following command prints the file named **report**:

```
$ lpr report
```

Because this command does not specify a printer, the output goes to the default printer, which is *the* printer when you have only one printer. Refer to Chapter 14 for information on setting up a printer and defining the default printer.

The next command line prints the same file on the printer named **mailroom**:

```
$ lpr -Pmailroom report
```

You can see what jobs are in the print queue by using the lpq utility:

```
$ lpq
lp is ready and printing
Rank  Owner   Job Files                 Total Size
active alex      86 (standard input)      954061 bytes
```

In this example, Alex has one job that is being printed; no other jobs are in the queue. You can use the job number, 86 in this case, with the lprm utility to remove the job from the print queue and stop it from printing:

```
$ lprm 86
```

You can send more than one file to the printer with a single command. The following command line prints three files on the printer named **laser1**:

```
$ lpr -Plaser1 05.txt 108.txt 12.txt
```

grep: **Finds a String**

The grep (global regular expression print[2]) utility searches through one or more files to see whether any contain a specified string of characters. This utility does not change the file it searches but displays each line that contains the string.

The grep command in Figure 5-4 searches through the file **memo** for lines that contain the string **credit** and displays a single line. If **memo** contained such words as **discredit, creditor,** or **accreditation,** grep would have displayed those lines as well because they contain the string it was searching for. You do not need to enclose the

```
$ cat memo

Helen:

In our meeting on June 6th we
discussed the issue of credit.
Have you had any further thoughts
about it?

                    Alex
$ grep 'credit' memo
discussed the issue of credit.
```

Figure 5-4   grep searches for a string

---

2. Originally it was a play on an ed—an original UNIX editor, available on Red Hat Linux—command: **g/re/p**. In this command the **g** stands for global, **re** is a regular expression delimited by slashes, and **p** is for print.

string you are searching for in single quotation marks, but doing so allows you to put SPACEs and special characters in the search string.

The grep utility can do much more than search for a simple string in a single file. Refer to the grep man page and Appendix A, Regular Expressions, for more information.

head: Displays the Beginning of a File

The head utility displays the first ten lines of a file. You can use head to help you remember what a particular file contains. If you have a file named **months** that lists the 12 months of the year in order, one to a line, head displays **Jan** through **Oct** (Figure 5-5).

The head utility can display any number of lines, so you can use it to look at only the first line of a file or at a screen or more. To specify the number of lines head displays, include a hyphen followed by the number of lines in the head command. For example, the following command displays only the first line of **months**:

```
$ head -1 months
Jan
```

The head utility can also display parts of a file based on a count of blocks or characters rather than lines. Refer to the head man page for more information.

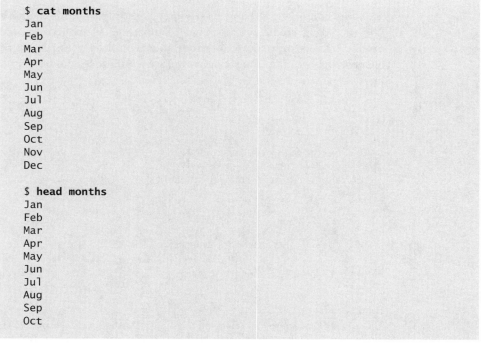

```
$ cat months
Jan
Feb
Mar
Apr
May
Jun
Jul
Aug
Sep
Oct
Nov
Dec

$ head months
Jan
Feb
Mar
Apr
May
Jun
Jul
Aug
Sep
Oct
```

Figure 5-5   head displays the first lines of a file

tail: Displays the End of a File

The tail utility is similar to head but by default displays the *last* ten lines of a file. Depending on how you invoke it, the tail utility can display fewer or more than ten lines, use a count of blocks or characters rather than lines to display parts of a file, and display lines being added to a file that is changing. The following command causes tail to display the last five lines, **Aug** through **Dec,** of the **months** file shown in Figure 5-5:

```
$ tail -5 months
Aug
Sep
Oct
Nov
Dec
```

The ability to display lines as they are added to the end of a file is a useful feature. You can monitor lines as they are added to the end of the growing file named **logfile** with the command

```
$ tail -f logfile
```

Press the interrupt key (usually CONTROL-C) to stop tail and return to the shell prompt. Refer to the tail man page for more information.

sort: Displays a File in Order

The sort utility displays the contents of a file in order by lines but does not change the original file. If you have a file named **days** that contains the name of each day of the week on a separate line, sort displays the file in alphabetical order (Figure 5-6).

```
$ cat days
Monday
Tuesday
Wednesday
Thursday
Friday
Saturday
Sunday
$ sort days
Friday
Monday
Saturday
Sunday
Thursday
Tuesday
Wednesday
```

Figure 5-6   sort displays a file in order

The sort utility is useful for putting lists in order. The **–u** option generates a sorted list in which each line is unique (no duplicates). The **–n** option puts a list of numbers in order. Refer to the sort man page for more information.

uniq: **Removes Duplicate Lines from a File**

The uniq (unique) utility displays a file, skipping adjacent duplicate lines, but does not change the original file. If a file contains a list of names and has two successive entries for the same person, uniq skips the extra line (Figure 5-7).

If a file is sorted before it is processed by uniq, uniq ensures that no two lines in the file are the same. (Of course, sort can do that all by itself with the **–u** option.) Refer to the uniq man page for more information.

```
$ cat dups
Cathy
Fred
Joe
John
Mary
Mary
Paula
$ uniq dups
Cathy
Fred
Joe
John
Mary
Paula
```

Figure 5-7   uniq removes duplicate lines

diff: **Compares Two Files**

The diff (difference) utility compares two files and displays a list of the differences between them. This utility does not change either file and is useful when you want to compare two versions of a letter or report or two versions of the source code for a program.

The diff utility with the **–u** (unified output format, Figure 5-8) option first displays two lines indicating which of the files you are comparing will be denoted by a plus sign (**+**) and which by a minus sign (**–**). Figure 5-8 shows that a minus sign indicates the **colors.1** file; a plus sign, the **colors.2** file.

The **diff –u** command breaks long, multiline text into *hunks*. Each hunk is preceded by a line starting and ending with two at signs (**@@**). This hunk identifier indicates the starting line number and the number of lines from each file for this hunk. In Figure 5-8, this line indicates that the hunk covers the section of the **colors.1** file (indicated by a minus sign) from the first line and continuing for six lines (for a total of

```
$ diff -u colors.1 colors.2
--- colors.1     Fri Nov 21 15:45:32 2003
+++ colors.2     Fri Nov 21 15:24:46 2003
@@ -1,6 +1,5 @@
 red
+blue
 green
 yellow
-pink
-purple
 orange
```

Figure 5-8   diff displaying the unified output format

seven lines). Similarly, the **+1,5** indicates that the hunk also covers **colors.2** from the first line through five subsequent lines.

Following these header lines, **diff –u** displays each line of text with a leading minus sign, plus sign, or nothing. The leading minus sign indicates that the line occurs only in the file denoted by the minus sign. The leading plus sign indicates that the line is from the file denoted by the plus sign. A line that begins with neither a plus sign nor a minus sign occurs in both files in the same location. Refer to the diff man page for more information.

file: Tests the Contents of a File

You can use the file utility to learn about the contents of any file on a Linux system without having to open and examine the file yourself. In the following example, file reports that **letter_e.gz** contains data that was compressed by the gzip utility (page 131):

```
$ file letter_e.gz
letter_e.gz: gzip compressed data, was "letter_e", from Unix
```

Refer to the file man page for more information.

| (Pipe): Communicates Between Processes

Because pipes are integral to the functioning of a Linux system, they are introduced here for use in examples. Pipes are covered in detail in on page 201.

A *process* is either the means by which Linux executes a utility or other program or the utility/program as Linux executes it (page 193). Communication between processes is one of the hallmarks of UNIX/Linux. A *pipe* (written as a vertical bar, |, on the command line and appearing as a solid or broken vertical line on keyboards) provides the simplest form of this kind of communication. Simply put, a pipe takes the output of one utility and sends that output as input to another utility. Using

UNIX/Linux terminology, a pipe takes standard output of one process and redirects it to become standard input of another process. Most of what a process displays on your screen is sent to standard output. Without being redirected, this output appears on your screen. Using a pipe, you can redirect that output so that it does not go to the screen but goes instead to standard input of another utility. (See page 194 for more information on standard input and output.) A utility such as head can take its input from a file whose name you specify on the command line following the word **head**, or it can take its input from standard input. For example, you can give the command shown in Figure 5-5 on page 124 as

```
$ cat months | head
Jan
Feb
Mar
Apr
May
Jun
Jul
Aug
Sep
Oct
```

You can use the following command to see the first line of the **months** file:

```
$ cat months | head -1
Jan
```

Four More Utilities

The echo and date utilities are two of the most frequently used from the large collection of Linux utilities. The script utility helps you record part of a session in a file, and mcopy makes a copy of a text file that can be read on a Windows machine.

echo: Displays Text

The echo utility copies anything you put on the command line, after **echo**, to the screen. Some examples are shown in Figure 5-9. The last example shows what the shell does with an unquoted asterisk (✳) on the command line: It expands it into a list of filenames in the directory.

The echo utility is a good tool for learning about the shell and other Linux programs. Some examples on page 208 use echo to illustrate how special characters, such as the asterisk, work. Throughout Chapters 9 and 28 echo helps explain shell variables and how to send messages from shell scripts to the screen.

date: Displays the Time and Date

The date utility displays the current date and time. An example of date is

```
$ date
Wed Mar 13 08:00:38 PST 2002
```

```
$ ls
memo  memo.0714  practice
$ echo Hi
Hi
$ echo This is a sentence.
This is a sentence.
$ echo star: *
star: memo memo.0714 practice
$
```

Figure 5-9   echo copies the command line (but not the word **echo**) to the screen

You can choose the format and select the contents of the output of date as in the following example. Refer to the date man page for more information.

```
$ date +"%A %B %d"
Wednesday March 13
```

script: **Records a Linux Session**

The script utility records all or part of a login session, including your input and the system's responses. This utility is useful only from character-based devices, such as a terminal or a terminal emulator. The utility does capture a session with vi, but because vi uses control characters to position the cursor and display different type-faces, such as bold, it will be difficult to read and may not be useful. When you cat a file that has captured a vi session, you will see the session pass before your eyes in a great hurry.

By default, script captures the session in a file named **typescript**. To use a different filename, follow the **script** command with a SPACE and the filename you want to use. To append to a file, use the **–a** option after **script** but before any filename; otherwise, script overwrites an existing file. Following is a session being recorded by script:

```
$ script
Script started, file is typescript
$ date
Wed Mar 13 08:10:51 PST 2002
$ who am i
alex      pts/4     Mar  8 22:15
$
$ apropos mtools
mtools                  (1)  - utilities to access DOS disks in Unix
mtools.conf [mtools] (5)  - mtools configuration files
mtoolstest              (1)  - tests and displays the configuration
$ exit
Script done, file is typescript
$
```

Use the exit command to terminate a script session. You can view the file you created with cat, less, more, or an editor. Following is the file that was created by the preceding script command:

```
$ cat typescript
Script started on Wed Mar 13 08:10:47 2002
$ date
Wed Mar 13 08:10:51 PST 2002
$ who am i
alex        pts/4     Mar  8 22:15
$
$ apropos mtools
mtools               (1)   - utilities to access DOS disks in Unix
mtools.conf [mtools] (5)   - mtools configuration files
mtoolstest           (1)   - tests and displays the configuration
$ exit
Script done on Wed Mar 13 08:11:07 2002
$
```

If you will be editing the file with the vi, emacs, or another Linux editor, you can use tr (translate) as shown in the following command to get rid of the ^M characters that appear at the ends of lines in the **typescript** file.

```
$ cat typescript | tr -d '\r' > typescript.good
```

Refer to the tr man page for more information.

mcopy: **Converts Linux Files to Windows Format**

The mcopy utility (part of the set of Mtools) converts a Linux text file so that it can be read by a DOS or Windows system. Give the following command to convert a file named **memo** (created with pico, vi, emacs, or another text editor) to a DOS-format file on the floppy in drive **a:** named **memo.txt**. The **–t** option converts the line-ending characters so that they are appropriate to the operating system that will read the file.

```
$ mcopy -t memo a:memo.txt
```

The original file is not changed. You can email the new file as an attachment to someone on an Windows system. You can also use mcopy to convert DOS files so they can be read on a Linux system:

```
$ mcopy -t a:memo.txt memo2
```

In order to change the format of a file with mcopy, you must read from or write to a DOS-format floppy disk. Refer to the mtools man page for more information.

You can also use tr to change a DOS file into a Linux text file. In the following example, the **–d** option causes tr to remove RETURNs (represented by **\r**) from the file:

```
$ cat memo | tr -d '\r' > memo.txt
```

Converting a file the other way without Mtools is not as easy. Refer to the tr man page for more information.

Compressing and Archiving a File

Large files use a lot of disk space and take longer than smaller files to transfer from one system to another over a network. If you do not need to look at the contents of a large file very often, you may want to save it on a magnetic tape, CD, or other medium and remove it from the hard disk. If you have a continuing need for the file, retrieving a copy from a tape may be inconvenient. To reduce the amount of disk space you use without removing the file entirely, you can compress the file without losing any of the information.

You frequently get a compressed file when you download files from the Internet. The utilities described following compress and decompress files by using various tools.

gzip: Compresses a File

The gzip (GNU zip) utility compresses a file by analyzing it and recoding it more efficiently. The new version of the file looks completely different. In fact, the new file contains many nonprinting characters so you cannot view it directly. The gzip utility works particularly well on files with a lot of repeated information, such as text and image data, although most image data is already in a compressed format. Red Hat stores manual pages in gzipped format to save disk space.

The following example shows a boring file. Each of the 8,000 lines of this file, named **letter_e**, contains 72 e's and a NEWLINE character marking the end of the line. The file occupies more than half a megabyte of disk storage.

```
$ ls -l
-rw-rw-r--  1 alex   speedy  584000 Jul 31 06:07 letter_e
```

The –l option causes ls to display more information about a file. Here, it shows that **letter_e** is 584,000 bytes long.

The --verbose (or –v) option causes gzip to report how much it was able to reduce the size of the file; in this case, it shrank the file by more than 99 percent.

```
$ gzip -v letter_e
letter_e:     99.6% -- replaced with letter_e.gz
$ ls -l
-rw-rw-r--  1 alex   speedy    2030 Jul 31 06:07 letter_e.gz
```

Now the file is only 2,030 bytes long. The gzip utility also renamed the file, appending **.gz** to the file's name. This naming convention helps to remind you that the file is compressed; you would not want to display or print it, for example, without first decompressing it. The gzip utility does not change the modification date associated with the file, even though it completely changes the file's contents.

In the following, more realistic example, the file **card2.bm** contains a complex computer graphics image:

```
$ ls -l
-rw-rw-r--  1 jenny   speedy  131092 Jul 31 10:48 card2.bm
```

Here gzip can reduce the disk storage for the file by about only 20 percent:

```
$ gzip -v card2.bm
card2.bm:        19.7% -- replaced with card2.bm.gz
$ ls -l
-rw-rw-r--  1 jenny   speedy  105261 Jul 31 10:48 card2.bm.gz
```

A second utility, compress, can also compress files but not as well as gzip. The compress utility marks a file it has compressed by adding a .Z to its name.

gunzip and zcat: Decompress a File

You can use the gunzip (GNU unzip) utility to restore a file that has been shrunk with gzip or compress:

```
$ gunzip letter_e.gz
$ ls -l
-rw-rw-r--  1 alex    speedy  584000 Jul 31 06:07 letter_e

$ gunzip card2.bm.gz
$ ls -l
-rw-rw-r--  1 jenny   speedy  131092 Jul 31 10:48 card2.bm
```

The zcat utility displays a file that has been compressed with either gzip or compress. The equivalent of cat for .gz and .Z files, zcat decompresses the compressed data and displays the contents of the decompressed file. Like cat, zcat does not change the source file. The pipe in the following example redirects the output of zcat so that instead of being displayed on the screen, it becomes the input to head, which displays the first two lines of the file:

```
$ zcat letter_e.gz | head -2
eeeeeeeeeeeeeeeeeeeeeeeeeeeeeeeeeeeeeeeeeeeeeeeeeeeeeeeeeeeeeeeeeeeeeee
eeeeeeeeeeeeeeeeeeeeeeeeeeeeeeeeeeeeeeeeeeeeeeeeeeeeeeeeeeeeeeeeeeeeeee
```

After zcat is run, the contents of **letter_e.gz** is unchanged; the file is still stored on the disk in compressed form.

caution ‖   gzip **versus** zip

Do not confuse gzip and gunzip with the zip and unzip utilities. These last two are used to pack and unpack zip archives containing several files compressed into a single file that has been imported from or is being exported to Windows. The zip utility constructs a zip archive, whereas unzip unpacks zip archives. The zip and unzip utilities are compatible with PKZIP, a Windows compress and archive program.

bzip2: Compresses/Decompresses a File

The bzip2 utility (sources.redhat.com/bzip2) is a highly efficient compression program that does a better job than any of the programs discussed previously. Its flags and operation are very similar to those of gzip (discussed in previous sections), and it supports limited recovery from media errors (bzip2recover). Use bzip2, bunzip2, and bzcat just as you would use gzip, gunzip, and zcat. Refer to the bzip2 man page and the *Bzip2 mini-HOWTO* (see page 98 for help finding this) for more information.

tar: Packs and Unpacks Files

The tar utility performs many functions. Its name is short for *tape archive*, as its original function was to create and read archive and backup tapes. Today it is used both to create a single file (called a *tar file*) from multiple files or directories containing any level of subdirectories and files and to extract files from a tar file.

In the following example, ls first shows the existence and sizes of the files **g**, **b**, and **d**. Next, tar uses the **–c** (create), **–v** (verbose), and **–f** (write to or read from a file) options[3] to create an archive named **all.tar** from these files. Each line of the output from tar starts with the letter **a** to indicate that it is appending to the archive. This letter is followed by the name of the file.

The tar utility does add overhead when it creates an archive. The next command shows that the archive file, **all.tar**, is about 9,700 bytes, whereas the sum of the sizes of the three files is about 6,000 bytes. This overhead is more appreciable on smaller files, such as the ones in this example:

```
$ ls -l g b d
-rw-r--r--  1 jenny    jenny       1302 Aug 20 14:16 g
-rw-r--r--  1 jenny    other       1178 Aug 20 14:16 b
-rw-r--r--  1 jenny    jenny       3783 Aug 20 14:17 d
$ tar -cvf all.tar g b d
a g
a b
a d
$ ls -l all.tar
-rw-r--r--  1 jenny    jenny       9728 Aug 20 14:17 all.tar
$ tar -tvf all.tar
-rw-r--r-- jenny/jenny     1302 2003-08-20 14:16 2003 g
-rw-r--r-- jenny/other     1178 2003-08-20 14:16 2003 b
-rw-r--r-- jenny/jenny     3783 2003-08-20 14:17 2003 d
```

---

3. Although the original UNIX tar did not use a leading hyphen to indicate an option on the command line, it now accepts hyphens. GNU tar described here will accept tar commands with or without a leading hyphen. This book uses the hyphen for consistency with most other utilities.

The final command in the preceding example uses the –t option to display a table of contents for the archive. Use –x in place of –t to extract files from a tar archive. Omit the –v option if you want tar to do its work silently.

You can use compress or gzip to compress tar files and make them easier to store and handle. Many files you download from the Internet are in one of these formats. Files that have been processed by tar and compressed by gzip frequently have a file-name extension of .tgz or .tar.gz. Those processed by tar and compress use .tar.Z.

You can unpack a tarred and gzipped file in two steps. (Follow the same procedure if the file was shrunk by compress, but use uncompress in place of gunzip.) The next example shows how to unpack the GNU make utility after it has been downloaded:

```
$ ls -l mak*
-rw-r--r--   1 sam      sam         634229 Oct 17 15:01 make-3.76.1.tar.gz
$ gunzip mak*
$ ls -l mak*
-rw-r--r--   1 sam      sam        2344960 Oct 17 15:01 make-3.76.1.tar
$ tar -xvf mak*
x make-3.76.1, 0 bytes, 0 tape blocks
x make-3.76.1/Makefile.in, 19129 bytes, 38 tape blocks
x make-3.76.1/AUTHORS, 1391 bytes, 3 tape blocks
...
x make-3.76.1/make.info-8, 42472 bytes, 83 tape blocks
x make-3.76.1/make.info-9, 10289 bytes, 21 tape blocks
```

The first of the preceding commands lists the downloaded tarred and gzipped file: **make-3.76.1.tar.gz** (about 0.6 megabytes). The asterisk (*) in the filename matches any characters in any filenames (page 208), so you end up with a list of files whose names begin with **mak**; in this case there is only one. Using an asterisk saves typing and can improve accuracy with long filenames. The gunzip command decompresses the file and yields **make-3.76.1.tar** (no .gz extension), which is about 2.3 megabytes. The tar command creates the **make-3.76.1** directory in the working directory and unpacks the files into it:

```
$ ls -ld mak*
drwxr-xr-x   4 sam      sam           2048 Sep 19  2003 make-3.76.1
-rw-r--r--   1 sam      sam        2344960 Oct 17 15:01 make-3.76.1.tar
$ ls make-3.76.1
total 4196
-rw-r--r--   1 sam      sam           1391 Aug 27  2003 AUTHORS
-rw-r--r--   1 sam      sam          18043 Dec 10  2002 COPYING
-rw-r--r--   1 sam      sam         153710 Sep 19  2003 ChangeLog
...
-rw-r--r--   1 sam      sam           5586 Jul 25  2002 vmsfunctions.c
-rw-r--r--   1 sam      sam          15653 Aug 27  2003 vmsify.c
-rw-r--r--   1 sam      sam          16320 Aug 27  2003 vpath.c
drwxr-xr-x   5 sam      sam            512 Sep 19  2003 w32
```

After tar extracts the files from the archive, the working directory contains two files whose names start with **mak**: **make-3.76.1.tar** and **make-3.76.1**. The –d option causes ls to display only file and directory names, not the contents of directories, which it normally does. The final ls command shows the files and directories in the **make-3.76.1** directory.

caution || **tar: –x Option May Extract a Lot of Files**

Some tar archives contain many files. Run tar with the **–t** option and the name of the tar file to list the files in the archive without unpacking them. In some cases you may want to create a new directory (mkdir [page 162]), move the tar file into that directory, and expand it there. That way the unpacked files do not mingle with your existing files, and there is no confusion. It makes it easier to delete the extracted files if you choose to do so. Some tar files automatically create a new directory and put the files into it. Refer to the preceding example.

caution || **tar: –x Option Can Overwrite Files**

The **–x** option to tar overwrites a file that has the same filename as a file you are extracting. Follow the suggestion in the preceding caution box to avoid overwriting a file.

You can combine the gunzip and tar commands on one command line with a pipe (I), which redirects the output of gunzip so that it becomes the input to tar:

```
$ gunzip -c make-3.76.1.tar.gz | tar -xvf -
```

The –c option causes gunzip to send its output through the pipe instead of creating a file. Refer to "Pipes" (page 201) and the gzip and tar man pages for more information about how this command line works.

A simpler solution is to use the –z option to tar. This option causes tar to call gunzip (or gzip when you are creating an archive) directly and simplifies the preceding command line to

```
$ tar -xvzf make-3.76.1.tar.gz
```

In a similar manner, the –j option calls bzip2 or bunzip2.

Locating Commands

The whereis and apropos utilities help you find a command whose name you have forgotten or whose location you do not know. When there are multiple copies of a utility/program, which can tell you which copy you will run. GNU made a utility named locate more secure and renamed it slocate. This utility builds a compressed database that speeds up searches. Refer to the slocate man page.

which, whereis: Locate a Utility

When you type the name of a utility on the command line (that is when you give Linux a command), the shell (Chapter 7) searches a list of directories for the program. This list of directories is called a *search path*; For information on how to change the search path, refer to "PATH: Where the Shell Looks for Programs" on page 283. If you do not change the search path, the shell searches only a standard set of directories and then stops searching. There are other directories on your system that contain useful utilities.

which **versus** whereis

Give it the name of a program you want to run, and which looks through the directories in your *search path,* in order, and locates the program. If more than one program with the name you specify is in your search path, which displays the name of only the first one (the one you will execute).

The whereis utility looks through a list of *standard directories* and works independently of your search path. Use whereis to locate a binary (executable) file, any manual pages, and source code for a program you specify.

The which utility helps you locate utilities (commands) by displaying the full pathname to the file for the utility. (Chapter 6 contains more information on pathnames and the structure of the Linux filesystem.) There may be multiple commands that have the same name on your system. When you type the name of a command, the shell searches for the command in your search path and runs the first one it finds. You can find out which copy of the program the shell runs by using which. In the following example, which reports the location of the tar command:

```
$ which tar
/bin/tar
```

The which utility can be helpful when a command seems to be working in unexpected ways. By running which, you may discover that you are running a nonstandard version of a tool or a different one than you expected. (Refer to "Important Standard Directories and Files" on page 167 for a list of standard locations for executable files.) For example, if tar is not working properly and you find that you are running **/usr/local/bin/tar** instead of **/bin/tar,** you might suspect that the local version is broken.

which, whereis, **and Builtin Commands**

Both the which and whereis utilities report only the names for commands as they are found on disk and do not report shell builtins (utilities that are built into a shell; see page 211). When you use whereis to try to find out where the echo command (which exists as both a utility program and a shell builtin) is kept, you get the following:

```
$ whereis echo
echo: /bin/echo /opt/../bin/echo /usr/man/man1/echo.1
```

The whereis utility does not display the echo builtin. Even the which utility reports the wrong information:

```
$ which echo
/bin/echo
```

The whereis utility also searches for copies of a utility by looking in a few standard locations instead of using your search path. For example, you can find the locations for versions of the tar command:

```
$ whereis tar
tar: /bin/tar /usr/include/tar.h /usr/share/man/man1/tar.1.gz
```

```
$ apropos who | sort
at.allow [at]         (5) - determine who can submit jobs via at or batch
at.deny [at]          (5) - determine who can submit jobs via at or batch
fwhois [whois]        (1) - query a whois or nicname database
w                     (1) - Show who is logged on and what they are doing
who                   (1) - show who is logged on
whoami                (1) - print effective userid
whois                 (1) - query a whois or nicname database
```

Figure 5-10   apropos displays man page headers that match a string

This whereis utility finds three references to tar. If it can find any man pages for the utility, whereis lists those too. In this case, the whereis utility has located tar, a tar header file, and the man page.

apropos: Searches for a Keyword

When you do not know the name of the command you need to carry out a particular task, you can use a keyword and the apropos[4] utility to search for it. This utility searches for the keyword in the short description line (the top line on a man page) of all of the man pages and displays those that contain a match. The man utility, with the –k (keyword) option, gives you the same output as apropos (it is actually the same command).

Figure 5-10 shows the output of apropos when you call it with the **who** keyword. The pipe redirects the output of apropos so that it becomes the input of sort, yielding a sorted list. The pipe includes the name of each command, the section of the manual that contains it, and the brief description from the top of the man page. This list includes the utility that you need (who) and also identifies other, related tools that you might find useful.

The whatis utility is similar to apropos but finds only complete word matches on the name of the utility. Try giving these commands to see the difference: **apropos grep** and **whatis grep**.

Obtaining User and System Information

This section covers utilities that display who is using the system, what most of the users are doing, and how the system is running. If you are running Linux on a workstation that is not connected to a network, you may want to skip the rest of this chapter. (If you are set up to send and receive email, read "Email" on page 144.)

---

4. The **whatis** database has to be set up with makewhatis in order for apropos to work. Refer to "Initializing Databases" on page 52.

```
$ who
root        console     Mar 27 05:00
alex        pts/4       Mar 27 12:23
alex        pts/5       Mar 27 12:33
jenny       pts/7       Mar 26 08:45
```

Figure 5-11   who lists who is logged in

To find out who is using the computer system, you can use one of several utilities that vary in the details they provide and the options they support. The oldest utility, who, produces a list of users who are logged in on your system, the terminal connection each person is using, and the time the person logged in.

Two newer utilities, w and finger, show more detail, such as each user's full name and the command line each user is running. You can use the finger utility (page 341) to retrieve information about users on remote systems if your computer is attached to a network.

Following these utilities, Table 5-1 on page 141 summarizes their output.

who: Lists Users on the System

The who utility displays a list of users who are logged in. In Figure 5-11 the first column of who shows that Alex and Jenny are logged in. (Alex is logged in from two locations.) The second column shows the designation of the terminal, workstation, or terminal emulator that each person is using. The third column shows the date and time the person logged in.

The information that who displays is useful when you want to communicate with a user at your installation. When the user is logged in, you can use write (page 141) to establish communication immediately. If who does not list the user or if you do not need to communicate immediately, you can send that person email (page 144).

If the output of who scrolls off your screen, you can redirect the output through a pipe (l [page 201]) so that it becomes the input to less, which displays the output one page at a time. You can also use a pipe to redirect the output through grep to look for a specific name.

If you need to find out which terminal you are using or what time you logged in, you can use the command **who am i**:

```
$ who am i
bravo.tcorp.com!alex        pts/5        Mar 27 12:33
```

finger: Lists Users on the System

You can use finger to display a list of the users who are logged in on the system. In addition to login names, finger supplies each user's full name, along with information

```
$ finger
Login     Name              Tty    Idle  Login Time   Office      Office
Phone
root      root               1     1:35  May 24 08:38
alex      Alex Watson       /0           Jun  7 12:46  (:0)
alex      Alex Watson       /1      19   Jun  7 12:47  (:0)
jenny     Jenny Chen        /2     2:24  Jun  2 05:33  (bravo.tcorp.com)
hls       Helen Simpson     */2      2   Jun  2 05:33  (bravo.tcorp.com)
```

Figure 5-12   finger I: lists who is logged in

about which terminal line the person is using, how recently the user typed something on the keyboard, when the user logged in, and where the user is located (if the terminal line appears in a system database). If the user has logged in over the network, the name of the remote system is shown as the user's location. In Figure 5-12, for example, the user **hls** is logged in from the remote system named **bravo**. The asterisk (✻) in front of the name of Helen's terminal (TTY) line indicates that she has blocked others from sending messages directly to her terminal (refer to "**mesg**: Denies or Accepts Messages" on page 144).

You can also use finger to learn more about a particular individual by specifying more information on the command line. In Figure 5-13, finger displays detailed information about the user named Alex. Alex is logged in and actively using his terminal; if he were not, finger would report how long he had been idle. You also learn from finger that if you want to set up a meeting with Alex, you should contact Jenny at extension 1693.

Most of the information in Figure 5-13 was collected by finger from system files. The information shown after the heading **Plan:**, however, was supplied by Alex. The finger utility searched for a file named **.plan**[5] in Alex's home directory and displayed its contents. You may find it helpful to create a **.plan** file for yourself; it can contain any information you choose, such as your typical schedule, interests, phone number, or address. In a similar manner, finger displays the contents of the **.project** file in your home directory. The **.forward** file contains the address that Alex's mail is forwarded to. If Alex had not been logged in, finger would have reported the last time he logged on, the last time he read his email, and his plan.

You can use finger to display a user's login name. For example, you might know that Helen's last name is Simpson but might not guess that her login name is **hls**. The finger utility can search for information on Helen, using her first or last name. (The finger utility is not case sensitive.) The following commands find the information you seek, along with information on other users whose names are Helen or Simpson.

---

5. Filenames that begin with a period are not normally listed by ls and are called invisible filenames (page 161).

```
$ finger alex
Login: alex                          Name: Alex Watson
Directory: /home/alex                Shell: /bin/ksh
On since Wed Jun  7 12:46 (PDT) on pts/0 from :0
    5 minutes 52 seconds idle
On since Wed Jun  7 12:47 (PDT) on pts/1 from bravo
Last login Wed Jun  7 12:47 (PDT) on 1 from bravo
New mail received Wed Jun  7 13:16 2000 (PDT)
      Unread since Fri May 26 15:32 2000 (PDT)Plan:
I will be at a conference in Hawaii all next week.  If you need
to see me, contact Jenny Chen, x1693.
```

Figure 5-13   finger II: lists details about one user

```
$ finger HELEN
Login: hls                              Name: Helen Simpson.
.
.
.
$ finger simpson
Login: hls                              Name: Helen Simpson.
.
.
.
```

security || finger **Can Be a Security Risk**

On systems where security is a concern, the system administrator may disable finger. This utility can give information that can help a malicious user break into the system.

w: Lists Users on the System

The w utility displays a list of the users who are logged in. As discussed in the section on who, the information that w displays is useful when you want to communicate with someone at your installation.

In Figure 5-14 the first column w displays shows that Alex, Jenny, and Scott are logged in. The second column shows the designation of the terminal that each person is using. The third column shows the time each person logged in. The fourth column indicates how long each person has been idle (how much time has elapsed since a key on the keyboard was pressed or the mouse was moved). The next two columns give measures of how much computer processor time each person has used during this login session and on the task that is running. The last column shows the command each person is running.

The first line that the w utility displays includes the time of day, how long the computer has been running (in days, hours, and minutes), how many users are logged in, and how busy the system is (load average). The three load average numbers represent the number of jobs waiting to run, averaged over the past 1, 5, and 15 minutes.

```
$ w
  8:20am  up 4 days,  2:28,  3 users,  load average: 0.04, 0.04, 0.00
 USER     TTY      FROM          LOGIN@   IDLE   JCPU   PCPU  WHAT
 alex     pts/4    :0            5:55am  13:45  0.15s  0.07s  w
 alex     pts/5    :0            5:55am     27   2:55   1:01  -ksh
 jenny    pts/7    bravo         5:56am  13:44  0.51s    30s  vi 3.txt
 scott    pts/12   bravo         7:17pm          1.00s  0:14s  run_bdgt
```

Figure 5-14   The w utility

Table 5-1 compares the w, who, and finger utilities.

table 5-1 ‖	Comparison of w, who, and finger		
Information Displayed	**w**	**who**	**finger**
User login name	X	X	X
Terminal-line identification (tty)	X	X	X
Login day and time	X		X
Login date and time		X	
Idle time	X		X
What program the user is executing	X		
Where the user logged in from			X
CPU time used		X	
Full name (or other information from **/etc/passwd**)			X
User-supplied vanity information			X
System up time and load average—use uptime for this information only	x		

Communicating with Other Users

The utilities discussed in this section exchange messages and files with other users either interactively or through email.

write: Sends a Message

The write utility sends a message to another user who is logged in. When you and another user use write to send messages to each other, you establish two-way com-

```
$ write alex
Hi Alex, are you there? o
```

Figure 5-15 The write utility I

munication. Initially, a write command (Figure 5-15) displays a banner on the other user's terminal, saying that you are about to send a message.

The syntax of a write command line is

write ***destination-user*** *[terminal]*

The ***destination-user*** is the login name of the user you want to communicate with. The ***terminal*** is the optional terminal name. You can display the login and terminal names of the users who are logged in on your system by using who, w, or finger.

To establish two-way communication with another user, you and the other user must each execute write, specifying the other's login name as the ***destination-user***. The write utility then copies text, line by line, from one keyboard/display to the other (Figure 5-16). Sometimes it helps to establish a convention, such as typing o (for over) when you are ready for the other person to type and typing oo (for over and out) when you are ready to end the conversation. When you want to stop communicating with the other user, press CONTROL-D at the beginning of a line. Pressing CONTROL-D tells write to quit, displays **EOF** (end of file) on the other user's terminal, and returns you to the shell. The other user must do the same.

If the **Message from ...** banner appears on your screen and obscures something you are working on, press CONTROL-L or CONTROL-R to refresh the screen and remove the banner. Then you can clean up, exit from your work, and respond to the person who is writing to you. You just have to remember who is writing to you as the banner will no longer be on your screen.

talk: **Communicates with Another User**

You can use the talk utility to carry on a two-way conversation with another person who is logged in on your system. If your system is connected to a network, you can also use talk to communicate with someone on a different computer. The talk utility splits your screen into two sections; once you establish contact with the other person, the messages that you type appear in the top half of your screen, and the mes-

```
$ write Alex
Hi Alex are you there? o
        Message from alex@bravo.tcorp.com on pts/0 at 16:23 ...
Yes Jenny, I'm here. o
```

Figure 5-16 The write utility II

sages from the other person are displayed in the bottom half. Each keystroke appears as you type it. In this example, Alex needs some information from Jenny:

```
$ talk jenny
```

Alex's display is immediately split into two sections, and the following message appears at the top of his screen:

```
[Waiting for your party to respond]
```

Meanwhile, the following message appears on Jenny's screen, and she responds. If she was unable to respond immediately, she could use CONTROL-L or CONTROL-R to refresh her screen and remove the banner (see the preceding discussion of talk):

```
Message from Talk_Daemon@bravo.tcorp.com at 9:22 ...
talk: connection requested by alex@bravo.
talk: respond with: talk alex@bravo
$ talk alex@bravo
```

Alex and Jenny are both using a computer named **bravo**; **alex@bravo** is Alex's network address, which is described in more detail in Chapter 7. Figure 5-17 shows what Jenny's and Alex's screens look like as they type their messages.

To end the talk session, one person interrupts by pressing CONTROL-C, and the following message appears before a new shell prompt is displayed:

```
[Connection closing. Exiting]
```

The other user must also press CONTROL-C to display a shell prompt. If you see the following message when you try to use talk to reach someone, the mesg command (see the next section) has been used to block interruptions:

```
[Your party is refusing messages]
```

Before the talk utility was available, people used the write command to interact with each other on the same computer. The talk utility has a few advantages over write: With talk the other person's messages appear on your screen, letter by letter, as they

```
Alex's screen:                              Jenny's screen:

[Connection established]                    [Connection established]
Did you finish the slides                   Hi, Alex, what's up?
for the 9:30 meeting today?                 Yes, they're all set.  Should
Sounds good, see you in a few               I just meet you in the conference
minutes!                                    room?
                                            Bye.
-----------------------------------         -----------------------------------
Hi, Alex, what's up?                        Did you finish the slides
Yes, they're all set.  Should               for the 9:30 meeting today?
I just meet you in the conference           Sounds good, see you in a few
room?                                       minutes!
Bye.
```

Figure 5-17   talk communicates with another user

are typed; write, on the other hand, sends only a whole line at a time. If you use write, sometimes you are not sure whether the person at the other end is disconnected or just a slow typist. Also, unlike write, talk has been extended to support communication over the network.

KDE has enhanced talk so that it has an answering machine and forwarding capability.

mesg: **Denies or Accepts Messages**

Give the following command when you do not wish to receive messages from another user:

```
$ mesg n
```

If Alex had given this command before Jenny tried to send him a message, she would have seen the following:

```
$ write alex
Permission denied
```

You can allow messages again by entering **mesg y**. Give the command **mesg** by itself to display **is y** (for yes, messages are allowed) or **is n** (for no, messages are *not* allowed).

Email

Email, or *electronic mail*, is similar to post office mail but is much quicker and does not involve any paper, stamps, or human intervention at various points along the way. You can use email to send and receive letters, memos, reminders, invitations, and even junk mail (unfortunately). Email can also transmit binary data, such as pictures or compiled code, as attachments. An *attachment* is a file that is attached to, but is not part of, a piece of email. Attachments are frequently opened by programs, including your Internet browser, that are called by your mail program, so you may not be aware that they are not an integral part of an email message.

You can use email to communicate with users on your system and, if your installation is part of a network, with other users on the network. If you are connected to the Internet, you can communicate electronically with users around the world.

Email utilities differ from write and talk in that email utilities can send a message when the recipient is not logged in. The email utilities can also send the same message to more than one user at a time.

Many mail programs are available for Linux, including the original character-based mail program, Netscape/Mozilla mail, pine, mail through emacs, Kmail, evolution, and exmh, which are supplied with Red Hat. Another popular graphical mail program is sylpheed (sylpheed.good-day.net).

You can use two programs to make any mail program easier to use and more secure. The procmail program (www.procmail.org) creates and maintains mail servers and mailing lists; preprocesses mail by sorting it into appropriate files and directories; starts various programs, depending on the characteristics of incoming mail; forwards mail; and so on. The GNU Privacy Guard (gpg or GNUpg, page 926) encrypts and decrypts email and makes it almost impossible for anyone else to read.

Refer to Chapter 20 (page 609) for more information on setting email clients and servers. See page 629 for instructions on setting up KMail to send and receive email.

Network addresses If your system is part of a LAN, you can generally send mail to and receive mail from users on other systems on the LAN by using their login names. Someone sending Alex email on the Internet would need to specify his domain name (page 352) along with his login name. Use this address to send the author email: **mgs@sobell.com**.

Tutorial: Creating and Editing a File with vim (vi)

This section explains how to start vim (a vi clone distributed by Red Hat), enter text, move the cursor, correct text, save the file to the disk, and exit from vim. The tutorial discusses two of the modes of operation of vim and how to go from one mode to the other. It also covers commands you can use to create a file and store it on disk. For additional help with vim, run the program named vimtutor: Give its name as a command to run it.

tip || **The vi Command Runs vim**

As installed on a Red Hat Linux system, the command **vi** runs vim in vi compatibility mode. In this mode, vim behaves similarly to the way vi behaves.

Specifying a Terminal

Because vim takes advantage of features specific to various kinds of terminals, you must tell it what type of terminal or terminal emulator you are using. On many systems, your terminal type is set for you automatically. If you need to specify your terminal type, refer to "Specifying a Terminal" on page 920.

Starting vim

Start vim with the following command line to create and edit a file named **practice**:

```
$ vim practice
```

When you press RETURN, the command line disappears, and the terminal screen looks similar to the one shown in Figure 5-18.

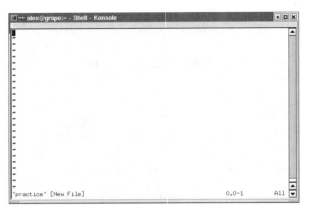

Figure 5-18   Starting vim

The tildes (~) at the left of the screen indicate the file is empty. They go away as you add lines of text to the file. If your screen looks like a distorted version of the one shown, your terminal type is probably not set correctly.

If you start vim with a terminal type that is not in the **terminfo** database, the following message is displayed for a few seconds, and the terminal type defaults to **ansi**, which works on many terminals. In the following examples, the user mistyped **vt100** and set the terminal type to **vg100**:

```
Terminal entry not found in terminfo
'vg100' not known. Available builtin terminals are:
    builtin_riscos
    builtin_amiga
    builtin_beos-ansi
    builtin_ansi
    builtin_pcansi
    builtin_win32
    builtin_vt320
    builtin_vt52
    builtin_xterm
    builtin_iris-ansi
    builtin_debug
    builtin_dumb
defaulting to 'ansi'
```

If you want to reset your terminal type, press ESCAPE, and then give the following command to exit from vim and get the shell prompt back:

:q!

When you enter the colon (:), vim moves the cursor to the bottom line of the screen. The characters **q!** tell vim to quit without saving your work. (You will not ordinarily exit from vim this way because you typically want to save your work.) You must press RETURN after you give this command. Once you get the shell prompt back, refer to "Specifying a Terminal" on page 920, and then start vim again.

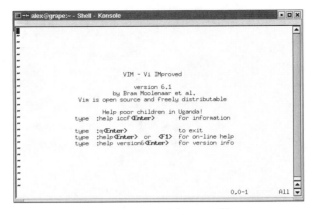

Figure 5-19   Starting vim without a filename

If you start it without a filename, vim assumes that you are a novice and tells you how to get started (Figure 5-19).

Continuing with the **practice** file example: The **practice** file is new, so it contains no text. The vim editor displays a message similar to the one shown in Figure 5-18 on the status (bottom) line of the terminal to show you are creating and editing a new file. Your version of vim may display a different message. When you edit an existing file, vim displays the first few lines of the file and gives status information about the file on the status (bottom) line.

Command and Input Modes

Two of the vim editor's modes of operation are *Command mode* and *Input mode* (Figure 5-20). While vim is in Command mode, you can give vim commands. For example, in Command mode you can delete text or exit from vim. You can also command vim to enter Input mode. In Input mode, vim accepts anything you enter as text and displays it on the screen. Press ESCAPE to return vim to Command mode.

By default the vim editor keeps you informed about which mode it is in: You will see --**INSERT**-- at the lower-left corner of the window while you are in Insert mode. The following command causes vim not to display the mode it is in while you are entering text:

    :set noshowmode

The colon (:) in this command puts vim into another mode, *Last Line mode*. While in this mode, vim keeps the cursor on the bottom line of the screen. When you finish the command by pressing RETURN, vim restores the cursor to its place in the text.

When you give vim a command, remember the editor is case sensitive. The vim editor interprets the same letter as two different commands, depending on whether you enter an upper- or lowercase character. Beware of the key that causes your keyboard

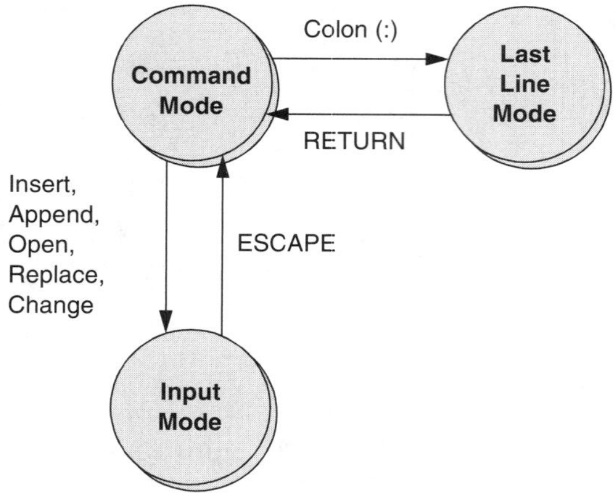

Figure 5-20   Modes in vim

to send only uppercase characters; it is typically labeled CAPS LOCK or SHIFTLOCK. If you set this key to enter uppercase text while you are in Input mode and then exit to Command mode, vim interprets your commands as uppercase letters. It can be very confusing when this happens because vim does not appear to be following the commands you are giving it.

Entering Text

When you start a new session with vim, you must put it in Input mode before you can enter text. To put vim in Input mode, press the **i** key (insert before the cursor) or the **a** key (append after the cursor).

If you are not sure whether vim is in Input mode, press the ESCAPE key; vim returns to Command mode if it was in Input mode or beeps/flashes if it is already in Command mode. You can put vim back in Input mode by pressing the **i** or **a** key again.

While vim is in Input mode, you can enter text by typing on the terminal. If the text does not appear on the screen as you type, you are not in Input mode.

Enter the sample paragraph shown in Figure 5-21, pressing the RETURN key to end each line. If you do not press RETURN before the cursor reaches the right side of the screen or window, vim will wrap the text so that it appears to start a new line: Physical lines will not correspond to logical lines, and editing will become more difficult.

While you are using vim, you can always correct any typing mistakes you make. If you notice a mistake on the line you are entering, you can correct it before you continue. Refer to "Getting Help" (following). You can correct other mistakes later. When you finish entering the paragraph, press ESCAPE to return vim to Command mode.

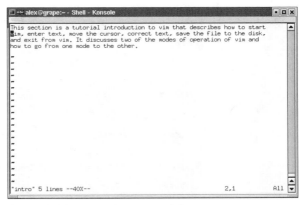

Figure 5-21   Entering text with vim

Getting Help

You can get help while you are using vim by typing **:help** [*feature*] followed by RETURN (you must be in Command mode). As before, the colon puts the cursor on the last line of the window. If you type **:help**, vim displays an introduction to vim Help (Figure 5-22). Each dark band near the bottom of the window names the file that is displayed above it. The **help.txt** file occupies most of the window while only a few lines of the file that was being edited (**intro**) are displayed. Give the command **:q!** to close the Help window.

Read through the introduction to Help by scrolling the Help window as you read. Pressing **j** or the DOWN ARROW key moves the cursor down one line at a time, whereas pressing CONTROL-D and CONTROL-U scroll the cursor down/up half a screen at a time. You can get help with the insert commands by giving the command **:help insert** while you are using vim in Command mode (Figure 5-23).

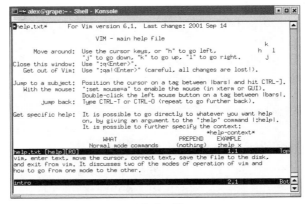

Figure 5-22   The main help file

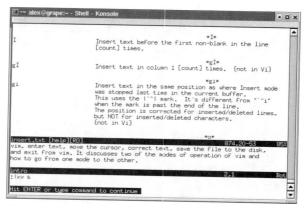

Figure 5-23   Help with insert

Correcting Text as You Insert It

The keys that back up and correct a shell command line serve the same functions when vim is in Input mode. These keys include the erase, line kill, and word kill keys (usually CONTROL-H, CONTROL-U, and CONTROL-W). Although vim may not remove deleted text from the screen as you back up over it, vim removes it when you type over it or press RETURN.

Moving the Cursor

When you are using vim, you need to move the cursor on the screen so you can delete, insert, and correct text. While vim is in Command mode, you can use the RETURN key, the SPACE bar, and the ARROW keys to move the cursor. If you prefer to keep your hand closer to the center of the keyboard, if your terminal does not have ARROW keys, or if the emulator you are using does not support them, you can use the **h, j, k,** and **l** (ell) keys to move the cursor left, down, up, and right, respectively.

Deleting Text

You can delete a single character by moving the cursor until it is over the character you want to delete and then giving the command **x**. You can delete a word by positioning the cursor on the first letter of the word and giving the command **dw** (delete word). You can delete a line of text by moving the cursor until it is anywhere on the line you want to delete and then giving the command **dd**.

Undoing Mistakes

If you delete a character, line, or word by mistake or give any command you want to undo, give the command **u** (undo) immediately after you give the command you want to undo; vim restores the text to the way it was before you gave the last command. If you give the **u** command again, vim undoes the command you gave before the one it just undid. You can use this technique to back up over many of your actions.

If you undo a command you did not mean to undo, give a redo command: Either CONTROL-R or **:red**, and vim will redo the undone command. As with undo, you can give this command many times in a row.

Inserting Additional Text

When you want to insert new text within text that you have already entered, move the cursor so that it is on the character that follows the new text you plan to enter. Then give the **i** (insert) command to put vim in Input mode, enter the new text, and press ESCAPE to return vim to Command mode. Or position the cursor on the character that precedes the new text, and use the **a** (append) command.

To enter one or more lines, position the cursor on the line above where you want the new text to go. Give the command **o** (open). The vim editor opens a blank line, puts the cursor on it, and goes into Input mode. Enter the new text, ending each line with a RETURN. When you are finished entering text, press ESCAPE to return vim to Command mode.

Correcting Text

To correct text, use **dd**, **dw**, or **x** to remove the incorrect text. Then use **i** or **o** to insert the correct text.

For example, one way to change the word **tutorial** to **section** in Figure 5-21 is to use the ARROW keys to move the cursor until it is on top of the **t** in **tutorial**. Then give the command **dw** to delete the word **tutorial**. Put vim in Input mode by giving an **i** command, enter the word **section** followed by a SPACE, and press ESCAPE. The word is changed, and vim is in Command mode, waiting for another command. A shorthand for the two commands **dw** followed by the **i** command is **cw** (change word). The command **cw** puts vim into Input mode.

tip || **Page Breaks for the Printer**

A CONTROL-L is a signal to a printer to skip to the top of the next page. You can enter this character anywhere in a document by pressing CONTROL-L. If a **^L** does not appear, press CONTROL-V before CONTROL-L.

Ending the Editing Session

While you are editing, vim keeps the edited text in an area named the *Work buffer*. When you finish editing, you must write out the contents of the Work buffer to a disk file so that the edited text is saved and available when you next want it.

Make sure that vim is in Command mode, and use the **ZZ** command (you must use uppercase Zs) to write your newly entered text to the disk and end the editing session. After you give the **ZZ** command, vim returns control to the shell. You can exit with **:q!** if you do not want to save your work.

caution ‖   **Do Not Confuse ZZ with** CONTROL-Z

When you exit from vim with **ZZ**, make sure that you use **ZZ** and not CONTROL-Z (typically the suspend key). When you press CONTROL-Z, vim disappears from your screen, almost as though you had exited from it. But vim will be running in the background with your file unsaved. Refer to "Job Control" on page 262. If you try to start editing the same file with a new vim command, vim displays a message about a swap file.

Chapter Summary

The utilities introduced in this chapter and the previous one are a small but powerful subset of the utilities available on a Red Hat Linux system. Because you will use them frequently and because they are integral to the following chapters, it is important that you become comfortable using them.

This chapter introduces some general file manipulation utilities that compress files and file archives, identify or locate utilities on the system, obtain information about other users, and communicate electronically with others.

The utilities listed in Table 5-2 manipulate, display, compare, and print files.

table 5-2 ‖	File Utilities
cp	Copies one or more files (page 121)
diff	Displays the differences between two files (page 126)
file	Displays information about the contents of a file (page 127)
grep	Searches a file for a string (page 123)
head	Displays the lines at the beginning of a file (page 124)
lpq	Displays a list of jobs in the print queue (page 123)
lpr	Places file(s) in the print queue (page 122)
lprm	Removes a job from the print queue (page 123)
mv	Renames file(s) or moves file(s) to another directory (page 122)
sort	Puts a file in order by lines (page 125)

table 5-2 ||	File Utilities (Continued)
tail	Displays the lines at the end of a file (page 125)
uniq	Displays the contents of a file, skipping successive duplicate lines (page 126)
vim	Creates and/or edits a file (page 145)

To reduce the amount of disk space a file occupies, you can compress it with the gzip utility. The compression works especially well on files that contain patterns, as do most text files, but reduces the size of almost all files. The inverse of gzip—gunzip—restores a file to its original, decompressed form. Table 5-3 lists utilities that compress and decompress files. The bzip2 utility is the most efficient of these.

table 5-3 ||	(De)Compression Utilities
compress	Compresses a file (not as well as gzip) (page 132)
gunzip	Returns a gzipped or compressed file to its original size and format (page 132)
gzip	Compresses a file (page 131)
zcat	Displays a compressed file (page 132)
bzip2, bunzip2, and bzcat	Compresses/decompresses/displays a file (better than gzip) (page 133)

An archive is a file, usually compressed, that contains a group of smaller, related files. The tar utility (Table 5-4) packs and unpacks archives. The filename extensions .tar.gz and .tgz identify compressed tar archive files and are often seen on software packages obtained over the Internet.

table 5-4 ||	Archive Utility
tar	Creates or extracts files from an archive file (page 133)

The utilities listed in Table 5-5 determine the location of a utility on your system. For example, they can display the pathname of a utility or a list of C++ compilers available on your system.

table 5-5 ||	Location Utilities
apropos	Searches the man page one-line descriptions for a keyword (page 137)
whereis	Displays the full pathnames of a utility, source code, or man page (page 135)

table 5-5 ||	Location Utilities (Continued)
which	Displays the full pathname of a command you can run (page 135)

Table 5-6 lists utilities that display information about other users. You can easily learn a user's full name, whether the user is logged in, the login shell of the user, and other items of information maintained by the system.

table 5-6 ||	User and System Information Utilities
finger	Displays detailed information about users who are logged in, including full names (page 138)
w	Displays detailed information about users who are logged in (page 140)
who	Displays information about users who are logged in (page 138)

The utilities shown in Table 5-7 can help you stay in touch with other users on your local network.

table 5-7 ||	User Communication Utilities
mesg	Permits or denies messages sent by write or talk (page 144)
talk	Sets up two-way communication with a local or remote user (page 142)
write	Sends a message to another user who is logged in (page 141)

Table 5-8 lists miscellaneous utilities.

table 5-8 ||	Miscellaneous Utilities
date	Displays the current date and time (page 128)
echo	Copies its *arguments* (page 957) to the terminal (page 128)

Exercises

1. What commands can you use to determine who is logged in on a specific terminal?

2. How can you keep other users from using write to communicate with you? Why would you want to?

3. What command sends the files **chapter1**, **chapter2**, and **chapter3** to the printer?

4. List some differences between talk and write. Why are three different communications utilities (talk, write, and an email client) useful? Describe a situation in which it makes sense to use

   a. A mail program instead of talk or write

   b. talk instead of write

   c. write instead of talk

5. What happens when you give the following commands if the file named **done** already exists?

   ```
   $ cp to_do done
   $ mv to_do done
   ```

6. How can you find out which utilities are available on your system for editing files? What utilities are there for editing on your system?

7. How can you find the phone number for Ace Electronics in a file named **phone** that contains a list of names and phone numbers? What command can you use to display the entire file in alphabetical order? How can you remove adjacent duplicate lines from the file?

8. What happens when you use diff to compare two binary files that are not identical? (You can use gzip to create the binary files.) Explain why the diff output for binary files is different from the diff output for ASCII files.

9. Create a **.plan** file in your home directory. Does finger on your system display the contents of your **.plan** file?

10. What is the result of giving the which utility the name of a command that resides in a directory that is *not* in your search path?

11. Are any of the utilities discussed in this chapter located in more than one directory on your system? If so, which ones?

12. Experiment by calling the file utility with names of files in **/usr/bin**. How many different types of files are there?

13. What command can you use to look at the first few lines of a file named **status.report**? What command can you use to look at the end of the file?

Advanced Exercises

14. Recreate the **colors.1** and **colors.2** files used in Figure 5-8 on page 127. Test your files by running **diff –u** on them, and see whether you get the same results as in the figure.

15. Try giving these two commands:

```
$ echo cat
$ cat echo
```

Explain the differences between them.

16. Repeat exercise 7 using the file **phone.gz**, a compressed version of the list of names and phone numbers. Try to consider more than one approach to each question, and explain how you chose your answer.

17. Find existing files or create files that

a. gzip compresses by more than 80 percent

b. get larger when compressed with gzip

Use **ls –l** to determine the sizes of the files in question. Can you characterize the files in a, b, and c?

18. Some mailers, particularly older ones, are not able to handle binary files. Suppose that you are mailing someone a file that has been compressed with gzip, which produces a binary file, and you do not know what mailer the recipient is using. Refer to the man page on uuencode, which converts a binary file to ASCII. Learn about the utility and how to use it.

a. Convert a compressed file to ASCII, using uuencode. Is the encoded file bigger or smaller than the compressed file? Explain.

b. Would it ever make sense to use uuencode on a file before compressing it? Explain.

The Linux Filesystem

6

A *filesystem* is a *data structure* (page 966) that usually resides on part of a disk. This chapter discusses the organization and terminology of the Linux filesystem, defines ordinary and directory files, and explains the rules for naming them. The chapter shows how to create and delete directories, move through the filesystem, and use pathnames to access files in various directories. This chapter also covers file access permissions which allow you to share selected files with other users. The final section describes links, which can make a single file appear in more than one directory.

The Hierarchical Filesystem

A *hierarchical* (page 974) structure frequently takes the shape of a pyramid. One example of this type of structure is found by tracing a family's lineage: A couple has a child who may have several children, each of whom may have more children. This hierarchical structure shown in Figure 6-1 is called a *family tree*.

Like the family tree it resembles, the Linux filesystem is also called a *tree*. It is composed of a set of connected files. This structure allows you to organize files so you can easily find any particular one. On a standard Linux system, each user starts with one directory. You can make as many subdirectories as you like from your single directory, dividing subdirectories into additional subdirectories. In this manner, you can continue expanding the structure to any level, according to your needs.

Typically, each subdirectory is dedicated to a single subject, such as a person, project, or event. The subject dictates whether a subdirectory should be subdivided

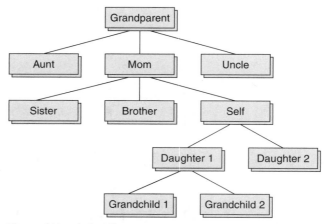

Figure 6-1   A family tree

further. For instance, Figure 6-2 shows a secretary's subdirectory named **corre-spond**. This directory contains three subdirectories: **business, memos,** and **personal.** The **business** directory contains files that store each letter the secretary types. If you expect many letters to go to one client, as is the case with **milk_co,** you can dedicate a subdirectory to that client.

One of the strengths of the Linux filesystem is its ability to adapt to users' needs. You can take advantage of this strength by strategically organizing your files so they are most convenient and useful for you.

Directory and Ordinary Files

Like a family tree, the tree representing the filesystem is usually pictured upside down, with its *root* at the top. Figures 6-2 and 6-3 show that the tree "grows"

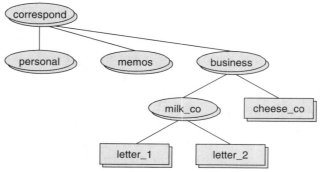

Figure 6-2   A secretary's directories

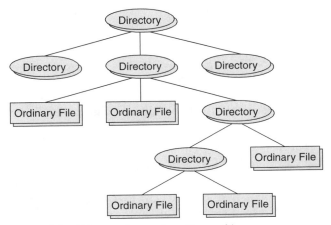

Figure 6-3   Directories and ordinary files

downward from the root, with paths connecting the root to each of the other files. At the end of each path is either an ordinary file or a directory file. *Ordinary files,* frequently just called *files,* are at the ends of paths that cannot support other paths. *Directory files,* usually referred to as *directories* or *folders,* are the points that other paths *can* branch off from. (Figures 6-2 and 6-3 show some empty directories.) When you refer to the tree, *up* is toward the root and *down* is away from the root. Directories directly connected by a path are called *parents* (closer to the root) and *children* (farther from the root). A *pathname* is a series of names that trace a path along branches from one file to another.

Filenames

Every file has a *filename.* The maximum length of a filename varies with the type of filesystem; Linux includes support for various types of filesystems. On most filesystems you can create files with names up to 255 characters in length, but some filesystems may restrict you to 14-character names. Although you can use almost any character in a filename, you will avoid confusion if you choose characters from the following list:

- Uppercase letters (A–Z)
- Lowercase letters (a–z)
- Numbers (0–9)
- Underscore (_)
- Period (.)
- Comma (,)

The **root** directory is always named **/** (slash) and referred to by this single character. No other file can use this name or have a **/** in its name. However, in a pathname, which is a string of filenames, including directory names, the slash *separates* filenames (page 165).

Like children of one parent, no two files in the same directory can have the same name. (Parents give their children different names because it makes good sense, but Linux requires it.) Files in different directories, like children of different parents, can have the same name.

The filenames you choose should mean something. Too often a directory is filled with important files with such names as **hold1**, **wombat**, and **junk**, not to mention **foo** and **foobar**. Such names are poor choices because they do not help you recall what you stored in a file. The following filenames conform to the suggested syntax *and* convey information about the contents of the file:

- **correspond**
- **january**
- **davis**
- **reports**
- **2001**
- **acct_payable**

When you share your files with users on other systems, you may need to make long filenames differ within the first 14 characters. If you keep the filenames short, they are easy to type; later you can add extensions to them without exceeding the 14-character limit imposed by some filesystems. The disadvantage of short filenames is that they are typically less descriptive than long filenames. When you share files with systems running DOS or older versions of Windows, you must respect the 8-character filename body length and 3-character filename extension length imposed by those systems.

Long filenames enable you to assign descriptive names to files. To help you select among files without typing entire filenames, shells support filename completion. See the "Filename Completion" tip on page 120.

You can use upper- and/or lowercase letters within filenames. Linux is case sensitive; thus files named **JANUARY**, **January**, and **january** represent three distinct files.

caution ‖   **Do Not Use SPACEs Within Filenames**

Although you can use SPACEs within filenames, it is a poor idea. Because a SPACE is a special character, you must quote it on a command line. Quoting a character on a command line can be difficult for a novice user and cumbersome for an experienced user. Use periods, underscores, or hyphens instead of SPACEs: **joe.02.04.26**, **for–sam**, **new_stuff**.

table 6-1 ‖	Filename Extensions
compute.c	A C programming language source file
compute.o	The object code for the program
compute	The same program as an executable file
memo.0410	A text file
memo.pdf	A PDF file; view with xpdf
memo.ps	A postscript file; view with gs
memo.Z	A file compressed with compress (page 132); use uncompress (or gunzip, page 132) to decompress
memo.tar.Z	A tar (page 133) archive of files compressed with compress (page 132)
memo.gz	A file compressed with gzip (page 131); view with zcat or decompress with gunzip (both on page 132)
memo.bz2	A file compressed with bzip2 (page 133); view with bzcat or decompress with bunzip2
memo.tgz or **memo.tar.gz**	A tar archive of files compressed with gzip (page 131)
memo.tbz2 or **memo.tar.bz2**	A tar archive of files compressed with bzip2 (page 133)
memo.html	A file meant to be viewed using a Web browser, such as Mozilla
photo.jpg or **photo.gif**	A file containing graphical information, such as a picture (also .jpeg)

Filename Extensions

In the filenames listed in Table 6-1, *filename extensions* help describe the contents of the file. A filename extension is the part of the filename following an embedded period. Some programs, such as the C programming language compiler, depend on specific filename extensions, but in most cases filename extensions are optional. Use extensions freely to make filenames easy to understand. If you like, you can use several periods within the same filename, for example, **notes.4.10.01** or **files.tar.gz**.

Invisible Filenames

A filename that begins with a period is called an *invisible filename* (or an *invisible file* or sometimes a *hidden file*) because ls does not normally display it. The command ls –a displays *all* filenames, even invisible ones. Startup files (page 164) are usually invisible so that they do not clutter a directory. The .plan file (page 139) is also invisible. Two special invisible entries—a single and double period (. and ..)—appear in every directory (page 167).

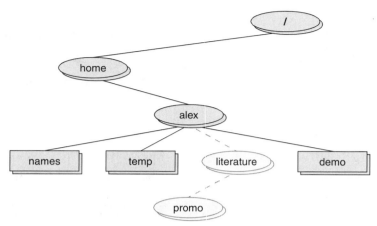

Figure 6-4   The file structure developed in the examples

mkdir: **Creates a Directory**

The mkdir utility creates a directory. The *argument* (page 957) to mkdir becomes the pathname of the new directory. The following examples develop the directory structure shown in Figure 6-4. The directories that are added are lighter than the others and are connected by dashes.

In Figure 6-5, ls shows the names of the files Alex has been working with in his home directory: **demo, names,** and **temp.** Next, using mkdir, Alex creates a directory named **literature** as a child of the **/home/alex** directory. When you use mkdir, enter the pathname of *your* home directory in place of **/home/alex.** The second ls verifies the presence of the new directory.

You can use the **–F** option with ls to display a slash after the name of each directory and an asterisk after each executable file (utility or program). When you call it with an argument that is the name of a directory, ls lists the contents of the directory. If no files are in the directory, ls does not display anything.

```
$ ls
demo   names   temp
$ mkdir /home/alex/literature
$ ls
demo   literature   names   temp
$ ls -F
demo   literature/   names   temp
$ ls literature
$
```

Figure 6-5   The mkdir utility

The Working Directory

While you are logged in on a character-based interface to a Linux system, you are always associated with one directory or another. The directory you are associated with, or are working in, is called the *working directory*, or *current directory*. Sometimes this association is referred to in a physical sense: "You are *in* (or *working in*) the **jenny** directory." The pwd command displays the pathname of the working directory.

To access any file in the working directory, you do not need a pathname but rather only a simple filename. To access a file in another directory, you *must* use a pathname.

Significance of the Working Directory

Typing a long pathname is tedious and increases the chance of making a mistake. This is less true under a GUI, where you click filenames or icons. You can choose a working directory for any particular task to reduce the need for long pathnames. Your choice of a working directory does not allow you to do anything you could not do otherwise but simply makes some operations easier.

Refer to Figure 6-6 as you read this paragraph. Files that are children of the working directory can be referenced by simple filenames. Grandchildren of the working directory can be referenced by short relative pathnames: two filenames separated by a slash. When you manipulate files in a large directory structure, short relative pathnames can save time and aggravation. If you choose a working directory that contains the files used most for a particular task, you need to use fewer long, cumbersome pathnames.

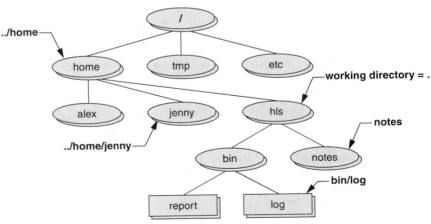

Figure 6-6   Relative pathnames

```
login: alex
Password:
Last login: Wed Oct 20 11:14:21 from zach
$ pwd
/home/alex
```

Figure 6-7   Log in

Home Directory

When you first log in on a Linux system, your working directory is your *home directory*. To display the absolute pathname of your home directory, use pwd just after you log in (Figure 6-7).

Without any arguments, the ls utility displays a list of the files in the working directory. Because your home directory has been the only working directory you have used so far, ls has always displayed a list of files in your home directory. (All the files you have created up to now were created in your home directory.)

cd: Changes to Another Working Directory

The cd (change directory) utility makes another directory the working directory but does *not* change the contents of the working directory. The first cd command in Figure 6-8 makes the **/home/alex/literature** directory the working directory, as verified by pwd.

Without an argument, cd makes your home directory the working directory, as it was when you first logged in. The second command in Figure 6-8 does not have an argument and makes Alex's home directory the working directory.

> tip || **The Working Directory versus Your Home Directory**
>
> The working directory is not the same as your home directory. Your home directory remains the same for the duration of your session and usually from session to session. Each time you log in, you are working in the same directory: your home directory.
>
> Unlike your home directory, your working directory can change as often as you like. You have no set working directory. That is why some people refer to it as the *current directory*. When you log in and until you change directories by using cd, your home directory is your working directory. If you were to change directories to Scott's home directory, then Scott's home directory would be your working directory.

Startup Files

Important files that appear in your home directory are *startup files*. They give the shell and other programs information about you and your preferences. Frequently,

```
$ cd /home/alex/literature
$ pwd
/home/alex/literature
$ cd
$ pwd
/home/alex
```

Figure 6-8   cd changes your working directory

one of these files tells the shell what kind of terminal you are using (page 920) and executes the stty (set terminal) utility to establish your line kill and erase keys.

Either you or the system administrator can put a shell startup file, containing shell commands, in your home directory. The shell executes the commands in this file, named **.bash_profile** (page 272), each time you log in. Because the startup files have invisible filenames, you must use the **ls –a** command to see whether one of these files is in your home directory. A GUI has many startup files. Usually you do not have to work with these files directly but can control startup sequences by using icons on your desktop.

Absolute Pathnames

Every file has a pathname. Figure 6-9 shows the pathnames of directories and ordinary files in part of a filesystem hierarchy.

An absolute pathname always starts with a slash (/), the name of the root directory. You can build the absolute pathname of a file by tracing a path from the root directory through all the intermediate directories to the file. String all the filenames in the

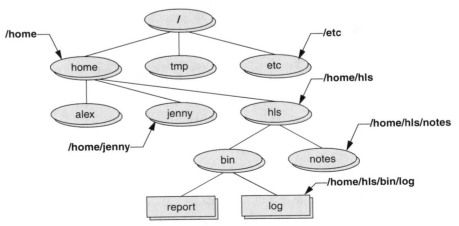

Figure 6-9   Absolute pathnames

path together, separating each from the next with a slash (**/**) and preceding the group of filenames with a slash (**/**).

This path of filenames is called an *absolute pathname* because it locates a file absolutely by tracing a path from the root directory to the file. The part of a pathname following the final slash is called a *simple filename*, or *filename*.

Another form of absolute pathname begins with a tilde (**~**), which represents a home directory. For more information, refer to "Special Pathnames" on page 171.

Relative Pathnames

A *relative pathname* traces a path from the working directory to a file. The pathname is *relative* to the working directory. Any pathname that does not begin with the root directory (**/**) or a tilde (**~**) is a relative pathname. Like absolute pathnames, relative pathnames can describe a path through many directories.

Alex could have created the **literature** directory in Figure 6-5 more easily by using a relative pathname:

```
$ pwd
/home/alex
$ mkdir literature
```

The pwd command shows that Alex's home directory (**/home/alex**) is the working directory. The mkdir utility displays an error message if a directory or file named **literature** exists: You cannot have two files or directories with the same name in one directory. The pathname used in this example is a simple filename. A simple filename is a kind of relative pathname that specifies a file in the working directory.

---

caution ‖   When Using a Relative Pathname, Know Which Is the Working Directory

The location of the file that you are accessing with a relative pathname is dependent on (relative to) the working directory. Always make sure you know which is the working directory before using a relative pathname. Use pwd to verify the directory: If you are using mkdir and you are not where you think you are in the file hierarchy, the new directory will end up in an unexpected location.

It does not matter which directory is the working directory when you use an absolute pathname.

The following commands show two ways to create the **promo** directory as a child of the newly created **literature** directory. The first way assumes that **/home/alex** is the working directory and uses a relative pathname:

```
$ pwd
/home/alex
$ mkdir literature/promo
```

The second way uses an absolute pathname:

```
$ mkdir /home/alex/literature/promo
```

Use the **−t** option to mkdir to create both the **literature** and **promo** directories with one command:

```
$ pwd
/home/alex
$ ls
demo  names  temp
$ mkdir -p literature/promo
```

or

```
$ mkdir -p /home/alex/literature/promo
```

The . and .. Directory Entries

The mkdir utility automatically puts two entries in every directory you create: a single period and a double period, representing the directory itself and the parent directory, respectively. These entries are invisible because each of their filenames begins with a period.

Because mkdir automatically places these entries in every directory, you can rely on their presence. The . is synonymous with the pathname of the working directory and can be used in its place; .. is synonymous with the pathname of the parent of the working directory.

The following example uses .. to copy **temp** to the parent directory (**/home/alex**) and then lists the contents of the **/home/alex** directory from **/home/alex/literature**, again to represent the parent directory:

```
$ pwd
/home/alex/literature
$ ls ..
demo  literature  names  temp
$ cp temp ..
$ ls ..
demo  temp  literature  names  temp
```

While working in his **promo** directory, Alex can use the following relative pathname to edit a file in his home directory. Before calling the editor, Alex checks which directory he is in:

```
$ pwd
/home/alex/literature/promo
$ vi ../../names
```

Virtually anywhere that a utility program requires a filename or pathname, you can use an absolute or relative pathname or a simple filename. This holds true for ls, vi, mkdir, rm, and most other Linux utilities.

Important Standard Directories and Files

Originally files on a Linux system were not located in standard places. That made it difficult to document and maintain a Linux system and just about impossible for someone to release a software package that would compile and run on various Linux systems. The first standard for the Linux filesystem, the FSSTND (Linux Filesystem Standard), was released on February 14, 1994. In early 1995, work was

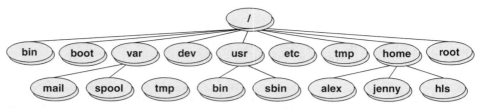

Figure 6-10   A typical FHS-based Linux system file structure

started on a broader standard covering many UNIX-like systems: FHS (Linux Filesystem Hierarchy Standard—www.pathname.com/fhs). More recently, FHS has been incorporated in LSB (Linux Standard Base—www.linuxbase.org), a workgroup of FSG (Free Standards Group—www.freestandards.org). Figure 6-10 shows the locations of some important directories and files as specified by FHS. The significance of many of these directories will become clear as you continue reading.

The following list describes the directories shown in Figure 6-10, along with some of the directories described by FHS, and some other directories. Red Hat Linux does not use all the directories specified by FHS. You cannot always determine the function of a directory by its name: Although **/opt** stores add-on software, **/etc/opt** stores configuration files for the software in **/opt**. See also "Important Files and Directories" on page 425.

/ **Root**   The root directory, present in all Linux system file structures, is the ancestor of all files in the filesystem.

/bin **Essential command binaries**   This directory holds the files needed to bring the system up and run it when it first comes up in single-user mode (page 387).

/boot **Static files of the boot loader**   This directory contains most of the files needed to boot the system.

/dev **Device files**   This directory contains all files that represent peripheral devices, such as disk drives, terminals, and printers.

/etc **Machine–local system configuration**   Administrative, configuration, and other system files are kept here. One of the most important is the **/etc/passwd** file, which contains a list of all users who have permission to use the system. See the list of the files in the **/etc** directory starting on page 427.

/etc/X11 **Machine–local configuration for the X Window System**

/etc/opt **Configuration files for add-on software packages kept in /opt**

/home **User home directories**   Each user's home directory is typically one of many subdirectories of the **/home** directory. As an example, assuming that users' directories are under **/home**, the absolute pathname of Jenny's home directory is **/home/jenny**. On some systems, the users' directories may not be under **/home** but instead might all be under **/inhouse**; some might be under **/inhouse** and others under **/clients**.

/lib   Shared libraries and kernel modules

/lib/modules   Loadable kernel modules

/mnt   Mount point for temporary mounting of filesystems

/opt   Add-on software packages (optional packages)

/proc   Kernel and process information virtual filesystem

/root   Home directory for root

/sbin   **Essential system binaries**   Utilities used for system administration are stored in **/sbin** and **/usr/sbin**. The **/sbin** directory includes utilities needed during the booting process, and **/usr/sbin** holds those utilities that are most useful after the system is up and running. In older versions of Linux, many system administration utilities were scattered through several directories that often included other system files (**/etc, /usr/bin, /usr/adm, /usr/include**).

/tmp   **Temporary files**   Many programs use this directory to hold temporary files.

/usr   **Second major hierarchy**   This directory traditionally includes subdirectories that contain information used by the system. Files in **/usr** subdirectories do not change often and may be shared by multiple systems.

/usr/bin   **Most user commands**   This directory contains the standard Linux utility programs: binaries that are not needed in single-user mode (page 387).

/usr/bin/X11   Symbolic link to **/usr/X11R6/bin**

/usr/games   Games and educational programs

/usr/include   Header files included by C programs

/usr/include/X11   Symbolic link to **/usr/X11R6/include/X11**

/usr/lib   Libraries

/usr/lib/X11   Symbolic link to **/usr/X11R6/lib/X11**

/usr/local   **Local hierarchy**   This directory holds locally important files and directories that are often added to Red Hat. Subdirectories of **/usr/local** include **bin, games, include, lib, sbin, share,** and **src**.

/usr/man   Online manuals

/usr/sbin   **Nonvital system administration binaries**   See **/sbin**.

/usr/share   **Architecture-independent data**   Subdirectories of **/usr/share** include **dict, doc, games, info, locale, man, misc, terminfo,** and **zoneinfo**.

/usr/share/doc   Miscellaneous documentation

/usr/share/info   GNU info system's primary directory

/usr/src   Source code

/usr/X11R6   X Window System, version 11 release 6.

/var   **Variable data**   Files with contents that vary as the system runs are found in sub-directories under **/var**. The most common examples are temporary files, system log files, spooled files, and user mailbox files. Subdirectories of **/var** include **cache, lib, lock, log, opt, run, spool, tmp,** and **yp.** Older versions of Linux scattered such files through several subdirectories of **/usr** (**/usr/adm, /usr/mail, /usr/spool, /usr/tmp**).

/var/log   **Log files**   This directory contains **lastlog** (record of the last login of each user), **messages** (system messages from **syslogd**), and **wtmp** (record of all logins/logouts).

/var/spool   **Spooled application data**   This directory contains **anacron, at, cron, lpd, mail, mqueue, news, samba,** and **uucp.** The file **/var/spool/mail** has a symbolic link in **/var.**

Working with Directories

This section covers deleting directories, copying and moving files between directories, and moving directories. It also describes how to use pathnames to make your work with Linux easier.

rmdir: Deletes a Directory

The rmdir (remove directory) utility deletes a directory. You cannot delete the working directory or a directory that contains other than . and .. entries. If you need to delete a directory with files in it, first use rm to delete the files and then delete the directory. You do not have to delete the . and .. entries; rmdir removes them automatically. The following command deletes the directory that was created in Figure 6-5:

```
$ rmdir /home/alex/literature
```

The rm utility has a –r option (**rm –r** *filename*) that recursively deletes files, including directories, within a directory and also deletes the directory itself.

---

caution || **Use rm –r Carefully, if at All**

Although **rm –r** is a handy command, you must use it carefully. Do not use it with an ambiguous file reference such as *. It is quite easy to wipe out your entire home directory with a single short command.

Pathnames

In the following example **/home/alex** is the working directory. The example uses a relative pathname to copy the file **letter** to the **/home/alex/literature/promo** directory. The copy of the file has the simple filename **letter.0610**:

```
$ pwd
/home/alex
$ cp letter literature/promo/letter.0610
```

Use a text editor to create a file named **letter** if you want to experiment with the examples that follow.

If Alex does not change to another directory, the following command allows him to edit the copy of the file he just made:

```
$ vi literature/promo/letter.0610
...
```

If Alex does not want to use a long pathname to specify the file, he can use cd to make the **promo** directory be the working directory before using vi:

```
$ cd literature/promo
$ pwd
/home/alex/literature/promo
$ vi letter.0610
...
```

If Alex wants to make the parent of the working directory (named **/home/alex/literature**) the new working directory, he can give the following command, which takes advantage of the .. directory entry:

```
$ cd ..
$ pwd
/home/alex/literature
```

optional ||

Special Pathnames

To save typing, the shells and some utilities, such as vi, recognize a few shortcuts in pathnames. The shell expands the characters ~/ (a tilde followed by a slash) at the start of a pathname into the pathname of your home directory. Using this shortcut, you can examine your **.bashrc** file with the following command, no matter which directory is your working directory:

```
$ less ~/.bashrc
```

A tilde quickly references paths that start with your or someone else's home directory. The shell expands a tilde followed by a login name at the beginning of a pathname into the pathname of that user's home directory. Assuming he has permission to do so, Alex can examine Scott's **.bashrc** file with

```
$ less ~scott/.bashrc
```

Refer to "~ Tilde Expansion" on page 311 for a discussion of this topic.

mv, cp: **Moves or Copies a File**

Chapter 5 discussed the use of mv to rename files. However, mv is more general than that: You can use mv to move files from one directory to another (change the pathname of a file) and to change a simple filename.

When used to move one or more files to a new directory, the syntax of the mv command is

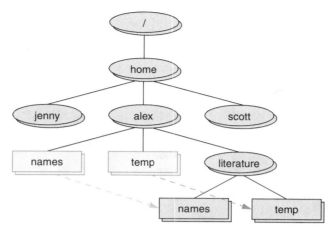

Figure 6-11   Directories and ordinary files

mv existing-file-list directory

If the working directory is **/home/alex**, Alex can use the following command to move the files **names** and **temp** from the working directory to the **literature** directory:

```
$ mv names temp literature
```

This command changes the absolute pathnames of the **names** and **temp** files from **/home/alex/names** and **/home/alex/temp** to **/home/alex/literature/names** and **/home/alex/literature/temp** (Figure 6-11). As with most Linux commands, mv accepts either absolute or relative pathnames.

As you work with Linux and create more and more files, you will need to create directories, using mkdir, to keep the files organized. The mv utility is a useful tool for moving files from one directory to another as you develop your file tree. The cp utility works the same way that mv does, but it makes copies of the *existing-file-list* in the specified *directory*.

mv: Moves a Directory

Just as it moves ordinary files from one directory to another, mv can also move directories. The syntax is similar except that you specify one or more directories, not ordinary files, to move:

mv existing-directory-list new-directory

If *new-directory* does not exist, the *existing-directory-list* must contain just one directory name, which mv changes to *new-directory* (mv renames the directory). Although directories can be renamed using mv, their contents cannot be copied with cp unless you use the **−r** option. Refer to the tar and cpio man pages for other ways to copy/move directories.

Figure 6-12   The columns displayed by the **ls –l** command

Access Permissions

Three types of users can access a file: the owner of the file (*owner*), a member of a group to which the owner belongs (*group;* see page 428 for more information on groups), and everyone else (*other*). A user can attempt to access an ordinary file in three ways: by trying to *read from, write to,* or *execute* it. Three types of users, each able to access a file in three ways, equals a total of nine possible ways to access an ordinary file.

ls –l: Displays Permissions

When you call **ls** with the **–l** option and the name of an ordinary file, **ls** displays a line of information about the file. The following example displays information for two files. The file **letter.0610** contains the text of a letter, and **check_spell** contains a shell script, a program written in a high-level shell programming language:

```
$ ls -l letter.0610 check_spell
-rw-r--r-- 1 alex  pubs  3355  May  2 10:52 letter.0610
-rwxr-xr-x 2 alex  pubs   852  May  5 14:03 check_spell
```

From left to right, the lines contain the following information (refer to Figure 6-12):

- The type of file (first character)
- The file's access permissions (the next nine characters)
- The number of links to the file (see page 177)
- The name of the owner of the file (usually the person who created the file)
- The name of the group that has group access to the file
- The size of the file in characters (bytes)
- The date and time the file was created or last modified
- The name of the file

The type of file (first column) for **letter.0610** is a hyphen (–) because it is an ordinary file (directory files have a **d** in this column).

The next three characters represent the access permissions for the *owner* of the file: **r** indicates read permission and **w** indicates write permission. The – in the next column indicates that the owner does *not* have execute permission; otherwise, you would see an **x** here.

In a similar manner the next three characters represent permissions for the *group*, and the final three characters represent permissions for *other* (everyone else). In the preceding example, the owner of the file **letter.0610** can read from and write to it, whereas group and others can only read from the file, and no one is allowed to execute it. Although execute permission can be allowed for any file, it does not make sense to assign execute permission to a file that contains a document, such as a letter. The **check_spell** file is an executable shell script, and execute permission is appropriate. (The owner, group, and others have execute access permission.)

chmod: **Changes Access Permissions**

The owner of a file controls which users have permission to access the file and how they can access it. When you own a file, you can use the chmod (change mode) utility to change access permissions for that file. In the following example, chmod adds (**+**) read and write permission (**rw**) for all (**a**) users:

```
$ chmod a+rw letter.0610
$ ls -l letter.0610
-rw-rw-rw- 1 alex  pubs    3355  May  2 10:52 letter.0610
```

tip ‖	You Must Have Read Permission to Execute a Shell Script

Because a shell needs to read a shell script (an ASCII file containing shell commands) before it can execute the commands within the script, you must have read permission to the file containing the script in order to execute it. You also need execute permission to execute a shell script directly on the command line. Binary (program) files do not need to be read; they are executed directly. You need only execute permission to run a binary (nonshell) program.

In the next example, chmod removes (**–**) read and execute (**rx**) permissions for users other (**o**) than the owner of the file (Alex) and members of the group associated with the file (**pubs** group):

```
$ chmod o-rx check_spell
$ ls -l check_spell
-rwxr-x--- 2 alex  pubs     852  May  5 14:03 check_spell
```

In addition to **a** (for *all*) and **o** (for *other*), you can use **g** (for *group*) and **u** (for *user*, although user refers to the owner of the file who may or may not be the user of the file at any given time) in the argument to chmod. Refer to page 254 for more information on chmod.

The Linux file access permission scheme lets you give other users access to the files you want to share and keep your private files confidential. You can allow other users to read from *and* write to a file (you may be one of several people working on a joint project). You can allow others only to read from a file (perhaps a project specification you are proposing). Or you can allow others only to write to a file (similar to an inbox or mailbox, where you want others to be able to send you mail but do not want them to read your mail). Similarly, you can protect entire directories from being scanned (covered shortly).

There is an exception to the access permissions just described. Anyone who knows the **root** password can log in as Superuser (page 371) and have full access to *all* files, regardless of owner or access permissions.

---

tip || chmod: **o** for Other, **u** for Owner

When using chmod, many people assume that the **o** stands for *owner;* it does not. The **o** stands for *other,* whereas **u** stands for *owner* (*user*).

---

security || Minimize Use of Setuid and Setgid Programs Owned by **root**

Executable files that are setuid and owned by **root** have Superuser privileges when they are run, even if they are not run by **root**. This type of program is very powerful because it can do anything that Superuser can do (that the program is designed to do). Similarly, executable files that are setgid and belong to the group **root** have extensive privileges.

Because of the power they hold and the potential destruction they can do, avoid creating and using setuid and setgid programs owned by or belonging to the group **root** indiscriminately. Because of the inherent dangers, many sites do not allow these programs on their machines at all. See page 372 for information on setuid and Superuser.

Setuid and Setgid Permissions

When you execute a file that has setuid (set user ID) permission, the process executing the file takes on the privileges of the owner of the file. For example, if you run a setuid program that removes all the files in a directory, you can remove files in any of the file owner's directories, even if you do not normally have permission to do so. In a similar manner, setgid (set group ID) permission means that the process executing the file takes on the privileges of the group the file is associated with. The ls utility shows setuid permission as an **s** in the owner's executable position and setgid as an **s** in the group's executable position:

```
$ ls -l program1
-rwxr-xr-x   1 alex        pubs         15828 Nov  5 06:28 program1
$ chmod u+s program1
$ ls -l program1
-rwsr-xr-x   1 alex        pubs         15828 Nov  5 06:28 program1
$ chmod g+s program1
$ ls -l program1
-rwsr-sr-x   1 alex        pubs         15828 Nov  5 06:28 program1
```

Directory Access Permissions

Access permissions have slightly different meanings when used with directories. Although the three types of users can read from or write to a directory, the directory cannot be executed. Execute access permission is redefined for a directory: It means that you can cd into the directory and/or examine files that you have permission to read from in the directory. It has nothing to do with executing a file.

When you have only execute permission for a directory, you can use ls to list a file in the directory if you know its name. You cannot use ls without an argument to list the contents of the directory. In the following exchange, Jenny first verifies that she is logged on as herself. Then she checks the permissions on Alex's **info** directory and cds into it. (You can view the access permissions associated with a directory by running ls with the –d [directory] and –l [long] options. The **d** at the left end of the line that ls displays indicates that **/home/alex/info** is a directory.) Because Jenny does not have read permission for the directory, the **ls –l** command without any arguments returns an error. The period (.) in the error message represents the working directory:

```
$ who am i
jenny      pts/7   Aug 21 10:02
$ ls -ld /home/alex/info
drwx-----x  2 alex      pubs           512 Aug 21 09:31 /home/alex/info
$ cd /home/alex/info
$ ls -l
.: Permission denied
total 2
```

When Jenny specifies the names of the files she wants information about, she is not reading new directory information, just searching for specific information, which she is allowed to do with execute access to the directory. She cannot display **financial** because she does not have read access to it. She does have read access to **notes**, so she has no problem using cat to display the file:

```
$ ls -l memo.1 memo.2 financial notes summary
-rw-------  1 alex      pubs            34 Aug 21 09:31 financial
-rw-r--r--  1 alex      pubs            21 Aug 21 09:31 memo.1
-rw-r--r--  1 alex      pubs            21 Aug 21 09:32 memo.2
-rw-r--r--  1 alex      pubs            30 Aug 21 09:32 notes
-rw-r--r--  1 alex      pubs            32 Aug 21 09:32 summary
$ cat financial
cat: cannot open financial
$ cat notes
This is the file named notes.
```

Next, Alex uses the following command to give everyone read access to his **info** directory:

```
$ chmod o+r /home/alex/info
```

When Jenny checks access permissions on **info**, she finds that she has both read and execute access to the directory. Now ls –l works just fine without arguments, but she still cannot read **financial**. (This is an issue of file permissions, not directory permissions.) Finally, she tries to create a file named **newfile** by redirecting output from cat (page 197). If Alex were to give her write permission to the **info** directory, she would be able to create new files in it:

```
$ ls -ld /home/alex/info
drwx---r-x    2 alex       pubs              512 Aug 21 09:31 /home/alex/info
$ ls -l
total 10
-rw-------    1 alex       pubs               34 Aug 21 09:31 financial
-rw-r--r--    1 alex       pubs               21 Aug 21 09:31 memo.1
-rw-r--r--    1 alex       pubs               21 Aug 21 09:32 memo.2
-rw-r--r--    1 alex       pubs               30 Aug 21 09:32 notes
-rw-r--r--    1 alex       pubs               32 Aug 21 09:32 summary
$ cat financial
cat: financial: Permission denied
$ cat > newfile
bash: newfile: Permission denied
```

Links

A *link* is a pointer to a file. Every time you create a file using vi or cp or by any other means, you are putting a pointer in a directory. This pointer associates a filename with a place on the disk. When you specify a filename in a command, you are indirectly pointing to the place on the disk where the information that you want is located.

Sharing files can be useful when two or more people are working on a project and need to share some information. You can make it easy for other users to access one of your files by creating additional links to the file.

To share a file with another user, first give the user permission to read from and write to the file. (In addition, you may have to change the access permission of the parent directory of the file to give the user read, write, and/or execute permission.) Once the permissions are appropriately set, the user can create a link to the file so that each of you can access the file from your separate file trees.

A link can also be useful to a single user with a large file tree. You can create links to cross-classify files in your file tree, using different classifications for different tasks. For example, if your file tree is the one depicted in Figure 6-2, you might have a file named **to_do** in each of the subdirectories of the **correspond** directory—that is, in **personal, memos,** and **business.** Then, if you find it difficult to keep track of everything you need to do, you can create a separate directory, named **to_do** in the

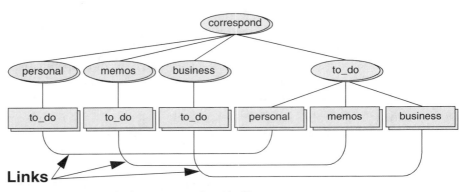

Figure 6-13   Using links to cross-classify files

correspond directory, and link each to-do list into that directory. You could link the file named **to_do** in the **memos** directory to a file named **memos** in the **to_do** directory. This set of links is shown in Figure 6-13.

Although this may sound complicated, this technique keeps all your to-do lists conveniently in one place. The appropriate list is also easily accessible in the task-related directory when you are busy composing letters, writing memos, or handling personal business.

tip || **About the Discussion of Hard Links**

There are two kinds of links: hard links and symbolic, or soft, links. Hard links, discussed first, are older and becoming dated. The section on hard links is marked optional; you can skip it, although it discusses inodes and gives you insight into how the filesystem is structured.

optional ||

Hard Links

A hard link appears as another file in the file structure. If the file appears in the same directory as the one the file is linked with, the links must have different filenames. This restriction does not apply if the linked file is in another directory.

ln: Creates a Hard Link

The ln (link) utility (without the **–s** or **––symbolic** option) creates an additional hard link to an existing file. The syntax for ln is

>   *ln existing-file new-link*

The following command makes the link shown in Figure 6-14 by creating a new link named **/home/alex/letter** to an existing file named **draft** in Jenny's home directory:

```
$ pwd
/home/jenny
$ ln draft /home/alex/letter
```

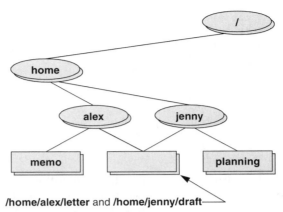

Figure 6-14 Two links to the same file: **/home/alex/letter** and **/home/jenny/draft**

The new link appears in the **/home/alex** directory with the filename **letter**. In practice, it may be necessary for Alex to change directory and file permissions as shown in the previous section in order to give Jenny the necessary permissions. Even though **/home/alex/letter** appears in Alex's directory, Jenny is the owner of the file.

The ln utility creates an additional pointer to an existing file but does *not* make another copy of the file. Because there is only one file, the file status information, such as access permissions, owner, and the time the file was last modified, is the same for all links. Only the filenames differ. When Jenny modifies **/home/jenny/draft**, Alex sees the changes in **/home/alex/letter**.

cp versus ln

The following commands verify that ln does not make an additional copy of a file. Create a file, use ln to make an additional link to the file, change the contents of the file through one link, and verify the change through the other link:

```
$ cat file_a
This is file A.
$ ln file_a file_b
$ cat file_b
This is file A.
$ vi file_b
.
.
.
$ cat file_b
This is file B after the change.
$ cat file_a
This is file B after the change.
```

If you try the same experiment using cp instead of ln and make a change to a *copy* of the file, the difference between the two utilities will become clearer. Once you change a *copy* of a file, the two files are different:

```
$ cat file_c
This is file C.
$ cp file_c file_d
$ cat file_d
This is file C.
$ vi file_d
.
.
.
$ cat file_d
This is file D after the change.
$ cat file_c
This is file C.
```

You can also use ls with the –l option, followed by the names of the files you want to compare, to see that the status information is the same for two links to a file and is different for files that are not linked. In the following example, the **2** in the links field (just to the left of **alex**) shows there are two links to **file_a** and **file_b**:

```
$ ls -l file_a file_b file_c file_d
-rw-r--r-- 2 alex pubs 33  May 24 10:52 file_a
-rw-r--r-- 2 alex pubs 33  May 24 10:52 file_b
-rw-r--r-- 1 alex pubs 16  May 24 10:55 file_c
-rw-r--r-- 1 alex pubs 33  May 24 10:57 file_d
```

Although it is easy to guess which files are linked to one another in this example, ls does not explicitly tell you.

Use ls with the –i option to determine without a doubt which files are linked. The –i option lists the *inode number* for each file. An *inode* is the control structure for a file. If the two filenames have the same inode number, they share the control structure and are links to the same file. Conversely, when two filenames have different inode numbers, they are different files. The following example shows that **file_a** and **file_b** have the same inode number and that **file_c** and **file_d** have different inode numbers:

```
$ ls -i file_a file_b file_c file_d
3534 file_a    3534 file_b    5800 file_c    7328 file_d
```

All links to a file are of equal value: The operating system cannot distinguish the order in which multiple links were made. When a file has two links, you can remove either one and still access the file through the remaining link. You can remove the link used to create the file and, as long as there is a remaining link, still access the file through that link.

Symbolic Link

The links that are described in the preceding optional section are *hard links*. In addition to hard links, Linux supports links called *symbolic links, soft links,* or *symlinks*. A hard link is a pointer to a file (directory entry → inode), whereas a symbolic link is an *indirect* pointer to a file. A symbolic link is a directory entry that contains the pathname of the pointed-to file (a pointer to the hard link to the file).

Symbolic links were developed because of the limitations of hard links. No one can create a hard link to a directory; anyone can create a symbolic link to a directory. Also, a symbolic link can point to any file, regardless of where it is located in the file structure, but a hard link to a file must be in the same filesystem as the other hard link(s) to the file.

Often the Linux file hierarchy is composed of several filesystems. Because each filesystem keeps separate control information (that is, separate inode tables) for the files it contains, it is not possible to create hard links between files in different filesystems. When you create links only among files in your own directories, you will not notice these limitations.

One of its big advantages over a hard link is that a symbolic link can point to a nonexistent file. This ability is useful if you need a link to a file that periodically gets removed and recreated. A hard link would keep pointing to the removed file, which the hard link would keep alive because of its being a hard link, even after a new file was created. A symbolic link would always point to the newly created file and would not interfere with deleting the old file. For example, a symbolic link could point to a file that gets checked in and out under the Source Code Control System, a .o file that is recreated by the C compiler each time you run make, or a log file that is periodically archived.

Although they are more general than hard links, symbolic links have some disadvantages. Whereas all hard links to a file have equal status, symbolic links do not have the same status as hard links. When a file has multiple hard links, it is like a person having multiple full legal names, as many married women do. In contrast, symbolic links are like nicknames. Anyone can have one or more nicknames, but nicknames have a lesser status than legal names. Some of the peculiarities of symbolic links are described in the following sections.

ln: Creates a Symbolic Link

Use ln with the --symbolic (or -s) option to create a symbolic link. The following example creates a symbolic link, **/tmp/s3**, to the file **sum** in Alex's home directory. When you use the ls -l command to look at the symbolic link, ls displays the name of the link and the name of the file it points to. The first character of the listing is l (for link):

```
$ ln --symbolic /home/alex/sum /tmp/s3
$ ls -l /home/alex/sum /tmp/s3
-rw-rw-r--   1 alex      alex              38 Jun 12 09:51 /home/alex/sum
lrwxrwxrwx   1 alex      alex              14 Jun 12 10:09 /tmp/s3 ->
/home/alex/sum
$ cat /tmp/s3
This is sum.
```

The sizes and times of the last modification of the two files are different. Unlike a hard link, a symbolic link to a file does not have the same status information as the file itself.

Use Absolute Pathnames with Symbolic Links

Symbolic links are literal and are not aware of directories: A link that points to a relative pathname, which includes simple filenames, assumes that the relative pathname is relative to the directory that the link was created *in* (and not the directory the link was created *from*). In the following example, the link points to the file named **sum** in the **/tmp** directory. Because there is no such file, cat gives an error message:

```
$ pwd
/home/alex
$ ln --symbolic sum /tmp/s3
$ ls -l sum /tmp/s3
lrwxrwxrwx  1 alex     alex               3 Jun 12 10:13 /tmp/s3 -> sum
-rw-rw-r--  1 alex     alex              38 Jun 12 09:51 sum
$ cat /tmp/s3
cat: /tmp/s3: No such file or directory
```

Similarly, you can use ln to create a symbolic link to a directory. When you use the **--symbolic** option, ln does not care whether the file you are creating a link to is a regular file or a directory.

cd and Symbolic Links

When you use a symbolic link as an argument to cd to change directories, the results can be confusing, particularly if you did not realize that you were using a symbolic link.

If you use cd to change to a directory that is represented by a symbolic link, the pwd builtin lists the name of the symbolic link. The pwd utility (**/bin/pwd**) lists the name of the linked-to directory, not the link, regardless of how you got there:

```
$ ln -s /home/alex/grades /tmp/grades.old
$ pwd
/home/alex
$ cd /tmp/grades.old
$ pwd
/tmp/grades.old
$ /bin/pwd
$/home/alex/grades
```

When you change directories back to the parent, you end up in the directory holding the symbolic link:

```
$ cd ..
$ pwd
/tmp
$ /bin/pwd
/tmp
```

rm: Removes a Link

When you create a file, there is one hard link to it. You can delete the file or, using Linux terminology, remove the link with the rm utility. When you remove the last hard link to a file, you can no longer access the information stored in the file, and the operating system releases for use by other files the space the file occupied on the disk.[1] The space is released even if symbolic links remain. When there is more than one hard link to a file, you can remove a hard link and still access the file from any remaining link.

When you remove all the hard links to a file, you will not be able to access the file through a symbolic link. In the following example, cat reports that the file **total** does not exist because it is a symbolic link to a file that has been removed:

```
$ ls -l sum
-rw-r--r-- 1 alex pubs 981  May 24 11:05 sum
$ ln -s sum total
$ rm sum
$ cat total
cat: total: No such file or directory
$ ls -l total
lrwxrwxrwx 1 alex pubs 6  May 24 11:09 total -> sum
```

When you remove a file, be sure to remove all symbolic links to it. Remove a symbolic link in the same way you remove other files:

```
$ rm total
```

Chapter Summary

Linux has a hierarchical, or treelike, file structure that makes it possible to organize files so that you can find them quickly and easily. The file structure contains directory files and ordinary files. Directories contain other files, including other directories, whereas ordinary files generally contain text, programs, or images. The ancestor of all files is the root directory named /.

Most Linux filesystems support 255-character filenames. Nonetheless, it is a good idea to keep filenames simple and intuitive. Filename extensions can help make filenames more meaningful.

An absolute pathname starts with the root directory and contains all the filenames that trace a path to a given file. Such a pathname starts with a slash representing the root directory and contains additional slashes between the other filenames in the path.

A relative pathname is similar to an absolute pathname, but it starts the path tracing from the working directory. A simple filename is the last element of a pathname and is a form of a relative pathname.

---

1. Unlike DOS/Windows, there is no easy way to undelete a file once you have removed it. A skilled hacker can, in some cases, piece the file together with time and effort.

When you are logged in, you are always associated with a working directory. Your home directory is your working directory from the time you first log in until you use cd to change directories.

A Linux filesystem contains many important directories, including **/usr/bin**, which stores most of the Linux utility commands, and **/dev**, which stores device files, many of which represent a physical piece of hardware. An important standard file is **/etc/passwd**; it contains information about users, such as the user ID and full name.

Among the attributes associated with each file are access permissions. These determine who can access the file and the manner in which the file may be accessed. Three groups of user(s) can access the file: the owner, members of a group, and all other users. A regular file can be accessed in three ways: read, write, and execute. The ls utility with the –l option displays these permissions. For directories, execute access is redefined to mean that the directory can be searched, meaning that it can be used as part of a pathname.

The owner of a file or Superuser can use the chmod utility to change the access permissions of a file at any time. This utility defines read, write, and execute permissions for the owner, the file's group, and all other users on the system.

A link is a pointer to a file. You can have several links to a single file so that you can share the file with other users or have the file appear in more than one directory. Because there is only one copy of a file with multiple links, changing the file through any one link causes the changes to appear in all the links. Hard links cannot link directories or span filesystems, whereas symbolic links can.

Table 6-2 lists the utilities introduced in this chapter.

table 6-2 ‖	Utilities Introduced in This Chapter
cd	Associates you with another working directory (page 164)
chmod	Changes the access permissions on a file (page 174)
ln	Makes a link to an existing file (page 178)
mkdir	Creates a directory (page 162)
pwd	Displays the pathname of the working directory (page 163)
rmdir	Deletes a directory (page 170)

Exercises

1. Is each of the following an absolute pathname, a relative pathname, or a simple filename?

    a. milk_co

    b. correspond/business/milk_co

    c. /home/alex

    d. /home/alex/literature/promo

    e. ..

    f. letter.0610

2. List the commands you can use to

    a. Make your home directory the working directory

    b. Identify the working directory

3. If your working directory is **/home/alex** with a subdirectory named **literature**, give three sets of commands that you can use to create a subdirectory named **classics** under **literature**. Also give several sets of commands you can use to remove the **classics** directory and its contents.

4. The df utility displays all mounted filesystems along with information about each. Use the df utility with the **–h** (humanly readable) option to answer the following questions.

    a. How many filesystems are on your Linux system?

    b. Which filesystem stores your home directory?

    c. Assuming that your answer to part 4a is two or greater, attempt to create a hard link to a file on another filesystem. What error message do you get? What happens when you attempt to create a symbolic link to the file instead?

5. Suppose that you have a file that is linked to a file owned by another user. What can you do so that changes to the file are no longer shared?

6. You should have read permission for the **/etc/passwd** file. To answer the following questions, use cat or less to display **/etc/passwd**. Look at the fields of information in **/etc/passwd** for the users on your system.

    a. What character is used to separate fields in **/etc/passwd**?

    b. How many fields are used to describe each user?

    c. How many users are on your system?

    d. How many different login shells are in use on your system? (*Hint:* Look at the last field.)

    e. The second field of **/etc/passwd** stores user passwords in encoded form. If the password field contains an **x**, your system uses shadow passwords and stores the encoded passwords elsewhere. Does your system use shadow passwords?

7. If **/home/jenny/draft** and **/home/alex/letter** are links to the same file and the following sequence of events occurs, what will be the date in the opening of the letter?

a. Alex gives the command **vi letter**.

b. Jenny gives the command **vi draft**.

c. Jenny changes the date in the opening of the letter to January 31, 2003, writes the file, and exits from vi.

d. Alex changes the date to February 1, 2003, writes the file, and exits from vi.

8. Suppose that a user belongs to a group that has all permissions on a file named **jobs_list**, but the user, as the owner of the file, has no permissions. Describe what operations, if any, the user can perform on **jobs_list**. What command that the user can give will grant the user all permissions on the file?

9. Does the root directory have any subdirectories that you cannot search? Does the root directory have any subdirectories that you cannot read? Explain.

10. Assume that you are given the directory structure shown in Figure 6-2 and the following directory permissions:

```
d--x--x---   3 jenny    pubs         512 Mar 10 15:16 business
drwxr-xr-x   2 jenny    pubs         512 Mar 10 15:16 business/milk_co
```

For each category of permissions—owner, group, and other—what happens when you run each of the following commands? Assume that the working directory is the parent of **correspond** and that the file **cheese_co** is readable by everyone.

a. **cd correspond/business/milk_co**

b. **ls –l correspond/business**

c. **cat correspond/business/cheese_co**

Advanced Exercises

11. Create a file named **–x** in an empty directory. Explain what happens when you try to rename it. How can you rename it?

12. Suppose that the working directory contains a single file named **andor**. What error message do you get when you run the following command line?

```
$ mv andor and\/or
```

Under what circumstances is it possible to run the command without producing an error?

13. The **ls** –**i** command displays a filename preceded by the inode number of the file (page 180). Write a command to output inode/filename pairs for the files in the working directory, sorted by inode number. (*Hint:* Use a pipe.)

14. Do you think that the system administrator has access to a program to decode user passwords? Why or why not (see exercise 6)?

15. Is it possible to distinguish a file from a hard link to a file? That is, given a filename, can you tell whether it was created using an **ln** command? Explain.

16. Explain the error messages displayed in the following sequence of commands:

```
$ ls -l
total 1
drwxrwxr-x   2 alex        bravo          1024 Mar  2 17:57 dirtmp
$ ls dirtmp
$ rmdir dirtmp
rmdir: dirtmp: Directory not empty
$ rm dirtmp/*
rm: No match.
```

17. How can you create a file named –**i**? Which techniques do not work, and why do they not work?

18. How can you remove a file named –**i**? Which techniques do not work, and why do they not work?

The Shell I

7

This chapter takes a look at the Bourne Again Shell (bash) and explains how to use some of its features. The chapter discusses command line syntax and how the shell processes a command line and initiates execution of a program. The chapter shows how to redirect input to and output from a command, construct pipes and filters on the command line, and run a command as a background task. The final section covers filename expansion and explains how you can use this feature in your everyday work. Refer to Chapter 9 for more information on bash and to Chapter 28 for information on writing and executing shell scripts.

tip ‖   **Run These Utilities and Commands from a Command Line**

This chapter describes command line, or text-based, utilities and commands. You can experiment with these utilities from a terminal emulator within a GUI (page 86) or from a virtual console (page 103).

The Command Line

The shell executes a program when you give it a command in response to its prompt. For example, when you give the ls command, the shell executes the utility program named ls. You can cause the shell to execute other types of programs— such as shell scripts, application programs, and programs you have written—in the same way. The line that contains the command, including any arguments, is called the *command line*. In this book, the term *command* refers to the characters you type on the command line, as well as to the program that action invokes.

Syntax

Command line syntax dictates the ordering and separation of the elements on a command line. When you press the RETURN key after entering a command, the shell scans the command line for proper syntax. The syntax for a basic command line is

> *command [arg1] [arg2] ... [argn]* RETURN

One or more SPACEs must appear between elements on the command line. The *command* is the command name, *arg1* through *argn* are arguments, and RETURN is the keystroke that terminates all command lines. The arguments in the command line syntax are enclosed in brackets to show that they are optional. Not all commands require arguments: Some commands do not allow arguments; other commands allow a variable number of arguments; and others require a specific number of arguments. Options, a special kind of argument, are usually preceded by a hyphen (also called a dash or minus sign: –). (No *smiley* [page 996] intended.)

Command Name

Some useful Linux command lines consist of only the name of the command without any arguments. For example, ls by itself lists the contents of the working directory. Most commands accept one or more arguments. Commands that require arguments typically give a short error message, called a *usage message,* when you use them without arguments, with incorrect arguments, or with the wrong number of arguments.

Arguments

On the command line each sequence of nonblank characters is called a *token,* or *word.* An *argument* is a token, such as a filename, string of text, number, or other object that a command acts on. For example, the argument to a vi or emacs command is the name of the file you want to edit.

The following command line shows cp copying the file named **temp** to **tempcopy**:

```
$ cp temp tempcopy
```

Arguments are numbered, starting with the command itself as argument zero. In this example, **cp** is argument zero, **temp** is argument one, and **tempcopy** is argument two. The cp utility requires two arguments on the command line. (The utility can take more but not fewer: See the cp man page.) Argument one is the name of an existing file, and argument two is the name of the file that cp is creating or overwriting. Here the arguments are not optional; both arguments must be present for the command to work. When you do not supply the right number or kind of arguments, cp displays a usage message. Try typing **cp** and then pressing RETURN.

Options

An *option* is an argument that modifies the effects of a command. You can frequently specify more than one option, modifying the command in several different

```
$ ls
alex   house   mark    office     personal  test
hold   jenny   names   oldstuff   temp
$ ls -r
test   personal  office  mark    house  alex
temp   oldstuff  names   jenny   hold
$ ls -x
alex      hold       house      jenny   mark   names
office    oldstuff   personal   temp    test
$ ls -rx
test   temp    personal   oldstuff   office   names
mark   jenny   house      hold       alex
```

Figure 7-1   Using options

ways. Options are specific to and interpreted by the program that the command line calls.

By convention, options are separate arguments that follow the name of the command. Most utilities require you to prefix options with a hyphen. However, this requirement is specific to the utility and not to the shell. GNU program options are frequently preceded by two hyphens in a row, with −−**help** generating a (sometimes extensive) usage message.

Figure 7-1 first shows what happens when you give an ls command without any options. By default, ls lists the contents of the working directory in alphabetical order, vertically sorted in columns. Next, you see that the −r (reverse order; because this is a GNU utility, you can also use −−**reverse**) option causes the ls utility to display the list of files in reverse alphabetical order, still sorted in columns. The −x option causes ls to display the list of files in horizontally sorted rows.

When you need to use several options, you can usually group multiple single-letter options into one argument that starts with a single hyphen; do not put SPACEs between the options. You cannot combine options that are preceded by two hyphens this way. Specific rules for combining options depend on the program you are running. Figure 7-1 shows both the −r and −x options with the ls utility. Together these options generate a horizontally sorted list of filenames in reverse alphabetical order. Most utilities allow you to list options in any order; **ls −xr** produces the same results as **ls −rx**. The command **ls −x −r** also generates the same list.

caution ‖   **The Human Readable Option**

Most utilities that report on file sizes tell you the size of a file in bytes. That is all right when you are dealing with smaller files, but the numbers can get difficult to read when you are working with file sizes that are measured in megabytes or gigabytes. Give the command **df**, which reports on the space available on your system (and possibly on other systems). Look at the **Used** and **Avail** columns. Now give the command **df −h** or **df − −human-readable**. See the difference? Many utilities that report on file sizes, including ls with the −l option, have this option.

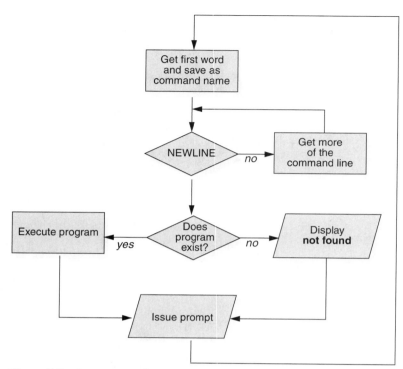

Figure 7-2   Processing the command line

Processing the Command Line

As you enter a command line, the Linux tty device driver (part of the Linux operating system kernel) examines each character to see whether it must take immediate action. When you press CONTROL-H (to erase a character) or CONTROL-U (to kill a line), the device driver immediately adjusts the command line as required; the shell never sees the character you erased or the line you killed. Often a similar adjustment occurs when you press CONTROL-W (to erase a word). When the character does not require immediate action, the device driver stores the character in a buffer and waits until it receives additional characters. When you press RETURN, the device driver passes the command line to the shell for processing.

When it processes a command line, the shell looks at the line as a whole and *parses* (breaks) it into its component parts (Figure 7-2). Next, the shell looks for the name of the command. Usually[1] the name of the command is the first thing on the command line after the prompt (argument zero), so the shell takes the first characters on the command line, up to the first blank (TAB or SPACE), and looks for a command with that name. The command name (the first token) can be specified on the command line either as a simple filename or as a pathname. For example, you can call the ls command in either of the following ways:

```
$ ls
```

or

```
$ /bin/ls
```

When you give an absolute pathname on the command line or a relative pathname that is not a simple filename (that is, any pathname that includes at least one slash), the shell looks in the specified directory (**/bin**, in this case) for a file that has the name **ls** and that you have permission to execute. When you give a simple filename, the shell searches through a list of directories for a filename that matches the name that you specified and that you have execute permission for. The shell does not look through all directories but rather through only the ones specified by the *shell variable* named **PATH**. Refer to page 283 for more information on **PATH**. Also refer to the discussion of which and whereis on page 135.

When it cannot find the executable file,[2] the shell displays a message such as the following:

```
$ abc
bash: abc: command not found
```

When the shell finds the program but cannot execute it (you do not have execute access to the file that contains the program), you see a message similar to

```
$ def
bash: ./def: Permission denied.
```

Executing the Command Line

If it finds an executable file with the same name as the command, the shell starts a new process. A *process* is the execution of a program (page 267). The shell makes each command line argument, including options and the name of the command, available to the called program. While the command is executing, the shell waits, inactive, for the process to finish. The shell is in a state called *sleep*. When the program finishes execution, the shell returns to an active state (wakes up), issues a prompt, and waits for another command.

---

1. The shell does not require that the name of the program appears as the first argument on the command line. You *can* structure a command line as follows:

```
$ >bb < aa cat
```

When the shell sees the redirect symbols (page 196), it recognizes and processes them and their arguments before finding the name of the program that the command line is calling. This is a properly structured, although uncommon, command line.

2. One reason the shell may not be able to find the executable file is that it is not in a directory in your **PATH**. Under bash, the following command adds the working directory (**.**) to your **PATH** temporarily:

```
$ PATH=$PATH:.
```

For reasons of security, you may not want to add the working directory to your **PATH** permanently; see the tip "**PATH** and Security" on page 284.

Figure 7-3   The command does not know where standard input comes from or where standard output and standard error go.

Because the shell does not process command line arguments but only hands them to the called program, the shell has no way of knowing whether a particular option or other argument is valid for a given program. Any error or usage messages about options or arguments come from the program itself. Some utilities ignore bad options.

---

tip || chsh: **Changes Your Login Shell**

The person who sets up your account determines which shell you will use when you first log in on the system or when you open a terminal emulator window in a GUI environment. You can run any shell you like once you are logged in. Enter the name of the shell you want to use (bash, tcsh, or zsh) and press RETURN; assuming the shell you requested is installed, the next prompt will be that of the new shell. Experiment with the shell as you like, and give an **exit** command to return to your previous shell. Because shells you call in this manner are nested (one runs on top of the other), you will be able to log out only from your original shell. When you have nested several shells, keep giving **exit** commands until you are back to your original shell. Then you will be able to log out.

Use the chsh utility when you want to change your login shell permanently: Give the command **chsh**. Then, in response to the prompts, enter your password and the absolute pathname of the shell you want to use (**/bin/bash**, **/bin/tcsh**, or **/bin/zsh**).

Standard Input and Standard Output

The *standard output* is a place that a program can send information, such as text. The command (program) never "knows" where the information it sends to standard output is going (Figure 7-3). The information can go to a printer, an ordinary file, or your screen. The following sections show that, by default, the shell directs standard output from a command to the screen[3] and describe how you can cause the shell to redirect this output to another file. Standard input is a place that a program gets information from. As with standard output, the command never "knows" where the information comes from. The following sections also explain how to redirect *standard input* to a command so that it comes from an ordinary file instead of from the keyboard (the default).

---

3. The term *screen* is used throughout to mean screen, terminal emulator window, and workstation: *Screen* refers to the device that you see the prompt and messages displayed on.

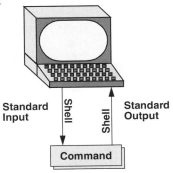

Standard Input   Shell   Shell   **Standard Output**

Command

Figure 7-4   By default, standard input comes from the keyboard, and standard output goes to the screen/window.

In addition to standard input and standard output, a running program normally has a place to send error messages: *standard error*. Refer to page 260 for more information on handling standard error.

The Screen as a File

Chapter 6 introduced ordinary files, directory files, and hard and soft links. Linux has an additional type of file: a *device file*. A device file resides in the Linux file structure, usually in the /dev directory, and represents a peripheral device, such as a terminal emulator window, screen, printer, or disk drive.

The device name that the who utility displays after your login name is the filename of your screen/window. When who displays the device name **pts/4**, the pathname of your screen/window is **/dev/pts/4**. When you work with multiple windows, each one has its own device name. You can also use the tty utility to display the name of the screen that you give the command from. Although you would not normally have occasion, you can read from and write to this file as though it were a text file. Writing to it displays what you wrote on the screen; reading from it reads what you entered on the keyboard.

The Screen/Keyboard as Standard Input and Standard Output

When you first log in, the shell directs standard output of your commands to the device file that represents your window/screen (Figure 7-4). Directing output in this manner causes it to appear on your screen. The shell also directs standard input to come from the same file, so that your commands receive anything you type on your keyboard as input.

The cat utility provides a good example of the way the screen/keyboard functions as standard input and standard output. When you use cat, it copies a file to standard output. Because the shell directs standard output to the screen, cat displays the file on the screen.

```
$ cat
This is a line of text.
This is a line of text.
Cat keeps copying lines of text
Cat keeps copying lines of text
until you press CONTROL-D at the beginning
until you press CONTROL-D at the beginning
of a line.
of a line.
CONTROL-D
$
```

Figure 7-5   The cat utility copies standard input to standard output.

Up to this point, cat has taken its input from the filename (argument) you specified on the command line. When you do not give cat an argument (that is, when you give the command cat followed immediately by a RETURN), cat takes input from standard input. The cat utility can now be described as a utility that, when called without an argument, copies standard input to standard output, one line at a time.

To see how cat works, type cat, and press RETURN in response to the shell prompt: Nothing happens. Enter a line of text and press RETURN. The same line appears just under the one you entered; the cat utility is working. When you type a line of text using the keyboard, the shell associates that line with cat's standard input. Then cat copies your line of text to standard output, which the shell associated with the screen. This exchange is shown in Figure 7-5.

The cat utility keeps copying until you enter CONTROL-D on a line by itself. Pressing CONTROL-D sends an EOF (end of file) signal to cat to indicate that it has reached the end of standard input and that there is no more text for it to copy. When you enter CONTROL-D, cat finishes execution and returns control to the shell, which gives you a prompt.

Redirection

The term *redirection* encompasses the various ways you can cause the shell to alter where standard input of a command comes from and where standard output goes. As the previous section demonstrated, by default, the shell associates standard input and standard output of a command with the keyboard and window/screen. You can cause the shell to redirect standard input and/or standard output of any command by associating the input or output with a command or file other than the device file representing the screen/keyboard. This section demonstrates how to redirect output to and input from ordinary text files and utilities.

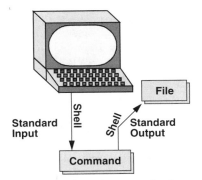

Figure 7-6   Redirecting standard output

Redirecting Standard Output

The *redirect output symbol* (**>**) instructs the shell to redirect the output of a command to the specified file instead of to the screen (Figure 7-6). The format of a command line that redirects output is

command [arguments] > filename

where **command** is any executable program (such as an application program or a utility), **arguments** are optional arguments, and **filename** is the name of the ordinary file the shell redirects the output to.

In Figure 7-7, cat demonstrates output redirection. This figure contrasts with Figure 7-3 on page 194, where both standard input *and* standard output are associated with the screen and keyboard. In Figure 7-7, only the input comes from the screen. The redirect output symbol on the command line causes the shell to associate cat's standard output with the file specified on the command line: **sample.txt**.

Now, the file **sample.txt** contains the text you entered. You can use cat with an argument of **sample.txt** to display the file. The next section shows another way to use cat to display the file.

caution ‖   **Redirecting Output Can Destroy a File I**

Use caution when you redirect output to a file. If the file exists, the shell overwrites it and destroys its contents. For more information, see the caution named "Redirecting Output Can Destroy a File II" on page 200.

Figure 7-7 shows that redirecting the output from cat is a handy way to make a file without using an editor. The drawback is that once you enter a line and press RETURN, you cannot edit the text. While you are entering a line, the erase and kill keys work to delete text. This procedure is useful for making short, simple files.

```
$ cat > sample.txt
This text is being entered at the keyboard.
Cat is copying it to a file.
Press CONTROL-D to indicate the
End of File.
CONTROL-D
$
```

Figure 7-7   cat with its output redirected

Figure 7-8 shows how to use cat and the redirect output symbol to *catenate* (join one after the other: the derivation of the name of the cat utility) several files into one larger file. The first three commands display the contents of three files: **stationery, tape,** and **pens.** The next command shows cat with three filenames as arguments. When you call it with more than one filename, cat copies the files, one at a time, to standard output. In this case, standard output is redirected to the file **supply_orders.** The final cat command shows that **supply_orders** contains the contents of all three files.

Redirecting Standard Input

Just as you can redirect standard output, you can redirect standard input. The *redirect input symbol* (<) instructs the shell to redirect a command's input from the specified file instead of the keyboard (Figure 7-9). The format of a command line that redirects input is

   command [arguments] < filename

where *command* is any executable program (such as an application program or a utility), *arguments* are optional arguments, and *filename* is the name of the ordinary file the shell redirects the input from.

```
$ cat stationery
2000 sheets letterhead ordered:    10/7/02
$ cat tape
1 box masking tape ordered:        10/14/02
5 boxes filament tape ordered:     10/28/02
$ cat pens
12 doz. black pens ordered:        10/4/02
$ cat stationery tape pens > supply_orders
$ cat supply_orders
2000 sheets letterhead ordered:    10/7/02
1 box masking tape ordered:        10/14/02
5 boxes filament tape ordered:     10/28/02
12 doz. black pens ordered:        10/4/02
$
```

Figure 7-8   Using cat to catenate files

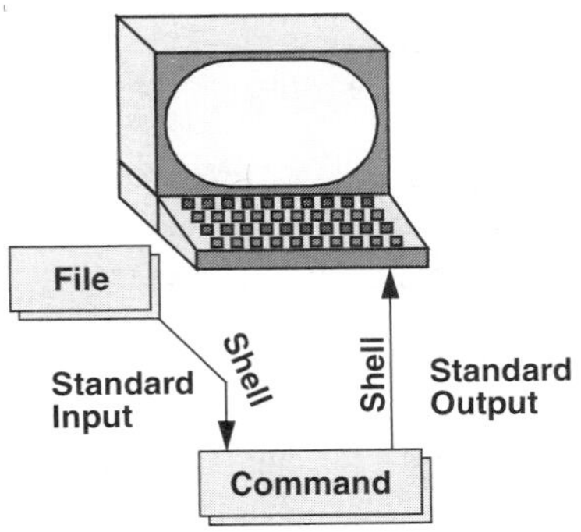

Figure 7-9   Redirecting standard input

Figure 7-10 shows cat with its input redirected from the **supply_orders** file that was created in Figure 7-8 and standard output going to the screen. This setup causes cat to display the sample file on the screen. The system automatically supplies an EOF (end of file) signal at the end of an ordinary file, so no CONTROL-D is necessary.

Giving a cat command with input redirected from a file yields the same result as giving a cat command with the filename as an argument. The cat utility is a member of a class of Linux utilities that function in this manner. Some of the other members of this class of utilities are lp, sort, and grep. These utilities first examine the command line that you use to call them. If you include a filename on the command line, the utility takes its input from the file you specify. If you do not specify a filename, the utility takes its input from standard input. It is the utility or program, not the shell or the operating system, that functions in this manner.

The shell provides a feature called **noclobber** (page 262) that stops you from inadvertently overwriting an existing file using redirection. When you enable this feature by setting the **noclobber** variable and you attempt to redirect output to an existing file, the shell presents an error message and does not execute the command. If the preceding examples result in one of the following messages, the **noclobber** feature is in effect. The following example sets **noclobber**, attempts to redirect the output from echo into an existing file, and then unsets **noclobber**:

```
$ set -o noclobber
$ echo "hi there" > tmp
bash: tmp: Cannot overwrite existing file
$ set +o noclobber
```

```
$ cat < supply_orders
2000 sheets letterhead ordered:    10/7/02
1 box masking tape ordered:        10/14/02
5 boxes filament tape ordered:     10/28/02
12 doz. black pens ordered:        10/4/02
```

Figure 7-10   cat with its input redirected

Redirecting Output Can Destroy a File II

Depending on how your environment has been set up, a command such as the following may give you undesired results:

```
$ cat orange pear > orange
cat: orange: input file is output file
```

Although cat displays an error message, the shell goes ahead and destroys the contents of the existing **orange** file. If you give the preceding command, the new **orange** file will have the same contents as **pear** because the first action the shell takes when it sees the redirection symbol (**>**) is to remove the contents of the original **orange** file. If you want to catenate two files into one, use cat to put the two files into a third, temporary file, and then use mv to rename the third file as you desire:

```
$ cat orange pear > temp
$ mv temp orange
```

What happens with the typo in the next example can be even worse. The user giving the command wants to search through files **a**, **b**, and **c** for the word **apple** and redirect the output from grep (page 123) to the file **a.output**. Instead, the user enters the filename as **a output**, omitting the period and leaving a SPACE in its place:

```
$ grep apple a b c > a output
grep: output: No such file or directory
```

The shell obediently removes the contents of **a** and then calls grep. The error message takes a moment to appear, giving you a sense that the command is running correctly. Even after you see the error message, it may take a while to realize that you destroyed the contents of **a**.

Appending Standard Output to a File

The *append output symbol* (**>>**) causes the shell to add new information to the end of a file, leaving intact any information that was there. This symbol provides a convenient way of catenating two files into one. The following commands demonstrate the action of the append output symbol. The second command accomplishes the catenation described in the preceding caution box:

```
$ cat orange
this is orange
$ cat pear >> orange
$ cat orange
this is orange
this is pear
```

You first see the contents of the **orange** file. Next, the contents of the **pear** file are added on to the end of (catenated with) the **orange** file. The final cat shows the result.

Figure 7-11 shows how to create a file that contains the date and time (the output from date), followed by a list of who is logged in (the output from who). The first line in Figure 7-11 redirects the output from date to the file named **whoson**. Then, cat displays the file. Next, the example appends the output from who to the **whoson** file. Finally, cat displays the file containing the output of both utilities.

```
$ date >whoson
$ cat whoson
Thu Mar 27 14:31:18 PST 2003
$ who >>whoson
$ cat whoson
Thu Mar 27 14:31:18 PST 2003
root        console      Mar 27 05:00(:0)
alex        pts/4        Mar 27 12:23(:0.0)
alex        pts/5        Mar 27 12:33(:0.0)
jenny       pts/7        Mar 26 08:45 (bravo.tcorp.com)
```

Figure 7-11   Redirecting and appending output

caution ‖   **Do Not Trust noclobber**

This technique is simpler to use than the two-step procedure just described, but you must be careful to include both greater than signs. If you accidentally use only one and the **noclobber** feature is not on, you will overwrite the **orange** file. Even if you have the **noclobber** feature turned on, it is a good idea to keep backup copies of files you are manipulating in these ways in case you make a mistake.

Although it protects you from making an erroneous redirection, **noclobber** cannot stop you from overwriting an existing file using cp or mv. These utilities include the **–i** (interactive) option that protects you from this type of mistake by verifying your intentions when you try to overwrite a file. For more information, see the Tip titled "cp Can Destroy a File" on page 121.

/dev/null: Data Sink

The **/dev/null** device is a *data sink*, commonly referred to as a *bit bucket*. You can redirect output that you do not want to keep or see to **/dev/null**. The output disappears without a trace:

```
$ echo "hi there" > /dev/null
$
```

When you read from **/dev/null**, you get a null string. Give the following cat command to truncate a file named **messages** to zero length while preserving the ownership and permissions of the file:

```
$ ls -l messages
-rw-r--r--   1 alex       pubs          25315 Oct 24 10:55 messages
$ cat /dev/null > messages
$ ls -l messages
-rw-r--r--   1 alex       pubs              0 Oct 24 11:02 messages
```

Pipes

The shell uses a *pipe* to connect standard output of one command directly to standard input of another command. A pipe (sometimes referred to as a *pipeline*) has

```
$ ls > temp
$ lpr temp
$ rm temp

or

$ ls | lpr
$
```

Figure 7-12   A pipe

the same effect as redirecting standard output of one command to a file and then using that file as standard input to another command. A pipe does away with separate
commands and the intermediate file. The symbol for a pipe is a vertical bar (|). The
syntax of a command line using a pipe is

> *command_a [arguments] | command_b [arguments]*

This command line uses a pipe to generate the same result as the following group of
command lines:

> *command_a [arguments] > temp*
> *command_b [arguments] < temp*
> *rm temp*

In the preceding sequence of commands, the first line redirects standard output
from *command_a* to an intermediate file named *temp*. The second line redirects
standard input for *command_b* to come from *temp*. The final line deletes *temp*. The
command using a pipe is not only easier to type, it is generally more efficient because it does not create a temporary file.

You can use a pipe with a member of the class of Linux utilities that accepts input
either from a file specified on the command line or from standard input. You can
also use pipes with commands that accept input only from standard input. For example, the tr (translate) utility takes its input from standard input only. In its simplest usage tr has the following format:

> *tr string1 string2*

The tr utility accepts input from standard input and looks for characters that match
one of the characters in *string1*. Finding a match, tr translates the matched character

```
$ who > temp
$ sort < temp
alex        pts/4        Mar 27 12:23
alex        pts/5        Mar 27 12:33
jenny       pts/7        Mar 26 08:45
root        console      Mar 27 05:00
$ rm temp
```

Figure 7-13   Using a temporary file to store intermediate results

```
$ who | sort
alex       pts/4        Mar 27 12:23
alex       pts/5        Mar 27 12:33
jenny      pts/7        Mar 26 08:45
root       console      Mar 27 05:00
```

Figure 7-14   A pipe doing the work of a temporary file

in *string1* to the corresponding character in *string2*. (The first character in *string1* translates into the first character in *string2*, and so forth.) In the following examples, tr displays the contents of the **abstract** file with the letters **a**, **b**, and **c** translated into **A**, **B**, and **C**, respectively:

```
$ cat abstract | tr abc ABC
```

or

```
$ tr abc ABC < abstract
```

The tr utility does not change the contents of the original file.

The lpr (line printer) utility is among the utilities that accept input from either a file or standard input. When you type the name of a file following lpr on the command line, it places that file in the print queue. When you do not specify a filename on the command line, lpr takes input from standard input. This feature enables you to use a pipe to redirect input to lpr. The first set of commands in Figure 7-12 shows how you can use ls and lpr, with an intermediate file (**temp**), to send a list of the files in the working directory to the printer. If the **temp** file exists, the first command overwrites its contents. The second set of commands sends the same list (with the exception of **temp**) to the printer, using a pipe.

The commands in Figure 7-13 redirect the output from the who utility to **temp** and then display this file in sorted order. The sort utility (page 125) takes its input from the file specified on the command line or, when a file is not specified, from standard input and sends its output to standard output. The sort command line in Figure 7-13 takes its input from standard input, which is redirected (<) to come from **temp**. The output that sort sends to the screen lists the users in sorted (alphabetical) order.

Because sort can take its input from standard input or from a filename on the command line, you can omit the < symbol from Figure 7-13 to yield the same results.

Figure 7-14 achieves the same result without creating the **temp** file. Using a pipe, the shell redirects the output from who to the input of sort. The sort utility takes input from standard input because no filename follows it on the command line.

When a lot of people are using the system and you want information about only one of them, you can send the output from who to grep (page 123), using a pipe. The grep utility displays the line containing the string you specify—**root** in the following example:

```
$ who | grep 'root'
root       console      Mar 27 05:00
```

Another way of handling output that is too long to fit on the screen, such as a list of files in a crowded directory, is to use a pipe to send the output through less (page 120):

```
$ ls | less
```

The less utility displays text one screen at a time.[4] To view another screen, press the SPACE bar. To view one more line, press RETURN. Press h for help and q to quit.

Filters

A *filter* is a command that processes an input stream of data to produce an output stream of data. A command line that includes a filter uses a pipe to connect standard output of one command to the filter's standard input. Another pipe connects the filter's standard output to standard input of another command. Not all utilities can be used as filters.

In the following example, sort is a filter, taking standard input from standard output of who and using a pipe to redirect standard output to standard input of lpr. The command line sends the sorted output of who to the printer:

```
$ who | sort | lpr
```

This example demonstrates the power of the shell combined with the versatility of Linux utilities. The three utilities, who, sort, and lpr, were not specifically designed to work with each other, but they all use standard input and standard output in the conventional way. By using the shell to handle input and output, you can piece standard utilities together on the command line to achieve the results you want.

tee: Sends Output in Two Directions

In a pipe, the tee utility sends the output of a command to a file and also to standard output. The utility is aptly named: It takes a single input and sends the output in two directions. In Figure 7-15, the output of who is sent via a pipe to standard input of tee. The tee utility saves a copy of standard input in a file named **who.out** and also sends a copy to standard output. Standard output of tee goes via a pipe to standard input of grep, which displays lines containing the string **root**.

Running a Program in the Background

In all the examples so far in this book, commands were run in the *foreground*. When you run a command in the foreground, the shell waits for it to finish before

---

4. Some utilities change the format of their output when you redirect it. Compare the output of ls by itself and when you send it through a pipe to less.

```
$ who | tee who.out | grep root
root        console      Mar 27 05:00
$ cat who.out
root        console      Mar 27 05:00
alex        pts/4        Mar 27 12:23
alex        pts/5        Mar 27 12:33
jenny       pts/7        Mar 26 08:45
```

Figure 7-15   Using tee

giving you another prompt and allowing you to continue. When you run a command in the *background*, you do not have to wait for the command to finish before you start running another command.

A *job* is a series of one or more commands connected by one or more pipes. You can have only one foreground job in a window or on a screen, but you can have many background jobs. By running more than one job at a time, you are using one of Linux's important features: multitasking. Running a command in the background can be useful when the command will be running for a long time and does not need supervision. The window/screen is free so that you can use it for other work. Of course, when you are using a GUI, you can simply open another window to run another job.

To run a command in the background, type an ampersand (&) just before the RETURN that ends the command line. The shell assigns a small number to the job and displays this *job number* between brackets. Following the job number, the shell displays the *process identification* (PID) number—a bigger number assigned by the operating system. Each of these numbers identifies the command running in the background. Then the shell gives you another prompt so you can enter another command. When the background job finishes running, the shell displays a message giving both the job number and the command line used to run the command.

The next example runs in the background and sends its output through a pipe to lpr, which sends it to the printer:

```
bash $ ls -l | lpr &
[1] 22092
bash $
```

The [1] following the command line indicates that the shell has assigned job number 1 to this job. The **22092** is the PID number of the first command in the job. When this background job completes execution, you see the message

```
[1]+ Done            ls -l | lpr
```

You can stop a foreground job from running by pressing the suspend key, usually CONTROL-Z. The shell stops the process and disconnects standard input from the screen keyboard. You can put a job in the background and start it running by using the bg command, followed by the job number. You do not need to use the job number when you have only one stopped job.

Only the foreground job can take input from the keyboard. To connect the keyboard to the program running in the background, you must bring it into the foreground: Type **fg** without any arguments when only one job is in the background. When more than one job is in the background, type **fg** (optional) followed by the number of the job you want to bring into the foreground. The shell displays the command you used to start the job, and you can enter any input the program requires to continue:

```
bash $ fg 1
[1] promptme
```

Redirect the output of a job you run in the background to keep it from interfering with whatever you are doing on the screen. Refer to "Separating and Grouping Commands" on page 256 for more detail about background tasks.

The interrupt key (usually CONTROL-C) cannot abort a process you are running in the background; you must use kill (page 375) for this purpose. Follow **kill** on the command line with either the PID number of the process you want to abort or a percent sign (%) followed by the job number.

If you forget the PID number, you can use the ps (process status [page 268]) utility to display it. The following example runs a **tail –f outfile** command (the –f option causes tail to watch **outfile** and display any new lines that are written to it) as a background job, uses ps to display the PID number of the process, and aborts the job with kill. So that it does not interfere with anything on the screen, the message saying that the job is terminated does not appear until you press RETURN after the RE-TURN that ends the kill command:

```
$ tail -f outfile &
[1] 22170
$ ps | grep tail
22170 pts/7    0:00 tail
$ kill 22170
$ RETURN
[1]+    Terminated          tail -f outfile
$
```

If you forget the job number, you can use the jobs command to display a list of job numbers. The following example is similar to the previous one but uses the job number in place of the PID number to kill the job:

```
$ tail -f outfile &
[1] 3339
$ bigjob &
[2] 3340
$ jobs
[1]  - Running             tail -f outfile
[2]  + Running             bigjob
$ kill %1
$RETURN
[1]+    Terminated          tail -f outfile
$
```

Filename Generation/Pathname Expansion

When you give the shell abbreviated filenames that contain special characters, also called *metacharacters,* the shell can generate filenames that match the names of existing files. These special characters are also referred to as *wildcards* because they act as jokers do in a deck of cards. When one of these special characters appears in an argument on the command line, the shell expands that argument in sorted order into a list of filenames and passes the list to the program that the command line calls. Filenames that contain these special characters are called *ambiguous file references* because they do not refer to any one specific file. The process that the shell performs on these filenames is called *pathname expansion,* or *globbing.*

Ambiguous file references refer to a group of files with similar names quickly, saving you the effort of typing the names individually, as well as a file whose name you do not remember in its entirety. If no filename matches the ambiguous file reference, the shell generally passes the unexpanded reference, special characters and all, to the command.

The ? Special Character

The question mark (?) is a special character that causes the shell to generate filenames. The question mark matches any single character in the name of an existing file. The following command uses this special character in an argument to the lpr utility:

```
$ lpr memo?
```

The shell expands the **memo?** argument and generates a list of files in the working directory that have names composed of **memo**, followed by any single character. The shell passes this list to lpr. The lpr utility never "knows" that the shell generated the filenames it was called with. If no filename matches the ambiguous file reference, the shell passes the string itself (**memo?**) to lpr, or, if it is set up to do so, the shell displays an error message.

The following example uses ls first to display the names of all of the files in the working directory and then to display the filenames that **memo?** matches:

```
$ ls
mem    memo12  memo9  memoalex  newmemo5
memo   memo5   memoa  memos
$ ls memo?
memo5   memo9   memoa  memos
```

The **memo?** ambiguous file reference does not match **mem**, **memo**, **memo12**, **memoalex**, or **newmemo5**. You can also use a question mark in the middle of an ambiguous file reference:

```
$ ls
7may4report   may4report      mayqreport   may_report
may14report   may4report.79   mayreport    may.report
$ ls may?report
may.report   may4report   may_report   mayqreport
```

To practice generating filenames, you can use echo and ls; echo displays the arguments that the shell passes to it:

```
$ echo may?report
may.report   may4report   may_report   mayqreport
```

The shell expands the ambiguous file reference into a list of all files in the working directory that match the string **may?report** and passes this list to echo, as though you had entered the list of filenames as arguments to echo. The echo utility responds by displaying the list of filenames. A question mark does not match a leading period (one that indicates an invisible filename). When you want to match filenames that begin with a period, you must explicitly include the period in the ambiguous file reference.

The * Special Character

The asterisk (*) performs a function similar to that of the question mark, but it matches any number of characters, *including zero characters,* in a filename. The following example shows all the files in the working directory and then shows three commands that display all the filenames that begin with the string **memo**, end with the string **mo**, and contain the string **alx:**

```
$ ls
amemo    memo          memoalx.0620   memosally   user.memo
mem      memo.0612     memoalx.keep   sallymemo
memalx   memoa         memorandum     typescript
$ echo memo*
memo memo.0612 memoa memoalx.0620 memoalx.keep memorandum memosally
$ echo *mo
amemo memo sallymemo user.memo
$ echo *alx*
memalx memoalx.0620 memoalx.keep
```

The ambiguous file reference **memo*** does not match **amemo, mem, sallymemo,** or **user.memo.** As with the question mark, an asterisk does not match a leading period in a filename.

The **–a** option causes ls to display invisible filenames. The command **echo *** does not display . (the working directory), .. (the parent of the working directory), **.aaa,** or **.profile.** The command **echo .*** displays only those four names:

```
$ ls
aaa memo.0612 memo.sally report sally.0612 saturday thurs
$ ls -a
.      aaa       memo.0612   .profile   sally.0612   thurs
..     .aaa      memo.sally  report     saturday
$ echo *
aaa memo.0612 memo.sally report sally.0612 saturday thurs
$ echo .*
. .. .aaa .profile
```

In the following example, .p✻ does not match **memo.0612**, **private**, **reminder**, or **report**. Following that, the **ls .✻** command causes ls to list **.private** and **.profile**, in addition to the entire contents of the . directory (the working directory) and the .. directory (the parent of the working directory). With the same argument, echo displays only the filenames from the working directory that begin with a dot (**.**):

```
$ ls -a
.          .private    memo.0612   reminder
..         .profile    private     report
$ echo .p✻
.private .profile
$ ls .✻
.private .profile

.:
memo.0612   private     reminder    report

..:
.
.
.
$ echo .✻
.private .profile
```

When you establish conventions for naming files, you can take advantage of ambiguous file references. For example, when you end all text filenames with **.txt**, you can reference that group of files with **✻.txt**. Following this convention, the next command sends all the text files in the working directory to the printer. The ampersand causes lpr to run in the background:

```
$ lpr ✻.txt &
```

The [ ] Special Characters

A pair of brackets surrounding a list of characters causes the shell to match filenames containing the individual characters. Whereas **memo?** matches **memo** followed by any character, **memo[17a]** is more restrictive, matching only **memo1**, **memo7**, and **memoa**. The brackets define a *character class* that includes all the characters within the brackets. The shell expands an argument that includes a character-class definition, substituting each member of the character class, *one at a time*, in place of the brackets and their contents. The shell passes the list of matching filenames to the program it is calling.

Each character-class definition can replace only a single character within a filename. The brackets and their contents are like a question mark that substitutes only the members of the character class.

The first of the following commands lists the names of all the files in the working directory that begin with **a**, **e**, **i**, **o**, or **u**. The second command displays the contents of the files named **page2.txt**, **page4.txt**, **page6.txt**, and **page8.txt**:

```
$ echo [aeiou]✻
. . .
$ less page[2468].txt
. . .
```

A hyphen within brackets defines a range of characters within a character-class definition. For example, [6–9] represents [6789], [a–z] represents all lowercase letters in English, and [a–zA–Z] represents all letters, upper- and lowercase, in English.

The following command lines show three ways to print the files named **part0**, **part1**, **part2**, **part3**, and **part5**. Each of the command lines causes the shell to call lpr with five filenames:

```
$ lpr part0 part1 part2 part3 part5
```

```
$ lpr part[01235]
```

```
$ lpr part[0-35]
```

The first command line explicitly specifies the five filenames. The second and third command lines use ambiguous file references, incorporating character-class definitions. The shell expands the argument on the second command line to include all files that have names beginning with **part** and ending with any of the characters in the character class. The character class is explicitly defined as **0**, **1**, **2**, **3**, and **5**. The third command line also uses a character-class definition but defines the character class to be all characters in the range **0–3** and **5**.

The following command line prints 39 files, **part0** through **part38**:

```
$ lpr part[0-9] part[12][0-9] part3[0-8]
```

The following two examples list the names of some of the files in the working directory. The first lists the files whose names start with **a** through **m**. The second lists files whose names end with **x**, **y**, or **z**:

```
$ echo [a-m]*
. . .
$ echo *[x-z]
. . .
```

optional ||

When an exclamation point (**!**) or a caret (**^**) immediately follows the opening bracket (**[**), the string enclosed by the brackets matches any character not between the brackets, so that [^ab]* matches any filename that does not begin with **a** or **b**. You can match a hyphen (**–**) or a closing bracket (**]**) by placing it immediately before the final closing bracket.

The following example demonstrates that the ls utility has no ability to interpret ambiguous file references. First, ls is called with an argument of ?old. The shell expands ?old into a matching filename, **hold**, and passes that name to ls. The second command is the same as the first, except the **?** is quoted (refer to "Special Characters" on page 118), so the shell does not recognize it as a special character and passes it on to ls. The ls utility generates an error message, saying that it cannot find a file named ?old (because there is no file named ?old):

> **tip ||**   **The Shell Expands Ambiguous File References**
>
> *The shell*, not the program that the shell runs, *does the expansion* when it processes an ambiguous file reference. In the examples in this section, *the utilities* (ls, cat, echo, lpr) *never see the ambiguous file references.* The shell expands the ambiguous file references and passes the utility a list of ordinary filenames. In the previous examples, echo shows this to be true because all it does is display its arguments; it never displays the ambiguous file reference.

```
$ ls ?old
hold
$ ls \?old
?old: No such file or directory
```

As with most utilities and programs, ls cannot interpret ambiguous file references; that work is left to the shell.

Builtins

A *builtin* is a utility (also called a *command*) that is built into a shell. When it runs a builtin, the shell does not fork a new process. Consequently, builtins run more quickly and can affect the environment of the current shell. Because builtins are used in the same way as utilities, you will not typically be aware of whether a utility is built into the shell or is a stand-alone utility.

The echo utility is a shell builtin. The shell always executes a shell builtin before trying to find a command/utility with the same name. Refer to "which, whereis, and Builtin Commands" on page 136 for information on using which and whereis to locate echo and other builtin commands. See page 892 for a list of bash builtins.

To get a complete list of bash builtins, give the command **help | less** from a bash shell prompt. You can also give the command **info bash** to display the top level info page on bash.[5] Next, give the command **m builtin** to display a menu of bash builtin commands. Use the DOWN ARROW key to move the cursor to the line that lists the builtin you are interested in. Press **m** RETURN to display the corresponding info page. Alternatively, after typing **info bash**, give the command **/builtin**, which searches the bash documentation for the string **builtin**. The cursor will rest on the word **Builtin** in a menu; press **m** RETURN to display a menu on builtins.

Chapter Summary

The shell is the Linux command interpreter. It scans the command line for proper syntax, picking out the command name and any arguments. The first argument is

---

5. Because bash was written by GNU, the info page has better information than the man page does.

referred to as argument one, the second as argument two, and so on. The name of the command itself is sometimes referred to as argument zero. Many programs use options to modify the effects of a command. Most Linux utilities identify an option by its leading one or two hyphens.

When you give it a command, the shell tries to find an executable program with the same name as the command. When it does, the shell executes the program. When it does not, the shell tells you that it cannot find or execute the program. If the command is expressed as a simple filename, the shell searches the directories given in the variable **PATH** in an attempt to locate the command.

When it executes a command, the shell assigns a file to the command's standard input and standard output. By default, the shell causes a command's standard input to come from the keyboard and standard output to go to the screen. You can instruct the shell to redirect a command's standard input from or standard output to any reasonable file or device. You can also connect standard output of one command to standard input of another using a pipe. A filter is a command that reads its standard input from standard output of one command and writes its standard output to standard input of another command.

When a command runs in the foreground, the shell waits for it to finish before it gives you another prompt and allows you to continue. When you put an ampersand (&) at the end of a command line, the shell executes the command in the background and gives you another prompt immediately. Put a command in the background when you think it may not execute quickly and you want to enter other commands at the shell prompt. The jobs builtin displays a list of background jobs and includes the job number of each.

The shell interprets shell special characters on a command line for filename generation: A question mark represents any single character, and an asterisk represents zero or more characters. A single character may also be represented by a character class: a list of characters within brackets. A reference that uses special characters (wildcards) to abbreviate a list of one or more filenames is called an ambiguous file reference.

Exercises

1. What does the shell ordinarily do while a command is executing? What should you do if you do not want to wait for a command to finish before running another command?

2. Using sort as a filter, rewrite the following sequence of commands:
   ```
   $ sort list > temp
   $ lpr temp
   $ rm temp
   ```

3. What is a PID number? Why are they useful when you run processes in the background?

4. Assume that the following files are in the working directory:

```
$ ls
intro     notesb    ref2      section1   section3   section4b
notesa    ref1      ref3      section2   section4a  sentrev
```

Give commands for each of the following, using wildcards to express filenames with as few characters as possible.

a. List all files that begin with **section**.

b. List the **section1**, **section2**, and **section3** files only.

c. List the **intro** file only.

d. List the **section1**, **section3**, **ref1**, and **ref3** files.

5. Refer to the man pages to determine what commands will

a. Output the number of lines in the standard input that contain the *word* **a** or **A**.

b. Output only the names of the files in the working directory that contain the pattern **$(** in the name of the file.

c. List the files in the working directory in their reverse alphabetical order.

d. Send a list of files in the working directory to the printer, sorted by size.

6. Give a command to

a. Redirect the standard output from a sort command into a file named **phone_list**. Assume that the input file is named **numbers**.

b. Translate all occurrences of characters [and { to the character (, and translate all occurrences of the characters] and } to the character) in the file **permdemos.c**. (*Hint:* Refer to the tr man page.)

c. Create a file named **book** that contains the contents of two other files: **part1** and **part2**.

7. The lpr and sort utilities accept input either from a file named on the command line or from standard input.

a. Name two other utilities that function in a similar manner.

b. Name a utility that accepts its input only from standard input.

8. Give an example of a command that uses grep

a. With both input and output redirected.

b. With only input redirected.

c. With only output redirected.

d. Within a pipe.

In which of the preceding is grep used as a filter?

9. Explain the following error message. What filenames would a subsequent ls display?

```
$ ls
abc  abd  abe  abf  abg  abh
$ rm abc ab*
rm: cannot remove 'abc': No such file or directory
```

Advanced Exercises

10. When you use the redirect output symbol (>) with a command, the shell creates the output file immediately, before the command is executed. Demonstrate that this is true.

11. In experimenting with shell variables, Alex accidentally deletes his **PATH** variable. He decides that he does not need the **PATH** variable. Discuss some of the problems he may soon encounter, and explain the reasons for these problems. How could he *easily* return **PATH** to its original value?

12. Assume that your permissions allow you to write to a file but not to delete it.

a. Give a command to empty the file without invoking an editor.

b. Explain how you might have permission to modify a file that you cannot delete.

13. If you accidentally create a filename with a nonprinting character, such as a CONTROL character in it, how can you rename the file?

14. Why can the **noclobber** variable *not* protect you from overwriting an existing file with cp or mv?

15. Why do command names and filenames usually not have embedded SPACEs? How would you create a filename containing a SPACE? How would you remove it? (This is a thought exercise, not a recommended practice. If you want to experiment, create and work in a directory with nothing but your experimental file in it.)

16. Create a file named **answers**, and give the following command:

```
$ > answers.0102 < answers cat
```

Explain what the command does and why. What is a more conventional way of expressing this command?

PART III
Digging Into Red Hat Linux

Linux GUIs: X, GNOME, and KDE

8

This chapter covers the Linux graphical user interface; it continues where Chapter 4 left off, going into more detail about the X Window System, the basis for the Linux GUI. It gives a brief history of GNOME and KDE and discusses some of the problems and benefits of having two major Linux desktops. The section on GNOME covers the Nautilus file manager, including its new spatial interface, and several important GNOME utilities. The final section covers KDE, presenting information about some of the more advanced features of Konqueror, as well as describing some KDE utilities.

X Window System

tip ‖   **Fedora Core 2 Replaces XFree86 X with X.org X**

With the introduction of Fedora Core 2, Red Hat replaced the XFree86 X Window System with the X.org Foundation X11R6.7.0 X Window System. See pages 62 and 218 for more information.

History of X   The X Window System (www.x.org) was created in 1984 at the Massachusetts Institute of Technology (MIT) by researchers working on a distributed computing project and a campuswide distributed environment, Project Athena. This system was not the first windowing software to run on a UNIX system, but it was the first to become widely available and accepted. In 1985, MIT released X (version 9) to the public, license free. Three years later, a group of vendors formed the X Consortium to support the continued development of X, under the leadership of MIT. By 1998, the X Consortium had become part of the Open Group, which, in 2001, released the current version of X, version 11, release 6.6 (commonly called X11R6.6).

217

X was inspired by the ideas and features found in earlier proprietary window systems but is written to be portable and flexible. X is designed to run on a workstation, typically attached to a LAN. The designers built X with the network in mind. If you can communicate with a remote computer over a network, running an X application on that computer and sending the results to your local display are straightforward.

While the X protocol has remained stable for quite a long time, additions in the form of extensions are quite common. One of the most interesting of these, which has not yet made its way into production, is the Media Application Server, which aims to provide the same level of network transparency for sound and video that X does for simple windowing applications.

XFree86 and X.org   Red Hat and Fedora used the XFree86 X server, which inherited its license from the original MIT X server, through release 4.3. Then, in early in 2004, just before the release of XFree86 4.4, the XFree86 license was changed to one that is more restrictive and not compatible with the GPL (page 4). A number of distributions, including Fedora, abandoned XFree86 and replaced it with a release of the X.org X server that is based on a prerelease version of XFree86 4.4, a release from before the XFree86 license was changed.

The X.org X server is functionally equivalent to the one distributed by XFree86 because most of the code is the same. Modules designed to work with one server work with the other. For historical reasons, the X.org server refers to itself as XFree86 in a number of places, including in the documentation and the names of the configuration files. Over time, these references may disappear.

tip || **Where Are the X Utilities?**

Many tools are not listed in KDE and GNOME's menus. You will find X utilities and application programs in many locations on a Linux system. One of the most popular is **/usr/X11R6/bin** (and **/usr/bin/X11**, which is a link to **/usr/X11R6/bin**); look on your system to familiarize yourself with the tools that are available. Read the manual pages for the tools you are not familiar with, or just experiment with them.

The X stack   The Linux GUI (graphical user interface) is built from a number of layers (Figure 8-1). At the bottom is the kernel, which provides the basic interfaces to the hardware. On top of the kernel is the X server, which is responsible for managing windows and drawing basic graphical primitives such as lines and bitmaps. Rather than directly generating X commands, most programs use Xlib, the next layer, which is a standard library for interfacing with an X server. Xlib is complicated and does not provide high-level abstractions, such as buttons and text boxes. Rather than using Xlib directly, most programs use a toolkit that provides high-level abstractions. Using a library not only makes programming easier, but has the added advantage of bringing consistency to applications.

The popularity of X has extended outside the UNIX community and beyond the workstation class of computers it was conceived for. X is available for Macintosh

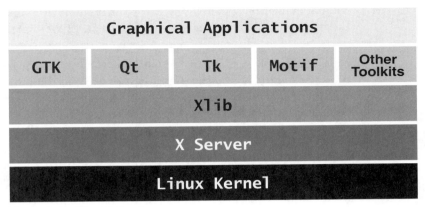

Figure 8-1   The X Stack

computers, as well as for PCs running Windows. It is also available on a special kind of display terminal, known as an X *terminal,* developed specifically to run X.

Client/server   Computer networks are central to the design of X. It is possible to run an application on one computer and display the results on a screen attached to a different computer; the ease with which this can be done distinguishes X from other window systems available today. Because X has this capability, a scientist can run a program on a powerful supercomputer in another building or another country and view the results on a personal workstation or laptop computer. For more information, refer to "Remote Computing and Local Displays" on page 220.

When you start an X Window System session, you set up a *client/server environment.* One process, called the X *server,* displays desktops and windows under X. Each application program and utility that makes a request of the X server is a *client* of that server. Examples of X clients are xterm, kwin, xclock, and such general applications as word processing and spreadsheet programs. A typical request from a client is to display an image or open a window.

caution ‖   **X Client and Server Are Reversed**

The terms *client* and *server,* when referring to X, are the opposite of how you might think of them intuitively: The server runs the mouse, keyboard, and display, while the application program is the client.

This disparity is even more apparent when you run an application program on a remote system. You might think of the system running the program as the server and the system providing the display as the client, but it is the other way around. With X, the system providing the display is the server, and the system running the program is the client.

Events   The server also monitors keyboard and mouse actions (*events*) and passes them on to the appropriate clients. For example, when you click the border of a window, this event is sent by the server to the window manager client. Characters you type into a terminal emulation window are sent to that terminal emulation client. The client takes appropriate action on receiving an event: In the preceding examples, that includes making a window active or displaying the typed character.

Separating the physical control of the display (the server) from the processes needing access to the display (the client) makes it possible to run the server on one computer and the client(s) on other(s). In general, this book discusses running the X server and client applications on a single system. Refer to "Remote Computing and Local Displays" on page 220 for information on using X in a distributed environment.

optional ||

You can run xev (X event) by giving the command **/usr/bin/X11/xev** from a terminal emulation window and watch the information flow from the client to the server and back again. This utility opens a window with a box in it and asks the X server to send it events each time anything happens, such as moving the mouse, clicking a mouse button, moving into the box, typing, resizing. Then xev displays information about each event in the window it opens. You can use xev as an educational tool: Start it and see how much information is being processed each time you move the mouse. Use CONTROL-C or close the Event Tester window to exit from xev.

Using X

This section provides some basic information about starting and configuring X from the command line.

Starting X from a Character-Based Display

Once you have logged in on a virtual console (page 103), you can start an X Window System server by using startx. See "Booting the System" on page 381 for information on changing the **initdefault** entry in the **/etc/inittab** file so Linux boots into character and not graphical mode. When you run startx, the X server displays an X screen, using one of the available virtual consoles. The following command causes startx to run in the background so that you can switch back to this virtual console and give other commands:

```
$ startx &
```

Remote Computing and Local Displays

There are two ways to identify the display that an X application should use. The most common method is to use the **DISPLAY** environment variable, which is a locally unique identification string that is automatically set by xinit when it starts the X server.

The **DISPLAY** shell environment variable contains the screen number of a display:

```
$ echo $DISPLAY
:0
```

The format of the complete (globally unique) ID string for a display is

hostname:display-number.screen-number

where *hostname* is the name of the machine running the X server, *display-number* is the number of the logical display (0 unless you are using virtual servers), and *screen-number* is 0 unless you have multiple displays. When you are working with a single physical screen, you can shorten the identification string. For example, you can use **bravo:0.0** or **bravo:0** to identify the only physical display on the machine named **bravo**. When the X server and the X clients are running on the same machine, you can shorten this identification string even further to **:0.0** or even **:0**.

If **DISPLAY** is empty or not set, the local computer is not using an X display screen. An application (the X client) uses the value of the **DISPLAY** variable to determine which display, keyboard, and mouse (all together, the X server) to use. One way to run an X application, such as xclock, on your local computer but have it use the X Window System display on a remote computer is to change the value of the **DISPLAY** variable on your local computer to identify the remote X server. If you get a refused/not authorized error, refer to the tip "xhost Grants Access to a Display" on page 222.

```
$ export DISPLAY=bravo:0.0
$ xclock &
```

The preceding example starts xclock with the default X server running on the computer **bravo**. After giving **DISPLAY** the ID of the **bravo** server, all X programs you start have their displays on **bravo**. If this is not what you want, you can also specify the display you want to use on the command line:

```
$ xclock -display bravo:0.0
```

Many X programs use the **–display** option, which affects only the one command you use it with. All other X-related commands will have their displays on the display whose ID is contained in the **DISPLAY** variable.

---

tip ‖   **When You Change the Value of DISPLAY**

Remember that when you change the value of the **DISPLAY variable**, all X programs send their output to the display named by **$DISPLAY**.

You can start multiple X servers on a single system. The most common reason for starting a second X server is to have a second display with a different number of bits allocated to each screen pixel. Most X servers available for Linux default to 24 or 32 bits per pixel, permitting the use of many millions of colors simultaneously. Starting an X server with 8 bits per pixel permits the use of any combination of 256 colors at the same time. The maximum number of bits per pixel you can use depends on the computer graphics hardware and X server. Having fewer bits per pixel means the system has to transfer less data, possibly making it more responsive. In addition, many games work only in 256 colors. The possible values are 8, 16, 24, and 32 bits per pixel, with the last two being the most common.

When you start multiple X servers, each must have a different ID string. The following command starts a second X server. Do not give this command from a terminal emulator; refer to "Using Virtual Consoles" on page 103 for information on how to switch to a virtual console to start a second server.

```
$ startx -- :1
```

The -- option (the - option but preceded by -, as are most options) to startx separates options to the startx command itself from options to be passed on to the X server. Any options that appear before the -- option are treated as options to startx, which passes options after -- to the X server. The following command starts a second X server running at 16 bits per pixel:

```
$ startx -- -depth 16 :1 &
```

Of course, you can use 16 bits per pixel with your first X server as well:

```
$ startx -- -depth 16 &
```

---

tip || xhost **Grants Access to a Display**

If you get an error message when you try to open a window on a remote display, you need to have the remote user run xhost to grant you access to the display. For example, if you are logged in on a system named **kudos** and you want to create a window on Alex's display, Alex needs to run the following command:

```
$ xhost +kudos
```

If Alex wants to allow anyone to create windows on his display, the following command line grants access to all hosts:

```
$ xhost +
```

If you frequently work with others over a network, you may find it convenient to add an xhost line to your **.bash_profile** file (page 272). Be selective about granting access to your X display with xhost; if you allow another machine to access your display, you may find that your work is often interrupted by others.

---

security || **Security and** xhost

Allowing a remote machine access to your display using xhost means that any user on the remote computer can watch everything you type in a terminal emulation window, including passwords. For this reason, some software packages, such as the Tcl/Tk development system (www.tcl.tk), restrict their own capabilities when xhost is used. If you are concerned about security or want to take full advantage of systems such as Tcl/Tk, you should use a safer means of granting remote access to your X session. See the xauth man page for information about a more secure replacement for xhost.

Stopping the X Server

How you terminate your window manager depends on which window manager you are running and how it is configured. When X does not respond, log in from another terminal or a remote system, or use telnet to gain access to the system. Then kill the process running **X**. Refer to "kill: Sends a Signal to a Process" on page 375. You can also press CONTROL-ALT-BACKSPACE to quit the X server. This method may not shut down the X session cleanly; use it only as a last resort.

Remapping Mouse Buttons

Throughout this chapter, each description of a mouse click has referred to the button by its position (left, middle, or right) because the position of a mouse button is more intuitive than an arbitrary name or number. X terminology numbers buttons starting at the left and continuing with the mouse wheel. The buttons on a three-button mouse are numbered 1 (left), 2 (middle), and 3 (right). If there is a mouse wheel it is 4 (up) and 5 (down). The buttons on a two-button mouse are 1 (left) and 2 (right).

If you are right-handed, you can conveniently press the left mouse button with your index finger; X programs take advantage of this by relying on button 1 for the most common operations. If you are left-handed, your index finger rests most conveniently on button 2 or 3 (the right button on a two- or three-button mouse).

When you are running GNOME, use the **Main menu: Preferences⇨Mouse** and put a mark in the check box labeled **Left-handed mouse**. From KDE, choose **Main menu: Preferences⇨More Preferences⇨Control Center⇨Peripherals⇨Mouse** and select **Right handed** or **Left handed** from the General tab.

You can also change how X interprets the mouse buttons by using xmodmap. If you are left-handed and using a three-button mouse with a wheel, the following command causes X to interpret the right button as button 1 and the left button as button 3:

```
$ xmodmap -e 'pointer = 3 2 1 4 5'
```

Omit the 4 and 5 if your mouse does not have a wheel. The following command works for a two-button mouse without a wheel:

```
$ xmodmap -e 'pointer = 2 1'
```

When you remap the mouse buttons, remember to reinterpret the descriptions in this chapter accordingly. When this chapter refers to the left button, use the right button instead.

Window Managers

Conceptually, X is very simple and does not provide some of the more common features found in GUIs, such as the ability to drag windows. The UNIX philosophy is one of modularity: X relies on a window manager, such as Metacity or kwin, to draw window borders and handle moving and resizing operations.

Unlike a window manager, which has a clearly defined task, a desktop environment does many things. In general, a desktop environment, such as KDE or GNOME, provides a means of launching applications and utilities, such as a file manager, that a window manager can use.

KDE and GNOME

The KDE project began in 1996, with the aim of creating a consistent, user-friendly desktop environment for free UNIX-like operating systems. KDE is based on the Qt toolkit made by Trolltech. When KDE development began, the Qt license was not compatible with the GPL (page 4) and the Free Software Foundation decided to support a different project, the GNU Network Object Model Environment (GNOME). More recently, Qt has been released under the terms of the GPL, removing one of the major early reasons for GNOME to exist.

KDE   KDE is written in C++ on top of the Qt framework. KDE tries to use existing technology, if it can be reused, but creates its own if nothing else is available or a superior solution is needed. For example, KDE implemented an HTML rendering engine long before the Mozilla project was born. Similarly, work on KOffice began a long time before StarOffice was open sourced as OpenOffice. In contrast, the GNOME office applications are stand-alone programs, which originated outside the GNOME project, and the GNOME Web browser uses the HTML rendering engine developed by the Mozilla project.

KDE's portability was recently demonstrated when a version of most of the core components, including Konqueror and KOffice, was released for MacOS X.

KParts   By itself, Konqueror has very little functionality; it is an application that uses other applications to do all its work. Konqueror takes advantage of KDE *i/o slaves* and *components* (KParts). The i/o slaves accept or gather input and change it to a standard format that a component can display. When you open Konqueror to view your home directory, Konqueror calls the File i/o slave, which gathers information about the filesystem and uses the Icon View component (**Konqueror menubar: View⇨View Mode⇨Icon View**) or the Text View component (**Konqueror menubar: View⇨View Mode⇨Text View**) to display the information it gets from the File i/o slave.

The i/o slaves are discrete modules; it is relatively easy to write a new one. Konqueror uses an i/o slave automatically when you put it in the directory structure (**$KDEDIR/lib/kde3/kio_***protocol*.***** and **$KDEDIR/share/services/***protocol***.desktop**). **$KDEDIR** is **/usr** by default, and *protocol* is the name of the protocol. Some examples of i/o slaves and their output format are FTP (virtual filesystem), POP3 (each retrieved piece of email appears as a file), and the audio CD browser (**kio_audiocd**, each track appears as a file).

The components display the information they receive from the i/o slaves. One i/o slave can feed several different components, and one component can receive input from several different i/o slaves. There must be both an i/o slave *and* a component pair to display information within a Konqueror view.

GNOME   GNOME is the default desktop environment for Red Hat Linux. It provides a simple, coherent user interface suitable for corporate use. GNOME uses GTK for drawing widgets. GTK, developed for the GNU Image Manipulation Program (GIMP), is written in C, although bindings for C++ and other languages are available.

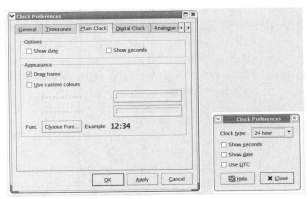

Figure 8-2   GNOME versus KDE clock settings

GNOME does not take much advantage of its component architecture; GNOME continues to support the traditional UNIX philosophy of having many small programs, each of which is good at doing a specific task.

Interoperability   Since version 2, GNOME has focussed on simplifying things for the user, removing options where they are deemed unnecessary, and aiming for a set of default settings, which the end user will not wish to change. KDE has moved in the opposite direction, emphasizing configurability. The difference between the two is exemplified by the clock provided with each one. If you bring up the settings dialog for the GNOME clock, you are greeted by a small window with few settings. In contrast, the KDE clock settings dialog requires six tabs. See Figure 8-2.

Having two desktop environments has lead to interoperability issues because programs written for one are likely to look and feel out of place in the other. Red Hat has helped smooth these issues by including the Blue Curve theme for both environments, making the KDE and GNOME desktops look very similar. From a user interface perspective, this unification is poor practice: GNOME and KDE applications behave differently; having them look the same removes an important visual cue that could help remind users which desktop they are using.

The freedesktop.org group (freedesktop.org), with members from both the GNOME and KDE projects, is improving interoperability and aims to produce standards that will allow the two environments to work together. One standard released by freedesktop.org allows applications to use the notification area of either the GNOME or KDE panels without being aware of which is in use.

GNUStep

The GNUStep project, which was started before both the KDE and GNOME projects, is creating an open source implementation of the OPENSTEP API and desktop environment. The result is a very clean, fast user interface.

The default look of windowmaker, the GNUStep window manager, is somewhat dated, but theme support is currently in beta and the user interface is widely regarded as one of the most intuitive of any UNIX platform. GNUStep is also lighter weight than KDE or GNOME, and so runs better on older hardware. If you are running Linux on hardware that struggles with GNOME and KDE or you would like to try a user interface that does not try to mimic Windows, try GNUStep.

TWM

The TWM (Tab Window Manager) is the default window manager included with XFree86. It provides minimal functionality and is not commonly used as a main window manager. If you are having problems logging in, you can use TWM as a minimal window manager for debugging, allowing you to use graphical configuration tools to diagnose your problem. TWM is also useful if you are using X11 over a low bandwidth link because it uses very little bandwidth to draw window borders and move or resize windows.

Using GNOME

This section discusses the Nautilus file manager and several GNOME utilities.

Using the Nautilus File Manager

Nautilus is a simple, powerful file manager. You can use it to create, open, view, move, and copy files and directories as well as execute programs and scripts. Nautilus gives you two ways to work with files: an innovative spatial view (*FEDORA*, Figure 8-3) and a traditional file browser view (*RHEL+FEDORA*, Figure 8-5 on page 228).

tip || **GNOME Desktop and Nautilus**

The GNOME Desktop is run from a backend process that runs as part of Nautilus. If that process stops running, it usually starts up again automatically. If it does not restart, start Nautilus by giving the command **nautilus** to restore your desktop. You do not have to keep the Nautilus window open to keep the desktop alive.

Spatial View

The Nautilus object window presents a spatial view (Figure 8-3); it has many simple, powerful features but may take some getting used to. The spatial (as in having the nature of space) view always provides one window per folder: Open a folder and you get a new window.

Open a spatial view of your home directory by double-clicking the home icon on the upper-left of the desktop and experiment as you read this section. Double-click

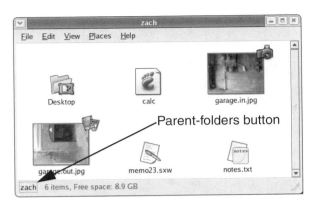

Figure 8-3   The Nautilus spatial view

the desktop icon in the spatial view and Nautilus opens a new window that displays the desktop folder.

A spatial view can display icons or a list of filenames; choose the display you prefer by choosing one of the **View as** selections from **View** on the menubar. To create files to experiment with, right click in the window (not on an icon) to display the Nautilus context menu and select **Create Folder** or **Create Document**.

---

tip || **Use** SHIFT **to Close the Current Window as You Open Another**

If you hold the SHIFT key down when you double-click to open a new window, Nautilus closes the current window as it opens the new one. This behavior may be more familiar and can help keep your desktop from getting cluttered. If you do not want to use the keyboard, you can get the same result by double-clicking the middle mouse button.

Window memory   Move the window by dragging the titlebar. The spatial view has *window memory*. The next time you open that folder, Nautilus opens it at the same size in the same location. Even the scrollbar will be in the same position.

Parent-folders button   The key to closing the current window and returning to the window of the parent directory is the Parent-folders button. See Figures 8-3 and 8-4. Click the Parent-folders button to display the Parent-folders pop-up menu and select the directory you want to open from this menu; Nautilus displays in a spatial view the directory you specified.

From a spatial view, you can open a folder in a traditional view by right clicking the folder and selecting **Browse Folder**.

Traditional View

Figure 8-5 shows the traditional, or file browser, window with a Side Pane (sometimes called a *sidebar*), View Pane, menubar, toolbar, and location bar. Open a browser view of your home directory by right clicking the home icon on the desktop and selecting **Browse Folder** or by selecting **Main menu: Browse Filesystem**.

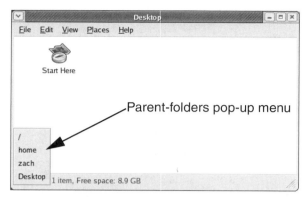

Figure 8-4   The Parent-folders pop-up menu

Side Pane

Click the box at the top of the Side Pane, just under the word **Location** on the Location bar to display the Side Pane menu. The box starts with the word **Information** in it. Select from this menu what you want Nautilus to display in the Side Pane: Information (shown), Emblems (drag emblems [page 231] to files in the View Pane), History (list of recent locations displayed by Nautilus), Notes, or Tree (displays the directory hierarchy).

View Pane

You can display icons or a list of filenames in the View Pane. Choose which you prefer by making a selection from the drop-down menu that appears on the right end of the location bar. **View as Icons** is shown in Figure 8-5 and **View as List** in Figure 8-6 (with the toolbar moved to the bottom of the window).

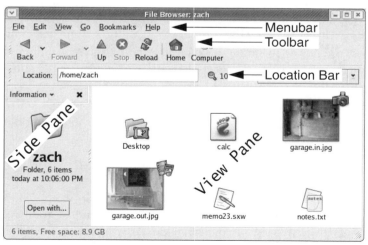

Figure 8-5   Nautilus traditional, or file browser, window

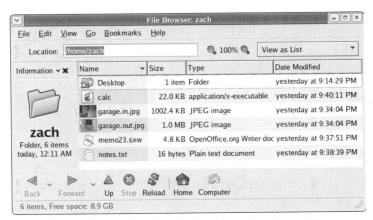

Figure 8-6   Nautilus displaying a list view with
the toolbar at the bottom of the window

Control Bars

This section discusses the three control bars—menubar, toolbar, and location bar—that initially appear at the top of a Nautilus browser window (Figure 8-6).

Menubar The menubar presents a drop-down menu when you click one of its selections. Nautilus varies the menu selections, depending on what it is displaying in the View Pane.

Toolbar The Nautilus toolbar holds navigation tool icons: Back, Forward, Up, Stop, Reload, Home, and Computer.

Location bar The Location bar text box displays the pathname of the directory that is displayed in the View Pane and highlighted in the Tree tab (when it is displayed). You can also use the Location bar text box, or press CONTROL-L to display a Location dialog box, to specify a local or remote directory or URL (FTP, HTTP, and so on) of a site that you want to display in the View Pane: Enter the absolute pathname of the directory or URL (an FTP address must be in the form **ftp://***address*) and press RETURN. Nautilus displays the contents of the directory or URL.

The location bar holds two tools in addition to the location bar text box: the magnification selector and the **View as** drop-down menu. To change the magnification of the display in the View Pane, click the plus or minus sign on either side of the magnification percentage; click the magnification percentage itself to return to 100% magnification. Click anywhere on **View as** (to the right of the magnifying glass) to display the viewing choices.

Tear-away bars One handy feature of Nautilus is the ability to reposition, or tear away, the toolbar and location bar. You can move either control bar onto the root window or position it at the top or bottom of the Nautilus window. Figure 8-6 shows the toolbar at the bottom of the Nautilus window. To return a bar to the window, drag it back and it snaps into place. You can also move the toolbar so that it is vertical on either side of

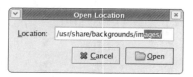

Figure 8-7   Location dialog box

the Nautilus window. Drag the toolbar handle, the striped vertical bar at the left or top end of one of the control bars, and you will drag the bar. To position the toolbar on one of the vertical sides of the window, drag the toolbar handle toward the middle of the side you want it on, and it snaps into place. Once the toolbar is vertical, you can move it to the root window and it will remain vertical.

Features Available from Both Spatial and Traditional Views

Location dialog box You can display deeply nested directories quickly using the Location dialog box (Figure 8-7). Press CONTROL-L while the cursor is over a Nautilus window (spatial or traditional) to display the Location dialog box. Enter the absolute pathname (starting with a slash) of the directory you want to display. Nautilus helps you type by completing directory names as you go. Press TAB to accept a suggested completion or keep typing to ignore it.

Zoom images Use the Location dialog box to display the **/usr/share/backgrounds/images** directory. Double-click an image file to display that file in a preview window. Position the mouse pointer over the image and use the mouse wheel to zoom the image.

Opening files By default, you double-click a file or icon to open it, or you can right click the file and choose **Open** from the pop-up menu. When you open a file, Nautilus tries to figure out which tool to use to open it, using MIME (page 89) to associate the filename extension with a MIME type and a program. For example, when you open a file with a filename extension of **ps**, Nautilus calls **gs** (ghostscript), which displays the PostScript file in a readable format. When you open an executable file such as Mozilla, Nautilus runs the executable. When you open a text file, Nautilus opens a text editor that displays and allows you to edit the file. When you open a directory, Nautilus displays its contents. When Nautilus does not know which tool to use to open a file, it asks you.

Properties

You can view information about a file, such as ownership, permission, size, and so on, by right clicking any filename or icon and selecting **Properties** from the drop-down menu. The Properties window initially displays some basic information; click the tabs at the top of the window to see additional information. Different types of files display different sets of tabs, depending on what is appropriate to the file (context menu). You can modify settings in this window only if you have permission to do so.

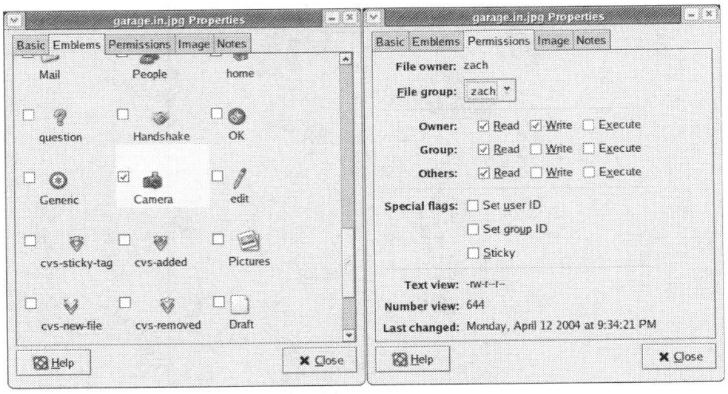

Figure 8-8   Properties window: Emblems tab left; Permissions tab right

Basic   The **Basic** tab displays information about the file and enables you to select a custom icon for the file or change its name. To change the name of the file, make your changes in the text box.

Emblems   The **Emblems** tab (Figure 8-8, left) allows you to add or remove emblems associated with the file by placing/removing a check mark next to an emblem. Figure 8-9 shows what the Important, New, and Special emblems look like on a file icon. Nautilus displays emblems in both its icon and list views. You can also place an emblem on an icon by dragging it from the Side Pane Emblems tab to an icon in the View Pane.

Permissions   The **Permissions** tab (Figure 8-8, right) allows you to change file permissions (page 173). When the **Read** button in the Owner row (*User* elsewhere, see the tip "**chmod: o** for Other, **u** for Owner" on page 175) has a check mark in it, the owner has permission to read from the file. When you click all the buttons in the Owner row so they all contain check marks, the owner has read, write, and execute permission. The owner of a file can change the group that the file is associated with to any other group the owner is associated with. When you run as Superuser, you can change the name of the user who owns the file and the group associated with the file. Directory permissions work as explained on page 176.

Start Here

You can display the Start Here window by double-clicking the Start Here icon on the root window or entering **start-here:** in the Nautilus location bar. Nautilus dis-

Figure 8-9   Emblems

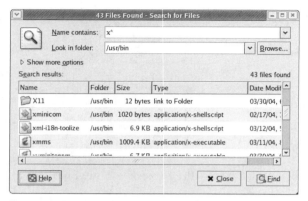

Figure 8-10   GNOME search tool: simple search

plays Start Here as a series of directories. Although Start Here is not strictly a menu, it is the root of a virtual directory structure that can help you in your day-to-day work on the system. In many areas, Start Here functions overlap those of the Main menu. The Preferences folder, a subdirectory of Start Here, duplicates exactly the **Preferences** item on the Main menu. Look around and experiment; you will not be allowed to do anything harmful to the system unless you are logged in as **root**.

GNOME Utilities

GNOME comes with many utilities that make your work on the desktop easier and more productive. This section covers several of the tools that are integral to the use of GNOME.

Search Tool

Display the GNOME Search tool (gnome-search-tool) by selecting **Main menu: Search for Files** (Figure 8-10). This tool is a front end for the find, grep, and locate utilities. A simple search is generally performed by slocate, an advanced search by find.

Simple Search

Enter a filename in the **Name contains** text box, enter an absolute pathname of a folder in the **Look in folder** text box, and click **Find**. The gnome-search-tool looks for files with the specified filename in the directory hierarchy, beginning at the specified folder. If you do not use wildcards (page 207) in the filename, the search matches files only with the exact name that you specify. Figure 8-10 shows a search for files in the **/usr/bin** directory hierarchy whose names match the pattern **x*** (simple filenames that begin with **x** or **X**, the search is not case sensitive).

Because it searches a prebuilt, compressed database of filenames, slocate performs more quickly than find. By default, the updatedb command that is located in

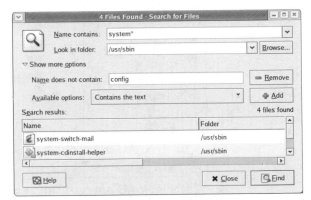

Figure 8-11   GNOME search tool: advanced search

/etc/cron.daily/slocate.cron recreates this database every night so a simple search frequently does not find files that were created during the day, since the last run of updatedb. If updatedb is not run regularly, a simple search will not work properly.

Advanced Search

When you click the triangle to the left of the words **Show more options**, gnome-search-tool expands the window (Figure 8-11). Click the down arrow at the right end of the **Available options** combo box, select the option you want to use, and click **Add**. If a text box appears, enter a value. Repeat this procedure until you have specified all the criteria you want to use. Each of the criteria you specify is ANDed with the others, so a file must meet all criteria to appear in the Search Results window. Refer to the find man page for more information on search criteria and how find works.

Figure 8-11 shows the **Name contains** as **system**❖ and the **Look in folder** as **/usr/sbin**. Additional options specify that the filename is not to contain **config**.

Font Preferences

Display the GNOME Font Preferences window (gnome-font-properties) by selecting **Main menu: Preferences⇨Font** (Figure 8-12). Click one of the four font bars at the top of the window to display the Pick a Font window (next section), and change the font that GNOME uses for applications, the desktop, window title, or terminal.

Look at the four boxes in the Font Rendering frame and select the one that looks best to you. **Subpixel smoothing** is usually best for LCD monitors. Click Details to refine the font rendering further. Again, pick the box in each of the frames that looks best to you.

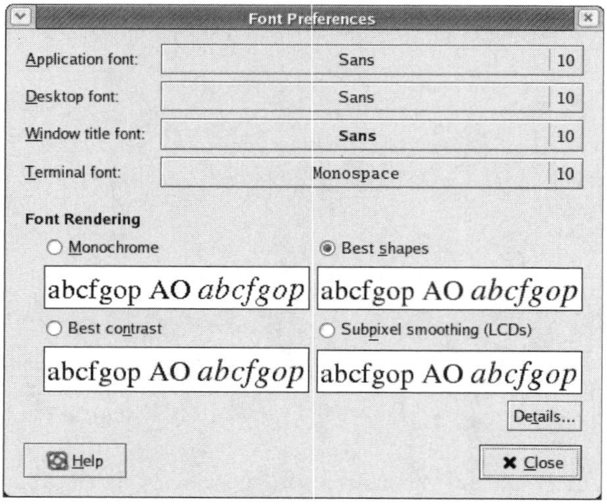

Figure 8-12   Font Preferences window

Pick a Font Window

The Pick a Font window (Figure 8-13) appears when you need to choose a font and when you select **Main menu: Preferences⇨Font**. Select a font family, a style, and a size you want to use. A preview appears in the **Preview** frame under the columns. Click **OK** when you are satisfied with your choice.

Pick a Color Window

The Pick a color window (Figure 8-14) appears when you need to choose a color, such as when you choose **Desktop menu: Change Desktop Background** and click

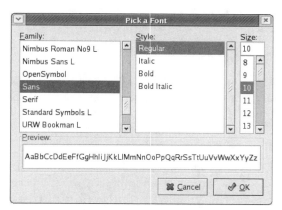

Figure 8-13   Pick a Font window

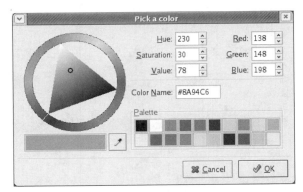

Figure 8-14   Pick a color window

the box down and to the right of **Desktop Colors**. When the window opens, the bar below the color circle displays the existing color. Click the color you want from the color ring, and click/drag the lightness of that color in the triangle. As you change the color, the right end of the bar displays the color you are selecting, and the left end keeps on displaying the existing color. Use the eyedropper to pick up a color from the workspace: Click the eyedropper, and then click the resulting crosshairs on the color you want. The color will be displayed in the Pick a color window.

Run Application Window

The Run Application window (Figure 8-15) enables you to run a program as though you had run it from a command line. Display the Run Application window by pressing Alt-F2 or by selecting **Run Application** from the Main menu. Enter a command in the text box; click **Run with File** to specify a filename to use as an argument to the command in the text box. Click **Run in terminal** to run text-based applications in a terminal emulator window.

File Types and Programs (MIME Types)

The File Types and Programs window (gnome-file-types-properties, Figure 8-16) displays and enables you to modify MIME types and their association to filename extensions (page 89). Display this window with **Main menu: Preferences⇨File types**

Figure 8-15   Run Application window

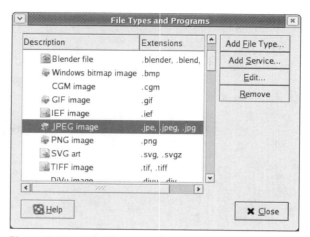

Figure 8-16   File Types and Programs window

and programs. Add a MIME type by clicking **Add File Type** and filling in the Add File Type window. Delete or modify a MIME type by selecting the MIME type/file-name extension combination you want to work with from the scroll list and clicking **Delete** or **Edit**. The **Add File Type** and **Edit** windows are similar. Enter or edit values in the text boxes as appropriate, change the icon by clicking the icon box at the top of the window, and change the default action by working with the items in the Actions frame.

GNOME Terminal Emulator/Shell

The GNOME terminal emulator (gnome-terminal, Figure 8-17) displays a window that mimics a character-based terminal (page 86). Bring up the terminal emulator by selecting **Open Terminal** from the Desktop menu or by selecting **Main menu: System Tools⇨Terminal**. When the GNOME terminal emulator is already displayed, you can select **Menubar: File⇨Open Terminal⇨Default** to display another, separate terminal emulator window.

As shown in Figure 8-17, you can display multiple terminal sessions within a single terminal emulator window. To open an additional terminal session, right click the window and select **Open Tab** from the context menu. A row of tabs appears below the menubar as gnome-terminal opens another terminal session on top of the existing terminal session. Add as many terminal sessions as you like; click the tabs to switch between sessions.

By default, additional sessions use the Default profile and appear the same as the first. You can add and modify profiles by selecting **Profiles** from the Menubar. Use **Menubar: Terminal⇨Change Profile** to change the profile that the displayed terminal session uses.

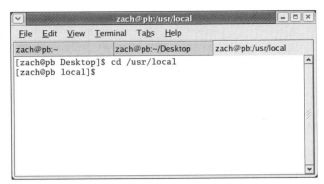

Figure 8-17   GNOME terminal emulator

Using KDE

Because KDE has so many features, associated utilities, and programs, this section cannot cover them all but attempts to familiarize you with the content and style of KDE. It is up to you to explore and find out more. One of the best ways to learn about KDE is to go through the online documentation and experiment. You can also look through the Main menu and browse www.kde.org.

tip ‖   **What Is a KDE Desktop?**

In KDE documentation, the term *desktop* refers to a single division of a larger area. This book, in conformance with the GNOME documentation, divides a desktop into workspaces. You will find a disparity between the terminology on the KDE desktop and that in this book.

Konqueror Browser/File Manager

Konqueror was introduced on page 87. This section describes some of Konqueror's advanced features.

Web Shortcuts

Web Shortcuts (different from regular shortcuts [page 242]) enable you to search for a keyword rapidly, using a default or specified search engine. "Search engines" can include dictionaries, bug-tracking systems, classic search engines, and more. For example, to look up the word **colocation** in the Free Online Dictionary of Computing, enter the shortcut **foldoc:colocation** in the location bar. To search for discussions about Samba on Google Groups, enter **groups:samba**. Other abbreviations that you may find useful are **gg** for Google (standard search), **webster** (Merriam-Webster Dictionary), and **fm** for Freshmeat.

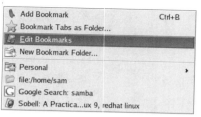

Figure 8-18   Konqueror Bookmarks menu

When you enter a keyword on the location bar without specifying a search engine, Konqueror looks it up using the default search engine. Use **Menubar: Settings⇨Configure Konqueror** and click **Web Shortcuts** from the column on the left to specify a default search engine and work with Web Shortcuts.

---

tip || **You Can Use Web Shortcuts by Pressing** Alt-F2

You can also use Web Shortcuts from the Run Command dialog box, which you can open by pressing Alt-F2. See page 245 for details.

Bookmarks

As with any browser, bookmarks give a name to a URL or local pathname and allow you to return to the bookmarked location by selecting the name from a menu. Figure 8-18 shows the Konqueror Bookmarks menu, available on the menubar. The bookmarks list appears below the standard entries in the Bookmarks menu (Add, Edit, and New Bookmark Folder). Click the bookmark of the location you want to visit, and Konqueror displays that location. In the figure, the **Personal** bookmark/menu choice is a folder that contains other bookmarks.

Choose **Konqueror menubar: Bookmarks⇨Add Bookmark** (or press CONTROL-B) to add to your bookmarks list the location displayed in the active view.

To open, check the status of, or edit the name of or location associated with a bookmark, open the KEditBookmarks window (**Konqueror menubar: Bookmarks⇨Edit Bookmarks**) and right click the entry you want to work with; choose the appropriate selection from the pop-up menu. You can also use the Bookmark Editor to change the order of the bookmarks: Use the mouse to drag the highlighted bookmark where you want it to appear in the list or use the up/down arrow keys to move the highlighted bookmark. The right/left arrow keys open/close directories/folders of bookmarks. **New Bookmark Folder** inserts a new folder below the highlighted bookmark.

Menubar

The menus on the menubar (Figure 8-19) change, depending on what Konqueror is displaying. A selection from the menubar produces a drop-down menu when you click it.

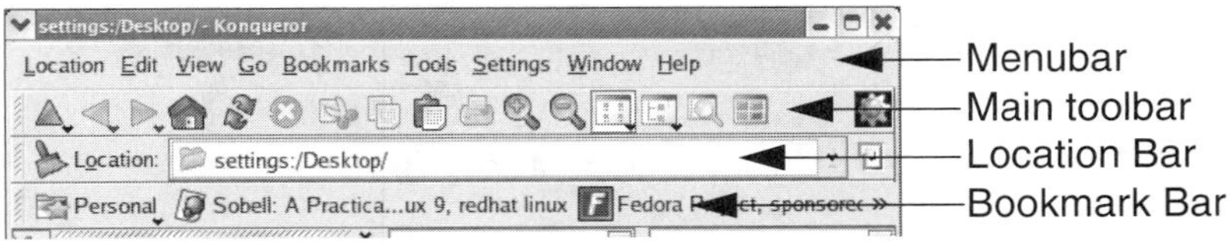

Figure 8-19   Konqueror Menubar and toolbars

Toolbars

Konqueror has four toolbars you can turn on and off from **Settings** on the Konqueror menubar: Main, Extra, Location, and Bookmark. Figure 8-19 shows three of these. Each of these toolbars has a toolbar handle (the shaded area, usually at the left end of the toolbar) that you can use to move the toolbar. Right click almost anywhere on a toolbar that has a handle to display the toolbar menu.

Main Toolbar

The Konqueror Main toolbar typically has a left and right arrow that take you linearly through what you have viewed with Konqueror. The **up** arrow takes you up in a directory hierarchy. Clicking the **house** displays your home directory; **reload** (the arrows going in a circle) reloads an image (typically used to reload a Web image that may be changing) or file structure (in case it has changed). Stop (the red **X**) halts the search for or loading of a Web page, and **Print** (the printer) sends the image in the active view to the printer.

Extra Window Toolbar

Choose **Konqueror menubar:**⇨**Settings**⇨**Toolbars**⇨**Show Extra Toolbar** to display the Extra toolbar. Use **Konqueror menubar:**⇨**Settings**⇨**Configure Toolbars**⇨**Extra Toolbar** to change the icons that appear on this toolbar.

Location Bar

The location bar has two items you can work with: the text box and the **Clear** button. The **Clear** button (the broom at the left end of the toolbar) clears the text box. You can enter a local or remote filename/URL, modify the text box, or click the **down** arrow at the right of this box and choose from the display of other locations you have visited.

Bookmark Toolbar

The bookmark toolbar gives you quick access to bookmarks (page 238). Display the Bookmark toolbar with **Konqueror: Settings**⇨**Toolbars**⇨**Show Bookmark Toolbar**.

kfind: Finds Files

Of the many ways to start kfind, the easiest is to use **Konqueror menubar: Tools**⇨**Find file.** Konqueror opens a new view that has three tabs: Name/Location,

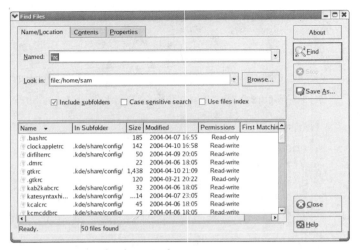

Figure 8-20   Find Files window

Contents, and Properties. The view opens to the Name/Location tab with a default filename to search for, *, which matches all filenames, *including* those that begin with a period, and your home directory as the place to start the search. In place of the *, kfind specifies the previous name you searched for, if you used kind previously in this session. In the Named text box, put the name of the file you want to search for (you can include wildcard characters) and in the **Look in** text box, put the directory you want to start the search in. The Browse button helps you locate the directory you want to start in. Put a check mark in the **Include subfolders** box to search through subdirectories. Click **Find** to start the search. The part of the window with the fields you just filled in dims as the results are tabulated and displayed in the lower part of the window. You can do whatever you want with the found files: copy, move, delete, edit, display, and so on.

Figure 8-20 shows a *case-sensitive* (page 961) search for all files whose names end with **rc** (*rc) in Sam's home directory and all subdirectories. Here the asterisk matches filenames that begin with a period.

In addition to or in place of filling in the Name/Location tab, you can click the Contents tab to specify a text string that the files you are looking for contain. Click **Case sensitive search** to perform a case-sensitive search for the text you put in the **Containing text** box. For a file to be found when you specify a text string, the file must match the Name/Location criteria *and* the Contents criteria.

In addition, you can use the Properties tab to specify the type, creation or modification date, owner, or size of the file.

You can save the results of your search to a file by clicking **Save As**, two buttons below **Find** on the right side of the window. You will be given a choice of filename, location, and type of file (text or HTML) you want to save.

Figure 8-21 Konqueror showing two views

Views II

Views, or subwindows, are key to taking advantage of Konqueror's power. This section expands on what was covered in "Views" on page 90 and covers some of the buttons, indicators, and menu choices that work with views.

Figure 8-21 shows two views side-by-side. Two indicators are important when you work with more than one view: the Active View indicator and the Link indicator (Figure 4-13, page 89).

Active View Indicator

A small circle at the lower-left of each view is green on the active view and white on other views. The active view has the input focus and is the object of all Konqueror menu commands. The location bar displays the location of the file displayed in the active view. Click within a view to make it the active view.

tip ‖   **Konqueror Terminology: View versus Window**

The Konqueror window is the entire window with four sides adjacent to the root window, the edge of the workspace, or other windows, usually with a menubar, location bar, and toolbar. The Konqueror window can house multiple views, the term used to describe subwindows within the Konqueror window. In addition to views, Konqueror can have a Navigation panel and a terminal emulator subwindow. Figure 8-21 shows a Konqueror window with two views.

Link Indicator

A small rectangle at the lower-right corner of each view has a small piece of a chain link fence in it in all views that are linked. Two linked views always show the same thing, with a useful exception, which is covered in the next paragraph. Although linked views display the same information, each may display it differently. For example, one may have an icon view, and the other, a detailed list view.

Figure 8-22   Configure Shortcuts window

Lock to Current Location/Unlock View

Choose **Konqueror menubar: View⇨Lock to Current Location** to cause the contents of the active view to remain constant, regardless of what links (URLs) you click in that view. With a normal (not locked) view, you click a link, and the view is replaced by the contents of that link. When you have two linked views, neither of which is locked, and you click a link in one, both views change to reflect the contents of the link. When a locked view is linked to an unlocked view and you click a link in the locked view, the contents of the link appear in the unlocked view. Click **Unlock view** to return the view to its normal, unlocked state.

Shortcuts

A *shortcut* (not a Web Shortcut [page 237]) is the connection between a key or keys (CONTROL-C, for example) that you hold/press at one time and an action that the system performs when you do so. Figure 8-22 shows the **Konqueror menubar: Settings⇨Configure Shortcuts** window with the action Copy at the top showing that CONTROL-C (**Ctrl+C**) is a shortcut for *copy* and that CONTROL-Insert is an alternate shortcut. The action **Find File** is highlighted in the figure with a shortcut of ALT-F. The bottom portion of the window shows that ALT-F is a Custom shortcut. When you highlight **Copy**, you see that CONTROL-C is a Default shortcut.

You can highlight any action and remove a shortcut by selecting **None** or revert to the default shortcut (if there is one) by selecting **Default**. Assign or change a custom binding by clicking the keycap button (the button with Alt+F in it in Figure 8-22) or the **Custom** radio button. The Configure Shortcuts window appears. To specify a

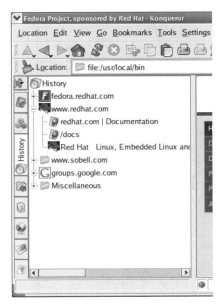

Figure 8-23   Navigation panel icons

shortcut, clear any existing shortcut by clicking the broom, press the key(s) you want to use for the shortcut, and click **OK**. The names of the keys that are now bound to the highlighted action appear on the keycap button.

The shortcuts you set in the Configure Shortcuts window apply to anything you do within Konqueror. You can set global and application shortcuts in a similar manner (**Control Center: Regional & Accessibility⇨Keyboard Shortcuts**). The bindings you establish in the Konqueror Configure Shortcuts window take precedence over other bindings that you set up.

Navigation Panel

The Konqueror Navigation panel is a view that displays a page of information. You select what information this view displays by clicking one of the icon/tabs that appears to the left of the page. On the active tab, text replaces the icon. Figure 8-23 shows a Navigation panel with the History tab active.

Toggle the Navigation panel on and off using **Konqueror menubar: Window⇨Show Navigation panel** or by pressing F9. Although the Navigation panel is a view, it has a different background from other views and cannot be active. When you click an entry in the Navigation panel, Konqueror opens, in the active view, the file/directory pointed to by that entry.

Click one of the icons in the Navigation panel to display a list of directories and files that corresponds to the icon. In the list, click a plus sign in a small box to expand a directory and see what is in it; click a minus sign in a box to collapse a directory. When you see an entry without a box next to it, click that entry to cause Konqueror to display it. When you click a directory in this manner, Konqueror displays a file manager view of the directory. When you click a URL of a Web site, Konqueror displays the Web site.

Each of the initial icons in the Navigation panel gives you a different perspective on the system and what you have been doing with it. You can modify, delete, and add to some of these icons by right clicking an icon. Click the tools button at the top of the column of icons to modify the Navigation panel.

KDE Utilities

Many utilities are available on the Main menu and on the KDE Web site. You can also use utilities, such as the GNOME utilities, that were not specifically designed with KDE in mind. This section lists a few of the most commonly used utilities.

konsole: Terminal Emulator

The KDE terminal emulator (konsole) displays a window that mimics a character-based terminal. Bring up a terminal emulator by selecting **Main menu: System Tools⇨Terminal**.

You can have multiple terminal sessions within a single Terminal window. With a KDE terminal emulator displayed, make a selection from **Menubar: Session** or click the yellow icon (on the toolbar, usually at the bottom of the window) to display another terminal emulator in place of the first. Click and hold the **New** icon for a few moments to display the Session menu, giving you a choice of sessions to start. Switch between terminals by clicking the terminal icons, also on the toolbar, or by holding SHIFT and pressing the right or LEFT ARROW key.

kcolorchooser: Selects a Color

The Select Color window (kcolorchooser, Figure 8-24) appears when you click a color bar, such as the two in the Background window (right click the root window, select **Configure Desktop**, then click **Background**; click one of the two color bars in the Options frame). The square centered on top of the line above the buttons always displays the selected color. When you click the **OK** button, this color is returned to the color bar that you initially clicked on.

There are several ways to select a color:

- Click the color/shade you want on the multicolored box at the upper-left of the window.

- Click the palette to the right of the **Add to Custom Colors** button. The mouse pointer turns into crosshairs. Position the crosshairs over the color

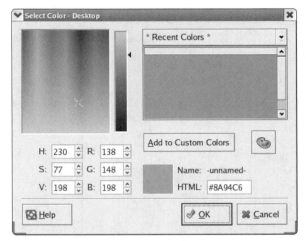

Figure 8-24 Select Color window

you want, anywhere on the workspace, and click. The color you click on becomes the selected color.

- Choose a line from the combo box at the upper-right corner of the window (Recent Colors in the figure). You have a choice of several groups of colors, including **Recent Colors** (an automatically generated list of colors you have selected) and **Custom Colors** (colors you have added to the list of custom colors by selecting and then clicking the **Add to Custom Colors** button). Then click a color in the area below the combo box.

- Enter the HTML specification for the color you want.

- Enter the appropriate numbers in the H, S, and V (hue, saturation, value) column of text boxes or in the R, G, and B (red, green, blue) column.

After you select a color, you can adjust its brightness by clicking the vertical bar to the right of the multicolor box or by dragging the pointer on the right side of this bar up or down. Click **OK** when you have selected the color you want.

Run Command

To run a character-based program, display the Run Command window by selecting **Run Command** from the Main menu or from any of several other menus or by pressing ALT-F2. Enter the name of the program in the Command text box, click **Options,** put a mark in the **Run in terminal window** box, and click **Run.** KDE runs the program in a Terminal Emulator window. When you run telnet in this manner, you see the **telnet>** prompt in a new window. Enter **quit,** telnet finishes, and the window closes. When you run who in this manner, you see a window flash on the screen for a moment and disappear. KDE ran who in a terminal emu-

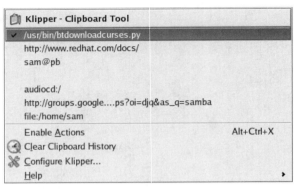

Figure 8-25   klipper pop-up menu

lator window, who finished, and KDE closed the window. When you want to run
who, you need to open a terminal emulator window (page 244) and give the command from the resulting window. When you call the terminal emulator in this
manner, it runs a shell that persists between commands so that you can see the
output of who. Alternatively, you can give the command **bash –c 'who;read'** from
the Run Command window. The **–c** option causes bash to execute the string that
follows the option. After it executes who, it executes read, which waits for you to
enter something at the keyboard, leaving the output of who visible until you press
a key.

You can also use the Run Command window to start graphical programs (enter the
name of the program) or view Web pages (enter the URL).

klipper: *Clipboard Utility*

The klipper utility is a sophisticated multiple-buffer cut-and-paste utility. In addition
to cutting and pasting from multiple buffers, klipper can execute a command based
on the contents of a buffer. To start klipper, choose **Main menu: Run Command**, enter **klipper,** and click **Run**. The klipper utility does not start a second occurrence of itself when it is already running. The klipper icon (a clipboard and pencil) appears at
the right of the Main panel.

Each time you highlight text, klipper copies it into its buffer. Click the klipper icon
or press CONTROL-ALT-V to display the klipper pop-up menu (Figure 8-25). The top part
of this menu lists the text that klipper has in its buffers. When the lines are too long
to fit in the width of the window, klipper uses ellipses (...) to indicate missing material. To paste the text from a buffer into a document, display the klipper pop-up
menu and click the line you want to paste; the pop-up menu closes. Move the
mouse pointer to the location you want to paste the text and middle click. In a
terminal emulator window, the text is always pasted at the location of the text
cursor.

Chapter Summary

The X Window System GUI is portable and flexible and makes it easy to write applications that work on many different types of systems without having to know low-level details about the individual systems. It can operate in a networked environment, allowing a user to run a program on a remote system and send the results to a local display. The concept of client and server is integral to the operation of the X Window System, with the X server responsible for fulfilling requests made of the X Window System applications or clients. Hundreds of clients run under X, and programmers can also write their own clients, using tools such as the Qt and KDE libraries to write KDE programs and the GTK+ and GTK+2 GNOME libraries to write GNOME programs.

The window managers, and virtually all X applications, are designed to permit users to tailor their work environments in simple or complex ways. You can designate applications that start automatically, set such attributes as colors and fonts, and even alter the way keyboard strokes and mouse clicks are interpreted.

Built on top of the X Window System, GNOME is a desktop manager that you can use as is or customize. It is a graphical user interface to system services (commands), the filesystem, applications, and more. Although not part of it, the Metacity window manager works closely with GNOME and is the default window manager for GNOME on Red Hat systems. The window manager controls all aspects of the windows: placement, decoration, grouping, minimizing and maximizing, sizing, moving, and so on.

GNOME also provides many graphical utilities that customize your desktop (pick a font, pick a color) and work with it (search tool, run a program, terminal emulator). GNOME also supports MIME extensions so that when you click on an icon, it generally knows which tool to use to open whatever is represented by the icon. In sum, GNOME is a powerful desktop manager that can make your job easier and more fun.

The KDE desktop environment presents an extensive array of tools, including multiple help systems; a flexible file manager and browser; an office package that includes word processing, spreadsheet, presentation, charting, and email packages; numerous panels and menus that you can configure in many ways; and enough options to please the most critical user.

Konqueror, the KDE file manager and browser, has very little functionality of its own. It is dependent on other programs to do its work. Konqueror opens these programs within its own window, giving the impression that it is very capable. It is a good example of seamless program integration. When you ask Konqueror to open a file (which can be a local or remote text, music, picture, or even an HTML file), it tries to figure out what kind of file it is (refer to "MIME/executing files" on page 89) so it knows which program to use to open/display it.

Panels and menus, which are closely related, give you the opportunity to select an object (which can be just about anything on the system) from a list. On a panel, you generally click an icon from a box of icons (the panel), whereas on a menu, you typically click text in a list.

The KDE environment provides the casual user, office worker, power user, and programmer/system designer a space to work in and a set of tools to work with. KDE also provides off-the-shelf productivity and almost limitless ways to customize its look, feel, and response.

Exercises

1. Regarding Konqueror the file manager,

   a. What is Konqueror?

   b. List four things that you can use it for.

   c. How do you use Konqueror to search for a file?

2. What is a terminal emulator? What does it allow you to do from a GUI that you would not be able to do without one?

3. What is klipper? How do you use it to cut and paste text?

4. What is Nautilus?

   a. List two ways that you can you open a file using Nautilus.

   b. How does Nautilus "know" what tool to use to open different types of files?

   c. Which are the three common Nautilus toolbars? What kinds of tools do you find on each?

   d. Discuss the use of the Nautilus Location bar.

Advanced Exercises

5. Discuss Konqueror's lack of functionality and how it performs so many tasks. What is a KPart?

6. Regarding Konqueror the Web browser,

   a. What is enhanced browsing and how do you use it?

b. How would you use Konqueror to transfer local files to a remote FTP site? Describe how you would do this using a Konqueror window with two views.

7. Describe three ways to

a. Change the size of a window.

b. Delete a window.

8. Explain the purpose of MIME. How does it facilitate your use of a GUI?

9. Write an xeyes command to display a window that is 600 pixels wide and 400 pixels tall, is located 200 pixels from the right edge of the screen and 300 pixels from the top of the screen, and contains orange eyes outlined in blue with red pupils. (*Hint:* Refer to the xeyes man page.)

The Shell II: The Bourne Again Shell

9

The Bourne Again Shell (bash) is a command interpreter and high-level programming language. As a command interpreter, bash processes commands that you enter on the command line in response to a prompt. When you use it as a programming language, a shell processes groups of commands stored in files called *shell scripts*. Like other languages, a shell has variables and control flow commands (for example, **for** loops and **if** statements).

---

tip || **Run These Utilities from a Command Line**

This chapter describes command line, or text-based, utilities. You can experiment with these utilities from a terminal emulator within a GUI (page 86) or from a virtual console (page 103).

Using a shell, you can customize the environment you work in. You can make your prompt display the name of the working directory, create a function or alias for cp that keeps it from overwriting certain kinds of files, take advantage of keyword variables to change aspects of how the shell works, and so on. You can also write shell scripts that do your bidding. A one-line script can store a long, complex command so you do not have to retype the command each time you run it. Longer scripts can run and print reports, mailing you a reminder when the job is done. Perhaps the script also mails the reports to the intended recipients. More complex shell scripts are themselves programs; they do not just run other programs (see Chapter 28 for examples).

Always make the Bourne Again Shell your primary root shell in single-user mode.[1] All system shell scripts are written to run under the Bourne Again Shell. If you will ever be working in single-user mode, as when you boot your system or do system maintenance, administration, or repair work, it is a good idea at least to become familiar with this shell.

Without repeating the material in "Filename Generation/Pathname Expansion" on page 207 of Chapter 7, this chapter expands on the interactive features of the shell described in Chapter 7, explains how to create and run simple shell scripts, introduces the basic aspects of shell programming, and describes command line expansion. Chapter 28 explores control flow commands and more advanced aspects of Bourne Again programming in detail.

---

tip ‖   **If You Are New to All This**

You may want to postpone reading the "Job Control" section (page 262) of this chapter and the sections beyond it until you are comfortable creating and running simple shell scripts. However, you should read "Parameters and Variables" (page 273). Besides user-created variables, the shell maintains several keyword variables that control important characteristics of the shell.

Background

The Bourne Again Shell is based on the Bourne Shell (an early UNIX shell that this book refers to as the *original Bourne Shell* to avoid confusion), which was written by Steve Bourne of AT&T's Bell Laboratories. Over the years, the original Bourne Shell has been expanded and is still the basic shell provided with many commercial versions of UNIX.

Because of its long and successful history, the Bourne Shell has been used to write many of the shell scripts that help manage UNIX systems. Some of these scripts appear in Linux as Bourne Again Shell scripts. Although bash includes many extensions and features not found in the Bourne Shell, bash maintains compatibility with the Bourne Shell so you can run Bourne Shell scripts under bash. Traditionally, the Bourne Shell is named sh. On Linux systems, sh is a symbolic link to bash so that scripts that require the presence of the Bourne Shell still run.

System V UNIX introduced the Korn Shell (ksh), written by David Korn. This shell extended many features of the Bourne Shell and then added many new features. Some of the features of the Bourne Again Shell, such as command aliases and command line editing, are based on similar features found in the Korn Shell.

The POSIX standardization group has defined a standard for shell functionality (POSIX 1003.2). The Bourne Again Shell provides the features that match the requirements of this POSIX standard. Efforts are under way to make the Bourne

---

1. You can use other shells, but it is not a good idea. The Bourne Again Shell is the only shell that is statically linked (**/sbin/bash**). If your machine crashes and the **/usr** filesystem is unavailable or some system libraries are corrupt, no other shell will work: You will not be able to boot your system and attempt to repair the damage because you will not have a shell to work with.

Again Shell fully comply with the POSIX standard. In the meantime, if you invoke bash with the **--posix** option, the behavior of the Bourne Again Shell will more closely match the POSIX requirements.

Shell Basics

This section covers variables and assignment statements and how to write a simple shell script and make it executable.

Assignment Statements

The shell allows you to create and use variables. The rules for naming and referring to variables are discussed in "Parameters and Variables" on page 273. You assign values to variables with the following syntax:

VARIABLE=value

There can be no whitespace on either side of the equal (=) sign. If you want to include SPACEs in the value of the variable, put quotation marks around the value or quote the SPACEs.

You reference the value of a variable by preceding the variable name with a dollar sign and enclosing it in braces, as in **${VARIABLE}**. The braces are optional unless the name of the variable is followed by a letter, digit, or underscore. Also, the Bourne Again Shell refers to the arguments on its command line by position, using the special variables **$1**, **$2**, **$3**, and so forth up to **$9**. If you wish to refer to arguments past the ninth, you must use braces, as in **${10}**. The name of the command is held in **$0**.

You can remove the variable's value and attributes, or unset, one or more variables with the unset builtin (page 211 has more information on builtins):

```
$ unset PREF SUFF
```

The Bourne Again Shell permits you to put variable assignments on a command line. These assignments are local to the command shell; that is, they apply to the command only. The following command runs **my_script** with the value of **TEMP-DIR** set to **~/temp**:

```
$ TEMPDIR=~/temp my_script
```

The **TEMPDIR** variable is set only in the shell that is spawned to execute **my_script**. It is not set, or if it is already set, it is not changed, in the interactive shell you are executing the script from.

Under bash, you can place the assignments anywhere on the command line.

Writing a Simple Shell Script

A *shell script* is a file that contains commands that the shell can execute. The commands in a shell script can be any commands you can enter in response to a shell prompt. For example, a command in a shell script might run a Linux utility, a compiled program you have written, or another shell script. As with commands you give on the command line, a command in a shell script can use ambiguous file references and can have its input or output redirected from/to a file or sent through a pipe (page 201). You can also use pipes and redirection with the input and output of the script itself.

In addition to the commands you would ordinarily use on the command line, *control flow* commands (also called *control structures*) find most of their use in shell scripts. This group of commands enables you to alter the order of execution of commands in a script as you would alter the order of execution of statements using a typical structured programming language. Refer to "Control Structures" on page 852 for specifics.

The easiest way to run a shell script is to give its filename on the command line. The shell then interprets and executes the commands in the script, one after another. By using a shell script, you can simply and quickly initiate a complex series of tasks or a repetitive procedure.

chmod: Makes a File Executable

To execute a shell script by giving its name as a command, you must have permission to read and execute the file that contains the script (refer to "Access Permissions" on page 173). Execute permission tells the shell and the system that the owner, group, or public has permission to execute the file; it implies that the content of the file is executable.

When you create a shell script using an editor, the file does not typically have its execute permission set. The following example shows a file, **whoson**, that is a shell script containing three command lines:

```
$ cat whoson
date
echo Users Currently Logged In
who

$ whoson
bash: ./whoson: Permission denied
```

When you create a file such as **whoson**, you cannot execute it by giving its name as a command because you do not have execute permission for the file.

The shell does not recognize **whoson** as an executable file and issues an error message when you try to execute it. You can execute it by giving the filename as an argument to bash (**bash whoson**). When you do this, bash takes the argument to be a

```
$ ls -l whoson
-rw-rw-r--   1 alex     group              40 May 24 11:30 whoson

$ chmod u+x whoson
$ ls -l whoson
-rwxrw-r--   1 alex     group              40 May 24 11:30 whoson

$ whoson
Sat May 24 11:40:49 PST 2003
Users Currently Logged In
jenny    pts/7    May 23 18:17
hls      pts/1    May 24 09:59
scott    pts/12   May 24 06:29 (bravo.tcorp.com)
alex     pts/4    May 24 09:08
```

Figure 9-1   Using chmod to make a shell script executable

shell script and executes it. In this case, bash is executable, and **whoson** is an argument that bash executes so you do not need to have permission to execute **whoson**.

You can use chmod (page 174) to change the access privileges associated with a file. Figure 9-1 shows ls with the –l option displaying the access privileges of **whoson** before and after chmod gives the owner execute permission.

tip || **Command Not Found?**

When you type **whoson** in response to a shell prompt and get an error message saying **bash: whoson: command not found**, your login shell is not set up to search for executable files in the working directory. Give this command:

```
$ ./whoson
```

The **./** explicitly tells the shell to look for an executable file in the working directory. To change your environment so that the shell searches the working directory automatically, refer to the **PATH** variable on page 283.

The first ls displays a hyphen (–) as the fourth character, indicating that the owner does not have permission to execute the file. Then chmod uses an argument to give the owner execute permission. The **u+x** causes chmod to add (**+**) execute permission (**x**) for the owner (**u**). (The **u** stands for *user*, although it means the owner of the file who may be the user of the file at any given time.) The second argument is the name of the file. The second ls shows an **x** in the fourth position, indicating that the owner now has execute permission.

If other users are going to execute the file, you must also change group and/or public access privileges. Any user must have execute access to a file to use the file's name as a command. If the file is a shell script (a shell command file), the user trying to execute the file must also have read access to the file. You do not need read access to execute a binary executable (compiled program). Finally, the shell executes the file when its name is given as a command. For more information refer to "Access Permissions" (page 173) and to the ls and chmod man pages.

Now you know how to write and execute simple shell scripts. The sections "Separating and Grouping Commands" (following) and "Redirecting Standard Error" (page 260) describe features that are useful when you are running commands either on a command line or from within a script. The section "Job Control" (page 262) explains the relationships between commands and Linux system processes.

Separating and Grouping Commands

Whether you give the shell commands interactively or write a shell script, you must separate commands from one another. This section reviews the ways that were covered in Chapter 7 and introduces a few new ones.

; and NEWLINE   Separate Commands

The NEWLINE character is a unique command separator because it initiates execution of the command preceding it. You have seen this throughout this book each time you press the RETURN key at the end of a command line.

The semicolon (;) is a command separator that *does not* initiate execution of a command and *does not* change any aspect of how the command functions. You can execute a series of commands sequentially by entering them on a single command line and separating them with a semicolon (;). You initiate execution of the sequence of commands by pressing RETURN:

```
$ x ; y ; z
```

If **x**, **y**, and **z** are commands, the preceding command line yields the same results as the next three commands. The difference is that in the next example, the shell issues a prompt after each of the commands (**x**, **y**, and **z**) finishes executing, whereas the preceding command line causes the shell to issue a prompt only after **z** is complete:

```
$ x
$ y
$ z
```

Although the whitespace around the semicolons in the earlier example makes the command line easier to read, it is not necessary. None of the command separators needs to be surrounded by SPACEs or TABs.

\   Continues a Command

When you enter a long command line and the cursor reaches the right side of your screen or window, you can use a backslash (\) character to continue the command on the next line. The backslash quotes, or escapes, the NEWLINE character that follows it so that the shell does not treat it as the command terminator (page 118).

| and &   Separate Commands and Do Something Else

Other command separators are the pipe symbol (|) and the background task symbol (&). These command separators *do not* start execution of a command, but they *do* change some aspect of how the command functions. The pipe symbol alters the source of standard input or the destination of standard output, and the background task symbol causes the shell to execute the task in the background so you get a prompt back right away and can continue working on other things.

Each of the following command lines initiates a single job comprising three tasks:

```
$ x | y | z
$ ls -l | grep tmp | less
```

In the first job, the shell directs the output from task **x** to task **y** and directs **y**'s output to **z**. Because the shell runs the entire job in the foreground, you do not get a prompt back until task **z** runs to completion: Task **z** does not finish until task **y** finishes, and task **y** does not finish until task **x** finishes. In the second job, task **x** is an **ls –l** command, task **y** is **grep tmp**, and task **z** is the pager, **less**. You end up with a long (wide) listing of the filenames of all the files in the working directory that contain the string **tmp**, piped through less.

The next command line executes tasks **d** and **e** in the background and task **f** in the foreground:

```
$ d & e & f
[1] 14271
[2] 14272
```

The shell displays the job number between brackets and the PID (process identification) number for each process running in the background. You get a prompt back as soon as **f** finishes.

Before displaying a prompt for a new command, the shell checks whether any background jobs have completed. For each job that has completed, the shell displays its job number, the word **Done**, and the command line that invoked the job; then the shell displays the prompt. When the job numbers are listed, the number of the last job started is followed by a **+** character, and the job number of the previous job is followed by a **–** character. Any other jobs listed show a SPACE character. After running the last command, the shell displays the following before issuing a prompt:

```
[1]-  Done                    d
[2]+  Done                    e
```

The following command line executes all three tasks as background jobs. You get a shell prompt immediately:

```
$ d & e & f &
[1] 14290
[2] 14291
[3] 14292
```

You can use pipes to send the output from one task to the next and an ampersand (&) to run the whole job as a background task. Again, the prompt comes back immediately. The shell regards the commands joined by a pipe as a single job. The shell treats all pipes as single jobs, no matter how many tasks are connected with the pipe (l) symbol or how complex they are:

```
% x | y | z &
[1] 14302 14304 14306
%
```

optional ||

Multitasking Demonstration

You can demonstrate sequential and concurrent processes running in both the foreground and the background. Create executable files named **a**, **b**, and **c**, and have each file echo its name over and over as file **a** does.

```
$ cat a
echo "aaaaaaaaaaaaaaaaaaaaaaaaaa"
echo "aaaaaaaaaaaaaaaaaaaaaaaaaa"
echo "aaaaaaaaaaaaaaaaaaaaaaaaaa"
echo "aaaaaaaaaaaaaaaaaaaaaaaaaa"
echo "aaaaaaaaaaaaaaaaaaaaaaaaaa"
```

Execute the files sequentially and concurrently, using the example command lines from this section. When you execute two of these shell scripts sequentially, the output of the second file follows the output of the first file. When you execute the two files concurrently, their output is interspersed as control is passed back and forth between the tasks (multitasking).[a] The results are not always identical because Linux schedules jobs slightly differently each time they run. Concurrent execution does not guarantee faster completion than sequential execution, and all background execution guarantees is a faster return of the prompt. Two sample runs are shown here:

```
$ a & b & c &
[1] 14717
[2] 14718
[3] 14719
$ aaaaaaaaaaaaaaaaaaaaaaaaaa
aaaaaaaaaaaaaaaaaaaaaaaaaa
aaaaaaaaaaaaaaaaaaaaaaaaaa
aaaaaaaaaaaaaaaaaaaaaaaaaa
bbbbbbbbbbbbbbbbbbbbbbbbbb
cccccccccccccccccccccccccc
aaaaaaaaaaaaaaaaaaaaaaaaaa
bbbbbbbbbbbbbbbbbbbbbbbbbb
bbbbbbbbbbbbbbbbbbbbbbbbbb
bbbbbbbbbbbbbbbbbbbbbbbbbb
bbbbbbbbbbbbbbbbbbbbbbbbbb
cccccccccccccccccccccccccc
cccccccccccccccccccccccccc
cccccccccccccccccccccccccc
cccccccccccccccccccccccccc
```

a. With faster computers and short programs, there may be no change of control back and forth: Each program may finish before it is time to change control. Try a similar script, with 1,000 or more echo commands, to see the switch. The command (a&b&c&) > **hold** redirects the output to the file named **hold** for easier viewing. See the next section for information about parentheses on the command line.

```
$ a & b & c &
[1] 14738
[2] 14739
[3] 14740
$ aaaaaaaaaaaaaaaaaaaaaaaaaa
bbbbbbbbbbbbbbbbbbbbbbbbbb
cccccccccccccccccccccccc
bbbbbbbbbbbbbbbbbbbbbbbbbb
bbbbbbbbbbbbbbbbbbbbbbbbbb
bbbbbbbbbbbbbbbbbbbbbbbbbb
cccccccccccccccccccccccc
cccccccccccccccccccccccc
cccccccccccccccccccccccc
cccccccccccccccccccccccc
aaaaaaaaaaaaaaaaaaaaaaaaaa
aaaaaaaaaaaaaaaaaaaaaaaaaa
aaaaaaaaaaaaaaaaaaaaaaaaaa
aaaaaaaaaaaaaaaaaaaaaaaaaa
bbbbbbbbbbbbbbbbbbbbbbbbbb
```

()   Groups Commands

You can use parentheses to group commands. The shell creates a copy of itself, called a *subshell*, for each group, treating each group of commands as a job and creating a new process to execute each of the commands (refer to "Process Structure" on page 268 for more information on creating subshells). Each subshell (job) has its own environment; among other things, this means that it has its own set of variables with values that can be different from those of other subshells.

The following command line executes commands **a** and **b** sequentially in the background while also executing **c** in the background. The shell prompt returns immediately:

```
$ (a ; b) & c &
15007
```

This example differs from the earlier example, a & b & c &, because tasks **a** and **b** are initiated sequentially, not concurrently.

Similarly, the following command line executes **a** and **b** sequentially in the background and, at the same time, executes **c** and **d** sequentially in the background. The subshell running **a** and **b** and the subshell running **c** and **d** run concurrently. The prompt returns immediately:

```
$ (a ; b) & (c ; d) &
15020
15021
$
```

In the following shell script, the second pair of parentheses creates a subshell to run the commands following the pipe. Because of these parentheses, the output of the first tar command is available for the second tar command, despite the intervening cd command. Without the parentheses, the output of the first tar command would be sent to cd and lost because cd does not process input from standard input. The **$1** and **$2** are shell variables that represent the first and second command line arguments (page 287). The first pair of parentheses, which creates a subshell to run the first two commands, is necessary so that users can call **cpdir** with relative pathnames. Without these parentheses, the first cd command would change the working directory of the script (and, consequently, the working directory of the second cd command); with the parentheses, only the working directory of the subshell is changed:

```
$ cat cpdir
(cd $1 ; tar -cf - . ) | (cd $2 ; tar -xvf - )
$ cpdir /home/alex/sources /home/alex/memo/biblio
```

This command line copies the files and subdirectories included in the **/home/alex/sources** directory to the directory named **/home/alex/memo/biblio**. This shell script is almost the same as using cp with the **-r** option. See "Process Structure" on page 268 for more information on creating subshells. Refer to the cp and tar man pages for more information.

Redirecting Standard Error

Chapter 7 covered the concept of standard output and explained how to redirect a command's standard output. In addition to standard output, commands can send their output to another place: *standard error*. A command can send error messages to standard error to keep them from getting mixed up with the information it sends to standard output. Just as it does with standard output, the shell sends a command's standard error to the screen/window unless you redirect it. Unless you redirect one or the other, you may not know the difference between the output a command sends to standard output and the output it sends to standard error.

When you execute a program, the process running the program opens three *file descriptors*, which are places the program sends its output to and gets its input from: 0 (standard input), 1 (standard output), and 2 (standard error). The redirect output symbol (> [page 197]) is shorthand for **1>**, which tells the shell to redirect standard output. Similarly, < (page 198) is short for **<0**, which redirects standard input. The symbols **2>** redirect standard error. The program does not "know" where its input comes from nor where its output goes; the shell takes care of that.

The following examples demonstrate how to redirect standard output and standard error to different files and to the same file. When you run cat with the name of a file that does not exist and the name of a file that does exist, cat sends an error message to standard error and copies the file that does exist to standard output. Unless you redirect them, both messages appear on the screen/window:

```
$ cat y
This is y.
$ cat x y
cat: x: No such file or directory
This is y.
```

When you redirect standard output of a command by using the greater than (>) symbol, output sent to standard error is not affected and still appears on the screen:

```
$ cat x y > hold
cat: x: No such file or directory
$ cat hold
This is y.
```

Similarly, when you send standard output through a pipe, standard error is not affected. The following example sends standard output of cat through a pipe to tr (translate), which in this example converts lowercase characters to uppercase. The text that cat sends to standard error is not translated because it goes directly to the screen/window rather than through the pipe:

```
$ cat x y | tr "[a-z]" "[A-Z]"
cat: x: No such file or directory
THIS IS Y.
```

The following example redirects standard output and standard error to different files. The notation 2> tells the shell where to redirect standard error (file descriptor 2). The 1> tells the shell where to redirect standard output (file descriptor 1). You can use > in place of 1>:

```
$ cat x y 1> hold1 2> hold2
$ cat hold1
This is y.
$ cat hold2
cat: x: No such file or directory
```

In the next example, 1> redirects standard output to **hold**. Then 2>&1 declares file descriptor 2 to be a duplicate of file descriptor 1. The result is that both standard output and standard error are redirected to **hold**:

```
$ cat x y 1> hold 2>&1
$ cat hold
cat: x: No such file or directory
This is y.
```

In the preceding example, **1> hold** precedes **2>&1**. If they had been listed in the opposite order, standard error would have been redirected to be a duplicate of standard output before standard output was redirected to **hold**. In that case, only standard output would have been redirected to the file **hold**.

The next example declares file descriptor 2 to be a duplicate of file descriptor 1 and sends the output for file descriptor 1 through a pipe to the tr command:

```
$ cat x y 2>&1 | tr "[a-z]" "[A-Z]"
CAT: X: NO SUCH FILE OR DIRECTORY
THIS IS Y.
```

You can also use **1>&2** to redirect standard output of a command to standard error. This technique is often used in shell scripts to send the output of echo to standard error. In the following script, standard output of the first echo is redirected to standard error:

```
$ cat message_demo
echo This is an error message. 1>&2
echo This is not an error message.
```

If you redirect standard output of **message_demo**, error messages such as the one produced by the first echo still go to the screen/window because you have not redirected standard error. Because standard output of a shell script is typically redirected to another file, this technique is often used so that error messages generated by the script are displayed on the screen. The **lnks** script (page 860) and several other scripts in the next chapter use this technique. You can also use the exec *builtin* to create additional file descriptors and to redirect standard input, standard output, and standard error of a shell script from within the script (page 887).

noclobber: Avoids Overwriting Files

Setting the **noclobber** variable prevents you from accidentally overwriting a file when you redirect output to the file. To override **noclobber**, put a pipe symbol after the symbol you use for redirecting or appending output (for example >| and >>|).

In the following example, the user creates or overwrites a file named **a** by redirecting the output of date to the file. Next, the user sets the **noclobber** variable and tries redirecting output to **a** again. The shell returns an error message. Then the user tries the same thing, but using a pipe symbol after the redirect symbol: The shell allows the user to overwrite the file. Finally, the user unsets **noclobber** (using a plus sign in place of the dash) and verifies that it is no longer set:

```
$ date > a
$ set -o noclobber
$ date > a
bash: a: Cannot overwrite existing file
$ date >| a
$ set +o noclobber
$ date > a
```

Job Control

A job is a command pipeline. You run a simple job whenever you give Linux a command (for example, type **date** on the command line and press RETURN: You have run a job). You can create several jobs with multiple commands on a single command line:

```
$ find . -print | sort | lpr & grep -l alex /tmp/* > alexfiles &
[1] 18839
[2] 18876
```

The portion of the command line up to the first & is one job, consisting of three processes: find, sort, and lpr, connected by pipes. The second job is a single process running grep. Both jobs have been put into the background by the trailing & characters, so bash does not wait for them to complete before giving you a prompt. Before the prompt, the shell displays information about each background job: its job number in brackets followed by the PID of the last process in the job.

Using job control, you can move commands from the foreground to the background and vice versa, stop commands temporarily, and get a list of the commands that are currently running or stopped.

jobs: Lists Jobs

The jobs builtin lists all background jobs. The following sequence demonstrates what happens when you give the command **jobs** from the Bourne Again Shell. In the following example, the sleep command run in the background creates a background job that jobs can report on, and jobs builtin displays job information:

```
$ sleep 60 &
[1] 7809
$ jobs
[1] + Running                    sleep 60&
```

fg: Brings a Job to the Foreground

The shell assigns a job number to commands that you run in the background (page 257). In the following example, several jobs are started in the background. For each, the Shell lists the job number and PID number immediately, just before it issues a prompt:

```
$ xclock &
[1] 1246
$ date &
[2] 1247
$ Sun Dec 7 11:44:40 PST 2003
[2]+ Done         date
$ find /usr -name ace -print > findout &
[2] 1269
$ jobs
[1]- Running          xclock &
[2]+ Running          find /usr -name ace -print > findout &
```

The jobs command lists the first job, xclock, as job 1. The date command does not appear in the jobs list because it completed before jobs was run. Because the date command completed before find was run, the find command became job 2.[2]

---

2. Job numbers are discarded when a job is finished and can be reused. When you start or put a job in the background, the shell assigns the lowest number that is not in use and is not less than a job number that is currently in use.

To move a background job into the foreground, use the fg builtin with a percent sign (%), followed by the job number as an argument. The following example moves job 2 into the foreground:

```
$ fg %2
```

You can also refer to a job by following the percent sign with a string that uniquely identifies the beginning of the command line used to start the job. Instead of the preceding command, for example, you could have used **fg %find** or **fg %f**, because either one uniquely identifies job 2. If you follow the percent sign with a question mark and a string, the string matches itself anywhere on the command line. In the preceding example, **%?ace** also refers to job 2.

Often the job you wish to bring into the foreground is the only job running in the background or is the job that jobs lists with a plus (**+**). In these cases, you can use fg without any arguments.

bg: Sends a Job to the Background

To put the foreground job into the background, you must first suspend the job by pressing the suspend key (usually CONTROL-Z). Pressing the suspend key stops the job immediately. Once the job is suspended, use the bg builtin to resume execution of the job, putting it in the background:

```
$ bg
```

If a background job attempts to read from the terminal, the shell stops it (that is, puts it to sleep [pages 193 and 270]) and notifies you that the job has been stopped and is waiting for input. When this happens, you must move the job into the foreground so that it can read from the terminal. The shell displays the command line as it moves the job into the foreground:

```
$ (sleep 5; cat > mytext) &
[1] 1343
$ date
Sun Dec 7 11:58:20 PST 2003
[1]+ Stopped (tty input)   ( sleep 5; cat >mytext )
$ fg
( sleep 5; cat >mytext )
Remember to let the cat out!
CONTROL-D
```

In this example, the shell displays the job number and PID number of the background job as soon as it starts, followed by a prompt. At this point, the user enters date, and its output appears on the screen. The shell waits until just before it issues a prompt (after date has finished) to notify you that job 1 is waiting for input. The reason for this delay is so that the notice does not disrupt your work: the default behavior of the shell. After the shell puts the job in the foreground, you can enter the input that the command was waiting for. Terminate the input with a CONTROL-D to signify EOF (end of file), and the shell displays another prompt.

The shell keeps you informed about changes in the status of a job, notifying you when a background job starts, completes, or is waiting for input from the terminal. The shell also lets you know when a foreground job is suspended. Because notices about a job being run in the background can disrupt your work, the shell delays these notices until it is ready to display a prompt.

If you try to leave a shell while jobs are stopped, the shell gives you a warning and does not allow you to exit. If, after the warning, you use jobs to review the list of jobs or you immediately try to leave the shell again, the shell allows you to leave and terminates your stopped jobs. Jobs that are running (not stopped) in the background continue to run. In the following example, find (job 1) continues to run after the second exit terminates the shell, but cat (job 2) is terminated:

```
$ find / -size +100k > $HOME/bigfiles 2>&1 &
[1] 1426
$ cat > mytest &
[2] 1428
$ exit
exit
There are stopped jobs.

[2]+ Stopped (tty input)    cat > mytext
$ exit

login:
```

Manipulating the Directory Stack

Using a shell, you can store a list of directories you are working with, enabling you to move easily among them. The list is referred to as a *stack*. You can think of it as a stack of dinner plates; you typically add plates to and remove plates from the top of the stack: a first-in last-out, or *FILO*, stack.

dirs: Displays the Stack

The dirs builtin displays the contents of the directory stack. If you call dirs when the directory stack is empty, it displays the name of the working directory:

```
$ dirs
~/literature
```

The dirs builtin uses a tilde (~) to represent the name of the user's home directory. The examples in the next several sections assume that you are referring to the directory structure shown in Figure 9-2.

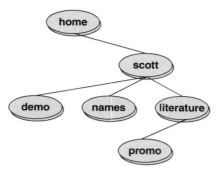

Figure 9-2   The directory structure in the examples

pushd: **Pushes a Directory on the Stack**

To change directories and at the same time add a new directory to the top of the stack, use the pushd (push directory) builtin. In addition to changing directories, the pushd builtin displays the contents of the stack. The following example is illustrated in Figure 9-3:

```
$ pushd ../demo
~/demo ~/literature
$ pwd
/home/scott/demo
$ pushd ../names
~/names ~/demo ~/literature
$ pwd
/home/scott/names
```

When you use pushd without an argument, it swaps the top two directories on the stack and makes the new top directory (which was the second directory) the new working directory (Figure 9-4):

```
$ pushd
~/demo ~/names ~/literature
$ pwd
/home/scott/demo
```

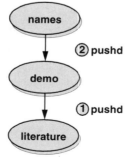

Figure 9-3   Creating a directory stack

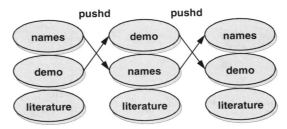

Figure 9-4   Using pushd to change working directories

Using pushd in this way, you can easily move back and forth between two directories. You can also use **cd –** to change to the previous directory. To access another directory in the stack, call pushd with a numeric argument preceded by a plus sign. The directories in the stack are numbered, starting with the top directory, which is number 0. The following pushd command changes the working directory to **literature** and moves it to the top of the stack:

```
$ pushd +2
~/literature ~/demo ~/names
$ pwd
/home/scott/literature
```

popd: **Pops a Directory Off the Stack**

To remove a directory from the stack, use the popd (pop directory) builtin. As Figure 9-5 shows, without an argument, popd removes the top directory from the stack and changes the working directory to the new top directory:

```
$ popd
~/demo ~/names
$ pwd
/home/scott/demo
```

To remove a directory other than the top one from the stack, use popd with a numeric argument preceded by a plus sign:

```
$ popd +1
~/demo
$ pwd
/home/scott/demo
```

If you remove a directory other than directory number 0 on the stack, this command does not change the working directory.

Processes

A *process* is the execution of a command by Linux. The shell that starts up when you log in is a command, or a process, like any other. Whenever you give the name of a Linux utility on the command line, you initiate a process. When you run a shell

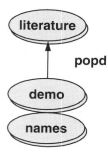

Figure 9-5   Using popd to remove a directory from the stack

script, another shell process is started, and additional processes are created for each command in the script. Depending on how you invoke the shell script, the script is run either by a new shell or by a subshell of the current shell. A process is not started when you run a shell builtin, such as cd, from the command line or within a script.

Process Structure

Like the file structure, the process structure is hierarchical, with parents, children, and even a *root*. A parent process *forks*[3] a child process, which in turn can fork other processes. (You can also use the term *spawn;* the words are interchangeable.) The operating system routine, or *system call,* that creates a new process is named **fork**. One of the first things Linux does to begin execution when a machine is started up is to start init, a single process, called a *spontaneous process,* with PID number 1. This process holds the same position in the process structure as the root directory does in the file structure: It is the ancestor of all processes that each user works with. When the system is in multiuser mode, init runs getty or mingetty processes, which display **login:** prompts on the virtual consoles. When someone responds to the prompt and presses RETURN, getty hands control over to a utility named login, which checks the user's name and password combination. After the user logs in, the login process becomes the user's shell process.

Process Identification

Linux assigns a unique PID number at the inception of each process. As long as a process exists, it keeps the same PID number. During one session, the same process is always executing the login shell. When you fork a new process—for example, when you use an editor—the PID number of the new (child) process is different from that of its parent process. When you return to the login shell, you will find that it is still being executed by the same process and has the same PID number as when you logged in.

---

3. The term *fork* is used to convey that, as with a fork in the road, one process turns into two. Initially, the two forks are identical except that one is identified as the parent and one as the child.

The following interaction shows that the process running the shell forked (is the parent of) the process running ps (page 206). When you call it with the –l option, ps displays a long listing of information about each process. The line of the ps display with **bash** in the **CMD** column refers to the process running the shell. The column headed by **PID** lists the PID number. The column headed PPID lists the PID number of the *parent* of each of the processes. From the PID and PPID columns, you can see that the process running the shell (PID 2168) is the parent of the process running sleep (PID 2191). The parent PID number of sleep is the same as the PID number of the shell (2168):

```
$ sleep 10 &
[1] 2891
$ ps -l
  F S   UID   PID  PPID  C PRI  NI ADDR    SZ WCHAN   TTY          TIME CMD
100 S   500  2168  2167  0  72   0   -    454 wait4   pts/1    00:00:00 bash
000 S   500  2891  2168  0  63   0   -    286 nanosl  pts/1    00:00:00 sleep
000 R   500  2892  2168  0  76   0   -    628 -       pts/1    00:00:00 ps
```

Refer to the ps man page for information on the columns it displays with the –l option. When you give another **ps –l** command, you can see that the shell is still being run by the same process but that it forked another process to run sleep:

```
$ sleep 10 &
[1] 2893
$ ps -l
  F S   UID   PID  PPID  C PRI  NI ADDR    SZ WCHAN   TTY          TIME CMD
100 S   500  2168  2167  0  71   0   -    454 wait4   pts/1    00:00:00 bash
000 S   500  2893  2168  0  63   0   -    286 nanosl  pts/1    00:00:00 sleep
000 R   500  2894  2168  0  75   0   -    628 -       pts/1    00:00:00 ps
```

You can also use pstree to see the parent/child relationship of processes. The next example shows the –p option to pstree, which causes it to display PID numbers:

```
$ pstree -p
init(1)-+-adsl-connect(1591)---pppd(1619)---pppoe(1620)
        |-apmd(832)
        |-atd(1148)
        |-crond(1089)
        |-gpm(1047)
        |-httpd(1070)-+-httpd(1088)
        |             '-httpd(1538)
        .
        .
        .
        |-ntpd(852)
        |-portmap(686)
        |-rhnsd(1170)
        |-rpc.mountd(989)
        |-rpc.rquotad(984)
        |-rpc.statd(714)
        |-rpciod(805)
        |-sendmail(1028)
        |-smbd(1107)---smbd(2118)
        |-sshd(909)
        |-syslogd(663)
        '-xinetd(942)
```

See the list starting on page 355 for information on some of the daemons listed by pstree. See "$$ PID Number" on page 291 for a description of how to instruct the shell to report on PID numbers.

Executing a Command

When you give it a command, the shell usually forks (spawns) a child process to execute the command. While the child process is executing the command, the parent process *sleeps*. While a process is sleeping, it does not use any computer time but remains inactive, waiting to wake up. When the child process finishes executing the command, it tells its parent of its success or failure via the exit status and dies. The parent process (which is running the shell) wakes up and prompts you for another command.

When you request that the shell run a process in the background by ending a command with an ampersand (&), the shell forks a child process without going to sleep and without waiting for the child process to run to completion. The parent process, executing the shell, reports the job number and PID number of the child and prompts you for another command. The child process runs in the background, independent of its parent.

Although the shell forks a process to run most of the commands you give it, some commands are built into the shell. The shell does not need to fork a process to run builtins. Each of the shell's info/man pages contains a list of builtin commands (page 211).

Within a given process, such as your login shell or a subshell, you can declare, initialize, read, and change variables. By default, however, a variable is local to a process. When a process forks a child process, the parent does not pass the value of a variable to the child. You can make the value of a variable available to child processes by using the export builtin (page 277).

Running a Shell Script

Whenever you give it a command on the command line, the shell **fork**s a new process, creating a duplicate of the shell process (a subshell). The new process attempts to **exec,** or execute, the command. Like **fork,** the **exec** routine is executed by the operating system (a system call). If the command is an executable program, such as a compiled C program, **exec** succeeds, and the system overlays the newly created subshell with the executable program. If the command is a shell script, **exec** fails. When **exec** fails, the command is assumed to be a shell script, and the subshell runs the commands in the script. Unlike your login shell, which expects input from the command line, the subshell takes its input from a file: the shell script.

As discussed earlier, if you have a shell script in a file that you do not have execute permission for, you can run the commands in the script by using a bash command to **exec** a shell to run the script directly. In the following example, bash creates a new shell that takes its input from the file named **whoson:**

```
$ bash whoson
```

Because the bash command expects to read a file containing commands, you do not need execute permission for **whoson**. (However, you do need read permission.) Although bash reads and executes the commands in the file **whoson**, standard input, standard output, and standard error are still connected to the terminal.

Although you can use bash to execute a shell script, this technique causes the script to run more slowly than giving yourself execute permission and directly invoking the script. Users typically prefer to make the file executable and run the script by typing its name on the command line. It is also easier simply to type the name, and it is consistent with the way other kinds of programs are invoked (so you do not need to know whether you are running a shell script or another kind of program). However, if bash is not your interactive shell or if you want to see how the script runs with different shells, you should give the bash (or the name of another shell) command, followed by the name of the file containing the script, as shown earlier.

---

caution || **sh Does Not Call the Original Bourne Shell**

The original Bourne Shell was invoked with the command **sh**. Although you can call bash with an **sh** command, it is not the original Bourne Shell. It is a symbolic link to **/bin/bash**, so it is simply another name for the **bash** command. When you call bash using the command **sh**, bash tries to mimic the behavior of the original Bourne Shell as closely as possible. It does not always succeed.

#!   Specifies a Shell

You can also put a special sequence of characters on the first line of a shell script to indicate to the operating system that it is a script or another type of file. Because the operating system checks the initial characters of a program before attempting to **exec** it, these characters save the system from making an unsuccessful attempt and also tell the system which utility to use (usually bash). If **#!** are the first two characters of a script, the system interprets the characters that follow as the absolute pathname of the program that should execute the script. This can be the pathname of any program, not just a shell. The following example specifies that the current script should be run by bash:

```
$ cat sh_script
#!/bin/bash
echo "This is a Bourne Again Shell script."
```

This feature is also useful if you have a script intended to be run with a shell other than bash. The following example shows a script that is intended to be executed by tcsh:

```
$ cat tcsh_script
#!/usr/bin/tcsh
echo "This is a tcsh script."
set person = jenny
echo "person is $person"
```

The script can be run from any shell, but tcsh must execute it. Because of the #! line, the operating system sees to it that tcsh executes the script no matter which shell you run it from.

Following is a demonstration program that displays the name of the shell it was run under:

```
$ cat whichshell
#!/bin/tcsh
ps -f | grep $0
$ whichshell
zach      5141  2168  0 14:36 pts/1     00:00:00 tcsh ./whichshell
zach      5143  5141  0 14:36 pts/1     00:00:00 grep ./whichshell
```

The –f option causes ps to display the full command line, which includes the name of the shell running the script. The $0 variable holds the name of the calling program so grep looks through the lines output by ps –f for the name of the program. It displays two lines: one for tcsh and the other for grep, which is running under tcsh.

If you do not follow the #! with the name of an executable program, the shell reports that it cannot find the command that you asked it to run. You can optionally follow #! with SPACEs. If you omit the #! line and try to run, for example, a tcsh script from bash, the shell generates error messages, or the script may just not run properly.

Begins a Comment

Comments make shell scripts and all code easier to read and maintain by you or by others.

If a pound sign (#) in the first character position of the first line of a script is not immediately followed by an exclamation point (!), or if a pound sign occurs in any other location in a script, the shell interprets it as the beginning of a comment and ignores everything between the pound sign and the end of the line (the next NEWLINE character).

Startup Files

When a shell starts, it runs certain startup files (scripts) with commands in them to initialize itself. Which files the shell runs depends on whether it is a login shell, an interactive shell that is not a login shell, or a noninteractive shell—one used to execute shell scripts.

When bash is started as a login shell or if you use the –login option when starting a bash shell, bash first reads /etc/profile for commands. Then a bash login shell looks in your home directory for .bash_profile and executes it. Otherwise, it executes .bash_login. If neither of these files exists, bash executes .profile file. When you log out, this same shell reads and executes commands from the .bash_logout file in your home directory, if it exists (Table 9-1).

When bash is started as a nonlogin interactive shell (such as you get by giving the command bash), bash reads only the .bashrc file. However, this shell inherits any environment (exported) variables from the parent shell, so environment variables set in **/etc/profile** and **.bash_profile** are passed to the nonlogin shell.

Finally, nonlogin, noninteractive shells (shells that have standard input and standard output not connected to your terminal) look for the environment variable **BASH_ENV** and then **ENV**, if **BASH_ENV** does not exist. If either of these environment variables has a filename as a value, the shell reads and executes commands from this file.

table 9-1 || **Order of Execution of bash Startup Files**

File	Interactive (Login) Shell	Noninteractive (Nonlogin) Shell
/etc/profile	First.	Not executed, but the shell inherits from the parent shell variables that were originally set by these files.
.bash_profile	Second.	
.bash_login	Second if no **.bash_profile**.	
.profile	Second if no **.bash_profile** or **.bash_login**.	
.bashrc	Executed only by interactive, nonlogin shells.	Not executed.
BASH_ENV or **ENV**	Not executed.	Execute the commands listed in the file named by one of these variables. When the shell is started in POSIX mode, the file named by **ENV** is executed using source. Otherwise, the file named by **BASH_ENV** is executed.
.bash_logout	Executed on logout.	Not executed.

Although the numbers of shell types and initialization files might seem confusing, many bash users have only **.bash_profile** and **.bashrc** in their home directories. Most of the commands that they want all instances of bash to execute are placed into **.bashrc**, whereas **.bash_profile** includes a command to load and run commands from **.bashrc**, as well as an assignment of the string **~/.bashrc** to the **ENV** variable. This way, **.bashrc** is executed, no matter how the shell gets started. You can put the following commands into **.bash_profile** to get this effect:

```
export ENV=~/.bashrc
if [ -f ~/.bashrc ]; then source ~/.bashrc; fi
```

Parameters and Variables

Within the shell, a *shell parameter* is associated with a value that is accessible to the user. There are several kinds of *shell parameters*. Parameters whose names consist of letters, digits, and underscores are often referred to as *.shell variables,* or simply *variables*. A variable name must start with a letter or underscore, not with a number. Thus **A76**, **MY_CAT**, and **___X___** are valid variable names, whereas **69TH_STREET** (starts with a digit) and **MY-NAME** (contains a hyphen) are not. Shell variables that you can name and assign values to are *user-created variables*. One convention is to use only uppercase letters for names of global variables (*environment variables*) and to use mixed-case or lowercase letters for other variables. You can change the values of user-created variables at any time, and you can make them *readonly* so that their value cannot be changed. You can also make user-created variables global. A global variable is available to all shells and other programs you fork from the original shell.

When you want to assign a value to a variable, use its name with no SPACEs on either side of the equal sign:

```
$ myvar=abc
```

When you want to use the value of a variable, use its name preceded by a dollar sign ($):

```
$ echo $myvar
abc
```

Variables that have special meaning to the shell are called *keyword shell variables* (or simply *keyword variables*) and usually have short, mnemonic names. When you start a shell (by logging in, for example), the shell inherits several keyword variables from the environment. Among these variables are **HOME**, which identifies your home directory, and **PATH**, which determines what directories the shell searches and in what order to locate a command that you give the shell. The shell creates and initializes (with default values) other keyword variables when you start it; still other variables do not exist until you set them.

You can change the values of most of the keyword shell variables at any time, although it is usually not necessary to change the values of keyword variables initialized in **/etc/profile**. If you need to change the value of a variable, do so in one of the files in your home directory listed in the Interactive column of Table 9-1 on page 273. Just as you can make user-created variables global, you can make keyword variables global; this is often done automatically when the shell starts. You can also make a keyword variable readonly.

The names of one group of parameters do not resemble variable names. Most of these parameters have one-character names (for example, **1**, **?**, and **#**) and are referenced (as are all variables) by preceding the name with a dollar sign (for example, **$1**, **$?**, and **$#**). The values of these parameters reflect different aspects of your ongoing interaction with the shell. For example, whenever you give a command on the command line, each argument on the command line becomes the value of a *positional parameter*. Positional parameters enable you to access command line arguments, a capability that you will often require when you write sophisticated shell scripts. Other frequently needed shell script values, such as the name of the last command executed, the number of command line arguments, and the status of the most recently executed command, are available as *special parameters*. With the exception of the set builtin (page 289), you cannot assign values to positional and special parameters.

User-Created Variables

As described earlier, you can declare any sequence of letters, digits, and underscores as the name of a variable, as long as the first character is not a number. The first line in the following example declares the variable named **person** and initializes it with the value **alex**:

```
$ person=alex
$ echo person
person
$ echo $person
alex
```

When you assign a value to a variable in bash, *you must not precede or follow the equal sign with a* SPACE *or* TAB. Because the echo builtin copies its arguments to standard output, you can use it to display the values of variables.

The second line shows that **person** does not represent **alex**. The string **person** is echoed as **person**. The shell substitutes the value of a variable only when you precede the name of the variable with a dollar sign ($). The command **echo $person** displays the value of the variable **person** but does not display **$person** because the shell does not pass **$person** to echo as an argument. Because of the leading **$**, the shell recognizes that **$person** is the name of a variable, *substitutes* the value of the variable, and passes that value to echo. The echo builtin displays the value of the variable, not its name, never knowing that you called it with a variable. The final command in the preceding example displays the value of the variable **person**.

You can prevent the shell from substituting the value of a variable by quoting the leading $:

```
$ echo $person
alex
$ echo "$person"
alex
$ echo '$person'
$person
$ echo \$person
$person
```

Double quotation marks do not prevent the substitution; single quotation marks or a backslash (\) do.

Because they do not prevent variable substitution but do turn off the special meanings of most other characters, double quotation marks are useful when you assign values to variables and when you use those values. To assign a value that contains SPACEs or

TABs to a variable, use double quotation marks around the value. Although double quotation marks may not be required, it is a good idea to place them around variables whose values you are using, as you can see from the second following example:

```
$ person="alex and jenny"
$ echo $person
alex and jenny
```

When you reference a variable that contains TABs or multiple adjacent SPACEs, you need to use quotation marks to preserve the spacing. If you do not quote the variable, echo collapses each string of nonblank characters into a single SPACE when it copies them to standard output:

```
$ person="alex    and    jenny"
$ echo $person
alex and jenny
$ echo "$person"
alex    and    jenny
```

When you execute a command with a variable as an argument, the shell replaces the name of the variable with the value of the variable and passes that value to the program being executed. If the value of the variable contains a special character, such as * or ?, the shell *may* expand that variable.

The first line in the following sequence of commands assigns the string **alex*** to the variable **memo**. The Bourne Again Shell does *not expand the string* because bash does not perform pathname expansion (page 207) when assigning a value to a variable. A shell processes a command line in a specific order. Within this order the Bourne Again Shell expands variables before it interprets commands. In the following echo command line, the double quotation marks quote the asterisk (*) and prevent the Bourne Again Shell from expanding the **memo** variable before passing its value to the echo command:

```
$ memo=alex*
$ echo "$memo"
alex*
```

The shell interprets special characters as special when you reference a variable containing a special character that is not quoted. In the following example, the shell expands the value of the **memo** variable because it is not quoted:

```
$ ls
alex.report
alex.summary
$ echo $memo
alex.report alex.summary
```

The preceding example shows that when you do not quote **memo**, the shell matches the value **alex*** to two files in the working directory: **alex.report** and **alex.summary**.

unset: Removes a Variable

Unless you remove a variable, it exists as long as the shell in which it was created exists. To remove the *value* of a variable but not the variable itself, set the value to null:

```
$ person=
$ echo $person

$
```

You can remove a variable with the unset builtin. To remove the variable **person**, give the following command:

```
$ unset person
```

readonly: Makes a Variable Permanent

You can use the readonly builtin to ensure that the value of a variable cannot be changed. The next example declares the variable **person** to be readonly. You must assign a value to a variable *before* you declare it to be readonly; you cannot change its value after the declaration. When you attempt to change the value of a readonly variable, the shell displays an error message:

```
$ person=jenny
$ echo $person
jenny
$ readonly person
$ person=helen
bash: person: readonly variable
```

If you use the readonly builtin without an argument, it displays a list of all readonly shell variables. This list includes keyword variables that are automatically readonly, as well as keyword or user-created variables that you have declared as readonly.

export: Makes a Variable Global

Variables are ordinarily local to the process in which they are declared: A shell script does not have access to variables declared in your login shell unless you explicitly make the variables available (global). You can use export to make a variable available to a child process.

Once you use the export builtin with a variable name as an argument, the shell places the value of the variable in the calling environment of child processes. This *call by value* gives each child process a copy of the variable for its own use.

The following **extest1** shell script assigns a value of **american** to the variable named **cheese** and then displays its filename (**extest1**) and the value of **cheese**. The **extest1** script then calls **subtest**, which attempts to display the same information. Then **subtest** declares a **cheese** variable and displays its value. When **subtest** finishes, it returns control to the parent process, which is executing **extest1**. Then **extest1** again displays the value of the original **cheese** variable.

```
$ cat extest1
cheese=american
echo "extest1 1: $cheese"
subtest
echo "extest1 2: $cheese"
```

```
$ cat subtest
echo "subtest 1: $cheese"
cheese=swiss
echo "subtest 2: $cheese"
$ extest1
extest1 1: american
subtest 1:
subtest 2: swiss
extest1 2: american
```

The **subtest** script never receives the value of **cheese** from **extest1**, and **extest1** never loses the value. Contrary to life, a child can never impact its parent's attributes. When it attempts to display the value of a variable that has not been declared, as is the case with **subtest**, a process displays nothing; the value of an undeclared variable is that of a null string.

The following script, **extest2**, is the same as **extest1** but uses export[4] to make **cheese** available to the **subtest** script:

```
$ cat extest2
export cheese
cheese=american
echo "extest2 1: $cheese"
subtest
echo "extest2 2: $cheese"
$ extest2
extest2 1: american
subtest 1: american
subtest 2: swiss
extest2 2: american
```

Here the child process inherits the value of **cheese** as **american** and, after displaying this value, changes *its copy* to **swiss**. When control is returned to the parent, the parent's copy of **cheese** still retains its original value: **american**.

declare: Sets Attributes and Values for a Shell Variable

The declare (same as typeset) builtin allows you to set attributes and values for shell variables. You can associate several attributes with a variable by using declare; five of these follow:

1. The **–a** option declares a variable as an array.

2. The **–f** option makes a variable a function name (functions are discussed on page 894).

3. The **–i** option marks a variable so that integer values are stored efficiently (this speeds up shell arithmetic involving the variable).

4. The **–r** option makes a variable readonly.

5. The **–x** option marks a variable for export.

---

4. Although it is rarely done, you can export a variable before you assign a value to it. Also, you do not need to export a variable a second time after you change its value.

The following commands declare several variables and set some attributes. The first line declares **person1** and assigns it a value of **alex**:

```
$ declare person1=alex
$ declare -r person2=jenny
$ declare -rx person3=helen
$ declare -x person4
```

The readonly and export builtins are synonyms for the commands **declare –r** and **declare –x**, respectively. It is legal to declare a variable without assigning a value to it, as the preceding declaration of the variable **person4** illustrates. This declaration makes **person4** available to all subshells, and, until an assignment is made to the variable, it has a null value whenever it is referenced.

You can list the options to declare separately in any order. The following is equivalent to the declaration of **person3**:

```
$ declare -x -r person3=helen
```

Also, you can use the **+** character in place of **–** if you want to remove an attribute from a variable. After the following command is given, making an assignment to the variable **person3** does not result in an error:

```
$ declare +r person3
```

If the declare builtin is given with options but no variable names as arguments, the command lists all shell variables that have the indicated attributes set. For example, the option **–r** with declare gives a list of all readonly shell variables. After the declarations in the preceding example have been given, the results are as follows:

```
$ declare -r
declare -ar BASH_VERSINFO='([0]="2" [1]="05b" [2]="0" [3]="1" ... )'
declare -ir EUID="500"
declare -ir PPID="936"
declare -r SHELLOPTS="braceexpand:emacs:hashall:histexpand:history:..."
declare -ir UID="500"
declare -r person2="jenny"
declare -rx person3="helen"
```

The first five entries are keyword variables that are automatically declared as readonly. Some of these variables are also stored as integers, as the option **–i** indicates. The **–a** option indicates that **BASH_VERSINFO** is stored as an array variable; the value of each element of the array is listed to the right of the equal sign. If you had used readonly to make a keyword variable readonly, the keyword variable would also appear in the list. Another way to get the same list of shell readonly variables is by using readonly with no arguments.

Without any arguments or options, the declare builtin lists all the shell variables. The same list is output when you run set (page 289) without any arguments. Another name for declare is typeset. You may see it often in shell scripts, including complex scripts that come with the Linux system.

read: Accepts User Input

As you begin writing shell scripts, you soon realize that one of the most common uses of user-created variables is storing information a user enters in response to a prompt. Using read, your scripts can accept input from the user and store the input in variables that you create. The read builtin reads one line from standard input and assigns the line to one or more variables:

```
$ cat read1
echo -n "Go ahead: "
read firstline
echo "You entered: $firstline"
$ read1
Go ahead: This is a line.
You entered: This is a line.
```

The first line of the read1 script uses echo to prompt the user to enter a line of text. The –n option suppresses the following NEWLINE, allowing you to enter a line of text on the same line as the prompt. The second line in read1 reads the text into the variable firstline. The third line verifies the action of read by displaying the value of firstline. The variable is quoted (along with the text string) in this example because you, as the scriptwriter, cannot anticipate what characters the user might enter in response to the prompt. Consider what would happen if the variable were not quoted and the user entered * in response to the prompt:

```
$ cat read1_no_quote
echo -n "Go ahead: "
read firstline
echo You entered: $firstline

$ read1_no_quote
Go ahead: *
You entered: read1 read1_no_quote script.1
$ ls
read1    read1_no_quote    script.1
```

The ls command lists the same words as the script, demonstrating that the shell expands the asterisk into a list of all the files in the working directory. When the variable $firstline is surrounded by double quotation marks, the shell does not expand the asterisk. Thus the read1 script behaves correctly:

```
$ read1
Go ahead: *
You entered: *
```

If you want the shell to interpret the special meanings of special characters, do not use quotation marks.

The read2 script prompts for a command line and reads it into the variable command. The script then executes the command line by placing $command on a line by itself. When it executes the script, the shell replaces the variable with its value and executes the command line as part of the script:

```
$ cat read2
echo -n "Enter a command: "
read command
$command
echo Thanks
```

In the following example, **read2** reads a command line that calls the echo builtin. The shell executes the command and then displays **Thanks**. Next, **read2** reads a command line that executes the who utility:

```
$ read2
Enter a command: echo Please display this message.
Please display this message.
Thanks
$ read2
Enter a command: who
alex      pts/4        Jun 17 07:50  (:0.0)
scott     pts/12       Jun 17 11:54  (bravo.tcorp.com)
Thanks
```

The following **read3** script reads values into three variables. The read builtin assigns one word (a sequence of nonblank characters) to each variable:

```
$ cat read3
echo -n "Enter something: "
read word1 word2 word3
echo "Word 1 is: $word1"
echo "Word 2 is: $word2"
echo "Word 3 is: $word3"
$ read3
Enter something: this is something
Word 1 is: this
Word 2 is: is
Word 3 is: something
```

When you enter more words than read has variables, read assigns one word to each variable, with all the leftover words going to the last variable. In fact, both **read1** and **read2** assigned the first word and all the leftover words to the one variable they each had to work with. In the following example, read accepts five words into three variables, assigning the first word to the first variable, the second word to the second variable, and the third through fifth words to the third variable:

```
$ read3
Enter something: this is something else, really.
Word 1 is:  this
Word 2 is:  is
Word 3 is:  something else, really.
```

$(...) or ` ... `   Command Substitution

Command substitution replaces a command with the output of the command. You can use command substitution to produce arguments for another command or assignment statement. Place a dollar sign and an open parenthesis before and a close parenthesis after the command whose output you want to use. This is the preferred method. Alternatively, you can enclose the command you want to substitute for between two back ticks, or grave accent marks. Thus **$(pwd)** is equivalent to `` `pwd` ``. The next chapter contains several scripts that use command substitution to assign values to variables (pages 860, 879, and 891).

Following, the shell executes pwd and substitutes the output of the command for the command and surrounding punctuation. Then the shell passes the output of the command, which is now an argument, to echo, which displays it as follows:

```
$ echo $(pwd)
/home/alex
```

The next shell script assigns the output of the pwd utility to the variable **where** and displays a message containing the value of this variable:

```
$ cat where
where=$(pwd)
echo "You are using the $where directory."
$ where
You are using the /home/jenny directory.
```

Although it illustrates how to assign the output of a command to a variable, this example is not realistic. You can more directly display the output of pwd without using a variable:

```
$ cat where2
echo "You are using the $(pwd) directory."
$ where2
You are using the /home/jenny directory.
```

Keyword Variables

Most keyword variables are either inherited or declared and initialized by the shell when it starts. You can assign values to these variables from the command line or from the **.bash_profile** or **.profile** file in your home directory. Typically, users want these variables to apply to any shells or subshells that they create, as well as to their login shell. Consequently, for those variables not automatically exported by the shell, you must use export to make them available to descendants.

HOME: Your Home Directory

By default, your home directory is your working directory when you log in. Your home directory is determined when you establish your account and is stored in the **/etc/passwd** file. When you log in, the shell inherits the pathname of your home directory and assigns it to the variable **HOME**.

When you give a **cd** command without an argument, cd makes the directory whose name is stored in **HOME** the working directory:

```
$ pwd
/home/alex/laptop
$ echo $HOME
/home/alex
$ cd
$ pwd
/home/alex
```

This example shows the value of the **HOME** variable and the effect of the cd utility. After you execute cd without an argument, the pathname of the working directory is the same as the value of **HOME** (your home directory).

In a similar manner, the shell uses **HOME** to expand pathnames that use the shorthand tilde (~) notation to denote a user's home directory. The following example illustrates the use of this shortcut, with ls listing the files in Alex's **laptop** directory:

```
$ ls ~/laptop
tester      count       lineup
```

PATH: Where the Shell Looks for Programs

When you give the shell an absolute or relative pathname rather than a simple filename as a command, it looks in the specified directory for an executable file with the appropriate filename. If the executable file does not have the exact pathname that you specify, the shell reports that it cannot find (or execute) the program. Alternatively, if you give it a simple filename as a command, the shell searches through certain directories for the program you want to execute. The shell looks in several directories for a file that has the same name as the command and that you have execute permission for (a compiled program) or read and execute permission for (a shell script). The **PATH** shell variable controls this search.

When you log in, the shell assigns a default value to the **PATH** variable. The shell gets this value from the **/etc/profile** file. Normally, the default specifies that the shell search your working directory and several system directories used to hold common commands. These system directories include **/bin** and **/usr/bin** and other directories that might be appropriate for your system. When you give a command, if the shell does not find the executable file named by the command in any of the directories listed in your **PATH** variable, the shell reports that it cannot find (or execute) the program.

The **PATH** variable specifies the directories in the order the shell is to search them. Each must be separated from the next by a colon. The following command sets **PATH** so that a search for an executable file starts with the **/usr/local/bin** directory. If it does not find the file in this directory, the shell looks in **/bin**, followed by **/usr/bin**. If the search in those directories also fails, the shell looks in **/home/alex/bin** and in the working directory last. A null value in the string indicates the working directory. There is a null value (nothing between the colon and the end of the line) as the last element of the string. The working directory is represented by a leading colon (not recommended; see the following security box), a trailing colon (as in the example), or two colons next to each other anywhere in the string. You can also represent the working directory explicitly with a period (.). The following command assigns a value to and exports the **PATH** variable. Exporting **PATH** makes its new value accessible to subshells that may be invoked during the login session:

```
$ export PATH=/usr/local/bin:/bin:/usr/bin:/home/alex/bin:
```

Because Linux stores many executable files in directories named **bin** (*binary*), users also typically put their executable files in their own **~/bin** directories. If you put your own **bin** directory at the end of your **PATH** as Alex has, the shell looks there for any commands that it cannot find in directories listed earlier in **PATH**.

---

security ‖   **PATH and Security**

Do not put the working directory first in your **PATH** when security is a concern. For example, most people type **ls** as the first command when entering a directory. If the owner of the directory has an executable file named **ls** in this directory, this file, instead of the system command ls, is executed, possibly with undesirable results. If you are running as Superuser, you should *never* put the working directory first in your **PATH**. In fact, it is common for Superuser **PATH** to omit the working directory entirely. You can always execute a file in the working directory by prepending a **./** to the name, as in **./ls**.

If you want to add directories to your **PATH**, you can reference the old value of the **PATH** variable while you are setting **PATH** to a new value. The following command adds **/usr/X11R6/bin** to the front of the current **PATH** and **/usr/bin** to the end:

```
$ PATH=/usr/X11R6/bin:$PATH:/usr/bin:
```

MAIL: Where Your Mail Is Kept

The **MAIL** variable contains the pathname of the file that your mail is stored in (your *mailbox*, usually **/var/spool/mail/***name*, where *name* is your login name).

The **MAILPATH** variable contains a list of filenames separated by colons. If this variable is set, the shell informs you when any one of the files is modified (for example, when mail arrives). You can follow any of the filenames in the list with a percent sign (%), followed by a message. The message replaces the **you have mail** message when you get mail while logged in.

The **MAILCHECK** variable specifies how often, in seconds, the shell checks for new mail. The default is 60 seconds. If you set this variable to zero, the shell checks before each prompt. If you unset **MAILCHECK** as follows, the shell does not check for mail at all:

```
$ unset MAILCHECK
```

PS1: User Prompt (Primary)

The **PS1** variable holds the prompt that the shell uses to let you know that it is waiting for a command. The bash prompt used in the examples throughout this chapter

is a **$** followed by a SPACE; your prompt may differ. When you change the value of
PS1 or **prompt**, you change the appearance of your prompt.

If you are working on more than one machine, it can be helpful to incorporate a
machine name into your prompt. The following example shows how to change the
prompt to the name of the machine you are using, followed by a colon and a SPACE (a
SPACE at the end of the prompt makes the commands that you enter following the
prompt easier to read):

```
$ PS1="`hostname`: "
bravo.tcorp.com: echo test
test
bravo.tcorp.com:
```

The preferred construct is

```
$ PS1="$(hostname): "
```

PS2: User Prompt (Secondary)

Prompt String 2 is a secondary prompt that the shell stores in **PS2**. On the first line
of the following example, an unclosed quoted string follows echo. The shell assumes
that the command is not finished and, on the second line, gives the default secondary prompt (>). This prompt indicates that the shell is waiting for the user to continue the command line. The shell waits until it receives the quotation mark that
closes the string and then executes the command:

```
$ echo "demonstration of prompt string
> 2"
demonstration of prompt string
2
$ PS2="secondary prompt: "
$ echo "this demonstrates
secondary prompt: prompt string 2"
this demonstrates
prompt string 2
```

The second command changes the secondary prompt to **secondary prompt:** followed by a SPACE. A multiline echo demonstrates the new prompt.

IFS: Separates Input Fields

The **IFS** variable holds the internal field separators. Refer to "Word Splitting" on
page 314.

CDPATH: Broadens the Scope of cd

The **CDPATH** variable allow you to use a simple filename as an argument to cd to
change your working directory to one that is not a child of your working directory. If
you have several directories you like to work out of, this variable can speed things up
and save you the tedium of using cd with longer pathnames to switch among them.

When **CDPATH** or **cdpath** is not set and you specify a simple filename as an argument to cd, cd searches the working directory for a subdirectory with the same name as the argument. If the subdirectory does not exist, cd issues an error message. When **CDPATH** or **cdpath** is set, cd searches for an appropriately named subdirectory in the directories in the **CDPATH** list. If cd finds one, that directory becomes the working directory. With **CDPATH** or **cdpath** set, you can use cd and a simple filename to change your working directory to a child of any of the directories listed in **CDPATH** or **cdpath**.

The **CDPATH** or **cdpath** variable takes on the value of a colon-separated list of directory pathnames (similar to the **PATH** variable) and is usually set in the **.bash_profile** or **.profile** file in your home directory with a command line such as the following:

```
export CDPATH=$HOME:$HOME/literature
```

This setup causes cd to search your home directory, the **literature** directory, and then your working directory when you give a cd command. If you do not include your working directory in **CDPATH** or **cdpath**, cd searches the working directory after the search of all the other directories in **CDPATH** or **cdpath** fails. If you want cd to search the working directory first (which you should never do when you are logged in as **root**—refer to the tip "**PATH** and Security" on page 284), include a null string, represented by two colons (::), as the first entry in **CDPATH**:

```
export CDPATH=::$HOME:$HOME/literature
```

If the argument to the cd builtin is an absolute filename—one starting with a slash (/)—the shell does not consult **CDPATH** or **cdpath**.

Running a Startup File with the . (dot) or source Builtin

After you edit your startup file (such as **.bash_profile**) to change the values of keyword shell variables, you do not have to wait until the next time you log in to put the changes into effect. You can run the startup file using the . (dot) builtin. As with all other commands, the . must be followed by a SPACE on the command line. Using the . or source builtin is similar to running a shell script, except that these commands run the script as part of the current process. Consequently, when you use . or source to run a script from your login shell, changes you make to the variables from within the script affect the login shell. You can use the . or source command to run any shell script, not simply a startup file, but undesirable side effects (such as having the value of shell variables you rely on changed) may occur. If you ran a startup file as a regular shell script and did not use the . or source builtin, the new variables would be in effect only in the subshell running the script. Refer to "export: Makes a Variable Global" on page 277.

In the following example, **.bash_profile** sets several variables and sets **PS1** to the machine name. The . builtin puts the new values into effect:

```
cat .bash_profile
TERM=vt100
PATH=/bin:/usr/bin:/usr/sbin:/home/alex/bin
export PS1="$(hostname -f): "
export CDPATH=:$HOME
stty kill '^u'
$ . .bash_profile
bravo.tcorp.com: $
```

Positional Parameters

When you call a shell script, the command name and arguments are the positional parameters. They are called positional because within a shell script, you refer to them by their position on the command line. Although you can reference them, only the set builtin allows you to change the values of positional parameters (page 289).

$0: Name of the Calling Program

The shell stores the name of the command you used to call a program in parameter $0. It is parameter number zero because it appears before the first argument on the command line:

```
$ cat abc
echo The name of the command used
echo to execute this shell script was $0
$ abc
The name of the command used
to execute this shell script was abc
```

This shell script uses echo to verify the name of the script you are executing.

$1–$n: Command Line Arguments

The first argument on the command line is represented by the parameter $1, the second argument by the parameter $2, and so on up to $x. The following script displays positional parameters that hold command line arguments:

```
$ cat display_5args
echo The first five command line
echo arguments are $1 $2 $3 $4 $5
$ display_5args jenny alex helen
The first five command line
arguments are jenny alex helen
```

The display_5args script displays the first five command line arguments. The shell assigns a null value to each of the parameters that represents an argument that is not present on the command line. The $4 and $5 variables have a null value.

The $* variable represents all the command line arguments, as the display_all program demonstrates:

```
$ cat display_all
echo All the command line arguments are:
echo $*
$ display_all a b c d e f g h i j k l m n o p
All the command line arguments are:
a b c d e f g h i j k l m n o p
```

When you refer to a positional parameter, enclose the reference between double quotation marks. The quotation marks are particularly important when using positional parameters as arguments to commands; without double quotation marks, a positional parameter with a null value disappears:

```
$ cat showargs
echo "I was called with $# arguments, the first is :$1:."
$ showargs a b c
echo I was called with 3 arguments, the first is :a:.
$ echo $3

$ showargs $3 a b c
echo I was called with 3 arguments, the first is :a:.
$ showargs "$3" a b c
echo I was called with 4 arguments, the first is ::.
```

The preceding example first calls **showargs** with three simple arguments. The **showargs** script displays the number of arguments and the value of the first argument enclosed between colons. The shell stores the number of arguments passed to it in the $# special parameter. (Refer to "$* and $@   Value of Command Line Arguments" on page 291 for more information.) The echo command demonstrates that the third positional parameter of the current shell ($3) has no value. In the final two calls to **showargs**, the first argument is $3. Because there is no value for this positional parameter, the shell replaces it with a null value. In the first case, the command line becomes **showargs a b c**; the shell passes **showargs** three arguments. In the second case, the command line becomes **showargs "" a b c**, which results in calling **showargs** with four arguments. The difference in the two calls to **showargs** illustrates a subtle potential problem that you must keep in mind when using positional parameters.

shift: Promotes Command Line Arguments

The shift builtin promotes each of the command line arguments. The first argument (which was $1) is discarded. The second argument (which was $2) becomes the first (now $1), the third becomes the second, the fourth becomes the third, and so on.

Using the command line variables ($1–$9), you can access only the first nine command line arguments from a shell script. The shift builtin gives you access to the tenth command line argument by making it the ninth. Successive shift commands make additional arguments available. The original first argument is discarded. Because there is no "unshift" command, it is not possible to bring back arguments that have been discarded.

The following **demo_shift** program is called with three arguments. Double quotation marks around the arguments to echo preserve the spacing of the output display. The program displays the arguments and shifts them repeatedly until there are no more arguments to shift:

```
$ cat demo_shift
echo "arg1= $1     arg2= $2     arg3= $3"
shift
echo "arg1= $1     arg2= $2     arg3= $3"
shift
echo "arg1= $1     arg2= $2     arg3= $3"
shift
echo "arg1= $1     arg2= $2     arg3= $3"
shift
$ demo_shift alice helen jenny
arg1= alice     arg2= helen     arg3= jenny
arg1= helen     arg2= jenny     arg3=
arg1= jenny     arg2=     arg3=
arg1=     arg2=     arg3=
```

In the original Bourne Shell, the positional parameters were limited to **$1–$9**, so shell scripts that accepted more than nine arguments were forced to use shift to get to later arguments. The Bourne Again Shell has no limit on the number of positional parameters, so this use of shift has declined. However, repeatedly using shift is a convenient way to loop over all the command line arguments in shell scripts that expect an arbitrary number of arguments. See page 857 for a sample shell program that uses this technique.

set: Initializes Command Line Arguments

When you call the set builtin with one or more arguments, it uses the arguments as values for positional parameters, starting with **$1**. The following script uses set to assign values to the positional parameters **$1**, **$2**, and **$3**:

```
$ cat set_it
set this is it
echo $3 $2 $1
$ set_it
it is this
```

Combining the use of command substitution (page 281) with the set builtin is a convenient way to get standard output of a command in a form that can be easily manipulated in a shell script. The following script shows how to use date and set to provide the date in a useful format. The first command shows the output of date. Then cat displays the contents of the **dateset** script. The first command in the script uses command substitution to set the positional parameters to the output of the date utility. The next command, **echo $***, displays all the positional parameters resulting from the previous set. Subsequent commands display the values of parameters **$1**, **$2**, **$3**, and **$4**. The final command displays the date in a format you can use in a letter or report:

```
$ date
Tue Apr 30 08:46:39 PDT 2002
$ cat dateset
set $(date)
echo $*
echo
echo "Argument 1: $1"
echo "Argument 2: $2"
echo "Argument 3: $3"
echo "Argument 6: $6"
echo
echo "$2 $3, $6"
$ dateset
Tue Apr 30 08:46:42 PDT 2002

Argument 1: Tue
Argument 2: Apr
Argument 3: 30
Argument 6: 2002

Apr 30, 2002
```

You can also use the **format** argument to date to modify the format of its output. Refer to the date man page for more information.

Without any arguments, set displays a list of the shell variables that are set, including user-created variables and keyword variables. This is the same output that declare gives when invoked without any arguments.

The set builtin also accepts a number of options that let you customize the behavior of the shell. When you replace the hyphen with a plus sign before one of these options, set turns off the option. The value of many of these options should be clear now; others are explained in the remainder of this chapter. Some of the more useful options and their effects are listed in Table 9-2.

table 9-2 ||

set Options

–a	(allexport)	Marks variables that you create or modify for automatic export.
–f	(noglob)	Stops bash from doing filename expansion (globbing).
–n	(noexec)	Causes bash to read and perform expansions on commands but not to execute them. This option is useful if you want to check a shell script for syntax errors; it is ignored for interactive shells.
–t	(exit)	Reads and executes a single command and then quits.
–u	(nounset)	Returns an error when you try to expand a variable that is not set. When this option is not set, bash expands variables that have not been set to a null string. When this option is set, shell scripts terminate when the shell attempts to expand an unset variable; interactive shells display **unbound variable** and do not execute the current command.

Special Parameters

Special parameters make it possible to access useful values pertaining to command line arguments and the execution of shell commands. You reference a shell special parameter by preceding a special character with a dollar sign ($). As with positional parameters, it is not possible to modify the value of a special parameter.

$* and $@   Value of Command Line Arguments

The $* parameter represents all the command line arguments, as the **display_all** script on page 288 demonstrates. The $@ and $* parameters are the same, except when they are enclosed within double quotation marks. Using "$*" yields a single argument (with SPACES between the positional parameters), whereas "$@" produces a list wherein each positional parameter is a separate argument. This difference makes $@ more useful than $* in shell scripts, as the **whos** script on page 867 demonstrates.

$#   Number of Command Line Arguments

As the **showargs** script on page 288 and the following example demonstrate, the $# parameter contains the number of arguments on the command line. This string parameter represents a decimal number:

```
$ cat num_args
echo "This shell script was called
with $# arguments."
$ num_args helen alex jenny
This shell script was called
with 3 arguments.
```

You can use test to perform logical tests on this number (for more information on test, see page 853).

The echo builtin in the preceding example displays a quoted string that spans two lines. Because the NEWLINE is quoted, the shell passes the entire string that is between the quotation marks, including the NEWLINE, to echo as an argument.

$$ PID Number

The shell stores in the $$ parameter the PID number of the process that is executing it. In the following interaction, echo displays the value of this variable, and the ps utility confirms its value (ps lists a lot more processes if you are running X). Both commands show that the shell has a PID number of 5209:

```
$ echo $$
5209
$ ps
  PID TTY          TIME CMD
 5209 pts/1     00:00:00 bash
 6015 pts/1     00:00:00 ps
```

The echo builtin keeps the shell from having to create another process when you give an echo command. However, the results are the same whether echo is a builtin or not, because the shell substitutes the value of $$ *before* it forks a new process to run a command. In the following example, the shell substitutes the value of $$ and passes that value to cp as a prefix for a new filename:

```
$ echo $$
8232
$ cp memo $$.memo
$ ls
8232.memo memo
```

This technique is useful for creating unique filenames when the meanings of the names do not matter; it is often used in shell scripts for creating names of temporary files. When two people are running the same shell script, these unique filenames keep them from inadvertently sharing the same temporary file.

The following example demonstrates that the shell creates a new shell process when it runs a shell script. The **id2** script displays the PID numbers of the process running it (not the process that called it; the substitution for $$ is performed by the shell that is forked to run **id2**):

```
$ cat id2
echo "$0 PID= $$"
$ echo $$
8232
$ id2
id2 PID= 8362
$ echo $$
8232
```

The first echo in the preceding example displays the PID number of the login shell. Then **id2** displays its name ($0) and the PID of the subshell that it is running in. The last echo shows that the current process is the login shell again.

The Bourne Again Shell stores the value of the PID number of the last process that you ran in the background in $!. The following example executes sleep as a background task and then uses echo to display the value of $!:

```
$ sleep 60 &
8376
$ echo $!
8376
```

$?   Exit Status

When a process stops executing for any reason, it returns an *exit status* to its parent process. The exit status is also referred to as a *condition code,* or *return code.* The $? variable stores the exit status of the last command.

By convention, a nonzero exit status represents a *false* value and means that the command failed. A zero is *true* and means that the command was successful. In the following example, the first ls command succeeds, whereas the second fails:

```
$ ls es
es
$ echo $?
0
$ ls xxx
ls: xxx: No such file or directory
$ echo $?
2
```

You can specify the exit status that a shell script returns by using the exit builtin, followed by a number, to terminate the script. If you do not use exit with a number to terminate a script, the exit status of the script is that of the last command the script ran. The following example shows that the number following the word **exit** specifies the exit status:

```
$ cat es
echo This program returns an exit status of 7.
exit 7
$ es
This program returns an exit status of 7.
$ echo $?
7
$ echo $?
0
```

The es shell script displays a message and then terminates execution with an exit command that returns an exit status of 7, the user-defined exit status in this script. Then echo displays the value of the exit status of es. The second echo displays the value of the exit status of the first echo. The value is zero because the first echo was successful.

You can include the exit status of the previous command as part of the shell prompt (page 284):

```
$ PS1='$ [$?] '
$ [0] ls xxx
ls: xxx: No such file or directory
$ [1] pwd
/home/mgs
$ [0]
```

History

The history mechanism, a feature adapted from the C Shell, maintains a list of recently issued command lines, also called *events*, providing a quick way to reexecute any of the events in the list. This mechanism also enables you to execute variations of previous commands and to reuse arguments from them. You can replicate complicated commands and arguments that you used earlier in this login session or in a previous one and enter a series of commands that differ from one another in minor ways. The history list is also useful as a record of what you have done. It can be helpful when you have made a mistake and are not sure what you did or when you want to keep a record of a procedure that involved a series of commands. The history builtin displays your history list. If it does not, read on; you need to set some variables.

tip || history **Can Help Track Down Mistakes**

When you have made a command line mistake (not an error within a script or program) and are not sure what you did wrong, you can look at the history list to review your recent commands. Sometimes this list can help you figure out what went wrong and how to fix things.

The value of the **HISTSIZE** variable determines the number of events preserved in the history list during a session. Although the default value for **HISTSIZE** is 500, you may want to set it to a more convenient value, such as 100.

When you exit from the shell, the most recently executed commands are saved in the file given by the **HISTFILE** variable (the default is **.bash_history** in your home directory). The next time you start the shell, this file initializes the history list. The value of the **HISTFILESIZE** variable (default 500) determines the number of lines of history saved in **HISTFILE** (not necessarily the same as **HISTSIZE**). **HISTSIZE** holds the number of events remembered during a session, **HISTFILESIZE** holds the number remembered between sessions, and file designated by **HISTFILE** holds the name of the file that holds the history list. See Table 9-3.

table 9-3 || **History Variables**

Function	Variable	Default
Maximum number of events saved during a session	HISTSIZE	500 events
Location of the history file	HISTFILE	**~/.bash_history**
Maximum number of events saved between sessions	HISTFILESIZE	500 events

The Bourne Again Shell assigns a sequential *event number* to each of your command lines. You can display this event number as part of the bash prompt (refer to "PS1: User Prompt (Primary)" on page 284). Examples in this section show numbered prompts when they help to illustrate the behavior of a command or group of commands.

Give the following command manually, or place it in your **.bash_profile** or **.profile** startup file (to affect all future sessions) to establish a history list of the 100 most recent events:

```
$ HISTSIZE=100
```

The following command causes bash to save the 100 most recent events across login sessions:

```
$ HISTFILESIZE=100
```

After you set **HISTFILESIZE**, you can log out and log in again, and the 100 most recent events from the previous login session appear in your history list.

Give the command **history** to display the events in the history list. The list of events is ordered from oldest events at the top of the list to the most recent at the bottom. The last event in the history list is the **history** command that displayed the list. The following history list includes a command to modify the bash prompt to display the history event number as well as the command number. To simplify the example, **HISTSIZE** has been set to the value 10 and **HISTFILESIZE** to 20. (The event number is 20 greater than the command number because the list of events includes those events that were saved from the last login session—20 in this case.)

```
32 $ history
   23   PS1="\! \# bash\$ "
   24   ls -l
   25   cat temp
   26   rm temp
   27   vi memo
   28   lpr memo
   29   vi memo
   30   lpr memo
   31   rm memo
   32   history
```

As you run commands and your history list becomes longer, it runs off the top of the screen when you use the history builtin. Pipe the output of history through less (page 120) to browse through it, or give the command **history 10** to look at the last ten commands the shell executed.

Editing the Command Line

You can reexecute any event in the history list. This feature can save you time, effort, and aggravation. Not having to reenter long command lines allows you to reexecute events more easily, quickly, and accurately than you could if you had to retype the entire command line. You can recall, modify, and reexecute previously executed events in three ways: You can use the fc builtin (covered next); the C Shell history mechanism (page 298); or the Readline Library, which uses a one-line vi- or emacs-like editor to edit and execute events (page 301).

fc: Displays, Edits, and Reexecutes Commands

The fc (fix command) builtin enables you to display the history file and to edit and reexecute previous commands. It provides many of the same capabilities as the command line editors.

Viewing the History List

When you call it with the **–l** option, **fc** displays commands from the history file on standard output. Without any arguments, **fc –l** lists the 16 most recent commands in a numbered list. The list of events is ordered from the oldest events at the top of the list to the most recent events at the bottom:

```
$ fc -l
190   lpr memor.0795
191   lpr memo.0795
192   mv memo.0795 memo.071195
193   cd
194   view calendar
195   cd Work
196   vi letter.adams01
197   aspell -c letter.adams01
198   nroff letter.admas01 > adams.out
199   nroff letter.adams01 > adams.out
200   less adams.out
201   lpr adams.out
202   rm adams.out
203   cd ../memos
204   ls
205   rm *0486
```

The **fc** builtin can take zero, one, or two arguments with the **–l** option. The arguments specify a part of the history list to be displayed. The syntax is

*fc –l [**first** [**last**]]*

The **fc** builtin lists commands beginning with the most recent event that matches the first argument. The argument can be the number of the event, the first few characters of the command line, or a negative number, which is taken to be the *n*th previous command. If you provide a second argument, **fc** displays all commands from the most recent event that matches the first argument through the most recent event that matches the second. The next command displays the history list from event 197 through event 205:

```
$ fc -l 197 205
197   aspell -c letter.adams01
198   nroff letter.admas01 > adams.out
199   nroff letter.adams01 > adams.out
200   less adams.out
201   lpr adams.out
202   rm adams.out
203   cd ../memos
204   ls
205   rm *0486
```

The following command lists the most recent event that begins with the string **view** through the most recent command line that begins with the letters **asp**:

```
$ fc -l view asp
194   view calendar
195   cd Work
```

```
196  vi letter.adams01
197  aspell -c letter.adams01
```

To list a single command from the history file, use the same identifier for the first and second arguments. The following command lists event 197:

```
$ fc -l 197 197
197  aspell -c letter.adams01
```

Editing and Reexecuting Previous Commands

You can use fc to edit and reexecute previous commands.

fc [-e editor] [first [last]]

When you call fc with the –e option followed by the name of an editor, fc calls the editor with event(s) in the Work Buffer. Without *first* and *last*, fc defaults to the most recent command. The next example invokes the vi editor to edit the most recent command:

```
$ fc -e vi
```

The fc builtin uses the stand-alone vi editor. If you set the **FCEDIT** variable, you do not need to use the –e option to specify an editor on the command line. Because the value of **FCEDIT** has been changed to **/usr/bin/pico** and fc has no arguments, the following command edits the most recent command with the pico editor.

```
$ export FCEDIT=/usr/bin/pico
$ fc
```

If you call it with a single argument, fc invokes the editor on the specified command. The following example starts the editor with event 21 in the Work Buffer. When you exit from the editor, the shell automatically executes the command:

```
$ fc 21
```

Again, you can identify commands with numbers or by specifying the first few characters of the command name. The following example calls the editor to work on events from the most recent event that begins with the letters **vi** through event number 206:

```
$ fc vi 206
```

caution ‖   **Clean Up the fc Buffer**

When you execute an fc command, the shell executes whatever you leave in the editor buffer, possibly with unwanted results. If you decide you do not want to execute a command, delete everything from the buffer before you leave the editor.

Reexecuting Commands Without Calling the Editor

You can reexecute previous commands without going into an editor. If you call fc with the –s option, it skips the editing phase and reexecutes the command. The following example reexecutes event 201:

```
$ fc -s 201
lpr adams.out
```

The next example reexecutes the previous command:

```
$ fc -s
```

When you reexecute a command, such as lpr in the previous example, you can tell fc to substitute one string for another. The next example substitutes the string **john** for the string **adams** in event 201 and executes the modified event:

```
$ fc -s adams=john 201
lpr john.out
```

Reexecuting an Event with the C Shell History Mechanism

The C Shell history mechanism, is frequently more cumbersome to use than fc, but it has some features you may want to use. For example, the **!!** command reexecutes the previous event, and the **!$** token represents the last word on the previous command line.

You can reference an event using C Shell commands in three ways: by its absolute event number, by its number relative to the current event, or by the text it contains. All references to events begin with an exclamation point (!). One or more characters follow the exclamation point to specify an event.

!!   Reexecutes the Previous Event

You can always reexecute the previous event by giving the **!!** command. In the following example, event 45 reexecutes event 44:

```
44 $ ls -l text
-rw-rw-r--    1 alex       group             45 Apr 30 14:53 text
45 $ !!
ls -l text
-rw-rw-r--    1 alex       group             45 Apr 30 14:53 text
```

This works whether or not your prompt displays an event number. As this example shows, when you use the history mechanism to reexecute an event, the shell displays the command it is reexecuting.

!n   Event Number

A number following an exclamation point refers to an event. If that event is in the history list, the shell executes it. If it is not in the history list, the shell gives you an error message. A negative number following an exclamation point references an event relative to the current event. The command **!–3** refers to the third preceding event. After you issue a command, the relative event number of a given event changes (event –3 becomes event –4). Both of the following commands reexecute event 44:

```
51 $ !44
ls -l text
-rw-rw-r--    1 alex      group            45 Nov 30 14:53 text
52 $ !-8
ls -l text
-rw-rw-r--    1 alex      group            45 Nov 30 14:53 text
```

!string   Event Text

When a string of text follows an exclamation point, the shell searches for and executes the most recent event that *began* with that string. If you enclose the string between question marks, the shell executes the most recent event that *contained* that string. The final question mark is optional if a RETURN would immediately follow it:

```
68 $ history
    59  ls -l text*    60   tail text5
    61  cat text1 text5 > letter
    62  vi letter
    63  cat letter
    64  cat memo
    65  lp memo
    66   jenny
    67  ls -l
    68  history
69 $ !1
ls -l
    .
    .
    .
70 $ !lp
lp memo
request id is printer_1-1016 (1 file)
71 $ !?letter?
cat letter
    .
    .
    .
```

optional ‖

!n:w   Word Within an Event

You can select any word or series of words from an event. The words are numbered starting with 0, representing the first word (usually the command) on the line, and continuing with 1, representing the first word following the command, through *n*, representing the last word on the line.

To specify a particular word from a previous event, follow the event designator (such as !14) with a colon and the number of the word in the previous event (for example, use !14:3 to specify the third word following the command from event 14). You can specify a range of words by separating two word designators with a hyphen. The first word following the command (word number 1) can be specified by a caret (^), and the last word by a dollar sign ($):

```
72 $ echo apple grape orange pear
apple grape orange pear
73 $ echo !72:2
echo grape
grape
74 $ echo !72:^
echo apple
apple
75 $ !72:0 !72:$
echo pear
pear
76 $ echo !72:2-4
echo grape orange pear
grape orange pear
77 $ !72:0-$
echo apple grape orange pear
apple grape orange pear
```

As the next example shows, !$ refers to the last word of the previous event. You can use this shorthand to edit, for example, a file you just displayed with cat:

```
$ cat report.718
...
$ vi !$
vi report.718
...
```

If an event contains a single command, the word numbers correspond to the argument numbers. If an event contains more than one command, this correspondence is not true for commands after the first. Event 78, following, contains two commands separated by a semicolon so that the shell executes them sequentially; the semicolon is word number 5.

```
78 $ !72 ; echo helen jenny barbara
echo apple grape orange pear ; echo helen jenny barbara
apple grape orange pear
helen jenny barbara
79 $ echo !78:7
echo helen
helen
80 $ echo !78:4-7
echo pear ; echo helen
pear
helen
```

!!:s/new/old   Modifies the Previous Event

On occasion, you may want to change an aspect of an event you are reexecuting. Perhaps you entered a complex command line with a typo or incorrect pathname, or you may want to specify a different argument in the reexecuted command. You can modify an event or a word of an event by following the event or word specifier with a colon and a modifier. The following example shows the substitute modifier correcting a typo in the previous event:

```
$ car /home/jenny/memo.0507 /home/alex/letter.0507
bash: car: command not found
$ !!:s/car/cat
cat /home/jenny/memo.0507 /home/alex/letter.0507
...
```

^old^new   Performs a Quick Substitution

An abbreviated form of the substitute modifier is the *quick substitution*. Use it to reexecute the most recent event while changing some of the event text. The quick substitution character is the caret (^). For example, this command

```
$ ^old^new^
```

produces the same results as

```
$ !!:s/old/new/
```

Thus substituting **cat** for **car** in the previous event could have been entered as

```
$ ^car^cat
cat /home/jenny/memo.0507 /home/alex/letter.0507
...
```

As with other command line substitutions, the shell displays the command line as it appears after the substitution. You can omit the final caret if it would be followed immediately by a RETURN. See Table 9-4 for a list of event modifiers and their effects.

table 9-4 ‖		Event Modifier
h		Removes the last element of a pathname
r (root)		Removes the filename extension
e (extension)		Removes all but the filename extension
t (tail)		Removes all elements of a pathname except the last
p (print)		Does not execute the modified event, just prints it
[g]s/*old*/*new*/ (substitute)		Substitutes *new* for the first occurrence of *old*; with the **g** option, substitutes all occurrences[a]

a. The **s** modifier substitutes the *first* occurrence of the old string with the new one. Placing a **g** before the **s** (as in **gs**/*old*/*new*/) causes a global substitution, replacing *all* occurrences of the old string. The **/** is the delimiter in these examples; you can use any character that is not in either the old or the new string. The final delimiter is optional if a RETURN would immediately follow it. Like the vi Substitute command, the history mechanism replaces an ampersand (**&**) in the new string with the old string. The shell replaces a null old string (**s**//*new*/) with the previous old string or string within a command that you searched for with **?***string***?**.

The Readline Library

The Bourne Again Shell's command line editing has been implemented through a package developed by the Free Software Foundation: the *Readline Library* (named after the bash readline function). This library is available to application writers using the C programming language for use in their applications. Any application that uses the Readline Library supports line editing consistent with that provided in bash.

You can choose one of two basic modes when using this type of command line editing in bash: emacs or vi. Both modes provide you with many of the commands available in these editors. The default mode is emacs, but you can switch to vi mode interactively in bash with the command

```
$ set -o vi
```

To switch back to emacs mode, give the command

```
$ set -o emacs
```

Familiarity with emacs makes it easy to use the emacs-like editing keystrokes, and the notation used in the documentation is similar. There is also the familiar concepts of a kill ring and yanking to reinsert text, both of which are present in emacs. Your keyboard keys have been bound to the commands available for command line editing. You can change these bindings in the .inputrc file in your home directory. Any application that uses the Readline Library first reads .inputrc, if it exists, to set the initial command bindings and any special configuration settings. See page 303 for more information about using .inputrc.

Use **bind –v** to see what key bindings are in effect. This command displays a list of all the available commands, and, if a command has been bound to a sequence of keystrokes, it also displays this sequence. The emacs mode is used in this discussion.

Basic Readline Commands

A number of categories of commands match those needed for general text editing:

- Moving back and forth in a command line
- Moving up and down through the history list
- Changing, deleting, and replacing text
- Undoing and redoing changes

Most of the commonly used emacs (or vi) commands for these operations are available, and you should experiment with those you have used to see how they work. You can also use the ARROW keys to move around. Up and down movements move you backward and forward through your history list.

Completion

You can use the TAB key to complete words you are entering on the command line. This facility is called *completion*. The type of completion depends on what you are typing.

If you are typing the name of a command (the first word on the command line), pressing TAB results in *command completion;* bash looks for a command whose name starts with the part of the word you have typed. If there is one, bash completes the rest of the command name for you. If there is more than one choice, bash beeps. Pressing TAB a second time causes bash to display a list of commands whose names start with the prefix you have typed and allows you to finish typing the command name.

If you are typing a filename, using TAB performs *filename completion*. If it can determine unambiguously what the name is, bash types the rest of the filename for you. As with command completion, you can use a second TAB to list alternatives. When typing in a variable name, pressing TAB results in *variable completion*, where bash tries to complete the name of the variable for you.

If you want to see a list of the possible completions at any time while you are entering a command, press ESCAPE ?.

Miscellaneous Commands

Table 9-5 lists some other useful Readline commands.

table 9-5 ‖	Miscellaneous Readline Commands
ESCAPE ~	The tilde-expand command tries to expand the current word into the name of a user that starts with that prefix. For example, typing **sc**TAB would result in **scott** if that is the only username that starts with **sc** on your system.
ESCAPE ^	The history-expand-line command performs history expansion on all history events in the current line.
ESCAPE-CONTROL-e	The shell-expand-line command does a full expansion on the current line, just as bash does when preparing to execute a command. The shell even performs alias and history expansions.

.inputrc

The Bourne Again Shell and other programs that use the Readline Library read **.inputrc** from your home directory for initialization information. This file is the default used if the **INPUTRC** environment variable is not set. If **INPUTRC** is set, its value is used as the name of the initialization file.

You can set variables in **.inputrc** to control the behavior of the Readline Library, using the following syntax:

    set *variable value*

Choose *variable* from the (partial) list in Table 9-6.

In addition to setting variables, you can specify bindings that map keystroke sequences to Readline commands, allowing you to change or extend the default

table 9-6 ‖	Readline Variables
editing-mode	Set to **vi** to start Readline in vi mode. Setting it to **emacs** starts Readline in emacs mode, which is the default.
expand-tilde	Set to **on** to cause Readline to perform tilde expansion whenever it tries to complete a word. Normally it is **off**.
horizontal-scroll-mode	Set to **on** to cause long lines to extend off the edge of the display area. Moving the cursor to the right when you are at the edge shifts the line to the left so you can see more of the line. You can shift the line back by moving the cursor back past the left edge. The default value is **off**, which causes long lines to be wrapped onto multiple lines of the display.
mark-modified-lines	Set to **on** to cause Readline to precede modified history lines with an asterisk. The default value is **off**.

bindings. As with emacs, Readline includes many commands that start with no binding to any keystroke sequence. To use any of these unbound commands, you must give a mapping, using one of the following two forms:

> *keyname: command_name*
> *"keystroke_sequence" : command_name*

In the first form, spell out the name for a single key. For example, CONTROL-u would be written as **control-u**. This form is useful for binding commands to single keys.

In the second form, you can give a string that describes a sequence of keys that are to be bound to the command. You can use the emacs-style escape sequences to represent the special keys CONTROL (\C), META (\M), and ESCAPE (\e). A backslash can be used by escaping it with another backslash, as in \\. Similarly, a double or single quotation mark can be escaped with a backslash, as in \" or \'.

Give the following command to bind the kill-whole-line command, which by default is unbound, to the keystroke sequence ESCAPE [11~:

```
"\e[11~": kill-whole-line
```

Because F1 (function key 1) generates this keystroke sequence (on the console running as terminal type **linux**), this binding turns F1 into a line-kill command key.

You can also bind text by enclosing it within double quotation marks:

```
"\e[12~": "The Linux Operating System"
```

This command inserts the string **The Linux Operating System** (without surrounding quotation marks) whenever you press F2.

Lines of **.inputrc** that are blank or that start with a pound sign (#) are treated as comments and are ignored.

Finally, you can conditionally select parts of the **.inputrc** file by using the **$if** directive. You can supply a test with this directive; the lines following the directive are used if the test is true. Otherwise, these lines, up to a **$else** or **$endif**, are ignored.

The **$else** directive works as you might expect: If the test used with the previous **$if** directive is false, the lines following the **$else** (up to a **$endif**) are used; otherwise, these lines are ignored.

The power of the **$if** directive lies in the three types of tests it can perform.

1. You can test to see which mode is currently set.

   `$if mode=vi`

   is *true* if the current Readline mode is vi and *false* otherwise.

2. You can test the type of terminal.

   `$if term=xterm`

   is *true* if you are using an xterm window.

3. You can test the application name.

   `$if bash`

   is *true* when you are running bash and not another program that uses the Readline Library.

All uses of **$if** should end with the **$endif** directive. These tests can customize the Readline Library based on the current mode, the type of terminal, and the application you are using. This gives you a great deal of power and flexibility when using the Readline Library with bash and with other programs.

Alias

The alias mechanism allows you to define new commands by letting you substitute any string for any command. The syntax of the alias builtin is

alias [name[=value]]

There are no SPACEs around the equal sign. If *value* contains SPACEs or TABs, you must enclose *value* within quotation marks. The alias mechanism is disabled for noninteractive shells (that is, shell scripts).

An alias cannot be recursive: The **name** of the alias may not appear within the **value** of the alias you are defining. You can nest aliases. To see a list of the current aliases, give the command **alias**. To view the alias for a particular name, use alias followed by the name and nothing else.

Quotation Marks: Single versus Double

Use of either double or single quotation marks is significant in the alias syntax. If you enclose *value* within double quotation marks, any variables that appear in *value* are expanded when the alias is created. If you enclose *value* within single quotation marks, variables are not expanded until the alias is used. The following example shows the difference:

```
$ alias p1="echo my prompt is $PS1"
$ alias p2='echo my prompt is $PS1'
$ PS1=">>>>>>>>>>>>>> "
>>>>>>>>>>>>>> p1
my prompt is $
>>>>>>>>>>>>>> p2
my prompt is >>>>>>>>>>>>>>
>>>>>>>>>>>>>>
```

Examples

You can use alias to create short names for commands that you use often. For example, the following alias allows you to type **r** to repeat the previous command or **r abc** to repeat the last command line that began with **abc**:

```
$ alias r='fc -s'
```

> **tip ‖**   **Prevent the Shell from Invoking an Alias**
>
> The shell checks only simple, unquoted commands to see if they are aliases. Commands given as relative or absolute pathnames and quoted commands are not checked. When you want to give a command that has an alias but do not want to use the alias, precede the command with a backslash, specify the command's absolute pathname, or give the command as *./command*.

If you use the command **ls –ltr** frequently, you can use the alias builtin to substitute **ls –ltr** when you give the command **l**:

```
$ alias l='ls -ltr'
$ l
total 41
-rw-r--r--   1 alex     group      30015 Mar  1 2002 flute.ps
-rw-r-----   1 alex     group       3089 Feb 11 2003 XTerm.ad
-rw-r--r--   1 alex     group        641 Apr  1 2003 fixtax.icn
-rw-r--r--   1 alex     group        484 Apr  9 2003 maptax.icn
drwxrwxr-x   2 alex     group       1024 Aug  9 17:41 Tiger/
drwxrwxr-x   2 alex     group       1024 Sep 10 11:32 testdir/
-rwxr-xr-x   1 alex     group        485 Oct 21 08:03 floor*
drwxrwxr-x   2 alex     group       1024 Oct 27 20:19 Test_Emacs/
```

Another common use of the alias mechanism is to protect yourself from mistakes. The following example uses an alias to substitute the interactive version of the rm utility when you give the command **zap**:

```
$ alias zap='rm -i'
$ zap f*
rm: remove 'fixtax.icn'? n
rm: remove 'flute.ps'? n
rm: remove 'floor'? n
```

The **–i** option causes rm to ask you to verify each file that would be deleted, to protect you from accidentally deleting the wrong file.

In the next example, alias causes the shell to substitute **ls –l** every time you give an **ll** command and **ls –F** when you use **ls:**

```
$ ls
Test_Emacs XTerm.ad  flute.ps  testdir
Tiger      fixtax.icn maptax.icn
$ alias ls='ls -F'
$ alias ll='ls -l'
$ ll
total 41
drwxrwxr-x  2 alex    group     1024 Oct 27 20:19 Test_Emacs/
drwxrwxr-x  2 alex    group     1024 Aug 9 17:41 Tiger/
-rw-r-----  1 alex    group     3089 Feb 11 2003 XTerm.ad
-rw-r--r--  1 alex    group      641 Apr 1 2003 fixtax.icn
-rw-r--r--  1 alex    group    30015 Mar 1 2002 flute.ps
-rwxr-xr-x  1 alex    group      485 Oct 21 08:03 floor*
-rw-r--r--  1 alex    group      484 Apr 9 2003 maptax.icn
drwxrwxr-x  2 alex    group     1024 Sep 10 11:32 testdir/
```

The **–F** option causes ls to print a slash (/) at the end of directory names and an asterisk (✻) at the end of the names of executable files. In this example, the string that replaces the alias **ll**, **ls –l**, itself contains an alias, **ls**. When it replaces an alias with its value, the shell looks at the first word of the replacement string to see whether it is an alias. In the preceding example, the replacement string contains the alias **ls**, so a second substitution occurs to produce the final command **ls –F –l**. (To avoid a *recursive plunge,* the **ls** in the replacement text, although an alias, is not expanded a second time.)

When given a list of aliases without the *=value* or *value* field, the alias builtin responds by displaying the value of each defined alias. The alias builtin reports an error if an alias has not been defined:

```
$ alias ll ls wx
alias ll='ls -l'
alias ls='ls -F'
alias: 'wx' not found
```

When you give an alias builtin without any arguments, the shell displays a list of all the defined aliases:

```
$ alias
alias ll='ls -l'
alias l='ls -ltr'
alias ls='ls -F'
alias zap='rm -i'
```

You can avoid alias substitution by preceding the aliased command with a backslash (\):

```
$ \ls
Test_Emacs XTerm.ad  flute.ps  maptax.icn
Tiger      fixtax.icn floor     testdir
```

Because the replacement of an alias name with the alias value does not change the rest of the command line, any arguments are still received by the command that gets executed:

```
$ ll f*
-rw-r--r--  1 alex    group        641 Apr  1 2003 fixtax.icn
-rw-r--r--  1 alex    group      30015 Mar  1 2002 flute.ps
-rwxr-xr-x  1 alex    group        485 Oct 21 08:03 floor*
```

You can remove an alias with the unalias builtin. When the **zap** alias is removed, it is no longer displayed with the alias builtin, and its subsequent use results in an error message:

```
$ unalias zap
$ alias
alias ll='ls -l'
alias l='ls -ltr'
alias ls='ls -F'
$ zap maptax.icn
bash: zap: command not found
```

Command Line Expansion

Before passing the command line to the program being called, the shell transforms the command line by using *command line expansion*. The shell also expands each line of a shell script as the shell executes the script. You can use a shell without knowing much about command line expansion, but you can make much better use of what it has to offer with an understanding of this topic.

Chapter 7 discussed one aspect of command line expansion in "Filename Generation/Pathname Expansion" on page 207. The following sections review several types of command line expansion you may be familiar with and introduce some new ones that bash uses. These sections also discuss the order in which the shell performs the various expansions and provide some examples. (Although bash provides history [page 293] and alias [page 305] expansion, they are not included in the following discussion because they are available only in interactive shells and therefore cannot be used in shell scripts.)

When the shell processes a command, it does not execute the command immediately. One of the first things the shell does is to *parse* (isolate strings of characters in) the command line into tokens or words. The shell then proceeds to scan each token for special characters and patterns that instruct the shell to take certain actions. These actions often involve substituting one word or words for another. When the shell parses the following command line, it breaks it into three tokens (**cp**, **~/letter**, and **.**):

```
$ cp ~/letter .
```

After separating tokens and before executing the command, the shell scans the tokens and performs *command line expansion*. You have seen many examples of command line expansion in this and previous chapters; a frequent one is the substitution of a list of filenames for an ambiguous file reference that includes any of the characters *, ?, [, and].

Order of Expansion

The Bourne Again Shell scans each token for the various types of expansion in the following order:

1. Brace expansion (page 309)

2. Tilde expansion (page 311)

3. Parameter expansion (page 311)

4. Variable expansion (page 312)

5. Command substitution (page 312)

6. Arithmetic expansion (page 313)

7. Word splitting (page 314)

8. Pathname expansion (page 315)

The order in which the various expansions take place is important; if the shell performed the expansions in a different order, a dramatically different result could occur. In the following example, if pathname expansion occurred prior to variable expansion, the asterisk (✳) would not be treated specially; after expansion, the argument given to echo would be **tmp✳**, and that would be the output of echo:

```
$ ls
tmp1 tmp2 tmp3
$ var=tmp✳
$ echo $var
tmp1 tmp2 tmp3
```

It is important to keep in mind that double and single quotation marks cause the shell to behave differently when performing expansions (page 275). Double quotation marks permit parameter and variable expansion but suppress other types of expansion. Single quotation marks suppress all types of expansion.

{}   Brace Expansion

Brace expansion, which originated in the original C Shell, provides a convenient way to specify filenames when pathname expansion does not apply. Although brace expansion is almost always used to specify filenames, the mechanism can be used to generate arbitrary strings; the shell does not attempt to match the brace notation with a list of the names of existing files. The following example illustrates the way that brace expansion works:

```
$ ls
$ echo chap_{one,two,three}.txt
chap_one.txt chap_two.txt chap_three.txt
```

The ls command shows that no files are in the working directory. The shell expands the comma-separated strings inside the braces into a SPACE-separated list of strings. Each string from the list is prepended with the string **chap_**, called the *preamble*, and appended with the string **.txt**, called the *postamble*. Both preamble and postamble are optional, and the left-to-right order of the strings within the braces is preserved in the expansion. For the shell to treat the left and right braces specially and for brace expansion to occur, at least one comma must be inside the braces with no unquoted whitespace characters. Brace expansions may be nested.

Brace expansion is useful when there is a long preamble or postamble. The following example copies the four files **main.c**, **f1.c**, **f2.c**, and **tmp.c**, which are located in the **/usr/local/src/C** directory, to the working directory:

```
$ cp /usr/local/src/C/{main,f1,f2,tmp}.c .
```

Brace expansion can also create directories with related names. Because the directories do not already exist, pathname expansion does not work in this case:

```
$ ls -l
total 3
-rw-rw-r--  1 alex     group         14 Jan 22 08:54 file1
-rw-rw-r--  1 alex     group         14 Jan 22 08:54 file2
-rw-rw-r--  1 alex     group         14 Jan 22 08:55 file3
$ mkdir version{A,B,C,D,E}
$ ls -l
total 8
-rw-rw-r--  1 alex     group         14 Jan 22 08:54 file1
-rw-rw-r--  1 alex     group         14 Jan 22 08:54 file2
-rw-rw-r--  1 alex     group         14 Jan 22 08:55 file3
drwxrwxr-x  2 alex     group       1024 Jan 25 13:27 versionA
drwxrwxr-x  2 alex     group       1024 Jan 25 13:27 versionB
drwxrwxr-x  2 alex     group       1024 Jan 25 13:27 versionC
drwxrwxr-x  2 alex     group       1024 Jan 25 13:27 versionD
drwxrwxr-x  2 alex     group       1024 Jan 25 13:27 versionE
```

If ambiguous file reference notation had been used to specify the directories instead of the preceding notation, the result would be very different (and not what was desired):

```
$ ls -l
total 3
-rw-rw-r--  1 alex     group         14 Jan 22 08:54 file1
-rw-rw-r--  1 alex     group         14 Jan 22 08:54 file2
-rw-rw-r--  1 alex     group         14 Jan 22 08:55 file3
$ mkdir version[A-E]
$ ls -l
total 4
-rw-rw-r--  1 alex     group         14 Jan 22 08:54 file1
-rw-rw-r--  1 alex     group         14 Jan 22 08:54 file2
-rw-rw-r--  1 alex     group         14 Jan 22 08:55 file3
drwxrwxr-x  2 alex     group       1024 Jan 25 13:38 version[A-E]
```

Because it found no filenames matching **version[A-E]**, the shell passed that string to mkdir, which created a directory with that name.

Braces are also useful to distinguish a variable from surrounding text without the use of a separator (for example, a SPACE):

```
$ prefix=Alex
$ echo $prefix is short for ${prefix}ander.
Alex is short for Alexander.
```

Without braces **prefix** would have to be separated from **ander** with a SPACE so that the shell would recognize **prefix** as a variable. This change would cause **Alexander** to become **Alex ander**.

~   Tilde Expansion

Chapter 6, page 171 showed a shorthand notation to specify your home directory or the home directory of another user. This section provides a more detailed explanation of *tilde expansion*.

The tilde (~) is a special character when it appears at the start of a token on a command line. When it sees this type of tilde, the shell looks at the following string of characters—up to the first slash (/) or to the end of the word if there is no slash—as a possible login name. If this possible login name is null (that is, if the tilde appeared as a word by itself or if it was immediately followed by a slash), the shell substitutes the value of the **HOME** variable for the tilde. In other words, the shell expands the tilde into the value of **HOME**. The following example demonstrates this substitution or expansion, with the last command copying the file named **letter** from Alex's home directory to the working directory:

```
$ echo $HOME
/home/alex
$ echo ~
/home/alex
$ echo ~/letter
/home/alex/letter
$ cp ~/letter .
```

If a string of characters forms a valid login name, the shell substitutes the path of the home directory associated with that login name for the tilde and name. If it is not null and not a valid login name, the shell does not make any substitution:

```
$ echo ~jenny
/home/jenny
$ echo ~root
/root
$ echo ~xx
~xx
```

$*n*   Parameter Expansion

Parameter expansion occurs when the shell replaces a dollar sign followed by one or more digits with the value of the positional parameter corresponding to the digits in the token.[5] Another type of parameter expansion occurs when a special character

---

5. In bash when you reference parameters greater than 9, the integer must be enclosed in braces, as in ${14}.

follows a dollar sign, in which case an aspect of the command or its arguments is substituted for the token (page 291).

$VARIABLE   Variable Expansion

Variable expansion takes place when the shell processes a token consisting of a dollar sign ($) followed by a variable name (user-defined or keyword), as in *$VARIABLE*, the token, where *VARIABLE* is the name of a variable that the shell replaces with the value of the variable.

optional ‖

The **$VARIABLE** syntax is a special case of the more general syntax **${VARIABLE}**, in which the variable name is enclosed by ${}. The braces insulate the variable name from what surrounds it. Braces are necessary when catenating a variable value with a string:

```
$ PREF=counter
$ WAY=$PREFclockwise
$ FAKE=$PREFfeit
$ echo $WAY $FAKE

$
```

The preceding example does not work as planned. Only a blank line is output. The reason is that the symbols **PREFclockwise** and **PREFfeit** are valid variable names, but they are not set. By default, the shell evaluates an unset variable as an empty (null) string and displays this value. To achieve the intent of these statements, refer to the **PREF** variable using braces:

```
$ PREF=counter
$ WAY=${PREF}clockwise
$ FAKE=${PREF}feit
$ echo $WAY $FAKE
counterclockwise counterfeit
```

$(...)   Command Substitution

Command substitution (page 281) allows you to use standard output of a command inline within a shell script. (Another way of using standard output is to send it to a file and read it back in.) Command substitution is another type of command line expansion that occurs after the tokens on the command line have been identified. The preferred syntax for command substitution is

>   *$(command)*

This notation instructs the shell to replace the token with standard output of *command*. To use standard output of *command*, the shell must first run *command* successfully.

Arithmetic Expansion

The shell performs *arithmetic expansion* by evaluating an arithmetic expression and then replacing it with the result. The syntax for arithmetic expansion is

$[expression]

The rules for forming an expression are the same as those found in the C programming language; all standard C arithmetic operators are available. Arithmetic in bash is done using integers, although often the shell must convert string-valued variables to integers for the purpose of the arithmetic evaluation.

The following example uses arithmetic expansion and command substitution to estimate the number of pages required to print the contents of the file **letter.txt**. The dollar sign and parentheses instruct the shell to perform command substitution; the dollar sign and brackets indicate arithmetic expansion:

```
$ echo $[$(wc -l letter.txt | cut -c1-7)/66 + 1]
6
```

The output of the wc utility with the –l option is the number of lines in the file, in columns 1 through 7, followed by a SPACE and the name of the file (the first command in the following example). The cut utility with the –c option extracts the first seven columns (the second command). Arithmetic expansion is then used to divide this count by 66, the number of lines in a page. A 1 is added at the end because the integer division results in any remainder being discarded (refer to the preceding example):

```
$ wc -l letter.txt
    351 letter.txt
$ wc -l letter.txt | cut -c1-7
    351
```

Refer to the cut and wc man pages for more information.

Another way to get the same result without using cut is to redirect the input to wc instead of having wc get its input from a file you name on the command line. When you redirect the input, wc does not display the name of the file:

```
$ wc -l < letter.txt
    351
```

It is common to assign the result of arithmetic expansion to a variable, as in

```
$ numpages=$[ $(wc -l < letter.txt)/66 + 1]
```

The let builtin allows you to evaluate arithmetic expressions without using arithmetic expansion, evaluating each argument you give it as an arithmetic expression. Thus the following is equivalent to the preceding expression:

```
$ let "numpages=$(wc -l < letter.txt)/66 + 1"
```

The double quotation marks keep the SPACEs (both those you can see and those that result from the command substitution) from separating the expression into separate arguments to let. The value of the last expression determines the exit status of let: If the *value* of the last expression is 0, the exit status of let is 1; otherwise, the exit status is 0.

You can give let multiple arguments on a single command line:

```
$ let a=5+3 b=7+2
$ echo $a $b
8 9
```

When you refer to variables when doing arithmetic expansion with either let or *$(expression)*, the shell does not require you to begin the variable name with a dollar sign (**$**), although it is a good practice to do so, because in most places you must. The following two expressions assign the same value to **numpages**:

```
$ let numpages=numpages+1
$ let numpages=$numpages+1
```

Word Splitting

The **IFS** (Internal Field Separators) shell variable specifies the characters that you can use to separate arguments on a command line and has the default value of SPACE TAB NEW-LINE. Regardless of what **IFS** is set to, you can always use one or more SPACE or TAB characters to separate arguments on the command line, provided that these characters are not quoted or escaped. When you assign **IFS** the value of characters, these characters can also separate fields, but only in the event that they undergo expansion. This type of interpretation of the command line is called *word splitting*. The following example demonstrates how setting **IFS** can affect the interpretation of a command line:

```
$ a=w:x:y:z
$ cat $a
cat: w:x:y:z: No such file or directory
$ IFS=":"
$ cat $a
cat: w: No such file or directory
cat: x: No such file or directory
cat: y: No such file or directory
cat: z: No such file or directory
```

The first time cat is called, the shell expands the variable **a**, interpreting the string **w:x:y:z** as a single token to be used as the argument to cat. The cat utility cannot find a file named **w:x:y:z** and reports an error for that filename. After **IFS** is set to a colon (**:**), the shell expands the variable **a** into four words as separate arguments to cat. This causes the cat utility to report an error on four separate files: **w**, **x**, **y**, and **z**. Word splitting based on the colon (**:**) takes place only *after* the variable **a** is expanded.

The shell splits all *expanded* words on a command line according to the separating characters found in **IFS**. When there is no expansion, there is no splitting. Consider the following commands:

```
$ IFS="p"
$ export IFS
```

Although IFS is set to **p**, nothing was expanded on the **export** command line, so the word **export** was not split. The following example uses variable expansion to produce the **export** command:

```
$ IFS=p
$ aa=export
$ $aa IFS
2 files to edit
ort: 2 files to edit: new file: line 1
:q
1 more files to edit
:q
$
```

This time there was expansion, and the character **p** in the token **export** was interpreted as a separator, so the effect of the command line is to start the **ex** editor with two filenames: **ort** and **IFS**. You cannot unset the **IFS** shell variable.

---

caution ‖   **Be Careful When Changing IFS**

Although sequences of SPACE or TAB characters are treated as single separators, *each occurrence* of another field-separator character acts as a separator.

Changing **IFS** has a variety of side effects, so change it cautiously. You may find it useful to save the value of **IFS** before changing it; that way you can easily restore it if you get unexpected results. Or you can fork a new shell with a **bash** command before experimenting with **IFS**; if you get into trouble, you can **exit** back to your old shell, where **IFS** is working properly. You can also set **IFS** to its default value with the following command:

```
$ IFS=$' \t\n'
```

Pathname Expansion

Pathname expansion (page 207) is the process of interpreting ambiguous file references and substituting the appropriate list of filenames. The shell performs this function when it encounters an ambiguous file reference—a token containing any of the characters *, ?, [, or]. If the shell is unable to locate any files that match the specified pattern, the token with the ambiguous file reference is left alone. The shell does not delete the token or replace it with a null string but passes it on to the program as is. In the first echo command in the following example, the shell expands the ambiguous file reference **tmp*** and passes three tokens (**tmp1**, **tmp2**, and **tmp3**) to echo, which displays the three filenames it was passed by the shell. After rm removes the three **tmp*** files, the shell finds no filenames that match **tmp*** when it tries to expand it and so passes the unexpanded string to the echo builtin, which displays the string it was passed:

```
$ ls
tmp1 tmp2 tmp3
$ echo tmp*
tmp1 tmp2 tmp3
$ rm tmp*
$ echo tmp*
tmp*
```

Putting double quotation marks around an argument causes the shell to suppress pathname and all other expansion except parameter and variable expansion. Putting single quotation marks around an argument suppresses all types of expansion. In the following example, the variable **$alex** is between double quotation marks, which allow parameter expansion, so the shell expands the variable to its value: **sonar**. This expansion does not occur when single quotation marks are used. Because neither single nor double quotation marks allow pathname expansion, the last two commands display the unexpanded argument **tmp***:

```
$ echo tmp* $alex
tmp1 tmp2 tmp3 sonar
$ echo "tmp* $alex"
tmp* sonar
$ echo 'tmp* $alex'
tmp* $alex
```

The shell distinguishes between the value of a variable and a reference to the variable and does not expand ambiguous file references if they occur in the value of a variable. This makes it possible for you to assign to a variable a value that includes special characters, such as an asterisk (*****).

In the next example, the working directory has three files whose names begin with **tmp**. When you assign the value **tmp*** to the variable **var**, the shell does not expand the ambiguous file reference because it occurs in the value of a variable (in the assignment statement for the variable). No quotation marks are around the string **tmp***. Context alone prevents the expansion. After the assignment, the set builtin (with the help of grep) shows the value of **var** to be **tmp***.

The three **echo** commands demonstrate three levels of expansion. When **$var** is quoted with single quotation marks, the shell performs no expansion and passes echo the character string **$var**, which echo displays. When you use double quotation marks, the shell performs only variable expansion and substitutes the value of the **var** variable for its name, preceded by a dollar sign. There is no filename expansion on this command because double quotation marks suppress it. In the final command, the shell, without the limitations of quotation marks, performs variable substitution and then pathname expansion before passing the arguments on to echo:

```
$ ls tmp*
tmp1   tmp2   tmp3
$ var=tmp*
$ set | grep var
var=tmp*
$ echo '$var'
$var
$ echo "$var"
tmp*
$ echo $var
tmp1 tmp2 tmp3
```

Chapter Summary

The shell is both a command interpreter and a programming language. As a command interpreter, the shell executes commands you enter in response to its prompt. When you use it as a programming language, the shell executes commands from files (shell scripts).

You typically run a shell script by giving its name on the command line. To run a script in this manner, you must have execute permission for the file holding the script. Otherwise, the shell does not know that the script is executable. Alternatively, you can execute the script by entering **bash** followed by the name of the file on the command line. Either way you need to have read permission for the file.

Job control is not part of the Bourne Again Shell but is included in the Job Shell, which is identical to the Bourne Again Shell in all other respects. A job is one or more commands connected by pipes. You can bring a job running in the background into the foreground with the fg builtin. A foreground job can be put into the background with the bg builtin, provided that it is first suspended by pressing the suspend key.

Each process has a unique identification, or PID, number and is the execution of a single Linux command. When you give it a command, the shell forks a new (child) process to execute the command, unless the command is built into the shell (see page 892 for a partial list of builtins). While the child process is running, the shell is in a state called sleep. By ending a command line with an ampersand (&), you can run a child process in the background and bypass the sleep state so that the shell prompt returns immediately after you press RETURN. Each command in a shell script forks a separate process, each of which may fork other processes. When a process terminates, it returns its exit status to its parent process: Zero signifies success, and nonzero signifies failure.

The shell allows you to define variables. You can declare and initialize a variable by assigning a value to it; you can remove a variable declaration by using unset. Variables are usually local to a process and must be exported by using the export builtin to make them available to child processes. The shell also defines some variables and parameters. The positional and special parameters are preceded by dollar signs in Table 9-7 to reflect the only manner in which you can reference them. Unlike shell variables, you cannot assign values to them.

When it processes a command line, the Bourne Again Shell may replace some words with expanded text. Most of the various types of command line expansion are invoked by the appearance of a special character within a word (for example, a leading dollar sign denotes a variable). See Table 9-8. The expansions take place in a specific order. The common expansions, in the order in which they occur, are parameter expansion, variable expansion, command substitution, and then pathname expansion.

table 9-7 ‖	Shell Variables/Parameters
CDPATH	List of directories for the shell to check when you give a cd builtin (page 285).
HISTFILE	Name of the file in which history events are saved between login sessions (page 293).
HISTFILESIZE	Maximum number of lines saved in HISTFILE (Table 9-3 on page 294).
HISTSIZE	Number of commands to remember in a given login session (number of commands that are displayed with the history builtin) (Table 9-3 on page 294).
HOME	Pathname of your home directory (page 282).
IFS	Internal Field Separators (page 285).
MAIL	Name of the file where the system stores your mail (page 284).
MAILCHECK	How often (in seconds) the shell checks your mailbox for new mail (page 284).
MAILPATH	List of other potential mailboxes (page 284).
PATH	Search path for commands (page 283).
PS1	Prompt String 1 (page 284).
PS2	Prompt String 2 (page 285).
$0	Name of the calling program (page 287).
$$n$	Value of the n^{th} command line argument (can be changed by set) (page 287).
$*	All command line arguments (can be changed by set) (page 291).
$@	All command line arguments (can be changed by set) (page 291).
$#	Count of the command line arguments (page 287).
$$	PID number of the current process (page 291).
$!	PID number of the most recent background task (page 291).
$?	Exit status of the last task executed by the shell (page 292).

Surrounding a word with double quotation marks suppresses all but parameter and variable expansion. Single quotation marks suppress all types of expansion, as does quoting (escaping) a special character by preceding it with a backslash.

table 9-8 || Special Characters

NEWLINE	Initiates execution of a command (page 256).
;	Separates commands (page 256).
( )	Groups commands for execution by a subshell or identifies a function (page 259).
&	Executes a command in the background (pages 204 and 257).
|	Pipe (page 257).
>	Redirects standard output (page 197).
>>	Appends standard output (page 200).
<	Redirects standard input (page 198).
<<	Here document (page 882).
*	Any string of characters in an ambiguous file reference (pages 208 and 257).
?	Any single character in an ambiguous file reference (page 207).
\	Quotes the following character (page 118).
'	Quotes a string, preventing all substitutions (page 118).
"	Quotes a string, allowing only variable and command substitutions (pages 118 and 275).
`. . .`	Performs command substitution (page 312).
[ ]	Character class in an ambiguous file reference (page 209).
$	References a variable (page 273).
. (dot builtin)	Executes a command (only at the beginning of a line) (page 286).
#	Begins a comment (page 862).
{ }	Command grouping (used to surround the contents of a function) (page 894).
: (null builtin)	Returns *true* exit status (page 891).
&& (Boolean AND)	Executes command on right only if command on left succeeds (returns a zero exit status).
|| (Boolean OR)	Boolean OR: executes command on right only if command on left fails (returns a nonzero exit status).
! (Boolean NOT)	Boolean NOT: reverses exit status of command.

table 9-8 ||	Special Characters (Continued)
$()	Performs command substitution (preferred form) (page 281).
[]	Evaluates arithmetic expression (page 313).

Exercises

1. The following shell script adds entries to a file named **journal-file** in your home directory. The script can help you keep track of phone conversations and meetings:

```
$ cat journal
# journal: add journal entries to the file
# $HOME/journal-file

file=$HOME/journal-file
date >> $file
echo -n "Enter name of person or group: "
read name
echo "$name" >> $file
echo >> $file
cat >> $file
echo "-----------------------------------------------------" >> $file
echo >> $file
```

   a. What do you have to do to the script in order to be able to execute it?

   b. Why does the script use the read builtin the first time it accepts input from the terminal and the cat utility the second time?

2. What are two ways you can execute a shell script when you do not have execute access permission to the file containing the script? Can you execute a shell script if you do not have read access permission?

3. What is the purpose of the **PATH** variable?

   a. Set up your **PATH** variable so that it causes the shell to search the following directories in order:

   - /usr/local/bin

   - /usr/bin/X11

   - /usr/bin

   - /bin

   - /usr/openwin/bin

   - Your own **bin** directory (usually **bin** or **.bin** in your home directory)

   - The working directory

    b. If a file named **whereis** is in **/usr/bin** and also in your **~/bin**, which one does **whereis** indicate will be executed? (Assume that you have execute permission for both of the files.)

    c. If your **PATH** variable is not set to search the working directory, how can you execute a program located there?

    d. What command can you use to add the directory **/usr/games** to the end of the list of directories in **PATH**?

4. Assume that you have made the following assignment:

    `$ person=jenny`

    Give the output of each of the following commands:

    a. echo $person

    b. echo ' $person '

    c. echo "$person"

5. Explain the unexpected following result:

```
$ whereis date
date: /bin/date
$ echo $PATH
.:/usr/local/bin:/usr/bin:/bin
$ cat > date
echo "This is my own version of date."
$ date
Wed Mar 12 09:11:54 MST 2003
```

6. Assume that the **/home/jenny/grants/biblios** and **/home/jenny/biblios** directories exist. For both (a) and (b), give Jenny's working directory after she executes the sequence of commands given. Explain.

    a.

```
$ pwd
/home/jenny/grants
$ CDPATH=$(pwd)
$ cd
$ cd biblios
```

    b.

```
$ pwd
/home/jenny/grants
$ CDPATH=$(pwd)
$ cd $HOME/biblios
```

7. Name two ways you can identify the PID of your login shell.

8. Give the following command:

    `$ sleep 30 | cat /etc/inittab`

    Is there any output from sleep? Where does cat get its input from? What has to happen before you get a prompt back?

Advanced Exercises

9. Write a sequence of commands or a script that demonstrates that parameter expansion occurs before variable expansion and that variable expansion occurs before pathname expansion.

10. Write a shell script that outputs the name of the shell that is executing it.

11. Type in the following shell scripts and run them:

```
$ cat report_dir
old_dir=$(pwd)
echo "Current working directory:  " $old_dir
go_home
echo "Current working directory:  " $(pwd)

$ cat go_home
cd
echo "New working directory:  " $(pwd)
echo "Last working directory: " $old_dir
```

12. The following is a modified version of the **read2** script from page 281. Explain why it behaves differently. For what type of input does it produce the same output as the original **read2** script?

```
$ cat read2
echo -n "Enter a command: "
read command
"$command"
echo "Thanks"
```

13. Explain the behavior of the following shell script:

```
$ cat quote_demo
twoliner="This is line 1.
This is line 2."
echo "$twoliner"
echo $twoliner
```

   a. How many arguments does each echo command see in this script? Explain.

   b. Redefine the **IFS** shell variable so that the output of the second echo is the same as the first.

Networking and the Internet

10

The communications facilities linking computers are continually improving, allowing faster and more economical connections. The earliest computers were unconnected stand-alone machines. To transfer information from one system to another, you had to store it in some form (usually magnetic tape, paper tape, or punch cards—called IBM or Hollerith cards), carry it to a compatible system, and read it back in. A notable advance occurred when computers began to exchange data over serial lines, although the transfer rate was slow (hundreds of bits per second). People quickly invented new ways to take advantage of this computing power, such as email, news retrieval, and bulletin board services. With the speed of today's networks, it is normal for a piece of email to cross the country or even travel halfway around the world in a few seconds.

It would be difficult to find a computer facility that does not include a LAN to link its systems. Linux systems are typically attached to an *Ethernet* (page 970) network. Wireless networks are becoming prevalent as well. Large computer facilities usually maintain several networks, often of different types, and almost certainly have connections to larger networks (company- or campuswide and beyond).

The Internet is a loosely administered network of networks (an *internetwork*) that links computers on diverse LANs around the globe. An internet (small *i*) is a generic network of networks that may share some parts in common with the public Internet. It is the Internet that makes it possible to send an email message to a colleague thousands of miles away and receive a reply within minutes. A related term, *intranet*, refers to the networking infrastructure within a company or other institution. Intranets are usually private; access to them from external networks may be limited and carefully controlled, typically using firewalls (page 331).

323

Network services Over the past decade many network services have emerged and become standard. On Linux systems, as on UNIX computers, special processes called *daemons* (page 966) support such services by exchanging specialized messages with other systems over the network. Several software systems have been created to allow computers to share filesystems with one another, making it appear as though remote files are stored on local disks. Sharing remote filesystems allows users to share information without knowing where the files physically reside, without making unnecessary copies, and without learning a new set of utilities to manipulate them. Because the files appear to be stored locally, you can use standard utilities (such as cat, vi, lpr, mv, or their graphical counterparts) to work with them.

Developers have been creating new tools and extending existing ones to take advantage of higher network speeds and to work within more crowded networks. The rlogin, rsh, and telnet utilities, designed long ago, have largely been supplanted by ssh (secure shell, page 563). The ssh utility allows a user to log in on or execute commands securely on a remote computer. Users rely on such utilities as scp and ftp to transfer files from one system to another across the network. Communication utilities, including email utilities and chat programs (such as talk, Internet Relay Chat [IRC], ICQ, and instant messenger [IM] programs, such as AOL's AIM and gaim) have become so prevalent that many people with very little computer expertise use them on a daily basis to keep in touch with friends and family.

Intranet An *intranet* is a network that connects computing resources at a school, company, or other organization but, unlike the Internet, typically restricts access to internal users. An intranet is very similar to a LAN but is based on Internet technology. An intranet can provide database, email, and Web page access to a limited group of people, regardless of their geographic location.

The fact that an intranet is able to connect dissimilar machines is one of its strengths. Think of all the machines that are on the Internet: Macs, PCs running different versions of Windows, various machines running UNIX and Linux, and so on. Each of these machines can communicate via IP (page 331), a common protocol. So it is with an intranet: Different machines can all talk to one another.

Another key difference between the Internet and an intranet is that the Internet transmits only one protocol suite: the IP protocol suite. An intranet can be set up to use a number of protocols, such as IP, IPX, Appletalk, DECnet, XNS, or various other protocols developed by vendors over the years. Although these protocols cannot be transmitted directly over the Internet, you can set up special gateway boxes at remote sites that tunnel or encapsulate these protocols into IP packets in order to use the Internet to pass them.

You can use an *extranet* (also called a *partner net*) or a virtual private network (VPN) to improve security. These terms describe ways to connect remote sites securely to a local site, typically by using the public Internet as a carrier and using encryption as a means of protecting data in transit.

As with the Internet, the communications potential of intranets is boundless. You can set up a private chat between people at remote locations, access a company database, see what is new at school, or read about the new university president. Companies that developed products for use on the Internet are investing more and more time and money developing intranet software applications as the intranet market explodes. Following are some words you may want to become familiar with before you read the rest of this chapter. Refer to the Glossary on page 955 for definitions.

ASP	bridge	extranet	firewall	gateway
hub	internet	Internet	intranet	ISP
packet	router	sneakernet	switch	VPN

Types of Networks and How They Work

Computers communicate over networks using unique addresses assigned by system software. A computer message, called a *packet, frame,* or *datagram,* includes the address of the destination computer and the sender's return address. The three most common types of networks are *broadcast, point-to-point,* and *switched.* Once popular token-based networks (such as FDDI and Token Ring) are rarely seen anymore.

Speed is important to the proper functioning of the Internet. Newer specifications (cat 6 and cat 7) are being standardized for 1000BaseT (one gigabit per second, called gigabit Ethernet, or GIG-E) and faster networking. Some of the networks that form the backbone of the Internet run at speeds up to almost 10 giga*bytes* per second (OC192) to accommodate the ever-increasing demand for network services. Table 10-1 lists some of the common specifications in use today.

table 10-1 ‖	Network Specifications
DS0	64 kilobits per second
ISDN	Two DS0 lines plus signaling (16 kilobits per second) or 128 kilobits per second
T-1	1.544 megabits per second (24 DS0 lines)
T-3	43.232 megabits per second (28 T-1s)
OC3	155 megabits per second (100 T-1s)
OC12	622 megabits per second (4 OC3s)
OC48	2.5 gigabits per seconds (4 OC12s)
OC192	9.6 gigabits per second (4 OC48s)

Broadcast

On a *broadcast network,* such as Ethernet, any of the many systems attached to the network cable can send a message at any time; each system examines the address in each message and responds only to messages addressed to it. A problem occurs on a broadcast network when multiple systems send data at the same time, resulting in a collision of the messages on the cable. When messages collide, they can become garbled. The sending system notices the garbled message and resends it after waiting a short but random amount of time. Waiting a random amount of time helps prevent those same systems from resending the data at the same moment and experiencing another collision. The extra traffic that results from collisions can put an extra load on the network; if the collision rate gets too high, retransmissions result in more collisions, and the network becomes unusable.

Point-to-Point

A point-to-point link does not seem like much of a network because only two endpoints are involved. However, most connections to WANs (wide area networks) are through point-to-point links, using wire cable, radio, or satellite links. The advantage of a point-to-point link is that because only two systems are involved, the traffic on the link is limited and well understood. A disadvantage is that each system can typically be equipped for a small number of such links, and it is impractical and costly to establish point-to-point links that connect each computer to all the rest.

Point-to-point links often use serial lines and modems but can use personal computer parallel ports for faster links between Linux systems. The use of a modem with a point-to-point link allows an isolated system to connect inexpensively into a larger network.

The most common types of point-to-point links are the ones used to connect to the Internet. When you use DSL[1] (digital subscriber line), you are using a point-to-point link to connect to the Internet. Serial lines, such as T-1, T-3, ATM links, and ISDN, are all point-to-point. Although it might seem like a point-to-point link, a cable modem is based on broadcast technology and in that way is similar to Ethernet.

Switched

A *switch* is a device that establishes a virtual path between source and destination hosts in such a way that each path appears to be a point-to-point link, much like a railroad roundhouse. The telephone network is a giant switched network. The switch brings up and tears down virtual paths as hosts need to communicate with each other. Each host thinks it has a direct point-to-point path to the host it is talk-

---

1. The term DSL incorporates the xDSL suite of technologies, including ADSL, XDSL, SDSL, and HDSL.

ing to. Contrast this with a broadcast network, where each host also sees traffic bound for other hosts. The advantage of a switched network over a pure point-to-point network is that each host requires only one connection: the connection to the switch. Using pure point-to-point connections, each host must have a connection to every other host. Scalability is provided by further linking switches.

LAN: Local Area Network

Local area networks (LANs) are confined to a relatively small area—a single computer facility, building, or campus. Today, most LANs run over copper or fiberoptic cable, but other, wireless technologies, such as infrared (similar to most television remote control devices) and radio wave (wireless, or Wi-Fi), are becoming more popular.

If its destination address is not on the local network, a packet must be passed on to another network by a router (page 328). A router may be a general-purpose computer or a special-purpose device attached to multiple networks to act as a gateway among them.

Ethernet

A Linux system connected to a LAN usually connects to a network using Ethernet. A typical Ethernet connection can support data transfer rates from 10 megabits per second to 1 gigabit per second, with speed enhancements planned. Owing to computer load, competing network traffic, and network overhead, file transfer rates on an Ethernet are always slower than the maximum, theoretical transfer rate.

Cables   An Ethernet network transfers data using copper or fiberoptic (glass) cable or wireless transmitters and receivers. Originally, each computer was attached to a thick coaxial cable (called *thicknet*) at tap points spaced at six-foot intervals along the cable. The thick cable was awkward to deal with, so other solutions, including a thinner coaxial cable called *thinnet*, or 10Base2,[2] were developed. Today, most Ethernet connections either are wireless or are made over unshielded twisted pair (referred to as UTP, Category 5 [cat 5], Category 5e [cat 5e], Category 6 [cat 6], 10BaseT, or 100BaseT) wire—similar to the type of wire used for telephone lines and serial data communications.

Switch   A *switched Ethernet* network is a special case of a broadcast network that works with a *network switch,* or just *switch,* which is a special class of hub that has intelligence. Instead of having a dumb repeater (passive hub) that broadcasts every packet it receives out of every port, a switch learns which devices are connected to which of its ports. A switch sorts packets so it sends traffic to only the machine the traffic is intended for. A switch also has buffers for holding and queuing packets.

---

2. Ethernet cables are classified as **XbaseY**, where *X* is the data rate in megabits per second, **base** means baseband (as opposed to radio frequency), and *Y* is the category of cabling.

Some Ethernet switches have enough bandwidth to communicate simultaneously, in full-duplex mode, with all the devices connected to it. A nonswitched (hub-based) broadcast network can run in only half-duplex mode. Full-duplex Ethernet further improves things by eliminating collisions. Each host on a switched network can transmit and receive simultaneously at 10/100/1000 megabits per second for an effective bandwidth between hosts of 20/200/2000 megabits per second, depending on the capacity of the switch.

Wireless

Wireless networks are becoming increasingly common. They are used in offices, homes, and public places, such as universities, coffee shops, and airports. Wireless access points provide functionality similar to an Ethernet hub. They allow multiple users to interact, using a common radio frequency spectrum. A wireless, point-to-point connection allows you to wander about your home or office with a laptop, using an antenna to link to a LAN or to the Internet via an in-house base station. Linux has drivers for many of the common wireless boards. A wireless access point connects a wireless network to a wired network so that no special protocol is required for a wireless connection. Refer to the *Linux Wireless LAN HOWTO* at www.hpl.hp.com/personal/Jean_Tourrilhes/Linux.

WAN: Wide Area Network

A wide area network (WAN) covers a large geographic area. The technologies (such as Ethernet) used for LANs were designed to work over limited distances and for a certain number of host connections. A WAN may span long distances over dedicated data lines (leased from a telephone company) or radio or satellite links. WANs are often used to interconnect LANs. Major Internet service providers rely on WANs to connect to customers within a country and around the globe.

Some networks do not fit into either the LAN or the WAN designation: A MAN (metropolitan area network) is one that is contained in a smaller geographic area, such as a city. Like WANs, MANs are typically used to interconnect LANs.

Internetworking Through Gateways and Routers

Gateway   A LAN connects to a WAN through a *gateway*, a generic term for a computer or a special device with multiple network connections that passes data from one network to another. A gateway converts the data traffic from the format used on the LAN to that used on the WAN. Data that crosses the country from one Ethernet to another over a WAN, for example, is repackaged from the Ethernet format to a different format that can be processed by the communications equipment that makes up the WAN backbone. When it reaches the end of its journey over the WAN, the data is converted by another gateway to the format appropriate for the receiving network. For the most part, these details are of concern only to the network administrators; the end user does not need to know anything about how the data transfer is carried out.

Router A *router* is the most common form of a gateway. Routers play an important role in internetworking. Just as you might study a map to plan your route when you need to drive to an unfamiliar place, a computer needs to know how to deliver a message to a system attached to a distant network by passing through intermediary systems and networks along the way. You can imagine using a giant network road map to choose the route that your data should follow, but a static map of computer routes is usually a poor choice for a large network. Computers and networks along the route you choose may be overloaded or down, without providing a detour for your message.

Routers communicate with one another dynamically, keeping each other informed about which routes are open for use. To extend the analogy, this would be like heading out on a car trip without consulting a map to find a route to your destination; instead you head for a nearby gas station and ask directions. Throughout the journey, you would continue to stop at one gas station after another, getting directions at each to find the next one. Although it would take a while to make the stops, each gas station would advise you of bad traffic, closed roads, alternative routes, and shortcuts.

The stops the data makes are much quicker than those you would make in your car, but each message leaves each router on a path chosen based on the most current information. Think of it as a GPS (global positioning system) setup that automatically gets updates at each intersection and tells you where to go next, based on traffic and highway conditions.

Figure 10-1 shows an example of how LANs might be set up at three sites interconnected by a WAN (the Internet). In network diagrams such as this, Ethernet LANs are drawn as straight lines, with devices attached at right angles; WANs are represented as clouds, indicating that the details have been left out; wireless connections are drawn as zigzag lines with breaks, indicating that the connection may be intermittent.

In Figure 10-1, a gateway or a router relays messages between each LAN and the Internet. Three of the routers in the Internet are shown (for example, the one closest to each site). Site A has a server, a workstation, a network computer, and a PC sharing a single Ethernet LAN. Site B has an Ethernet LAN that serves a printer and four Linux workstations. A firewall permits only certain traffic between the Internet router and the site's local router. Site C has three LANs linked by a single router, perhaps to reduce the traffic load that would result if they were combined or to keep workgroups or locations on separate networks. Site C includes a wireless access point that enables wireless communication with nearby computers.

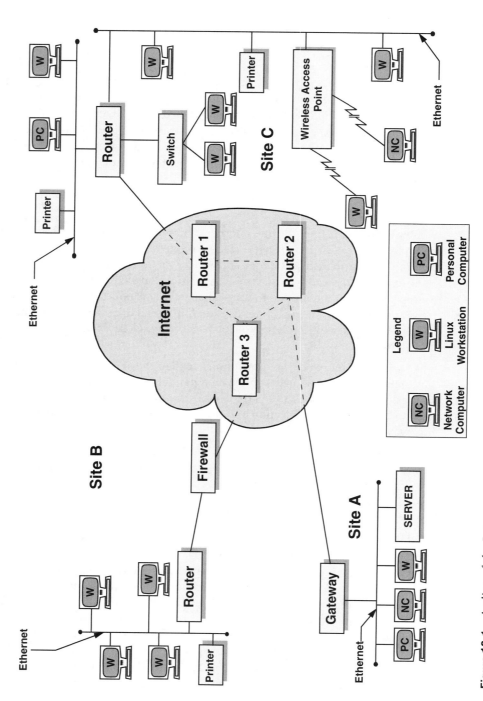

Figure 10-1   A slice of the Internet

Firewall

A firewall in a car separates the engine compartment from the passenger compartment, protecting the driver and passengers from engine fires, noise, and fumes. Computer firewalls separate computers from malicious and unwanted users.

A *firewall* prevents certain types of traffic from entering or leaving a network. A firewall might prevent traffic from your IP address from leaving the network and prevent anyone except users from select domains from using FTP to retrieve data from the network. The implementations of firewalls vary widely, from Linux machines with two *interfaces* (page 977) running custom software to a *router* (page 994) with simple access lists to esoteric, vendor-supplied firewall appliances. Most larger installations have at least one kind of firewall in place. A firewall is often accompanied by a proxy server/gateway (page 357) to provide an intermediate point between you and the host you are communicating with.

In addition to those found in multipurpose computers, firewalls are becoming increasingly common in consumer appliances. Firewalls are built into cable modems, wireless gateways, routers, and stand-alone devices.

When your need for privacy is critical, you can meet with a consulting firm that will discuss your security needs, devise a strategy, produce a written implementation policy, and design a firewall from scratch for you. Typically, a single Linux machine can include a minimal firewall. A small group of Linux machines may have a cheap, slow Linux machine with two network interfaces and packet-filtering software functioning as a dedicated firewall. One of the interfaces connects to the Internet, modems, and other outside data sources, whereas the other connects, normally through a hub or switch, to the local network's machines. Refer to Chapter 25, page 737, for information on iptables and setting up a firewall and to Appendix C for a discussion of security.

Network Protocols

To exchange information over a network, computers must communicate using a common language, or *protocol* (page 990). The protocol determines the format of message packets. The predominant network protocols used by Linux systems are TCP and IP, referred to as TCP/IP[3] (Transmission Control Protocol and Internet Protocol). Network services that need highly reliable connections, such as ssh and scp, tend to use TCP/IP. Another protocol used for some system services is UDP (User Datagram Protocol). Network services that do not require guaranteed delivery, such as RealAudio and RealVideo, operate satisfactorily with the simpler UDP.[4]

---

3. All references to IP imply *IPv4* (page 978).

IP: Internet Protocol

Layering was introduced to facilitate protocol design: Layers distinguish functional differences between adjacent protocols. A grouping of layers can be standardized into a protocol model. IP is a protocol and has a corresponding model for what distinguishes protocol layers. The IP model differs from the ISO seven-layer protocol model (also called the OSI model) often illustrated in networking textbooks. IP uses the following simplified five-layer model:

1. The first layer of the IP protocol, called the *physical layer,* describes the physical medium (copper, fiber, wireless) and the data encoding used to transmit signals on that medium (pulses of light, electrical waves, or radio waves, for instance).

2. The second layer, called the *data link layer,* covers media access by network devices and describes how to put data into packets, transmit the data, and check it for errors. Ethernet is at this layer, as is *802.11* (page 955) wireless.

3. The third layer, called the *network layer,* frequently uses IP and addresses and routes packets.

4. The fourth layer, called the *transport layer,* is where TCP and UDP exist. This layer provides a means for applications to communicate with each other. Common functions of the transport layer include guaranteed delivery, delivery of packets in the order of transmission, flow control, error detection, and error correction. The transport layer is responsible for dividing data streams into packets. This layer also performs port addressing, which allows it to distinguish among different services using the same transport protocol. Port addressing keeps the data from multiple applications using the same protocol (for example, TCP) separate.

5. Anything above the transport layer is the domain of the application and is part of the fifth layer. Unlike the ISO model, the Internet model does not distinguish among application, presentation, and session layers. All the upper-layer characteristics, such as character encoding, encryption, GUI, and so on, are part of the application. Applications choose the transport characteristics they require and choose the corresponding transport layer protocol to send and receive data.

---

4. Voice and video protocols are delay sensitive, not integrity sensitive. The human ear and eye accept and interpolate loss in an audio stream but cannot deal with variable delay. The guaranteed delivery that TCP provides introduces delay on a busy network when packets get retransmitted. This delay is not acceptable for video and audio transmissions, whereas less than 100 percent integrity is acceptable.

TCP: Transmission Control Protocol

TCP is most frequently run on top of IP in a combination referred to as TCP/IP. TCP provides error recovery and guaranteed delivery in packet transmission order and works with multiple ports so that it can handle more than one application. TCP is a *connection-oriented protocol* (page 964), also known as a stream-based protocol. Once established, a TCP connection looks like a stream of data, not individual IP packets. The connection is assumed to remain up and be uniquely addressable. Every piece of information you write to the connection always goes to the same destination and arrives in the order it was sent. Because TCP is connection oriented and establishes what you can think of as a *virtual circuit* between two machines, TCP is not suitable for one-to-many transmissions (see UDP, following). TCP has builtin mechanisms for dealing with congestion (or flow) control over busy networks and throttles back (slows the speed of data flow) when it has to retransmit dropped packets. TCP can also deal with acknowledgments, wide area links, high delay links, and other situations.

UDP: User Datagram Protocol

UDP runs at layer 4 of the IP stack, just as TCP does, but is much simpler. Like TCP, UDP works with multiple ports/multiple applications. It has checksums for error detection but does not automatically retransmit *datagrams* (page 966) that fail the checksum. UDP is a datagram-oriented protocol: Each datagram must carry its own address and port information. Each router along the way examines each datagram to determine the destination one hop at a time. You can broadcast or multicast UDP datagrams to many destinations at the same time by using special addresses.

PPP: Point-to-Point Protocol

PPP provides serial line point-to-point connections that support IP. PPP compresses data to make the most of the limited bandwidth available on serial connections. PPP, which replaces SLIP[5] (Serial Line IP), acts as a point-to-point layer 2/3 transport that many other types of protocols can ride on. PPP is used mostly for IP-based services and connections, such as TCP or UDP.

Xremote and LBX

Two protocols that speed up work over serial lines are Xremote and LBX. Xremote compresses the X Window System protocol so that it is more efficient over slower serial lines. LBX (low-bandwidth X) is based on the Xremote technology and is part of the X Window System release X11R6.

---

5. SLIP was one of the first serial line implementations of IP and has slightly less overhead than PPP, but PPP supports multiple protocols (such as Appletalk and IPX), whereas SLIP supports only IP.

Host Address

Each computer interface is identified by a unique address, or host number, on its network. A system attached to more than one network has multiple interfaces, one for each network, each with a unique address.

Each packet of information that is broadcast over the network has a destination address. All hosts on the network must process each broadcast packet to see whether it is addressed to that host.[6] If the packet is addressed to a given host, that host continues to process it. If not, the host ignores it.

The network address of a machine is an IP address, which, under IPv4, is represented as one number broken into four segments separated by periods (for example, 192.168.184.5). Domain names and IP addresses are assigned through a highly distributed system coordinated by ICANN (Internet Corporation for Assigned Names and Numbers—www.icann.org) via many registrars (see www.internic.net). ICANN is funded by the various domain name registries and registrars and by IP address registries, which supply globally unique identifiers for hosts and services on the Internet. Although you may not deal with any of these agencies directly, your Internet service provider does.

How a company uses IP addresses is determined by the system or network administrator. For example, the leftmost two sets of numbers in an IP address might represent a large network (campus- or companywide); the third set might specify a subnetwork (perhaps a department or a single floor in a building); and the rightmost number, an individual computer. The operating system uses the address in a different, lower-level form, converting it to its binary equivalent, a series of 1s and 0s. See the following Optional section for more information. Refer to "Private address space" on page 554 for information about addresses you can use on a LAN without registering them.

Static versus Dynamic IP Addresses

A static IP address is one that remains the same. A dynamic IP address is one that can change each time you connect to the network. A dynamic address remains the same during a single login session. Any server (mail, Web, and so on) must have a static address so clients can find the machine that is the server. End user machines usually work well with dynamic addresses. During a given login session, they can function as a client (your Web browser, for example) because they have a constant IP address. When you log out and log in again, it does not matter that you have a different IP address because your computer, acting as a client, establishes a new connection with a server. The advantage of dynamic addressing is that it allows inactive addresses to be reused, reducing the total number of IP addresses needed.

---

6. Contrast broadcast packets with unicast packets: Ethernet hardware on a computer filters out unicast packets that are not addressed to that machine; the operating system on that machine never sees them.

IP Classes

To facilitate routing on the Internet, IP addresses are divided into *classes*. Classes, labeled *class A* through *class E,* allow the Internet address space to be broken into blocks of small, medium, and large networks that are designed to be assigned based on the number of hosts within a network.

When you need to send a message to an address outside the local network, your system looks up the address block/class in its routing table and sends the message to the next router on the way to the final destination. Every router along the way does a similar lookup to forward the message. At the destination, local routers direct the message to the specific address. Without classes and blocks, your host would have to know every network and subnetwork address on the Internet before it could send a message. This would be impractical because of the number of addresses on the Internet.

Each of the four numbers in the IP address is in the range of 0–255 because each segment of the IP address is represented by 8 bits (an *octet*), each bit capable of taking on two values; the total number of values is $2^8 = 256$. When you start counting at 0, 1–256 becomes 0–255.[7] Each IP address is divided into a net address (*netid*) portion, which is part of the class, and a host address (*hostid*) portion. See Table 10-2.

table 10-2 || **IP Classes**

Class	Start Bits	Address Range	All Bits (including start bits)			
			0-7	8-15	16-23	24-31
Class A	0	001.000.000.000-126.000.000.000	0-netid-	========hostid========		
Class B	10	129.000.000.000-191.255.000.000	10-------netid-----	=====hostid=====		
Class C	110	192.000.000.000-223.255.255.000	110---------netid-----------	=hostid=		
Class D (Multicast)	1110	224.000.000.000-239.255.255.000	1110			
Class E (Reserved)	11110	240.000.000.000-255.255.255.000	11110			

The first set of addresses, defining class A networks, is for extremely large corporations, such as General Electric (3.0.0.0) and Hewlett-Packard (15.0.0.0), or for ISPs. One start bit (0) in the first position designates a class A network, 7 bits holds the network portion of the address (netid), and 24 bits holds the host portion of the address (hostid, Table 10-2). This means that GE can have 2^{24}, or ap-

---

7. Internally, the IP address is represented as a set of four unsigned 8-bit fields, or a 32-bit unsigned number, depending on how programs are using it. The most common format in C is to represent it as a union of an unsigned 32-bit long integer, four unsigned chars, and two unsigned short integers.

proximately 16 million hosts on its network. Unused address space and *subnets* (page 999) lower this number quite a bit. The 127.0.0.0 subnet (page 339) is reserved, as are 128.0.0.0 and several others.

Two start bits (10) in the first two positions designates a class B network, 14 bits holds the network portion of the address (**netid**), and 16 bits holds the host portion of the address, for a potential total of 65,534 hosts.[8] A class C network uses 3 start bits (100), 21 netid bits (2 million networks), and 8 hostid bits (254 hosts). Today, a new large customer will not receive a class A or B network but is likely to receive a class C or several (usually contiguous) class C networks, if merited.

Several other classes of networks exist. Class D networks are reserved for *multicast* (page 984) networks. When you run **netstat –nr** on a Linux system, you can see whether the machine is a member of a multicast network. A 224.0.0.0 in the Destination column that netstat displays indicates a class D, multicast address (Table 10-2). A multicast is like a broadcast, but only hosts that subscribe to the multicast group receive the message. To use Web terminology, a broadcast is like a push. A host pushes a broadcast on the network, and every host on the network must check each packet to see whether it contains relevant data. A multicast is like a pull. A host will see a multicast only if it registers itself as subscribed to a multicast group or service and pulls the appropriate packets from the network.

Table 10-3 shows some of the computations for IP address 131.204.027.027. Each address is shown in decimal, hexadecimal, and binary. Binary is the easiest to work with for bitwise (binary) computations. The first three lines show the IP address. The next three lines show the *subnet mask* (page 999) in three bases. Next, the IP address and the subnet mask are ANDed together bitwise to yield the *subnet number* (page 999), which is shown in three bases. The last three lines show the *broadcast address* (page 960), which is computed by taking the subnet number and turning the hostid bits to 1s. The subnet number is the name/number of the local network. The subnet number and the subnet mask determine what range the IP address of the machine must be in. They are also used by routers to segment traffic; see *network segment* (page 985). A broadcast on this network goes to all hosts in the range 131.204.27.1 through 131.204.27.254 but will be acted on only by hosts that have a use for it.

---

8. A 16-bit (class B) address can address 2^{16} = 65,536 hosts, yet the potential number of hosts is two less than that because the first and last addresses on any network are reserved. In a similar manner, an 8-bit (class C) address can address only 254 hosts ($2^8 - 2$ = 254). The 0 host address (for example, 194.16.100.0 for a class C or 131.204.0.0 for a class B) is reserved as a designator for the network itself. Several older operating systems use this as a broadcast address. The 255 host address (for example, 194.16.100.255 for a class C or 131.204.255.255 for a class B) is reserved as the IP broadcast address. An IP packet (datagram) that is sent to this address is broadcast to all hosts on the network.

The **netid** portion of a subnet does not have the same limitations. Often you are given the choice of reserving the first and last networks in a range as you would a **hostid**, but this is rarely done in practice. More often, the first and last network in the netid range are used to provide more usable address space. Refer to "Subnets" on the following page.

Subnets

Each host on a network must process each broadcast packet to determine whether the information in the packet is useful to that host. If a lot of hosts are on a network, each host must process many packets. To maintain efficiency, most networks, particularly shared media networks such as Ethernet, need to be split into subnetworks, or *subnets*.[9] The more hosts on a network, the more dramatically network performance is impacted. Organizations use router and switch technology called VLANs (virtual local area network) to group similar hosts into broadcast domains (subnets) based on function. It's not uncommon to see a switch with different ports being part of different subnets. See page 400 for information on how to specify a subnet.

A *subnet mask* (or *address mask*) is a bit mask that identifies which parts of an IP address correspond to the network address and subnet portion of the address. This mask has 1s in positions corresponding to the network and subnet numbers and 0s in the host number positions. When you perform a bitwise AND on an IP address and a subnet mask (Table 10-3), the result is an address that contains everything but the host address (**hostid**) portion.

There are several ways to represent a subnet mask: A network could have a subnet mask of 255.255.255.0 (decimal), FFFFFF00 (hexadecimal), or /24 (the number of bits used for the subnet mask). If it were a class B network (of which 16 bits are already fixed), this yields 2^8 (24 total bits − 16 fixed bits = 8 bits, 2^8 = 256) networks[10] with $2^8 - 2$ (256 − 2 = 254) hosts[11] on each network.

For example, when you divide the class C address 192.25.4.0 into eight subnets, you get a subnet mask of 255.255.255.224, FFFFFFE0, or /27 (27 1s). The eight resultant networks are 192.25.4.0, 192.25.4.32, 192.25.4.64, 192.25.4.96, 192.25.4.128, 192.25.4.160, 192.25.4.192, and 192.25.4.224. You can use a Web-based subnet mask calculator to calculate subnet masks (page 919). To use this calculator to determine the preceding subnet mask, use an IP host address of 192.25.4.0. Go to www.telusplanet.net/public/sparkman/netcalc.htm for a nice subnet calculator.

CIDR: Classless Inter-Domain Routing

CIDR (pronounced *cider*) allows groups of addresses that are smaller than a class C block to be assigned to an organization or ISP and further subdivided and parceled out. In addition, it helps to alleviate the potential problem of routing tables on major Internet backbone and peering devices becoming too large to manage.

---

9. This is also an issue with other protocols, particularly Appletalk.

10. The first and last networks are reserved in a manner similar to the first and last host, although the standard is flexible. You can configure router(s) to reclaim the first and last networks in a subnet. Different routers have different techniques for reclaiming these networks.

11. Subtract 2 because the first and last host addresses on every network are reserved.

table 10-3 ||　　　　　　　　　　　　　　**Computations for IP address 131.204.027.027**

	----------Class B----------		netid	hostid
IP Address	131	.204	.027	.027 decimal
	8C	CC	1B	1B hexadecimal
	1000 1100	1100 1100	0001 1011	0001 1011 binary
Subnet Mask	255	.255	.255	.000 decimal
	FF	FF	FF	00 hexadecimal
	1111 1111	1111 1111	1111 1111	0000 0000 binary
IP Address Bitwise AND	1000 1100	1100 1100	0001 1011	0001 1011
Subnet Mask	1111 1111	1111 1111	1111 1111	0000 0000 binary
= Subnet Number	1000 1100	1100 1100	0001 1011	0000 0000
Subnet Number	131	.204	.027	.000 decimal
	83	CC	1B	00 hexadecimal
	1000 1100	1100 1100	0001 1011	0000 0000 binary
Broadcast Address (Set host bits to 1)	131	.204	.27	.255 decimal
	83	CC	1B	FF hexadecimal
	1000 0011	1100 1100	0001 1011	1111 1111 binary

The pool of available IPv4 addresses has been depleted to the point that no one gets a class A address anymore. The trend is to reclaim these huge address blocks, if possible, and recycle them into groups of smaller addresses. Also, as more class C addresses are assigned, routing tables on the Internet are filling up and causing memory overflows. The solution is to aggregate[12] groups of addresses into blocks and allocate them to ISPs, which in turn subdivide these blocks and allocate them to customers. The address class designations (A, B, and C) described in the previous section are used less today, although subnets are still used. When you request an address block, your ISP usually gives as many addresses as you need and no more. The ISP aggregates several contiguous smaller blocks and routes them to your location. This aggregation is CIDR. Without CIDR, the Internet as we know it would not function.

---

12. *Aggregate* means to join. In CIDR, the aggregate of 208.178.99.124 and 208.178.99.125 is 208.178.99.124/23 (the aggregation of two class Cs).

For example, you might be allocated the 192.168.5.0/22 IP address block, which could support 2^{10} hosts (32 − 22 = 10). Your ISP would set its routers so that any packets going to an address in that block would be sent to your network. Internally, your own routers might further subdivide this block of 1024 potential hosts into subnets, perhaps into four networks. Four networks require an additional two bits of addressing (2^2 = 4). You could set up your router to have four networks with this allocation: 192.168.5.0/24, 192.168.6.0/24, 192.168.7.0/24, and 192.168.8.0/24. Each of these networks could have 254 hosts. CIDR lets you arbitrarily divide networks and subnetworks into ever smaller blocks along the way. Each router has enough memory to keep track of the addresses it needs to direct and aggregates the rest. This scheme uses memory and address space efficiently. You could take 192.168.8.0/24 and further divide it into 16 networks with 14 hosts each. The 16 networks require four more bits (2^4 = 16), so you would have 192.168.8.0/28, 192.168.8.16/28, 192.168.8.32/28, and so on to the last subnet of 192.168.8.240/16, which would have the hosts 192.168.8.241 through 192.168.8.254.

Hostnames

People generally find it easier to work with names than numbers, and Linux provides several ways to associate hostnames with IP addresses. The oldest method is to consult a list of names and addresses that are stored in the **/etc/hosts** file:

```
$ cat /etc/hosts
127.0.0.1       localhost
130.128.52.1    gw-example.example.com   gw-example
130.128.52.2    bravo.example.com        bravo
130.128.52.3    hurrah.example.com       hurrah
130.128.52.4    kudos.example.com        kudos
```

localhost = 127.0.0.1   The address 127.0.0.1 is reserved for the special hostname **localhost,** which serves as a hook for the system's networking software to operate on the local machine without going onto a physical network. The names of the other systems are shown in two forms: in a *fully qualified domain* (FQDN) format that is unique on the Internet and as a nickname that is locally unique.

As more hosts joined networks, storing these name-to-address mappings in a text file proved to be inefficient and inconvenient. The file grew ever larger and impossible to keep up-to-date. Linux supports NIS (Network Information Service, page 354), which was developed for use on Sun computers. NIS stores information in a database, making it easier to find a specific address, but it is useful only for host information within a single administrative domain. Hosts outside the domain cannot access the information.

The solution is DNS (Domain Name Service, page 352). DNS effectively addresses the efficiency and update issues by arranging the entire network naming space as a hierarchy. Each domain in the DNS manages its own name space (addressing and name resolution), and each domain can easily query for any host or IP address by following the tree up or down the name space until the appropriate domain is found. By providing a hierarchical naming structure, DNS distributes name administration across the entire Internet.

IPv6

The explosive growth of the Internet has uncovered deficiencies in the design of the current address plan, most notably lack of addresses. Over the next few years, a revised protocol, named IPng (IP Next Generation), or IPv6 (IP version 6),[13] will be phased in (it may take longer; the phase-in is going quite slowly). This new scheme is designed to overcome the major limitations of the current approach and can be phased in gradually because it is compatible with the existing address usage. IPv6 makes it possible to assign many more unique Internet addresses (2^{128}, or 340 *undecillion* [10^{36}]) and supports security and performance control features.

IPv6

- Enables autoconfiguration. With IPv4, autoconfiguration is available using optional DHCP (page 408). With IPv6, autoconfiguration is mandatory, making it easy for hosts to configure their IP addresses automatically.

- Reserves 24 bits in the header for advanced services, such as resource reservation protocols, better backbone routing, and improved traffic engineering.

- Makes multicast protocols mandatory and uses them extensively. In IPv4, multicast, which improves scalability, is optional.

- Aggregates address blocks more efficiently because of the huge address space. This aggregation obsoletes *NAT* (page 984), which decreased scalability and introduced protocol issues.

- Provides a simplified packet header that allows hardware accelerators to work better.

A sample IPv6 address is fe80::a00:20ff:feff:5be2/10. Each group of four hexadecimal digits is equivalent to a number between 0 and 65536 (16^4). A pair of adjacent colons indicates a hex value of 0x0000; leading 0s need not be shown. With eight sets of hexadecimal groupings, there are $65,536^8 = 2^{128}$ possible addresses. In an IPv6 address on a host with the default autoconfiguration, the first characters in the address are always fe80. The last 64 bits hold an interface ID designation, which is often the *MAC address* (page 981) of the Ethernet controller on the system.

---

13. IPv5 referred to an experimental real-time stream protocol named ST thus the jump from IPv4 to IPv6.

Communicate over a Network

Many commands that you can use to communicate with other users on a single computer system have been extended to work over a network. Examples of extended utilities are electronic mail programs, information-gathering utilities (such as finger, page 138), and communications utilities (such as talk, page 142). These utilities are examples of the UNIX philosophy: Instead of creating a new, special-purpose tool, modify an existing one.

Many utilities understand a convention for the format of network addresses: **user@host** (spoken as *user at host*). When you use an @ sign in an argument to one of these utilities, the utility interprets the text that follows as the name of a remote host. When it does not include an @ sign, a utility assumes that you are requesting information from or corresponding with someone on the LAN.

The prompts shown in the examples in this chapter include the hostname of the system you are using. When you frequently use more than one system over a network, you may find it difficult to keep track of which system you are using at any particular moment. If you set your prompt to include the hostname of the current system, it will always be clear which system you are using. To identify the computer you are using, run hostname or **uname –n**:

```
$ hostname
kudos
```

See page 284 for information on how you can change the prompt.

finger: Displays Information About Remote Users

The finger utility displays information about one or more users on a system. This utility was designed for local use, but when networks became popular, it was obvious that finger should be enhanced to reach out and collect information remotely. In the following examples, finger displays information about all the users logged in on the system named **bravo**:

```
[kudos]$ finger @bravo
[bravo.example.com]
Login     Name           Tty   Idle  Login Time    Office     Office Phone
root      root           *1    1:35  Oct 22  5:00
alex      Alex Watson    4           Oct 22 12:23 (kudos)
alex      Alex Watson    5      19   Oct 22 12:33 (:0)
jenny     Jenny Chen     7     2:24  Oct 22  8:45 (:0)
hls       Helen Simpson  11     2d   Oct 20 12:23 (:0)
```

A user's login name in front of the @ sign causes finger to display information from the remote system for the specified user only. If there are multiple matches for that name on the remote system, finger displays the results for all of them:

```
[kudos]$ finger alex@bravo
[bravo.example.com]
Login      Name           Tty  Idle  Login Time   Office      Office Phone
alex       Alex Watson    4          Oct 22 12:23 (kudos)
alex       Alex Watson    5     19   Oct 22 12:33 (:0)
```

The finger utility works by querying a standard network service, the **fingerd** dae-mon, that runs on the system being queried. Although this service is supplied with Red Hat Linux, some sites choose not to run it to minimize the load on their systems, reduce security risks, or maintain privacy. When you use finger to obtain information about someone at such a site, you will see an error message or nothing at all. It is the remote **fingerd** daemon that determines how much information to share and in what format. As a result, the report displayed for any given system may differ from the preceding examples.

<table>
<tr><td>security ||</td><td>**The fingerd Daemon**</td></tr>
</table>

The finger daemon (**fingerd**) gives away system account information that can aid a malicious user. Some sites disable finger or randomize user account IDs to make a malicious user's job more difficult. Disable finger by giving the following command as **root**: **chkconfig finger off**.

The information for remote finger looks much the same as it does when finger runs on the local system, with one difference: Before displaying the results, finger reports the name of the remote system that answered the query (**bravo**, as shown in brackets in the preceding example). The name of the host that answers may be different from the system name you specified on the command line, depending on how the finger daemon service is configured on the remote system. In some cases, several hostnames may be listed if one finger daemon contacts another to retrieve the information.

Sending Mail to a Remote User

Given a user's login name on a remote system and the name of the remote system or its domain, you can use an email program to send a message over the network or the Internet, using the @ form of an address:

    jenny@bravo

or

    jenny@example.com

Although the @ form of a network address is recognized by many Linux utilities, you may find that you can reach more remote computers with email than with the other networking utilities described in this chapter. The reason for this disparity is that the mail system can deliver a message to a host that does not run IP, even though it appears to have an Internet address. The message may be routed over the network, for example, until it reaches a remote system that has a point-to-point, dial-up connection to the destination system. Other utilities, such as talk, rely on IP and operate only between networked hosts.

Mailing List Servers

A mailing list server (listserv[14]) allows you to create, manage, and administrate an email list. An electronic mailing list provides a means for people interested in a topic to participate in an electronic discussion and for a person to disseminate information periodically to a potentially large mailing list. One of the most powerful features of most list servers is the ability to archive email postings to the list, create an archive index, and allow users to retrieve postings from the archive based on keywords or discussion threads. Typically, you can subscribe and unsubscribe from the list with or without human intervention. The owner of the list can restrict who can subscribe, unsubscribe, and post messages to the list. Popular list servers include LISTSERV (www.lsoft.com), Lyris (www.lyris.com), Majordomo (www.greatcircle.com/majordomo), Mailman (www.list.org and see page 627), and ListProc (www.listproc.net). Red Hat maintains quite a few mailing lists and list archives for those lists (www.redhat.com/mailman/listinfo). Use Google to search on **linux mailing list** to find other lists.

Network Utilities

To make use of a networked environment, it made sense to extend certain tools, some of which have already been described. Networks also created a need for new utilities to control and monitor them; this led to ideas for new tools that took advantage of network speed and connectivity. This section describes concepts and utilities for systems attached to a network; without a network connection, they are of little use.

Trusted Hosts

Some commands, including rcp and rsh, work only if the remote system trusts your local computer (that is, the remote system knows your local computer and believes that it is not pretending to be a system that it is not). The **/etc/hosts.equiv** file lists trusted systems. For reasons of security, Superuser account does not rely on this file to identify trusted Superusers from other systems.

Host-based trust is largely obsolete. Because there are many ways to subvert trusted host security, including subverting DNS systems and *IP spoofing* (page 978), authentication based on IP address is widely regarded as insecure and obsolete. In a small homogeneous network of machines with local DNS control, it can be "good enough." The ease of use in these situations may outweigh the security concerns.

---

14. Although the term *listserv* is sometimes used generically to include many different list server programs, it is a specific product and a registered trademark of L-soft International, Inc.: LISTSERV (for information go to www.lsoft.com).

OpenSSH Tools

The OpenSSH project provides a set of tools that replace rcp, rsh, and others with secure equivalents. These are installed by default and can be used as drop-in replacements for their insecure counterparts. The OpenSSH tool suite is covered in detail in Chapter 18 (page 563).

telnet: Logs in on a Remote System

You can use the TELNET protocol to interact with a remote computer. The telnet utility, a user interface to this protocol, is older than ssh and is not secure, but it may work where ssh (page 570) is not available (there is more non-UNIX support for TELNET access than there is for ssh access). In addition, many legacy devices, such as terminal servers and network devices, do not support ssh.

```
[bravo]$ telnet kudos
Trying 172.19.52.2...
Connected to kudos.example.com
Escape character is '^]'.

Welcome to SuSE Linux 7.3 (i386) - Kernel 2.4.10-4GB (2).
kudos login: watson
Password:
You have old mail in /var/mail/watson.
Last login: Mon Feb 25 14:46:55 from bravo.example.com
watson@kudos:~>
.
.
.
watson@kudos:~> logout
Connection closed by foreign host.
[bravo]$
```

telnet versus ssh   When you connect to a remote UNIX or Linux system using telnet, you are presented with a regular, textual **login:** prompt. Unless you specify differently, the ssh utility assumes that your login name on the remote system matches that on the local system. Because telnet is designed to work with non-UNIX/Linux systems, it makes no such assumptions.

telnet Is Not Secure

Whenever you enter sensitive information, such as your password, while you are using telnet, it is transmitted in cleartext and can be read by someone who is listening in on the session.

Another difference between these two utilities is that telnet allows you to configure many special parameters, such as how RETURNs or interrupts are processed. When using telnet between two UNIX/Linux systems, you rarely need to change any parameters.

When you do not specify the name of a remote host on the command line, telnet runs in an interactive mode. The following example is equivalent to the previous telnet example:

```
[bravo]$ telnet
telnet> open kudos
Trying 172.19.52.2...
Connected to kudos.example.com
Escape character is '^]'.
...
```

Before connecting you to a remote system, telnet tells you what the *escape character* is; in most cases, it is ^] (the ^ represents the CONTROL key). When you press CONTROL-], you escape to telnet's interactive mode. Continuing the preceding example:

```
[kudos]$ CONTROL-]
telnet> ?
```

(displays help information)

```
telnet> close
Connection closed.
[bravo]$
```

When you enter a question mark in response to the **telnet>** prompt, telnet lists its commands. The **close** command ends the current telnet session, returning you to the local system. To get out of telnet's interactive mode and resume communication with the remote system, press RETURN in response to a prompt.

While telnet is no longer commonly used to access remote systems, it is still used extensively as a debugging tool. The telnet utility allows you to communicate directly with any TCP server and can often be used to diagnose problems quickly. If you are having a problem with a network server, attempting to connect to it using telnet is often a good first step.

It has been possible to use telnet to access special remote services at sites that have chosen to make such services available. However, many of these services, such as the U.S. Library of Congress Information System (LOCIS), have moved to the Web, so you can now obtain the same information using a Web browser.

ftp: Transfers Files over a Network

The File Transfer Protocol (FTP) is a method of downloading files from and uploading files to another system using TCP/IP over a network. FTP is not a secure protocol; use it only for downloading public information from a public server. Chapter 19 (page 583) covers FTP clients and servers.

ping: Tests a Network Connection

The ping[15] utility (http://ftp.arl.mil/~mike/ping.html) sends an ECHO_REQUEST packet to a remote computer. This packet causes the remote system to send back a reply. This is a quick way to verify that a remote system is available, as well as to check how well the network is operating, such as how fast it is or whether it is dropping data packets. The protocol ping uses is ICMP (Internet Control Message Protocol). Without any options, ping tests the connection once per second until you abort the execution with CONTROL-C.

```
$ ping tsx-11.mit.edu
PING tsx-11.mit.edu (18.7.14.121) 56(84) bytes of data.
64 bytes from TSX-11.MIT.EDU (18.7.14.121): icmp_seq=0 ttl=45 time=97.2 ms
64 bytes from TSX-11.MIT.EDU (18.7.14.121): icmp_seq=1 ttl=45 time=96.1 ms
64 bytes from TSX-11.MIT.EDU (18.7.14.121): icmp_seq=2 ttl=45 time=95.7 ms
64 bytes from TSX-11.MIT.EDU (18.7.14.121): icmp_seq=3 ttl=45 time=96.3 ms
CONTROL-C

--- tsx-11.mit.edu ping statistics ---
4 packets transmitted, 4 received, 0% packet loss, time 3001ms
rtt min/avg/max/mdev = 95.755/96.361/97.202/0.653 ms, pipe 2
```

This example shows that the remote system named **tsx-11.mit.edu** is up and available over the network.

By default, ping sends packets containing 64 bytes (56 data bytes and 8 bytes of protocol header information). In the preceding example, four packets were sent to the system **tsx-11.mit.edu** before the user interrupted ping by pressing CONTROL-C. The four-part number in parentheses on each line is the remote system's IP address. A packet sequence number (called **icmp_seq**) is also given. If a packet is dropped, a gap occurs in the sequence numbers. The round-trip time is listed last, in microseconds; this represents the time that elapsed from when the packet was sent from the local system to the remote system until the reply from the remote system was received by the local system. This time is affected by the distance between the two systems, as well as by network traffic and the load on both computers. Before it terminates, ping summarizes the results, indicating how many packets were sent and

---

15. The name ping mimics the sound of a sonar burst used by submarines to identify and communicate with each other. The word ping also expands to Packet Internet Groper.

received, as well as the minimum, average, maximum, and mean deviation round-trip times it measured.

traceroute: Traces a Route over the Internet

The traceroute utility, supplied with Red Hat Linux, traces the route an IP packet follows, including all the intermediary points traversed (called *network hops*), to its destination (the argument to traceroute—an Internet host). It displays a numbered list of hostnames, if available, and IP addresses, together with the round-trip time it took for a packet to get to each router along the way and an acknowledgment to get back. You can put this information to good use when you are trying to determine where a network bottleneck is.

The traceroute utility has no concept of the path from one host to the next; it simply sends out packets with increasing *TTL* values. TTL is an IP header field that indicates how many more hops the packet should be allowed to make before being discarded or returned. In the case of a traceroute packet, the packet is returned by the host that has the packet when the TTL value is zero. The result is a list of hosts that the packet travels through to get to its destination.

The traceroute utility can help you solve routing configuration problems and routing path failures. When you cannot reach a host, use traceroute to see what path the packet follows, how far it gets, and what the delay is.

The next example is the output of traceroute following a route from a local computer to **www.linux.org**. The first line tells you the IP address of the target, the maximum number of hops that will be traced, and the size of the packets that will be used. Each numbered line contains the name and IP address of the intermediate destination, followed by the time it takes a packet to make a round-trip to that destination and back. The traceroute utility sends three packets to each destination; thus there are three times on each line. Line 1 shows the statistics when a packet is sent to the local gateway (under 3 ms). Lines 4–6 show it bouncing around Mountain View (California) before it goes to San Jose. Between hops 13 and 14 the packet travels across the United States (San Francisco to somewhere in the East). By hop 18 the packet has found **www.linux.org**. The traceroute utility displays asterisks when it does not receive a response. Each asterisk indicates that traceroute has waited three seconds.

```
$ /usr/sbin/traceroute www.linux.org
traceroute to www.linux.org (198.182.196.56), 30 hops max, 38 byte packets
 1  gw.localco.com. (204.94.139.65)  2.904 ms  2.425 ms  2.783 ms
 2  covad-gw2.meer.net (209.157.140.1)  19.727 ms  23.287 ms  24.783 ms
 3  gw-mv1.meer.net (140.174.164.1)  18.795 ms  24.973 ms  19.207 ms
 4  d1-4-2.a02.mtvwca01.us.ra.verio.net (206.184.210.241)  59.091 ms d1-10-0-0-200.a03.
      mtvwca01.us.ra.verio.net (206.86.28.5)  54.948 ms  39.485 ms
 5  fa-11-0-0.a01.mtvwca01.us.ra.verio.net (206.184.188.1)  40.182 ms  44.405 ms 49.362 ms
 6  p1-1-0-0.a09.mtvwca01.us.ra.verio.net (205.149.170.66)  78.688 ms  66.266 ms 28.003 ms
 7  p1-12-0-0.a01.snjsca01.us.ra.verio.net (209.157.181.166)  32.424 ms 94.337 ms 54.946 ms
 8  f4-1-0.sjc0.verio.net (129.250.31.81)  38.952 ms  63.111 ms  49.083 ms
 9  sjc0.nuq0.verio.net (129.250.3.98)  45.031 ms  43.496 ms  44.925 ms
10  mae-west1.US.CRL.NET (198.32.136.10)  48.525 ms  66.296 ms  38.996 ms
11  t3-ames.3.sfo.us.crl.net (165.113.0.249)  138.808 ms  78.579 ms  68.699 ms
12  E0-CRL-SFO-02-E0X0.US.CRL.NET (165.113.55.2)  43.023 ms  51.910 ms  42.967 ms
13  sfo2-vva1.ATM.us.crl.net (165.113.0.254)  135.551 ms  154.606 ms  178.632 ms
14  mae-east-02.ix.ai.net (192.41.177.202)  158.351 ms  201.811 ms  204.560 ms
15  oc12-3-0-0.mae-east.ix.ai.net (205.134.161.2)  202.851 ms  155.667 ms  219.116 ms
16  border-ai.invlogic.com (205.134.175.254)  214.622 ms  *  190.423 ms
17  router.invlogic.com (198.182.196.1)  224.378 ms  235.427 ms  228.856 ms
18  www.linux.org (198.182.196.56)  207.964 ms  178.683 ms  179.483 ms
```

host and dig: Queries Internet Nameservers

The host utility looks up an IP address given a name or vice versa. This utility is easy to use and replaces nslookup in its simplest case. The following example shows how to use host to look up the domain name of a machine, given an IP address:

```
$ host 140.174.164.2
2.164.174.140.in-addr.arpa. domain name pointer ns.meer.net.
```

You can also use host to determine the IP address of a domain name:

```
$ host ns.meer.net
ns.meer.net. has address 140.174.164.2
```

The dig (domain information groper) utility queries DNS servers and individual machines for information about a domain. A powerful utility, dig has many features that you may never use. It is more involved than host and replaces nslookup in its complex cases.

The chapter on DNS (page 699) has many examples of the use of host and dig.

whois: Looks Up Information About an Internet Site

The whois utility queries a whois server for information about an Internet site. This utility returns site contact and InterNIC or other registry information that can help you track down the person responsible for a site: Perhaps that person is sending you or your company *spam* (page 997). Many sites on the Internet are easier to use and faster than whois. Use a browser and search engine to search on **whois** or go to www.networksolutions.com/en_US/whois or www.ripe.net/perl/whois to get started.

When you search by name, whois may return more than one entry. In the following example, whois returns **SOBELL.NET** and **SOBELL.COM** when queried for **sobell**:

```
$ whois sobell
[whois.crsnic.net]

Whois Server Version 1.3

Domain names in the .com, .net, and .org domains can now be registered
with many different competing registrars. Go to http://www.internic.net
for detailed information.

SOBELL.NET
SOBELL.COM

To single out one record, look it up with "xxx", where xxx is one of the
of the records displayed above. If the records are the same, look them up
with "=xxx" to receive a full display for each record.

>>> Last update of whois database: Tue, 26 Feb 2002 05:22:08 EST <<<

The Registry database contains ONLY .COM, .NET, .ORG, .EDU domains and
Registrars.
```

When you do not specify a whois server, whois defaults to **whois.crsnic.net**. Set the **NICNAMESERVER** or **WHOISSERVER** shell variables, or use the **–h** option to whois to specify a different whois server.

To obtain information on a domain name, specify the complete domain name as in the following example:

```
$ whois sobell.com
[whois.crsnic.net]

Whois Server Version 1.3

Domain names in the .com, .net, and .org domains can now be registered
with many different competing registrars. Go to http://www.internic.net
for detailed information.

   Domain Name: SOBELL.COM
   Registrar: NETWORK SOLUTIONS, INC.
   Whois Server: whois.networksolutions.com
   Referral URL: http://www.networksolutions.com
   Name Server: NS.MEER.NET
   Name Server: NS2.MEER.NET
   Updated Date: 05-nov-2001
>>> Last update of whois database: Tue, 26 Feb 2002 05:22:08 EST <<<

The Registry database contains ONLY .COM, .NET, .ORG, .EDU domains and
Registrars.

Registrant:
Sobell Associates Inc (SOBELL-DOM)
```

```
            PO Box 1089
            Menlo Park, CA 94026
            US

            Domain Name: SOBELL.COM

            Administrative Contact, Billing Contact:
               Sobell, Mark  (MS989)  sobell@MEER.NET
               Sobell Associates Inc
               PO Box 1089
               Menlo Park, CA 94026
       [No phone]
            Technical Contact:
               meer.net hostmaster  (MN85-ORG)  hostmaster@MEER.NET
               meer.net
               po box 390804
               Mountain View, CA 94039
               US
               +1.888.844.6337
               Fax- +1.888.844.6337

            Record last updated on 09-Apr-2000.
            Record expires on 08-Apr-2004.
            Record created on 07-Apr-1995.
            Database last updated on 26-Feb-2002 01:57:00 EST.

            Domain servers in listed order:

            NS.MEER.NET                  140.174.164.2
            NS2.MEER.NET                 216.206.136.2
```

Several top-level registries serve various regions of the world. The ones you are most likely to use are

North American Registry	whois.arin.net
European Registry	www.ripe.net
Asia-Pacific Registry	www.apnic.net
American Military	whois.nic.mil
American Government	www.nic.gov

Distributed Computing

When many similar systems are on a network, it is often desirable to share common files and utilities among them. For example, a system administrator might choose to keep a copy of the system documentation on one computer's disk and to make those files available to remote systems. In this case, the system administrator configures the files so users who need to access the online documentation are not aware that the files are stored on a remote system. This type of setup, which is an example of *distributed computing*, not only conserves disk space but also allows you to update

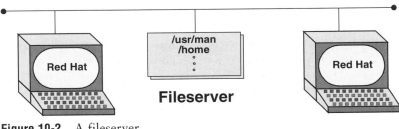

Figure 10-2   A fileserver

one central copy of the documentation rather than tracking down and updating copies scattered throughout the network on many different systems.

Figure 10-2 illustrates a *fileserver* that stores the system manual pages and users' home directories. With this arrangement, a user's files are always available to that user—no matter which system the user logs in on. Each system's disk might contain a directory to hold temporary files, as well as a copy of the operating system. Chapter 22 (page 655) contains instructions for setting up NFS clients and servers in networked configurations such as this.

The Client/Server Model

Mainframe model
The client/server model was not the first computational model. First came the mainframe, which follows a one-machine-does-it-all model. All the intelligence is in one system, including the data and the program that manipulates and reports on the data. Users connect to a mainframe using terminals.

File-sharing model
With the introduction of PCs, file-sharing networks were introduced. Data was downloaded from a shared location to a user's PC where a program manipulated the data. The file-sharing model ran into problems as networks expanded and more users needed access to the data.

Client/server model
In the client/server model, a client uses a protocol, such as FTP, to request services, and a server provides the services that the client requests. Rather than providing data files as the file-sharing model does, the server in a client/server relationship is a database that provides only the pieces of information that the client needs or requests.

The client/server model dominates UNIX and Linux system networking and underlies most of the network services described in this book. FTP, NFS, DNS, email, and HTTP (the web browsing protocol) all rely on the client/server model. Some servers, such as Web servers and browser clients, are designed to interact with specific utilities. Other servers, such as those supporting DNS, communicate with one another, in addition to answering queries from a variety of clients. Clients and servers can reside on the same or different systems running the same or different operating systems. The systems can be proximate or thousands of miles apart. A system that is a server to one system can turn around and be a client to another. A server can reside on a single system or, as is the case with DNS, be distributed among thousands of geographically separated systems running many different operating systems.

Peer-to-peer model   Contrast the client/server model to the peer-to-peer (PTP) model in which either program can initiate a transaction. PTP protocols are common on small networks. Microsoft's Network Neighborhood and Apple's AppleTalk both rely on broadcast-based PTP protocols for browsing and automatic configuration. The Zeroconf multicast DNS protocol is a PTP alternative DNS for small networks. The highest profile PTP networks are those used for file sharing, such as Kazaa and GNUtella. Many of these networks are not pure PTP topologies. Pure PTP networks do not scale well, so networks such as Napster and Kazaa employ a hybrid approach.

DNS: Domain Name Service

DNS is a distributed service: Nameservers on thousands of machines around the world cooperate to keep the database up-to-date. The database itself, which contains the information that maps hundreds of thousands of alphanumeric hostnames into numeric IP addresses, does not exist in one place. That is, no system has a complete copy of the database. Instead, each system that runs DNS knows about the hosts that are local to that site and how to contact other nameservers to learn about other, nonlocal hosts.

Like the Linux filesystem, DNS is organized hierarchically. Each country has an ISO (International Standards Organization) country code designation as its domain name. (For example, **AU** represents Australia, **IL** is Israel, and **JP** is Japan; see www.iana.org/cctld/cctld.htm for a complete list.) Although the United States is represented in the same way (**US**) and uses the standard two-letter Postal Service abbreviations to identify the next level of the domain, only governments and a few organizations use these codes. Schools in the **US** domain are represented by a third- (and sometimes second-) level domain: **k12**. For example, the domain name for My-school in New York state could be www.myschool.k12.ny.us.

Following is a list of the six original, common, top-level domains. These domains are used extensively within the United States and, to a lesser degree, by users in other countries:

COM	Commercial enterprises
EDU	Educational institutions
GOV	Nonmilitary government agencies
MIL	Military government agencies
NET	Networking organizations
ORG	Other (often nonprofit) organizations

As this book was being written, the following additional top-level domains had been approved for use:

AERO	Air-transport industry
BIZ	Business
COOP	Cooperatives

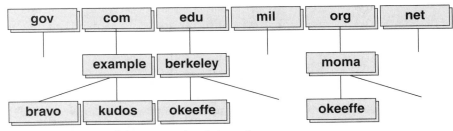

Figure 10-3 United States top-level domains

INFO	Unrestricted use
MUSEUM	Museums
NAME	Name registries

As with Internet addresses, domain names used to be assigned by the Network Information Center (NIC, page 334). Now they are assigned by several companies. A system's full name, referred to as its *fully qualified domain name* (FQDN), is unambiguous in the way that a simple hostname cannot be. The system **okeeffe.berkeley.edu** at the University of California, Berkeley (Figure 10-3) is not the same as one named **okeeffe.moma.org**, which might represent a host at the Museum of Modern Art. The domain name not only tells you something about where the system is located but also adds enough diversity to the name space to avoid confusion when different sites choose similar names for their systems.

Unlike the filesystem hierarchy, the top-level domain name in the United States appears last (reading from left to right). Also, domain names are not case sensitive. The names **okeeffe.berkeley.edu**, **okeeffe.Berkeley.edu**, and **okeeffe.Berkeley.EDU** refer to the same computer. Once a domain has been assigned, the local site is free to extend the hierarchy to meet local needs.

With DNS, mail addressed to **user@example.com** can be delivered to the computer named **example.com** that handles the corporate mail and knows how to forward messages to user mailboxes on individual machines. As the company grows, the site administrator might decide to create organizational or geographical subdomains. The name **delta.ca.example.com** might refer to a system that supports California offices, with **alpha.co.example.com** dedicated to Colorado. Functional subdomains might be another choice, with **delta.sales.example.com** and **alpha.dev.example.com** representing the sales and development divisions, respectively.

On Linux systems, the most common interface to the DNS is BIND (Berkeley Internet Name Domain). BIND follows the client/server model. On any given local network, one or more systems may be running a nameserver, supporting all the local hosts as clients. When it wants to send a message to another host, a system queries the nearest nameserver to learn the remote host's IP address. The client, called a *resolver*, may be a process running on the same computer as the nameserver, or it may pass the request over the network to reach a server. To reduce network traffic and accelerate name lookups, the local nameserver has some knowledge of distant hosts.

If the local server has to contact a remote server to pick up an address, when the answer comes back, the local server adds that to its internal table and reuses it for a while. The nameserver deletes the nonlocal information before it can become outdated. Refer to "TTL" on page 1002.

How the system translates symbolic hostnames into addresses is transparent to most users; only the system administrator of a networked system needs to be concerned with the details of name resolution. Systems that use DNS for name resolution are generally capable of communicating with the greatest number of hosts—more than would be practical to maintain in an **/etc/hosts** file or private NIS database. Chapter 24 (page 699) covers setting up and running a DNS server.

Three common sources are used for host name resolution: NIS, DNS, and system files (such as **/etc/hosts**). Linux does not ask you to choose among these sources; rather, the **nsswitch.conf** file (page 413) allows you to choose any of these sources, in any combination, and in any order.

NIS: Network Information Service

NIS (Network Information Service) simplifies the administration of common administrative files by maintaining them in a central database and having clients contact the database server to retrieve information from the database. Just as DNS addresses the problem of keeping multiple copies of **hosts** files up-to-date, NIS deals with the issue of keeping system-independent configuration files (such as **/etc/passwd**) current. Refer to Chapter 21 (page 637) for coverage of NIS.

NFS: Network Filesystem

The NFS (Network Filesystem) protocol allows a server to share selected local directory hierarchies with client systems on a heterogeneous network. Files on the remote fileserver appear as if they are present on the local system. NFS is covered in Chapter 22 (page 655).

optional ‖

Internet Services

Linux Internet services are provided by daemons that run continuously or by a daemon that is started automatically by the **xinetd** daemon (page 357) when a service request comes in. The **/etc/services** file lists network services (for example, **telnet, ftp, ssh**) and their associated numbers. Any service that uses TCP/IP or UDP/IP uses an entry in this file. IANA (Internet Assigned Numbers Authority) maintains a database of all permanent, registered services. The **/etc/services** file usually lists a small, commonly used subset of services. Go to www.rfc.net/rfc1700.html for more information and a complete list of registered services.

Most of the daemons (the executable files) are stored in **/usr/sbin**. By convention, the names of many daemons end with the letter **d** to distinguish them from utilities (one common daemon whose name does not end in **d** is **sendmail**). The prefix **in.** or **rpc.** is often used for daemon names. Look at **/usr/sbin/*d** to see a list of many of the daemon programs on the local system. Refer to "Init Scripts: Start and Stop System Services" on page 381 and service: Configures Services I on page 383 for information about starting and stopping these daemons.

As an example of how a daemon works, when you run ssh, the local system contacts the ssh daemon (**sshd**) on the remote system to establish the connection. The two systems negotiate the connection according to a fixed protocol. Each system identifies itself to the other, and then they take turns asking each other specific questions and waiting for valid replies. Each network service follows its own protocol.

In addition to the daemons that support the utilities described up to this point, many other daemons support system-level network services that you will not typically interact with. Some of these daemons are listed in Table 10-4.

table 10-4 ‖   **Common Daemons**

Daemon	Used For or By	Function
apmd	Advanced power management	Reports and takes action on specified changes in system power, including shutdowns. Useful with machines, such as laptops, that run on batteries.
atd	at	Executes a command once at a specific time and date. See **crond** for periodic execution of a command.
automount	Automatic mounting	Automatically mounts filesystems when they are accessed. Automatic mounting is a way of demand-mounting remote directories without having to hard-configure them into **/etc/fstab**.
crond	cron	Used for periodic execution of tasks, this daemon looks in the **/var/spool/cron** directory for files with filenames that correspond to users' login names. It also looks at the **/etc/crontab** file and at files in the **/etc/cron.d** directory. When a task comes up for execution, crond executes it as the user who owns the file that describes the task.
dhcpcd	DHCP	DHCP client daemon (page 410).
dhcpd	DHCP	Assigns Internet address, subnet mask, default gateway, DNS, and other information to hosts. This protocol answers DHCP requests and, optionally, BOOTP requests. Refer to "DHCP" on page 408.
fingerd	finger	Handles requests for user information from the finger utility. Launched by **xinetd**.

table 10-4 ||		Common Daemons (Continued)
Daemon	**Used For or By**	**Function**
ftpd	FTP	Handles FTP requests. Refer to "ftp: Transfers Files over a Network" on page 346. See also **vsftpd** (page 583). Launched by **xinetd**.
gpm	General-purpose mouse or GNU paste manager	Allows you to use a mouse to cut and paste text on console applications.
httpd	HTTP	The Web server daemon (Apache, page 759).
inetd		Deprecated in favor of **xinetd**.
lpd	line printer spooler daemon	Launched by **xinetd** when printing requests come to the machine. Not used with CUPS.
named	DNS	Supports DNS (page 699).
nfsd, statd, lockd, mountd, rquotad	NFS	These five daemons operate together to handle NFS (page 655) operations. The **nfsd** daemon handles file and directory requests. The **statd** and **lockd** daemons implement network file and record locking. The **mountd** daemon takes care of converting a filesystem name request from the mount utility into an NFS handle and checks access permissions. Finally, if disk quotas are enabled, **rquotad** handles those.
ntpd	NTP	Synchronizes time on network computers. Requires a **/etc/ntp.conf** file. For more information go to www.ntp.org.
portmap	RPC	Maps incoming requests for RPC service numbers to a TCP or UDP port numbers on the local machine. Refer to "RPC Network Services" on page 358.
pppd	PPP	For a modem, this protocol controls the pseudointerface represented by the IP connection between the local computer and a remote computer. Refer to "PPP: Point-to-Point Protocol" on page 333.
rexecd	rexec	Allows a remote user with a valid username and password to run programs on a machine. Its use is generally deprecated because of security, but certain programs, such as PC-based X servers, may still have it as an option. Launched by **xinetd**.
routed	Routing tables	Manages the routing tables so your system knows where to send messages that are destined for remote networks. If your system does not have a **/etc/defaultrouter** file, **routed** is started automatically to listen to incoming routing messages and to advertise outgoing routes to other systems on the local network. A newer daemon, the Gateway daemon (**gated**), offers enhanced configurability and support for more routing protocols and is proportionally more complex.

table 10-4 ‖		Common Daemons (Continued)
Daemon	**Used For or By**	**Function**
sendmail	Mail programs	The **sendmail** daemon came from Berkeley UNIX and has been available for a long time. The de facto mail transfer program on the Internet, the **sendmail** daemon always listens on port 25 for incoming mail connections and then calls a local delivery agent, such as **/bin/mail**. Mail user agents, such as Kmail and Mozilla mail, typically use **sendmail** to deliver mail messages.
smbd, nmbd	Samba	Allow Windows PCs to share files and printers with UNIX/Linux computers (page 675).
sshd	ssh, scp	Enables secure logins between remote machines (page 574).
syslogd	System log	Transcribes important system events and stores them in files and/or forwards them to users or another host running the **syslogd** daemon. This daemon is configured with **/etc/syslog.conf** and used with the syslog utility. See page 546.
talkd	talk	Allows you to have a conversation with another user on the same or a remote machine. The **talkd** daemon handles the connections between the machines. The talk utility on each machine contacts the **talkd** daemon on the other machine for a bidirectional conversation. Launched by **xinetd**.
telnetd	TELNET	One of the original Internet remote access protocols (page 344). Launched by **xinetd**.
tftpd	TFTP	Used to boot a system or get information from a network. Examples include network computers, routers, and some printers. Launched by **xinetd**.
timed	Time server	On a LAN synchronizes time with other computers that are also running **timed**.
xinetd	Internet *Superserver*	Listens for service requests on network connections and starts up the appropriate daemon to respond to any particular request. Because of **xinetd**, a system does not need the daemons running all the time in order to handle various network requests. For more information, refer to "The xinetd Super Server" on page 403.

Proxy Server

A *proxy* is a network service that is authorized to act for a system while not being part of that system. A proxy server or proxy gateway provides proxy services; it is a transparent intermediary, relaying communications back and forth between an application, such as a browser and a server, usually outside of a LAN and frequently on the Internet. When more than one process uses the proxy gateway/server, it must keep track of which processes are connecting to which hosts/servers so that it can route the return messages to the proper process. The most common proxies you will encounter are email and Web proxies.

A proxy server/gateway insulates the local computer from all other computers or from specified domains by using at least two IP addresses: one to communicate with your local computer and one to communicate with a server. The proxy server/gateway examines and changes the header information on all packets it handles so it can encode, route, and decode them properly. The difference between a proxy gateway and a proxy server is that the proxy server usually includes *cache* (page 961) to store frequently used Web pages so that the next request for that page is available locally and quickly; a proxy gateway usually does not use cache. The terms proxy server and proxy gateway are frequently interchanged.

Proxy servers/gateways are available for such common Internet services as HTTP, HTTPS, FTP, SMTP, and SNMP. When an HTTP proxy sends queries from local machines, it presents a single organization-wide IP address (the external IP address of the proxy server/gateway) to all servers. It funnels all user requests to servers and keeps track of them. When the responses come back, it fans them out to the appropriate applications, using each machine's unique IP address, protecting local addresses from remote/specified servers. Proxy servers/gateways are generally just one part of an overall firewall strategy to prevent intruders from stealing information or damaging an internal network. Other functions, which can be combined with or be separate from the proxy server/gateway, are packet filtering, which blocks traffic based on origin and type, and user activity reporting, which helps management learn how the Internet is being used.

RPC Network Services

Much of the client/server interaction over a network is implemented using the RPC (remote procedure call) protocol, which is implemented as a set of library calls that make network access transparent to the client and server. RPC specifies and interprets messages and does not concern itself with transport protocols; RPC runs on top of TCP/IP and UDP/IP. Services that use RPC include NFS and NIS. RPC was developed by Sun as ONC RPC (Open Network Computing Remote Procedure Calls) and differs from Microsoft RPCs.

In the client/server model, a client contacts a server on a specific *port* (page 989) to avoid any mix up between services, clients, and servers. To avoid maintaining a long list of port numbers and to enable new clients/servers to start up without registering a port number with a central registry, when a server that uses RPC starts, the server specifies the port it expects to be contacted on. Common RPC servers have port numbers that are defined by Sun. If a server does not use a predefined port number, it picks an arbitrary number.

The server then registers this port with the RPC portmapper (the **portmap** daemon) on the local system. The server tells the daemon which port number it is listening on and which RPC program numbers it serves. Because of these exchanges, the **portmap** daemon knows the location of every registered port on the host and which programs are available on each of these ports. The **portmap** daemon, which always listens on port 111 for both TCP and UDP, must be running in order to make RPC calls.

Files The **/etc/rpc** file (page 433) maps RPC services to RPC numbers and the **/etc/services** file (page 433) lists system services.

RPC client/server communication The sequence of events for communication between an RPC client and server is shown following:

1. The client program on the client system makes an RPC call to obtain data from a (remote) server system. (The client issues a read record from a file request.)

2. If RPC has not yet established a connection with the server system for the client program, it contacts **portmap** on port 111 of the server and asks which port the desired RPC server is listening on (for example, **rpc.nfsd**).

3. The **portmap** daemon on the remote server looks in its tables and returns a UDP or TCP port number to the local system, the client (typically 2049 for **nfs**).

4. The RPC libraries on the server system receive the call from the client and pass the request to the appropriate server program. The origin of the request is transparent to the server program. (The filesystem receives the read record from file request.)

5. The server responds to the request. (The filesystem reads the record.)

6. The RPC libraries on the remote server return the result over the network to the client program. (The read record is returned to the calling program.)

Because standard RPC servers are normally started by the **xinetd** daemon (page 369), the **portmap** daemon must be started before the **xinetd** daemon is invoked. The init scripts (page 381) make sure **portmap** starts before **xinetd**; look at the numbers associated with **/etc/rc.d/*/S*portmap** and **/etc/rc.d/*/S*/xinetd**. If the **portmap** daemon stops, you must restart all RPC servers on the local system.

Usenet

One of the earliest information services available on the Internet, Usenet is an electronic bulletin board that allows users with common interests to exchange information.

Usenet is an informal, loosely connected network of systems that exchange email and news items (commonly referred to as *netnews*). Usenet was formed in 1979 when a few sites decided to share some software and information on topics of common interest. They agreed to contact one another and to pass the information along over dial-up telephone lines (at that time running at 1200 baud at best), using UNIX's uucp utility (UNIX-to-UNIX copy program).

The popularity of Usenet led to major changes in uucp to handle the ever-escalating volume of messages and sites. Today, much of the news flows over network links using a sophisticated protocol designed especially for this purpose: NNTP (Network News Transfer Protocol). The news messages are stored in a standard format, and the many public domain programs available let you read them. An old, simple interface is named readnews. Others, such as rn, its X Window System cousin xrn, tin, nn, and xvnews have many features that help you browse through and reply to the articles that are available or create articles of your own. In addition, Netscape and Mozilla include an interface that you can use to read news (Netscape/Mozilla News) as part of their Web browsers. One of the easiest ways to read netnews is to go to groups.google.com. The program you select to read netnews is largely a matter of personal taste.

Because programs to read netnews articles have been ported to non-UNIX/Linux systems, the community of netnews users has diversified. In the UNIX tradition, categories of netnews groups are structured hierarchically. The top level includes such designations as **comp** (computer-related), **misc** (miscellaneous), **rec** (recreation), **sci** (science), **soc** (social issues), and **talk** (ongoing discussions). Usually at least one regional category is at the top level, such as **ba** (San Francisco Bay Area), and includes information about local events. Many new categories are continually being added to the more than 30,000 newsgroups. The names of newsgroups resemble domain names but are read from left to right (like Linux filenames): **comp.os.UNIX.misc, comp.lang.c, misc.jobs.offered, rec.skiing, sci.med, soc.singles, talk.politics** are a few. The following article appeared in **linux.redhat.install**:

```
> I have just installed Fedora 2 and when i try to start X I get the
> following error message:
>
>
> Fatal Server Error.
> no screens found
>
>
> XIO: Fatal IO err 104 (connection reset by peer) on X server ",0.0" after
> 0 requests (0 known processed) with 0 events remaining.
>
> How can i solve this problem?
>
> Thanks,
> Fred
```

```
Fred,
It would appear that your X configuration is incorrect or missing.  You
should run system-config-display and set up the configuration for your
video card and monitor.  You may also have to run mouseconfig to set it up.

Carl
```

A great deal of useful information is available on Usenet, but you need patience and perseverance to find what you are looking for. You can ask a question, as the user did in the previous example, and someone from halfway around the world may answer it. Before posing such a simple question and causing it to appear on thousands of systems around the world, ask yourself whether you can get help in a less invasive way. Try the following:

- Refer to the man pages and info.

- Look through the files in **/usr/share/doc**.

- Ask the system administrator or another user for help.

- All the popular newsgroups have FAQs (lists of frequently asked questions). Consult these lists and see whether your question has been answered. FAQs are periodically posted to the newsgroups; in addition, all the FAQs are archived at sites around the Internet, including the Usenet newsgroup **comp.answers** and ftp://ftp.uu.net (see the **index/info** directory for a list).

- Because someone has probably asked the same question earlier, search the netnews archives for an answer: Try looking at groups.google.com, which has a complete netnews archive.

- Use a search engine to find an answer. One good way to get help is to search on an error message.

- Review support documents at **www.redhat.com**.

- Contact a Red Hat Linux users' group.

Use the worldwide Usenet community as a last resort. If you are stuck on a Linux question and cannot find any other help, try submitting it to one of these newsgroups:

- **linux.redhat.install**

- **linux.redhat.misc**

For more generic questions, try these lists:

- **comp.os.linux.misc**

- **comp.os.linux.networking**

- **comp.os.linux.security**

- **comp.os.linux.setup**

- **linux.redhat.rpm**

One way to find out about new tools and services is to read Usenet news. The **comp.os.linux** hierarchy is of particular interest to Linux users; for example, news about newly released software for Linux is posted to **comp.os.linux.announce**. People often announce the availability of free software there, along with instructions on how to get a copy for your own use using anonymous FTP (page 589). Other tools to help you find resources, both old and new, exist on the network; see Appendix B.

WWW: World Wide Web

The World Wide Web (WWW, W3, or the Web) provides a unified, interconnected interface to the vast amount of information stored on computers around the world. The idea that created the World Wide Web came from the mind of Tim Berners-Lee of the European Particle Physics Laboratory (CERN) in response to a need to improve communications throughout the High Energy Physics community. The first generation was a notebook program named Enquire, short for *Enquire Within Upon Everything* (the name of a book from Berners-Lee's childhood), that he created in 1980 and that provided for links to be made between named nodes. It was not until 1989 that the concept was proposed as a global hypertext project to be known as the World Wide Web. In 1990, Berners-Lee wrote a proposal for a Hyper-Text project, which eventually produced HTML, HyperText Markup Language, the common language of the Web. The World Wide Web program became available on the Internet in the summer of 1991. By designing the tools to work with existing protocols, such as FTP and gopher, the researchers who created the Web created a system that is generally useful for many types of information and across various types of hardware and operating systems.

The WWW is another example of the client/server paradigm. You use a WWW client application, or *browser*, to retrieve/display information stored on a server that may be located anywhere on your local network or the Internet. WWW clients can interact with many types of servers; for example, you can use a WWW client to contact a remote FTP server and display the list of files it offers for anonymous FTP. Most commonly, you use a WWW client to contact a WWW server, which offers support for the special features of the World Wide Web that are described in the remainder of this chapter.

The power of the Web is in its use of *hypertext*, a way to navigate through information by following cross-references (called *links*) from one piece of information to another. To use the Web effectively, you need to be able to run interactive network applications. The first GUI for browsing the Web was a tool named Mosaic, released in February 1993. It was designed at the National Center for Supercomputer Applications at the University of Illinois and sparked a dramatic increase in the number of users of the World Wide Web. Marc Andreessen, who participated in the

Mosaic project at the University of Illinois, later cofounded Netscape Communications with the founder of Silicon Graphics, Jim Clark. They created Netscape Navigator, a Web client program that was designed to perform better and support more features than the Mosaic browser. Netscape Navigator has enjoyed immense success and has become a popular choice for users exploring the World Wide Web. Important for Linux users is fact that from the beginning, Netscape has provided versions of its tools that run on Linux. Also, Netscape created Mozilla (mozilla.org) as an open-source browser project.

Mozilla and the Netscape Navigator provide GUIs that allow you to listen to sounds, watch Web events or live news reports, and display pictures as well as text, giving you access to *hypermedia*. A picture on your screen may be a link to more detailed, nonverbal information, such as a copy of the same picture at a higher resolution or a short animation. When you run Mozilla or Netscape on a system that is equipped for audio, you can to listen to audio clips that have been linked to a document.

URL: Uniform Resource Locator

Consider the URL http://www.w3.org/pub/WWW. The first component in the URL indicates the type of resource, in this case, **http** (HTTP—HyperText Transfer Protocol). Other valid resource names, such as **https** (HTTPS—secure HTTP) and **ftp** (FTP—File Transfer Protocol), represent information available on the Web, using other protocols. Next comes a colon and double slash (**://**). Frequently the **http://** string is omitted from a URL in print, as you seldom need to enter it to get to the URL. Following this is the full name of the host that acts as the server for the information (**www.w3.org/**). The rest of the URL is a relative pathname to the file that contains the information (**pub/WWW**). Enter a URL in the location bar text box of a Web browser, and the Web server returns the page, frequently an *HTML* (page 975) file, pointed to by this URL.

By convention, many sites identify their WWW servers by prefixing a host or domain name with **www**. For example, you can reach the Web server at the New Jersey Institute of Technology at www.njit.edu. When you use a browser to explore the World Wide Web, you may never need to use a URL directly. However, as more information is published in hypertext form, you cannot help but find URLs everywhere—not just online in mail messages and Usenet articles, but also in newspapers, advertisements, and on product labels.

Browsers

Mozilla (www.mozilla.org) is the open-source counterpart to Netscape. Mozilla was first released in March 1998, and was based on Netscape 4 code. Since that time, Mozilla has been under development by employees of Netscape (now a division of

AOL), Red Hat, and other companies and by contributors from the community. KDE offers Konqueror, an all-purpose file manager and Web browser (page 87). Other browsers include epiphany (www.gnome.org/projects/epiphany) and Opera (www.opera.com). Although each Web browser is unique, they all allow you to move about the Internet, viewing HTML documents, listening to sounds, and retrieving files. If you do not use the X Window System, try a text browser, such as lynx or links. The lynx browser works well with a braille terminal.

Search Engine

Search engine is a name that applies to a group of hardware and software tools that help you find World Wide Web sites that have the specific information you are looking for. A search engine relies on a database of information collected by a *Web crawler,* a program that regularly looks through the millions of pages that make up the World Wide Web. A search engine must also have a way of collating the information the Web crawler collects so that you can access it quickly, easily, and in a manner that makes it most useful to you. This part of the search engine, called an *index*, allows you to search for a word, a group of words, or a concept and returns the URLs of Web pages that pertain to what you are searching for. Many different types of search engines are on the Internet. Each type of search engine has its own set of strengths and weaknesses.

Chapter Summary

A Linux system attached to a network is probably communicating on an Ethernet, which may be linked to other local area networks (LANs) and wide area networks (WANs). Communication between LANs and WANs requires the use of gateways and routers. Gateways translate the local data to a format suitable for the wide area network, and routers make decisions about optimal routing of the data along the way. The most widely used network, by far, is the Internet.

Basic networking tools allow Linux users to log in and run commands on remote systems (ssh, telnet) and copy files quickly from one system to another (scp, ftp/sftp). Many tools that were originally designed to support communication on a single-host computer (for example, finger and talk) have been extended to recognize network addresses, thus allowing users on different systems to interact with one another. Other features, such as the Network Filesystem (NFS), were created to extend the basic UNIX model and to simplify information sharing.

Concern is growing for the security and privacy of machines connected to networks and of data transmitted over networks. Toward this end, many new tools and protocols have been created: ssh, scp, HTTPS, IPv6, firewall hardware and software,

VPN, and so on. Many of these tools take advantage of newer, more impenetrable encryption techniques. In addition, some concepts, such as that of trusted hosts, and some tools, such as finger and rwho, are being discarded in the name of security.

Two major advantages of computer networks over other ways of connecting computers are that they enable systems to communicate at high speeds and require few physical interconnections (typically one per system, often on a shared cable). The Internet Protocol (IP), the universal language of the Internet, has made it possible for dissimilar computer systems around the world to communicate easily with one another. Technological advances continue to improve the performance of computer systems and the networks that link them.

One way to gather information on the Internet is Usenet news (netnews). Many Linux users routinely read Usenet news to learn about the latest resources available for their systems. Usenet news is organized into newsgroups that cover a wide range of topics, computer-related and otherwise. To read Usenet news, you need to have access to a news server and the appropriate client software. Many modern mailers, such as Mozilla and Netscape, can display netnews.

The rapid increase of network communication speeds in recent years has encouraged the development of many new applications and services. The World Wide Web provides access to vast information stores on the Internet and makes extensive use of hypertext links to promote efficient searching through related documents. The World Wide Web adheres to the client/server model so pervasive in networking; typically the WWW client is local to a site or is made available through an Internet service provider. WWW servers are responsible for providing the information requested by their many clients.

Netscape Navigator is a WWW client program that has enormous popular appeal. Netscape and Mozilla use a GUI to give you access to text, picture, and audio information: Making extensive use of these hypermedia simplifies access to and enhances the presentation of information.

Exercises

1. Describe the similarities and differences among these utilities:

   a. scp and ftp

   b. ssh and telnet

   c. rsh and ssh

2. Assuming rwho is disabled on the systems on your LAN, describe two ways to find out who is logged in on some of the other machines attached to your network.

3. Explain the client/server model and give three examples of services on Linux systems that take advantage of this model.

4. A software implementation of chess was developed by GNU and is free software. How can you use the Internet to find a copy and download it?

5. What is the difference between the World Wide Web and the Internet?

6. If you have access to the World Wide Web, answer the following:

   a. What browser do you use?

   b. What is the URL of the author of this book's home page? How many links does it have?

   c. Does your browser allow you to create bookmarks? If so, how do you create a bookmark? How can you delete one?

7. Give one advantage and two disadvantages of using a wireless network.

Advanced Exercises

8. Suppose the link between Routers 1 and 2 is down in the Internet shown in Figure 10-1 on page 330. What happens if someone at Site C sends a message to a user on a workstation attached to the Ethernet cable at Site A? What happens if the router at Site A is down? What does this tell you about designing network configurations?

9. If you have a class B network and want to divide it into subnets, each with 126 hosts, what subnet mask should you use? How many networks will be available? What are the four addresses (broadcast and network number) for the network starting at 131.204.18?

10. Suppose you have 300 hosts and want to have no more than about 50 hosts per subnet. What size address block should you request from your ISP? How many class C-equivalent addresses would you need? How many subnets would you have left over from your allocation?

11. On your system, find two daemons running that are not listed in this chapter, and explain what purpose they serve.

   Review what services/daemons are automatically started on your system, and consider which you might turn off. Are there any services/daemons in the list in Table 10-4 on page 355 that you would consider adding?

PART IV
System Administration

System Administration: Core Concepts

11

The job of a system administrator is to keep one or more systems useful and convenient for users. On a Linux system, the administrator and user may both be you, with you and a single computer only a few feet apart. Or the system administrator may be halfway around the world, supporting a network of systems, with you simply one of thousands of users. A system administrator can be one person who works part time taking care of a system and perhaps is also a user of the system. Or the administrator can be several people, all working full-time to keep many systems running.

A well-maintained system

- Runs quickly enough so users do not get too frustrated waiting for the system to respond or complete a task.

- Has enough storage to accommodate users' reasonable needs.

- Provides a working environment appropriate to each user's abilities and requirements.

- Is secure from malicious and accidental acts altering its performance or compromising the security of the data it holds and exchanges with other systems.

- Is backed up regularly with recently backed-up files readily available to users.

- Has recent copies of the software that users need to get their jobs done.

- Is easier to administer than a poorly maintained system.

In addition, a system administrator should be available to help users with all types of system-related problems, from logging in to obtaining and installing software updates to tracking down and fixing obscure network issues.

Part V of this book breaks system administration into the following 7 chapters:

- Chapter 11 (this chapter) covers the core concepts of system administration, including Superuser, system operation, the Red Hat configuration tools and other useful utilities, general information about setting up and securing a server (including a section on DHCP), and PAM.

- Chapter 12 (page 425) covers files, directories, and filesystems from an administrator's point of view.

- Chapter 13 (page 453) covers installing software on the system, including how to use Red Hat Network (RHN), up2date, Apt, yum, BitTorrent, and wget.

- Chapter 14 (page 485) discusses how to set up local and remote printers that use the CUPS printing system.

- Chapter 15 (page 507) explains how to rebuild the Linux kernel.

- Chapter 16 (page 521) covers additional system administrator tasks and tools, including setting up users and groups, backing up files, scheduling tasks, printing system reports, and general problem solving.

- Chapter 17 (page 551) goes into detail about how to set up a LAN, including setting up and configuring the hardware and configuring the software.

Because Linux is configurable and runs on various platforms (Sun SPARC, DEC/Compaq Alpha, Intel x86, AMD, PowerPC, and more), this chapter cannot discuss every system configuration or every action you will have to take as a system administrator. This chapter familiarizes you with the concepts you need to understand and the tools you need to use to maintain a Red Hat Enterprise Linux or Fedora Core system. Where it is not possible to go into depth about a subject, the chapter provides references to other sources.

This chapter assumes that you are familiar with the following terms. Refer to the glossary (page 955) for definitions.

block (device)	environment	mount (a device)	spawn
daemon	filesystem	process	system console
device	fork	root filesystem	X server
device filename	kernel	runlevel	
disk partition	login shell	signal	

System Administrator and Superuser

Much of what a system administrator does is work that ordinary users do not have permission to do. When doing one of these tasks, the system administrator logs in as **root** (or uses another method; see the list starting on page 372) in order to have systemwide powers that are beyond those of ordinary users: A user with **root** privileges is referred to as *Superuser*. The username is **root** by default. Superuser has the following powers and more:

- Some commands, such as those that add new users, partition hard drives, and change system configuration, can be executed only by **root**. Superuser can use certain tools, such as sudo, which is covered shortly, to give specific users permission to perform tasks that are normally reserved for Superuser.

- Read, write, and execute file access and directory access permissions do not affect **root**: Superuser can read from, write to, and execute all files, as well as examine and work in all directories.

- Some restrictions and safeguards that are built into some commands do not apply to **root**. For example, **root** can change any user's password without knowing the old password.

When you are running with **root** (Superuser) privileges, the shell by convention displays a special prompt to remind you of your status. By default, this prompt is or ends with a pound sign (#).

To lessen the chance that a user other than Superuser will try to use them by mistake, many of the commands that Superuser runs are kept in the **/sbin** and **/usr/sbin** directories, rather than in **/bin** and **/usr/bin**. (Many of these commands can be run by ordinary users.) You can execute these commands by giving their full pathnames on the command line (for example, **/sbin/runlevel**). When you log in as **root**, these directories are in your **PATH** (page 283) by default.

caution ‖   **Least Privilege**

When you are working on the computer, especially when you are working as the system administrator, perform any task by using the least privilege possible. When you can perform a task logged in as an ordinary user, do so. When you must be logged in as Superuser, do as much as you can as an ordinary user, log in or use su so that you have **root** privileges, do as much of the task that has to be done as Superuser, and revert to being an ordinary user as soon as you can. Because you are more likely to make a mistake when you are rushing, this concept becomes more important when you have less time to apply it.

You can gain or grant Superuser privileges in a number of ways:

1. When you bring the system up in single-user mode (page 387), you are Superuser.

2. Once the system is up and running in multiuser mode (page 388), you can log in as **root**: When you supply the proper password, you will be Superuser.

3. You can give an su (substitute user) command while you are logged in as yourself, and, with the proper password, you will have Superuser privileges. For more information, refer to "su: Gives You Another User's Privileges" on page 373.

4. You can use sudo selectively to give users Superuser privileges for a limited amount of time on a per-user and per-command basis. The sudo utility is controlled by the **/etc/sudoers** file, which must be set up by **root**. Refer to the sudo man page for more information.

---

security || **root-Owned Setuid Programs Are Extremely Dangerous**

Because a **root**-owned setuid program allows someone who does not know the **root** password to have the powers of Superuser, it is a tempting target for a malicious user. Your site should have as few of these programs as necessary. You can disable setuid programs at the filesystem level by mounting a filesystem with the **nosuid** option (page 443).

---

5. Any user can create a *setuid* (Set User ID) file (page 175). Setuid programs run on behalf of the owner of the file and have all the access privileges that the owner has. While you are running as Superuser, you can change the permissions of a file owned by **root** to setuid. When an ordinary user executes a file that is owned by **root** and has setuid permissions, the program has *full root privileges*. In other words, the program can do anything that **root** can do and that the program does or allows the user to do. The user's privileges do not change. When the program finishes running, all user privileges are back to the way they were before the program was started. Setuid programs that are owned by **root** are extremely powerful and are also extremely dangerous to system security, which is why very few of them are on the system. Examples of setuid programs that are owned by **root** include passwd, at, and crontab. The following example shows two ways for Superuser to give a program setuid privileges:

```
# ls -l my*
-rwxr-xr-x   1 root      other      24152 Apr 29 16:30 myprog
-rwxr-xr-x   1 root      other      24152 Apr 29 16:31 myprog2
# chmod 4755 myprog
# chmod u+s myprog2
# ls -l my*
-rwsr-xr-x   1 root      other      24152 Apr 29 16:30 myprog
-rwsr-xr-x   1 root      other      24152 Apr 29 16:31 myprog2
```

The **s** in the owner execute position of the **ls –l** output (page 173) indicates that the file has setuid permission.

6. Some programs ask you for a password (either your password or the **root** password, depending on the particular command and the configuration of the system) when they start. When you provide the **root** password, the program runs with Superuser privileges.

When a program requests the **root** password when it starts, you stop running as the privileged user when you quit using the program. This setup helps keep you from remaining logged in as Superuser when you do not need/intend to be. Refer to "**consolehelper**: Runs Programs as Root" on page 375.

Some techniques limit the number of ways to become Superuser. PAM (page 416) controls the who, when, and how of logging in. The **/etc/securetty** file controls which terminals (ttys) a user can log in on as **root**. The **/etc/security/access.conf** file adds another dimension to login control (see the file for details).

security ‖	Do Not Allow root Access over the Internet

Prohibiting **root** logins using login over a network is the default policy of Red Hat Enterprise Linux and Fedora and is implemented by the PAM **securetty** module. The **/etc/security/access.conf** file must contain the names of all the users and terminals/workstations that you want a user to be able to log in on as **root**. Initially, every line in **access.conf** is commented out.

If you need **root** access to a system over a network, use **ssh** (page 563). As shipped by Red Hat, **ssh** does not follow the instructions in **securetty** or **access.conf**. Also, in **/etc/ssh/sshd_config**, Red Hat sets **PermitRootLogin** to YES to permit **root** to log in using **ssh** (page 578).

System Administration Tools

Many tools can help you be an efficient and thorough system administrator. A few of these tools/utilities are described in this section, another group of administration utilities is described starting on page 393, and many others are scattered throughout the system administration chapters.

su: Gives You Another User's Privileges

The **su** (substitute user) utility can create a shell or execute a program with the identity and permissions of a specified user. Follow **su** on the command line with the name of a user; if you are **root** or if you know that user's password, you take on the identity of that user. When you give an **su** command without an argument, **su** defaults to Superuser so that you take on the identity of **root** (you have to know the **root** password).

To be sure that you are using the system's official version of su (and not one planted on your system by a malicious user), specify su's absolute pathname (**/bin/su**) when you use it. (Of course, if someone has compromised your system enough to have you run a fake su command, you are in serious trouble anyway, but using an absolute pathname for su is still a good idea.)

When you give an su command to become Superuser, you spawn a new shell, which displays the # prompt. You return to your normal status (and your former shell and prompt) by terminating this shell: Press CONTROL-D, or give an **exit** command. Giving an su command by itself changes your user and group IDs but makes minimal changes to your environment. You still have the same **PATH** you did when you logged in as yourself. When you run a utility that is normally run by **root** (those in **/sbin** and **/usr/sbin**), you need to specify an absolute pathname for the utility (as in **/sbin/service**). When you give the command **su –** (you can use **–l** or **––login** in place of the dash), you get a **root** login shell: It is as though you logged in as **root**. Not only are your user and group IDs those of **root**, but your entire environment is that of **root**. The login shell executes the appropriate start-up scripts before giving you a prompt, and your **PATH** is set to what it would be if you had logged in as **root**, typically including **/sbin** and **/usr/sbin**.

Use the id utility to display the changes in your user and group IDs and in the groups you are associated with:

```
$ id
uid=500(alex) gid=500(alex) groups=500(alex)
$ su
Password:
# id
uid=0(root) gid=0(root) groups=0(root),1(bin),2(daemon),3(sys), ...
```

You can use su with the –c option to run a single command with **root** privileges, returning to your original shell when the command finishes executing. The following example first shows that a user is not permitted to kill a process. With the use of **su –c** and the **root** password, the user is permitted to kill (page 375) the process. The quotation marks are necessary because **su –c** takes its command as a single argument.

```
$ kill -15 4982
-bash: kill: (4982) - Operation not permitted
$ su -c "kill -15 4982"
Password:
$
```

security || Superuser, PATH, and Security

The fewer directories you keep in your **PATH** when you are **root**, the less likely you will be to execute an untrusted program as **root**. If possible, keep only the default directories, along with **/sbin** and **/usr/sbin**, in **root**'s **PATH**. *Never include the working directory (as . or : : anywhere in PATH, or : as the last element of PATH).* For more information, refer to "PATH: Where the Shell Looks for Programs" on page 283.

consolehelper: Runs Programs as Root

The consolehelper utility can make it easier for someone who is logged in on the system console but not logged in as **root** to run system programs that normally can be run only by **root**. PAM (page 416) authenticates users and can be set to trust all console users, to require user passwords (not the **root** password), or to require **root** passwords before granting trust. As shipped, Red Hat sets up PAM to require a **root** password for consolehelper. The concept behind consolehelper is that you may want to consider as trustworthy anyone who has access to the console. You can turn this feature on, so, for example, Alex could log in on the console as himself and run halt without knowing the **root** password. For more information refer to the discussion of consolehelper on page 391 and to the consolehelper man page.

kill: Sends a Signal to a Process

The kill builtin sends a signal to a process. This signal may or may not terminate (kill) the process, depending on the signal sent and how the process is designed. Refer to "trap: Catches a Signal" on page 889 for a discussion of the various signals and how a process receives them. Running kill is not the first method a user or system administrator should try when a process needs to be aborted.

---

caution ‖   **kill: Method of Last Resort**

Because of its inherent dangers, using kill is a method of last resort, especially when you are running as Superuser. One kill command issued by **root** can bring the system down without warning.

When you do need to use kill, send the termination signal (**kill –TERM** or **kill –15**) first. Only when that does not work should you attempt to use the kill signal (**kill –KILL** or **kill –9**).

Usually a user can kill a process from another window or by logging in on another terminal. Sometimes you may have to log in as **root** (or use su) to kill a process for a user. To kill a process, you need to know the PID of the process. The ps utility can give you this information once you know the name of the program the user is running and/or the username of the user. The top utility (page 534) can also be helpful in finding and killing (see top's **k** command) a runaway process.

In the following example, Alex complains that xmms is stuck and that he cannot do anything from the xmms window, not even close it. A more experienced user could open another window and kill the process, but in this case, you kill it for Alex. First, use ps with the **–u** option, followed by the name of the user and the **–f** (full/wide) option to view all the processes associated with that user.

```
$ ps -u alex -f
UID        PID  PPID  C STIME TTY          TIME CMD
alex      2841  2840  0 19:39 tty1     00:00:00 -bash
alex      2896  2841  0 19:40 tty1     00:00:00 /bin/sh /usr/X11R6/bin/startx
alex      2903  2896  0 19:40 tty1     00:00:00 xinit /etc/X11/xinit/xinitrc --
alex      2908  2903  0 19:40 tty1     00:00:00 /bin/bash /usr/bin/startkde
```

```
alex      2974      1   0 19:41 ?          00:00:00 kdeinit:dcopserver --nosid
alex      2977      1   0 19:41 ?          00:00:00 kdeinit:klauncher
alex      2980      1   0 19:41 ?          00:00:00 kdeinit:kded
alex      3002      1   0 19:41 ?          00:00:03 /usr/bin/artsd -F 10 -S 4096 -s 60
alex      3008      1   0 19:41 ?          00:00:00 kdeinit:knotify
alex      3009      1   0 19:41 ?          00:00:00 kdeinit:Running...
alex      3010   2908   0 19:41 tty1       00:00:00 ksmserver --restore
alex      3012   3009   0 19:41 ?          00:00:00 kdeinit:kwin
alex      3014      1   0 19:41 ?          00:00:00 kdeinit:kdesktop
alex      3019      1   0 19:41 ?          00:00:01 kdeinit:kicker
alex      3024      1   0 19:41 ?          00:00:00 kdeinit:klipper -icon klipper
alex      3028      1   0 19:41 ?          00:00:00 kdeinit:kwrited
alex      3029      1   0 19:41 ?          00:00:00 alarmd
alex      3030   3028   0 19:41 pts/2      00:00:00 /bin/cat
alex      3040   3009   0 19:41 ?          00:00:00 kdeinit:konsole -icon konsole
alex      3041   3040   0 19:41 pts/3      00:00:00 /bin/bash
alex      3069      1   0 19:41 ?          00:00:00 kdeinit:kcontrol -caption Control
alex      3074   3041   0 19:42 pts/3      00:00:03 xmms
alex      3101   3074   0 19:42 pts/3      00:00:00 (dns helper)
alex      3121   3014  33 19:49 ?          00:00:41 kscience.kss -window-id 4194310
```

This list is fairly short, and the process running xmms is easy to find. Another way to go about searching is to use ps to produce a long list of all the processes and use grep to find all the processes running xmms.

```
$ ps -ef | grep xmms
alex      3074      1   1 10:22 tty1       00:00:01 xmms
alex      3157   2573   0 10:25 pts/1      00:00:00 grep xmms
```

Many people may be running xmms, and you may need to look in the left column to find the name of the user so you can kill the right process. You can combine the two commands as **ps –u alex –f | grep xmms**.

Now that you know the PID of Alex's process running xmms is 3074, you can use kill to terminate it. The safest way to do this is to log in as Alex (perhaps allow him to log in for you or su to alex [**su alex**] if you are logged in as **root**) and give the command

```
$ kill -TERM 3074
```

Only if this command fails should you send the kill signal as

```
$ kill -KILL 3074
```

The –KILL option instructs kill to send a **SIGKILL** signal, which the process cannot ignore. You can give the same command while you are logged in as **root**, but a typing mistake can have much more far-reaching consequences than when you make the mistake while you are logged in as an ordinary user. A user can kill only her or his own processes, whereas Superuser can kill any process, including system processes.

As a compromise between speed and safety, you can combine the su and kill utilities by using the –c option to su. The following command runs the part of the command line following the –c with the identity of Alex:

```
# su alex -c "kill -TERM 3074"
```

Two useful utilities related to kill are killall and pidof. The first is very similar to kill but uses a command name in place of a PID number. To kill all your processes that are running xmms or vi, you can give the command

```
$ killall xmms vi
```

When **root** gives this command, all processes that are running xmms or vi on the system are killed.

The pidof utility displays the PID number of each of the processes running the command you specify. Because this utility resides in **/sbin**, you must give the absolute pathname if you are not running as **root**:

```
$ /sbin/pidof httpd
567 566 565 564 563 562 561 560 553
```

Refer to the man pages for each of these utilities for more information, including lists of available options.

Rescue Mode

Rescue mode is an environment you can use to fix a system that does not boot normally. To bring a system up in rescue mode, boot the system from the first installation CD or the rescue CD. From the **boot:** prompt, give the command **linux rescue** from the first installation CD or press RETURN without entering a command from the rescue CD. The system comes up in rescue mode.

In rescue mode, you can change or replace configuration files, check and repair partitions using fsck, rewrite boot information, and more. The rescue setup first asks if you want to set up the network interface. You may want to copy files from other systems on the LAN or download files from the Internet. When you choose to set up the network interface, you need to choose whether to use DHCP to automatically configure the network connection or supply the IP address and netmask of the interface, as well as the IP addresses of the gateway and up to three DNS addresses.

If the rescue setup finds an existing Linux installation, you can choose to mount it under **/mnt/sysimage**, optionally in readonly mode. With the existing installation mounted, once the system displays a shell prompt (similar to **2.05b#**), you can give the command **chroot /mnt/sysimage** to mount the existing installation as it would be if you booted normally, with the existing installation's root mounted at **/** (root). See page 406 for more information on chroot. If you choose not to mount the existing installation, you are running a rescue system with standard tools mounted in standard locations (**/bin**, **/usr/bin** and so on). Partitions from your local installation are available for fixing or mounting. When you exit from the rescue shell, the system reboots. Remove the CD if you want to boot from the hard drive.

Avoiding a Trojan Horse

A *Trojan horse* is a program that does something destructive or disruptive to your system while appearing to be benign. As an example, you could store the following script in an executable file named mkfs:

```
while true
    do
        echo 'Good Morning Mr. Jones. How are you? Ha Ha Ha.' > /dev/console
    done
```

If you are running as Superuser when you run this command, it would continuously write a message to the console. If the programmer were malicious, it could do worse. The only thing missing in this plot is access permissions.

A malicious user could implement this Trojan horse by changing Superuser's **PATH** variable to include a publicly writable directory at the start of the **PATH** string. (The catch is that you need to be able to write to **/etc/profile**—where the **PATH** variable is set for **root**—and only **root** can do that.) Then you would need to put the bogus mkfs program file in that directory. Because the fraudulent version appears in a directory mentioned earlier than the real one in **PATH**, the shell runs it. The next time Superuser tries to run mkfs, the fraudulent version would run.

Trojan horses that wait for and take advantage of the misspellings that most people make are one of the most insidious types. For example, you might type **sl** instead of **ls**. Because you do not regularly execute a utility named **sl** and you may not remember typing the command **sl**, it is more difficult to track down this type of Trojan horse than one that takes the name of a utility you are familiar with.

A good way to prevent executing a Trojan horse is to make sure that your **PATH** variable does not contain a single colon (:) at the beginning or end of the **PATH** string or a period (.) or double colon (::) anywhere in the **PATH** string. A common way to check for a Trojan horse is to examine the filesystem periodically for files with setuid (refer to item 5 on page 372). The following command lists these files:

```
# find / -perm -4000 -exec ls -lh {} \; 2> /dev/null
-rwsr-xr-x  1 root root 54K Apr  5 16:17 /usr/bin/lppasswd
-rwsr-xr-x  1 root root 111K Feb 17 10:26 /usr/bin/crontab
-rwsr-xr-x  1 root root 7.0K Apr 13 08:26 /usr/bin/kpac_dhcp_helper
-rws--x--x  1 root root 18K Mar 23 12:05 /usr/bin/chfn
-rws--x--x  1 root root 6.8K Mar 23 12:05 /usr/bin/newgrp
-rwsr-xr-x  1 root root 39K Apr 15 12:26 /usr/bin/at
-rwsr-xr-x  1 root root 42K Mar 30 13:45 /usr/bin/gpasswd
-r-s--x--x  1 root root 91K Feb 15 10:04 /usr/bin/passwd
-rwsr-xr-x  1 root root 17K Feb 17 09:12 /usr/bin/rlogin
---s--x--x  1 root root 96K Apr  1 08:19 /usr/bin/sudo
-rwsr-xr-x  1 root root 6.8K Apr 13 08:26 /usr/bin/kgrantpty
-rwsr-xr-x  1 root root 18K Feb 17 09:12 /usr/bin/rcp
-rwsrwxr-x  1 root root 364K Mar 16 13:32 /usr/bin/tvtime
-rwsr-xr-x  1 root root 40K Mar 30 13:45 /usr/bin/chage
-rwsr-xr-x  1 root root 9.6K Feb 17 09:12 /usr/bin/rsh
-rws--x--x  1 root root 19K Mar 23 12:05 /usr/bin/chsh
...
```

This command uses find to locate all the files that have their setuid bits set (mode 4000). The hyphen preceding the mode causes find to report on any file that has this bit set, regardless of how the other bits are set. The output sent to standard error is redirected to **/dev/null** so that it does not clutter the screen.

You can also set up a program, such as AIDE (Advanced Intrusion Detection Environment), that will take a snapshot of your system and check it periodically as you specify. See www.cs.tut.fi/~rammer/aide.html for more information.

Getting Help

Your distribution comes with extensive documentation (page 94). Red Hat maintains a page that points toward many useful support documents: www.redhat.com/apps/support. You can also find help on the System Administrator's Guild site (www.sage.org). In addition, the Internet is a rich source of information on managing a Linux system; refer to Appendix B (page 913) and to the author's home page (www.sobell.com) for pointers to useful sites.

You do not need to act as a Red Hat system administrator in isolation; a large community of Linux/Red Hat experts is willing to assist you in getting the most out of your system, although you will get better help if you have already tried to solve a problem yourself by reading the available documentation. If you are unable to solve a problem through the documentation, a well thought-out question to the appropriate newsgroup, such as **comp.os.linux.misc**, or mailing list can often provide useful information. Be sure you describe the problem and identify your system carefully. Include information about your version of Red Hat Enterprise Linux or Fedora Core and any software packages and hardware that you think relate to the problem. The newsgroup **comp.os.linux.answers** contains postings of solutions to common problems and periodic postings of the most up-to-date versions of FAQ and HOWTO documents. See www.catb.org/~esr/faqs/smart-questions.html for a good paper by Eric S. Raymond and Rick Moen titled "How to Ask Questions the Smart Way."

SELinux (*FEDORA*)

Traditional Linux security, called *Discretionary Access Control* (DAC), is based on users and groups. A process run by a user has access to anything the user has access to, making fine-grained access control difficult. Fine-grained access control is particularly important on servers, which often require root privileges to run.

SELinux (Security Enhanced Linux) implements *Mandatory Access Control* (MAC), wherein you can define a security policy that controls all objects, such as files and devices, and all subjects, such as processes and users. Using SELinux, you can grant a program only the permissions it needs.

Under SELinux, users are assigned roles that determine the primary function of the user. SELinux roles are conceptually similar to groups, except that under SELinux, a user must actively switch between permitted roles. You can use system-config-users (page 521) to assign roles to users.

SELinux can be in one of three states:

- **Enforcing/Active**   The SELinux security policy is enforced. You will not be able to do anything not permitted by the security policy.

- **Permissive/Warn**   SELinux sends warning messages to a log but does not enforce. You can use the log to build a security policy that matches your requirements.

- **Disabled**   SELinux does not enforce because no policy is loaded.

Running SELinux in permissive or enforcing mode degrades system performance between five and ten percent. SELinux is usually of no benefit on a single-user system. You may want to consider SELinux for a server that connects to the Internet. If you are unsure whether to use SELinux or not, selecting permissive mode allows you to change to disabled or enforcing mode easily at a later date.

To disable SELinux, change the **SELINUX=** line in **/etc/sysconfig/selinux** to **SELINUX=disabled**. The following listing shows SELinux disabled:

```
$ cat /etc/sysconfig/selinux
# This file controls the state of SELinux on the system.
# SELINUX= can take one of these three values:
#         enforcinfg - SELinux security policy is enforced.
#         permissive - SELinux prints warnings instead of enforcing.
#         disabled - No SELinux policy is loaded.
SELINUX=disabled
```

If you are going to use SELinux in the future but not now, turn it on when you install Linux, and run it in permissive mode. Permissive mode writes the required extended information to inodes, but it does not stop you from doing anything on the system. Because SELinux sets extended attributes on files, it is an involved process to turn on SELinux after you install Linux. If you decide you are never going to use SELinux, you can disable it. For more information, see the Fedora SELinux FAQ at people.redhat.com/kwade/fedora-docs/selinux-faq-en.

system-config-securitylevel

Under Fedora Core 2 and later, you can use system-config-securitylevel to set the state of SELinux. From the Security Level Configuration window, click the SELinux tab and choose Active, Warm, or Disabled from the combo box. Click **OK**. See page 741 for information on the Firewall Options tab.

System Operation

This section covers the basics of how the system functions and how you can make intelligent decisions as a system administrator. This section does not cover every aspect of system administration in the depth necessary to set up or modify all system functions. It provides a guide to bringing a system up and keeping it running from day to day.

Booting the System

Booting a system is the process of reading the Linux *kernel* (page 979) into system memory and starting it running. Refer to "Boot Loader" on page 514 for more information on the initial steps of bringing a system up.

As the last step of the boot procedure, Linux runs the init program as PID number 1. The init program is the first genuine process to run after booting and is the parent of all system processes. (That is why when you run as **root** and kill process **1**, the system dies.)

initdefault The **initdefault** entry in the **/etc/inittab** file (page 429) tells init what runlevel to bring the system to (Table 11-1). Set **initdefault** to 3 to cause the system to present a text login message when it boots; set **initdefault** to 5 to present a graphical login screen.

table 11-1 ‖				Runlevels
Number	**Name**	**Login**	**Network**	**Filesystems**
0	Halt			
1 (not **S** or **s**)	Single user	Text	Down	Not mounted
2	Undefined			
3	Multiuser	Text	Up	Mounted
4	Undefined			
5	Multiuser with X	Graphics	Up	Mounted
6	Reboot			

Init Scripts: Start and Stop System Services

The first script that init runs is **/etc/rc.d/rc.sysinit**, which runs initlog to set up command logging for the duration of the boot process. The **rc.sysinit** script also performs basic system configuration, including setting the system clock, hostname, and keyboard mapping; setting up swap partitions; checking the filesystems for errors; and turning on quota management (page 545).

Next, the **/etc/rc.d/rc** init script runs the scripts that handle the services that need to be started when you first bring the system up and that need to be started or stopped when the system goes from single-user to multiuser mode and back down again.

tip || **List the Kernel Boot Messages**

To save a list of kernel boot messages, give the following command immediately after booting the system and logging in:

    $ dmesg > dmesg.boot

This command saves the kernel messages in the **dmesg.boot** file. This list can be educational. It can also be useful when you are having a problem with the boot process. For more information, refer to "dmesg: Display Kernel Messages" on page 517.

The **init** (initialization) scripts, also called **rc** (run command) scripts, are shell scripts located in the **/etc/rc.d/init.d** directory and run via symbolic links in the **/etc/rc.d/rc*n*.d** directory, where *n* is the runlevel the system is entering.

The **/etc/rc.d/rc*n*.d** directories contain scripts whose names begin with **K** (**K15httpd, K72autofs, K30sendmail,** and so on) and scripts whose names begin with **S** (**S05kudzu, S10network, S13portmap,** and so on). When entering a new runlevel, each of the **K** (kill) scripts is executed with an argument of **stop**, and then each of the **S** (start) scripts is executed with an argument of **start**. Each of the **K** files is run in numerical order. The **S** files are run similarly. This setup allows the person who sets up these files to control which services are stopped and which are started and in what order, whenever the system enters a given runlevel. Using scripts with **start** and **stop** arguments is flexible because it allows one script to both start and kill a process, depending on the argument it is called with.

To customize system initialization, you can add shell scripts to the **/etc/rc.d/init.d** directory and add links to the files in **init.d** from the **/etc/rc.d/rc*n*.d** directories. The following example shows several links to the **cups** script. These links are called to run the **cups** init script to start or stop the **cupsd** daemon at various runlevels:

```
$ pwd
/etc/rc.d
$ ls -l */*cups
-rwxr-xr-x  1 root root 2312 Apr  5 16:17 init.d/cups
lrwxrwxrwx  1 root root   14 Apr 28 21:40 rc0.d/K10cups -> ../init.d/cups
lrwxrwxrwx  1 root root   14 Apr 28 21:40 rc1.d/K10cups -> ../init.d/cups
lrwxrwxrwx  1 root root   14 May  2 22:44 rc2.d/S55cups -> ../init.d/cups
lrwxrwxrwx  1 root root   14 May  2 22:44 rc3.d/S55cups -> ../init.d/cups
lrwxrwxrwx  1 root root   14 May  2 22:44 rc4.d/S55cups -> ../init.d/cups
lrwxrwxrwx  1 root root   14 May  2 22:44 rc5.d/S55cups -> ../init.d/cups
lrwxrwxrwx  1 root root   14 Apr 28 21:40 rc6.d/K10cups -> ../init.d/cups
```

Each link in **/etc/rc.d/rc*n*.d** should point to a file in **/etc/rc.d/init.d**. The file **/etc/rc.d/rc1.d/K10cups** is a link to the file named **cups** in **/etc/rc.d/init.d**. (The numbers that are part of the filenames of the links in the **/etc/rc.d/rc*n*.d** directories may change from one OS release to the next, but the scripts in **/etc/rc.d/init.d** always have the same names.) The names of files in the **/etc/rc.d/init.d** directory are functional. When you want to turn NFS services on or off, use the **nfs** script. When you want to turn basic network services on or off, run the **network** script. The **cups** script controls the printer daemon. Each of the scripts takes an argument of **stop** or start, depending on what you want to do. Some of the scripts also take arguments of **restart, reload, status,** and some others. Run a script without an argument to display a usage message telling you which arguments it accepts.

Following are three examples of calls to init scripts. You may find it easier to use service (next) in place of the pathnames in these calls:

```
# /etc/rc.d/init.d/nfs stop
# /etc/rc.d/init.d/network start
# /etc/rc.d/init.d/network restart
```

The first example stops all processes related to serving filesystems over the network, using NFS. The second example starts all processes related to basic network services. The third example stops and then starts these same processes.

tip || **Maintain the Links in the /etc/rc✳.d Hierarchy**

Refer to page 385 for information about using chkconfig to maintain the symbolic links in the **/etc/rc✳.d** hierarchy.

The **/etc/rc.d/rc.local** file is executed after the other **init** scripts. Put commands that customize the system in **rc.local.** You can add any commands you like to **rc.local;** however, it is best to run them in the background so that if they hang, they do not stop the boot process.

service: Configures Services I

Red Hat provides service, a handy script that reports on or changes the status of any of the system services in **/etc/rc.d/init.d.** In place of the commands toward the end of the previous section, you can give the following commands from any directory:

```
# /sbin/service nfs stop
# /sbin/service network start
# /sbin/service network restart
```

The command **/sbin/service ––status–all** displays the status of all system services.

system-config-services: Configures Services II

The system-config-services (*FEDORA*) and redhat-config-services (*RHEL*) graphical utilities (Figure 11-1) each have two distinct functions: They turn system services on and off, and they control which services are stopped and started when the system enters and leaves runlevels 3, 4 (not used), and 5. The line below the toolbar gives you two pieces of information: the current runlevel of the system and the runlevel that you will edit. The [system|redhat]-config-services utilities control two groups of services: independent services listed in **/etc/rc.d/init.d** and those controlled by **xinetd** (page 403) and listed in **/etc/xinetd.d** (or as specified in **/etc/xinetd.conf**). Scroll to and highlight the service you are interested in; a short description appears in the

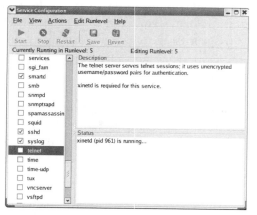

Figure 11-1   The Service Configuration window

text box at the upper-right of the window. When the description includes **xinetd is required for this service**, the highlighted service is dependent on **xinetd**; otherwise, it is an independent service. The lower text box has status information.

The **xinetd** superserver is an independent service. You must make sure that **xinetd** is turned on for the runlevels at which you want to run services that are dependent on it. It is usually on for runlevels 3, 4, and 5.

The [system|redhat]-config-services utilities do the following:

- **Turn independent services on and off.**   When you highlight an independent service, you can click the toolbar or make a selection from Actions in the menubar to stop, start, or restart (stop and start) the service. The system turns on/off the service immediately; the change does not affect whether the service will run the next time you bring up the system, enter another runlevel, or reenter the current runlevel.

- **Turn xinetd-controlled services on and off.**   When you highlight a service that is controlled by **xinetd**, the Start, Stop, and Restart buttons on the toolbar are grayed out. Until you click the box to the left of the service, the **Save** and **Cancel** buttons are grayed out too. The only things you can do are to turn this service off or on. Click the small box, and click the **Save** button to change the state of the service. You are changing the **yes/no** parameter of the **disable** line discussed on page 404. When you click **Save**, the system restarts **xinetd** with the service status change you requested. This change affects all runlevels and will stay in effect through changes in runlevels and reboots unless you change it again.

- **Controls future execution of independent services in runlevels 3, 4, and 5.**   Select the runlevel you want to affect, using the Edit Runlevel selection from the menubar. Highlight an independent service, and click the box next to it to indicate whether you want the service on or off at the specified runlevel. Click the **Save** button. When you enter that runlevel in the future, the service will be on or off as you specified. The current state of the service is not changed. See the first item in this list when you want to change the state of the service.

chkconfig: **Configures Services III**

The chkconfig character-based utility duplicates much of what [system|redhat]-config-services does: It makes it easier for a system administrator to maintain the **/etc/rc.d** directory hierarchy. This utility can add, remove, list start-up information, and check the state of system services; it changes the configuration only, it does not change the current state of any service. To see a list of all services, give the following command:

```
# chkconfig --list
dhcrelay        0:off   1:off   2:off   3:off   4:off   5:off   6:off
dhcpd           0:off   1:off   2:off   3:off   4:off   5:off   6:off
syslog          0:off   1:off   2:on    3:on    4:on    5:on    6:off
atd             0:off   1:off   2:off   3:on    4:on    5:on    6:off
gpm             0:off   1:off   2:on    3:on    4:on    5:on    6:off
...
xinetd based services:
        chargen-udp:    off
        rsync:  off
        chargen:        off
        daytime-udp:    off
        daytime:        off
...
```

All the services that run their own daemons are listed, one to a line, followed by their configured state for each runlevel. Following that list, chkconfig displays each of the **xinetd**-based services and their current status. You can check on how a specific daemon is configured by adding its name to the previous command:

```
# chkconfig --list sshd
sshd            0:off   1:off   2:on    3:on    4:on    5:on    6:off
```

In the next example, chkconfig configures the **/etc/rc.d** directory hierarchy so that **sshd** will be off in runlevels 2, 3, 4, and 5 and then confirms the change:

```
# chkconfig --level 2345 sshd off
# chkconfig --list sshd
sshd            0:off   1:off   2:off   3:off   4:off   5:off   6:off
```

For convenience, you can omit the **–level 2345**. When you specify an init script and **on** or **off**, chkconfig defaults to runlevels 2, 3, 4, and 5. The following command is equivalent to the first of the preceding commands:

```
# chkconfig sshd off
```

Following, both ps and service confirm that even though chkconfig set things up so that **sshd** would be off in all runlevels, it is still running. The chkconfig utility did not shut down **sshd**. In the following example, the second command line shows that when you give a service command followed by the name of an init script, you get the usage message from the script:

```
# ps -ef | grep sshd
root       697     1  0 Oct01 ?        00:00:00 /usr/sbin/sshd
root     17185 21650  0 15:15 pts/4    00:00:00 grep sshd
# /sbin/service sshd
Usage: /etc/init.d/sshd {start|stop|restart|reload|condrestart|status}
# /sbin/service sshd status
sshd (pid 697) is running...
```

When you reboot the system, **sshd** will not start, but you can stop it more easily using service:

```
# /sbin/service sshd stop
Stopping sshd:                                          [  OK  ]
# ps -ef | grep sshd
root     17209 21650  0 15:16 pts/4    00:00:00 grep sshd
# /sbin/service sshd status
sshd is stopped
```

Emergency Mode

When you use lilo or grub to boot, you can set the emergency kernel flag that gets passed to init and causes init to run sulogin (single-user login). Also see "Rescue Mode" on page 377 for booting the system when it will not boot normally. To bring the system up in emergency mode when you are booting using lilo, enter **linux emergency**, and press RETURN in response to the **Boot:** prompt.

When you are using grub, you need to press e as soon as the grub screen appears so you can edit the boot commands. If the grub screen shows multiple bootable kernels, move the highlight to the one you want to boot before pressing e. After pressing e, use the up/down ARROW keys to move the highlight to the line that starts with **kernel**. Press e to bring up the grub editor; the cursor will be at the end of the **kernel** command line. Type SPACE **emergency**, press RETURN to return to the previous grub screen, and then press **b** to boot the system.

With either grub or lilo, when the boot process hands control to init, init runs sulogin, which displays the following message:

```
Give root password for system maintenance
(or type Control-D for normal startup):
```

Enter the **root** password, and you will see the **root** shell prompt. At this point the only mounted filesystem is root (**/**), and possibly **/proc** (page 434); root is mounted as a readonly filesystem (despite what the mount command says). If **/proc** is not mounted, give the command

```
# mount /proc
```

The ps, top, fsck, and other programs require the **/proc** filesystem. The **–L** and **–U** mount options, as well as the LABEL= and UUID= specifications in the **/etc/fstab** file (page 445), also require **/proc**.

Now you can safely use fsck to check the integrity of the root filesystem:

```
# fsck /
```

With most types of filesystems, you can use the **–f** option with fsck to force a check when the filesystem appears to be clean.

If you need to write any files to the root filesystem, you need to remount it in read-write mode:

```
# mount -n -o remount,rw /
```

The **–n** argument keeps mount from trying to write to the **/etc/mtab** file first. If it were to attempt to write to a readonly filesystem, mount would fail, and the filesystem would remain mounted in readonly mode. If you remount the root filesystem as shown, you may need to remount it in readonly mode before you can continue booting the system:

```
# mount -o remount,rw /
```

When you are ready to bring the system up to multiuser mode, exit from the shell. Linux will either continue booting or reboot to the default runlevel (as specified by **initdefault** in **/etc/inittab** [page 381]).

Single-User Mode

When the system is in single-user mode, only the system console is enabled. You can run programs from the console in single-user mode as you would from any terminal in multiuser mode. The differences are that not all filesystems may be mounted, so you may not be able to access some files, and few of the system daemons will be running. The **root** filesystem is always mounted in single-user mode. The scripts in **/etc/rc.d/rc1.d** are run as part of single-user initialization.

With the system in single-user mode, you can perform system maintenance that requires filesystems unmounted or just a quiet system—no one except you using it, so that no user programs interfere with disk maintenance and backup programs. The classical UNIX term for this state is *quiescent*. See "Backing Up Files" on page 524 for a discussion of one of the most important and often neglected areas of system administration.

Going Multiuser

After you have determined that all is well with all filesystems, you can bring the operating system up to multiuser mode. When you exit from the single-user shell, init brings the system to the default runlevel—usually **3** or **5** (page 381). Or, the following command in response to the Superuser prompt brings the system to (textual) multiuser mode (use **5** to go to graphics [multiuser] mode):

```
# telinit 3
```

The telinit utility tells init what runlevel to enter. The telinit executable is a symbolic link to the init executable, but, by convention, running telinit is preferred to running init directly.

When it goes from single- to (textual) multiuser mode, the system executes the **K** (kill or stop) scripts and then the **S** (start) scripts in **/etc/rc.d/rc3.d**. For more information, refer to "Init Scripts: Start and Stop System Services" on page 381. Use chkconfig (page 385) to stop one of these scripts from running.

Runlevel **2** is referred to as multiuser mode, and runlevel **3** is extended multiuser mode. But because runlevel **2** is rarely used, this chapter uses the term *multiuser* to refer to runlevel **3**. Runlevel **4** is not used, and runlevel **5** is graphics or X11 mode.

Multiuser/Graphics Mode

Multiuser/graphics mode is the normal state for a Linux system. All appropriate filesystems are mounted, and users can log in from all connected terminals, dial-in lines, and network connections. All support services and daemons are enabled and running. Once the system is in multiuser/graphics mode, you will see a login screen or prompt. Most systems are set up to boot directly to multiuser/graphics mode without stopping at single-user mode.

Logging In

With a text login, the system uses init, mingetty, and login to allow a user to log in; login uses PAM modules (page 416) to authenticate users. Once the system is in multiuser mode, init is responsible for spawning a mingetty process on each of the lines that a user can log in on.

When you enter your username, mingetty establishes the characteristics of your terminal and then overlays itself with a login process and passes to the login process whatever you entered in response to the **login:** prompt. The login program consults the **/etc/passwd** file to see whether a username matches the username you entered. This program then consults the **/etc/shadow** file to see whether a password is associated with the username. If there is, login prompts you for a password; if not, it continues without requiring a password. When your username requires a password, login verifies the password you enter by checking the **/etc/shadow** file again. If either your username or password is not correct, login displays **Login incorrect** and prompts you to log in again.

All passwords in the **/etc/shadow** file are encrypted or hashed using *MD5* (page 982). It is not feasible to recover an encrypted password. When you log in, the login process encrypts/hashes the password you type at the prompt and compares it to the encrypted/hashed password in **/etc/shadow**. If it matches, you are authenticated.

With a graphical login, the init process spawns gdm (the GNOME display manager) on the first free virtual terminal, providing features similar to mingetty and login. The gdm utility starts an X server and presents a login window. The gdm display manager then uses PAM to authenticate the user and runs the scripts in the **/etc/X11/gdm/PreSession** directory. The scripts inspect the user's **~/.dmrc** file, which stores the user's default session and language, and launch the user's session. GNOME and KDE desktop environments store the state of the last login and attempt to recreate it when the user logs back in.

With NIS, login compares your username and password with the information in the appropriate naming service instead of (or in addition to) the **passwd** and **shadow** files. If the system is configured to use both of these methods (**/etc/passwd** and NIS), it checks the **/etc/nsswitch.conf** file (page 413) to see which order to consult them in.

PAM (page 416), the Pluggable Authentication Module facility, allows you greater control over user logins than the **/etc/passwd** and **/etc/shadow** files do. Using PAM, you can specify multiple levels of authentication, mutually exclusive authentication methods, or parallel methods that are each in themselves sufficient to grant access to the system. For example, you can have a different authentication method for console logins and for TELNET logins. And you can require that modem users authenticate themselves via two or more methods (such as a smartcard or badge reader and a password). PAM modules also provide security technology vendors with a convenient way to interface their hardware or software products with a system.

When the username and password are correct, login or the scripts in **PreSession** consult the appropriate services to initialize your user and group IDs, establish your home directory, and determine which shell or desktop manager you will be working with.

The login utility/**PreSession** scripts assign values to the **HOME, PATH, LOGNAME, SHELL, TERM**, and **MAIL** variables. They look in the **/etc/group** file (page 428) to identify the groups the user belongs to. When login has finished its work, it overlays itself with the login shell, which inherits the variables login has set. In a graphical environment, the **PreSession** scripts start the desktop manager.

During a textual login, the login shell assigns values to additional shell variables and executes the commands in the system start-up shell script(s) **/etc/profile** and **/etc/bashrc**. Some systems have additional system start-up shell scripts. Exactly what these scripts do is system dependent, but they usually display the contents of the **/etc/motd** (message of the day) and **/etc/issue** files, let you know that you have mail, and set umask (page 398), the file-creation mask.

After executing the system start-up commands, the shell executes the commands from the personal start-up shell scripts in your home directory. For a list of these scripts, refer to page 272. Because the shell executes these scripts *after* the system script, a sophisticated user can override any variables or conventions that were established by the system, whereas a new user can remain uninvolved in these complications.

Running a Program and Logging Out

When you see a shell prompt, you can execute a program or exit from the shell. If you exit from a shell, the process running the shell dies and the parent process wakes up. When the shell is a child of another shell, the parent shell wakes up and displays a prompt. Exiting from a login shell causes the operating system to send init a signal that one of its children has died. Upon receiving this signal, init takes action based on the contents of the /etc/inittab file. In the case of a process controlling a line for a terminal, init informs mingetty that the line is free for another user.

When you are at runlevel 5 and exit from a GUI, the GNOME display manager, gdm, takes care of initiating a new login display.

Bringing the System Down

The shutdown and halt utilities perform all the tasks needed to bring the system down safely. These utilities can restart the system, prepare the system to be turned off, put the system in single-user mode, and on some hardware, power down the system. The poweroff and reboot utilities are linked to halt. When you call halt when the system is not shutting down (runlevel 0) or rebooting (runlevel 6), halt calls shutdown. (When you are running as other than Superuser, the link is through console-helper [page 375].)

You must tell shutdown when you would like to bring the system down. This can be expressed as an absolute time of day, as in 19:15, which causes the shutdown to occur at 7:15 P.M. Alternatively, you can give the number of minutes from the present time, as in +15, which means fifteen minutes from now. To bring the system down immediately (recommended for emergency shutdowns only or when you are the only user logged in), you can give the argument +0, or its synonym: **now**. For shutdown times longer than 5 minutes, all non**root** logins are disabled for the last 5 minutes before shutdown.

Calling shutdown with the **-r** option causes the system to reboot (same as the reboot command except that reboot implies **now**). Adding the **-f** option forces a fast reboot, where filesystem checking is disabled (see the shutdown man page for details). Using **-h** instead of **-r** forces the system to halt (same as the halt command except that halt implies **now**). A message appears once the system has been safely halted: **System halted**, although most ATX systems turn off automatically after shutdown, so you will not see the message

Because Linux is a multiuser system, shutdown warns all users before taking any action. This gives users a chance to prepare for the shutdown, perhaps by writing out editor files or exiting from networking applications. You can replace the default shutdown message with one of your own by following the time specification on the command line with a message:

```
# /sbin/shutdown -h 09:30 Going down 9:30 to install disk, up by 10am.
```

caution || **Do Not Turn the Power Off Before Bringing the System Down**

Avoid rebooting your Linux system without first bringing it down as described here. Linux, like UNIX system, speeds up disk access by keeping an in-memory collection of disk buffers that are written to the disk periodically or when system use is momentarily low. When you turn off or reset the computer without writing the contents of these disk buffers to the disk, you lose any information in the buffers. Running **shutdown** forces these buffers to be written. You can force the buffers to be written at any time by issuing a **sync** command. However, **sync** does not unmount filesystems, nor does it bring the system down.

CONTROL-ALT-DEL: Reboots the System

By default, the **/etc/inittab** file on an Intel-based computer has the entry

```
ca::ctrlaltdel:/sbin/shutdown -t3 -r now
```

This entry allows any user[1] to reboot the computer safely by pressing the key sequence CONTROL-ALT-DEL (also referred to as the *three-finger salute*, or the *Vulcan death grip*) from a textual login on the console. (Although it is not recommended, you can press CONTROL-ALT-BACKSPACE from a graphical session to kill the X server; once the X server is killed, you can use CONTROL-ALT-DEL.) Because of its hooks into the keyboard driver, this key sequence sends a SIGINT signal to the init process, which in response runs shutdown. Because it runs as **root**, init causes shutdown to run as **root** also, even if the key sequence is initiated by an ordinary user. You can disable CONTROL-ALT-DEL by deleting the preceding line from **/etc/inittab** (or putting a # at the left end of the line) and then sending init a HUP signal (**kill –HUP 1**), which causes it to reread the **/etc/inittab** file.

consolehelper: Allows an Ordinary User to Run a Privileged Command

As shown following, there are two executable **halt** files:

```
$ file /sbin/halt /usr/bin/halt
/sbin/halt:    ELF 32-bit LSB executable, Intel 80386, version 1 (SYSV)...
/usr/bin/halt: symbolic link to 'consolehelper'
```

The one in **/sbin** runs the halt utility, whereas the one in **/usr/bin** is a link to consolehelper. In **root**'s **PATH** variable, **/sbin** normally precedes **/usr/bin** so that when someone running as **root** gives a halt command, the shell executes **/sbin/halt** (the halt utility). Normally, **/sbin** does not appear in an ordinary user's **PATH**; when an ordi-

---

1. When you include the **–a** option in the shutdown command in **/etc/inittab** and the **/etc/shutdown.allow** file exists, one of the users whose name appears in this file (or **root**) must be logged in on one of the virtual consoles in order for a non**root** user to run shutdown from a virtual console.

nary user gives a halt command, the shell follows the link from **/usr/bin/halt** and executes **/usr/bin/consolehelper**.

What consolehelper does depends on how PAM is set up (see **/etc/pam.d/halt** for the modules it calls and **/usr/share/doc/pam-*/txts/*** for descriptions of the modules). Refer to "PAM" on page 416 for more information. As shipped by Red Hat, consolehelper prompts for the **root** password; when you supply it, consolehelper proceeds to shut the system down.

Going Single-user

Because going from multiuser to single-user mode can affect other users, you must be Superuser to make this change. Make sure that you give other users enough warning before going to single-user mode; otherwise, they may lose whatever they were working on.

Following is a method of manually bringing the system down to single-user mode—the point where it is safe to turn the power off. You must be running as Superuser to perform these tasks.

1. Use **wall** (write all) to warn everyone who is using the system to log out.

2. If you are sharing files via NFS, use **exportfs –ua** to disable network access to the shared filesystems. (Use **exportfs** without an argument to see what filesystems are being shared.)

3. Use **umount –a** to unmount all mounted devices. (Use **mount** without an argument to see what devices are mounted.)

4. Give the command **telinit 1** to bring the system down to single-user mode.

Turning the Power Off

Once the system is in single-user mode, shutting it down is quite straightforward. Give the command **telinit 0** (preferred) or **halt** to bring the system down. You can build a kernel with apm so it turns the machine off at the appropriate time. If your machine is not set up this way, turn the power off when the appropriate prompt appears or when the system starts rebooting.

Crash

A *crash* occurs when the system suddenly stops/fails when you do not intend it to. A crash may result from software or hardware problems or a loss of power. As a running system loses power, nothing is regular or predictable. In a fraction of a second, some components are supplied with enough voltage; others are not. Buffers are not flushed, corrupt data may be written to the hard disk, and so on. IDE drives do not behave as predictably as SCSI drives under these circumstances. After a crash, you must bring the operating system up carefully to minimize possible damage to the filesystems. Frequently there will be little or no damage.

Repairing a Filesystem

Although the filesystems are checked automatically during the boot process if needed, you will have to check them manually if a problem cannot be repaired automatically. To check the filesystems manually after a crash, boot the system up to emergency mode (page 386). *Do not* mount any devices other than root, which Linux mounts automatically. Run fsck on all the local filesystems that were mounted at the time of the crash, repairing them as needed. Depending on how your system is set up, when fsck cannot repair a filesystem automatically, the system enters emergency mode so you can run fsck manually. Make note of any ordinary files or directories that you repair (and can identify), and inform their owners that they may not be complete or correct. Look in the **lost+found** directory *in each filesystem* for missing files. After successfully running fsck, type **exit** to exit from the single-user shell and resume booting.

If files are not correct or are missing altogether, you may have to recreate them from a backup copy of the filesystem. For more information, refer to "Backing Up Files" on page 524.

When the System Does Not Boot

When you cannot boot the computer from the hard drive, boot the system into rescue mode. For more information, refer to "Rescue Mode" on page 377. If that works, run fsck on the root filesystem and try rebooting from the hard drive again.

When all else fails, go through the install procedure, and perform an "upgrade" to your current version of Linux. Red Hat Linux/Fedora Core can perform a nondestructive upgrade and can fix quite a bit in the process. For more information, refer to "Upgrade Examine" on page 48.

Useful Utilities

This section briefly describes a few of the many utilities that can help you perform system administration tasks. Read the man/info pages for the utilities described in "Linux Utilities" on page 396 to learn more about using them. Some of these utilities are incorporated as part of the Main menu, and some are useful to users other than the system administrator.

Red Hat Configuration Tools

The Red Hat configuration tools, most of which are named redhat-config-✷ in all older releases of Red Hat Linux, including Red Hat Enterprise Linux and Fedora Core 1, were renamed system-config-✷ in Fedora Core 2. Many of these tools bring up a graphical display when called from a GUI and a textual display when called from a non-GUI command line. In general, these tools, which are listed Table 11-2, are simple to use and require little explanation beyond what the tool presents. Some have Help selections on their toolbar; most do not have man pages.

table 11-2 ‖	Red Hat Configuration Tools
system-config-bind (*FEDORA*) redhat-config-bind (*RHEL*)	Displays the Domain Name Service window. For more information, refer to "JumpStart II: system-config-bind: Setting Up a Domain" on page 712.
system-config-boot (*FEDORA*)	Displays the Boot Configuration window, which allows you to specify which boot entry in **/etc/grub.conf** (page 514) you want the system to boot from.
system-config-date (*FEDORA*) redhat-config-date (*RHEL*)	Displays the Date/Time Properties window with two tabs: Date & Time and Time Zone. You can set the date and time or enable NTP (network time protocol) from the first tab. The Time Zone tab allows you to specify the time zone of the system clock or whether you want the system clock set to *UTC* (page 1004).
system-config-display (*FEDORA*) redhat-config-xfree86 (*RHEL*)	Brings up the Display settings window with three tabs: Settings, Hardware, and Dual head. For more information, refer to "system-config-display: Configuring the Display" on page 63.
system-config-httpd (*FEDORA*) redhat-config-httpd (*RHEL*)	Displays the HTTP window with four tabs: Main, Virtual Hosts, Server, and Performance Tuning. For more information, refer to "JumpStart II: Setting Up Apache with system-config-httpd" on page 764.
system-config-keyboard (*FEDORA*) redhat-config-keyboard (*RHEL*)	Displays the Keyboard window, which allows you to select the type of keyboard attached to the system. This is the utility you use to select the keyboard when you install the system.
system-config-kickstart (*FEDORA*) redhat-config-kickstart (*RHEL*)	Displays the Kickstart Configurator window, which allows you to create a Kickstart script. For more information, refer to "Using the Kickstart Configurator" on page 57.
system-config-language (*FEDORA*) redhat-config-language (*RHEL*)	Displays the Language Selection window, which allows you to specify the default system language from among those that are installed. This is the utility you use to select the system language when you install the system.
redhat-config-mouse (*RHEL*)	Displays the Mouse Configuration window, which allows you to specify the type of mouse that is attached to the system. This is the utility you use to select the system mouse when you install the system.

table 11-2 ‖	Red Hat Configuration Tools (Continued)
redhat-config-netboot (*RHEL*)	Displays the Network Installation and Diskless Environment window, which allows you to configure network installation or a diskless environment. The first time you run this utility, it displays the First Time Druid window.
system-config-network (*FEDORA*) redhat-config-network (*RHEL*)	Displays the Network Configuration window. For more information, refer to "system-config-network: Configuring the Hardware" on page 555.
system-config-network-cmd (*FEDORA*) redhat-config-network-cmd (*RHEL*)	Displays the parameters that system-config-network uses.
system-config-nfs (*FEDORA*) redhat-config-nfs (*RHEL*)	Displays the NFS Server Configuration window. For more information, refer to "JumpStart: system-config-nfs: Configures an NFS Server" on page 664.
system-config-packages (*FEDORA*) redhat-config-packages (*RHEL*)	Displays the Package Management window. This is the utility you use to customize the list of packages you install when you install the system. For more information, refer to "system-config-packages: Adds and Removes Software Packages" on page 453.
system-config-printer (*FEDORA*) redhat-config-printer (*RHEL*)	Displays the Printer configuration window, which allows you to set up printers and edit printer configurations. For more information, refer to "JumpStart I: Configuring a Local Printer Using system-config-printer" on page 487.
system-config-proc (*FEDORA*) redhat-config-proc (*RHEL*)	Displays the Kernel Tuning window, which allows you to tune the kernel by working with the **/proc** filesystem (page 434). Be sure you know what you are doing if you modify **/proc**, as you can cause the system to fail by changing kernel parameters.
system-config-rootpassword (*FEDORA*) redhat-config-rootpassword (*RHEL*)	Displays the Root Password window, which allows you to change the **root** password. While logged in as **root**, you can also use passwd from a command line to change the **root** password.
system-config-samba (*FEDORA*) redhat-config-samba (*RHEL*)	Displays the Samba Server Configuration window, which can help you configure Samba. For more information, refer to "JumpStart: system-config-samba: Configuring a Samba Server" on page 679.
system-config-securitylevel (*FEDORA*) redhat-config-securitylevel (*RHEL*)	Displays the Security Level Configuration window with two tabs: Firewall Options and SELinux (*FEDORA*). Refer to "JumpStart: Using system-config-securitylevel to Build a Firewall" on page 741 for more information about configuring a firewall. See page 379 for information about SELinux.

table 11-2 ||	Red Hat Configuration Tools (Continued)
system-config-services (*FEDORA*) redhat-config-services (*RHEL*)	Displays the Service Configuration window, which allows you to specify which daemons (services) run at each of the runlevels. For more information, refer to "system-config-services: Configures Services II" on page 383.
system-config-soundcard (*FEDORA*) redhat-config-soundcard (*RHEL*)	Displays the Audio Devices window, which tells you which audio device the system detected and gives you the option of playing a sound.
system-config-users (*FEDORA*) redhat-config-users (*RHEL*)	Displays the User Manager window, which allows you to work with users and groups. For more information, refer to "system-config-users: Manages User Accounts" on page 521.
system-logviewer (*FEDORA*) redhat-logviewer (*RHEL*)	Displays the System Logs window, which can display any of various system logs.
system-switch-mail (*FEDORA*) redhat-switch-mail (*RHEL*)	Displays the system-switch-mail window, which allows you to choose between the **sendmail** (page 609) and Postfix (page 633) MTAs.

Linux Utilities

This section lists and explains a few command line system administration tools you may find useful.

chsh   Changes the login shell for a user. When you call chsh without an argument, you change your own login shell. Superuser can change the shell for any user by calling chsh with that user's username as an argument. When changing a login shell with chsh, you must specify an installed shell that is listed in the file **/etc/shells**; other entries are rejected. Also, you must give the pathname to the shell exactly as it appears in **/etc/shells**. In the following example, Superuser changes Alex's shell to tcsh:

```
# chsh alex
Changing the login shell for alex
Enter the new value, or press return for the default

Login Shell [/bin/bash]: /bin/tcsh
```

clear   Clears the screen. You can also use CONTROL-L from the bash shell to clear the screen. The value of the environment variable **TERM** is used to determine how to clear the screen.

dmesg   Displays recent system log messages (page 517).

e2label   Displays or creates a volume label on an ext2 or ext3 disk partition. The format of an e2label command is shown following:

e2label device [newlabel]

where ***device*** is the name of the device (**/dev/hda2**, **/dev/sdb1**, **/dev/fd0**, and so on) you want to work with. When you include the optional ***newlabel*** parameter, e2label changes the label on ***device*** to ***newlabel***. Without this parameter, e2label displays the label. You can also create a volume label with the –L option of tune2fs (page 447).

kudzu The kudzu utility finds new and changed hardware and configures it. This utility determines which hardware is new by probing all devices on internal and external buses and comparing the results to the **/etc/sysconfig/hwconf** database. In the default configuration, the **/etc/rc.d/init.d/kudzu** script runs and calls kudzu as the machine enters runlevels 3 and 5. When it finds new or changed hardware, kudzu gives you a chance to configure it and permits you to deconfigure any hardware that you have removed.

mkfs Makes a New Filesystem. This utility is a front end for many utilities, each of which builds a a different type of filesystem. By default, mkfs builds an **ext2** filesystem and works on either a hard disk partition or a floppy diskette. Although it can take many options and arguments, you can use mkfs simply as

```
# mkfs device
```

where *device* is the name of the device (**/dev/hda2**, **/dev/sdb1**, **/dev/fd0**, and so on) you want to make a filesystem on. Use the –t option to specify a type of filesystem. The following command creates an **ext3** filesystem on *device:*

```
# mkfs -t ext3 device
```

ping Sends packets to a remote system. This utility determines if you can reach a remote system through the network and the time it takes to exchange messages with the remote system. Refer to "ping: Tests a Network Connection" on page 346.

reset (link to tset) Resets terminal characteristics. The value of the environment variable **TERM** (page 920) is used to determine how to reset the screen. The screen is cleared, the kill and interrupt characters are set to their default values, and character echo is turned on. From a graphical terminal emulator, this command also changes the size of the window to its default. The reset utility is useful to restore your screen to a sane state after it has been corrupted. Similar to an **stty sane** command.

setserial Gets and sets serial port information; it is used by Superuser to configure a serial port. The following command sets the input address of **/dev/ttys0** to 0x100, the interrupt (IRQ) to 5, and the baud rate to 115,000 baud:

```
# setserial /dev/ttys0 port 0x100 irq 5 spd_vhi
```

You can also check the configuration of a serial port with setserial:

```
# setserial /dev/ttyS0
/dev/ttyS0, UART: 16550A, Port: 0x0100, IRQ: 5, Flags: spd_vhi
```

Normally, setserial is called while the system is being booted if any of the serial ports needs to be set up specially.

umask   A shell builtin that specifies a mask the system uses to set up access permissions when you create a file. The format of a umask command is shown following:

umask [mask]

where ***mask*** is a three-digit octal number or a symbolic value such as you would use with chmod (page 174). The ***mask*** specifies the permissions that are *not* allowed. When ***mask*** is an octal number, the digits correspond to the permissions for the owner of the file, members of the group the file is associated with, and everyone else. Because the ***mask*** specifies the permissions that are *not* allowed, the system subtracts each of these from 7 when you create a file. The result is three octal numbers that specify the access permissions for the file (the numbers you would use with chmod). A ***mask*** that you specify as a symbolic value also specifies the permissions that are not allowed.

Most utilities and applications do not attempt to create files with execute permissions, regardless of the value of ***mask***; they assume you do not want an executable file. The effective result is that when a utility or application, such as touch, creates a file, the system subtracts each of the digits in ***mask*** from 6. An exception is mkdir, which assumes that you want the execute (access in the case of a directory) bit set.

The following commands set the file-creation permissions mask and display the mask and its effect when you create a file and a directory. The mask of 022, when subtracted from 777, gives permissions of 644 (rw-r--r--) for a file and 755 (rwxr-xr-x) for a directory.

```
$ umask 022
$ umask
0022
$ touch afile
$ mkdir adirectory
$ ls -ld afile adirectory
drwxr-xr-x  2 sam sam 4096 May  2 23:57 adirectory
-rw-r--r--  1 sam sam    0 May  2 23:57 afile
```

The next example sets the same mask value symbolically.

```
$ umask g=rx,o=rx
$ umask
0022
```

uname   Displays information about the system. When you run uname without any arguments, it displays the name of the operating system (**Linux**). Giving uname a –a (all) option causes it to display the operating system name, the hostname, the version number and release date of the operating system, and the type of hardware you are using:

```
# uname -a
Linux pb 2.6.3-2.1.253.2.1 #1 Fri Mar 12 14:01:55 EST 2004 i686 athlon i386 GNU/Linux
```

Setting Up a Server

This section discusses issues that are common to setting up most servers: rules for writing configuration files; how to specify hosts and subnets; how to use **portmap,** rpcinfo, **xinetd,** TCP wrappers (**hosts.allow** and **hosts.deny**); and how to set up a chroot jail. Setting up specific servers is covered in Chapters 14 and 18–26. Setting up a LAN is covered in Chapter 17 (page 551).

Standard Rules in Configuration Files

Most configuration files, typically named *.conf, rely on the following conventions:

- Blank lines are ignored.

- A # anywhere on a line starts a comment which continues to the end of the line. Comments are ignored.

- When a name contains a SPACE, you must quote the SPACE by preceding it with a backslash (\) or by enclosing the entire name within single or double quotation marks.

- To make long lines easier to read and edit, you can break them into several shorter lines. Break a line by inserting a backslash (\) immediately followed by a NEWLINE (press RETURN in a text editor). When you insert the NEWLINE before or after a SPACE, you can indent the following line to make it easier to read. Do not break lines in this manner while editing on a Windows machine, as the NEWLINEs may not be properly escaped (Windows uses RETURN-LINEFEEDs to end lines).

Configuration files that do not follow these conventions are noted in the text.

Specifying Clients

Table 11-3 shows some of the common ways to specify a host or a subnet (next section). Most of the time you can specify multiple hosts or subnets by separating the host or subnet specifications with SPACES.

table 11-3 ‖	Specifying a Client
Client Name Pattern	**Matches**
n.n.n.n	One IP address
name	One hostname, either local or remote
name that starts with .	Matches a host name that ends with the specified string. For example, **.tcorp.com** matches the systems **kudos.tcorp.com** and **speedy.tcorp.com**, among others.

table 11-3 || **Specifying a Client (Continued)**

Client Name Pattern	Matches
IP address that ends with .	Matches a host address that starts with the specified numbers. For example, **192.168.0.** matches **192.168.0.0 – 192.168.0.255**. If you omit the trailing period, this format does not work.
starts with @	Specifies a netgroup.
n.n.n.n/m.m.m.m *or* n.n.n.n/mm	An IP address and subnet mask specify a subnet (next section).
starts with /	An absolute pathname of a file containing one or more names or addresses as specified in this table.
Wildcards	
* *and* ?	Matches one (?) or more (*) characters in a simple hostname or IP address. These wildcards do not match periods in a domain name.
ALL	Always matches.
LOCAL	Matches any hostname that does not contain a period.
Operator	
EXCEPT	Matches anything in the preceding list that is not in the following list. For example, **a b c d EXCEPT c** matches **a**, **b**, and **d**. So you could use 192.168. EXCEPT 192.168.0.1 to match all IP addresses that start with 192.168. except 192.168.0.1.

Examples   Each of the following examples specifies one or more systems:

10.10.	Matches all systems with IP addresses that start with **10.10.**.
.redhat.com	Matches all named hosts on the Red Hat network.
localhost	Matches the local system.
127.0.0.1	The loopback address; always resolves to the local host.
192.168.*.1	Could match all routers on a network of /24 subnets.

Specifying a Subnet

When you set up a server, you frequently need to specify the clients that are allowed to connect to the server. Sometimes, it is convenient to specify a range of IP addresses, a subnet. The discussion on page 337 explains what a subnet is and how to use a subnet mask to specify a subnet. Usually, you can specify a subnet as

n.n.n.n/m.m.m.m

or

n.n.n.n/mbits

where *n.n.n.n* is the base IP address and the subnet is represented by *m.m.m.m* (the subnet mask) or *mbits* (the number of bits used for the subnet mask). For example, **192.168.0.1/255.255.255.0** represents the same subnet as **192.168.0.1/24**. In binary, decimal **255.255.255.0** is represented by 24 ones followed by eight zeros. The **/24** is shorthand for a subnet mask with 24 ones. Each line in Table 11-4 presents two notations for the same subnet followed by the range of IP addresses that the subnet includes.

table 11-4 ‖		Different Ways to Represent a Subnet
Bits	Mask	Range
10.0.0.0/8	10.0.0.0/255.0.0.0	10.0.0.0 - 10.255.255.255
172.16.0.0/12	172.16.0.0/255.240.0.0	172.16.0.0 - 72.31.255.255
192.168.0.0/16	192.168.0.0/255.255.0.0	192.168.0.0 - 192.168.255.255

rpcinfo: **Displays Information About portmap**

The rpcinfo utility can display information about programs registered with **portmap** and can make RPC calls to programs to see if they are alive. For more information on **portmap**, refer to "RPC Network Services" on page 358. The rpcinfo utility takes the following options and arguments:

rpcinfo –p [host]
rpcinfo [–n port] –u | –t host program [version]
rpcinfo –b | –d program version

–p **probe**   Lists all RPC programs registered with **portmap** on *host* or on the local system if *host* is not specified.

–n **(port) number**   With –t or –u, uses port *number* in place of the port number specified by **portmap**.

–u **UDP**   Makes a UDP RCP call to *version* (if specified) of *program* on *host* and reports whether there was a response.

–t **TCP**   Makes a TCP RCP call to *version* (if specified) of *program* on *host* and reports whether there was a response.

–b **broadcast**   Makes an RPC broadcast to *version* of *program* and lists hosts that respond.

–d **delete**   Removes local RPC registration for *version* of *program*. Superuser only.

Give the following command to see which RPC programs are registered with the **portmap** daemon on the system named **peach**:

```
$ /usr/sbin/rpcinfo -p peach
   program vers proto    port
    100000    2   tcp     111   portmapper
    100000    2   udp     111   portmapper
    100024    1   udp   32768   status
    100024    1   tcp   32768   status
    100021    1   udp   32769   nlockmgr
    100021    3   udp   32769   nlockmgr
...
```

Use the **–u** option to display a list of versions of a daemon, such as **ypserv**, registered on a remote system (**peach**):

```
$ /usr/sbin/rpcinfo -u peach ypserv
program 100004 version 1 ready and waiting
program 100004 version 2 ready and waiting
```

Specify **localhost** to display a list of versions of a daemon registered on the local system:

```
$ /usr/sbin/rpcinfo -u localhost nfs
program 100003 version 2 ready and waiting
program 100003 version 3 ready and waiting
```

Locking down portmap   As the **portmap** daemon holds information about which servers are running on the local system and which port each is running on, it is important that only trusted systems have access to this information. One way to ensure that only selected systems have access to **portmap** is to lock it down in the **/etc/hosts.allow** and **/etc/hosts.deny** files (page 404). Put the following line in **hosts.deny** to prevent all systems from using portmap on the local (server) system:

```
portmap: ALL
```

Test this setup from a *remote* system with the following command:

```
$ rpcinfo -p hostname
No remote programs registered.
```

Replace *hostname* with the name of the remote system that you changed the **hosts.deny** file on. The change is immediate; you do not need to kill/restart a daemon.

Next, add the following line to the **hosts.allow** file on the server system:

```
portmap: host-IP
```

where *host-IP* is the IP address of the trusted, remote system that you gave the preceding rpcinfo command from. Use only IP addresses with **portmap** in **hosts.allow**; do not use system names that **portmap** could get stuck trying to resolve. Give the same rpcinfo command, and you should see a list of the servers that RPC knows about, including **portmap**. See page 642 for more examples.

---

caution || **Set the Clocks**

The **portmap** daemon relies on the client's and server's clocks being synchronized. A simple *DoS attack* (page 968) can be initiated by setting the server's clock to the wrong time.

The xinetd Super Server

The **xinetd** daemon is a more secure replacement for the **inetd** super server that originally shipped with 4.3BSD. The Internet super server listens for network connections and, when one is made, launches a specified server daemon and forwards the data from the socket (page 439) to the daemon's standard input. The **xinetd** super server performs these tasks and provides additional features to control access.

The version of **xinetd** distributed with Red Hat Linux is linked against **libwrap.a,** so it is capable of using the **/etc/hosts.allow** and **/etc/hosts.deny** files for access control (see "TCP Wrappers," page 404 for more information). Using TCP Wrappers can simplify configuration but hides some of the more advanced features of **xinetd.**

The base configuration for **xinetd** is stored in the **/etc/xinetd.conf** file. The file supplied by Red Hat is shown following:

```
$ cat /etc/xinetd.conf
# Simple configuration file for xinetd
defaults
{
        instances               = 60
        log_type                = SYSLOG authpriv
        log_on_success          = HOST PID
        log_on_failure          = HOST
        cps                     = 25 30
}
includedir /etc/xinetd.d
```

The **defaults** section specifies the default configuration of **xinetd;** the files in the included directory, **/etc/xinetd.d,** specify server-specific configurations. Defaults can be overridden by server-specific configuration files.

In the preceding file, the **instances** directive specifies that no daemon may run more than 60 copies of itself at one time. The **log_type** directive specifies that **xinetd** send messages to the system log daemon (**syslogd,** page 546) using the **authpriv** facility. The next two lines specify what to log on success and on failure. The **cps** (connections per second) directive specifies that no more than 25 connections to a specific service should be made per second and that the service should be disabled for 30 seconds if this limit is exceeded.

The following **xinetd** configuration file allows telnet connections from the local system and any system with an IP address that starts with **192.168..** This configuration file does not rely on TCP wrappers and so does not rely on the **hosts.allow** and **hosts.deny** files.

```
$ cat /etc/xinetd.d/telnet
service telnet
{
        socket_type     = stream
        wait            = no
        user            = root
        server          = /usr/sbin/in.telnetd
        only_from       = 192.168.0.0/16 127.0.0.1
        disable         = no
}
```

The **socket_type** indicates whether the socket uses TCP or UDP. TCP-based protocols establish a connection between the client and the server and are identified by the type **stream**. UDP-based protocols rely on the transmission of individual datagrams and are identified by the type **dgram**.

When **wait** is set to **no**, **xinetd** handles multiple, concurrent connections to this service. Setting **wait** to **yes** causes **xinetd** to wait for the server process to complete before handling the next request for that service. In general, UDP services should be set to **yes** and TCP services to **no**. If you were to set **wait** to **yes** for a service such as telnet, only one person would be able to use the service at a time.

The **user** specifies the user that the server runs as. If the user is a member of multiple groups, you can also specify the group on a separate line using the keyword **group**. The **user** directive is ignored if **xinetd** is run as other than **root**. The **server** provides the pathname of the server program that **xinetd** runs for this service.

The **only_from** specifies which systems **xinetd** allows to use the service. Use IP addresses only because using hostnames can make the service unavailable if DNS fails. Zeros at the right of an IP address are treated as wildcards: **192.168.0.0** allows access from any system in the **192.168** subnet.

The **disable** line can disable a service without removing the configuration file. As shipped by Red Hat, a number of services include an **xinetd** configuration file with **disable** set to **yes**. To run one of these services, you must change **disable** to **no** in the appropriate file in **xinetd.d** and restart **xinetd**:

```
# /sbin/service xinetd restart
Stopping xinetd:                                      [  OK  ]
Starting xinetd:                                      [  OK  ]
```

Securing a Server

This section discusses how to secure a server using TCP wrappers or by setting up a chroot jail.

TCP Wrappers: Client/Server Security (hosts.allow and hosts.deny)

When you open a local system to access from remote systems, you must ensure that you

- Open the local system only to systems you want to allow to access it.
- Allow each remote system to access only the data you want it to access.
- Allow each remote system to access data only in the manner you want it to (read only, read/write, write only).

As part of the client/server model, TCP Wrappers, which can be used for any daemon that is linked against **libwrap.a**, uses the **/etc/hosts.allow** and **/etc/hosts.deny** files to form the basis of a simple access control language. This access control language defines rules that selectively allow clients to access server daemons on a local system based on the client's address and the daemon the client tries to access.

Each line in the **hosts.allow** and **hosts.deny** files has the following format:

daemon_list : client_list [: command]

where *daemon_list* is a comma-separated list of one or more server daemons (such as **portmap, vsftpd, sshd**), *client_list* is a comma-separated list of one or more clients (see Table 11-3, "Specifying a Client," on page 399), and the optional *command* is the command that is executed when a client from *client_list* tries to access a server daemon from *daemon_list*.

When a client requests a connection with a local server, the **hosts.allow** and **hosts.deny** files are consulted as follows until a match is found. The first match determines whether the client is allowed to access the server.

1. If the daemon/client pair matches a line in **hosts.allow**, access is granted.

2. If the daemon/client pair matches a line in **hosts.deny**, access is denied.

3. If there is no match in either the **hosts.allow** or the **hosts.deny** files, access is granted.

When either the **hosts.allow** or the **hosts.deny** file does not exist, it is as though that file were empty. Although it is not recommended, you can allow access to all daemons for all clients by removing both files.

Examples   For a more secure system, put the following line in **hosts.deny** to block all access:

```
$ cat /etc/hosts.deny
...
ALL : ALL : echo '%c tried to connect to %d and was blocked' >> /var/log/tcpwrappers.log
```

This line blocks any client attempting to connect to any service, unless specifically permitted in **hosts.allow**. When this rule is matched, it adds a line to the **/var/log/tcpwrappers.log** file. The **%c** expands to client information and the **%d** expands to the name of the daemon the client attempted to connect to.

With the preceding **hosts.deny** file in place, you can put lines in **hosts.allow** explicitly to allow access to certain services and systems. For example, the following **hosts.allow** file allows anyone to connect to the OpenSSH daemon (ssh, scp, sftp) but allows telnet connections only from the same network as the local system and users on the 192.168. subnet:

```
$ cat /etc/hosts.allow
sshd : ALL
in.telnet : LOCAL
in.telnet : 192.168.? 127.0.0.1
...
```

The first line in the preceding file allows connection from any system (ALL) to **sshd**. The second line allows connection from any system in the same domain as the server (LOCAL). The third line matches any system whose IP address starts **192.168.** and the local system.

Setting Up a chroot Jail

On early UNIX systems, the root directory was a fixed point in the file system. On modern UNIX variants, including Linux, you can define the root directory on a per-process basis. The chroot utility allows you to run a process with a root directory other than **/**.

The root directory is the top of the directory hierarchy and has no parents: A process cannot access any files above the root directory (because they do not exist). If, for example, you run a program (process) and specify its root directory as **/home/sam/jail**, the program would have no concept of any files in **/home/sam** or above: **jail** is the program's root directory and is labeled **/** (not **jail**).

By creating an artificial root directory, frequently called a (chroot) jail, you prevent a program from being able to access and modify, possibly maliciously, files outside the directory hierarchy starting at its root. You must set up a chroot jail properly in order to increase security: If you do not set up a chroot jail correctly, you can make it easier for a malicious user to gain access to a system than if there were no chroot jail.

Using chroot

Creating a chroot jail is simple: Working as **root**, give the command **/usr/sbin/chroot** *directory*. The *directory* becomes the root directory and the process attempts to run the default shell. Working as **root** from the **/home/sam** directory, the following example attempts to set up a chroot jail in the (existing) **/home/sam/jail** directory:

```
# /usr/sbin/chroot jail
/usr/sbin/chroot: /bin/bash: No such file or directory
```

In the preceding example, chroot sets up the chroot jail, but when it attempts to run a the bash shell, it fails. Once the jail is set up, the directory that was named **jail** takes on the name of the root directory: **/** and chroot cannot find the file identified by the pathname **/bin/bash**. The chroot jail is working perfectly but is not very useful.

Getting a chroot jail to work the way you want is more complicated. To get the preceding example to run bash in a chroot jail, you need to create a **bin** directory in **jail** (**/home/sam/jail/bin**) and copy **/bin/bash** to this directory. Because the bash binary is dynamically linked to shared libraries (page 813), you need to copy these libraries into **jail** too. The libraries go in **/lib**. The following example creates the necessary directories, copies **bash**, uses ldd to display the shared library dependencies of bash, and copies the necessary libraries into **lib**:

```
$ pwd
/home/sam/jail
$ mkdir bin lib
$ cp /bin/bash bin
$ ldd bin/bash
        libtermcap.so.2 => /lib/libtermcap.so.2 (0x4002a000)
        libdl.so.2 => /lib/libdl.so.2 (0x4002f000)
        libc.so.6 => /lib/tls/libc.so.6 (0x42000000)
        /lib/ld-linux.so.2 => /lib/ld-linux.so.2 (0x40000000)
$ cp /lib/libtermcap.so.2 lib
$ cp /lib/libdl.so.2 lib
$ cp /lib/tls/libc.so.6 lib
$ cp /lib/ld-linux.so.2 lib
```

Now that everything is set up, you can try starting the chroot jail again. All the setup can be done by an ordinary user; you have to run chroot as Superuser:

```
$ su
Password:
# /usr/sbin/chroot .
bash-2.05b# pwd
/
bash-2.05b# ls
bash: ls: command not found
bash-2.05b#
```

This time the chroot finds and starts **bash**, which displays its default prompt (**bash-2.05b#**). The pwd command works because it is a shell builtin (page 211). However, bash cannot find the ls utility (it is not in the chroot jail). You can copy **/bin/ls** and its libraries into the jail if you want users in the jail to be able to use ls.

To set up a useful chroot jail, you need to determine which utilities the users of the chroot jail are going to need. Then, you can copy the binaries and their libraries into the jail, or you can build static copies of the binaries and put them in the jail without the need for separate libraries. (The statically linked binaries are considerably larger than their dynamic counterparts. The base system with bash and the core utilities is over 50 megabytes.) You can find the source code for most of the common utilities you need in the **bash** and **coreutils** SRPMS (source rpm) packages.

Whichever technique you choose, you must put a copy of su in the jail. The su command is required to run programs as a user other than **root**. Because **root** can break out of a chroot jail, it is imperative that you run a program in the chroot jail as a user other than **root**.

The dynamic version of su that Red Hat distributes requires PAM and will not work within a jail. You need to build a copy of su from the source to use in a jail. By default, a copy of su you build does not require PAM. Refer to "GNU Configure and Build System" on page 459 for instructions on how to build packages such as **coreutils** (which includes su).

In order to be able to use su, you need to copy the relevant lines from the **/etc/passwd** and **/etc/shadow** files into files with the same names in the **etc** directory inside the jail.

---

tip ‖   **Keeping Multiple** chroot **Jails**

If you are going to deploy multiple chroot jails, it is a good idea to keep a clean copy of the **bin** and **lib** files somewhere other than in one of the active jails.

Running a Service in a *chroot* Jail

Running a shell inside a jail has limited use. You are more likely to need to run a specific service inside the jail. To run a service inside a jail, you need make sure all the files needed by that service are inside the jail. The format of a command to start a service in a chroot jail is

```
# /usr/sbin/chroot jailpath /bin/su user daemonname &
```

Where *jailpath* is the pathname of the jail directory, *user* is the username that runs the daemon, and *daemonname* is the path (inside the jail) of the daemon that provides the service.

Several servers are set up to take advantage of chroot jails. The system-config-bind utility (page 712) automatically sets up DNS so **named** runs in a jail and the **vsftpd** FTP server can automatically start chroot jails for clients (page 598).

Security Considerations

Some services need to be run as **root**, but they release their **root** privilege once started (Procmail and **vsftpd** are examples). If you are running such a service, you do not need to put su inside the jail.

It is possible for a process run as **root** to escape from a chroot jail. For this reason, you should always su to another user before starting a program running inside the jail. Also, be careful about what setuid (page 175) binaries you allow inside a jail because a security hole in one of these can compromise the security of the jail. Also, make sure the user cannot access executable files that she uploads.

DHCP

Instead of having network configuration information stored in local files on each system, DHCP (Dynamic Host Configuration Protocol) enables client systems to retrieve network configuration information each time they connect to the network. A DHCP server assigns temporary IP addresses from a pool of addresses to clients as needed.

This technique has several advantages over storing network configuration information in local files:

- DHCP makes it possible for a new user to set up an Internet connection without having to work with IP addresses, netmasks, DNS addresses, and other technical details. DHCP also makes it faster for an experienced user to set up a connection.

- DHCP facilitates assignment and management of IP addresses and related network information by centralizing the process on a server. A system administrator can configure new systems, including laptops that connect to the network from different locations, to use DHCP, which assigns IP addresses only when each system connects to the network. The pool of IP addresses is managed as a group on the DHCP server.

- DHCP enables IP addresses to be used by more than one system, reducing the number of IP addresses needed overall. This conservation of addresses is important as the Internet is quickly running out of IPv4 addresses. Although one IP address can be used by only one system at a time, many end-user systems require addresses only occasionally, when they connect to the Internet. By reusing IP addresses, DHCP lengthens the life of the IPv4 protocol. DHCP applies to IPv4 only, as IPv6 forces systems to configure their IP addresses automatically (called autoconfiguration) when they connect to a network (page 340).

DHCP is particularly useful for administrators responsible for a large number of systems because it removes the requirement for individual systems to store unique configuration information. DHCP allows an administrator to set up a master system and deploy new systems with a copy of the master's hard disk. In educational establishments and other open access facilities, it is common to store the hard disk image on a shared drive and have each workstation automatically restore itself to pristine condition at the end of each day.

More Information

Web   www.dhcp.org

FAQ   www.dhcp-handbook.com/dhcp_faq.html

HOWTO   *DHCP Mini HOWTO*

How DHCP Works

The client daemon, **dhclient**, contacts the server daemon, **dhcpd**, to obtain the IP address, netmask, broadcast address, nameserver address, and other networking parameters. The server provides a *lease* on the IP address to the client. The client can request specific terms of the lease, including its duration, and the server can limit these terms. While connected to the network, a client typically requests extensions of its lease as necessary so its IP address remains the same. The lease can expire once the client is disconnected from the network; the server can give the client a new IP address when it requests a new lease. You can also set up a DHCP server to provide static IP addresses for specific clients (refer to "Static versus Dynamic IP Addresses" on page 334).

DHCP is broadcast based, so the client and server must be on the same subnet (page 337).

DHCP Client

A DHCP client requests network configuration parameters from the DHCP server and uses those parameters to configure its network interface.

Prerequisites

Install the following package:

- **dhclient**

dhclient: The DHCP Client

When a DHCP client system connects to the network, dhclient requests a lease from the DHCP server and configures the client's network interface(s). Once a DHCP client has requested and established a lease, it stores information about the lease in **/etc/dhclient.leases**. This information is used to reestablish a lease when either the server or client needs to reboot. The DHCP client configuration file, **/etc/dhclient.conf**, is required only for custom configurations. The following **dhclient.conf** file specifies a single interface, **eth0**:

```
$ cat /etc/dhclient.conf
interface "eth0"
{
send dhcp-client-identifier 1:xx:xx:xx:xx:xx:xx;
send dhcp-lease-time 86400;
}
```

In the preceding file, the 1 in the **dhcp-client-identifier** specifies an Ethernet network and **xx:xx:xx:xx:xx:xx** is the *MAC address* (page 981) of the device controlling that interface. See page 412 for instructions on how to display a MAC address. The **dhcp-lease-time** is the duration, in seconds, of the lease on the IP address. While the client is connected to the network, dhclient automatically renews the lease each time half of the lease is up. The choice of 86400 seconds, or one day, is a reasonable choice for a workstation.

DHCP Server

The DHCP server maintains a list of IP addresses and other configuration parameters. When requested, the DHCP server provides configuration parameters to a client.

Prerequisites

Install the following package:

• dhcpd

Run chkconfig to cause **dhcpd** to start when the system goes multiuser:

```
# /sbin/chkconfig dhcpd on
```

Start **dhcpd**:

```
# /sbin/service dhcpd start
```

dhcpd: The DHCP Daemon

A simple DCHP server allows you to add clients to a network without maintaining a list of assigned IP addresses. A simple network, such as a home LAN sharing an Internet connection, can use DHCP to assign a dynamic IP address to almost all nodes. The exceptions are servers and routers, which must be at known network locations in order to be able to receive connections. If servers and routers are configured without DHCP, you can specify a simple DHCP server configuration in **/etc/dhcpd.conf**:

```
$ cat /etc/dhcpd.conf
default-lease-time 600;
max-lease-time 86400;

option subnet-mask 255.255.255.0;
option broadcast-address 192.168.1.255;
option routers 192.168.1.1;
option domain-name-servers 192.168.1.1;

subnet 192.168.1.0 netmask 255.255.255.0 {
    range 192.168.1.2 192.168.1.200;
}
```

The preceding configuration file specifies a LAN where the router and DNS are both located on **192.168.1.1**. The **default-lease-time** specifies the number of seconds a dynamic IP lease will be valid if the client does not specify a duration. The **max-lease-time** is the maximum time allowed for a lease.

The information in the **option** lines is sent to each client when it connects. The names following the word **option** specify what the following argument represents. For example, the **option broadcast-address** line specifies the broadcast address of the network. The **routers** and **domain-name-servers** options allow multiple values separated by commas.

The **subnet** section includes a **range** line that specifies the range of IP addresses that the DHCP server can assign. If you define multiple subnets, you can define options, such as **subnet-mask**, inside the **subnet** section. Options defined outside all **subnet** sections are global and apply to all subnets.

The preceding configuration file assigns addresses in the range between 192.168.1.2 and 192.168.1.200. The DHCP server starts at the bottom of the range and attempts to assign a new IP address to each new client. Once the DHCP server reaches the top of the range, it starts reassigning IP addresses that have been used, but are not currently in use. If you have fewer systems than IP addresses, the IP address of each system should remain fairly constant. You cannot use the same IP address for more than one system at a time.

Once you have configured a DHCP server, you can start or restart it using the **dhcpd** init script:

```
# /sbin/service dhcpd restart
```

Once the server is running, clients configured to obtain an IP address from the server using DHCP should be able to do so.

Static IP Addresses

As mentioned earlier, routers and servers typically require static IP addresses. While you can manually configure IP addresses for these systems, it may be more convenient to have the DHCP server provide them with static IP addresses.

When a system that requires a specific static IP address connects to the network and contacts the DHCP server, the server needs a way to identify the system so it can assign the proper IP address. The DHCP server uses the *MAC address* (page 981) of the system's Ethernet card (NIC) to identify the system. When you set up the server, you must know the MAC addresses of each of the systems that requires a static IP address.

Displaying a MAC address — You can use ifconfig to display the MAC addresses of the Ethernet boards (NICs) in a system. The MAC address is the colon-separated series of hexadecimal number pairs following **HWaddr**:

```
$ /sbin/ifconfig | grep -i hwaddr
eth0      Link encap:Ethernet   HWaddr BA:DF:00:DF:C0:FF
eth1      Link encap:Ethernet   HWaddr 00:02:B3:41:35:98
```

Run ifconfig on each system that requires a static IP address. Once you have determined the MAC address of each system that requires a static IP address, you can add a **host** section to the **/etc/dhcpd.conf** file for each of these systems, instructing the DHCP server to assign a specific address to each system. The following **host** section assigns the address **192.168.1.1** to the system with the MAC address of **BA:DF:00:DF:C0:FF**:

```
$ cat /etc/dhcpd.conf
...
host router {
    hardware ethernet BA:DF:00:DF:C0:FF;
    fixed-address 192.168.1.1;
    option host-name router;
}
```

The name following **host** is used internally by **dhcpd**, while the name specified after **option host-name** is passed to the client and can be a hostname or a FQDN.

After making changes to **dhcpd.conf**, restart **dhcpd** using service and the **dhcpd** init script (page 411).

nsswitch.conf: Which Service to Look at First

With the advent of NIS and DNS, it was no longer a simple matter of searching a local file for user and system information. Where you used to look in **/etc/passwd** to get user information and look in **/etc/hosts** to find system address information, you can now use several methods to find this type of information. The **/etc/nsswitch.conf** (name service switch configuration) file specifies which methods to use and the order to use them in when looking for a certain type of information. You can also specify what action the system takes based on whether a method works or fails.

Format   Each line in **nsswitch.conf** specifies how to search for a piece of information, such as a user's password. The format of a line in **nsswitch.conf** is

> *info:*   *method [[action]] [method [[action]]...]*

where *info* specifies the type of information that the line describes (discussed following), *method* is the method used to find the information (described following), and *action* is the response to the return status of the preceding *method*. The action is enclosed within square brackets.

How nsswitch.conf Works

When called upon to supply information that **nisswitch.conf** describes, the system examines the line with the appropriate *info* field. The system uses the methods specified on the line starting with the method on the left. By default, when the information is found, the system stops searching. Without an *action* specification, when a method fails to return a result, the next action is tried. It is possible for the search to end without finding the requested information.

Information

The **nisswitch.conf** file commonly controls searches for users (in **passwd**), passwords (in **shadow**), host IP address, and group information. The following list describes most of the types of information (*info* in the format discussed earlier) that **nsswitch.conf** controls searches for.

automount	Automount (**/etc/auto.master** and **/etc/auto.misc**, page 671)
bootparams	Diskless and other booting options. See the **bootparam** man page.
ethers	*MAC address* (page 981)

group	Groups of users (**/etc/group**, page 428)
hosts	System information (**/etc/hosts**, page 428)
netgroup	Netgroup information (**/etc/netgroup**, page 430)
networks	Network information (**/etc/networks**)
passwd	User information (**/etc/passwd**, page 430)
protocols	Protocol information (**/etc/protocols**, page 432)
publickey	Used for NFS running in secure mode
rpc	RPC names and numbers (**/etc/rpc**, page 433)
services	Services information (**/etc/services**, page 433)
shadow	Shadow password information (**/etc/shadow**, page 433)

Methods

Following is a list of the types of information that **nsswitch.conf** controls searches for (*method* in the format on page 413). For each type of information, you can specify one or more of the following methods:[2]

files	Searches local files such as **/etc/passwd** and **/etc/hosts**.
nis	Searches the NIS database; **yp** is an alias for **nis**.
dns	Queries the DNS (**hosts** queries only).
compat	± syntax in **passwd, group, and shadow** files (page 416).

Search Order

The information provided by two or more methods may overlap: For example, **files** and **nis** can each provide password information for the same user. With overlapping information, you need to consider which method you want to be authoritative (take precedence), and put that method at the left of the list of methods.

The default **nsswitch.conf** file lists methods without actions, assuming no overlap (which is normal). In this case, the order is not critical: When one method fails, the system goes to the next one; all that is lost is a bit of time for a failure. Order becomes critical when you use actions between methods, or when you have overlapping entries that differ.

The first of the following lines from **nisswitch.conf** causes the system to search for password information in **/etc/passwd** and, if that fails, to use NIS to find the information. If the user you are looking for is listed in both places, the information in the local file would be used and therefore would be authoritative. The second line uses NIS and, if that fails, searches **/etc/hosts** and, if that fails, checks with DNS to find host information.

---

2. There are other, less commonly used methods. See the default **/etc/nisswitch.conf** file and the nisswitch.conf man page for more information. Although NIS+ belongs in this list, it is not implemented for Linux and is not discussed in this book.

```
passwd          files nis
hosts           nis files dns
```

Action Items

Each method can optionally be followed by an action item that specifies what to do if the method succeeds or fails for one of a number of reasons. The format of an action item is

[[!]STATUS=action]

where the opening and closing square brackets are part of the format and do not indicate that the contents are optional; *STATUS* (by convention uppercase although it is not case sensitive) is the status being tested for; and *action* is the action to be taken if *STATUS* matches the status returned by the preceding method. The leading exclamation point (!) is optional and negates the status.

Values for *STATUS* are

NOTFOUND   The method worked, but the value being searched for was not found. Default action is **continue**.

SUCCESS   The method worked, and the value being searched for was found; no error was returned. Default action is **return**.

UNAVAIL   The method failed because it is permanently unavailable. For example, the required file may not be accessible or the required server may be down. Default action is **continue**.

TRYAGAIN   The method failed because it is temporarily unavailable. For example, a file may be locked or a server overloaded. Default action is **continue**.

Values for *action* are

return   Returns to the calling routine with or without a value.

continue   Continues with the next method. Any returned value is overwritten by a value found by the next method.

For example, the following line from **nsswitch.conf** causes the system first to use DNS to search for the IP address of a given host. The action item following the DNS method tests to see if the status returned by the method is not (!) UNAVAIL.

```
hosts           dns [!UNAVAIL=return] files
```

The system takes the action associated with the *STATUS* (**return**) if the DNS method did not return UNAVAIL (!UNAVAIL), that is, if DNS returned SUCCESS, NOTFOUND, or TRYAGAIN. The result is that the following method (**files**) is used only when the DNS server is unavailable: If the DNS server is *not un*available (read the two negatives as "is available,"), the search returns the domain name or reports the domain name was not found. The search uses the **files** method (check the local **/etc/hosts** file) only if the server is not available.

compat Method: ± in passwd, group, and shadow files

You can put special codes in the **/etc/passwd**, **/etc/group**, and **/etc/shadow** files that cause the system, when you specify the **compat** method in **nisswitch.conf**, to combine and modify entries in the local files and the NIS maps.

A plus sign (+) at the beginning of a line in one of these files adds NIS information; a minus sign (–) removes information. For example, to use these codes in the **passwd** file, specify **passwd: compat** in **nisswitch.conf**. The system then goes through the **passwd** file in order, adding or removing the appropriate NIS entries when it gets to each line that starts with a + or –.

Although you can put a plus sign at the end of the **passwd** file and specify **passwd: compat** in **nsswitch.conf** to search the local **passwd** file and then go through the NIS map, it is more efficient to put **passwd: file nis** in **nsswitch.conf** and not modify the **passwd** file.

PAM

PAM (actually Linux-PAM, or Linux Pluggable Authentication Modules) allows a system administrator to determine how various applications use *authentication* (page 957) to verify the identity of a user. PAM provides shared libraries (page 813) of modules (located in **/lib/security**) that, when called by an application, authenticate a user. Pluggable refers to the ease with which you can add and remove modules from the authentication stack. The configuration files kept in the **/etc/pam.d** directory determine the method of authentication and contain a list, or stack, of calls to the modules. PAM may also use other files, such as **/etc/passwd**, when necessary.

Instead of building the authentication code into each application, PAM provides shared libraries to keep the authentication code separate from the application code. The techniques of authenticating users stay the same from application to application. PAM enables a system administrator to change the authentication mechanism for a given application without touching the application.

PAM provides authentication for a variety of system-entry services (login, ftp, and so on). You can take advantage of PAM's ability to stack authentication modules to integrate system-entry services with different authentication mechanisms, such as RSA, DCE, Kerberos, and smart cards.

From login through using su to shutting the system down, whenever you are asked for a password (or not asked for a password because the system trusts that you are who you say you are), PAM makes it possible for systems administrators to configure the authentication process and makes the configuration process essentially the same for all applications that use PAM to do their authentication.

The configuration files stored in **/etc/pam.d** describe the authentication procedure for each application. These files usually have names that are the same as or similar to the name of the application that they configure. For example, authentication for the login utility is configured in **/etc/pam.d/login**. The name of the file is the name of the PAM service[3] that the file configures. Occasionally, one file may serve two programs. PAM accepts only lowercase letters in the names of files in the **/etc/pam.d** directory.

---

tip ‖   **Do Not Lock Yourself Out of the System**

Editing PAM configuration files correctly takes care and attention. It is easy to lock yourself out of the computer with a single mistake. To avoid this type of problem, always keep backup copies of the PAM configuration files you edit, test every change thoroughly, and make sure you can still log in once the change is installed. Keep a Superuser session open until you are done testing. When a change fails and you cannot log in, use the Superuser session to replace the newly edited files with their backup copies.

PAM warns you about any errors it encounters, logging them to the **/var/log/messages** or **/var/log/secure** files. Look in these files if you are trying to figure out why a changed PAM file is not working properly. In order to prevent possibly giving unnecessary information to a malicious user, PAM sends error messages to a file rather than to the screen.

More Information

Local   **/usr/share/doc/pam-*/html/index.html**

Web   www.kernel.org/pub/linux/libs/pam/Linux-PAM-html/pam.html (*Linux-PAM System Administrators' Guide*)

HOWTO   *User Authentication HOWTO*

Configuration File, Module Type, and Control Flag

Following is an example of a PAM configuration file. Comment lines begin with a pound sign (#):

Login module
```
$ cat /etc/pam.d/login
#%PAM-1.0
auth        required      pam_securetty.so
auth        required      pam_stack.so service=system-auth
auth        required      pam_nologin.so
account     required      pam_stack.so service=system-auth
password    required      pam_stack.so service=system-auth
session     required      pam_selinux.so multiple
session     required      pam_stack.so service=system-auth
session     optional      pam_console.so
```

---

3. There is no relationship between PAM services and the **/etc/services** file. The name of the PAM service is an arbitrary string that each application gives to PAM; PAM then looks up the configuration file with that name and uses it to control how it does authentication. There is no central registry of PAM service names.

The first line is a special comment; it will become significant only if another PAM format is released. Do not use **#%** other than its use in the first line of the preceding example.

The rest of the lines tell PAM to do something as part of the authentication process. The first word on each line is a module type indicator: **account, auth, password,** or **session** (Table 11-5). The second is a control flag (Table 11-6), which indicates what type of action to take if authentication fails. The rest of the line contains the pathname of a PAM module and any arguments for that module. The PAM library itself uses the **/etc/pam.d** files to determine which modules to delegate work to.

table 11-5 || **Module Type Indicators**

Module Type	Description	Controls
account	Account management	Determining whether an already authenticated user is allowed to use the service he/she is trying to use. (That is, has the account expired? Is the user allowed to use this service at this time of day?)
auth	Authentication	Proving that the user is authorized to use the service. This may be done using passwords or another mechanism.
password	Password changing	Updating authentication mechanisms such as user passwords.
session	Session management	Setting things up when the service is started (for example, when the user logs in) and breaking them down when the service is terminated (for example, when the user logs out).

You can use one of the Control Flag keywords listed in Table 11-6 to set the control flags.

table 11-6 || **Control Flag**

required	Success is required for authentication to succeed. Control and a failure result are returned after all the modules in the stack have been executed. The technique of delaying the report to the calling program until all modules have been executed may keep attackers from knowing what caused their authentication attempts to fail and tell them less about the system, making it more difficult for them to break in.
requisite	Success is required for authentication to succeed. Further module processing is aborted, and control is returned immediately after a module fails. This technique may expose information about the system to an attacker. On the other hand, if it prevents a user from giving a password over an insecure connection, it might keep information out of the hands of an attacker.

table 11-6 ||	Control Flag (Continued)
sufficient	Success indicates that this module type has succeeded, and no subsequent required modules of this type are executed. Failure is not fatal to the stack of this module type. This technique is generally used when one form or another of authentication is good enough: If one fails, PAM tries the other. For example, when you use rsh to connect to another computer, **pam_rhosts** first checks to see whether your connection can be trusted without a password. If the connection can be trusted, the **pam_rhosts** module reports success, and PAM immediately reports success to the rsh daemon that called it. You will not be asked for a password. If your connection is not considered trustworthy, PAM starts the authentication over, asking for a password. If this second authentication succeeds, PAM ignores the fact that the **pam_rhosts** module reported failure. If both modules fail, you will not be able to log in.
optional	Result is generally ignored. An optional module is relevant only when it is the only module on the stack for a particular service.

PAM uses each of the module types as requested by the application. That is, the application will ask PAM separately to authenticate, check account status, manage sessions, and change the password. PAM will use one or more modules from the **/lib/security** directory to accomplish each of these tasks.

The configuration files in **/etc/pam.d** list the set of modules to be used for each application to do each task. Each such set of the same module types is called a *stack*. PAM calls the modules one at a time in order, from the top of the stack (the first module listed in the configuration file) to the bottom. The modules report success or failure back to PAM. When all the stacks of modules (there are exceptions) within a configuration file have been called, the PAM library reports success or failure back to the application.

Example

Part of the login service's authentication stack follows as an example:

```
$ cat /etc/pam.d/login
#%PAM-1.0
auth        required        /lib/security/pam_securetty.so
auth        required        /lib/security/pam_stack.so service=system-auth
auth        required        /lib/security/pam_nologin.so
...
```

The login program first asks for a user name and then asks PAM to run this stack to authenticate the user. Refer to the Table 11-5 on page 418 and Table 11-6 on page 418.

1. PAM first calls the **pam_securetty** (secure tty) module to make sure that the **root** user logs in only from an allowed terminal (by default, **root** is not

allowed to run login over the network; this policy helps prevent security breaches). The **pam_securetty** module is *required* to succeed in order for the authentication stack to succeed. The **pam_securetty** module reports failure only if someone is trying to log in as **root** from an unauthorized terminal. Otherwise (if the user name being authenticated is not **root** or if the user name is **root** and the login attempt is being made from a secure terminal), the **pam_securetty** module reports success.

Success and failure within PAM are opaque concepts that apply only to PAM. They do not equate to true and false as used elsewhere in the operating system.

2. The **pam_stack.so** module diverts the PAM stack to another module, returning the success or failure as the other module returns to it. The **service=system-auth** gives the name of the other module, in this case **system-auth** in /etc/pam.d. This module checks that the user who is logging in is authorized to do so, including checks on the username and password.

3. Next, the **pam_nologin** module makes sure that if the **/etc/nologin.txt** file exists, only the **root** user is allowed to log in. (That is, the **pam_nologin** module reports success only if **/etc/nologin.txt** does not exist or if the **root** user is logging in.) Thus when a shutdown has been scheduled for some time in the near future, the system administrator can keep users from logging in on the system only to experience a shutdown moments later.

The **account** module type works like the **auth** module type but is called after the user has been authenticated; it is an additional security check or requirement for a user to gain access to the system. For example, account modules can enforce a requirement that a user can log in only during business hours.

The **session** module type sets up and tears down the session (perhaps mounting and unmounting the user's home directory). One common **session** module on a Red Hat system is the **pam_console** module, which sets the system up especially for users who log in at the physical console, not for those who log in remotely. A local user is able to access the floppy and CD drives, the sound card, and sometimes other devices as defined by the system administrator.

The **password** module type is a bit unusual: All the modules in the stack are called once and told to get all the information they need to store the password to persistent memory, such as a disk, but not actually to store it. If it determines that it cannot or should not store the password, a module reports failure. If all the password modules in the stack report success, they are called a second time and told to store to persistent memory the password they obtained on the first pass. The **password** module is responsible for updating the authentication information (that is, changing the user's password).

Any one module can act as more than one module type; many modules can act as all four module types.

caution || **Brackets ([]) in the Control Flags Field**

You can set the control flags in a more complex way. When you see brackets ([ ]) in the control flags position in a PAM configuration file, the newer, more complex method is in use. Each comma-delimited argument is a **value=action** pair. When the return from the function matches **value**, **action** is evaluated. Refer to the *PAM System Administrator's Guide* (**/usr/share/doc/pam-*/txts/pam.txt**) for more information.

Modifying the PAM Configuration

Some UNIX systems require that a user be a member of the **wheel** group in order to use the su command. Although Red Hat is not configured this way by default, PAM allows you to change the default by editing the **/etc/pam.d/su** file:

```
$ cat /etc/pam.d/su
#%PAM-1.0
auth       sufficient   /lib/security/$ISA/pam_rootok.so
# Uncomment the following line to implicitly trust users in the "wheel" group.
#auth      sufficient   /lib/security/$ISA/pam_wheel.so trust use_uid
# Uncomment the following line to require a user to be in the "wheel" group.
#auth      required     /lib/security/$ISA/pam_wheel.so use_uid
auth       required     /lib/security/$ISA/pam_stack.so service=system-auth
account    required     /lib/security/$ISA/pam_stack.so service=system-auth
password   required     /lib/security/$ISA/pam_stack.so service=system-auth
session    required     /lib/security/$ISA/pam_stack.so service=system-auth
session    optional     /lib/security/$ISA/pam_selinux.so multiple
session    optional     /lib/security/$ISA/pam_xauth.so
```

The third through sixth lines of the **su** module contain comments that include the lines necessary to permit members of the **wheel** group to run su without supplying a password (sufficient) and to permit only users who are in the **wheel** group to use su (required). Uncomment one of these lines when you want your system to follow one of these rules.

caution || **Do Not Create /etc/pam.conf**

You may have encountered PAM on other systems where all configuration is arranged in a single file (**/etc/pam.conf**). This file does not exist on Red Hat systems. Instead, the **/etc/pam.d** directory contains individual configuration files, one per application that uses PAM. This setup makes it easy to install and uninstall applications that use PAM without having to modify the **/etc/pam.conf** file each time. If you create a **/etc/pam.conf** file on a system that does not use this file, your PAM configuration may become confused. Do not use PAM documentation from a different system. Also, the **requisite** control flag is unavailable on some systems that support PAM.

Chapter Summary

A system administrator is someone who keeps the system useful and convenient for its users. This chapter describes many of the files and programs you will work with to maintain a Red Hat system. Much of the work you do as the system administrator requires you to log in as **root**. The **root** user, called Superuser, has extensive systemwide powers that normal users do not have. Superuser can read from and write to any file and can execute programs that ordinary users are not permitted to execute.

When you bring up the system, it is sometimes in single-user mode. In this mode, only the system console is functional, and not all the filesystems are mounted. When the system is in single-user mode, you can back up files and use fsck to check the integrity of filesystems before you mount them. The telinit utility brings the system to its normal multiuser state. With the system running in multiuser mode, you can still perform many administration tasks, such as adding users and printers.

The chapter describes system operation: booting up, running init scripts, single-user mode, emergency mode, multiuser mode, bringing the system down, and what to do when the system crashes.

The chapter covers the Red Hat configuration tools (redhat-config-* under Red Hat Enterprise Linux and system-config-* under Fedora) and other tools that are useful to the system administrator. The section on setting up a server discusses the **xinetd** superserver which starts daemons as needed and can be used to help secure a system by controlling who can use which services. You can also use TCP wrappers to control who can use which system services by editing the **hosts.allow** and **hosts.deny** files in the /etc directory. By limiting the portion of the filesystem a user sees, setting up a chroot jail can help control the damage a malicious user can do.

The section on DHCP describes how to set up a DHCP server so you do not have to configure each system on a network manually. It details setting up both static and dynamic IP addresses using DHCP. Whether a system uses as the source of certain information NIS, DNS, local files, or a combination, and in what order, is determined by /etc/nsswitch.conf. The final section of this chapter discusses Linux-PAM, which allows you to maintain fine-grain control over who can access the system, how they can access it, and what they can do.

Exercises

1. How does single-user mode differ from multiuser mode?

2. How would you communicate each of the following messages?

   a. The system is coming down tomorrow at 6:00 in the evening for periodic maintenance.

   b. The system is coming down in 5 minutes.

   c. Jenny's jobs are slowing the system down drastically, and she should postpone them.

   d. Alex's wife just had a baby girl.

3. What do the letters of the su command stand for? (*Hint:* It is not Superuser.) What can you do with su besides give yourself Superuser privileges? How would you log in as Alex if you did not know his password but knew the **root** password? How would you establish the same environment that Alex has when he first logs on?

4. How would you allow a user to execute privileged commands without giving the user the Superuser password?

5. Assume you are working as Superuser. How do you kill process 1648? How do you kill all processes running kmail?

6. How can you disable SELinux?

   Put the following line in **/etc/sysconfig/selinux**:

   ```
   SELINUX=disabled
   ```

7. Develop a strategy for coming up with a password that an intruder would not be likely to guess but that you will be able to remember.

Advanced Exercises

8. Give the command

   ```
   $ /sbin/fuser -uv /
   ```

   What is this a list of? Why is it so long? Give the same command as **root** (or ask the system administrator to do so and mail you the results). How does this list differ from the first? Why is it different?

9. When it puts files in a **lost+found** directory, fsck has lost the directory information for the files and thus has lost the names of the files. Each file is given a new name, which is the same as the inode number for the file:

```
$ ls -lg lost+found
-rw-r--r-- 1 alex pubs    110 Jun 10 10:55 51262
```

What can you do to identify these files and restore them?

10. Take a look at **/usr/bin/lesspipe.sh**, and explain what it does and six ways it works.

11. Why are setuid shell scripts inherently unsafe?

12. When a user logs in, you would like the system to check for a username in the local **/etc/passwd** file first and then check NIS. How do you implement this strategy?

13. Some older kernels contain a vulnerability that allows a local user to gain **root** privileges. Explain how this kind of vulnerability negates the value of a chroot jail.

Files, Directories, and Filesystems

12

Filesystems hold directories of files. These structures store user data and system data that are the basis of users' work on the system and the system's existence. This chapter discusses important files and directories, various types of files and how to work with them, and the use and maintenance of filesystems.

Important Files and Directories

This section details the most common files used to administer the system. Also refer to "Important Standard Directories and Files" on page 167.

~/.bash_profile Contains an individual user login shell initialization script. The shell executes the commands in this file in the same environment as the shell each time a user logs in. The file must be located in a user's home directory.

The default Red Hat **.bash_profile** file executes the commands in **~/.bashrc**. You can use **.bash_profile** to specify a terminal type (for vi, terminal emulators, and other programs), run stty to establish the terminal characteristics a user desires, and perform other housekeeping functions when a user logs in.

A typical **.bash_profile** file specifying a vt100 terminal and CONTROL-H as the erase key follows:

```
$ cat .bash_profile
export TERM=vt100
stty erase '^h'
```

For more information, refer to "Startup Files" on page 272.

425

~/.bashrc   Contains an individual user, interactive, nonlogin shell initialization script. The shell executes the commands in this file in the same environment as the (new) shell each time a user creates a new interactive shell. The **.bashrc** script differs from **.bash_profile** in that it is executed each time a new shell is spawned, not only when a user logs in. For more information, refer to "Startup Files" on page 272.

/dev/null   Output sent to this file disappears; also called a *bit bucket*. The **/dev/null** file is a device file and must be created with mknod. Input that you redirect to come from this file appears as nulls, creating an empty file. You can create an empty file named **nothing** by giving the following command:

```
$ cat /dev/null > nothing
```

or

```
$ cp /dev/null nothing
```

or, without explicitly using **/dev/null**

```
$ > nothing
```

This last command redirects the output of a null command to the file with the same result as the previous commands. You can use this technique to truncate an existing file to zero length without changing its permissions. You can also use **/dev/null** to get rid of output that you do not want:

```
$ grep portable * 2>/dev/null
```

The preceding command looks for the word **portable** in all files in the working directory. Any output to standard error (page 260), such as permission or directory errors, is discarded, while output to standard output appears on the screen.

/dev/pts   The **/dev/pts** pseudofilesystem is a hook into the Linux kernel and is part of the pseudoterminal support. Pseudoterminals are used by remote login programs, such as ssh, telnet, and xterm and other graphical terminal emulators. The following sequence of commands demonstrates that the user is logged in on **/dev/pts/1**. After using **who am i** to verify the line the user is logged in on and using ls to show that that line exists, the user redirects the output of an echo command to **/dev/pts/1**, whereupon the output appears on the user's screen:

```
$ who am i
bravo.example.com!alex      pts/1    May 10 13:03
$ ls /dev/pts
0   1   2
$ echo Hi there > /dev/pts/1
Hi there
```

/dev/zero   Input you take from this file contains an infinite string of zeros (numerical zeros, not ASCII zeros). You can fill a file (such as a swap file, page 435) or overwrite a file with zeros with a command such as the following. The od utility shows the contents of the new file:

```
$ dd if=/dev/zero of=zeros bs=1024 count=10
10+0 records in
10+0 records out
```

```
$ ls -l zeros
-rw-rw-r--    1 alex      alex          10240 Dec  3 20:26 zeros
$ od -c zeros
0000000  \0  \0  \0  \0  \0  \0  \0  \0  \0  \0  \0  \0  \0  \0  \0  \0
*
0024000
```

When you try to do with **/dev/zero** what you can do with **/dev/null**, you quickly fill the partition you are working in:

```
$ cp /dev/zero bigzero
cp: writing 'bigzero': No space left on device
$ rm bigzero
```

/etc/aliases   Used by the mail delivery system (typically sendmail) to hold **aliases** for users. Edit this file to suit local needs. For more information, refer to "/etc/aliases" on page 614.

/etc/at.allow, /etc/at.deny, /etc/cron.allow, and /etc/cron.deny   By default, users can use the at and cron utilities. The **at.allow** file lists the users who are allowed to use at. The **cron.allow** file works in the same manner for cron. The **at.deny** and **cron.deny** files specify users who are not permitted to use the corresponding utilities. As Red Hat is configured, an empty **at.deny** file and the absence of an **at.allow** file allows anyone to use at; the absence of **cron.allow** and **cron.deny** files allows anyone to use cron. To prevent anyone except Superuser from using at, remove the **at.allow** and **at.deny** files. To prevent anyone except Superuser from using cron, create a **cron.allow** file with the single entry **root**. Refer to "Scheduling Tasks" on page 531.

/etc/dumpdates   Contains information about the last execution of dump. For each filesystem, it stores the time of the last dump at a given dump level. The dump utility uses this information to determine which files to back up when executing at a particular dump level. Refer to "Backing Up Files" on page 524 and the dump man page for more information. Following is a sample **/etc/dumpdates** file from a system with four filesystems and a backup schedule that uses three dump levels:

```
/dev/hda1          5 Thu Apr 23 03:53:55 2004
/dev/hda8          2 Sun Apr 19 08:25:24 2004
/dev/hda9          2 Sun Apr 19 08:57:32 2004
/dev/hda10         2 Sun Apr 19 08:58:06 2004
/dev/hda1          2 Sun Apr 19 09:02:27 2004
/dev/hda1          0 Sun Mar 22 22:08:35 2004
/dev/hda8          0 Sun Mar 22 22:33:40 2004
/dev/hda9          0 Sun Mar 22 22:35:22 2004
/dev/hda10         0 Sun Mar 22 22:43:45 2004
```

The first column contains the device name of the dumped filesystem. The second column contains the dump level and the date of the dump.

/etc/fstab   **filesystem (mount) table**   Contains a list of all mountable devices as specified by the system administrator. Programs do not write to this file but only read from it. Refer to "fstab: Keeps Track of Filesystems" on page 445.

/etc/group Groups allow users to share files or programs without allowing all system users access to them. This scheme is useful if several users are working with files that are not public. The **/etc/group** file associates one or more user names with each group (number).

An entry in the **/etc/group** file has four fields in the following format:

group-name:password:group-ID:login-name-list

The *group-name* is the name of the group. The *password* is an optional encrypted password. This field is rarely used and frequently contains an **x**, indicating that group passwords are not used. The **group-ID** is a number, with 1–499 reserved for system accounts. The *login-name-list* is a comma-separated list of users who belong to the group. If an entry is too long to fit on one line, end the line with a backslash (\), which quotes the following RETURN, and continue the entry on the next line. A sample entry from a **group** file follows. The group is named **pubs**, has no password, and has a group ID of 503:

```
pubs:x:503:alex,jenny,scott,hls,barbara
```

Each user has a primary group, which is the group that user is assigned in the **/etc/passwd** file. By default, Red Hat Linux has user private groups: Each user's primary group has the same name as the user. In addition, a user can belong to other groups, depending on which *login-name-list*s the user appears on in the **/etc/group** file. In effect, you simultaneously belong to both your primary group and any groups you are assigned to in **/etc/group**. When you attempt to access a file you do not own, the operating system checks whether you are a member of the group that has access to the file. If you are, your access permissions are controlled by the group access permissions for the file. If you are not a member of the group that has access to the file and you do not own the file, you are subject to the public access permissions for the file.

When you create a new file, it is assigned to the group associated with the directory the file is being written into, assuming that you belong to the group. If you do not belong to the group that has access to the directory, the file is assigned to your primary group.

Refer to page 523 for information on using system-config-users to work with groups.

/etc/hosts The **/etc/hosts** file stores the name, IP address, and optional alias of the other systems that your system knows about. At the very least, the file must have the hostname and IP address that you have chosen for your local system and a special entry for **localhost**. This entry is for the *loopback service,* which allows the local system to talk to itself (for example, for RPC services). The IP address of the loopback service is always 127.0.0.1. Following is a simple **/etc/hosts** file:

```
$ cat /etc/hosts
127.0.0.1       localhost
192.168.0.1     gateway
```

```
192.168.0.2    mp3server
192.168.0.3    workstation
192.168.0.4    windowsbox
...
```

If you are not using NIS or DNS to look up hostnames (called *hostname resolution*), you must include in **/etc/hosts** all the systems that you want the local system to be able to contact. The order in which hostname resolution services are checked is controlled by the **hosts** entry in the **/etc/nsswitch.conf** file (page 413).

/etc/inittab **initialization table** Controls how the init process behaves. Each line in **inittab** has four colon-separated fields:

id:runlevel:action:process

The *id* uniquely identifies an entry in the **inittab** file. The *runlevel* is the system runlevel(s) at which *process* is executed. The *runlevel(s)* are zero or more characters chosen from 0123456S. If more than one runlevel is listed, the associated *process* is executed at each of the specified runlevels. When you do not specify a runlevel, init executes *process* at all runlevels. When the system changes runlevels, the *processes* specified by all entries in **inittab** that do not include the new runlevel are sent the SIGTERM signal to allow them to terminate gracefully. After 5 seconds, these *processes* are killed with SIGKILL if they are still running. The *process* is any bash command line.

The *action* is one of the following keywords: **respawn, wait, once, boot, bootwait, ondemand, powerfail, powerwait, powerokwait, powerfailnow, ctrlaltdel, kbrequest, off, ondemand, initdefault,** or **sysinit.** This keyword controls how the *process* is treated when it is executed. The most commonly used keywords are **wait** and **respawn.**

The **wait** keyword instructs init to start *process* and wait for it to terminate. All subsequent scans of **inittab** ignore this **wait** entry. Because a **wait** entry is started only once (on entering *runlevel*) and is not executed again while the system remains at *runlevel*, it is often used to redirect init output to the console.

The **respawn** entry tells init to start *process* if it does not exist but not to wait for it to terminate. If *process* does exist, init goes on to the next entry in the **inittab.** The init utility continues to rescan **inittab,** looking for processes that have died. When a *process* dies, a **respawn** entry causes init to restart it.

The **initdefault** entry tells init what runlevel to bring the system to (see Table 11-1 on page 381). Without this information, init prompts for a runlevel on the system console. The value of the **initdefault** entry is set when you configure the system or when you edit **inittab** directly.

Each virtual console (page 103) has in **inittab** a **mingetty** entry that includes a unique terminal identifier (such as **tty1,** which is short for **/dev/tty1**). Add or remove **mingetty** lines to add or remove virtual consoles. Remember to leave a virtual console for each X window that you want to run. Following is the **mingetty** entry for **/dev/tty2:**

```
2:2345:respawn:/sbin/mingetty tty2
```

The *id* on a **mingetty** line corresponds to the **tty** number.

All the *actions* are documented in the **inittab** man page. For more information, refer to "Booting the System" on page 381.

/etc/motd   Contains the message of the day, which can be displayed each time someone logs in using a textual login. This file typically contains site policy and legal information. Keep this file short because users tend to see the message many times.

/etc/mtab   When you call mount without any arguments, it consults this file and displays a list of mounted devices. Each time you (or an **init script**) call mount or umount, these utilities make the necessary changes to **mtab**. Although this is an ASCII text file, you should not edit it. See also **/etc/fstab**.

/etc/netgroup   Defines netgroups, which are used for checking permissions when performing remote logins and remote mounts and when starting remote shells.

/etc/nsswitch.conf   Specifies whether a system uses as the source of certain information NIS, DNS, local files, or a combination, and in what order (page 413).

/etc/pam.d   Files in this directory specify the authentication methods used by PAM (page 416) applications.

/etc/passwd   Describes users to the system. Do not edit this file directly, but instead, use one of the utilities discussed in "Configuring User and Group Accounts" on page 521. Each line in **passwd** has seven colon-separated fields that describe one user:

login-name:dummy-password:user-ID:group-ID:info:directory:program

The *login-name* is the user's login name—the name you enter in response to the **login:** prompt or GUI login screen. The value of the *dummy-password* is the character **x**. An encrypted/hashed password is stored in **/etc/shadow** (page 433). For security, every account should have a password. By convention, disabled accounts have an asterisk (✻) in this field.

The *user-ID* is a number, with 0 indicating Superuser and 1–499 reserved for system accounts. The *group-ID* identifies the user as a member of a group. It is a number, with 0–499 reserved for system accounts; see **/etc/group**. You can change these values and set maximum values in **/etc/login.defs**.

The *info* is information that various programs, such as accounting programs and email, use to identify the user further. Normally it contains at least the first and last name of the user. It is referred to as the *GECOS* (page 972) field.

The *directory* is the absolute pathname of the user's home directory. The *program* is the program that runs once the user logs in. If *program* is not present, **/bin/bash** is assumed. You can put **/bin/tcsh** here to log in using the TC Shell or **/bin/zsh** to log in using the Z Shell. The chsh utility (page 396) changes this value.

The *program* is usually a shell, but it can be any program. The following line in the **passwd** file creates a "user" whose only purpose is to execute the who utility:

```
who:x:1000:1000:execute who:/usr:/usr/bin/who
```

Using **who** as a login name causes the system to log you in, execute the who utility, and log you out. The output of who flashes by in a hurry as the new login prompt clears the screen immediately after who finishes running. This entry in the **passwd** file does not provide a shell; there is no way for you to stay logged in after who finishes executing.

This technique is useful for providing special accounts that may do only one thing. For instance, sites may create an FTP (page 583) account in order to enable anonymous FTP access to their systems. Because no one logs in on this account, set the shell to **/bin/false** (which returns a false exit status) or to **/sbin/nologin** (which does not permit the user to log in). When you put a message in **/etc/nologin.txt**, nologin displays that message (except it has the same problem as the output of who: It is removed so quickly that you cannot see it).

---

security ‖   **Do Not Replace a Login Shell with a Shell Script**

Do not use shell scripts as replacements for shells in **/etc/passwd**. A user may be able to interrupt a shell script, giving him or her full shell access when you did not intend to do so. When installing a dummy shell, use a compiled program, not a shell script.

/etc/printcap   The printer capability database. This file describes system printers and is derived from 4.3BSD UNIX.

/etc/profile   Contains a systemwide interactive shell initialization script for environment and start-up programs. When you log in, the first thing the shell does is to execute the commands in this file in the same environment as the shell. (For more information on executing a shell script in this manner, refer to the discussion of the . [dot] command on page 286.) This file allows the system administrator to establish system-wide environment parameters that individual users can override. Using this file, you can set shell variables, execute utilities, and take care of other housekeeping tasks. See also "~/.bash_profile" on page 425.

Following is an example of a **/etc/profile** file that displays the message of the day (the **/etc/motd** file), sets the file-creation mask (umask), and sets the interrupt character to CONTROL-C:

```
# cat /etc/profile
cat /etc/motd
umask 022
stty intr '^c'
```

See the **/etc/profile** file on your system for a more complex example.

/etc/protocols   Provides protocol numbers, aliases, and brief definitions for DARPA Internet TCP/IP protocols. Do not modify.

/etc/rc.d   Holds the system init scripts, also called run command (**rc**) scripts. The init program executes several init scripts each time it changes state or runlevel. The **/etc/rc.d/init.d** directory holds all the scripts. Each runlevel has a dedicated directory within **/etc/rc.d**. For example, runlevel 3 has the **/etc/rc.d/rc3.d** directory. The files in each of these directories are links to the files in **init.d**. The **init script**s perform such tasks as mounting filesystems (when the system goes multiuser), removing temporary files after the filesystems are mounted, and unmounting filesystems when the system is returned to single-user mode or brought down. For more information, refer to "Init Scripts: Start and Stop System Services" on page 381.

/etc/resolv.conf   The resolver (page 701) configuration file, used to provide access to DNS.

The following example shows the **resolv.conf** file for the **example.com** domain. A **resolv.conf** file usually has at least two lines: a domain line and a nameserver line:

```
# cat /etc/resolv.conf
domain example.com
nameserver 10.0.0.50
nameserver 10.0.0.51
```

The first line (optional) specifies the domain name. A **resolv.conf** file may use **search** in place of **domain:** In the simple case, the two perform the same function. In either case, this domain name is appended to all hostnames that are not fully qualified. See *FQDN* on page 972.

The **domain** keyword takes a single domain name as an argument: This name is appended to all DNS queries, shortening the time to query hosts at your site. When you put **domain example.com** in **resolv.conf**, any reference to a host within the **example.com** domain or a subdomain (such as **marketing.example.com**) can use the abbreviated form of the host: Instead of **ping speedy.marketing.example.com**, you can use **ping speedy.marketing**.

This **search** keyword is similar to **domain** but can contain multiple domain names. The domains are searched in order in the process of resolving a hostname. The following line in **resolv.conf** causes the **marketing** subdomain to be searched first, followed by **sales**, and finally the whole **example.com** domain:

```
search marketing.example.com sales.example.com example.com
```

Put the most frequently used domain names first to try to outguess possible conflicts. If both **speedy.marketing.example.com** and **speedy.example.com** exist, the order of the search determines which one you get when you invoke DNS. Do not overuse this feature. The longer the search path (three or four names is typically enough), the more network DNS requests are generated, and the slower the response is.

The **nameserver** line(s) indicate which systems the local system should query to resolve hostnames to IP addresses and vice versa. These machines are consulted in the order they appear with a 10-second timeout between queries. The preceding file causes this machine to query 10.0.0.50, followed by 10.0.0.51 when the first machine does not answer within 10 seconds. The **resolv.conf** file may be automatically updated when a PPP- (Point to Point Protocol) or DHCP- (Dynamic Host Configuration Protocol) controlled interface is activated. Refer to the **resolv.conf** and **resolver** man pages for more information.

/etc/rpc   Maps RPC services to RPC numbers. The three columns in this file show the name of the server for the RPC program, the RPC program number, and aliases.

/etc/services   Lists system services. The three columns in this file show the friendly name of the service, the port number/protocol the service frequently uses, and aliases for the service. This file does not specify which services are running on the local machine, nor is it used to map services to port numbers. The **services** file is used internally to map port numbers to services for display purposes.

/etc/shadow   Contains encrypted or *MD5* (page 982) hashed user passwords. Each entry occupies one line composed of nine fields, separated by colons:

login-name:password:last-mod:min:max:warn:inactive:expire:flag

The *login-name* is the user's login name—the name that the user enters in response to the **login:** prompt or GUI login screen. The *password* is an encrypted or hashed password that passwd puts into this file. When setting up new user accounts manually, run passwd as Superuser to assign a password to a new user.

The *last-mod* field indicates when the password was last modified. The *min* is the minimum number of days that must elapse before the password can be changed; *max* is the maximum number of days before the password must be changed. The *warn* specifies how much advance warning (in days) to give the user before the password expires. The account will be closed if the number of days between login sessions exceeds the number of days specified in the *inactive* field. The account will also be closed as of the date in the *expire* field. The last field in an entry, *flag*, is reserved for future use. You can use the Password Info tab in system-config-users ("Modifying a user" on page 522) to modify these fields.

The **shadow** password file should be owned by **root** and should not be publicly readable or writable, making it more difficult for someone to break into your system by identifying accounts without passwords or by using specialized programs that try to match hashed passwords.

A number of conventions exist for making special **shadow** entries. An entry of *LK* or **NP** in the *password* field indicates *locked* and *no password*, respectively. *No password* is different from an empty password, implying that this is an administrative account that nobody ever logs in on directly. Occasionally, programs will run with the privileges of this account for system maintenance functions. These accounts are set up under the principle of least privilege.

Entries in the **shadow** file must appear in the same order as in the **passwd** file. There must be one and only one **shadow** entry for each **passwd** entry.

/etc/sysconfig   A directory containing a hierarchy of system configuration files. For more information, refer to the **/usr/share/doc/initscripts*/sysconfig.txt** file.

/proc   The **/proc** pseudofilesystem provides a window into the Linux kernel. Through **/proc** you can obtain information on any process running on your computer, including its current state, memory usage, CPU usage, terminal, parent, group, and more. You can also use **/proc** to modify the kernel as with the system-config-proc utility (page 395). You can extract information directly from the files in **/proc**. An example follows:

```
$ sleep 10000 &
[1] 17924
$ cd /proc/17924
$ ls -l
total 0
-r--r--r--  1 alex   alex     0 Feb  2 17:13 cmdline
lrwx------  1 alex   alex     0 Feb  2 17:13 cwd -> /home/alex
-r--------  1 alex   alex     0 Feb  2 17:13 environ
lrwx------  1 alex   alex     0 Feb  2 17:13 exe -> /bin/sleep
dr-x------  2 alex   alex     0 Feb  2 17:13 fd
pr--r--r--  1 alex   alex     0 Feb  2 17:13 maps
-rw-------  1 alex   alex     0 Feb  2 17:13 mem
lrwx------  1 alex   alex     0 Feb  2 17:13 root -> /
-r--r--r--  1 alex   alex     0 Feb  2 17:13 stat
-r--r--r--  1 alex   alex     0 Feb  2 17:13 statm
-r--r--r--  1 alex   alex     0 Feb  2 17:13 status
$ cat status
Name:   sleep
State:  S (sleeping)
Pid:    17924
PPid:   17909
TracerPid:    0
Uid:    0      0      0      0
Gid:    0      0      0      0
```

```
FDSize: 256
Groups: 0 1 2 3 4 6 10
VmSize:      1144 kB
VmLck:          0 kB
VmRSS:        420 kB
VmData:        20 kB
...
```

In this example, bash creates a background process (PID 17924) for sleep. Next, the user changes directories to the directory in **/proc** that has the same name as the PID of the subject background process (**cd /proc/17924**). This directory holds information about the process for which it is named. In this case, it holds information about the sleep process. The **ls –l** command shows that some of the entries in this directory are links (**cwd** is a link to the directory the process was started from, and **exe** is a link to the executable file that this process is running), and some appear to be regular files. All appear to be empty. When you cat one of these pseudofiles (**status** in the example), you get the output shown. Obviously this is not a regular file.

/sbin/shutdown A utility that brings the system down (see page 390).

swap Even though **swap** is not a file, swap space can be added and deleted from the system dynamically. Swap space is used by the virtual memory subsystem. When it runs low on real memory (RAM), the system writes memory pages from RAM to the swap space on the disk. Which pages are written and when they are written are controlled by finely tuned algorithms in the Linux kernel. When needed by running programs, these pages are brought back into RAM. This technique is called *paging* (page 987). When a system is running very short on memory, an entire process may be paged out to disk.

Running an application that requires a large amount of virtual memory may result in the need for additional swap space. If you run out of swap space, you can use mkswap to create a new swap file and swapon to enable it. Normally, you use a disk partition as swap space, but you can also use a file.

If you are using a file as swap space, first use df to make sure that you have enough space in the partition for the file. In the following sequence of commands, the administrator first uses dd and **/dev/zero** (page 426) to create an empty file (do not use cp as you may create a file with holes, which may not work) in the working directory. Next, mkswap takes an argument of the name of the file created in the first step to set up the swap space. For security, change the file so that it cannot be read from or written to by anyone but **root**. Use swapon with the same argument to turn the swap file on, and then use **swapon –s** to confirm that the swap space is available. The final two commands turn off the swap file and remove it:

```
# dd if=/dev/zero of=swapfile bs=1024 count=65536
65536+0 records in
65536+0 records out
# mkswap swapfile
Setting up swapspace version 1, size = 67104768 bytes
```

```
# chmod 600 swapfile
# swapon swapfile
# swapon -s
Filename                    Type        Size     Used    Priority
/dev/hda12                  partition   265032   38216   -1
/var/swapfile               file        65528    0       -2
...
# swapoff swapfile
# rm swapfile
```

/usr/share/magic   Most files begin with a unique identifier called a *magic number*. This file is a text database listing all known magic numbers on the system. When you use the file utility, it consults **/usr/share/magic** to determine the type of a file. Occasionally, you will acquire a new tool that creates a new type of file that is unrecognized by the file utility: You need to update the **/usr/share/magic** file; refer to the **magic** man page for details. See also "magic number" on page 982.

/var/log   Holds system log files. You can use system-logviewer (*FEDORA*) or redhat-logviewer (*RHEL*) to view log messages.

/var/log/messages   Contains messages from daemons, the Linux kernel, and security programs. For example, you will find **filesystem full** warning messages, error messages from system daemons (NFS, syslog, printer daemons), SCSI and IDE disk error messages, messages from such security-related programs as su, and more in **messages**. Check **/var/log/messages** periodically to keep informed about important system events. Much of the information displayed on the system console is also sent to **messages**. If the system has a problem and you do not have access to the console, check this file for messages about the problem.

File Types

Linux supports many types of files. The following sections discuss these types of files:

- Ordinary Files, Directories, Links, and Inodes (following)
- Symbolic links (page 437)
- Special Files (page 437)
- FIFO Special File (Named Pipe) (page 438)
- Sockets (page 439)
- Block and Character Devices (page 439)
- Raw Devices (page 440)

Ordinary Files, Directories, Links, and Inodes

Ordinary and directory files   An *ordinary* file stores user data, such as textual information, programs, or an image, such as a **jpeg** or **tiff** file. A *directory* is a standard-format disk file that stores information, including names, about ordinary files and other directory files.

Inodes An *inode* is a *data structure* (page 966), stored on disk, that defines a file's existence and is identified by an inode number. A directory relates each of the filenames it stores to a specific inode. An inode contains critical information, such as the name of the owner of the file, where it is physically located on the disk, and how many hard links point to it. In addition, SELinux (page 379) stores extended information about files in inodes.

When you move (mv) a file within a filesystem, you change the filename portion of the directory entry associated with the inode that describes the file. You do not create a new inode. If you move a file to another filesystem, mv first creates a new inode on the destination filesystem and then deletes the original inode. You can also use mv to move a directory recursively, in which case all the files are copied and deleted.

When you make an additional hard link (ln, page 178) to a file, you create another reference (an additional filename) to the inode that describes the file. You do not create a new inode.

When you remove (rm) a file, you delete the directory entry that describes the file. When you remove the last hard link to a file, the operating system puts all the blocks the inode pointed to back in the *free list* (the list of blocks that are available for use on the disk) and frees the inode to be used again.

The . and .. directory entries Every directory has at least two entries (. and ..). The . entry is a link to the directory itself. The .. entry is a link to the parent directory. In the case of the root directory, there is no parent, and the .. entry is a link to the root directory itself. It is not possible to create hard links to directories.

Symbolic links Because each filesystem has a separate set of inodes, you can create hard links to a file only from within the filesystem that holds that file. To get around this limitation, Linux provides symbolic links, which are files that point to other files. Files that are linked by a symbolic link do not share an inode: You can create a symbolic link to a file from any filesystem. You can also create a symbolic link to a directory, device, or other special file. For more information, refer to "Symbolic Link" on page 180.

Special Files

Special files represent Linux kernel routines that provide access to an operating system feature. FIFO (first in, first out) special files allow unrelated programs to exchange information. Sockets allow unrelated processes on the same or different computers to exchange information. One type of socket, the UNIX domain socket, is a special file. Symbolic links are another type of special file.

Device files Device files, which include block and character special files, represent device drivers that let you communicate with peripheral devices, such as terminals, printers, and hard disks. By convention, device files appear in the /dev directory and its subdirectories. Each device file represents a device: You read from and write to the file to read from and write to the device it represents. For example, using cat to send an audio file to /dev/dsp plays the file. The following example shows part of the output an ls –l command produces for the /dev directory:

```
$ ls -l /dev
crw-------   1 root    sys      14,    4 Apr 17  2004 audio
crw-------   1 root    root      5,    1 Jan 22 08:31 console
crw-------   1 root    root      5,   64 May  5  2004 cua0
crw-------   1 root    root      5,   65 May  5  2004 cua1
brw-rw----   1 root    floppy    2,    0 May  5  2004 fd0
brw-rw----   1 root    floppy    2,   12 May  5  2004 fd0D360
brw-rw----   1 root    floppy    2,   16 May  5  2004 fd0D720
brw-rw----   1 root    floppy    2,   28 May  5  2004 fd0H1440
brw-rw----   1 root    floppy    2,   12 May  5  2004 fd0H360
brw-rw----   1 root    disk      3,    0 May  5  2004 hda
brw-rw----   1 root    disk      3,    1 May  5  2004 hda1
brw-rw----   1 root    disk      3,    2 May  5  2004 hda2
brw-rw----   1 root    disk      3,    3 May  5  2004 hda3
brw-rw----   1 root    disk      3,    4 May  5  2004 hda4
brw-rw----   1 root    disk      3,    5 May  5  2004 hda5
brw-rw----   1 root    disk      3,    6 May  5  2004 hda6
...
```

The first character of each line is always –, b, c, d, l, or p, representing ordinary (plain), block, character, directory, symbolic link, or named pipe (see the following section). The next nine characters represent the permissions for the file, followed by the number of hard links and the names of the owner and group. Where the number of bytes in a file would appear for an ordinary or directory file, a device file shows its *major* and *minor device numbers* (page 439) separated by a comma. The rest of the line is the same as any other ls –l listing (page 173).

FIFO Special File (Named Pipe)

A *FIFO special* file, also called a *named pipe*, represents a pipe: You read from and write to the file to read from and write to the pipe. The term *FIFO* stands for *first in, first out*—the way any pipe works. The first information that you put in one end is the first information that comes out the other end. When you use a pipe on a command line to send the output of a program to the printer, the printer prints the information in the same order that the program produced it and sent it into the pipe.

Unless you are writing sophisticated programs, you will not be working with FIFO special files. However, programs that you use on Linux use named pipes for interprocess communication. You can create a pipe using mkfifo:

```
# mkfifo AA
# ls -l AA
prw-rw-r--   1 root    root            0 Apr 26 13:11 AA
```

The **p** at the left end of the output of ls –l indicates that the file is a pipe.

The UNIX and Linux systems have had pipes for many generations. Without named pipes, only processes that were children of the same ancestor could use pipes to exchange information. Using named pipes, *any* two processes on a single system can exchange information. One program writes to a FIFO special file. Another program reads from the same file. The programs do not have to run at the same time or be aware of each other's activity. The operating system handles all buffering and information storage. The term *asynchronous (async)* applies to this type of communication because programs on the ends of the pipe do not have to be synchronized.

Sockets

Like a FIFO special file, a socket allows asynchronous processes that are not children of the same ancestor to exchange information. Sockets are the central mechanism of the interprocess communication that is the basis of the networking facility. When you use networking utilities, pairs of cooperating sockets manage the communication between the processes on the local computer and the remote computer. Sockets form the basis of such utilities as ssh and scp.

Major and Minor Device Numbers

A *major device number* represents a class of hardware devices: terminal, printer, tape drive, hard disk, and so on. In the list of the **/dev** directory on page 438, all the hard disk partitions have a major device number of 3.

A *minor device number* represents a particular piece of hardware within a class. Although all the hard disk partitions are grouped together by their major device number, each has a different minor device number (**hda1** is 1, **hda2** is 2, and so on). This setup allows one piece of software (the device driver) to service all similar hardware and to be able to distinguish among different physical units.

Block and Character Devices

This section describes typical device drivers. Because device drivers can be changed to suit a particular purpose, the descriptions in this section do not pertain to every system.

A *block device* is an I/O (input/output) device that is characterized by

- Being able to perform random access reads.
- Having a specific block size.
- Handling only single blocks of data at a time.
- Accepting only transactions that involve whole blocks of data.
- Being able to have a filesystem mounted on it.
- Having the Linux kernel buffer its input and output.
- Appearing to the operating system as a series of blocks numbered from 0 through $n - 1$, where n is the number of blocks on the device.

The common block devices on a Linux system are hard disks, floppy diskettes, and CD-ROMs.

A *character device* is any device that is not a block device. Some examples of character devices are printers, terminals, tape drives, and modems.

The device driver for a character device determines how a program reads from and writes to the device. For example, the device driver for a terminal allows a program to read the information you type on the terminal in two ways. A program can read single characters from a terminal in *raw* mode (that is, without the driver doing any interpretation of the characters). This mode has nothing to do with the *raw device* described in the following section. Alternatively, a program can read a line at a time. When a program reads a line at a time, the driver handles the erase and kill characters so the program never sees corrected typing mistakes. In this case, the program reads everything from the beginning of a line to the RETURN that ends a line; the number of characters in a line can vary.

Raw Devices

Device driver programs for block devices usually have two entry points so they can be used in two ways: as block devices *or* as character devices. The character device form of a block device is called a *raw* device. A raw device is characterized by

- Direct I/O (no buffering through the Linux kernel).
- A one-to-one correspondence between system calls and hardware requests.
- Device-dependent restrictions on I/O.

An example of a utility that uses a raw device is fsck. It is more efficient for fsck to operate on the disk as a raw device, not restricted by the fixed size of blocks in the block device interface. Because it has full knowledge of the underlying filesystem structure, fsck can operate on the raw device using the largest possible units. When a filesystem is mounted, processes normally access the disk through the block device interface, which explains why it is important to allow fsck to modify only an unmounted filesystem. On a mounted filesystem, there is the danger that, while fsck is rearranging the underlying structure through the raw device, another process would change a disk block using the block device, resulting in a corrupted filesystem.

Filesystems

Table 12-1 lists some of the types of filesystems available under Linux.

table 12-1 ‖	Filesystems
adfs	The Acorn Disc Filing System.
affs	The Amiga Fast Filesystem(FFS).
autofs	Automounting filesystem (page 671).
coda	The CODA distributed filesystem (developed at Carnegie Mellon).
devpts	A pseudofilesystem for pseudoterminals (page 426).
ext2	A standard filesystem for Red Hat systems, usually with the **ext3** extension.

table 12-1 ‖	**Filesystems (Continued)**
ext3	A journaling (page 978) extension to the **ext2** filesystem; greatly improves recovery time from crashes (it takes a lot less time to run fsck), promoting increased availability. As with any filesystem, a journaling filesystem can lose data during a system crash or hardware failure.
hfs	Hierarchical Filesystem: used by older Macintoshes. Newer Macs use **hfs+**.
hpfs	High Performance Filesystem: the native filesystem for IBM's OS/2.
iso9660	The standard filesystem for CDs.
minix	Very similar to Linux, the filesystem of a small operating system that was written for educational purposes by Prof. Andrew S. Tanenbaum (www.cs.vu.nl/~ast/minix.html).
msdos	The filesystem used by DOS and subsequent Microsoft operating systems. Do not use **msdos** for mounting Windows filesystems; it does not read vfat attributes.
ncpfs	Novell NetWare NCP Protocol Filesystem: used to mount remote filesystems under NetWare.
nfs	Network Filesystem: Developed by Sun Microsystems, a protocol that allows a computer to access remote files over a network as if they were local (page 655).
ntfs	NT Filesystem: the native filesystem of Windows NT. Still *very* experimental; use caution.
proc	An interface to several Linux kernel *data structures* (page 966) that behaves like a filesystem (page 434).
qnx4	The QNX 4 Operating System filesystem.
reiserfs	A journaling (page 978) filesystem, based on balanced-tree algorithms. See **ext3** for more on journaling filesystems.
romfs	A dumb, readonly filesystem used mainly for *RAM disks* (page 991) during installation.
software RAID	RAID implemented in software. Refer to "RAID Filesystem" on page 449.
smbfs	Samba Filesystem (page 675).
sysv	System V UNIX filesystem.
ufs	Default filesystem under Sun's Solaris Operating System and other UNIXs.
umsdos	A full-feature UNIX-like filesystem that runs on top of a DOS FAT filesystem.
vfat	Developed by Microsoft, a standard that allows long filenames on FAT partitions.
xfs	SGI's journaled filesystem (ported from Irix)

mount: **Mounts a Filesystem**

The mount utility connects directory hierarchies, typically filesystems, to the Linux directory hierarchy. These directory hierarchies can be on remote and local disks, CDs, and floppy diskettes. Linux also allows you to mount *virtual filesystems* that have been built inside regular files, filesystems built for other operating systems, and the special **/proc** filesystem (page 434), which maps useful Linux kernel information to a pseudodirectory.

The *mount point* for the filesystem/directory hierarchy that you are mounting is a directory in the local filesystem. The directory must exist before mounting; its contents disappear as long as a filesystem is mounted on it and reappear when you unmount the filesystem.

Without any arguments, mount lists the currently mounted filesystems, showing the physical device holding each filesystem, the mount point, the type of filesystem, and any options set when each filesystem was mounted:

```
$ mount
none on /proc type proc (rw)
/dev/hdb1 on / type ext2 (rw)
/dev/hdb4 on /tmp type ext2 (rw)
/dev/hda5 on /usr type ext3 (rw)
/dev/sda1 on /usr/X386 type ext2 (rw)
/dev/sda3 on /usr/local type ext2 (rw)
/dev/hdb3 on /home type ext3 (rw)
/dev/hda1 on /dos type msdos (rw,umask=000)
tuna:/p04 on /p04 type nfs (rw,addr=192.168.0.8)
/dev/scd0 on /mnt/cdrom type iso9660 (ro,noexec,nosuid,nodev)
```

The mount utility gets this information from the **/etc/mtab** file (page 430). This section covers mounting local filesystems; refer to page 655 for information on using NFS to mount remote directory hierarchies.

The first entry in the preceding example shows the **/proc** pseudofilesystem (page 434). The next six entries show disk partitions holding standard Linux **ext2** and **ext3** filesystems. Disk partitions are on three disks: two IDE disks (**hda, hdb**) and one SCSI disk (**sda**). Disk partition **/dev/hda1** has a DOS (**msdos**) filesystem mounted at the directory **/dos** in the Linux filesystem. You can access the DOS files and directories on this partition as if they were Linux files and directories, using Linux utilities and applications. The line starting with **tuna** shows a mounted, remote NFS filesystem. The last line shows a CD mounted on a SCSI CD drive (**/dev/scd0**).

On occasion the list of files in **/etc/mtab** may not be synchronized with the partitions that are mounted. You can remedy this situation by rebooting the system, or you can refer to the contents of the **/proc/mounts** file, which may have slightly different information than **mtab** but is always correct. You can even replace **mtab** with a symbolic link to **/proc/mounts**:

```
# rm /etc/mtab
# ln -s /proc/mounts /etc/mtab
```

Always mount network directory hierarchies and removable devices at least one level below the
root level of the filesystem. The root filesystem is mounted on /; you cannot mount two filesystems in the same place. If you were to try to mount something on /, all the files, directories, and
filesystems that were under root would no longer be available, and the system would crash.

When you add a line for a filesystem to the **/etc/fstab** file (page 427), you can
mount that filesystem by giving the associated mount point (or the device) as the argument to mount. For example, the SCSI CD listed earlier was mounted using the
following command:

```
$ mount /mnt/cdrom
```

This command worked because **/etc/fstab** contains the additional information
needed to mount the file:

```
/dev/scd0 /mnt/cdrom iso9660 user,noauto,ro
```

You can also mount filesystems that do not appear in **/etc/fstab**. For example, when
you insert a floppy diskette that holds a DOS filesystem into the floppy diskette
drive, you can mount that filesystem using the following command:

```
# mount -t msdos /dev/fd0 /mnt/floppy
```

The **–t msdos** specifies a filesystem type of **msdos**. You can mount DOS filesystems
only if you have configured your Linux kernel (page 507) to accept DOS filesystems. You do not need to mount a DOS filesystem in order to read from and write
to it, such as when you use mcopy (page 130). You do need to mount a DOS filesystem to use Linux commands (other than Mtools commands) on files on the diskette.

Mount Options

The mount utility takes many options which you can specify on the command line or
in the **/etc/fstab** file (page 445). For a complete list of mount options for local filesystems, see the mount man page; for remote directory hierarchies, the nfs man page.

The **noauto** option causes Linux not to mount the filesystem automatically. The
nosuid option forces mounted setuid executables to run with regular permissions
(no effective user ID change) on the local system (the system that mounted the filesystem). Always mount removable devices **nosuid** so a malicious user does not, for
example, put a setuid copy of bash on a disk and have a **root** shell.

Unless you specify the **user, users,** or **owner** option, only Superuser can mount and
unmount a filesystem. The **user** option means that any user can mount the filesystem, but it must be unmounted by the same user who mounted it; **users** means that
any user can mount and unmount the filesystem. These options are frequently used
for CD and floppy drives. The **owner** option, used only under special circumstances,
is similar to the **user** option except that the user mounting the device must own the
device.

Mounting a Linux Floppy Diskette

Mounting a Linux floppy diskette is similar to mounting a partition of a hard disk. Put an entry similar to the following in **/etc/fstab** for a diskette in the first floppy drive. Specifying a filesystem type of **auto** causes the system to probe the filesystem to determine its type and allows users to mount a variety of diskettes.

```
/dev/fd0    /mnt/floppy    auto    noauto,users              0 0
```

Create the **/mnt/floppy** directory if necessary. Insert a diskette and try to mount it. The diskette must be formatted (use fdformat). In the following examples, the error message following the first command usually indicates there is no filesystem on the diskette: Use mkfs (page 397) to create a filesystem, but be careful, because mkfs destroys all data on the diskette:

```
# mount /dev/fd0
mount: wrong fs type, bad option, bad superblock on /dev/fd0,
       or too many mounted file systems

# mkfs /dev/fd0
mke2fs 1.35 (28-Feb-2004)
Filesystem label=
OS type: linux
Block size=1024 (log=0)
Fragment size=1024 (log=0)
184 inodes, 1440 blocks
72 blocks (5.00%) reserved for the super user
First data block=1
1 block group
8192 blocks per group, 8192 fragments per group
184 inodes per group

Writing inode tables: done
Writing superblocks and filesystem accounting information: done

This filesystem will be automatically checked every 28 mounts or
180 days, whichever comes first.  Use tune2fs -c or -i to override.
```

Try the mount command again:

```
# mount /dev/fd0
# mount
.
.
.
/dev/fd0 on /mnt/floppy type ext2 (rw,nosuid,nodev)

# df -h /dev/fd0
Filesystem          Size  Used Avail Use% Mounted on
/dev/fd0            1.4M   13K  1.3M   1% /mnt/floppy
```

The mount command without any arguments and **df /dev/fd0** show the floppy is mounted and ready for use.

umount: **Unmounts a Filesystem**

The umount utility unmounts a filesystem as long as it does not house any files or directories that are in use (open). For example, a logged-in user's working directory must not be on the filesystem you want to unmount. The next command unmounts the CD shown earlier:

```
$ umount /mnt/cdrom
```

Unmount a floppy or a remote directory hierarchy the same way you would unmount a partition of a hard drive.

The umount utility consults **/etc/fstab** to get the necessary information and then unmounts the appropriate filesystem from its server. When a process has a file open on the filesystem that you are trying to unmount, umount displays a message similar to the following:

```
umount: /home: device is busy
```

tip ‖   **When You Cannot Unmount a Device Because It Is in Use**

When a process has a file open on a device you need to unmount, use fuser to determine which process has the file opened and to kill it. For example, when you want to unmount the floppy, give the command **fuser –ki /mnt/floppy**, which, after checking with you, kills the process using the floppy.

Use the **–a** option to umount in order to unmount all filesystems, except for the one mounted at **/**, which can never be unmounted. You can combine **–a** with the **–t** option to unmount filesystems of a given type (**ext3**, **nfs**, or others). For example, use the following command to unmount all mounted **nfs** directory hierarchies that are not being used:

```
# umount -at nfs
```

fstab: **Keeps Track of Filesystems**

The system administrator maintains the **/etc/fstab** file, which lists local and remote directory hierarchies, most of which the system mounts automatically when it boots. The **fstab** file has six columns; a dash keeps the place of a column that has no value. The six columns are

1. **Name**   The name of the block device (page 439) or remote directory hierarchy. A remote directory hierarchy appears as *hostname:pathname*, where *hostname* is the name of the host that houses the filesystem, and *pathname* is the absolute pathname of the directory that is to be mounted. You can substitute the volume label of a local filesystem by using the form **LABEL=**xx, where *xx* is the volume label. Refer to e2label on page 396.

2. **Mount point**   The name of a directory file that the filesystem/directory hierarchy is to be mounted over. If it does not exist, create this directory with mkdir.

3. **Type**   The type of filesystem/directory hierarchy that is to be mounted. Local filesystems are generally **ext2** or **ext3**, and remote directory hierarchies are **nfs**. See Table 12-1 on page 440 for a list of filesystem types.

4. **Mount options**   A comma-separated list of mount options, such as whether the filesystem is mounted for reading and writing (**rw**, the default) or readonly (**ro**). Refer to the mount and nfs man pages for lists of options.

5. **Dump**   Used by dump (page 529) to determine when to back up the filesystem.

6. **Fsck**   Determines which filesystem fsck should check first. Root (**/**) should have a **1** in this column, other filesystems that need to be checked should have a **2**, and filesystems/directory hierarchies that do not need to be checked (for example, remotely mounted directory hierarchies or a CD) should have a **0**.

The following example shows a typical **fstab** file:

```
# cat /etc/fstab
LABEL=/              /               ext3     defaults            1 1
LABEL=/boot          /boot           ext2     defaults            1 2
LABEL=/home          /home           ext3     defaults            1 2
/dev/cdrom           /mnt/cdrom      iso9660  noauto,owner,ro     0 0
/dev/hda7            /tmp            ext2     defaults            1 2
/dev/hda6            /usr            ext3     defaults            1 2
/dev/hda11           swap            swap     defaults            0 0
/dev/fd0             /mnt/floppy     ext2     noauto,owner        0 0
none                 /proc           proc     defaults            0 0
none                 /dev/pts        devpts   gid=5,mode=620      0 0
bravo:/home          /bravo_home     nfs      defaults            0 0
kudos:/home/alex     /kudos_alex     nfs      defaults            0 0
```

tip ‖   **Exporting Symbolic Links and Device Files**

When you export a symbolic link, make sure the object of the link is available on the client (remote) system. If the object of the link does not exist on a client system, you must export and mount it along with the exported link; otherwise, it will not point to the file it points to on the server.

A device file refers to a Linux kernel interface. When you export a device file, you export that interface. If the client system does not have the same type of device, the exported device will not work.

A mounted filesystem with a mount point within an exported filesystem will not be exported with the exported filesystem. You need to export each filesystem that you want exported, even if it resides within an already exported filesystem. When you have two filesystems, **/opt/apps** and **/opt/apps/oracle**, residing on two partitions to export, you must export each explicitly, even though **oracle** is a subdirectory of **apps**. Most other subdirectories and files are exported automatically.

fsck: Checks Filesystem Integrity

The fsck (filesystem check) utility verifies the integrity of filesystems and, if possible, repairs any problems it finds. Because many filesystem repairs can destroy data, particularly on a non*journaling filesystem* (page 978), such as **ext2**, fsck asks you for confirmation, by default, before making each repair.

caution ‖	Do Not Run fsck on a Mounted Filesystem

Do not run fsck on a mounted filesystem (except **/**). When you attempt to check a mounted file-system, fsck warns you and asks you whether you want to continue. Reply **no**. You can run fsck with the **–N** option on a mounted filesystem as it will not write to the filesystem, so no harm will come of running it.

The following command checks all the filesystems that are marked to be checked in **/etc/fstab** (page 427) except for the root filesystem:

```
# fsck -AR
```

The **–A** option causes fsck to check filesystems listed in **fstab**, and **–R** skips the **root** filesystem. You can check a specific filesystem with a command similar to one of the following:

```
# fsck /home
```

or

```
# fsck /dev/hda6
```

Crash flag   The **/etc/rc.d/rc.sysinit** start-up script looks for two flags in the root directory of each partition to help determine whether fsck needs to be run on that partition before it is mounted. The **.autofsck** flag (the *crash flag*) indicates that the partition should be checked. By default, the person bringing up the system has 5 seconds to respond to a prompt with a **y**, or the check is skipped. The other flag, **forcefsck**, is also in the root directory of a partition. When this flag is set, the user is given no choice; fsck is automatically run on the partition. These checks are in addition to those established by tune2fs (next section). The **.autofsck** flag is present while the system is running and is removed when the system is properly shut down. When the system crashes, the flag is present when the system is brought up. The **forcefsck** flag is placed on the filesystem when a hard error is on the disk and the disk must be checked.

tune2fs: Changes Filesystem Parameters

The tune2fs utility displays and modifies filesystem parameters on **ext2** filesystems and on **ext3** filesystems, as they are modified **ext2** filesystems. This utility can also set up journaling on an **ext2** filesystem, turning it into an **ext3** filesystem. With more reliable hardware and software, the system is rebooted less frequently and it becomes more important to check filesystems regularly. By default, fsck is run on each partition while the system is brought up, before the partition is mounted. (The checks scheduled by tune2fs are separate and scheduled differently from the checks that are done following a system crash or hard disk error [see the previous section].) Depending on the flags, fsck may do nothing more than display a message saying that the filesystem is clean. The larger the partition, the more time it takes to check it, assuming a nonjournaling filesystem. These checks are frequently unnecessary. The tune2fs utility helps you to find a happy medium between checking filesystems each time you reboot the system and never checking them. It does this by scheduling when fsck checks a filesystem (these checks occur only when the system is booted).[1] You can use two scheduling patterns: time elapsed since the last check and number of mounts since the last check. The following command causes **/dev/hda6** to be checked when fsck runs after it has been mounted eight times or after 15 days have elapsed since its last check, whichever happens first:

```
# tune2fs -c 8 -i 15 /dev/hda6
tune2fs 1.35 (28-Feb-2004)
Setting maximal mount count to 8
Setting interval between check 1296000 seconds
```

The next tune2fs command is similar except that it works on a different partition and sets the current mount count to 4. When you do not specify a current mount count, as in the previous example, it is assumed to be zero:

```
# tune2fs -c 8 -i 15 -C 4 /dev/hda10
tune2fs 1.35 (28-Feb-2004)
Setting maximal mount count to 8
Setting current mount count to 4
Setting interval between check 1296000 seconds
```

The **–l** option displays a list of information about the partition. You can combine this option with others. Below the **Maximum mount count** is –1, which means that the mount count information is ignored by fsck and the kernel. A mount count of 0 works the same way:

```
# tune2fs -l /dev/hda5
tune2fs 1.35 (28-Feb-2004)
Filesystem volume name:    /free1
Last mounted on:           <not available>
Filesystem UUID:           f93d69a8-a419-11d4-944c-e77d13cd6039
Filesystem magic number:   0xEF53
Filesystem revision #:     1 (dynamic)
Filesystem features:       has_journal filetype needs_recovery sparse_super
Filesystem state:          clean
Errors behavior:           Continue
Filesystem OS type:        Linux
Inode count:               513024
```

---

1. For systems whose purpose in life is to run continuously, this kind of scheduling does not work. You must come up with a schedule that is not based on system reboots but rather on a clock. Each filesystem must be unmounted periodically, checked with fsck (preceding section), and remounted.

```
Block count:              1024135
...
Last mount time:          Mon Feb  2 01:54:30 2004
Last write time:          Mon Feb  2 01:54:30 2004
Mount count:              6
Maximum mount count:      -1
Last checked:             Mon Feb  2 01:54:30 2004
Check interval:           0 (<none>)
```

Set the filesystem parameters on your system so that they are appropriate to the way you use your computer. Using the **–C** option to stagger the checks ensures that all the checks do not occur at the same time. Always check new and upgraded filesystems to make sure that they have checks scheduled as you desire.

To change an **ext2** filesystem to an **ext3** filesystem, you must put a *journal* (page 978) on the filesystem, and the kernel must support **ext3** filesystems. Use the **–j** option to set up a journal on an unmounted filesystem:

```
# tune2fs -j /dev/hdd3
tune2fs 1.35 (28-Feb-2004)
Creating journal inode: done
This filesystem will be automatically checked every -1 mounts or
0 days, whichever comes first.  Use tune2fs -c or -i to override.
```

Before you can use **fstab** (page 427) to mount the changed filesystem, you must modify its entry in the **fstab** file to reflect its new type. Change the third column to **ext3**.

The following command changes an unmounted **ext3** filesystem to an **ext2** filesystem:

```
# tune2fs -O ^has_journal /dev/hdd3
tune2fs 1.35 (28-Feb-2004)
```

Refer to the tune2fs man page for more details.

RAID Filesystem

RAID (Redundant Arrays of Inexpensive/Independent Disks) spreads information across several disks to combine several physical disks into one larger virtual device. RAID improves performance and creates redundancy. There are more than six types of RAID configurations. Using Red Hat tools, you can set up *software* RAID. *Hardware* RAID requires hardware that is designed to implement RAID and is not covered here.

caution || **Do Not Replace Backups with RAID**

Do not use RAID as a replacement for regular backups. If your system undergoes a catastrophic failure, RAID will be useless. Earthquake, fire, theft, and so on may leave your entire system inaccessible (if your hard drives are destroyed or missing). RAID does not take care of something as simple as replacing a file when you delete it by accident. In these cases a backup on removable media (that has been removed) is the only way you will be able to restore a filesystem.

RAID can be an effective *addition* to a backup. Red Hat has RAID software that you can install when you install your Red Hat system or as an afterthought. The Linux kernel can automatically detect RAID disk partitions at boot time if the partition ID is set to 0xfd, which fdisk recognizes as Linux **raid autodetect**.

The kernel disk code implements software RAID so it is much cheaper than a hardware RAID. Not only does it avoid specialized RAID disk controllers, but it also works with both the less expensive IDE disks as well as SCSI disks. For more information refer to the *Software-RAID HOWTO*.

Chapter Summary

This chapter covers the Linux filesystem, which was introduced in Chapter 6, from a system administrator's point of view. It lists many important system files and directories, explaining what each does. The section on file types explains the difference between ordinary and directory files and the inodes that hold each. It also covers the use of hard and symbolic links.

Special files provide access to operating system features. The section covering these files details major and minor device numbers, which the kernel uses to identify classes of devices and specific devices within each class, and character and block devices, which represent I/O devices such as hard disks and printers.

The section on the filesystem discusses how to mount and unmount a filesystem, how to edit **/etc/fstab** to mount filesystems automatically when the system boots, and how to verify or repair a filesystem with fsck.

Exercises

1. What is the function of the **/etc/hosts** file? What services can you use in place of, or to supplement, the **hosts** file?

2. What does the **/etc/resolv.conf** file do? What does the **nameserver** line in this file do?

3. What is an inode? What happens to the inode when you move a file within a filesystem?

4. What does the .. entry in a directory point to? What does this entry point to in the root (/) directory?

5. What is a device file? Where can you find device files?

6. What is a FIFO? What does FIFO stand for? What is another name for a FIFO? How does a FIFO work?

Advanced Exercises

7. Write a line for **/etc/fstab** file that would mount the **/dev/hdb1 ext3** filesystem on **/extra** with the following characteristics: The filesystem will not be mounted automatically when the system boots, and anyone can mount and unmount the filesystem.

8. Without using rm, how can you delete a file? (*Hint:* How do you rename a file?)

9. After burning an ISO image file named **image.iso** to a CD on **/dev/hdc,** how can you can verify the copy from the command line?

10. Why should **/var** be on a separate partition from **/usr**?

11. Suggest a way to ensure that deleted files can not be recovered.

12. How would you mount an ISO image so that you could copy files from it without burning it to a CD?

Downloading and Installing Software

13

A software package is the collection of scripts, programs, files, and directories required to run a software application, including system software. Using packages makes it easier to transfer, install, and uninstall applications. A package contains either executable files or source code files that you need to compile and install. Executable files are precompiled for a specific processor and operating system, whereas source files need to be compiled but will run on a wide range of machines and operating systems.

Software for your system can come in different kinds of packages, such as rpm (page 455), the GNU Configure and Build System (page 459), tar, compressed tar, and others. The most popular package is rpm. Other packages (such as tar), which were popular before the introduction of rpm, are used less now because they require more work on the part of the installer (you) and do not provide the depth of prerequisite and compatibility checking that rpm offers. Newer programs such as yum (page 469) and Apt (page 472) not only check for compatibility but obtain over the Internet additional software required to install a given software package.

system-config-packages: Adds and Removes Software Packages

Red Hat has made the process of adding and removing software packages that they supply much easier with the system-config-packages (*FEDORA*) and redhat-config-packages (*RHEL*) package management utilities (Figure 13-1). These are the same tools you use during installation when you choose to select packages manually.

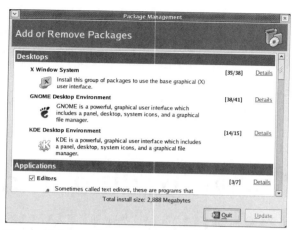

Figure 13-1   Package Management window

These utilities divide software packages into five categories: Desktops, Applications, Servers, Development, and System. Within each category are package groups. Figure 13-1 shows the Desktops category and a little bit of the Applications category. The Desktops category has three package groups. The pair of numbers in brackets to the left of each of the Details buttons tells you how many packages are (to be) installed and how many are available. Before you make any changes, the first of each of these pairs of numbers tells you how many packages are installed; after you make changes, it tells you how many packages will be installed after you click **Update**.

Boxes to the left of the names of the package groups, such as the one next to Editors in the Application category, indicate whether a group is selected (with a check mark) or not (no check mark). Click a box to add or remove a package group.

The Desktop package groups cannot be removed (there are no boxes to the left of the group names), although they can be added if they were not installed when the system was first configured. All other package groups can be removed.

Once a package group is selected, you can click **Details** to display the Package Details window. Figure 13-2 shows the Details window for the KDE package group. Within a package group are two sets of packages: those that are standard when you select the group (Standard Packages) and those that are optional (Extra Packages). Click the triangle to the left of the name of the package set to hide or display the list of packages in that set. Put check marks in the boxes next to the names of the Extra Packages you want on the system. Remove check marks next to Extra Packages you do not want. Click **Close** to return to the Package Management window when you finish selecting packages. Click **Update** to install/remove the packages you specified. The package manager asks you for the installation CDs it needs.

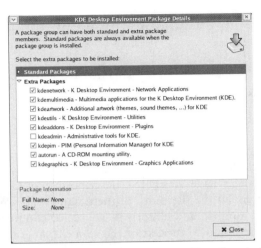

Figure 13-2   Package Management, Details window

rpm: **Red Hat Package Manager**

The rpm (Red Hat Package Manager) utility works only with software packages that have been built for processing by rpm; it installs, uninstalls, upgrades, queries, and verifies rpm packages. Because Red Hat released rpm under the GPL (page 4), rpm is used by several distributions. Together with information contained within software packages assembled for use with rpm (named *.rpm), the rpm utility keeps track of where software packages should be installed, the versions of the packages that you have installed, and the dependencies between the packages.

Source rpm packages are frequently found in a directory named **SRPMS** (source rpms), whereas binary rpm packages are in **RPMS**. When you download binary packages, make sure that they are relevant to your operating system (both distribution and release—for example, **Fedora Core 2**) and were compiled on the appropriate architecture (**i386** covers all Intel- and most AMD-based systems; **i586** covers Pentium-class processors and above; **i686** refers to Pentium II or better, and includes MMX extensions; **S390** is for IBM System/390; **ia64** is for the 64-bit Intel processor; **alpha** is for the DEC/Compaq Alpha chip; **athlon** denotes the AMD Athlon family; x86-64, x86_64, and AMD64 for AMD64 technology; **ppc** is for the Power PC chip; and **sparc** covers the Sun Sparc processor).[1] The name of the rpm file contains almost all the necessary information. Each of the following lines from a search for **sendmail** on www.rpmfind.net gives you the information you need:

---

1. Many rpm packages run on releases and even distributions other than the ones they were compiled on/for. However, installing packages intended for other distributions can create problems. In particular, Mandrake packages are rarely compatible with other systems.

```
sendmail-8.12.10-1mdk.src.html ...      Mandrake Cooker              sendmail-8.12.10-1mdk.src.rpm
sendmail-8.12.10-1.src.html ...         PLD Linux Distribution       sendmail-8.12.10-1.src.rpm
sendmail-8.12.9-7mdk.src.html ...       Mandrake                     sendmail-8.12.9-7mdk.src.rpm
sendmail-8.12.9-7mdk.i586.html ...      Mandrake                     sendmail-8.12.9-7mdk.i586.rpm
sendmail-8.12.8-9.90asp.i386.html...    ASPLinux                     sendmail-8.12.8-9.90asp.i386.rpm
                                ...     RedHat-9 Updates for i386    sendmail-8.12.8-9.90.i386.rpm
                                ...     Red Hat Linux 9 Updates Sources  sendmail-8.12.8-9.90.src.rpm
                                ...     RedHat-8.0 Updates for i386  sendmail-8.12.8-9.80.i386.rpm
sendmail-8.12.8-5.90asp.src.html...     ASPLinux                     sendmail-8.12.8-5.90asp.src.rpm
sendmail-8.12.8-5.90.src.html...        Netwinder.Org                sendmail-8.12.8-5.90.src.rpm
                                ...     SuSE Linux 8.2 Updates for i386  sendmail-8.12.7-77.i586.rpm
                                ...     SuSE Linux 8.1 Updates for i386  sendmail-8.12.6-159.src.rpm
                                ...     RedHat-8.0 for i386          sendmail-8.12.5-7.i386.rpm
sendmail-8.11.6-3a.src.html     ...     Yellow Dog PPC               sendmail-8.11.6-3a.src.rp
```

Click the **html** filename at the left to display the information about the file. Not all packages have an HTML description file. Click the **rpm** filename at the right to download the file. Both of these names tell you the name of the program, its version number, and its format (source or compiled for **i386**, **alpha**, **ia64**, and so on). The column to the left of the **rpm** filename tells you which distribution the file is from/for.

Packages marked **noarch**, short for *no architecture*, contain resources, such as images or scripts, which are run by an interpreter. You can install and run **noarch** packages on any architecture. Another site to search for rpm (and non-rpm) files is www.rpmseek.com.

Querying Packages and Files

The rpm utility can be run from a command line. Use **rpm –qa** to get a list of one-line summaries of all packages installed on the system (any user can run this utility). Use **rpm –q**, followed by the name of the package, to get more information about a particular package. For instance, **rpm –q nis** tells you whether NIS is installed and if so, which version. Use the **–ql** options to get a list of files in a package:

```
$ rpm -q nis
package nis is not installed
$ rpm -ql logrotate
/etc/cron.daily/logrotate
/etc/logrotate.conf
/etc/logrotate.d
/usr/sbin/logrotate
/usr/share/doc/logrotate-3.7
/usr/share/doc/logrotate-3.7/CHANGES
/usr/share/man/man8/logrotate.8.gz
/var/lib/logrotate.status
```

When you run rpm with the **–qi** options, you get quite a bit of information about a package:

```
$ rpm -qi logrotate
Name        : logrotate                    Relocations: (not relocatable)
```

```
Version      : 3.7                    Vendor: Red Hat, Inc.
Release      : 4.1                 Build Date: Sun Feb 15 05:58:51 2004
Install Date: Tue Mar 30 18:34:53 2004  Build Host: tweety.devel.redhat.com
Group        : System Environment/Base  Source RPM: logrotate-3.7-4.1.src.rpm
Size         : 46526                   License: GPL
Signature    : DSA/SHA1, Wed Mar 17 11:20:06 2004, Key ID da84cbd430c9ecf8
Packager     : Red Hat, Inc. <http://bugzilla.redhat.com/bugzilla>
Summary      : Rotates, compresses, removes and mails system log files.
Description :
The logrotate utility is designed to simplify the administration of
log files on a system which generates a lot of log files.  Logrotate
allows for the automatic rotation compression, removal and mailing of
log files.  Logrotate can be set to handle a log file daily, weekly,
monthly or when the log file gets to a certain size.  Normally,
logrotate runs as a daily cron job.

Install the logrotate package if you need a utility to deal with the
log files on your system.
```

Installing, Upgrading, and Removing Packages

You can use rpm to install or upgrade a package. Log in as, or su to, **root**. (Although you can run rpm as a nonprivileged user, you will not have permission to write to the necessary directories during an install or uninstall, and the install/uninstall will fail. During a query, you do not need this permission, so you can and should work as a nonprivileged user.) Use the **–U** option, followed by the name of the file that contains the rpm version of the package you want to install. The **–U** option upgrades existing packages and installs new packages (as though you had used the **–i** option). For kernels, use **–i**, not **–U** in order to leave the old kernel intact when you install a new kernel. Add the **–v** (verbose) option to get more information about what is going on and the **–h** (or **––hash**) option to see hash marks as the package is unpacked and installed. For example, while logged in as **root**, use the following command to add samba to your system:

```
# rpm -Uvh samba-3.0.0-15.i386.rpm
warning: samba-3.0.0-15.i386.rpm: V3 DSA signature: NOKEY, key ID 4f2a6fd2
Preparing...               ######################################### [100%]
    1:samba                ######################################### [100%]
```

When you install a package, your working directory must be the directory that contains the rpm file, or you must use a pathname that points to the file.

To remove the same package, give the following command from any directory:

```
# rpm -e samba
```

The rpm utility queries its database to find out the information it needs to uninstall the package and removes links, unloads device drivers, and stops daemons as necessary. Refer to the rpm man page for more rpm options.

Installing a Linux Kernel Binary

The following steps install a new Linux kernel binary. Refer to Chapter 15 when you want to configure and rebuild a kernel, not to install a new, prebuilt kernel binary. Rebuilding a kernel is more involved than installing a new one.

1. Run rpm with the –i option to install the new kernel. Do not use the –U option. You are installing a new kernel that has a name different from the old kernel: You are not upgrading the existing kernel.

2. Make sure the new kernel works before you remove the old kernel. To verify that the new kernel works, reboot the system using the new kernel.

3. Remove the old kernel by removing the files that contain the release number (and EXTRAVERSION number [page 511], if applicable) in their filenames from **/boot** or **/** (root). Remove information about the old kernel from **lilo.conf** or **grub.conf**. Remember to run lilo if you modify **lilo.conf** (*RHEL* only). You may want to wait a while before removing the old kernel to make sure that there are no problems with the new one. Instead of removing the old kernel manually, you may be able to remove it using the tool you used to install it (rpm, yum, Apt, or other).

Installing Non-rpm Software

Most software that does not come in rpm format comes with detailed instructions on how to configure, build (if necessary), and install it. Some binary distributions (those containing prebuilt executables that run on Red Hat) require you to unpack the software from the root directory.

The /opt and /usr/local Directories

Some newer application packages include scripts to install themselves automatically into a directory hierarchy under **/opt**, with files in a **/opt** subdirectory that is named after the package and executables in **/opt/bin** or **/opt/***package***/bin**. These scripts are relatively new additions to Red Hat but are familiar to Sun Solaris users.

Other software packages allow you to choose where you unpack them. Because the software available for Linux is developed by many different people, there is no consistent method for doing installations. As you acquire local software, you should install it on your system in as consistent and predictable a manner as possible. The standard Linux file structure has a directory hierarchy under **/usr/local** for binaries (**/usr/local/bin**), manual pages (**/usr/local/man**), and so forth. To prevent confusion later and to avoid overwriting or losing the software when you install standard software upgrades in the future, avoid installing nonstandard software in standard system directories (such as **/usr/bin**). On a multiuser system, make sure that users know where to find the local software, and make an announcement whenever you install, change, or remove local tools.

GNU Configure and Build System

The GNU Configure and Build System makes it easy to build a program that is distributed as source code (see autoconf at developer.gnome.org/tools/build.html). This two-step process does not require special tools other than a shell, make, and gcc (the GNU C compiler). You do not need to work with **root** privileges for either of these steps.

The following example assumes you have downloaded the GNU chess program (www.gnu.org/software/chess/chess.html) to the working directory. First, unpack and decompress the file and cd to the new directory:

```
$ tar -xvzf gnuchess*
gnuchess-5.03/
gnuchess-5.03/book/
gnuchess-5.03/book/README
...
$ cd gnuchess*
```

After reading the **README** and **INSTALL** files, run the configure script, which finds out about your system and generates the **Makefile** file:

```
$ ./configure
checking for a BSD compatible install... /usr/bin/install -c
checking whether build environment is sane... yes
checking for mawk... mawk
checking whether make sets ${MAKE}... yes
checking for gcc... gcc
checking for C compiler default output... a.out
checking whether the C compiler works... yes

...
checking for memset... yes
configure: creating ./config.status
config.status: creating Makefile
config.status: creating src/Makefile
config.status: creating src/config.h
```

Refer to the configure info page, specifically the **--prefix** option, which causes the install phase to place the software in a directory other than **/usr/local**. The second step is to run make.

```
$ make
Making all in src
make[1]: Entering directory '/hdd4/gnuchess-5.03/src'
cd .. \
&& CONFIG_FILES= CONFIG_HEADERS=src/config.h \
/bin/sh ./config.status
config.status: creating src/config.h
```

```
config.status: src/config.h is unchanged
make  all-am
make[2]: Entering directory '/hdd4/gnuchess-5.03/src'
source='atak.c' object='atak.o' libtool=no \
depfile='.deps/atak.Po' tmpdepfile='.deps/atak.TPo' \
depmode=gcc3 /bin/sh ../depcomp \
gcc -DHAVE_CONFIG_H -I. -I. -I.      -g -O2 -c 'test -f atak.c || echo './''atak.c
.
.
.
gcc  -g -O2   -o gnuchess  atak.o book.o cmd.o epd.o eval.o genmove.o hash.o hung.o init.o
iterate.o main.o move.o null.o output.o players.o pgn.o quiesce.o random.o repeat.o
search.o solve.o sort.o swap.o test.o ttable.o util.o version.o  -lreadline -lncurses -lm
make[2]: Leaving directory '/hdd4/gnuchess-5.03/src'
make[1]: Leaving directory '/hdd4/gnuchess-5.03/src'
make[1]: Entering directory '/hdd4/gnuchess-5.03'
make[1]: Nothing to be done for 'all-am'.
make[1]: Leaving directory '/hdd4/gnuchess-5.03'
$ ls src/gnuchess
src/gnuchess
```

After make finishes, the gnuchess executable is in the **src** directory. If you want to install it, give the following command while running with **root** privileges:

```
# make install
Making install in src
make[1]: Entering directory '/hdd4/gnuchess-5.03/src'
make[2]: Entering directory '/hdd4/gnuchess-5.03/src'
/bin/sh ../mkinstalldirs /usr/local/bin
/usr/bin/install -c gnuchess /usr/local/bin/gnuchess
make[2]: Nothing to be done for 'install-data-am'.
...
```

You can run the two steps and install the software with this command line:

```
# ./configure && make && make install
```

The Boolean operator **&&** (AND) allows the execution of the next step only if the previous step returned a successful exit status.

Keeping Software Up-to-Date

Of the many reasons to keep the software on your system up-to-date, one of the most important is security. Although you hear about software-based security breaches, you do not hear about the fixes that were available but never installed before the breach. Timely installation of software updates is critical to system security. Linux Open Source software is the ideal environment to find and fix bugs and make repaired software available quickly. When you keep your system and application software up-to-date, you keep abreast of bug fixes, new features, support for new hardware, speed enhancements, and more.

Bugs

A *bug* is an unwanted and unintended program property, especially one that causes the program to malfunction (definition courtesy www.foldoc.org). Bugs have been around forever, in many types of systems, machinery, thinking, and so on. All sophisticated software contains bugs. Bugs in system software or application packages can crash the system or cause programs not to run correctly. Security holes (a type of bug) can compromise the security of the system, allowing malicious users to read and write files, send mail to your contacts in your name, or destroy all the data on the system, rendering the system useless. If the engineers fixed all the bugs, there would still be feature requests as long as anyone used the software. Bugs, feature requests, and security holes are here to stay; they must be properly tracked if developers are to fix the most dangerous/important bugs first, users are to research and report bugs in a logical manner, and administrators are to be able to apply the developer's fixes quickly and easily.

Early on, Netscape used an internal bug-tracking system named BugSplat. Later, after Netscape created Mozilla (mozilla.org) as an Open Source browser project, the Mozilla team decided that it needed its own bug-tracking system. Netscape's IS department wrote a very short-lived version of Bugzilla. Then Terry Weissman, who had been maintaining BugSplat, wrote a new, Open Source version of Bugzilla in Tcl, rewriting it in Perl a couple of months later.

Bugzilla belongs to a class of programs formally known as Defect Tracking Systems, of which Bugzilla is now preeminent. It is the tool that almost all Linux developers use to track problems and enhancement requests for their software. Red Hat uses Bugzilla to track bugs and bug fixes for its Linux distributions; Red Hat Network takes advantage of Bugzilla to notify users of and distribute these fixes.

Errata

For both Red Hat Enterprise Linux and Fedora, Red Hat processes security, bugfix, and new feature (enhancement) updates. The easiest way to learn about new updates and to obtain and install them is to use up2date (page 462).

As the Linux community, including Red Hat, finds and fixes operating system and software package bugs, including security holes, Red Hat generates rpm files (page 455) that contain the code that fixes the problems. Installing a new version of a package is almost the same as installing the package in the first place. When running rpm, use the –U (upgrade) option, not –i. The upgrade option is the same as the install option except that it removes the earlier version of the package. When you upgrade a system software package, rpm renames modified configuration files with a .rpmsave extension. You must manually merge the changes you made to the original files into the new files.

RHEL   Lists of errata for all recent releases of Red Hat Enterprise Linux are available at www.redhat.com/security. However, if you are running *RHEL*, you probably have a subscription to RHN (page 467) and can use this service to find and download updates.

FEDORA   For information on Fedora Core updates, point a browser at fedora.redhat.com and click **Download⇨Updates**. Information about updates is posted to the Fedora Announce List (www.redhat.com/mailman/listinfo/fedora-announce-list). You can use up2date, yum, or Apt to find and download updates.

Fedora, Red Hat Enterprise Linux, Red Hat Network, and up2date

Before Red Hat introduced Fedora, RHN (Red Hat Network), for a fee, provided updates for software on Red Hat systems (page 467). The tool used to download and install the updates was up2date (page 462), which used yum/Apt-like tools to download rpm files. The round button on the panel that changed colors to let you know when updates were available was called the RHN Alert Notification Tool (page 466).

When Red Hat split its product line, RHN, a Red Hat profit center, went with Red Hat Enterprise Linux. The up2date utility went with both Red Hat Enterprise Linux and Fedora. Although up2date remained the same, its configuration files changed: Under Fedora, up2date uses yum (and optionally Apt) to download updated rpm files from the Fedora site. Also under Fedora, the round button that lets you know when updates are available has the same name and works the same way, except when it calls up2date (up2date does not use RHN). The letters **rhn** appear in Fedora filenames (for example, **/etc/sysconfig/rhn**), even though Fedora does not use RHN. See page 469 for information on yum and page 472 for Apt.

up2date: Updates Packages

The up2date utility downloads and optionally installs rpm packages. It works with many files and directories, in graphical and character-based modes, and has many options.

RHEL   The up2date utility works with the RHN server.

FEDORA   The up2date utility uses yum (and optionally Apt) to download files from the Fedora and other repositories.

The **−−configure** option generates **/etc/sysconfig/rhn/up2date**, up2date's system profile file. The up2date-config utility (next section) is a link to up2date with the **−−configure** option. You do not normally use this option because up2date configures itself (creates the up2date system profile) when necessary. The **−−nox** option (also up2date-nox) runs up2date in character-based mode. Refer to the up2date man page for more information.

In addition to updating packages on the system, up2date can download and install Red Hat packages that are not on the system. In the following example, a Fedora user calls links, the character-based browser program, finds it is not on the system, and confirms that finding with whereis. Then, up2date, with the **−−whatprovides** option, queries the Fedora repository to find that the **elinks** package provides links. Finally, up2date, with an argument of the rpm package to be installed, downloads the **elinks** package. In this case, up2date installs the package because that is what the up2date profile is set up to do. The same commands work under Red Hat Enterprise Linux when you are subscribed to RHN. You must run up2date as Superuser to install or upgrade a package.

```
# links
bash: links: command not found
# whereis links
links:
# up2date --whatprovides links
http://fedora.redhat.com/download/up2date-mirrors/fedora-core-2
using mirror: http://ftp.dulug.duke.edu/pub/fedora/linux/core/development/i386/
elinks-0.9.1-1
# up2date elinks
http://fedora.redhat.com/download/up2date-mirrors/fedora-core-2
using mirror: http://ftp.dulug.duke.edu/pub/fedora/linux/core/development/i386/

Fetching Obsoletes list for channel: fedora-core-2...

Fetching rpm headers...
#####################################

Name                                        Version      Rel
-------------------------------------------------
elinks                                      0.9.1        1            i386


Testing package set / solving RPM inter-dependencies...
#####################################
Preparing               ########################################## [100%]

Installing...
   1:elinks              ########################################## [100%]
```

When you give it a command, up2date determines where to look for the file you request by looking at the **/etc/sysconfig/rhn/sources** configuration file. In the preceding example, up2date says it is looking in **fedora.redhat.com/download/up2date-mirrors/fedora-core-2**, a list of Fedora repository mirrors. Then up2date displays the URL of the repository it is using following the words **using mirror**.

up2date-config: Configures up2date

The up2date-config utility sets parameters in **/etc/sysconfig/rhn/up2date**, the up2date profile file. You can run up2date-config from a command line, but it is not usually

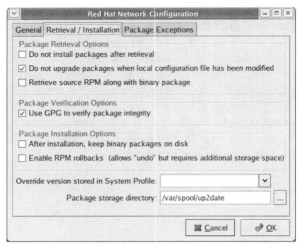

Figure 13-3   Configuring up2date, Retrieval/Installation tab

tip || (*FEDORA*) **When You Do Not Want** up2date **to Run RHN**

When the following line appears uncommented anywhere in **/etc/sysconfig/rhn/sources**, up2date tries to contact RHN and fails; up2date ignores other repositories listed in the file:

```
up2date default
```

Registering with RHN can put this line in **sources**, but up2date still will not work. Remove this line or comment it out by putting a **#** at the beginning of the line to cause up2date to contact Fedora or other repositories.

required because up2date configures itself as necessary the first time you run it. In a graphical environment, this tool displays a window with three tabs: General, Retrieval/Installation (Figure 13-3), and Package Exceptions. See Table 13-1.

table 13-1 || **Configuring** up2date

General/Network Settings

Select a Red Hat Network Server to use	This text box is already filled in. Do not change it unless you have reason to do so. Works for RHN (*RHEL*), Fedora, and other repositories.
Enable HTTP Proxy	If you need to use a proxy server, enter the HTTP proxy server in the required format.
Use Authentication	Select Use Authentication and fill in the Username and Password text boxes when the proxy server requires authentication. These spaces are for the proxy server, *not* for the RHN username and password.

table 13-1 ‖	Configuring up2date (Continued)
Retrieval/Installation	
Package Retrieval Options	
Do not install packages after retrieval	Download, but do not install packages. You will need to install the new packages manually.
Do not upgrade packages when local configuration file has been modified	Do not download or install packages that have been customized. This option is not necessary unless you are using other than the standard Red Hat packages.
Retrieve source RPM along with binary package	Download the source code (*.**src.rpm**) file in addition to the binary file (*.***arch**.**rpm**) that is to be installed. The up2date utility does nothing with the source file except download it.
Package Verification Options	
Use GPG to verify package integrity	Uses Red Hat's GPG signature to verify the authenticity of the files you are downloading. If the Red Hat signature is not on the local system, up2date asks if you want the system to download it for you. This is a critical security link; it is a good idea to select this option.
Package Installation Options	
After installation, keep binary packages on disk	Normally, binary rpm files are removed once the files they contain have been installed. Select this option if you want them left on the system in the Package storage directory (following).
Enable RPM rollbacks (allows "undo" but requires additional storage space)	By using extra disk space, up2date can store information so it can uninstall a package it has installed and reinstall the version that was installed previously.
Override version stored in System Profile	Downloads and installs packages for a version of Red Hat that you specify in the text box, overriding the version number that is stored in the system profile.
Package storage directory	Specifies a directory to store the downloaded files in. By default, they are stored in **/var/spool/up2date**.
Package Exceptions	Specifies packages and files that you do not want to download. These names can include wildcard characters.
Package Names to Skip	By default **kernel**٭ appears in this list box, meaning that no rpm packages whose names begin with the letters **kernel** will be downloaded. Installing a new kernel is an important event, and Red Hat assumes you do not want this to happen without your knowledge. Use the Add, Edit, and Remove buttons to adjust the list box to meet your requirements. Normally, you do not have to make any changes here.
File Names to Skip	Similar to Package Names to Skip except you can specify filenames you want to skip here.

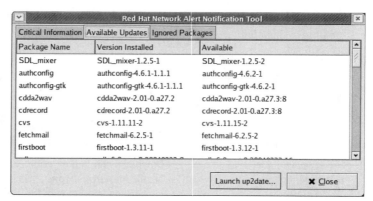

Figure 13-4   RHN Alert Notification Tool, Available Updates tab

Red Hat Network Alert Notification Tool

RHEL+FEDORA   The Red Hat Network Alert Notification Tool can take care of everything you need to do from your system to set up and run up2date to keep a system up to date. Although its title includes the words **Red Hat Network**, you can use it on a Fedora system to control up2date without using RHN. The Red Hat Network Alert Notification Tool is represented by a round button on both the GNOME and KDE Main panel. It shows one of four icons:

- Blue with a check mark indicates that all is well: There are no pending downloads.

- Red with an exclamation point indicates that files need to be downloaded. Click the button to display the window shown in Figure 13-4.

- Green with half arrows pointing left and right indicates that the system is communicating with the server.

- Grey with a question mark indicates that there has been an error. Click the icon to display the error message.

If the button is not on the Main panel, run rhn-applet-gui from Run Application on the GNOME Main menu or Run Command on the KDE Main menu to display it. Table 13-2 describes the selections in the Red Hat Network Alert Notification Tool panel icon menu (right click).

table 13-2 ||	Red Hat Network Alert Notification Tool Icon Menu
Check for updates	Runs up2date (page 462) in the background to check for updates. The green icon with arrows on the Red Hat Network Alert Notification button shows that the system is communicating with the server.

table 13-2 ‖	Red Hat Network Alert Notification Tool Icon Menu (Continued)
Launch up2date	Runs up2date (page 462) in the foreground, opening a series of windows that does not give you many options.
Configuration	Opens a series of windows that displays the Terms of Service, allows you to configure a proxy, and checks for updates.
RHN Website	Opens a Mozilla window displaying the RHN Website.

Red Hat Network (*RHEL*)

RHN (Red Hat Network, rhn.redhat.com), a service provided by Red Hat, is an Internet-based system that can keep the software on one or more of your Red Hat Enterprise Linux systems up-to-date with minimal work on your part. You must subscribe to this service in order to use it. Red Hat uses the term *entitle* to indicate that a system is subscribed to RHN: Your system must be entitled before you can use RHN. To date, Red Hat allows each user to register one system for free. You can choose to make RHN more or less automated, giving you various degrees of control over the update process.

The systems that are entitled are the clients; Red Hat maintains the RHN server. The RHN Server is much more than a single server; it involves many systems and databases that are replicated and located in different areas. For the purpose of understanding how to use the client tools on your system, picture the RHN Server as a single server. For additional information, refer to the Red Hat Network manuals at www.redhat.com/docs/manuals/RHNetwork.

Red Hat built RHN with security as a priority. Any time you allow a remote system to put a program on your system and run it, the setup must be very close to the theoretical ideal of absolutely secure. Toward this end, RHN never initiates communication with your system. Once a program running on your system sends a message to the RHN server, the server can respond and your system can trust the response.

Subscribing to Red Hat Network (*RHEL*)

Perform the following tasks to subscribe to and start using RHN.

- Give the command rhn_register to open the RHN registration window.
  - Read the Welcome page and click **Forward**.
  - Step 1: Review the Red Hat Privacy Statement window opens. If you are comfortable with the information in this window, click **Forward**.

- Step 2: Login window opens. Choose whether you want to Create New Account or Use Existing Account. Fill in the requested information. Click **Forward**.

- Step 3: Register a System Profile - Hardware window opens. This window establishes a profile name for your computer. The default name is your node (system) name. You can put any information to help you identify this system in this text box. The window also confirms that you want to include the hardware and network information in the profile information that you will send to RHN at the end of this process. When you click **Forward**, the program compiles a list of the rpm packages installed on your system.

- Step 3: Register a System Profile - Packages window opens (there are two Step 3 windows). This window confirms that you want to include a list of installed rpm packages as part of the system profile and gives you the option of removing packages from the profile so they do not get updated. Click **Forward**.

- Click **Forward** to send your profile to RHN; or click **Cancel**, and nothing will be sent.

- Entitle the system. The error: **Service not enabled for server profile: "profilename"** means that your system is not entitled. If you get this message, go to rhn.redhat.com, and log in with the username and password you set up in Step 2.

  Click the Systems tab at the top of the page, and then click the System Entitlements box at the left. The system you just registered should be listed. Change the entry in the combo box (in the Entitlement column) on the line with the proper system name to **Update**. You can click **Buy them now** at the top of the page to buy an entitlement, if necessary.

- Check for updates. Run up2date, or choose **Red Hat Network Alert Notification Tool Icon menu: Check for updates** (page 466) to see if the RHN server downloads files to or exchanges information with the local system. Alternatively, give the command **up2date - -list** to see whether any packages are available for the system, thereby testing your connection with the RHN server.

  You can start the flow of updates from the system or from the Web site. From the system, run up2date. From the Web site, log in, click the Systems tab, click the name of the system in the table, click **update now** if applicable, and click **Apply Errata**. In either case, the next time the **rhnsd** daemon (next) on the local system contacts the RHN server, you will get updates per the up2date profile (installed or not, left on the system or not, source code or not, and so on).

rhnsd: RHN Daemon

The RHN daemon (**rhnsd**) is a background service that periodically queries the RHN server to find out whether any new packages are available to be downloaded. This daemon is one of the keys to RHN security; it is the component that initiates contact with the RHN server so the server never has to initiate contact with the local system. Refer to "service: Configures Services I" on page 383 to start, stop, or display the status of **rhnsd** immediately; refer to "system-config-services: Configures Services II" on page 383 or to "chkconfig: Configures Services III" on page 385 to start or stop **rhnsd** at specified runlevels.

Keeping the System Up-to-Date

Apt and yum both fill the same role: They install and update software packages. Apt is slightly faster, especially on slow connections, and supports a few more features, such as undoing upgrades. The yum utility is installed by default and is easier to configure and use than Apt. If you are familiar with Debian systems or find yum lacks some features you need, try using Apt; otherwise use yum.

yum: Updates and Installs Packages

Early releases of RedHat Linux did not include a tool for managing updates. The RPM tool could install or upgrade individual software packages, but it was up to the user to locate the packages and the packages they were dependent on. When Terra Soft produced their RedHat-based Linux distribution for the PowerPC, they created the Yellow Dog Updater to fill this gap. This program has since been ported to other architectures and distributions. The result, Yellow Dog Updater, Modified (yum), is included with Fedora Core.

Configuring yum

The yum utility is designed to be easy to use. The configuration file, **/etc/yum.conf**, has two parts: The [main] section contains general settings and the rest of the file holds a list of servers.

The [main] section must be present for yum to function. The **cachedir** specifies the directory yum should store downloaded packages in and **logfile** specifies where yum keeps its log. The amount of information logged is specified by **debuglevel**, with a value of 10 producing the most information.

```
$ cat /etc/yum.conf
[main]
cachedir=/var/cache/yum
debuglevel=2
logfile=/var/log/yum.log
```

```
pkgpolicy=newest
distroverpkg=fedora-release
tolerant=1
exactarch=1
...
```

The **pkgpolicy** defines which version of a software package yum installs; always set to **newest** to install the newest version of a package. You can also configure yum to try to install from a specific server, falling back to other servers on failure, ignoring package versions. The **distroverpkg** specifies the distribution the system is running. You should not need to change this setting.

With **tolerant** set to **1**, yum automatically corrects simple command line errors, such as attempting to install a package already on the system. Setting **tolerant** to **0** tuns this feature off. Setting **exactarch** to **1** causes yum to update packages only with packages of the same architecture, preventing an i686 package from replacing an i386 one, for example.

The last three sections contain lists of servers holding updates. The first, [base], contains the packages present on the installation CDs. The second, [updates-released], contains updated versions of packages considered to be stable, and the last, [updates-testing], contains updates that are not ready for release. The last section is commented out; do not uncomment it unless you are testing unstable packages. Never uncomment on production systems.

```
$ cat /etc/yum.conf
...
[base]
name=Fedora Core $releasever - $basearch - Base
baseurl=http://fedora.redhat.com/releases/fedora-core-$releasever

[updates-released]
name=Fedora Core $releasever - $basearch - Released Updates
baseurl=http://fedora.redhat.com/updates/released/fedora-core-$releasever

#[updates-testing]
#name=Fedora Core $releasever - $basearch - Unreleased Updates
#baseurl=http://fedora.redhat.com/updates/testing/fedora-core-$releasever
```

Each server section contains a **name** and a **baseurl**. The **name** provides a friendly name for the server and is displayed by up2date when listing possible servers. The **baseurl** indicates the location of the server. These definitions use two variables: yum sets **$basearch** to the architecture of the system and **$releasever** to the version of the release. Refer to the **yum.conf** man page for more options.

Using yum

Working as **root**, you can run yum from a command line. The behavior of yum depends on the options you specify. The **update** option updates all installed packages:

It downloads package headers for installed packages, prompts you to proceed, and downloads and installs the updated packages.

```
# yum update
Gathering header information file(s) from server(s)
Server: Fedora Core 2 - i386 - Base
Server: Fedora Core 2 - i386 - Released Updates
Finding updated packages
Downloading needed headers
getting /var/cache/yum/updates-released/headers/pango-0-1.2.54.i386.hdr
pango-0-1.2.5-4.i386.hdr    100% |=========================| 6.5 kB 00:00
...
[update: rhn-applet 2.1.4-3.i386]
Is this ok [y/N]: y
Getting pango-1.2.5-4.i386.rpm
pango-1.2.5-4.i386.rpm      100% |=========================| 341 kB 00:06
...
```

You can update individual packages by specifying the names of the packages on the command line following the word **update**.

To install a new package together with the packages it is dependent on, give the command **yum install**, followed by the name of the package:

```
# yum install tcsh
Gathering header information file(s) from server(s)
Server: Fedora Core 1 - i386 - Base
Server: Fedora Core 1 - i386 - Released Updates
Finding updated packages
Downloading needed headers
getting /var/cache/yum/base/headers/tcsh-0-6.12-5.i386.hdr
tcsh-0-6.12-5.i386.hdr      100% |========================| 3.8 kB    00:00
Resolving dependencies
Dependencies resolved
I will do the following:
[install: tcsh 6.12-5.i386]
Is this ok [y/N]: y
Getting tcsh-6.12-5.i386.rpm
tcsh-6.12-5.i386.rpm        100% |========================| 443 kB    00:10
Running test transaction:
Test transaction complete, Success!
tcsh 100 % done 1/1
Installed:  tcsh 6.12-5.i386
Transaction(s) Complete
```

You can also use yum to remove packages, using a similar syntax.

```
# yum remove tcsh
Gathering header information file(s) from server(s)
Server: Fedora Core 1 - i386 - Base
Server: Fedora Core 1 - i386 - Released Updates
Finding updated packages
Downloading needed headers
Resolving dependencies
Dependencies resolved
I will do the following:
```

```
[erase: tcsh 6.12-5.i386]
Is this ok [y/N]: y
Running test transaction:
Test transaction complete, Success!
Erasing: tcsh 1/1
Erased:  tcsh 6.12-5.i386
Transaction(s) Complete
```

Apt: An Alternative to yum

The Apt (Advanced Package Tool) utility can help with the issue of dependencies: Apt tries to resolve package dependencies automatically by looking for the packages that the package you are installing is dependent on. Starting life as part of the Debian Linux distribution using Debian's **.deb** package format, Apt has been ported to rpm-based distributions, including Red Hat; download it from ayo.freshrpms.net.

The Apt utility uses repositories of rpm files as the basis for its actions. It can use public repositories, such as those maintained by freshrpms.com, or you can create a private repository as explained on page 478. To make things quicker, Apt keeps locally a list of packages that are on each of the repositories it uses. Any software you want to install or update must reside in a repository.

The only connection between Apt repositories and Red Hat is that the repositories include rpm files produced by Red Hat.

When you give Apt a command to install a package, Apt looks for the package in its local package list. If the package is in the list, Apt fetches the package and the packages that the package you are installing is dependent on and calls rpm to install the packages. Because Apt calls rpm, it maintains the rpm database.

Using Apt on Your System

This section shows how to configure Apt to use an external repository and how to create a local repository.

Installing and Setting Up Apt

Once you have downloaded the **apt∗.rpm** file, install it as shown following (your Apt version number will be different):

```
# rpm -Uvh apt-0.5.15cnc6-1.1.fc2.fr.i386.rpm
Preparing...           ###########################################[100%]
   1:apt               ###########################################[100%]
```

Update the local package list   The primary Apt command is apt-get; its arguments determine what the command does. After you install Apt, you need to give the command **apt-get update** to update the local package list:

```
# apt-get update
Get:1 http://ayo.freshrpms.net fedora/linux/2/i386 release [1991B]
Fetched 1991B in 0s (4922B/s)
Get:1 http://ayo.freshrpms.net fedora/linux/2/i386/core pkglist [1445kB]
```

```
Get:2 http://ayo.freshrpms.net fedora/linux/2/i386/core release [151B]
Get:3 http://ayo.freshrpms.net fedora/linux/2/i386/updates pkglist [251kB]
Get:4 http://ayo.freshrpms.net fedora/linux/2/i386/updates release [157B]
Get:5 http://ayo.freshrpms.net fedora/linux/2/i386/freshrpms pkglist [98kB]
Get:6 http://ayo.freshrpms.net fedora/linux/2/i386/freshrpms release [161B]
Fetched 1847kB in 28s (64.7kB/s)
Reading Package Lists... Done
Building Dependency Tree... Done
```

Because the available packages change frequently, it is a good idea to create a cron job (page 531) to update the local package list automatically. Create the following file to perform this task daily:

```
$ cat /etc/cron.daily/apt-update
apt-get update
```

Check the dependency tree   The Apt utility does not tolerate a broken rpm dependency tree. To check the status of your dependency tree, run **apt-get check**:

```
# apt-get check
Reading Package Lists... Done
Building Dependency Tree... Done
```

The easiest way to fix errors that apt-get reveals is to erase the offending packages and then reinstall them using Apt.

At the time of writing, Apt was incompatible with the Ximian Desktop.

Update the system   There are two arguments to apt-get that upgrade all packages on the system: **upgrade**, which upgrades all packages on the system that do not require new packages to be installed, and **dist-upgrade**, which upgrades all packages on the system, installing new packages as needed.

The following command updates all rpm-based packages on the system that depend only on packages that are already installed:

```
# apt-get upgrade
Reading Package Lists... Done
Building Dependency Tree... Done
The following packages will be upgraded
  bash binutils dia ethereal foomatic gaim gdm ghostscript gimp-print
...
  rhn-applet rsync sed slocate strace vnc-server yum
The following packages have been kept back
  gstreamer-plugins gthumb rhythmbox
57 upgraded, 0 newly installed, 0 removed and 3 not upgraded.
Need to get 59.7MB/87.9MB of archives.
After unpacking 11.8MB of additional disk space will be used.
Do you want to continue? [Y/n]
```

Enter **Y** to upgrade the listed packages; otherwise enter **N**. Packages that are not upgraded because they depend on packages that are not already installed are listed as **kept back**.

Use **dist-upgrade** to upgrade all packages, including packages that are dependent on packages that are not installed. Also installs dependencies:

```
# apt-get dist-upgrade
Reading Package Lists... Done
Building Dependency Tree... Done
Calculating Upgrade... Done
The following packages will be upgraded
  gstreamer-plugins gthumb rhythmbox
The following NEW packages will be installed:
  Hermes flac libexif libid3tag
3 upgraded, 4 newly installed, 0 removed and 0 not upgraded.
Need to get 4510kB of archives.
After unpacking 6527kB of additional disk space will be used.
Do you want to continue? [Y/n]
```

Adding and Removing Individual Packages

The format of a command to install a specific software package and the packages it is dependent on is shown following:

*apt-get install **package***

where **package** is the name of the package, such as **zsh**, not the name of the rpm, which usually includes version and architecture information (for example, **zsh-1.2.i386.rpm**).

```
# apt-get install zsh
Reading Package Lists... Done
Building Dependency Tree... Done
The following NEW packages will be installed:
  zsh
0 upgraded, 1 newly installed, 0 removed and 0 not upgraded.
Need to get 1435kB of archives.
After unpacking 2831kB of additional disk space will be used.
Get:1 http://ayo.freshrpms.net fedora/linux/1/i386/core zsh 4.0.7-1.1 [1435kB]
Fetched 1435kB in 21s (66.0kB/s)
Committing changes...
Preparing...              ######################################### [100%]
   1:zsh                  ######################################### [100%]
Done.
```

Remove a package the same way you install a package, substituting **remove** for **install**:

```
# apt-get remove zsh
Reading Package Lists... Done
Building Dependency Tree... Done
The following packages will be REMOVED:
  zsh
0 upgraded, 0 newly installed, 1 removed and 0 not upgraded.
Need to get 0B of archives.
After unpacking 2831kB disk space will be freed.
Do you want to continue? [Y/n] y
Committing changes...
Preparing...              ######################################### [100%]
Done.
```

So that you can later reinstall a package with the same configuration, the **apt-get remove** command does not remove configuration files from the **/etc** directory hierarchy. Although it is not recommended, you can use the **--purge** option to remove all files, including configuration files. Alternatively, you can move these files to an archive so you can restore them if you want to.

apt.conf: *Configuring Apt*

The **/etc/apt/apt.conf** file contains Apt configuration information and is split into three sections: Apt, which contains global settings for the Apt tools; Acquire, which describes settings related to the package-fetching mechanism; and RPM, which contains rpm specific settings. In this file, semicolons (;) separate statements, and double forward slashes (**//**) introduce comments.

APT section   The APT section is shown following:

```
$ cat /etc/apt/apt.conf
APT {
    Clean-Installed "false";
    Get {
        Assume-Yes "false";
        Download-Only "false";
        Show-Upgraded "true";
        Fix-Broken "false";
        Ignore-Missing "false";
        Compile "false";
    };
};
...
```

When you set **Clean-Installed** to TRUE, Apt removes packages that are no longer in the repository. This option is useful if Apt is keeping a number of systems in the same state using a private repository: You can uninstall a package from all the systems by deleting the package from the repository.

The options in the **Get** subsection, listed following, apply to the apt-get utility. (The apt-get utility has command line arguments with the same names.)

Assume-Yes   TRUE runs apt-get in batch mode, automatically answering YES whenever it would otherwise prompt you for input.

Download-Only   TRUE retrieves packages from the repository but does not install them. FALSE retrieves and installs the packages.

Show-Upgraded   TRUE displays a list of upgraded packages.

Fix-Broken   TRUE attempts to fix dependency tree problems with varying degrees of success. FALSE quits if it finds a dependency tree problem.

Ignore-Missing   TRUE holds back missing or corrupt packages and continues to install other packages. FALSE aborts the entire install or upgrade upon finding a missing or corrupt
package.

Compile   TRUE compiles and installs source rpm (SRPM) packages that you ask apt-get to retrieve. FALSE downloads these files without compiling or installing them.

Acquire section   The Acquire section controls options related to fetching packages:

```
$ cat /etc/apt/apt.conf
...
Acquire {
Retries "0";
Http {
Proxy ""; // http://user:pass@host:port/
}
};
...
```

The **Retries** option specifies the number of times Apt attempts to fetch a package
when an attempt failed. The **Http Proxy** setting specifies the proxy to use when
fetching packages using HTTP. The argument to this option is blank by default, indicating that Apt is not to use a proxy. An example proxy is shown as a comment.

RPM section   Following is the RPM section of **apt.conf**:

```
$ cat /etc/apt/apt.conf
...
RPM {
    Ignore { };
    Hold { };
    Allow-Duplicated { "^kernel$"; "^kernel-"; "^kmodule-"; "^gpg-pukey$"
};
    Options { };
    Install-Options "";
    Erase-Options "";
    Source {
        Build-Command "rpmbuild --rebuild";
    };
};
```

The **Ignore** and **Hold** options perform similar functions and contain lists of packages that Apt ignores or holds (does not upgrade) respectively. These are usually
blank.

The **Allow-Duplicated** section lists packages that can have more than one version
on the system at one time. In general, you do not want multiple versions of the same
package. The kernel is an exception because it is good practice to leave the old kernel installed when you install a new kernel in case you are unable to boot the new
one.

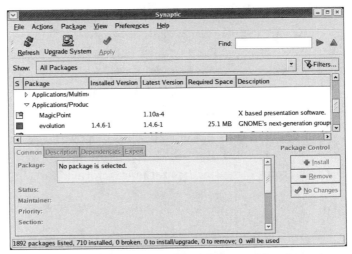

Figure 13-5 Synaptic, a graphical front end for Apt

The **Options** section contains options that are passed to rpm. The **Install-Options** and **Erase-Options** sections contain options passed to rpm whenever it is used to install or erase a package.

Finally, the **Source Build-Command** option specifies the command that Apt uses to build a source rpm file.

synaptic: The Apt GUI

The GNU project has produced for Apt a graphical front-end named synaptic (Figure 13-5), which you can install using apt-get:

```
# apt-get install synaptic
...
Committing changes...
Preparing...          ########################################[100%]
    1:synaptic         ########################################[100%]
Done.
```

The synaptic utility supports most of the features of the command line apt-get utility. Once installed, synaptic can be launched from the Main menu or the command line:

```
# synaptic &
```

Each time you run synaptic, it pauses for up to several minutes as it creates a dependency tree.

The synaptic utility lists packages hierarchically, providing a nice way of browsing the packages available in the repositories. From the hierarchy, you can select packages to upgrade, install, and remove.

Creating a Repository

If you are maintaining systems on a network, you may want to set up a private Apt repository, which has a number of advantages over a public repository:

- Updates do not require each system to connect to the Internet.
- You can test packages before deploying them.
- You can add custom packages to the repository.

An Apt repository is a directory hierarchy with a specific layout. The repository can be local, mounted using NFS or Samba, or shared using FTP or HTTP.

Refer to freshrpms.net/apt for more information.

BitTorrent

BitTorrent is the name of a protocol that implements a hybrid client-server and *P2P* (page 987) file transfer mechanism. BitTorrent efficiently distributes large amounts of static data, such as the Fedora installation ISO images (page 35). BitTorrent can replace protocols such as anonymous FTP, where client authentication is not required. Each BitTorrent client that downloads a file provides additional bandwidth for uploading the file, reducing the load on the initial source. In general, BitTorrent downloads proceed faster than FTP downloads.

Unlike protocols such as FTP, BitTorrent groups multiple files into a single package called a *torrent*. For example, you can download the Fedora Core ISO images, together with the release notes and MD5 values, as a single torrent.

BitTorrent, like other P2P systems, does not use a dedicated server. The functions of a server are performed by the tracker, peers, and seeds. The *tracker* allows clients to communicate with each other. A client, called a *peer* when it has downloaded part of the torrent and a *seed* once it has downloaded the entire torrent, acts as an additional source for the torrent. As with a P2P network, each peer and seed that downloads a torrent uploads to other clients the sections of the torrent it already has. There is nothing special about a seed: It can be removed at any time once the torrent is available for download from other seeds.

The first step in downloading a torrent using BitTorrent is to locate or acquire a **.torrent** file. A **.torrent** file contains the information about the torrent, such as its size and the location of the tracker. You can use a **.torrent** file using its *URI* (page 1003), or you can acquire it via the Web, an email attachment, or other means. The next step is for your BitTorrent client to connect to the tracker to learn the locations of other clients that it can download the torrent from.

Once you have downloaded a torrent, it is good manners to allow BitTorrent to continue to run so another clients can upload *at least* as much information as you downloaded.

Prerequisites

BitTorrent is not distributed with Red Hat Linux; you can download the rpm files from torrent.dulug.duke.edu/btrpms. If there is no rpm file for your version of Linux, use an rpm file for a similar version. Because BitTorrent is written in Python and runs on any platform with a Python interpreter, it is not dependent on system architecture. The **noarch** in the name of the RPM file stands for no architecture.

In order to run, BitTorrent requires Python, which is installed as /usr/bin/python on most Red Hat systems. Python is available in the **python** rpm package.

How BitTorrent Works

The official BitTorrent distribution includes three client applications. You can use any of these applications to download BitTorrent files:

- **btdownloadheadless.py**   A text-based client that writes the status to standard output. Good for unattended downloads where the output is redirected to a file.

- **btdownloadcurses.py**   A text-based client that provides a pseudographical interface. Good for attended downloads to machines not running a GUI.

- **btdownloadgui.py**   A graphical client (Figure 13-6).

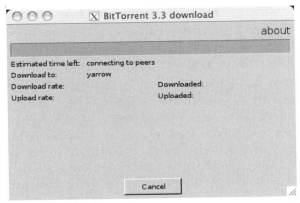

Figure 13-6   The graphical BitTorrent client

In addition to the official clients, there are other clients that provide additional features. Some of these clients are available on sourceforge.net.

Using BitTorrent

First locate the **.torrent** file for the torrent you want to download. You can copy the **.torrent** file to the working directory (first format following) or specify it with a

--url option (second format). The simplest BitTorrent command lines have the following formats:

> $ *btdownloadheadless.py --responsefile **tfile.torrent** --saveas **savefile***

or

> $ *btdownloadheadless.py --url **http://domain/tfile.torrent** --saveas **savefile***

Where **tfile.torrent** is the name of, or **http://domain/tfile.torrent** is the URI for, the **.torrent** file, and **savefile** is the location to save the torrent in. In the case of torrents containing a single file, the file is saved as **savefile**. For torrents containing multiple files, the files are saved in a directory named **savefile**. If you omit the **--saveas** argument, the files are saved in the name specified in the **.torrent** file. Because each of the **btdownload*.py** applications takes the same arguments, the preceding formats work for all three applications.

The following example shows how to download Fedora Core 2 ISO images. These are large files and take a while to download. See page 35 for information about burning installation CDs from ISO images. Go to fedora.redhat.co/download to find the location of the latest **.torrent** file. To start the download, give the following command. Because the command line is long, it is broken by a backslash (\). Make sure no character follows the backslash, or the backslash will not quote the following RETURN, and the command will fail. (The shell supplies the > on the second line.)

```
$ btdownloadheadless.py --max_upload_rate 8 \
> --url http://torrent.dulug.duke.edu/tettnang-binary-i386-iso.torrent
```

The preceding command uses a URI to specify a **.torrent** file and saves the downloaded files in a directory named **tettnang** (the name of the Fedora release) as specified by the **.torrent** file.

The **--max_upload_rate 8** option prevents BitTorrent from using more than 8 kilobytes per second of upstream bandwidth. BitTorrent usually gives higher download rates to clients that upload more, so feel free to increase this value if you have spare bandwidth. You need to leave enough free upstream bandwidth for the acknowledgement packets from your download to get through, or your download will be very slow. By default, the client uploads to a maximum of 7 other clients at once. You can change this value by specifying the **--max_uploads** argument, followed by the number of concurrent uploads you wish to permit. The default value of 7 is about right for most consumer broadband connections.

After you give the preceding command, the screen quickly fills with output that looks similar to the following:

```
saving: tettnang-binary-i386-iso (2179.7 MB)
percent done: 0.0
time left: 9 hour 27 min 28 sec
download to: tettnang-binary-i386-iso
download rate: 34.08 kB/s
upload rate: 4.48 kB/s
```

```
download total: 0.8 MiB
upload total: 0.1 MiB
```

The file size is that of all the files you are downloading: four ISO images and several smaller files.

You can abort the download by pressing CONTROL-C. The download will automatically resume from where it left off when you download the same torrent to the same location again.

Use the following command to perform the same download as in the previous example, throttling the rate and number of uploads to values sensible for modem users. (The shell supplies the > on the second line, you do not enter it.)

```
$ btdownloadcurses.py --max_upload_rate 3 --max_uploads 2 \
> --url http://torrent.dulug.duke.edu/tettnang-binary-i386-iso.torrent
```

The preceding command displays output similar to the following:

```
------------------------------------------------------
| file: tettnang-binary-i386-iso                     |
| size: 2,285,617,943 (2.1 GB)                       |
| dest: /home/mark/tettnang-binary-i386-iso          |
| progress: _____ |
| status: finishing in 1:17:56 (11.7%)               |
| speed: 450.3 KB/s down -   3.1 KB/s up             |
| totals: 256.0 MB   down -   2.0 MB   up            |
| error(s):                                          |
|                                                    |
------------------------------------------------------
```

wget: Download Files Noninteractively

The wget utility is a noninteractive, command line utility that can retrieve files from the Web using HTTP, HTTPS, and FTP.

The following simple example of wget downloads Red Hat's home page, named **index.html**, to a file with the same name.

```
$ wget http://www.redhat.com
--18:03:34--  http://www.redhat.com/
           => 'index.html'
Resolving www.redhat.com... done.
Connecting to www.redhat.com[66.187.232.50]:80... connected.
HTTP request sent, awaiting response... 200 OK
Length: 29,537 [text/html]
100%[================================>] 29,537     54.32K/s   ETA 00:00
18:03:35 (54.32 KB/s) - 'index.html' saved [29537/29537]
```

Use the **–b** option to run wget in the background and to redirect its standard error to a file named **wget-log**:

```
$ wget -b http://example.com/big_file.tar.gz
Continuing in background, pid 10752.
Output will be written to 'wget-log'.
```

If you download a file that would overwrite a local file, wget appends a dot followed by a number to the filename. In the same way, subsequent background downloads are logged to **wget-log.1**, **wget-log.2**, and so on.

The **–c** option continues an interrupted download. The next command continues the download from the previous example:

```
$ wget -b -c http://example.com/big_file.tar.gz
```

Chapter Summary

As a system administrator, you need to keep application and system software current. Of the many reasons to keep the software on a system up-to-date, one of the most important is system security. Red Hat has made the process of adding and removing the software packages they supply much easier with the system-config-packages (FEDORA) and redhat-config-packages (RHEL) package management utilities. In addition, you can use the rpm utility to install, uninstall, upgrade, query, and verify rpm packages. For packages distributed as source code, the GNU Configure and Build System makes it easy to build executable files.

For both Red Hat Enterprise Linux and Fedora, Red Hat processes security, bugfix, and new feature (enhancement) updates. The easiest way to learn about new updates is to use up2date. The up2date utility downloads and optionally installs rpm packages. It works with many files and directories, in graphical and character-based modes, and has many options.

Red Hat Network (RHN), a service provided by Red Hat, is an Internet-based system that can keep the software on one or more Red Hat Enterprise Linux systems up-to-date.

For Fedora systems, yum and Apt both fill the same role of installing and updating software packages. Apt is slightly faster, especially on slow connections, and supports a few more features, such as undoing upgrades. The yum utility is installed by default and is easier to configure and use than Apt. The GNU Project distributes for Apt a graphical front-end named synaptic, which is easy to use.

BitTorrent is a good tool for downloading large static data files such as the Fedora installation ISO images. BitTorrent can replace protocols such as anonymous FTP, where client authentication is not required.

Exercises

1. Why would you use HTTP or FTP instead of BitTorrent for downloading large files?

2. What command would you give to perform a complete upgrade using

a. up2date?

b. yum?

c. Apt?

3. Why would you build a package from source when a (binary) rpm file is available?

4. Suggest two advantages rpm files have over source distributions.

5. Why would you choose to use RHN instead of yum or Apt? (*RHEL* only)

Advanced Exercises

6. What are some steps you should take before performing an upgrade on a mission-critical server?

7. When should you use **rpm –i** instead of rpm –U?

8. The system-config-packages utility does not allow you to remove KDE. If you decide that you no longer wish to have KDE installed, how would you remove it?

9. When you compile a package yourself, not from an rpm file, which directory hierarchy should you put it in?

Printing with CUPS   14

A *printing system* handles the tasks involved in getting a print job from an application (or the command line) through the appropriate *filters* (page 971) into a queue for a suitable printer and getting it printed. While handling a job, a printing system can keep track of billing information so that the proper accounts can be charged for printer use. When a printer fails, the printing system can redirect jobs bound for that printer to other, similar printers.

Introduction

LPD and LPR   Traditionally, UNIX had two printing systems: the BSD Line Printer Daemon (LPD) and the System V Line Printer system (LPR). Linux adopted those systems at first, and both UNIX and Linux have seen modifications to and replacements for these systems. Today, CUPS is the default printing system under Red Hat Linux.

CUPS   CUPS (Common UNIX Printing System) is a cross-platform print server built around IPP (Internet Printing Protocol), which is based on HTTP. CUPS provides a number of printer drivers and can print different types of files including PostScript. Because it is built on IPP and written to be portable, CUPS runs under many operating systems, including Linux and Windows. Other UNIX variants, including MacOS X, use CUPS, and recent versions of Windows include the ability to print to IPP printers, making CUPS an ideal solution for printing in a heterogeneous environment. CUPS provides System V and BSD command line interfaces and, in addition to IPP, supports LPD/LPR, HTTP, SMB, and JetDirect (socket) protocols, among others.

IPP   The IPP project (www.ietf.org/html.charters/ipp-charter.html) was started in 1996 when Novell and several other companies decided to design a protocol for printing over the Internet. The IPP enables users to

- Determine the capabilities of a printer
- Submit jobs to a printer
- Determine the status of a printer
- Determine the status of a print job
- Cancel a print job

IPP is a client/server protocol in which the server side can be a print server or a network capable stand-alone printer.

Printers and queues   On a modern computing system, when you "send a job to the printer," you actually add the job to the list of jobs waiting their turn to be printed on a printer. The list is called a *print queue* or simply a *queue*. The phrase *configuring* (or *setting up*) a *printer* is often used to mean *configuring a (print) queue*. This chapter uses the phrases interchangeably.

Prerequisites

Install the following packages:

- **cups**
- **system-config-printer** (*FEDORA*) or **redhat-config-printer** (*RHEL*) (optional)
- **kdebase** (optional, provides kprinter)
- **printman** (optional, provides gnome-print-manager)

Run chkconfig to cause CUPS (the **cupsd** daemon) to start when the system goes multiuser:

```
# /sbin/chkconfig cups on
```

Start CUPS:

```
# /etc/rc.d/init.d/cups start
```

To use the Web interface to CUPS, you need an X server and a Web browser.

More Information

Local   CUPS Documentation   With the CUPS Web interface up (page 493), point a local browser at localhost:631/documentation.html.

Web   www.linuxprinting.org   information on printers and printing under Linux; hosts a support database with details about many printers, including notes and driver information, also forums, articles, and a HOWTO on printing
CUPS home page   www.cups.org

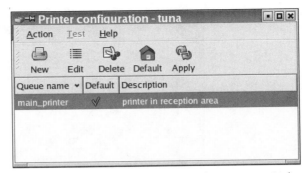

Figure 14-1   The main Printer configuration window

IPP information   www.pwg.org/ipp
www.ietf.org/html.charters/ipp-charter.html

HOWTO   *SMB HOWTO* has a section named "Sharing a Windows Printer with Linux Machines."

JumpStart I: Configuring a Local Printer Using system-config-printer

This JumpStart configures a printer that is connected directly to the local system. The fastest way to add a new printer is to use system-config-printer (*FEDORA*) or redhat-config-printer (*RHEL*), a simple wrapper script that launches either the textual or the graphical version of printconf-gui, depending on whether it detects an X server. You can run [system|redhat]-config-printer from a command line or from the Gnome or K (Red Hat) menus: **System Setting->Printing.**

From the [system|redhat]-config-printer **Printer configuration** window (Figure 14-1), click the **New** button to display the **Add a new print queue** wizard. Click **Forward** to display **Queue name** window (Figure 14-2). Enter a name for, and a short de-

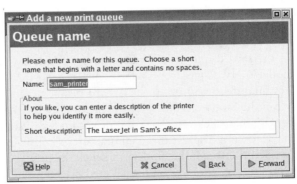

Figure 14-2   The Queue name window

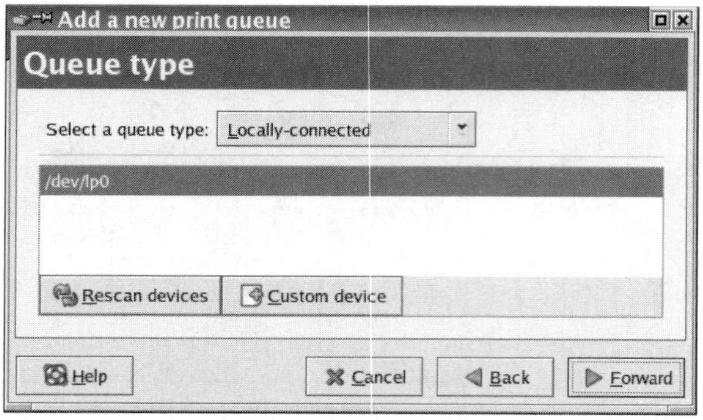

Figure 14-3   The Queue type window

scription of, the printer. The name is a short identifier that starts with a letter and does not contain any SPACEs. The description can be a short sentence. Click **Forward**.

The next window, **Queue type**, asks you to specify the printer connection (Figure 14-3). By default, the **Locally-connected** queue type is selected in the combo box at the top of the window.

Most printers connect to a parallel or USB port, although older printers may connect to a serial port. The default list in the box in the middle of the window lists the system's parallel ports. Under Linux, a parallel port is identified as **/dev/lp***n*, where *n* is the number that identifies the port. The first parallel port (LPT1 under Windows) is **/dev/lp0**. Unless you have several parallel ports on the local system, the printer is probably connected to **/dev/lp0**.

USB devices appear in the **/dev/usb** directory. USB printers appear as standard parallel printers within the **usb** directory hierarchy. The first USB printer port is **/dev/usb/lp0**, with subsequent printers appearing as **lp1**, **lp2**, and so on, exactly as parallel ports do. The first serial port (COM1 under DOS or Windows) is **/dev/tty0**.

If your device is not listed, click **Custom device** and enter the pathname of the device as **/dev/***xxx*.

Click to highlight the line that names the port the printer you are installing is connected to and click **Forward**.

The wizard displays the **Printer model** window (Figure 14-4). Specifying the printer model is a two-step process: First, click the bar that has the words **Generic (click to select manufacturer)** on it; the wizard displays a long pop-up menu of manufacturers. Move the mouse pointer over the menu until the manufacturer of your printer is highlighted; then click. The wizard replaces the words in the bar with the name of the manufacturer and displays that manufacturer's known printer models in the box below the bar. Scroll through the models and click the printer that is attached to the system. Click **Notes** to display notes on the selected printer from the Linux Printing Database.

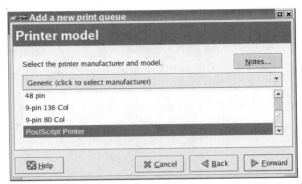

Figure 14-4   The Printer model window

If your printer is not listed, check to see if it can emulate another printer (if it has an *emulation mode*). If it can, check to see if the printer it can emulate is listed and set it up that way. If all else fails, reselect **Generic** in the bar and choose a generic printer from the list in the box. Choose **PostScript Printer** if your printer is Post-Script capable. If there is no match, select **Text Only Printer**; you will not be able to print graphics, but you should be able to print text.

FEDORA   If you are using a winprinter, select **GCI Printer** from the list of Generic printers.

Click **Forward** to display the **Finish, and create the new print queue** window. The wizard has not saved any information at this point; you can click **Cancel** to abort the process or **Apply** to create the new print queue.

Next, the wizard asks you if you want to print a test page; do so to ensure that the configuration was successful. Printing the test page automatically commits the configuration changes. If you do not print a test page, select **Apply** from the **Action** drop down menu to commit the changes.

If you have more than one print queue and want to make the new print queue the default one, highlight the print queue and select **Set as default** from the **Action** drop-down menu.

JumpStart II: Configuring a Remote Printer Using CUPS

This JumpStart uses the Web interface to CUPS to configure either a printer that is connected to a different UNIX/Linux system that provides IPP support or an LPD/LPR queue, or a printer connected directly to the network.

If the printer you are configuring is on an older Linux system or another UNIX-like operating system that does not run CUPS, the system is probably running LPD/LPR. Newer versions of Linux and UNIX variants that support CUPS (including Mac OS

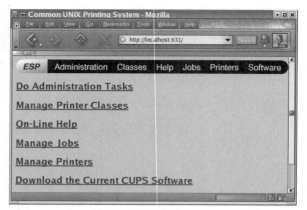

Figure 14-5   CUPS Web interface: main page

X) support IPP. Most devices that connect printers directly to a network support LPR/LPD and may support IPP.

Printers connected directly to a network are functionally equivalent to printers connected to a system running a print server: They listen on the same ports as systems running print servers and queue jobs.

Connect to the Web interface to CUPS by pointing a Web browser at **localhost:631** on the system you are configuring the printer on (Figure 14-5).

Click **Printers** on the navigation bar at the top of the page; then click **Add Printer** to display the **Admin->Add New Printer** page (Figure 14-6). If you are prompted for a username and password, enter **root** and the **root** password. The **Name** field holds the system name for the printer; it must start with a letter and not contain any SPACES. Fill in the **Location** and **Description** fields with text that will help users identify the printer and click **Continue**.

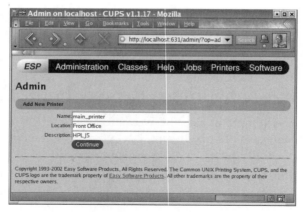

Figure 14-6   CUPS Web interface: Admin->Add New Printer

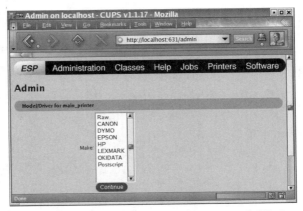

Figure 14-7   CUPS Web interface: Admin->Model/Driver page

The next page asks you to select the device that the printer is attached to. Click the down arrow at the right of the Device combo box to display the list of printer devices. Select **Internet Printing Protocol (ipp)** or an **LPD/LPR Host or Printer**, depending on what the printer is attached to. Select **AppSocket/HP JetDirect** for an HP JetDirect compatible network printer. Click **Continue**.

The next page asks for the URI (location on the network) of the printer. For an LPD printer, use the form **lpd://*hostname*/*queue*;** for an IPP printer, use **ipp://*hostname*/ipp;** for an HP JetDirect compatible network printer, use **socket://*hostname*.** Replace *hostname* with the name of the host that the printer is attached to or the name of printer for a network printer. You can specify an IP address in place of *hostname*. Replace *queue* with the name of the queue on the remote system. Enter the URI of the printer and click **Continue**.

Next is the first of two **Model/Driver** pages (Figure 14-7). Highlight the brand of printer and click **Continue**. If the printer is PostScript capable and it is not listed, select **Postscript**. If the printer is not PostScript capable and is not listed, check to see if the printer supports PCL; if it does, select another, similar PCL printer. If all else fails, determine which listed printer is most similar to the one you are configuring and specify that printer. You can also try configuring the printer using [system|redhat]-config-printer (page 487) which offers a different choice of models.

The final page in this process is the second Model/Driver page. Select the model of the printer from the scrollable list and click **Continue**.

If the printer was configured properly, when you select a printer and click **Continue**, you will get a message saying that the printer was added successfully. Click the name of the printer on this page or click **Printers** at the top of the page to display the Printer page (Figure 14-8). Once you have set up the printer, it is a good idea to print a test page.

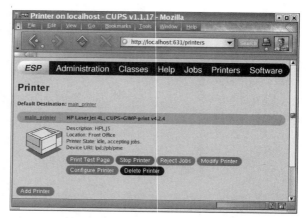

Figure 14-8   CUPS Web interface: Printer page

Traditional UNIX Printing

Before the advent of GUIs and *wysiwyg* (page 1006) word processors, UNIX users would create documents using an editor such as vi and a typesetting markup language such as TeX or nroff/troff, convert the resulting files to PostScript using an interpreter, and send the PostScript files to the printer using lp (System V) or lpr (BSD). Red Hat Linux implements both BSD and System V command line printing utilities for compatibility: These utilities are now wrappers around the equivalent functionality in CUPS rather than core components of the printing system. The corresponding utilities are functionally equivalent; use whichever you prefer (Table 14-1).

table 14-1 || **BSD and System V Command Line Utilities**

BSD/SysV	Purpose
lpr/lp	Sends job(s) to the printer.
lpq/lpstat	Displays the status of the print queue.
lprm/cancel	Removes job(s) from the print queue.

From the command line, you can print a text or PostScript file using lp:

```
$ lp memo.txt
request id is MainPrinter-25 (1 file(s))
```

The preceding command adds **memo.txt** to the print queue of the default printer as job 25. When this printer is available, it prints the file.

You can specify a printer using the **–d** option:

```
$ lp -d colorprinter graph.ps
request id is colorprinter-26 (1 file(s))
```
The **–P** option to lpr is equivalent to the **–d** option to lp.

Without an argument, lp (and lpr) sends its standard input to the printer:

```
$ cat memo2.txt | lp
request id is MainPrinter-27 (1 file(s))
```
The lpq and lpstat commands display information about the print queue:

```
$ lpstat
MainPrinter-25       mark        13312   Sun Feb 22 18:28:38 2004
ColorPrinter-26      mark        75776   Sun Feb 22 18:28:48 2004
MainPrinter-27       mark         8192   Sun Feb 22 18:28:57 2004
```
Use cancel or lprm to remove jobs from the print queue. Only the owner of a print job or **root** can remove a job.

```
$ cancel 27
$ lpstat
MainPrinter-25       mark        13312   Sun Feb 22 18:28:38 2004
ColorPrinter-26      mark        75776   Sun Feb 22 18:28:48 2004
```
Use **cancel –a** or **lprm –** to remove all your jobs from the print queue.

Configuring Printers Using CUPS

You can use the Web interface or the command line interface to CUPS to manage printers and queues.

The CUPS Web Interface

CUPS, designed for Internet printing, provides a Web interface to configure printers. To connect to this interface, point a Web browser running on the local system at **localhost:631**.

Setting Up and Modifying a Printer

"JumpStart II: Configuring a Remote Printer Using CUPS" (page 489) discusses how to set up a remote printer using CUPS. The procedure for setting up a local printer is similar. The major difference is the second step: specifying the device that the printer is connected to.

A local printer is generally connected to **USB Port #1** or **Parallel Port #1**. After specifying one of these devices, the Web interface displays the page on which you specify the brand of the printer; you do not specify a URI for a local printer. If you are setting up a serial printer, you will need to specify characteristics of the printer, including its baud rate. After these steps, the procedure is the same as explained in JumpStart II.

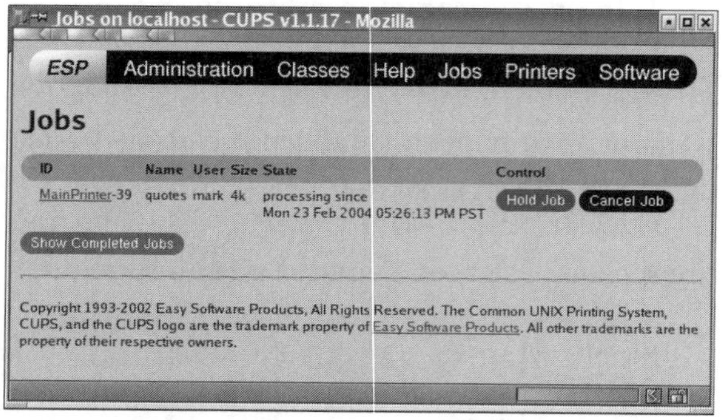

Figure 14-9   CUPS Web interface: Jobs page

To modify a printer, click **Printers** from the Web interface navigation bar and click the **Modify Printer** button adjacent to the printer you want to modify. The Web interface takes you through the same steps as setting up a new printer.

Click the red **Stop Printer** button to pause the printer. Click the **Reject Jobs** button to prevent jobs from being added to the printer's queue.

Jobs

The Jobs page (Figure 14-9) lists jobs in the print queues. From this page you can hold (pause), release (unpause), and cancel print jobs. Click Show Complete Jobs to display a list of recently completed jobs; in some cases, you can restart completed jobs from this page.

Classes

CUPS allows you to group similar printers; this group is called a *class*. A print job sent to a class will be printed on the first available printer in the class. For example, you may be able to divide your print jobs into black and white and color. If you have more than one printer that can fulfil each role, you can allow users to select a printer manually, or you can define two printer classes (black and white and color) and have users send jobs to a class of printers.

tip || **Plan for the Future**

If you expect to add printers to the network, you may want to configure classes containing the existing printers when you set up the network. You can then add printers later without having to change printer configuration on client systems.

Adding printers to a class is a two-step process. First, you need to define a class. Second, you need to add existing printers to the class. To define a class, click **Classes** from the navigation bar at the top of the page and then click **Add Class**. To clients, a class of printers appears as a single printer; for each class, you need to specify a

name, location, and description. Once you have defined a class, you can add printers to the class. Repeat this process for the classes you want to define. A printer can
belong to more than one class.

CUPS on the Command Line

In addition to using the Web interface, you can control CUPS and manage print
queues from the command line. This section details utilities that enable you to manage printers and print queues and establish printing quotas.

lpinfo: Display Available Drivers

The lpinfo utility provides information about the printer drivers and interfaces available to CUPS. The **–m** option displays the list of available PostScript Printer Definition (PPD) files/drivers.

PPD files
```
$ /usr/sbin/lpinfo -m
raw Raw Queue
dymo.ppd.gz DYMO Label Printer CUPS v1.1
epson9.ppd.gz EPSON 9-Pin Series CUPS v1.1
epson24.ppd.gz EPSON 24-Pin Series CUPS v1.1
stcolor2.ppd.gz EPSON New Stylus Color Series CUPS v1.1
stphoto2.ppd.gz EPSON New Stylus Photo Series CUPS v1.1
stcolor.ppd.gz EPSON Stylus Color Series CUPS v1.1
stphoto.ppd.gz EPSON Stylus Photo Series CUPS v1.1
deskjet.ppd.gz HP DeskJet Series CUPS v1.1
laserjet.ppd.gz HP LaserJet Series CUPS v1.1
deskjet2.ppd.gz HP New DeskJet Series CUPS v1.1
okidata9.ppd.gz OKIDATA 9-Pin Series CUPS v1.1
okidat24.ppd.gz OKIDATA 24-Pin Series CUPS v1.1
...
postscript.ppd.gz Generic postscript printer
```

CUPS uses *URIs* (page 1003) to identify printer ports by location and type, just as a
Web browser identifies documents by location and protocol. A parallel port has a URI
with the format: **parallel:/dev/lp0;** a remote LPD printer uses this format:
lpd://192.168.0.101. With the **–v** option, lpinfo provides a list of available connections.

```
$ lpinfo -v
network socket
network http
network ipp
network lpd
direct parallel:/dev/lp0
direct scsi
serial serial:/dev/ttyS0?baud=115200
...
serial serial:/dev/ttyS31?baud=115200
direct usb:/dev/usb/lp0
...
direct usb:/dev/usb/lp15
network smb
```

The the –v option to lpinfo does not display every possible network address for the socket, HTTP, IPP, LPD, and SMB protocols; there are more than four billion of these addresses in the IPv4 address space.

lpadmin: Configure Printers

The lpadmin utility can add and remove printers from the system, modify printer configurations, and manage printer classes. It has three major options: –d (set the default printer), –x (remove a printer), and –p (add or modify a printer). The first two options are simple; examples are shown after the next section. Each of the options takes an argument of the name of a printer. The name of the printer must start with a letter and cannot contain SPACEs.

Adding or Modifying a Printer

Add a printer or modify an existing printer by giving the following command:

```
# /usr/sbin/lpadmin -p printer options
```

where *printer* is the name of the printer and *options* is a combination of options from the following list:

–c *class* Adds the printer to the class *class*, creating the class if necessary.

–D *info* The *info* is a string that describes the printer for users. This string has no meaning to the system. Enclose *info* within quotation marks if it contains SPACEs.

–E **enable** Enables the printer and instructs it to accept jobs.

–L *loc* The *loc* is a string that physically locates the printer for users (office, building, floor, and so on). This string has no meaning to the system. Enclose *loc* within quotation marks if it contains SPACEs.

–m *model* **The** *model* is the name of the PPD file (page 495) that describes the printer. Use **lpinfo –m** to display a list of all of the installed PPD files. If you have a manufacturer-provided PPD file, copy it to **/usr/share/cups/model**. Use the **–P** option to specify the pathname of the file. Specifying **–m postscript.ppd.gz** is the same as specifying **–P /usr/share/cups/model/postscript.ppd.gz**.

–P *file* The *file* is the absolute pathname of the PPD file (page 495) that holds the printer driver. See **–m** for an alternative way to specify a PPD file.

–r *class* Removes the printer from the class *class*. This option removes the class if after removing the printer the class would be left empty.

–v *URI* The *URI* is the device to which the printer is attached. Use **lpinfo –v** to list possible devices.

Example lpadmin *commands*

At a minimum, you need to provide a device and a model when you add a printer to the system. The following command adds an Epson Stylus Color printer to the system and enables it for use. The printer is connected locally to the first parallel port and is named **ColorPrinter**.

```
# lpadmin -p ColorPrinter -E -v parallel:/dev/lp0 -m stcolor.ppd.gz
```

The printer information generated by the preceding command is stored in the **/etc/cups/printers.conf** file.

```
# cat /etc/cups/printers.conf
# Printer configuration file for CUPS v1.1.17
# Written by cupsd on Mon 23 Feb 2004 03:08:58 AM GMT
<Printer ColorPrinter>
Info ColorPrinter
DeviceURI parallel:/dev/lp0
State Idle
Accepting Yes
JobSheets none none
QuotaPeriod 0
PageLimit 0
KLimit 0
</Printer>
```

The printer driver information from **/usr/share/cups/model/stcolor.ppd.gz** is uncompressed and copied to **/etc/cups/ppd**. The resulting file is given the printer's name: **/etc/cups/ppd/ColorPrinter.ppd**.

You can modify a printer configuration with lpadmin using the same options that you used to add it: When you specify the name of a printer that exists, lpadmin modifies the printer rather than creating a new one.

The next command configures an HP LaserJet compatible printer with a JetDirect interface that is connected directly to the LAN at 192.168.1.103 and names it HPLJ. Specifying **socket** in the protocol part of the URI instructs CUPS to use the JetDirect protocol, a proprietary protocol developed by HP for printers connected directly to a network.

```
# lpadmin -p HPLJ -E -v socket://192.168.1.103 -m laserjet.ppd.gz
```

The lpstat utility with the **–d** option displays the name of the default printer:

```
$ lpstat -d
system default destination: MainPrinter
```

CUPS automatically makes the first printer you defined the default printer. The following command makes HPLJ the default printer:

```
# lpadmin -d HPLJ
```

The following command removes the configuration for the printer named **Color-Printer**:

```
# lpadmin -x ColorPrinter
```

Printing Quotas

CUPS provides rudimentary printing quotas. You can define two forms of quotas: page count and file size. File size quotas are almost meaningless because a small

PostScript file can take a long time to interpret and can use a lot more ink than a large one. Page quotas are more useful, although their implementation is flawed. To determine the number of pages in a document, CUPS examines the PostScript input. If a job is submitted in the printer's native language, such as PCL, CUPS bypasses this accounting mechanism. Also, if mpage is used to create a PostScript file with multiple pages printed on each sheet, CUPS counts each page in the original document, rather than each sheet of paper it prints on.

Use the **job-quota-period** and either **job-page-limit** or **job-k-limit** to establish a quota for each user on a given printer. The **job-quota-period** option specifies the number of seconds that the quota is valid. The following command establishes a quota of 20 pages per day per user for the printer named HPLJ:

```
$ lpadmin -p HPLJ -o job-quota-period=86400 -o job-page-limit=20
```

The **job-k-limit** option works similarly but defines a file size limit in kilobytes. The limit is the total number of kilobytes that each user can print over the quota period. Once a user has exceeded her quota, she will not be allowed to print until the next quota period.

Managing Print Queues

When a printer is operating normally, it accepts jobs into its print queue and prints them in the order received. Two factors determine how a printer handles a job: if the printer is accepting jobs and if it is enabled. Table 14-2 shows what happens in each of the four combinations of the two factors.

table 14-2 ‖		Printer Status
	Enabled	**Disabled**
Accepting Jobs	Accepts new jobs into the queue.	Accepts new jobs into the queue.
	Prints jobs from the queue.	Does not print jobs from the queue until the printer is enabled.
Rejecting Jobs	Rejects new jobs.	Rejects new jobs.
	Prints jobs from the queue.	Does not print jobs from the queue until the printer is enabled.

The utilities that change these factors are disable, enable, reject, and accept. Each of these utilities takes the name of a printer as an argument. The following commands disable and then enable the printer named HPLJ:

```
# /usr/bin/disable HPLJ
# /usr/bin/enable HPLJ
```

The next commands cause HPLJ to reject and then accept jobs:

```
# /usr/sbin/reject HPLJ
# /usr/sbin/accept HPLJ
```

The enable and disable utilities are located in **/usr/bin**, while reject and accept are located in **/usr/sbin**. Depending on how the **PATH** environment variable (page 283) is set, you may need to specify absolute pathnames for disable, reject, and accept. Because enable is a bash builtin (page 211), you always need to specify the absolute pathname of this utility. You may want to create easier-to-use aliases (page 305) for these commands.

Sharing CUPS Printers

IPP is designed for remote printing. By default, CUPS binds to **localhost** and accepts connections from the local system only. To allow other systems to connect to CUPS on the local system, you need to instruct CUPS to bind to an IP address that the other computers can reach. The **Listen** directive in the CUPS configuration file, **/etc/cups/cupsd.conf**, specifies which IP address CUPS binds to and accepts requests on. The format of the **Listen** directive follows:

Listen IP:port

where *IP* is the IP address that CUPS accepts connections on and *port* is the port number that CUPS listens on for connections on *IP*. CUPS typically uses port 631. For example, the following directive causes CUPS to listen on IP address 192.168.0.10, port 631:

```
Listen 192.168.0.10:631
```

After you change **cupsd.conf**, you need to restart the CUPS daemon:

```
# /sbin/service cups restart
Stopping cups:                                          [  OK  ]
Starting cups:                                          [  OK  ]
```

Once you restart the CUPS daemon, remote systems can print on the local system's printers using the IP address and port number specified with **Listen** directive. Make sure the system's firewall allows LAN users to connect to port 631 on the local system and does not allow systems outside the LAN to connect.

Alternatively, you can use CUPS's access control list to permit only selected machines to connect to local printers. An access control list is defined inside a **<Location>** container. The following example allows only the system at IP 192.168.1.101 and the local system to print to the specified printer:

```
<Location /printers>
Order Deny,Allow
Allow from 192.168.1.101
Allow from @LOCAL
</Location>
```

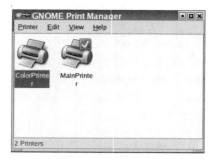

Figure 14-10   The GNOME Print Manager

The **/printers** indicates that this container refers to all local printers. Alternatively, you can control access on a per-printer basis by specifying **/printers/***name*, where *name* is the printer name, or by specifying **/printers/***path*.**ppd**, where *path*.**ppd** is the full pathname of the PPD file (page 495) that the printer uses.

The Order Deny,Allow line denies print requests by default and allows requests only from explicitly specified addresses. Specifying Order Allow,Deny allows print requests by default and denies requests from explicitly specified addresses.

Allow from specifies the IP addresses that CUPS accepts connections from. Use **Deny from** with Order Allow,Deny to specify IP addresses that CUPS will not accept connections from.

The **@LOCAL** macro specifies the local machine: It accept jobs from any address that resolves to the local machine. Specifying **127.0.0.1** in place of **@LOCAL** would work as long as no application tried to print to the print server using its external IP address. Do not use the machine's external IP address. Most processes use the loopback device (127.0.0.1) to connect to the printer, and the loopback device does not allow connections to any IP other than itself. You can also use domain names, including wildcards, and IP ranges with either wildcards or netmasks in **Allow from** and **Deny from** directives.

The GNOME Print Manager

The GNOME Print Manager (Figure 14-10) is similar to the Windows printer control panel; by default, it displays an icon for each printer. You can run the GNOME Print Manager from the GNOME (Red Hat) menu: **System Tools -> Print Manager** or from a virtual terminal.

From the GNOME Print Manager window, double-click an icon to display the print queue for the printer represented by the icon. From this list you can cancel a job by highlighting it, right clicking, and clicking **Cancel Documents**.

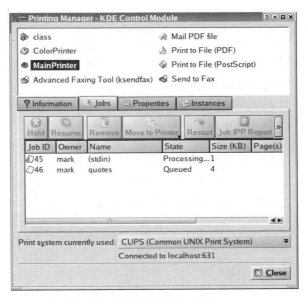

Figure 14-11   The KDE Printing Manager

```
$ gnome-print-manager &
```

When you ask the GNOME Print Manager to configure or add a printer and when you start it when no printers are configured, it calls [system|redhat]-config-printer (page 487).

The KDE Printing Manager

KDE includes a printing abstraction layer (**kprinter**) that provides the print dialog box for KDE applications and a utility for managing printers (Figure 14-11). Give the command **kcmshell printmgr** to display the Printing Manager window; this is the same window that **Control Center: Peripherals -> Printers** displays. You can use the related kprinter utility to print files.

The **kprinter** abstraction layer is not a stand-alone program and does not replace CUPS. Rather, **kprinter** is an interface between an application or user submitting a print job and the printing system. KDE's Printing Manager provides much of the same functionality as CUPS and can use CUPS as a printing mechanism. With proper permissions, the Printing Manager

- **Starts print jobs**   You can start a print job with the Printing Manager, as well as from a command line or within an application.
- **Controls print jobs**   The Printing Manager can display information on each of your print jobs. From these windows, you can cancel print jobs

(even when they have started printing), hold and release print jobs, and move print jobs to different queues (as long as they have not started printing). You can also send a print job as a fax or save it as a PDF or PostScript file.

- **Works with printers**   You can add, remove, and modify printers and their properties.

- **Works with multiple printing systems**   The Printing Manager works with CUPS, LPRng, RLPR, PDQ, and other printing systems.

- **Works with filters**   The Printing Manager allows you to import existing printing *filters* (page 971) or to install new ones.

The benefits of the Printing Manager are such that you may wish to use it from non-KDE applications. For example, the Mozilla Web browser, as shipped by Red Hat, prints using lpr. You can change Mozilla so that it uses kprinter by following these steps:

- Start Mozilla and select **File -> Print** from the Menubar.
- Click **Properties** in the Printer frame to display the Mozilla Printer Properties window.
- Change the command that starts with **lpr** in the Print Command text box to **kprinter --stdin**. This command runs kprinter and causes it to take its input from standard input.
- Click **OK**.

With these changes, when you print from Mozilla, kprinter opens a window that allows you to control where the be printed output goes. Select the printer you want to use at the top of the window, make any other changes in the window as appropriate, and click **Print**.

Refer to the *KDEPrint Handbook* (click "Help" from the kprinter window) for more information.

Integration with Windows

This section explains how to use Linux printers from Windows computers and how to use Windows printers from Linux systems.

Printing from Windows

This section assumes that Samba (page 675) is installed and working on the Linux system that controls the printer you want to use from Windows. Samba must be set up so that the Windows user who will be printing is mapped to a Linux user (including mapping the Windows **guest** user to the Linux user **nobody**). Make sure that these users have Samba passwords. Refer to "Samba Users, User Maps, and Passwords" on page 677.

Windows supports printer sharing via SMB, allowing a printer to be shared transparently between Windows systems using the same mechanism as file sharing. Samba allows Windows users to use printers connected to Linux systems just as they use any other shared printers. Because all Linux printers traditionally appear to be PostScript printers, the Linux print server appears to share a PostScript printer. Windows does not include a generic PostScript printer driver. Instead, Windows users must select a printer driver for a PostScript printer. The Apple Color LaserWriter driver is a good choice.

When you use rpm to install Samba, it creates a directory named **/var/spool/samba** that is owned by **root** and that anyone can read from and write to. The sticky bit (page 998) is set for this directory, allowing a Windows user who starts a print job as a Linux user to be able to delete that job, but not allowing users to delete print jobs of other users. Make sure this directory is in place and has the proper ownership and permissions:

```
$ ls -ld /var/spool/samba
drwxrwxrwt   2 root     root          4096 Feb 24 12:29 /var/spool/samba
```

Put the following two lines in the [global] section of the **/etc/smb.conf** file:

```
[global]
...
printing = cups
printcap name = cups
```

The printer's share is listed in the [printers] section in **smb.conf**. Following, the **path** is the path Samba uses as a spool directory and is not a normal share path. The following settings allow anyone, including **guest**, to use the printer. Setting **use client driver** to YES causes Windows systems to use their own drivers. Not setting this option, or setting it to NO, can cause printing from Windows not to work. Make sure the [printers] section in **smb.conf** has the following entries:

```
[printers]
comment = All Printers
path = /var/spool/samba
printer admin = root
guest ok = Yes
printable = Yes
use client driver = Yes
browseable = No
```

Ideally, each user who is going to print should have an account. When multiple users share the same account (for example, the **nobody** account), these users can delete each other's print jobs.

Modern versions of Windows (2000 and later) support IPP and, as a result, can communicate directly with CUPS. To use this feature, you must have CUPS configured on the Linux print server to allow remote IPP printing and you need to create a new printer on the Windows system that points to the IP address of the Linux print server. The details involved in configuring a Windows machine are beyond the scope of this book. You can use testparm (page 694) and testprns to check the syntax of the Samba setup.

Printing to Windows

CUPS views a printer on a Windows computer exactly the same way it views any other printer. The only difference is the URI you need to specify when connecting it. To configure a printer connected to a Windows machine, go to the Printers page in the CUPS Web interface. From here, select **Add Printer**, as you would for a local printer.

When you are asked to select the device, choose **Windows Printer via SAMBA**. Next, enter the URI of the printer using the following format: **smb://*windows_system*/*printer_name***. Once you have added the printer, you can use it as you would any other printer.

Chapter Summary

A printing system such as CUPS sets up printers and moves a print job from an application or the command line through the appropriate filters into a queue for a suitable printer and prints it.

CUPS is a cross-platform print server built around the IPP printing protocol. CUPS handles setting up and sending jobs through print queues. The easiest way to work with CUPS is to use the Web interface which you can connect to by pointing a Web browser at **localhost:631** on the printer system connected to the printer. From the Web interface, you can configure print queues and modify print jobs in the queues.

You can use the traditional UNIX commands from a command line to send jobs to a printer (lpr/lp), display a print queue (lpq/lpstat), and remove jobs from a print queue (lprm/cancel). In addition, CUPS provides the lpinfo and lpadmin utilities to configure printers from the command line.

Samba enables you to print on a Linux printer from a Windows system and vice versa.

Exercises

1. What commands can you use from a command line to send a file to the default printer?

2. What command would you give to cancel all your print jobs?

3. What commands list your outstanding print jobs?

4. What is the purpose of sharing a Linux printer using Samba?

5. Name three printing protocols that CUPS supports. Which is the CUPS native protocol?

Advanced Exercises

6. What command lists the installed printer drivers available to CUPS?

7. How would you send a text file to a printer connected to the first parallel port without using a print queue? Why is doing this not a good idea?

8. Assume you have a USB printer with a manufacturer-supplied PostScript printer definition file named **newprinter.ppd.** What command would you use to add this printer to the system on the first USB port with the name **USBPrinter**?

9. How would you define a quota that would allow each user to print up to 50 pages per week to the printer named **LaserJet**?

10. Define a set of access control rules for a <Location> container inside **/etc/cups/cupsd.conf** that would allow anyone to print to all printers as long as they were either on the local machine or in the **mydomain.com** domain.

Rebuilding the Linux Kernel

15

Once you have installed Red Hat Enterprise Linux or Fedora Core, you may want to reconfigure and rebuild the Linux kernel. Red Hat comes with a prebuilt kernel that simplifies the installation process. This kernel may not be properly configured for all your system's features. By reconfiguring and rebuilding the kernel, you can build one that is customized for your system and needs.

tip ‖   **Maybe You Just Need to Install a New Linux Kernel Binary?**

Refer to "Installing a Linux Kernel Binary" on page 458 when you want to install a Linux kernel binary that you do not need to configure or build.

Because recent releases of the Linux kernel are modular, you do not usually need to rebuild them. You can dynamically change many things that used to require rebuilding the kernel. Two ways to make these changes are using boot options or modifying /etc/sysctl.conf, which is used by sysctl when the system is booted.

grub   If you are using grub, append *string* to the **kernel** line in **/boot/grub/grub.conf** or to its symbolic link, **/etc/grub.conf**. For example, **norelocate** prevents the substitution of CPU-specific optimizations and **selinux=0** turns off SELinux.

lilo   The **append** kernel configuration parameter in **/etc/lilo.conf** appends a string to the parameter line that is passed to the kernel. You can use this parameter to specify parameters so you do not have to rebuild the kernel, parameters that cannot be detected automatically, and parameters you do not want to probe for. The following example turns off the Advanced Power Management BIOS:

```
append="apm=off"
```

See the *BootPrompt HOWTO* for more information.

sysctl   The sysctl utility modifies kernel parameters while the system is running. This utility uses the facilities of **/proc/sys**, which defines the parameters that sysctl can modify.

You can get a complete list of sysctl parameters with a **sysctl −a** command. An example of displaying and changing the **domainname** kernel parameter follows. The quotation marks are not required in this example but will quote any characters that would otherwise be interpreted by the shell.

```
# /sbin/sysctl kernel.domainname
kernel.domainname = tcorp.com
# /sbin/sysctl -w kernel.domainname="testing.com"
kernel.domainname = testing.com
```

caution ‖   **Have the First Installation CD at Hand When You Rebuild the Kernel**

When you rebuild the Linux kernel to install a new version or to change the configuration of the existing version, make sure that you have the First Installation CD handy. This disk allows you to reboot your computer, even when you have destroyed your system software completely. (You can also use the rescue CD. See page 39.) Always follow these instructions; having this CD can make the difference between momentary panic and a full-scale nervous breakdown. Refer to "Rescue Mode" on page 377 for instructions on bringing the system up in rescue mode.

Rebuilding a Linux kernel is fairly straightforward. When you do need to rebuild the kernel, perform the steps described in this chapter.

Preparing the Source Code

Before you can start, you must locate/install and clean the source code. If you want code that has not been customized (patched) by Red Hat, go to kernel.org.

Locating the Source Code

When you have the kernel source on your system, the **/usr/src** directory will look something like the following:

```
$ ls -l /usr/src
total 8
drwxr-xr-x  19 root root 4096 Apr 28 21:49 linux-2.6.5-1.327
drwxr-xr-x   7 root root 4096 Apr 28 21:47 redhat
```

In the preceding example, the name **linux-2.6.5-1.327** means that the directory contains version 2.6 of the Linux kernel, release 5-1.327. If the source code is present on your system, skip to "Cleaning the Source Tree" on page 509.

Installing the Source Code

When the source is not present on your system, you need to install it. The easiest way to install the kernel source is by giving the command **up2date kernel-source**. See page 462 for more information on up2date.

Alternatively, you can load the kernel source from the installation CD set or the Red Hat/Fedora Web site. You need **kernel-source*.rpm**. The kernel used in the examples comes from **kernel-source-linux-2.6.5-1.327.i386.rpm**. You need to work as **root** to use rpm to install the kernel package. You can also use yum (page 469) or Apt (page 472) to download and install the kernel source.

Once you have located the **kernel-source** rpm package, give an rpm command to install it. The following command installs the **kernel-source** rpm package from the directory that contains the package (refer to "rpm: Red Hat Package Manager" on page 455 for more information on using rpm):

```
$ rpm -ivh kernel-source*.rpm
```

Do not use the –U option as it overwrites the source for the existing kernel. You generally want to keep old kernel source code around for a while after you install a new kernel in case you need to go back to the old kernel.

---

tip ‖   **Now the Working Directory Is /usr/src/linux***

All commands in this section on building a kernel are given relative to the top-level directory that holds the kernel source. Make sure that this directory is your working directory before proceeding. The working directory for the examples in this chapter is **/usr/src/linux-2.6.5-1.327**.

Read the Documentation

The kernel package includes the latest documentation, some of which may not be available in other documents. Review the **README** file and the relevant files in the **Documentation** directory. Read the *Linux Kernel-HOWTO* for an excellent, detailed generic guide to installing and configuring the Linux kernel.

Configuring and Compiling the Linux Kernel

This section describes how to configure the kernel to meet your needs and how to compile it.

Cleaning the Source Tree

If you want to save the existing configuration file (**/usr/src/linux*/.configure**), copy it to another directory (such as your home directory) before you proceed, because the following command removes it. Purge the source tree (all the subdirectories and files within **/usr/src/linux***) of all configuration and potentially stale ***.o** files by giving the following command:

```
$ make mrproper
```

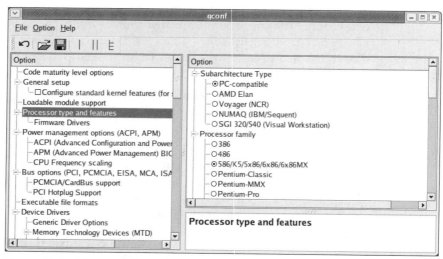

Figure 15-1   The qconf window as displayed by **make xconfig** on Fedora

Configuring the Linux Kernel

Before you can compile the code and create the Linux kernel, you must decide and specify what features you want the kernel to support. A kernel can support most features in two ways: by building the feature into the kernel or by specifying the feature as a loadable kernel module (page 512), which is loaded into the kernel only as needed. Trade off the size of the kernel against the time it takes to load a module. Make the kernel as small as possible while minimizing how often modules have to be loaded. Do not make the SCSI driver modular unless you have reason to do so.

The **configs** directory has sample configuration files for various processors, multiple processors, and configurations. You may want to look at these before you get started or even use one of these as your starting point. To use one of these files, copy it from the **configs** directory to the **linux**✷ directory and rename it .config.

The three standard commands to configure the Linux kernel are

```
$ make config
$ LANG=C make menuconfig
$ make xconfig
```

FEDORA   The **LANG=C** is required before the **make menuconfig** command because the default encoding in Fedora is UTF8, which the kernel's build routines do not understand. The **make xconfig** command uses Qt (www.trolltech.com), which is normally installed with KDE or GNOME under Fedora. If you prefer to use GTK+ (www.gtk.org) and it is installed on the system, give the command **make gconfig**.

RHEL   Under Red Hat Enterprise Linux, the **make xconfig** command uses Tk.

Each command asks the same questions and produces the same result, given the same responses. The first and second commands work in character-based environ-

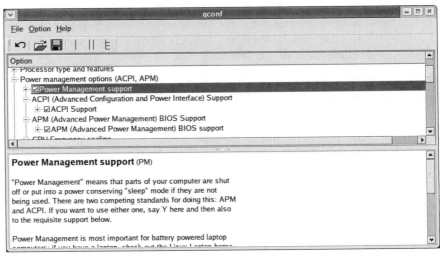

Figure 15-2   The qconf Processor Type submenu

ments; the second and third commands work in graphical environments. For most administrators in most situations, the third (graphical) method is the easiest to use (Figures 15-1, and 15-2). The figures show the windows displayed by Fedora; the Red Hat Enterprise Linux windows look different but perform the same function.

The **make xconfig** command displays the qconf window. You can view the qconf window in three configurations: single, split, or full view. Choose a view by clicking one of the three icons to the right of the floppy diskette on the toolbar. Figure 15-1 shows the default split view. In the split view, the left frame shows the options and the top-right view lists the features for each option. The bottom-right view describes the highlighted option or feature. Figure 15-2 shows the full view.

In any view, click the boxes and circles next to the choices and subchoices: An empty box/circle indicates the feature is disabled, a check mark indicates it is to be included in the kernel, and a dot means it is to be compiled as a module. Select **Menubar: Options⇨Show All Options** to display all options and features.

Go through the options and mark the features as you would like them to be configured in the new kernel. At any time during the configuration process, you can store the currently defined configuration to a file, load a configuration from a file, or exit with or without saving. See the selections in File on the Menubar. When you are done, select **Menubar: File⇨Save** and close the window.

EXTRAVERSION Number

To prevent overwriting existing kernel files and to identify various compilations of the kernel, you can use the **EXTRAVERSION** variable in **Makefile**. This variable is initially set to a dash and the release number, followed by the word **custom** (for example –2.6.5-1.327custom). Whatever value you assign to this variable is placed at the end of the kernel name. It is a good idea to keep the original release number, but you can append the date or time to ensure a unique name for each kernel you build. You can also make note of patches you applied to the kernel in this string to help people track down problems later on.

Compiling the Linux Kernel

Before compiling the kernel, make sure, once again, that no files are in the source tree from previous work:

```
$ make clean
```

Then give the following command to compile the kernel:

```
$ make bzImage
CHK     include/linux/version.h
UPD     include/linux/version.h
SYMLINK include/asm -> include/asm-i386
SPLIT   include/linux/autoconf.h -> include/config/*
HOSTCC  scripts/basic/fixdep
HOSTCC  scripts/basic/split-include
HOSTCC  scripts/basic/docproc
...
```

Using Loadable Kernel Modules

A *loadable kernel module* (page 980) (sometimes called a *module* or *loadable module*) is an object file, part of the kernel, that is linked into the kernel at runtime. Modules are compiled separately from the kernel and can be inserted into and removed from a running kernel at almost any time except when the module is being used. This ability gives the kernel the flexibility to be as small as possible at any given time. Modules are a good way to code some kernel features, including drivers that are not used all the time (such as a tape driver).

tip ‖   **Module Filename Extensions Have Changed**

Filenames of modules in the 2.4 and earlier kernels ended in **.o**. Starting with the 2.6 kernel (Fedora Core 2 and greater), module filenames end in **.ko**.

If you are not using loadable kernel modules, skip to "Installing the Kernel and Associated Files" on page 513. If you do not know for a fact that you are *not* using loadable modules, you probably are, so continue with this section.

When you configure the kernel to support loadable modules, you need to build and install the modules. Give the following command to compile the modules that you specified when you configured the kernel:

```
$ make modules
```

The next command installs the modules in the **/lib/modules/*kernel-versionEXTRA-VERSION*** directory. Run this command as **root** even when you did not build any modules:

```
# make modules_install
```

Table 15-1 lists some of the tools that can help you work with modules. Refer to the corresponding man pages for options and more information.

table 15-1 ‖	Tools for Working with Modules
depmod	Works with dependencies for modules.
insmod	Loads modules in a running kernel.
lsmod	Lists information about all loaded modules.
modinfo	Lists information about a module.
modprobe	Loads, unloads, and reports on modules. When it loads a module, it also loads dependencies.
rmmod	Unloads modules from a running kernel.

Installing the Kernel and Associated Files

Next, copy the compiled kernel and associated files to the appropriate directory, usually either root (**/**) or **/boot**. When you have a **boot** partition, the files are kept in the root of this partition (**/boot**). Without a **boot** partition, the files are kept in the root directory. Run the following command as **root** to install the new kernel files in the proper directory:

```
# make install
```

Changing lilo.conf (RHEL)

If you are using lilo (Fedora Core does not support lilo), edit **/etc/lilo.conf**, and add a section giving the absolute pathname of the new kernel image and, when you use modules, the pathname of the **initrd** file. Run lilo to make your changes to **lilo.conf** take effect. Refer to "lilo: The Linux Loader (**RHEL**)" on page 516 for details.

grub.conf

When using grub, you do not have to make any changes to **/etc/grub.conf**.

Rebooting

Reboot the computer by logging out and selecting **Reboot** from the login screen (Figure 4-1, page 77). If you are working at the console, you can press CONTROL-ALT-DEL or give a **reboot** command.

Boot Loader

A boot loader is a very small program that takes its place in the *bootstrap* (page 960) process, which brings a computer from off or reset to a fully functional state. It frequently resides on the starting sectors of a hard disk called the MBR (Master Boot Record).

The *BIOS* (page 959), stored in an *EEPROM* (page 969) on the system's motherboard, gains control of a system when you turn it on or reset it. After testing the hardware, the BIOS transfers control to the MBR, which usually passes control to the partition boot record. This transfer of control starts the boot loader, which is responsible for locating the operating system kernel (kept in the **/** or **/boot** directory), loading that kernel into memory and starting it running. Refer to "Booting the System" on page 381 for more information on what happens from this point forward.

You can place the **/boot** directory on a very small filesystem that is near the beginning of the hard drive where the BIOS can access it. With this setup, the root (**/**) filesystem can be anywhere on any hard drive that Linux can access and that perhaps the BIOS cannot.

grub: The Linux Loader

The term grub (see the grub info page and www.gnu.org/software/grub) stands for Grand Unified Boot Loader. The grub loader is a product of the GNU project and conforms to the *multiboot specification* (page 984), which allows it to load many free operating systems directly, as well as *chain loading* (page 962) proprietary operating systems. In many ways, grub is more flexible than lilo. The grub loader can recognize various types of filesystems and kernel executable formats, allowing it to load an arbitrary operating system: You must specify the kernel's filename and location (drive and partition). You can pass this information to grub by using either the command line or the menu interface. When you boot the system, grub displays a menu of choices that is generated by the **/boot/grub/grub.conf** file (or see its symbolic link, **/etc/grub.conf**). At this point you can modify the menu, choose which operating system to boot, or do nothing and allow grub to boot the default system.

When you install a Red Hat Enterprise Linux, you have the choice of using grub or lilo. Fedora runs grub only. When you install grub at the time you install Linux on a system, the installation program configures grub, and you do not have to.

The **/boot/grub/grub.conf** file is the default grub configuration file and is similar in function to **/etc/lilo.conf**. The **grub.conf** file following is from a system that had its kernel replaced (there are two versions of **vmlinuz** and **initrd**). The system has a separate **boot** partition so that all kernel and **initrd** (for systems using loadable modules, page 512) image paths are relative to **/boot/** (see the NOTICE in the file). Without a separate **boot** partition, the boot files reside in the root partition (**/**) so that kernel and **initrd** paths are relative to **/**. (Thus you would specify the kernel as **kernel /vmlinuz-*version***, replacing ***version*** with the version number of the kernel.)

The file starts with comments that Anaconda, the graphical installer, puts there, followed by three assignments. The **default** is the section number of the default boot specification. The numbering starts with 0. The following example includes two boot specifications. The first, numbered 0, is for the **2.6.5-1.327custom** kernel, and the second, numbered 1, is for the **2.6.5-1.327** kernel. The **timeout** is the number of seconds that grub waits after it has prompted you for a boot specification before it boots the system with the default boot specification. The **splashimage** is the grub menu interface background that you see when you boot the system.

```
$ cat /etc/grub.conf
# grub.conf generated by anaconda
#
# Note that you do not have to rerun grub after making changes to this file
# NOTICE:  You have a /boot partition.  This means that
#          all kernel and initrd paths are relative to /boot/, eg.
#          root (hd0,0)
#          kernel /vmlinuz-version ro root=/dev/hda10
#          initrd /initrd-version.img
default=1
timeout=10
splashimage=(hd0,0)/grub/splash.xpm.gz
title Fedora Core (2.6.5-1.327custom)
        root (hd0,0)
        kernel /vmlinuz-2.6.5-1.327custom ro root=LABEL=/ rhgb quiet
        initrd /initrd-2.6.5-1.327custom.img
title Fedora Core (2.6.5-1.327)
        root (hd0,0)
        kernel /vmlinuz-2.6.5-1.327 ro root=LABEL=/ rhgb quiet
        initrd /initrd-2.6.5-1.327.img
```

Following the **splashimage** assignment in the preceding example are two boot specifications, differentiated by the **title** lines as explained previously. The three lines following the title line in each specification specify the location of the **root** (drive 0, partition 0), **kernel**, and **initrd** images. In this case, because there is a **/boot** partition, the pathnames are relative to **/boot**. For the default boot specification (the second one, numbered 1), the absolute pathname of the kernel is **/boot/vmlinuz-2.6.5-1.327custom**, which is specified with the options **ro root=LABEL=/ rhgb quiet**.

These options tell grub that it is to be mounted readonly and that root (**/**) is mounted on the device labeled **/** in **/etc/fstab** (page 445). The **rhgb** (Red Hat graphical boot) is the software that generates a graphical display that tells you what is going on as the system boots. The **quiet** option produces less debugging output so it is easier to tell what is happening. You specify the **initrd** (initialize *RAM disk,* page 991) image in a manner similar to the kernel. Substitute your kernel and **initrd** names and version numbers for the ones in the example. Make sure that when you install a new kernel manually, its **title** line is different from the others present in **grub.conf.**

lilo: **The Linux Loader** (*RHEL*)

The term lilo (Linux loader) applies to both the Linux loader utility and the boot loader that lilo writes to the beginning of the active partition on the hard drive or to a floppy. Although written to support Linux, lilo is a general-purpose boot loader that can start many operating systems, including DOS, OS/2, Windows, and versions of BSD. You can configure lilo to select from various operating systems and versions of the Linux kernel each time you start your system (called *dual booting*).

When you run lilo without any options, it reads **/etc/lilo.conf** to determine which operating systems are to be made available at boot time. Then it writes this information to the MBR. You must run lilo to reinstall the boot loader whenever you change **/etc/lilo.conf**, as when you rebuild the Linux kernel.

The **/etc/lilo.conf** file gives you a great deal of control over lilo:

```
$ cat /etc/lilo.conf
# lilo configuration file
boot=/dev/hda
map=/boot/map
install=/boot/boot.b
prompt
timeout=50
default=linux

image=/boot/vmlinuz-2.4.18-14custom
        label=linux
        initrd=/boot/initrd-2.4.18-14custom.img
        read-only
        root=/dev/hda12
```

Comments in the **lilo.conf** file start with a pound sign (#) and run through the end of the line, just as they do in a shell script. In the example, the first line that is not a comment identifies the disk that holds the Master Boot Record: **/dev/hda**. The next line gives the location of the map file. The **install** line tells lilo where to find the file it is to install as the boot loader. The **prompt** presents the user with a **boot:** prompt, whereas **timeout** gives the time (in tenths of a second) that the system will wait before booting automatically. When you set **prompt** and do not set **timeout**, the system cannot boot automatically. Press TAB in response to the **boot:** prompt to see the choices.

Protect lilo.conf Too

When you protect the images specified in **lilo.conf** with passwords, also change permissions on **lilo.conf** to 600, as anyone can read it with its default permissions.

The lilo boot loader allows you to specify more than one boot image. The **default** line specifies the label of the image to boot if none is specified, such as when you press RETURN in response to the **boot:** prompt. In this example, the label of the default (and only) image is **linux** (see the **label** line). The **image** line specifies the boot image of the Linux kernel. The **initrd** line initializes the boot loader *RAM disk* (page 991), which is used in the first phase of the system boot when you use loadable modules (page 512). Specify the **read-only** line for *every* image on a Linux system so it is safe to run fsck automatically as you bring the system up.

You can add lines to **lilo.conf** to pass arguments to the Linux kernel, adjust for strange disk geometries, require passwords to start specific kernels, and add many other options. See the **lilo.conf** man page for the technical details and the **/usr/share/doc/lilo**＊**/doc** directory for the User and Technical Guides. View the ＊**.ps** files with gs (ghostscript).

Before you modify an existing **lilo.conf** file, save the existing configuration as **lilo.conf.old** or **lilo.conf.1**. Then edit **lilo.conf** and create a new section that looks similar to the preceding example. Use the kernel version number and **EXTRAVER-SION** (page 511) in place of **2.4.18-14custom**.

If you use modules, set up the appropriate **initrd** line in **lilo.conf**:

```
initrd=/boot/initrd-2.4.18-14custom.img
```

When you are finished editing **lilo.conf**, run lilo to write the new information to the MBR.

LOADLIN: A DOS-Based Linux Loader

The LOADLIN loader, a DOS utility that loads Linux from DOS and some versions of Windows, can load big kernels (**bzImage**) and RAM disk images (**initrd**). Refer to elserv.ffm.fgan.de/~lermen, where you can find the *LOADLIN Users Guide* and other information. See also the *Loadlin+Win95/98/ME mini-HOWTO*.

dmesg: Display Kernel Messages

The dmesg utility displays the kernel-ring buffer, where the kernel stores messages. When the system boots, the kernel fills this buffer with messages regarding hardware and module initialization. Messages in the kernel-ring buffer are often useful for diagnosing system problems. Run dmesg to view the messages:

```
$ dmesg
...
VFS: Disk quotas vdquot_6.5.1
Detected PS/2 Mouse Port.
pty: 2048 Unix98 ptys configured
Serial driver version 5.05c (2001-07-08) with MANY_PORTS MULTIPORT
SHARE_IRQ SER
IAL_PCI ISAPNP enabled
ttyS0 at 0x03f8 (irq = 4) is a 16550A
ttyS1 at 0x02f8 (irq = 3) is a 16550A
Real Time Clock Driver v1.10e
NET4: Frame Diverter 0.46
RAMDISK driver initialized: 16 RAM disks of 8192K size 1024 blocksize
...
```

The dmesg utility, which is frequently used with grep, is useful if you are having hardware-related problems. If you find that your hard disks are performing poorly, you can use dmesg to check that they are running in DMA mode:

```
$ dmesg | grep DMA
...
ide0: BM-DMA at 0xa400-0xa407, BIOS settings: hda:pio, hdb:DMA
ide1: BM-DMA at 0xa408-0xa40f, BIOS settings: hdc:DMA, hdd:DMA
...
```

The preceding lines tell you which mode each IDE device is operating in.

If you are having problems with the Ethernet connection, search the dmesg log for eth:

```
$ dmesg | grep eth
eth0: RealTek RTL8139 Fast Ethernet at 0xe4d05000, 00:d0:70:01:a0:64, IRQ 5
eth0:  Identified 8139 chip type 'RTL-8139C'
eth0: link up, 100Mbps, full-duplex, lpa 0x45E1
```

If everything is working properly, dmesg displays the hardware configuration information for each network card. If you have configured a system service incorrectly, the dmesg log quickly fills up with errors; it is a good place to start when diagnosing faults.

Chapter Summary

This chapter describes how to rebuild the Linux kernel. Sometimes you do not need to rebuild the kernel; you can dynamically change many things by using boot options in **/etc/lilo.conf** or **/etc/grub.conf**, or by modifying **/etc/sysctl.conf**.

Before you can rebuild the kernel, you must have the kernel source files on the system. These files are located in **/usr/src/linux***. The chapter discusses the steps involved in compiling and installing both the kernel and loadable modules. It concludes with a discussion of the dmesg utility, which displays the kernel-ring buffer, where the kernel stores messages.

Exercises

1. What is the purpose of the kernel?
2. How would you display a list of all loaded modules in the current kernel?
3. What command would you give to upgrade the kernel from an rpm file, and how is this different from upgrading other packages?
4. How would you display information from the kernel about the hard disk on the first IDE channel?
5. The **noreplacement** kernel argument tells the kernel not to use CPU-specific sections of code. How would you use this argument?
6. What is a boot loader?

Advanced Exercises

7. What is the EXTRAVERSION variable? Where is it used and what is it used for?
8. You have just installed an Adaptec SCSI card. How can you find out if it has been recognized and which entry in **/dev** represents it?
9. When you install an experimental kernel for testing, how do you instruct grub not to load it by default?
10. How would you obtain a list of all network-related kernel parameters?

Administration Tasks 16

The system administrator has many responsibilities. This chapter discusses tasks not covered in Chapter 11, including configuring user and group accounts, backing up files, scheduling tasks, general problem solving, and using the system log daemon, **syslogd**.

Configuring User and Group Accounts

More than a login name is required for a user to be able to log in and use the system. A user should have the necessary files, directories, permissions, and usually a password in order to log in. Minimally, a user must have an entry in the **/etc/passwd** and **/etc/shadow** files and a home directory. The following sections describe several ways you can work with user accounts. Refer to page 354 and the *NIS-HOWTO* when you want to run NIS to manage the **passwd** database.

system-config-users: Manages User Accounts

The system-config-users (*FEDORA*) and redhat-config-users (*RHEL*) utilities display the User Manager window and enable you to add, delete, and modify system users and groups. The User Manager Window has two tabs: Users and Groups, each tab displaying information appropriate to its name. Figure 16-1 shows the Users tab.

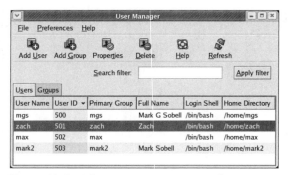

Figure 16-1   The User Manager window

Search filter   The Search filter, located just below the toolbar, selects users or groups whose names match the string, which can include wildcards that you enter in the Search filter text box. The string matches the beginning of a name. For example, *nob matches **nobody** and **nfsnobody**, whereas **nob** matches only **nobody**. After you enter the string, click **Apply filter** or press RETURN. If you have only a few users, you will not need to use the Search filter.

Adding a user   To create a new user, click the **Add User** button on the toolbar. The User Manager displays the Create New User window, which holds the same information as the User Data tab of the User Properties window (Figure 16-2). Enter the information for the new user and click **OK**. Refer to page 379 for information on SELinux. Once you create a user, you can modify the user to add/change/remove information.

Modifying a user   To modify a user, highlight the user in the User Manager window and click **Properties** on the toolbar; the utility displays the User Properties window (Figure 16-2). The User Properties window has four tabs: User Data, Account Info, Password Info, and Groups. The User Data tab holds basic user information such as name and password. The Account Info tab allows you to specify an expiration date for the account and to lock the account so the user cannot log in. The Password Info tab

Figure 16-2   The User Properties window, User Data tab

allows you to turn on password expiration and specify various related parameters. In the Groups tab, you can specify the groups that the user is a member of.

Working with groups Click the **Groups** tab in the User Manager window to work with groups. To create a group, click **Add Group** on the toolbar and specify the name of the group. To change the name of a group or add or remove users from a group, highlight the group and click Properties on the toolbar. Click the appropriate tab, make the changes you want, and click **OK**.

Help The User Manager has extensive help: Click **Help** on the toolbar.

When you are done working with users and groups, close the window.

useradd: **Adds a User Account**

The useradd utility (and the link to it, named adduser) adds new user accounts to the system. By default, useradd assigns the next highest unused user ID to a new account and specifies the bash as the user's login shell. The following example creates the user's home directory (in **/home**), specifies the user's group ID, and puts the user's full name in the comment field:

```
# useradd -g 500 -c "Alex Watson" alex
```

Based on the **/etc/login.defs** file, the system creates a home directory for the new user. When useradd creates a home directory, it copies the contents of **/etc/skel**, which contains bash and other startup files, to that directory. For more information on adding and modifying user information, see the useradd and usermod man pages. Once you have added a user, use passwd to give the user a password.

userdel: **Removes a User Account**

If appropriate, make a backup copy of the files belonging to the user before deleting them. The userdel utility deletes user accounts. The following command removes **alex**'s account, his home directory, and all his files:

```
# userdel -r alex
```

To turn off a user's account temporarily, you can use usermod to change the expiration date for the account. Because it specifies that his account expired in the past (December 31, 2003), the following command line prevents **alex** from logging in:

```
# usermod -e "12/31/03" alex
```

groupadd: **Adds a Group**

Just as useradd adds a new user to the system, groupadd adds a new group by adding an entry to **/etc/group**. The following example creates a new group, named **rtfm**:

```
# groupadd -g 1024 rtfm
```

Unless you use the –g option to assign a group ID, the system picks the next available sequential number greater than 500. The –o option allows the group ID to be nonunique if you want to have multiple names for the same group ID.

The analogue of userdel for groups is groupdel, which takes a group name as an argument. You can also use groupmod to change the name or group ID of a group, as in the following examples:

```
# groupmod -g 1025 rtfm
# groupmod -n manuals rtfm
```

The first example gives the previously created **rtfm** group a new group ID number. The second example renames the **rtfm** group **manuals**.

---

caution || **Group ID Cautions**

The groupmod utility does not change group numbers in **/etc/passwd** when you renumber a group. You must edit **/etc/passwd** and change the entries yourself. If you change the number of a group, files that belonged to the group will no longer belong to the group. They may belong to no group or to another group with the old group ID number.

Backing Up Files

One of the most neglected tasks of system administration is making backup copies of files on a regular basis. The backup copies are vital in three instances: when the system malfunctions and files are lost, when a catastrophic disaster (fire, earthquake, and so on) occurs, and when a user or the system administrator deletes or corrupts a file by accident. Even when you set up RAID (page 31), you still need to back up files. Although RAID is useful for fault tolerance (disk failure), it does not help in a catastrophic disaster or when a file is accidentally removed or corrupted. It is a good idea to have a written backup policy and to keep copies of backups offsite (in another building, at home, or at a completely different facility or campus) in a fireproof vault or safe.

The time to start thinking about backups is when you partition the disk. Refer to "Partitioning a Disk" on page 29. Make sure the capacity of the backup device and your partition sizes are in line. Although you can back up a partition onto multiple volumes, it is easier not to and much easier to restore from a single volume.

You must back up filesystems on a regular basis. Backup files are usually kept on magnetic tape or other removable media. Exactly how often you should back up which files depends on your system and needs. The criterion is: If the system crashes, how much work are you willing to lose? Ideally, you would back up all the files on the system every few minutes so you would never lose more than a few minutes of work.

The tradeoff is: How often are you willing to back up the files? The backup procedure typically slows down the system for other users, takes a certain amount of your time, and requires that you have and store the media (tape or disk) you keep the backup on. Avoid backing up an active filesystem; the results may be inconsistent, and restoring from the backup may be impossible. This requirement is a function of the backup program and the filesystem you are backing up.

Another question is when to run the backup. Unless you kick the users off and bring the system down to single-user mode (not a very user-friendly practice), you want to do it when the machine is at its quietest. Depending on the use of the system, sometime in the middle of the night can work well. Then the backup is least likely to impact the users, and the files are not likely to change as they are being read for backup.

A *full* backup makes copies of all files, regardless of when they were created or accessed. An *incremental* backup makes copies of the files that have been created or modified since the last (usually full) backup.

The more people using the machine, the more often you should back up the filesystems. A common schedule might have you perform an incremental backup one or two times a day and a full backup one or two times a week.

Choosing a Backup Medium

Traditionally, personal computers used floppy diskettes for performing backups. However, the large, hard disks now available for computers makes this impractical. If you have a ninety gigabyte disk on your system, you would need more than 72,000 floppy diskettes to do a full backup. Even if files are compressed as you back them up, the number of diskettes required would be unmanageable. If your computer is connected to a network, you can write your backups to a tape drive on another system. This is often done with networked computers to avoid the cost of having a tape drive on each computer in the network and to simplify management of doing backups for many computers in a network. Most likely you want to use a tape system for backing up your computer. Because tape drives to hold many gigabytes of data are available, using tape simplifies the task of backing up the system, making it more likely that you regularly do this important task. Other options for holding backups are writable CDs, DVDs, and removable hard disks. These devices, although not as cost-effective or able to store as much information as tape systems, offer convenience and improved performance over using tapes.

Backup Utilities

A number of utilities help you back up the system, and most work with any media. Most Linux backup utilities are based on one of the archive programs—tar or cpio—and augment these basic programs with bookkeeping support for managing backups conveniently.

You can use any one of the tar, cpio, or dump/restore utilities to construct full or partial backups of the system. Each utility constructs a large file that contains, or archives, other files. In addition to file contents, an archive includes header information for each file it holds. This header information can be used when extracting files from the archive to restore file permissions and modification dates. An archive file can be saved to disk, written directly to tape, or shipped across the network while it is being created.

In addition to helping you back up your system, these programs are convenient for bundling files for distribution to other sites. The tar program is often used for this purpose, and some software packages available on the Internet are bundled as tar archive files.

The amanda (Advanced Maryland Automatic Network Disk Archiver— www.amanda.org) utility, one of the more popular backup systems, uses dump or tar and takes advantage of Samba to back up Windows systems. The amanda utility backs up a LAN of heterogeneous hosts to a single tape drive. It is available under Red Hat; refer to the amanda man page for details.

tar: Archives Files

The tar (tape archive) utility stores and retrieves files from an archive and can compress the archive to conserve space. You can specify an archive device with the –f option. If you do not specify an archive device, tar uses /dev/rmt0 (which may not exist on the local system). With the –f option, tar uses the argument to –f as the name of the archive device. You can use this option to refer to a device on another system on the network. Although a lot of options are available with tar, you need only a few in most situations. The following command displays a complete list of options:

```
# tar --help | less
```

Most options for tar can be given either in a short form (a single letter) or as a descriptive word. Descriptive-word options are preceded by two dashes, as in --help. Single-letter options can be combined into a single command line argument and do not need to be preceded by a dash (for consistency with other utilities, it is good practice to use the dash anyway).

Although the following two commands look quite different, they specify the same tar options in the same order. The first version combines single-letter options into a single command line argument; the second version uses descriptive words for the same options:

```
# tar -ztvf /dev/st0
# tar --gzip --list --verbose --file /dev/st0
```

Both commands tell tar to generate a (v, verbose) table of contents (t, list) from the tape on /dev/st0 (f, file), using gzip (z, gzip) to decompress the files. Unlike the original UNIX tar, the GNU version strips the leading / from absolute pathnames.

The options in Table 16-1 tell the tar program what you want it to do. You must include exactly one of these options whenever you use tar.

table 16-1 || **The tar Utility**

Option	Effect
--append (-r)	Appends files to an archive.
--catenate (-A)	Adds one or more archives to the end of an existing archive.
--create (-c)	Creates a new archive.
--delete	Deletes files in an archive (not on tapes).
--dereference (-h)	Follows symbolic links.
--diff (-d)	Compares files in an archive with disk files.
--extract (-x)	Extracts files from an archive.
--help	Displays a help list of tar options.
--list (-t)	Lists the files in an archive.
--update (-u)	Like the **-r** option, but the file is not appended if a newer version is already in the archive.

The **-c**, **-t**, and **-x** options are used most frequently. You can use many other options to change how tar operates. The **-j** option compresses/decompresses the file by filtering it through bzip2 (page 133).

cpio: Archives Files

The cpio (copy in/out) program is similar to tar but can use archive files in a variety of formats, including the one used by tar. Normally, cpio reads the names of the files to insert into the archive from standard input and produces the archive file as standard output. When extracting files from an archive, cpio reads the archive as standard input.

As with tar, some options can be given in both a short, single-letter form and a more descriptive word form. However, unlike tar, the syntax of the two forms differs when the option must be followed by additional information. In the short form, you must, use a SPACE between the option and the additional information; with the word form, you must separate the two with an equal sign and no SPACEs.

Running cpio with **--help** displays a full list of options, although not as nice a list as tar.

Performing a Simple Backup

When you prepare to make a major change to a system, such as replacing a disk drive or updating the Linux kernel, it is a good idea to archive some or all of the files so you can restore any that are damaged if something goes wrong. For this type of backup, tar or cpio works well. For example, if you have a SCSI tape drive as device /dev/st0 that is capable of holding all your files on a single tape, you can use the following commands to construct a backup tape of the entire system:

```
# cd /
# tar -cf /dev/st0 .
```

This command creates an archive (c) on the device /dev/st0 (f). All the commands in this section start by using cd to change to the root directory so you are sure to back up the entire system. If you would like to compress the archive, replace the preceding tar command with the following command, which uses j to call bzip2:

```
# tar -cjf /dev/st0 .
```

You can back up your system with a combination of find and cpio. The following commands create an output file and set the I/O block size to 5120 bytes (the default is 512 bytes):

```
# cd /
# find . -depth | cpio -oB > /dev/st0
```

The next command restores all the files in the /home directory from the preceding backup. The options extract files from an archive (–i) in verbose mode, keeping the modification times and creating directories as needed.

```
# cd /
# cpio -ivmd /home/\* < /dev/st0
```

---

tip ‖   **Exclude Some Directories from a Backup**

In practice, you exclude some directories from the backup process. For example, not backing up /tmp or /var/tmp (or its link, /usr/tmp) can save room in the archive. Also, do not back up the files in /proc. Because the /proc filesystem is not a disk filesystem but rather a way for the Linux kernel to provide you with information about the operating system and system memory, you need not back up /proc; you cannot restore it later. You do not need to back up filesystems that are mounted from disks on other computers in your network. Do not back up FIFOs; the results are unpredictable. If you plan on using a simple method, similar to those just shown, create a file naming the directories to exclude from the backup, and use the appropriate option with the archive program to read the file.

Although any of the archive programs works well for such simple backups, only amanda provides a sophisticated backup and restore system. For example, to determine whether a file is in an archive requires you to read the entire archive. If the archive is split across several tapes, this is particularly tiresome. More sophisticated utilities, including amanda, assist you in several ways, including keeping a table of contents of the files in a backup.

dump, restore: **Back Up and Restore Filesystems**

The dump utility, first seen in UNIX version 6, backs up an entire filesystem, or only those files that have changed since the last dump. The restore utility restores an entire filesystem, an individual file, or a directory hierarchy. You will get the best results if you perform a backup on a quiescent system so that the files are not changing as you make the backup.

The following command performs a complete backup of all files (including directories and special files) on the **root** (**/**) partition onto SCSI tape 0. Frequently, there is a link to the active tape drive, named **/dev/tape**, which you can use in place of the actual entry in the **/dev** directory.

```
# dump -0uf /dev/st0 /
```

The option specifies that the whole filesystem is to be backed up (a full backup). There are ten dump levels: 0–9. Zero is the highest (most complete) level and always backs up the entire filesystem. Each additional level is incremental with respect to the level above it. For example, 1 is incremental to 0 and backs up only files that have changed since the last level 0 dump. Level 2 is incremental to 1 and backs up only files that have changed since the last level 1 dump, and so on. You can construct a very flexible schedule by using this scheme. Also, you do not need to use sequential numbers for backup levels. You can perform a level 0 dump, followed by level 2 and 5 dumps.

The **u** option updates the **/etc/dumpdates** file (page 427) with filesystem, date, and dump level information for use by the next incremental dump. The **f** option and its argument (**/dev/st0**) write the backup to the file named **/dev/st0**.

The following command makes a partial backup containing all the files that have changed since the last level 0 dump. The first argument is a 1, specifying a level 1 dump.

```
# dump -1uf /dev/st0 /
```

To restore an entire filesystem from a tape, first restore the most recent complete (level 0) backup. Do this carefully because restore can overwrite the existing filesystem. When you are logged in as Superuser, cd to the directory the filesystem is mounted on, and give the following command:

```
# restore -if /dev/st0
```

The **i** option invokes an interactive mode that allows you to choose which files and directories you would like to restore. As with dump, the **f** option specifies the name of the device that the backup tape is mounted on. When restore finishes, load the next lower-level (higher number) dump tape and issue the same restore command. If you have multiple incremental dumps at a particular level, always restore with the most recent one. You do not need to invoke restore with any special arguments to restore an incremental dump; it will restore whatever is on the tape.

You can also use restore to extract individual files from a tape using the **x** option and specifying the filenames on the command line. Whenever you restore a file, the restored file will be in your working directory. Before restoring files, make sure you are working in the right directory. The following commands restore the **etc/xinetd.conf** file from the tape in **/dev/st0**. The filename of the dumped file does not begin with a **/** because all dumped pathnames are relative to the filesystem that you dumped—in this case **/**. Because the restore command is given from the **/** directory, the file will be restored to its original location: **/etc/xinetd.conf**:

```
# cd /
# restore -xf /dev/st0 etc/xinetd.conf
```

If you use the **x** option without specifying a file or directory name to extract, the entire dumped filesystem is extracted. Use the **r** option to restore an entire filesystem without using the interactive interface. The following command restores the filesystem from the tape on **/dev/st0** into the working directory without interaction:

```
# restore -rf /dev/st0
```

You can also use dump and restore to access a tape drive on another system. Specify the file/directory as *host:file,* where *host* is the hostname of the system the tape drive is on and *file* is the file/directory you want to dump/restore.

Occasionally, restore may prompt you with

```
You have not read any volumes yet.
Unless you know which volume your file(s) are on you should start
with the last volume and work towards the first.
Specify next volume #:
```

Enter **1** (one) in response to this prompt. If the filesystem spans more than one tape or disk, this prompt allows you to switch tapes.

At the end of the dump, you will receive another prompt:

```
set owner/mode for '.'? [yn]
```

Answer **y** to this prompt when restoring entire filesystems or files that have been accidentally removed. Doing so will restore the appropriate permissions to the files and directories being restored. Answer **n** if you are restoring a dump to a directory other than the one it was dumped from; the working directory permissions and owner will be set to those of the person doing the restore (typically **root**).

Various device names can access the **/dev/st0** device. Each name accesses a different minor device number that controls some aspect of how the tape drive is used. After you complete a dump when you use **/dev/st0**, the tape drive automatically rewinds the tape to the beginning. Use the nonrewinding SCSI tape device (**/dev/nst0**) to keep the tape from rewinding on completion. This feature allows you to back up multiple filesystems to one volume. Following is an example of backing up a system where the **/home**, **/usr**, and **/var** directories are on different filesystems:

```
# dump -0uf /dev/nst0 /home
# dump -0uf /dev/nst0 /usr
# dump -0uf /dev/st0 /var
```

The preceding example uses the nonrewinding device for the first two dumps. If you use the rewinding device, the tape rewinds after each dump, and you are left with only the last dump on the tape. For more information, refer to the mt (magnetic tape) man page.

You can use mt to manipulate files on a multivolume dump tape. The following mt command positions the tape (**fsf 2** instructs mt to skip forward *past* two files, leaving the tape at the start of the third file). The restore command restores the **/var** filesystem from the previous example:

```
# mt -f /dev/st0 fsf 2
# restore rf /dev/st0
```

Scheduling Tasks

It is a good practice to schedule certain routine tasks to run automatically. For example, you may want to remove old core files once a week, summarize accounting data daily, and rotate system log files monthly.

cron **and** crontab: **Schedule Routine Tasks**

Using crontab, you can submit a list of commands in a format that can be read and executed by cron. As Superuser, you can put commands in one of the **/etc/cron.** * directories to be run at intervals specified by the directory name, such as **cron.daily**.

---

tip || cron **Stops for No One; Try** anacron

The cron utility assumes the system it is running on is always running. A similar utility, anacron, does not make that assumption and is well suited to portable and home computers that are frequently turned off. The anacron utility takes its instructions from the **/etc/anacrontab** file unless you specify otherwise. Refer to the anacron and anacrontab man pages for more information.

---

at: **Runs Occasional Tasks**

Like the cron utility, at allows you to run a job sometime in the future. Unlike cron, at runs a job only once. For instance, you can schedule an at job that will reboot the system at 3 A.M. (when all users are logged off):

```
# at 3am
at> reboot
at> CONTROL-D <EOT>
job 1 at 2004-02-01 03:00
```

It is also possible to run an at job from within an at job. For instance, you could have an at job that would check for new patches every 18 days, something that would be more difficult with cron.

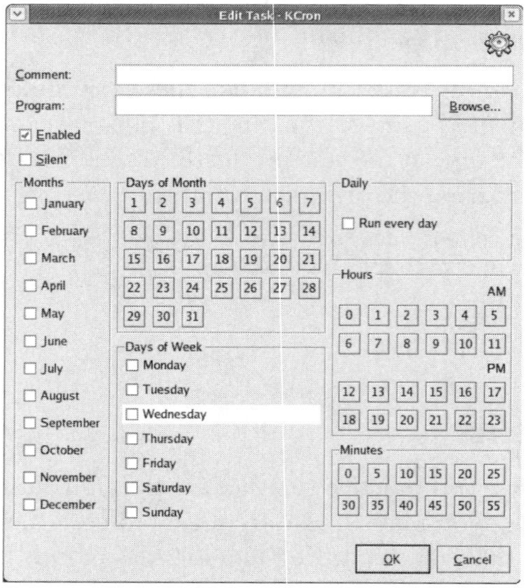

Figure 16-3   The kcron Task Scheduler

kcron: **Schedules Tasks**

The kcron utility provides an easy-to-use GUI to cron, allowing you to create and modify **crontab** files. Scheduling tasks with kcron is a matter of clicking buttons (Figure 16-3).

Run kcron when you are logged in as yourself to view and modify your personal **crontab** file. When you run kcron as **root**, you can modify any **crontab** file on the system. To start, kcron displays a window that lists Users (when you are running as **root**), Tasks, and Variables. The Description column of this window is very wide and does not fit in the window. Use the right-left scroll bar to view its contents. If you are running as **root**, you need to double-click a user to display the **Tasks** folder. To create a new **crontab** entry, highlight **Tasks**, and select **New** from **Edit** on the menubar (or from the right-click menu). To modify an entry, highlight the entry, and select **Modify** from **Edit** on the menubar. From the resulting window, enter the name of the program you want to run in the **Program** text box, and depress buttons or place check marks corresponding to the dates and times you want to run the program. Unless you redirect it, output from the program that kcron runs is mailed to you.

System Reports

Many utilities report on one thing or another. The who, finger, ls, ps, and other utilities generate simple end user reports. In some cases, these reports can help you with system administration. This section describes utilities that generate more in-depth reports that can usually be of more help with system administration tasks. Linux has many other report utilities, including sar (system activity report), iostat (input/output and CPU statistics), netstat (network report), mpstat (processor statistics), and nfsstat (NFS statistics).

vmstat: **Reports Virtual Memory Statistics**

The vmstat utility generates virtual memory information along with (limited) disk and CPU activity data. The following example shows virtual memory statistics in 3-second intervals for seven iterations (from the arguments 3 7). The first line covers the time since the system was last booted; the rest of the lines cover the period since the previous line:

```
$ vmstat 3 7
procs -----------memory---------- ---swap-- -----io---- --system-- ----cpu----
 r  b   swpd   free   buff  cache   si   so    bi    bo    in    cs us sy id wa
 0  2      0 684328  33924 219916    0    0   430   105  1052   134  2  4 86  8
 0  2      0 654632  34160 248840    0    0  4897  7683  1142   237  0  5  0 95
 0  3      0 623528  34224 279080    0    0  5056  8237  1094   178  0  4  0 95
 0  2      0 603176  34576 298936    0    0  3416   141  1161   255  0  4  0 96
 0  2      0 575912  34792 325616    0    0  4516  7267  1147   231  0  4  0 96
 1  2      0 549032  35164 351464    0    0  4429    77  1120   210  0  4  0 96
 0  2      0 523432  35448 376376    0    0  4173  6577  1135   234  0  4  0 95
```

The following list explains the column heads displayed by vmstat.

- **procs**   process information
  - **r**   number of waiting, runnable processes
  - **b**   number of blocked processes (in uninterruptable sleep)
- **memory**   memory information in kilobytes
  - **swpd**   used virtual memory
  - **free**   idle memory
  - **buff**   memory used as buffers
  - **cache** memory used as cache
- **swap**   system paging activity in kilobytes per second
  - **si**   memory swapped in from disk
  - **so**   memory swapped out to disk
- **io**   system I/O activity in blocks per second
  - **bi**   blocks received from a block device
  - **bo**   blocks sent to a block device
- **system**   values are per second
  - **in**   interrupts (including the clock)
  - **cs**   context switches

- **cpu**   percentage of total CPU time spent in each of these states

    - **us**   user (nonkernel)

    - **sy**   system (kernel)

    - **id**   idle (*RHEL* includes I/O wait time)

    - **wa**   waiting for I/O (*RHEL* shows zeroes)

top: Lists Processes Using the Most Resources

The top utility is a useful supplement to ps. At its simplest, top displays system information at the top and the most CPU-intensive processes below the system information. The top utility updates itself periodically; type **q** to quit. Although you can use command line options, the interactive commands are often more useful. Refer to Table 16-2 and to the top man page for more information.

```
$ top
top - 21:30:26 up 18 min,  2 users,  load average: 0.95, 0.30, 0.14
Tasks:  63 total,   4 running,  58 sleeping,   1 stopped,   0 zombie
Cpu(s): 30.9% us, 22.9% sy, 0.0% ni,  0.0% id, 45.2% wa, 1.0% hi, 0.0%si
Mem:   1036820k total,  1032276k used,    4544k free,   40908k buffers
Swap:  2048276k total,        0k used, 2048276k free,  846744k cached

  PID USER      PR  NI  VIRT  RES  SHR S %CPU %MEM    TIME+  COMMAND
 1285 root      25   0  9272 6892 1312 R 29.3  0.7  0:00.88 bzip2
 1276 root      18   0  3048  860 1372 R  3.7  0.1  0:05.25 cp
    7 root      15   0     0    0    0 S  0.7  0.0  0:00.27 pdflush
    6 root      15   0     0    0    0 S  0.3  0.0  0:00.11 pdflush
    8 root      15   0     0    0    0 S  0.3  0.0  0:00.06 kswapd0
  300 root      15   0     0    0    0 S  0.3  0.0  0:00.24 kjournald
 1064 mgs2      16   0  8144 2276 6808 S  0.3  0.2  0:00.69 sshd
 1224 root      16   0  4964 1360 3944 S  0.3  0.1  0:00.03 bash
 1275 mgs2      16   0  2840  936 1784 R  0.3  0.1  0:00.15 top
 1284 root      15   0  2736  668 1416 S  0.3  0.1  0:00.01 tar
    1 root      16   0  2624  520 1312 S  0.0  0.1  0:06.51 init
```

table 16-2 || **top: InteractiveCommands**

A	Sorts processes by age (newest first).
h or **?**	Displays a help screen.
k	Prompts for a PID number and type of signal and sends the process that signal. Defaults to signal 15 (SIGTERM); specify 9 (SIGKILL) only when 15 does not work.
M	Sorts processes by memory usage.
P	Sorts processes by CPU usage (default).
q	Quits.

table 16-2 ‖	top: Interactive Commands (Continued)
s	Prompts for time between updates in seconds. Use 0 for continuous updates.
SPACE	Updates display immediately.
T	Sorts tasks by time.
W	Writes a startup file named ~/.toprc so that next time you start top, it uses the same parameters it is currently using.

Keeping Users Informed

One of your primary responsibilities as system administrator is communicating with the system users. You need to make announcements, such as when the system will be down for maintenance, when a class on some new software will be held, and how users can access the new system printer. You can even start to fill the role of a small local newspaper, letting users know about new employees, RIFs, births, the company picnic, and so on.

Different communications have different priorities. Information about the company picnic in two months is not as time sensitive as the fact that you are bringing the system down in 5 minutes. To meet these differing needs, Linux provides different ways of communicating. The most common methods are described and contrasted in the following list. All these methods are generally available to everyone, except for the message of the day, which is typically reserved for Superuser.

write   Use write to communicate with a user who is logged in on the local system. You might use it to ask a user to stop running a program that is bogging down the system. The user might reply that he will be done in 3 minutes. Users can also use write to ask the system administrator to mount a tape or restore a file.

talk   The talk utility performs the same function as write but is more advanced. Although talk uses a character-based interface, it has a graphical appearance, showing what each user is typing as it is being typed. Unlike write, you can use talk to have a discussion with someone on another machine on the network.

wall   The wall (write all) utility effectively communicates immediately with all users who are logged in. It works similarly to write, except users cannot use wall to write back to only you. Use wall when you are about to bring the system down or are in another crisis situation. Users who are not logged in do not get the message.

Use wall while you are Superuser *only* in crisis situations; it interrupts anything anyone is doing.

email   Email is useful for communicating less urgent information to one or more system and/or remote users. When you send mail, you have to be willing to wait for each user to read it. The email utilities are useful for reminding users that they are forgetting to log out, bills are past due, or they are using too much disk space.

Users can easily make permanent records of messages they receive via email, as opposed to messages received via write or talk, so they can keep track of important details. It would be appropriate to use email to inform users about a new, complex procedure, so each user could keep a copy of the information for reference.

message of the day   Users see the message of the day each time they log in in a textual environment. You can edit the **/etc/motd** file to change the message. The message of the day can alert users to upcoming periodic maintenance, new system features, or a change in procedures.

Creating Problems

Even experienced system administrators make mistakes; new system administrators make more mistakes. Even though you can improve your odds by carefully reading and following the documentation provided with your software, many things can still go wrong. A comprehensive list is not possible, no matter how long, as new and exciting ways to create problems are discovered every day. A few of the more common techniques are described here.

Failing to Perform Regular Backups

Few feelings are more painful to a system administrator than realizing that important information is lost forever. If your system supports multiple users, having a recent backup may be your only protection from a public lynching. If it is a single-user system, having a recent backup certainly keeps you happier when you lose a hard disk.

Not Reading and Following Instructions

Software developers provide documentation for a reason. Even when you have installed a software package before, you should carefully read the instructions again. They may have changed, or you may simply remember them incorrectly. Software changes more quickly than books are revised, so no book should be taken as offering foolproof advice; look for the latest documentation online.

Failing to Ask for Help When Instructions Are Not Clear

If something does not seem to make sense, try to find out what does make sense; do not guess. Refer to "Help" on page 913.

Deleting or Mistyping a Critical File

One sure way to give yourself nightmares is to execute the command

```
# rm -rf /etc
```
←do not do this

Perhaps no other command renders a Linux system useless so quickly. The only recourse is to reboot into rescue mode (page 377) using the first installation CD and restore the missing files from a recent backup. Although this example is extreme, many files are critical to proper operation of a system. Deleting one of these files or mistyping information in one of them is almost certain to cause problems. If you directly edit **/etc/passwd**, for example, entering the wrong information in a field can make it impossible for one or more users to log in. Do not use **rm –rf** with an argument that includes wildcard characters; do pause after typing the command, and read it before you press RETURN. Check everything you do carefully, and make a copy of a critical file before you edit it.

Solving Problems

As the system administrator, it is your responsibility to keep the system secure and running smoothly. When a user is having a problem, it usually falls to the administrator to help the user get back on track. This section suggests ways to keep users happy and the system functioning at its peak.

Helping When a User Cannot Log In

When a user has trouble logging in on the system, the problem may be a user error or a problem with the system software or hardware. The following steps can help you determine where the problem is:

- Determine if only that one user or only that one user's terminal/ workstation has a problem or if the problem is more widespread.

- Check that the user's Caps Lock key is not on.

- Make sure the user's home directory exists and corresponds to that user's entry in the **/etc/passwd** file. Verify that the user owns his or her home directory and startup files and that they are readable (and, in the case of the home directory, executable). Confirm that the entry for the user's login shell in the **/etc/passwd** file is valid (that is, that the entry is accurate and that the shell exists as specified).

- Change the user's password if there is a chance that he or she has forgotten the correct password.

- Check the user's startup files (.**profile**, .**login**, .**bashrc**, and so on). The user may have edited one of these files and introduced a syntax error that prevents login.

- Check the terminal or monitor data cable from where it plugs into the terminal to where it plugs into the computer (or as far as you can follow it). Finally, try turning the terminal or monitor off and then turning it back on.

- When the problem appears to be widespread, check if you can log in from the system console. If you can, make sure that the system is in multiuser mode. If you cannot log in, the system may have crashed; reboot it and perform any necessary recovery steps (the system usually does quite a bit automatically).

- Check the **/etc/inittab** file to see that it is starting the appropriate login service (usually some form of getty, such as mingetty).

- Check the **/var/log/messages** file. This file accumulates system errors, messages from daemon processes, and other important information. It may indicate the cause or more symptoms of a problem. Also, check the system console. Occasionally messages about system problems that do not get written to **/var/log/messages** (for instance, if the disk is full) get displayed on the console.

- If the user is logging in over a network connection, use "system-config-services: Configures Services II" on page 383 to make sure that the service the user is trying to use (such as telnet or ssh) is enabled.

- Use df to check for full filesystems. Sometimes, if the **/tmp** filesystem or the user's home directory is full, login fails in unexpected ways. In some cases you may be able to log in to a textual environment but not a graphical one. When applications that start when the user logs in cannot create temporary files or cannot update files in the user's home directory, the login process itself may terminate.

Speeding Up the System

When the system is running slowly for no apparent reason, perhaps a process did not exit when a user logged out. Symptoms include poor response time and a system load, as shown by w or uptime, that is greater than 1.0. Use **ps –ef** to list all processes. The top utility is excellent for quickly finding rogue processes. One thing to look for in **ps –ef** output is a large number in the **TIME** field. For example, if you find a Netscape process that has a **TIME** field over 100.0, this process has likely run amok. However, if the user is doing a lot of Java work and has not logged out for a long time, this value may be normal. Look at the **STIME** field to see when the process was started. If the process has been running for longer than the user has been logged in, it is a good candidate to be killed.

When a user gets stuck and leaves his or her terminal unattended without notifying anyone, it is convenient to kill (page 375) all processes owned by that user. If the user is running a window system, such as GNOME or KDE on the console, kill the window manager process. Manager processes to look for include **startkde, gnome-**

session, or another process name that ends in **wm.** Usually the window manager is either the first or the last thing to be run, and exiting from the window manager logs the user out. If killing the window manager does not work, try killing the X server process itself. This process is typically listed as **/etc/X11/X.** If that fails, you can kill all processes owned by a user by running **kill –1 –1,** or equivalently **kill –TERM –1** as the user. Using **–1** (one) in place of the process ID tells kill that it should send the signal to all processes that are owned by that user. For example, as **root** you could type

```
# su jenny -c 'kill -TERM -1'
```

If this does not kill all processes (sometimes TERM does not kill a process), you can use the KILL signal. The following line will definitely kill all processes owned by Jenny and will not be friendly about it:

```
# su jenny -c 'kill -KILL -1'
```

(If you do not use **su jenny –c,** the same command brings the system down.)

lsof: Finds Open Files

The name lsof is short for ls open files; this utility locates open files. Its options let you look only at certain processes, look only at certain file descriptors of a process, or show certain network connections (network connections use file descriptors just as normal files do and lsof can show those as well). Once you have identified a suspect process using **ps –ef,** run the following command:

```
# lsof -sp pid
```

Replace *pid* with the process ID of the suspect process; lsof displays a list of all file descriptors that process *pid* has open. The **–s** option displays the size of all open files. The size information may be helpful in determining whether the process has a very large file open. If it does, contact the owner of the process or, if necessary, kill the process. The **–r**n option redisplays the output of lsof every n seconds.

Keeping a Machine Log

A machine log that includes the information shown in Table 16-3 can help you find and fix system problems. Note the time and date for each entry in the log. Avoid the temptation to keep the log *only* on the computer because it will be most useful to you at times when the machine is down. Another good idea is to keep a record of all email about user problems. One way to do this is to save all this mail to a separate file or folder as you read it. Another way is to set up a special mail alias that users send mail to when they have problems. This alias can then forward mail to you and also store a copy in an archive file. Following is an example of an entry in the **/etc/aliases** file (page 614) that sets up this type of alias:

```
trouble: admin,/var/mail/admin.archive
```

Email sent to the **trouble** alias will be forwarded to the **admin** user and also stored in the file **/var/mail/admin.archive.**

table 16-3 ||	Machine Log
Hardware modifications	Keep track of the system hardware configuration: which devices hold which partitions, the model of the new NIC you added, and so on.
System software modifications	Keep track of the options used when building Linux. Print such files as **/usr/src/linux∗/.config** (Linux kernel configuration), **/etc/modules.conf** (*RHEL*), and the X11 configuration file **/etc/X11/XF86Config** (*RHEL*) or **/etc/X11/xorg.conf** (*FEDORA*). The file hierarchy under **/etc/sysconfig** contains valuable information about network configuration and so on.
Hardware malfunctions	Keep as accurate a list as possible of any problems with the system. Make note of any error messages or numbers that the system displays on the system console and what users were doing when the problem occurred.
User complaints	Make a list of all reasonable complaints made by knowledgeable users (for example, "machine is abnormally slow").

Keeping the System Secure

No system with dial-in lines or public access to terminals is absolutely secure. You can make a system as secure as possible by changing the Superuser password frequently and choosing passwords that are difficult to guess. Do not tell anyone who does not *absolutely* need to know the Superuser password. You can also encourage system users to choose difficult passwords and to change them periodically.

By default, passwords on Red Hat Linux use *MD5* (page 982) hashing, which makes them more difficult to break than DES (page 924) encrypted passwords. It makes little difference how well encrypted your password is if you make it easy for someone to find out or guess what it is.

A password that is difficult to guess is one that someone else would not be likely to think you would have chosen. Do not use words from the dictionary (spelled forward or backward); names of relatives, pets, or friends; or words from a foreign language. A good strategy is to choose a couple of short words, include some punctuation (for example, put a ^ between them), mix the case, and replace a couple of the letters in the words with numbers. If it were not printed in this book, an example of a good password would be **C&yGram5** (candygrams). Ideally you would use a random combination of ASCII characters, but that would be difficult to remember.

You can use one of several excellent password-cracking programs to find users who have chosen poor passwords. These programs work by repeatedly encrypting words from dictionaries, phrases, names, and other sources. If the encrypted password matches the output of the program, then the program has found the password of the user. Two programs that crack passwords are crack and cops. These and many other security tips and programs are available from CERT (www.cert.org), which was originally called the *computer emergency response team*. Specifically look at www.cert.org/tech_tips.

Make sure that no one except Superuser can write to files containing programs that are owned by **root** and run in setuid mode (for example, mail and su). Also make sure that users do not transfer programs that run in setuid mode and are owned by **root** onto the system by means of mounting tapes or disks. These programs can be used to circumvent system security. One technique that prevents users from having setuid files is to use the **–nosuid** flag to mount, which you can set in the flags section in the **fstab** file. Refer to "fstab: Keeps Track of Filesystems" on page 445.

The BIOS in many machines gives you some degree of protection from an unauthorized person modifying the BIOS or rebooting the system. When you set up the BIOS, look for a section named *Security*. You can probably set up a BIOS password. If you depend on the BIOS password, lock the computer case. It is usually a simple matter to reset the BIOS password with access to a jumper on the motherboard.

Log Files and Mail for **root**

Users frequently email **root** and **postmaster** to communicate with the system administrator. If you do not forward **root**'s mail to yourself (refer to "/etc/aliases" on page 614), remember to check **root**'s mail periodically. You will not receive reminders about mail that arrives for **root** when you use su to perform system administration tasks. However, after using su to become **root**, you can give the command **mail –u root** to look at **root**'s mail.

Look at the system log files regularly for evidence of problems. Two important files are **/var/log/messages**, where the operating system and some applications record errors, and **/var/log/maillog**, which contains errors from the mail system. You can use system-logviewer (*FEDORA*) or redhat-logviewer (*RHEL*) to view many of the system logs.

The logwatch utility (**/usr/sbin/logwatch** points to the **/etc/log.d/scripts/logwatch.pl** Perl script) is a report writer that sends email reports on log files. By default, the script is run daily (**/etc/cron.daily/00-logwatch** also points to **/etc/log.d/scripts/logwatch.pl**) and emails its output to **root**. Refer to the logwatch man page and to the script itself for more information.

Monitoring Disk Usage

Sooner or later, you will probably start to run out of disk space. Do not fill up a disk; Linux can write to files significantly faster if at least 5 to 30 percent of the disk space in a given filesystem is free. The result is that using more than the maximum optimal disk space in a filesystem can degrade system performance.

Fragmentation   When the filesystem becomes full, it can become fragmented. This is similar to the DOS concept of fragmentation but is not nearly as pronounced and is typically rare on modern Linux filesystems; by design Linux filesystems are resistant to fragmentation. Keep filesystems from running near full capacity, and you may never need to worry about fragmentation. If there is no space on a filesystem, you cannot write to it at all.

To check on fragmentation, you can unmount the filesystem and run fsck on it. As part of fsck execution, fragmentation is computed and displayed. You can defragment a filesystem by backing it up, using mkfs (page 397) to make a clean, empty image, and then restoring the filesystem. The utility that you use to do your backup and restore is irrelevant and completely up to you. You can use dump/restore, tar, cpio, or a third-party backup program.

Reports   Linux provides several programs that report on who is using how much disk space on what filesystems. Refer to the du, quot, and df man pages and the –size option in the find utility man page. In addition to these utilities, you can use the disk quota system to manage disk space.

The main ways to increase the amount of free space on a filesystem are to compress files, delete files, grow filesystems, and condense directories. This section contains some ideas on ways to maintain a filesystem so that it does not get overloaded.

Files that grow quickly   Some files, such as log files and temporary files, grow over time. Core dump files take up space and are rarely needed. Also, users occasionally run programs that accidentally generate huge files. As the system administrator, you must review these files periodically so that they do not get out of hand.

If a filesystem is running out of space quickly (that is, over a period of an hour rather than weeks or months), first figure out why it is running out of space. Use a **ps –ef** command to determine whether a user has created a runaway process that is creating a huge file. In evaluating the output of ps, look for a process that has used a large amount of CPU time. If such a process is running and creating a large file, the file will continue to grow as you free up space. If you remove the huge file, the space it occupied will not be freed until the process terminates, so you need to kill the process. Try to contact the user running the process, and ask the user to kill it. If you cannot contact the user, log in as **root** and kill the process. Refer to kill on page 375 for more information.

You can also truncate a large log file rather than removing it, although you can better deal with this recurring situation with logrotate. For example, if the **/var/log/messages** file has become very large because a system daemon is misconfigured, you can use **/dev/null** to truncate it:

```
# cp /dev/null /var/log/messages
```

or

```
# cat /dev/null > /var/log/messages
```

or, without spawning a new process,

```
# : > /var/log/messages
```

If you remove **/var/log/messages**, you have to restart the **syslogd** daemon. Without restarting **syslogd**, the space on the filesystem is not released.

When no single process is consuming the disk space but it has instead been used up gradually, locate unneeded files and delete them. You can archive them by using cpio, dump, or tar before you delete them. You can safely remove most files named core that have not been accessed for several days. The following command line performs this function without removing necessary files named **core** (such as **/dev/core**):

```
# find / -type f -name core | xargs file | grep 'B core file' | sed 's/:ELF.*//g' | xargs rm -f
```

The find command lists all ordinary files named **core** and sends its output to xargs, which runs file on each of the files in the list. The file utility displays a string that includes **B core file** for files created as the result of a core dump. These files need to be removed. The grep command filters out from file lines that do not contain this string. Finally, sed removes everything following the colon so that all that is left on the line is the pathname of the **core** file; xargs removes the file.

Look through the **/tmp** and **/var/tmp** directories for old temporary files and remove them. Keep track of disk usage in **/var/mail**, **/var/spool**, and **/var/log**.

logrotate: **Manages Log Files**

Rather than deleting or truncating log files, you may want to keep the contents around for a while in case you need to refer to them. The logrotate utility helps you manage system log (and other) files automatically by *rotating* (page 994), compressing, mailing, and removing each as you specify. The logrotate utility is controlled by the **/etc/logrotate.conf** file, which sets default values and can optionally specify files to be rotated. Typically, **logrotate.conf** has an include statement that points to utility-specific specification files in **/etc/logrotate.d**. Following is the default **logrotate.conf** file:

```
$ cat /etc/logrotate.conf
# see "man logrotate" for details
# rotate log files weekly
weekly

# keep 4 weeks worth of backlogs
rotate 4

# create new (empty) log files after rotating old ones
create

# uncomment this if you want your log files compressed
#compress

# RPM packages drop log rotation information into this directory
include /etc/logrotate.d

# no packages own wtmp -- we'll rotate them here
/var/log/wtmp {
    monthly
    create 0664 root utmp
    rotate 1
}

# system-specific logs may be also be configured here.
```

The **logrotate.conf** file sets default values for common parameters. Whenever logrotate runs into another value for one of these parameters, it resets the default value. You have a choice of rotating files **daily, weekly,** or **monthly**. The number following the **rotate** keyword specifies the number of rotated log files that you want to keep. The **create** keyword causes logrotate to create a new log file with the same name and attributes as the newly rotated log file. The **compress** keyword (commented out in the default file) causes log files to be compressed using gzip. The **include** keyword specifies the standard **/etc/logrotate.d** directory for program-specific logrotate specification files. When you install a program using rpm (page 455), rpm puts the logrotate specification file (if it is part of the package) in this directory.

The last set of instructions in **logrotate.conf** takes care of the **/var/log/wtmp** log file (wtmp holds login records; you can view this file with the command **who /var/log/wtmp**). The keyword **monthly** overrides the default value of **weekly** *for this utility only* (because the value is within brackets). The **create** keyword is followed by the arguments establishing the permissions, owner, and group for the new file. Finally, **rotate** establishes that one rotated log file should be kept.

The **/etc/logrotate.d/samba** file is an example of a utility-specific logrotate specification file:

```
$ cat /etc/logrotate.d/samba
/var/log/samba/*.log {
    notifempty
    missingok
    sharedscripts
    copytruncate
    postrotate
        /bin/kill -HUP `cat /var/run/smbd.pid /var/run/nmbd.pid /var/run/winbindd.pid
2> /dev/null` 2> /dev/null || true
    endscript
}
```

This file, which is incorporated in **/etc/logrotate.d** because of the **include** statement in **logrotate.conf**, works with each of the files in **/var/log/samba** that has a filename extension of **log** (***.log**). The **notifempty** keyword causes logrotate not to rotate the log file if it is empty, overriding the default action of rotating empty log files. The **missingok** keyword means that no error will be issued when the file is missing. The **sharedscripts** keyword causes logrotate to execute the command(s) in the **prerotate** and **postrotate** sections one time only, not one time for each log that is rotated. The **copytruncate** keyword causes logrotate to truncate the original log file immediately after it copies it. This keyword is useful for programs that cannot be instructed to close and reopen their log files because they might continue writing to the original file even after it has been moved. The commands between **postrotate** and **endscript** are executed after the rotation is complete. Similarly, commands between **prerotate** and **endscript** are executed before the rotation is started.

The logrotate utility has many keywords, and many of these take arguments and have side effects. Refer to the logrotate man page for details.

Removing Unused Space from Directories

A directory with too many filenames in it is inefficient. The point at which a directory on an **ext2** or **ext3** filesystem becomes inefficient varies, depending partly on the length of the filenames it contains. Keep your directories relatively small. Having fewer than a few hundred files (or directories) in a directory is generally a good idea, and having more than a few thousand is generally a bad idea. Additionally, Linux uses a caching mechanism for frequently accessed files to speed the process of locating an inode from a filename. This caching mechanism works only on filenames of up to 30 characters in length, so avoid extremely long filenames for frequently accessed files.

When you find a directory that is too large, you can usually break it into several smaller directories by moving its contents into new directories. Make sure that you remove the original directory once you have moved its contents.

Because Linux directories do not shrink automatically, removing a file from a directory does not shrink the directory, even though it makes more space on the disk. To remove unused space and make a directory smaller, you must copy or move all the files into a new directory and remove the original directory.

The following procedure removes unused directory space. First, remove all unneeded files from the large directory. Then create a new, empty directory. Next, move or copy all the remaining files from the old large directory to the new empty directory. Remember to copy hidden files. Finally, delete the old directory and rename the new directory:

```
# mkdir /home/alex/new
# mv /home/alex/large/* /home/alex/large/.[A-z]* /home/alex/new
# rmdir /home/alex/large
# mv /home/alex/new /home/alex/large
```

optional ‖

Disk Quota System

The disk quota system limits the disk space and number of files owned by individual users. You can choose to limit each user's disk space, the number of files each user can own, or both. Each resource that is limited has two limits. The lower limit, or *quota*, can be exceeded by the user, although a warning is presented each time the user logs in when he or she is above the quota. After a certain number of warnings (set by the system administrator), the system will behave as if the user had reached the upper limit. Once the upper limit is reached or the user has received the specified number of warnings, the user will not be allowed to create any more files or use any more disk space. The user's only recourse at that point is to remove some files.

Users can review their usage and limits with the quota command. Superuser can use quota to obtain information about any user.

First, you must decide which filesystems to limit and how to allocate space among users. Typically, only filesystems that contain users' home directories, such as **/home**, are limited. Use the edquota command to set the quotas, and then use quotaon to start the quota system. You will probably want to put the quotaon command into the appropriate init script so that the quota system will be enabled when you bring up the system (page 381). Unmounting a filesystem automatically disables the quota system for that filesystem.

syslogd: Logs System Messages

Traditionally, UNIX programs sent log messages to standard error. If a more permanent log was required, the output was redirected to a file. Because of the limitations of this approach, 4.3BSD introduced the system log daemon (**syslogd**) that Linux uses. This daemon listens for log messages and stores them in the **/var/log** hierarchy. In addition to providing logging facilities, **syslogd** allows a single machine to serve as a log repository for a network and allows arbitrary programs to process specific log messages.

syslog.conf   The **/etc/syslog.conf** file stores configuration information for **syslogd**. Each line in this file contains a *selector* and an *action*, separated by whitespace. The selector defines the origin and type of the message and the action specifies how **syslogd** is to process the message. Sample lines from **syslog.conf** follow (a **#** indicates a comment):

```
# Log all kernel messages to the console.
kern.*                                  /dev/console
# Log all the mail messages in one place.
mail.*                                  /var/log/maillog
# Log cron stuff
cron.*                                  /var/log/cron
# Everybody gets emergency messages
*.emerg                                 *
# Save boot messages also to boot.log
local7.*                                /var/log/boot.log
```

Selectors   A selector is split into two parts, a *facility* and a *priority*, separated by a period. The facility indicates the origin of the message; for example, **kern** messages come from the kernel and **mail** messages come from the mail subsystem. Following is a list of facility names used by **syslogd** and the systems that generate these messages:

auth	Authorization and security systems including login
authpriv	Same as **auth**, but should be logged to a secure location
cron	cron
daemon	System and network daemons without their own categories
kern	Kernel
lpr	Printing subsystem
mail	Mail subsystem

news	Network news subsystem
user	Default facility; all user programs use this
uucp	The UNIX to UNIX copy protocol subsystem
local0 to local7	Reserved for local use

The priority indicates the severity of the message. The following list of the priority names and the conditions they represent is in priority order:

debug	Debugging information
info	Information not requiring intervention
notice	Conditions that may require intervention
warning	Warnings
err	Errors
crit	Critical conditions such as hardware failures
alert	Conditions requiring immediate attention
emerg	Emergency conditions

A selector consisting of a single facility and priority, such as **kern.info,** causes the corresponding action to be applied to every message from that facility with that priority *or higher* (more urgent). Use .= to specify a single priority (**kern.=info** applies the action to kernel messages of **info** priority). An exclamation point specifies that a priority is not matched, so **kern.!info** matches kernel messages with a priority lower than **info** and **kern.!=info** matches kernel messages with a priority other than **info.**

A line with multiple selectors, separated by semicolons, applies the action if any of the selectors is matched. Each of the selectors on a line with multiple selectors constrains the match, with subsequent selectors frequently tightening the constraints. For example, the selectors **mail.info;mail.!err** match mail subsystem messages with **info, notice,** or **warning** priorities.

You can replace either part of the selector with an asterisk to match anything. Similarly, the keyword **none** in either part of the selector indicates no match is possible. The selector ***.crit;kern.none** matches all critical or higher messages, except those from the kernel.

Actions The action specifies how **syslogd** processes a message that matches the selector. The simplest actions are regular files, specified by an absolute pathname; **syslogd** appends messages to these files. Because a terminal is represented by a device file, you can specify **/dev/console** to have messages sent to the system console. If you want a hard copy record of messages you can specify a device file that represents a dedicated printer.

You can write important messages to a specific user's terminal by specifying a username, such as **root,** or a comma-separated list of usernames. Very important messages can be written to every logged-in terminal by using an asterisk.

To forward messages to **syslogd** on a remote system, specify the name of the system preceded by @. It is a good idea to forward critical messages from the kernel to another system because these messages often precede a system crash and may not be saved to the local disk. The following line from **syslog.conf** sends critical kernel messages to **grape**:

```
kern.crit       @grape
```

Chapter Summary

This chapter starts by describing how to use system-config-users (*FEDORA*) and redhat-config-users (*RHEL*) to add new users and groups to the system and how to modify existing users' accounts. It also explains how to use the equivalent command line tools to work with user accounts. The section on making backups explains how to use the tar, cpio, dump, and restore utilities to back up and restore files.

The section on scheduling tasks discusses cron, the system scheduling daemon, and how to schedule tasks using crontab, at, and KDE's kcron. The system reports section covers vmstat, which details virtual memory, I/O, and CPU statistics, and top, a useful tool to see how the system is performing from moment to moment and help you figure out what might be slowing it down. The final sections cover general problem solving, discussing several tools that can help track down system problems. One of the most important of these tools is **syslogd**, the system log daemon. Using **/etc/syslogd.conf**, you can control which error messages appear on the console, which are sent as email, and which go to one of several log files.

Exercises

1. How would you list all the processes running vi?

2. How would you use kill to cause a server process to reread its configuration files?

3. From the command line, how would you create a user named John Doe who has the username **jd** and who belongs to group 65535?

4. How would you notify the users of the system that you are going to reboot the system in ten minutes?

5. Give a command that will create a level 0 dump of the **/usr** filesystem on the first tape device on the system. What command would you use to take advantage of a drive that supports compression? What command would place a level 3 dump of the **/var** filesystem immediately after the level 0 dump on the tape?

Advanced Exercises

6. If your system is not as responsive as it usually is, what is a good first step in figuring out where the problem is?

7. A process stores its PID in a file named **process.pid**. What command line will terminate the process?

8. Working as **root,** you are planning to delete some files but want to make sure that the wildcard expression you will use is correct. Suggest two ways you could make sure that you deleted the correct files.

9. Create a cron file that will regularly perform the following backups:

   a. Performs a level 0 backup once per month.

   b. Performs a level 2 dump one day per week.

   c. Performs a level 5 dump every day that neither a level 0 nor a level 2 dump is performed.

   In the worst case, how many restores would you have to perform to recover a file that was dumped using the preceding schedule?

Configuring a LAN

17

Networks allow computers to communicate and share resources. A local area network (LAN) connects together computers at one site, such as an office, home, or library, and can allow the connected computers to share an Internet connection and a printer. Of course, one of the most important reasons to set up a LAN is to allow systems to communicate while users play multiplayer games.

This chapter covers the two aspects of configuring a LAN: setting up the hardware and configuring the software. This chapter is not necessarily organized in the order you will perform the tasks involved in setting up a particular LAN: Read the chapter through, figure out how you are going to set up the LAN, then read the parts of the chapter in the order appropriate to your setup.

Setting Up the Hardware

Each system, or node, on a LAN must have a network interface card (NIC). NICs can be connected to the network with cables or radio waves (wireless); in either case, there must be a hub that each of the systems connects to. If the network is connected to another network, such as the Internet, it must also have a router, or gateway. The router can be one of the systems on the LAN or a dedicated piece of hardware.

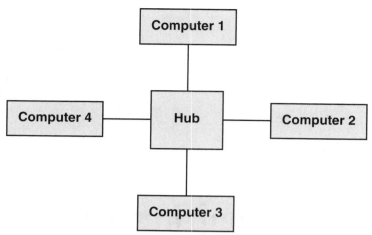

Figure 17-1   A simple network

Connecting the Computers

A modern Ethernet-based LAN has a connection between each computer and a central hub. There are two kinds of hubs: passive (sometimes just called a *hub*) and switching (called a *switch*). A passive hub simply connects all systems together and shares the network bandwidth among the systems. A switching hub puts each system on its own network with the switch and routes packets between those networks, providing each system with the full network bandwidth.

In the simple network shown in Figure 17-1, four computers are connected to a single hub. Assuming the hub is passive, when computers 1 and 2 are communicating at the same time as computers 3 and 4, each conversation is limited to a maximum of half the network bandwidth. If the hub were a switch, each conversation could use the full network bandwidth.

Usually, hubs are less expensive than switches. If you are planning on using a network for sharing an Internet connection and light file sharing, a hub is likely to be fast enough. If systems on the network are going to exchange files regularly, a switch may be more appropriate. Refer to "Ethernet" on page 327 for a discussion of switches, hubs, and cables.

Each computer on a LAN must be connected to the hub. If you are using use more than one hub, connect the port labeled uplink on one to a normal port on another.

Wireless access point (WAP)   A wireless access point (WAP) connects a wireless network to a wired one. Typically, a WAP acts as a transparent bridge, forwarding packets between the two networks as if they were one. If you connect multiple WAPs in different locations to the same wired network, it is possible for wireless clients to roam transparently between the WAPs.

Wireless networks do not require a hub, although a WAP can optionally fill a similar role. In a wireless network, the bandwidth is shared among all the nodes within range of each other; the maximum speed is limited by the slowest node.

Gateways and Routers

If the LAN you are setting up is connected to another network, such as the Internet, you need a router, sometimes called a gateway. A router can perform several functions, the most common of which is allowing several systems to share a single Internet connection and IP address (masquerading). When a router masquerades packets, the packets from each system on the LAN appear to come from a single IP address; return packets are passed back to the correct system.

There are several choices for routers:

- A simple hardware router is relatively cheap and does most things required by a small network.
- You can set up a Red Hat Linux system as a router. The Linux kernel can use iptables to route packets between network adapters.
- You can use a Linux distribution tailored for use as a router. For example, SmoothWall (www.smoothwall.org) provides a browser-based configuration in the style of a hardware router.

Network Interface Card (NIC)

Each system's NIC may be a separate Ethernet card (wired or wireless) or it may be built into the motherboard.

Supported NICs   Linux supports most wired Ethernet NICs. Fewer wireless NICs are supported. See "More Information" on page 559 for references.

Unsupported wireless NICs   If a wireless network card is not supported under Linux directly, you may be able to get it to work with NdisWrapper (ndiswrapper.sourceforge.net), which uses Win32 drivers. NdisWrapper is a kernel module that provides a subset of the Windows network driver API.

Wireless bridge   An alternative to a wireless NIC is a wireless bridge. A wireless bridge forwards packets between wired and wireless interfaces, eliminating the need for wireless drivers. It is a simple device with an ethernet port that plugs into a NIC and an 802.11 (wireless) controller. While carrying a bridge around is usually not possible for mobile users, it is an easy way to migrate a desktop computer to a wireless configuration.

Mode   Wireless networks operate in either ad hoc or infrastructure mode. In ad hoc mode, individual nodes in the network communicate directly with each other. In infrastructure mode, nodes communicate via a WAP (page 552). Infrastructure mode is generally more reliable if the wireless LAN communicates with a wired LAN.

If you do not want to use a WAP, it may be possible to set up a WLAN card so it acts as a WAP; consult the NIC/driver documentation.

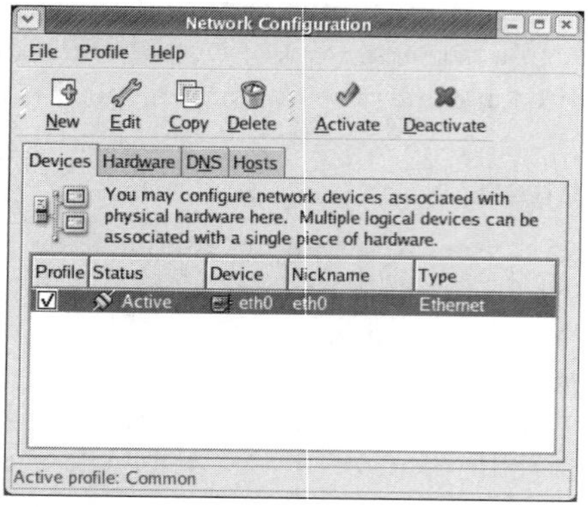

Figure 17-2   The Network Configuration window, Devices tab

Configuring the Systems

kudzu Once the hardware is in place, you need to configure each system so that it knows about the NIC that connects it to the network. Normally, kudzu, the Red Hat utility that detects and configures new hardware, gives the system the information it needs about the NIC. The kudzu utility probes the NIC when you install Red Hat Linux or the first time you boot after you install a NIC.

You can use system-config-network (next) to augment the information kudzu collects and to activate the NIC. When it prompts you for information, kudzu allows you to specify only one nameserver. It is a good idea to specify at two or three nameservers; you can use system-config-network to add additional nameservers.

System information In addition to information about the NIC, each system must also have the following information:

- The system's IP address
- The netmask (subnet mask) for the system's address (pages 337 and 400)
- The IP address of the gateway
- The IP addresses of the nameservers (DNS addresses)
- The system's hostname (set when you install Red Hat Linux)

If you set up a DHCP server (page 408) to distribute network configuration information to systems on the LAN, you do not need to specify the preceding information on each system; you just specify that the system is using DHCP to obtain this information. You need to specify this information when you set up the DHCP server.

Private address space When you set up a LAN, the IP addresses of the systems on the LAN are generally not made public on the Internet. There are special IP addresses, part of the *private*

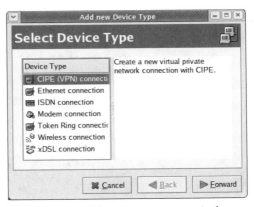

Figure 17-3 Select Device Type window

address space defined by *IANA* (page 976), that are reserved for private use and are appropriate to use on a LAN (Table 17-1). Unless you have been assigned IP addresses for the systems on the LAN, choose addresses from the private address space.

table 17-1 ‖		Private IP Ranges
Range of IP Addresses	From IP Address	To IP Address
10.0.0.0/8	10.0.0.0	10.255.255.255
172.16.0.0/12	172.16.0.0	172.31.255.255
192.168.0.0/16	192.168.0.0	192.168.255.255

system-config-network: Configuring the Hardware

The system-config-network (*FEDORA*) and redhat-config-network (*RHEL*) utilities display the Network Configuration window (Figure 17-2) with tabs to specify hosts (**/etc/hosts**, page 428) and DNS servers (**/etc/resolv.conf**, page 432), as well as to configure network hardware and logical devices associated with the hardware.

Adding a device Normally, kudzu identifies and adds new hardware to the system, after which you can then use [system|redhat]-config-network to edit the configuration information. If you do need to add a NIC to the system, click the Devices tab; then click **New** on the toolbar. The utility displays the Select Device Type window (Figure 17-3).

The Select Device Type window can set up seven types of connections (most of which do not pertain to setting up a LAN): *CIPE* (page 963), Ethernet (page 327), *ISDN* (page 978), modem, *token ring* (page 1002), wireless, and *xDSL* (page 1006). CIPE, ISDN, modem, wireless, and xDSL are PPP (Point-to-Point Protocol) connections. PPP is a serial line protocol that establishes a connection between two systems, putting them on the same network. PPP is capable of handling several protocols, the

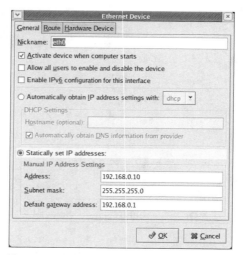

Figure 17-4   The Ethernet Device window

most common of which is TCP/IP, which provides compression for increased efficiency. The two systems can then run **ssh**, X, or any other network application between them. Ethernet and token ring are used to connect to LANs.

Choose the type of connection you want to establish and click **Forward**. Some selections probe for information. You can accept entries in the text boxes that are filled
in in the following window. Fill in blank text boxes as appropriate. When you have
finished setting up the device, click **Apply**. The Select Device Type window closes,
leaving the Network Configuration window displaying the device you just added.
Follow the instructions in the next paragraph to edit the configuration information
or click the **Devices** tab, highlight the new device, click **Menubar: File⇨Save**, and
click **Activate** to bring the new device on line.

Editing a device   The Network Configuration window (Figure 17-2) has four tabs; two pertain to
hardware devices and two to the system. The Hosts tab modifies the **/etc/hosts** file
(page 428) and the DNS tab modifies the system's hostname and **/etc/resolv.conf**
file (page 432). Make changes in these tabs as necessary.

To modify the configuration of network hardware, such as a NIC, click the **Hardware** tab, highlight the description of the hardware, and click **Edit** on the toolbar.
The utility displays the Network Adapters Configuration window. In this window,
you can change the name of the device (**eth0**, **eth1**, and so on) and the resources it
uses. Typically, you will change only the name. Click **OK** to accept the changes and
close the window.

To modify the device represented by a piece of hardware, click the **Devices** tab, highlight the device, and click **Edit** on the toolbar. The utility displays a window appropriate
to the device you are editing. For example, if you are working with an Ethernet NIC,
[system|redhat]-config-network displays the Ethernet Device window (Figure 17-4).

From this window, you can set up the device to use DHCP or manually specify the necessary IP addresses. The Hardware Device tab allows you to associate the device with a piece of hardware and specify a *MAC address* (page 981). When you are finished making changes, click **OK**, click the **Devices** tab, highlight the new device, and click **Menubar: File⇨Save**. Activate the device if necessary.

iwconfig: **Configuring a Wireless NIC**

You can configure a wireless NIC using system-config-network (page 555) or iwconfig. The iwconfig utility is based on ifconfig and configures elements of a wireless NIC not supported by ifconfig, such as setting up Master mode and binding a card to a WAP.

The most common parameters you will change with iwconfig are the encryption key, the mode, and the name of the network. Most devices support a minimum of 40-bit Wired Equivalent Privacy (WEP) encryption. The encryption key is defined by a string of 10 hexadecimal digits. The contents of the string are arbitrary, but must be the same on all nodes.

```
# iwconfig eth1 key 19FEB47A5B
```

The algorithm used by WEP is known to be flawed; using it does not give much protection. If you require privacy, use an encrypted protocol, such as SSH or HTTPS. If you are have difficulty connecting, disable encryption on all nodes:

```
# iwconfig eth1 key off
```

The **mode** defines whether you are connecting to an ad hoc or an infrastructure network. Normally, you can set **mode** to **Auto**, which selects the correct mode automatically:

```
# iwconfig eth1 mode Auto
```

The exception is if you want to use the NIC as a WAP, in which case you need to set **mode** to **Master**. Not all wireless NICs are capable of acting as masters.

```
# iwconfig eth1 mode Master
```

The network name is defined by the ESSID (Extended Service Set ID), an arbitrary string. With the ESSID set (it must be the same on every node, including the WAP), you should be able to roam between any set of nodes with the same network name:

```
# iwconfig eth1 essid "My Wireless Network"
```

See the iwconfig man page for more information.

Setting Up Servers

Setting up local clients and servers can make a LAN easier to use and more useful. The following list briefly describes some of these tools and references the pages that describe them in detail.

- **NIS**   NIS can provide a uniform login regardless of which system you log in on. The NIS authentication server is covered on page 645 and the client on page 640. NIS is often combined with home directories mounted using NFS.

- **NFS**   NFS allows you to share directory hierarchies. Sharing directories using NFS requires that the server export the directory hierarchy (page 665) and the clients mount the hierarchy (page 658).

  Using NFS, you can store all home directories on one system and mount them from other systems as needed. This configuration works well with NIS login authentication. With this setup, it can be convenient to create a world-writable directory, for example **/home/shared**, which users can use to exchange files. If you set the sticky bit (page 998) on this directory (**chmod 1777 /home/shared**), users are able to delete only files they created. If you do not set the sticky bit, any user can delete any file.

- **OpenSSH**   OpenSSH tools include ssh (logs in on a remote system, page 570) and scp (copies files to/from a remote system, page 572). You can also set up automatic logins with OpenSSH: If you set up a shared home directory with NFS, each user's **~/.ssh** directory (page 565) is the same on each system; a user who sets up a personal authentication key (page 575) will be able to use OpenSSH tools between systems without entering a password. See page 575 to set up an OpenSSH server. You can just use the ssh and scp clients; you do not have to set them up.

- **DHCP**   DHCP enables a client system to retrieve network configuration information from a server each time it connects to a network. See page 408 for more information.

- **Samba**   Samba allows Linux systems to participate in a Windows network, sharing directories and printers, and accessing those shared by Windows systems. Samba includes a special share for accessing users' home directories. For more information, refer to "The [homes] Share: Sharing Users' Home Directories" on page 691.

  You can also use Samba to set up a shared directory similar to the one described under "NFS." To share a Linux directory with Windows computers, place the following code in **/etc/smb.conf** (page 685). Any Windows user can access this share; it can be used to exchange files between users and between Linux and Windows systems:

```
[public]
    comment = Public file space
    path = /home/shared
    read only = no
    public = yes
    browseable = yes
```

More Information

Web SmoothWall Linux distribution   www.smoothwall.org
     NdisWrapper   ndiswrapper.sourceforge.net
     Hardware compatibility list   hardware.redhat.com

HOWTOs *Linux Wireless Lan HOWTO*   www.hpl.hp.com/personal/Jean_Tourrilhes/Linux
     Wireless HOWTO

Summary

A local area network (LAN) connects together computers at one site and can allow the connected computers to share an Internet connection and a printer. Each system, or node, on a LAN must have a network interface card (NIC). NICs can be connected to the network with cables or radio waves (wireless).

An Ethernet-based LAN has a connection between each computer and a central hub. There are two kinds of hubs: passive (sometimes just called a *hub*) and switching (faster, called a *switch*). A wireless access point (WAP) connects a wireless network to a wired one. If the LAN you are setting up is connected to another network, such as the Internet, you need a router (gateway). A router can perform several functions, the most common of which is allowing several systems to share a single Internet connection and IP address, called masquerading.

You can set up the LAN to use NIS as a login server so that you do not have to set up accounts on each system. You can use NFS, which allows you to mount remote directory hierarchies, to set up a universal home directory. Samba is an important part of many LANs: It allows Linux systems to participate in a Windows network, sharing directories and printers, and accessing those shared by Windows systems.

Exercises

1. What advantage does a switch have over a passive hub?
2. What server would you set up to allow users to log in with the same username and password on all computers on a LAN?
3. Name two servers that allow you to share directories between systems.
4. What is a WAP and what does it do?
5. What is a common function of a router? What is this function called?

6. What does a wireless bridge do?

7. What is kudzu? What does it do when you install a new NIC?

8. What is the private address space? When would you use a private address?

Advanced Exercises

9. If you set a system's subnet mask to 255.255.255.0, how many computers can you put on the network without using a router?

10. Which file stores information about which DNS servers the system uses?

PART V

Using Clients and Setting Up Servers

OpenSSH: Secure Network Communication

18

OpenSSH is a suite of secure network connectivity tools that replaces telnet, rcp, rsh/rshd, rlogin/rlogind, and ftp/ftpd. Unlike the tools it replaces, OpenSSH tools encrypt all traffic, including passwords, thwarting malicious users who would eavesdrop, hijack connections, and steal passwords.

This chapter covers the following OpenSSH tools:

scp   Copies files to/from another system
sftp   Copies files to/from other systems (a secure replacement for ftp)
ssh   Runs a command on or logs in on another system
sshd   The OpenSSH daemon (runs on the server)
ssh-keygen   Creates RSA or DSA host/user authentication keys

Introduction

Using public-key encryption (page 923), OpenSSH provides two levels of authentication: server and client/user. First, the client verifies that it is connected to the correct server. Then, OpenSSH encrypts communication between the systems. Second, once a secure, encrypted connection has been established, OpenSSH makes sure that the user is authorized to log in on or copy files from/to the server. Once the system and user have been verified, OpenSSH allows different services to be passed through the connection. These services include interactive shell sessions (ssh), remote command execution (ssh and scp), X11 client/server connections, and TCP/IP port tunneling.

SSH1 versus SSH2   SSH protocol version 2 (SSH2) is a complete rewrite of the SSH protocol version 1 (SSH1) with improved security, performance, and portability. The two protocols are not compatible. Because SSH1 is being rapidly supplanted by SSH2 and because SSH1 is subject to a person in the middle attack (footnote 3 on page 926), this chapter does not discuss SSH1. Because version 2 is floating-point intensive, version 1 does have a place on systems without FPUs (floating-point units or accelerators), such as old 486SX systems. As initially installed, the OpenSSH tools supplied with Red Hat support both protocols; you need run only one server to communicate with systems using either protocol.

ssh   The ssh utility allows you to log in on a remote system over a network. You might choose to use a remote system to access a special-purpose application or to use a device that is available only on that system, or you might use a remote system because you know that it is faster or not as busy as the local computer. While traveling, many people use ssh on a laptop to log in on a system at headquarters. From a GUI you can use several systems simultaneously by logging in on each from a different terminal emulator window.

X11 forwarding   With X11 forwarding turned on, as it is when you install Red Hat Linux, it is a simple matter to run an X11 program over an ssh connection: Run ssh from a terminal emulator running in a GUI and give an X11 command such as **xclock**; the graphical output appears on the local display. For more information, refer to "Forwarding X11" on page 580.

About OpenSSH

This section discusses configuration files that OpenSSH clients and servers use, describes how OpenSSH works, and provides additional OpenSSH resources.

Files

OpenSSH clients and servers rely on many files. Global files are kept in **/etc/ssh** and user files in **~/.ssh**. In the description of each file, the first word indicates whether the client or the server uses the file.

---

caution ‖   **rhost Authentication Is a Security Risk**

Although OpenSSH can get authentication information from **/etc/hosts.equiv**, **/etc/shosts.equiv**, **~/.rhosts**, and **~/.shosts**, this chapter does not cover the use of these files because they are security risks and the default settings in the **/etc/ssh/sshd_config** configuration file prevent their use.

/etc/ssh: Global Files

Global files listed in this section effect all users but can be overridden by files in a user's ~/.ssh directory.

moduli   client and server   Contains key exchange information that is used to establish a secure connection. Do not modify this file.

ssh_config   client   The global OpenSSH configuration file (page 573). Entries here can be overridden by entries in a user's ~/.ssh/config file.

sshd_config   server   The configuration file for **sshd** (page 577).

ssh_host_dsa_key, ssh_host_dsa_key.pub
  server   SSH protocol version 2 DSA host keys. Both files should be owned by **root**. The **ssh_host_dsa_key.pub** public file should be readable by anyone but writable only by its owner (644 permissions). The **ssh_host_dsa_key** private file should not be readable or writable by anyone except its owner (600 permissions).

ssh_host_rsa_key, ssh_host_rsa_key.pub
  server   SSH protocol version 2 RSA host keys. Both files should be owned by **root**. The **ssh_host_rsa_key.pub** public file should be readable by anyone but writable only by its owner (644 permissions). The **ssh_host_rsa_key** private file should not be readable or writable by anyone except its owner (600 permissions).

ssh_known_hosts   client   Contains public RSA (by default) keys of hosts that users on the local system can connect to. This file contains information similar to ~/.ssh/known_hosts, except it is set up by the administrator and is available to all users. This file should be owned by **root** and should be readable by anyone but writable only by its owner (644 permissions).

sshrc   server   Contains initialization routines. If ~/.ssh/rc is not present, this script is run after ~/.ssh/environment and before the user's shell is started.

~/.ssh: User Files

OpenSSH creates the ~/.ssh directory and the **known_hosts** file therein automatically when you connect to a remote system.

authorized_keys   server   Enables you to log in on or copy files from/to another system without supplying a password (page 575). No one except the owner should be able to write to this file.

config   client   A user's private OpenSSH configuration file (page 573). Entries here override those in /etc/ssh/ssh_config.

environment   server   Contains commands that are executed when a user logs in with ssh. Similar in function to ~/.bashrc for a local bash shell.

id_dsa, id_dsa.pub client   User authentication DSA keys generated by ssh-keygen (page 576). Both files should be owned by the user in whose home directory they appear. The **id_dsa_key.pub** public file should be readable by anyone but writable only by its owner (644 permissions). The **id_dsa_key** private file should not be readable or writable by anyone except its owner (600 permissions).

id_rsa, id_rsa.pub client   User authentication RSA keys generated by ssh-keygen (page 576). Both files should be owned by the user in whose home directory they appear. The **id_rsa_key.pub** public file should be readable by anyone but writable only by its owner (644 permissions). The **id_rsa_key** private file should not be readable or writable by anyone except its owner (600 permissions).

known_hosts client   Contains public RSA keys (default) of hosts that the user has connected to. OpenSSH automatically adds entries each time the user connects to a new server (page 568). Refer to "HostKeyAlgorithms" (page 574) for information on using DSA keys.

rc server   Contains initialization routines. This script is run after **environment** and before the user's shell is started. If this file is not present, OpenSSH runs **/etc/ssh/sshrc**; if that file does not exist, OpenSSH runs xauth.

How OpenSSH Works

When OpenSSH starts, it first establishes an encrypted connection and then authenticates the user. Once these two tasks are taken care of, OpenSSH allows the two systems to send information back and forth.

OpenSSH uses two key pairs to negotiate an encrypted session: a *host key* pair and a *session key* pair. The host key pair is a set of public/private keys that is established the first time the server system runs **sshd** (page 575). The session key pair is a set of public/private keys that changes hourly.

The first time an OpenSSH client connects with an OpenSSH server, you are asked to verify that it is connected to the correct server (see "JumpStart: Using ssh and scp" on page 567). After verification, the client makes a copy of the server's public host key. On subsequent connections, the client compares the key provided by the server with the key it stored. Although this test is not foolproof, the next one is quite secure.

Next, the client generates a random key, which it encrypts with both the server's public host key and the session key. The client then sends this encrypted key to the server. The server uses its private keys to decrypt the key. This process creates a key that is known only to the client and server and is used to encrypt the rest of the session.

More Information

Local man pages   ssh scp ssh-keygen ssh_config sshd sshd_config

Web OpenSSH home page   www.openssh.com
Search tldp.org for **ssh** for various HOWTOs and other documents.

Books *Implementing SSH: Strategies for Optimizing the Secure Shell* by Dwivedi; John Wiley & Sons (October 2003)
SSH, The Secure Shell: The Definitive Guide by Barrett & Silverman; O'Reilly & Associates, 1st edition (February 15, 2001)

OpenSSH Clients

This section covers setting up and using the ssh, scp, and sftp clients.

Prerequisites

Install the following packages:

* **openssh**
* **openssh-clients**

There are no startup commands for OpenSSH clients.

JumpStart: Using ssh and scp

The ssh and scp clients do not require setup beyond installing the requisite packages, although you can create/edit files that facilitate their use. In order to run a secure shell on, or securely copy a file to/from a remote system, the remote system must be running the OpenSSH daemon (**sshd**); you must have an account on the remote system; and the server must positively identify itself to the client. The following example shows a user logging in on **grape** as **zach** and then giving an **exit** command to return to the shell on the local system:

```
$ ssh zach@grape
zach@grape's password:
[zach@grape zach]$ exit
Connection to grape closed.
$
```

You can omit **user@** (**zach@** in the preceding example) from the command line if you have the same username on both systems. The first time you connect to a remote OpenSSH server, ssh or scp asks you to make sure that you are connected to the right system. Refer to "Message on initial connection to a server" on page 568.

Following is an example of copying a file to a remote system using scp:

```
$ scp ty1 zach@grape:
zach@grape's password:
ty1                    100% |*******************************|  1311      00:00
```

Setup

This section describes how to set up OpenSSH on the client side.

Recommended Settings

X11 forwarding   The configuration files provided by Red Hat provide a mostly secure system and may or may not meet your needs. The important OpenSSH default value that the Red Hat configuration files override is ForwardX11, which is set to **yes** in the Red Hat **/etc/ssh/ssh_config** configuration file (page 578). See page 580 for more information on X11 forwarding.

Server Authentication/Known Hosts

known_hosts,
ssh_known_hosts   There are two files that list the hosts the local system has connected to and positively identified: **~/.ssh/known_hosts** (user) and **/etc/ssh/ssh_known_hosts** (global). No one except the owner (**root** in the case of the second file) should be able to write to either of these files. No one except the owner should have any access to a **~/.ssh** directory.

When you connect to an OpenSSH server for the first time, the OpenSSH client prompts you, following, to confirm that you are connected to the right system. This checking can help prevent a person-in-the-middle attack (footnote 3 on page 926).

Message on initial
connection to a server
```
The authenticity of host 'grape (192.168.0.3)' can't be established.
RSA key fingerprint is c9:03:c1:9d:c2:91:55:50:e8:19:2b:f4:36:ef:73:78.
Are you sure you want to continue connecting (yes/no)? yes
Warning: Permanently added 'grape,192.168.0.3' (RSA) to the list of
known hosts.
```

Before you respond to the preceding query, make sure you are logging in on the correct system and not on an imposter. If you are not sure, a telephone call to someone who logs in on that system locally can help verify that you are on the intended system. When you answer **yes** (you must spell it out), the client appends the server's public host key (the single line in the **/etc/ssh/ssh_host_rsa_key.pub** or **/etc/ssh/ssh_host_dsa_key.pub** file on the server) to the user's **~/ssh/known_hosts** file on the local client, creating the **~/.ssh** directory if necessary. So that it can keep track of which line in **known_hosts** applies to which server, OpenSSH prepends the name of the server and the server's IP address (by default) to the line.

Subsequently, when you use OpenSSH to connect to that server, the client verifies that it is connected to the correct server by comparing this key to the one the server supplies.

The **known_hosts** file uses one very long line to identify each host it keeps track of. Each line starts with the hostname and IP address of the system the line corresponds to, followed by the type of encryption being used and the server's public host key. The following line (it is one logical line wrapped on to three physical lines) from **known_hosts** is used to connect to **grape** at 192.168.0.3 using *RSA* (page 994) encryption.

known_hosts file
```
$ cat ~/.ssh/known_hosts
grape,192.168.0.3 ssh-rsa AAAAB3NzaClyc2EAAAABIwAAAIEArinPGsaLUtnSL4V7b
T51ksF7KoScsIk7wqm+2sJEC43rxVNS5+MO/O64UXp5qQOHBmeLCCFCsIJg8xseuVkg9iwO
BKKOd1ZdBNVqFS7tnJdBQTFf+ofPIDDip8w6ftHOdM8hZ/diQq5gXqMH+Mpac31pQXAxXgY
SP8NYIgb3X18=
```

OpenSSH automatically stores keys from servers it has connected to in user-private files (**~/.ssh/known_hosts**). These files work only for the user whose directory they appear in. Working as **root** and using a text editor, you can copy lines from a user's private list of known hosts to the public list in **/etc/ssh/ssh_known_hosts** to make a server known globally on the local system.

If, after you have a remote system's private key stored in one of the known hosts files, the remote system supplies a different fingerprint when you attempt to connect, OpenSSH displays the following message and does not complete the connection:

```
@@@@@@@@@@@@@@@@@@@@@@@@@@@@@@@@@@@@@@@@@@@@@@@@@@@@@@@@@@@
@    WARNING: REMOTE HOST IDENTIFICATION HAS CHANGED!     @
@@@@@@@@@@@@@@@@@@@@@@@@@@@@@@@@@@@@@@@@@@@@@@@@@@@@@@@@@@@
IT IS POSSIBLE THAT SOMEONE IS DOING SOMETHING NASTY!
Someone could be eavesdropping on you right now (man-in-the-middle attack)!
It is also possible that the RSA host key has just been changed.
The fingerprint for the RSA key sent by the remote host is
f1:6f:ea:87:bb:1b:df:cd:e3:45:24:60:d3:25:b1:0a.
Please contact your system administrator.
Add correct host key in /home/sam/.ssh/known_hosts to get rid of this message.
Offending key in /home/sam/.ssh/known_hosts:1
RSA host key for grape has changed and you have requested strict checking.
Host key verification failed.
```

When you see this message, it is possible that you are the subject of a person-in-the-middle attack. It is more likely that something on the remote system changed, causing it to supply a new fingerprint. Check with the remote system's administrator. If all is well, remove the offending key from the specified file (the third line from the bottom in the preceding example points to the line you need to remove) and try connecting again. You will see the "Message on initial connection to a server" (page 568) again as OpenSSH verifies that you are connecting to the correct system. Follow the same steps as when you initially connected to the remote host.

ssh: Connect to and Execute Commands on a Remote System

The format of an ssh command line is

ssh [user@]host [command]

where *host,* the name of the OpenSSH server you want to connect to, is the only required argument. The *host* can be a local system name, an FQDN of a system on the Internet, or an IP address. Give the command ssh *host* to log in on the remote system *host* with the same username that you are using on the local system. Include *user@* when you want to log in with a username other than the one you are using on the local system. Depending on how things are set up, you may need to supply your password.

Opening a remote shell   When you do not include *command,* ssh logs you in on *host.* You get a shell prompt and can run commands on *host.* Give the command exit to close the connection to *host* and return to the local system's prompt.

```
[bravo]$ ssh speedy
alex@speedy's password:
Last login: Sat Sep 14 06:51:59 from bravo
Have a lot of fun...
You have new mail.
[speedy]$
...
[speedy]$ exit
Connection to speedy closed.
[bravo]$
```

Running a remote command   When you include *command,* ssh logs in on *host,* executes *command,* closes the connection to *host,* and returns control to the local system; you never get the remote system's prompt.

The following example runs ls in the **memos** directory on the remote system **speedy**. The example assumes that the user running the command (Alex) has a login on **speedy** and that the **memos** directory is in Alex's home directory on **speedy**:

```
[bravo]$ ssh speedy ls memos
alex@speedy's password:
memo.0921
memo.draft
[bravo]$
```

For the next example, assume a file named **memo.new** is in the working directory on the local system (**bravo**) and you cannot remember whether it contains certain changes or you made these changes to the file named **memo.draft** on **speedy**. You could copy **memo.draft** to the local system and run diff (page 126) on the two files, but then you would have three similar copies of the file spread across two systems. If you are not careful about removing the old copies when you are done, you may be confused again in a few days. Instead of copying the file, you can use ssh:

```
[bravo]$ ssh speedy cat memos/memo.draft | diff memos.new -
```

When you run ssh, standard output of the command run on the remote system is passed to the local shell as though the command had been run in place on the local system. As with all shell commands, you must quote special characters that you do not want interpreted by the local system. In the preceding example, the output of the cat command on **speedy** is sent through a pipe on **bravo** to diff (running on **bravo**), which compares the local file **memos.new** to standard input (–). The following command line has the same effect but causes diff to run on the remote system:

```
[bravo]$ cat memos.new | ssh speedy diff - memos/memo.draft
```

Standard output from diff on the remote system is sent to the local shell, which displays it on the screen (because it is not redirected).

Options

This section lists some of the options you can use with ssh.

–C **compression**   Enables compression. (In the commercial version of ssh, **–C** *dis*ables compression and **+C** *en*ables compression.)

–f **not foreground**   Sends ssh to the background after asking for a password and before executing the *command*. Useful when you want to run the *command* in the background but must supply a password. Implies **–n**.

–L   Forwards a port on the local client to a remote system. For more information, refer to "Tunneling/Port Forwarding" on page 579.

–l *user* **login** (ell)   Attempts to log in as *user*.

–n **null**   Redirects standard input to ssh to come from **/dev/null**. Required when running ssh in the background.

–o *option* **option**   Specifies *option* in the format used in configuration files (page 573).

–p **port**   Specifies the port on the remote host that the connection is made to. Using the **host** declaration (page 573) in the configuration file, you can specify a different port for each system you connect to.

–R   Forwards a port on the remote system to the local client. For more information, refer to "Tunneling/Port Forwarding" on page 579.

–v **verbose**   Displays debugging messages about the connection and transfer. Useful if things are not going as expected.

–X **X11**   Turns on X11 forwarding. You do not need this option if you turn on X11 forwarding in the configuration file (page 568).

–x **X11**   Turns off X11 forwarding.

scp: Copying a File from/to a Remote System

The scp (secure copy) utility copies a file from one computer to another on a network, using the same authentication mechanism as ssh and therefore providing the same security. As does ssh, scp asks you for a password when it is needed. The format of an scp command is

scp [[user@]fromhost:]source-file [[user@]tohost:]destination-file

where *source-file* is the file you want to copy and *destination-file* is the resulting copy. A simple or relative filename is assumed to be relative to your home directory on the remote system and relative to your working directory on the local system. An absolute pathname describes a path from the root directory on either system. Make sure that you have read permission to the file you are copying and write permission for the directory you are copying it into.

The *fromhost:* and *tohost:* are the names of the systems that (will) hold the files. When you do not specify *fromhost* or *tohost*, each defaults to the local system. The *fromhost* and *tohost* can be local system names, *FQDNs* (page 972) of a systems on the Internet, or IP addresses. You can copy from or to the local system or between two remote systems.

Sam has an alternate username, **sls**, on **grape**. In the following example, Sam uses scp to copy **memo.txt** from the home directory of his **sls** account on **grape** to the **allmemos** directory in the working directory on the local system. If **allmemos** were not the name of a directory, **memo.txt** would be copied to a file named **allmemos** in the working directory.

```
$ scp sls@grape:memo.txt allmemos
sls@grape's password:
memo.txt            100% |*******************************| 14664      00:00
```

As the transfer progresses, the percent and number of bytes transferred increase and the time remaining decreases. The asterisks provide a visual representation of the progress of the transfer.

The next example shows Sam, working from **peach**, copying the same file as in the previous example to the directory named **old** in Sam's home directory on **speedy**. For this example to work, Sam must be able to use ssh to log in on **speedy** from **grape** without using a password. For more information, refer to "Authorized Keys: Automatic Login" on page 575.

```
$ [sam@peach] scp sls@grape:memo.txt speedy:old
sam@grape's password:
```

Options

This section lists some of the options you can use with scp.

–C **compression**   Enables compression.

–o *option* **option**   Specifies *option* in the format used in configuration files (next section).

–P *port*   **port**   Connects to port *port* on the remote host.

    –p **preserve**   Preserves the modification and access times as well as the modes of the original file.

    –q **quiet**   Does not display the progress meter.

    –r **recursive**   Recursively copies a directory hierarchy.

    –v **verbose**   Displays debugging messages about the connection and transfer. Useful if things are not going as expected.

sftp: A Secure FTP Client

As part of OpenSSH, Red Hat provides sftp, a secure alternative to ftp (page 583). Functionally the same as ftp, sftp maps ftp commands into OpenSSH commands. You can replace ftp with sftp when you are logging into a server that is running the OpenSSH daemon, **sshd**. Once you are connected to a system with sftp, give the command **?** to display a list of commands. For secure communication, use sftp or scp for all file transfers requiring authentication. Refer to the sftp man page for more information.

~/.ssh/config and /etc/ssh/ssh_config Configuration Files

It is usually not necessary to modify OpenSSH client configuration files. For a given user there are two configuration files: **~/.ssh/config** (user) and **/etc/ssh/ssh_config** (global). These files are read in this order and, for a given parameter, the first one found is the one that is used. A user can override a global parameter setting by setting the same parameter in his user configuration file. Parameters given on the ssh or scp command line take precedence over parameters set in either of these files.

Lines in the configuration files contain declarations that start with a keyword, which is not case sensitive, followed by whitespace, and end with case-sensitive arguments.

You can use the Host keyword to cause declarations to apply to a specific system. A **Host** declaration applies to all the lines that follow it until the next Host declaration. You can use ✻ and ? wildcards within a hostname.

Host *hostnames*   Specifies that the following declarations, until the next Host declaration, apply to *hostnames* only. The *hostnames* should be in the same form you would use on a command line and can contain ? and ✻ wildcards. Use a single ✻ to specify all hosts.

CheckHostIP yes | no

    Uses an IP address in addition to a hostname to identify a system in the **known_hosts** file when set to **yes** (default). Set to **no** to use a hostname only.

ForwardX11 yes | no

Automatically forwards X11 connections over a secure channel and sets the DIS-PLAY shell variable when set to **yes**. (Alternatively, you can use **–X** on the command to redirect X11 connections.) The default is **no**, but the Red Hat configuration files set ForwardX11 to **yes**. In order for X11 forwarding to work, X11Forwarding must also be set to **yes** in the **/etc/sshd_config** file on the server (page 578). For more information, refer to "Forwarding X11" on page 580.

HostbasedAuthentication yes | no

Tries **rhosts** authentication when set to **yes**. For a more secure system, set to **no** (default).

HostKeyAlgorithms *algorithms*

The *algorithms* is a comma-separated list of algorithms that the client wants to use in order of preference. Choose *algorithms* from: **ssh-rsa**, **ssh-dss** (default is **ssh-rsa**, **ssh-dss**).

KeepAlive yes | no   Periodically checks to see if a connection is alive when set to **yes** (default). Checking causes the **ssh** or **scp** connection to be dropped when the server crashes or the connection dies for another reason, even if it is only temporary. Setting this parameter to **no** causes the client not to check if the connection is alive.

This declaration uses the TCP **keepalive** option, which is not encrypted and is susceptible to *IP spoofing* (page 978). Refer to ClientAliveInterval on page 577 for a server-based nonspoofable alternative.

StrictHostKeyChecking yes | no | ask

Determines whether and how OpenSSH adds host keys to a user's **known_hosts** file. Set to **ask** (default) to ask whether to add a host key when connecting to a new system, **no** to add a host key automatically, and **yes** to require that host keys be manually added. The **yes** and **ask** arguments cause OpenSSH to refuse to connect to a system whose host key has changed. For a more secure system, set to **yes** or **ask**.

User *name*   Specifies a username to use when logging in on a system. Specify systems with the **Host** declaration. Avoids having to enter a username on the command line when you are using a username that differs from your username on the local system.

sshd: OpenSSH Server

This section discusses how to set up an OpenSSH server.

Prerequisites

Install the following packages:

- openssh

- openssh-server

Run chkconfig to cause **sshd** to start when the system goes multiuser:

```
# /sbin/chkconfig sshd on
```

See "Starting **sshd** for the First Time," following, for information on starting the server for the first time.

JumpStart: Starting the sshd Daemon

Install the requisite packages and start the **sshd** daemon as described following. Look in **/var/log/messages** to make sure everything is working properly.

Recommended Settings

The configuration files provided by Red Hat establish a mostly secure system and may or may not meet your needs. The Red Hat **/etc/ssh/sshd_config** file turns on X11 forwarding (page 580). For a more secure system, you can set PermitRootLogin to **no**, thereby removing a known-name, privileged account that is exposed to the outside world with only password protection.

Starting sshd for the First Time

When you start the **sshd** OpenSSH daemon for the first time, generally when you boot the system, it creates host key files (page 565) in **/etc/ssh**:

```
# /sbin/service sshd start
Generating SSH1 RSA host key:                              [  OK  ]
Generating SSH2 RSA host key:                              [  OK  ]
Generating SSH2 DSA host key:                              [  OK  ]
Starting sshd:                                             [  OK  ]
```

OpenSSH uses the files it creates to identify the server.

Authorized Keys: Automatic Login

You can configure OpenSSH so you do not have to enter a password each time you connect to a remote system. To set things up, you need to generate a personal authentication key, place the public part of the key on the remote server, and keep the private part of the key on the local client. When you connect, the remote system issues a challenge based on the public part of the key. The private part of the key is required to respond properly to the challenge. When the local system provides the proper response, the remote system logs you in.

The first step in setting up an automatic login is to generate your personal authentication keys. Check to see if authentication keys are already in place: Look in

~/.ssh for either **id_dsa** and **id_dsa.pub** or **id_rsa** and **id_rsa.pub**. If one of these pairs of files is present, skip the next step (do not create a new key).

The ssh-keygen utility creates the public and private parts of an RSA key:

ssh-keygen
```
$ ssh-keygen -t rsa
Generating public/private rsa key pair.
Enter file in which to save the key (/home/sam/.ssh/id_rsa):RETURN
Enter passphrase (empty for no passphrase):RETURN
Enter same passphrase again:RETURN
Your identification has been saved in /home/sam/.ssh/id_rsa.
Your public key has been saved in /home/sam/.ssh/id_rsa.pub.
The key fingerprint is:
f2:eb:c8:fe:ed:fd:32:98:e8:24:5a:76:1d:0e:fd:1d sam@peach
```

Replace **rsa** with **dsa** to generate DSA keys. In this example, the user pressed RETURN in response to each of the queries. You have the option of specifying a passphrase (10–30 characters is a good length) to encrypt the private part of the key. There is no way to recover a lost passphrase. See the following security tip for more information about the passphrase. The ssh-keygen utility generates two keys: A private key or identification in **~/.ssh/id_rsa** and a public key in **~/.ssh/id_rsa.pub**. No one except the owner should be able to write to either of these files. Only the owner should be able to read from the private key file.

authorized_keys
To enable you to log in on or copy files from/to another system without supplying a password, first create a **~/.ssh** directory with permissions set to 700 on the remote system. Automatic login will fail if anyone except the owner has permission to read from or write to the **~/.ssh** directory on either system. Next, copy **~/.ssh/id_rsa.pub** on the local system to a file named **~/.ssh/authorized_keys** on the remote system. No one except the owner should be able to read from or write to this file. Now when you run ssh or scp to access the remote system, you do not have to supply a password.

security || **Encrypt Your Personal Key**

The private part of the key is kept in a file that only you can read. If a malicious user compromises your account or the **root** account on the local system, that user then has access to your account on the remote system because she can read the private part of your personal key.

Encrypting the private part of your personal key protects the key and, therefore, access to the remote system should someone compromise your local account. However, if you encrypt your personal key, you have to supply the passphrase you used to encrypt the key each time you use the key, negating the benefit of not having to type a password in order to log in on the remote system. Also, most passphrases that you can remember can be cracked quite quickly by a powerful computer.

A better idea is to store the private keys on a removable medium, such as a USB flash drive, and have your **~/.ssh** directory as the mountpoint for the filesystem stored on this drive.

Command Line Options

Command Line options override declarations in the configuration files (following). Following is a list of some of the more useful **sshd** options.

-d debug Sets debug mode wherein **sshd** sends debugging messages to the system log and the server stays in the foreground. You can specify this option up to three times to increase the verbosity of the output. See also **-e**. (The ssh client uses **-v** for debugging, page 571.)

-e error Sends output to standard error, not to the system log. Useful with **-d**.

-f *file* **file** Specifies the file with the pathname *file* as the default configuration file in place of **/etc/ssh/sshd_config**.

-t test Checks the configuration file syntax and the sanity of the key files.

-D noDetach Keeps **sshd** in the foreground. Useful for debugging, implied by **-d**.

/etc/ssh/sshd_config Configuration File

Lines in the **/etc/ssh/sshd_config** configuration file contains declarations that start with a keyword, which is not case sensitive, followed by whitespace, and end with case-sensitive arguments.

AllowUsers *userlist* The *userlist* is a SPACE-separated list of usernames that specifies users who are allowed to log in using **sshd**. The list can include * and ? wildcards. You can specify a user as *user* or *user@host*. If you use the second format, make sure that you specify the host as returned by hostname. Without this declaration, any user who can log in locally can log in using an OpenSSH client.

ClientAliveInterval *n*

Sends a message through the encrypted channel after *n* seconds of not receiving a message from the client. See ClientAliveCountMax. Default is 0, meaning that no messages are sent.

This declaration passes messages over the encrypted channel and is not susceptible to *IP spoofing* (page 978). This declaration differs from KeepAlive, which uses the TCP **keepalive** option and is susceptible to IP spoofing.

ClientAliveCountMax *n*

The *n* specifies the number of client alive messages that can be sent without receiving a response before **sshd** disconnects from the client. See ClientAliveInterval. Default is 3.

HostbasedAuthentication yes | no

Tries **rhosts** authentication when set to **yes**. For a more secure system, set to **no** (default).

IgnoreRhosts yes | no

> Ignores **.rhosts** and **.shosts** files for authentication. Does not affect the use of **/etc/hosts.equiv** and **/etc/ssh/shosts.equiv** files for authentication. For security, set to **no** (default).

KeepAlive yes | no   Periodically checks to see if a connection is alive when set to **yes** (default). Checking causes the **ssh** or **scp** connection to be dropped when the client crashes or the connection dies for another reason, even if it is only temporary. Setting this parameter to **no** causes the server not to check if the connection is alive.

> This declaration uses the TCP **keepalive** option, which is not encrypted and is susceptible to *IP spoofing* (page 978). Refer to ClientAliveInterval (page 577) for a nonspoofable alternative.

LoginGraceTime *n*   Waits *n* seconds for a user to log in on the server before disconnecting. A value of 0 means there is no time limit. The default is 120.

LogLevel *val*   Specifies how detailed the log messages are. Choose *val* from QUIET, FATAL, ERROR, INFO, and VERBOSE. The default is INFO.

PermitEmptyPasswords

> Permits a user to log in to an account that has an empty password. The default is **no**.

PermitRootLogin   Permits root to log in using an OpenSSH client. For a more secure system, set to **no**. The default is **yes**.

StrictModes yes | no   Checks modes and ownership of user's home directory and files. Login fails if directories and/or files can be written to by anyone. For security, set to **yes** (default).

VerifyReverseMapping yes | no

> Checks to see that the client's IP address reverse maps (page 708) to the host name the user is logging in from. The default is **no**.

X11Forwarding yes | no

> Allows X11 forwarding when set to **yes**. The default is **no**, but the Red Hat configuration files set **X11Forwarding** to **yes**. In order for X11 forwarding to work, **ForwardX11** must also be set to **yes** in either the **~/.ssh/config** or the **/etc/ssh/ssh_config** client configuration file (page 574). For security, do not allow untrusted users to open X11 connections.

Troubleshooting

Log files   There are several places to look for clues when you have problems connecting with **ssh** or **scp**. First, look for **sshd** entries in **/var/log/secure** and **/var/log/messages** on the server. Following are messages you may see when you are using an **AllowUsers** declaration but have not included the user who is trying to log in (page 577).

```
# grep sshd /var/log/secure
grape sshd[16]: User sam not allowed because not listed in AllowUsers
grape sshd[16]: Failed password for illegal user sam from 192.168.0.6 port 59276 ssh2
```

The next messages originate with PAM (page 416) and indicate that the user is not known to the system.

```
# grep sshd /var/log/messages
grape sshd(pam_unix)[2817]: check pass; user unknown
grape sshd(pam_unix)[2817]: authentication failure; logname= uid=0
euid=0 tty=NODEVssh ruser= rhost=peach.sobell.com
```

Debug the client   If entries in these files do not help solve the problem, try connecting with the **–v** option (ssh or scp, the results should be the same). OpenSSH displays a lot of messages and one of them may help you figure out what the problem is.

```
$ ssh -v grape
OpenSSH_3.1p1, SSH protocols 1.5/2.0, OpenSSL 0x0090602f
debug1: Reading configuration data /etc/ssh/ssh_config
debug1: Applying options for *
debug1: Rhosts Authentication disabled, originating port will not be trusted.
debug1: restore_uid
debug1: ssh_connect: getuid 500 geteuid 0 anon 1
debug1: Connecting to grape [192.168.0.3] port 22.
debug1: temporarily_use_uid: 500/500 (e=0)
...
debug1: Host 'grape' is known and matches the RSA host key.
debug1: Found key in /home/sam/.ssh/known_hosts:1
debug1: bits set: 1617/3191
debug1: ssh_rsa_verify: signature correct
...
debug1: authentications that can continue: publickey,password,keyboard-interactive
debug1: next auth method to try is publickey
debug1: try privkey: /home/sam/.ssh/identity
debug1: try privkey: /home/sam/.ssh/id_rsa
debug1: try privkey: /home/sam/.ssh/id_dsa
debug1: next auth method to try is keyboard-interactive
debug1: authentications that can continue: publickey,password,keyboard-interactive
debug1: next auth method to try is password
sam@grape's password:
```

Debug the server   You can debug from the server side by running **sshd** with the **–de** options. The server will run in the foreground and its display may help you solve the problem.

Tunneling/Port Forwarding

The ssh utility allows you to forward a port (*port forwarding*, page 989) through the encrypted connection it establishes. Because the data sent across the forwarded port uses the encrypted ssh connection as its data link layer (page 332), the term *tunneling* (page 1002) is applied to this type of connection: "The connection is tunneled through ssh." You can secure protocols including POP, X, IMAP, and WWW by tunneling them through ssh.

Forwarding X11   The ssh utility makes it easy to tunnel the X11 protocol. In order for X11 tunneling to work, you must enable it in both the server and the client. Red Hat enables X11 tunneling in its default setup. If necessary, you can enable X11 tunneling on the server by setting the **X11Forwarding** declaration to yes in the **/etc/ssh/sshd_config** file (page 578). On the client, you can use the –X option to ssh on the command line or set the ForwardX11 declaration to yes in the ~/.ssh/config or /etc/ssh/ssh_config file (page 574) to enable X11 tunneling.

With X11 forwarding turned on, ssh tunnels the X11 protocol, setting the $DIS-PLAY environment variable on the system it connects to and forwarding the required port. You must be running from a GUI, which usually means that you are using ssh on a terminal emulator to connect to a remote system. When you give an X11 command from an ssh prompt, OpenSSH creates a new secure channel that carries the X11 data. The graphical output from the X11 program appears on your screen.

```
[peach] $ ssh -X speedy
[speedy] $ echo $DISPLAY
localhost:10.0
```

By default, ssh uses X Window System display numbers 10 and higher (port numbers 6010 and higher) for forwarded X sessions. Once you connect to a remote system using ssh –X, you can give a command to run an X application and it will run on the remote system with its display on the local system: It appears to run locally.

Port forwarding   You can forward arbitrary ports using the –L and –R options. The –L option forwards a local port to a remote system, so that a program that tries to connect to the forwarded port on the local system transparently connects to the remote system. The –R option does the reverse, forwarding remote ports to the local system. The –N option, which prevents ssh from executing remote commands, is generally used with –L and –R. When you specify –N, ssh works only as a private network to forward ports. The format of an ssh command line using one of these options follows:

$ ssh –N –L | –R *local-port:remote-host:remote-port target*

where

local-port is the number of the local port that is being forwarded to or from *remote-host*.

remote-host is the name or IP address of the system that *local-port* gets forwarded to or from.

remote-port is the number of the port on *remote-host* that is being forwarded from or to the local system.

target is the name or IP address of the system ssh connects to.

As an example, assume that there is a POP mail client on the local system and that the POP server is on a remote network, on a system named **pophost**. POP is not a secure protocol; passwords are sent in cleartext each time the client connects to the server. You can make it more secure by tunneling POP through ssh. (POP-3 connects on port 110; port 1550 is an arbitrary port on the local system.)

```
$ ssh -N -L 1550:pophost:110 pophost
```

After giving the preceding command, you can point the POP client at localhost:1550, and the connection between the client and the server will be encrypted. (When you set up an account on the POP client, specify the location of the server as **localhost, port 1550**; details vary with different mail clients.) In this example, *remote-host* and *target* are the same system.

Firewalls The system specified for port forwarding (*remote-host*) does not have to be the same as the destination of the ssh connection (*target*). For example, assume the POP server is behind a firewall and you cannot connect to it via ssh. If you can connect to the firewall via the Internet using ssh, you can encrypt the part of the connection over the Internet.

```
$ ssh -N -L 1550:pophost:110 firewall
```

In the preceding example, *remote-host,* the system receiving the port forwarding, is **pophost**, and *target,* the system that ssh connects to, is **firewall**.

You can also use ssh when you are behind a firewall (that is running **sshd**) and want to forward a port into your system without modifying the firewall settings.

```
$ ssh -R 1678:localhost:80 firewall
```

The preceding command forwards connections from the outside to port 1678 on your firewall back to the local Web server. Forwarding connections in this manner allows you to use a Web browser to connect to port 1678 on your firewall in order to connect to the Web server on your machine. This setup would be useful if you ran a Webmail program (page 625) on your system because it would allow you to check your mail from anywhere using an Internet connection.

Compression Compression, enabled with the –C option, can speed up communication over a low-bandwidth connection. This option is commonly used with port forwarding. Compression can increase latency to an extent that may not be desirable for an X session forwarded over a high-bandwidth connection.

Chapter Summary

OpenSSH is a suite of secure network connectivity tools that encrypts all traffic, including passwords, thwarting malicious users who would eavesdrop, hijack connections, and steal passwords. The components discussed in this chapter are **sshd** (the server daemon), ssh (runs a command on or logs in on another system), scp (copies files to/from another system), sftp (securely replaces ftp) and **ssh-keygen** (creates authentication keys).

In order to ensure secure communications, when an OpenSSH client opens a connection, it first verifies that it is connected to the correct server. Then OpenSSH encrypts communication between the systems. Finally, OpenSSH makes sure that the user is authorized to log in on or copy files from/to the server.

OpenSSH also enables secure X11 forwarding. With this feature, you can run securely a graphical program on a remote system and have the display appear on the local system.

Exercises

1. What is the difference between the scp and sftp utilities?
2. How can you use ssh to find out who is logged in on a remote system?
3. How would you use scp to copy your ~/.bashrc file from **bravo** to the local system?
4. How would you use ssh to run xterm on **bravo** and show the display on the local system?
5. What problem can enabling compression present when using ssh to run remote X11 applications on a local display?
6. When you try to connect to another system using an OpenSSH client and you see a message warning you that the remote host identification has changed, what has happened? What should you do?

Advanced Exercises

7. What scp command would you use to copy your home directory from **bravo** to the local system?
8. What single command could you give to log in as **root** on the remote system named **bravo**, if **bravo** has remote **root** logins disabled?
9. How could you use ssh to compare the contents of the ~/memos directories on **bravo** and the local system?

```
$ ls ~/memos > filelist
$ ssh bravo ls ~/memos | diff filelist -
```

FTP: Transferring Files Across a Network

19

The ftp File Transfer Protocol (FTP) is a method of downloading files from and uploading files to another system using TCP/IP over a network. File Transfer Protocol is the name of a client/server protocol (FTP) and a client utility (ftp) that invokes the protocol. In addition to the original ftp utility, there are many line-oriented and graphical FTP client programs, including most browsers, that run under many different operating systems. There are also many FTP server programs.

Introduction

First implemented under 4.2BSD, FTP has played an essential role in the propagation of Linux; it is the protocol/program frequently used to distribute free software. The term *FTP site* refers to an FTP server that is connected to a network, usually the Internet. FTP sites can be public, allowing anonymous users to log in and download software and documentation. Private FTP sites require you to log in with a username and password. Some sites allow you to upload programs.

ftp and vsftpd   Although most FTP clients are similar, the servers differ quite a bit. This chapter describes the ftp client with references to sftp, a secure FTP client, and it covers the FTP server that Red Hat uses internally and offers as part of its distribution, **vsftpd** (very secure FTP).

Security   FTP is not a secure protocol. All usernames and passwords exchanged in setting up an FTP connection are sent in cleartext, data exchanged over an FTP connection is not encrypted, and the connection is subject to hijacking. FTP is best used for downloading public files. In most cases, the OpenSSH clients, ssh (page 570), scp (page 572), and sftp (page 573), offer secure alternatives to FTP.

You can use scp for almost all FTP functions other than allowing anonymous users to download information. Because scp uses an encrypted connection, user passwords and data cannot be sniffed. See page 570 for more information on scp.

The **vsftpd** server does *not* make usernames, passwords, data, and connections more secure. The **vsftpd** server is secure in that it is harder for a malicious user to compromise directly the system running it, even if **vsftpd** is poorly implemented. One of the features that makes **vsftpd** more secure than, for example **ftpd**, is that it does not run with **root** privileges. See also "Security" on page 595.

ftp utility   The ftp utility is a user interface to the standard File Transfer Protocol (FTP), which transfers files between systems that can communicate over a network.

sftp utility   Part of the OpenSSH suite, sftp is a secure alternative to ftp. See page 573 for more information.

FTP connections   FTP uses two connections: one for control (you establish this connection when you log in on an FTP server) and one for data transfer (FTP sets this up when you ask it to transfer a file). An FTP server listens for incoming connections on port 21 by default and handles user authentication and file exchange.

Passive versus active connections   A client can ask an FTP server to establish either a PASV (passive, default) or a PORT (active) connection for data transfer. Some servers are limited to one type of connection or the other. The difference between a passive and an active FTP connection is in whether the client or server initiates the data connection. In passive mode, the client initiates the connection to the server (on port 20 by default), while in active mode the server initiates the connection (there is no default port; see "Connection Parameters" on page 603 for the parameters that determine which ports are used). Neither is inherently more secure. The reasons that passive connections are more common are that a client behind a NAT (page 738) can connect to a passive server and it is simpler to program a scalable passive server.

The parameters that control the type of connection that **vsftpd** server allows are discussed under "Connection Parameters" on page 603.

More Information

Local   Type **help** or ? at any **ftp>** prompt to see a list of commands; follow the ? with a SPACE and an **ftp** command for information about the command
man pages   ftp netrc vsftpd.conf

Web   **vsftpd** home page   vsftpd.beasts.org

HOWTO   *FTP mini-HOWTO*

FTP Client

ftp   Red Hat supplies several different FTP clients including ftp (an older version of the BSD ftp utility). This section discusses ftp as most other FTP clients provide a superset of ftp commands.

sftp   Part of the OpenSSH suite, sftp is a secure alternative to ftp. See page 573 for more information.

gftp   Red Hat also provides gftp, a graphical client that works with FTP, SSH, and HTTP servers. This client has many useful features, including the ability to resume an interrupted file transfer. See the gftp man page for more information.

ncftp   *FEDORA* includes ncftp, a text-based client with many more features than ftp, including filename completion and command line editing. See the ncftp man page for details.

Prerequisites

The ftp and sftp utilities are installed on most Red Hat systems. You can check for their presence by giving either of these utilities' names as commands:

```
$ ftp
ftp> quit

$ sftp
usage: sftp [-vC1] [-b batchfile] [-o option] [-s subsystem|path] ...
            [-F config] [-P direct server path] [-S program]
            [user@]host[:file [file]]
```

Install the **ftp** or **openssh-clients** (contains sftp, see [page 567] for information on installing OPENssh) rpm package if needed.

JumpStart: Downloading Files Using ftp

This JumpStart section is broken into two parts: a description of the basic commands and a tutorial session that shows a user working with ftp.

Basic Commands

Give the command

```
$ ftp hostname
```

where *hostname* is the name of the FTP server you want to connect to. If you have an account on the server, log in with your username and password. If it is a public system, log in as user **anonymous** (or **ftp**) and give your email address as your password. Use the **ls** and **cd** ftp commands on the server as you would use the corresponding utilities from a shell. The **get** *file* command copies *file* from the server to the local system, **put** *file* copies *file* from the local system to the server, **status** displays information about the FTP connection, and **help** displays a list of commands.

The preceding instructions, except for **status**, also work from sftp and ncftp.

Tutorial Session

Following are two ftp sessions wherein Alex transfers files from and to a **vsftpd** server named **bravo**. When Alex gives the command **ftp bravo**, the local ftp client connects to the server, which asks for a username and password. Because he is logged in on his local system as **alex**, ftp suggests that he log in on **bravo** as **alex**. To log in as **alex**, he could just press RETURN; but his username on **bravo** is **watson**, so he types **watson** in response to the **Name (bravo:alex):** prompt. Alex responds to the **Password:** prompt with his normal system password, and the **vsftpd** server greets him and informs him that it is **Using binary mode to transfer files**. With ftp in binary mode, Alex can transfer ASCII and binary files (page 589).

Connect and log in

```
$ ftp bravo
Connected to bravo.
220 (vsFTPd 1.2.0)
530 Please login with USER and PASS.
530 Please login with USER and PASS.
KERBEROS_V4 rejected as an authentication type
Name (bravo:alex): watson
331 Please specify the password.
Password:
230 Login successful.
Remote system type is UNIX.
Using binary mode to transfer files.
ftp>
```

After logging in, Alex uses the ftp **ls** command to see what is in his remote working directory, which is his home directory on **bravo**. Then he **cd**s to the **memos** directory and displays the files there.

ls and cd

```
ftp> ls
227 Entering Passive Mode (192,168,0,6,79,105)
150 Here comes the directory listing.
drwxr-xr-x    2 500        500          4096 Oct 10 23:52 expenses
drwxr-xr-x    2 500        500          4096 Oct 10 23:59 memos
drwxrwxr-x   22 500        500          4096 Oct 10 23:32 tech
226 Directory send OK.

ftp> cd memos
250 Directory successfully changed.

ftp> ls
227 Entering Passive Mode (192,168,0,6,114,210)
150 Here comes the directory listing.
-rw-r--r--    1 500        500          4770 Oct 10 23:58 memo.0514
-rw-r--r--    1 500        500          7134 Oct 10 23:58 memo.0628
-rw-r--r--    1 500        500          9453 Oct 10 23:58 memo.0905
-rw-r--r--    1 500        500          3466 Oct 10 23:59 memo.0921
-rw-r--r--    1 500        500          1945 Oct 10 23:59 memo.1102
226 Directory send OK.
```

Next, Alex uses the ftp **get** command to copy **memo.1102** from the server to the local system. Binary mode ensures that he will get a good copy of the file regardless of whether it is binary or ASCII. The server gives him confirmation that the file was copied successfully and tells him the size of the file and how long it took to copy. Alex then copies the local file **memo.1114** to the remote system. The file is copied into his remote working directory, **memos**.

get and put

```
ftp> get memo.1102
local: memo.1102 remote: memo.1102
227 Entering Passive Mode (192,168,0,6,194,214)
150 Opening BINARY mode data connection for memo.1102 (1945 bytes).
226 File send OK.
1945 bytes received in 7.1e-05 secs (2.7e+04 Kbytes/sec)

ftp> put memo.1114
local: memo.1114 remote: memo.1114
227 Entering Passive Mode (192,168,0,6,174,97)
150 Ok to send data.
226 File receive OK.
1945 bytes sent in 2.8e-05 secs (6.8e+04 Kbytes/sec)
```

After a while, Alex decides he wants to copy all the files in the **memo** directory on **bravo** to a new directory on his local system. He gives an **ls** command to make sure he is going to copy the right files, but ftp has timed out. Instead of exiting from ftp and giving another ftp command from the shell, he gives ftp an **open bravo** command to reconnect to the server. After logging in, he uses the ftp **cd** command to change directories to **memos** on the server.

timeout and open

```
ftp> ls
421 Timeout.
Passive mode refused.
ftp> open bravo
Connected to bravo (192.168.0.6).
220 (vsFTPd 1.1.3)
...
ftp> cd memos
250 Directory successfully changed.
```

local cd (lcd) At this point, Alex realizes he has not created the new directory to hold the files he wants to download. Giving an ftp **mkdir** command would create a new directory on the server, but Alex wants a new directory on his local system. He uses an exclamation point (!) followed by a **mkdir memos.hold** command to invoke a shell and run mkdir on his local system, creating a directory named **memos.hold** in his working directory on the local system. (You can display the name of your working directory on the local system with **!pwd**.) Next, because he wants to copy files from the server to the **memos.hold** directory on his local system, he has to change his working directory on the local system. Giving the command **!cd memos.hold** will not accomplish what Alex wants to do because the exclamation point spawns a new shell on the local system and the **cd** command would be effective only in the new shell, which is not the shell that ftp is running under. For this situation, ftp provides the **lcd** (local cd) command, which changes the working directory for ftp and reports on the new local working directory.

```
ftp> !mkdir memos.hold
```

```
ftp> lcd memos.hold
Local directory now /home/alex/memos.hold
```

Alex uses the ftp **mget** (multiple get) command followed by the asterisk (*) wildcard to copy all the files from the remote **memos** directory to the **memos.hold** directory on the local system. When ftp prompts him for the first file, he realizes that he forgot to turn off prompts, responds with **n**, and presses CONTROL-C to stop copying files in response to the second prompt. The server checks if he wants to continue with his **mget** command.

Next, he gives the ftp **prompt** command, which toggles the prompt action (turns it off if it is on and turns it on if it is off). Now when he gives a **mget** * command, ftp copies all the files without prompting him. After getting the files he wants, Alex gives a **quit** command to close the connection with the server, exit from ftp, and return to the local shell prompt.

mget and prompt

```
ftp> mget *
mget memo.0514? n
mget memo.0628? CONTROL-C
Continue with mget? n
```

```
ftp> prompt
Interactive mode off.
```

```
ftp> mget *
local: memo.0514 remote: memo.0514
227 Entering Passive Mode (192,168,0,6,53,55)
150 Opening BINARY mode data connection for memo.0514 (4770 bytes).
226 File send OK.
4770 bytes received in 8.8e-05 secs (5.3e+04 Kbytes/sec)
local: memo.0628 remote: memo.0628
227 Entering Passive Mode (192,168,0,6,65,102)
150 Opening BINARY mode data connection for memo.0628 (7134 bytes).
226 File send OK.
...
150 Opening BINARY mode data connection for memo.1114 (1945 bytes).
226 File send OK.
1945 bytes received in 3.9e-05 secs (4.9e+04 Kbytes/sec)
ftp> quit
221 Goodbye.
```

Notes

A Linux system running ftp can exchange files with any of the many operating systems that support the FTP protocol. Many sites offer archives of free information on an FTP server, although for many it is just an alternate to an easier-to-access Web site (see for example, ftp://ftp.ibiblio.org/pub/Linux and http://www.ibiblio.org/pub/Linux). Most browsers can connect to and download files from FTP servers. Many systems that permit anonymous access store interesting files in the **pub** directory.

The ftp utility makes no assumptions about filesystem naming or structure because you can use ftp to exchange files with non-UNIX/Linux systems (whose filenaming conventions may be different).

Anonymous FTP

Many systems, notably those that allow you to download free software, allow you to log in as **anonymous**. Most systems that support anonymous logins accept the name **ftp** as an easier-to-spell and quicker-to-enter synonym for **anonymous**. An anonymous user is usually restricted to a portion of a filesystem set aside to hold files that are to be shared with remote users. When you log in as an anonymous user, the server prompts you to enter a password. Although any password may be accepted, by convention you are expected to supply your email address.

Automatic Login

You can store server specific FTP username and password information so that you do not have to enter it each time you visit an FTP site. Each line of **~/.netrc** identifies a server. When you connect to an FTP server, ftp reads the **~/.netrc** file to determine whether you have an automatic login set up for that server. The format of a line in **~/.netrc** is

> machine **server** login **username** password **passwd**

where **server** is the name of the server, **username** is your username and **passwd** is your password on **server**. Replace **machine** with **default** on the last line of the file to specify a username and password for systems not listed in **~/.netrc**. The **default** line is useful for logging in on anonymous servers. A sample **~/.netrc** file follows:

```
$ cat ~/.netrc
machine bravo login alex password mypassword
default login anonymous password alex@tcorp.com
```

Protect the account information in **.netrc** by making it readable by only the user whose home directory it appears in. Refer to the **netrc** man page for more information.

Binary versus ASCII Transfer Mode

The **vsftpd** FTP server can, but does not always, provide two modes to transfer files. Binary mode transfers always copy an exact, byte-for-byte image of a file and never changes line endings. Transfer all binary files using binary mode. Unless you need to convert line endings, use binary mode to transfer ASCII files too.

ASCII files, such as text or program source code, created under Linux with a text editor such as vi, use a single NEWLINE character (CONTROL-J, written as \n) to mark the end of each line. Other operating systems mark the ends of lines differently. Windows marks the end of each such line with a RETURN (CONTROL-M, written as \r) followed by a NEWLINE (two characters). Apple uses a RETURN by itself. These descriptions do not apply to files created by word processors such as Word or OpenOffice as these programs generate binary files.

The **vsftpd** FTP server can map Linux line endings to Windows line endings as you upload files and Windows line endings to Linux line endings as you download files. Although these features should arguably be on the client and not the server, they are incorporated in **vsftpd** where the ASCII download feature can be a security risk.

To use ASCII mode on an FTP server that allows it, give an **ascii** command (page 592) after you log in and set **cr** to ON (the default, page 592). If the server does not allow you to change line endings as you transfer a file, you can use the unix2dos or dos2unix utilities before/after you transfer a file in binary mode.

Security   When run against a very large file, the ftp **size** command, which displays the size of a file, consumes a lot of server resources and can be used to initiate a *DoS attack* (page 968). For security, by default, **vsftpd** transfers every file in binary mode, even when it appears to be using ASCII mode. On the server side, you can enable *real* ASCII mode transfers by setting the **ascii_upload_enable** and **ascii_download_enable** parameters (page 601) to YES. With the server set to allow ASCII transfers, the client controls whether line endings are mapped by using the **ascii**, **binary**, and **cr** commands (page 592).

ftp Specifics

This section covers the details of using ftp.

Format

The format of an ftp command line is shown following:

ftp [options] [ftp-server]

where *options* is one or more options from the list in the next section and *ftp-server* is the name or network address of the FTP server that you want to exchange files with. If you do not specify an *ftp-server*, you will need to use the ftp **open** command to connect to a server once ftp is running.

Command Line Options

–i   interactive   Turns off prompts during file transfers with **mget** (page 591) and **mput** (page 592). See also **prompt** (page 593).

–g   globbing   Turns off globbing. See **glob** (page 592).

–v verbose Tells you more about how ftp is working. Responses from the remote computer are displayed, and ftp reports information on how quickly files are transferred. See also **verbose** (page 594).

–n no automatic login Disables automatic logins as described on page 589.

ftp Commands

The ftp utility is interactive: After you start ftp, it prompts you to enter commands to set parameters or transfer files. You can abbreviate commands as long as the abbreviations are unique. Enter a question mark (**?**) in response to the **ftp>** prompt to display a list of commands. Follow the question mark by a SPACE and a command to display a brief description of what the command does:

```
ftp> ? mget
mget            get multiple files
```

Shell Command

![*command*] Escapes to (spawns) a shell on the local system (use CONTROL-D or **exit** to return to ftp when you are finished using the local shell). Follow the exclamation point with a command to execute that command only; ftp returns you to the **ftp>** prompt when the command completes executing. Because the shell that ftp spawns with this command is a child of the shell that is running ftp, no changes you make in this shell are preserved when you return to ftp. Specifically, when you want to copy files to a local directory other than the directory that you started ftp from, you need to use the ftp **lcd** command to change your local working directory: Issuing a **cd** command in the spawned shell will not make the change you desire. See "local cd (lcd)" on page 587 for an example.

Transfer Files

In the following descriptions, the *remote-file* and *local-file* can be pathnames.

append *local-file* [*remote-file*]
Appends *local-file* to the file of the same name on the remote system or to *remote-file* if specified.

get *remote-file* [*local-file*]
Copies *remote-file* to the local system under the name *local-file*. Without *local-file*, ftp uses *remote-file* as the filename on the local system.

mget *remote-file-list* **multiple get** The **mget** command copies several files to the local system, each maintaining its original filename. You can name the remote files literally or use wildcards (see **glob**, page 592). See **prompt** (page 593) to turn off prompts during transfers.

mput *local-file-list*   **multiple put**   The **mput** command copies several files to the server, each maintaining its original filename. You can name the local files literally or use wildcards (see **glob**, page 592). See **prompt** (page 593) to turn off prompts during transfers.

put *local-file* [*remote-file*]

Copies *local-file* to the remote system under the name *remote-file*. Without *remote-file*, ftp uses *local-file* as the filename on the remote system.

newer *remote-file* [*local-file*]

If the modification time of *remote-file* is more recent than that of *local-file* or if *local-file* does not exist, copies *remote-file* to the local system under the name *local-file*. Without *local-file*, ftp uses *remote-file* as the filename on the local system. Similar to **get**.

reget *remote-file* [*local-file*]

If *local-file* exists and is smaller than *remote-file*, assumes that a previous **get** of *local-file* was interrupted and continues from where the previous **get** left off. This command can save you time when a **get** of a large file fails part way through the transfer.

Status

ascii   Sets the file transfer type to ASCII. The **cr** command must be ON for **ascii** to work (page 589).

binary   Sets the file transfer type to binary (page 589).

bye   Closes the connection to the server and terminates ftp. Same as **quit**.

case   Toggles and displays case mapping status. Default is OFF. When ON, for **get** and **mget** commands, maps filenames that are all uppercase on the server to all lowercase on the local system.

close   Closes the connection to the server without exiting from ftp.

cr   **Carriage** RETURN   Toggles and displays (carriage) RETURN stripping status. Effective only when file transfer type is **ascii**. Set **cr** to ON (default) to remove RETURN characters from RETURN/LINEFEED line termination sequences used by Windows, yielding the standard Linux line termination of LINEFEED. Set **cr** to OFF to leave line ending unmapped (page 589).

debug [*n*]   Toggles/sets and displays debugging status/level. The *n* is the debugging level. OFF or 0 (zero) is the default. When *n* > 0, displays each command ftp sends to the server.

glob   Toggles and displays filename expansion (page 207) status for **mdelete** (page 593), **mget** (page 591), and **mput** (page 592) commands.

hash   Toggles and displays pound sign (#, also called a hash mark) display status. When ON, ftp displays one pound sign for each 1024-byte data block it transfers.

open   Interactively specifies the name of the server. Useful when a connection times out or otherwise fails.

passive   Toggles between active (PORT, default) and passive (PASV) transfer modes and displays the transfer mode. For more information, refer to "Passive versus active connections" on page 584.

prompt   Toggles and displays the prompt status. When ON (default), **mdelete** (page 593), **mget** (page 591), and **mput** (page 592) ask for verification before transferring each file. Turn OFF to turn off these prompts.

quit   Closes the connection to the server and terminates ftp. Same as **bye**.

umask [*nnn*]   Changes the umask (page 398) applied to files created on the server to *nnn*. Without an option, displays the umask.

user [*username*] [*password*]
Prompts for or accepts the *username* and *password* that enable you to log in on the server. Unless you call it with the **–n** option, ftp prompts you for a username and password automatically.

Directories

cd *remote-directory*   Changes the working directory on the server to *remote-directory*.

cdup   Changes the working directory on the server to the parent of the working directory.

lcd [*local_directory*]   **local change directory**   Changes the working directory on the local system to *local_directory*. Without an argument, this command changes the working directory on the local system to your home directory (just as the cd shell builtin does without an argument). See "local cd (lcd)" on page 587 for an example.

Files

chmod *mode remote-file*
Changes access permissions of *remote-file* on the server to *mode*. See chmod on (page 174) for more information on how to specify *mode*.

delete *remote-file*   Removes *remote-file* from the server.

mdelete *remote-file-list*
multiple delete   Deletes the files specified by *remote-file-list* from the server.

Display Information

dir [*remote-directory*] [*file*]
Displays a listing of *remote-directory* from the server. Displays the working directory when you do not specify *remote-directory*. When you specify *file*, the listing is saved on the local system in a file named *file*.

help   Displays a list of local ftp commands.

ls [*remote-directory*] [*file*]

Similar to **dir** but produces a more concise listing from some servers.

pwd   Displays the pathname of the working directory on the server. Use **!pwd** to display the pathname of the local working directory.

status   Displays ftp connection and status information.

verbose   Toggles and displays verbose mode, which displays responses from the server and reports on how quickly files are transferred. Same as specifying the **–v** option on the command line.

FTP Server (vsftpd)

This section discusses the **vsftpd** server as supplied and installed under Red Hat Linux.

Prerequisites

Install the following packages:

• **vsftpd**

Run chkconfig to cause **vsftpd** to start when the system goes multiuser.

```
# /sbin/chkconfig vsftpd on
```

Start **vsftpd**. If you change the **vsftpd.conf** configuration file, you need to restart **vsftpd**.

```
# /sbin/service vsftpd start
```

Notes

The **vsftpd** server can run in normal mode (the **xinetd** daemon [page 403] calls **vsftpd** each time a client tries to make a connection) or it can run in standalone mode (**vsftpd** runs as a daemon and handles connections directly).

Standalone mode   Although by default **vsftpd** runs in normal mode, Red Hat sets it up to run in standalone mode by setting the **listen** parameter (page 596) to YES in the **vsftpd.conf** file. Under Red Hat Linux, with **vsftpd** running in standalone mode, you start and stop the server using service and the **vsftpd** init script.

Normal mode   You must install an **xinetd** control file (page 403) if you want to run **vsftpd** in normal mode. There is a sample file at **/usr/share/doc/vsftpd*/vsftpd.xinetd**. Copy the sample file to **/etc/xinetd.d**, rename it **vsftpd,** and edit the file to change the **disable** parameter to **no**. With the **listen** parameter set to NO, **xinetd** will take care of starting **vsftpd** as needed.

Security The safest policy is not to allow users to authenticate against FTP: Use FTP for anonymous access only. If you do allow local users to authenticate and upload files to the server, be sure to put local users in a chroot jail (page 598). Because FTP sends usernames and passwords in cleartext, a malicious user can easily *sniff* (page 997) them. With a username and password, the same user can impersonate a local user, upload a *Trojan horse* (page 1002), and compromise the system.

JumpStart: Starting a vsftpd Server

As **vsftpd** is installed from the Red Hat rpm file, local and anonymous users can log in on the server; there is no guest account. You do not have to configure anything.

Testing the Setup

Make sure **vsftpd** is working by logging in from the system running the server. You can refer to the server as **localhost** or by using its hostname on the command line. Log in as **anonymous**; use any password.

```
$ ftp localhost
Connected to localhost.localdomain.
220 (vsFTPd 1.2.0)
530 Please login with USER and PASS.
530 Please login with USER and PASS.
KERBEROS_V4 rejected as an authentication type
Name (bravo:alex): anonymous
331 Please specify the password.
Password:
230 Login successful.
Remote system type is UNIX.
Using binary mode to transfer files.
ftp> quit
221 Goodbye.
```

If you are not able to connect to the server, check the following:

Make sure the server is running.

```
# /sbin/service vsftpd status
vsftpd (pid 3091) is running...
```

Check that permissions on **/var/ftp**, or the home directory of ftp as specified in **/etc/passwd**, are set to 755. If the **ftp** user can write to **/var/ftp**, connections will fail.

```
# ls -ld /var/ftp
drwxr-xr-x    4 root     root         4096 Aug 27 23:54 /var/ftp
```

Once you are able to log in from the local system, log in from another system, either one on your LAN or another system with access to the server. On the command line, use the hostname from within your LAN or the *FQDN* (page 972) from outside your LAN. The dialog should appear the same as in the previous example. If you cannot log in from a system that is not on your LAN, use ping (page 346) to test the connection and make sure your firewall is set up to allow FTP access. See "FTP connections" on page 584 for a discussion of active and passive modes and the ports that each uses.

vsftpd.conf: Configuring vsftpd

The configuration file for **vsftpd**, **/etc/vsftpd/vsftpd.conf**, lists Boolean, numeric, and string name-value pairs of configuration parameters, called directives. Each name-value pair is joined by an equal sign with no SPACEs on either side. Red Hat provides a well-commented **/etc/vsftpd/vsftpd.conf** file that changes many of the compiled-in defaults. This section covers most of the options, noting their default values and their values as specified in the **vsftpd.conf** file supplied by Red Hat.

Set Boolean options to YES or NO and numeric options to a nonnegative integer. Octal numbers, useful for setting umask options, must have a leading 0 (zero), or the number will be treated as base ten. Following are examples from **vsftpd.conf** of setting each type of option:

```
anonymous_enable=YES
local_umask=022
xferlog_file=/var/log/vsftpd.log
```

Where Red Hat has overridden the default value by putting a different value in **vsftpd.conf**, both the default and Red Hat values are noted. The directives are broken into the following groups:

- Standalone Mode (page 596)
- Logging In (page 597)
- Working Directory and the chroot Jail (page 598)
- Downloading and Uploading Files (page 600)
- Messages (page 602)
- Display (page 602)
- Logs (page 603)
- Connection Parameters (page 603)

Standalone Mode

Refer to "Notes" on page 588 for a discussion of normal and standalone modes. This section describes the parameters that affect standalone mode.

listen YES runs **vsftpd** in standalone mode; NO runs it in normal mode.

Default: NO
Red Hat: YES

listen_port   In standalone mode, specifies the port that **vsftpd** listens on for incoming connections.

Default: 21

listen_address   In standalone mode, specifies the IP address of the local interface that **vsftpd** listens on for incoming connections. When not set, **vsftpd** uses the default network interface.

Default: none

max_clients   In standalone mode, specifies the maximum number of clients. Zero (0) indicates unlimited clients.

Default: 0

max_per_ip   In standalone mode, specifies the maximum number of clients from the same IP address. Zero (0) indicates unlimited clients from the same IP address.

Default: 0

Logging In

There are three classes of users who can log in on a **vsftpd** server: anonymous, local, and guest. The guest user is rarely used and is not covered in this chapter. Local users log in with their system username and password, while anonymous users log in with **anonymous** or **ftp**, using their email address as a password. You can control whether each of these classes of users can log in on the server and what they can do once they log in. You can specify what a local user can do on a per-user basis; refer to **user_config_dir** on page 606.

Local Users

userlist_enable   The **/etc/vsftpd.user_list** file (page 606), or other file specified by **userlist_file**, contains a list of zero or more users. YES consults the list and takes action based on **userlist_deny**, either granting or denying users in the list permission to log in on the server. To prevent the transmission of cleartext passwords, access is denied immediately after the user enters his/her username. NO does not consult the list. For a more secure system, set to NO.

Default: NO
Red Hat: YES

userlist_deny   YES prevents users listed in **/etc/vsftpd.user_list** (page 606) from logging in on the server. NO allows *only* users listed in **/etc/vsftpd.user_list** to log in on the server. Use **userlist_file** to change the name of the file that this parameter consults. This parameter is checked only when **userlist_enable** is set to YES.

Default: YES

userlist_file   The name of the file consulted when **userlist_enable** is set to YES.

Default: **/etc/vsftpd.user_list**

local_enable   YES permits local users (users listed in **/etc/passwd**) to log in on the server.

Default: NO
Red Hat: YES

Anonymous Users

anonymous_enable   YES allows anonymous logins.

Default: YES

no_anon_password   YES skips asking anonymous users for passwords.

Default: NO

deny_email_enable   YES checks to see if the password (email address) that an anonymous user enters is listed in **/etc/vsftpd.banned_emails** or other file specified by **banned_email_file**. If it is, the user is not allowed to log in on the system. NO does not perform this check. Using iptables (page 737) to block specific hosts is generally more productive than using this parameter.

Default: NO

banned_email_file   The name of the file consulted when **deny_email_enable** is set to YES.

Default: (**/etc/vsftpd.banned_emails**)

Working Directory and the chroot Jail

When a user logs in on a **vsftpd** server, standard filesystem access permissions control which directories and files the user can access and how the user can access them. There are three basic parameters that control a user who is logged in on a **vsftpd** server. They are the user's

- User ID (UID)
- Initial working directory
- Root directory

By default, the **vsftpd** server sets the user ID of a local user to that user's login name and sets the user ID of an anonymous user to **ftp**. A local user starts in her home directory and an anonymous user starts in **/var/ftp**.

By default, anonymous users are placed in a chroot jail for security; local users are not. For example, when an anonymous user logs in on a **vsftpd** server, his home directory is **/var/ftp**. But all that user sees is that his home directory is **/**. The user sees the directory at **/var/ftp/upload** as **/upload**. The user cannot see, nor work with, for example, the **/home**, **/usr/local**, or **/tmp** directories. The user is in a chroot jail. For more information, refer to "Setting Up a chroot Jail" on page 406.

You can use the **chroot_local_user** option to put each local user in a chroot jail whose root is the user's home directory. You can use **chroot_list_enable** to put selected local users in chroot jails.

chroot_list_enable Upon login, YES checks to see whether a local user is listed in **/etc/vsftpd.chroot_list** (page 606) or other file specified by **chroot_list_file**.

When a user is in the list and **chroot_local_user** is set to NO, the user is put in a chroot jail in his home directory. Only users listed in **/etc/vsftpd.chroot_list** are put in chroot jails.

When a user is in the list and **chroot_local_user** is set to YES, that user is not put in a chroot jail. Users not listed in **/etc/vsftpd.chroot_list** are put in chroot jails.

Default: NO

chroot_local_user See **chroot_list_enable**. Set to NO for a more open system, but remember to add new users to the **chroot_list_file** as needed as you add users to the system. Set to YES for a more secure system. New users are automatically restricted unless you add them to **chroot_list_file**.

Default: NO

chroot_list_file The name of the file consulted when **chroot_list_enable** is set to YES.

Default: **/etc/vsftpd.chroot_list**

passwd_chroot_enable

YES enables you to change the location of the chroot jail that the **chroot_list_enable** and **chroot_local_user** settings impose on a local user.

The location of the chroot jail can be moved up the directory structure by including a */./* within the home directory string for that user in **/etc/passwd**. This change has no effect on the standard system login, just as **cd .** has no effect on your working directory.

For example, changing the home directory field in **/etc/passwd** (page 430) for Sam from **/home/sam** to **/home/./sam** allows Sam to cd to **/home** after logging in using **vsftpd**. Given the proper permissions, this ability can allow Sam to view files and possibly collaborate with another user.

Default: NO

secure_chroot_dir The name of an empty directory that is not writable by user **ftp**. The **vsftpd** server uses this directory as a secure chroot jail when the user does not need access to the filesystem.

Default: **/usr/share/empty**

local_root   After a local user logs in on the server, this directory becomes the user's working directory. No error results if the specified directory does not exist.

Default: none

Downloading and Uploading Files

By default, any user, local or anonymous, can download files from the server, assuming proper filesystem access and permissions. You must change **write_enable** from NO (default) to YES to permit local users to upload files. By default, **local_umask** is set to 022, giving uploaded files 644 permissions (page 173).

Security   Refer to "Security" on page 595 for information on the security hole that is created when you allow local users to upload files.

The following actions set up **vsftpd** to allow anonymous users to upload files:

1. Set **write_enable** (page 600) to YES.

2. Create a directory under **/var/ftp** that an anonymous user can write to but not read from (mode 333). You do not want a malicious user to be able to see, download, modify, and upload a file that another user originally uploaded. The following commands create a **/var/ftp/uploads** directory that anyone can write to but no one can read from:

```
# mkdir /var/ftp/uploads
# chmod 333 /var/ftp/uploads
```

Because of the security risk, **vsftpd** prevents anonymous connections when an anonymous user (**ftp**) can write to **/var/ftp**.

3. Set **anon_upload_enable** (page 601) to YES.

4. See other options in this section.

Download/Upload for Local Users

local_umask   The umask (page 398) setting for local users.

Default: 077
Red Hat: 022

file_open_mode   Uploaded file permissions for local users. The umask (page 398) is applied to this value. Change to 0777 to make uploaded files executable.

Default: 0666

write_enable   YES permits users to create and delete files and directories (assuming appropriate filesystem permissions). NO prevents users from making changes to the filesystem.

Default: NO
Red Hat: YES

Anonymous Users

anon_mkdir_write_enable

> YES permits an anonymous user to create new directories when **write_enable**=YES and the anonymous user has permission to write to the parent directory.
>
> Default: NO

anon_other_write_enable

> YES grants an anonymous user write permission in addition to the permissions granted by **anon_mkdir_write_enable** and **anon_upload_enable**. For example, YES allows an anonymous user to delete and rename files, assuming permission to write to the parent directory. Not recommended for secure sites.
>
> Default: NO

anon_root   After an anonymous user logs in on the server, this directory becomes the user's working directory. No error results if the specified directory does not exist.

> Default: none

anon_umask   The umask (page 398) setting for anonymous users. The default setting gives only anonymous users access to files uploaded by anonymous users; set to 022 to give everyone read access to these files.

> Default: 077

anon_upload_enable

> YES allows anonymous users to upload files when **write_enable**=YES and the anonymous user has permission to write to the directory.
>
> Default: NO

anon_world_readable_only

> YES limits the files that a user can *download* to those that are readable by the owner, group, and others. It may not be desirable to allow one anonymous user to download a file that another anonymous user uploaded. Setting this parameter to YES can prevent this scenario.
>
> Default: YES

ascii_download_enable

> YES allows a user to download files using ASCII mode. Setting this parameter to YES can create a security risk (page 590).
>
> Default: NO

ascii_upload_enable YES allows a user to upload files using ASCII mode (page 589).

> Default: NO

chown_uploads   YES causes files uploaded by anonymous users to be owned by **root** (or other user specified by **chown_username**).

> Default: NO

chown_username   See **chown_uploads**.

Default: **root**

ftp_username   The login name of anonymous users.

Default: **ftp**

nopriv_user   The name of the user with minimal privileges, as used by **vsftpd**. For security, because other programs use **nobody**, replace **nobody** with the name of a dedicated user such as **ftp**.

Default: **nobody**

Messages

You can replace the standard greeting banner that **vsftpd** displays when a user logs in on the system (**banner_file** and **ftpd_banner**) and you can display a message each time a user enters a directory (**dirmessage_enable** and **message_file**). When you set **dirmessage_enable=YES**, each time a user enters a directory using cd, **vsftpd** displays the contents of the file in that directory named **.message** (or other file specified by **message_file**).

dirmessage_enable   YES displays **.message** or other file specified by **message_file** as an ftp user enters a new directory by giving a **cd** command.

Default: NO
Red Hat: YES

message_file   See **dirmessage_enable**.

Default: **.message**

banner_file   The absolute pathname of the file that is displayed when a user connects to the server. Overrides **ftpd_banner**.

Default: none

ftpd_banner   This string overrides the standard **vsftpd** greeting banner displayed when a user connects to the server.

Default: none, uses standard **vsftpd** banner

Display

This section describes parameters that can improve security and performance by controlling how **vsftpd** displays information.

hide_ids   YES lists all users and groups in directory listings as **ftp**. NO lists real owners.

Default: NO

setproctitle_enable   NO causes **ps** to display the process running **vsftpd** as **vsftpd**. YES causes **ps** to display what **vsftpd** is currently doing (uploading and so on). Set to NO for a more secure system.

Default: NO

text_userdb_names   NO improves performance by displaying numeric UIDs and GIDs in directory listings. YES displays names.

Default: NO

use_localtime   NO causes **ls, mls,** and **modtime** FTP commands to display *UTC* (page 1004); YES causes these commands to display local times.

Default: NO

ls_recurse_enable   YES permits allows users to give **ls –R** commands. Setting this parameter to YES may pose a security risk because giving an **ls –R** command at the top of a large directory hierarchy can consume a lot of system resources.

Default: NO

Logs

By default, logging is turned off. However, the **vsftpd.conf** file that Red Hat supplies turns it on. This section describes parameters that control the detail and location of logs.

log_ftp_protocol   YES logs FTP requests and responses, provided that **xferlog_std_format** is set to NO.

Default: NO

xferlog_enable   YES maintains a transfer log in **/var/log/vsftpd.log** (or other file specified by **xferlog_file**). NO does not create a log.

Default: NO

xferlog_std_format   YES causes a transfer log (not covering connections) to be written in standard **xferlog** format, as used by **wu-ftpd**, as long as **xferlog_file** is explicitly set. The default **vsftpd** log format is more readable than **xferlog** format, but it cannot be processed by programs that generate statistical summaries of **xferlog** files. Search for **xferlog** on the Internet for more information.

Default: NO

xferlog_file   See **xferlog_enable** and **xferlog_std_format**.

Default: **/var/log/vsftpd.log**

Connection Parameters

You can allow clients to establish passive and/or active connections (page 584). Setting timeouts and maximum transfer rates can improve server security and perfor-

mance. This section describes parameters that control types of connections that a
client can establish, the length of time **vsftpd** will wait while establishing a connection, and the speeds of connections for different types of users.

Passive (PASV) Connections

pasv_enable   NO prevents the use of PASV connections.

Default: NO

pasv_promiscuous   NO causes PASV to perform a security check that ensures that the data and control
connections originate from a single IP address. YES disables this check and is not
recommended for a secure system.

Default: NO

pasv_max_port   The highest port number that **vsftpd** will allocate for a PASV data connection, useful in setting up a firewall.

Default: 0 (use any port)

pasv_min_port   The lowest port number that **vsftpd** will allocate for a PASV data connection, useful
in setting up a firewall.

Default: 0 (use any port)

pasv_address   Specifies an IP address other than the one used by the client to contact the server.

Default: none, the address is the one used by the client

Active (PORT) Connections

port_enable   NO prevents the use of PORT connections.

Default: YES

port_promiscuous   NO causes PORT to perform a security check that ensures that outgoing data connections connect only to the client. YES disables this check and is not recommended
for a secure system.

Default: NO

connect_from_port_20

YES specifies port 20 (**ftp-data,** a privileged port) on the server for PORT connections, as required by some clients. NO allows **vsftpd** to run with fewer privileges (on
a nonprivileged port).

Default: NO
Red Hat: YES

ftp_data_port   With **connect_from_port_20** set to NO, specifies the port that **vsftpd** uses for PORT
connections.

Default: 20

Timeouts

accept_timeout The number of seconds the server waits for a client to establish a PASV data connection.

Default: 60

connect_timeout The number of seconds the server waits for a client to respond to a PORT data connection.

Default: 60

data_connection_timeout

The number of seconds the server waits for a stalled data transfer to resume before disconnecting.

Default: 300

idle_session_timeout

The number of seconds the server waits between FTP commands before disconnecting.

Default: 300

local_max_rate For local users, the maximum data transfer rate in bytes per second. Zero indicates no limit.

Default: 0

anon_max_rate For anonymous users, the maximum data transfer rate in bytes per second. Zero indicates no limit.

Default: 0

one_process_model YES establishes one process per connection, improving performance but degrading security. NO allows multiple processes per connection. NO is recommended for a more secure system.

Default: NO

Miscellaneous

This section describes parameters not discussed elsewhere.

pam_service_name The name of the PAM service **vsftpd** uses.

Default: **ftp**
Red Hat: **vsftpd**

tcp_wrappers YES causes incoming connections to use **tcp_wrappers** (page 404) if **vsftpd** was compiled with **tcp_wrappers** support. When **tcp_wrappers** sets the environment variable **VSFTPD_LOAD_CONF**, **vsftpd** loads the configuration file specified by this variable, allowing per-IP configuration.

Default: NO

Red Hat: YES

user_config_dir   Specifies a directory that contains files named for local users. Each of these files, which mimics **vsftpd.conf**, contains parameters that override, on a per-user basis, default parameters and those specified in **vsftpd.conf**. For example, assume that **user_config_dir** is set to **/etc/vsftpd_user_conf**. If the default configuration file, **/etc/vsftpd/vsftpd.conf**, sets **idlesession_timeout=300** and Sam's individual configuration file, **/etc/vsftpd_user_conf/sams**, sets **idlesession_timeout=1200**, all users' sessions, except for Sam's, will timeout after 300 seconds of inactivity. Sam's sessions will timeout after 1200 seconds.

Default: none

Files

In addition to **/etc/vsftpd.conf**, the following files control the functioning of **vsftpd**. The directory hierarchy that **user_config_dir** points to is not included in this list as it has no default name.

/etc/vsftpd.ftpusers   Lists users, one per line, who are never allowed to log in on the FTP server, regardless of how **userlist_enable** (page 597) is set and regardless of the users listed in **vsftpd.user_list**. The default file lists **root**, **bin**, **daemon**, and others.

/etc/vsftpd.user_list   Lists either the only users who can log in on the server or the users who are not allowed to log in on the server. The **userlist_enable** (page 597) option must be set to YES for **vsftpd** to examine the list of users in this file. Setting **userlist_enable** to YES and **userlist_deny** (page 597) to YES (or not setting it) prevents listed users from logging in on the server. Setting **userlist_enable** to YES and **userlist_deny** to NO permits only the listed users to log in on the server.

/etc/vsftpd.chroot_list

Depending on the **chroot_list_enable** (page 599) and **chroot_local_user** (page 599) settings, this file lists either users who are forced into a chroot jail in their home directories or users who are not placed in a chroot jail.

/var/log/vsftpd.log   Log file. For more information, refer to "Logs" on page 603.

Chapter Summary

FTP, a protocol for downloading files from and uploading files to another system over a network, is the name of both a client/server protocol (FTP) and a client utility (ftp) that invokes the protocol. FTP is not a secure protocol and should be used only to download public information. You can run the **vsftpd** FTP server in the restricted environment of a chroot jail to make it significantly less likely that a malicious user can compromise the system.

There are many servers and clients that implement the FTP protocol. The ftp utility is the original client implementation; sftp is a secure implementation that uses the facilities of OpenSSH to encrypt the connection. The **vsftpd** daemon is a secure FTP server; it is secure in that it better protects the server from malicious users than do other FTP servers.

Public FTP servers allow you to log in as **anonymous** or **ftp**. Convention has you supply your email address as a password when you log in as an anonymous user. Public servers frequently have interesting files in the **pub** directory.

FTP provides two modes of transferring files: binary and ASCII. It is safe to use binary mode to transfer all types of files, including ASCII files. If you transfer a binary file using ASCII mode, the transfer will not be successful.

Exercises

1. What changes does FTP make to an ASCII file when you download it in ASCII mode to a Windows machine from a Linux server? What changes are made when you download the file to a Mac?

2. What happens if you transfer an executable program file in ASCII mode?

3. When would ftp be better than sftp?

4. How would you prevent local users logging in on the **vsftpd** server using their system username and password?

5. What advantage does sftp have over ftp?

6. What is the difference between cd and lcd in ftp?

Advanced Exercises

7. Why might you have problems connecting to an FTP server in PORT mode?

8. Why is it advantageous to run **vsftp** in a chroot jail?

9. After downloading a file, you find that it does not match the MD5 checksum provided. Downloading it again gives the same incorrect checksum. What have you done wrong and how would you fix it?

10. How would you configure **vsftpd** to run through **xinetd**, and what would be the main advantage of doing this?

sendmail: Setting Up Mail Clients, Servers, and More

20

Sending and receiving email require three pieces of software. At each end, there is a client, called an MUA (Mail User Agent), which is a bridge between a user and the mail system. Common MUAs are mutt, Kmail, Mozilla Mail, and Outlook. When you send an email, the MUA hands it to an MTA (a Mail Transfer Agent such as **sendmail**), which transfers it to the destination server. At the destination, an MDA (a Mail Delivery Agent such as **procmail**) puts the mail in the recipient's mailbox file. On Linux systems, the MUA on the receiving system either reads the mailbox file or retrieves mail from a remote MUA or MTA, such as an ISP's SMTP (mail) server, using POP (Post Office Protocol) or IMAP (Internet Message Access Protocol).

Most Linux MUAs expect a local copy of **sendmail** will deliver outgoing email. On some systems, including those with a dialup connection to the Internet, **sendmail** relays email to an ISP's mail server. Because **sendmail** uses SMTP (Simple Mail Transfer Protocol) to deliver email, **sendmail** is often referred to as an SMTP server.

In the default Red Hat setup, the **sendmail** MTA uses **procmail** as the local MDA. By default, **procmail** writes email to the end of the recipient's mailbox file. You can also use **procmail** to sort email according to a set of rules, either on a per-user basis or globally. The global filtering function is useful for systemwide filtering to detect spam and for other tasks, but the per-user feature is largely superfluous on a modern system. Traditional UNIX MUAs were simple programs that could not filter mail and delegated this function to MDAs such as **procmail**. Modern MUAs incorporate this functionality.

caution || **You Do Not Need to Set Up sendmail to Send and Receive Email**

Most MUAs can use POP or IMAP for receiving email. These protocols do not require an MTA such as **sendmail**. Thus you do not need to install or configure **sendmail** (or other MTA) to receive email. You still need SMTP to send email. However, the SMTP server can be at a remote location, such as your ISP, so you do not need to concern yourself with it.

Introduction

When the network that was to evolve into the Internet was first set up, it connected a few computers, each serving a large number of users and running several services. Each computer was capable of sending and receiving email and had a unique host name, which was used as a destination for email.

Today, the Internet has a large number of transient clients. Because these clients do not have fixed IP addresses or hostnames, they cannot receive email directly. Users on these systems usually have an account on an email server run by their employer or an ISP, and they collect email from this account using POP or IMAP. Unless you own a domain that you want to receive email at, you will not need to set up **send-mail** as an incoming SMTP server.

You can set up **sendmail** on a client system so all it does is relay outbound mail to an SMTP server. This configuration is required by organizations that use firewalls to prevent email from being sent out on the Internet from any system other than the company's official mail servers. As a partial defense against spreading viruses, some ISPs block outbound port 25 to prevent their customers from sending email directly to a remote computer. This configuration is required by these ISPs.

You can also set up **sendmail** as an outbound server that does not use an ISP as a re-lay. In this configuration, **sendmail** connects directly to the SMTP servers for the do-mains receiving the email. An ISP set up as a relay is configured this way.

You can set up **sendmail** to accept email for a registered domain name as specified in the domain's DNS MX record (page 706). However, most mail clients (MUAs) do not interact directly with **sendmail** to receive email. Instead, they use POP or IMAP, protocols that include features for managing mail folders, leaving messages on the server, and reading only the subject of an email without downloading the en-tire message. If you want to collect your email from a system other than the one running the incoming mail server, you may need to set up a POP or IMAP server, as discussed on page 628.

Prerequisites

Install the following packages:

- sendmail (required)
- sendmail-cf (required to configure **sendmail**)
- squirrelmail (optional, provides Webmail, page 625)
- spamassassin (optional, provides spam filtering, page 622)
- **mailman** (optional, provides mailing list support, page 627)
- imap (optional, provides IMAP and POP incoming mail server daemons)

Run chkconfig to cause **sendmail** to start when the system goes multiuser (by default, **sendmail** does not run in single user mode):

```
# /sbin/chkconfig sendmail on
```

Start **sendmail**. Because **sendmail** is normally running, you need to restart it to cause **sendmail** to reread its configuration files. The following restart command works even when **sendmail** is not running; it just fails to shut down **sendmail**:

```
# /sbin/service sendmail restart
Shutting down sendmail:                          [  OK  ]
Shutting down sm-client:                         [  OK  ]
Starting sendmail:                               [  OK  ]
Starting sm-client:                              [  OK  ]
```

Run chkconfig to cause the spamassassin daemon, **spamd,** to start when the system goes multiuser (spamassassin is normally installed in this configuration):

```
# /sbin/chkconfig spamassassin on
```

As with **sendmail**, spamassassin is normally running; restart it to cause **spamd** to reread its configuration files:

```
# /sbin/service spamassassin restart
Starting spamd:                                  [  OK  ]
```

The IMAP and POP protocols are implemented as several different daemons that are controlled by **xinetd.** See page 628 for information on these daemons and how to start them.

More Information

Web   **sendmail**   www.sendmail.org
IMAP   www.imap.org
SquirrelMail   www.squirrelmail.org
Postfix   www.postfix.org/docs.html
Qmail   www.qmail.org
Mailman   www.list.org
procmail   www.procmail.org
SpamAssassin   spamassassin.org
Spam database   razor.sourceforge.net

JumpStart I: Configuring sendmail on a Client

This JumpStart configures an outbound **sendmail** server. This server

- Uses a remote SMTP server, typically an ISP, to relay email to its destination

- Sends to the SMTP server email originating from the local system only; it does not forward email originating from other systems

- Does not handle inbound email; as is frequently the case, you need to use POP or IMAP to receive email

To set up this server, you must edit **/etc/mail/sendmail.mc** and restart **sendmail**.

Change sendmail.mc   The **dnl** at the start of the following line in **sendmail.mc** says that the line is a comment:

```
dnl define('SMART_HOST', 'smtp.your.provider')
```

To specify a remote SMTP server, you must open **sendmail.mc** in an editor and change the preceding line, deleting **dnl** from the beginning of the line and replacing **smtp.your.provider** with the FQDN of your ISP's SMTP server (obtain this name from your ISP). Be careful not to alter the back tick (`) preceding or the single quotation mark (') following the FQDN. If your ISP's SMTP server is at **smtp.my-isp.com**, you would change the line:

```
dnl define('SMART_HOST', 'smtp.your.provider')
```

Restart sendmail   When you restart it, **sendmail** regenerates the **sendmail.cf** file from the **sendmail.mc** file you edited:

```
# /sbin/service sendmail restart
```

Test   Test **sendmail** with the following command:

```
$ echo "my sendmail test" | /usr/sbin/sendmail user@remote.host
```

Replace *user@remote.host* with an email address on another system where you receive email. You need to send email to a remote system to make sure that **sendmail** is relaying your email.

JumpStart II: Configuring sendmail on a Server

If you want to receive inbound email sent to a registered domain that you own, you need to set up **sendmail** as an incoming mail server; this JumpStart describes how to set up such a server. This server

- Accepts outbound email from the local system only

- Delivers outbound email directly to the recipient's system, without using a relay

- Accepts inbound email from any system

This server does not relay outbound email originating on other systems. Refer to "access: Setting Up a Relay Host" on page 620 if you want the local system to act as a relay. For this configuration to work, you must be able to make outbound connections from, and receive inbound connections to, port 25.

The line in **sendmail.mc** that limits **sendmail** to accept inbound email from the local system only is

```
DAEMON_OPTIONS(`Port=smtp,Addr=127.0.0.1, Name=MTA')dnl
```

To allow **sendmail** to accept inbound email from other systems, remove the parameter **Addr=127.0.0.1,** from the preceding line, leaving the following line:

```
DAEMON_OPTIONS(`Port=smtp, Name=MTA')dnl
```

By default sendmail does not use a remote SMTP server to relay email, so there is nothing to change to cause sendmail to send email directly to recipients' systems. (JumpStart I set up a SMART_HOST to relay email.)

Once you have restarted **sendmail**, it will accept mail addressed to the local system, as long as there is a DNS MX record (page 706) pointing at the local system. If you are not running a DNS server, you must ask your ISP to set up an MX record.

How sendmail Works

Outbound email   When you send email, the MUA passes the email to **sendmail**, which creates in the **/var/spool/mqueue** directory two files that hold the message while **sendmail** processes it. In order to generate unique filenames for a particular piece of email, **sendmail** generates a random string for each piece of email and uses the string in filenames pertaining to the email. The **sendmail** daemon stores the body of the message in a file named **df** (data file) followed by the generated string. It stores the headers and other information in a file named **qf** (queue file) followed by the generated string.

If a delivery error occurs, sendmail creates a temporary copy of the message that it stores in a file whose name starts with **tf** and logs errors in a file whose name starts **xf**. Once an email has been sent successfully, **sendmail** removes all files pertaining to that email from **/var/spool/mqueue**.

Incoming email   By default, the MDA stores incoming messages in users' files in the mail spool directory, **/var/spool/mail**, in **mbox** format (next paragraph). Within this directory, each user has a mail file named with the user's username. Mail remains in these files until it is collected, typically by an MUA. Once an MUA collects the mail from the mail spool, the MUA stores the mail as directed by the user, usually in the user's home directory hierarchy.

mbox versus maildir   The **mbox** format, which **sendmail** uses, stores all messages for a user in a single file. To prevent corruption, the file must be locked while a process is adding messages to or deleting messages from the file; you cannot delete a message at the same time the MTA is adding messages. A competing format, **maildir**, stores each message in a separate file. This format does not use locks, allowing an MUA to read and delete messages at the same time as new mail is delivered. In addition, the **maildir** format is better able to handle larger mailboxes. The downside is that the **maildir** format adds overhead when using a protocol such as IMAP to check messages. Qmail (page 633) uses **maildir** format mailboxes.

Mail logs

The **sendmail** daemon stores log messages in **/var/log/maillog**. Other mail servers, such as the **imapd** and **ipop3d** daemons may log information to this file. Following is a sample log entry:

/var/log/maillog

```
# cat /var/log/maillog
...
Mar  3 16:25:33 MACHINENAME sendmail[7225]: i23GPXvm007224:
to=<user@localhost.localdomain>, ctladdr=<root@localhost.localdomain>
(0/0), delay=00:00:00, xdelay=00:00:00, mailer=local, pri=30514,
dsn=2.0.0, stat=Sent
```

Each log entry starts with a timestamp, the name of the system sending the email, the name of the mail server (**sendmail**), and a unique identification number. The address of the recipient follows the **to=** label and the address of the sender follows **ctladdr=**. Additional fields provide the name of the mailer and the time it took to send the message. If a message is sent correctly, the **stat=** label is followed by **Sent**.

A message is marked **Sent** when **sendmail** sends it; **Sent** does not indicate that the message has been delivered. If a message is not delivered due to an error down the line, the sender usually receives an email saying that it was not delivered, giving a reason why.

If you get a lot of email, the **maillog** file can grow quite large; the **syslog** logrotate (page 543) entry is set up to archive and rotate the **maillog** files regularly.

Aliases and Forwarding

There are three files that can forward email: **.forward** (page 615), **aliases** (next), and **virtusertable** (page 621). See page 621 for a table comparing the three files.

/etc/aliases   Most of the time when you send email, it goes to a specific person; the recipient, **user@system**, maps to a specific, real user on the specified system. Sometimes you may want email to go to a class of user and not to a specific recipient. Examples of classes of users are **postmaster, webmaster, root, tech_support**, and so on. Different users may receive this email at different times or the email may be answered by a group of users. You can use the **/etc/aliases** file to map inbound addresses to local users, files, commands, and remote addresses.

Each line in **/etc/aliases** contains the name of a local pseudouser, followed by a colon, whitespace, and a comma-separated list of destinations. The default installation includes a number of aliases that redirect messages for certain pseudousers to **root**. These have the form

```
system:      root
```

Sending messages to the **root** account is a good way of making them easy to review, but, because it is rare that anyone checks **root**'s email, you may want to send copies to a real user. The following line forwards mail sent to **abuse** on the local system to **root** and **alex**:

```
abuse:       root, alex
```

You can create simple mailing lists with this type of alias. For example, the following alias sends copies of all email sent to **admin** on the local system to several users, including Zach, who is on a different system:

```
admin:       sam, helen, mark, zach@tcorp.com
```

You can direct email to a file by specifying an absolute pathname in place of a destination address. The following alias, which is quite popular among less conscientious system administrators, redirects email sent to **complaints** to **/dev/null** (page 426) where they disappear:

```
complaints:  /dev/null
```

You can also send email to standard input of a command by preceding the command with a pipe character (|). This technique is commonly used with mailing list software such as Mailman (page 627). For each list it maintains, Mailman has entries, such as the following entry for **mylist**, in the **aliases** file:

```
mylist:      "|/var/mailman/mail/mailman post mylist"
```

newaliases   After you edit **/etc/aliases**, you must either run newaliases as **root** or restart **sendmail** to recreate the **aliases.db** file that **sendmail** reads.

praliases   You can use praliases to list aliases currently loaded by **sendmail**:

```
# /usr/sbin/praliases | head -5
postmaster:root
daemon:root
adm:root
lp:root
shutdown:root
```

~/.forward   Systemwide aliases are useful in many cases, but non**root** users cannot make or change them. Sometimes you may want to forward your own mail: Maybe you want to have mail from several systems go to one address or perhaps you just want to forward your mail while you are at another office for a week. The **~/.forward** file allows ordinary users to forward their email.

Lines in a **.forward** file are the same as the right column of the **aliases** file explained previously: Destinations are listed one per line and can be a local user, a remote email address, a filename, or a command preceded by a pipe character (|).

Mail that you forward does not go to your local mailbox. If you want to forward mail and keep a copy in your local mailbox, you must specify your local username preceded by a backslash to prevent an infinite loop. The following example sends Sam's email to himself on the local system and on the system at **tcorp.com**:

```
$cat ~sam/.forward
sams@tcorp.com
\sam
```

Related Programs

sendmail   The **sendmail** distribution includes several programs. The primary program, **sendmail**, reads from standard input and sends an email to the recipient specified by its argument. You can use **sendmail** from the command line to check that the mail delivery system is working and to email the output of scripts:

```
$ echo "sample email" | /usr/sbin/sendmail sams@tcrop.net
```

mailq   The mailq utility displays the status of the outgoing mail queue and normally reports there are no messages in the queue. Messages in the queue usually indicate a problem with the local or remote **sendmail** configuration or a network problem.

```
# /usr/bin/mailq
/var/spool/mqueue is empty
                Total requests: 0
```

mailstats   The mailstats utility reports on the number and sizes of messages **sendmail** has sent and received since the date it displays on the first line:

```
# /usr/sbin/mailstats
Statistics from Sat Dec 22 16:02:34 2001
M    msgsfr   bytes_from    msgsto     bytes_to   msgsrej  msgsdis  Mailer
0        0          0K      17181       103904K        0        0  prog
4   368386    4216614K     136456      1568314K    20616        0  esmtp
9   226151   26101362K     479025     12776528K     4590        0  local
=================================================================
T   594537   30317976K     632662     14448746K    25206        0
C   694638                 499700                  146185
```

In the preceding output, each mailer is identified by the first column, which displays the mailer number, and by the last column, which displays the name of the mailer. The second through fifth columns display the number and total sizes of messages sent and received by the mailer. The sixth and seventh columns display the number of messages rejected and discarded respectively. The row that starts with **T** lists the column totals and the row that starts with **C** lists the number of TCP connections.

makemap   The makemap utility processes text configuration files in **/etc/mail** into the database format that sendmail reads (✳**.db** files). You do not need to run makemap manually; it is invoked by the **sendmail** init script when you start or restart **sendmail**.

Configuring sendmail

The **sendmail** configuration files reside in **/etc/mail** where the primary configuration file is **sendmail.cf**. This directory contains other text configuration files, such as **access**, **mailertable**, and **virtusertable**. The **sendmail** daemon does not read these files but reads the corresponding ∗.db files in the same directory.

You can use makemap or give the command **make** from the **/etc/mail** directory to generate all the ∗.db files, although this step is not usually necessary. The **sendmail** init script automatically generates these files when you restart **sendmail**:

```
# /sbin/service sendmail restart
```

The sendmail.mc and sendmail.cf Files

This **sendmail.cf** file is not intended to be edited by hand and contains a large warning to this effect:

```
$ cat /etc/mail/sendmail.cf
...
#########################################################
#####
#####    DO NOT EDIT THIS FILE!  Only edit the source .mc file.
#####
#########################################################
...
```

Editing sendmail.mc and Generating sendmail.cf

The **sendmail.cf** file is generated from **sendmail.mc** using the m4 macro processor. It can be helpful to use a text editor that supports syntax highlighting, such as vim, to edit **sendmail.mc**.

dnl Many of the lines in **sendmail.mc** start with **dnl**, which stands for **delete to new line**, and instructs m4 to delete from the **dnl** to the end of the line (the next NEWLINE character). Because m4 ignores anything on a line after a **dnl** instruction, you can use **dnl** to introduce comments; it works the same way as a # does in a shell script.

Many of the lines in **sendmail.mc** *end* with **dnl**. Because NEWLINES immediately follow these **dnl**s, these **dnl**s are superfluous; you can remove them if you like.

After editing **sendmail.mc**, you need to regenerate **sendmail.cf** and restart **sendmail** to make your changes take effect. You can give the command **make** from the **/etc/mail** directory to regenerate **sendmail.cf**, although this step is not usually necessary. The **sendmail** init script automatically regenerates **sendmail.cf** when you restart **sendmail**.

About sendmail.mc

Lines near the beginning of **sendmail.mc** provide basic configuration information.

```
divert(-1)dnl
include('/usr/share/sendmail-cf/m4/cf.m4')dnl
VERSIONID('setup for Red Hat Linux')dnl
OSTYPE('linux')dnl
```

The line that starts with **divert** tells m4 to discard extraneous output it may generate when processing this file.

The **include** statement, which tells m4 where to find the macro definition file that it will use to process the rest of this file, points to the file named **cf.m4**. The **cf.m4** file contains other **include** statements that include parts of the **sendmail** configuration rule sets.

The **VERSIONID** statement defines a string that indicates the version of this configuration. You can change this string to include a brief comment about the changes you make to this file or other information. The value of this string is not significant to **sendmail**.

Do not change the **OSTYPE** statement unless you are migrating a **sendmail.mc** file from another operating system.

Other statements you may want to change are explained in the following sections and in the **sendmail** documentation.

---

tip || **Quoting m4 Strings**

The m4 macro processor, which converts **sendmail.mc** to **sendmail.cf**, requires strings to be preceded by a back tick (`) and closed with a single quotation mark (').

Masquerading

Typically, you want your email to appear to come from the user and the domain where you receive email; sometimes the outbound server is in a different domain than the inbound server. You can cause **sendmail** to alter outbound messages so that they appear to come from a user and/or domain other than the one they are sent from: You *masquerade* (page 982) the message.

There are several lines in **sendmail.mc** that pertain to this type of masquerading; each is commented out in the file that Red Hat distributes:

```
dnl MASQUERADE_AS('mydomain.com')dnl
dnl MASQUERADE_DOMAIN(localhost)dnl
dnl FEATURE(masquerade_entire_domain)dnl
```

The MASQUERADE_AS statement causes email that you send from the local system to appear to come from the domain specified within the single quotation marks (**mydomain.com** in the commented out line in the distributed file). Remove the leading **dnl** and change **mydomain.com** to the domain name that you want mail to appear to come from.

The MASQUERADE_DOMAIN statement causes email from the specified system or domain to be masqueraded, just as local email is. That is, email from the system specified in this statement is treated as though it came from the local system: It is changed to appear to come from the domain specified in the MASQUERADE_AS statement. Remove the leading **dnl** and change **localhost** to the name of the system or domain that sends the email that you want to masquerade. If the name you specify has a leading period, it specifies a domain; if there is no leading period, it specifies a system or host. You can have as many MASQUERADE_DOMAIN statements as necessary.

The **masquerade_entire_domain** feature statement causes sendmail also to masquerade subdomains of the domain specified in the MASQUERADE_DOMAIN statement. Remove the leading **dnl** to masquerade entire domains.

Accepting Email from Unknown Hosts

As shipped by Red Hat, **sendmail** is configured to accept email from domains that it cannot resolve (and that may not exist). To turn this feature off and cut down the amount of spam you receive, add **dnl** to the beginning of the following line:

```
FEATURE(`accept_unresolvable_domains')dnl
```

When this feature is off, **sendmail** uses DNS to look up the domains of all email it receives; if it cannot resolve the domain, it rejects the email.

Setting Up a Backup Server

You can set up a backup mail server to hold email when the primary mail server experiences problems. For maximum coverage, the backup server should be on a different connection to the Internet from the primary server.

Setting up a backup server is easy: Remove the leading **dnl** from the following line in the *backup* mail server's **sendmail.mc** file:

```
dnl FEATURE(`relay_based_on_MX')dnl
```

DNS MX records (page 706) specify where email for a domain should be sent. You can have multiple MX records for a domain, each pointing to a different mail server. When a domain has multiple MX records, each record usually has a different priority; priority is specified by a two-digit number with lower numbers specifying higher priorities.

When attempting to deliver email, an MTA first tries to deliver email to the highest priority server. Failing that delivery, it tries to deliver to a lower-priority server. If you activate the **relay_based_on_MX** feature and point a low-priority MX record at a secondary mail server, the mail server will accept email for the domain. The mail server will then forward email to the server identified by the highest priority MX record for the domain when that server becomes available.

Other Files in /etc/mail

The **/etc/mail** directory holds most of the files that control **sendmail**. This section discusses three of those files: **mailertable**, **access**, and **virtusertable**.

mailertable: Forwarding Email from One Domain to Another

When you run a mail server, you may want to send mail destined for one domain to a different location. The **sendmail** daemon uses the **/etc/mail/mailertable** file for this purpose. Each line in **mailertable** holds the name of a domain and a destination mailer separated by whitespace; when **sendmail** receives email for the specified domain, it forwards it to the mailer specified on the same line. Red Hat enables this feature by default: Put an entry in the **mailertable** file and restart **sendmail** to use it.

The following line in **mailertable** forwards email sent to **tcorp.com** to the mailer at **bravo.com**:

```
$ cat /etc/mail/mailertable
tcorp.com          smtp:[bravo.com]
```

The square brackets in the example instruct **sendmail** not to use MX records but to send email directly to the SMTP server. Without the brackets, email could be put in an infinite loop.

A period in front of a domain name acts as a wildcard and causes the name to match any domain that ends in the specified name. For example, **.tcorp.com** matches **sales.tcorp.com**, **mktg.tcrop.com**, and so on.

The **sendmail** init script regenerates **mailertable.db** from **mailertable** each time you run it, as when you restart **sendmail**.

access: Setting Up a Relay Host

On a LAN, you may want to set up a single server to process outbound mail, keeping local mail inside the network. A system that processes outbound mail for other systems is called a *relay host*. The **/etc/mail/access** file specifies which systems the local server relays email for. As distributed by Red Hat, this file lists only the local system:

```
$ cat /etc/mail/access
...
# by default we allow relaying from localhost...
localhost.localdomain          RELAY
localhost                      RELAY
127.0.0.1                      RELAY
```

You can add systems to the list in **access** by adding an IP address followed by whitespace and the word **RELAY**. The following line adds the 192.168. subnet to the list of hosts that the local system relays mail for:

```
192.168.                       RELAY
```

The **sendmail** init script regenerates **access.db** from **access** each time you run it, as when you restart **sendmail**.

virtusertable: Serving Email to Multiple Domains

When the DNS MX records are set up properly, a single system can serve email to multiple domains. On a system that serves mail to many domains, you need a way to sort the incoming mail so that it goes to the right places. The **virtusertable** file can forward inbound email addressed to different domains (**aliases** cannot do this).

As **sendmail** is shipped by Red Hat, **virtusertable** is enabled; you need to put forwarding instructions in the **/etc/mail/virtusertable** file and restart **sendmail** to get it to work. The **virtusertable** file is similar to the **aliases** file (page 614), except the left column contains full email addresses, not just local ones. Each line in **virtusertable** has the address that the email was sent to, followed by whitespace and the address **sendmail** will forward the email to. As with **aliases**, the destination can be a local user, an email address, a file, or a pipe symbol (|), followed by a command.

The following line from **virtusertable** forwards mail addressed to **zach@tcorp.com** to **zcs**, a local user:

```
zach@tcorp.com      zcs
```

You can also forward email for a user to a remote email address:

```
sams@bravo.com      sams@tcorp.com
```

You can forward all email destined for a domain to another domain without specifying each user individually. To forward email for every user at **bravo.com** to **tcorp.com**, specify **@bravo.com** as the first address on the line. When **sendmail** forwards email, it replaces **%1** in the destination address with the name of the recipient. The next rule forwards all email addressed to **bravo.com** to **tcorp.com**, keeping the original recipients' names:

```
@bravo.com      %1@tcorp.com
```

Finally, you can specify that email intended for a specific user should be rejected by using the **error:** namespace in the destination. The next example bounces email addressed to **spam@tcorp.com** with the message **5.7.0:550 Invalid address**:

```
spam@tcorp.com      error:5.7.0:550 Invalid address
```

.forward, aliases, and virtusertable   The **.forward** (page 615), **aliases** (page 614), and **virtusertable** files do the same thing: They forward email addressed to one user to another user. They can also redirect email to a file or as input to a program. The difference between them is scope and ownership; see Table 20-1.

table 20-1 ‖			Comparison of Forwarding Techniques
	.forward	**aliases**	**virtusertable**
Controlled by	non**root** user	**root**	**root**
Forwards email addressed to	non**root** user	Any real or virtual user on the local system	Any real or virtual user on any domain recognized by **sendmail**
Order of precedence	Third	Second	First

In Addition to sendmail

This section covers SpamAssassin, Webmail, and mailing lists. In addition, it discusses how to set up IMAP and POP3 servers and a KMail client.

SpamAssassin

Spam, or more correctly, UCE (Unsolicited Commercial Email), accounts for about half of all email. SpamAssassin evaluates each piece of incoming email and assigns it a number that indicates how likely it is that the email is spam. The higher the number, the more likely it is that the email is spam. You can filter the email based on its rating. SpamAssassin is effective as installed or you can modify its configuration files to make it better meet your needs.

How SpamAssassin works   You can set up SpamAssassin on a mail server so that it rates all inbound email before it is sent to users. Or individual users can run it from their mail clients. Either way, you run the Spamassassin **spamd** daemon and filter email through it using the spamc client.

SpamAssassin uses several techniques to identify spam:

- **Header analysis** Checks for tricks that people who send spam use to make you think email is legitimate
- **Text analysis** Checks the body of an email for characteristics of spam
- **Blacklists** Checks various lists to see if the sender is known for sending spam
- **Database** Checks the signature of the message against Vipul's Razor (razor.sourceforge.net), a spam-tracking database

With **spamd** running, you can see how spamc works by sending it a simple string:

```
$ echo "hi there" | spamc
X-Mail-Format-Warning: Bad RFC2822 header formatting in hi there
X-Spam-Checker-Version: SpamAssassin 2.63 (2004-01-11) on
speedy.tcorp.com
X-Spam-Level: **
X-Spam-Status: No, hits=2.9 required=5.0
tests=DATE_MISSING,FROM_NO_LOWER
        autolearn=no version=2.63
```

Of course, SpamAssassin complains because the string you gave it did not have standard email headers. The logical line that starts with X-Spam-Status contains the heart of the report on the string **hi there**. First, it says **No** (it does not consider the message to be spam). SpamAssassin uses a rating system that assigns a number of hits to a piece of email. If the email receives over the required number of hits (5.0 by default), SpamAssassin marks it as spam. The tests the string failed, because it did not have standard email headers, are DATE_MISSING and FROM_NO_LOWER (the From line in the header had no lowercase characters [because there was no From line]). The following listing is from a real piece of spam processed by SpamAssassin. It received 24.5 hits, indicating that it is almost certainly spam.

```
X-Spam-Status: Yes, hits=24.5 required=5.0
    tests=DATE_IN_FUTURE_06_12,INVALID_DATE_TZ_ABSURD,
        MSGID_OE_SPAM_4ZERO,MSGID_OUTLOOK_TIME,
        MSGID_SPAMSIGN_ZEROES,RCVD_IN_DSBL,RCVD_IN_NJABL,
        RCVD_IN_UNCONFIRMED_DSBL,REMOVE_PAGE,VACATION_SCAM,
        X_NJABL_OPEN_PROXY
    version=2.55
X-Spam-Level: ************************
X-Spam-Checker-Version: SpamAssassin 2.55 (1.174.2.19-2003-05-19-exp)
X-Spam-Report:   This mail is probably spam.  The original message has been attached
 along with this report, so you can recognize or block similar unwanted
 mail in future.  See http://spamassassin.org/tag/ for more details.
 Content preview:  Paradise SEX Island Awaits! Tropical 1 week vacations
 where anything goes! We have lots of WOMEN, SEX, ALCOHOL, ETC! Every
 man's dream awaits on this island of pleasure. [...]
 Content analysis details:   (24.50 points, 5 required)
 MSGID_SPAMSIGN_ZEROES (4.3 points)  Message-Id generated by spam tool (zeroes variant)
 INVALID_DATE_TZ_ABSURD (4.3 points)  Invalid Date: header (timezone does not exist)
 MSGID_OE_SPAM_4ZERO (3.5 points)  Message-Id generated by spam tool (4-zeroes variant)
 VACATION_SCAM       (1.9 points)  BODY: Vacation Offers
 REMOVE_PAGE         (0.3 points)  URI: URL of page called "remove"
 MSGID_OUTLOOK_TIME (4.4 points)  Message-Id is fake (in Outlook Express format)
 DATE_IN_FUTURE_06_12 (1.3 points)  Date: is 6 to 12 hours after Received: date
 RCVD_IN_NJABL       (0.9 points)  RBL: Received via a relay in dnsbl.njabl.org
 [RBL check: found 94.99.190.200.dnsbl.njabl.org.]
 RCVD_IN_UNCONFIRMED_DSBL (0.5 points)  RBL: Received via a relay in unconfirmed.dsbl.org
 [RBL check: found 94.99.190.200.unconfirmed.dsbl.org.]
 X_NJABL_OPEN_PROXY (0.5 points)  RBL: NJABL: sender is proxy/relay/formmail/spam-source
 RCVD_IN_DSBL        (2.6 points)  RBL: Received via a relay in list.dsbl.org
 [RBL check: found 211.157.63.200.list.dsbl.org.]
X-Spam-Flag: YES
Subject: [SPAM] re: statement
```

Because SpamAssassin considered the preceding email to be spam, it modified the Subject line by adding [SPAM] at the beginning of the line.

Configuration   You can configure SpamAssassin globally by editing **/etc/mail/spamassassin/local.cf**. Users can override the global options and add their own options in **~/.spamassassin/user_prefs**. You can put the options discussed in this section in either of these files. Use **perldoc** to display the configuration document that lists all the options:

Documentation $ **perldoc Mail::SpamAssassin::Conf**

As shown in the preceding example, SpamAssassin rewrites the Subject line of email that it rates as spam. The **rewrite_subject** keyword in the configuration files controls this behavior. A **1** following this keyword indicates that SpamAssassin will rewrite Subject lines. Change the **1** to a **0** (zero) to turn off this behavior:

```
rewrite_subject 0
```

The **required_hits** keyword specifies the minimum number of hits a piece of email must receive before SpamAssassin considers it to be spam. The default is 5.0. With a higher number, SpamAssassin marks fewer pieces of email as spam.

```
required_hits 5.00
```

Sometimes, mail from addresses that should be marked as spam is not, or mail from addresses that should not be marked as spam is. Use the **whitelist_from** keyword to specify addresses that should never be marked as spam and **blacklist_from** to specify addresses that should always be marked as spam:

```
whitelist_from sams@tcorp.com
blacklist_from spammer.net
```

You can specify multiple addresses, separated by SPACEs, on the **whitelist_from** and **blacklist_from** lines and each address can include wildcards. You can also use multiple lines.

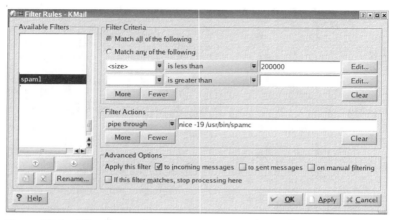

Figure 20-1   The first rule passes messages through SpamAssassin

Using SpamAssassin with a mail server

To add these headers to every email that arrives on the system, you need to configure your MDA to pipe email through the **spamc**. The first step is to make sure you have **procmail** configured as your MDA. The first of the following lines in **sendmail.mc** specifies the **procmail** command, its path and flags. The MAILER line defines **procmail** as the mailer. You should not have to change either of these lines.

```
FEATURE(local_procmail, `', `procmail -t -Y -a $h -d $u')dnl
MAILER(procmail)dnl
```

The **procmail** configuration file, **/etc/procmailrc**, may not exist on the server. If the file does not exist, create it so that it is owned by **root** and has 644 permissions and the following contents. If it does exist, append the last two lines from the following file to it:

```
$ cat /etc/procmailrc
DROPPRIVS=yes
:0 fw
| /usr/bin/spamc
```

The first line of this file ensures that **procmail** runs with the least possible privileges. The next two lines implement a rule that pipes each user's incoming email through spamc. The :0 tells **procmail** that a rule follows. The f flag indicates a filter and the w causes **procmail** to wait for the filter to complete and check the exit code. The last line specifies the **/usr/bin/spamc** file as the filter.

With the preceding changes in place, all email that comes into the system passes through SpamAssassin, which rates it according to the options in the global configuration file. For users who have home directories on the server system, SpamAssassin allows users' configuration files to override the global file.

When you run SpamAssassin on a server, you typically want to rate the email more conservatively so fewer pieces of good email are marked as spam. Setting **required_hits** in the range of 6–10 is generally appropriate. Also, you do not want

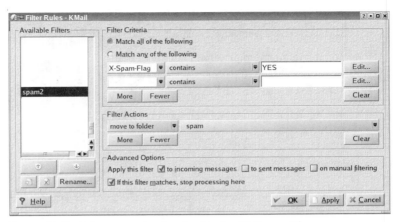

Figure 20-2   The second rule checks the X-Spam-Flag

to remove any email automatically as there is a chance that you could prevent a user from getting a piece of nonspam email. When the server marks email that is potentially spam, users can manually or automatically filter the spam and decide what to do with it.

Using SpamAssassin
with a mail client

With the SpamAssassin (**spamd**) daemon running and the configuration files set up, you are ready to have SpamAssassin filter your email. You need to set up two rules in your mail client: The first passes each piece of email through SpamAssassin using spamc (page 622) and the second filters email based on whether the X-SPAM-Flag line has a YES or NO on it.

In general, you do not want to pass very large pieces of email through SpamAssassin. This example, which uses Kmail, passes messages smaller than 200,000 bytes through SpamAssassin. The first filter rule (Figure 20-1) processes all messages where the size is less than 200000 (bytes). The action the rule takes is to pipe the message through **/usr/bin/spamc**. This rule uses nice to conserve system resources. Use nice or not as your system requires. The rule is applied to incoming messages and filtering does not stop if the message matches this rule.

The first rule adds an X-Spam-Flag line to each piece of email it processes. The second rule checks the value of the flag on this line. If the X-Spam-Flag line contains YES, the second rule moves the email to a folder named **spam** (Figure 20-2). Because the **If this filter matches, stop processing here** box is checked, Kmail does not further process messages marked as spam. Messages not marked as spam can be processed by other rules.

Webmail

Traditionally, you read email using a dedicated email client such as Kmail. Recently it has become more common to use a Web application to read email. If you have an

Figure 20-3   SquirrelMail login page

email account with a commercial provider such as HotMail or Yahoo! Mail, you use a Web browser to read email. Email read in this manner is called *Webmail*. Unlike email you read on a dedicated client, you can read Webmail from anywhere you can open a browser on the Internet: You can check your email from an Internet cafe or a friend's computer.

SquirrelMail, distributed with Red Hat, provides Webmail services; the Squirrel-Mail files reside in **/usr/share/squirrelmail**. If you want to run SquirrelMail, you must run IMAP (page 628) because SquirrelMail uses IMAP to receive and authenticate email. You must also run Apache, Chapter 26, so a user can use a browser to connect to SquirrelMail.

SquirrelMail is modular: You can easily add functionality using plugins. There are plugins that allow you to share a calendar and plugins that give you the ability to change passwords using the Webmail interface. See the plugins section of the Squir-relMail Web site for more information.

Create the following link to make SquirrelMail accessible from the Web:

```
# ln -s /usr/share/squirrelmail /var/www/html/mail
```

With this link in place, you can point a Web browser at **http://localhost/mail** to display the SquirrelMail login page (Figure 20-3).

Next, use the **conf.pl** script in **/usr/share/squirrelmail/config** to configure Squirrel-Mail:

```
# cd /usr/share/squirrelmail/config
# ./conf.pl
SquirrelMail Configuration : Read: config.php (1.4.0)
---------------------------------------------------------
Main Menu --
1. Organization Preferences
2. Server Settings
3. Folder Defaults
```

```
4. General Options
5. Themes
6. Address Books (LDAP)
7. Message of the Day (MOTD)
8. Plugins
9. Database

D. Set pre-defined settings for specific IMAP servers

C. Turn color off
S  Save data
Q  Quit

Command >>
```

The only item that you must set to get SquirrelMail to work is the server's domain name (from the Server Settings page). SquirrelMail provides several themes; if you do not like the way SquirrelMail looks, choose another theme from the Themes page.

Mailing Lists

A mailing list can be an asset if you regularly send email to the same, large group of people. A mailing list provides advantages over listing numerous recipients in the To or Cc field of an email or sending the same email individually to many people:

- **Anonymity**   None of the recipients of the email can see the addresses of the other recipients.

- **Archiving**   Email sent to the list is stored in a central location where list members or the public, as specified by the list administrator, can browse through it.

- **Access control**   You can easily specify who can send email to the list.

- **Consistency**   When you send mail to a group of people using To or Cc, it is easy to leave people who want to be on the list off and leave people who want to be off the list on.

- **Efficiency**   A mailing list application spreads sending email over time so it does not overload the mail server.

Mailman, included with Red Hat, provides mailing list support. Mailman resides in **/var/mailman**; the configuration file is **/var/mailman/Mailman/mm_cfg.py**. Before you can use Mailman, you need to change the two following lines in **mm_cfg.py** so that they point to your domain:

```
DEFAULT_URL_HOST   = 'mm_cfg_has_not_been_edited_to_set_host_domains'
DEFAULT_EMAIL_HOST = 'mm_cfg_has_not_been_edited_to_set_host_domains'
```

After making these changes, create a new mailing list with the **newlist** script:

```
# /var/mailman/bin/newlist
Enter the name of the list: painting_class
Enter the email of the person running the list: helen@tcorp.com
Initial list password:
To finish creating your mailing list, you must edit your /etc/aliases (or equivalent)
file by adding the following lines, and possibly running the 'newaliases' utility:
## list mailing list
list:                  "|/var/mailman/mail/mailman post list"
list-admin:            "|/var/mailman/mail/mailman admin list"
list-bounces:          "|/var/mailman/mail/mailman bounces list"
list-confirm:          "|/var/mailman/mail/mailman confirm list"
list-join:             "|/var/mailman/mail/mailman join list"
list-leave:            "|/var/mailman/mail/mailman leave list"
list-owner:            "|/var/mailman/mail/mailman owner list"
list-request:          "|/var/mailman/mail/mailman request list"
list-subscribe:        "|/var/mailman/mail/mailman subscribe list"
list-unsubscribe:      "|/var/mailman/mail/mailman unsubscribe list"
Hit enter to notify painting_class owner...
```

Before the list can receive email, you need to copy the lines generated by newlist to the end of **/etc/aliases** (page 614) and run newaliases.

Mailman includes a Web configuration interface that you can enable by configuring a Web server to run the scripts in **/var/mailman/cgi-bin**. An entry such as the following in **/etc/httpd/conf/httpd.conf** (page 767) sets up this interface (pipermail is the archive manager that Mailman uses):

```
# Mailman configs
ScriptAlias /mailman/ /var/mailman/cgi-bin/
Alias /pipermail/ /var/mailman/archives/public/
<Directory /var/mailman/archives>
    Options +FollowSymLinks
</Directory>
```

Setting Up an IMAP or POP3 Server

There are two protocols that allow users to retrieve email remotely: IMAP (Internet Message Access Protocol) and POP (Post Office Protocol). The **imap** package that Red Hat ships includes the **imapd** and **ipop3d** daemons that implement these protocols.

The **imapd** and **ipop3d** daemons run through the **xinetd** super server (page 403). The **imap** package includes the **imap**, **imaps**, **ipop3**, and **ipop3s xinetd** control files in the **/etc/xinetd.d** directory. The files whose names end in **s** control the SSL versions of the protocols. By default, each of these protocols is disabled in its **xinetd** control file.

To start one of these daemons, change the **yes** following **disable** = to **no** in the control file that corresponds to the service you want to enable and restart **xinetd**.

If you enable an insecure protocol, you may want to restrict access to the local system by adding the following line to the control file:

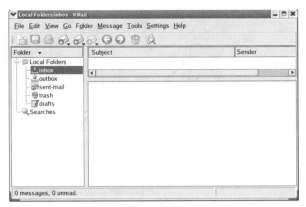

Figure 20-4   The initial KMail window

```
only_from = 127.0.0.1.
```
To use one of these protocols from a mail client, tell the mail client which protocol you are using and whether the server is running SSL.

Setting Up KMail

KMail is the graphical email client for KDE and is compatible with the MIME, SMTP, POP3, and IMAP standards. To start KMail, give the command **kmail** from a terminal emulator window or from a Run Command window (press ALT-F2 to open this window). Or you can choose **Internet⇨KMail** from the KDE main menu. You can run KMail from any desktop environment, including GNOME. Figure 20-4 shows the initial KMail window.

Selecting **Configure KMail** from the Settings menu on the menubar displays the Configure KMail window (Figure 20-5). This window has buttons along the left side; click the buttons to display different configuration pages on the right.

Identity   KMail sets up a minimal identity for you. Click the **Identities** button to display the Identities page where you can specify your email address, a reply-to address (if it is different from your email address), a signature that KMail automatically appends to your outgoing email messages, and more.

Help   KMail provides help in setting up KMail to send and receive email. Click the **Help** button at the lower-left of any KMail window to display the appropriate page of the online Configure KMail manual (part of the KDE Help Center).

Once you have an identity, you need to set up incoming and outgoing accounts. Click the **Network** button to display the Network page where you can set up accounts for sending and receiving messages. This page has two tabs: Sending and Receiving.

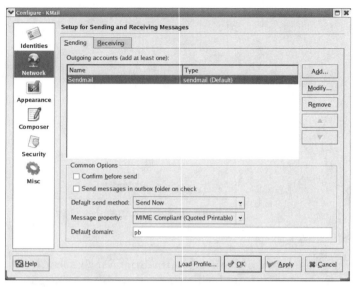

Figure 20-5   The Configure KMail window

Outgoing account   Click the **Sending** tab on the Network page to display the outgoing accounts. The outgoing account defaults to **sendmail** on the local system. If you use the local **sendmail,** you need to configure it as explained in "Jumpstart I: Configuring sendmail on a Client" on page 612. If you are using SMTP, you need to remove the **sendmail** account and add an SMTP account: Highlight the **sendmail** account and click **Remove**; next, click **Add** to display the Add Transport window where you can select **sendmail** or SMTP.

Incoming account   Click the **Receiving** tab on the Network page to display the incoming accounts; there is no default incoming account. Click Add to display the Add Account window where you can select a type of account such as Local mailbox, POP3, or IMAP. If you receive mail locally and from an ISP, you need to set up two accounts. For a POP3 or IMAP account you need to specify the server (host) and your login name and password on the server. If you want KMail to check for mail periodically, turn on **Enable interval mail checking** and specify how often you want KMail to check for mail.

You do not have to change any settings on other pages. Following is a summary of what you will find on each of the Configure KMail pages:

- **Identities**   Specify one or more email identities including name, email addresses, signature, and if you are using PGP or GnuPG (page 926), you can specify your OpenPGP key in the Advanced tab.

- **Network**   Specify outgoing and incoming email accounts.

- **Appearance**   Specify how KMail looks, including fonts, colors, layout, and headers.

- **Compose**   Specify what outgoing messages look like and what headers are included when you reply to or forward a message.

- **Security**   Specify various security features including whether you want to receive HTML messages in HTML or plain text. Receiving HTML messages in HTML can make a system less secure.

- **Misc**   Specify various KMail options including which warnings you receive, how messages you read are marked, and what happens when you exit from KMail.

KMail has a lot of options and features. Use the Help button to get assistance. It is easy to set up KMail for basic use. As you become more comfortable using it, you can configure KMail to take care of more tasks for you.

Authenticated Relaying

If you travel with a portable computer such as a laptop, you may connect to the Internet through a different connection at each location you work. Perhaps you travel for work, or maybe you just bring your laptop home at night.

This section does not apply if you always dial into the network through your ISP. In that case, you are always connected to your ISP's network and it is as though you never moved your computer.

On a laptop you do not use a local instance of **sendmail** to send email: you use SMTP to connect to an ISP or to a company's SMTP server, which relays the outgoing mail. To avoid relaying email for anyone, including those who would send spam, SMTP servers restrict whom they relay email for, based on IP address. By implementing authenticated relaying, you can cause the SMTP server to authenticate, based on user identification. In addition, SMTP can encrypt communication when you send mail from your email client and use the SMTP server.

An authenticated relay provides these advantages over a plain connection:

- You can send email from any Internet connection.

- The secure connection makes it more difficult to intercept email as it traverses the Internet.

- The outgoing mail server requires authentication, preventing it from being used for spam.

You set up authenticated relaying by creating an SSL certificate (or using an existing one), enabling SSL in sendmail, and telling your email client to connect to the SMTP server using SSL. If you have an SSL certificate from a company such as Verisign, you can skip the next step, in which you create a self-signed certificate.

Creating a Self-Signed Certificate

The default location for SSL certificates is **/usr/share/ssl/certs**. Working as **root**, you can use the **Makefile** in this directory to generate the required certificates. Apache uses a similar procedure for creating a certificate (page 796).

```
# cd /usr/share/ssl/certs
# make sendmail.pem
...
Generating a 1024 bit RSA private key
..................................................++++++
...............++++++
writing new private key to '/tmp/openssl.OK6561'
-----
You are about to be asked to enter information that will be incorporated
into your certificate request.
What you are about to enter is what is called a Distinguished Name or a DN.
There are quite a few fields but you can leave some blank
For some fields there will be a default value,
If you enter '.', the field will be left blank.
-----
Country Name (2 letter code) [GB]:US
State or Province Name (full name) [Berkshire]:California
Locality Name (eg, city) [Newbury]:San Francisco
Organization Name (eg, company) [My Company Ltd]:Sobell Associates Inc.
Organizational Unit Name (eg, section) []:
Common Name (eg, your name or your server's hostname) []:sobell.com
Email Address []:mgs@sobell.com
```

You can enter any information you wish, with one exception. TLS/SSL negotiation fails if the hostname you specify does not match that of the server.

Enabling SSL in sendmail

Once you have a certificate, instruct **sendmail** to use it. First, add the following lines to **sendmail.mc**. The first of these lines tells **sendmail** to allow authenticated users to relay. The next two lines specify the authentication mechanisms.

The first option for confAUTH_OPTIONS, **A**, instructs **sendmail** to use the AUTH parameter when sending mail only if authentication succeeded. The second option, **p**, instructs **sendmail**, for connections that are not secure, not to allow authentication methods that could be cracked by a packet sniffer.

```
define('confAUTH_OPTIONS', 'A p')
TRUST_AUTH_MECH('EXTERNAL DIGEST-MD5 CRAM-MD5 LOGIN PLAIN')
define('confAUTH_MECHANISMS', 'EXTERNAL GSSAPI DIGEST-MD5 CRAM-MD5 LOGIN PLAIN')
```

Next, add the following lines to **sendmail.mc** to tell **sendmail** where the certificate is:

```
define('CERT_DIR', '/usr/share/ssl/certs')
define('confCACERT_PATH', 'CERT_DIR')
define('confCACERT', 'CERT_DIR/sendmail.pem')
define('confSERVER_CERT', 'CERT_DIR/sendmail.pem')
```

```
define( 'confSERVER_KEY',  'CERT_DIR/sendmail.pem')
define( 'confCLIENT_CERT', 'CERT_DIR/sendmail.pem')
define( 'confCLIENT_KEY',  'CERT_DIR/sendmail.pem')
```

Encrypted connections are made in one of two ways: SSL (simpler) and TLS. SSL requires a dedicated port and has the client and server negotiate a secure connection and continue the transaction as if the connection were unencrypted. TLS has the client connect to the server using an insecure connection and then issue a STARTTLS command to negotiate a secure connection. TLS runs over the same port as an unencrypted connection. Because many clients support only SSL, it is a good idea to instruct sendmail to listen on the SMTPS port. The final line that you need to add to **sendmail.mc** instructs **sendmail** to listen on the SSL port:

```
DAEMON_OPTIONS( 'Port=smtps, Name=TLSMTA, M=s')
```

Enabling SSL in the Mail Client

Enabling SSL in a mail client is usually quite simple. For example, the Kmail setup provides a Security tab that allows you to choose the type of encryption you want to use: **None**, **SSL**, or **TLS**.

Alternatives to sendmail

Over its years, **sendmail** has grown to be enormously complex. Its complexity makes it hard to configure if you want to set up something more than a simple mail server. And its size and complexity add to its vulnerability. For optimum security, make sure you run the latest version of **sendmail** and always keep **sendmail** up to date. Or, consider using one of the following alternatives.

Postfix   Postfix, which is included with Red Hat, is an alternative MTA. Postfix attempts to be fast and easy to administer while, at the same time, being **sendmail** compatible enough to not upset **sendmail** users. Postfix has a good reputation for ease of use and security and is a drop-in replacement for **sendmail**. Documentation for Postfix is at www.postfix.org/docs.html.

Qmail   Qmail is a direct competitor of Postfix and has the same objectives. By default, Qmail stores email using the **maildir** format as opposed to the **mbox** format that other MTAs use (page 614). The Qmail Web site is www.qmail.org.

Chapter Summary

The **sendmail** daemon is an MTA (Mail Transfer Agent). When you send a message, **sendmail** works with other software to get it to the proper recipients. You can set up

sendmail to relay email to an SMTP server that sends it on to its destination or you can have **sendmail** send email directly to the SMTP servers for the domains receiving the email. By default, **sendmail** stores incoming messages in the mail spool directory, **/var/spool/mail**.

The file that controls many aspects of how sendmail works is **sendmail.cf**. You edit **sendmail.mc** and when you restart **sendmail**, the **sendmail** init script generates **sendmail.cf**. The system administrator can use the **/etc/aliases** file and ordinary users can use **~/.forward** files to reroute email to one or more local or remote addresses, to files, or as input to programs.

You can use a program such as SpamAssassin to grade and mark email as to the likelihood of it being spam. You can then decide what to do with the marked email: You can either look at each piece of potential spam and decide where to put it or have your MUA automatically put potential spam in a special mailbox for spam.

Exercises

1. By default, email addressed to **system** goes to **root**. How would you also save a copy in **/var/logs/systemmail**?

2. How would Max store a copy of his email in **~/mbox** and send a copy to **max@bravo.com**?

3. If your firewall allowed only the machine with the IP address 192.168.1.1 to send email outside the network, how would you instruct your local copy of **sendmail** to use this server as a relay?

4. What does **dnl** stand for in the m4 macro language; what are **dnl** commands used for?

5. SpamAssassin is installed on your mail server, with the threshold set to an unusually low value of 3, resulting in a lot of false positives. What rule could you give to your mail client to allow it to identify spam with a score of 5 or above?

6. Describe the software and protocols used when Max sends an email to Sam on a remote Linux system.

Advanced Exercises

7. Your company's current mail server runs on a commercial UNIX server, and you are planning on migrating it to Linux. After copying the

configuration files across to the Linux box, you find that it does not work. What might you have forgotten to change?

8. Assume you have a script that sends its output to standard output. How would you modify the script to send the output in an email to a user specified by the first argument on the command line? (You may assume that the data is stored in $RESULT.)

9. Give a simple way of reading your email that does not involve the use of an MUA.

10. If you accidentally delete the **/etc/aliases** file, how could you easily recreate it (assuming that you had not restarted **sendmail**)?

NIS: Network Information Service

21

NIS (Network Information Service) simplifies the administration of common administrative files by maintaining them in a central database and having clients contact the database server to retrieve information from the database. Developed by Sun Microsystems, NIS is an example of the client/server paradigm.

Just as DNS addresses the problem of keeping multiple copies of **/etc/hosts** files up-to-date, NIS deals with the issue of keeping system-independent configuration files (such as **/etc/passwd**) current. Most networks today are *heterogeneous* (page 974), and even though they run different varieties of UNIX or Linux, they have certain common attributes, such as a **passwd** file.

Introduction to NIS

A primary goal of a LAN administrator is to make the network transparent to users. One aspect of this transparency is presenting users with similar environments, including username and password, when they log in on different machines. From the administrator's perspective, the information that supports a user's environment should not be replicated but should be kept in a central location and distributed as requested. NIS simplifies this task.

As with DNS, users need not be aware that NIS is managing system configuration files. Setting up and maintaining NIS databases are tasks for the system administrator; individual users and users on single-user Linux systems rarely need to work directly with NIS.

637

Yellow pages   NIS used to be called the *Yellow Pages,* and people still refer to it by this name. Sun renamed the service because another corporation holds the trademark to that name. The names of NIS utilities and files, however, are reminiscent of the old name: ypcat displays an NIS file, ypmatch searches, and the server is named ypserv.

How NIS Works

NIS domain   NIS makes a common set of information available to systems on a network. The network, referred to as an *NIS domain,* is characterized by each system having the same *NIS domain name* (different than a *domain name* [page 968]).

Master and slave servers   Each NIS domain must have exactly one master server; larger networks may have slave servers. Each slave server holds a copy of the NIS database from the master. The need for slave servers is based on the size of the NIS domain and the reliability of the systems and network. A system can belong to only one NIS domain at a time.

When a client determines that a server is down or is not responding fast enough, it selects another server, as specified in the configuration file. If it cannot reach a server, ypbind terminates with an error.

nsswitch.conf   Whether a system uses NIS, DNS, local files, or a combination as the source of certain information, and in what order, is determined by **/etc/nsswitch.conf** (page 413). When it needs information from the NIS database, a client requests the information from the NIS server. For example, when a user attempts to log in, the client may authenticate the user with name and password information from the server.

You can configure **nsswitch.conf** to cause **/etc/passwd** to override NIS password information for the local machine. When you do not export the **root** account to NIS (and you should not), this setup allows you to have a unique **root** password for each system.

Source files   Under Red Hat Linux, NIS derives the information it offers, such as login names and passwords, and local system names and IP addresses, from local, ASCII configuration files such as **/etc/passwd** and **/etc/hosts**. These files are called *source files* or *master files.* (Some administrators avoid confusion by using different files for local configuration and NIS source information.) An NIS server can include information from as many of the following source files as is appropriate:

/etc/group	Defines groups and their members
/etc/gshadow	Provides shadow passwords for groups
/etc/hosts	Maps local systems and IP addresses
/etc/netgrp	Defines net groups and their members
/etc/passwd	Lists user information
/etc/printcap	Lists printer information
/etc/rpc	Maps RPC program names and numbers
/etc/services	Maps system service names and port numbers
/etc/shadow	Provides shadow passwords for users

The information that NIS offers is based on files that change from time to time; NIS is responsible for making this changing information available in a timely manner to all systems in the NIS domain.

NIS maps   Before NIS can store the information contained in a source file, it must be converted to *dbm* (page 966) format files, called *maps*. Each map is indexed on one field (column); records (rows) from a map can be retrieved by specifying a value from the indexed field. Some files generate two maps, each indexed on a different field. For example, the **/etc/passwd** file generates two maps, one indexed by username, the other by UID. The maps are named **passwd.byname** and **passwd.byuid**.

optional ||

> NIS maps correspond to C library functions. The **getpwnam()** and **getpwuid()** functions obtain user name and UID information from **/etc/passwd** on non-NIS systems. On NIS systems, these functions place RPC calls to the NIS server in a process that is transparent to the application calling the function.

Map names   The names of maps that NIS uses correspond to the files in the **/var/yp/***nisdomainname* directory on the master server, where *nisdomainname* is the name of the NIS domain:

```
$ ls /var/yp/mgs
group.bygid    mail.aliases    protocols.byname     services.byname
group.byname   netid.byname    protocols.bynumber   services.byservicename
hosts.byaddr   passwd.byname   rpc.byname           ypservers
hosts.byname   passwd.byuid    rpc.bynumber
```

Map nicknames   To make it easier to refer to NIS maps, you can assign nicknames to maps. The **/var/yp/nicknames** file contains a list of commonly used nicknames. View the **nicknames** file or give the command **ypcat –x** to display the list of nicknames:

```
$ cat /var/yp/nicknames
passwd          passwd.byname
group           group.byname
networks        networks.byaddr
hosts           hosts.byname
protocols       protocols.bynumber
services        services.byname
aliases         mail.aliases
ethers          ethers.byname
```

Each line in **nicknames** contains a nickname followed by whitespace and the name of the map the nickname refers to. You can add, remove, or modify nicknames by changing the **nicknames** file.

Displaying maps   The ypcat and ypmatch utilities display information from the NIS maps. Using the nickname **passwd**, the following command displays the information contained in the **passwd.byname** map:

```
$ ypcat passwd
mark:$1$X4JAzD0.$c.64fRCLPvQNSmq9qrfYv/:500:500:Mark Sobell:/home/mark:/bin/bash
...
```

By default, NIS stores passwords only for users with UIDs >= 500 (see MINUID on page 648), so you will not see lines for **root, bin,** and other system entries. You can display password information for a single user with ypmatch:

```
$ ypmatch mark passwd
mark:$1$X4JAzD0.$c.64fRCLPvQNSmq9qrfYv/:500:500:Mark Sobell:/home/mark:/bin/bash
```

You can retrieve the same information by filtering the output of ypcat through grep, but ypmatch is more efficient because it searches the map directly, using a single process. The ypmatch utility works on the key for the map only. To match members of the group or other fields not in a map, such as the *GECOS* (page 972) field in **passwd,** you need to use ypcat with grep:

```
$ ypcat passwd | grep -i sobell
mark:$1$X4JAzD0.$c.64fRCLP9qrfYv/:500:500:Mark Sobell:/home/mark:/bin/bash
```

Terminology   This chapter uses the following definitions:

NIS source files   The ASCII files that NIS obtains information from
NIS maps   The dbm format files created from the NIS source files
NIS database   The collection of NIS maps

More Information

Local   man pages   domainname makedbm **netgroup** revnetgroup ypbind ypcat ypinit ypmatch yppoll yppush ypset **ypserv ypserv.conf** ypwhich ypxfr **ypxfrd**

Web   www.linux-nis.org

NIS Client Setup

This section discusses how to set up an NIS client on the local system.

Prerequisites

Install the following packages:

- **yp-tools**
- **ypbind**

Run chkconfig to cause ypbind to start when the system goes multiuser:

```
# /sbin/chkconfig ypbind on
```

After you have configured ypbind, start it with service:

```
# /sbin/service ypbind start
Binding to the NIS domain:                              [  OK  ]
Listening for an NIS domain server.
```

Notes

If there is no NIS server for your NIS domain, you need to set one up (page 645). If there is an NIS server, you need to know the name of the NIS domain the system belongs to and optionally the name or IP address of one or more NIS servers for your NIS domain.

An NIS client can run on the same system as an NIS server.

Step-by-Step

This section lists the steps involved in setting up and starting an NIS client.

Specify the System's NIS Domain Name

tip ‖   **A DNS Domain Name Is Different from an NIS Domain Name**

The DNS domain name is used throughout the Internet to refer to a group of systems. DNS maps these names to IP addresses to enable systems to communicate.

The NIS domain name is used strictly to identify systems that share an NIS server and is normally not seen or used by users and other programs. Some administrators use one name as both a DNS domain name and an NIS domain name, although this practice can degrade security.

Specify the system's NIS domain name by adding the following line to the **/etc/sys-config/network** file:

> *NSDOMAIN=nisdomainname*

where **nisdomainname** is the name of the NIS domain that the local system belongs to. The **xinetd** (page 403) super server reads the **network** file when the network is brought up. When you specify the NIS domain name in the **network** file, it is established in the proper sequence when networking is started. You can use the nisdomainname utility to set or view the NIS domain name, but setting it in this manner does not maintain the name when the system is rebooted:

```
# nisdomainname
(none)
# nisdomainname mgs
# nisdomainname
mgs
```

caution ‖   **To Avoid Confusion, Use nisdomainname, Not domainname**

The domainname and nisdomainname utilities do the same thing: They display or set a system's NIS domain name. Use nisdomainname to avoid confusion when working with DNS domain names.

caution || **You Must Specify an NIS Domain Name**

If you do not specify the NIS domain name, when you start ypbind, it sends a message to **syslogd** (page 546) and quits.

/etc/yp.conf: Specify an NIS Server

Edit **/etc/yp.conf** to specify one or more NIS servers (masters and/or slaves). As explained by comments in the file, you can use one of three formats to specify each server:

> *domain* **nisdomain** *server* **server_name**
>
> *domain* **nisdomain** *broadcast* (**do not use**)
>
> *ypserver* **server_hostname**

where **nisdomain** is the name of the name of an NIS domain that the client system belongs to and **server_name** is the hostname of the NIS server the system queries. The second format is less secure than the first and third as it exposes the system to rogue servers by broadcasting a request for a server to identify itself.

You can use multiple lines to specify multiple servers for one or more domains. Specifying multiple servers for a single domain allows the system to change to another server when its current server is slow or down.

When you specify more than one NIS domain, you must set the system's NIS domain name before starting **ypbind** so the client queries the proper server. Specifying the NIS domain name in **/etc/sysconfig/network** (page 641) before booting the system takes care of this issue. You can use nisdomainname to change the system's NIS domain name while the system is up.

Start ypbind

The Red Hat **ypbind** daemon is **ypbind-mt** renamed, a newer, multithreaded version of the older **ypbind** daemon. Use chkconfig to cause **ypbind** to start each time the system goes multiuser and service to start **ypbind** immediately. For more information, refer to "Prerequisites" on page 640.

Test the Setup

Use nisdomainname to make sure the correct NIS domain name is set. Refer to "Specify the System's NIS Domain Name" on page 641 if you need to set the NIS domain name. Next, check that the system is set up to connect to the proper server:

```
$ ypwhich
peach
```

The name of the server is set in **/etc/yp.conf** (page 642).

Next, make sure the NIS server is up and running (replace *server* with the name of the server that ypwhich returned):

```
$ /usr/sbin/rpcinfo -u server ypserv
program 100004 version 1 ready and waiting
program 100004 version 2 ready and waiting
```

After starting **ypbind**, check that it has registered with **portmap**:

```
$ /usr/sbin/rpcinfo -u localhost ypbind
program 100007 version 1 ready and waiting
program 100007 version 2 ready and waiting
```

If rpcinfo does not report that **ypbind** is **ready and waiting**, check that **ypbind** is running:

```
$ /sbin/service ypbind status
ypbind (pid 28689 28688 28687 28683) is running...
```

If NIS is still not working properly, use the init script to stop **ypbind**. Next, start it again with debugging turned on:

```
# /sbin/service ypbind stop
Shutting down NIS services:                            [  OK  ]
# /sbin/ypbind -debug
...
```

The –debug option keeps **ypbind** in the foreground and causes it to send error messages and debugging output to standard error.

yppasswd: Changing NIS Passwords

The yppasswd utility, not to be confused with the **yppasswdd** daemon (two **d**'s, page 651) that runs on the NIS server, replaces the functionality of passwd on clients when you are using NIS for passwords. Where passwd changes password information in the /etc/shadow file on the local system, yppasswd changes password information in the /etc/shadow file on the NIS master server *and* in the NIS **shadow.byname** map. Optionally, yppasswd can also change user information in the /etc/passwd file and **passwd.byname** map.

The yppasswd utility changes the way you log in on all systems in the NIS domain that use NIS for passwords. The yppasswd utility cannot change **root** and system passwords; by default, NIS does not store passwords of users with UIDs < 500. You have to use passwd to change these users' passwords locally.

In order to use yppasswd, the **yppasswdd** daemon must be running on the NIS master server.

passwd versus yppasswd

When a user, who is authenticated using NIS passwords, runs passwd to change her password, all appears to work properly, yet the user's password is not changed: The user needs to use yppasswd. Yet **root** and system accounts must use passwd to change their passwords. A common solution to this problem is first to rename passwd, for example, to rootpasswd, and then to change its permissions so only **root** can execute it.[1] Second, create a link to yppasswd named passwd:

```
# ls -l /usr/bin/passwd
-r-s--x--x    1 root      root   16336 Feb 13  2003 /usr/bin/passwd
# mv /usr/bin/passwd /usr/bin/rootpasswd
# chmod 700 /usr/bin/rootpasswd
# ln -s /usr/bin/yppasswd /usr/bin/passwd
# ls -l /usr/bin/{yppasswd,passwd,rootpasswd}
lrwxrwxrwx    1 root      root      17 Oct  8 15:32 /usr/bin/passwd -> /usr/bin/yppasswd
-rwx------    1 root      root   16336 Feb 13  2003 /usr/bin/rootpasswd
-r-xr-xr-x    3 root      root   18544 Jan 25  2003 /usr/bin/yppasswd
```

With this setup, a nonroot user changing her password using passwd will run yp-passwd, which is appropriate. If root or a system account user runs passwd (really yppasswd), yppasswd displays an error which will hopefully remind the administrator to run rootpasswd.

Modifying User Information

As long as **yppasswdd** is running on the NIS master server, a user can use yppasswd from an NIS client to change his NIS password and **root** can change any user's password (except that of a **root** or system account user). If the **yppasswdd** daemon permits it, a user can also use yppasswd to change her login shell and *GECOS* (page 972) information. Refer to "yppasswdd: NIS Password Update Daemon" on page 651 for information on how to configure **yppasswdd** to permit users to change these fields. Use the –f option with yppasswd to change GECOS information; use –l to change the login shell:

```
$ yppasswd -f
Changing NIS account information for mark on peach.
Please enter password:

Changing full name for mark on peach.
To accept the default, simply press return. To enter an empty
field, type the word "none".
Name [MSobell]: Mark G Sobell
Location []: SF
Office Phone []:
Home Phone []:

The GECOS information has been changed on peach.

$ ypmatch mark passwd
mark:$1$X49qrfYv/:500:500:Mark G Sobell,SF:/home/mark:/bin/bash
```

Adding and Removing Users

There are several ways to add and remove users from the NIS **passwd** map. The easiest is to keep the **/etc/passwd** file on the NIS master server synchronized with the

1. The passwd utility has setuid permission with execute permission for all users. If, after changing its name and permissions, you want to restore its original name and permissions, first change its name, and then give the command **chmod 4511 /usr/bin/passwd**.

passwd map. You can keep these files synchronized by making changes to the passwd file using standard tools such as passwd and running ypinit to update the map (page 649).

NIS Server Setup

This section discusses how to set up an NIS server.

Prerequisites

Decide on an NIS domain name. Some sites use their DNS domain name as the NIS domain name. Choosing a different name is more secure.

Install the following package:

- **ypserv**

Run chkconfig to cause **ypserv** to start when the system goes multiuser:

```
# /sbin/chkconfig ypserv on
```

On the master server only, run chkconfig to cause the map server, **ypxfrd** (page 650), to start when the system goes multiuser:

```
# /sbin/chkconfig ypxfrd on
```

In addition, on the master server only, run chkconfig to cause the NIS password update daemon, **yppasswdd** (page 651), to start when the system goes multiuser:

```
# /sbin/chkconfig yppasswdd on
```

After configuring **ypserv**, start it with the **ypserv** init script:

```
# /sbin/service ypserv start
Starting YP server services:
```

After starting **ypserv**, start the **ypxfrd** daemon (page 650) on the system running the master server:

```
# /sbin/service ypxfrd start
Starting YP map server:                                [  OK  ]
```

After starting **ypserv**, start the **yppasswdd** daemon (page 651) on the system running the master server:

```
# /sbin/service yppasswdd start
Starting YP passwd service:                            [  OK  ]
```

Notes

An NIS client can run on the same system as an NIS server.

There must be only one master server per domain.

You can run multiple NIS domain servers (for different domains) on a single system.

An NIS server serves the NIS domains listed in **/var/yp**. For a more secure system, remove the maps directories from **/var/yp** when disabling an NIS server.

Step-by-Step

This section lists the steps involved in setting up and starting an NIS server.

Specify the System's NIS Domain Name

Specify the system's NIS domain name by adding the following line to the **/etc/sysconfig/network** file:

>   *NSDOMAIN=nisdomainname*

where ***nisdomainname*** is the name of the NIS domain that the local system belongs to. For more information, refer to "Specify the System's NIS Domain Name" on page 641.

Edit /etc/ypserv.conf to Configure the Server

The **/etc/ypserv.conf** file, which holds NIS server configuration information, specifies options and access rules. Option rules specify server options and have the following format:

>   *option: value*

Options

Following is a list of ***option***s and their default ***value***s:

files   Specifies the maximum number of map files that **ypserv** caches. Set to 0 to turn off caching. Default is 30.

trusted_master   On a slave server, the name/IP address of the master server that new maps will be accepted from. Default is no master server, meaning no new maps are accepted.

xfer_check_port   YES (default) requires the master server to run on a *privileged port* (page 990). NO allows it to run on any port.

Access Rules

Access rules, which specify which hosts and domains can access which maps, have the following format:

>   **host:domain:map:security**

where *host* and *domain* specify the IP address and NIS domain this rule applies to; *map* is the name of the map that this rule applies to; and *security* is **none** (always allows access), **port** (allows access from a privileged port), or **deny** (never allows access).

The following lines appear in the **ypserv.conf** file that Red Hat provides:

```
$ cat /etc/ypserv.conf
...
# Not everybody should see the shadow passwords, not secure, since
# under MSDOG everbody is root and can access ports < 1024 !!!
*                       : *       : shadow.byname     : port
*                       : *       : passwd.adjunct.byname : port
...
```

These lines restrict the **shadow.byname** and **passwd.adjunct.byname** (the passwd map with shadow [asterisk] entries) maps to access from ports less than 1024. But, as the comment points out, anyone using a DOS or early Windows system on the network can read the maps as they can access ports less than 1024.

The following example describes a LAN with some addresses that you want to grant NIS access from and some that you do not; perhaps you have a wireless segment or some public network connections that you do not want to expose to NIS. You can list the systems or an IP subnet that you want to grant access to in **ypserv.conf**. Anyone logging in on another IP address will be denied NIS services. The following line from **ypserv.conf** grants access to anyone logging in from an IP address in the range of 192.168.0.1 to 192.168.0.255 (specified as 192.168.0.1 with a subnet mask [page 400] of /24):

```
$ cat /etc/ypserv.conf
...
  192.168.0.1/24 : * : * : none
```

Create /var/yp/securenets

To enhance system security, create the **/var/yp/securenets** file, which prevents unauthorized systems from sending RPC requests to the NIS server and retrieving NIS maps. Notably, **securenets** prevents unauthorized users from retrieving the **shadow** map, which contains encrypted passwords. When **securenets** does not exist or is empty, an NIS server accepts requests from any system.

Each line of **securenets** lists a netmask and IP address. NIS accepts requests from systems whose IP address is specified by one of the lines in **securenets** and ignores and logs requests from other addresses. You must include the (local) server system as localhost (127.0.0.1) in **securenets**. A simple **securenets** file follows:

```
$ cat /var/yp/securenets
# you must accept requests from localhost
255.255.255.255        127.0.0.1
#
# accept requests from IP addresses 192.168.0.1 - 192.168.0.62
255.255.255.192        192.168.0.0
#
# accept requests from IP addresses starting with 192.168.14
255.255.255.0          192.168.14.0
```

Edit /var/yp/Makefile

The make utility (page 816), controlled by **/var/yp/Makefile**, uses makedbm to create the NIS maps that hold the information that NIS distributes. When you run ypinit (next) on the master server, ypinit calls make: You do not need to run make manually.

Edit **/var/yp/Makefile** to set options and specify which maps to create. The following sections discuss **/var/yp/Makefile** in more detail.

Variables

Following is a list of variables you can set in **/var/yp/Makefile**. The values following the words **Red Hat** are the values set in the file distributed by Red Hat.

B   Do not change.

Red Hat: not set

NOPUSH   Specifies that **ypserv** is not to copy (push) maps to slave servers. Set to TRUE if you do not have any slave NIS servers; FALSE to cause NIS to copy maps to slave servers.

Red Hat: TRUE

MINUID
MINGID   Specifies the lowest UID and GID numbers to include in NIS maps. In the **/etc/passwd** and **/etc/group** files, lower ID numbers belong to **root** and system accounts and groups. For security, NIS does not distribute password and group information about these users and groups. Set MINUID to the lowest UID number you want to include in the NIS maps and set MINGID to the lowest GID number you want to include.

Red Hat: 500/500

NFFSNOBODYUID
NFFSNOBODYGID   Specifies the UID and GID of the user named **nfsnobody**. NIS does not export values for this user. Set to 0 to export maps for **nfsnobody**.

Red Hat: 65534/65534

MERGE_PASSWD
MERGE_GROUP   TRUE merges the **/etc/shadow** and **/etc/passwd** files and the **/etc/gshadow** and **/etc/group** files in the **passwd** and **group** maps, enabling shadow user passwords and group passwords.

Red Hat: TRUE/TRUE

File Locations

The next sections of **/var/yp/Makefile** specify file locations. These locations are standard; you do not normally need to change them. This part of the makefile is broken into the following groups:

Commands   Locates awk and make and sets a value for umask (page 398)
Source directories   Locates directories that contain NIS source files (next)
NIS source files   Locates NIS source files used to build the NIS database
Servers   Locates the file that lists NIS servers

The all: Target

The **all:** target in **/var/yp/Makefile** specifies the maps that make is to build for NIS.

```
all:   passwd group hosts rpc services netid protocols mail \
         # netgrp shadow publickey networks ethers bootparams printcap \
         # amd.home auto.master auto.home auto.local passwd.adjunct \
         # timezone locale netmasks
```

The first line of the **all:** target lists the maps that make builds by default. This line starts with the word **all**, followed by a colon (:) and a TAB. Because each of the first three lines of the **all:** target ends with a backslash, each of the four physical lines in the **all:** target is part of one long logical line. The last three physical lines are commented out. Uncomment lines and delete/move map names until the list is appropriate for your needs.

As your needs change, you can edit the **all:** target in **Makefile** and run make in the **/var/yp** directory to modify the list of maps that NIS distributes.

ypinit: Build or Import the Maps

The ypinit utility builds or imports and then installs the NIS database. On the master server, ypinit gathers information from the **passwd, group, hosts, networks, services, protocols, netgroup,** and **rpc** files in **/etc** and builds the database. On a slave, ypinit copies the database from the master server.

You must run ypinit by giving its absolute pathname (**/usr/lib/yp/ypinit**). Use the **–m** option to create the domain subdirectory under **/var/yp** and build the maps that go in it on the master server; use the **–s** *master* option on slave servers to import maps from *master* (the master server). Following, ypinit asks for the names of each of the slave servers; it already has the name of the master server as that is the system this command is run on. Terminate the list with CONTROL-D on a line by itself. After you respond to the query about the list of servers being correct, ypinit builds the **ypservers** map and calls make with **/var/yp/Makefile**, which builds the maps specified in **Makefile**.

```
# /usr/lib/yp/ypinit -m
```

At this point, we have to construct a list of the hosts which will run NIS
servers. peach is in the list of NIS server hosts. Please continue to add
the names for the other hosts, one per line. When you are done with the
list, type a <control D>.
next host to add: **speedy**
next host to add: CONTROL-D
The current list of NIS servers looks like this:

peach
speedy

Is this correct? [y/n: y] **y**
We need a few minutes to build the databases...
Building /var/yp/mgs/ypservers...
Running /var/yp/Makefile...
gmake[1]: Entering directory `/var/yp/mgs'
Updating passwd.byname...
Updating passwd.byuid...
Updating group.byname...
Updating group.bygid...
Updating hosts.byname...
Updating hosts.byaddr...
Updating rpc.byname...
Updating rpc.bynumber...
Updating services.byname...
Updating services.byservicename...
Updating netid.byname...
Updating protocols.bynumber...
Updating protocols.byname...
Updating mail.aliases...
gmake[1]: Leaving directory `/var/yp/mgs'

peach has been set up as a NIS master server.

Now you can run ypinit -s peach on all slave server.

Start the Servers

Start the master server and then the slave servers after completing the preceding
steps. Use chkconfig to cause **ypserv** to start each time the system goes multiuser and
service to start **ypserv** immediately. For more information, refer to "Prerequisites"
on page 645.

ypxfrd: the map server   The **ypxfrd** daemon speeds up the process of copying large NIS databases from
servers to slaves. It allows slaves to copy the maps, avoiding the need for each slave
to copy the raw data and then compile the maps. When an NIS slave receives from
the server a message that there is a new map, it starts ypxfr, which reads the map
from the server.

The **ypxfrd** daemon runs on the master server only; it is not necessary to run it on slave servers. Use chkconfig to cause **ypxfrd** to start each time the system goes multiuser and service to start **ypxfrd** immediately. For more information, refer to "Prerequisites" on page 645.

Testing

First, from the server, check that **ypserv** is connected to portmap:

```
# rpcinfo -p | grep ypserv
    100004    2   udp    849   ypserv
    100004    1   udp    849   ypserv
    100004    2   tcp    852   ypserv
    100004    1   tcp    852   ypserv
```

Again from the server system, make sure the NIS server is up and running:

```
$ /usr/sbin/rpcinfo -u localhost ypserv
program 100004 version 1 ready and waiting
program 100004 version 2 ready and waiting
```

If the server is not working properly, use service to stop **ypserv**. Next, start it again with debugging turned on:

```
# /sbin/service ypserv stop
Stopping YP server services:                        [  OK  ]
# /usr/sbin/ypserv --debug
...
```

The **--debug** option keeps **ypserv** in the foreground and causes it to send error messages and extra debugging output to standard error.

yppasswdd: NIS Password Update Daemon

The NIS password update daemon, **yppasswdd**, runs only on the master server; it is not necessary to run it on slave servers. (If the master server is down and you try to change your password from a client, you get an error message.) When a user runs yppasswd (page 643) on a client, yppasswd exchanges information with the **yppasswdd** daemon to update the user's password (and optionally other) information in the NIS **shadow** (and optionally **passwd**) map and in the **/etc/shadow** (and optionally **/etc/passwd**) file on the NIS master server. Password change requests are sent to **syslogd** (page 546).

Start yppasswdd

Use chkconfig to cause **yppasswdd** to start each time the system goes multiuser and **service** to start **yppasswdd** immediately. For more information, refer to "Prerequisites" on page 645.

Allow GECOS and Login Shell Modification

By default, **yppasswdd** does not allow users to change *GECOS* (page 972) information or the login shell when they run yppasswd from a client. You can allow users to change this information with options on the command line when you start **yppasswdd** or, more conveniently, by modifying the **/etc/sysconfig/yppasswdd** configuration file. The **–e chfn** option to **yppasswdd** allows users to change their GECOS information; **–e chsh** allows users to change their login shell. When you set the options in the **/etc/sysconfig/yppasswdd** file, they are set automatically each time the network starts:

```
$ cat /etc/sysconfig/yppasswdd
...
YPPASSWDD_ARGS="-e chfn -e chsh"
```

Chapter Summary

NIS (Network Information Service) simplifies the administration of common administrative files by maintaining them in a central database and having clients contact the database server to retrieve information from the database. The network that NIS serves is called an *NIS domain*. Each NIS domain has one master server; larger networks may have slave servers.

Under Red Hat Linux, NIS derives the information it offers from local configuration files, such as **/etc/passwd** and **/etc/hosts**. These files are called *source files* or *master files*. Before NIS can store the information contained in a source file, it must be converted to dbm format files, called maps. The ypcat and ypmatch utilities display information from NIS maps.

The yppasswd utility runs on the NIS server and replaces the functionality of passwd on clients when you are using NIS for passwords. The **/etc/ypserv.conf** file, which holds NIS server configuration information, specifies options and access rules for the NIS server. To enhance system security, you can create the **/var/yp/securenets** file, which prevents unauthorized systems from sending RPC requests to the NIS server and retrieving NIS maps.

Exercises

1. What is the difference between the passwd and yppasswd commands?

2. How would you prevent NIS from exporting **root** and other system users to clients?

3. How would you make NIS user information override local user information on client systems?

4. Why does the **/etc/passwd** file need two NIS maps?

Advanced Exercises

5. How can you use NIS to mirror the functionality of a private DNS server for a small network? Why should NIS not be used this way on a large network?

6. How can you find out if the working directory is the home directory of an NIS user?

7. What advantage does NIS provide when you use it with NFS?

8. Suggest a way to implement NIS maps so they can be indexed on more than one field.

NFS: Sharing Filesystems

22

The NFS (Network Filesystem) protocol, a de facto standard originally developed by Sun Microsystems, allows a server to share selected local *directory hierarchies* (page 967) with client systems on a heterogeneous network. NFS runs on UNIX, DOS, Windows, VMS, Linux, and more. Files on the remote computer (the *fileserver*) appear as if they are present on the local system (the client). The physical location of a file is irrelevant to an NFS user.

NFS reduces storage needs and system administration. As an example, each system in a company traditionally holds its own copy of an application program. In order to upgrade the program, the administrator needs to upgrade it on each of the systems. NFS allows you to store a copy of a program on one system and give other users access to it over the network. This scenario uses less storage by reducing the number of locations that the same data needs to be maintained. In addition to efficiency, NFS gives users on the network access to the same data (not just application programs), improving data consistency and reliability. By consolidating data, NFS reduces administrative overhead and provides a convenience to users.

Introduction

Figure 22-1 shows the flow of data from a client to a server in a typical NFS client/server setup. An NFS directory hierarchy appears to users and application programs as just another directory hierarchy. By looking at it, you cannot tell that a given directory holds a remotely mounted NFS directory hierarchy and not a local **ext3** filesystem. The NFS server translates commands from the client into operations on the server's filesystem.

655

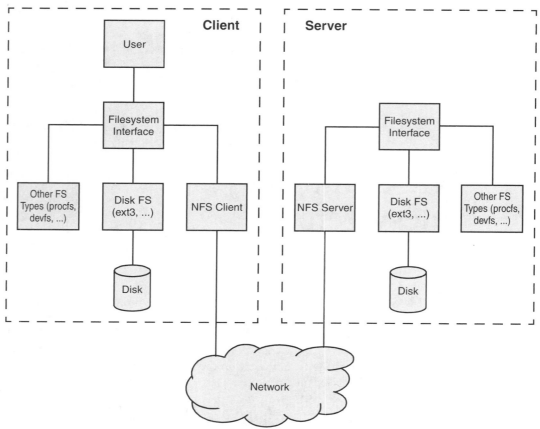

Figure 22-1   Flow of data in a typical NFS client/server setup

Diskless   In many computer facilities, user files are stored on a central fileserver equipped with many large-capacity disk drives and devices that quickly and easily make backup copies of the data. A *diskless* system boots from a fileserver (netboots, next paragraph), a CD, or a floppy diskette and loads system software from a fileserver. The Linux Terminal Server Project (LTSP.org) Web site says it all: "Linux makes a great platform for deploying diskless workstations that boot from a network server. The LTSP is all about running thin client computers in a Linux environment." Because a diskless workstation does not require a lot of computing power, you can give older, retired computers a second life by using them as diskless systems.

Netboot/PXE   You can *netboot* (page 985) systems that are appropriately set up. Red Hat includes the PXE (Preboot Execution Environment) server package for netbooting Intel systems. Older systems sometimes use tftp (trivial file transfer protocol) for netbooting. Non-Intel architectures have historically included netboot capabilities that Red Hat Linux also supports. You can build the Linux kernel so that it mounts **root** (**/**) using NFS. Of the many ways to set up your system, the one you choose depends on what you want to do. See the *Remote-boot mini HOWTO* for more information.

Dataless Another type of Linux system is a *dataless* system, in which the client has a disk but stores no user data (only Linux and the applications are kept on the disk). Setting up this type of system is a matter of choosing which directory hierarchies are mounted remotely.

df shows where directory hierarchies are mounted The df utility displays a list of the directory hierarchies available on your system, along with the amount of disk space, free and used, on each. The **–h** (human) option makes the output more intelligible. Directory hierarchy names that are prepended with **hostname:** are available through NFS.

```
[bravo]$ cd;pwd
/speedy.home/jenny
[bravo]$ df -h
Filesystem      Size  Used Avail Use% Mounted on
/dev/hda1       981M  287M  645M  31% /
/dev/hda6        20G  2.7G   16G  15% /usr
/dev/hda7       9.7G  384M  8.8G   5% /home
grape:/gc1      985M   92M  844M  10% /grape.gc1
grape:/gc5      3.9G  3.0G  738M  81% /grape.gc5
speedy:/home    3.9G  2.4G  1.4G  64% /speedy.home
```

In the preceding example, Jenny's home directory, **/home/jenny**, is on the remote system **speedy**. Using NFS, the **/home** filesystem on **speedy** is mounted on **bravo**; to make it easy to recognize, it is mounted as **/speedy.home**. The **/gc1** and **/gc5** filesystems on **grape** are mounted on **bravo** as **/grape.gc1** and **/grape.gc5**.

You can use the **–T** option to df to add a Type column to the display. The following command uses **–t nfs** to display NFS filesystems only:

```
[grape]$ df -ht nfs
Filesystem      Size  Used Avail Use% Mounted on
grape:/gc1      985M   92M  844M  10% /grape.gc1
grape:/gc5      3.9G  3.0G  738M  81% /grape.gc5
speedy:/home    3.9G  2.4G  1.4G  64% /speedy.home
```

Errors At times you may lose access to remote files. A network problem or a remote system crash may make these files temporarily unavailable: When you try to access a remote file, you get an error message, such as **NFS server speedy not responding.** When the local system can contact the remote server again, you see a message, such as **NFS server speedy OK.** Setting up a stable network and server (or not using NFS) is the best defense against these kinds of problems.

Security NFS is based on the trusted-host paradigm (page 343) and therefore has all the security shortcomings that plague services based on this paradigm. In addition, NFS is not encrypted. Because of these issues, you should implement NFS on a single LAN segment only, where you can be (reasonably) sure that systems on a LAN segment are the systems they claim to be. Make sure a firewall blocks NFS traffic from outside the LAN and never use NFS over the Internet.

To improve security, make sure UIDs and GIDs are the same on server and clients (page 668).

More Information

Web   nfs.sourceforge.net

HOWTO   *NFS HOWTO*
   Netboot and PXE   *Remote-boot mini HOWTO*

Book   *NFS Illustrated* by Callaghan, Addison-Wesley; 1st edition (December 17, 1999)

NFS Client

This section covers setting up a NFS client, mounting remote directory hierarchies, and improving NFS performance.

Prerequisites

Install the following packages:

- **nfs-utils**
- **system-config-nfs** (*FEDORA*) or **redhat-config-nfs** (*RHEL*) (optional)

The portmap utility (refer to "RPC Network Services" on page 358) must be running to enable reliable file locking.

There are no daemons to start for NFS clients.

JumpStart: Mounting a Remote Directory Hierarchy

To set up an NFS client, mount the remote directory hierarchy the same way you mount a local directory hierarchy (page 442). The following sections detail the process.

mount: Mounts a Remote Directory Hierarchy

The following examples show two ways to mount a remote directory hierarchy, assuming that **speedy** is on the same network as the local system and is sharing **/home** and **/export** with the local system. The **/export** directory on **speedy** holds two directory hierarchies that you want to mount: **/export/progs** and **/export/oracle**. The example mounts **speedy**'s **/home** directory on **/speedy.home** on the local system, **/export/progs** on **/apps**, and **/export/oracle** on **/oracle**.

First, use mkdir to create the directories that are the mount points for the remote directory hierarchies:

```
# mkdir /speedy.home /apps /oracle
```

You can mount any directory from an exported directory hierarchy: In this example, **speedy** exports **/export** and the local system mounts **/export/progs** and **/export/oracle**.

The following commands manually mount the directory hierarchies one time. The error **mount: RPC: Program not registered** may mean NFS is not running on the server.

```
# mount speedy:/home /speedy.home
# mount -o r,nosuid speedy:/export/progs /apps
# mount -o r speedy:/export/oracle /oracle
```

By default, directory hierarchies are mounted read-write, assuming the NFS server is exporting them with read-write permissions. The first preceding command mounts the **/home** directory hierarchy from **speedy** on the local directory **/speedy.home**. The second and third mount lines use the **−o r** option to force a read-only mount. The second mount line adds the **nosuid** option, which forces setuid (page 175) executables in the mounted directory hierarchy to run with regular permissions on the local system.

nosuid option Giving a user the ability to run a setuid program can give that user the power of Superuser and should be limited. Unless you know that a user will need to run a program with setuid permissions from a mounted directory hierarchy, always mount a directory hierarchy with the **nosuid** option. An example of when you would need to mount a directory hierarchy with setuid privileges is a diskless workstation that has its root partition mounted using NFS.

nodev option Mounting a device file creates another potential security hole. Although the best policy is not to mount untrustworthy directory hierarchies, it is not always possible to implement this policy. Unless a user needs to use a device on a mounted directory hierarchy, mount directory hierarchies with the **nodev** option, which prevents character and block special files (page 439) on the mounted directory hierarchy from being used as devices.

fstab If you mount directory hierarchies frequently, you can add entries for the directory hierarchies to the **/etc/fstab** file (page 663). (Alternatively, you can use **automount**, page 671.) The following **/etc/fstab** entries automatically mount the same directory hierarchies as the previous example at the same time as the system mounts the local filesystems:

```
speedy:/home           /speedy.home   nfs    -          0 0
speedy:/export/progs   /apps          nfs    r,nosuid   0 0
speedy:/export/oracle  /oracle        nfs    r          0 0
```

A file that is mounted using NFS is always type **nfs** on the local system, regardless of what type it is on the remote system. Typically, you never run fsck on or back up an NFS directory hierarchy. The entries in the third, fifth, and sixth columns of **fstab** are usually **nfs** (filesystem type), 0 (do not back up this directory hierarchy with dump, page 529), and 0 (do not run fsck [page 447] on this directory hierarchy). The options for mounting an NFS directory hierarchy differ from those for mounting an **ext3** or other type of filesystem. See the next section for details.

umount: **Unmounts a Remote Directory Hierarchy**

Use umount to unmount a remote directory hierarchy the same way you would unmount a local one.

mount: **Mounts a Directory Hierarchy**

The mount utility (page 442) associates a directory hierarchy with a mount point (a directory). You can use mount to mount an NFS (remote) directory hierarchy. This section describes some mount options and lists default options first and nondefault options, enclosed in parentheses, second. You can use these options on the command line or in **/etc/fstab** (page 663). For a complete list of options, refer to the mount and nfs man pages.

Attribute Caching

File attributes, stored in a file's inode (page 437), are information about a file, such as file modification time, size, links, and owner. File attributes do not include the data stored in a file. Typically, file attributes do not change very often for an ordinary file and change less often for a directory file. Even the size attribute does not change with every write instruction: When a client is writing to an NFS-mounted file, several write instructions may be given before the data is actually transferred to the server. Finally, many file accesses, such as that performed by ls, are read-only and do not change the file's attributes or its contents. Thus a client can cache attributes and avoid costly network reads.

The kernel uses the modification time of the file to determine when its cache is out of date. If the time the attribute cache was saved is later than the modification time of the file itself, the data in the cache is current. The attribute cache of an NFS-mounted file must be periodically refreshed from the server to see if another process has modified the file. This period is specified as a minimum and maximum number of seconds for ordinary and directory files. Following is a list of options that affect attribute caching.

ac (noac)   **attribute cache**   Permits attribute caching (default). The **noac** option disables attribute caching. Although **noac** slows the server, it avoids stale attributes when two NFS clients actively write to a common directory hierarchy.

acdirmax=*n*   **attribute cache directory file maximum**   The number of seconds, at a maximum, that NFS waits before refreshing directory file attributes (default is 60 seconds).

acdirmin=*n*   **attribute cache directory file minimum**   The number of seconds, at a minimum, that NFS waits before refreshing directory file attributes (default is 30 seconds).

acregmax=*n*   **attribute cache regular file maximum**   The number of seconds, at a maximum, that NFS waits before refreshing regular file attributes (default is 60 seconds).

acregmin=*n*   **attribute cache regular file minimum**   The number of seconds, at a minimum, that NFS waits before refreshing regular file attributes (default is 3 seconds).

actimeo=*n*   **attribute cache timeout**   Sets **acregmin**, **acregmax**, **acdirmin**, and **acdirmax** to *n* (without this option, each individual option takes on its default value).

Error Handling

The following options control what NFS does when the server does not respond or there is an I/O error. To allow for a mount point located on a mounted device, a missing mount point is treated as a timeout.

fg (bg)   **foreground**   Retries failed NFS mount attempts in the foreground (default). The **bg** (background) option retries failed NFS mount attempts in the background.

hard (soft)   Displays **server not responding** on the console on a major timeout and keeps retrying (default). The **soft** option reports an I/O error to the calling program on a major timeout. In general, it is not advisable to use **soft**. The mount man page says of **soft**, "Usually it just causes lots of trouble." For more information, refer to "Improving Performance" on page 662.

nointr (intr)   **no interrupt**   Does not allow a signal to interrupt a file operation on a hard mounted directory hierarchy when a major timeout occurs (default). The **intr** option allows this type of interrupt.

retrans=*n*   **retransmission value**   After *n* minor timeouts, NFS generates a major timeout (default is 3). A major timeout aborts the operation or displays **server not responding** on the console, depending on whether **hard** or **soft** is set.

retry=*n*   **retry value**   The number of minutes that NFS retries a mount operation before giving up (default is 10,000).

timeo=*n*   **timeout value**   The number of tenths of a second that NFS waits before retransmitting following an RPC, or minor, timeout (default is 7). The value is increased at each timeout to a maximum of sixty seconds or until a major timeout occurs (see **retrans**). On a busy network, a slow server, or when the request passes through multiple routers/gateways, increasing this value may improve performance.

Miscellaneous Options

Following are additional, useful options:

lock (nolock)   Permits NFS locking (default). The **nolock** option disables NFS locking (does not start the **lockd** daemon) and is useful with older servers that do not support NFS locking.

mounthost=*name*   The name of the host running **mountd**, the NFS mount daemon.

mountport=*n*   The port that **mountd** uses.

nodev   **no device**   Causes mounted device files not to function as devices (page 659).

port=*n*   The port used to connect to the NFS server (defaults to 2049 if the NFS daemon is not registered with portmap). When **n=0** (the default), NFS queries portmap on the server to determine the port.

rsize=*n*   **read block size**   The number of bytes read at one time from an NFS server. The default block size is 4096. Refer to "Improving Performance" on page 662.

wsize=*n*   **write block size**   The number of bytes written at one time to an NFS server. The default block size is 4096. Refer to "Improving Performance" on page 662.

tcp   Use TCP in place of the default UDP protocol for an NFS mount. This option may improve performance on a congested network.

udp   Use the default UDP protocol for an NFS mount.

Improving Performance

hard/soft   There are several parameters that can affect the performance of NFS, especially over slow connections such as a line with a lot of traffic or one controlled by a modem. If you have a slow connection, make sure **hard** (page 661) is set (this is the default) so that timeouts do not abort program execution.

Block size   One of the easiest ways to improve NFS performance is to increase the block size, the number of bytes NFS transfers at a time. The default of 4096 is low for a fast connection using modern hardware. Try increasing **rsize** (page 662) and **wsize** (page 662) to 8192 or higher. Experiment until you find the optimal block size. Unmount and mount the directory hierarchy each time you change an option. See the NFS-HOWTO for more information on testing different block sizes.

Timeouts   NFS waits the amount of time specified by the **timeo** (timeout, page 661) option for a response to a transmission. If it does not receive a response in this amount of time, it sends another transmission. The second transmission uses bandwidth that, over a slow connection, may slow things down further. You may be able to increase performance by increasing **timeo**.

The default value of **timeo** is 7 tenths of a second or 700 milliseconds. After a timeout, NFS doubles the time it waits to 1400 milliseconds. On each timeout it doubles the amount of time it waits to a maximum of 60 seconds. You can test the speed of a connection with the size packets you are sending (**rsize** (page 662) and **wsize** [page 662]) using ping with the –s (size) option:

```
$ ping -s 4096 speedy
PING speedy.tcorp.com (192.168.0.1) 4096(4124) bytes of data.
4104 bytes from speedy.tcorp.com (192.168.0.1): icmp_seq=0 ttl=64 time=1.43 ms
4104 bytes from speedy.tcorp.com (192.168.0.1): icmp_seq=1 ttl=64 time=1.17 ms
4104 bytes from speedy.tcorp.com (192.168.0.1): icmp_seq=2 ttl=64 time=1.17 ms
```

```
...
4104 bytes from speedy.tcorp.com (192.168.0.1): icmp_seq=26 ttl=64 time=1.16 ms
4104 bytes from speedy.tcorp.com (192.168.0.1): icmp_seq=27 ttl=64 time=1.16 ms
4104 bytes from speedy.tcorp.com (192.168.0.1): icmp_seq=28 ttl=64 time=1.16 ms
4104 bytes from speedy.tcorp.com (192.168.0.1): icmp_seq=29 ttl=64 time=1.26 ms

--- speedy.tcorp.com ping statistics ---
30 packets transmitted, 30 received, 0% packet loss, time 29281ms
rtt min/avg/max/mdev = 1.154/1.192/1.431/0.067 ms
```

The preceding example uses Red Hat's default packet size of 4096 bytes and shows a fast average packet round-trip time of just over 1 millisecond. Over a modem line, you can expect times of several seconds. If there is other traffic on the connection, the time will be longer. Run the test during a period of heavy traffic. Try increasing **timeo** to three or four times the average round-trip time (to allow for unusually bad network conditions, as when the connection is made) and see if things improve. Remember that the **timeo** value is tenths of a second (100 milliseconds = 1 tenth of a second).

/etc/fstab: Mounts Directory Hierarchies Automatically

The **/etc/fstab** file (page 445) lists directory hierarchies that the system mounts automatically as it comes up. You can use the options discussed in the preceding section on the command line or in the **fstab** file.

The first example line from **fstab** mounts **grape**'s **/gc1** filesystem on the **/grape.gc1** mount point. A mount point should be an empty, local directory. (Files in a mount point are hidden when a directory hierarchy is mounted on it.) The type of a filesystem mounted using NFS is always **nfs**, regardless of its type on the local system. You can increase the **rsize** and **wsize** options to improve performance. Refer to "Improving Performance" on page 662.

```
grape:/gc1              /grape.gc1      nfs     rsize=8192,wsize=8192          0 0
```

The next example from **fstab** mounts a filesystem from **speedy**. Because the local system connects to **speedy** over a slow connection, **timeo** is increased to 5 seconds (50 tenths of a second). Refer to "Timeouts" on page 662. In addition, **hard** is set to make sure that NFS keeps trying to communicate with the server after a major timeout. Refer to "hard/soft" on page 662.

```
speedy:/export          /speedy.export nfs     timeo=50,hard                 0 0
```

The final example from **fstab** shows a remote-mounted home directory. Because **speedy** is a local server and is connected via a reliable, high-speed connection, **timeo** is decreased and **rsize** and **wsize** are increased substantially.

```
speedy:/export/home     /home          nfs     timeo=4,rsize=16384,wsize=16384  0 0
```

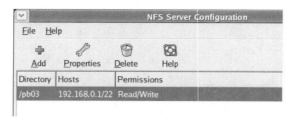

Figure 22-2   NFS Server Configuration window

NFS Server

Prerequisites

Install the following package:

- **nfs-utils**

Run chkconfig to cause nfs to start when the system goes multiuser:

```
# /sbin/chkconfig nfs on
```

Start **nfs**:

```
# /etc/rc.d/init.d/nfs start
```

The **nfs** init script starts **mountd**, **nfsd**, and **rquotad**.

The portmap utility (page 358) must be running to enable file locking.

JumpStart: system-config-nfs: **Configures an NFS Server**

You can generate an **/etc/exports** file, which is almost all there is to setting up an NFS server, using system-config-nfs (*FEDORA*) or redhat-config-nfs (*RHEL*). These utilities display the NFS Server Configuration window (Figure 22-2), which allows you to specify which directory hierarchies are shared and how they are shared using NFS. You use the same window to add and modify directory hierarchies; in the first case it is named Add NFS Share and in the second it is named Edit NFS Share.

The Add/Edit NFS Share window has three tabs: Basic, General Options, and User Access. Figure 22-3 shows the Basic tab where you can specify the pathname of the root of the directory hierarchy you want to share, the names or IP addresses of the systems (hosts) you want to share the hierarchy with, and whether you want users from the specified systems to be able to write to the shared files.

The selections in the other two tabs correspond to options that you can use in the **/etc/exports** file. Following is a list of the check box descriptions in these tabs and

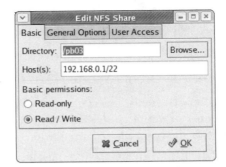

Figure 22-3 Edit NFS Share window

the options each corresponds to. Refer to the options starting on page 666 for more information.

General Options tab Allow connections from ports 1023 and higher **insecure**
Allow insecure file locking **no_auth_nlm** or **insecure_locks**
Disable subtree checking **no_subtree_check**
Sync write operations on request **sync**
Force sync of write operations immediately **no_wdelay**

User Access tab Treat remote root user as local root **no_root_squash**
Treat all client users as anonymous users **all_squash**
Specify local user ID for anonymous users **anonuid**
Specify local group ID for anonymous users **anongid**

After making the changes you want, click **OK** to close the Add/Edit NFS Share window and click **OK** again to close the NFS Server Configuration window. There is no need to restart any daemons.

Exporting a Directory Hierarchy

Exporting a directory hierarchy makes the directory hierarchy *available* for mounting by designated systems via a network. Exported does not mean mounted: When a directory hierarchy is exported, it is placed in the list of directory hierarchies that can be mounted by other systems. An exported directory hierarchy may be mounted or not at any given time. A server holds three lists of exported directory hierarchies:

- **/etc/exports**   Access control list for exported directory hierarchies (next section). The system administrator can modify this file by editing it or by running [system|redhat]-config-nfs.

- **/var/lib/nfs/xtab**   Access control list for exported directory hierarchies. Initialized from **/etc/exports** when the system is brought up. Read by mountd when a client asks to mount a directory hierarchy. Modified by exportfs (page 670) as directory hierarchies are mounted and unmounted by NFS.

- Kernel's export table   List of active exported directory hierarchies. The kernel obtains this information from **/var/lib/nfs/xtab**. You can display this table by giving the command **cat /proc/fs/nfs/exports**.

/etc/exports: List of Exported Directory Hierarchies

The **/etc/exports** file is the access control list for exported directory hierarchies that NFS clients can mount and is the only file you need to edit to set up an NFS server. The **exports** file controls

- Which clients can access files on the server
- Which directory hierarchies on the server each client can access
- How each client can access each directory hierarchy
- How client usernames are mapped to server usernames
- Various NFS parameters

The format of each line in the **exports** file is

> *export-point client1(options)* [*client2(options)* ...]

Where *export-point* is the absolute pathname of the root directory of the directory hierarchy to be exported, *client1-n* is the name of one or more clients or is one or more IP addresses, separated by SPACEs, that are allowed to mount the *export-point*. The *options*, described in the following section, apply to the preceding *client*.

Either you can use system-config-nfs (page 664) to make changes to **exports** or you can edit this file directly. The following simple **exports** file gives **grape** read and write access and gives **speedy** read-only access to the files in **/home**. In each case, access is implicitly granted for all subdirectories. For historical reasons, exportfs complains when you do not specify either **sync** or **async**.

```
# cat /etc/exports
/home grape(rw,sync)
/home speedy(ro,sync)
```

You can use IP addresses and include more than one system on a line:

```
# cat /etc/exports
/home grape(rw,sync) speedy(ro,sync) 192.168.0.22(rw,sync)
```

General Options

This section lists default options first and nondefault options, enclosed in parentheses, second.

auth_nlm (no_auth_nlm) *or* secure_locks (insecure_locks)

Causes the server to require authentication of lock requests (using the NLM [NFS Lock Manager] protocol). Use **no_auth_nlm** for older clients when you find that only files that anyone can read can be locked.

nohide (hide)   When a server exports two directory hierarchies, one of which is mounted on the other, a client has to mount both directory hierarchies explicitly in order to access both. When the second, or child directory hierarchy is not explicitly mounted, its mount point appears as an empty directory and the directory hierarchy is hidden. The **nohide** option causes the second directory hierarchy to appear without being explicitly mounted, but does not work in all cases.

caution ‖   **Exporting Symbolic Links and Device Files**

When you export a directory hierarchy that contains a symbolic link, make sure that the object of the link is available on the client (remote) system. Either the object of the link must exist on a client system, or you must export and mount the object along with the exported link, otherwise the symbolic link will not point to the file it points to on the server.

A device file refers to a Linux kernel interface. When you export a device file, you export that interface. If the client system does not have the same type of device, the exported device will not work. From a client, you can use mount's **nodev** option (page 659) to prevent device files on mounted directory hierarchies from being used as devices.

ro (rw)   **read only**   Permits only read requests on an NFS directory hierarchy. Use **rw** to permit read and write requests.

secure (insecure)   Requires that NFS requests originate on a secure port (<1024) so that a program without **root** permissions cannot mount a directory hierarchy. This option does not guarantee a secure connection.

subtree_check
(no_subtree_check)   Checks subtrees for valid files. Assume that you have an exported directory hierarchy that has its root below the root of the filesystem that holds it (that is, an exported subdirectory of a filesystem). When the NFS server receives a request for a file in that directory hierarchy, it performs a subtree check to make sure the file is in the exported directory hierarchy.

Subtree checking can cause problems with files that are renamed while opened and, when **no_root_squash** is used, files that only **root** can access. The **no_subtree_check** option disables subtree checking and can improve reliability in some cases.

For example, you may need to disable subtree checking for home directories. Home directories are frequently subtrees (of **/home**), written to often, and can have files within them frequently renamed. You would probably not need to disable subtree checking for directory hierarchies that contain files that are mostly read, such as **/usr**.

sync (async)   **synchronize**   Specifies that the server is to reply to requests only after it has written to disk changes made by the request. The **async** option specifies that the server does not have to wait for information to be written to disk and can improve performance at the cost of possible data corruption if the server crashes or the connection is interrupted.

Because the default changed with release 1.0.0 of **nfs-utils**, exportfs displays a warning when you do not specify either **sync** or **async**.

wdelay   **write delay**   Causes the server to delay committing write requests when it antici-
(no_wdelay)   pates that another, related request follows, improving performance by committing
multiple write requests within a single operation. The **no_wdelay** option does not
delay committing write requests and can improve performance when the server receives multiple, small, unrelated requests.

User ID Mapping Options

Each user has a UID number and a primary GID number on the local system. The
local **/etc/passwd** and **/etc/group** files map these numbers to names. When a user
makes a request of an NFS server, the server uses these numbers to identify the user
on the remote system, raising several issues:

- The user may not have the same ID numbers on both systems and may
therefore have owner access to files of another user (see "NIS and NFS,"
following, for a solution).

- You may not want the **root** user on the client system to have owner access
to **root**-owned files on the server.

- There are some important system files that are not owned by **root** (such as
those owned by **bin**) that you may not want a remote user to have owner
access to.

security ‖   **Critical Files in NFS-Mounted Directories Should Be Owned by root**

Despite the mapping done by the **root-squash** option, the **root** user on a client system can use su
to take on the identity of any user on the system and then access that user's files on the server.
Thus, without resorting to **all-squash**, you can protect only files owned by **root** on an NFS server.
Make sure that **root**, and not **bin** or another user, owns and is the only user who can modify or
delete all critical files within any NFS-mounted directory hierarchy.

The preceding precaution does not completely protect against an attacker with **root** privileges, but
it can help protect a system from less experienced malicious users.

Owner access to a file means that the remote user can execute, remove, or, worse,
modify the file. NFS gives you two ways to deal with these cases:

- You can use the **root_squash** option to map the ID number of the **root** user
on a client to the **nfsnobody** user on the server.

- You can use the **all-squash** option to map all NFS users on the client to
nfsnobody on the server.

The **/etc/passwd** file shows that **nfsnobody** has a UID and GID of 65534. You can
use the **anonuid** and **anongid** options to override these values.

NIS and NFS   When you use NIS (page 637) for user authorization, users automatically have the
same UIDs on both systems. If you are using NFS on a large network, it is a good
idea to use a directory service such as *LDAP* (page 980) or NIS for authorization.

Without such a service, you will have to synchronize the **passwd** files on all the systems manually.

root_squash Maps requests from **root** on a remote system to appear to come from the UID for
(no_root_squash) **nfsnobody**, an unprivileged user on the local system, or as specified by **anonuid**. Does not affect other sensitive UIDs such as **bin**. The **no_root_squash** option turns off this mapping so that requests from **root** appear to come from **root**.

no_all_squash Does not change the mapping of users making requests of the NFS server. The
(all_squash) **all_squash** option maps requests from all users, not just **root**, on remote systems to appear to come from the UID for **nfsnobody**, an unprivileged user on the local system, or as specified by **anonuid**. This option is useful for controlling access to exported public FTP, news, and other directories.

anonuid=*un* and Set the UID or GID of the anonymous account to *un* or *gn*, respectively. NFS uses
anongid=*gn* these accounts when it does not recognize an incoming UID or GID and when instructed to do so by **root_squash** or **all_squash**.

showmount: Displays NFS Status Information

Without any options, the showmount utility displays a list of systems that are allowed to mount local directories. To display information for a remote system, give the name of the remote system as an argument. You typically use showmount to display a list of directory hierarchies that a server is exporting. The information that showmount provides may not be complete because it depends on **mountd** and trusts that remote servers are reporting accurately.

In the following example, **bravo** and **grape** can mount local directories, but you do not know which ones:

```
# /usr/sbin/showmount
Hosts on localhost:
bravo.tcorp.com
grape.tcorp.com
```

If showmount displays an error such as **RPC: Program not registered**, NFS is not running on the server. Start NFS on the server with the **nfs** init script (page 664).

–a **all** Tells which directories are exported to which remote systems. This information is stored in **/etc/exports**.

```
# /usr/sbin/showmount -a
All mount points on localhost:
bravo.tcorp.com:/home
grape.tcorp.com:/home
```

–e **exports** Displays the export list. Displays the same information as **–a** from another vantage point: The local **/home** directory is exported to **bravo** and **grape**:

```
# /usr/sbin/showmount -e
Export list for localhost:
/home bravo.tcorp.com,grape.tcorp.com
```

exportfs: Maintains the List of Exported Directory Hierarchies

The exportfs utility maintains the kernel's list of exported directory hierarchies. Without changing /etc/exports, exportfs can add or remove from the list of exported directory hierarchies. The format of an exportfs command follows:

/usr/sbin/exportfs [options] [client:dir ...]

Where *options* is one or more options as detailed in the next section, *client* is the name of the system that *dir* is exported to, and *dir* is the absolute pathname of the directory at the root of the directory hierarchy being exported.

The system executes the following command when it comes up (it is in the **nfs** init script); it reexports the entries in **/etc/exports** and removes invalid entries from **/var/lib/nfs/xtab** (page 665) so that **/var/lib/nfs/xtab** is synchronized with **/etc/exports**:

```
# exportfs -r
```

Replace the –r with –a to export only the entries in **/etc/exports**. Remove an exported directory hierarchy with the –u option and remove all exported directory hierarchies with the –ua options.

Options

–a **all**   Exports directory hierarchies specified in **/etc/exports**. This option does not *unexport* entries you have removed from **exports** (that is, it does not remove invalid entries from **/var/lib/nfs/xtab**); use –r to do this.

–i **ignore**   Ignores **/etc/exports**; uses what is specified on the command line only.

–o **options**   Specifies options. You can specify options following –o the same way you do in the **exports** file. For example, **exportfs –i –o ro speedy:/home/sam** exports **/home/sam** on the local system to **speedy** for readonly access.

–r **reexport**   Reexports the entries in **/etc/exports** and removes invalid entries from **/var/lib/nfs/xtab** so that **/var/lib/nfs/xtab** is synchronized with **/etc/exports**.

–u **unexport**   Makes an exported directory hierarchy no longer exported. If a directory hierarchy is mounted when you unexport it, you see the message **Stale NFS file handle** when you try to access the directory hierarchy from the remote system.

–v **verbose**   Provides more information. Displays export options when you use exportfs to display export information.

Testing the Server Setup

From the server, run the **nfs** init script with an argument of **status**. If all is well, the system displays something similar to the following:

```
# /sbin/service nfs status
rpc.mountd (pid 15795) is running...
nfsd (pid 15813 15812 15811 15810 15809 15808 15807 15806) is running...
rpc.rquotad (pid 15784) is running...
```

Next, from the server, use rpcinfo to make sure NFS is registered with portmap.

```
$ /usr/sbin/rpcinfo -p localhost | grep nfs
    100003    2   udp   2049  nfs
    100003    3   udp   2049  nfs
```

Repeat the preceding command from the client, replacing **localhost** with the name of the server. The results should be the same.

Finally, try mounting directory hierarchies from remote systems and verify access.

automount: **Mounting Directory Hierarchies Automatically**

With distributed computing, when you log in on any system on the network, all your files, including startup scripts, are available. A distributed computing environment commonly has all systems able to mount all directory hierarchies on all servers: Whichever system you log in on, your home directory is waiting for you.

As an example, assume that **/home/alex** is a remote directory hierarchy that is mounted on demand. When you issue the command ls **/home/alex**, autofs goes to work: It looks in the **/etc/auto.home** map, finds that **alex** is a key that says to mount **bravo:/export/homes/alex**, and mounts the remote directory hierarchy. Once the directory hierarchy is mounted, ls displays the list of files you want to see. If after this mounting sequence you give the command ls **/home**, ls shows that **alex** is present within the **/home** directory. The df utility shows that **alex** is mounted from **bravo**.

Prerequisites

Install the following package:

- **autofs**

Run chkconfig to cause **autofs** to start when the system goes multiuser:

```
# /sbin/chkconfig autofs on
```

Start **autofs**:

```
# /sbin/service nfs start
```

More Information

Local   man pages   autofs, automount, and **auto.master**

Web   tutorial   www.linuxhq.com/lg/issue24/nielsen.html

HOWTO   *Automount mini-HOWTO*

autofs: Automatically Mounts Directory Hierarchies

An **autofs** directory hierarchy is like any other directory hierarchy, but remains unmounted until it is needed, at which time the system mounts it automatically (*demand mounting*). The system unmounts an **autofs** directory hierarchy when it is no longer needed: by default after five minutes of inactivity. Automatically mounted directory hierarchies are an important part of administrating a large collection of systems in a consistent way. The automount utility is particularly useful when there is a large number of servers or a large number of directory hierarchies. It also helps to remove server-server dependencies (following).

When you boot a system that uses traditional **fstab**-based mounts and an NFS server is down, the system can take a long time to come up as it waits for the server to time out. Similarly, when you have two servers, each mounting directory hierarchies from the other and both systems are down, both may hang as they are brought up and each tries to mount a directory hierarchy from the other. This situation is called a *server-server dependency*. The automount facility gets around these issues by mounting a directory hierarchy from another system only when a process tries to access it.

When a process attempts to access one of the directories within an unmounted **autofs** directory hierarchy, the kernel notifies the **automount** daemon, which mounts the directory hierarchy. You have to give a command, such as **cd /home/alex**, that accesses the **autofs** mount point (in this case **/home/alex**) in order to create the demand that causes **automount** to mount the **autofs** directory hierarchy so you can see it. Before you issue the cd command, **alex** does not appear to be in **/home**.

The main file that controls the behavior of automount is **/etc/auto.master**. A simple example follows:

```
# cat /etc/auto.master
/free1 /etc/auto.misc  --timeout 60
/free2 /etc/auto.misc2 --timeout 60
```

The **auto.master** file has three columns: The first column names the parent of the **autofs** *mount point*—the location where the **autofs** directory hierarchy is to be mounted (**/free1** and **/free2** in the example are not mount points but will hold the mount points when the directory hierarchies are mounted). The second column names the files, called *map files*, that store supplemental configuration information. The optional third column holds mount options for map entries that do not specify an option.

The map files can have any names, but one is traditionally named **auto.misc**. Following are the two map files specified in **auto.master**:

```
# cat /etc/auto.misc
sam             -fstype=ext3        :/dev/hda8

# cat /etc/auto.misc2
helen           -fstype=ext3        :/dev/hda9
```

The first column of a map file holds the relative **autofs** mount point (**sam** and **helen**). This mount point is appended to the corresponding **autofs** mount point from column one of the **auto.master** file to create the absolute **autofs** mount point. In this example, **sam** (from **auto.misc**) is appended to **/free1** (from **auto.master**) to make **/free1/sam**. The second column holds the options, and the third column shows the server and directory hierarchy to be mounted. This example shows local drives; an NFS-mounted device would have the hostname of the remote system before the colon (for example, **grape:/home/sam**).

Before the new setup can work, you have to create directories for the parents of the mount points (**/free1** and **/free2** in the preceding example) and start or restart the **automount** daemon using the **autofs** init script. The following command displays information about configured and active **autofs** mount points:

```
# /sbin/service autofs status
```

Chapter Summary

NFS allows a server to share selected local directory hierarchies with client systems on a heterogeneous network, reducing storage needs and administrative overhead. NFS defines a client/server relationship in which a server provides directory hierarchies that clients can mount.

On the server, the **/etc/exports** file lists the directory hierarchies that the system exports. Each line in **exports** lists the systems that are allowed to mount the hierarchy and specifies the options for each hierarchy (read only, read-write, and so on). Give an **exportfs –r** command to cause NFS to reread this file.

From a client, you can give a mount command to mount an exported NFS directory hierarchy or you can put an entry in **/etc/fstab** to have the system automatically mount the directory hierarchy when it comes up.

Automatically mounted directory hierarchies help administrate large groups of systems with many servers and filesystems in a consistent way and can help remove server-server dependencies. The **automount** daemon automatically mounts **autofs** directory hierarchies when they are needed and unmounts them when they are no longer needed.

Exercises

1. List three reasons to use NFS.
2. What command would you give to mount on the local system the **/home** directory hierarchy that resides on the file server named **bravo**? Assume

the mounted directory hierarchy will appear as **/bravo.home** on the local system. How would you mount the same directory hierarchy if it resided on the fileserver at 192.168.1.1? How would you unmount **/home**?

3. How would you list the mount points on the remote system named **bravo** that the local system named **grape** can mount?

4. What command line lists the currently mounted NFS directory hierarchies?

5. What does the **/etc/fstab** file do?

   The **fstab** file facilitates mounting directory hierarchies. You can use **fstab** to mount automatically directory hierarchies when the system comes up and to allow an ordinary user to mount a directory hierarchy.

6. From a server, how would you allow read-only access to **/opt** for any system in **example.com**?

Advanced Exercises

7. When is it a good idea to disable attribute caching?

8. Describe the difference between the **root_squash** and the **all_squash** options in **/etc/exports**.

9. Why does the **secure** option in **/etc/exports** not really provide any security?

10. Some diskless workstations use NFS as swap space. Why is this useful? What is the downside?

11. NFS maps client users to users on the server. Explain why this mapping is a security risk.

12. What does the mount **nosuid** option do? Why would you want to do this?

Samba: Integrating Linux and Windows

23

Samba is a free suite of programs that enables UNIX-like operating systems, including Linux, Solaris, FreeBSD, and MacOS X, to work with other operating systems, such as OS/2 and Windows, as both a server and a client.

As a server, Samba shares Linux files and printers with Windows systems. As a client, Samba gives Linux users access to files on Windows systems. Its ability to share files across operating systems makes Samba an ideal tool in a heterogeneous computing environment.

Refer to "Integration with Windows" on page 502 for information about printing using Samba.

Which Version of Samba?

FEDORA Fedora Core 2 provides Samba 3.

RHEL Red Hat Enterprise Linux version 3 provides Samba 2.

Samba changed significantly between versions 2 and 3. Most of the changes are internal; however some may require you to change configuration parameters.

The primary focus when developing Samba 3 was to provide a migration path for organizations running a Windows NT 4 primary domain controller. Windows NT 4 is officially unsupported at the end of 2004, and Samba on top of Linux is now a viable alternative to Windows 2000 as an upgrade path.

If you are migrating from Samba version 2 to version 3, read the Samba HOWTO, Chapter 30, "Upgrading from Samba-2.x to Samba-3.0.0," which you can find at www.samba.org/samba/docs/man/upgrading-to-3.0.html.

675

Introduction

This chapter starts with a technical discussion of Samba followed by some basic information. The JumpStart section discusses how to set up a Samba server using system-config-samba, a minimal GUI. The next section covers how to use swat, a Web-based advanced GUI configuration tool, to set up a Samba server. The final server section discusses how to set up a Samba server by hand, using text editor to edit manually the files that control Samba. The next two sections, "Accessing Linux Shares from Windows" (page 691) and "Accessing Windows Shares from Linux" (page 692), explain how to work with Linux and Windows files and printers. The final section of the chapter, "Troubleshooting" (page 694), discusses what to do if you have a problem setting up or using Samba.

Table 23-1 lists the utilities and daemons that make up the Samba suite of programs.

table 23-1 ||	Samba Utilities and Daemons
make_smbcodepage	Makes SMB a codepage definition file. Used in Samba internationalization features. Maps upper- to lowercase and vice versa for characters > ASCII 127.
net	*FEDORA* Samba 3 includes a new utility: net. This utility has the same syntax as the Windows net command and, over time, will eventually replace other Samba utilities such as smbpasswd.
nmbd	The NetBIOS nameserver program, run as a daemon by default. Provides NetBIOS over IP naming services for Samba clients. Also provides browsing (as in the Windows Network Neighborhood or My Network Places view) support.
nmblookup	Makes NetBIOS name queries (page 695).
smbclient	Displays shares on a Samba server such as a Windows machine (page 692).
smbd	The Samba program, run as a daemon by default. Provides file and print services for Samba clients.
smbpasswd	Changes Windows NT password hashes on Samba and Windows NT servers (page 678).
smbstatus	Displays information about current **smbd** connections.
smbtree	Displays a hierarchical diagram of available shares (page 692).
swat	Samba Web Administration Tool. A graphical editor for the **smb.conf** file (page 681).
testparm	Checks syntax of the **smb.conf** file (page 694).
testprns	Checks printer names in the **printcap** file.

About Samba

This section covers the packages you need to install to run Samba, where you can get more information, and users and passwords under Samba.

Prerequisites

Install the following packages:

- **samba**
- **samba-client**
- **samba-common**
- **system-config-samba** (*FEDORA*) or **redhat-config-samba** (*RHEL*) (optional)
- **samba-swat** (optional, but a good idea)

Run chkconfig to cause **smb** to start when the system goes multiuser:

```
# /sbin/chkconfig smb on
```

Start **smb**:

```
# /sbin/service smb start
```

If you want to use swat, modify **/etc/xinetd.d/swat**, as explained in "swat: Configuring a Samba Server" on page 681, and restart **xinetd**:

```
# /sbin/service xinetd restart
```

More Information

Local Documentation Samba/swat home page has links to local Samba documentation (page 681) **/usr/share/doc/samba-***

Web Samba   www.samba.org (mailing lists, documentation, downloads, and more)
CIFS   www.samba.org/cifs

HOWTO *Unofficial Samba HOWTO*   hr.uoregon.edu/davidrl/samba
Samba HOWTO Collection   point a browser at
/usr/share/doc/samba-*/docs/htmldocs/index.html

Samba Users, User Maps, and Passwords

In order for a Windows user to gain access to Samba services on a Linux system, you must provide a Windows username and a Samba password. In some cases, Windows supplies the username and password for you. It is also possible to authenticate using other methods. Samba can use *LDAP* (page 980) or PAM (page 416) in place of the default password file. Refer to the Samba documentation for more information on authentication methods.

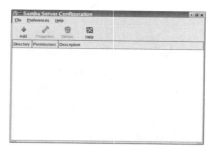

Figure 23-1   Samba Server Configuration window

Usernames   The supplied username must be the same as a Linux username or must map to a Linux username. Samba keeps the username maps in **/etc/samba/smbusers.** Users with the same username on Linux and Samba do not need to appear in this file, but they still need a Samba password.

When you install Samba, **smbusers** has two entries:

```
$ cat /etc/samba/smbusers
# Unix_name = SMB_name1 SMB_name2 ...
root = administrator admin
nobody = guest pcguest smbguest
```

The first entry maps the two Windows usernames (**administrator** and **admin**) to the Linux username **root.** The second entry maps three Windows usernames, including **guest,** to the Linux username **nobody:** When a Windows user attempts to log in on the Samba server as **guest,** Samba authenticates the Linux user named **nobody.**

Passwords   Samba uses Samba passwords, not Linux passwords, to authenticate users. By default, Samba keeps passwords in **/etc/samba/smbpasswd.** As Samba is installed, authentication for **root** or **nobody** would fail because Samba is installed without any passwords: The **smbpasswd** file does not exist.

Each of the configuration techniques described in this chapter allows you to add users to **smbusers** and passwords to **smbpasswd.** You can always use smbpasswd (see "Example," following) to add and change passwords in **smbpasswd.**

Note   When you attempt to connect from Windows to a Samba server, Windows presents your Windows username and password to Samba. If your Windows username is the same as, or maps to, your Linux username and if your Windows and Samba passwords are the same, you do not have to enter a username or password to connect to the Samba server.

Example   You can add the following line to **smbusers** to map the Windows username **sam** to the Linux username **sls:**

```
sls = sam
```

You can add a password for **sls** to **smbpasswd** with the following command:

```
# smbpasswd -a sls
New SMB password:
Retype new SMB password:
Added user sls.
```

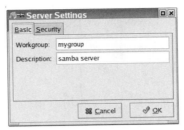

Figure 23-2   Server Settings window, Basic tab

Now, when Sam logs in on the Samba server as **sam**, Samba maps **sam** to **sls** and looks up **sls** in **smbpasswd**. Assuming Sam provides the correct password, he logs in on the Samba server as **sls**.

JumpStart: system-config-samba: Configuring a Samba Server

The system-config-samba (*FEDORA*) and redhat-config-samba (*RHEL*) utilities can set up only basic features of a Samba server. They are, however, the best tool to use if you are not familiar with Samba and you want to set up a simple Samba server quickly. The [system|redhat]-config-samba utility has three basic functions: configuring the server, configuring users, and setting up shares or directories that are exported to the Windows machines.

The [system|redhat]-config-samba utility edits the **/etc/samba/smb.conf** file; make a copy of this file for safekeeping before you start. Start this tool by giving the command [system|redhat]-config-samba from a terminal emulator command line. The utility displays the Samba Server Configuration window (Figure 23-1).

Select **Menubar: Preferences⇨Server Settings** to display the Server Settings window Basic tab (Figure 23-2). Change the workgroup to the one in use on your Windows machines. Change the description of the server if you like. Click the **Security** tab and make sure Authentication Mode is set to **User**; you do not need to specify an Authentication Server. If you are using Windows 98 or newer, set Encrypt Passwords to **Yes**. When you specify a username in Guest Account, anyone logging into the Samba server as **guest** maps to that user's ID. Typically, the **guest** account maps to the UID of the Linux user named **nobody**. Click OK.

Samba users   Select **Menubar: Preferences⇨Samba Users** to display the Samba Users window (Figure 23-3). If the user you want to log in as is not already specified in this window, click **Add User**. With the proper permissions, the Create New Samba User window displays a combo box next to Unix Username that allows you to select a Linux user. Otherwise, your username is displayed as the Unix Username. The Windows Username is the Windows username that you want to map to the specified Linux (UNIX) username. The Samba Password is the password this user or Windows enters to gain access to the Samba server.

Figure 23-3   Samba Users window

If Sam has accounts named **sam** on both the Windows and Linux systems, you
would select **sam** from the Unix Username combo box, enter **sam** in the Windows
Username text box, and enter Sam's Windows password in the two Samba Password text boxes.

tip || **Adding a Samba Password for the Linux User nobody**

Because the user nobody exists in **smbusers** when you install Samba, you cannot add the user
nobody, nor can you add a password for **nobody** from system-config-samba; you must use
smbpasswd from the command line as follows:

```
# smbpasswd -a nobody
New SMB password:
Retype new SMB password:
```

Normally, the user **nobody** does not have a password because it is the guest login. Just press
RETURN (without typing any characters) in response to each of the **SMB password** prompts to
add **nobody** to the password file without a password.

Click **OK** to close the Create New Samba User window and click **OK** to close the Samba Users window.

Linux shares   Next, you need to add a *share*, which is the directory you export from the Linux
system to the Windows system. Click **Add** on the Toolbar to display the Create
Samba Share window Basic tab (Figure 23-4). In the Directory text box, enter the
absolute pathname of the directory you want to share (**/tmp** is an easy directory to
practice with). Enter a description if you like. It can be useful to enter the Linux
hostname and the pathname of the directory you are sharing here. Specify Readonly or Read/Write as suits your purpose. Click the **Access** tab and specify if you
want to limit access to specified users or if you want to allow anyone to access this
share. Click **OK**. Close the Samba Server Configuration window.

There is no need to restart the Samba server; you should be able to access the share
from a Windows machine (page 691).

caution || **Make a Copy of smb.conf**

Before you run swat, make a copy of **/etc/samba/smb.conf** because swat overwrites it.

Figure 23-4   Create Samba Share window, Basic tab

swat: **Configuring a Samba Server**

The swat (Samba Web Administration Tool) utility is a browser-based graphical editor for the **smb.conf** file. For each of the configurable parameters, it provides help links, default values, and a text box to change the value. The swat utility is a well-designed tool in that it remains true to the lines in the **smb.conf** file you edit: You can use and learn from swat and the transition to using a text editor on **smb.conf** will be straightforward.

The swat utility is run from **xinetd** (page 403). Before you can run swat, you need to edit **/etc/xinetd.d/swat**, as shown following:

```
$ cat /etc/xinetd.d/swat
# Default: off
# description: SWAT is the Samba Web Admin Tool. Use swat \
#              to configure your Samba server. To use SWAT, \
#              connect to port 901 with your favorite web browser.
service swat
{
        port             = 901
        socket_type      = stream
        wait             = no
        only_from        = 127.0.0.1
        user             = root
        server           = /usr/sbin/swat
        log_on_failure  += USERID
        disable          = yes
}
```

First, you must turn swat on by changing the **yes** that follows **disable =** to **no**. If you want to access swat from other than the local system, add the names or IP addresses of the other systems you want to access swat from on the line that starts with **only_from**. Separate the system names or IP addresses with SPACEs. Finally, you need to restart **xinetd** so that it rereads its configuration files:

```
# /etc/rc.d/init.d/xinetd restart
Stopping xinetd:                                        [  OK  ]
Starting xinetd:                                        [  OK  ]
```

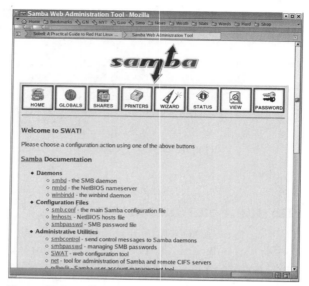

Figure 23-5   The local swat home page

Alternatively, you can give the command **killall –HUP xinetd**.

After making these changes and restarting **xinetd**, you should be able to run swat. From the local system, open a browser, enter **http://127.0.0.1:901** or **http://localhost:901** in the location bar, and give the username **root** and the **root** password in response to swat's request for a username and password. From a remote system, replace **127.0.0.1** with the IP address of the server in the preceding command.

---

security || **Do Not Allow Remote Access to** swat

Do not allow access to swat from a remote system. When you do so and log in, your password is sent in cleartext over whatever connection you are using and can easily be sniffed.

The browser displays the local Samba/swat home page (Figure 23-5). This page has links to local Samba documentation and the following buttons:

HOME   Links to local Samba documentation. When you click the word **Samba** (not the logo, but the one just before the word **Documentation** on the HOME window), swat displays the Samba man page, which defines each Samba program.

GLOBALS   Edits global variables (parameters) in **smb.conf**.

SHARES   Edits share information in **smb.conf**.

PRINTERS   Edits printer information in **smb.conf**.

WIZARD   Rewrites the **smb.conf** file, removing all comment lines and lines that specify default values.

STATUS   Shows the active connections, active shares, and open files. Stops and restarts **smbd** and **nmbd**.

VIEW   Displays a subset or all of the configuration parameters as determined by default values and settings in **smb.conf**.

PASSWORD   Manages passwords.

It is quite easy to establish a basic Samba setup so that you can see a Linux directory from a Windows system (any version of Windows from 3.1 on). More work is required to set up a secure connection or one with special features. The following example creates a basic setup based on the sample **smb.conf** file that is included with Red Hat.

swat Help and defaults   Each of the variables/parameters in swat has a link named **Help** next to it. Click **Help** and a new browser window containing an explanation of the parameter appears. Each variable/parameter also has a **Set Default** button that you can click to reset the variable/parameter to its default value.

For this example, do not click any of the **Set Default** buttons. Make sure to click **Commit Changes** at the top of each page after you finish making changes on a page and before you click a menu button at the top of the window; otherwise, swat will not keep your changes.

GLOBALS   First, click the **GLOBALS** button at the top of the Samba/swat home page. Leave everything at its current setting except **workgroup, hosts allow,** and **hosts deny.** Set **workgroup** to the workgroup used on your Windows systems. (If you followed the preceding JumpStart, the workgroup is already set.) Scroll to the bottom of the Security Options and set **hosts allow** to the names or IP addresses of machines that you want to be able to access the local system's shares and printers (including localhost [127.0.0.1]). Set **hosts deny** to **ALL.** See page 686 for more information on various ways you can set **hosts allow.** Click **Commit Changes** when you are done with the GLOBALS page.

---

tip || **If You Can No Longer Use** swat...

If you can no longer use swat, you probably changed the **hosts allow** setting incorrectly. If this is the case, you need to edit **/etc/samba/smb.conf** and fix the line with the words **hosts allow** in it:

```
# grep hosts smb.conf
        hosts allow = 127.0.0.1, 192.168.0.8
        hosts deny = ALL
```

The preceding entries allow access from the local system and from 192.168.0.8 only.

SHARES   Next, click the **SHARES** button at the top of the page. Three buttons and two text boxes appear in addition to the two **Change View To** buttons (Figure 23-6). In the box adjacent to the **Create Share** button, enter the name you want to assign to the share you are setting up. This name can be anything you want; it is the name that a Windows' user sees and selects when working with the share. Click **Create Share.**

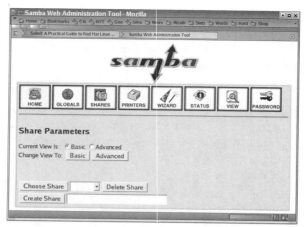

Figure 23-6   The Share Parameters page

When you want to modify an existing share, bring up the name of the share in the combo box adjacent to **Choose Share**, and click **Choose Share**. Either of these actions displays the complete Share Parameters window.

Leave everything at its default setting except **path**, which specifies the absolute pathname on the local Linux system of the share, and optionally **comment**, which you can use to specify the Linux system and directory that this share points to. The values for **hosts allow** and **hosts deny** are taken from the global variables that you set previously. Click **Commit Changes** when you are done with the SHARES page. If you want to see how many parameters there really are, click the **Advanced** button near the top of the page.

tip || **You Do Not Need to Restart Samba When You Change smb.conf**

Samba rereads its configuration files each time a client connects; you do not need to restart Samba when you change **smb.conf**.

Now, from a Windows machine, you should be able to access the share you just created (page 691).

Manually Configuring a Samba Server

The **/etc/samba/smb.conf** file controls most aspects of how Samba works and is divided into sections, each beginning with a line that starts with an open bracket ([), includes some text, and ends with a close bracket (]). The text within the brackets identifies the section. Typical sections are

[globals]   defines global parameters
[printers]   defines printers

[homes]   defines shares in the **homes** directory

[*share name*]   defines a share (you can have more than one of these sections)

Installing Samba using the Red Hat rpm files creates a sample configuration file (**/etc/samba/smb.conf**), which has extensive comments and commented-out examples. Comment lines in **smb.conf** can start with a pound sign (#) or a semicolon (;). The sample file uses pound signs to begin lines that are intended to remain as comments and semicolons to begin lines that you may want to mimic or use as is by removing the semicolons. In the following segment of **smb.conf**, there are two lines of true comments and seven lines beginning with semicolons that you may want to uncomment and make changes to:

```
# A private directory, usable only by fred. Note that fred requires
# write access to the directory.
;[fredsdir]
;    comment = Fred's Service
;    path = /usr/somewhere/private
;    valid users = fred
;    public = no
;    writable = yes
;    printable = no
```

Assuming the global parameters in **smb.conf** are set properly, you need to add a share to get a Windows system to be able to access a directory on the local Linux system. Add the following simple share to the end of the **smb.conf** file to enable a user on a Windows system to be able to read from/write to the local **/tmp** directory:

```
[tmp]
        comment = temporary directory
        path = /tmp
        writeable = yes
        guest ok = yes
```

The name of the share under Windows is **tmp**; the path under Linux is **/tmp**. Any Windows user, including **guest**, who can log in on Samba, can read from/write to the directory, assuming that that user's Linux permissions allow it. The Linux permissions that apply to a Windows user using Samba are the permissions that apply to the Linux user that the Windows user maps to.

Parameters in the smbd.conf File

The the **smb.conf** man page and the help feature of swat list all the parameters you can set in **smb.conf**. The following sections list some of the parameters you are likely to want to change.

Global Parameters

interfaces   A SPACE separated list of the networks that Samba uses. Specify as interface names such as **eth0** or IP address/net mask pairs (page 400).

Default: all active interfaces except 127.0.0.1

printing The printing system in use on the server. On a Red Hat system, you will normally set to CUPS. Other choices are BSD, LPRNG, and SYSV. You can set this parameter on a per-printer basis. See page 502 for information about printing under Samba.

Default: none

server string The string that is displayed in various places on the Windows machine. Within the string, Samba replaces **%v** with the Samba version number and **%h** with the hostname.

Default: Samba %v
Red Hat: Samba Server

workgroup The workgroup that the server belongs to. Set to the same workgroup as the Windows clients who use the server. This parameter controls the domain name that Samba uses when **security** (page 687) is set to DOMAIN.

Default: WORKGROUP
Red Hat: MYGROUP

Security Parameters

encrypt passwords YES accepts only encrypted passwords from clients. Windows 98 and Windows NT 4.0 Service Pack 3 and above use encrypted passwords by default. Uses **smbpasswd** to authenticate passwords unless you set **security** to SERVER or DOMAIN, in which case Samba authenticates using another server.

Default: YES

FEDORA Samba 3 defaults to storing encrypted passwords in the **smbpasswd** file if you do not set up **passdb** (a password database). Storing passwords in the **smbpasswd** file is sensible on servers with under 250 users. For high-load servers, consult the Samba HOWTO collection for information about configuring a database back end.

guest account The username that is assigned to users logging in as **guest** or mapped to **guest**; applicable only when **guest ok** (page 690) is set to YES. This username should be present in **/etc/passwd** but should not be able to log in on the system. Typically, **guest account** is assigned a value of **nobody** because the user **nobody** can access only files that any user can access. If you are using the **nobody** account on the Linux system, set this variable to a name other than **nobody**.

Default: **nobody**

hosts allow Analogous to the **/etc/hosts.allow** file (page 404), this parameter specifies hosts that are allowed to connect to the server. Overrides hosts specified in **hosts deny**. A good strategy is to specify ALL in **hosts deny** and specify the hosts you want to grant access to in this file. Specify hosts in the same manner as **hosts.allow**.

Default: none (all hosts permitted access)

hosts deny Analogous to the **/etc/hosts.deny** file (page 404), this parameter specifies hosts that are not allowed to connect to the server. Overridden by hosts specified in **hosts allow**. If you specify ALL in this file, remember to include the local machine (127.0.0.1) in **hosts allow**. Specify hosts in the same manner as **hosts.deny**.

Default: none (no hosts excluded)

map to guest Defines when a failed login is mapped to the **guest account**.

Never: Allows **guest** to login only when the user explicitly provides **guest** as the username and a blank password.

Bad User: Treats any attempt to log in as a user who does not exist as a **guest** login. This parameter is a security risk because it allows a malicious user to retrieve a list of users on the system quickly.

Bad Password: Silently log in as **guest** any user who incorrectly enters his or her password. This parameter may confuse a user when she mistypes her password and is unkowingly logged in as **guest** because she will suddenly see fewer shares than she is used to.

Default: Never

passwd chat The chat script that Samba uses to converse with the passwd program. If the script is not followed, Samba does not change the password. Used only when **unix password sync** is set to YES.

Default: *new*password* %n\n ... *changed*,
Red Hat: *New*UNIX*password* %n\n ... *successfully*

passwd program The program Samba uses to set Linux passwords. Samba replaces **%u** with the user's username.

Default: **/usr/bin/passwd %u**

security Specifies if and how clients transfer user and password information to the server. Choose one of the following:

USER: Causes Samba to require a username and password from Users or Windows when logging in on the Samba server. With this setting you can use

- **username map** (page 688) to map usernames to other names
- **encrypt passwords** (page 686) to encrypt passwords (recommended)
- **guest account** (page 686) to map users to the **guest** account

SHARE: Causes Samba not to authenticate clients on a per-user basis. Instead, Samba uses the system found in Windows 9x where each share can have an individual password for either read or full access. This option is not compatible with more recent versions of Windows.

SERVER: Causes Samba to use another SMB server to validate usernames and passwords. Failing remote validation, the local Samba server tries to validate as though **security** were set to USER.

DOMAIN: Samba passes an encrypted password to a Windows NT Domain Controller for validation.

FEDORA **ADS:** Samba 3 adds this parameter, which instructs Samba to use an Active Directory Server for authentication, allowing a Samba server to participate as a native

Active Directory member. (Active Directory is the centralized information system that Windows 2000 and later uses. It replaces Windows Domains used by Windows NT and earlier.)

Default: USER

unix password sync YES causes Samba to change a user's Linux password when the associated user changes the encrypted Samba password.

Default: NO

update encrypted YES allows users to migrate from cleartext passwords to encrypted passwords without logging in on the server and using smbpasswd. To migrate users, set to YES and set **encrypt passwords** to NO. As each user logs in on the server with a cleartext Linux password, smbpasswd encrypts and stores the password in **/etc/samba/smbpasswd**. Set to NO and set **encrypt passwords** to YES after all users have been converted.

Default: NO

username map The name of the file that maps usernames from a client to those of the server. Each line of the map file starts with a server username, followed by a SPACE, an equal sign, another SPACE, and one or more SPACE-separated client usernames. An asterisk (∗) on the client side matches any client username. This file frequently maps Windows usernames to Linux usernames and/or maps multiple Windows usernames to a single Linux username to facilitate file sharing. A sample map file is shown following:

```
$ cat /etc/samba/smbusers
# Unix_name = SMB_name1 SMB_name2 ...
root = administrator admin
nobody = guest
sam = sams
```

Default: no map
Red Hat **/etc/samba/smbusers**

Logging Parameters

log file The name of the Samba log file; Samba replaces **%m** with the name of the client system, allowing you to generate a separate log file for each client.

Default: **/var/log/samba/%m.log**

log level Sets the log level, with 0 (zero) being off and higher numbers being more verbose.

Default: 0 (off)

max log size An integer specifying the maximum size of the log file in kilobytes. A 0 (zero) specifies no limit. When a file reaches this size, Samba appends a **.old** to the filename and starts a new log, deleting any old log file.

Default: 5000, Red Hat 50

Browser Parameters

The *domain master browser* is the system that is responsible for maintaining the list of machines on a network used when browsing a Windows Network Neighborhood or My Network Places. SMB uses weighted elections every 11–15 minutes to determine which machine will be the domain master browser.

Whether a Samba server wins this election depends on two parameters: First, setting **domain master** to YES instructs the Samba server to enter the election. Second, the **os level** determines how much weight the Samba server's vote receives. Setting **os level** to 2 should cause the Samba server to win against any Windows 9x machines. NT Server series domain controllers, including Windows 2000, XP, and 2003, use an **os level** of 32. The maximum setting for **os level** is 255, although setting it to 65 should ensure that the Samba server wins.

domain master   YES causes **nmbd** to attempt to be the domain master browser. If a domain master browser exists, then local master browsers will forward copies of their browse lists to it. If there is no domain master browser, then browse queries may not be able to cross subnet boundaries. A Windows PDC (Primary Domain Controller) will always try to become the domain master and may behave unexpectedly if it fails. Refer to the preceding discussion.

Default: AUTO

local master   YES causes **nmbd** to enter elections for the local master browser on a subnet. A local master browser stores a cache of the NetBIOS names of entities on the local subnet, allowing browsing. Windows computers automatically enter elections; for browsing to work, you need on a network at least one Windows computer or one Samba server with **local master** set to YES. It is poor practice to set **local master** to NO. If you do not want a computer to act as a local master, set its **os level** to a lower number, allowing it to be used as the local master, if all else fails.

Default: YES

os level   An integer that controls how much Samba advertises itself for browser elections and how likely **nmbd** is to become the local master browser for its workgroup. A higher number increases the chances of the local server becoming the local master browser. Refer to the discussion at the beginning of this section.

Default: 20

preferred master   YES forces **nmbd** to hold an election for local master and enters the local system with a slight advantage. With **domain master** set to YES, this parameter helps ensure that the local Samba server becomes the domain master. Setting this parameter to YES on more than one server causes the servers to keep competing to become master, generating a lot of network traffic and sometimes causing unpredictable results. A Windows PDC (Primary Domain Controller) automatically acts as if this parameter is set.

Default: AUTO

Communication Parameters

dns proxy   When acting as a WINS server, YES causes **nmbd** to use DNS if NetBIOS resolution fails.

Default: YES
Red Hat: NO

socket options   Tunes network parameters used when exchanging data with a client. The Red Hat setting is appropriate in most cases.

Default: TCP_NODELAY,
Red Hat: TCP_NODELAY SO_RCVBUF=8192 SO_SNDBUF=8192

wins server   The IP address of the WINS server that **nmbd** should register with.

Default: not enabled

wins support   YES specifies that **nmbd** act as a WINS server.

Default: NO

Share Parameters

Each of the following parameters can appear many times in **smb.conf**, once in each share definition.

available   YES specifies the share as active. Set to NO to disable the share, but continue logging requests for it.

browseable   Determines whether the share can be browsed, for example, in Windows My Network Places.

Default: YES
Red Hat: NO

comment   A description of the share, shown when browsing the network from Windows.

Default: none
Red Hat: various

guest ok   Allows a user who logs in as **guest** to access this share.

Default: NO

path   The path of the directory that is being shared.

Default: none
Red Hat: various

read only   Does not allow write access.

Default: YES
Red Hat: YES

The [homes] Share: Sharing Users' Home Directories

Frequently, users want to share their Linux home directories with a Windows machine. To make this task easier, Samba provides the [homes] share. When you define this share, each user's home directory is shared with the specified parameters. In most cases, the following parameters are adequate:

```
[homes]
        comment = Home Directories
        read only = No
        browseable = No
        guest ok = No
```

These settings prevent users other than the owners from browsing home directories, while allowing logged-in owners full access.

Accessing Linux Shares from Windows

Browsing Shares

To access a share on a Samba server, open My Computer or Explorer on the Windows system and, in the Address text box, enter \\ followed by the NetBIOS name (or just the hostname if you have not assigned a different NetBIOS name) of the Samba server. Windows displays the directories that the Linux system is sharing. To view the shares on the Linux system named **bravo**, you would enter **\\bravo**. From this window, you can view and browse the shares available on the Linux system. If you set a share so that it is not browseable, you need to enter the path of the share using the format *servername**sharename*.

Mapping a Share

Another way to access a share on a Samba server is by mapping a share: Open My Computer or Explorer on the Windows system and click **Map Network Drive** from one of the drop-down menus on the Menubar (it is on the **Tools** menu on Windows XP). Windows displays the Map Network Drive window. Select an unused Windows drive letter from the Drive combo box and enter the Windows path to the share you just created. (When you use system-config-samba to create a share, the share has the same name as the name of the directory you are sharing.) The format of the windows path is *hostname**sharename*. For example, to map **/tmp** on **bravo** to Windows drive J, assuming the share is named **tmp** on the Linux system, select **J** in the Drive combo box, enter **\\bravo\tmp** in the Folder text box, and click **Finish**. You should be able to access the **/tmp** directory from **bravo** as **J** (**tmp**) on the Windows machine. If you cannot map the drive, see "Troubleshooting" on page 694.

Accessing Windows Shares from Linux

As a client, Samba enables you to view and work with files on a Windows system from a Linux system. This section discusses several ways of accessing Windows files from Linux.

smbtree: Displaying Windows Shares

The smbtree utility displays a hierarchical diagram of available shares. When you run smbtree, it prompts you for a password; do not enter a password if you want to browse shares visible to the **guest** user. The password allows you to view restricted shares, such as a user's home directory in the [**homes**] share. Following is sample output from smbtree:

```
$ smbtree
Password:
MGS
        \\PB                               pb Samba
                \\PB\mark                  Home Directories
                \\PB\MainPrinter           MainPrinter
                \\PB\ADMIN$                IPC Service (pb Samba)
                \\PB\IPC$                  IPC Service (pb Samba)
                \\PB\tmp                   mgs temp
```

In the preceding output, **MGS** is the name of the workgroup, **PB** is the name of the Windows machine, **mark** and **tmp** are directory shares, and **MainPrinter** is a shared printer. Workgroup and machine names are always shown in capitals. Refer to the smbtree man page for more information.

smbclient: Connecting to Windows Shares

The smbclient utility functions similarly to ftp (page 583) and connects to a Windows share; smbclient uses Linux-style forward slashes (/) as path separators rather than Windows-style backslashes (\). The next example connects to one of the shares displayed in the preceding example:

```
$ smbclient //PB/mark
Password:
Domain=[PB] OS=[Unix] Server=[Samba 3.0.2-7.FC1]
smb: \> ls
  .                         D        0   Wed Feb 25 15:10:03 2004
  ..                        D        0   Mon Feb  2 12:40:17 2004
  .kde                      DH       0   Tue Feb  3 22:24:17 2004
  .xemacs                   DH       0   Mon Feb  2 10:12:45 2004
  .bash_logout              H       24   Tue Oct 28 06:15:04 2003
  .bash_profile             H      191   Tue Oct 28 06:15:04 2003
  .bashrc                   H      124   Tue Oct 28 06:15:04 2003
  ...
```

You can use most ftp commands from smbclient. Refer to "Tutorial Session" on page 586 for some examples or give the command **help** to display a list of commands.

Figure 23-7   Nautilus displaying a Windows share

Browsing Windows Networks

Browsing Windows shares using smbtree and smbclient is quite cumbersome compared with the ease of browsing a network from Windows; Gnome and KDE provide much more user friendly alternatives. From either Konqueror or Nautilus (the KDE and Gnome file managers), enter **smb:///** in the Location bar to browse the Windows shares on the network (Figure 23-7).

Because both Konqueror and Nautilus use virtual filesystem add-ons, which are part of the respective desktop environments and not part of the native Linux system, only native Gnome or KDE applications can open files on remote shares; normal Linux programs cannot. For example, gedit and kedit will be able to open files on remote shares, while OpenOffice, mplayer, and xedit will not be able to.

smbmount: **Mounting Windows Shares**

The smbmount utility mounts Windows shares just as mount mounts a Linux directory hierarchy. When you mount a Windows share, you can write to the files on the share; you cannot write to files on a share using smbclient.

The syntax of a smbmount command is the same as that of a mount command (page 442):

> # *smbmount //host/share dir*

where *host* is the name of the system that the share is on, *share* is the name of the Windows share that you want to mount, and *dir* is the absolute pathname of the Linux directory that you are mounting the share on.

The following command, run as **root**, mounts the share used in the preceding example on the **/share** directory:

```
# smbmount  //PB/mark /share -o username=mark
Password:
# ls /share
Desktop      mansmbconf                              smb.conf  smbout
httpd.conf   NVIDIA-Linux-x86-1.0-5336-pkg1.run      smbhold   x
```

Troubleshooting

Samba provides three utilities that can help troubleshoot a connection: The smbstatus utility displays a report on open Samba connections; testparm checks the syntax of **/etc/samba/smb.conf** and displays its contents; and testprns checks the validity of the name of a printer.

The following steps can help you narrow down the problem when you cannot get Samba to work.

1. Restart the **smbd** and **nmbd** daemons. Make sure the last two lines of output end with **OK**.

```
# /etc/rc.d/init.d smb restart
Shutting down SMB services:                          [  OK  ]
Shutting down NMB services:                          [  OK  ]
Starting SMB services:                               [  OK  ]
Starting NMB services:                               [  OK  ]
```

testparm

2. Run testparm to check that your **smb.conf** file is syntactically correct.

```
$ testparm
Load smb config files from /etc/samba/smb.conf
Processing section "[homes]"
Processing section "[printers]"
Processing section "[tmp]"
Loaded services file OK.
Press enter to see a dump of your service definitions
...
```

If you misspell a keyword in **smb.conf**, you get an error such as the following:

```
# testparm
Load smb config files from /etc/samba/smb.conf
Unknown parameter encountered: "workgruop"
Ignoring unknown parameter "workgruop"
...
```

ping

3. Use ping (page 346) from both sides of the connection to make sure your network is up.

net view

4. From a Windows command prompt, use net view to display a list of shares available from the server (**pb** in this example):

```
C:>net view \\pb
Shared resources at \\pb

pb Samba

Share name   Type    Used as  Comment

------------------------------------------------------------
MainPrinter  Print            MainPrinter
mark         Disk    (UNC)    Home Directories
tmp          Disk             mgs temp
The command completed successfully.
```

net use 5. See if you can map the drive from a Windows command prompt. The following command attempts to mount the share named **tmp** on **pb** as drive X:

```
C:>net use x: \\pb\tmp
The command completed successfully.
```

nmblookup 6. From the server, query the **nmbd** server, using the special name **__SAMBA__**, for the server's NetBIOS name. The **–d 2** option turns the debugger on at level 2, which generates a moderate amount of output.

```
$ nmblookup -d 2 -B pb __SAMBA__
added interface ip=192.168.0.10 bcast=192.168.0.255
nmask=255.255.255.0
querying __SAMBA__ on 192.168.0.10
Got a positive name query response from 192.168.0.10 ( 192.168.0.10 )
192.168.0.10 __SAMBA__<00>
```

nmblookup 7. From the server, query the **nmbd** server for the client's NetBIOS name. (The machine named **jam** is the Windows client.)

```
$ nmblookup -B jam \*
querying * on 192.168.0.9
192.168.0.9 *<00>
```

Omit the **–B jam** option to query for all NetBIOS names.

smbclient 8. From the server, use smbclient with the **–L** option to generate a list of shares offered by the server.

```
$ smbclient -L pb
Password:
Domain=[PB] OS=[Unix] Server=[Samba 3.0.2-7.FC1]

        Sharename       Type       Comment
        ---------       ----       -------
        tmp             Disk       mgs temp
        IPC$            IPC        IPC Service (pb Samba)
        ADMIN$          IPC        IPC Service (pb Samba)
        MainPrinter     Printer    MainPrinter
        mark            Disk       Home Directories
Domain=[PB] OS=[Unix] Server=[Samba 3.0.2-7.FC1]
```

```
Server              Comment
---------           -------

Workgroup           Master
---------           -------
MGS                 TUNAER
```

nmblookup   9. To query for the master browser from the server, run nmblookup with the
    −M option followed by the name of the workgroup:

```
$ nmblookup -M MGS
querying MGS on 192.168.0.255
192.168.0.8 MGS<1d>
```

Chapter Summary

Samba is a suite of programs that enables Linux to work with Windows to share directories and printers. A directory or printer that is shared between Linux and Windows systems is called a *share*. In order to access a share on a Linux system, a
Windows user must supply a username and password. Usernames must correspond
to Linux usernames either directly or as mapped by the **/etc/samba/smbusers** file.
Samba passwords are generated by smbpasswd and kept in **/etc/samba/smbpasswd**.

The main Samba configuration file is **/etc/samba/smb.conf**, which you can edit using a text editor, swat (a Web-based administration utility), or system-config-samba
(a minimal configuration GUI). The swat utility is a powerful configuration tool
that provides integrated online documentation and clickable default values to help
set up Samba.

From a Windows machine, you can access a share on a Linux Samba server by
opening My Computer or Explorer and, in the Address text box, entering \\ followed by the name of the server. Windows displays the shares on the server and you
can work with them as though they were Windows files.

From a Linux system, you can use any of several Samba tools to access Windows
shares. These tools include smbtree (displays shares), smbclient (similar to ftp), and
smbmount (mounts shares). In addition, you can enter **smb:///** in the Location bar of
Konqueror or Nautilus and browse the shares.

Samba is a suite of tools that makes heterogeneous computing a reality.

Exercises

1. What two daemons are part of the Samba suite? What does each do?

2. What steps are required for mapping a Windows user to a Linux user?

3. How would you allow access to swat only from machines on the 192.168.1.0/8 subnet?

4. What is the purpose of the [homes] share?

Advanced Exercises

5. Describe how Samba's handling of users differs from that of NFS.

6. What configuration changes would you need to apply to your routers if you wanted to allow SMB/CIFS browsing across multiple subnets without configuring master browsers?

7. How could you use SWAT securely from a remote location?

8. WINS resolution allows hosts to define their own names. Suggest a way that Samba could be used to assign names from a centralized list.

DNS/BIND: Tracking Domain Names and Addresses

24

DNS (Domain Name System) maps domain names to IP addresses and vice versa and reduces the need for humans to work with IP addresses, which, with the introduction of IPv6, are complex. The DNS specification defines secure, general-purpose databases that hold Internet host information. It also specifies a protocol that is used to exchange this information. Further, DNS defines library routines that implement the defined protocol. Finally, DNS provides a means for routing email. Under DNS, *nameservers* work with clients, called *resolvers,* to distribute host information in the form of *resource records* in a timely manner as needed.

This chapter describes BIND (Berkeley Internet Name Domain) version 9, a popular, open-source implementation of DNS. BIND is part of the Red Hat distribution and includes the DNS server daemon (**named**), a DNS resolver library, and tools for working with DNS. Although DNS can be used for private networks, this chapter covers DNS as used by the Internet.

Introduction to DNS

You frequently use DNS when you display a Web page. For example, to display Red Hat's home page, you enter its name, www.redhat.com, in a browser and the browser displays the page you want. You never enter or see the IP address for the displayed page. However, without the IP address, the browser could not display the page; DNS works behind the scenes to find the IP address when you enter the name in the browser. The DNS database is

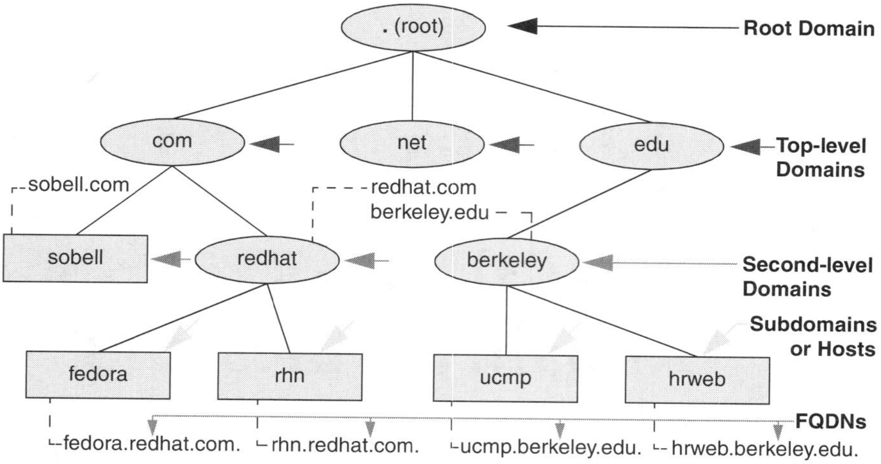

Figure 24-1   The DNS domain structure

- **Hierarchical** for quick responses to queries: DNS has a root, branches, and nodes.

- **Distributed** for fast access to servers. The DNS databases are spread across thousands of systems worldwide; each system is referred to as a *DNS server* (or a *domain server* or *nameserver*).

- **Replicated** for reliability. Because many systems hold the same information, when some systems fail, DNS does not stop functioning.

As implemented, DNS is

- **Secure** so that your browser or email is directed to the correct location.

- **Flexible** in order to adapt to new names, deleted names, and names whose information changes.

- **Fast** so that Internet connections are not delayed by slow DNS lookups.

History   The mapping that DNS does was originally done statically in a **/etc/hosts** file (page 428) on each system on a network. Small LANs still make use of this file. As networks, specifically the Internet, grew, a dynamic mapping system was required. DNS was specified in 1983 and BIND became part of BSD in 1985.

Security   BIND is by far the most popular implementation of a DNS. However, recently there has been concern about its security. You may want to run BIND inside a chroot jail (page 724) and use transaction signatures (TSIG, page 722) to improve security.

host and dig   The host and dig utilities (page 348) query DNS servers. The host utility is simpler, is easier to use, and returns less information than dig. This chapter uses both tools to explore DNS.

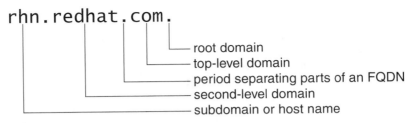

Figure 24-2   An FQDN (Fully Qualified Domain Name)

Nodes, Domains, and Subdomains

Each node in the hierarchical DNS database is called a domain and is labeled with a (domain) name. As with the Linux file structure, the node at the top of the DNS hierarchy is called the *root node,* or *root domain.* While the Linux file structure separates the nodes (directory and ordinary files) with slashes (/) and labels the root node (directory) with a slash, the DNS structure uses periods (Figure 24-1).

You read an absolute pathname in a Linux filesystem from left to right: It starts with the root directory (/) at the left and, as you read to the right, describes the path to the file being identified (for example, **/var/named/named.ca**). Unlike a Linux pathname, you read a DNS domain name from right to left: It starts with the root domain at the right (represented by a period [.]) and, as you read to the left, works its way down through the top-level and second-level domains to a subdomain or host. Frequently, the name of the root domain (the period at the right) is omitted from a domain name. The term *domain* refers both to a single node in the DNS domain structure and to a catenated, period-separated list (path) of domain names that describes the location of a domain.

FQDN   An FQDN (fully qualified domain name) is the DNS equivalent of a filesystem's absolute pathname: It is a pointer that positively locates a domain on the Internet. As you (and Linux) can identify an absolute pathname by its leading slash (/) that names the root directory, an FQDN can be identified by its trailing period (.) that names the root domain (Figure 24-2).

Resolver   The resolver comprises the routines that turn an unqualified domain name into an FQDN that is passed to DNS to be mapped into an IP address. The resolver can append several domains, one at a time, to an unqualified domain name, producing several FQDNs that it passes, one at a time, to DNS. For each FQDN, DNS reports success (it found the FQDN and is returning the corresponding IP address) or failure (the FQDN does not exist).

The resolver always appends the root domain (.) to an unqualified domain name first, allowing you to type **www.redhat.com** instead of **www.redhat.com.** (with the trailing period specifying the root domain) in a browser. You can specify other domains for the resolver to try if the root domain fails. Put the domain names, in the order you want them tried, after the **search** keyword in **/etc/resolv.conf** (page 432).

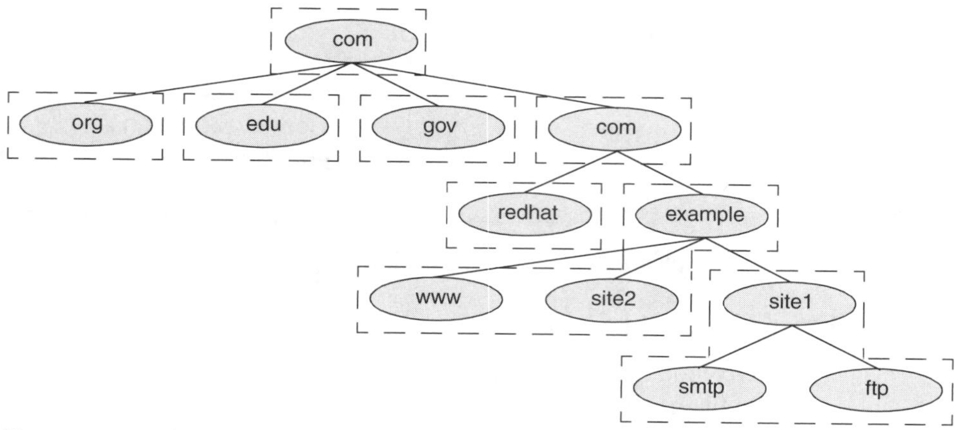

Figure 24-3 DNS structure showing zones

For example, if your search domains include **redhat.com.**, then the domains **rhn** and **rhn.redhat.com.** resolve to the same address.

Subdomains Each node in the domain hierarchy is a domain. Each domain that has a parent (that is, every domain except the root domain) is also a subdomain, regardless of whether it has children. All subdomains *can* resolve to hosts, even those with children. For example, the **redhat.com.** domain resolves to the host that serves the Red Hat Web site, without preventing its children, domains such as **fedora.redhat.com.**, from resolving. The left-most part of an FQDN is often called the *hostname*.

Hostnames Until recently, hostnames could contain only characters from the set a–z, A–Z, 0–9, and –. As of March 2004, you should be able to use various accents, umlauts, and so on. DNS considers upper- and lowercase letters the same, so www.sobell.com is the same as WWW.sObEll.coM. Contrasted with the zone files, **named.conf** does not use periods at the ends of domain names.

Zones

For administrative purposes, domains are grouped into zones that extend downward from a domain (Figure 24-3). A single DNS server is responsible for (holds the information required to resolve) all domains within a zone. The DNS server for a zone also holds pointers to DNS servers that are responsible for the zones immediately below the zone it is responsible for. Information about zones originates in zone files, one zone per file.

Root domain The highest zone, the one containing the root domain, does not contain any hosts. Instead, this domain delegates to the DNS servers for the top-level domains (Figure 24-1, page 700).

Authority Each zone has at least one authoritative DNS server. This server holds all the information about the zone. A DNS query returns information about a domain and specifies which DNS server(s) is authoritative for that domain.

DNS employs a hierarchical structure to keep track of names and authority. At the top or root of the structure is the root domain, which employs 13 authoritative nameservers. These are the only servers that are authoritative for the root and top-level domains.

Delegation of authority

When referring to DNS, the term *delegation* means *delegation of authority*. ICANN (Internet Corporation for Assigned Names and Numbers, www.icann.org) delegates authority to the root and top-level domains. In other words, ICANN says which servers are authoritative for these domains. Authority is delegated to each domain below the top-level domains by the authoritative server at the next higher-level domain. ICANN is not authoritative for most second-level domains. For example, Red Hat is authoritative for the redhat.com domain. This scheme of delegating authority allows local control over segments of the DNS database while making all segments available to the public.

Queries

Iterative query

There are two types of DNS queries: *iterative* and *recursive*.[1] An iterative query sends a domain name to a DNS server and asks the server to return either the IP address of the domain or the name of the DNS server that is authoritative for the domain or one of its parents: The server does not query other servers in determining an answer.

Recursive query

A recursive query sends a DNS server a domain name and asks the server to return the IP address of the domain: The server may need to query other servers to get the answer. Both types of queries can fail with the server returning a message saying it is unable to locate the domain.

When a client, such as a browser, needs the IP address that corresponds to a domain name, the client queries a resolver. Most resolvers are quite simple and require a DNS server to do most of the work: They send recursive queries. The resolver communicates with a single DNS server, which can perform multiple iterative queries in response to the resolver's recursive query.

All DNS servers must answer iterative queries. DNS servers can also be set up to answer recursive queries. A DNS server that is not set up to answer recursive queries treats recursive queries as though they were iterative queries.

Figure 24-4 shows the resolver on a client system trying to discover the address of the server ftp.site1.example.com. on the network with the DNS layout shown in Figure 24-3 on page 702. The resolver on the client sends a recursive query to its primary DNS server. This server interrogates the root server and one additional

---

1. There is a third type of query that is not covered in this book: inverse queries. This type of query provides a domain name given a resource record. Reverse name resolution (page 708), not inverse queries, is used to query for a domain name given an IP address.

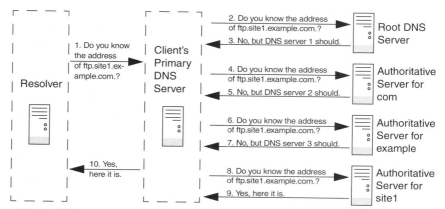

Figure 24-4   A Recursive Query that starts several iterative queries to find the answer

server for each zone, until it gets the answer, which it returns to the resolver on the client. In practice, the query would not start with the root server because most servers usually have the location of the authoritative nameserver for the **com.** domain stored in cache (memory).

Servers

There are three main types of DNS servers: primary (master), secondary (slave), and caching:

- A *primary master server,* also called a *primary server* or *master server,* is the authoritative server that holds the master copy of zone data. This server copies information from the *zone* or *master file,* a local file that the server administrator maintains. For security and efficiency, primary master servers should provide iterative answers only. A primary master server that provides recursive answers is more easily subverted by a *DoS attack* (page 968) than one that provides iterative answers.

- *Slave servers,* also called *secondary servers,* are authoritative and copy zone information from the primary master server or another slave server. On some systems, when information on the primary master server changes, the primary master server sends a message to the slave servers. When a slave receives such a message, it uses a process called *zone transfer* to copy the new zone information to itself.

- *DNS caches,* also called *caching servers,* are not authoritative. These servers store answers to previous queries in cache (memory). When a DNS cache receives a query, it answers it from cache if it can. If the DNS cache does not have the answer in cache, it forwards the query to an authoritative server.

It is possible, but for reasons of security not recommended, for the same server to be the primary master server (authoritative) for some zones and a DNS cache for others.

With the same server acting as both a DNS cache and a master, if a malicious local user or malfunctioning resolver on the local network floods the DNS cache with more traffic than it can handle (a DoS attack), users may be prevented from accessing your public servers. Conversely, if your authoritative server is compromised, the attacker can also subvert all traffic leaving your network.

DNS Database

Information about nodes (domains) in the DNS database is stored in resource records. There are over 30 types of resource records, ranging from common types, such as address records that store the address of a host, to those that contain geographical information. This section covers the types of resource records you are most likely to work with.

Resource Records

A resource record has the following fields (the TTL field is not present in all resource records):

- Name   The domain name or IP address
- TTL   Time to Live (page 1002)
- Class Always 1 for IN Internet (the only class that DNS supports)
- Type   Record type (next section)
- Data   Varies with record type

If the Name field is missing, the resource record inherits the name from the previous resource record. The zone is that which the zone file containing the resource record defines.

A **Address**   Maps a domain name to the IPv4 address of a host. There must be at least one address record for each domain; you can have multiple address records pointing to the same IP address. The Name field holds the domain name, assumed to be in the same zone as the domain. The Data field holds the IP address associated with the name. The following address resource record maps the **ns** domain in the zone to 192.168.0.1:

```
ns    IN    A    192.168.0.1
```

AAAA **Address**   Maps a domain name to the IPv6 address of a host. The following address resource record maps the **ns** domain in the zone to an IPv6 address:

```
ns    IN    AAAA    2001:630:d0:131:a00:20ff:feb5:ef1e
```

CNAME **Canonical Name**   Maps an alias or nickname to a domain name. The Name field holds the alias or nickname. The Data field holds the official or canonical name. CNAME is useful for specifying an easy-to-remember name or multiple names for the same domain. It is also good when a system changes names or IP addresses: The alias can always point to a real name that must resolve to an IP address.

When a query returns a CNAME, a client or DNS tool performs a DNS lookup on the domain name returned with the CNAME. It is not poor practice to provide multiple levels of CNAME records. The following resource record maps **ftp** in the zone to the www.sam.net.:

```
ftp     IN    CNAME   www.sam.net.
```

MX Mail Exchange Specifies a destination for mail addressed to the domain. The Name field holds the domain name, assumed to be in the zone. The Data field holds the name of a mail server preceded by its priority. Unlike A records, MX records contain a priority number that allows mail delivery agents to fall back gracefully to a backup server in case the primary is down. Several mail servers can be ranked in priority order with the lowest number having the highest priority. DNS selects randomly from among mail servers with the same priority. The following resource records forward mail sent to **speedy** in the zone first to **mail** in the zone and then, if that fails, to **mail.sam.net..** The value of **speedy** in the Name field on the second line is implicit.

```
speedy          MX      10 mail
                MX      20 mail.sam.net.
```

NS NameServer Specifies the name of the system that provides domain service (DNS records) for the domain. The Name field holds the domain name; the Data field holds name of the DNS server. Each domain must have at least one NS record. DNS servers do not need to reside in the domain, and, in fact, it is better if at least one does not. The system name **ns** is frequently used to specify a nameserver, but this name is not required and does not have any significance beyond assisting humans in identifying a nameserver. The following resource record specifies ns.max.net as a nameserver for peach in the zone:

```
peach           NS      ns.max.net.
```

PTR Pointer Maps an IP address to a domain name and is used for reverse name resolution. The Name field holds the IP address; the Data field holds the domain name. Do not use with aliases. The following resource record maps 3 in a reverse zone (for example, **0.168.192.in-addr.arpa**) to **grape** in the zone. For more information, refer to "Reverse Name Resolution" on page 708.

```
3       IN      PTR     grape
```

SOA Start of Authority Designates the start of a zone. Each zone must have exactly one SOA record. An authoritative server maintains the SOA record for the zone it is authoritative for.

All zone files must have one SOA resource record which must be the first resource record in the file. The Name field holds the name of the domain at the start of the zone. The Data field holds the name of the host the data was created on, the email address of the person responsible for the zone, and the following information enclosed within parentheses. The opening parenthesis must appear on the first physical line of an SOA record.

serial A value in the range 1-2147483647. A change in this number indicates that the zone data has changed. By convention, this field is set to the string yyyymmddnn (year, month, day, change number). Along with the date, the final two digits, the change number, should be incremented each time you change the SOA record.

refresh The elapsed time after which the primary master server notifies secondary and slave servers to refresh the record; the time between updates.

retry The time to wait after a refresh fails.

expiry The elapsed time after which the zone is no longer authoritative and the root servers must be queried. The expiry applies to slave and secondary servers only.

minimum The minimum amount of time that data stays in a slave server's cache (TTL).

The following two SOA resource records are equivalent:

```
@ IN SOA ns.zach.net. mgs@sobell.com. ( 2003111247 8H 2H 4W 1D )
    @       IN     SOA      ns.zach.net. mgs@sobell.com. (
                            2003111247      ; serial
                            8H              ; refresh
                            2H              ; retry
                            4W              ; expire
                            1D )            ; minimum
```

The second format is more readable because of its layout and the comments it contains. The at symbol (**@**) at the start of the SOA resource record stands for the origin (**zach.net** in this case because that is how it is referred to in the **named.conf** configuration file [page 715] that locates the zone file that contains this SOA record). You could rewrite the first line as

```
    zach.net.  IN  SOA      ns.zach.net. mgs@sobell.com. (
```

The host utility returns something closer to the first format with each of the times specified in seconds:

```
$ host -t soa zach.net
zach.net. SOA ns.zach.net. mgs\@sobell.com. 03111 28800 7200 2419200 86400
```

TXT Text Associates a character string with a domain. The Name field holds the domain name. The data field can contain up to 256 characters and must be enclosed within quotation marks. TXT records can contain any arbitrary text value. As well as general information, they can also be used for things such as public key distribution.

DNS Query and Response

Query A DNS query has three parts:

1. **Name** Domain name, FQDN, or IP address for reverse name resolution

2. Type   Type of record requested (page 705).

3. Class   Always 1 for IN or Internet class

Cache   Most DNS servers store in cache memory query responses from other DNS servers. When a DNS server receives a query, it first tries to resolve the query from its cache. Failing that, the server may query other servers to get an answer.

Because DNS uses cache, when you make a change to a DNS record, the change takes time, sometimes a matter of days, to propagate through DNS.

Response   A DNS message, sent in response to a query, has the following structure:

- Header record   Information about this message

- Query record   Repeats the query

- Answer records   Resource records that answer the query

- Authority records   Resource records for servers that have authority for the answers

- Additional records   Additional resource records, such as NS records

An example query and response follow.

```
$ dig fedora.redhat.com
...
;; QUESTION SECTION:
;fedora.redhat.com.              IN      A

;; ANSWER SECTION:
fedora.redhat.com.      600     IN      CNAME   www.redhat.com.
www.redhat.com.         330     IN      A       209.132.177.50

;; AUTHORITY SECTION:
redhat.com.             409     IN      NS      ns1.redhat.com.
redhat.com.             409     IN      NS      ns2.redhat.com.
redhat.com.             409     IN      NS      ns3.redhat.com.

;; ADDITIONAL SECTION:
ns1.redhat.com.         300     IN      A       66.187.233.210
ns2.redhat.com.         600     IN      A       66.187.224.210
ns3.redhat.com.         600     IN      A       66.187.229.10
...
```

Reverse Name Resolution

In addition to normal or forward name resolution, DNS provides *reverse name resolution,* also referred to as *inverse mapping* or *reverse mapping,* so that you can look up domain names given an IP address. Because resource records in the forward DNS database are indexed hierarchically by domain name, DNS cannot perform an efficient search by IP address on this database.

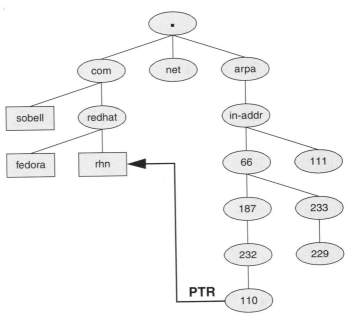

Figure 24-5   Reverse name resolution and the **in-addr.arpa** domain

DNS implements reverse name resolution by means of a special domain named **in-addr.arpa**. Resource records in this domain have Name fields that hold IP addresses; the records are indexed hierarchically by IP address. The Data fields hold the FQDN that corresponds to the IP address.

Reverse name resolution can be used to verify that someone is who he says he is or at least from the domain they say he says he is from. In general, it allows a server to retrieve and record the domain names of the clients it provides services to. For example, legitimate mail contains the domain of the sender and the IP address of the sending machine. A mail server can verify the stated domain of a sender by checking the domain associated with the IP address. It is also used by anonymous FTP servers to verify that a domain specified in an email address used as a password is legitimate.

For example, to determine the domain name that corresponds to an IP address of 66.187.232.110, a resolver would query DNS for information about the domain named 110.232.187.66.in-addr.arpa (Figure 24-5).

The following example uses dig to query DNS for the IP address that corresponds to rhn.redhat.com, which is 66.187.232.110. The second command line uses dig to query the same IP address, reversed, and appended with **.in-addr.arpa**: **110.232.187.66.in-addr.arpa** for a PTR resource record. The data portion of the resultant resource record is the domain name from the original query: rhn.redhat.com.

```
$ dig rhn.redhat.com
...
;; QUESTION SECTION:
;rhn.redhat.com.                              IN      A

;; ANSWER SECTION:
rhn.redhat.com.          93      IN      A       66.187.232.110
...
$ dig 110.232.187.66.in-addr.arpa PTR
...
;; QUESTION SECTION:
;110.232.187.66.in-addr.arpa.     IN      PTR

;; ANSWER SECTION:
110.232.187.66.in-addr.arpa. 540 IN      PTR      rhn.redhat.com.
...
```

Instead of reformatting the IP address as in the preceding example, you can use the
–x option to dig to perform a reverse query:

```
$ dig -x 66.187.232.110
...
;; QUESTION SECTION:
;110.232.187.66.in-addr.arpa.     IN      PTR

;; ANSWER SECTION:
110.232.187.66.in-addr.arpa. 552 IN      PTR      rhn.redhat.com.
...
```

Or you can just use host:

```
$ host 66.187.232.110
110.232.187.66.in-addr.arpa domain name pointer rhn.redhat.com.
```

About DNS

This section discusses how DNS works and provides resources for additional information on DNS.

How DNS Works

Application programs do not issue DNS queries directly but rather use the **gethostbyname**() system call. How the system comes up with the corresponding IP address is transparent to the calling program. The **gethostbyname**() call examines the **hosts** line in **/etc/nsswitch.conf** file (page 413) to determine which files it should examine and/or which services it should query in what order to get an IP address that corresponds to a domain name. When it needs to query DNS, the local system, which is the DNS client, queries the DNS database by calling the resolver library on the local system. This call returns the required information to the application program.

Prerequisites

Install the following packages:

- **bind**
- **bind-utils**
- **caching-nameserver**
- **system-config-bind** (*FEDORA*) or **redhat-config-bind** (*RHEL*) (optional)
- **bind-chroot** (if you want to run BIND in a chroot jail)

Run chkconfig to cause **named** to start when the system goes multiuser:

```
# /sbin/chkconfig named on
```

Do not start **named** until you have configured it (see "Start named" on page 712).

More Information

"DNS for Rocket Scientists" is an excellent site that makes good use of links to present information on DNS in a very digestible form.

Local *Bind Administrator Reference Manual* **/usr/share/doc/bind✱/arm/Bv9ARM.html**

Web DNS for Rocket Scientists www.zytrax.com/books/dns
Bind   www.isc.org/products/BIND
DNS   www.mscs.mu.edu/~doug/spectral/Networks2001F/dns/c1.htm
DNS security   www.sans.org/rr/papers/index.php?id=1069

HOWTO *DNS HOWTO*

Book DNS & BIND by Albitz & Liu O'Reilly & Associates; 4th edition (April 1, 2001)

JumpStart I: Setting Up a DNS Cache

As explained earlier, a DNS cache is a bridge between a resolver and authoritative DNS servers: It is not authoritative; it simply stores the results of its queries in memory. Most ISPs provide a DNS cache for the use of their customers. Setting up a local cache can reduce the traffic between the LAN and the outside world and improve response times. While it is possible to set up a DNS cache on each system on a LAN, setting up a single DNS cache on a LAN prevents multiple systems on the LAN from having to query a remote server for the same information.

After installing BIND, including the **caching-nameserver** package, you have most of a caching nameserver ready to run. Refer to "A DNS Cache" (page 717) for an explanation of the files that this nameserver uses and how it works. Before you start the DNS cache, put the following line in **/etc/resolv.conf** (page 432), before any other **nameserver** lines:

```
nameserver 127.0.0.1
```

This line tells the resolver to use the local system (localhost or 127.0.0.1) as the primary nameserver. To experiment with using the local system as the only nameserver, comment out other nameserver lines in **resolv.conf** by preceding each with a pound sign (#).

Start named   Next, start the **named** daemon using service and the **named** init script:

```
# /sbin/service named start
Starting named:                                          [  OK  ]
```

Refer to "Troubleshooting" on page 724 for ways to check that the DNS cache is working. Once **named** is running, you can see the effect of the cache by using dig to look up the IP address of www.redhat.com, a remote system:

```
$ dig www.redhat.com

; <<>> DiG 9.2.1 <<>> www.redhat.com
;; global options:  printcmd
;; Got answer:
;; ->>HEADER<<- opcode: QUERY, status: NOEresource recordOR, id: 2941
;; flags: qr rd ra; QUERY: 1, ANSWER: 1, AUTHORITY: 3, ADDITIONAL: 0

;; QUESTION SECTION:
;www.redhat.com.IN A

;; ANSWER SECTION:
www.redhat.com.300INA       66.187.232.50

;; AUTHORITY SECTION:
redhat.com.600 IN  NS  ns2.redhat.com.
redhat.com.600 IN  NS  ns3.redhat.com.
redhat.com.600 IN  NS  ns1.redhat.com.

;; Query time: 748 msec
;; SERVER: 127.0.0.1#53(127.0.0.1)
;; WHEN: Tue Nov  4 10:28:27 2003
;; MSG SIZE  rcvd: 102
```

The fourth line from the bottom shows that the query took 748 milliseconds or about three-quarters of a second. When you run the same query again, it runs more quickly because the DNS cache has saved the information in memory:

```
$ dig www.redhat.com
...
;; Query time: 1 msec
;; SERVER: 127.0.0.1#53(127.0.0.1)
;; WHEN: Tue Nov  4 10:28:36 2003
;; MSG SIZE  rcvd: 102
```

JumpStart II: system-config-bind: Setting Up a Domain

Running system-config-bind (*FEDORA*) or redhat-config-bind (*RHEL*) displays the Domain Name Service window (Figure 24-6), which you can use to set up a DNS server. This section explains how to use [system|redhat]-config-bind but does not go into de-

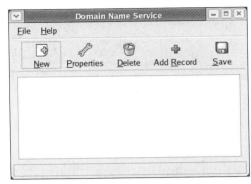

Figure 24-6 The Domain Name Service window

tail about what each of the files and settings does; that is covered elsewhere in this chapter.

tip ‖ system-config-bind **Sets Up Files in a** chroot **Jail**

FEDORA The files that system-config-bind creates are located in the **/var/named/chroot** directory hierarchy so you can run **named** in a chroot jail. See page 724 for more information.

Click **New** on the toolbar to set up a new zone (page 702); [system|redhat]-config-bind displays the Select a zone type window, which allows you to specify a domain name and choose between a forward master zone, a reverse master zone (page 708), and a slave zone. For more information, refer to "Servers" on page 704. After you make your selections and click **OK**, [system|redhat]-config-bind displays the Name to IP Translations window (Figure 24-7).

Fill in the text boxes in this window, making sure to put a period at the end of the name of the primary nameserver. Click **Time Settings** if you want to change the times associated with the SOA record (page 706). See "SOA" on page 706 for an

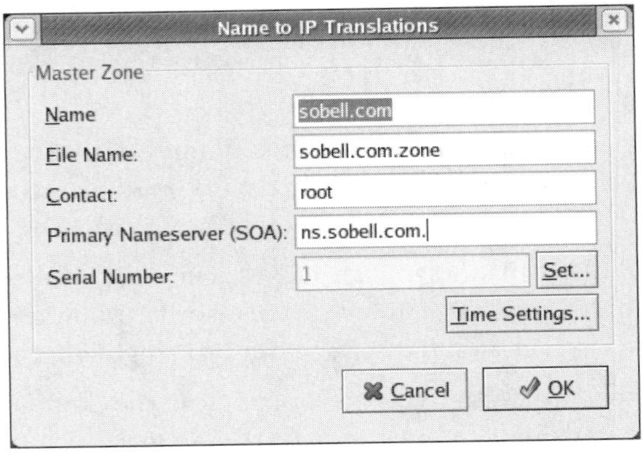

Figure 24-7 The Name to IP Translations window

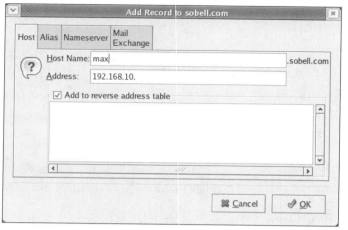

Figure 24-8   The Add Record to window

explanation of the serial number and the times in the SOA record. When you click **OK**, you have set up an SOA record for the new zone.

With the domain you want to work with highlighted in the Domain Name Service window, click **Add Record** on the toolbar to display the Add Record to window (Figure 24-8).

Using the Host tab of the Add Record to window, add the names of the systems (hosts) in the domain you are setting up. You can add only one system at a time in this window. Add a system, click **OK**, then open the window again and add another system until all the systems in the domain are listed in the Domain Name Service window.

With the systems added, you can use the Add Record to window to add alias (CNAME, page 705), nameserver (NS, page 706), and mail exchange (MX, page 706) records to the zone file. To add any of these records, first, in the Domain Name Service window, highlight the domain you want to work with. Next, click **Add Record** on the toolbar.

To add an alias, click the **Alias** tab. In the Host Name box highlight the hostname you want to create the alias for, enter the name of the alias in the Alias text box, and click **OK**.

To add a nameserver, click the **Nameserver** tab. In the Domain Name text box, enter the name of the domain that is served by the nameserver. Enter the address of the nameserver in the Served by text box. Click **OK**.

To add a mail exchange record, click the **Mail Exchange** tab. Enter the name you want to assign to the server, the priority of the server (a lower number means a higher priority), and, in the Mail Server box, highlight the name of the mail server. Click **OK**.

Click Save when you are done, close the Domain Name Service window, and start the **named** daemon as explained on page 712.

Setting Up BIND

This section discusses the **named.conf** file, zone files, how to implement a DNS cache, and running DNS inside a chroot jail.

named.conf

Configuration information for **named**, including the names and locations of zone files, is kept in **/etc/named.conf**. By default, the zone files are kept in **/var/named**. A sample **named.conf** file is included with the **caching-nameserver** package (page 718).

IP-list

The *IP-list* is a semicolon-separated list of IP addresses, each optionally followed by a slash and subnet mask length (page 400). You can prefix an *IP-list* with an exclamation point (!) to negate it. Builtin names that you can use in *IP-list* include **any**, **none**, and **localhost**. You must enclose builtin names in double quotation marks.

Comments

Within **named.conf**, you can specify a comment by preceding it with a pound sign (#) as in a perl or shell program, preceding it with a double-slash (//) as in a C++ program, or enclosing it between /* and */ as in a C program.

Options Section

Option statements can appear within two sections of **named.conf**: Options and Zone. Option statements within the Options section apply globally. When an option statement appears in a Zone section, the option applies to the zone and overrides any corresponding global option within that zone. An Options section starts with the keyword **options** and continues with braces surrounding the statements. Following is a list of some statements that can appear in the Options section. Statements that can appear only in an Options section are so noted.

allow-query {*IP-list***}** Allows queries from *IP-list* only. Without this option, the server responds to all queries.

allow-recursion {*IP-list***}**

Specifies systems that this server will perform recursive queries (page 703) for. For systems not in *IP-list*, the server performs iterative queries only. Without this option, the server performs recursive queries for any system.

allow-transfer {*IP-list***}**

Specifies systems that are allowed to perform zone transfers from this server. Specify an IP-list of **"none"** (include the quotation marks) to prevent zone transfers.

directory *path*   Specifies the absolute pathname of the directory containing the zone files; under Red Hat Linux, this directory is initially **/var/named**. Filenames specified in this **named.conf** file are relative to this directory. Options section only.

forward ONLY|FIRST

ONLY forwards all queries. FIRST forwards all queries and, if a query does not receive an answer, attempts to find an answer using additional queries. Valid with **forwarders** statement only.

forwarders {*IP* [*port*] [; ...]}

Specifies IP addresses and optionally port numbers that queries are forwarded to. See the **forward** statement.

notify YES|NO   YES sends a message to slave servers for the zone when zone information changes. Master servers only.

recursion YES|NO   YES (default) provides recursive queries (page 703) if the client requests. NO provides iterative queries only (page 703). An answer is always returned if it appears in the server's cache. Options section only.

Zone Section

A Zone section defines a zone and can include any of the statements listed for the Options section except as noted. A Zone section starts with the keyword **zone** and continues with braces surrounding the zone statements being specified. Following is a list of some zone statements:

allow-update {*IP-list*}

Specifies systems that are allowed to update this zone dynamically. This may be useful when hosting a master DNS server for a domain owned by someone other than yourself because it allows a remote user to update the DNS entry without granting the user access to your server.

file *filename*   Specifies the *zone file*, the file that specifies the characteristics of the zone. The *filename* is relative to the directory specified by the **directory** statement in the Options section. The **file** statement is mandatory for master and hint zones and a good idea for slave zones (see **type**).

masters (*IP-list*)   Specifies systems that a slave zone can use to update zone files. Slave zones only.

type *ztype*   Specifies the type of zone that this section defines. Specify *ztype* from the following list:

- **forward**   Specifies a forward zone, which forwards queries directed to this zone. See the **forward** and/or **forwarders** statements in the Options section.

- **hint**   Specifies a hint zone. A hint zone lists root servers that the local server queries when it starts and when it cannot find an answer in its cache.

- **master**   Specifies the local system as a primary master server (page 704) for this zone.

- **slave**   Specifies the local system as a slave server (page 704) for this zone.

Zone Files

Zone files, kept in **/var/named** by default, define zone characteristics.

Time Formats

All times in BIND files are in seconds, unless they are followed by one of the following letters (upper- or lowercase): S (seconds), M (minutes), H (hours), D (days), or W (weeks). You can combine formats: The time 2h25m30s means two hours, 25 minutes, and 30 seconds and is the same as 8730 seconds.

Domain Qualification

An unqualified domain in a zone file is assumed to be in the current zone (the zone being defined by the zone file). The name **zach** in the zone file for **myzone.com** would be expanded to the FQDN **zach.myzone.com.**. Use an FQDN (include the trailing period) to specify a domain that is not in the current zone. Any name that does not end in a period is regarded as a subdomain of the current zone.

Zone File Directives

The following directives can appear within a zone file. Each directive is identified by a leading dollar sign. The $TTL directive is mandatory and must be the first entry in a zone file.

$TTL   Defines the default time to live for all resource records in the zone. Any resource record can include a TTL to override this value.

$ORIGIN   Changes the zone name from that specified in the **named.conf** file. This name replaces an @ sign in the Name field of a resource record. It is also used to complete unqualified domain names.

$INCLUDE   Includes a file as though it were part of the zone file. The scope of an $ORIGIN directive within an included file is the included file. That is, an $ORIGIN directive within an included file does not affect the file it is included in.

A DNS Cache

You install a DNS cache, also called a resolving, caching nameserver, when you install the Red Hat BIND packages, including **caching-nameserver**. The section "JumpStart I: Setting Up a DNS Cache" (page 711) explains how to run this server.

This section explains how the files Red Hat provides implement this server. The default **named.conf** file is shown following:

```
$ cat /etc/named.conf
// generated by named-bootconf.pl

options {
    directory "/var/named";
    /*
     * If there is a firewall between you and nameservers you want
     * to talk to, you might need to uncomment the query-source
     * directive below.  Previous versions of BIND always asked
     * questions using port 53, but BIND 8.1 uses an unprivileged
     * port by default.
     */
    // query-source address * port 53;
};

//
// a caching only nameserver config
//
controls {
    inet 127.0.0.1 allow { localhost; } keys { rndckey; };
};
zone "." IN {
    type hint;
    file "named.ca";
};

zone "localhost" IN {
    type master;
    file "localhost.zone";
    allow-update { none; };
};

zone "0.0.127.in-addr.arpa" IN {
    type master;
    file "named.local";
    allow-update { none; };
};

include "/etc/rndc.key";
```

Options section   The Options section specifies the directory that all filenames in this file are relative to. Specifically, the files named in the Zone sections are in the **/var/named** directory. The comments in the Options section of the **named.conf** file supplied by Red Hat suggest that you uncomment the **query-source address** option if you are having trouble getting the DNS server to work through a firewall. If the local firewall does not allow the nameserver to make connections from arbitrary ports, uncommenting this line and opening port 53 outbound in the firewall will allow the nameserver to work.

Controls section   The Controls section has two statements that set up rndc (see following) control: **inet** and **keys**. The **inet** statement opens a control channel on 127.0.0.1, allowing local, nonprivileged users to manage the nameserver. The keys statement allows a key to be defined to secure rndc communications.

Zone sections   There are three Zone sections, one each for the hints zone, the normal server on the local system, and the reverse name resolution server on **in-addr.arpa**.

The hints zone specifies that when the server starts or when it does not know which server to query, it should look in the **/var/named/named.ca** (**ca** stands for cache) file to find the addresses of authoritative servers for the root domain.

The localhost and 0.0.127.in-addr.arpa zones specify a zone file in **/var/named** and specify that dynamic updates of the zone are not allowed.

A nameserver almost never has to answer queries in the 127.0.0.1 and localhost zones. Most operating systems include this information in **/etc/hosts** (or the operating system equivalent) to prevent them from having to perform a remote lookup to connect to the local system.

include/rndc   The rndc (Remote Name Daemon Control) utility allows the system administrator to control BIND remotely (from the local or a remote system). You can use rndc to start and stop the daemon, force the daemon to reread the configuration files, and view diagnostic information. See the rndc man page for more information.

The **include** section of **named.conf** on the nameserver incorporates the **/etc/rndc.key** file as though it appeared within **named.conf**. (By putting the rndc key information in a file separate from the **named.conf** file, the rndc key information can be kept private using file permissions, while the **named.conf** file can be read by anyone.) The rndc key is a secret shared between the nameserver and the remote control program. The **/etc/rndc.key** file must also be included in the **/etc/rndc.conf** file on the controlling system. If you wish to use rndc on a system other than the local one, you must copy **rndc.key** to the remote machine and add the remote host to the control section in the **named.conf** file on the server.

Zone Files

The root zone:
named.ca   There are three zone files in **/var/named**. The file for the hints zone, **named.ca**, is a copy of ftp.internic.net/domain/named.cache, which does not change frequently. The **named.ca** file specifies authoritative servers for the root domain. The DNS server initializes its cache from this file and can determine an authoritative server for any domain from this information.

The root zone is required only for servers answering recursive queries: If a server responds to recursive queries, it needs to perform a series of iterative queries starting at the root domain. Without the root domain hints file, it will not know the location of the root domain servers.

```
$ cat /var/named/named.ca
;        This file holds the information on root name servers needed to
;        initialize cache of Internet domain name servers
;        (e.g. reference this file in the "cache  .  <file>"
;        configuration file of BIND domain name servers).
;
;        This file is made available by InterNIC
;        under anonymous FTP as
;             file                  /domain/named.cache
;             on server             FTP.INTERNIC.NET
;
;        last update:   Nov 5, 2002
;        related version of root zone:   2002110501
;
;
; formerly NS.INTERNIC.NET
;
.                            3600000  IN  NS   A.ROOT-SERVERS.NET.
A.ROOT-SERVERS.NET.          3600000      A    198.41.0.4
;
; formerly NS1.ISI.EDU
;
.                            3600000      NS   B.ROOT-SERVERS.NET.
B.ROOT-SERVERS.NET.          3600000      A    128.9.0.107
;
; formerly C.PSI.NET
;
.                            3600000      NS   C.ROOT-SERVERS.NET.
C.ROOT-SERVERS.NET.          3600000      A    192.33.4.12
...
; End of File
```

localhost.zone   The **localhost.zone** file starts with a $TTL directive and holds three resource records: SOA, NS, and A. The $TTL directive in the following file specifies that the default time to live for the resource records specified in this file is 86400 seconds (24 hours). In the file, each resource record specifies a TTL, but that value is redundant as it specifies the same value as the default (24 hours). You can leave a TTL field blank to use the default TTL.

```
$ cat /var/named/localhost.zone
; zone "localhost"
;
$TTL    86400
$ORIGIN localhost.
@       1D IN   SOA     @ root (
                            42              ; serial
                            3H              ; refresh
                            15M             ; retry
                            1W              ; expiry
                            1D )            ; minimum

        1D IN   NS      @
        1D IN   A       127.0.0.1
```

The $ORIGIN directive specifies the suffix that is appended to unqualified domain names. This value is redundant because the Zone section in **named.conf** specifies the origin of the zone as localhost (**zone "localhost" IN {}**). As explained earlier, the @ at the start of the SOA resource record stands for the origin which is **localhost**.

The last two lines in the preceding file are the NS resource record that specifies the nameserver for the zone as localhost and the A resource record that specifies the address of the host as 127.0.0.1. Because the NS and A resource records have blank Name fields, they each inherit this value from the preceding resource record, in this case, @.

named.local   The **named.local** zone file provides information about the 0.0.127.in-addr.arpa reverse lookup zone. It follows the same pattern as the **localhost** zone file, except the TTL field is blank in all three resource records, causing BIND to use the value from the $TTL directive at the beginning of the file. In place of the A resource record, this file has a PTR record that provides the name that the zone associates with the IP address. The PTR resource record specifies the name 1, which equates the system at address 1 in the origin (0.0.127.in-addr.arpa) with the name **localhost**.

```
$ cat /var/named/named.local
$TTL    86400
@       IN    SOA    localhost. root.localhost.    (
                          1997022700    ; Serial
                          28800         ; Refresh
                          14400         ; Retry
                          3600000       ; Expire
                          86400)        ; Minimum
        IN    NS     localhost.

1       IN    PTR    localhost.
```

Once you start **named** (page 712), you can use the tests described under "Troubleshooting" on page 724 to make sure the server is working.

DNS Glue

It is common to put the nameserver for a zone inside the zone it serves. For example, you might put the nameserver for the zone starting at site1.example.com (Figure 24-3, page 702) in ns.site1.example.com. When a DNS cache tries to resolve www.site1.example.com, the authoritative server for example.com gives it the NS record pointing at ns.site1.example.com. In an attempt to resolve ns.site1.example.com, the DNS cache again queries the authoritative server for example.com, which points back to ns.site1.example.com. This loop does not allow ns.site1.example.com to be resolved.

The simplest solution to this problem is not to allow any nameserver to reside inside the zone it points to. Because every zone is a child of the root zone, this solution would mean that every domain would have to be served by the root server and would not scale at all. The solution is *glue* records. A glue record is an A record for a nameserver that is returned in addition to the NS record when an NS query is performed. Because the A record provides an IP address for the nameserver, it does not need to be resolved and does not create the problematic loop.

The nameserver setup for redhat.com illustrates the use of glue records. When you query for NS records for redhat.com, DNS returns three NS records. In addition, it returns three A records that provide the IP addresses for the hosts that the NS records point to:

```
$ dig -t NS redhat.com
...
;; QUESTION SECTION:
;redhat.com.                    IN     NS

;; ANSWER SECTION:
redhat.com.            600      IN     NS       ns3.redhat.com.
redhat.com.            600      IN     NS       ns1.redhat.com.
redhat.com.            600      IN     NS       ns2.redhat.com.

;; ADDITIONAL SECTION:
ns1.redhat.com.        300      IN     A        66.187.233.210
ns2.redhat.com.        600      IN     A        66.187.224.210
ns3.redhat.com.        600      IN     A        66.187.229.10
.
.
.
```

You can create a glue record by providing an A record for the nameserver inside the delegating domain's zone information file:

```
site1.example.com              IN     NS       ns.site1.example.com
ns.site1.example.com           IN     A        1.2.3.4
```

TSIG (Transaction Signatures)

Interaction between DNS components is based on the query-response model: One part queries another and receives a reply. Traditionally, a server determines whether and how to reply to a query based on the IP address of the client. *IP spoofing* (page 978) is relatively easy, making this situation less than ideal. Recent versions of BIND support transaction signatures (TSIG), which allow two entities to establish a trust relationship by establishing a *shared secret key*.

TSIG can provide an additional layer of authentication between master and slave servers for a zone. When a slave server is located on a different site than the master (as it should be), a malicious person operating a router between the sites can spoof the IP of the master server and change the DNS data on the slave. With TSIG, this person would need to know the secret key to change the DNS data on the slave.

Creating a Secret Key

The secret key is an encoded string of up to 512 bytes; you can use dnssec-keygen, included with BIND, to generate this key. The following command generates a 512-bit random key using md5, a *one-way hash function* (page 986):

```
$ /usr/sbin/dnssec-keygen -a hmac-md5 -b 512 -n HOST keyname
Kkeyname.+157+47586
```

Replace *keyname* with something unique yet meaningful. This command creates a key in a file whose name is similar to **Kkeyname.+157+47586.private**, where *keyname* is replaced by the name of the key, **+157** indicates the algorithm used, and **+47586** is a hash of the key. If you run the same command again, the hash part will be different. The key file is not used directly. Use the following command to display the algorithm and key information you will need in the next step:

```
$ cat Kkeyname.+157+47586.private
Private-key-format: v1.2
Algorithm: 157 (HMAC_MD5)
Key: uNPDouqVwR7fvo/zFyjkqKbQhcTd6Prm...
```

Using the Shared Secret

The next step is to tell the nameservers about the shared secret by inserting the following code into the **/etc/named.conf** file on both servers. This code is a top-level section in **named.conf**; you can insert it following the options section.

```
key keyname {
    algorithm "hmac-md5";
    secret "uNPDouqVwR7fvo/zFyjkqKbQhcTd6Prm...";
};
```

Replace *keyname* with the name of the key you created. The **algorithm** is the string that appears within parentheses in the output from **cat**, preceding. The **secret** is the string that follows **Key:** in the preceding output. You must enclose each string within double quotation marks. Be careful when you copy the key as it is long; do not break it into two lines.

Because key names are unique, you can insert any number of key sections into **named.conf**. In order to keep the key a secret, make sure users other than **root** cannot read it: Either give **named.conf** permissions so that no one except **root** has access to it, or put the key in a file that only **root** can read and include in **named.conf** using an **include** statement (page 717).

Once both servers know about the key, use the **server** statement in **named.conf** to tell them when to use it.

```
server 1.2.3.4 {
# 1.2.3.4 is the IP address of the other server using this key
    keys {
        "keyname";
    };
};
```

Each server must have a server section, each containing the IP address of the other. The servers will now communicate with each other only if they first authenticate each other using the secret key.

Running BIND Inside a chroot Jail

To increase security, you can run BIND in a chroot jail. See page 406 for information about the security advantages of, and how to set up, a chroot jail. The **bind-chroot** package, which is required to run BIND in a chroot jail, creates a directory named **/var/named/chroot** that should take the place of the root directory (**/**) for all BIND files.

RHEL You must manually move the file hierarchy that is normally in **/var/named** to **/var/named/chroot/var/named** and move the **named.conf** file, normally located in **/etc**, to **/var/named/chroot/etc**.

FEDORA service-config-bind creates all files in **/var/named/chroot** to make it easier to run BIND in a chroot jail.

To get the **named** init script to run BIND in a chroot jail, the **ROOTDIR** shell variable needs to be set to **/var/named/chroot**. When you install the **bind-chroot** package, the installation process should place the following line, which sets this variable, just below the introductory comments in the **/etc/rc.d/init.d/named** file:

```
ROOTDIR=/var/named/chroot
```

Make sure this line is present in the file; add the line if it is not there.

Troubleshooting

When you start a DNS cache, the **/var/log/messages** file contains lines similar to the following. Other types of DNS servers display similar messages.

```
10:06:31 peach named[28437]: starting BIND 9.2.1 -u named
10:06:31 peach named[28437]: using 1 CPU
10:06:31 peach named[28437]: loading configuration from '/etc/named.conf'
10:06:31 peach named[28437]: no IPv6 interfaces found
10:06:31 peach named[28437]: listening on IPv4 interface lo, 127.0.0.1#53
10:06:31 peach named[28437]: listening on IPv4 interface eth0, 192.168.0.6#53
10:06:31 peach named: named startup succeeded
10:06:31 peach named[28437]: command channel listening on 127.0.0.1#953
10:06:31 peach named[28437]: zone 0.0.127.in-addr.arpa/IN: loaded serial 3747054700
10:06:31 peach named[28437]: zone localhost/IN: loaded serial 25
10:06:31 peach named[28437]: running
```

With an argument of **status**, the **named** init script displays useful information:

```
# /sbin/service named status
number of zones: 4
debug level: 0
```

```
xfers running: 0
xfers deferred: 0
soa queries in progress: 0
query logging is OFF
server is up and running
```

When you create or update DNS information, you can use dig or host to test that the server works the way you planned. The most useful part of the output from dig is usually the answer section, which gives you the nameserver's reply to your query:

```
$ dig example.com
...
;; ANSWER SECTION:
example.com.            22198   IN      A       192.0.34.166
...
```

The preceding output shows that the example.com. domain has a single A record and that record points to 192.0.34.166. The TTL of this record, which tells you how long the record can be held in cache, is 22198 seconds (a little over 6 hours). You can also use dig to query other record types by specifying –t followed by the type of record you want to query for (–t works with host too):

```
$ dig -t MX redhat.com
...
;; ANSWER SECTION:
redhat.com.            551   IN      MX      20 mx2.redhat.com.
redhat.com.            551   IN      MX      50 mx3.redhat.com.
redhat.com.            551   IN      MX      10 mx1.redhat.com.
...
```

If you query for a domain that does not exist, dig returns the SOA record for the authority section of the highest-level domain in your query that does exist:

```
$ dig domaindoesnotexist.info
...
;; AUTHORITY SECTION:
info. 7200   IN      SOA      tld1.ultradns.net.domadmin.ultradns.net. ...
...
```

Because it tells you the last zone that was queried correctly, this information can be useful in tracing faults.

TSIG If two servers using TSIG (page 722) fail to communicate, check the time on each. The TSIG authentication mechanism is dependent on the current time. If the clocks on the two servers are not synchronized, TSIG will fail. Consider setting up *NTP* (page 986) on the servers to prevent this problem.

A Full-functioned Nameserver

The IP addresses used in this example are part of the *private address space* (page 989) so you can copy the example and run the server without affecting global

DNS. Also, to prevent contamination of the global DNS, each of the zones has the notify option set to NO. When you build a nameserver that is integrated with the Internet, you will want to use IP addresses that are particular to your installation. You may want to change the settings of the **notify** statements.

named.conf   The **named.conf** file in this example limits the IP addresses that **named** answers queries from and sets up logging:

```
$ cat /etc/named.conf
options {
    directory "/var/named";
    allow-query {127.0.0.1; 192.168.0.0/24;};};

zone "." IN {
    type    hint;
    file    "named.ca";};

zone "0.168.192.in-addr.arpa" IN {
    type    master;
    file    "named.local";
    notify  NO;
};

zone "sam.net" IN {
    type    master;
    file    "sam.net";
    notify  NO;
};

logging{
    channel "misc" {
        file "/var/log/bind/misc.log" versions 4 size 4m;
        print-time YES;
        print-severity YES;
        print-category YES;
    };
    channel "query" {
        file "/var/log/bind/query.log" versions 4 size 4m;
        print-time YES;
        print-severity NO;
        print-category NO;
    };
    category default {
        "misc";
    };
    category queries {
        "query";
    };
};
```

The **allow-query** statement in the Options section specifies the IP addresses of the systems that the server will answer queries from. You must include the local system as 127.0.0.1 if it will be querying the server. The zone that this server is authoritative for is **sam.net**; the zone file for sam.net is **/var/named/sam.net**.

Logging   Logging is turned on by the Logging section. This file opens two logging channels: one that logs information to **/var/log/bind/misc.log** and one that logs to **/var/log/bind/query.log**. When one of these logs grows to 4 megabytes (**size 4m** in the **file** statement), it is renamed by appending a **.1** to its filename and a new log is started. The numbers at the ends of other, similarly named logs are incremented. Any log that would be numbered over the number specified by the **versions** clause (**4** in the example) is removed. See logrotate (page 543) for another way to maintain log files. The **print** statements determine whether the time, severity, and category of the information are sent to the log; specify each as YES or NO. The category determines what information is logged to the channel. In the example, default information is sent to the **misc** channel and queries are sent to the **query** channel. Refer to the named.conf man page for more choices.

named.local   The origin for the reverse zone file (**named.local**) is 0.168.192.in-addr.arpa (see the Zone section that refers to this file in **named.conf**). Following the SOA and NS resource records, the first three PTR resource records equate address 1 in the subnet 0.168.192.in-addr.arpa (192.168.0.1) with the names gw.sam.net., www.sam.net., and ftp.sam.net.. The next three PTR resource records equate 192.168.0.3 with mark.sam.net., 192.168.0.4 with mail.sam.net., and 192.168.0.6 with ns.sam.net.

```
$ cat named.local
; zone "0.168.192.in-addr.arpa"
;
$TTL    3D
@       IN      SOA     ns.sam.net. mgs@sobell.com. (
                        2003110501      ; serial
                        8H              ; refresh
                        2H              ; retry
                        4W              ; expire
                        1D)             ; minimum
        IN      NS      ns.sam.net.
1       IN      PTR     gw.sam.net.
1       IN      PTR     www.sam.net.
1       IN      PTR     ftp.sam.net.
3       IN      PTR     mark.sam.net.
4       IN      PTR     mail.sam.net.
6       IN      PTR     ns.sam.net.
```

sam.net   The zone file for sam.net takes advantage of many BIND features and includes TXT (page 707), CNAME (page 705), and MX (page 706) resource records. When you query for resource records, **named** returns the TXT resource record along with the records you requested. The first of the two NS records specifies an unqualified name (**ns**) to which BIND appends the zone name (**sam.net**), yielding an FQDN of ns.sam.net. The second nameserver is specified with a FQDN name that BIND does not alter. The MX records specify mail servers in a similar manner and include a priority number at the start of the data field; lower numbers indicate preferred servers.

```
$ cat sam.net
; zone "sam.net"
;
$TTL    3D
@       IN      SOA     ns.sam.net. mgs@sobell.com. (
                                200311051       ; serial
                                8H              ; refresh
                                2H              ; retry
                                4W              ; expire
                                1D )            ; minimum

                TXT     "Sobell Associates Inc."
                NS      ns              ; Nameserver address(unqualified)
                NS      ns.max.net.; Nameserver address (qualified)
                MX      10 mail     ; Mail exchange (primary/unqualified)
                MX      20 mail.max.net.; Mail exchange (2nd/qualified)

localhost IN    A       127.0.0.1

www     IN      CNAME   ns
ftp     IN      CNAME   ns

gw      IN      A       192.168.0.1
                TXT     "Router"

ns      IN      A       192.168.0.6
                MX      10 mail
                MX      20 mail.max.net.

mark    IN      A       192.168.0.3
                MX      10 mail
                MX      20 mail.max.net.
                TXT     "MGS"

mail    IN      A       192.168.0.4
                MX      10 mail
                MX      20 mail.max.net.
```

Some resource records have a value in the Name field; those without a name inherit the name from the previous resource record. The previous resource record may have an inherited name value, and so on. The five resource records following the SOA resource record inherit the @, or origin, from the SOA resource record. These resource records pertain to the zone as a whole. In the preceding example, the TXT resource record inherits its name from the SOA resource record; it is the TXT resource record for the sam.net zone (use **host –t TXT sam.net** to display the TXT resource record).

Following these five resource records are resource records that pertain to a domain within the zone. For example, the MX resource records that follow the A resource record with the Name field set to **mark** are resource records for the mark.sam.net. domain.

The A resource record for localhost is followed by two CNAME resource records that specify www(.sam.net.) and ftp(.sam.net.) as aliases for the nameserver ns.sam.net.. For example, a user connecting to ftp.sam.net will connect to 192.168.0.6. The resource records named **gw**, **ns**, **mark**, and **mail** specify resource records for domains within the sam.net zone.

Log files   Before restarting **named**, create the directory for the log files and give it permissions and ownership as follows:

```
# mkdir /var/log/bind
# chmod 744 /var/log/bind
# chown named /var/log/bind
# ls -ld /var/log/bind
drwxr--r--   2 named     root          4096 Nov  5 19:41 /var/log/bind
```

With the log directory in place, **named.conf** in **/etc**, and the **named.ca**, **named.local**, and **sam.net** zone files in **/var/named**, restart **named** and check the log files. The **/var/log/messages** file should show something like the following:

```
22:55:27 peach named[4502]: starting BIND 9.2.1 -u named
22:55:27 peach named[4502]: using 1 CPU
22:55:27 peach named[4502]: loading configuration from '/etc/named.conf'
22:55:27 peach named[4502]: no IPv6 interfaces found
22:55:27 peach named[4502]: listening on IPv4 interface lo, 127.0.0.1#53
22:55:27 peach named[4502]: listening on IPv4 interface eth0, 192.168.0.6#53
22:55:27 peach named[4502]: command channel listening on 127.0.0.1#953
22:55:27 peach named: named startup succeeded
```

The **misc.log** file may show errors that do not appear in the **messages** file.

```
# cat /var/log/bind/misc.log
22:55:27.047 general: info: zone 0.168.192.in-addr.arpa/IN: loaded serial 2003110501
22:55:27.048 general: info: zone sam.net/IN: loaded serial 200311051
22:55:27.049 general: info: running
```

A Slave Server

To set up a slave server, copy the **/etc/named.conf** file from the master server to the slave server, replacing the **type master** statement with **type slave**. Remove any zones that the slave server will not be acting as a slave for, including the root (.) zone, if the slave server will not respond to recursive queries. Create the **/var/log/bind** directory for log files as explained on page 729.

notify statement   Slave servers copy zone information from the primary master server or another slave server. The **notify** statement specifies whether you want a master server to notify slave servers when information on the master server changes: Set the (global) value of **notify** in the Options section or set it within a Zone section, which overrides a global setting for a given zone. The format is *notify YES | NO | EXPLICIT*

where *YES* causes the master server to notify all slaves listed in NS resource records for the zone, as well as servers at IP addresses listed in an **also-notify** statement. When you set notify to *EXPLICIT*, the server notifies servers listed in the **also-notify** statement only. *NO* turns off notification.

When you start **named**, it copies the zone files to **/var/named**. If you specify **notify YES** on the master server, the zone files on the slave server will be updated each time you change the serial field of the SOA resource record in a zone. You must manually distribute changes to the **/etc/named.conf** file.

A Split Horizon Server

Assume you want to set up a LAN that provides all its systems and services to local users on internal systems, which may be behind a firewall, and only certain, public services, such as Web, FTP, and mail, to Internet (public) users. A *split horizon*, or *DMZ*, DNS server takes care of this situation by treating queries from internal systems differently from queries from public systems (systems on the Internet).

View sections   BIND 9 introduced in **named.conf** View sections, which facilitate the implementation of a split DNS server. Each view provides a different perspective of the DNS namespace to a group of clients. Previous examples have not had explicit View sections. When there is no View section, all zones specified in **named.conf** are part of the implicit default view.

Assume an office with several systems on a LAN and public Web, FTP, DNS, and mail servers. The single connection to the Internet is NATed (page 984) so that it is shared by the local systems and the servers. The gateway system, the one connected directly to the Internet, is a router, firewall, and server. This scenario takes advantage of View sections in **named.conf** and supports separate secondary nameservers for local and public users. Although public users need access to the DNS server as the authority on the domain that supports the servers, they do not require the DNS server to support recursive queries. Not supporting recursion for public users limits the load on the DNS server and the Internet connection. For security, public users must not have access to information about local machines other than the server. Local users should have access to information about local systems and should be able to use the DNS server recursively.

Figure 24-9 shows that the server responds differently to queries from the LAN and the Internet.

The iptables utility (page 737) controls which ports on which systems users on internal and external systems can access. DNS controls which systems are advertised to which users.

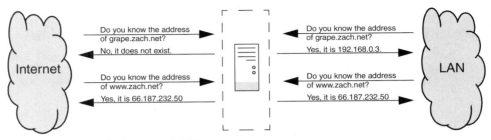

Figure 24-9   A split horizon DNS

The **named.conf** file has four sections: Options, two View sections, and Logging. The Options section specifies that the zone files are in the **/var/named** directory. The View sections specify the characteristics and zones that a resolver is given access to depending on its address. One zone is for use by the LAN/local users and the other by Internet/public users. The Logging section sets up the **misc2.log** file for default messages.

There are several ways to specify which clients see a view; the following **named.conf** file uses **match-clients** statements:

```
$ cat /etc/named.conf
options {
    directory "/var/named";
}; //end options


view "local" IN {                        // start local view
match-clients { 127.0.0.1; 192.168.0.0/24;};
recursion YES;

zone"zach.net" IN {
    type    master;
    file    "local.net";
    notify YES;
};

zone "0.168.192.in-addr.arpa" IN {
    type    master;
    file    "named.local";
    notify YES;
};

zone "." IN {
    type    hint;
    file    "named.ca";
};

};                  // end local view
```

```
view "public" IN {                        // start public view
match-clients { "all";
};
recursion NO;

zone"zach.net" IN {
    type    master;
    file    "public.net";
    notify  YES;
};

zone "0.168.192.in-addr.arpa" IN {
    type    master;
    file    "named.public";
    notify  YES;
};

zone "." IN {
    type    hint;
    file    "named.ca";
};

};                                         // end public view

logging{
    channel "misc" {
        file "/var/log/bind/misc2.log" versions 2 size 1m;
        print-time YES;
        print-severity YES;
        print-category YES;
    };
    category default {
        "misc";
    };
};                                         //end logging
```

The ordering of View sections within **named.conf** is critical: The view that is presented to a client is the first view that the client matches. The preceding **named.conf** file holds two View sections: one for local users and one for public users, in that order. Local users are defined to be those on the 192.168.0.0/24 subnet or localhost (127.0.0.1); public users are defined to be any users. If you reversed the order of the View sections, all users, including local users, would get the view intended for the public and no users would see the local view.

Many statements from the Options section can be used within View sections where they override statements in the (global) Options section. The **recursion** statement, which can appear within an Options section, appears in each of the View sections. This **named.conf** file sets up a server that provides recursive answers to queries that originate locally and iterative answers to queries from the public. This setup provides quick, complete answers to local users, limiting the network and processor bandwidth that are devoted to other users while still providing authoritative name service for the local servers.

To make **named.conf** easier to understand and maintain, zones in different View sections can have the same name while having different zone files. Both the local and public View sections in the example have zones named **zach.net**: The public zach.net zone file is named **public.net**, while the local one is **local.net**.

The Logging section is described on page 727.

The zone files defining **zach.net** are similar to the ones in the previous examples; the public file is a subset of the local one. Following the SOA resource record in both files is a TXT, two NS, and two MX resource records. Next are three CNAME resource records that direct queries addressed to www.zach.net, ftp.zach.net, and mail.zach.net to the system named ns.zach.net. The next three resource records specify the address and two mail servers for the ns.zach.net domain.

The final four resource records appear in the local zach.net zone file and not in the public zone file. These are address (A) resource records for local systems. Instead of keeping this information in **/etc/hosts** files on each system, you can keep it on the DNS server where it can be updated easily. When you use DNS in place of **/etc/hosts**, you must change the **hosts** line in **/etc/nsswitch.conf** (page 413).

```
$ cat local.net
; zach.net local zone file
;
$TTL    3D
@       IN      SOA     ns.zach.net. mgs@sobell.com. (
                        200311118       ; serial
                        8H              ; refresh
                        2H              ; retry
                        4W              ; expire
                        1D )            ; minimum

        IN      TXT     "Sobell Associates Inc."
        IN      NS      ns          ; Nameserver address (unqualified)
        IN      NS      ns.speedy.net.; Nameserver address (qualified)
        IN      MX      10 mail     ; Mail exchange (primary/unqualified)
        IN      MX      20 mail.max.net.; Mail exchange (2nd/qualified)

www     IN      CNAME   ns
ftp     IN      CNAME   ns
mail    IN      CNAME   ns

ns      IN      A       192.168.0.1
        IN      A       192.168.0.6
        IN      MX      10 mail
        IN      MX      20 mail.max.net.

speedy  IN      A       192.168.0.1
grape   IN      A       192.168.0.3
potato  IN      A       192.168.0.4
peach   IN      A       192.168.0.6
```

```
$ cat public.net
; zach.net public zone file
;
$TTL    3D
@       IN      SOA     ns.zach.net. mgs@sobell.com. (
                                200311118       ; serial
                                8H              ; refresh
                                2H              ; retry
                                4W              ; expire
                                1D )            ; minimum

        IN      TXT     "Sobell Associates Inc."
        IN      NS      ns              ; Nameserver address(unqualified)
        IN      NS      ns.speedy.net.; Nameserver address (qualified)

        IN      MX      10 mail ; Mail exchange (primary/unqualified)
        IN      MX      20 mail.max.net.; Mail exchange (2nd/qualified)

www     IN      CNAME   ns
ftp     IN      CNAME   ns
mail    IN      CNAME   ns

ns      IN      A       192.168.0.1
        IN      A       192.168.0.6
        IN      MX      10 mail
        IN      MX      20 mail.max.net.
```

There are two reverse zone files, each of which starts with SOA and NS resource records followed by PTR resource records for each of the names of the servers. The local version of this file (following) also lists the names of the local systems.

```
$ cat named.local
;"0.168.192.in-addr.arpa" reverse zone file
;
$TTL    3D
@       IN      SOA     ns.zach.net. mgs@sobell.com. (
                                2003110501      ; serial
                                8H              ; refresh
                                2H              ; retry
                                4W              ; expire
                                1D)             ; minimum
        IN      NS      ns.zach.net.
        IN      NS      ns.speedy.net.
1       IN      PTR     gw.zach.net.
1       IN      PTR     www.zach.net.
1       IN      PTR     ftp.zach.net.
1       IN      PTR     mail.zach.net.
1       IN      PTR     speedy.zach.net.
3       IN      PTR     grape.zach.net.
4       IN      PTR     potato.zach.net.
6       IN      PTR     peach.zach.net.
```

Chapter Summary

DNS, which maps domain names to IP addresses and vice versa, is implemented as a hierarchical, distributed, and replicated database on the Internet. Although BIND, which implements DNS, has security issues, you can improve its security by running it inside a chroot jail and using transaction signatures (TSIG).

When a program on the local system needs to look up an IP address that corresponds to a domain name, it calls the resolver. The resolver queries local DNS cache, if available, and then queries DNS servers on the LAN or Internet. There are two types of queries: iterative and recursive. When a server responds to an iterative query, it returns whatever information it has at hand; it does not query other servers. Recursive queries cause a server to query other servers if necessary to come up with an answer.

There are three types of servers: Master servers, which hold the master copy of zone data, are authoritative for a zone; slave servers are also authoritative and copy their data from a master server or other slave; and DNS caches, which are not authoritative and either answer queries from cache or forward queries to another server.

The DNS database holds resource records for domains. There are many types of resource records including A (address), MX (mail exchange), NS (nameserver), PTR (pointer for performing reverse name resolution), and SOA (start of authority, which describes the zone).

Exercises

1. What kind of server responds to recursive queries?
2. What kind of DNS record is likely to be returned when a Web browser tries to resolve the domain part of a URI?
3. What are MX resource records for?
4. How would you find the IP address of example.com from the command line?
5. How would you instruct a Linux system to use the local network's DNS cache, located at 192.168.1.254, or the ISP's DNS cache, located on 1.2.3.4, if the LAN nameserver was unavailable?
6. How would you instruct a DNS server to respond only to queries from the 137.44.* IP range?

7. List the possible ways a resolver might attempt to find the IP address of the **example** domain.

Advanced Exercises

8. How would you start to set up a private domain name hierarchy that does not include any of the official InterNIC-assigned domain names?

9. What part of DNS is most vulnerable to attack and why?

10. It is often irritating to have to wait for DNS records to update around the world when you change DNS entries. You could prevent this delay by setting the TTL to a small number. Why is setting the TTL to a small number a bad idea?

11. Outline a method by which DNS could be used to support encryption.

iptables: Setting Up a Firewall

25

The iptables utility builds and manipulates network packet filtering rules in the Linux kernel. You can use iptables to set up a firewall to protect your system from malicious users and to set up *NAT* (Network Address Translation, page 984), which can allow multiple systems to share a single Internet connection. The iptables utility is flexible and extensible, allowing you to set up simple or complex network packet filtering solutions. It provides connection tracking (stateful packet filtering), allowing you to handle packets based on the state of their connection. For example, you can set up rules that reject inbound packets trying to open a new connection and accept inbound packets that are responses to locally initiated connections. Features not included in the base iptables package are available as patches via the patch-o-matic program. See page 740 for links to more information.

Some of the concepts involved in fully understanding iptables are beyond the scope of this book. You can use iptables at different levels and this chapter attempts to present the fundamentals. There are, however, some sections of this chapter that delve into areas that may require additional understanding or explanation. If a concept is not clear, refer to one of the resources in "More Information" on page 740.

How iptables Works

netfilter and iptables   What is frequently referred to as iptables is actually composed of two components: **netfilter** and iptables. Running in *kernelspace* (page 979), the **netfilter** component is a set of tables that hold rules that the kernel uses to control packet filtering. Running in *userspace* (page 1003), the iptables utility sets up, maintains, and displays the rules stored by **netfilter**.

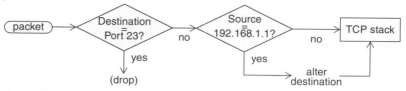

Figure 25-1   Example of how rules work

Rules, matches, targets, and chains
A *rule* comprises one or more criteria (*matches* or *classifiers*) and a single action (a *target*). If, when a rule is applied to a packet, the packet matches all the criteria, the action is applied to the packet. Rules are stored in *chains*. Each of the rules in a chain is applied, in order, to a packet, until there is a match. If there is no match, the chain's *policy*, or default action, is applied to the packet (page 745).

History
In the kernel, iptables replaces the earlier ipchains as a method of filtering network packets and provides multiple chains for increased filtration flexibility. The iptables utility also provides stateful packet inspection (page 740).

Example rules
As an example of how rules work, assume that a chain has two rules (Figure 25-1). The first rule tests to see if a packet's destination is port 23 (FTP) and drops the packet if it is. The second rule tests to see if a packet was received from the IP address 192.1681.1 and alters the packet's destination if it was. When a packet is processed by the example chain, the kernel first applies the first rule in the chain to see if the packet arrived on port 23. If yes, the packet is dropped and that is the end of processing for that packet. If no, the kernel applies the second rule in the chain to see if the packet is from the specified IP address. If yes, the destination in the packet's header is changed and the modified packet is sent on its way. If no, the packet is sent on without being changed.

Chains are collected in three tables: Filter, NAT, and Mangle. Each of the tables has builtin chains as described following. You can create additional, user-defined chains in Filter, the default table.

Filter
The default table. This table is mostly used to DROP or ACCEPT packets based on their content and does not alter packets. Builtin chains are INPUT, FORWARD, and OUTPUT. All user-defined chains go in this table.

NAT
The Network Address Translation table. Packets that create new connections are routed through this table, which is used exclusively to translate the source or destination field of the packet. Builtin chains are PREROUTING, OUTPUT, and POSTROUTING. Use with DNAT, SNAT, and MASQUERADE targets only.

- **DNAT** (Destination NAT) alters the destination IP address of the first inbound packet in a connection so it is rerouted to another host. Subsequent packets in the connection are automatically DNATed. Useful for redirecting packets from the Internet that are bound for a firewall or a NATed server (page 755).

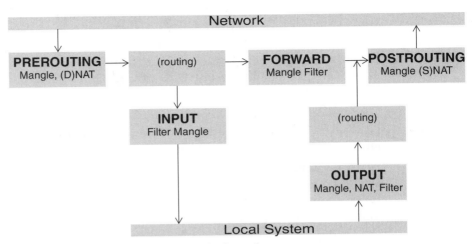

Figure 25-2   Filtering a packet in the kernel

- **SNAT** (Source NAT) alters the source IP address of the first outbound packet in a connection so that it appears to come from a fixed IP address, for example, a firewall or router. Subsequent packets in the connection are automatically SNATed. Replies to SNATed packets are automatically De-SNATed so they go back to the original sender. SNAT is useful for hiding LAN addresses from systems outside the LAN and using a single IP address to serve multiple, local hosts. See also MASQUERADE, following.

- **MASQUERADE** differs from SNAT only in that it checks for an IP address to apply to each outbound packet, making it suitable for use with dynamic IP addresses such as those provided by DHCP (page 408). MASQUERADE is slightly slower than SNAT.

Mangle   Used exclusively to alter TOS (Type of Service), TTL (Time To Live), and MARK fields in a packet. Builtin chains are PREROUTING and OUTPUT.

Network packet   When a packet from the network enters the kernel's network protocol stack, it is given some basic sanity tests, including checksum verification. After passing these tests, the packet goes through the PREROUTING chain where it can have its destination address changed (Figure 25-2).

Next, the packet is routed, based on its destination address. If it is bound for the local system, it first goes through the INPUT chain where it can be filtered (accepted, dropped, or sent to another chain) or altered. If the packet is not addressed to the local system (the local system is forwarding the packet), it goes through the FORWARD and POSTROUTING chains where it can again be filtered or altered.

Packets that are created locally pass through the OUTPUT and POSTROUTING chains where they can be filtered or altered before being sent on the network.

State   The connection tracking machine or, as it is sometimes called, the state machine, gives you information on the state of a packet, allowing you to define rules that match on the state of the connection the packet is part of. For example, when a connection is opened, the first packet is part of a NEW connection, while subsequent packets are part of an ESTABLISHED connection. Connection tracking is handled by the **conntrack** module.

The OUTPUT chain handles connection tracking for locally generated packets. The PREROUTING chain handles connection tracking for all other packets. For more information, refer to "State" on page 748.

Before the advent of connection tracking, it was sometimes necessary to open many or all nonprivileged ports to make sure that you accepted all RETURN and RELATED traffic. Because connection tracking allows you to identify these kinds of traffic, you can keep many more ports closed to general traffic, making a system more secure.

Jumps and targets   A *jump* or *target* specifies the action the kernel takes if a packet matches all the match criteria for the rule being processed (page 748).

About iptables

This section contains information about iptables: resources, prerequisites for running iptables, and notes.

More Information

Web   Documentation, HOWTOs, FAQs, patch-o-matic, security information   netfilter.org
Tutorial   www.faqs.org/docs/iptables
Scripts and more   www.linuxguruz.com/iptables

HOWTO   *KernelAnalysis-HOWTO*
IP Masquerade HOWTO (contains useful scripts)
Netfilter Extensions HOWTO at netfilter.org and
www.iptables.org/documentation/HOWTO/netfilter-extensions-HOWTO.html

Book   *TCP Illustrated* by W. Richard Stevens, Addison-Wesley, 1993.

Prerequisites

Install the following package:

• **iptables**

Run chkconfig to cause iptables to start when the system comes up:

```
# /sbin/chkconfig iptables on
```

To ensure maximum protection, the init script (page 381) starts packet filtering by running iptables very soon after entering runlevels 2–5 while runlevels 0, 1, and 6 do not stop packet filtering almost until the system leaves the runlevel.

Notes

The iptables utility differs from most other Linux utilities in its setup and use. Where other Linux utilities such as Apache, **vsftpd**, and **sshd** read the data that controls their operation from a configuration file, iptables requires that you give a series of iptables commands to build a set of packet filtering rules that are kept in the kernel.

There are two ways to set up reliably the same set of rules each time you bring the system up. First, you can put iptables commands in a script and run that script each time the system comes up. You can call this script from **/etc/rc.d/rc.local**.

Second, you can put the arguments to the iptables commands you want to execute in **/etc/sysconfig/iptables**. The system-config-securitylevel utility (page 751), as well as the Anaconda installer (page 46), uses this technique, building sets of rules and storing the corresponding iptables command arguments in **/etc/sysconfig/iptables**.

For information on copying packet filtering rules to and from the kernel, refer to "Copying Rules to and from the Kernel" on page 750. You can run iptables with the –L option or you can run **service iptables status** to display the packet filtering rules the kernel is using.

Resetting iptables   If you have a problem with firewall rules, you can return packet processing rules in the kernel to their default state without rebooting by giving the following commands:

```
# iptables --flush && iptables --delete-chain
```

These commands flush all chains and delete any user-defined chains, leaving the system without a firewall. In an emergency you can give the following command to unload all iptables modules from the kernel and set a policy of DROP for all tables:

```
# /sbin/service iptables panic
```

JumpStart: Using system-config-securitylevel to Build a Firewall

The system-config-securitylevel (*FEDORA*) and redhat-config-securitylevel (*RHEL*) utilities (Figure 25-3) build an extremely simple firewall. It cannot deal with complex setups; it cannot even deal with NFS. The system-config-securitylevel utility has two tabs; the SELinux tab is discussed on (page 380). The Firewall Options tab displays a few more choices than redhat-config-securitylevel and is discussed here.

From the Security level combo box, select **Enable firewall**. The firewall automatically allows packets that originate locally through to the outside (generally the Internet) and allows responses to those packets back in.

Figure 25-3   The Security Level Configuration window

Click the check boxes of the services you want to provide; these boxes set up a firewall that allows the local system to be one or more of the following types of servers: HTTP (Web), FTP, SSH, TELNET, and SMTP (mail).

Click the check box next to any devices you trust. The sit0 device is a virtual device that can be used for tunneling IPv6 over IPv4; you can ignore this device if you have not configured IPv6. Do not specify a device that connects directly or indirectly to the Internet as a trusted device. You can enter the numbers of other ports you want to open in the Other ports text box.

Click **OK** and [system|redhat]-config-securitylevel sets up and turns on the firewall. For more information, refer to "A Rule Set Generated by system-config-securitylevel" on page 751.

Anatomy of an iptables Command

The command line   This section lists the components of an iptables command line that follow the name of the utility, iptables. Except as noted, the iptables utility is not sensitive to the position of arguments on the command line. The examples in this chapter reflect a generally accepted syntax that allows commands to be easily read, understood, and maintained. Not all commands have all components.

Many tokens on an iptables command line have two forms: a short form, consisting of a single letter preceded by a single hyphen, and a long form, consisting of a word preceded by two hyphens. Most scripts use the short forms for brevity; lines using the long forms can get unwieldy. The following iptables command lines are equivalent and are used as examples in this section:

```
# iptables --append FORWARD --in-interface eth1 --out-interface eth0 --jump ACCEPT
# iptables -A FORWARD -i eth1 -o eth0 -j ACCEPT
```

Table Specifies the name of the table the command operates on: FILTER, NAT, or MAN-GLE. You can specify a table name in any iptables command. When you do not specify a table name, the command operates on the FILTER table. Most of the examples in this chapter do not specify table names and, therefore, work on the FILTER table. Specify a table as **–t** *tablename* or **––table** *tablename.*

Command Tells iptables what to do with the rest of the command line: for example, add or delete a rule, display rules, or add a chain. The example commands, **–A** or **––append**, append the rule specified by the command line to the specified table and chain. See (page 744) for a list of commands.

Chain Specifies the name of the chain that this rule belongs to or that this command works on. The chain is INPUT, OUTPUT, FORWARD, PREROUTING, POSTROUTING, or the name of a user-defined chain. Specify a chain by putting the name of the chain on the command line without preceding hyphens. The examples at the beginning of this section work with the FORWARD table.

There are two kinds of match criteria: *packet match* criteria that match a network packet and *rule match* criteria that match an existing rule.

Packet match criteria Packet match criteria identify network packets and implement rules that take action on packets that match the criteria. Packet match criteria and an action together are called a *rule specification.* Rule specifications form the basis for packet filtering. The first example at the beginning of this section uses the **––in-interface eth1 ––out-interface eth0** rule match criteria; the second example uses the short form of the same criteria: **–i eth1 –o eth0.** Both of these rules forward packets that come in on device **eth1** to device **eth0.**

Rule match criteria Rule match criteria identify existing rules. An iptables command can modify, remove, or position a new rule adjacent to a rule specified by a rule match criterion. There are two ways to identify an existing rule. You can use the same rule specification that was used to create the rule or you can use the rule's ordinal number, called a *rule number.* Rule numbers begin with 1, the first rule in a chain, and can be displayed with **iptables –L ––line-numbers.** The first of the following commands deletes the rule listed at the beginning of this section; the second replaces rule number 3 in the INPUT chain with a rule that rejects all packets from IP address 192.168.0.10.

```
# iptables --delete -A FORWARD -i eth1 -o eth0 -j ACCEPT
# iptables -R INPUT 3 -source 192.168.0.10 -jump REJECT
```

A *jump* or *target* specifies what action the kernel takes on packets that match all the match criteria for this rule. Specify a jump or target as **–j** *target* or **––jump** *target.* The examples at the beginning of this section specify the ACCEPT target using the following commands: **––jump ACCEPT** and **–j ACCEPT.**

Jumps A jump transfers control to a different chain within the same table. The following command adds (**––append**) a rule to the INPUT chain that transfers packets that use the TCP protocol (**--protocol tcp**) to a user-defined chain named **tcp_rules** (**--jump tcp_rules**).

```
# iptables --append INPUT --protocol tcp --jump tcp_rules
```

When the packet finishes traversing the **tcp_rules** chain, assuming it has not been dropped or rejected, it continues traversing the INPUT chain from the rule following the one it jumped from.

Targets A target specifies an action the kernel takes on the packet; the simplest actions are ACCEPT and DROP or REJECT. The following command adds a rule to the FORWARD chain that rejects packets coming from the FTP port (**/etc/services**, the file iptables consults to determine which port to use, shows that FTP uses port 22).

```
# iptables --append FORWARD --sport ftp --jump REJECT
```

Some targets, such as LOG, are *non-terminating:* Control passes to the next rule after the target is executed. See page 748 for information on how to use targets.

Building a Set of Rules

To specify a table, it is common practice to put the table declaration on the command line immediately following **iptables**. For example, the following command flushes (deletes all the rules from) the NAT table:

```
# iptables -t NAT -F
```

Commands

Following is a list of iptables commands:

--append –A Adds rule(s) specified by *rule-specifications* to the end of *chain*. When a packet matches *rule-specifications, target* processes it.

> *iptables –A chain rule-specification –jump target*

--delete –D Removes one or more rules, as specified by *rule-numbers* or *rule-specifications*.

> *iptables –D chain rule-number | rule-specification*

--insert –I Adds rule(s) specified by *rule-specifications* and *target* to the location in *chain* specified by *rule-number*. If you do not specify *rule-number*, it defaults to 1, the head of the chain.

> *iptables –I chain rule-number rule-specification –jump target*

--replace –R Replaces rule number *rule-number* with *rule-specification* and *target*. Command fails if *rule-specification* resolves to more than one address.

> *iptables –R chain rule-number | rule-specification –jump target*

−−list **−L** Displays rules in *chain*. Omit *chain* to display rules for all chains. Use **−−line-numbers** to display rule numbers.

>   *iptables −L [chain] display-options*

−−flush **−F** Deletes all rules from *chain*. Omit *chain* to delete all rules from all chains.

>   *iptables −F [chain]*

−−zero **−Z** Change to 0 the value of all packet and byte counters in *chain* or in all chains when you do not specify *chain*. Use with **−L** to display the counters before clearing them.

>   *iptables −Z [−L] [chain]*

−−delete-chain **−X** Removes the user-defined chain named *chain*. If you do not specify *chain*, removes all user-defined chains. You cannot delete a chain that a targets point to.

>   *iptables −X chain*

−−policy **−P** Sets the default target or policy for a builtin chain. This policy is applied to packets that do not match any rule in the chain. If a chain does not have a policy, unmatched packets are ACCEPTed.

>   *iptables −P **builtin-chain builtin-target***

−−rename-chain **−E** Changes the name of chain *old* to *new*.

>   *iptables −E old new*

−−help **−h** Displays a summary of iptables command syntax.

>   *iptables −h*

Follow a match extension protocol with **−h** to display options you can use with that protocol. For more information, refer to "Help with extensions" on page 746.

Packet Match Criteria

>   The following criteria match network packets. When you precede a criterion with an exclamation point (!), the rule matches packets that do not match the criterion.

−−protocol [!] *proto* −p Matches on protocol. This is a match extension (page 746).

−−source [!] *address[/mask]*

>   **−s** or **−−src** Matches if the packet came from *address*. The *address* can be a name or IP address. See (page 400) for formats of the optional *mask* that you can use only with an IP address.

−−destination [!] *address[/mask]*

>   **−d** or **−−dst** Matches if the packet is going to *address*. The *address* can be a name or IP address. See (page 400) for formats of the optional *mask*, which you can use only with an IP address.

--in-interface [!] *iface*[+]

> **-i** For the INPUT, FORWARD, and PREROUTING chains, matches if *iface* is the name of the interface the packet was received from. Append a plus sign (+) to *iface* to match any interface whose name begins with *iface*. When you do not specify **in-interface**, the rule matches packets coming from any interface.

--out-interface [!] *iface*[+]

> **-o** For the FORWARD, OUTPUT, and POSTROUTING chains, matches if *iface* is the interface the packet will be sent to. Append a plus sign (+) to *iface* to match any interface whose name begins with *iface*. When you do not specify **out-interface**, the rule matches a packet going to any interface.

[!] --fragment -f Matches the second and subsequent fragments of fragmented packets. Because these packets do not contain source or destination information, they do not match any other rules.

Display Criteria

> The following criteria display information. All packets match these criteria.

--verbose -v Displays additional output.

--numeric -n Displays IP addresses and port numbers as numbers, not names.

--exact -x Use with –L to display exact packet and byte counts instead of rounded values.

--line-numbers Display line numbers when listing rules. The line numbers are also the rule numbers that you can use in rule match criteria (page 743).

Match Extensions

> Rule specification (packet match criteria) extensions, called *match extensions,* add matches based on protocols and state to matches described previously. Each of the protocol extensions is kept in a module that must be loaded before the match extension can be used. The command that loads the module must appear in the same rule specification as, and to the left of, the command that uses the module. There are two types of match extensions: implicit and explicit.

Implicit Match Extensions

Help with extensions Implicit extensions are loaded (somewhat) automatically when you use a **--protocol** command (following). Each protocol has its own extensions. Follow the protocol with –h to display extensions you can use with that protocol. For example, **iptables –p tcp –h** displays TCP extensions at the end of the help output.

--protocol [!] *proto*

> **-p** Loads the *proto* module and matches if the packet uses *proto*. The *proto* can be a name or number from **/etc/protocols**, including **tcp**, **udp**, and **icmp** (page 976).

Specifying **all** or 0 (zero) matches any of **tcp**, **udp**, or **icmp** and is the same as not including this match in a rule.

The following criteria load the TCP module and match TCP protocol packets coming from port 22 (ssh packets):

```
--protocol tcp --source-port 22
```

The following command expands the preceding match to cause iptables to drop all incoming ssh packets. This command uses **ssh**, which iptables looks up in **/etc/services**, in place of **22**.

```
# iptables --protocol tcp --source-port ssh -jump DROP
```

This section does not describe all extensions; use **–h**, described preceding, for a complete list.

TCP

––destination-port [!] [*port*][:*port*]]

> ––**dport**   Matches a destination port number or service name (see **/etc/services**). You can also specify a range of port numbers, :*port* to specify ports 0 through *port*, or *port*: to specify ports *port* through 65535.

––source-port [!] [*port*][:*port*]]

> ––**sport**   Matches a source port number or service name (see **/etc/services**). You can also specify a range of port numbers, :*port* to specify ports 0 through *port*, or *port*: to specify ports *port* through 65535.

> [!] ––syn   Matches packets with the SYN bit set and ACK and FIN bits cleared. This match extension is shorthand for **––tcp-flags SYN,RST,ACK SYN**.

––tcp-flags [!] *mask comp*

> Defines TCP flag settings that constitute a match. Valid flags are SYN, ACK, FIN, RST, URG, PSH, ALL, NONE. The *mask* is a comma-separated list of flags to be examined and *comp* is a comma-separated subset of *mask* that specifies the flags that must be set for there to be a match. Flags not specified in *mask* must be unset.

––tcp-option [!] *n*   Matches TCP options based on their decimal value (*n*).

UDP

You can specify a source and/or destination port in the same manner as described under "TCP," preceding.

ICMP

ICMP (page 976) packets carry messages only.

––icmp-type [!] *name*

> Matches when the packet is an ICMP packet of type *name*. The *name* can be a numeric ICMP type or one of the names returned by

```
# iptables -p icmp -h
```

Explicit Match Extensions

Explicit match extensions differ from implicit match extensions in that you must use a –m or ––match option to specify a module before you can use the extension. There are many explicit match extension modules; this chapter covers **state**, one of the most important.

State

This match extension matches on the state of the connection the packet is part of (page 740).

––state *state*   Matches a packet whose state is defined by *state*, a comma-separated list of states from the following list:

ESTABLISHED   Any packet, within a specific connection, following the exchange of packets in both directions for that connection.

INVALID   A stateless or unidentifiable packet.

NEW   The first packet within a specific connection, typically a SYN packet.

RELATED   Any packets exchanged in a connection spawned from an ESTAB-LISHED connection. For example, an FTP data connection might be related to the FTP control connection. (You need the **ip_conntrack_ftp** module for FTP connection tracking.)

The following command establishes a rule that matches and drops invalid packets as well as packets from new connections:

```
# iptables --match state --state INVALID,NEW -jump DROP
```

Targets

All targets are built in; there are no user-defined targets. This section lists some of the targets available with iptables as distributed by Red Hat. Applicable target options are listed following each target.

ACCEPT   Continues processing the packet.

DNAT   **Destination Network Address Translation**   Rewrites the destination address of the packet.

––to-destination *ip[-ip][:port-port]*
Same as SNAT with **to-source**, except changes the destination addresses of packets to the specified address(es) and port(s) and is valid only in the PREROUTING or OUTPUT chains of the NAT table and any user-defined chains called from those chains. The following command adds to the PREROUTING chain of the NAT table a rule that changes the destination in the headers of TCP packets with a destination of 66.187.232.50 to 192.168.0.10.

```
# iptables -t NAT -A PREROUTING -p tcp -d 66.187.232.50 -j DNAT --to-destination 192.168.0.10
```

DROP   Ends the packet's life without notice.

LOG   Turns on logging for the packet being processed. The kernel uses **syslogd** (page 546) to process output generated by this target. LOG is a nonterminating target; processing continues with the next rule. Use two rules to LOG packets that you REJECT, one each with the targets LOG and REJECT, with the same matching criteria.

--og-level *n*
Specifies a logging level as per **syslog.conf** (page 546).

--log-prefix *string*
Prefixes log entries with *string*, which can be up to 14 characters.

--log-tcp-options
Logs options from the TCP packet header.

--log-ip-options
Logs options from the IP packet header.

MASQUERADE   Similar to SNAT with **--to-source**, except the IP information is grabbed from the interface on the specified port. For use on systems with dynamically assigned IP addresses, such as those that use DHCP, including most dial-up lines. Valid only in rules in the POSTROUTING chain of the NAT table.

--to-ports *port[-port]*
Specifies the port for the interface you want to masquerade. Forgets connections when the interface goes down, as is appropriate for dial-up lines. You must specify a TCP or UDP protocol (**--protocol tcp** or **udp**) with this target.

REJECT   Similar to DROP, except it notifies the sending system that the packet was blocked.

--reject-with *type*
Returns the error *type* to the originating system. The *type* can be one of the following, which returns the appropriate *ICMP* (page 976) error: **icmp-net-unreachable, icmp-host-unreachable, icmp-port-unreachable, icmp-proto-unreachable, icmp-net-prohibited,** or **icmp-host-prohibited.** You can specify *type* as **echo-reply** from rules that specify an ICMP ping packet to return a ping reply. You can specify **tcp-reset** from rules in or called from the INPUT chain to return a TCP RST packet. Valid in the INPUT, FORWARD, and OUTPUT chains and user-defined chains called from these chains.

RETURN   Stops traversing this chain and returns the packet to the calling chain.

SNAT   **Source Network Address Translation**   Rewrites the source address of the packet. Appropriate for hosts on a LAN that share an Internet connection.

--to-source *ip[-ip][:port-port]*
Alters the source IP address of an outbound packet, and all future packets in this connection, to *ip*. Skips additional rules, if any. Returning packets are automatically

de-SNATed so they return to the originating host. Valid only in the POSTROUT-ING chain of the NAT table.

When you specify a range of IP addresses (*ip-ip*), or use multiple **to-source** targets, iptables assigns the addresses in a round-robin fashion, cycling through the addresses, one for each new connection.

When the rule specifies the TCP or UDP protocol (**–p tcp** or **–p udp**), you can specify a range of ports. When you do not specify a range of ports, the rule matches all ports. Every connection on a NATed subnet must have a unique IP address and port combination. If two computers on a NATed subnet try to use the same port, the kernel maps one of the ports to another (unused) one. Ports less than 512 are mapped to other ports less than 512, ports from 512 to 1024 are mapped to other ports from 512 to 1024, and ports above 1024 are mapped to other ports above 1024.

Copying Rules to and from the Kernel

The iptables-save utility copies packet filtering rules from the kernel to standard output so you can save them in a file. The iptables-restore utility copies rules from standard input, as written by iptables-save, to the kernel. Sample output from iptables-save follows:

```
# iptables-save
# Generated by iptables-save v1.2.8 on Sun Mar 14 20:41:37 2004
*filter
:INPUT ACCEPT [0:0]
:FORWARD ACCEPT [0:0]
:OUTPUT ACCEPT [0:0]
:RH-Firewall-1-INPUT - [0:0]
-A INPUT -j RH-Firewall-1-INPUT
-A FORWARD -j RH-Firewall-1-INPUT
-A RH-Firewall-1-INPUT -i lo -j ACCEPT
...
COMMIT
```

Most of the lines that iptables-save writes are iptables command lines without the **iptables** at the beginning. Lines that begin with a pound sign (#) are comments. Lines that start with an asterisk are names of tables that the following commands work on; all the preceding commands work on the Filter table. The COMMIT line must appear at the end of all the commands for a table; it executes the preceding commands. Lines that begin with colons specify chains in the following format:

> :*chain policy [packets:bytes]*

Where *chain* is the name of the chain, *policy* is the policy (default target) for the chain, and *packets* and *bytes* are the packet and byte counters. The square brackets must appear in the line; they do not indicate optional parameters. Refer to www.faqs.org/docs/iptables/iptables-save.html for more information.

A Rule Set Generated by system-config-securitylevel

This section describes a set of rules generated by system-config-securitylevel (page 741) when you ask it to create a default firewall. The redhat-config-securitylevel works the same way. The system-config-securitylevel utility, which replaces gnome-lokkit, writes the rules in the format used by iptables-save (see the preceding section) to **/etc/sysconfig/iptables**, so the firewall is implemented each time the system boots.

In the following listing, ✳**filter** indicates that the following commands work on the FILTER table and the first line that begins with a colon specifies that the policy for the INPUT chain in the FILTER table is ACCEPT. FORWARD and OUTPUT chains are specified similarly. Because the counters for all the chains are zero, the counters will be reset to zero each time the system boots and starts iptables from this file.

The system-config-securitylevel utility creates a user-defined chain that is named RH-Firewall-1-INPUT. No policy is specified because user-defined chains cannot have policies.

```
# cat /etc/sysconfig/iptables
# Firewall configuration written by system-config-securitylevel
# Manual customization of this file is not recommended.
*filter
:INPUT ACCEPT [0:0]
:FORWARD ACCEPT [0:0]
:OUTPUT ACCEPT [0:0]
:RH-Firewall-1-INPUT - [0:0]
-A INPUT -j RH-Firewall-1-INPUT
-A FORWARD -j RH-Firewall-1-INPUT
-A RH-Firewall-1-INPUT -i lo -j ACCEPT
-A RH-Firewall-1-INPUT -p icmp --icmp-type any -j ACCEPT
-A RH-Firewall-1-INPUT -p 50 -j ACCEPT
-A RH-Firewall-1-INPUT -p 51 -j ACCEPT
-A RH-Firewall-1-INPUT -m state --state ESTABLISHED,RELATED -j ACCEPT
-A RH-Firewall-1-INPUT -j REJECT --reject-with icmp-host-prohibited
COMMIT
```

The first two lines that begin with **–A** add rules to the INPUT and FORWARD chains that cause control to transfer to the RH-Firewall-1-INPUT chain. The subsequent lines append rules to the RH-Firewall-1-INPUT chain. COMMIT executes the preceding commands. Following is a description of what the rest of the lines do:

```
-A RH-Firewall-1-INPUT -i lo -j ACCEPT
```

The preceding line accepts packets from the local interface.

```
-A RH-Firewall-1-INPUT -p icmp --icmp-type any -j ACCEPT
```

The preceding line accepts all ICMP packets.

```
-A RH-Firewall-1-INPUT -p 50 -j ACCEPT
-A RH-Firewall-1-INPUT -p 51 -j ACCEPT
```

The preceding lines accept packets that match protocol 50 and 51, which **/etc/protocols** lists as IPv6-Crypt, an encryption header for IPv6, and IPv6-Auth, an encryption header for IPv6.

```
-A RH-Firewall-1-INPUT -m state --state ESTABLISHED,RELATED -j ACCEPT
```

The preceding line uses **–m** to specify the **state** module and accepts ESTABLISHED and RELATED packets.

```
-A RH-Firewall-1-INPUT -j REJECT --reject-with icmp-host-prohibited
```

The preceding line rejects all packets that have not been accepted and returns ICMP error **icmp-host-prohibited** to the system that sent the packet.

With the preceding rules loaded, you can use iptables to list the rules and see the defaults that iptables puts in place.

```
# iptables -L
Chain INPUT (policy ACCEPT)
target        prot opt source                  destination
RH-Firewall-1-INPUT  all  --  anywhere                    anywhere

Chain FORWARD (policy ACCEPT)
target        prot opt source                  destination
RH-Firewall-1-INPUT  all  --  anywhere                    anywhere

Chain OUTPUT (policy ACCEPT)
target        prot opt source                  destination

Chain RH-Firewall-1-INPUT (2 references)
target        prot opt source                  destination
ACCEPT        all  --  anywhere              anywhere
ACCEPT        icmp --  anywhere              anywhere               icmp any
ACCEPT        ipv6-crypt--  anywhere              anywhere
ACCEPT        ipv6-auth--  anywhere              anywhere
ACCEPT        all  --  anywhere              anywhere               state RELATED,ESTABLISHED
REJECT        all  --  anywhere              anywhere               reject-with icmp-host-prohibited
```

Sharing an Internet Connection Using NAT

On the Internet there are a lot of scripts available that set up Internet connection sharing using iptables. Each of the scripts boils down to the same few basic iptables commands with minor differences. This section discusses those few statements to explains how a connection can be shared. You can use the statements presented in this section or refer to the *Linux IP Masquerade HOWTO* for complete scripts, the simplest of which is at tldp.org/HOWTO/IP-Masquerade-HOWTO/firewall-examples.html.

There are two ways you can share a single connection to the Internet (one IP address). Both involve setting up *NAT* to alter addresses in and forward packets. The first allows clients (browsers, mail readers, and so on) on several systems on a LAN to share a single IP address to connect to servers on the Internet. The second allows servers (mail, web, FTP, and so on) on different systems on a LAN to provide their services over a single connection to the Internet. You can use iptables to set up one or both of these configurations. In both cases, you need to set up a system that is a router: It must have two network connections—one connected to the Internet and the other to the LAN.

For optimum security, use a dedicated system as a router. Because data transmission over a connection to the Internet, even a broadband connection, is relatively slow, using an slower, older system as a router does not generally slow down a LAN. This setup gives you some defense against intrusion from the Internet. A workstation on the LAN *can* also function as a router, but this setup means you have data on a system that is directly connected to the Internet. The following sections discuss the security of each setup.

The examples in this section assume that the device named **eth0** connects to the Internet on 10.255.255.255 and that **eth1** connects to the LAN on 192.168.0.1. Substitute the devices and IP addresses that your systems use. If you use a modem to connect to the Internet, you need to substitute **ppp0** (or another device) for **eth0** in the examples.

In order for the examples in this section to work, you must turn on IP forwarding. First, give the following command and make sure everything is working:

```
# /sbin/sysctl -w net.ipv4.ip_forward=1
```

Once you know that iptables is working the way you want, change the 0 to a **1** in the following line in **/etc/sysctl.conf** to make the kernel always perform IP forwarding:

```
net.ipv4.ip_forward = 0
```

Connecting Several Clients to a Single Internet Connection

Configuring the kernel of the router system to allow clients on multiple, local systems on the LAN to connect to the Internet requires you to set up *IP masquerading*, or *SNAT* (source NAT). IP masquerading translates the source and destination addresses in the headers of network packets that originate on local systems and the packets that remote servers send in response to those packets. These packets are part of connections that originate on a local system. The example in this section does nothing to packets that are part of connections that originate on the remote systems (on the Internet): These packets cannot get past the router system, providing a degree of security.

The point of rewriting the packet headers is to allow systems with different local IP addresses to share a single IP address on the Internet. The router system translates the source or origin address of packets from local systems to that of the Internet connection, so that all packets passing from the router to the Internet appear to come from a single system, 10.255.255.255 in the example. All packets sent in response by remote systems on the Internet to the router system have the address of the Internet connection, 10.255.255.255 in the example, as their destination address. The router system remembers each connection and alters the destination address on each response packet to that of the local, originating system.

The router system is established by four iptables commands, one of which sets up a log of masqueraded connections. The first command puts the first rule in the FORWARD chain of the FILTER (default) table (–A FORWARD):

```
# iptables -A FORWARD -i eth0 -o eth1 -m state --state ESTABLISHED,RELATED -j ACCEPT
```

To match this rule, a packet must be

1. Received on **eth0** (coming in from the Internet): **–i eth0**.
2. Going to be sent out on **eth1** (going out to the LAN): **–o eth1**.
3. Part of an established connection or a connection that is related to an established connection: **––state ESTABLISHED,RELATED**.

The kernel accepts (**–j ACCEPT**) packets that meet these three criteria. Accepted packets pass to the next appropriate chain/table. Packets that are not accepted pass to the next rule in the FORWARD chain. Packets from the Internet that attempt to create a new connection are not accepted by this rule.

The second command puts the second rule in the FORWARD chain of the FILTER table:

```
# iptables -A FORWARD -i eth1 -o eth0 -j ACCEPT
```

To match this rule, a packet must be

1. Received on **eth1** (coming in from the LAN): **–i eth1**.
2. Going to be sent out on **eth0** (going out to the Internet): **–o eth0**.

The kernel accepts packets that meet these two criteria, which means that all packets that originate locally and are going to the Internet are accepted. Accepted packets pass to the next appropriate chain/table. Packets that are not accepted pass to the next rule in the FORWARD chain.

The third command puts the third rule in the FORWARD chain of the FILTER table:

```
# iptables -A FORWARD -j LOG
```

This rule has no match criteria so it acts on all packets it processes. This rule's action is to log packets, which means it logs packets from the Internet that attempt to create a new connection.

Packets that get to the end of the FORWARD chain of the FILTER table are done with the rules set up by iptables and are handled by the local tcp stack. Packets from the Internet that attempt to create a new connection on the router system are accepted or returned, depending on whether the service they are trying to connect to is available on the router system.

The fourth command puts the first rule in the POSTROUTING chain of the NAT table. Only packets that are establishing a new connection are passed to the NAT table. Once a connection has been set up for SNAT or MASQUERADE, the headers on all subsequent ESTABLISHED and RELATED packets are altered the same way as the first packet. Packets that are sent in response to these packets automatically have their headers adjusted so that they return to the originating local system.

```
# iptables -t NAT -A POSTROUTING -o eth0 -j MASQUERADE
```

To match this rule, a packet must be

1. Establishing a new connection (otherwise it would not have come to the NAT table).

2. Going to be sent out on **eth0** (going out to the Internet): **–o eth0**.

The kernel MASQUERADEs all packets that meet these criteria, which means that all locally originating packets that are establishing new connections have their source address changed to the address that is associated with **eth0** (10.255.255.255 in the example).

Following are the four commands together:

```
# iptables -A FORWARD -i eth0 -o eth1 -m state --state ESTABLISHED,RELATED -j ACCEPT
# iptables -A FORWARD -i eth1 -o eth0 -j ACCEPT
# iptables -A FORWARD -j LOG
# iptables -t NAT -A POSTROUTING -o eth0 -j MASQUERADE
```

You can put these commands in **/etc/rc.local** or in a script called by this file on the router system to have them executed each time the system boots. Or you can put them in **/etc/sysconfig/iptables**, leaving off the iptables command at the start of each line. When you put the commands in the **iptables** file, they are be executed by the **iptables** init script each time it is called. For more information, refer to "Copying Rules to and from the Kernel" on page 750.

To limit the local systems that can connect to the Internet, you can add a **–s** (source) match criterion to the last command as shown following:

```
# iptables -t NAT -A POSTROUTING -o eth0 -s 192.168.0.0-192.168.0.32 -j MASQUERADE
```

In the preceding command, **–s 192.168.0.0-192.168.0.32** causes only packets from an IP address in the specified range to be MASQUERADEd.

Connecting Several Servers to a Single Internet Connection

DNAT (destination NAT) can set up rules to allow clients from the Internet to send packets to servers on the LAN. This example sets up an SMTP mail server on 192.168.1.33 and an HTTP (Web) server on 192.168.1.34. Both protocols use TCP; SMTP uses port 25 and HTTP uses port 80, so the rules match TCP packets with destination ports of 25 and 80. The example assumes the mail server does not make outgoing connections and uses another server on the LAN for DNS and mail relaying. Both commands put rules in the PREROUTING chain of the NAT table (–A PREROUTING –t NAT):

```
# iptables -A PREROUTING -t NAT -p tcp --dport 25 --to-source 192.168.0.33:25 -j DNAT
# iptables -A PREROUTING -t NAT -p tcp --dport 80 --to 192.168.0.34:80 -j DNAT
```

To match these rules, the packet must use the TCP protocol (**–p tcp**) and have a destination port of 25 (first rule, **––dport 25**) or 80 (second rule, **––dport 80**).

The **––to-source** is a target specific to the PREROUTING and OUTPUT chains of the NAT table; it alters the destination address and port of matched packets as specified. As with MASQUERADE and SNAT, subsequent packets in the same and related connections are appropriately altered.

The fact that the servers cannot originate connections means that neither server can be exploited to participate in a *DDoS attack* (page 966) on systems on the Internet and cannot send private data from the local system back to a malicious user's system.

Chapter Summary

The iptables utility is used to set up firewalls that help to prevent unauthorized access to a system or network. An iptables command sets up or maintains in the kernel rules that control the flow of network packets; rules are stored in chains. Each rule has a criteria part and an action part, called a target. When the criteria part matches a network packet, the kernel applies the action from the rule to the packet.

There are three tables that hold chains: Filter, NAT, and Mangle. Filter, the default table, DROPs or ACCEPTs packets based on their content. NAT, the Network Address Translation table, translates the source or destination field of packets. Mangle is used exclusively to alter TOS (Type of Service), TTL (Time To Live), and MARK fields in a packet. The connection tracking machine, handled by the **conntrack** module, defines rules that match on the state of the connection a packet is part of.

In an emergency you can give the following command to unload all iptables modules from the kernel and set a policy of DROP for all tables.

```
# /sbin/service iptables panic
```

Exercises

1. How would you remove all iptables rules and chains?

2. How would you list all current iptables rules?

3. How is configuring iptables different from configuring most Linux services?

4. Define an iptables rule that will reject incoming connections on the TELNET port.

5. What does NAT stand for? What does the NAT table do?

Advanced Exercises

6. What does the **conntrack** module do?

7. What do rule match criteria do? What are they used for?

8. What do packet match criteria do? What are they used for?

9. What utilities copy packet filtering rules to and from the kernel? How do they work?

10. Define a rule that will silently block incoming SMTP connections from **spmr.com**.

Apache (httpd): Setting Up a Web Server

26

The World Wide Web, WWW or Web for short, is a collection of servers that hold material, called *content*, that Web browsers, or just browsers, can display. Each of the servers on the Web is connected to the Internet, a network of networks (an *internetwork*). Much of the content on the Web is coded in HTML (Hypertext Markup Language, page 975). *Hypertext*, the code behind the links that you click on a Web page, allows browsers to display and react to links that point to other Web pages on the Internet.

Apache is the most popular Web server on the Internet today. It is robust and extensible. The ease with which you can install, configure, and run it in the Linux environment makes it an obvious choice for publishing content on the World Wide Web. The Apache server and related projects are developed and maintained by the Apache Software Foundation (ASF), a not-for-profit corporation formed in June of 1999. The ASF grew out of The Apache Group, which was formed in 1995 to develop the Apache server.

This chapter starts with introductory information about Apache, followed by the first JumpStart section, which describes the minimum you need to do to get Apache up and running. The second JumpStart section covers the use of the Red Hat system-config-httpd configuration script. Following these sections is "Filesystem Layout," which tells you where the various Apache files are located.

Configuration directives, a key part of Apache, are discussed starting on page 767. This section includes coverage of contexts and containers, two features/concepts that are critical to understanding Apache. The next section explains the main Apache configuration file, **httpd.conf**, as modified by Red Hat. The final pages of the chapter cover virtual hosts, troubleshooting, and modules you can use with Apache, including CGI and SSL.

Introduction

Apache is a server that responds to requests from Web browsers, or *clients*, such as Mozilla, Netscape, lynx, and Internet Explorer. When you enter the address of a Web page (a *URI* [page 1003]) in a Web browser's location bar, the browser sends a request over the Internet to the (Apache) server at that address. In response, the server sends the requested content back to the browser. The browser then displays or plays the content, which might be a song, picture, video clip, or other information.

Content   Aside from add-on modules that can interact with the content, Apache is oblivious to the content itself. Server administration and content creation are two different aspects of bringing up a Web site. This chapter concentrates on setting up and running an Apache server and spends little time discussing content creation.

Modules   Apache, like the Linux kernel, uses external modules to increase load-time flexibility and allow parts of its code to be recompiled without recompiling the whole program. Not part of the Apache binary, modules are stored as separate files that can be loaded when Apache is started.

Apache uses external modules, called Dynamic Shared Objects or DSOs, for basic and advanced functions; there is not much to Apache without these modules. Apache also uses modules to extend its functionality: There are modules that can process scripts written in Perl, PHP, Python, and other languages, use several different methods to authenticate users, facilitate publishing content, and process nontextual content, such as audio. The list of modules written by the Apache group and third-party developers is always growing. For more information, refer to "Modules" on page 793.

About Apache

This section describes the packages you need to install and provides references for the programs this chapter covers. The "Notes" section on page 762 covers terminology and other topics that will help you make better sense of this chapter. The next section, "JumpStart I" on page 762, gets Apache up and running as quickly as possible.

Prerequisites

Minimal Installation   Install the following packages:

- **httpd**
- **apr** (Apache portable runtime, *FEDORA*)
- **apr-util** (library, *FEDORA*)

Starting Apache   Run chkconfig to cause **httpd** to start when the system goes multiuser:

```
# /sbin/chkconfig httpd on
```

After you configure Apache, use service to start **httpd**:

```
# /sbin/service httpd start
```

After changing the Apache configuration, restart **httpd** with the following command, which will not disturb clients connected to the server:

```
# /sbin/service httpd graceful
```

Optional Packages   You can install the following optional packages:

- **httpd-manual**   The Apache manual (*FEDORA*)
- **webalizer**   Web server log analyzer (page 799)
- **mod_perl**   Embedded Perl scripting language
- **mod_python**   Embedded Python scripting language
- **mod_ssl**   Secure Sockets Layer extension (page 795)
- **php**   Embedded PHP scripting language, including IMAP & LDAP support
- **mrtg**   MRTG traffic monitor (page 799).
- **net-snmp** and **net-snmp-utils**   SNMP, required for MRTG (page 799).

More Information

Local   The Apache *Reference Manual* and *Users' Guide*   **/var/www/manual** Point a browser at **http://localhost/manual** or **/var/www/manual/index.html.en** (**en** is for English, substitute for **en: fr** [French], **ja.jis** [Japanese], or **ko.euc-kr** [Korean] as needed). On Fedora, present only if you installed the **httpd-manual** package.

Web   Apache Documentation   httpd.apache.org/docs-2.0
Apache Directives List   httpd.apache.org/docs-2.0/mod/directives.html
Apache Software Foundation (newsletters, mailing lists, projects, module registry, and more)   www.apache.org

mod_perl   perl.apache.org

mod_python   www.modpython.org

mod_php   www.php.net

mod_ssl   www.modssl.org (page 795)

MRTG   mrtg.hdl.com/mrtg.html

SNMP   net-snmp.sourceforge.net

SSI   httpd.apache.org/docs-2.0/howto/ssi.html

webalizer   www.mrunix.net/webalizer.

Notes

Terms: Apache and httpd
Apache is the name of a server that serves HTTP content, among others. The Apache daemon is named **httpd** as it is an HTTP server daemon. This chapter uses the terms *Apache* and *httpd* interchangeably.

Terms: server and process
An Apache *server* is the same thing as an Apache *process:* an Apache child process exists to handle incoming client requests, hence it is referred to as a server.

Running as root
Because Apache serves content on privileged ports, you must start it as **root**. For security, the processes that Apache spawns run as the user and group **apache**.

Document root
The root of the directory hierarchy that Apache serves content from is called the *document root*. As shipped by Red Hat, the document root is **/var/www/html**. You can use the DocumentRoot directive (page 770) to change the location of the document root.

Modifying content
As shipped, only **root** can add or modify content in **/var/www/html**. To avoid having people work as **root** when working with content, create a group (**webwork**, for example), put people who need to work with Web content in this group, and make the directory hierarchy starting at **/var/www/html** (or other document root) writable by that group. In addition, if you make the directory hierarchy setgid (**chmod g+s** *filename*), all new files created in the hierarchy will belong to the group, making sharing files easy. See page 523 for information about working with groups.

JumpStart I: Getting Apache Up and Running

To get Apache up and running, you should modify the **/etc/httpd/conf/httpd.conf** configuration file. "Directives I: Directives You May Want to Modify As You Get Started" on page 768 explains more about this file and explores other changes you may want to make to it.

Modifying the httpd.conf Configuration File

Apache runs as installed, but it is best if you add the two lines described in this section to the **/etc/httpd/conf/httpd.conf** configuration file before starting Apache. If you do not add these lines, Apache assigns values that may not work for you.

The ServerName line establishes a name for the server; add one of the following lines to **httpd.conf** to set the name of the server to the domain name of the server or, if you do not have a domain name, to the IP address of the server:

> *ServerName example.com*

or

> *ServerName IP_address*

where *example.com* is the domain name of the server and *IP_address* is the IP address of the server. If you are not connected to a network, you can use the localhost address, 127.0.0.1, so you can start the server and experiment with it.

When a client has trouble getting information from a server, the server frequently displays an error page that says what the problem is. For example, when Apache cannot find a requested page, it displays a page that says **Error 404: Not Found**. Each error page has a link that the user can click on to send mail to the administrator of the server. ServerAdmin specifies the email address that the server displays on error pages. Add a ServerAdmin line to **httpd.conf** that follows this format:

> *ServerAdmin email_address*

where *email_address* is the email address of the person who needs to know if people are having trouble using the server. Make sure that someone checks this email account frequently.

After making the changes to **httpd.conf**, start or restart **httpd** as explained on page 761.

Testing Apache

Once you start the **httpd** daemon, you can check that Apache is working by pointing a browser on the local system to **http://localhost/**. From a remote system, point a browser to **http://** followed by the ServerName you specified in **httpd.conf**. For example, you might use either of these URIs: **http://192.168.0.16** or **http://example.org**. The browser should display the Red Hat/Apache test page. This test page is actually an error page that says there is no content. For more information, refer to "Red Hat test page" on page 789.

If you are having problems getting Apache to work, see "Troubleshooting" on page 792.

Putting Your Content in Place

Place the content you want Apache to serve in **/var/www/html**. Apache automatically displays the file named **index.html** in this directory. Working as **root** (or as a member of the group [**webwork**] you set up for this purpose), give the following command to create such a page:

```
# cat > /var/www/html/index.html
<html><body><p>This is my test page.</p></body></html>
CONTROL-D
```

After creating this file, refresh the browser, if it is still running from testing, or start it again and point it at the server. The browser should display the page you just created.

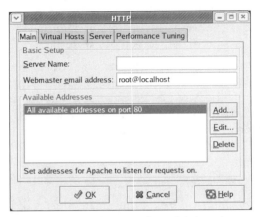

Figure 26-1   HTTP window, Main tab

JumpStart II: Setting Up Apache with system-config-httpd

You can use the system-config-httpd (*FEDORA*) and redhat-config-httpd (*RHEL*) utilities to display the HTTP window, which can help you set up Apache. The HTTP window has four tabs: Main, Virtual Hosts, Server, and Performance Tuning. The Virtual Hosts tab has buttons that open other, extensive windows. Each of the fields in these tabs/windows corresponds to a directive in the **/etc/httpd/conf/httpd.conf** file. This section discusses some of the basic directives you can change with [system|redhat]-config-httpd. For more information, click **Help** at the bottom of the HTTP window.

Main tab   The Main tab (Figure 26-1) allows you to establish an *FQDN* (page 972) as the name of the server (ServerName, page 769), an email address for the server administrator (ServerAdmin, page 769), and the ports and addresses that Apache listens for requests on (Listen, page 768). Highlight an entry in the Available Addresses subwindow, and click **Edit** to edit that entry or **Add** to add a new entry. Both actions bring up a window that allows you to specify a port and select whether you want to listen to all IP addresses on that port or listen to a specific address.

Default settings   The Virtual Hosts tab can establish default settings for Apache and set up virtual hosts (page 791). Click the **Virtual Hosts** tab, and then click **Edit Default Settings** to configure default values for the Apache server (Figure 26-2). The entries in the frame at the left of the window work like tabs: Click an entry, such as **Logging**, to display the corresponding selections on the right. You do not have to change most of the values in this window. When you are done making changes, click **OK** to close the window.

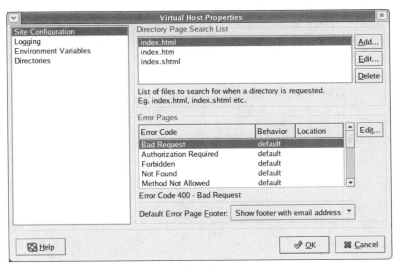

Figure 26-2   Establishing default values for Apache

Virtual Hosts   Click the **Virtual Hosts** tab, highlight an entry in the Virtual Hosts subwindow, and click either **Edit** to edit the entry or **Add** to add a new virtual host. Both actions bring up the Virtual Hosts Properties window for a specific virtual host (Figure 26-3). This window is similar to the one you used to establish default settings, except it pertains to a specific virtual host and has more entries in the frame at the left. You do not have to change most of the values in this window. Click **OK** when you are done making changes in this window.

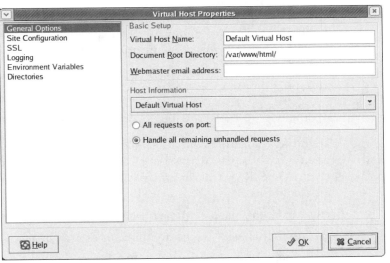

Figure 26-3   Virtual Hosts Properties window for a specific virtual host

Server tab   Usually, you do not need to change the values in this tab. You can specify the path-name of the lock file (LockFile directive), the PID file (PidFile directive), and the directory that Apache stores core dumps in (CoreDumpDirectory). The lower portion of the tab allows you to specify a user (User, page 785) and group (Group, page 783) that Apache runs as.

Performance Tuning tab   The selections in this tab control the maximum number of connections that Apache allows (MaxClients, page 776), the number of seconds after which a connection will disconnect (Timeout, page 778), the maximum number of requests Apache allows per connection (MaxRequestsPerChild, page 776), and whether to allow persistent connections (KeepAlive directive). Initially, the values in this tab do not need to be changed. Click **OK** when you are done making changes and restart httpd as discussed on page 761.

Filesystem Layout

This section tells you where you can find many of the files you may need to work with as you set up and modify an Apache server.

Binaries, scripts, and modules   The Apache server and related binary files are kept in several directories:

/usr/bin/httpd   The Apache server (daemon)

/usr/sbin/apachectl   Starts and stops Apache, the **httpd** init script that service executes calls apachectl.

/usr/bin/htpasswd   Creates and maintains password files used by the Apache authentication module (page 797).

/usr/bin/rotatelogs   Rotates Apache log files so the files do not get too large. See logrotate (page 543) for more information about rotating log files.

/etc/httpd/modules   Module binaries, including **mod_perl.so** and **mod_python.so** are kept in this directory (a symbolic link to **/usr/lib/httpd/modules**, page 793).

Configuration files   Apache configuration files are kept in the **/etc/httpd/conf** directory and in the **/etc/httpd/conf.d** directory hierarchy:

/etc/httpd/conf/httpd.conf   The main Apache configuration file; contains configuration directives. The discussion of configuration directives starts on page 767. Refer to "The Red Hat httpd.conf File" on page 788 for a description of the **httpd.conf** file.

/etc/httpd/conf/magic   Mime file type identification; generally not changed.

/etc/httpd/conf/ssl.*   Files and directories used by **mod_ssl** (page 795).

/etc/httpd/conf.d   Configuration files for modules including **php** and **mod_perl**.

Logs   Logs are kept in **/var/log/httpd** (there is a symbolic link at **/etc/httpd/logs**):

/var/log/httpd/access_log   Requests made to the server.

/var/log/httpd/error_log   Request and run-time server errors.

/var/log/httpd/ssl_*_log   Logs for **mod_ssl**.

Web documents   Web documents, including the Web pages displayed by client browsers, custom error messages, and CGI scripts are kept in **/var/www** by default:

/var/www/cgi-bin   CGI scripts (page 794).

/var/www/error   Multilanguage default error documents. You can modify these documents to conform to the style of your Web site: See ErrorDocument (page 780).

/var/www/icons   Icons used to display directory entries.

/var/www/manual   *FEDORA* The Apache *Reference Manual* and *Users' Guide*. On Fedora, present only if you installed the **httpd-manual** package.

Document root   By default, the document root (page 762) is **/var/www/html**. You can change this location with the DocumentRoot directive (page 770). In addition to content for the Web pages Apache serves, this directory can house the **usage** directory, which holds webalizer (page 799) output.

.htaccess files   A **.htaccess** file contains configuration directives and can appear in any directory in the document root hierarchy. The location of a **.htaccess** file is critical: The directives in a **.htaccess** file apply to all files in the hierarchy rooted at the directory that holds the **.htaccess** file. You must use the AllowOverride directive (page 786) to cause Apache to examine **.htaccess** files. Clients cannot read **.htaccess** files; based on the Red Hat **httpd.conf** file, Apache does not answer requests for files whose names start with **.ht**.

Configuration Directives

Configuration directives, or simply *directives*, are lines in a configuration file that control some aspect of how Apache functions. A configuration directive is composed of a keyword followed by one or more arguments (values) separated by SPACEs. For example, the following configuration directive sets **Timeout** to 300 (seconds):

```
Timeout 300
```

You must enclose arguments that contain SPACEs within double quotation marks. Keywords are not case-sensitive, but arguments (pathnames, filenames, and so on) often are.

httpd.conf   The most important file that holds Apache configuration directives is, by default, **/etc/httpd/conf/httpd.conf**. This file holds global directives that affect all content served by Apache. An Include directive (page 783) within **httpd.conf** can incorporate the contents of another file as though it was part of **httpd.conf**.

.htaccess   Local directives can appear in **.htaccess** files (page 767). A **.htaccess** file can appear in any directory within the document root hierarchy and affects files in the directory hierarchy rooted at the directory the **.htaccess** file appears in.

Pathnames   When you specify an absolute pathname in a configuration directive, the directive uses that pathname without modifying it. When you specify a relative pathname, including a simple filename or the name of a directory, Apache prepends to the name the value specified by the ServerRoot (page 782) directive (**/etc/httpd** by default).

Directives I: Directives You May Want to Modify As You Get Started

When it starts, Apache reads the **/etc/httpd/conf/httpd.conf** configuration file (by default) for instructions governing every aspect of how Apache runs and delivers content. The **httpd.conf** file shipped by Red Hat is over a thousand lines long. This section details some of the lines in this file you may want to change as you are getting started with Apache. You can use each of the following directives in **httpd.conf**; the Context line in each explanation shows which other files the directives can appear in. Context is explained on page 772. The section titled "Directives II" on page 776 describes more directives.

Listen   *Specifies the port(s) that Apache listens for requests on.*

Listen [IP-address:]portnumber

where **IP-address** is the IP address that Apache listens on, and **portnumber** is the number of the port that Apache listens on for the given **IP-address**. When **IP-address** is absent, or set to 0.0.0.0, Apache listens on all network interfaces.

There must be at least one Listen directive in **httpd.conf** or Apache will not work. The following minimal directive from the Fedora **httpd.conf** file listens for requests on all interfaces on port 80:

```
Listen 80
```

Red Hat Enterprise Linux uses the following Listen directive, which is equivalent to the preceding one, in its **httpd.conf** file:

```
Listen 0.0.0.0:80
```

The next directive changes the port from the default value of 80 to 8080:

```
Listen 8080
```

When you specify a port other than 80, each request to the server must include a port number (as in **www.example.org:8080**), or the kernel will return a **Connection Refused** message. Use multiple Listen directives to cause Apache to listen on multiple IP addresses and ports. For example,

```
Listen 80
Listen 192.168.1.1:8080
Listen 192.168.1.2:443
```

accepts connections on all network interfaces on port 80, on 192.168.1.1 on port 8080, and on 192.168.1.2 on port 443.

Context: server config
Default: none (Apache will not start without this directive)
Red Hat: Listen 0.0.0.0:80

ServerAdmin   *Sets the email address displayed on error pages.*

ServerAdmin **email-address**

where **email-address** is the email address of the person responsible for Web content. This address appears on Apache-generated error pages, except in Fedora Core 2, where Red Hat has removed email addresses from error pages. Make sure **email-address** points to an email account that someone checks frequently. Users can use this address to get help with the Web site or to inform the administrator of errors. There is no default value for ServerAdmin; if you do not use this directive, the value is undefined and no email address appears on error pages.

Red Hat provides the following ServerAdmin template in its **httpd.conf** file:

```
#    ServerAdmin webmaster@dummy-host.example.com
```

Copy this line, remove the #, and substitute the email address of the person responsible for Web content in place of **webmaster@dummy-host.example.com**. Because **webmaster** is a common name, you can use **webmaster** at your domain and use the **/etc/aliases** file (page 614) to forward mail that is sent to **webmaster** to the person responsible for maintaining the Web site.

Contexts: server config, virtual host
Default: none
Red Hat: none

ServerName   *Specifies the server's name and the port it listens on.*

ServerName **FQDN** [:**port**]

where **FQDN** is the fully qualified domain name or IP address of the server and **port** is the optional port number Apache listens on. The domain name of the server must be able to be resolved by DNS and may be different from the hostname of the system running the server. If you do not specify a ServerName, Apache performs a DNS reverse name resolution (page 708) on the IP address of the system and assigns that value to ServerName. If the reverse lookup fails, Apache assigns the IP address of the system to ServerName.

Red Hat provides the following ServerName template in its **httpd.conf** file:

```
#    ServerName dummy-host.example.com
```

Copy this line, remove the #, and substitute the FQDN or IP address of the server in place of **dummy-host.example.com**. Append to this name or number a colon and the port number Apache listens on if you are using other than port 80.

The ports specified by ServerName and Listen (page 768) must be the same if you want the FQDN specified by ServerName tied to the IP address specified by Listen.

Apache uses ServerName to construct a URI when it redirects a client (page 790).

Context: server config, virtual host
Default: none
Red Hat: none

DocumentRoot *Points to the root of the directory hierarchy that holds the server's content.*

DocumentRoot **dirname**

where **dirname** is the absolute pathname of the directory at the root of the directory hierarchy that holds the content Apache serves. Do not use a trailing slash. You can put the document root wherever you like, as long as the user **apache** has read access to the ordinary files and execute access to the directory files in the directory hierarchy. The FHS (page 167) specifies **/srv** as the top-level directory for this purpose. The following directive puts the document root at **/home/www**:

```
DocumentRoot /home/www
```

Context: server config, virtual host
Default: **/usr/local/apache/htdocs**
Red Hat: **/var/www/html**

UserDir *Allows users to publish content from their home directories*

UserDir **dirname** | *disabled* | *enabled* **user-list**

where **dirname** is the name of a directory which, if it appears in a local user's home directory, Apache publishes to the Web. The *disabled* keyword prevents content from being published from users' home directories, and *enabled* causes content to be published from the home directories of users specified in the SPACE separated **user-list**. When you do not specify a directory, Apache publishes to **~/public_html**.

Apache combines the effects of multiple UserDir directives. Assume the following directives:

```
UserDir disabled
UserDir enabled user1 user2 user3
UserDir web
```

The first of the preceding directives turns off user publishing for all users. The second directive enables user publishing for three users. The third directive makes **web** the name of the directory which, if it appears in one of the specified users' home directories, Apache publishes to the Web.

To cause a browser to display the content published by a user, specify in the Location bar the name of the Web site followed by a **/~** and the user's username. For example, if Sam published content in the **public_html** directory in his home directory and the URI of the Web site was **www.example.com**, you would enter http://www.example.com/~sam to display his Web page. To display a user's Web page, Apache must have execute permission (as user **apache**) to the user's home directory and the directory holding the content, and read permission to the content files.

Red Hat provides the following ServerName directive and template in its **httpd.conf** file:

```
UserDir disable
#UserDir public_html
```

Put a pound sign (#) in front of the first line and remove the pound sign from the second line to allow users to publish content from directories named **public_html** in their home directories.

Context: server config, virtual host
Default: public_html
Red Hat: disabled

DirectoryIndex   *Specifies which file to display when a user asks for a directory.*

DirectoryIndex filename [filename ...]

where *filename* is the name of the file that Apache serves.

This directive specifies a list of filenames. When a client requests a directory, Apache attempts to find a file in the specified directory whose name matches that of a file in the list. When Apache finds a match, it returns that file. When this directive is absent or when none of the files specified by this directive exists in the specified directory, Apache displays a directory listing as specified by the IndexOptions directive (page 780).

Red Hat provides the following DirectoryIndex directive in its **httpd.conf** file:

```
DirectoryIndex index.html index.html.var
```

This directive causes Apache to return from the specified directory the file named **index.html** and, if that file does not exist, the file named **index.html.var**.

The **index.html** is the name of the standard, default HTML document. If you supply PHP or CGI documents, you may want to add the **index.php** or **index.cgi** values to this directive. The name **index** is standard but arbitrary.

The **.var** filename extension denotes a content-negotiated document that allows Apache to serve the Apache manual and other documents in one of several languages as specified by the client. If you are not using the local copy of the Apache manual and do not provide content in different languages, you can remove **index.html.var** from this directive.

Context: server config, virtual host
Default: index.html
Red Hat: index.html index.html.var

Contexts and Containers

To make it flexible and easy to customize, Apache uses configuration directives, contexts, and containers. Configuration directives are covered starting on page 767. This section discusses contexts and containers, which are critical to managing an Apache server.

Contexts

There are four locations, called *contexts,* that define where a configuration directive can appear. This chapter marks each configuration directive to indicate which context(s) it can appear in. Table 26-1 lists the contexts with a description of each.

table 26-1 || Contexts

Context	Location(s) Directives Can Appear In
server config	Directive can appear in the **httpd.conf** file only, but not inside <VirtualHost> or <Directory> containers (next section) unless so marked.
virtual host	Directive can appear inside <VirtualHost> containers in the **httpd.conf** file only.
directory	Directive can appear inside <Directory>, <Location>, and <Files> containers in the **httpd.conf** file only.
.htaccess	Directive can appear in **.htaccess** files (page 767) only.

Directives in files incorporated by means of the Include directive (page 783) are part of the context they are included in and must be allowed in that context.

Putting a directive in the wrong context generates a configuration error and can cause Apache to serve content incorrectly or not start.

Containers

Containers, or *special directives,* are directives that group other directives. Containers are delimited by XML-style tags. Three examples are shown following:

```
<Directory> ... </Directory>
<Location> ... </Location>
<VirtualHost> ... </VirtualHost>
```

Look in **httpd.conf** for examples of containers. Containers are limited, just as other directives, to use within specified contexts. This section describes some of the more frequently used containers.

<Directory>   *Applies directives to directories within specified directory hierarchies.*

*<Directory **directory**> ... </Directory>*

where *directory* is an absolute pathname specifying the root of the directory hierarchy that holds the directories the directives in the container apply to. The ***directory*** can include wildcards; a * does not match a /.

A <Directory> container provides the same functionality as a .htaccess file. While an administrator can use a <Directory> container in the **httpd.conf** file, regular users cannot. Regular users can use .htaccess files to control access to their own directories.

The directives in the following <Directory> container apply to the **/var/www/html/corp** directory hierarchy: The Deny directive denies access to all clients, the Allow directive grants clients from the 192.168.10. subnet access, and the AllowOverride directive (page 786) enables the use of .htaccess files in the hierarchy:

```
<Directory /var/www/html/corp>
    Deny from all
    Allow from 192.168.10.
    AllowOverride All
</Directory>
```

Contexts: server config, virtual host

<Files> *Applies directives to specified ordinary files.*

*<Files **directory**> ... </Files>*

where ***directory*** is an absolute pathname specifying the root of the directory hierarchy that holds the ordinary files the directives in the container apply to. The ***directory*** can include wildcards; a * does not match a /. This container is similar to <directory> but applies to ordinary files and not to directories.

The following directive, from the Red Hat **httpd.conf** file, denies access to all files whose filenames start with **.ht**. The tilde (~) changes how Apache interprets the following string. Without a tilde, the string is a simple shell match that interprets shell special characters (page 207). With a tilde, Apache interprets the string as a regular expression (page 903):

```
<Files ~ "^\.ht">
    Order allow,deny
    Deny from all
</Files>
```

Contexts: server config, virtual host, directory, .htaccess

<IfModule> *Applies directives if a specified module is loaded.*

*<IfModule [!]**module-name**> ... </IfModule>*

where ***module-name*** is the name of the module (page 793) that is tested for. Apache executes the directives in this container if ***module-name*** is loaded or, with !, if ***module-name*** is *not* loaded.

Apache will not start if you specify a configuration directive that is specific to a module that is not loaded.

The following <IfModule> container from the Red Hat **httpd.conf** file depends on the **mod_mime_magic.c** module being loaded. If the module is loaded, Apache runs the MIMEMagicFile directive, which tells the **mod_mime_magic.c** module where its hints file is located.

```
<IfModule mod_mime_magic.c>
    MIMEMagicFile conf/magic
</IfModule>
```

See page 788 for another example of the <IfModule> container.

Contexts: server config, virtual host, directory, .htaccess

<Limit>   *Limits access control directives to specified HTTP methods.*

*<Limit **method** [**method**] ... > ... </Limit>*

where ***method*** is an HTTP method. An HTTP method specifies what action is to be performed on a URI. The most frequently used methods are GET, POST, and PUT and are case-sensitive. GET is the default method; it sends any data indicated by the URI. PUT stores data from the body section of the communication at the specified URI. POST creates a new document containing the body of the request at the specified URI.

This container binds a group of access-control directives to specified HTTP methods: Only methods named by the <Limit> container are affected by this group of directives.

The following example disables HTTP uploads (PUTs) from systems not in a subdomain of **example.com**:

```
<Limit PUT>
order deny,allow
deny from all
allow from .example.com
</Limit>
```

caution ‖   **Use <LimitExcept> in Place of <Limit>**

It is safer to use the <LimitExcept> container in place of the <Limit> container, as it protects against arbitrary methods. When you use <Limit>, you must be careful to name explicitly all possible methods that the group of directives could affect.

It is safer still not to put access control directives in any container.

Contexts: server config, virtual host, directory, .htaccess

<LimitExcept>   *Limits access control directives to all but specified HTTP methods.*

*<LimitExcept **method** [**method**] ... > ... </LimitExcept>*

where ***method*** is an HTTP method. See <Limit> for a discussion of methods.

This container causes a group of access control directives *not* to be bound to specified HTTP methods: Methods *not* named in <LimitExcept> are affected by this group of directives.

The access control directives within the following <LimitExcept> container affect HTTP methods other than GET and POST. You could put this container in a <Directory> container to limit its scope:

```
<LimitExcept GET POST>
        Order deny,allow
        Deny from all
    </LimitExcept>
```

Contexts: server config, virtual host, directory, .htaccess

<Location> *Applies directives to specified URIs*

<Location URI | URI> ... </Location>

where *URI* is a URI that points to content and specifies a file or the root of the directory hierarchy that the directives in the container apply to. While the <Directory> container points within the local filesystem, <Location> points outside the local file system. The *URI* can include wildcards; a * does not match a /.

The following <Location> container limits access to **http://*server*/pop**, where ***server*** is the FQDN of the server, to clients from the **example.net** domain:

```
<Location /pop>
    Order deny,allow
    Deny from all
    Allow from .example.net
</Location>
```

Contexts: server config, virtual host

caution ‖   **Use <Location> with Care**

Use this powerful container with care. Do not use it in place of the <Directory> container: When several URIs point to the same location in a filesystem, a client may be able to circumvent the desired access control by using a URI not specified by this container.

<LocationMatch> *Applies directives to matched URIs.*

<LocationMatch regexp> ... </LocationMatch>

where *regexp* is a regular expression that matches one or more URIs. This container works the same way as <Location>, except it applies to any URIs that *regexp* matches:

```
# Disable autoindex for the root directory and present a
# default welcome page if no other index page is present.
#
<LocationMatch "^/$">
Options -Indexes
ErrorDocument 403 /error/noindex.html
</LocationMatch>
```

Contexts: server config, virtual host

<VirtualHost>   *Applies directives to a specified virtual host.*

*<VirtualHost **addr[:port]** [addr[:port]] ... > ... </VirtualHost>*

where **addr** is an FQDN or IP address of the virtual host and **port** is the port that Apache listens on for the virtual host. This container holds commands that Apache applies to a virtual host. For an example and more information, refer to "Virtual-Hosts" on page 791.

Context: server config

Directives II

This section discusses configuration directives that you may want to use after you have gained some experience with Apache.

Directives That Control Processes

MaxClients   *Specifies the maximum number of child processes.*

*MaxClients **num***

where **num** is the maximum number of child processes (servers) Apache runs at one time, including idle processes and those serving requests. When Apache is running **num** processes and there are no idle processes, Apache issues **server too busy** errors to new connections; it does not start new child processes. A value of 150 is usually sufficient, even for moderately busy sites.

Context: server config
Default: 256
Red Hat: 150

MaxRequestsPerChild

Specifies the maximum number of requests a child process can serve.

*MaxRequestsPerChild **num***

where **num** is the maximum number of requests a child process (server) can serve during its lifetime. After a child process serves **num** requests, it does not process any more requests but dies after it finishes processing its current requests. At this point additional requests are processed by other processes from the server pool.

Set **num** to 0 so as not to set a limit on the number of requests a child can process, except for the effects of MinSpareServers. By limiting the life of processes, this directive can prevent memory leaks from consuming too much system memory. However, setting MaxRequestsPerChild to a small value can hurt performance by causing Apache to create new child servers constantly.

Context: server config
Default: 10000
Red Hat: 1000

MaxSpareServers *Specifies the maximum number of idle processes.*

MaxSpareServers **num**

where **num** is the maximum number of idle processes (servers) Apache keeps running to serve requests as they come in. Do not set this number too high as each process consumes system resources.

Context: server config
Default: 10
Red Hat: 20

MinSpareServers *Specifies the minimum number of idle processes.*

MinSpareServers **num**

where **num** is the minimum number of idle processes (servers) Apache keeps running to serve requests as they come in. More idle processes occupy more computer resources; increase this value for busy sites only.

Context: server config
Default: 5
Red Hat: 5

StartServers *Specifies the number of child processes that Apache starts with.*

StartServers **num**

where **num** is the number of child processes, or servers, that Apache starts when it is brought up. This value is significant only when Apache starts; MinSpareServers and MaxSpareServers control the number of idle processes once Apache is up and running. Starting Apache with multiple servers ensures a pool of servers waiting to serve requests immediately.

Context: server config
Default: 5
Red Hat: 8

Networking Directives

HostnameLookups *Specifies whether Apache puts a client's hostname or IP address in its logs.*

HostnameLookups On | Off | Double

where

On: Performs DNS reverse name resolution (page 708) to determine the hostname of each client for logging.

Off: Logs each client's IP address.

Double: For security, performs DNS reverse name resolution (page 708) to determine the hostname of each client, performs a forward DNS lookup to verify the original IP address, and logs the hostname.

Contexts: server config, virtual host, directory
Default: Off
Red Hat: Off

tip || **Lookups Can Consume a Lot of System Resources**

Use the **On** and **Double** options with caution as they can consume a lot of resources on a busy system. You can use a program such as logresolve to perform reverse name resolution offline for statistical purposes.

If you perform host name resolution offline, you run the risk that the name has changed; you usually want the name that was current at the time of the request. To minimize this problem, perform the host name resolution as soon as possible after writing the log.

Timeout   *Specifies the time Apache waits for network operations to complete.*

Timeout **num**

where **num** is the number of seconds that Apache waits for network operations to complete. You can usually set this directive to a lower value; five minutes is a long time to wait on a busy server. The Apache documentation says that the default is not lower, "...because there may still be odd places in the code where the timer is not reset when a packet is sent."

Context: server config
Default: 300
Red Hat: 300

UseCannonicalName

Specifies the method the server uses to identify itself

UseCannonicalName On | Off | DNS

On: Apache uses the value of the ServerName directive (page 769) as its identity.

Off: Apache uses the name and port from the incoming request as its identity.

DNS: Apache performs a DNS reverse name resolution (page 708) on the IP address from the incoming request and uses the result as its identity. Rarely used.

This directive is important when a server has more than one name and needs to perform a redirect. Red Hat sets this directive to OFF because the ServerName directive (page 769) is commented out. Once you set ServerName, change UseCannonicalName to ON. See page 790 for a discussion of redirects and this directive.

Contexts: server config, virtual host, directory
Default: ON
Red Hat: OFF

Logging Directives

ErrorLog   *Specifies where Apache sends error messages.*

ErrorLog **filename** *| syslog[:facility]*

where

filename: Specifies the name of the file, relative to ServerRoot (page 782), that Apache sends error messages to.

syslog: Specifies that Apache send errors to **syslogd** (page 546).

facility: Specifies which **syslogd** facility to use. The default facility is **local7**.

Contexts: server config, virtual host
Default **logs/error_log**
Red Hat **logs/error_log**

LogLevel *Specifies the level of error messages that Apache logs.*

*LogLevel **level***

where **level** specifies that Apache logs errors of that level and higher (more urgent). Choose **level** from the following list, which is in order of decreasing urgency and increasing verbosity:

emerg   System unusable messages
alert   Need for immediate action messages
crit   Critical condition messages
error   Error condition messages
warn   Nonfatal warning messages
notice   Normal but significant messages
info   Operational messages and recommendations
debug   Messages for finding and solving problems

Contexts: server config, virtual host
Default: warn
Red Hat: warn

Directives That Control Content

AddHandler *Creates a mapping between filename extensions and a builtin Apache handler.*

*AddHandler **handler extension** [**extension**] ...*

where **handler** is the name of a builtin handler and **extension** is a filename extension that maps to the **handler**. Handlers are actions that are built into Apache and are directly related to loaded modules. Apache uses a handler when a client requests a file with a specified filename extension.

For example, the following AddHandler directive causes Apache to process files that have a filename extension of **.cgi** with the **cgi-script** handler:

```
AddHandler cgi-script .cgi
```

Contexts: Server config, virtual host, directory, htaccess
Default: none
Red Hat: imap-file map, type-map var

Alias   *Maps a URI to a directory or file.*

*Alias **alias pathname***

where **alias** must match part of the URI that the client requested in order to invoke the alias and **pathname** is the absolute pathname of the target of the alias, usually a directory.

For example, the following alias in **httpd.conf** causes Apache to serve **/usr/local/pix/milk.jpg** when a client requests **http://www.example.com/pix/milk.jpg**:

```
Alias /pix /usr/local/pix
```

In some cases, you need to use a <Directory> container (page 772) to grant access to aliased content.

Contexts: server config, virtual host
Default: None
Red Hat (provides two aliases, one for **/icons/** and one for **/error/**)

ErrorDocument   *Specifies the action Apache takes when the specified error occurs.*

*ErrorDocument **code action***

where **code** is the error code (page 799) that this directive defines a response for and **action** is one of the following:

string: Defines the message that Apache returns to the client.

absolute pathname: Points to a local script or other content that Apache redirects the client to.

URI: Points to an external script or other content that Apache redirects the client to.

When you do not specify this directive for a given error code, Apache returns a hard-coded error message when that error occurs. See (page 789) for an explanation of how an ErrorDocument directive returns the Red Hat test page when the system is first installed.

Some examples of ErrorDocument directives follow:

```
ErrorDocument 403 "Sorry, access is forbidden."
ErrorDocument 403 /cgi-bin/uh-uh.pl
ErrorDocument 403 http://errors.example.com/not_allowed.html
```

Contexts: server config, virtual host, directory, .htaccess
Default: none: Apache returns hard-coded error messages.
Red Hat: 403 /error/noindex.html; refer to "Red Hat test page" on page 789.

IndexOptions   Specifies how Apache displays directory listings.

IndexOptions [±]option [[±]option] ...

where **option** can be any combination of the following:

DescriptionWidth=*n*: Sets the width of the description column to *n* characters. Use * in place of *n* to accommodate the widest description.

FancyIndexing: In directory listings, displays column headers that are links. When you click one of these links, Apache sorts the display based on the content of the column. Clicking a second time reverses the order.

FoldersFirst: Sorts the listing so that directories come before plain files. Use only with FancyIndexing.

IconsAreLinks: Makes the icons clickable. Use only with FancyIndexing.

IconHeight=n: Sets the height of icons to n pixels. Use only with IconWidth.

IconWidth: Sets the width of icons to n pixels. Use only with IconHeight.

IgnoreCase: Ignores case when sorting names.

IgnoreClient: Ignores options the client supplied in the URI.

NameWidth=n: Sets the width of the filename column to n characters. Use * in place of n to accommodate the widest filename.

ScanHTMLTitles: Extracts and displays titles from HTML documents. Use only with FancyIndexing. Not normally used because it is CPU and disk intensive.

SuppressColumnSorting: Suppresses clickable column headings that can be used for sorting columns. Use only with FancyIndexing.

SuppressDescription: Suppresses file descriptions. Use only with FancyIndexing.

SuppressHTMLPreamble: Suppresses the contents of the file specified by the HeaderName directive, even if that file exists.

SuppressIcon: Suppresses icons. Use only with FancyIndexing.

SuppressLastModified: Suppresses the modification date. Use only with FancyIndexing.

SuppressRules: Suppresses horizontal lines. Use only with FancyIndexing.

SuppressSize: Suppresses file sizes. Use only with FancyIndexing.

VersionSort: Sorts version numbers (in filenames) in a natural way; character strings, except for substrings of digits, are not affected.

When a client requests a URI that points to a directory (such as **http://www.example.com/support/**) and none of the files specified by the DirectoryIndex directive (page 771) is present in that directory and, if the directory hierarchy is controlled by a **.htaccess** file, AllowOverride (page 786) has been set to allow indexing, then Apache displays a directory listing according to the options specified by this directive.

When this directive appears more than once within a directory, Apache merges the options from the directives. Use + and – to merge options with options from higher-level directories. (Unless you use + or – with all options, Apache discards any options set in higher-level directories.) For example, the following directives and containers set the options for **/custsup/download** to VersionSort; Apache discards

FancyIndexing and IgnoreCase in the **download** directory because there is no **+** or **−** before VersionSort in the second <Directory> container.

```
<Directory /custsup>
    IndexOptions FancyIndexing
    IndexOptions IgnoreCase
</Directory

<Directory /custsup/download>
    IndexOptions VersionSort
</Directory>
```

Because of the **+** before VersionSort, the next directives and containers set the options for **/custsup/download** to FancyIndexing, IgnoreCase, and VersionSort.

```
<Directory /custsup>
    IndexOptions FancyIndexing
    IndexOptions IgnoreCase
</Directory

<Directory /custsup/download>
    IndexOptions +VersionSort
</Directory>
```

Contexts: server config, virtual host, directory, .htaccess
Default: None. Lists only filenames.
Red Hat: FancyIndexing VersionSort NameWidth=*

ServerRoot   *Specifies the root directory for server files (not content).*

ServerRoot **directory**

where **directory** specifies the pathname of the root directory for files that make up the server; Apache prepends **directory** to relative pathnames in **httpd.conf**. This directive does not specify the location of the content that Apache serves; the DocumentRoot directive (page 770) performs that function. Do not change this value unless you move the server files.

Context: server config
Default: /usr/local/apache
Red Hat: /etc/httpd

ServerTokens   *Specifies the server information that Apache returns to a client.*

ServerTokens Prod | Major | Minor | Min | OS | Full

Prod: Returns the product name (**Apache**). Also *ProductOnly*.

Major: Returns the major release number of the server (**Apache/2**).

Minor: Returns the major and minor release numbers of the server (**Apache/2.0**).

Minimal: Returns complete version (**Apache/2.0.40**). Also *Min*.

OS: Returns the name of the operating system and the complete version (**Apache/2.0.40 (Red Hat Linux)**). Provides less information that might help a malicious user then *Full* does.

Full: Same as *OS,* plus sends the names and versions of non-Apache group modules (**Apache/2.0.40 (Red Hat Linux) PHP/4.2.2**).

Unless there is a reason you want to let clients know the details of the software you are running, set ServerTokens to reveal as little as possible.

Contexts: server config
Default: Full
Red Hat: OS

ServerSignature *Adds a line to server generated pages.*

ServerSignature On | Off | EMail

On: Turns the signature line on. The signature line contains the server version as specified by the ServerTokens directive (page 782) and the name specified by the <VirtualHost> container (page 776).

Off: Turns the signature line off.

EMail: To the signature line, adds a **mailto:** link to the server email address. This option produces output that can attract spam.

Contexts: server config, virtual host, directory, .htaccess
Default: Off
Red Hat: On

Configuration Directives

Group *Sets the GID of the processes that run the servers.*

Group #grouprid | groupname

where *groupid* is a GID value, preceded by a **#**, and *groupname* is the name of a group. The processes (servers) that Apache spawns are run as the group specified by this directive. See the User directive (page 785) for more information.

Context: server config
Red Hat: apache
Default: #–1

Include *Loads directives from files.*

Include filename | directory

where *filename* is the relative pathname of a file that contains directives. Apache prepends ServerRoot (page 782) to *filename.* The directives in *filename* are included in the file holding this directive at the location of the directive. Because *filename* can include wildcards, it can specify more than one file.

And where *directory* is the relative pathname that specifies the root of a directory hierarchy that holds files containing directives. Apache prepends ServerRoot to *directory.* The directives in ordinary files in this hierarchy are included in the file holding this directive at the location of the directive. The *directory* can include wildcards.

When you install Apache and its modules, rpm puts configuration files, which have a filename extension of **conf**, in the **conf.d** directory within the ServerRoot directory. The Include directive in the Red Hat **httpd.conf** file incorporates module configuration files for whichever modules are installed.

Contexts: server config, virtual host, directory
Default: None.
Red Hat: **conf.d/*.conf**

LoadModule   *Loads a module.*

LoadModule **module filename**

where **module** is the name of an external DSO module and **filename** is the relative pathname of the named module. Apache prepends ServerRoot (page 782) to **filename**. Apache loads the external module specified by this directive. For more information, refer to "Modules" on page 793.

Context: server config
Default: None. Nothing is loaded by default if omitted.
Red Hat: Loads over 40 modules, refer to **httpd.conf** for the list.

Options   *Controls server features by directory.*

*Options [±]**option** [[±]**option** ...]*

This directive controls which server features are enabled for a directory hierarchy. The directory hierarchy is specified by the container this directive appears in. A + or the absence of a – turns an option on and a – turns it off.

where **option** is one of the following:

None   None of the features this directive can control are enabled.

All   All of the features this directive can control are enabled, except for MultiViews, which you must explicitly enable.

ExecCGI   Apache can execute CGI scripts (page 794).

FollowSymLinks   Apache follows symbolic links.

Includes   Permits SSIs (server side includes). SSIs are containers embedded in HTML pages and evaluated on the server before the content is passed to the client.

IncludesNOEXEC   The same as **Includes** but disables the **#exec** and **#exec cgi** commands that are part of SSIs. Does *not* prevent the **#include** command from referencing CGI scripts.

Indexes   Generates a directory listing if DirectoryIndex (page 771) is not set.

MultiViews   Allows multiviews (page 791).

SymLinksIfOwnerMatch   The same as FollowSymLinks but follows the link only if the file or directory being pointed to has the same owner as the link.

The following Options directive from the Red Hat **httpd.conf** file sets the Indexes and FollowSymLinks options and, because the <Directory> container specifies the **/var/www/html** directory hierarchy (the document root), affects all content:

```
<Directory "/var/www/html">
    Options Indexes FollowSymLinks
...
    <Directory>
```

Contexts: directory
Default: All
Red Hat: None

ScriptAlias   *Maps a URI to a directory or file and declares the target a server (CGI) script.*

*ScriptAlias **alias pathname***

where ***alias*** must match part of the URI the client requested in order to invoke the ScriptAlias and ***pathname*** is the absolute pathname of the target of the alias, usually a directory. Similar to the Alias directive, this directive specifies the target is a CGI script (page 794).

The following ScriptAlias directive from the Red Hat **httpd.conf** file maps client requests that include **/cgi-bin/** to the **/var/www/cgi-bin** directory (and indicates that these requests will be treated as CGI requests):

```
ScriptAlias /cgi-bin/ "/var/www/cgi-bin/"
```

Contexts: server config, virtual host
Default: None
Red Hat: /cgi-bin/ "/var/www/cgi-bin"

User   *Sets the UID of the processes that run the servers.*

*User #**userid** | **username***

where ***userid*** is a UID value, preceded by a **#**, and ***username*** is the name of a local user. The processes (servers) that Apache spawns are run as the user specified by this directive.

Apache must start as **root** in order to listen on a privileged port. For reasons of security, Apache's child processes (servers) run as nonprivileged users. The default UID of −1 does not map to a user under Red Hat. Instead, Red Hat's **httpd** rpm creates a user named **apache** during installation and sets User to that user.

security ‖   **Do Not Set User to root or 0**

For a more secure system, do not set User to **root** or **0** (zero) and do not allow the Apache user to have write access to the DocumentRoot directory hierarchy (except as needed for storing data), especially not to configuration files.

Context: server config
Red Hat: apache
Default: #−1

Security Directives

Allow   *Specifies which clients can access specified content.*

*Allow from All | **host** [**host** ...] | env=var [env=var ...]*

This directive, which must be written as **Allow from**, grants to specified clients access to a directory hierarchy. The directory hierarchy is specified by the container or **.htaccess** file this directive appears in.

All: Serves content to any client.

host: Serves content to the client(s) specified by ***host,*** which can take several forms: ***host*** can be an FQDN, a partial domain name (such as **example.com**), an IP address, a partial IP address, or a network/netmask pair.

var: Serves content when the environment variable named ***var*** is set. You can set a variable with the SetEnvIf directive. See the Order directive for an example.

Contexts: directory, .htaccess
Default: none; default behavior depends on the Order directive
Red Hat: All

AllowOverride   *Specifies the classes of directives that are allowed in* **.htaccess** *files.*

*AllowOverride All | None | **directive-class** [**directive-class** ...]*

This directive specifies whether Apache reads **.htaccess** files in the directory hierarchy specified by its container. If Apache does read **.htaccess** files, this directive specifies which kinds of directives are valid within **.htaccess** files.

None: Ignores **.htaccess** files.

All: Allows all classes of directives in **.htaccess** files.

where ***directive-class*** is one of the following directive class identifiers:

AuthConfig: Class of directives that control authorization (AuthName, AuthType, Require, and so on). This class is used mostly in **.htaccess** files when requiring a username and password to access the content. For more information, refer to "Authentication Modules and .htaccess" on page 797.

FileInfo: Class of directives that controls document types (DefaultType, ErrorDocument, SetHandler, and so on).

Indexes: Class of directives relating to directory indexing (DirectoryIndex, FancyIndexing, IndexOptions, and so on).

Limit: Class of client access directives (Allow, Deny, and Order).

Options: Class of directives controlling directory features.

Context: directory
Default: All
Red Hat: None

Deny   *Specifies which clients are not allowed to access specified content.*

Deny from All | host [host ...] | env=var [env=var ...]

This directive, which must be written as **Deny from,** denies to specified clients access to a directory hierarchy. The directory hierarchy is specified by the container or **.htaccess** file this directive appears in. See the Order directive for an example.

All: Denies content to all clients.

host: Denies content to the client(s) specified by *host*, which can take several forms: *host* can be an FQDN, a partial domain name (such as **example.com**), an IP address, a partial IP address, or a network/netmask pair.

var: Denies content when the environment variable named *var* is set. You can set a variable with the SetEnvIf directive.

Contexts: directory, .htaccess
Default: none
Red Hat: none

Order   *Specifies default access and the order Allow and Deny directives are evaluated in.*

Order Deny,Allow | Allow,Deny

Deny,Allow: Allows access by default: Denies access only to clients specified in Deny directives. (First evaluates Deny directives, then evaluates Allow directives.)

Allow,Deny: Denies access by default: Allows access only to clients specified in a Allow directives. (First evaluates Allow directives, then evaluates Deny directives.)

Access granted or denied by this directive applies to the directory hierarchy specified by the container or **.htaccess** file this directive appears in.

There must not be SPACEs on either side of the comma. Although Red Hat has a default of Allow,Deny, which denies access to all clients not specified by Allow directives, the next directive in **httpd.conf, Allow from all,** grants access to all clients:

```
Order allow,deny
Allow from all
```

You can restrict access by specifying Deny,Allow to deny all access and then specifying the clients you want to grant access to in an Allow directive. The following directives grant access to clients from the **example.net** domain only and would typically appear within a <Directory> container (page 772):

```
Order deny,allow
Deny from all
Allow from .example.net
```

Contexts: directory, .htaccess
Default: Deny,Allow
Red Hat: Allow,Deny

The Red Hat httpd.conf File

This section highlights some of the important features of the Red Hat **httpd.conf** file, which is based on the **httpd.conf** file distributed by Apache. This heavily commented file is broken into the following parts (as is this section):

1. **Global Environment:** Controls the overall functioning of the Apache server.

2. **Main Server Configuration:** Configures the default server (as opposed to virtual hosts) and provides default configuration information for virtual hosts.

3. **Virtual Hosts:** Configures virtual hosts. For more information, refer to "VirtualHosts" on page 791.

Section 1: Global Environment

ServerTokens   The ServerTokens directive (page 782) is set to **OS**, which causes Apache, when queried, to return the name of the operating system and the complete version number of Apache:

```
ServerTokens OS
```

ServerRoot   The ServerRoot directive (page 782) is set to **/etc/httpd**, which is the pathname that Apache prepends to relative pathnames in **httpd.conf**.

```
ServerRoot "/etc/httpd"
```

\<IfModule>   Multiprocessing Modules (MPMs) allow you to change the way Apache works by changing modules it uses. The <IfModule> containers (page 773) allow you to use the same **httpd.conf** file with different modules: The directives in an <IfModule> container are executed only if the specified module is loaded.

The section of **httpd.conf** that starts with the comment

```
## Server-Pool Size Regulation (MPM specific)
```

holds two <IfModule> containers (page 773) that configure Apache, depending on which module, **prefork** or **worker**, is loaded. Red Hat ships Apache with the **prefork** module loaded; this section does not discuss the <IfModule> container for the **worker** module.

The **prefork** <IfModule> container, shown following, holds directives that control the functioning of Apache when it starts and as it runs:

```
<IfModule prefork.c>
StartServers        8
MinSpareServers     5
MaxSpareServers    20
MaxClients        150
MaxRequestsPerChild  1000
</IfModule>
```

Listen   The Listen directive (page 768) does not specify an IP address (the 0.0.0.0 is the same as no IP address) and so Apache listens on all network interfaces:

```
Listen 80 FEDORA
Listen 0.0.0.0:80 RHEL
```

LoadModule   There are quite a few LoadModule directives (page 784); these directives load the Apache DSO modules (page 793).

Include   The Include directive (page 783) includes the files that match *.conf in the /etc/httpd/conf.d directory, as though they were part of httpd.conf:

```
Include conf.d/*.conf
```

Red Hat test page   When you first install Apache, there is no index.html file in /var/www/html; when you point a browser at the local Web server, Apache generates an error 403, which returns the Red Hat test page. The mechanism by which this page is returned is convoluted: The Red Hat httpd.conf file holds an Include directive that includes all files in the conf.d directory that is in the ServerRoot directory (page 782). The welcome.conf file in this directory has an ErrorDocument 403 directive (page 780) that redirects users who receive this error to error/noindex.html in the DocumentRoot directory (page 770). The noindex.html is the Red Hat test page that confirms the server is working but there is no content to display.

Section 2: Main Server Configuration

ServerAdmin   As shipped, the ServerAdmin and ServerName directives are commented out.
ServerName   Change them to useful values as suggested in ServerAdmin (page 769) and Server-Name (page 769).

DocumentRoot   The DocumentRoot directive (page 770) appears as follows:

```
DocumentRoot "/var/www/html"
```

You need to modify this directive only if you want to put your content somewhere other than /var/www/html.

<Directory>   The following <Directory> container (page 772) sets up restrictive environment for the entire local filesystem (specified by /):

```
<Directory />
    Options FollowSymLinks
    AllowOverride None
</Directory>
```

The preceding Options directive (page 784) allows Apache to follow symbolic links but disallows many options. The AllowOverride directive (page 786) causes Apache to ignore .htaccess files. You must explicitly enable less restrictive options if you want them, but doing so can expose the root filesystem and compromise the system.

Next, another <Directory> container sets up less restrictive options for the DocumentRoot (/var/www/html). The code in httpd.conf is interspersed with many comments. Without the comments it looks like this:

```
<Directory "/var/www/html">
    Options Indexes FollowSymLinks
    AllowOverride None
    Order allow,deny
    Allow from all
</Directory>
```

The Indexes option in the Options directive allows Apache to display directory listings. The Order (page 787) and Allow (page 786) directives combine to allow requests from all clients. This container is slightly less restrictive than the preceding one, although it still does not allow Apache to follow directives in **.htaccess** files.

DirectoryIndex As explained on page 771, the DirectoryIndex directive causes Apache to return the file named **index.html** from a requested directory and, if that file does not exist, to return **index.html.var**. Because Options Indexes is specified in the preceding <Directory> container, if neither of these files exists in a queried directory, Apache returns a directory listing:

```
DirectoryIndex index.html index.html.var
```

There are many more directives in this part of the **httpd.conf** file. The comments in the file provide a guide to what they do. There is nothing here you need to change as you get started using Apache.

Section 3: Virtual Hosts

All lines in this section are comments or commented out directives. If you want to set up virtual hosts, see page 791.

Redirects

Apache can respond to a request for a URI by asking the client to request a different URI. This response is called a *redirect*. A redirect works because redirection is part of the HTTP implementation: Apache sends the appropriate response code and the new URI, and a compliant browser requests the new location.

The Redirect directive can establish an explicit redirect that sends a client to a different page when a Web site is moved. Or, when a user enters the URI of a directory in a browser but leaves off the trailing slash, Apache automatically redirects the client to the same URI terminated with a slash.

UseCannonicalName The ServerName directive (page 769), which establishes the name of the server, and UseCannonicalName directive (page 778) are important when a server has more than one name and needs to perform an automatic redirect. For example, assume the server with the name **zach.example.com** and an alias of **www.example.com** has ServerName set to **www.example.com**. When a client specifies a URI of a directory but leaves off the trailing slash (**zach.example.com/dir**), Apache has to perform a redirect to determine the URI of the requested directory. When UseCannonicalName is set to ON, Apache uses the value of ServerName and returns **www.example.com/dir/**. With UseCannonicalName set to OFF, Apache uses the name from the incoming request and returns **zach.example.com/dir/**.

Multiviews

Multiviews is a way to represent a page in different ways, most commonly in different languages. Using request headers, a browser can request a specific language from a server. Servers that cannot handle these requests ignore them.

Multiviews is demonstrated by the Apache manual, which can be installed locally in **/var/www/manual**. When you point a browser to **http://*server*/manual/index.html**, the browser displays the page in the browser's default language. If you change the browser's default language setting and reload the page, the browser displays the page in the new language. The browser can display the pages in different languages because the server has a copy of the page for each language. For example, the files **index.html.en** and **index.html.fr** both exist in the **/var/www/manual** directory.

Server Generated Directory Listings (Indexing)

When a client requests a directory, Apache configuration determines what it returns to the client. Apache can return a file as specified by the DirectoryIndex directive (page 771), a directory listing if there is no file matching DirectoryIndex and the Options Indexes directive (page 784) is set, or an error message if there is no file matching DirectoryIndex and Options/Indexes is not set.

VirtualHosts

Apache supports *virtual hosts*, which means one instance of Apache can respond to requests directed to multiple IP addresses or hostnames as though it were multiple servers. Each IP address or hostname can provide different content and be configured differently.

There are two types of virtual hosts: *host-by-name* and *host-by-IP*. Host-by-name relies on the FQDN the client uses in its request to Apache; for example, **www.example.com** versus **www2.example.com**. Host-by-IP examines the IP address the host resolves as and responds according to that match.

Host-by-name is useful if there is only one IP address, but Apache must support multiple FQDNs. You can use host-by-IP if a given Web server has aliases, but Apache should serve the same content regardless of which name is used.

Virtual hosts inherit their configuration from **httpd.conf** Section 1 (page 788) and Section 2 (page 789). Then, in Section 3, <VirtualHost> containers create the virtual hosts and specify directives that override inherited and default values. You can specify many virtual hosts for a single instance of Apache.

The following <VirtualHost> container sets up a Host-by-name for the site named **intranet.example.com**. This virtual host handles requests that Apache receives directed to **intranet.example.com**.

```
<VirtualHost intranet.example.com>
    ServerName intranet.example.com
    DocumentRoot /usr/local/www
    ErrorLog /var/log/httpd/intra.error_log
    CustomLog /var/log/httpd/intra.server_log
    <Directory /usr/local/www>
        Order deny,allow
        Deny from all
        Allow from 192.168.  # allow from private subnet only
    </Directory>
</VirtualHost>
```

Troubleshooting

You can use service and the **httpd** init script to check the syntax of the Apache configuration files:

```
# service httpd configtest
Syntax OK
```

Once you start the **httpd** daemon, you can check that Apache is working by pointing a browser on the local system at **http://localhost/**. From a remote system, use **http://*server/***, substituting the hostname of the server for *server*. Apache displays the Red Hat test page.

If the browser does not display the test page, it will display one of two errors: **Connection refused** or an error page. If you get a connection refused error, make sure port 80 is not blocked by iptables and check that the server is running:

```
# /sbin/service httpd status
httpd (pid 21406 21405 21404 21403 21402 21401 13622) is running...
```

If the server is running, check that you did not specify a port other than 80 in a Listen directive. If you did, the URI you specify in the browser must reflect this port number. Otherwise, check the error log (**/var/log/httpd/error_log**) for information on what is not working.

To make sure the browser is not at fault, use telnet to try to connect to port 80 of the server:

```
$ telnet www.example.com 80
Trying 192.0.34.166...
Connected to www.example.com.
Escape character is '^]'.
CONTROL-]
telnet> quit
Connection closed.
```

If you see **Connection refused,** you have verified that you cannot get through to the server.

Modules

Apache is a skeletal program that uses external modules, called Dynamic Shared Objects (DSOs), for most of its functionality. This section lists these modules and discusses some of the more important ones. In addition to the modules included with Red Hat, there are many other modules. See httpd.apache.org/modules for more information.

Module List

The following Apache modules are included with Red Hat:

access (mod_access.so) Controls access based on client characteristics.

actions (mod_actions.so) Allows execution of CGI scripts based on request method.

alias (mod_alias.so) Allows outside directories to be mapped to DocumentRoot.

asis (mod_asis.so) Allows sending files that contain their own headers.

auth (mod_auth.so) Provides user authentication using **.htaccess.**

auth_anon (mod_auth_anon.so) Provides anonymous user access to restricted areas.

auth_dbm (mod_auth_dbm.so) Uses DBM files for authentication.

auth_digest (mod_auth_digest.so) Uses MD5 digest for authentication.

autoindex (mod_autoindex.so) Allows directory indexes to be generated.

cern_meta (mod_cern_meta.so) Allows the use of CERN httpd metafile semantics.

cgi (mod_cgi.so) Allows the execution of CGI scripts.

dav (mod_dav.so) Allows Distributed Authoring and Versioning.

dav_fs (mod_dav_fs.so) Provides a filesystem for mod_dav.

dir (mod_dir.so) Allows directory redirects and listings as index files.

env (mod_env.so) Allows CGI scripts to access environment variables.

expires (mod_expires.so) Allows generation of Expires HTTP headers.

headers (mod_headers.so) Allows customization of request and response headers.

imap   (mod_imap.so) Allows image maps to be processed on the server side.

include   (mod_include.so) Provides server side includes (SSIs).

info   (mod_info.so) Allows the server configuration to be viewed.

log_config   (mod_log_config.so) Allows logging of requests made to the server.

mime   (mod_mime.so) Allows association of file extensions with content.

mime_magic   (mod_mime_magic.so) Determines MIME types of files.

negotiation   (mod_negotiation.so) Allows content negotiation.

proxy   (mod_proxy.so) Allows Apache to act as a proxy server.

proxy_connect   (mod_proxy_connect.so) Allows connect request handling.

proxy_ftp   (mod_proxy_ftp.so) Provides an FTP extension proxy.

proxy_http   (mod_proxy_http.so) Provides an HTTP extension proxy.

rewrite   (mod_rewrite.so) Allows on-the-fly URI rewriting based on rules.

setenvif   (mod_setenvif.so) Sets environment variables based on a request.

speling   (mod_speling.so) Auto-corrects spelling if requested URI has incorrect capitalization and one spelling mistake.

status   (mod_status.so) Allows the server status to be queried and viewed.

unique_id   (mod_unique_id.so) Generates a unique ID for each request.

userdir   (mod_userdir.so) Allows users to have content directories (public_html).

usertrack   (mod_usertrack.so) Allows tracking of user activity on a site.

vhost_alias   (mod_vhost_alias.so) Allows the configuration of virtual hosting.

mod_cgi and CGI Scripts

The CGI (Common Gateway Interface) allows external application programs to interface with Web servers. Any program can be a CGI program if it runs in real time (at the time of the request) and relays its output to the requesting client. Various kinds of scripts, including shell, Perl, Python, and PHP, are the most common CGI programs because a script can call a program and reformat its output in HTML for a client.

Apache can handle requests for CGI programs in different ways. The most common method is to put a CGI program in the **cgi-bin** directory and enable its execution from that directory only. The location of the **cgi-bin** directory, as specified by the ScriptAlias directive (page 785), is **/var/www/cgi-bin**. Alternatively, an AddHandler directive (page 779) can identify filename extensions of scripts, such as **.cgi** or **.pl**, within the regular content (for example, **AddHandler cgi-script .cgi**). If you use an AddHandler, you must also specify the ExecCGI option within an Options directive within the appropriate <Directory> container. The **mod_cgi** module must be loaded in order to access and execute CGI scripts.

The following Perl CGI script displays the Apache environment. This script should be used for debugging only as it presents a security risk if outside clients can access it.

```
#!/usr/bin/perl
##
##   printenv -- demo CGI program which just prints its environment
##
print "Content-type: text/plain\n\n";
foreach $var (sort(keys(%ENV))) {
    $val = $ENV{$var};
    $val =~ s|\n|\\n|g;
    $val =~ s|"|\\"|g;
    print "${var}=\"${val}\"\n";
}
```

mod_ssl

SSL (Secure Socket Layer), which is implemented by the **mod_ssl** module, has two functions: It allows a client to verify the identity of a server and it enables secure two-way communication between a client and server. SSL is used on Web pages with forms that require passwords, credit card numbers, or other sensitive data.

Apache uses the HTTPS protocol, not HTTP, for SSL communication. When Apache uses SSL, it listens on a second port (443 by default) for a connection and performs a handshaking sequence before sending the requested content to the client.

Server verification is critical for financial transactions; you do not want to give your credit card number to a fraudulent Web site posing as a known company. SSL uses a certificate to positively identify a server. Over a public network such as the Internet, the identification is reliable only if the certificate has a digital signature from an authoritative source such as VeriSign or Thawte. SSL Web pages are denoted by a URI beginning with **https://**.

Data encryption prevents malicious users from evesdropping on Internet connections and copying personal information. To encrypt communication, SSL sits between the network and an application and encrypts communication between the server and client.

Setting Up mod_ssl

The **/etc/httpd/conf.d/ssl.conf** file configures **mod_ssl**. The first few directives in this file load the **mod_ssl** module, instruct Apache to listen on port 443, and set various parameters for SSL operation. About a third of the way through the file is a section labeled **SSL Virtual Host Context** that sets up virtual hosts (page 791).

A <VirtualHost> container in **ssl.conf** is similar to one in **httpd.conf**. As with any <VirtualHost> container, it holds directives such as ServerName and ServerAdmin that need to be configured. In addition, it holds some SSL-related directives.

Using a Self-Signed Certificate for Encryption

If you require SSL for encryption and not verification, that is, if the client already trusts the server, it is possible to generate and use a self-signed certificate and bypass the time and expense of obtaining a digitally signed certificate. Self-signed certificates generate a warning when you connect to the server: Most browsers display a dialog box that allows you to examine and accept the certificate. The **sendmail** daemon also uses certificates (page 632).

To generate the private key that the encryption relies on, cd to **/etc/httpd/conf** and give the following command:

```
# cd /etc/httpd/conf
# make server.key
umask 77 ; \
/usr/bin/openssl genrsa -des3 1024 > server.key
Generating RSA private key, 1024 bit long modulus
..................................++++++
.......++++++
e is 65537 (0x10001)
Enter pass phrase:
Verifying - Enter pass phrase:
```

The preceding command generates a file named **server.key** that is protected by the pass phrase you entered; *you will need this pass phrase to start the server*. Keep the **server.key** file secret.

The next command generates the certificate. This process uses the private key you just created; you need to supply the same pass phrase you entered when you created the private key.

```
# make server.crt
umask 77 ; \
/usr/bin/openssl req -new -key server.key -x509 -days 365 -out server.crt
Enter pass phrase for server.key:
You are about to be asked to enter information that will be incorporated
into your certificate request.
What you are about to enter is what is called a Distinguished Name or a DN.
There are quite a few fields but you can leave some blank
For some fields there will be a default value,
If you enter '.', the field will be left blank.
-----
Country Name (2 letter code) [GB]:US
State or Province Name (full name) [Berkshire]:California
Locality Name (eg, city) [Newbury]:San Francisco
Organization Name (eg, company) [My Company Ltd]:Sobell Associates Inc.
Organizational Unit Name (eg, section) []:Executive
Common Name (eg, your name or your server's hostname) []:www.sobell.com
Email Address []:mgs@sobell.com
```

The answers to the first five questions are arbitrary: They can help clients identify you when they examine the certificate. The answer to the sixth question (**Common Name**) is critical. Because certificates are tied to the name of the server, it is important you enter your server's FQDN accurately. If you mistype this information, the server name and that of the certificate will not match and the browser will generate a warning message each time a connection is made.

The preceding commands created two files in the working directory; move **server.key** into the **ssl.key** directory, and **server.crt** into the **ssl.crt** directory. After you restart Apache, the new certificate will be in use.

Notes on Certificates

- Although the server name is part of the certificate, the SSL connection is tied to the IP address of the server: You can have only one certificate per IP address. In order for multiple virtual hosts to have separate certificates, you must specify host-by-IP rather than host-by-name virtual hosts (page 791).

- As long as the server is identified by the name for which the certificate was issued, you can use the certificate on another server and/or IP address.

- A root certificate (root CA) is the certificate that signs the server certificate. Every browser contains a database of the public keys for the root certificates of the major signing authorities including VeriSign and Thawte.

- It is possible to generate a root certificate (root CA) and sign all your server certificates with this root CA. Regular clients can import the public key of the root CA so that they recognize every certificate signed by that root CA. This setup is convenient for a server with multiple SSL-enabled virtual hosts and no commercial certificates. For more information see www.modssl.org/docs/2.8/ssl_faq.html#ToC29.

- You cannot use a CA you generate if clients need to verify the identity of the server.

Authentication Modules and .htaccess

To restrict access to a Web page, Apache and third parties provide authentication modules and methods that can verify a user's credentials, such as a username and password. Some modules enable authentication against various databases including *LDAP* (page 980) and NIS (page 637).

Commonly, user authentication directives are placed in a **.htaccess** file. A basic **.htaccess** file that uses the Apache default authentication module (mod_auth) follows. Substitute appropriate values for the local server.

```
# cat .htaccess
AuthUserFile /var/www/.htpasswd
AuthGroupFile /dev/null
AuthName "Browser dialog box query"
AuthType Basic
require valid-user
```

The **/var/www/.htpasswd** is a typical absolute pathname of a **.htpasswd** file and **Browser dialog box query** is the string that the user will see as part of the dialog box that requests a username and password.

The second line of the preceding **.htaccess** file turns off the group function. The fourth line specifies the user authentication type **Basic,** which is implemented by the default **mod_auth** module. The last line tells Apache which users can access the protected directory. The entry **valid-user** grants access to the directory to any user who is in the Apache password file and who enters the correct password. You can also specify Apache usernames separated by SPACEs.

You can put the Apache password file anywhere on the system, as long as Apache can read it. It is safe to put this file in the same directory as the **.htaccess** file as, by default, Apache will not answer any requests for files whose names start with **.ht**.

The following command creates a **.htpasswd** file for Sam:

```
$ htpasswd -c .htpasswd sam
New password:
Re-type new password:
Adding password for user sam
```

Omit the **–c** option to add a user or to change a password in an existing **.htpasswd** file. Remember to use an AllowOverride directive (page 786) to permit Apache to read the **.htaccess** file.

Scripting Modules

Apache can process content before serving it to a client. In earlier versions of Apache, only CGI scripts could process content; in the current version, *scripting modules* can work with scripts that are embedded in HTML documents.

Scripting modules manipulate content before Apache serves it to a client. Because they are built into Apache, they are fast. Scripting modules are especially efficient at working with external data sources such as relational databases. Clients can pass data to a scripting module that modifies the information that Apache serves.

Contrast scripting modules with CGI scripts that are run external to Apache: CGI scripts do not allow client interaction and are slow because of the external calls.

RedHat provides packages that allow you to embed Perl, Python, and PHP code in HTML content. Perl and Python, general-purpose scripting languages, are encapsulated for use directly in Apache and are implemented in the **mod_perl** and **mod_python** modules.

PHP, developed for manipulating Web content, outputs HTML by default. PHP, implemented in the **mod_php** module, is easy to set up, has a syntax similar to Perl and C, and comes with a large number of Web-related functions.

webalizer: Analyzing Web Traffic

The webalizer package, which is typically installed as part of Apache, creates a directory at **/var/www/usage** and a cron file (page 531) at **/etc/cron.daily/00webalizer**. Once a day, the cron file generates usage data and puts it in the **usage** directory; you can view the data by pointing a browser at **http://*server*/usage/** where *server* is the hostname of the server.

The **/etc/webalizer.conf** file controls the behavior of the webalizer utility. If you change the location of the DocumentRoot or log files, you must edit this file to reflect those changes. For more information on webalizer, refer to the webalizer man page and the sites listed under "More Information" on page 761.

MRTG: Monitoring Traffic Loads

Multi Router Traffic Grapher (MRTG) is an open source application that graphs statistics available through SNMP (Simple Network Management Protocol). SNMP information is available on all high-end routers and switches, as well as on some other networked equipment, such as printers and wireless access points. You can use the **net-snmp** and **net-snmp-utils** rpm packages supplied by Red Hat to install SNMP on a system. You also need to install the **mrtg** package.

Once MRTG and SNMP are installed and running, you can view the reports at **http://*server*/mrtg** where *server* is the FQDN of your server. For more information, see the mrtg man page and the sites listed under "More Information" on page 761.

Error Codes

Following is a list of Apache error codes:

100 Continue
101 Switching Protocols
200 OK
201 Created
202 Accepted
203 Non-Authoritative Information
204 No Content
205 Reset Content
206 Partial Content
300 Multiple Choices

301 Moved Permanently
302 Moved Temporarily
303 See Other
304 Not Modified
305 Use Proxy
400 Bad Request
401 Unauthorized
402 Payment Required
403 Forbidden
404 Not Found
405 Method Not Allowed
406 Not Acceptable
407 Proxy Authentication Required
408 Request Time-out
409 Conflict
410 Gone
411 Length Required
412 Precondition Failed
413 Request Entity Too Large
414 Request-URI Too Large
415 Unsupported Media Type
500 Internal Server Error
501 Not Implemented
502 Bad Gateway
503 Service Unavailable
504 Gateway Time-out
505 HTTP Version not supported

Chapter Summary

Apache is the most popular Web server on the Internet today. It is robust and extensible. The **/etc/httpd/conf/httpd.conf** configuration file controls many aspects of how Apache runs. The Red Hat **httpd.conf** file, based on the **httpd.conf** file distributed by Apache, is heavily commented and broken into three parts: Global Environment, Main Server Configuration, and Virtual Hosts. You can use the system-config-httpd (*FEDORA*) and redhat-config-httpd (*RHEL*) utilities to modify **httpd.conf**.

Content to be served must be placed in **/var/www/html,** called the document root. Apache automatically displays the file named **index.html** in this directory.

Configuration directives, or simply directives, are lines in a configuration file that control some aspect of how Apache functions. There are four locations, called contexts, that define where a configuration directive can appear: server config, virtual host, directory, and .htaccess. Containers, or special directives, are directives that group other directives.

To restrict access to a Web page, Apache and third parties provide authentication modules and methods that can verify a user's credentials, such as a username and password. Some modules enable authentication against various databases including LDAP and NIS.

Apache can respond to a request for a URI by asking the client to request a different URI. This response is called a redirect. Apache can also process content before serving it to a client using scripting modules that work with scripts embedded in HTML documents.

Apache supports virtual hosts, which means that one instance of Apache can respond to requests directed to multiple IP addresses or hostnames as though it were multiple servers. Each IP address or hostname can provide different content and be configured differently.

The CGI (Common Gateway Interface) allows external application programs to interface with Web servers. Any program can be a CGI program if it runs in real time and relays its output to the requesting client.

SSL (Secure Socket Layer) has two functions: It allows a client to verify the identity of a server and it enables secure two-way communication between a client and server.

Exercises

1. How would you tell Apache that your content is in **/usr/local/www**?

2. How would you instruct an Apache server to listen on port 81 instead of port 80?

3. How would you enable Sam to publish Web pages from his **~/website** directory but not allow anyone else to publish to the Web?

4. Apache must be started as **root**. Why? Why does this not present a security risk?

Advanced Exercises

5. If you are running Apache on a firewall system, perhaps to display a Web front end for firewall configuration, how would you make sure that it is accessible only from inside the local network?

6. Why is it more efficient to run scripts using mod_php or mod_perl than through CGI?

7. What two things does SSL provide and how does this differ if the certificate is self-signed?

8. Some Web sites generate content by retrieving data from a database and inserting it into a template using PHP or CGI each time the site is accessed. Why is this often a poor practice?

9. Assume you want to provide Webmail access for employees on the same server that hosts the corporate Web site. The Web site address is example.com, you want to use mail.example.com for Webmail, and the Webmail application is located in **/var/www/webmail**. Describe two ways you can set this up.

10. Part of a Web site is a private intranet and is accessed as http://example.com/intranet. Describe how you would prevent people outside the company accessing this site. Assume the company uses the 192.168.0.0/16 subnet internally.

PART VI
Programming

Programming Tools 27

With its rich set of languages and development tools, the Linux operating system provides an outstanding environment for programming. C is one of the most popular system programming languages to use with Linux, in part because the operating system itself is written mostly in C. Using C, programmers can easily access system services using function libraries and system calls. In addition, a variety of tools can make the development and maintenance of programs easier.

This chapter explains how to compile and link C programs. It introduces the GNU gdb debugger and tools that provide feedback about memory, disk, and CPU resources. It also covers some of the most useful software development tools: the make utility and the Concurrent Versions System (CVS) source code management system. The make utility helps you keep track of which modules of a program have been updated and helps to ensure that when you compile a program, you use the latest versions of all program modules. Source code management systems track the versions of files involved in a project.

Programming in C

One of the main reasons the Linux system provides an excellent C programming environment is that C programs can easily access the services of the operating system. The system calls—the routines that make operating system services available to programmers—can be called from C programs. The system calls provide such services as creating files, reading from and writing to files, collecting information about files, and sending signals to processes. When you write a C program, you can use the system calls in the same way you use ordinary C program modules, or *functions*, that you have written. For more information, refer to "System Calls" on page 834.

A variety of *libraries* of functions have been developed to support programming in C. The libraries are collections of related functions that you can use just as you use your own functions and the system calls. Many of the library functions access basic operating system services through the system calls, providing the services in ways that are more suited to typical programming tasks. Other library functions, such as the math library functions, serve special purposes.

This chapter describes the processes of writing and compiling C programs. However, it will *not* teach you to program in C.

Checking Your Compiler

Give the following command to see if you have access to the gcc compiler (www.gnu.org/software/gcc/gcc.html):[1]

```
$ gcc --version
bash: gcc: command not found
```

If you get a response other than version information, the compiler is not installed, or your **PATH** variable does not contain the necessary pathname (usually gcc is installed in **/usr/bin**). If you get version information from the gcc command, the GNU C compiler is installed.

Next, make sure that the compiler is functioning: As a simple test, create a file named **Makefile** with the following lines. The line that starts with **gcc** must be indented by using a TAB, not SPACEs.

```
$ cat Makefile
morning: morning.c
TAB gcc -o morning morning.c
```

Next, create a source file named **morning.c** with the lines

```
$ cat morning.c
#include <stdio.h>
int main(int argc, char** argv) {
    printf("Good Morning\n");
    return 0;
}
```

Compile the file with the command **make morning**. When it compiles successfully, run the program by giving the command **morning** or **./morning**. When you get output from this program, you know that you have a working C compiler.

---

1. The C compiler in common use on Linux is GNU gcc, which comes as part of Red Hat distributions. If it is not on your system, you need to install the **gcc*.rpm** package.

A C Programming Example

You must use an editor, such as pico, emacs, or vi, to create or change a C program. The name of the C program file must end in .c. Entering the source code for a program is similar to typing a memo or shell script. Although emacs and vim "know" that you are editing a C program, many editors do not know whether your file is a C program, a shell script, or an ordinary text document. You are responsible for making the contents of the file syntactically suitable for the C compiler to process.

```
 1  /* convert tabs in standard input to spaces in */
 2  /* standard output while maintaining columns */
 3
 4  #include        <stdio.h>
 5  #define         TABSIZE         8
 6
 7  /* prototype for function findstop */
 8  int findstop(int *);
 9
10  int main()
11  {
12  int c;              /* character read from stdin */
13  int posn = 0;       /* column position of character */
14  int inc;            /* column increment to tab stop */
15
16  while ((c = getchar()) != EOF)
17          switch(c)
18                  {
19                  case '\t':                  /* c is a tab */
20                          inc = findstop(&posn);
21                          for( ; inc > 0; inc-- )
22                                  putchar(' ');
23                          break;
24                  case '\n':                  /* c is a newline */
25                          putchar(c);
26                          posn = 0;
27                          break;
28                  default:                    /* c is anything else */
29                          putchar(c);
30                          posn++;
31                          break;
32                  }
33  return 0;
34  }
35
36  /* compute size of increment to next tab stop */
37
38  int findstop(int *col)
39  {
40  int retval;
41  retval = (TABSIZE - (*col % TABSIZE));
42
43  /* increment argument (current column position) to next tabstop */
44  *col += retval;
45
46  return retval;              /* main gets how many blanks for filling */
47  }
```

- **Comments**
- **Preprocessor Directives**
- **Function Prototype**
- **Main Function**
- **Function**

Figure 27-1 A simple C program (**tabs.c**—the line numbers are not part of the source code)

Figure 27-1 illustrates the structure of a simple C program named **tabs.c**. The first two lines of the program are comments that describe what the program does. The string **/*** identifies the beginning of the comment, and the string ***/** identifies the end; the C compiler ignores all the characters between them. Because a comment can span two or more lines, the ***/** at the end of the first line and the **/*** at the beginning of the second are not necessary but are included for clarity. As the comment explains, the program reads standard input, converts TAB characters into the appropriate number of spaces, and writes the transformed input to standard output. Like many Linux utilities, this program is a filter.

Following the comments at the top of **tabs.c** are *preprocessor directives*, which are instructions for the C preprocessor. During the initial phase of compilation, the C preprocessor expands the directives, making the program ready for the later stages of the compilation process. Preprocessor directives begin with the pound sign (#) and may, optionally, be preceded by SPACE and TAB characters.

You can use the **#define** preprocessor directive to define symbolic constants and/or macros. *Symbolic constants* are names that you can use in your programs in place of constant values. For example, **tabs.c** uses a **#define** preprocessor directive to associate the symbolic constant **TABSIZE** with the constant 8. **TABSIZE** is used in the program in place of the constant 8 as the distance between TAB stops. By convention, the names of symbolic constants are composed of all uppercase letters.

By defining symbolic names for constant values, you can make your program easier to read and easier to modify. If you later decide to change a constant, you need to change only the preprocessor directive rather than the value everywhere it occurs in your program. If you replace the **#define** directive for **TABSIZE** in Figure 27-1 with the following directive, the program will place TAB stops every four columns rather than every eight:

```
#define    TABSIZE    4
```

Symbolic constants are one type of *macro,* the mapping of a symbolic name to *replacement text*. Macros are handy when the replacement text is needed at multiple points throughout the source code or when the definition of the macro is subject to frequent change. The process of substituting the replacement text for the symbolic name is called *macro expansion*.

You can also use **#define** directives to define macros with arguments. Use of such a macro resembles a function call. Unlike C functions, however, macros are replaced with C code prior to compilation into object files.

The following macro computes the distance to the next TAB stop, given the current column position, **curcol**:

```
#define NEXTTAB(curcol) (TABSIZE - ((curcol) % TABSIZE))
```

The definition of this macro uses the macro TABSIZE, whose definition must appear prior to NEXTTAB in the source code. The macro NEXTTAB could be used in **tabs.c** to assign a value to **retval** in the function **findstop**:

```
retval = NEXTTAB(*col);
```

When various modules of a program use several macro definitions, the definitions are typically collected together in a single file called a *header file*, or an *include file*. Although the C compiler does not put constraints on the names of header files, by convention they end in .h. The name of the header file is then listed in an **#include** preprocessor directive in each program source file that uses any of the macros. The program in Figure 27-1 uses **getchar** and **putchar**, which are macros defined in **stdio.h**. The **stdio.h** header file defines a variety of general-purpose macros and is used by many C library functions.

The angle brackets (< and >) that surround **stdio.h** in **tabs.c** instruct the C preprocessor to look for the header file in a standard list of directories (such as **/usr/include**). If you want to include a header file from another directory, you can enclose its pathname between double quotation marks. You can specify an absolute pathname within the double quotation marks, or you can give a relative pathname. If you give a relative pathname, searching begins with the working directory and is followed by the same directories that are searched when the header file is surrounded by angle brackets. By convention, header files that you supply are surrounded by double quotation marks.

Another way to specify directories to be searched for header files is to use the **–I** option to the C compiler. Assume that Alex wants to compile the program **deriv.c**, which contains the following preprocessor directive:

```
#include "eqns.h"
```

If the header file **eqns.h** is located in the subdirectory **myincludes**, Alex can compile **deriv.c** with the **–I** option to tell the C preprocessor to look for the file **eqns.h** there:

```
$ gcc -I./myincludes deriv.c
```

With this command, when the C preprocessor encounters the **#include** directive in the file **deriv.c** file, it look for **eqns.h** in the **myincludes** subdirectory of the working directory.

tip || **Use Relative Pathnames for Include Files**

Using absolute pathnames for include files does not work if the location of the header file within the filesystem changes. Using relative pathnames for header files works as long as the location of the header file relative to the working directory remains the same. Relative pathnames also work with the **–I** option on the gcc command line and allow header files to be moved.

Preceding the definition of the function **main** is a *function prototype*, a declaration that tells the compiler what type a function returns, how many arguments a function expects, and what the types of those arguments are. In **tabs.c** the prototype for the function **findstop** informs the compiler that **findstop** returns type *int* and that it expects a single argument of type *pointer to int*. Once the compiler has seen this declaration, it can detect and flag inconsistencies in the definition and the uses of the function.

For example, suppose that the reference to **findstop** in **tabs.c** was replaced with the following statement:

```
inc = findstop();
```

The prototype for **findstop** would cause the compiler to detect a missing argument and issue an error message. The programmer could then easily fix the problem. When a function is present in a separate source file or is defined after it is referenced in a source file (as **findstop** is in the example), the function prototype helps the compiler check that the function is being called properly. Without the prototype, the compiler would not issue an error message, and the problem would manifest itself as unexpected behavior during execution. At this late point, finding the bug might be difficult and time-consuming.

Although you can call most C functions anything you want, each program must have exactly one function named **main**. The function **main** is the control module: Your program begins execution with the function **main**, which typically calls other functions in turn, which may call yet other functions, and so forth. By putting different operations into separate functions, you can make a program easier to read and maintain. The program in Figure 27-1 uses a function, **findstop**, to compute the distance to the next TAB stop. Although the few statements of **findstop** could easily have been included in the **main** function, isolating them in a separate function draws attention to a key computation.

Functions can make both development and maintenance of the program more efficient. By putting a frequently used code segment into a function, you avoid entering the same code into the program over and over again. Later when you want to make changes to the code, you need to change it only once.

If your program is long and involves several functions, you may want to split it into two or more files. Regardless of its size, you may want to place logically distinct parts of your program in separate files. A C program can be split into any number of different files; however, each function must be wholly contained within a single file.

---

tip || **Use a Header File for Multiple Source Files**

When you are creating a program that takes advantage of multiple source files, put **#define** preprocessor directives into a header file, and use an include statement with the name of the header file in any source file that uses the directives.

Compiling and Linking a C Program

To compile **tabs.c**, give the following command:

```
$ gcc tabs.c
```

The gcc utility calls the C preprocessor, the C compiler, the assembler, and the linker. The four components of the compilation process are shown in Figure 27-2.

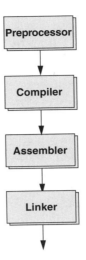

Figure 27-2   The compilation process

The C preprocessor expands macro definitions and also includes header files. The compilation phase creates assembly language code, corresponding to the instructions in the source file. Then the assembler creates machine-readable object code. One object file is created for each source file. Each object file has the same name as the source file, except that the .c extension is replaced with a .o. The previous example creates a single object file, **tabs.o**. However, after successfully completing all phases of the compilation process for a program, the C compiler creates the executable file and then removes any .o files.

During the final phase of the compilation process, the linker searches specified libraries for functions your program uses and combines object modules for those functions with your program's object modules. By default, the C compiler links the standard C library, **libc.so** (usually found in **/lib**), which contains functions that handle input and output and provides many other general-purpose capabilities. If you want the linker to search other libraries, you must use the −l (ell) option to specify the libraries on the command line. Unlike most options to Linux system utilities, the −l option does not come before all filenames on the command line but usually comes after all the filenames of all modules that it applies to. In the next example, the C compiler searches the math library, **libm.so** (usually found in **/lib**):

```
$ gcc calc.c -lm
```

As you can see from the example, the −l option uses abbreviations for library names, appending the letter following −l to **lib** and adding a **.so** or **.a** extension. The **m** in the example stands for **libm.so**.

Using the same naming mechanism, you can have a graphics library named **libgraphics.a**, which could be linked on the command line with

```
$ gcc pgm.c -lgraphics
```

When this convention is used to name libraries, gcc knows to search for them in **/usr/lib** and **/lib**. You can have gcc also search other directories with the **–L** option:

```
$ gcc pgm.c -L. -L/usr/X11R6/lib -lgraphics
```

The preceding command causes gcc to search for the library file **libgraphics.a** in the working directory and in **/usr/X11R6/lib** before searching **/usr/lib** and **/lib**.

As the last step of the compilation process, the linker creates by default an executable file named **a.out**. Object files are deleted after the executable is created. In the next example, the **–O3** option causes gcc to use the C compiler *optimizer*. The optimizer makes object code more efficient so that the executable program runs more quickly. Optimization has many facets, including locating frequently used variables and taking advantage of processor-specific features. The number after the **–O** indicates the level of optimization: A higher number specifies more optimization. See the gcc info page for specifics. The following example also shows that the **.o** files are not present after **a.out** is created:

```
$ ls
acctspay.c  acctsrec.c  ledger.c
$ gcc -O3 ledger.c acctspay.c acctsrec.c
$ ls
a.out        acctspay.c  acctsrec.c  ledger.c
```

You can use the executable **a.out** in the same way you use shell scripts and other programs: by typing its name on the command line. The program in Figure 27-1 on page 807 expects to read from standard input, so once you have created the executable, **a.out**, you can use a command such as the following to run it:

```
$ ./a.out < mymemo
```

If you want to save the **a.out** file, you should change the name to a more descriptive one. Otherwise, you might accidentally overwrite it during a later compilation:

```
$ mv a.out accounting
```

To save the trouble of renaming **a.out** files, you can specify the name of the executable file when you use gcc. The **–o** option causes the C compiler to give the executable the name of your choice rather than **a.out**. In the next example, the executable is named **accounting**:

```
$ gcc -o accounting ledger.c acctspay.c acctsrec.c
```

Assuming that **accounting** does not require arguments, you can run it with the following command:

```
$ accounting
```

You can suppress the linking phase of compilation by using the **–c** option with the gcc command. The **–c** option is useful because it does not treat unresolved external references as errors; this capability enables you to compile and debug the syntax of the modules of a program as you create them. Once you have compiled and debugged all the modules, you can run gcc again with the object files as arguments to produce an executable program. In the next example, gcc produces three object files but no executable:

```
$ gcc -c ledger.c acctspay.c acctsrec.c
$ ls
acctspay.c  acctspay.o  acctsrec.c  acctsrec.o  ledger.c    ledger.o
```

If you then run gcc again, naming the object files on the command line, gcc will produce the executable. Because it recognizes the filename extension .o, the C compiler knows that the files need only to be linked. You can also include both .c and .o files on a single command line, as in this example:

```
$ gcc -o accounting ledger.o acctspay.c acctsrec.o
```

The C compiler recognizes that the .c file needs to be preprocessed and compiled, whereas the .o files do not. The C compiler also accepts assembly language files ending in .s and treats them appropriately (that is, gcc assembles and links them). This feature makes it easy to modify and recompile a program.

You can use separate files to divide a project into functional groups. You might put graphics routines in one file, string functions in another, and database calls in a third. Multiple files can enable several engineers to work on the same project concurrently and can speed up compilation. If all the functions are in one file and you make a change, the compiler must recompile all the functions in the file. That means that the entire program will be recompiled, which may take considerable time for a small change. When you use separate files, only the file that you make a change in must be recompiled. For large programs with many source files (for example, the C compiler or emacs), the time lost by recompiling one huge file for every small change would be enormous. For more information, refer to "make: Keeps a Set of Programs Current" on page 816.

---

tip || **What Not to Name Your Program**

Do not name your program **test** or any other name of a builtin or other executable on your system. If you do, you will likely execute the builtin or other program in place of the program you intend to run. Use which (page 135) to determine which program you will run when you give a command.

Using Shared Libraries

Most modern operating systems use *shared* libraries, also called *dynamic* libraries, which are not linked into a program at compile time but rather are loaded when the program starts or later in some cases. The names of files housing shared libraries end with the filename extension .so (shared object). An example is **libc.so**. Usually **libaaa.so** is a symbolic link to **libaaa.so.x**, where x is a small number representing the version of the library. Many of these libraries are kept in **/usr/lib**: A typical

Linux installation has more than 300 shared libraries in **/usr/lib** and more than 30 in **/usr/X11R6/lib**. Applications can have their own shared libraries; for example, the gcc compiler might keep its libraries in **/usr/lib/gcc-lib/i386-redhat-linux/3.2**.

Contrasted with shared libraries are the older, *statically linked* libraries (with a **.a** filename extension), also called *archived* libraries. Archived libraries are added to the executable file during the last (link) phase of compilation. This addition can make a program run slightly faster the first time it is run, at the expense of program maintainability and size. Together, the combined size of several executables that use a shared library and the size of the shared library is smaller than the combined size of the same executables with static libraries. Alternatively, when a running program has already loaded a dynamic library, a second program that requires the same dynamic library starts slightly faster.

Reducing memory usage and increasing maintainability are the primary reasons for using shared object libraries; they have largely replaced statically linked libraries as the library type of choice. Consider what happens when you discover an error in a library. If it is a static library, you need to relink every program that uses the library, once the library has been fixed and recompiled. With a dynamic library, you need to fix and recompile only the library itself.

Shared object libraries also make dynamic loading of program libraries on the fly possible (for example, perl, python, and/or tcl extensions and modules). The Apache (HTTP) Web server specifies modules in the **httpd.conf** file that it loads as needed.

The ldd (list dynamic dependencies) utility tells you which shared libraries a program needs. For example, the following shows that cp uses **libacl**, the Access Control Lists library; **libc**, the C library; **libattr**, the Extended Attributes library; and **ld-linux**, the runtime linker:

```
$ ldd /bin/cp
        libacl.so.1 => /lib/libacl.so.1 (0x40026000)
        libc.so.6 => /lib/i686/libc.so.6 (0x42000000)
        libattr.so.1 => /lib/libattr.so.1 (0x4002d000)
        /lib/ld-linux.so.2 => /lib/ld-linux.so.2 (0x40000000)
```

Running ldd on **/usr/bin/gnome-session** (a program that starts a GNOME session) lists 59 libraries from **/usr/lib**, **/usr/X11R6/lib**, and **/lib**.

The program that does the dynamic runtime linking, ld-linux.so, always looks in **/usr/lib** for libraries. The other directories that ld looks in varies, depending on how ld is set up. You can add directories for ld to look in by specifying a search path at compile (actually link) time, using the **–r** option followed by a colon-separated list of directories (do not put a SPACE after the **–r**). Use only absolute pathnames in the search path. Although you use this option on the gcc command line, it is passed to the linker (ld). The gnome-session desktop manager was likely linked with a command such as the following:

gcc **flags** *–o gnome-session* **objects** *–r/lib:/usr/X11R6/lib* **libraries**

This command line allows ld.so (and ldd) to search **/lib** and **/usr/X11R6/lib** in addition to the standard **/usr/lib** for the libraries the executable needs.

The compiler needs to see the shared libraries at link time to make sure that the needed functions and procedures are there as promised by the header (.h) files. Use the –L option to tell the compile-time linker to look in the directory **mylib** for shared or static libraries: –L **mylib**. Unlike the search path, –L can use relative pathnames, such as –L **../lib**. This is handy when a program builds its own shared library. The library can be in one location at build time (–L) but in another location at runtime (after it is installed) (–r*path*). (The SPACE after the –L is optional and is usually omitted. The –r must not be followed by a SPACE. You can repeat the –L and the –r options multiple times on the link line.)

Fixing Broken Binaries

The command line search path is a fairly new idea. The old way to create the search path was to use the **LD_LIBRARY_PATH** and, more recently, **LD_RUN_PATH** environment variables. These variables have the same format as **PATH** (page 283). The directories in **LD_LIBRARY_PATH** are normally searched before the usual library locations. Newer Linux releases extend the function of **LD_LIBRARY_PATH** to specify directories to be searched either before or after the normal locations. See the ld man page for details. The **LD_RUN_PATH** variable behaves similarly to **LD_LIBRARY_PATH**, but if you use –r, **LD_LIBRARY_PATH** supersedes anything in **LD_RUN_PATH**.

The use of **LD_LIBRARY_PATH** has several problems. Because there is only one environment variable, it has to be shared among all programs. If two programs have the same name for a library or use different, incompatible versions of the same library, only the first will be found, and one of the programs will not run or, worse, will not run correctly.

security || **LD_LIBRARY_PATH**

Under certain circumstances, a malicious user can create a Trojan horse named **libc.so** and place it in a directory that is searched before **/usr/lib** (any directory in **LD_LIBRARY_PATH**, which appears before **/usr/lib**). The fake **libc** will then be used instead of the real **libc**.

LD_LIBRARY_PATH still has its place in scripts, called *wrappers*, used to fix broken binaries. Suppose that the broken binary **bb** uses the shared library **libbb.so**, which you want to put in **/opt/bb/lib** and not in **/usr/lib**, as the bb programmer requested. The command **ldd bb** will tell you which libraries are missing. Not a problem; rename **bb** to **bb.broken**, and create a **/bin/sh** wrapper named **bb**:

```
#!/bin/sh
LD_LIBRARY_PATH=/opt/bb/lib
export LD_LIBRARY_PATH
exec bb.broken "$@"
```

(The **$@** rather than **$*** preserves SPACEs in the parameters. See page 291.) This wrapper can also be used to install programs in arbitrary locations.

Creating Shared Libraries

Building a dynamically loadable shared library is not trivial: It involves using reentrant function calls, defining a library entrance routine, and performing other tasks. When you want to create a shared object library, you must, at a minimum, compile the source files with the –fPIC (position-independent code) option and link the resulting object files into the lib*xx*.so file, using the –shared –x options to the linker (for example, ld –shared –x –o libmylib.so *.o). The best resource for investigating shared library construction and usage is existing code on the Internet. You can start by looking at the source files for such programs as zlib (www.gzip.org/zlib).

C++ files have special needs, and libraries (shared or not) often have to be made by the compiler rather than ld or ar. Shared libraries can depend on other shared libraries and have their own search paths. If you set **LD_LIBRARY_PATH**, add the –i flag to the link phase when compiling to ignore the current **LD_LIBRARY_PATH**, or you may have unexpected results. Ideally, you would not have **LD_LIBRARY_PATH** set at all on a global level but would use it only in wrappers as needed.

make: Keeps a Set of Programs Current

tip || **This Chapter Covers the GNU make Program**

This chapter describes the GNU make program. There are other make tools (BSN make, GNUStep make, Borland make, and so on), as well as similar tools such as ant (the Apache build tool). Make files created for GNU make are often incompatible with other make tools which can be problematic if you are trying to compile code targeted for another platform.

When you have a large program with many source and header files, the files typically depend on one another in complex ways. When you change a file that other files depend on, you *must* recompile all dependent files. For example, you might have several source files, all of which use a single header file. When you make a change to the header file, each of the source files must be recompiled. The header file might depend on other header files, and so forth. Figure 27-3 shows a simple example of dependency relationships. Each arrow in this figure points from a file to another file that depends on it.

When you are working on a large program, it can be difficult, time-consuming, and tedious to determine which modules need to be recompiled because of their dependency relationships. The make utility automates this process.

In its simplest use, make looks at *dependency lines* in a file named **Makefile** or **makefile** in the working directory. The dependency lines indicate relationships among files, specifying a *target file* that depends on one or more *prerequisite files*. If you have modified any of the prerequisite files more recently than their target file,

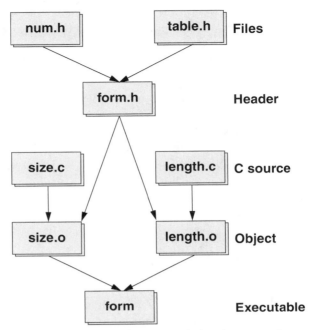

Figure 27-3   Dependency graph for the target **form**

make updates the target file based on construction commands that follow the dependency line. The make utility normally stops if it encounters an error during the construction process.

The file containing the updating information for the make utility is called a *makefile*. See page 806 for a trivial example. A simple makefile has the following syntax:

> *target: prerequisite-list*
> TAB *construction-commands*

The dependency line is composed of the *target* and the *prerequisite-list*, separated by a colon. Each *construction-commands* line (you may have more than one) must start with a TAB and must follow the dependency line. Long lines can be continued with a BACKSLASH (\) as the last character on the line.

The *target* is the name of the file that depends on the files in the *prerequisite-list*. The *construction-commands* are regular commands to the shell that construct (usually compile and/or link) the target file. The make utility executes the *construction-commands* when the modification time of one or more of the files in the *prerequisite-list* is more recent than that of the target file.

The following example shows the dependency line and construction commands for the file named **form** in Figure 27-3. The example depends on the prerequisites **size.o** and **length.o**. An appropriate gcc command constructs the **target**:

```
form: size.o length.o
TAB     gcc -o form size.o length.o
```

Each of the prerequisites on one dependency line can be a target on another dependency line. For example, both **size.o** and **length.o** are targets on other dependency lines. Although the example in Figure 27-3 is simple, the nesting of dependency specifications can create a complex hierarchy that specifies relationships among many files.

The following makefile (named **Makefile**) corresponds to the complete dependency graph shown in Figure 27-3. The executable file **form** depends on two object files, and the object files each depend on their respective source files and a header file, **form.h**. In turn, **form.h** depends on two other header files:

```
$ cat Makefile
form: size.o length.o
    gcc -o form size.o length.o
size.o: size.c form.h
    gcc -c size.c
length.o: length.c form.h
    gcc -c length.c
form.h: num.h table.h
    cat num.h table.h > form.h
```

Although the last line would not normally be seen in a makefile, it illustrates the fact that you can put any shell command on a construction line. Because makefiles are processed by the shell, the command line should be one that you could input in response to a shell prompt.

The following command builds the default target **form** if its prerequisites are more recent or if the target does not exist:

```
$ make
```

Thus, if the file **form** has been deleted, make will rebuild it, regardless of the modification dates of its prerequisite files. The first target in a makefile is the default and is built when you call make without any arguments.

If you want make to rebuild a target other than the first in the makefile, you must provide the target as an argument to make. The following command rebuilds only **form.h** if it does not exist or if its prerequisites are more recent:

```
$ make form.h
```

Implied Dependencies

You can rely on *implied* dependencies and construction commands to make your job of writing a makefile easier. For instance, if you do not include a dependency line for an object file, make assumes that it depends on a compiler or assembler source code file. Thus, if a prerequisite for a target file is **xxx.o** and there is no dependency line with **xxx.o** as a target, make looks at the extension to try to determine how to build the .o file. If it finds an appropriate source file, make provides a default construction command line that calls the proper compiler or the assembler to create the object file. Table 27-1 lists some of the filename extensions that make recognizes and the type of file that corresponds to the suffix.

table 27-1 ‖	**Filename Extensions**
filename.c	C programming language source code
filename.C, filename.cc, filename.cxx, filename.c++, filename.cpp	C++ programming language source code
filename.f	FORTRAN programming language source code
filename.h	Header file
filename.l	flex, lex lexical analyzer generator source code
filename.o	Object module
filename.s	Assembler code
filename.sh	Shell scripts
filename.y	bison, yacc parser generator source code

C and C++ are traditional programming languages that are available with Red Hat Linux. The bison and flex tools create command languages.

The next example shows a makefile that keeps a file named **compute** up-to-date. The make utility ignores any line that begins with a pound sign (#). Thus the first three lines of the following makefile are comment lines. The first dependency line shows that **compute** depends on two object files: **compute.o** and **calc.o**. The corresponding construction line gives the command make needs to produce **compute**. The next dependency line shows that **compute.o** depends not only on its C source file but also on a header file, **compute.h**. The construction line for **compute.o** uses the C compiler optimizer (−O3 option). The third set of dependency and construction lines is not required. In their absence, make infers that **calc.o** depends on **calc.c** and produces the command line needed for the compilation:

```
$ cat Makefile
#
# Makefile for compute
#
compute: compute.o calc.o
        gcc -o compute compute.o calc.o

compute.o: compute.c compute.h
        gcc -c -O3 compute.c

calc.o: calc.c
        gcc -c calc.c

clean:
    rm *.o *core* *~
```

There are no prerequisites for the last target, **clean**, in the preceding makefile. This target is commonly used to get rid of extraneous files that may be out-of-date or no longer needed, such as .o files.

Following are some sample executions of make, based on the previous makefile. As the ls command that follows shows, **compute.o**, **calc.o**, and **compute** are not up-to-date. Consequently, the make command runs the construction commands that recreate them:

```
$ ls -ltr
total 22
-rw-rw----  1 alex  pubs   311 Jun 21 15:56 makefile
-rw-rw----  1 alex  pubs   354 Jun 21 16:02 calc.o
-rwxrwx---  1 alex  pubs  6337 Jun 21 16:04 compute
-rw-rw----  1 alex  pubs    49 Jun 21 16:04 compute.h
-rw-rw----  1 alex  pubs   880 Jun 21 16:04 compute.o
-rw-rw----  1 alex  pubs   780 Jun 21 18:20 compute.c
-rw-rw----  1 alex  pubs   179 Jun 21 18:20 calc.c
$ make
gcc -c -O3 compute.c
gcc -c calc.c
gcc -o compute compute.o calc.o
```

If you run make once and then run it again without making any changes to the prerequisite files, make indicates that the program is up-to-date and does not execute any commands:

```
$ make
make: 'compute' is up to date.
```

The following example uses the touch utility to change the modification time of a prerequisite file. This simulation shows what happens when you make a change to the file. The make utility executes only the commands necessary to make the out-of-date targets up-to-date:

```
$ touch calc.c
$ make
gcc -c calc.c
gcc -o compute compute.o calc.o
```

In the next example, touch changes the modification time of **compute.h**. The make utility recreates **compute.o** because it depends on **compute.h** and recreates the executable because it depends on **compute.o**:

```
$ touch compute.h
$ make
gcc -c -O3 compute.c
gcc -o compute compute.o calc.o
```

As these examples illustrate, touch is useful when you want to fool make into recompiling programs or into *not* recompiling them. You can use touch to update the modification times of all the source files so that make considers that nothing is up-to-date. The make utility will then recompile everything. Alternatively, you can use touch or the **–t** option to make to touch all relevant files so that make considers everything to be up-to-date. Using touch in this manner is useful if the modification times of files have changed, yet the files are all up-to-date (as happens when you copy a set of files from one directory to another). If you want to see what make *would* do if you ran it, run make with the **–n** option. The **–n** option shows the commands that make would execute, but it does not execute them.

Once you are satisfied with the program you have created, you can use the makefile to clean out the files you no longer need. It is useful to keep intermediate files around while you are writing and debugging your program so that you need to rebuild only the ones that change. If you will not be working on the program again for a while, though, you should release the disk space. The advantage of using a **clean** target in your makefile is that you do not have to remember all the little pieces that can safely be deleted. The example that follows simply removes all the object (**.o**) files:

```
$ make clean
rm *.o
```

Macros

The make utility's macro facility enables you to create and use macros within a makefile. The syntax of a macro definition is

ID = list

Replace *ID* with an identifying name, and replace *list* with a list of filenames. After this macro definition, **$(ID)** represents *list* in the makefile.

You can use a macro so that you can compile a program with any of several C compilers, making only a minor change to the makefile. By using the **CC** macro and replacing all occurrences of **gcc** in the makefile on page 819 with **$(CC)**, you need to assign a value only to **CC** to use the compiler of your choice:[2]

```
$ cat Makefile
#
# Makefile for compute
#
CC=gcc
compute: compute.o calc.o
        $(CC) -o compute compute.o calc.o

compute.o: compute.c compute.h
        $(CC) -c -O3 compute.c

calc.o: calc.c
        $(CC) -c calc.c

clean:
        rm *.o
```

---

2. This example assumes that the compiler/loader flags are the same across compilers/loaders. In a more complex situation, you will need to create macros for these flags or stay with the default values.

(There are commercial, high-performance compilers available for Linux. The compiler from the Portland Group, pgcc, could be specified by replacing the **CC=gcc** assignment with **CC=pgcc**.)

If you do not assign a value to the **CC** macro, it defaults to gcc under Linux. The **CC** macro invokes the C compiler with only the options that you specify.

Additional macro definitions are commonly used in programs. The **CFLAGS** macro sends arguments to the C compiler, **LDFLAGS** sends arguments to the linker (ld, or **gcc –o**), and **CPPFLAGS** sends arguments to the C preprocessor and programs that use it, including gcc. The **COMPILE.c** macro expands to **$(CC) –c $(CFLAGS) $(CPPFLAGS)**, and **LINK.c** expands to **$(CC) $(CFLAGS) $(CPPFLAGS) $(LDFLAGS)**.

By default, make invokes the C compiler without any options (except the **–c** option when it is appropriate to compile but not to link a file). You can use the **CFLAGS** macro definition, shown next, to cause make to call the C compiler with specific options. Replace *options* with the options you want to use:

> *CFLAGS = options*

The following makefile uses macros, as well as implied dependencies and constructions:

```
# makefile: report, print, printf, printh
#
CC=gcc
CFLAGS = –O3
# comment out the two lines above and uncomment the
# two below when you are using the Portland Group's compiler
#CC=pgcc
#CFLAGS = -fast
FILES = in.c out.c ratio.c process.c tally.c
OBJECTS = in.o out.o ratio.o process.o tally.o
HEADERS = names.h companies.h conventions.h

report: $(OBJECTS)
        $(LINK.c) –o report $(OBJECTS)

ratio.o: $(HEADERS)

process.o: $(HEADERS)

tally.o: $(HEADERS)

print:
    pr $(FILES) $(HEADERS) | lp

printf:
    pr $(FILES) | lp

printh:
    pr $(HEADERS) | lp
```

Following the comment lines, the makefile uses the **CFLAGS** macro to cause make always to use the optimizer (**–O3** option) when it invokes the C compiler as the result of an implied construction. (The **CC** and **CFLAGS** definitions for the pgcc C compiler perform the same functions when they are uncommented and you are using pgcc, except that you use **–fast** with pgcc in place of **–O3** with gcc.) Whenever you put a construction line in a makefile, the construction line overrides the corresponding implied construction line, if one exists. If you want to apply a macro to a construction command, you must include the macro in that command. This was done, for example, with **OBJECTS** in the construction command for the **report** target. Following **CFLAGS**, the makefile defines the **FILES**, **OBJECTS**, and **HEADERS** macros. Each of these macros defines a list of files.

The first dependency line shows that **report** depends on the list of files that **OBJECTS** defines. The corresponding construction line links the **OBJECTS** and creates an executable file named **report**.

The next three dependency lines show that three object files depend on the list of files that **HEADERS** defines. There are no construction lines, so when it is necessary, make looks for a source code file corresponding to each of the object files and compiles it. These three dependency lines ensure that the object files are recompiled if any of the header files is changed.

Finally, the **LINK.c** macro is invoked to link the executable file. If you specify any **LDFLAGS**, they are used in this step.

You can combine several targets on one dependency line, so these three dependency lines could have been combined into one line as follows:

```
ratio.o process.o tally.o: $(HEADERS)
```

The three final dependency lines send source and header files to the printer. They have nothing to do with compiling the **report** file. None of these targets (**print**, **printf**, and **printh**) depends on anything. When you call one of these targets from the command line, make executes the construction line following it. The following command prints all the source files that **FILES** defines:

```
$ make printf
```

You can override macros in a makefile by specifying them on the command line, causing debugging symbols to be added to all object files:

```
$ make CFLAGS=-g ...
```

Debugging C Programs

The C compiler is liberal about the kinds of constructs it allows in programs. In keeping with the UNIX philosophy that "no news is good news" and that the user knows what is best, gcc, like many other Linux utilities, accepts almost anything that is logically possible according to the definition of the language. Although this approach gives the programmer a great deal of flexibility and control, it can make debugging difficult.

Figure 27-4 shows **badtabs.c**, a flawed version of the **tabs.c** program discussed earlier. It contains some errors and does not run properly, but illustrates some debugging techniques.

```
 1   /* convert tabs in standard input to spaces in */        | Comments
 2   /* standard output while maintaining columns */
 3
 4   #include        <stdio.h>                                 | Preprocessor
 5   #define         TABSIZE        8                          | Directives
 6
 7   /* prototype for function findstop */                     | Function
 8   int findstop(int *);                                      | Prototype
 9
10   main()                                                    | Main
11   {                                                         | Function
12   int c;          /* character read from stdin */
13   int posn = 0;   /* column position of character */
14   int inc;        /* column increment to tab stop */
15
16   while ((c = getchar()) != EOF)
17       switch(c)
18           {
19           case '\t':                /* c is a tab */
20                   inc = findstop(&posn);
21                   for( ; inc > 0; inc-- )
22                           putchar(' ');
23                   break;
24           case '\n':                /* c is a newline */
25                   putchar(c);
26                   posn = 0;
27                   break;
28           default:                  /* c is anything else */
29                   putchar(c);
30                   posn++;
31                   break;
32           }
33
34   }
35
36   /* compute size of increment to next tab stop */          | Function
37
38   int findstop(int *col)
39   {
40   int colindex, retval;
41   retval = (TABSIZE - (*col % TABSIZE));
42
43   /* increment argument (current column position) to next tabstop * /
44   *col += retval;
45
46   return retval;          /* main gets how many blanks for filling */
47   }
```

Figure 27-4 The **badtabs.c** program (The line numbers are not part of the source code; the arrows point to errors in the program.)

In the following example, **badtabs.c** is compiled and then run with input from the **testtabs** file. Inspection of the output shows that the TAB character has not been replaced with the proper number of SPACES:

```
$ gcc -o badtabs badtabs.c
$ cat testtabs
abcTABxyz
$ badtabs < testtabs
abc    xyz
```

One way to debug a C program is to insert **print** statements at critical points throughout the source code. To learn more about the behavior of **badtabs.c** when it runs, you can replace the contents of the **switch** statement with

```
case '\t':                /* c is a tab */
    fprintf(stderr, "before call to findstop, posn is %d\n", posn);
    inc = findstop(&posn);
    fprintf(stderr, "after call to findstop, posn is %d\n", posn);
    for( ; inc > 0; inc-- )
        putchar(' ');
    break;
case '\n':                /* c is a newline */
    fprintf(stderr, "got a newline\n");
    putchar(c);
    posn = 0;
    break;
default:                   /* c is anything else */
    fprintf(stderr, "got another character\n");
    putchar(c);
    posn++;
    break;
```

The **fprintf** statements in this code send their messages to standard error, so if you redirect standard output of this program, it will not be interspersed with the output sent to standard error. Following is an example that demonstrates the operation of this program on the input file **testtabs**:

```
$ gcc -o badtabs badtabs.c
$ badtabs < testtabs > testspaces
got another character
got another character
got another character
before call to findstop, posn is 3
after call to findstop, posn is 3
got another character
got another character
got another character
got a newline
$ cat testspaces
abcTABxyz
```

The **fprintf** statements provide additional information about the execution **of tabs.c**, especially that the value of the variable **posn** is not incremented in **findstop**, as it should be. This might be enough to lead you to the bug in the program. If not, you might attempt to "corner" the offending code by inserting **fprintf** statements in **findstop**.

For simple programs or when you have an idea of what is wrong with your program, adding **print** statements that trace the execution of the code can often help you solve the problem quickly. A better strategy may be to switch to one of the tools that Linux provides to help you debug programs.

gcc: **Compiler Warning Options Find Errors in Programs**

The gcc compiler has many of the features of lint, the classic C program verifier,[3] built into it and then some. This compiler is able to identify many C program constructs that pose potential problems, even for programs that conform to the syntax rules of the language. For instance, if you request, the compiler can report whether a variable is declared but not used, a comment is not properly terminated, or a function returns a type not permitted in older versions of C. Options that enable this stricter compiler behavior all begin with the uppercase letter **W** (Warning).

Among the **–W** options is a class of warnings that typically result from programmer carelessness or inexperience. The constructs causing these warnings are generally easy to fix and easy to avoid. Table 27-2 lists some of these options.

table 27-2 ‖   **gcc –W Options**

Option	Reports These Errors
–Wimplicit	When a function or parameter is not explicitly declared
–Wreturn-type	When a function that is not void does not return a value or when the type of a function defaults to **int**
–Wunused	When a variable is declared but not used
–Wcomment	When the characters /∗, which normally begin a comment, are seen within a comment
–Wformat	When certain input/output statements contain format specifications that do not match the arguments

To get warnings about all the preceding errors, along with others in this class, use the **–Wall** option.

The program **badtabs.c** is syntactically correct (it compiles without generating an error). However, if you compile (**–c** causes gcc to compile but not to link) it with the **–Wall** option, you see several problems:[4]

---

3. Not available for Red Hat Linux; use splint (secure programming lint, www.splint.org) instead.

```
$ gcc -c -Wall badtabs.c
badtabs.c:47: warning: '/*' within comment
badtabs.c:11: warning: return-type defaults to 'int'
badtabs.c: In function 'main':
badtabs.c:34: warning: control reaches end of non-void function
badtabs.c: In function 'findstop':
badtabs.c:40: warning: unused variable 'colindex'
badtabs.c:49: warning: control reaches end of non-void function
```

The first warning message references line 47. Inspection of the code for **badtabs.c** around that line reveals a comment that is not properly terminated. The compiler sees the string /* in the following line as the beginning of a comment:

```
/* increment argument (current column position) to next tabstop * /
```

However, because the characters * and / at the end of the line are separated by a SPACE, they do not signify the end of the comment to the compiler. Instead the compiler interprets all the statements, including the statement that increments the argument, through the string */ at the very end of the **findstop** function as part of the comment.

Compiling with the **–Wall** option can be very helpful when debugging a program. By removing the SPACE between the characters * and /, **badtabs** produces the correct output.

The next few paragraphs discuss the remaining warning messages. Although most do not cause problems in the execution of **badtabs**, programs can generally be improved by rewriting parts of the code that produce warnings.

Because the definition of the function **main** does not include an explicit type, the compiler assumes type **int**, the default. This results in the warning message referencing line 11 in **badtabs.c**, the top of the function **main**. An additional warning is given when the compiler encounters the end of the function **main** (line 34) without seeing a value returned.

If a program runs successfully, it should, by convention, return a zero value; if no value is returned, the exit code is undefined. Although it is common to see C programs that do not return a value, the oversight can cause problems when the program is executed. When you add the following statement at the end of the function **main** in **badtabs.c**, the warning referencing line 34 disappears:

```
return 0;
```

Line 40 of **badtabs.c** contains the definition for the local variable **colindex** in the function **findstop**. The warning message referencing that line occurs because the **colindex** variable is never used. Removing its declaration gets rid of the warning message.

The final warning message, referencing line 49, results from the improperly terminated comment discussed earlier. The compiler issues the warning message because

---

4. Warning messages do not stop the program from compiling, whereas error messages do.

it never sees a return statement in **findstop**. (The compiler ignores commented text.) Because the function **findstop** returns type **int**, the compiler expects a return statement before reaching the end of the function. The warning disappears when the comment is properly terminated.

Many other **–W** options are available with the gcc compiler. The ones not covered in the **–Wall** class often involve portability differences; modifying the code causing these warnings may not be appropriate. The warnings usually result from programs written in different C dialects as well as from constructs that may not work well with other (especially older) C compilers. The **–pedantic-errors** option turns warnings into errors, causing a build to fail if it contains items that would cause warnings. To learn more about these and other warning options, refer to the gcc info page.

Symbolic Debugger

Many debuggers are available to tackle problems that evade the simpler methods involving print statements and compiler warning options. These debuggers include gdb, kdbg, xxgdb mxgdb, ddd, and ups, which are available from the Web (refer to Appendix B). All are high-level symbolic debuggers, enabling you to analyze the execution of a program in terms of C language statements. The debuggers also provide a lower-level view for analyzing the execution of a program in terms of the machine instructions. Except for gdb, each of the debuggers mentioned in this paragraph provides a GUI.

A debugger enables you to monitor and control the execution of a program. You can step through a program line by line while you examine the state of the execution environment. A debugger also allows you to examine *core* files. (Core files are named **core**.) When a serious error occurs during the execution of a program, the operating system can create a core file containing information about the state of the program and the system when the error occurred. This file is a dump of the computer's memory (it used to be called *core memory;* thus the term *core dump*) that was being used by the program. To conserve disk space, your system may be set up so that core files are not saved. You can use the ulimit builtin to enable core files to be saved. If you are running bash, the following command allows core files of unlimited size to be saved to disk:

```
$ ulimit -c unlimited
```

The operating system advises you when it dumps core. You can use a symbolic debugger to read information from the core file to identify the line in the program where the error occurred, to check the values of variables at that point, and so forth. Because core files tend to be large and take up disk space, be sure to remove them when you are done.

gdb: Symbolic Debugger

The following examples demonstrate the use of the GNU gdb debugger. Other symbolic debuggers offer a different interface but operate in a similar manner. To make full use of a symbolic debugger with a program, it is necessary to compile the program with the –g option. The –g option causes gcc to generate additional information that the debugger uses. This information includes a *symbol table*—a list of variable names used in the program and associated values. Without the symbol table information, the debugger is unable to display the values and types of variables. If a program is compiled without the –g option, gdb is unable to identify source code lines by number, as many gdb commands require.

tip || **Always Use –g**

It can be helpful always to use the **–g** option, even when releasing software. Including debugging symbols makes the binaries a bit bigger. It does not make them any slower, but it does make it a lot easier to find problems identified by users.

The following example uses the –g option when creating the executable file **tabs** from the C program **tabs.c**, discussed at the beginning of this chapter:

```
$ gcc -g tabs.c -o tabs
```

Input for **tabs** is contained in the file **testtabs**, which consists of a single line:

```
$ cat testtabs
xyzTABabc
```

tip || **Avoid Using Optimization Flags with the Debugger**

Limit the optimization flags to **–0** or **–02** when you compile a program for debugging. Because debugging and optimizing inherently have different goals, it may be best to avoid combining the two.

tip || **Optimization Should Work**

Turning optimization off completely can sometimes eliminate errors. Eliminating errors in this way should not be seen as a solution. When optimization is not enabled, the compiler may automatically initialize variables and perform certain other checks for you, resulting in more stable code. Correct code should work correctly when compiled with at least **–0**, and almost certainly **–02**. The **–03** setting often includes experimental optimizations, so it may not generate correct code in all cases.

You cannot specify the input file to **tabs** when you first call the debugger. Specify the input file once you have called the debugger and started execution with the **run** command.

To run the debugger on the sample executable, give the name of the executable file on the command line when you run gdb. You will see some introductory statements about gdb, followed by the gdb prompt (**gdb**). The debugger is ready to accept commands. The **list** command displays the first ten lines of source code. A subsequent **list** command displays the next ten lines of source code:

```
$ gdb tabs
GNU gdb 4.18
GNU gdb Red Hat Linux (6.0post-0.20040223.14rh)
Copyright 2004 Free Software Foundation, Inc.
GDB is free software, covered by the GNU General Public License, and you are
welcome to change it and/or distribute copies of it under certain
conditions. Type "show copying" to see the conditions. There is absolutely
no warranty for GDB.  Type "show warranty" for details.
This GDB was configured as "i386-redhat-linux-gnu".
(gdb) list
4         #include      <stdio.h>
5         #define       TABSIZE        8
6
7         /* prototype for function findstop */
8         int findstop(int *);
9
10        int main()
11        {
12        int c;           /* character read from stdin */
13        int posn = 0;    /* column position of character */
(gdb) list
14        int inc;         /* column increment to tab stop */
15
16        while ((c = getchar()) != EOF)
17                switch(c)
18                        {
19                        case '\t':               /* c is a tab */
20                                inc = findstop(&posn);
21                                for( ; inc > 0; inc-- )
22                                        putchar(' ');
23                                break;
(gdb)
```

One of the most important features of a debugger is the ability to run a program in a controlled environment. You can stop the program from running whenever you want. While it is stopped, you can check on the state of an argument or variable. The **break** command can be given a source code line number, an actual memory address, or a function name as an argument. The following command tells gdb to stop the process whenever the function **findstop** is called:

```
(gdb) break findstop
Breakpoint 1 at 0x804849f: file tabs.c, line 41.
(gdb)
```

The debugger acknowledges the request by displaying the breakpoint number, the hexadecimal memory address of the breakpoint, and the corresponding source code line number (41). The debugger numbers breakpoints in ascending order as you create them, starting with 1.

Having set a breakpoint, you can issue a **run** command to start execution of **tabs** under the control of the debugger. The **run** command syntax allows you to use angle brackets to redirect input and output (just as the shells do). Following, the **testtabs** file is specified as input. When the process stops (at the breakpoint), you can use the **print** command to check the value of *col. The **backtrace** (or **bt**) command displays the function stack. The example shows that the currently active function has been assigned the number 0. The function that called **findstop** (**main**) has been assigned the number 1:

```
(gdb) run < testtabs
Starting program: /home/mark/book/14/tabs < testtabs

Breakpoint 1, findstop (col=0xbffffc70) at tabs.c:41
41      retval = (TABSIZE - (*col % TABSIZE));
(gdb) print *col
$1 = 3
(gdb) backtrace
#0  findstop (col=0xbffffc70) at tabs.c:41
#1  0x804843a in main () at tabs.c:20
(gdb)
```

You can examine anything in the current scope, including variables and arguments in the active function as well as globals. The following example shows that the request to examine the value of the variable **posn** at breakpoint 1 results in an error. The error results because the variable **posn** is defined locally in the function **main**, not in the function **findstop**:

```
(gdb) print posn
No symbol "posn" in current context.
```

The **up** command changes the active function to the caller of the currently active function. Because **main** calls the function **findstop**, the function **main** becomes the active function when the **up** command is given. (The **down** command does the inverse.) The **up** command may be given an integer argument specifying the number of levels in the function stack to backtrack, with **up 1** meaning the same as **up**. (You can use the **backtrace** command, if necessary, to determine the argument to use with **up**.)

```
(gdb) up
#1  0x804843a in main () at tabs.c:20
20                          inc = findstop(&posn);
(gdb) print posn
$2 = 3
(gdb) print *col
No symbol "col" in current context.
(gdb)
```

The **cont** (continue) command causes the process to continue running from where it left off. The **testtabs** file contains only one line; the process finishes executing, and the results appear on the screen. The debugger reports the exit code of the program. A **cont** command given after a program has finished executing reminds you that execution of the program has completed. Following, the debugging session is ended with a **quit** command:

```
(gdb) cont
Continuing.
abc     xyz

Program exited normally.
(gdb) cont
The program is not being run.
(gdb) quit
$
```

The **gdb** utility supports many commands that are designed to make debugging easier. Type **help** at the **(gdb)** prompt to get a list of the command classes available under **gdb**:

```
(gdb) help
List of classes of commands:

aliases -- Aliases of other commands
breakpoints -- Making program stop at certain points
data -- Examining data
files -- Specifying and examining files
internals -- Maintenance commands
obscure -- Obscure features
running -- Running the program
stack -- Examining the stack
status -- Status inquiries
support -- Support facilities
tracepoints -- Tracing of program execution without stopping the program
user-defined -- User-defined commands

Type "help" followed by a class name for a list of commands in that class.
Type "help" followed by command name for full documentation.
Command name abbreviations are allowed if unambiguous.
(gdb)
```

As given in the instructions following the list, entering **help** followed by the name of a command class or command name will give more information. The following lists the commands in the class **data**:

```
(gdb) help data
Examining data.

List of commands:

call -- Call a function in the program
delete display -- Cancel some expressions to be displayed when program stops
disable display -- Disable some expressions to be displayed when program stops
disassemble -- Disassemble a specified section of memory
display -- Print value of expression EXP each time the program stops
enable display -- Enable some expressions to be displayed when program stops
inspect -- Same as "print" command
output -- Like "print" but don't put in value history and don't print newline
print -- Print value of expression EXP
printf -- Printf "printf format string"
ptype -- Print definition of type TYPE
set -- Evaluate expression EXP and assign result to variable VAR
```

```
set variable -- Evaluate expression EXP and assign result to variable VAR
undisplay -- Cancel some expressions to be displayed when program stops
whatis -- Print data type of expression EXP
x -- Examine memory: x/FMT ADDRESS

Type "help" followed by command name for full documentation.
Command name abbreviations are allowed if unambiguous.
(gdb)
```

The following requests information on the command **whatis**, which takes a variable name or other expression as an argument:

```
(gdb) help whatis
Print data type of expression EXP.
```

Graphical Symbolic Debuggers

There are several GUIs to gdb. Two interfaces that are similar are xxgdb and mxgdb (a Motif-based interface that requires that you have Motif installed on your system). These graphical versions of gdb provide you with a number of windows, including a Source Listing window, a Command window that contains a set of commonly used commands, and a Display window for viewing the values of variables. The left mouse button selects commands from the Command window. You can click the desired line in the Source Listing window to set a breakpoint, and you can select variables by clicking them in the Source Listing window. Selecting a variable and clicking **print** in the Command window display the value of the variable in the Display window. You can view lines of source code by scrolling (and resizing) the Source Listing window.

The ddd debugger also provides a GUI to gdb. Unlike xxgdb and mxgdb, ddd can graphically display complex C structures and the links between them. This display makes it easier to see errors in these structures. Otherwise, the ddd interface is very similar to that of xxgdb and mxgdb.

Unlike xxgdb and mxgdb, ups was designed from the ground up to work as a debugger with a GUI; the graphical interface was not added after the debugger was complete. The result is an interface that is simple yet powerful. For example, ups automatically displays the value of a variable when you click it and has a built-in C interpreter that allows you to attach C code to the program you are debugging. Because this attached code has access to the variables and values in the program, you can use it to perform sophisticated checks, such as following and displaying the links in a complex *data structure* (page 966).

Threads

A *thread* is a single sequential flow of control within a process. Threads are the basis for multithreaded programs, which allow a single program to control concurrently running threads, each performing a different task. Multithreaded programs generally use *reentrant* code (code that multiple threads can use simultaneously) and are most valuable when run on multiple CPU machines. Under Linux, multi-threaded servers, such as NFS, can provide a cleaner interface and may be easier to write than multiple server processes. When applied judiciously, multithreading can also serve as a lower-overhead replacement for the traditional fork-exec idiom for spawning processes. See the FAQ at tldp.org/FAQ/Threads-FAQ.

tip ||	Multiple Threads Are Not Always Better

If you write a multithreaded program with no clear goal or division of effort for a single CPU machine (for example, a parallel-server process), you are likely to end up with a program that runs more slowly than a nonthreaded program on the same machine.

System Calls

Three fundamental responsibilities of the Linux kernel are to control processes, manage the filesystem, and operate peripheral devices. As a programmer you have access to these kernel operations through system calls and library functions. This section discusses system calls at a general level; a detailed treatment is beyond the scope of this book.

As the name implies, a system call instructs the system (kernel) to perform some work directly on your behalf. The request is a message that tells the kernel what work needs to be done and includes the necessary arguments. For example, a system call to open a file includes the name of the file. A library routine is indirect; it issues system calls for you. The advantages of a library routine are that it may insulate you from the low-level details of kernel operations and that it has been written carefully to make sure that it performs efficiently.

For example, it is straightforward to use the standard I/O library function **fprintf( )** to send text to standard output or standard error. Without this function, you would need to issue several system calls to achieve the same result. The calls to the library routines **putchar( )** and **getchar( )** in Figure 27-1 ultimately use the **write( )** and **read( )** system calls to perform the I/O operations.

strace: Traces System Calls

The strace utility is a debugging tool that prints out a trace of all the system calls made by a process or program. Because you do not need to recompile the program that you want to trace, you can use strace on binaries that you do not have source for.

System calls are events that take place at the interface (boundary) between user code and kernel code. Examining this boundary can help you isolate bugs, track down race conditions, and perform sanity checking. The Linux kernel does not fully cooperate with strace. See the strace home page (www.liacs.nl/~wichert/strace) for kernel patches that improve kernel cooperation with strace.

Controlling Processes

When you enter a command line at a shell prompt, the shell process calls the **fork** system call to create a copy of itself (spawn a child) and then uses an **exec** system call to overlay that copy in memory with a different program (the command you asked it to run). Table 27-3 lists system calls that affect processes.

table 27-3 ‖	System Call: Processes Control
fork()	Creates a copy of a process
exec()	Overlays a program in memory with another
getpid()	Returns the process ID of the calling process
wait()	Causes the parent process to wait for the child to finish running before it resumes execution
exit()	Causes a process to exit
nice()	Changes the priority of a process
kill()	Sends a signal to a process

Accessing the Filesystem

Many operations take place when a program reads from or writes to a file. The program needs to know where the file is located; the filename must be converted to an inode number on the correct filesystem. Your access permissions must be checked not only for the file itself but also for all the intervening directories in the path to the file. The file is not stored in one continuous piece on the disk; all the disk blocks that contain pieces of the file must be located. The appropriate kernel device driver must be called to control the operation of the disk. Finally, once the file has been found, the program may need to find a particular location within the file rather than working with it sequentially from beginning to end. Table 27-4 lists some of the most common system calls in filesystem operations.

Access to peripheral devices on a UNIX/Linux system is handled through the filesystem interface. Each peripheral device is represented by one or more special files, usually located under **/dev**. When you read or write to one of these special files, the kernel passes your requests to the appropriate kernel device driver. As a result, you can use the standard system calls and library routines to interact with these devices; you do not need to learn a new set of specialized functions. This is one of the most powerful features of a UNIX/Linux system because it allows users to use the same basic utilities on a wide range of devices.

table 27-4 ||	System Call: Filesystem
stat( )	Gets status information from an inode, such as the inode number, the device on which it is located, owner and group information, and the size of the file
lseek( )	Moves to a position in the file
creat( )	Creates a new file
open( )	Opens an existing file
read( )	Reads a file
write( )	Writes a file
close( )	Closes a file
unlink( )	Unlinks a file (deletes a name reference to the inode)
chmod( )	Changes file access permissions
chown( )	Changes file ownership

The availability of standard system calls and library routines is the key to the portability of Linux tools. For example, as an applications programmer, you can rely on the read and write system calls working the same way on different versions of the Linux system and on different types of computers. The systems programmer who writes a device driver or ports the kernel to run on a new computer, however, must understand the details at their lowest level.

Source Code Management

When you work on a project involving many files that evolve over long periods of time, it can be difficult to keep track of the versions of the files, particularly if several people are updating the files. This problem frequently occurs in large software development projects. Source code and documentation files change frequently as you fix bugs, enhance programs, and release new versions of the software. It becomes even more complex when more than one version of each file is active. Frequently customers are using one version of a file while a newer version is being modified. You can easily lose track of the versions and accidentally undo changes or duplicate earlier work.

To help avoid these kinds of problems, Linux includes CVS (Concurrent Versions System, www.cvshome.org) for managing and tracking changes to files. Although CVS can be used on any file, it is most often used to manage source code and software documentation. CVS is based on RCS and is designed to control the concurrent access and modification of source files by multiple users.

A graphical front end to CVS, tkCVS (www.twobarleycorns.net/tkcvs.html), simplifies the use of CVS, especially if you do not use it frequently enough to memorize its many commands and options.

All three programs/interfaces control who is allowed to update files. For each update, the programs record who made the changes and include notes about why the changes were made. Because they store the most recent version of a file and the information needed to recreate all previous versions, it is possible to regenerate any version of a file.

A set of file versions for several files may be grouped together to form a *release*. An entire release can be recreated from the change information stored with each file. Saving the changes for a file rather than saving a complete copy of the file generally conserves a lot of disk space, well in excess of the space required to store each update in the CVS files themselves.

The following sections provide overviews of CVS and tkCVS. See the *CVS-RCS-HOW-TO Document for Linux* for more information.

CVS: Concurrent Versions System

CVS (Concurrent Versions System—www.cvshome.org) treats collections of files as single units, making it easy to work on large projects and permitting multiple users to work on the same file. CVS also provides valuable self-documenting features for utilities in the CVS system.

Built-in CVS Help

CVS uses a single utility, cvs, for all its functions. To display the instructions for getting help, use the --**help** option:

```
$ cvs --help
Usage: cvs [cvs-options] command [command-options-and-arguments]
  where cvs-options are -q, -n, etc.
    (specify --help-options for a list of options)
  where command is add, admin, etc.
    (specify --help-commands for a list of commands
      or --help-synonyms for a list of command synonyms)
  where command-options-and-arguments depend on the specific command
    (specify -H followed by a command name for command-specific help)
  Specify --help to receive this message
```

The Concurrent Versions System (CVS) is a tool for version control.
For CVS updates and additional information, see
    the CVS home page at http://www.cvshome.org/ or Pascal Molli's CVS
    site at http://www.loria.fr/~molli/cvs-index.html

To get help with a cvs command, use the **--help** option followed by the name of the utility. The following example shows how to get help with the log command:

```
$ cvs --help log
Usage: cvs log [-lRhtNb] [-r[revisions]] [-d dates] [-s states]
    [-w[logins]] [files...]
        -l          Local directory only, no recursion.
        -R          Only print name of RCS file.
        -h          Only print header.
        -t          Only print header and descriptive text.
        -N          Do not list tags.
        -b          Only list revisions on the default branch.
        -r[revisions]    Specify revision(s)s to list.
           rev1:rev2    Between rev1 and rev2, including rev1 and rev2.
           rev1::rev2   Between rev1 and rev2, excluding rev1 and rev2.
           rev:         rev and following revisions on the same branch.
           rev::        After rev on the same branch.
           :rev         rev and previous revisions on the same branch.
           ::rev        Before rev on the same branch.
           rev          Just rev.
           branch       All revisions on the branch.
           branch.      The last revision on the branch.
        -d dates        Specify dates (D1<D2 for range, D for latest before).
        -s states       Only list revisions with specified states.
        -w[logins]      Only list revisions checked in by specified logins.
(Specify the --help global option for a list of other help options)
```

Options for individual cvs commands (command options) go to the *right* of the individual command names. However, options to the cvs utility itself, such as the **--help** option to the log command, go to the *left* of all the individual command names (that is, they follow the word **cvs** on the command line). The two types of options sometimes use the same letter yet may have an entirely different meaning.

How CVS Stores Revision Files

With CVS, revision files are kept in a common area called a *source repository*. This area is identified by the value of the environment variable **CVSROOT**, which holds the absolute pathname of the repository. Your system administrator can tell you what value of **CVSROOT** to use, or you can create your own private repository.

The source repository is organized as a hierarchical collection of files and directories. In CVS you are not limited to checking out one file at a time; you can check out an entire subdirectory containing many files—typically all the files for a particular project. A subdirectory of **CVSROOT** that can be checked out as a single unit is called a *module*. Several people can check out and simultaneously modify the files within a single module.

It is common practice for CVS users to store all the modules they are currently working on in a special directory. If you want to follow this practice, you must use cd to make that special directory your working directory before you check out a module. When you check out a module, *CVS replicates the module's tree structure in the working directory.* Multiple developers can check out and edit CVS files simultaneously because the originals are retained in the source repository; the files in the repository undergo relatively infrequent modification in a controlled manner.

Basic CVS Commands

Although there are many cvs commands, a handful of commands allows a software developer to use the CVS system and to contribute changes to a module. A discussion of some useful commands follows. All examples assume that the appropriate modules have been installed in the CVS source repository. "Adding a Module to the Repository" (page 843) explains how to install a module.

Of the commands discussed in this section, the cvs commit command is the only one that changes the source repository. The other commands affect only the files in the working directory.

To simplify examples in the following sections, the pathname of the working directory is given by the variable **CVSWORK**; all modules can be assumed to be subdirectories of **CVSWORK**. Although this variable has no special meaning to CVS, you may find it helpful to define such a variable for your own work.

Checking Out Files from the Source Repository

To check out a module from the CVS source repository, use the cvs checkout command. The following example checks out the **Project2** module, which consists of four source files. First, use cd to change working directories to the directory you want the module copied into (**CVSWORK** in this case); cvs always copies into the working directory:

```
$ cd $CVSWORK
$ ls
Project1
$ cvs checkout Project2
cvs checkout: Updating Project2
U Project2/adata.h
U Project2/compute.c
U Project2/randomfile.h
U Project2/shuffle.c
$ ls
Project1 Project2
$ ls Project2
CVS adata.h compute.c randomfile.h shuffle.c
```

The name of the module, **Project2**, is given as an argument to **cvs checkout**. Because the **Project2** directory does not already exist, cvs creates it in the working directory and places copies of all source files for the **Project2** module into it: The name of the module and the name of the directory holding the module are the same. The check-out command preserves the tree structure of the cvs module, creating subdirectories as needed.

The second ls command after checkout reveals, in addition to the four source files for **Project2**, a directory named **CVS**. The CVS system uses this directory for administrative purposes; it is not normally accessed by the user.

Once you have your own copies of the source files, you can edit them as you see fit. You can make changes to files within the module, even if other developers are making changes to the same files at the same time.

Making Your Changes Available to Others

To check in your changes so that others have access to them, you need to run the cvs commit command. When you give this command, cvs prompts you for a brief log message describing the changes, unless you use the **−m** option. With this option, cvs uses the string following the option as the log message. The file or files that you want to commit follow the optional log message on the command line:

```
$ cvs commit -m "function shuffle inserted" compute.c
cvs commit: Up-to-date check failed for `compute.c'
cvs [commit aborted]: correct above errors first!
```

The cvs utility reports an error because the version of **compute.c** that you modified is not up-to-date. A newer version of **compute.c** has been committed by someone else since you last checked it out of the source repository. After informing you of the problem, cvs exits without storing your changes in the source repository.

To make your version of **compute.c** current, you need to run the update command (see the next section). A subsequent commit will then succeed, and your changes will apply to the latest revision in the source repository.

Updating Your Copies with Changes by Others

As the preceding example shows, CVS does not notify you when another developer checks in a new revision of a file since you checked out your working copy. You learn this only when you attempt to commit your changes to the source repository. To incorporate up-do-date revisions of a CVS source file, use the cvs update command:

```
$ cvs update compute.c
RCS file: /usr/local/src/master/Project2/compute.c,v
retrieving revision 1.9
retrieving revision 1.10
Merging differences between 1.9 and 1.10 into compute.c
M compute.c
```

The changes made to the working copy of **compute.c** remain intact because the update command merges the latest revision in the source repository with the version specified on the update command line. The result of the merge is not always perfect. The cvs update command will inform you if it detects overlapping changes.

Adding New Files to the Repository

You can use the cvs add command to schedule new files to be added to the source repository as part of the module you are working on. Once you have moved to the directory containing the files, give the cvs add command, listing the files you want to add as arguments:

```
$ cd $CVSWORK/Project2
$ ls
CVS compute.c shuffle.c tabout2.c
adata.h randomfile.h tabout1.c
$ cvs add tabout[1-2].c
cvs add: scheduling file 'tabout1.c' for addition
cvs add: scheduling file 'tabout2.c' for addition
cvs add: use 'cvs commit' to add these files permanently
```

The add command marks the files **tabout1.c** and **tabout2.c** for entry into the repository. The files will not be available for others until you give a commit command. This staging allows you to prepare several files before others incorporate the changes into their working copies with the cvs update command.

Removing Files from the Repository

The cvs remove command records the fact that you wish to remove a file from the source repository and, like the add command, does not affect the source repository. To delete a file from the repository, you must first delete your working copy of the file, as the following example shows:

```
$ cvs remove shuffle.c
cvs remove: file 'shuffle.c' still in working directory
cvs remove: 1 file exists; use 'rm' to remove it first
$ rm shuffle.c
$ cvs remove shuffle.c
cvs remove: scheduling 'shuffle.c' for removal
cvs remove: use 'cvs commit' to remove this file permanently
```

After using rm to remove the working copy of **shuffle.c**, invoke the cvs remove command. Again, you must give the commit command before the file is actually removed from the source repository.

Other CVS Commands

Although the commands given earlier are sufficient for most work on a module, you may find some other commands that are useful as well.

Tagging a Release

You can apply a common label, or *tag,* to the files in a module as they currently exist. Once you have tagged files of a module, you can recreate them in exactly the same form, even if they have been modified, added, or deleted since that time. This enables you to *freeze* a release and still allows development to continue on the next release:

```
$ cvs rtag Release_1 Project1
cvs rtag: Tagging Project1
```

Here the **Project1** module has been tagged with the label **Release_1**. You can use this tag with the cvs export command (see the following) to extract the files; they were frozen at this time.

Extracting a Release

The cvs export command lets you extract files as they were frozen and tagged:

```
$ cvs export -r Release_1 -d R1 Project1
cvs export: Updating R1
U R1/scm.txt
```

This command works like the cvs checkout command but does not create the CVS support files. You must give either the –r option to identify the release (as shown) or a date with the –D option. The –d R1 option instructs cvs to place the files for the module into the directory R1 instead of using the module name as the directory.

Removing Working Files

When you are finished making changes to the files you have checked out of the repository, you may decide to remove your copy of the module from your working directory. One simple method is to move into the working directory and recursively remove the module. For example, if you want to remove your working copy of **Project2**, you could use the following commands:

```
$ cd $CVSWORK
$ rm -rf Project2
```

The repository will not be affected. However, if you had made changes to the files but had not yet committed those changes, they would be lost if you use that approach. The cvs release command is helpful in this situation:

```
$ cd $CVSWORK
$ cvs release -d Project2
```

The release command also removes the working files but first checks each one to see whether it has been marked for addition into the repository but has not been committed. If that is the case, the release command warns you and asks you to verify your intention to delete the file. If you want, you can fix the problem at this point and redo the release command. The release command also warns you if the repository holds a newer version of the file than the one in your working directory. This gives you the opportunity to update and commit your file before deleting it. (Without the –d option, your working files will not be deleted, but the same sequence of warning messages will be given.)

Adding a Module to the Repository

The discussion of CVS to this point assumes that a module is already present in the CVS source repository. If you want to install a directory hierarchy as a new module in the repository or update an existing module with a new release that was developed elsewhere, go to the directory that holds the files for the project and run the cvs import command. The following example installs the files for **Project1** in the source repository:

```
$ cvs import -m "My first project" Project1 ventag reltag
```

The **−m** option allows you to enter a brief description of the module on the command line. Following the description is the directory or the pathname of the directory under **CVSROOT** that you want to hold the module. The last two fields are symbolic names for the vendor branch and the release. Although they are not significant here, they can be useful when releases of software are supplied by outside sources. You can now use the cvs checkout command to check out the **Project1** module:

```
$ cvs checkout Project1
```

CVS Administration

Before you install a CVS repository, think about how you would like to administer it. Many installations have a single repository where separate projects are kept as separate modules. You may choose to have more than one repository. The CVS system supports a single repository that is shared across several computer systems using NFS.

Inside a repository is a module, named CVSROOT, that contains administrative files (here CVSROOT is the name of a module and is different from the **CVSROOT** directory). Although the files in this module are not required to use CVS, they can simplify access to the repository.

Do not change any of the files in the CVSROOT module by editing them directly. Instead, check out the file you want to change, edit the checked-out copy, and then check it back in, just as you would with files in any other module in the repository. For example, to check out the **modules** file from the CVSROOT module, use the command

```
$ cvs checkout CVSROOT/modules
```

This command creates the directory **CVSROOT** in your working directory and places a checked out copy of **modules** into that directory. After checking it out, you can edit the **modules** file in the **CVSROOT** directory:

```
$ cd CVSROOT
$ vi modules
```

After you edit the **modules** file, check it back into the repository:

```
$ cd ..
$ cvs checkin CVSROOT/modules
```

Of the administrative files in the CVSROOT module, the **modules** file is the most important. You can use the **modules** file to attach symbolic names to modules in the repository, allow access to subdirectories of a module as if they were themselves modules, and specify actions to take when checking specific files in or out.

As an example, most repositories start with a **modules** file that allows you to check out the **modules** file with the following command, instead of the one shown earlier:

```
$ cvs checkout modules
```

Here CVS creates a subdirectory named **modules** within your working directory, instead of one named **CVSROOT**. The **modules** file is checked out into this directory.

The following is an example of a **modules** file (the lines that start with a # are comment lines and, along with blank lines, are ignored by CVS):

```
# The CVS modules file
#
# Three different line formats are valid:
#   key -a aliases...
#   key [options] directory
#   key [options] directory files...
#
# Where "options" are composed of:
#   -i prog     Run "prog" on "cvs commit" from top-level of module.
#   -o prog     Run "prog" on "cvs checkout" of module.
#   -t prog     Run "prog" on "cvs rtag" of module.
#   -u prog     Run "prog" on "cvs update" of module.
#   -d dir      Place module in directory "dir" instead of module name.
#   -l          Top-level directory only -- do not recurse.
#
# And "directory" is a path to a directory relative to $CVSROOT.
#
# The "-a" option specifies an alias.  An alias is interpreted as if
# everything on the right of the "-a" had been typed on the command line.
#
#
# You can encode a module within a module by using the special '&'
# character to interpose another module into the current module.  This
# can be useful for creating a module that consists of many directories
# spread out over the entire source repository.


# Convenient aliases
world       -a .

# CVSROOT support; run mkmodules whenever anything changes.
CVSROOT     -i mkmodules CVSROOT
modules     -i mkmodules CVSROOT modules
loginfo     -i mkmodules CVSROOT loginfo
commitinfo  -i mkmodules CVSROOT commitinfo
rcsinfo     -i mkmodules CVSROOT rcsinfo
editinfo    -i mkmodules CVSROOT editinfo
# Add other modules here...
```

```
testgen      testgen
testdata1    testdata1
testdata2    testdata2
testdata3    testdata3
testdata4    testdata4
testcode     testgen/_code
cvs          cvs
```

The lines after the comment and blank lines define symbolic names for many modules. For example, the following line defines the name **world** to be an alias for the root of the CVS repository:

```
world        -a .
```

You can use such names in CVS commands as the names of modules, so the following command checks out the entire repository (probably not a good idea):

```
$ cvs checkout world
```

In the sample **modules** file shown, the administrative files have been given definitions that attach both a symbolic name to the file and an action (**–i mkmodules**) to take when each file is checked into the repository. The **–i mkmodules** action causes CVS to run the mkmodules program when the file is checked in. This program ensures that a copy of the checked-in file exists in a location where CVS can locate it.

Following the action is the name of the subdirectory in **CVSROOT** where the file (or files) associated with the symbolic name are located. Any remaining arguments on the line are the names of specific files within that directory.

The following line identifies the name CVSROOT as the module name for the module in the directory **$CVSROOT/CVSROOT**; that is, all the administrative files for CVS:

```
CVSROOT      -i mkmodules CVSROOT
```

Similarly, the following line associates the module named **modules** with the **modules** file within the **CVSROOT** directory:

```
modules      -i mkmodules CVSROOT modules
```

This line that allows the following command to find and check out the **modules** file:

```
$ cvs checkout modules
```

The last set of lines in the sample **modules** file associates symbolic module names with directories and files in the repository.

Using tkcvs

The CVS utility is useful enough that an X Window System interface, tkcvs, has been written for it, using the Tk extension to the Tcl programming language (tcl.sourceforge.net). This utility provides a convenient point-and-click interface to CVS (Figure 27-5). After you have downloaded and installed tkcvs, start it by using cd to change to the directory you want to work in and entering the following command:

```
$ tkcvs &
```

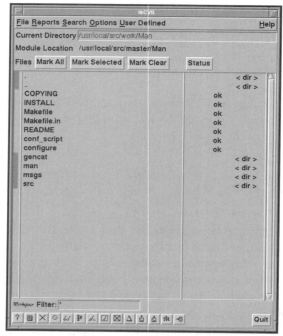

Figure 27-5   The tkCVS utility

All operations are available through the pull-down menus at the top of the window. Along the bottom are buttons for accessing the most common actions. Because the icons on the buttons may not make sense to you, a longer description of the action bound to a button appears when you position the mouse pointer on top of a button.

In the middle of the window is a *browse list*. Move into a subdirectory by double-clicking the left mouse button while the mouse pointer is on the directory name in the list. Edit a file by double-clicking the filename. To select more than one file, drag the mouse pointer across several names while holding down the left mouse button. Clicking the right mouse button will *mark* all selected files. Some of the operations (such as viewing the revision log messages) will work on all marked files.

The Help pull-down menu in the upper-right corner is an excellent way to learn how tkCVS works. For example, when you select the Help menu item **CVS modules file...**, an explanation of the lines that you can add to the CVS **modules** file to support the tkCVS utility better appears in a window. If you choose not to add these lines to the **modules** file, some of the tkCVS commands, such as browsing the repository, may not display all available modules.

Chapter Summary

The operating system interface to C programs and a variety of software development tools make the Linux system well suited to programming in C. The C libraries provide general-purpose C functions that make operating system services and other functionality available to C programmers. The standard C library, **libc**, is always accessible to C programs, and you can specify other libraries by using the –l option to the gcc compiler.

You can write a C program by using a text editor, such as pico, vi, or emacs. C programs always have a function named **main** and often have several other functions. Preprocessor directives define symbolic constants and macros and instruct the preprocessor to include header files.

When you use gcc, it calls the C preprocessor followed by the C compiler and the assembler. The compiler creates assembly language code, which the assembler uses to create object modules. Finally, the linker combines the object modules into an executable file. You can use the –**Wall** option to gcc to detect *risky* constructs—ones that are legal but suggest the possibility of later problems. Other options to gcc can help locate areas of your code that might not be portable.

Although using **printf** statements and the –**Wall** option can help in tracking program bugs, it is a good practice to compile C programs routinely with the –**g** option. This option causes information that can be interpreted by gdb, a symbolic debugger, to be generated with your executable file. When you run your program under the control of gdb, you can specify points where you want gdb to pause your program, inquire about the values of variables, display the program stack, and use a wide range of debugger commands to learn about many other aspects of your program's behavior.

The make utility uses a file named **Makefile** (or **makefile**) that documents the relationships among files. It keeps track of which modules of a program are out-of-date and compiles files in order to keep all modules up-to-date. The dependency line, which specifies the exact dependency relationship between target and prerequisite files, is the key to the operation of a makefile. A dependency line not only specifies a relationship but also gives the construction commands that make the target up-to-date. Implied dependencies and construction commands, as well as the make macro facility, are available to simplify the writing of complex makefiles.

The Linux system includes utilities that assist in keeping track of groups of files that undergo multiple revisions, often by multiple developers. These source code management systems include CVS. CVS, the Concurrent Versions System, is built on top of RCS but provides a much more extensive set of operations for managing directories of files that may be accessed and modified by many users. It is a better choice for large-scale projects and for maintaining software releases that are sent to and from other sites.

Exercises

1. What function does every C program have? Why should you split large programs into several functions?

2. What command could you use to compile **prog.c** and **func.c** into an executable named **cprog**?

3. Show two ways to instruct the C preprocessor to include the header file **/usr/include/math.h** in your C program. Assuming that the **declar.h** header file is located in the subdirectory named **headers** of your home directory, describe two ways to instruct the C preprocessor to include this header file in your C program.

4. How are the names of system libraries abbreviated on the gcc command line? Where does gcc search for libraries named in this manner? Describe how to specify your own library on the gcc command line.

5. Write a **makefile** that reflects the following relationships:

   a. The C source files **transactions.c** and **reports.c** are compiled to produce an executable **accts**.

   b. Both **transactions.c** and **reports.c** include a header file **accts.h**.

   c. The header file **accts.h** is composed of two other header files: **trans.h** and **reps.h**.

6. If you retrieve Version 4.1 of the file **answers** for editing and then attempt to retrieve the same version again, what will CVS do? Why is CVS set up this way?

Advanced Exercises

7. Modify the **badtabs.c** program (page 824) so that it exits cleanly (with a specific return value). Compile the program, and run it using the dbx or another debugger. What values does the debugger report when the program finishes executing?

8. For the following makefile,

```
$ cat Makefile
leads: menu.o users.o resellers.o prospects.o
        gcc -o leads menu.o users.o resellers.o prospects.o

menu.o: menu.h dialog.h inquiry.h

users.o: menu.h dialog.h

prospects.o: dialog.h
```

Identify:

a. Targets

b. Construction commands

c. Prerequisites

9. Refer to **Makefile** in exercise 8 to answer the following questions:

   a. If the target **leads** is up-to-date and you then change **users.c,** what happens when you run make again? Be specific.

   b. Rewrite the makefile to include the following macros:
```
OBJECTS = menu.o users.o resellers.o prospects.o
HFILES = menu.h dialog.h
```

10. Review the make info page to answer the following questions:

    a. What does the **–t** option do?

    b. If you have files named **makefile** and **Makefile** in the working directory, how can you instruct make to use **Makefile**?

    c. Give two ways to define a variable so that you can use it inside a makefile.

11. Refer to the makefile for **compute** on page 819. Suppose that a file in the working directory is named **clean**. What is the effect of giving the following command. Explain.
```
$ make clean
```
The discussion of the makefile on page 818 states that the following command is not normally seen in makefiles:
```
cat num.h table.h > form.h
```

    a. Discuss the effect of removing this construction command from the makefile while retaining the dependency line.

    b. The preceding construction command works only because the file **form.h** is made up of **num.h** and **table.h**. More often **#include** directives in the target define the dependencies. Suggest a more general technique that updates **form.h** whenever **num.h** or **table.h** has a more recent modification date.

Programming the Bourne Again Shell

28

Chapters 7 and 9 introduced the Bourne Again Shell. This chapter describes additional commands, builtins, and concepts that carry shell programming to a point where it can be useful. The first programming constructs covered are control structures, or control flow constructs. These structures allow you to write scripts that can loop over command line arguments, make decisions based on the value of a variable, set up menus, and more. The Bourne Again Shell uses the same constructs found in such high-level programming languages as C.

This chapter goes on to explain how the Here document makes it possible for you to redirect input to a script to come from the script itself, rather than from the terminal or other file. "Expanding Null or Unset Variables" (page 884) shows you various ways to set default values for a variable. The section on the **exec** builtin demonstrates how it provides an efficient way to execute a command by replacing a process and how you can use it to redirect input and output from within a script. The next section covers the **trap** builtin, which provides a way to detect and respond to operating system signals (or interrupts, such as the one that is generated when you press CONTROL-C). Finally, the section on functions gives you a clean way to execute code similar to scripts much more quickly and efficiently.

This chapter contains many examples of shell programs. Although they illustrate certain concepts, most use information from earlier examples as well. This overlap not only reinforces your overall knowledge of shell programming but also demonstrates how commands can be combined to solve complex tasks. Running, modifying, and experimenting with the examples are good ways to become comfortable with the underlying concepts.

This chapter illustrates concepts with simple and more complicated examples. The more complex scripts illustrate traditional shell programming practices and introduce some Linux utilities often used in scripts. The first time you read the chapter, you can skip these sections without loss of continuity. Return to them later when you feel comfortable with the basic concepts.

Control Structures

The *control flow* commands alter the order of execution of commands within a shell script. Control structures include the **if...then, for...in, while, until,** and **case** statements. In addition, the **break** and **continue** statements work in conjunction with the control flow structures to alter the order of execution of commands within a script.

if...then

The syntax of the **if...then** control structure is

> *if test-command*
> > *then*
> > > **commands**
> > *fi*

The ***bold*** words in the syntax description are the items you supply to cause the structure to have the desired effect. The *nonbold* words are the keywords the shell uses to identify the control structure.

Figure 28-1 shows that the **if** statement tests the status returned by the ***test-command*** and transfers control based on this status. The end of the **if** structure is marked by a **fi** statement, which is *if* spelled backwards. The following script prompts you for two words, reads them in, and then uses an **if** structure to evaluate the result returned by the test builtin when it compares the two words. The test builtin returns a status of *true* if the two words are the same and *false* if they are not. Double quotation marks around $word1 and $word2 make sure that test works properly if you enter a string that contains a SPACE or other special character:

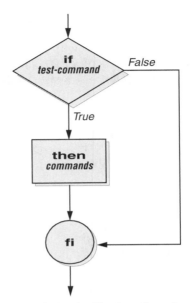

Figure 28-1   An **if...then** flowchart

```
$ cat if1
echo -n "word 1: "
read word1
echo -n "word 2: "
read word2

if test "$word1" = "$word2"
    then
        echo "Match"
fi
echo "End of program."

$ if1
word 1: peach
word 2: peach
Match
End of program.
```

test   In the preceding example, the *test-command* is **test "$word1" = "$word2"**. The **test** builtin returns a *true* status if its first and third arguments have the relationship specified by its second argument. If this command returns a *true* status (= 0), the shell executes the commands between the **then** and **fi** statements. If the command returns a *false* status (not = 0), the shell passes control to the statement after **fi** without executing the statements between **then** and **fi**. The effect of this **if** statement is to display **Match** if the two words match. The script always displays **End of program**.

In the Bourne Again Shell, test is a builtin—part of the shell. It is also a stand-alone utility kept in **/usr/bin/test**. This chapter discusses and demonstrates many Bourne Again Shell builtins. You usually use the builtin version if it is available and the utility if it is not. Each version of a command may vary slightly from one shell to the next and from the utility to any of the shell builtins. To locate documentation, first determine whether you are using a builtin or a stand-alone utility. Use the type builtin for this purpose:

```
$ type test cat echo who if
test is a shell builtin
cat is hashed (/bin/cat)
echo is a shell builtin
who is /usr/bin/who
if is a shell keyword
```

To get more information on a stand-alone utility, use the man or info command followed by the name of the utility. Refer to "Builtins" on page 211 for instructions on how to find information on a builtin command.

The next program uses an **if** structure at the beginning of a script to check that you supplied at least one argument on the command line. The **–eq** test operator compares two integers. This structure displays a message and exits from the script if you do not supply an argument:

```
$ cat chkargs
if test $# -eq 0
    then
        echo "You must supply at least one argument."
        exit 1
fi
echo "Program running."
$ chkargs
You must supply at least one argument.
$ chkargs abc
Program running.
```

A test like the one shown in **chkargs** is a key component of any script that requires arguments. To prevent the user from receiving meaningless or confusing information from the script, the script needs to check whether the user has supplied the appropriate arguments. Sometimes the script simply tests whether arguments exist (as in **chkargs**). Other scripts test for a specific number or specific kinds of arguments.

You can use test to ask a question about the status of a file argument or the relationship between two file arguments. After verifying that at least one argument has been given on the command line, the following script tests whether the argument is the name of a regular file (not a directory or other type of file) in the working directory. The test builtin with the **–f** option and the first command line argument (**$1**) check the file:

```
$ cat is_regfile
if test $# -eq 0
    then
        echo "You must supply at least one argument."
        exit 1
fi
if test -f "$1"
    then
        echo "$1 is a regular file in the working directory"
    else
        echo "$1 is NOT a regular file in the working directory"
fi
```

With test and various options, you can test many other characteristics of a file. Some of the options are listed in Table 28-1

table 28-1 || **Options to the test Utility**

Option	Test Performed on File
−d	Exists and is a directory file
−e	Exists
−f	Exists and is a regular file
−r	Exists and is readable
−s	Exists and has a length greater than 0
−w	Exists and is writable
−x	Exists and is executable

Other test options provide a way to test for a relationship between two files, such as whether one file is newer than another. Refer to later examples in this chapter, as well as the test man page, for more detailed information. (Although test is a builtin, the utility described on the test man page functions similarly.)

tip || **Always Test the Arguments**

To keep the examples in this and subsequent chapters short and focused on specific concepts, the code to verify arguments is often omitted or abbreviated. It is a good practice to include tests for argument verification in your own shell programs. Doing so will result in scripts that are easier to run and debug.

The following example, another version of **chkargs**, checks for arguments in a way that is more traditional for Linux shell scripts. The example uses the bracket ([]) synonym for test. Rather than using the word test in scripts, you can surround the arguments to test with brackets, as shown. The brackets must be surrounded by whitespace (SPACEs or TABs).

```
$ cat chkargs2
if [ $# -eq 0 ]
    then
        echo "Usage: chkargs2 argument..." 1>&2
        exit 1
fi
echo "Program running."
exit 0
$ chkargs2
Usage: chkargs2 arguments
$ chkargs2 abc
Program running.
```

The error message that **chkargs2** displays is called a *usage message* and uses the
1>&2 notation to redirect its output to standard error (page 260). After issuing the
usage message, **chkargs2** exits with an exit status of 1, indicating that an error has
occurred. The **exit 0** command at the end of the script causes **chkargs2** to exit with
a 0 status after the program runs without an error.

The usage message is a common notation to specify the type and number of arguments the script takes. Many Linux utilities provide usage messages similar to the
one in **chkargs2**. When you call a utility or other program with the wrong number
or kind of arguments, you often see a usage message. Following is the usage message that cp displays when you call it without any arguments:

```
$ cp
cp: missing file arguments
Try `cp --help' for more information.
```

if...then...else

The introduction of the **else** statement turns the **if** structure into the two-way
branch shown in Figure 28-2. The syntax of the **if...then...else** control structure is

*if **test-command***
    then
        commands
    else
        commands
fi

Because a semicolon (;) ends a command just as a NEWLINE does, you can place **then** on
the same line as **if** by preceding it with a semicolon. (Because **if** and **then** are separate builtins, they require a command separator between them; a semicolon and NEW-
LINE work equally well.) Some people prefer this notation for aesthetic reasons;
others, because it saves space:

*if **test-command**; then*
        commands
    else
        commands
fi

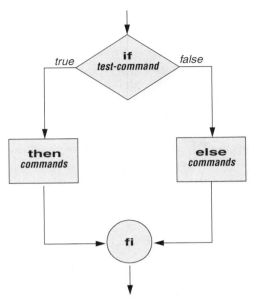

Figure 28-2   An **if...then...else** flowchart

If the *test-command* returns a *true* status, the **if** structure executes the commands between the **then** and **else** statements and then diverts control to the statement following **fi**. If the *test-command* returns a *false* status, the **if** structure executes the commands following the **else** statement.

The next script builds on **chkargs2**. When you run **out** with arguments that are filenames, it displays the files on the terminal. If the first argument is a **–v** (called an option in this case), **out** uses less (page 120) to display the files one page at a time. After determining that it was called with at least one argument, **out** tests its first argument to see whether it is **–v**. If the result of the test is *true* (if the first argument is **–v**), **out** shifts the arguments to get rid of the **–v** and displays the files using less. If the result of the test is *false* (if the first argument is *not* **–v**), the script uses cat to display the files:

```
$ cat out
if [ $# -eq 0 ]
    then
        echo "Usage: out [-v] filenames..." 1>&2
        exit 1
fi
if [ "$1" = "-v" ]
    then
        shift
        less -- "$@"
    else
        cat -- "$@"
fi
```

optional ‖

In **out**, the −− argument to cat and less tells the utility that no more options follow on the command line and not to consider leading hyphens (–) in the following list as indicating options. Thus −− allows you to view a file with a name that starts with a hyphen. Although not common, filenames beginning with a hyphen do occasionally occur. (One way to create such a file is to use the command **cat >** **–fname**.) The −− argument works with all Linux utilities that use the getopts function, a bash builtin, to parse their options. It does not work with all Linux utilities (for example, more). It is particularly useful with rm to remove a file whose name starts with a hyphen (**rm −− –fname**), including any that you create while experimenting with the −− argument.

if...then...elif

The format of the **if...then...elif** control structure, shown in Figure 28-3, is as follows:

> *if **test-command***
> > *then*
> > > *commands*
> > *elif **test-command***
> > > *then*
> > > > *commands*
>
> .
> .
>
> > > *else*
> > > > *commands*
> *fi*

The **elif** statement combines the **else** statement and the **if** statement and allows you to construct a nested set of **if...then...else** structures (Figure 28-3). The difference between the **else** statement and the **elif** statement is that each **else** statement must be paired with a **fi** statement, whereas multiple nested **elif** statements require only a single closing **fi** statement.

The following example shows an **if...then...elif** control structure. This shell script compares three words that the user enters. The first **if** statement uses the AND operator (−a) as an argument to test. The test builtin returns a *true* status only if the first and the second logical comparisons are true (that is, if **word1** matches **word2** and **word2** matches **word3**). If **test** returns a *true* status, the program executes the command following the next **then** statement and passes control to the **fi** statement, and the script terminates:

```
$ cat if3
echo -n "word 1: "
read word1
echo -n "word 2: "
read word2
echo -n "word 3: "
```

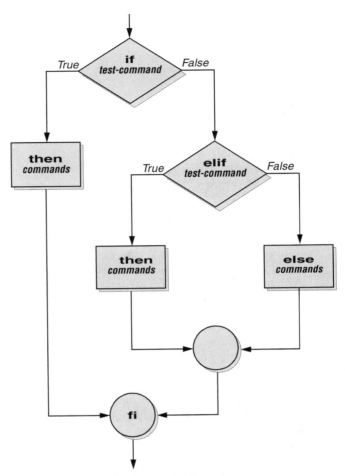

Figure 28-3   An **if**...**then**...**elif** flowchart

```
read word3
if [ "$word1" = "$word2" -a "$word2" = "$word3" ]
    then
        echo "Match: words 1, 2, & 3"
    elif [ "$word1" = "$word2" ]
    then
        echo "Match: words 1 & 2"
    elif [ "$word1" = "$word3" ]
    then
        echo "Match: words 1 & 3"
    elif [ "$word2" = "$word3" ]
    then
        echo "Match: words 2 & 3"
    else
        echo "No match"
fi
```

```
$ if3
word 1: apple
word 2: orange
word 3: pear
No match
$ if3
word 1: apple
word 2: orange
word 3: apple
Match: words 1 & 3
$ if3
word 1: apple
word 2: apple
word 3: apple
Match: words 1, 2, & 3
```

If the three words are not the same, the structure passes control to the first **elif**, which begins a series of tests to see if any pair of words is the same. As the nesting continues, if any one of the **if** statements is satisfied, the structure passes control to the next **then** statement and subsequently to the statement after **fi**. Each time an **elif** statement is not satisfied, the structure passes control to the next **elif** statement. In the **if3** script, the double quotation marks around the arguments to echo that contain ampersands (&) prevent the shell from interpreting the ampersands as special characters.

The lnks Script

The following script, **lnks**, demonstrates the **if...then** and **if...then...elif** control structures. This script finds hard links to its first argument, a filename. If you provide a name of a directory as the second argument, **lnks** searches for links in that directory and all subdirectories. If you do not specify a directory, **lnks** searches the working directory and its subdirectories.

```
$ cat lnks
#!/bin/bash
# Identify links to a file
# Usage: lnks file [directory]

if [ $# -eq 0 -o $# -gt 2 ]; then
    echo "Usage: lnks file [directory]" 1>&2
    exit 1
fi
if [ -d "$1" ]; then
    echo "First argument cannot be a directory." 1>&2
    echo "Usage: lnks file [directory]" 1>&2
    exit 1
else
    file="$1"
fi
```

```
if [ $# -eq 1 ]; then
    directory="."
elif [ -d "$2" ]; then
    directory="$2"
else
    echo "Optional second argument must be a directory." 1>&2
    echo "Usage: lnks file [directory]" 1>&2
    exit 1
fi

# Check to make sure file exists and is a regular file:
if [ ! -f "$file" ]; then
    echo "lnks: $file not found or special file" 1>&2
    exit 1
fi
# Check link count on file
set -- $(ls -l "$file")

linkcnt=$2
if [ "$linkcnt" -eq 1 ]; then
    echo "lnks: no other link to $file" 1>&2
    exit 0
fi

# Get the inode of the given file
set $(ls -i "$file")

inode=$1

# Find and print the files with that inode number
echo "lnks: using find to search for links..." 1>&2
find "$directory" -xdev -inum $inode -print
```

In the following example, Alex uses **lnks** while he is in his home directory to search for links to a file named **letter** in the working directory. The **lnks** script reports that **/home/alex/letter** and **/home/jenny/draft** are links to the same file:

```
$ lnks letter /home
lnks: using find to search for links...
/home/alex/letter
/home/jenny/draft
```

In addition to the **if...then...elif** control structure, **lnks** introduces other features that are commonly used in shell programs. The following discussion describes **lnks** section by section.

The first line of the **lnks** script specifies the shell to execute the script (refer to "#! Specifies a Shell" on page 271):

```
#!/bin/bash
```

In this chapter the **#!** notation appears only in more complex examples. It ensures that the proper shell executes the script, even if the user is currently running a different shell. It also works correctly if invoked within another shell script.

The second and third lines of **lnks** are comments; the shell ignores the text that follows pound signs up to the next NEWLINE character. These comments in **lnks** briefly identify what the file does and how to use it.

```
# Identify links to a file
# Usage: lnks file [directory]
```

The first **if** statement in **lnks** tests whether **lnks** was called with zero arguments or more than two arguments:

```
if [ $# -eq 0 -o $# -gt 2 ]; then
    echo "Usage: lnks file [directory]" 1>&2
    exit 1
fi
```

If either of these conditions is true, **lnks** sends a usage message to standard error and exits with a status of 1. The double quotation marks around the usage message prevent the shell from interpreting the brackets as special characters. The brackets in the usage message indicate to the user that the **directory** argument is optional.

The second **if** statement tests to see whether **$1** is a directory (the **–d** argument to test returns a *true* value if the file exists and is a directory):

```
if [ -d "$1" ]; then
    echo "First argument cannot be a directory." 1>&2
    echo "Usage: lnks file [directory]" 1>&2
    exit 1
else
    file="$1"
fi
```

If it is a directory, **lnks** presents a usage message and exits. If it is not a directory, **lnks** saves the value of **$1** in the **file** variable because later in the script **set** resets the command line arguments. If the value of **$1** is not saved before the **set** command is issued, its value is lost.

The next section of **lnks** is an **if...then...elif** statement:

```
if [ $# -eq 1 ]; then
    directory="."
elif [ -d "$2" ]; then
    directory="$2"
else
    echo "Optional second argument must be a directory." 1>&2
    echo "Usage: lnks file [directory]" 1>&2
    exit 1
fi
```

The first *test-command* determines whether the user specified a single argument on the command line. If the *test-command* returns 0 (*true*), the user-created variable named **directory** is assigned the value of the working directory (.). If the *test-command* returns a *false* value, the **elif** statement tests whether the second argument is a directory. If it is a directory, the **directory** variable is set equal to the second command line argument, **$2**. If **$2** is not a directory, **lnks** sends a usage message to standard error and exits with a status of 1.

The next **if** statement in **lnks** tests whether **$file** does not exist. This is an important inquiry because it would be pointless for **lnks** to spend time looking for links to a nonexistent file.

The test builtin with the three arguments, **!**, **−f**, and **$file**, evaluates to *true* if the file **$file** does *not* exist:

```
[ ! -f "$file" ]
```

The **!** operator preceding the **−f** argument to test negates its result, yielding *false* if the file **$file** *does* exist and is a regular file.

Next, **lnks** uses set and **ls −l** to check the number of links **$file** has:

```
# Check link count on file
set -- $(ls -l "$file")
linkcnt=$2
if [ "$linkcnt" -eq 1 ]; then
    echo "lnks: no other links to $file" 1>&2
    exit 0
fi
```

The set builtin uses command substitution (page 281) to set the positional parameters to the output of **ls −l**. In the output of **ls −l**, the second field is the link count, so the user-created variable **linkcnt** is set equal to **$2**. The **−−** used with set prevents set from interpreting as an option the first argument that **ls −l** produces (the first argument is the access permissions for the file, and it is likely to begin with **−**). The **if** statement checks whether **$linkcnt** is equal to 1; if it is, **lnks** displays a message and exits. Although this message is not truly an error message, it is redirected to standard error. The way **lnks** has been written, all informational messages are sent to standard error. Only the final product of lnks—the pathnames of links to the specified file—is sent to standard output, so you can redirect the output as you please.

If the link count is greater than one, **lnks** goes on to identify the inode (page 436) for **$file**. As explained in Chapter 6 (page 180), comparing the inodes associated with filenames is a good way to determine whether the filenames are links to the same file. The **lnks** script uses set again to set the positional parameters to the output of **ls −i**. The first argument to set is the inode number for the file, so the user-created variable named **inode** is set to the value of **$1**:

```
# Get the inode of the given file
set $(ls -i "$file")
inode=$1
```

Finally, **lnks** uses the find utility to search for filenames having inodes that match **$inode**.

```
# Find and print the files with that inode number
echo "lnks: using find to search for links..." 1>&2
find "$directory" -xdev -inum $inode -print
```

The find utility searches for files that meet the criteria specified by its arguments, beginning its search with the directory specified by its first argument (**$directory** in this case) and searching all subdirectories. The last three arguments to find specify that the filenames of files having inodes matching **$inode** should be sent to standard output. Because files in different filesystems can have the same inode number and not be linked, find must search only directories in the same filesystem as **$file** for accurate results. The **–xdev** argument to find prevents the search of subdirectories on other filesystems. Refer to page 177 and page 436 for more information about filesystems and links. Refer to the find man page for more information on find.

The echo above the find command in **lnks**, which tells the user that find is running, is included because find frequently takes a long time to run. Because **lnks** does not include a final exit statement, the exit status of **lnks** is that of the last command it runs, find.

Debugging Shell Scripts

When you are writing a script such as **lnks**, it is easy to make mistakes. While you are debugging a script, you can use the shell's **–x** option, which causes the shell to display each command before it runs the command. This trace of a script's execution can give you a lot of information about where the problem is.

Suppose that Alex wants to run **lnks** as in the previous example, while displaying each command before it is executed. He can either set the **–x** option for the current shell (**set –x**) so that all scripts display commands as they are run or use the **–x** option to affect only the script he is currently executing:

```
$ bash -x lnks letter /home
```

Each command that the script executes is preceded by a plus sign (**+**) so that you can distinguish the output of the trace from any output that your script produces. You can also set the **–x** option of the shell running the script by putting the following set command at the top of the script:

```
set -x
```

Turn off the debug option with a plus sign:

```
set +x
```

for...in

The **for...in** structure has the following format:

for loop-index in argument-list
do
        commands
done

This structure (Figure 28-4) assigns the value of the first argument in the *argument-list* to the *loop-index* and executes the *commands* between the **do** and **done** statements. The **do** and **done** statements mark the beginning and end of the **for** loop.

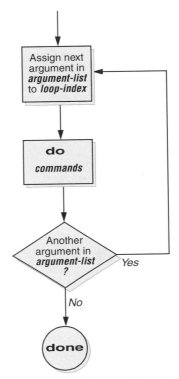

Figure 28-4   A **for...in** flowchart

After it passes control to the **done** statement, the structure assigns the value of the second argument in the *argument-list* to the *loop-index* and repeats the *commands*. The structure repeats the *commands* between the **do** and **done** statements: once for each argument in the *argument-list*. When the structure exhausts the *argument-list*, it passes control to the statement following **done**.

The following **for...in** structure assigns **apples** to the user-created variable **fruit** and then displays the value of **fruit**, which is **apples**. Next the structure assigns **oranges** to **fruit** and repeats the process. When it exhausts the argument list, the structure transfers control to the statement following **done**, which displays a message:

```
$ cat fruit
for fruit in apples oranges pears bananas
do
    echo "$fruit"
done
echo "Task complete."
```

```
$ fruit
apples
oranges
pears
bananas
Task complete.
```

The next script lists the names of the directory files in the working directory by looping over all the files, using test to determine which are directory files:

```
$ cat dirfiles
for i in *
do
    if [ -d "$i" ]
        then
            echo "$i"
    fi
done
```

The ambiguous file reference character * stands for all files (except invisible files) in the working directory. Prior to executing the **for** loop, the shell expands the * and uses the resulting list to assign successive values to the index variable **i**.

for

The **for** control structure has the following format:

> *for **loop-index***
> *do*
> > ***commands***
> *done*

In the **for** structure the *loop-index* automatically takes on the value of each of the command line arguments, one at a time. It performs a sequence of commands, usually involving each argument in turn.

The following shell script shows a **for** structure displaying each of the command line arguments. The first line of the shell script, **for arg**, implies **for arg in "$@"**, where the shell expands "$@" into a list of quoted command line arguments "$1" "$2" "$3".... The balance of the script corresponds to the **for...in** structure:

```
$ cat for_test
for arg
do
    echo "$arg"
done

$ for_test candy gum chocolate
candy
gum
chocolate
```

The whos Script

The following script, **whos**, demonstrates the usefulness of the implied **"$@"** in the **for** structure. You give **whos** one or more **ids** for users as arguments (for example, a user's name or login name), and **whos** displays information about the users. The **whos** script gets the information it displays from the first and fifth fields in the **/etc/passwd** file. The first field always contains a user's login name, and the fifth field typically contains the user's name. You can use a login name as an argument to **whos** to identify the user's name or you can use a name as an argument to identify the login name. The **whos** script is similar to the finger utility, although **whos** provides less information:

```
$ cat whos
#!/bin/bash
# adapted from finger.sh by Lee Sailer
# UNIX/WORLD, III:11, p. 67, Fig. 2

if [ $# -eq 0 ]
    then
        echo "Usage: whos id..." 1>&2
        exit 1
fi
for i
do
    gawk -F: '{print $1, $5}' /etc/passwd |
    grep -i "$i"
done
```

In the following script, **whos** identifies the user whose login is **chas** and the user whose name is **Marilou Smith**:

```
$ whos chas "Marilou Smith"
chas Charles Casey
msmith Marilou Smith
```

The **whos** script uses a **for** statement to loop through the command line arguments. In this script, the implied use of **"$@"** in the **for** loop is particularly useful because it causes the **for** loop to treat as a single argument an argument containing a SPACE. In this example, the user quotes **Marilou Smith**, which causes the shell to pass it to the script as a single argument. Then the implied **"$@"** in the **for** statement causes the shell to regenerate the quoted argument **Marilou Smith** so that it is again treated as a single argument.

For each command line argument, **whos** searches for **id** in the **/etc/passwd** file. Inside the **for** loop, gawk extracts the first (**$1**) and fifth (**$5**) fields from the lines in **/etc/passwd** (which contain the user's login name and information about the user, respectively). The **$1** and **$5** are arguments that the gawk command sets and uses; they are included within single quotation marks and are not interpreted by the shell. (Do not confuse them with the positional parameters, which correspond to the command line arguments.) The first and fifth fields are sent, via a pipe, to grep. The grep

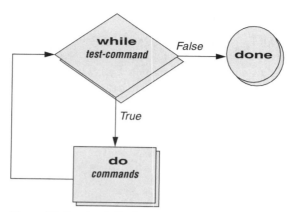

Figure 28-5   A while flowchart

utility searches for **$i** (which has taken on the value of a command line argument) in its input. The **–i** option causes grep to ignore case as it searches for and displays each line in its input that contains **$i**.

An interesting syntactical exception that the shell gives the pipe symbol (I) is shown on the line with the gawk command. You do not have to quote a NEWLINE that immediately follows a pipe symbol (that is, a pipe symbol that is the last thing on a line) to keep the NEWLINE from executing a command. You can see this if you give the command **who I** and press RETURN. The shell displays a secondary prompt. If you then enter **sort** followed by another RETURN, you see a sorted who list. The pipe works even though a NEWLINE follows the pipe symbol.

Because it gets its information from the **/etc/passwd** file, information that the **whos** script displays is only as informative and accurate as the information in **/etc/passwd**. See page 430 for more information about **/etc/passwd**. Refer to the gawk and grep man pages for more information.

while

The **while** control structure (Figure 28-5) has the following syntax:

while **test-command**
do
       commands
done

As long as the **test-command** returns a *true* exit status, the structure continues to execute the series of **commands** delimited by the **do** and **done** statements. Before each loop through the **commands**, the structure executes the **test-command**. When the exit status of the **test-command** is *false*, the structure passes control to the statement after the **done** statement.

The following shell script first initializes the **number** variable to a value of zero. The test builtin then determines whether the value of **number** is less than 10. The script uses test with the **–lt** argument to perform a numerical test. For numerical comparisons, you must use **–ne** (not equal), **–eq** (equal), **–gt** (greater than), **–ge** (greater than or equal to), **–lt** (less than), or **–le** (less than or equal to). For string comparisons, use = (equal) or != (not equal) when you are working with test. The test builtin has an exit status of 0 (*true*) as long as **number** is less than 10. As long as test returns *true,* the structure executes the commands between the **do** and **done** statements:

```
$ cat count
#!/bin/bash
number=0
while [ "$number" -lt 10 ]
    do
        echo -n "$number"
        number=$( expr $number + 1)
    done
echo
$ count
0123456789
$
```

The first command following **do** displays the string represented by **number**. The next command uses the expr utility to increment the value of **number** by one. Here expr converts its arguments to numbers, adds them, converts the result to characters, and sends them to standard output. The $(...) causes the enclosed command to be replaced by the output of the command (command substitution). This value is assigned to the variable **number**. The first time through the loop, number has a value of zero, so expr converts the strings 0 and 1 to numbers, adds them, and converts the result back to a string (**1**). The shell then assigns this value to the variable **number**. The **done** statement closes the loop and returns control to the **while** statement to start the loop over again. The final echo causes **count** to send a NEWLINE character to standard output so that the next prompt occurs in the leftmost column on the display (rather than immediately following **9**).

The spell_check Script

The aspell utility checks the words in a file against a dictionary of correctly spelled words. With the **–l** option, aspell runs in list mode: Input comes from standard input, and aspell displays each potentially misspelled word on standard output. The following command produces a list of possible misspellings in the file **letter.txt**:

```
$ aspell -l < letter.txt
```

The next shell script, **spell_check**, shows another use of a **while** structure. To find the incorrect spellings in a file, you can use **spell_check**, which uses aspell to check your file against a system dictionary but goes a step further: It enables you to specify your own list of correct words and removes these words from the output of aspell. This script is useful for removing words that you use frequently, such as names and technical terms, that are not in a standard dictionary.

Although you can duplicate the functionality of **spell_check** using aspell, **spell_check** is included here for its instructive value.

The **spell_check** script requires two filename arguments: The first file contains your list of correctly spelled words, and the second file is the one you want to check. The first **if** statement verifies that the user specified two arguments, and the next two **if** statements verify that both arguments are readable files. (The exclamation point negates the sense of the following operator; the –**r** operator causes test to determine whether a file is readable. The result is a test that determines whether a file is *not readable*.)

```
$ cat spell_check
#!/bin/bash
# remove correct spellings from aspell output

if [ $# -ne 2 ]
    then
        echo "Usage: spell_check file1 file2" 1>&2
        echo "file1: list of correct spellings" 1>&2
        echo "file2: file to be checked" 1>&2
        exit 1
fi

if [ ! -r "$1" ]
    then
        echo "spell_check: $1 is not readable" 1>&2
        exit 1
fi

if [ ! -r "$2" ]
    then
        echo "spell_check: $2 is not readable" 1>&2
        exit 1
fi

aspell -l < "$2" |
while read line
do
    if ! grep "^$line$" "$1" > /dev/null
        then
            echo $line
    fi
done
```

The **spell_check** script sends the output from aspell (with the –**l** option so that it produces a list of misspelled words on standard output) through a pipe to standard input of a **while** structure, which reads one line at a time (each line has one word on it in this case) from standard input. The *test-command* (that is, **read line**) returns a *true* exit status as long as it receives a line from standard input. Inside the **while** loop, an **if** statement[1] monitors the return value of grep, which determines whether the line that was read is in the user's list of correctly spelled words. The pattern that grep searches for (the value of **$line**) is preceded and followed by special characters that specify the beginning and end of a line (**^** and **$**, respectively). These special characters are used so that grep finds a match only if the **$line** variable matches an entire line in the file of correctly spelled words. (Otherwise, grep would match a string, such as **paul**, in the output of aspell, if the file of correctly spelled words contained the word **paulson**.) These special characters, together with the value of the **$line** variable, form a regular expression (page 903). The output of grep is redirected to **/dev/null** (page 201) because the output is not needed; only the exit code is important. The **if** statement checks the negated exit status of grep (the leading exclamation point negates or changes the sense of the exit status—*true* becomes *false* and vice versa), which is 0 or *true* (*false* when negated), only if a matching line was found. If the exit status is *not* 0 or *false* (*true* when negated), the word was *not* in the file of correctly spelled words. The echo builtin displays a list of words that are not in the file of correctly spelled words on standard output. Once it detects the EOF (end of file), the read builtin returns a *false* exit status, control is passed out of the **while** structure, and the script terminates.

Before you use **spell_check**, create a file of correct spellings containing words that you use frequently but that are not in a standard dictionary. For example, if you work for a company named **Blankenship and Klimowski, Attorneys,** you would put **Blankenship** and **Klimowski** into the file. The following example shows how **spell_check** checks the spelling in a file named **memo** and removes **Blankenship** and **Klimowski** from the output list of incorrectly spelled words:

```
$ aspell -l < memo
Blankenship
Klimowski
targat
hte
$ cat word_list
Blankenship
Klimowski
$ spell_check word_list memo
targat
hte
```

Point a browser at /usr/share/doc/aspell/man-html/index.html (*FEDORA*) or at /usr/share/doc/aspell-0.*/man-html/index.html (*RHEL*) more information on aspell.

---

1. This **if** statement can also be written as

```
if ! grep -qw "$line" "$1"
```

The **–q** option suppresses the output from grep so only an exit code is returned, and the **–w** option causes grep to match only a whole word.

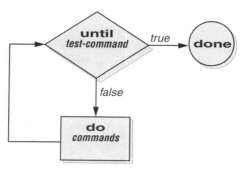

Figure 28-6   An **until** flowchart

until

The **until** and **while** structures are very similar, differing only in the sense of the test at the top of the loop. Figure 28-6 shows that **until** continues to loop *until* the *test-command* returns a *true* exit status. The **while** structure loops *while* the *test-command* continues to return a *true* or nonerror condition. The **until** structure is as follows:

> *until* **test-command**
> *do*
> > *commands*
>
> *done*

The following script demonstrates an **until** structure that includes read. When the user enters the correct string of characters, the *test-command* is satisfied, and the structure passes control out of the loop:

```
$ cat until1
secretname=jenny
name=noname
echo "Try to guess the secret name!"
echo
until [ "$name" = "$secretname" ]
do
    echo -n "Your guess: "
    read name
done
echo "Very good."

$ until1
Try to guess the secret name!

Your guess: helen
Your guess: barbara
Your guess: rachael
Your guess: jenny
Very good
```

The following **locktty** script is similar to the lock command on Berkeley UNIX and the **Lock Screen** menu selection in GNOME. The script prompts the user for a key (password) and uses an **until** control structure to "lock" the terminal. The **until** statement causes the system to ignore any characters typed at the keyboard until the user types in the key on a line by itself, which unlocks the terminal. The **locktty** script can keep people from using your terminal while you are away from it for short periods of time. It saves you from having to log out if you are concerned about other users using your login:

```
$ cat locktty
#! /bin/bash
# UNIX/WORLD, III:4

trap '' 1 2 3 18
stty -echo
echo -n "Key: "
read key_1
echo
echo -n "Again: "
read key_2
echo
key_3=
if [ "$key_1" = "$key_2" ]
    then
        tput clear
        until [ "$key_3" = "$key_2" ]
        do
            read key_3
        done
    else
        echo "locktty: keys do not match" 1>&2
fi
stty echo
```

tip || **Forget Your Password?**

If you forget your key (password), you will need to log in from another (virtual) terminal and kill (page 375) the process running **locktty**.

The trap builtin (page 889) at the beginning of the **locktty** script stops a user from being able to terminate the script by sending it a signal (for example, by pressing the interrupt key). Trapping signal 18 means that no one can use CONTROL-Z (job control, a stop from a tty) to defeat the lock. See Table 28-5 on page 889 for a list of signals. The **stty -echo** command causes the terminal not to display characters typed at the keyboard. This prevents the key that the user enters from appearing on the screen. After turning off echo, the script prompts the user for a key, reads it into the user-created variable **key_1**, prompts the user to enter the same key again, and then saves it in the user-created variable **key_2**. The statement **key_3=** creates a variable with a NULL value. If **key_1** and **key_2** match, **locktty** clears the screen (with the tput command) and starts an **until** loop. The **until** loop keeps attempting to read from the terminal and assigning the input to the **key_3** variable. Once the user types in a string that matches one of the original keys (**key_2**), the **until** loop terminates, and echo is turned back on.

break and continue

You can interrupt a **for, while,** or **until** loop with a **break** or **continue** statement. The **break** statement transfers control to the statement after the **done** statement, terminating execution of the loop. The **continue** command transfers control to the **done** statement, which continues execution of the loop.

The following script demonstrates the use of these two statements. The **for...in** structure loops through the values 1–10. The first **if** statement executes its commands when the value of the index is less than or equal to 3 (**$index –le 3**). The second **if** statement executes its commands when the value of the index is greater than or equal to 8 (**$index –ge 8**). In between the two **ifs**, echo displays the value of the index. For all values up to and including 3, the first **if** displays **continue** and executes a **continue** statement that skips **echo $index** and the second **if** and continues with the next **for.** For the value of 8, the second **if** displays **break** and executes a **break** that exits from the **for** loop. The echo builtin displays the values of **index**:

```
$ cat brk
for index in 1 2 3 4 5 6 7 8 9 10
    do
        if [ $index -le 3 ] ; then
            echo "continue"
            continue
        fi
#
    echo $index
#
    if [ $index -ge 8 ] ; then
        echo "break"
        break
    fi
done

$ brk
continue
continue
continue
4
5
6
7
8
break
```

case

Figure 28-7 shows the **case** structure, a multiple-branch decision mechanism. The path taken through the structure depends on a match or lack of a match between the *test-string* and one of the *patterns*.

The **case** structure is

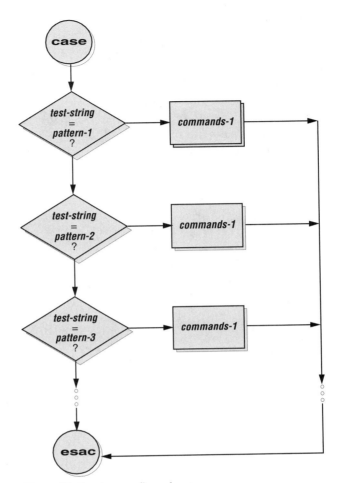

Figure 28-7 A case flowchart

```
case test-string in
      pattern-1)
          commands-1
          ;;
      pattern-2)
          commands-2
          ;;
      pattern-3)
          commands-3
          ;;
...
esac
```

The following **case** structure uses the character that the user enters as the ***test-string***. This value is held in the variable **letter**. If the ***test-string*** has a value of **A**, the structure executes the command following the ***pattern*** **A**. The right parenthesis is part of the **case** control structure, not part of the ***pattern***. If the ***test-string*** has a value of **B** or **C**, the structure executes the command following the matching ***pattern***. The asterisk (*) indicates *any string of characters* and serves as a catchall in case there is no match. If no ***pattern*** matches the ***test-string*** and if there is no catchall (*) ***pattern***, control passes to the command following the **esac** statement, without the **case** structure taking any action. The second sample execution of **case1** shows the user entering a lowercase **b**. Because the ***test-string*** **b** does not match the uppercase **B** ***pattern*** (or any other ***pattern*** in the **case** statement), the program executes the commands following the catchall ***pattern*** and displays a message:

```
$ cat case1
echo -n "Enter A, B, or C: "
read letter
case "$letter" in
    A)
        echo "You entered A"
        ;;
    B)
        echo "You entered B"
        ;;
    C)
        echo "You entered C"
        ;;
    *)
        echo "You did not enter A, B, or C"
        ;;
esac

$ case1
Enter A, B, or C: B
You entered B
$ case1
Enter A, B, or C: b
You did not enter A, B, or C
```

The ***pattern*** in the **case** structure is analogous to that of an ambiguous file reference. The ***pattern*** can include any of the special characters and strings shown in Table 28-2.

table 28-2 ‖   **Patterns**

*	Matches any string of characters. Use it for the default case.
?	Matches any single character.
[...]	Defines a character class. Any characters enclosed within brackets are tried, one at a time, in an attempt to match a single character. A hyphen between two characters specifies a range of characters.
|	Separates alternative choices that satisfy a particular branch of the **case** structure.

The next script accepts upper- and lowercase letters:

```
$ cat case2
echo -n "Enter A, B, or C: "
read letter
case "$letter" in
    a|A)
        echo "You entered A"
        ;;
    b|B)
        echo "You entered B"
        ;;
    c|C)
        echo "You entered C"
        ;;
    *)
        echo "You did not enter A, B, or C"
        ;;
esac

$ case2
Enter A, B, or C: b
You entered B
$
```

The following example shows how you can use the **case** structure to create a simple menu.[2] The **command_menu** script uses echo to present menu items and prompt the user for a selection. The **case** structure executes the appropriate utility, depending on the user's selection:

```
$ cat command_menu
#!/bin/bash
# menu interface to simple commands

echo -e "\n        COMMAND MENU\n"
echo "   a.   Current date and time"
echo "   b.   Users currently logged in"
echo "   c.   Name of the working directory"
echo -e "   d.   Contents of the working directory\n"
echo -n "Enter a, b, c, or d: "
read answer
echo
case "$answer" in
    a)
        date
        ;;
    b)
        who
        ;;
    c)
        pwd
        ;;
    d)
        ls
        ;;
```

---

2. The Bourne Again Shell has a menu control structure that automatically takes care of a lot of the work that this program does. See **select** on page 881.

```
            *)
                echo "There is no selection: $answer"
                ;;
    esac
```

$ **command_menu**

```
                COMMAND MENU

    a.  Current date and time
    b.  Users currently logged in
    c.  Name of the working directory
    d.  Contents of the working directory

Enter a, b, c, or d: a

Mon Jun 14 10:58:05 PDT 2004
```

The −e option causes echo to interpret the \ns (toward the beginning of **command_menu**) as NEWLINE characters. If you do not include this option, echo does not output the extra blank lines that make the menu easy to read but instead outputs the (literal) two-character sequence \n. The −e option causes echo to interpret several other backslash-quoted characters as well (Table 28-3). Remember to quote (with double quotation marks around the string) the backslash-quoted character so that the shell does not interpret it but passes the backslash and the character on to echo.

table 28-3 || **Quoted Arguments to echo**

Quoted Character	echo Displays
\a	Alert (bell)
\b	BACKSPACE
\c	Suppress trailing NEWLINE
\f	FORMFEED
\n	NEWLINE
\r	RETURN
\t	Horizontal TAB
\v	Vertical TAB
\\	Backslash
nnn	The character with the ASCII octal code *nnn*. If *nnn* is not valid, echo displays the string literally.

You can also use the **case** control structure to take various actions in a script, depending on how many arguments the script is called with. The following script, **safedit**, uses a **case** structure that branches based on the number of command line arguments ($#). The **safedit** script saves a backup copy of a file you are editing with vi:

```
$ cat safedit
#!/bin/bash
# UNIX/WORLD, IV:11

PATH=/bin:/usr/bin
script=$(basename $0)
case $# in

    0)
        vi
        exit 0
        ;;

    1)
        if [ ! -f "$1" ]
            then
                vi "$1"
                exit 0
            fi
        if [ ! -r "$1" -o ! -w "$1" ]
            then
                echo "$script: check permissions on $1" 1>&2
                exit 1
            else
                editfile=$1
            fi
        if [ ! -w "." ]
            then
                echo "$script: backup cannot be " \
                    "created in the working directory" 1>&2
                exit 1
            fi
        ;;
    *)
        echo "Usage: $script [file-to-edit]" 1>&2
        exit 1
        ;;
esac
tempfile=/tmp/$$.$script
cp $editfile $tempfile
if vi $editfile
    then
        mv $tempfile bak.$(basename $editfile)
        echo "$script: backup file created"
    else
        mv $tempfile editerr
        echo "$script: edit error--copy of " \
            "original file is in editerr" 1>&2
    fi
```

If you call **safedit** without any arguments, the **case** structure executes its first branch and calls vi without a filename argument. Because an existing file is not being edited, **safedit** does not create a backup file. If the user calls **safedit** with one argument, **safedit** runs the commands in the second branch of the **case** structure and verifies that the file specified by **$1** does not yet exist or is the name of a file for which the user has read and write permission. The **safedit** script also verifies that the user has write permission for the working directory. If the user calls **safedit** with more than one argument, the third branch of the **case** structure presents a usage message and exits with a status of 1.

In addition to the use of a **case** structure for branching based on the number of command line arguments, the **safedit** script introduces several other features. First, at the beginning of the script, the **PATH** variable is set to search **/bin** and **/usr/bin**. This ensures that the commands executed by the script are standard utilities, which are kept in those directories. By setting **PATH** inside a script, you can avoid the problems that might occur if users have set up **PATH** to search their own directories first and have scripts or programs with the same names as utilities the script uses.

Second, the following line creates a variable named **script** and assigns the simple filename of the script to it:

```
script=$(basename $0)
```

The **basename** utility sends the simple filename component of its argument to standard output, which is assigned to the **script** variable, using command substitution. No matter which of the following commands the user calls the script with, the output of basename is the simple filename **safedit**:

```
$ /home/alex/bin/safedit memo
$ ./safedit memo
$ safedit memo
```

After the **script** variable is set, it is used in place of the filename of the script in usage and error messages. By using a variable that is derived from the command that invoked the script rather than a filename that is hardcoded (typed directly) into the script, you can create links to the script or rename it, and the usage and error messages will still provide accurate information.

A third significant feature of **safedit** is the use of the **$$** variable in the name of a temporary file. The statement following the **esac** statement creates and assigns a value to the **tempfile** variable. This variable contains the name of a temporary file that is stored in the **/tmp** directory, as are many temporary files. The temporary filename begins with the PID number of the current shell and ends with the name of the script. The PID number is used because it ensures that the filename is unique, and **safedit** will not attempt to overwrite an existing file, as might happen if two people were using **safedit** at the same time and not using unique filenames. The name of the script is appended so that, should the file be left in **/tmp** for some reason, you can figure out where it came from.

The PID is used in front of rather than after **$script** in the filename because of the 14-character limit on filenames on some filesystems on older versions of UNIX. Linux systems do not have this limitation. Because the PID ensures the uniqueness of the filename, it is placed first so that it cannot be truncated. (If the **$script** component is truncated, the filename is still unique.) For the same reason, when a backup file is created inside the **if** control structure a few lines down in the script, the filename is composed of the string **bak.** followed by the name of the file being edited. On an older system, if **bak** were used as a suffix rather than a prefix and the original filename were 14 characters, **.bak** might be lost, and the original file would be overwritten. The basename utility extracts the simple filename of **$editfile** before it is prefixed with **bak.**.

Fourth, **safedit** uses an unusual *test-command* in the **if** structure: **vi $editfile**. The *test-command* calls vi to edit **$editfile**. When you finish editing the file and exit from vi, vi returns an exit code that is the basis for branching by the **if** control structure. If the editing session completed successfully, vi returns a **0**, and the statements following the **then** statement are executed. If vi does not terminate normally (as would occur if the user used the kill utility to terminate the vi process), vi returns a nonzero exit status, and the script executes the statements following **else**.

select

The Bourne Again Shell's **select** control structure, based on the one found in the Korn Shell, displays a menu, assigns a value to a variable based on the user's choice of items, and executes a series of commands. The syntax of a **select** structure is

> *select **varname** [in **arg** ...]*
> *do*
> > ***commands***
> *done*

First, **select** generates and displays a menu of the *arg* items. The menu is formatted with numbers before each item. For example, a **select** structure that begins with

```
select fruit in apple banana blueberry kiwi orange watermelon STOP
```

displays the following menu:

```
1) apple      3) blueberry   5) orange      7) STOP
2) banana     4) kiwi        6) watermelon
```

You can have many items in the list of **args**. The **select** structure uses the values of the **LINES** and **COLUMNS** variables to determine the size of the display. (**LINES** has a default value of 24; **COLUMNS**, a default of 80.) With **COLUMNS** set to 20, the menu looks like this:

```
1) apple
2) banana
3) blueberry
4) kiwi
5) orange
6) watermelon
7) STOP
```

After displaying the menu, **select** displays the value of **PS3**, the special **select** prompt. The default value of **PS3** is the characters ?#, but typically you would set **PS3** to a more meaningful value.

If, in the preceding menu, you enter a valid number (one in the menu range), **select** sets the value of *varname* to the argument corresponding to the number entered and executes the commands between **do** and **done**. The **select** structure then reissues the **PS3** prompt and waits for another entry, doing this repeatedly until something causes it to exit from the statements between **do** and **done**, typically a **break**, **return**, or **exit** statement. The **break** statement exits from the loop. From within a function, **return** returns control to the program that called the function. The **exit** statement exits from the current shell. The following script illustrates the use of **select**:

```
$ cat fruit2
#!/bin/bash
PS3="Choose your favorite fruit from these possibilities: "
select FRUIT in apple banana blueberry kiwi orange watermelon STOP
do
if [ $FRUIT = STOP ]; then

echo "Thanks for playing!"
break
fi
echo "You chose $FRUIT as your favorite."
echo "That is choice number $REPLY."
echo
done
$ fruit2
1) apple        3) blueberry    5) orange       7) STOP
2) banana       4) kiwi         6) watermelon

Choose your favorite fruit from these possibilities: 3
You chose blueberry as your favorite.
That is choice number 3.

Choose your favorite fruit from these possibilities:
```

As the syntax indicates, you can omit the keyword **in** and the list of arguments. If you do, **select** uses the current values of the positional parameters $@.

Here Document

A Here document allows you to redirect input to a shell script from within the shell script itself. A Here document is so called because it is *here,* immediately accessible in the shell script, instead of *there,* perhaps in another file.

The following script, **birthday,** contains a Here document. The two less than (<<) symbols in the first line indicate to the shell that a Here document follows. One or more characters that delimit the Here document follow the less than symbols—this example uses plus signs. Whereas the opening delimiter can occur adjacent to the less than symbols, the closing delimiter must occur on a line by itself. The shell sends everything between the two delimiters to the process as standard input. In the following example, it is as though you had redirected standard input to grep from a file, except that the file is embedded in the shell script:

```
$ cat birthday
grep -i "$1" <<+
Alex     June 22
Barbara  February 3
Darlene  May 8
Helen    March 13
Jenny    January 23
Nancy    June 26
+
$ birthday Jenny
Jenny    January 23
$ birthday June
Alex     June 22
Nancy    June 26
```

When you run **birthday**, it lists all the Here document lines that contain the argument you called it with. In the preceding example, the first time **birthday** is run, it displays Jenny's birthday because it is called with an argument of **Jenny**. The second run displays all the birthdays in June.

The next script, **bundle**, includes a clever use of a Here document. The **bundle**[3] script is an elegant example of a script that creates a shell archive (or **shar**) file. The **bundle** program creates a file that is itself a shell script containing several other files as well as the code to recreate the original files.

Just as the shell does not treat special characters that occur in standard input of a shell script as special, the shell does not treat the special characters that occur between the delimiters in a Here document as special:

```
$ cat bundle
#!/bin/bash
# bundle:  group files into distribution package

echo "# To unbundle, bash this file"
for i
do
    echo "echo $i 1>&2"
    echo "cat >$i <<'End of $i'"
    cat $i
    echo "End of $i"
done
```

As the following example shows, the output that **bundle** creates is a shell script, which is redirected to a file named **bothfiles**. It contains the contents of each file

---

3. Brian W. Kernighan and Rob Pike, *The Unix Programming Environment* (Englewood Cliffs, N.J.: Prentice-Hall, 1984), 98. Reprinted with permission.

given as an argument to **bundle** (**file1** and **file2** in this case) inside a Here document. To extract the original files from **bothfiles**, the user simply runs it. Before each Here document is a cat command that causes the Here document to be written to a new file when **bothfiles** is run:

```
$ cat file1
This is a file.
It contains two lines.
$ cat file2
This is another file.
It contains
three lines.
$ bundle file1 file2 > bothfiles
$ cat bothfiles
# To unbundle, bash this file
echo file1 1>&2
cat >file1 <<'End of file1'
This is a file.
It contains two lines.
End of file1
echo file2 1>&2
cat >file2 <<'End of file2'
This is another file.
It contains
three lines.
End of file2
```

Following, **file1** and **file2** are removed before **bothfiles** is run. The **bothfiles** script echoes the names of the files it creates as it creates them. Finally, the ls command shows that **bothfiles** has recreated **file1** and **file2**:

```
$ rm file1 file2
$ bash bothfiles
file1
file2
$ ls
bothfiles
file1
file2
```

Expanding Null or Unset Variables

The expression ${name} (or just $name if it is not ambiguous) expands to the value of the **name** variable (page 312). If **name** is null or not set, the shell expands ${Name} to a null string. The shell provides the following alternatives to accepting the expanded null string as the value of the variable:

- Use a default value for the variable.
- Use a default value and assign that value to the variable.
- Display an error.

You can choose one of these alternatives by using a modifier with the variable name.

:–   Uses a Default Value

The **:–** modifier uses a default value in place of a null or unset variable while allowing a nonnull variable to represent itself:

${name:–default}

The shell interprets the **:–** as: "If *name* is null or unset, expand ***default*** and use the expanded value in place of *name;* else use *name*." The following command lists the contents of the directory named by the **LIT** variable; if **LIT** is null or unset, it lists the contents of **/home/alex/literature**:

```
$ ls ${LIT:-/home/alex/literature}
```

The default can itself have variable references that are expanded:

```
$ ls ${LIT:-$HOME/literature}
```

You can supply defaults for unset variables but leave null variables unchanged by omitting the colon:

```
$ ls ${LIT-$HOME/literature}
```

:=   Assigns a Default Value

The **:–** modifier does not change the value of a variable. You may want to change the value of a null or unset variable to its default in a script. You can do this with the **:=** modifier:

${name:=default}

The shell expands the expression **${name:=default}** in the same manner as it expands **${name:–default}** but also sets the value of *name* to the expanded value of ***default***. When you omit the : from the **:=**, bash assigns a value to an unset variable but not a null one. If your script contains a line such as the following and **LIT** is unset or null at the point where this line is executed, it is assigned the value **/home/alex/literature**:

```
$ ls ${LIT:=/home/alex/literature}
```

Shell scripts frequently start with the : (colon) builtin followed on the same line by the **:=** expansion modifier in order to set any variables that may be null or unset. The : builtin evaluates each token in the remainder of the command line but does not execute any commands. Without the leading colon (:), the shell evaluates and attempts to execute the "command" that results from the evaluation. The order of evaluation is such that if a variable is a command and you name that variable, it is executed. If it is not a valid command, the shell displays an error.

Use the following syntax to set a default for a null or unset variable in a shell script (there is a SPACE following the colon):

```
:   ${name:=default}
```

When your script needs a directory for temporary files and uses the value of **TEMPDIR** for the name of this directory, the following line makes **TEMPDIR** default to **/tmp**:

```
: ${TEMPDIR:=/tmp}
```

:?   Displays an Error Message

Sometimes a script needs the value of a variable, and there is no reasonable default that you can supply at the time you write the script. If the variable is null or unset, you can cause the script to display an error message and terminate with an exit status of 1. The modifier for this purpose is :?:

${name:?message}

If **TESTDIR** in the following command is null or unset, the shell displays the expanded value of **mesg3** on standard error and terminates the script:

```
$ cd ${TESTDIR:?mesg3}
```

You must quote **message** if it contains SPACEs. If you omit *message*, the shell displays the default error message (**parameter not set**). If you omit the colon (**:**), an error occurs only if the variable is unset; a null variable remains null. Interactive shells do not exit when you use :?.

String Pattern Matching

The shell provides a powerful set of string pattern-matching operators that manipulate pathnames and other strings. These operators can delete from strings prefixes or suffixes that match patterns. The four operators are listed in Table 28-4.

table 28-4 ‖	String Operators
#	Removes minimal matching prefixes
##	Removes maximal matching prefixes
%	Removes minimal matching suffixes
%%	Removes maximal matching suffixes

The syntax for these operators is

${varname op pattern}

In this syntax *op* is one of the operators listed in Table 28-4, and *pattern* is a match pattern similar to that used for filename generation. These operators are commonly used to manipulate pathnames to extract or remove components or to change suffixes:

```
$ SOURCEFILE=/usr/local/src/prog.c
$ echo ${SOURCEFILE#/*/}
local/src/prog.c
$ echo ${SOURCEFILE##/*/}
prog.c
$ echo ${SOURCEFILE%/*}
/usr/local/src
```

```
$ echo ${SOURCEFILE%%/*}

$ echo ${SOURCEFILE%.c}
/usr/local/src/prog
$ CHOPFIRST=${SOURCEFILE#/*/}
$ echo $CHOPFIRST
local/src/prog.c
$ NEXT=${CHOPFIRST%%/*}
$ echo $NEXT
local
```

Filename Generation

An important feature of the shell is the ability to refer to files by giving a pattern that describes one or more filenames. For example, the shell uses *.c as a pattern describing all filenames that end in .c. The shell expands this pattern into a list of filenames that match the pattern. This process of matching filenames to a pattern is called *globbing*. Globbing is useful for specifying many files with a single pattern and long filenames with a short string.

Setting the **noglob** (**set –o noglob**) option turns off all pattern matching so that you will have to give filenames exactly: *.c will refer only to a file whose name consists of the three-character sequence *, ., and c. See "Filename Generation/Pathname Expansion" on page 207.

Builtins

Commands that are built into a shell do not fork a new process when you execute them. The following sections discuss the exec and trap builtins and are followed by Table 28-6 on page 892, which lists many of the shell builtins.

exec: Executes a Command

The exec builtin has two primary purposes: to run a command without creating a new process and to redirect standard input, output, or error of a shell script from within the script. When the shell executes a command that is not built into the shell, it typically creates a new process. The new process inherits environment (global or exported) variables from its parent but does not inherit variables that are not exported by the parent. Refer to "export: Makes a Variable Global" (page 277). In contrast, exec executes a command in place of (overlays) the current process.

Insofar as exec runs a command in the environment of the original process, it is similar to the . (dot) command (page 286). However, unlike the . command, which can run only scripts, exec can run both scripts and compiled programs. Also, whereas the . command returns control to the original script when it finishes running, exec does not. Finally, whereas the . command gives the new program access to local variables, exec does not. The syntax of the exec builtin is

exec command arguments

Because the shell does not create a new process when you use exec, the command runs more quickly. However, because exec does not return control to the original program, the exec builtin can be used only with the last command that you want to run in a script. The following script shows that control is not returned to the script:

```
$ cat exec_demo
who
exec date
echo This echo builtin is never executed.
$ exec_demo
jenny    pts/7    May 30   7:05 (bravo.tcorp.com)
hls      pts/1    May 30   6:59 (:0.0)
Mon Jun 14 10:58:05 PDT 2004
```

The next example, a modified version of the **out** script (page 857), uses exec to execute the final command the script runs. Because **out** runs either cat or less and then terminates, the new version, **out2**, uses exec with both cat and less:

```
$ cat out2
if [ $# -eq 0 ]
    then
        echo "Usage: out2 [-v] filenames" 1>&2
        exit 1
fi
if [ "$1" = "-v" ]
    then
        shift
        exec less "$@"
    else
        exec cat -- "$@"

fi
```

The second major use of exec is to redirect standard input, output, or error from within a script. Following the next command in a script, all the input to the script is redirected to come from the file named **infile**:

```
exec < infile
```

Similarly, the following command redirects standard output and error to **outfile** and **errfile**, respectively:

```
exec > outfile 2> errfile
```

When you use exec in this manner, the current process is not replaced with a new process, and exec can be followed by other commands in the script. When a script prompts the user for input, it is useful to redirect the output from within the script to go to the terminal. This redirection ensures that your prompt appears on the user's terminal, even if the user has redirected the output from the script. When redirecting the output in a script, you can use **/dev/tty** as a synonym for the user's terminal. The **/dev/tty** device is a pseudonym the system maintains for the terminal or window the user is using. This pseudonym enables you to refer to the user's terminal without knowing which device it is.[4] By redirecting the output from a script to **/dev/tty**, you ensure that prompts go to the user's terminal, regardless of which terminal the user is logged in on. The following command redirects the output from a script to the terminal the user is on:

```
exec > /dev/tty
```

Using exec to redirect the output to **/dev/tty** has one disadvantage: All subsequent output is redirected, unless you use exec again in the script. If you do not want to redirect the output from all subsequent commands in a script, you can redirect the individual echo commands that display prompts:

```
echo -n "Please enter your name: " > /dev/tty
```

You can also redirect the input to read to come from **/dev/tty**:

```
read name < /dev/tty
```

trap: Catches a Signal

A *signal* is a report to a process about a condition. Linux uses signals to report interrupts generated by the user (for example, by pressing the interrupt key), as well as bad system calls, broken pipes, illegal instructions, and other conditions. The trap builtin catches, or traps, one or more signals, allowing you to direct the actions a script takes when it receives a specified signal.

This discussion covers the six signals that are significant when you work with shell scripts. Table 28-5 lists the signals, the signal numbers that systems often ascribe to them, and the conditions that usually generate each signal.

table 28-5			Signals*
Type	**Name**	**Number**	**Generating Condition**
Not a real signal		0	Exit because of exit command or reaching the end of the program (not an actual signal but useful in trap).
Hang up	SIGHUP	1	Disconnect line.
Terminal interrupt	SIGINT	2	Press the interrupt key (usually CONTROL-C).

---

4. The actual device appears in the second column of the output of who am i but lacks the leading **/dev/**. The tty utility returns the name of the screen/window device you are using.

table 28-5 ‖   Signals* (Continued)

Type	Name	Number	Generating Condition
Quit	SIGQUIT	3	Press the quit key (usually CONTROL-SHIFT-| or CONTROL-SHIFT-\).
Kill	SIGKILL	9	The kill command (page 375) with the **−9** option (cannot be trapped; use only as a last resort).
Software termination	SIGTERM	15	Default of the kill command (page 375).
Stop	SIGTSTP	20	Press the suspend key (usually CONTROL-Z).

* Give the command **kill –l** or **man 7 signal** for a list of signal names; for a complete list of signal names and numbers, see **/usr/include/bits/signum.h**.

When it traps a signal, a script takes whatever action you specify: remove files or finish any other processing as needed, display a message, terminate execution immediately, or ignore the signal. If you do not use trap in a script, any of the six signals in Table 28-5 terminates the script while it is running in the foreground. Because a process cannot trap the KILL signal, you can use **kill –KILL** (or **kill –9**) as a last resort to terminate a script or any other process. Refer to the kill man page for more information. The format of trap is

> *trap ['commands'] [signal-numbers]*

The trap builtin does not require the single quotation marks shown, but it is a good practice to use them. The single quotation marks cause shell variables within the *commands* to be expanded when the signal occurs, not when the shell evaluates the arguments to trap. Even if you do not use any shell variables in the *commands*, you need to enclose any command that takes arguments within either single or double quotation marks. Quoting the *commands* causes the shell to pass trap the entire command as a single argument.

The *signal-numbers* are the numbers of the signals that trap catches. The *commands* part is optional. If it is not present, trap resets the trap to its initial condition, which is usually to exit from the script. If the *commands* part is present, the shell executes the *commands* when it catches one of the specified signals. After executing the *commands*, the shell resumes executing the script where it left off. If you want trap to prevent a script from exiting when it receives a signal but not to run any commands explicitly, you can use trap with a null (empty) builtin, as shown in the **locktty** script (page 873). The following command traps signal number 15, and the script continues:

```
trap '' 15
```

If you call trap without any arguments, the command displays a list of commands associated with each signal. The following script demonstrates how the trap builtin can catch the terminal interrupt signal (2). You can use SIGINT, INT, or 2 to specify the signal. The script returns an exit status of 1:

```
$ cat inter
#!/bin/bash
trap 'echo PROGRAM INTERRUPTED; exit 1' INT
while true
do
    echo "Program running."
    sleep 1
done
$ inter
Program running.
Program running.
Program running.
CONTROL-C
PROGRAM INTERRUPTED
$
```

Null builtin   The second line of **inter** sets up a trap for the terminal interrupt signal, using INT. When trap catches the signal, the shell executes the two commands between the single quotation marks in the trap command. The echo builtin displays the message **PROGRAM INTERRUPTED**. Then the exit builtin terminates the shell running the script, and the parent shell displays a prompt. If exit were not there, the shell would return control to the **while** loop after displaying the message. The **while** loop repeats continuously until the script receives a signal because the true utility always returns a *true* exit status. In place of true, you can use the null builtin, which is written as a colon (:) and always returns a 0, or *true*, status. The **while** statement would then be **while** : instead of **while true**.

The trap builtin frequently removes temporary files when a script is terminated prematurely. Thus the files are not left around, cluttering up the filesystem.

The following shell script, **addbanner**, uses two traps to remove a temporary file when the script terminates normally or owing to a hangup, software interrupt, quit, or software termination signal:

```
$ cat addbanner
#!/bin/bash
script=`basename $0`

if [ ! -r "$HOME/banner" ]
    then
        echo "$script: need readable $HOME/banner file" 1>&2
        exit 1
fi

trap 'exit 1' 1 2 3 15
trap 'rm /tmp/$$.$script 2> /dev/null' 0
```

```
for file
do
    if [ -r "$file" -a -w "$file" ]
        then
            cat $HOME/banner $file > /tmp/$$.$script
            cp /tmp/$$.$script $file
            echo "$script: banner added to $file" 1>&2
        else
            echo "$script: need read and write permission for $file" 1>&2
    fi
done
```

When called with one or more filename arguments, **addbanner** loops through the files, adding a header to the top of each. This script is useful when you use a standard format at the top of your documents, such as a standard layout for memos, or when you want to add a standard header to shell scripts. The header is kept in a file named **banner** in the user's home directory. The **HOME** variable contains the pathname of the user's home directory so that **addbanner** can be used by several users without modification. If Alex had written the script with **/home/alex** in place of **$HOME** and then given the script to Jenny, either she would have had to change it, or **addbanner** would have used Alex's **banner** file when Jenny ran it.

The first trap in **addbanner** causes it to exit with a status of 1 when it receives a hangup, software interrupt (terminal interrupt or quit signal), or software termination signal. The second trap uses a 0 in place of **signal-number,** which causes trap to execute its command argument *whenever* the script exits because of an exit command or because it reached its end. Together these traps remove a temporary file whether the script terminates normally or prematurely. Standard error of the second trap is sent to **/dev/null** for cases in which trap attempts to remove a nonexistent temporary file. In those cases, rm sends an error message to standard error. Because the standard error is redirected to **/dev/null**, the user does see the message.

A Partial List of Builtins

Table 28-6 lists some of the shell builtins. See "Builtins" on page 211 for instructions on how to find complete lists of builtins for each of the shells.

table 28-6 ‖	Builtin
:	Returns 0 or *true* (the null builtin, page 891)
.	Executes a program or shell script as part of the current process (page 286)
bg	Puts a job in the background (page 264)
break	Exits from **for, while,** or **until** loop (page 874)

table 28-6 || **Builtin (Continued)**

cd	Changes to another working directory (page 164)
continue	Starts with next iteration of **for**, **while**, or **until** loop (page 874)
echo	Displays arguments (page 128)
eval	Scans and evaluates the command line (page 895)
exec	Executes a program in place of the current process (page 887)
exit	Exits from the current shell (usually the same as CONTROL-D) (page 293)
export	Places the value of a variable in the calling environment (makes it global) (page 277)
fg	Brings a job into the foreground (page 263)
getopts	Parses arguments to a shell script
jobs	Displays list of current jobs in the foreground and background (page 263)
kill	Sends a signal to a process or job (page 375)
pwd	Prints the name of the working directory (page 163)
read	Reads a line from standard input (page 280)
readonly	Declares a variable to be readonly (page 277)
set	Sets shell flags or command line argument variables; with no argument **set** lists all variables (page 289)
shift	Promotes each command line argument (page 288)
test	Compares arguments (page 853)
times	Displays total times for the current shell and its children (**times** man page)
trap	Traps a signal (page 889)
type	Displays how each argument would be interpreted as a command (page 854)
umask	Returns the value of the file-creation mask (page 398)
unset	Removes a variable or function (page 276)
wait	Waits for a background process to terminate

Functions

A shell function is similar to a shell script, storing a series of commands for execution at a later time. However, because the shell stores a function in the computer's main memory (RAM) instead of in a file on the disk, you can access it more quickly than you can access a script. Also, the shell preprocesses (parses) a function so that it starts up more quickly than a script. Finally, the shell executes a shell function in the same shell that called it.

You can declare a shell function in your **.bash_profile** file, in the script that uses it, or directly from the command line. You can remove functions with the unset builtin. The shell does not keep functions once you log out.

tip || **Removing Variables and Functions**

If you have a shell variable and a function with the same name, using unset removes the shell variable. If you then use unset again with the same name, it removes the function.

The syntax that declares a shell function is

function-name ()
{
   commands
}

The *function-name* is the name you use to call the function. The *commands* comprise the list of commands the function executes when you call it. These *commands* can be anything you would include in a shell script, including calls to functions.

The next example shows how to create a simple function that displays the date, a header, and a list of the people who are using the system. This function runs the same commands as the **whoson** script described on page 254:

```
$ whoson ()
{
    date
    echo "Users Currently Logged On"
    who
}
$ whoson
Fri Aug  8 15:44:58 PDT 2003
Users Currently Logged On
hls        console      Aug  6 08:59  (:0)
alex       pts/4        Aug  6 09:33  (0.0)
jenny      pts/7        Aug  6 09:23  (bravo.tcorp.com)
```

If you want to have the **whoson** function always available, without having to enter it each time you log in, put its definition in your **.bash_profile** (page 164) file. After adding **whoson** to your **.bash_profile** file, run **.bash_profile**, using the . (dot) command to put the changes into effect immediately:

```
$ cat .bash_profile
TERM=vt100
export TERM
stty kill '^u'
whoson ()
{
    date
    echo "Users Currently Logged On"
    who
}
$ . .bash_profile
```

You can specify arguments when you call a function. Within the function, these arguments are available as positional parameters. The following example shows the **arg1** function entered from the keyboard. In this sequence, the two greater–than (**>**) signs are secondary shell prompts (**PS2**); do not enter them.

```
$ arg1( ) {
> echo "$1"
> }
$ arg1 my_first_arg
my_first_arg
```

The following function allows you to export variables, using the syntax provided by the C Shell, under the Bourne Again Shell. The set builtin lists all environment variables and their values and verifies that **setenv** has worked correctly:

```
$ cat .bash_profile
.
.
.
# setenv - keep csh users happy
setenv()
{
    if [ $# -eq 2 ]
        then
            eval $1=$2
            export $1
        else
            echo "Usage: setenv NAME VALUE" 1>&2
    fi
}
$ . .bash_profile
$ setenv TCL_LIBRARY /usr/local/lib/tcl
$ set | grep TCL_LIBRARY
TCL_LIBRARY=/usr/local/lib/tcl
```

This function uses the eval builtin to force bash to scan the command **$1=$2** *twice*. Because **$1=$2** begins with a dollar sign (**$**), the shell treats the entire string as a single token—a command. With variable substitution performed, the command name becomes **TCL_LIBRARY=/usr/local/lib/tcl**, which results in an error. Using eval, a second scanning, which splits the string into the three desired tokens, is done, and the correct assignment occurs.

Chapter Summary

The shell is a programming language. Programs written in this language are called shell scripts, or simply scripts. Shell scripts provide the decision and looping control structures present in high-level programming languages while allowing easy access to system utilities and user programs. Shell scripts can also use functions to modularize and simplify complex tasks.

The control structures that use decisions to select alternatives are **if...then**, **if...then...else**, and **if...then...elif**. The **case** control structure provides a multiway branch and can be used when you want to express alternatives, using a simple pattern-matching syntax.

The **test** builtin can evaluate an expression in a shell script. The expression is often a comparison of two quantities or files or an inquiry about the status of a file. As with all decisions within Linux shell scripts, a *true* status is represented by the value zero; *false*, by any nonzero value.

The looping control structures are **for...in**, **for**, **until**, and **while**. These structures perform one or more tasks repetitively.

The **break** and **continue** control structures alter control within loops; **break** transfers control out of a loop, and **continue** transfers control immediately to the top of a loop.

The **trap** builtin catches a signal sent by Linux to the process running the script and allows you to specify actions to be taken on receipt of one or more signals. The **trap** builtin might be used, for instance, to ignore the signal sent when the user presses the interrupt key.

The **exec** builtin executes a command without creating a new process. The new command overlays the current process, assuming the same environment and PID number of that process. This builtin executes user programs and other Linux commands, when it is *not* necessary to return control to the calling process.

The Here document allows input to a command in a shell script to come from within the script itself.

A shell function is a series of commands that, unlike a shell script, are parsed prior to being stored in main memory. Shell scripts are parsed at runtime and are stored on disk. Shell functions run faster than shell scripts and can be used repeatedly. A function can be defined on the command line or within a shell script; if you want the function definition to remain in effect across login sessions, you can define it in your **.bash_profile** file. Like the functions of a programming language, a shell function is called by giving its name along with any arguments.

In addition to the use of control structures, builtins, functions, and the like, useful shell scripts generally use Linux utilities. The **find** utility, for instance, is commonplace in shell scripts that involve a search for files in the system hierarchy and can perform a vast range of tasks, from simple to complex.

A well-written shell script adheres to the use of standard techniques, such as specifying the shell to execute the script on the first line of the script, verifying the number and type of arguments that the script is called with, displaying a standard usage message to report command line errors, and redirecting all informational messages to standard error.

Exercises

1. Rewrite the **journal** script of Chapter 9 (example 1, page 320) by adding commands to verify that the user has write permission for a file named **journal-file** in the user's home directory, if such a file exists. The script should take appropriate actions if **journal-file** exists and the user does not have write permission to the file. Verify that the modified script works.

2. The special parameter **$@** is referenced twice in the **out** script (page 857). Explain what would be different if the parameter **$*** were used in its place.

3. Write a filter that takes a list of files as input and outputs the basename (page 880) of each file in the list.

4. Write a function that takes a single filename as an argument and adds execute permission to the file for the user.

   a. When might such a function be useful?

   b. Revise the script so that it takes one or more filenames as arguments and adds execute permission for the user for each file argument.

   c. What can you do to make the function available every time you log in?

   d. What if, in addition to having the function available on subsequent login sessions, you want to make the function available now in your current shell?

5. When might it be necessary or advisable to write a shell script instead of a shell function? Give as many reasons as you can think of.

6. Write a shell script that will display the names of all directory files, but no other types of files, in the working directory.

7. If your Linux system runs the X Window System, open a small window on your screen, and write a script to display the time in that window every 15 seconds. Read the date man page and display the time, using the **%r** field descriptor. Clear the window (using the clear command) each time before you display the time.

8. Enter the following script named **savefiles**, and give yourself execute permission to the file:

```
$ cat $HOME/bin/savefiles
#! /bin/bash
echo "Saving files in current directory in file savethem."
exec > savethem
for i in *
do
echo "==========================================================="
echo "File: $i"
echo "==========================================================="
cat "$i"
done
```

a. What error message do you get when you execute this script? Rewrite the script so that the error does not occur, making sure the output still goes to **savethem**.

b. What might be a problem with running this script twice in the same directory? Discuss a solution to this problem.

9. Read the bash info page, try some examples, and then describe

a. How to export a function.

b. What the hash builtin does.

c. What happens if the argument to exec is not executable.

10. Using the find utility, perform the following steps:

a. List all files in the working directory that have been modified within the last day.

b. List all files on the system that are bigger than 1 megabyte.

c. Remove all files named **core** from the directory structure rooted at your home directory.

d. List the inode numbers of all files in the working directory whose filenames end in .c.

e. List all files on the root filesystem that have been modified in the last month.

11. Write a short script that tells you whether the permissions for two files, whose names are given as arguments to the script, are identical. If the permissions for the two files are identical, output the common permission field. Otherwise, output each filename, followed by its permission field. (*Hint:* Try using the cut utility.)

12. Write a script that takes the name of a directory as an argument and searches the file hierarchy rooted at that directory for zero-length files.

Write the names of all zero-length files to standard output. If there is no option on the command line, have the script delete the file after displaying its name, asking the user for confirmation, and receiving positive confirmation. A –f option on the command line indicates that the script should display the filename but not ask for confirmation before deleting the file.

Advanced Exercises

13. Write a function that takes a colon-separated list of items and outputs the items, one per line, to standard output (without the colons).

14. Generalize the function written in exercise 13 so that the character separating the list items is given as an argument to the function. If this argument is absent, the separator should default to a colon.

15. Write a function named **funload** that takes as its single argument the name of a file containing other functions. The purpose of **funload** is to make all functions in the named file available in the current shell; that is, **funload** loads the functions from the named file. To locate the file, **funload** searches the colon-separated list of directories given by the environment variable **FUNPATH**. Assume that the format of **FUNPATH** is the same as **PATH** and that searching **FUNPATH** is similar to the shell's search of the **PATH** variable.

16. If your Linux system runs X Windows, write a script that turns the root window a different color when the amount of free disk space in any filesystem reaches a certain threshold. (*Hint:* See the df man page.) Both the threshold and the color should be specified as arguments. Check disk usage every 30 minutes. Start the script executing when your X Windows session starts.

17. Enhance the **spell_check** script (page 870) to accept an optional third argument. If given, this argument specifies a list of words to be added to the output of **spell_check**. You can use a list of words like this to cull usages you do not want in your documents. For example, if you decide that you want to use **disk** rather than **disc** in your documents, you can add **disc** to the list of words, and **spell_check** will complain if you use **disc** in a document. Make sure that you include appropriate error checks and usage messages.

18. Rewrite **bundle** (page 883) so that the script it creates takes an optional list of filenames as arguments. If one or more filenames are given on the command line, only those files should be recreated; otherwise, all files in

the shell archive should be recreated. For example, suppose that all files with the filename extension **.c** are bundled into an archive named **srcshell**, and you want to unbundle just the files **test1.c** and **test2.c**. The following command will unbundle just these two files:

```
$ bash srcshell test1.c test2.c
```

19. Using a single command line (pipes are all right), find all the unique shells in the **/etc/passwd** file, and print out two columns listing each shell followed by the username for every user who logs into that shell. (*Hint:* Use gawk.)

20. What kind of links will the **lnks** script (page 860) not find? Why?

PART VII

Appendixes

Regular Expressions

A regular expression defines a set of one or more strings of characters. Several of the Linux utilities, including vi, emacs, grep, gawk, and sed, use regular expressions to search for and replace strings. A simple string of characters is a regular expression that defines one string of characters: itself. A more complex regular expression uses letters, numbers, and special characters to define many different strings of characters. A regular expression is said to *match* any string it defines.

This appendix describes the regular expressions used by ed, vi, emacs, grep, gawk, and sed. The regular expressions used in ambiguous file references with the shell are different and are described in "Filename Generation/Pathname Expansion" on page 207.

Characters

As used in this appendix, a *character* is any character *except* a NEWLINE. Most characters represent themselves within a regular expression. A *special character* is one that does not represent itself. If you need to use a special character to represent itself, refer to "Quoting Special Characters" on page 907.

Delimiters

A character called a *delimiter* usually marks the beginning and end of a regular expression. The delimiter is always a special character for the regular expression it delimits (that is, it does not represent itself but marks the beginning and end of the expression). Although vi permits the use of other characters as a delimiter and grep does not use delimiters at all, the regular expressions in this appendix use a forward slash (/) as a delimiter. In some unambiguous cases, the second delimiter is not required. For example, you can sometimes omit the second delimiter when it would be followed immediately by RETURN.

Simple Strings

The most basic regular expression is a simple string that contains no special characters except the delimiters. A simple string matches only itself (Table A-1). In the examples in this appendix, the strings that are matched look like this.

table A-1 ‖		Simple Strings
Regular Expression	**Matches**	**Examples**
/ring/	ring	ring, spring, ringing, stringing
/Thursday/	Thursday	Thursday, Thursday's
/or not/	or not	or not, poor nothing

Special Characters

You can use special characters within a regular expression to cause the regular expression to match more than one string. A regular expression that includes a special character always matches the longest possible string, starting as far toward the beginning (left) of the line as possible.

Periods

A period (.) matches any character (Table A-2).

table A-2 || **Period**

Regular Expression	Matches	Examples
/ .alk/	All strings consisting of a SPACE followed by any character followed by <u>alk</u>	will <u>talk</u>, may <u>balk</u>
/.ing/	All strings consisting of any character preceding <u>ing</u>	<u>sing</u> song, <u>ping</u>, before <u>inglenook</u>

Brackets

Brackets ([]) define a *character class*[1] that matches any single character within the brackets (Table A-3). If the first character following the left bracket is a caret (^), the brackets define a character class that matches any single character not within the brackets. You can use a hyphen to indicate a range of characters. Within a character class definition, backslashes and asterisks (described in the following sections) lose their special meanings. A right bracket (appearing as a member of the character class) can appear only as the first character following the left bracket. A caret is special only if it is the first character following the left bracket, and a dollar sign is special only if it is followed immediately by a right bracket.

table A-3 || **Brackets**

Regular Expression	Matches	Examples
/[bB]ill/	Member of the character class <u>b</u> and <u>B</u> followed by <u>ill</u>	<u>bill</u>, <u>Bill</u>, <u>bill</u>ed
/t[aeiou].k/	<u>t</u> followed by a lowercase vowel, any character, and a <u>k</u>	<u>talk</u>ative, <u>stink</u>, <u>teak</u>, <u>tank</u>er
/# [6–9]/	<u>#</u> followed by a SPACE and a member of the character class <u>6</u> through <u>9</u>	<u># 60</u>, <u># 8</u>:, get <u># 9</u>
/[^a–zA–Z]/	Any character that is not a letter (ASCII character set only)	<u>1</u>, <u>7</u>, <u>@</u>, <u>.</u>, <u>}</u>, Stop<u>!</u>

---

1. GNU documentation calls these List Operators and defines Character Class operators as expressions that match a predefined group of characters, such as all numbers.

Asterisks

An asterisk can follow a regular expression that represents a single character (Table A-4). The asterisk represents *zero* or more occurrences of a match of the regular expression. An asterisk following a period matches any string of characters. (A period matches any character, and an asterisk matches zero or more occurrences of the preceding regular expression.) A character class definition followed by an asterisk matches any string of characters that are members of the character class.

table A-4 ‖		**Asterisks**
Regular Expression	**Matches**	**Examples**
/ab∗c/	a followed by zero or more b's followed by a c	ac, abc, abbc, debbcaabbbc
/ab.∗c/	ab followed by zero or more characters followed by c	abc, abxc, ab45c, xab 756.345 x cat
/t.∗ing/	t followed by zero or more characters followed by ing	thing, ting, I thought of going
/[a–zA–Z]∗/	A string composed only of letters and SPACES	1. any string without numbers or punctuation!
/(.∗)/	As long a string as possible between (and)	Get (this) and (that);
/([^)]∗)/	The shortest string possible that starts with (and ends with)	(this), Get (this and that)

Carets and Dollar Signs

A regular expression that begins with a caret (^) can match a string only at the beginning of a line. In a similar manner, a dollar sign at the end of a regular expression matches the end of a line. The caret and dollar sign are called anchors because they force (anchor) a match to the beginning or end of a line (Table A-5).

table A-5 ‖		**Carets and Dollar Signs**
Regular Expression	**Matches**	**Examples**
/^T/	A T at the beginning of a line	This line..., That Time..., In Time
/^+[0–9]/	A plus sign followed by a digit at the beginning of a line	+5 +45.72, +759 Keep this...
/:$/	A colon that ends a line	...below:

Quoting Special Characters

You can quote any special character (but not a digit or a parenthesis) by preceding it with a backslash (Table A-6). Quoting a special character makes it represent itself.

table A-6 ‖		Quoted Special Characters
Regular Expression	**Matches**	**Examples**
/end\./	All strings that contain <u>end</u> followed by a period	The <u>end.</u>, <u>send.</u>, pret<u>end.</u>mail
/\\/	A single backslash	\
/*/	An asterisk	<u>*</u>.c, an asterisk (<u>*</u>)
/\[5\]/	<u>[5]</u>	it was five <u>[5]</u>
/and \/or/	<u>and/or</u>	<u>and/or</u>

Rules

The following rules govern the application of regular expressions.

Longest Match Possible

As stated previously, a regular expression always matches the longest possible string, starting as far toward the beginning of the line as possible. For example, given the following string,

```
This (rug) is not what it once was (a long time ago), is it?
```

the expression **/Th.*is/** matches

```
This (rug) is not what it once was (a long time ago), is
```

and **/(.*)/** matches

```
(rug) is not what it once was (a long time ago)
```

However, **/([^)]*)/** matches

```
(rug)
```

Given the following string,

```
singing songs, singing more and more
```

the expression **/s.*ing/** matches

```
singing songs, singing
```

and **/s.*ing song/** matches

```
singing song
```

Empty Regular Expressions

Within some utilities, such as vi and less, but not grep, an empty regular expression represents the last regular expression that you used. For example, if you give vi the following Substitute command:

```
:s/mike/robert/
```

and then want to make the same substitution again, you can use the following command:

```
:s//robert/
```

Alternatively, you can use the following commands to search for the string **mike** and then make the substitution

```
/mike/
:s//robert/
```

The empty regular expression (**//**) represents the last regular expression you used (**/mike/**).

Bracketing Expressions

You can use quoted parentheses, \(and \), to *bracket* a regular expression. The string that the bracketed regular expression matches can be recalled, as explained in "Quoted Digit," following. A regular expression does not attempt to match quoted parentheses. Thus a regular expression enclosed within quoted parentheses matches what the same regular expression without the parentheses would match. The expression /\(**rexp**\)/ matches what /**rexp**/ would match, and /**a**\(**b**∗\)**c**/ matches what /**ab**∗**c**/ would match.

You can nest quoted parentheses. The bracketed expressions are identified only by the opening \(, so there is no ambiguity in identifying them. The expression /\([a–z]\([A–Z]∗\)x\)/ consists of two bracketed expressions, one within the other. In the string **3 t dMNORx7 l u**, the preceding regular expression matches **dMNORx**, with the first bracketed expression matching **dMNORx** and the second matching **MNOR**.

The Replacement String

The vi and sed editors use regular expressions as search strings within Substitute commands. You can use the ampersand (**&**) and quoted digits (**\n**) special characters to represent the matched strings within the corresponding replacement string.

Ampersand

Within a replacement string, an ampersand (&) takes on the value of the string that the search string (regular expression) matched. For example, the following vi Substitute command surrounds a string of one or more digits with **NN**. The ampersand in the replacement string matches whatever string of digits the regular expression (search string) matched:

    :s/[0-9][0-9]*/NN&NN/

Two character class definitions are required because the regular expression [0–9]* matches *zero* or more occurrences of a digit, and *any* character string is zero or more occurrences of a digit.

Quoted Digit

Within the search string, a quoted regular expression, \(**xxx**\), matches what the regular expression would have matched without the quotes. Within the replacement string, a quoted digit, *n*, represents the string that the bracketed regular expression (portion of the search string) beginning with the *n*th \(matched. For example, you can take a list of people in the form

    last-name, first-name initial

and put it in the following form:

    first-name initial last-name

with the following vi command:

    :1,$s/\([^,]*\), \(.*\)/\2 \1/

This command addresses all the lines in the file (**1,$**). The Substitute command (**s**) uses a search string and a replacement string delimited by forward slashes. The first bracketed regular expression within the search string, \([^,]*\), matches what the same unbracketed regular expression, [^,]*, would match: zero or more characters not containing a comma (the **last-name**). Following the first bracketed regular expression are a comma and a SPACE that match themselves. The second bracketed expression, \(.*\), matches any string of characters (the **first-name** and **initial**).

The replacement string consists of what the second bracketed regular expression matched (\2), followed by a SPACE and what the first bracketed regular expression matched (\1).

Extended Regular Expressions

The three utilities egrep, grep when run with the –E option (similar to egrep), and gawk provide all the special characters that are included in ordinary regular expressions, except for \(and \), as well as several others. The vi (vim) editor includes the additional characters as well as \(and \). Patterns using the extended set of special characters are called *full regular expressions,* or *extended regular expressions.*

Two of the additional special characters are the plus sign (+) and question mark (?). They are similar to the *, which matches *zero* or more occurrences of the previous character. The plus sign matches *one* or more occurrences of the previous character, whereas the question mark matches *zero* or *one* occurrence. You can use any one of the special characters *, +, and ? following parentheses, causing the special character to apply to the string surrounded by the parentheses. Unlike the parentheses in bracketed regular expressions, these parentheses are not quoted (Table A-7).

table A-7 || **Extended Regular Expressions**

Regular Expression	Matches	Examples
/ab+c/	a followed by one or more b's followed by a c	yabcw, abbc57
/ab?c/	a followed by zero or one b followed by c	back, abcdef
/(ab)+c/	One or more occurrences of the string ab followed by c	zabcd, ababc!
/(ab)?c/	Zero or one occurrence of the string ab followed by c	xc, abcc

In full regular expressions, the vertical bar (I) special character is an OR operator. Within vim, you must quote the vertical bar by preceding it with a backslash to make it special (\I). A vertical bar between two regular expressions causes a match with strings that match the first expression or the second expression or both. You can use the vertical bar with parentheses to separate from the rest of the regular expression the two expressions that are being ORed (Table A-8).

table A-8 || **Full Regular Expressions**

Regular Expression	Meaning	Examples
/ab|ac/	Either ab or ac	ab, ac, abac *(abac is two matches of the regular expression)*
/^Exit|^Quit/	Lines that begin with Exit or Quit	Exit, Quit, No Exit
/(D|N)\. Jones/	D. Jones or N. Jones	P.D. Jones, N. Jones

Appendix Summary

A regular expression defines a set of one or more strings of characters. A regular expression is said to match any string it defines.

Special Characters

In a regular expression, a special character is one that does not represent itself. Table A-9 lists special characters.

table A-9 ||	Special Characters
Character	**Meaning**
.	Matches any single character
*	Matches zero or more occurrences of a match of the preceding character
^	Forces a match to the beginning of a line
$	A match to the end of a line
\	Used to quote special characters
\<	Forces a match to the beginning of a word
\>	Forces a match to the end of a word

Character Classes and Bracketed Regular Expressions

Table A-10 lists ways of representing character classes and bracketed regular expressions.

table A-10 ||	Character Classes and Bracketed Regular Expressions
Class	**Defines**
[*xyz*]	Defines a character class that matches *x*, *y*, or *z*
[^ *xyz*]	Defines a character class that matches any character except *x*, *y*, or *z*
[*x–z*]	Defines a character class that matches any character *x* through *z* inclusive
\(*xyz*\)	Matches what *xyz* matches (a bracketed regular expression)

Extended Regular Expressions

In addition to the preceding special characters and strings (excluding quoted parentheses, except in vim), the following characters are special within full, or extended, regular expressions.

table A-11 || **Extended Regular Expressions**

Expression	Matches
+	Matches one or more occurrences of the preceding character
?	Matches zero or one occurrence of the preceding character
(*xyz*)+	One or more occurrences of what *xyz* matches
(*xyz*)?	Zero or one occurrence of what *xyz* matches
(*xyz*) *	Zero or more occurrences of what *xyz* matches
xyz|*abc*	Either what *xyz* or what *abc* matches (use \\| in vim)
(*xy*|*ab*)*c*	Either what *xyc* or what *abc* matches (use \\| in vim)

Replacement Strings

The following characters are special within a replacement string in sed and vim.

table A-12 || **Replacement Strings**

String	Represents
&	Represents what the regular expression (search string) matched
n	A quoted number, *n*, represents what the *n*th bracketed regular expression in the search string matched

B

Help

You need not act as a Red Hat user or administrator in isolation; a large community of Linux/Red Hat experts is willing to assist you in learning about, helping you solve your problems with, and getting the most out of your Linux system. Before you ask for help, make sure you have done everything you can to solve the problem by yourself. No doubt, someone has had the same problem before you and the answer to your question is written down somewhere on the Internet. Your job is to find it. This appendix lists resources and describes methods that can help you in that task.

Solving a Problem

Following is a list of steps that can help you solve a problem without asking someone else for help. Depending on your understanding of and experience with the hardware and software involved, these steps may lead you to a solution.

1. Red Hat Linux comes with extensive documentation (page 94). Read the documentation on the specific hardware/software you are having a problem with. If it is a GNU product, use info; otherwise, use man to find local information.

2. When the problem involves some type of error or other message, use a search engine, such as Google (www.google.com) or Google Groups (groups.google.com), to look up the message on the Internet. If the message is long, pick a unique part of the message to search for; 10 to 20

characters should be enough. Enclose the search string within double quotation marks.

3. Check whether the Linux Documentation Project (www.tldp.org) has a HOWTO or mini-HOWTO on the subject in question. Search on keywords that relate directly to the product and your problem. Read the FAQs.

4. See Table B-1 on page 915 for other sources of documentation.

5. Use Google or Google Groups to search on keywords that relate directly to the product and your problem.

6. When all else fails, or perhaps before you try anything else, look at the system logs in **/var/log**. Running as Superuser, first look at the end of the **messages** file using the following command:

```
# tail -20 /var/log/messages
```

If **messages** contains nothing useful, run the following command, which displays the most recent log files at the bottom of the list:

```
$ ls -ltr /var/log
```

If your problem involves a network connection, look at the **secure** log file on the local and remote machines. Also look at **messages** on the remote machine.

7. The **/var/spool** directory contains subdirectories with useful information: **cups** holds the print queues, **mail** holds the user's mail files, and so on.

If you are unable to solve a problem yourself, a well-thought-out question to an appropriate newsgroup (page 917) or mailing list (page 917) can elicit useful information. When you send or post a question, make sure you describe the problem and identify your system carefully. Include the version numbers of Red Hat Linux and any software packages you think relate to the problem. Describe your hardware, if appropriate. For a fee, Red Hat provides many different types of support.

The author's home page (www.sobell.com) contains an up-to-date version of the tables in this appendix, corrections to this book, answers to some chapter exercises, as well as pointers to other Linux sites.

Finding Linux-Related Information

Distributions of Linux come with reference pages stored online. You can read these documents by using the info or man utilities (page 94). You can read man and info pages to get more information about specific topics while reading this book or to determine what features are available with Linux. You can search for topics by using apropos (see page 137 or give the command **man apropos**).

Documentation

Good books are available on various aspects of using and administrating UNIX systems in general and Linux systems in particular. In addition, you may find the sites listed in Table B-1 useful.[1]

table B-1 || **Documentation**

Site	About the Site	URL
freedesktop.org	Creates standards for interoperability between open source desktop environments.	freedesktop.org
GNOME	GNOME home page.	www.gnome.org
GNU Manuals	GNU manuals. GNU manual on info.	www.gnu.org/manual www.gnu.org/software/texinfo/manual/info
Internet FAQ Archives	Searchable FAQ archives.	www.faqs.org
Info	Instructions for using the info utility.	www.gnu.org/manual/info/html_mono/info.html
KDE News	KDE news.	dot.kde.org
KDE Documentation	KDE documentation.	/kde.org/documentation
Red Hat Documentation and Support	This site has a search engine that looks through the Red Hat Knowledgebase to help answer your questions. The site also has links to online documentation for Red Hat products and a section named Quickhelp that links to common topics of interest.	www.redhat.com/apps/support
RFCs	Request for Comments; see *RFC* (page 993). Download **rfc-index** for a list of RFCs.	ftp://ftp.uu.net/inet/rfc
System Administrators Guild (SAGE)	SAGE is a group for system administrators.	www.sage.org

1. The right-hand columns of most of the tables in this appendix show Internet addresses (URLs). All sites have an implicit http:// prefix unless ftp:// or https:// is shown. Refer to "URLs (Web Addresses)" on page 19.

table B-1 ‖		Documentation (Continued)
Site	**About the Site**	**URL**
The Linux Documentation Project	All things related to Linux documentation (in many languages): HOWTOs, guides, FAQs, man pages, and magazines. This is the best overall source for Linux documentation. Make sure to visit their Links page.	www.tldp.org
Linux Documentation	The usual along with e-zines, books, journals, standards, and logos. In English and German.	www.fokus.gmd.de/linux/linux-doc.html

Useful Linux Sites

Sometimes the sites listed in Table B-2 are so busy that you cannot log in. When this happens, you are usually given a list of alternative, or *mirror*, sites to try.

table B-2 ‖		Useful Linux Sites
Site	**About the Site**	**URL**
GNU	GNU Project web server.	www.gnu.org
ibiblio	A large library and digital archive. Formerly Metalab, formerly Sunsite.	www.ibiblio.org www.ibiblio.org/pub/Linux www.ibiblio.org/pub/historic-linux
Linux Knowledge Portal	A configurable site that gathers information from other sites and sources and presents it in a well-organized format. Sources include KDE News, GNOME News, slashdot, and many more. In English and German.	www.linux-knowledge-portal.org
Linux Standard Base (LSB)	A group dedicated to standardizing Linux.	www.linuxbase.org
Sobell	The author's home page contains useful links, errata for this book, code for many of the examples in this book, and so on.	www.sobell.com
USENIX	A large, well-established UNIX group. This site has many links, including a list of conferences.	www.usenix.org
X.Org	The X Window System home. Click **Download** for software.	www.x.org

Linux Newsgroups

One of the best ways of getting specific information is through a newsgroup (see "Usenet" on page 359). Frequently, you can find the answer to your question just by reading postings to the newsgroup. Try using Google Groups to search through newsgroups (groups.google.com) to see whether your question has already been asked and answered. Or open a newsreader program and subscribe to appropriate newsgroups. If necessary, you can post your question for someone to answer. Before you post it, make sure you are posting to the correct group and that your question has not been answered. There is an etiquette to posting questions—see www.catb.org/~esr/faqs/smart-questions.html for a good paper by Eric S. Raymond and Rick Moen titled "How To Ask Questions the Smart Way."

The newsgroup **comp.os.linux.answers** contains postings of solutions to common problems and periodic postings of the most up-to-date versions of the FAQ and HOWTO documents. The **comp.os.linux.misc** newsgroup has answers to miscellaneous Linux-related questions.

Mailing Lists

Subscribing to a mailing list (page 343) allows you to participate in an electronic discussion. With most lists, you can send and receive email dedicated to a specific topic to and from a group of users. Moderated lists do not tend to stray as much as unmoderated lists, assuming the list has a good moderator. The disadvantage of a moderated list is that some discussions may be cut off when they get interesting if the moderator deems that the discussion has gone on for too long. Mailing lists described as bulletins are strictly unidirectional: You cannot post information to these lists but can only receive periodic bulletins. If you have the subscription address for a mailing list but are not sure how to subscribe, put the word **help** in the body and/or header of email that you send to the address. You will usually receive instructions via return email. Red Hat hosts several mailing lists; go to www.redhat.com/mailman/listinfo for more information. You can also use a search engine to search for **mailing list linux**.

Words

Many dictionaries, thesauruses, and glossaries are online. Table B-3 lists a few of them.

table B-3 || **Looking Up Words**

Site	About the Site	URL
ARTFL Project: ROGET'S Thesaurus	Thesaurus	humanities.uchicago.edu/forms_unrest/ROGET.html
DICT.org	Multiple database search for words	www.dict.org
Dictionary.com	Everything related to words	www.dictionary.com
DNS Glossary	DNS Glossary	www.menandmice.com/online_docs_and_faq/glossary/glossarytoc.htm?dynamic.ip.address.htm
FOLDOC (The Free On-line Dictionary of Computing)	Computer terms	www.foldoc.org
Merriam-Webster	English language	www.m-w.com
OneLook	Multiple-site word search with a single query	www.onelook.com
The Jargon File	An online version of *The New Hacker's Dictionary*	www.catb.org/~esr/jargon
Webopedia	Commercial technical dictionary	www.webopedia.com
Wikipedia	An open source (user-contributed) encyclopaedia project.	wikipedia.org
Wordsmyth	Dictionary and thesaurus	www.wordsmyth.net
Yahoo Reference	Search multiple sources at the same time	education.yahoo.com/reference

Software

There are many ways to learn of interesting software packages and where they are available on the Internet. Table B-4 lists sites that you can download software from. For security-related programs, refer to Table C-1 on page 937. Another way to learn about software packages is through a newsgroup (page 917).

table B-4 || **Software**

Site	About the Site	URL
Free Software Directory	Categorized, searchable lists of free software	www.gnu.org/directory savannah.gnu.org
Freshmeat	A large index of UNIX and cross-platform software, themes, and Palm OS software	freshmeat.net

table B-4 || **Software (Continued)**

Site	About the Site	URL
Free Software Directory	Free Software Foundation (FSF) and UNESCO directory of over 3000 free software packages	www.gnu.org/directory
GNOME Project	Links to all the GNOME projects	www.gnome.org/projects
IceWALKERS	Categorized, searchable lists of free software	www.icewalkers.com
Linux Software Map	A database of packages written for, ported to, or compiled for Linux	www.boutell.com/lsm
linuxapps	Categorized, searchable list of free software	www.linuxapps.com
Network Calculators	Subnet mask calculator and more	www.telusplanet.net/public/sparkman/netcalc.htm
rpmfind.net	Searchable list of rpm files for various Linux distributions and versions	rpmfind.net/linux/RPM
SourceForge	A development Website with a large repository of Open Source code and applications	sourceforge.net
Tucows-Linux	Commercial, categorized, searchable list of software	linux.tucows.com

Office Suites and Word Processors

Several office suites and many word processors are available for Linux. Table B-5 lists a few of them. If you are exchanging documents with people using Windows make sure the import from/export to MS Word functionality covers your needs.

table B-5 || **Office Suites and Word Processors**

Product Name	What It Does	URL
AbiWord	Word processor (free)	www.abisource.com
KOffice	Integrated suite of office applications including the Kword word processing program (free, KDE based)	www.koffice.org
OpenOffice	An open source version of StarOffice	www.openoffice.org www.gnome.org/projects/ooo
Xcoral	A programmer's multiwindow mouse-based editor that runs under X (free)	xcoral.free.fr

Specifying a Terminal

Because vi, emacs, konsole, and other programs take advantage of features that are specific to various kinds of terminals and terminal emulators, you must tell these programs the name of the terminal you are using or the terminal that your terminal emulator is emulating. On many systems, your terminal name is set for you. If your terminal name is not specified or is not specified correctly, your screen will look strange, or, when you start a program, the program will ask for this information.

Terminal names describe the functional characteristics of your terminal or terminal emulator to programs that require this information. Although terminal names are referred to as either Terminfo or Termcap names, the difference is in the method the two systems use to store the terminal characteristics internally, not in the manner that you specify the name of your terminal. Terminal names that are often used with Linux terminal emulators and with graphical monitors while they are run in text mode are **ansi**, **linux**, **vt100**, **vt102**, **vt220**, and **xterm**.

When you are running a terminal emulator, you can specify the type of terminal you want to emulate. Set the emulator to either **vt100** or **vt220**, and set **TERM** to the same value (following).

When you log in, you may be prompted to identify the type of terminal you are using:

```
TERM = (vt100)
```

There are two ways to respond to this prompt: You can press RETURN to set your terminal type to the name in parentheses. When that name does not describe the terminal you are using, you can enter the correct name before you press RETURN:

```
TERM = (vt100) ansi
```

You can also receive the following prompt:

```
TERM = (unknown)
```

This prompt indicates that the system does not know what type of terminal you are using. If you are going to be running programs that require this information, enter the name of your terminal or terminal emulator before you press RETURN.

If you do not receive a prompt, you can give the following command to check whether your terminal type has been set:

```
$ echo $TERM
```

If the system responds with the wrong name, a blank line, or an error message, set or change the terminal name. From the Bourne Again Shell (bash), enter a command similar to the following to identify the type of terminal you are using:

export TERM=name

Replace *name* with the terminal name for your terminal, making sure that you do not put a SPACE before or after the equal sign. If you always use the same type of terminal, you can place this command in your **.bashrc** file. This causes the shell to set the terminal type each time you log in (page 272).

For example, give the following command to set your terminal name to **vt100**:

```
$ export TERM=vt100
```

Security

Security is a major part of the foundation of any system that is not totally cut off from other machines and users. Some aspects of security have a place even on isolated machines. Examples are periodic system backups, BIOS or power-on passwords, and self-locking screensavers.

A system that is connected to the outside world requires other mechanisms to secure it: tools to check files (tripwire), audit tools (tiger/cops), secure access methods (kerberos/ssh), services that monitor logs and machine states (swatch/watcher), packet-filtering and routing tools (ipfwadm/iptables/ipchains), and more.

System security has many dimensions. The security of your system as a whole depends on the security of individual components, such as your email, files, network, login and remote access policies, as well as the physical security of the host itself. These dimensions frequently overlap, and their borders are not always static or clear. For instance, email security is affected by the security of files and your network. If the medium (the network) over which you send and receive your email is not secure, you must take extra steps to ensure the security of your messages. If you save your secure email into a file on your local system, you rely on the filesystem and host access policies for file security. A failure in any one of these areas can start a domino effect, diminishing reliability and integrity in other areas and potentially compromising system security as a whole.

This short appendix cannot cover all the facets of system security, but it does provide an overview of the complexity of setting up and maintaining a secure system. This appendix provides some specifics, concepts, guidelines to consider, and many pointers to security resources (Table C-1 on page 937).

security || **Other Sources of System Security Information**

Depending on how important system security is to you, you may want to purchase one or more of the books dedicated to system security, read from some of the Internet sites that are dedicated to security, or hire someone who is an expert in the field.

Do not rely on this appendix as your sole source of information on system security.

Encryption

One of the building blocks of security is encryption, which provides a means of scrambling data for secure transmission to other parties. In cryptographic terms, the data or message to be encrypted is referred to as *plaintext,* and the resulting encrypted block of text as *ciphertext.* Processes exist for converting plaintext into ciphertext through the use of *keys,* which are essentially random numbers of a specified length used to *lock* and *unlock* data. This conversion is achieved by applying the keys to the plaintext by following a set of mathematical instructions, referred to as the *encryption algorithm.*

Developing and analyzing strong encryption software is extremely difficult. There are many nuances and standards governing encryption algorithms, and a background in mathematics is requisite. Also, unless an algorithm has undergone public scrutiny for a significant period of time, it is generally not considered secure; it is often impossible to know that an algorithm is completely secure but possible to know that one is not secure. Time is the best test of an algorithm. Also, a solid algorithm does not guarantee an effective encryption mechanism, as the fallibility of an encryption scheme frequently lies in problems with implementation and distribution.

An encryption algorithm uses a key that is a certain number of bits long. Each bit you add to the length of a key effectively doubles the *key space* (the number of combinations allowed by the number of bits in the key—2 to the power of the length of the key in bits[1]) and means that it will take twice as long for an attacker to decrypt your message (assuming that there are no inherent weaknesses or vulnerabilities to exploit in the scheme). However, it is a mistake to compare algorithms based only on the number of bits used. An algorithm that uses a 64-bit key can be more secure than an algorithm that uses a 128-bit key.

The two primary classifications of encryption schemes are *public key encryption* and *symmetric key encryption.* Public key encryption, also called *asymmetric encryption,* uses two keys: a public key and a private key; these keys are uniquely associated with a specific individual user. Symmetric key encryption, also called

---

1. A 2-bit key would have a key space of 4 (2^2), a 3-bit key would have a key space of 8 (2^3), and so on.

symmetric encryption, or *secret key encryption,* uses one key that you and the person you are communicating with (hereafter, referred to as your *friend*) share as a secret. Public key algorithm keys typically have a length of 512 bits to 2,048 bits, whereas symmetric key algorithms use keys in the range of 64 bits to 512 bits.

When you are choosing an encryption scheme, realize that security comes at a price. There is usually a trade-off between resilience of the cryptosystem and ease of administration.

security ‖   Hard to Break? Hard to Use!

The more difficult an algorithm is to crack, the more difficult it is to maintain and to get people to use properly. The paramount limitations of most respectable cryptosystems lie not in weak algorithms but rather in users' failure to transmit and store keys in a secure manner.

The practicality of a security solution is a far greater factor in encryption, and in security in general, than most people realize. With enough time and effort, nearly every algorithm can be broken. In fact, you can often unearth the mathematical instructions for a widely used algorithm by flipping through a cryptography book, reviewing a vendor's product specifications, or performing a quick search on the Internet. The challenge is to ensure that the effort required to follow the twists and turns taken by an encryption algorithm and its resulting encryption solution outweighs the worth of the information it is protecting.

tip ‖   How Much Time and Money Should You Spend on Encryption?

When the cost of obtaining the information exceeds the value realized by its possession, the solution is an effective one.

Public Key Encryption

In order to use public key encryption, you must generate two keys: a public key and a private key. You keep the private key for yourself and give the public key to the world. In a similar manner, your friends will generate a pair of keys and give you their public keys. Public key encryption is marked by two distinct features:

1. When you encrypt data with someone's public key, only that person's private key can decrypt it.

2. When you encrypt data with your private key, anyone else can decrypt it with your public key.

You may wonder why the second point is useful at all: Why would you want everybody else to be able to decrypt something you just encrypted? The answer lies in the purpose of the encryption. Although encryption changes the original message into unreadable ciphertext, the purpose of this encryption is to provide a *digital signa-*

ture. If the message decrypts properly with your public key, *only you* could have encrypted it with your private key, proving that the message is authentic. Combining these two modes of operation yields privacy and authenticity. You can sign something with your private key so that it is verified as authentic, and then you can encrypt it with your friend's public key so that only your friend can decrypt it.

Public key encryption has three major shortcomings:

1. Public key encryption algorithms are generally much slower than symmetric key algorithms and usually require a much larger key size and a way to generate large prime numbers to use as components of the key, making them more resource intensive.

2. The private key must be stored securely and its integrity safeguarded. If a person's private key is obtained by another party, that party can encrypt, decrypt, and sign messages impersonating the original owner of the key. If the private key is lost or becomes corrupted, any messages previously encrypted with it are also lost, and a new keypair must be generated.

3. It is difficult to authenticate the origin of a key, that is, to prove whom it originally came from. This is known as the key-distribution problem and is the raison d'être for such companies as VeriSign (www.verisign.com).

Algorithms such as RSA, Diffie-Hellman, and El-Gamal implement public key encryption methodology. Today, a 512-bit key is considered barely adequate for RSA encryption and offers marginal protection; 1,024-bit keys are expected to withhold determined attackers for several more years. Keys that are 2,048 bits long are now becoming commonplace and rated as *espionage strength*. A mathematical paper published in late 2001 and reexamined in the spring of 2002 describes how a machine can be built—for a very large sum of money—that could break 1,024-bit RSA encryption in seconds to minutes (the article at www.schneier.com/crypto-gram-0203.html#6 debates this point). Although the cost of such a machine is beyond the reach of most individuals and smaller corporations, it is well within the reach of large corporations and governments.

Symmetric Key Encryption

Symmetric key encryption is generally fast and simple to deploy. First, you and your friend agree on which algorithm to use and a key that you will share. Then either of you can decrypt or encrypt a file with the same key. Behind the scenes, symmetric key encryption algorithms are most often implemented as a network of black boxes, which can involve hardware components, software, or a combination of the two. Each box imposes a reversible transformation on the plaintext and passes it on to the next box, where another reversible transformation further alters the data. The security of a symmetric key algorithm relies on the difficulty of determining which boxes were used and the number of times the data was fed through the set of boxes.

A good algorithm will cycle the plaintext through a given set of boxes many times before yielding the result, and there will be no obvious mapping from plaintext to ciphertext.

The disadvantage of symmetric key encryption is that it depends heavily on a secure channel to send the key to your friend. For example, you would not use email to send your key; if your email is intercepted, a third party is in possession of your secret key, and your encryption is useless. You could relay the key over the phone, but your call could be intercepted if your phone were tapped or someone overheard your conversation.

Common implementations of symmetric key algorithms are DES (Data Encryption Standard), 3-DES (triple DES), IDEA, RC5, Blowfish, and AES (Advanced Encryption Standard). AES is the new Federal Information Processing Standard (FIPS-197) algorithm endorsed for governmental use and chosen to replace DES as the de facto encryption algorithm. AES uses the Rijndael algorithm (www.rijndael.com), chosen after a thorough evaluation of 15 candidate algorithms by the cryptographic research community.

None of the aforementioned algorithms has undergone more scrutiny than DES, which has been in use since the late 1970s. However, the use of DES has drawbacks, and it is no longer considered secure, as the weakness of its 56-bit key makes it unreasonably easy to break. With advances in computing power and speed since DES was developed, the small size of its key renders it inadequate for operations requiring more than basic security for a relatively short period of time. For a few thousand dollars, you can link off-the-shelf computer systems so that they can crack DES keys in a few hours.

The 3-DES application of DES is intended to combat its degenerating resilience by running the encryption three times; it is projected to be secure for years to come. DES is probably sufficient for such tasks as sending email to a friend when you need it to be confidential, or secure, for only a few days (for example, to send a notice of a meeting that will take place in a few hours). It is unlikely that anyone is sufficiently interested in your email to invest the time and money to decrypt it. Because of 3-DES's wide availability and ease of use, it is advisable to use it instead of DES.

Encryption Implementation

In practice, most commercial software packages use both public and symmetric key encryption algorithms, taking advantage of the strengths of each and avoiding the weaknesses. The public key algorithm is used first, as a means of negotiating a randomly generated secret key and providing for message authenticity. Then a secret key algorithm, such as 3-DES, IDEA, AES, or Blowfish, encrypts and decrypts the data on both ends for speed. Finally, a hash algorithm, such as DSA (Digital Signature Algorithm), generates a message digest that provides a signature that can alert you to tampering. The digest is digitally signed with the sender's private key.

GnuPG/PGP

The most popular personal encryption packages available today are GnuPG (GNU Privacy Guard—www.gnupg.org) and PGP (Pretty Good Privacy—www.pgp.com). GNU Privacy Guard was designed as a free replacement for PGP, a security tool that made its debut during the early 1990s. Phil Zimmerman developed PGP as a Public Key Infrastructure (PKI), featuring a convenient interface, ease of use and management, and the security of digital certificates. One critical characteristic set PGP apart from the majority of cryptosystems then available: PGP functions entirely without certification authorities (CA). Until the introduction of PGP, PKI implementations were built around the concept of CAs and centralized key management controls.

PGP and GnuPG use the notion of a ring of trust:[2] If you trust someone and that person trusts someone else, the person you trust can provide an introduction to the third party. When you trust someone, you perform an operation called *key signing*. By signing someone else's key, you are verifying that that person's public key is authentic and safe for you to use to send email. When you sign a key, you are asked whether you trust this person to introduce other keys to you. It is common practice to assign this trust based on several criteria, including your knowledge of a person's character or a lasting professional relationship with the person. The best practice is to sign someone's key only after you have met face to face to avert any chance of a person-in-the-middle[3] scenario. The disadvantage of this scheme is the lack of a central registry for associating with people you do not already know.

PGP is available without cost for personal use, but its deployment in a commercial environment requires you to purchase a license. This was not always the case: Soon after its introduction, PGP was available on many bulletin board systems, and users could implement it in any manner they chose. PGP rapidly gained popularity in the networking community, which capitalized on its encryption and key management capabilities for secure transmission of email.

After a time, attention turned to the two robust cryptographic algorithms, RSA and IDEA, which are an integral part of PGP's code. These algorithms are privately owned. The wide distribution and growing user base of PGP sparked battles over patent violation and licenses, resulting in the eventual restriction of PGP's use.

---

2. For more information, see the section of *The GNU Privacy Handbook* (www.gnupg.org/docs.html) titled "Validating Other Keys on Your Public Keyring."

3. Person in the middle: If Alex and Jenny try to carry on a secure email exchange over a network, Alex first sends Jenny his public key. However, suppose that Mr. X sits between Alex and Jenny on the network and intercepts Alex's public key. Mr. X then sends *his own* public key to Jenny. Jenny then sends her public key to Alex, but once again Mr. X intercepts it and substitutes *his* public key and sends that to Alex. Without some kind of active protection (a piece of shared information), Mr. X, the *person in the middle*, can decrypt all traffic between Alex and Jenny, reencrypt it, and send it on to the other party.

Enter GnuPG, which supports most of the features and implementations made available by PGP and complies with the OpenPGP Message Format standard. Because GnuPG does not use the patented IDEA algorithm but uses BUGS (www.gnu.org/directory/bugs.html) instead, you can use it almost without restriction: It is released under the GNU GPL (refer to "The Code Is Free" on page 4). The two tools are considered to be interchangeable and interoperable. The command sequences for and internal workings of PGP and GnuPG are very similar.

tip || **The GnuPG System Includes the gpg Program**

GnuPG is frequently referred to as gpg, but gpg is actually the main program for the GnuPG system.

GNU has a good introduction to privacy, *The GNU Privacy Handbook*, available in several languages, listed at www.gnupg.org/documentation.html. Listed on the same Web page is the *Gnu Privacy Guard (GnuPG) Mini Howto*, which steps through the setup and use of gpg. And, of course, there is a gpg info page.

In addition to encryption, gpg is useful for authentication. For example, you can use it to verify that the person who signed a piece of email is the one who sent it.

File Security

From an end user's perspective, file security is one of the most critical areas of security. Some file security is built into Linux: chmod (page 174) gives you basic security control. ACLs (Access Control Lists) allow more fine-grained control of file access permissions. ACLs are part of Solaris, Windows NT/2000/XP, VAX/VMS, and mainframes OSs. Fedora Core 2 supports ACLs; refer to the acl man page for more information. Even these tools are insufficient when your account is compromised (for example, by someone watching your fingers on the keyboard as you type your password). To provide maximum file security, you must encrypt your files. Then even someone who knows your password cannot read your files. (Of course, if someone knows your key, that person can decrypt your files if he or she can get to them.)

Email Security

Email security overlaps file security and, as discussed later, network security. GnuPG is the most frequently used tool for email security, although you can also use PGP. PEM (Privacy Enhanced Mail) is a standard rather than an algorithm and is used less frequently.

MTAs (Mail Transfer Agents)

An increasingly commonplace MTA is STARTTLS (Start Transport Layer Security—www.sendmail.org/~ca/email/starttls.html). TLS itself usually refers to SSL (Secure Socket Layer) and has become the de facto method for encrypting TCP/IP traffic on the Internet. The **sendmail** utility can be built to support STARTTLS, and much documentation exists on how to do so. STARTTLS enhancements also exist for qmail and postfix and other popular MTAs. It is important to note that this capability provides encryption between two mail servers but not necessarily between your machine and the mail server. Also, the advantages of using TLS are negated if the email has to go through a relay that does not support TLS.

MUAs (Mail User Agents)

Many popular mail user agents, such as mutt, elm, and emacs, include the ability to use PGP or GnuPG for encryption. This has become the default way to exchange secure email.

Network Security

Network security is vital to the security of a computing site. However, without the right infrastructure, providing network security is difficult, if not impossible. For example, if you run a shared network topology,[4] such as Ethernet, and have in public locations jacks that allow anyone to plug in to the network at will, how can you prevent someone from plugging in a machine and capturing all the *packets* (page 987) that traverse the network?[5] You cannot, so you have a potential security hole. Another common security hole is the use of telnet for logins. Because telnet sends and receives cleartext, anyone "listening in" on the line can easily capture login names and passwords, compromising security.

Do not allow unauthenticated PCs (any PC that does not require users to supply a local name and password) on your network. With a Windows 9x PC, any user on the network is effectively Superuser for the following reasons:

- On a PC there is no concept of **root**; all users, by default, have access to and can watch the network, capture packets, and send packets.

---

4. Shared network topology: A network in which each packet may be seen by machines other than its destination. "Shared" means that the 100 megabits per second bandwidth is shared by all users.

5. Do not make the mistake of assuming that you have security just because you have a switch. Switches are designed to allocate bandwidth, not to guarantee security.

- On UNIX/Linux, only Superuser can put the network interface in promiscuous mode and collect packets. On UNIX and Linux, ports numbered less than 1,024[6] are privileged. That is, normal user protocols cannot bind to these ports. This is an important but regrettable means of security for some protocols, such as NIS, NFS, RSH, and LPD. Normally, a data switch on your LAN automatically protects your machines from people snooping on your network for data. In high-load situations, switches have been known to behave unpredictably, directing packets to the wrong ports. There are programs that can overload the switch tables that hold information about which machine is on which port. When these tables are overloaded, the switch becomes a repeater and broadcasts all packets to all ports. The attacker on the same switch as you can potentially see all the traffic your system sends and receives.

Network Security Solutions

One solution to the shared-network problems is to encrypt messages that travel between machines. IPSec (Internet Protocol Security Protocol) provides just such a technology. IPSec is commonly used to establish a secure point-to-point virtual network, called a *VPN* (page 1004), that allows two hosts to communicate securely over an insecure channel, such as the Internet. IPSec provides integrity, confidentiality, authenticity, and flexibility of implementation that supports multiple vendors.

IPSec is an amalgamation of protocols (IPsec = AH + ESP + IPComp + IKE):

- **Authentication Header** (AH) A cryptographically secure, irreversible *checksum* (page 962) for an entire packet. AH guarantees that the packet is authentic.

- **Encapsulating Security Payload** (ESP) Encrypts a packet to make the data unreadable.

- **IP Payload Compression** (IPComp) Compresses a packet. Encryption can increase the size of a packet, and IPComp counteracts this increase in size.

- **Internet Key Exchange** (IKE) Provides a way for the endpoints to negotiate a common key securely. For AH to work, the two ends must use the same key to prevent a "person in the middle" (see footnote 3 on page 926) from spoofing the connection.

---

6. The term *port* has many meanings. Here it is a number assigned to a program. The number links incoming data with a specific service. For example, port 21 is used by ftp traffic, and port 23 is used by telnet.

While IPSec is an optional part of IPv4, IPv6 (page 340) mandates its use. However, it may be quite some time before IPv6 is widely implemented. See page 948 for information about the implementation of IPSec in the 2.6 kernel.

Network Security Guidelines

Some general guidelines for establishing and maintaining a secure system follow. The list is not complete but rather is only a guide.

• Fiberoptic cable is more secure than copper cable. Copper is subject to active and passive eavesdropping. With access to copper cable, all a data thief needs to monitor your network traffic is a passive device for measuring magnetic fields. It is much more difficult to tap a fiberoptic cable without interrupting the signal. Sites requiring top security keep fiberoptic cable in pressurized conduits, where a change in pressure signals that the physical security of the cable has been breached.

• Avoid leaving unused ports in public areas. If a malicious user can plug a laptop into the network without being detected, you are at risk of a serious security problem. Network drops that are to remain unused for extended periods should be disabled at the switch, preventing them from accepting or passing network traffic.

• Many network switches have provisions for binding a hardware address to a port for enhanced security. If someone unplugs a machine and plugs in another machine to capture traffic, chances are that that machine will have a different hardware address. When it detects a device with a different hardware address, the switch can disable the port. Even this solution is no guarantee, as there are programs that enable you to change or mask the hardware address of a network interface.

security || **Install a Small Kernel and Run Only the Programs You Need**

Linux systems contain a huge number of programs that, although useful, significantly reduce the security of the host. Install the smallest operating system kernel that meets your needs. For Web and FTP servers, install only the needed components. Users usually require additional packages.

• Do not allow NFS or NIS access outside of your network. Otherwise, it is a simple matter for a malicious user to steal your entire password map. Default NFS security is marginal to nonexistent and should not be allowed outside your network to machines that you do not trust. Experimental versions of NFS for Linux that support much better authentication algorithms are now becoming available. A common joke is that NFS stands for No File Security. Use IPSec, an experimental NFSv4 with improved authentication, or firewalls to provide access outside of your domain.

- Support for VPN configuration is often built into new firewalls or provided as a separate product, enabling you to join securely with customers or partners. If you must allow business partners, contractors, or other outside parties to access your files, consider using a secure filesystem, such as NFS with *Kerberos* (page 979), secure NFS (encrypts authentication, not traffic), NFS over a VPN such as IPSec, or cfs (cryptographic filesystem).

- Specify **/usr** as readonly (**ro**) in **/etc/fstab**. This may cause your machine to be difficult to update, so use this tactic with care. For example,

```
/dev/hda6      /usr      ext2      ro      0    0
```

- Mount filesystems other than **/** and **/usr nosuid** to prevent setuid programs from executing on this filesystem. For example,

```
/dev/hda4      /var        ext3      nosuid    0    0
/dev/hda5      /usr/local  ext3      nosuid    0    0
```

- Use a barrier or firewall product between your network and the Internet. Several valuable mailing lists cover firewalls: the **comp.security.firewalls** newsgroup and the free firewalls Web site, www.freefire.org. Red Hat Linux includes iptables (page 737), which allows you to implement a firewall.

Host Security

Your host must be secure. Simple security steps include preventing remote logins and leaving the **/etc/hosts.equiv** and individual users' **~/.rhosts** files empty (or not having them at all). Complex security steps include installing IPSec for VPNs between hosts. Many common security measures are between these two extremes. A few of these follow. See Table C-1 on page 937 for URLs.

- Although potentially tricky to implement and manage, Intrusion Detection Systems (IDSs) are an excellent way to keep an eye on the integrity of a device. An IDS can warn of possible attempts at subverting security on the host on which it runs. The great-granddaddy of intrusion detection systems is tripwire. This host-based system checks modification times and integrity of files by using strong algorithms (cryptographic checksums or signatures) that can detect even the most minor modification. There is also a commercial version of tripwire. Another commercial IDS is DragonSquire. Other free, popular, and flexible IDSs include samhain and AIDE. These last two offer even more features and means of remaining invisible to users than tripwire does. Commercial IDSs that are popular in enterprise environments include Cisco Secure IDS (formerly NetRanger), Enterasys Dragon, and ISS RealSecure.

- Keep Fedora systems up to date by downloading and installing the latest updates. Go to fedora.redhat.com/download/updates.html for more information.

- Red Hat Network (RHN, page 467), yum (page 469), or Apt (page 472) can automatically or semiautomatically keep one or more systems up-to-date, preventing your system from becoming prey to fixed security bugs.

- Complementing host-based intrusion detection systems are network-based intrusion detection systems. These programs monitor the network and nodes on the network and report suspicious occurrences (attack signatures) via user-defined alerts. These signatures can be matches on known worms, overflow attacks against programs, or unauthorized scans of network ports. Such programs as snort, klaxon, and NFR are used in this capacity. Commercial programs, such as DragonSentry, also fill this role.

- Provided with Red Hat Linux is PAM, which allows you to set up different methods and levels of authentication in many ways (page 416).

- Process accounting, a good supplement to system security, can provide a continuous record of user actions on your system. See the accton man page for more information.

- Emerging standards for such things as Role Based Access Control (RBAC) allow tighter delegation of privileges along defined organizational boundaries. You can delegate each user a role or roles appropriate to the access required.

- General mailing lists and archives are an extremely useful repository of security information, statistics, and papers. The most useful are the bugtraq mailing list and CERT.[7] The bugtraq site and email provide immediate notifications about specific vulnerabilities, whereas CERT provides notice of widespread vulnerabilities and useful techniques to fix them, as well as links to vendor patches.

- The syslog facility (provided with Red Hat Linux) can direct messages from system daemons to specific files such as those in /var/log. On larger groups of systems, you can send all important syslog information to a secure host, where that host's only function is to store syslog data so that it cannot be tampered with. See page 357 and the syslogd man page.

Login Security

Without a secure host, good login security cannot add much protection. Table C-1, "Security Resources," on page 937 lists some of the best login security tools, includ-

---

7. CERT is slow but useful as a medium for coordination between sites. It acts as a tracking agency to document the spread of security problems.

ing replacement daemons for **telnetd, rlogind**, and **rshd**. The current choice of most sites is ssh, which comes as both freeware and a commercially supported package that works on UNIX/Linux, Windows, and Macintosh platforms.

The PAM facility (page 416) allows you to set up multiple authentication methods for users in series or in parallel. In-series PAM requires multiple methods of authentication for a user. In-parallel PAM uses any one of a number of methods for authentication.

Although not a frequent choice, you can configure your system to take advantage of one-time passwords. S/Key is the original implementation of one-time passwords by Bellcore. OPIE (one-time passwords in everything), developed by the U.S. Naval Research Labs, is an improvement over the original Bellcore system. In one permutation of one-time passwords, the user gets a piece of paper listing a set of one-time passwords. Each time a user logs in, the user enters a password from the piece of paper. Once used, a password becomes obsolete, and the next password in the list is the only one that will work. Even if a malicious user compromises the network and sees your password, it will be of no use because the password can be used only one time. This setup makes it very difficult for someone to log in as you but does nothing about protecting the data you type at the keyboard. One-time passwords are a good solution if you are at a site where no encrypted login is available. A truly secure (or paranoid) site will combine one-time passwords and encrypted logins.

Another type of secure login that is becoming more common is facilitated by a token or a *smart card*. Smart cards are credit-card-like devices that use a challenge-response method of authentication. Smart card and token authentication rely on something you have (the card) and something you know (a pass phrase, user ID, or pin). For example, you might enter your login name in response to the login prompt and get a password prompt. In response, you enter your PIN and the number displayed on the access token. The token has a unique serial number that is stored in a database on the authentication server. The token and the authentication server use this serial number as a means of computing a challenge every 30 to 60 seconds. If the pin and token number you enter match what it should be as computed by the access server, you are granted access to the system.

Remote Access Security

Issues and solutions surrounding remote access security overlap those pertaining to login and host security. Local logins may be secure with simply a login name and password, whereas remote logins (and all remote access) should be made more secure. Many breakins can be traced back to reusable passwords. It is a good idea to use an encrypted authentication client, such as ssh or kerberos. You can also use smart cards for remote access authentication.

Modem pools can also be an entry point. Most people are aware of how easy it is to monitor a network line. But people take for granted the security of the public switched telephone network (PSTN, aka POTS—plain old telephone service). You may want to set up an encrypted channel after dialing in to a modem pool. One way to do this is by running ssh over PPP.

There are ways to provide stringent modem authentication policies so that unauthorized users are not able to use your modems. The most common techniques are PAP (password authentication protocol), CHAP (challenge handshake authentication protocol), and Radius. PAP and CHAP are relatively weak when compared with Radius, so the latter has rapidly gained in popularity. Cisco also provides a method of authentication called TACACS/TACACS+ (Terminal Access Controller Access Control System).

One or more of these authentication techniques are available in a RAS (remote access server—in a network a computer that provides network access to remote users via modem). Before purchasing a RAS, check what kind of security it provides and decide whether that level of security meets your needs.

Two other techniques for remote access security can be built into a modem (or RAS if it has integrated modems). One is callback: After you dial in, you get a password prompt. Once you type in your password, the modem hangs up and calls you back at a phone number it has stored internally. But this technique is not foolproof. Some modems have a built-in callback table with about ten entries. This works for small sites with only a few modems. If you use more modems, you will need to have callback provided by the RAS software.

The second technique is to use CLID (caller line ID) or ANI (automatic number identification) to decide whether to answer the call. Depending on your wiring and the local phone company, you may or may not be able to use ANI. ANI information is provided before the call, whereas CLID information is provided along with the call.

Viruses and Worms

Examples of UNIX/Linux viruses are the Bliss virus/worm released in 1997 and the RST.b virus discovered in December 2001. Both are discussed in detail in articles on the Web. Viruses spread through systems by infecting executable files. In the cases of Bliss and RST.b, the Linux native executable format, ELF, was used as a propagation vector.

Just after 5 P.M. on November 2, 1988, Robert T. Morris Jr., a graduate student at Cornell University, released the first big virus onto the Internet. This virus was called an Internet worm and was designed to propagate copies of itself over many machines on the Internet. The worm was a piece of code that exploited four vulnerabilities, including one in finger, to get a buffer to overflow on a system. Once the buffer overflowed, the code was able to get a shell and then to recompile itself on the remote machine. The worm spread around the Internet very quickly and was not disabled, despite many people's efforts, for 36 hours.

The chief characteristic of a worm is propagation over a public network, such as the Internet. A virus propagates by infecting executables on the machine, but a worm tends to prefer exploiting known security holes in network servers to gain **root** access and then trying to infect other machines in the same way.

UNIX/Linux file permissions help to inoculate against many viruses. Windows NT is resistant for similar reasons. You can easily protect your system against many viruses and worms by keeping your system patches up-to-date, not executing untrusted binaries from the Internet, limiting your path to include only necessary system directories, and doing as little as possible while enabled with Superuser privileges. You can prevent a disaster in case of a virus by backing up your system frequently.

Physical Security

Physical security, often overlooked as a defense against intrusion, covers access to the computer itself and to the console or terminal attached to the machine. If the machine is unprotected in an unlocked room, there is very little hope for physical security. (A simple example of physical vulnerability is someone walking into the room where the computer is, removing the hard drive from the computer, taking it home, and analyzing it.) You can take certain steps to improve the physical security of your computer.

- Keep servers in a locked room with limited access. A key, a combination, or a swipe card should be required to gain access. Protect windows as well as doors. Maintain a single point of entry. (Safety codes may require multiple exits, but only one must be an entry.)

- For public machines, use a security system, such as a fiberoptic security system, which can secure a lab full of machines. With this system, you run a fiberoptic cable through each of the machines such that the machine cannot be removed (or opened) without cutting the cable. When the cable is cut, an alarm goes off. Some machines are much more difficult to secure than others. PCs with plastic cases are difficult to secure. Although this is not a perfect solution, it may improve your security enough to cause a would-be thief to go somewhere else.

- Most modern PCs have a BIOS password. You can set the order in which a PC searches for a boot device, preventing the PC from being booted from a floppy disk or CD. Some BIOSs can prevent the machine from booting altogether without a proper password. The password protects the BIOS from unauthorized modification. Beware, however; many BIOSs have well-known *back doors* (page 958). Research this issue if the BIOS password is an important feature for you. In addition, you can blank the BIOS password by setting the clear-CMOS jumper on a PC motherboard; if you are relying on a BIOS password, lock the case.

- Run only fiberoptic cable between buildings. This is not only more secure but also safer in the event of lightning strikes and is required by many commercial building codes.

- Maintain logs of who goes in and out of secure areas. Sign-in/out sheets are useful only if everyone uses them. Sometimes a guard is warranted. Often, a simple proximity badge or smart card can tell when anyone has entered or left an area and keep logs, although these can be expensive to procure and install.

- Anyone who has access to the physical hardware has the keys to the palace. Someone with direct access to a computer system can do such things as swap components, insert boot media, and so on, that are security threats.

- Avoid activated, unused network jacks in public places. Such jacks provide unnecessary risk.

- Many modern switches can lock a particular switch port so that it accepts only traffic from an NIC (network interface card) with a particular hardware address and shuts down the port if another address is seen. However, commonly available programs allow one to reset this address.

- Make periodic security sweeps. Check doors for proper locking. If you must have windows, make sure that they are locked or are permanently sealed.

- Waste receptacles are a common source of information for intruders. Have policies for containment and disposal of sensitive documents.

- Use a UPS (uninterruptable power supply). Without a clean source of power, your system is vulnerable to corruption.

Security Resources

Many free and commercial programs can enhance system security. Some of these are listed in Table C-1.

table C-1 ||

Tool	What It Does	Where to Get It
AIDE	Advanced Intrusion Detection Environment. Similar to tripwire with extensible verification algorithms.	sourceforge.net/projects/aide
Argus	Audits network transactions.	ciac.llnl.gov/ciac/ToolsUnixNetMon.html#Argus
bugtraq	A moderated mailing list for the announcement and detailed discussion of all aspects of computer security vulnerabilities.	www.securityfocus.com
CERT	Computer Emergency Response Team. A repository of papers and data about major security events and a list of security tools.	www.cert.org http://www.cert.org/tech_tips/security_tools.html
chkrootkit	Checks for signs of a rootkit indicating that the machine has been compromised.	www.chkrootkit.org
cops	Checks password files for bad passwords and other vulnerabilities.	www.fish.com/cops
dsniff	Sniffing and network audit tool suite. Free.	naughty.monkey.org/~dugsong/dsniff/
ethereal	Network protocol analyzer. Free.	www.ethereal.com
freefire	Supplies free security solutions and supports developers of free security solutions.	www.freefire.org
fwtk	Firewall toolkit. A set of proxies that can be used to construct a firewall.	www.fwtk.org
GIAC	A security certification and training Web site.	www.giac.org
hping	Multipurpose network auditing and packet analysis tool. Free.	www.hping.org
John	John the Ripper: a fast, flexible, weak password detector.	www.openwall.com/john

table C-1 || **Security Resources (Continued)**

Tool	What It Does	Where to Get It
Kerberos	Complete, secure network authentication system.	web.mit.edu/kerberos/www
klaxon	Launches out of **xinetd** and allows you to put alarms on unused services.	ftp://ftp.cerias.purdue.edu/pub/tools/unix/logutils/klaxon
L6	Verifies file integrity; similar to tripwire.	www.pgci.ca/l6.html
LIDS	Intrusion detection and active defense system.	www.lids.org
logdaemon	Has portable, secure replacements for **telnetd**, **login**, **ftpd**, **rexecd**. Requires tcp_wrappers.	ftp://ftp.cerias.purdue.edu/pub/tools/unix/logutils/logdaemon
mason	Builds Linux firewalls.	www.dreamwvr.com/fwtk.org/mason/
nessus	A plugin-based remote security scanner that can perform more than 370 security checks. Free.	www.nessus.org
netcat	Explores, tests, and diagnoses networks.	freshmeat.net/projects/netcat
netsys	A full-disclosure unmoderated security mailing list.	lists.netsys.com
nmap	Scans hosts to see what ports are available. It can perform stealth scans, determine OS type, find open ports, and so on.	www.insecure.org/nmap
OPIE	Provides one-time passwords for system access.	inner.net/opie
RBAC	Role Based Access Control. Assigns roles and privileges associated with the roles.	csrc.nist.gov/rbac
SAINT	Security Administrator's Integrated Network Tool. Assesses and analyzes network vulnerabilities. This tool follows satan.	www.wwdsi.com/saint

table C-1 ‖		Security Resources (Continued)
Tool	**What It Does**	**Where to Get It**
samhain	A file integrity checker. Has a GUI configurator, client/server capability, and real-time reporting capability.	samhain.sourceforge.net
SARA	The Security Auditor's Research Assistant security analysis tool.	www-arc.com/sara
SecurityFocus	Home for security tools, mail lists, libraries, and cogent analysis.	www.securityfocus.com
sentry	Detects port scans.	ftp.cerias.purdue.edu/pub/tools/unix/logutils/sentry
sfingerd	A secure, configurable replacement for the **fingerd** daemon.	ftp.cerias.purdue.edu/pub/tools/unix/daemons/sfingerd
skey	One-time disposable passwords for login.	See logdaemon earlier in this list.
snort	A flexible IDS.	www.snort.org
srp	Secure Remote Password. Upgrades common protocols, such as TELNET and FTP to use secure password exchange.	srp.stanford.edu
ssh	A secure rsh, rdist, rlogin replacement with encrypted sessions and other options. Supplied with Red Hat Linux.	www.ssh.org openssh.org
sudo	Gives very limited Superuser capabilities on an as-needed basis to system operators. Supplied with Red Hat Linux.	ftp://ftp.courtesan.com/pub/sudo
swatch	A Perl-based log parser and analyzer.	www.oit.ucsb.edu/~eta/swatch
tcp_wrappers	Monitor, filter, and log incoming requests for the systat, finger, ftp, telnet, rlogin, rsh, exec, tftp, talk, and other network services by wrapping system daemons. Supplied with Red Hat Linux.	ftp://ftp.porcupine.org/pub/security/index.html

table C-1 || **Security Resources (Continued)**

Tool	What It Does	Where to Get It
tct	The Coroner's Toolkit. Performs post-breakin forensic analysis.	www.fish.com/tct
titan	Audits and fixes potential security issues. Originally coded for Solaris, it is being ported to Linux.	www.fish.com/titan
tklogger	Visualizes logs. Requires Tcl/Tk.	ftp://ftp.cerias.purdue.edu/pub/tools/unix/logutils/tklogger
Treachery	A collection of tools for security and auditing.	www.treachery.net/tools
tripwire	Checks for possible signs of intruder activity. Supplied with Red Hat Linux.	ftp://ftp.cerias.purdue.edu/pub/tools/unix/ids/tripwire

Appendix Summary

Security is inversely proportional to usability. There must be a balance between the requirements that your users have to get their work done and the amount of security that is implemented. It is often unnecessary to provide top security for a small business with only a few employees. On the other hand, if you work for a government military contractor, you are bound to have extreme security constraints and an official audit policy to determine whether your security policies are being implemented correctly.

Review your own security requirements periodically. Several of the tools mentioned in this appendix are designed to help you do this. Such tools as nessus, samhain, and SAINT all provide an auditing mechanism.

Some companies specialize in security and auditing. Hiring one of them to examine your site can be costly but may result in specific recommendations for areas that you may have overlooked in your initial setup. When you hire someone to audit your security, you may be providing both physical and Superuser access to your systems. Make sure the company that you hire has a good history, has been in business for several years, and has impeccable references. Check on them periodically: Things change over time. Avoid the temptation to hire former system crackers as consultants. Security consultants should have an irreproachable ethical background, or you will always have doubts about their intentions.

Your total security package is based on your risk assessment of your vulnerabilities. Strengthen those areas that are most important for your business. For example, many sites will rely on a firewall to protect them completely from the Internet, whereas internal hosts receive little or no security attention. Crackers refer to this as "the crunchy outside surrounding the soft chewy middle." Yet this is entirely sufficient to protect some sites. Perform your own risk assessment and address your needs accordingly. If need be, hire a full-time security administrator whose job it is to design and audit your security policies.

The Free Software Definition

D

[Croatian | Czech | Danish | Dutch | English | French | Galician | German | Hungarian | Indonesian | Italian | Japanese | Korean | Norwegian | Polish | Portuguese | Russian | Slovenian | Spanish | Turkish][1]

We maintain this free software definition to show clearly what must be true about a particular software program for it to be considered free software.

"Free software" is a matter of liberty, not price. To understand the concept, you should think of "free" as in "free speech," not as in "free beer."

Free software is a matter of the users' freedom to run, copy, distribute, study, change and improve the software. More precisely, it refers to four kinds of freedom, for the users of the software:

- The freedom to run the program, for any purpose (freedom 0).

- The freedom to study how the program works, and adapt it to your needs (freedom 1). Access to the source code is a precondition for this.

- The freedom to redistribute copies so you can help your neighbor (freedom 2).

---

1. This material is at www.gnu.org/philosophy/free-sw.html on the GNU Web site. Because GNU requests a verbatim copy, links remain in place (underlined). View the document on the Web to ensure you are reading the latest copy and to follow the links.

- The freedom to improve the program, and release your improvements to the public, so that the whole community benefits. (freedom 3). Access to the source code is a precondition for this.

A program is free software if users have all of these freedoms. Thus, you should be free to redistribute copies, either with or without modifications, either gratis or charging a fee for distribution, to anyone anywhere. Being free to do these things means (among other things) that you do not have to ask or pay for permission.

You should also have the freedom to make modifications and use them privately in your own work or play, without even mentioning that they exist. If you do publish your changes, you should not be required to notify anyone in particular, or in any particular way.

The freedom to use a program means the freedom for any kind of person or organization to use it on any kind of computer system, for any kind of overall job, and without being required to communicate subsequently with the developer or any other specific entity.

The freedom to redistribute copies must include binary or executable forms of the program, as well as source code, for both modified and unmodified versions. (Distributing programs in runnable form is necessary for conveniently installable free operating systems.) It is ok if there is no way to produce a binary or executable form (since some languages don't support that feature), but you must have the freedom to redistribute such forms should you find or develop a way to make them.

In order for the freedoms to make changes, and to publish improved versions, to be meaningful, you must have access to the source code of the program. Therefore, accessibility of source code is a necessary condition for free software.

In order for these freedoms to be real, they must be irrevocable as long as you do nothing wrong; if the developer of the software has the power to revoke the license, without your doing anything to give cause, the software is not free.

However, certain kinds of rules about the manner of distributing free software are acceptable, when they don't conflict with the central freedoms. For example, copyleft (very simply stated) is the rule that when redistributing the program, you cannot add restrictions to deny other people the central freedoms. This rule does not conflict with the central freedoms; rather it protects them.

Thus, you may have paid money to get copies of GNU software, or you may have obtained copies at no charge. But regardless of how you got your copies, you always have the freedom to copy and change the software, even to sell copies.

"Free software" does not mean "non-commercial". A free program must be available for commercial use, commercial development, and commercial distribution. Commercial development of free software is no longer unusual; such free commercial software is very important.

Rules about how to package a modified version are acceptable, if they don't effectively block your freedom to release modified versions. Rules that "if you make the program available in this way, you must make it available in that way also" can be acceptable too, on the same condition. (Note that such a rule still leaves you the choice of whether to publish the program or not.) It is also acceptable for the license to require that, if you have distributed a modified version and a previous developer asks for a copy of it, you must send one.

In the GNU project, we use "copyleft" to protect these freedoms legally for everyone. But non-copylefted free software also exists. We believe there are important reasons why it is better to use copyleft, but if your program is non-copylefted free software, we can still use it.

See Categories of Free Software (18k characters) for a description of how "free software," "copylefted software" and other categories of software relate to each other.

Sometimes government export control regulations and trade sanctions can constrain your freedom to distribute copies of programs internationally. Software developers do not have the power to eliminate or override these restrictions, but what they can and must do is refuse to impose them as conditions of use of the program. In this way, the restrictions will not affect activities and people outside the jurisdictions of these governments.

When talking about free software, it is best to avoid using terms like "give away" or "for free", because those terms imply that the issue is about price, not freedom. Some common terms such as "piracy" embody opinions we hope you won't endorse. See Confusing Words and Phrases that are Worth Avoiding for a discussion of these terms. We also have a list of translations of "free software" into various languages.

Finally, note that criteria such as those stated in this free software definition require careful thought for their interpretation. To decide whether a specific software license qualifies as a free software license, we judge it based on these criteria to determine whether it fits their spirit as well as the precise words. If a license includes unconscionable restrictions, we reject it, even if we did not anticipate the issue in these criteria. Sometimes a license requirement raises an issue that calls for extensive thought, including discussions with a lawyer, before we can decide if the requirement is acceptable. When we reach a conclusion about a new issue, we often update these criteria to make it easier to see why certain licenses do or don't qualify.

If you are interested in whether a specific license qualifies as a free software license, see our list of licenses. If the license you are concerned with is not listed there, you can ask us about it by sending us email at <licensing@gnu.org>.

Other Texts to Read

Another group has started using the term "open source" to mean something close (but not identical) to "free software". We prefer the term "free software" because, once you have heard it refers to freedom rather than price, it calls to mind freedom.

[Croatian | Czech | Danish | Dutch | English | French | Galician | German | Hungarian | Indonesian | Italian | Japanese | Korean | Norwegian | Polish | Portuguese | Russian | Slovenian | Spanish | Turkish]

Return to GNU's home page.

Please send FSF & GNU inquiries & questions to gnu@gnu.org. There are also other ways to contact the FSF.

Please send comments on these web pages to webmasters@gnu.org, send other questions to gnu@gnu.org.

Copyright (C) 1996, 1997, 1998, 1999, 2000, 2001 Free Software Foundation, Inc., 59 Temple Place - Suite 330, Boston, MA 02111, USA

Verbatim copying and distribution of this entire article is permitted in any medium, provided this notice is preserved.

Updated: $Date: 2002/08/26 22:02:14 $ $Author: rms $

The Linux 2.6 Kernel

E

The Linux 2.6 kernel was released on December 17, 2003. A new major release of a Linux kernel is not an everyday occurrence: The last kernel, Linux 2.4, was released in January of 2001. This appendix lists features that are new to the 2.6 kernel.

Linux kernel revisions alternate between stable and unstable versions, so 2.4 was the previous stable version, and 2.5 was the development branch, which later became 2.6. For each of the major revisions, there is a series of minor revisions. Usually, minor revisions do not contain major changes, although one minor revision to the 2.4 kernel replaced the entire virtual memory subsystem, a major part of the kernel.

FEDORA   Fedora Core 2 and above include the 2.6 kernel.

RHEL   Red Hat maintains its own fork (version) of the 2.4 kernel for Red Hat Enterprise Linux. Red Hat's version of the kernel includes features from the 2.6 kernel that Red Hat considers are stable enough for enterprise use. Once the 2.6 kernel is more stable, Red Hat will use it as the basis for its commercial offerings.

See www.kniggit.net/wwol26.html if you want more information on the Linux 2.6 kernel than this appendix provides.

Native Posix Thread Library (NPTL)

Classically, programs start execution at the beginning of a series of instructions and execute them in sequence. While this technique works well for simple programs running on single CPU systems, it is often better to allow a program to execute different parts of itself simultaneously in parallel. Most programs with a GUI benefit from this functionality as it can prevent the user interface from freezing while the program performs computations.

The traditional way of writing parallel code under UNIX is to execute a **fork**() system call (page 834), which creates a copy of the running program in memory and starts it executing at the same point as the original. At the point **fork**() is called, the two copies of the program are indistinguishable, except for the fact that they receive different return values from their **fork**() call. One disadvantage of this procedure is that each time **fork**() is called, the system must create a complete copy of the process, which takes a relatively long time and causes parallel applications to use a lot of memory. (This description is not quite accurate because copy-on-write functionality in a modern operating system actually copies only those parts of memory that would be different.)

A more efficient solution to this problem is to allow a single process to run multiple threads. A thread exists in the same memory space as other threads, and so has a much smaller overhead than a single program running multiple processes. The disadvantage of threads is that multithreaded applications must be designed more carefully and thus take more time to write than multiprocessor ones. Operating systems, such as Solaris, rely heavily on threads to provide scalability to very large SMP (symmetric multiprocessing) systems. The new threading support in the 2.6 kernel uses the same industry standard POSIX APIs as Solaris for implementing threads and provides high-performance processing.

RHEL This feature has been back-ported to the Red Hat Enterprise Linux kernel.

IPSecurity (IPSec)

IPSec is a network layer protocol suite that secures Internet connections by encrypting IP packets. IPSec is an optional part of IPv4 (page 978) and a required part of IPv6 (page 978). See page 929 for more information on IPSec.

Kernel integration of IPSec means that any kernel module or application can use IPSec in the same way that it would use unsecured IP.

RHEL This feature has been back-ported to the Red Hat Enterprise Linux kernel.

Asynchronous I/O (AIO)

Without AIO, when an application needs to get data from a hardware device or a network connection, it can either poll the connection until the data is available or spawn a thread for the connection that waits for the data. Neither of these techniques is efficient.

Asynchronous I/O allows the kernel to notify an application when it has data ready to be read. This feature is most useful to large servers but can provide moderate performance gains in almost any application.

RHEL This feature has been back-ported to the Red Hat Enterprise Linux kernel.

O(1) Scheduler

One of the responsibilities of the kernel is to make sure that each execution thread gets a reasonable amount of time on the CPU(s). The scheduling algorithm used in the 2.4 kernel gradually decreased performance as more processes were added and additional CPUs were brought online, making it hard to use Linux on large SMP systems. The 2.6 scheduling algorithm runs in O(1) time, a term that indicates that a process takes the same time to run under all conditions, making Linux better able to run large numbers of processes and scale to large systems.

RHEL This feature has been back-ported to the Red Hat Enterprise Linux kernel.

OProfile

It is often said that a program spends 90% of its time executing 10% of the code. Programmers use profiling tools to identify bottlenecks in code and target this 10% for optimization. OProfile is an advanced profiling tool that identifies common programming inefficiencies. Because of its close relationship to the kernel, OProfile is able to identify hardware-specific efficiency problems, such as cache misses, which are often not possible to identify from source code.

RHEL This feature has been back-ported to the Red Hat Enterprise Linux kernel.

kksymoops

When something goes wrong in the kernel, it generates an error message called an *OOPS*. This is an in-joke from the Linux Kernel Mailing List, where developers would start bug reports with, "Oops, we've found a bug in the kernel." An OOPS provides debugging information that can help kernel developers track down the offending code or indicate that the OOPS was caused by hardware failure.

The **kksymoops** functionality provides detailed debugging information, allowing a developer to determine the line of code in the kernel that caused the OOPS. While this does not directly benefit the end user, it allows developers to find kernel bugs more quickly, resulting in a more stable kernel.

RHEL This feature has been back-ported to the Red Hat Enterprise Linux kernel.

Reverse Map Virtual Memory (rmap VM)

Virtual memory (VM) allows each process to exist in its own memory space. Every time a process attempts to access a portion of memory, the kernel translates the memory location from an address in the process's own address space to one in real memory. The reverse map allows the kernel to perform this process in reverse: Given a location in physical memory, the kernel can determine which process owns it. The reverse map allows pages to be unallocated quickly, giving the system more free memory, fewer page faults, and less overhead when quitting a program.

RHEL This feature has been back-ported to the Red Hat Enterprise Linux kernel.

HugeTLBFS (Translation Look-Aside Buffer File System)

The kernel allocates memory by pages. Virtual memory uses these pages to map between the virtual and real memory address spaces. Older versions of the Linux kernel set the size of these pages to 4 kilobytes. In cases where a lot of virtual memory is used, such as large database servers, this small size can cause a heavy load on the VM subsystem. HugeTLBFS allows much larger pages, which provides a significant performance increase under heavy VM load.

RHEL This feature has been back-ported to the Red Hat Enterprise Linux kernel.

Remap_file_pages

When retrieving data from or writing data to a file, it is common to map the file on disk to an area of memory. The system translates accesses to that area of memory directly into accesses to disk.

For additional flexibility, large database systems map different parts of a file to different parts of memory. Each mapping results in an additional load on the kernel and VM subsystems. The **remap_file_pages**() system call can perform a nonuniform mapping, meaning that a file needs to be mapped only once, significantly improving the performance of large database servers.

RHEL   This feature has been back-ported to the Red Hat Enterprise Linux kernel.

2.6 Network Stack Features (IGMPv3, IPv6, and Others)

The 2.6 kernel includes a large number of improvements in the area of networking, including support for IPv6 (page 978) and enhanced multicast (page 984) support. These features do not immediately benefit end users, but they do allow the development and deployment of network services that will not require significant modification for integration with future technologies.

RHEL   These features have been back-ported to the Red Hat Enterprise Linux kernel.

Internet Protocol Virtual Server (IPVS)

IPVS implements transport-layer switching inside the kernel for load balancing. This feature enables a single machine to distribute connections to a server farm, allowing transparent load balancing.

RHEL   This feature has been back-ported to the Red Hat Enterprise Linux kernel.

Access Control Lists (ACLs)

The traditional UNIX permission system allows three permissions to be assigned to each file: controlling access by the owner, by a single group, and by everyone else. ACLs provide much finer-grained access control. In theory, ACLs can increase security, although they make setting correct permissions more complicated, encouraging administrators to establish weaker controls than they should.

RHEL   This feature has been back-ported to the Red Hat Enterprise Linux kernel.

4GB-4GB Memory Split: Physical Address Extension (PAE)

Although Red Hat speaks of the 4GB-4GB Memory Split in its discussion of the 2.6 kernel, it has nothing to do with the new kernel. This memory split is a Red Hat enhancement to the Enterprise and Fedora kernels; it is not integrated into the main source tree (it is not part of the 2.6 kernel).

32-bit CPUs are limited to being able to address 2^{32} bytes (4 gigabytes) of memory. With the Pentium Pro, Intel introduced a work-around to this limitation called Physical Address Extension (PAE), allowing the operating system to address up to 64 gigabytes of memory. 32-bit programs, which are limited to addressing 4 gigabytes each, cannot access this much memory. A Linux kernel from the main tree is able to allocate up to 1 gigabyte for the kernel and 3 gigabytes for each *userspace* (page 1003) process.

RHEL+FEDORA   The kernels shipped with both Red Hat Enterprise Linux and Fedora Core 2 are patched to allow the kernel to allocate up to 4 gigabytes for itself and 3.7 gigabytes for each userspace process. These limitations affect Linux on 32-bit architectures only. A 64-bit Linux kernel on a 64-bit CPU, such as a SPARC64, UltraSparc, Alpha, or Opteron is able to access up to 16 *exabytes* (16×2^{60} bytes) of RAM.

Scheduler Support for HyperThreaded CPUs

Both the 2.6 kernel and the Red Hat Enterprise Linux kernel support Intel's Hyper-Threading. The 2.6 kernel treats each virtual CPU as the equivalent of a physical CPU.

RHEL   Prior to the release of the 2.6 kernel, Red Hat had implemented support for Hyper-Threaded CPUs. Although Red Hat Enterprise Linux supports these features, it does so differently than Fedora.

Block I/O (BIO) Block Layer

The 2.6 kernel includes a completely redesigned interface to drivers for block devices (page 439). While this conveys a number of benefits, it also means that these device drivers need to be rewritten and tested.

RHEL   Red Hat is allowing this feature time to stabilize before including it in Red Hat Enterprise Linux.

Support for > 2TB Filesystem

The 2.6 kernel includes SGI's XFS journaling file system, which supports file systems of up to 9 exabytes (9×2^{60} bytes).

RHEL The 2.4 kernel, including the Red Hat branch, supports disks of under a terabyte only.

New I/O Elevators

I/O elevators control how long I/O requests can be queued to allow them to be re-ordered for optimal device performance. The 2.6 kernel includes some additional settings that allow I/O elevators to be tuned for specific high device-load situations.

RHEL Red Hat is allowing this feature time to stabilize before including it in Red Hat Enterprise Linux.

Interactive Scheduler Response Tuning

The new scheduler in the 2.6 kernel prioritizes I/O bound processes. Because most user interface processes spend most of their time waiting for input from the user, this tuning should result in a more responsive system under high system load.

RHEL Red Hat is allowing this feature time to stabilize before including it in Red Hat Enterprise Linux.

Glossary

All entries marked with <small>FOLDOC</small> are based on definitions in the Free Online Dictionary of Computing (www.foldoc.org), Denis Howe, editor. Used with permission.

10.0.0.0 See *private address space* on page 989.

172.16.0.0 See *private address space* on page 989.

192.168.0.0 See *private address space* on page 989.

802.11 A family of specifications developed by IEEE for wireless LAN technology, including 802.11 (1–2 megabits per second), 802.11a (54 megabits per second), 802.11b (11 megabits per second), and 802.11g (20+ megabits per second).

absolute pathname A pathname that starts with the root directory (/). An absolute pathname locates a file without regard to the working directory.

access In computer jargon, a verb meaning to use, read from, or write to. To access a file means to read from or write to the file.

Access Control List See *ACL*.

access permission Permission to read from, write to, or execute a file. If you have write access permission to a file, you can write to the file. Also, *access privilege*.

ACL Access Control List.   A system that performs a function similar to file permissions but with much finer-grain control. Refer to "File Security" on page 927.

active window

On a desktop, the window that receives the characters you type on the keyboard. Same as *focus, desktop* (page 971).

address mask

See *subnet mask* on page 999.

alias

A mechanism of a shell that enables you to define new commands.

alphanumeric character

One of the characters, either upper- or lowercase, from A to Z and 0 to 9, inclusive.

ambiguous file reference

A reference to a file that does not necessarily specify any one file but can be used to specify a group of files. The shell expands an ambiguous file reference into a list of filenames. Special characters represent single characters (?), strings of zero or more characters (*), and character classes ([]) within ambiguous file references. An ambiguous file reference is a type of *regular expression* (page 992).

angle bracket

A left angle bracket (<) and a right angle bracket (>). The shell uses < to redirect a command's standard input to come from a file and > to redirect the standard output. Also, the shell uses the characters << to signify the start of a here document and >> to append output to a file.

animate

When referring to a window action, means that the action is slowed down so the user can view it. For example, when you minimize a window, it can disappear all at once (not animated), or it can slowly telescope into the panel so you can get a visual feel for what is happening (animated).

antialiasing

Adding gray pixels at the edge of a diagonal line to get rid of the jagged appearance and thereby make the line look smoother. Antialiasing sometimes makes type on a screen look better and sometimes worse; it works best on small and large fonts and is less effective on fonts from 8–15 points. See also *subpixel hinting* (page 999).

API

Application Program Interface. The interface (calling conventions) by which an application program accesses an operating system and other services. An API is defined at the source code level and provides a level of abstraction between the application and the kernel (or other privileged utilities) to ensure the portability of the code.FOLDOC

append

To add something to the end of something else. To append text to a file means to add the text to the end of the file. The shell uses >> to append a command's output to a file.

applet

A small program that runs within a larger program. Examples are Java applets that run in a browser and panel applets that run from a desktop panel.

argument

A number, letter, filename, or another string that gives some information to a command and is passed to the command when it is called. A command line argument is anything on a command line following the command name that is passed to the command. An option is a kind of argument.

arithmetic expression

A group of numbers, operators, and parentheses that can be evaluated. When you evaluate an arithmetic expression, you end up with a number. The Bourne Again Shell uses the expr command to evaluate arithmetic expressions; the TC Shell uses @, and the Z Shell uses let.

array

An arrangement of elements (numbers or strings of characters) in one or more dimensions. The TC and Z Shells and gawk can store and process arrays.

ASCII

American Standard Code for Information Interchange.   A code that uses seven bits to represent both graphic (letters, numbers, and punctuation) and CONTROL characters. You can represent textual information, including program source code and English text, in ASCII code. Because ASCII is a standard, it is frequently used when exchanging information between computers. See the file **/usr/pub/ascii**, or give the command **man ascii** to see a list of ASCII codes.

Extensions of the ASCII character set use eight bits. The seven-bit set is common; the eight-bit extensions are still coming into popular use. The eighth bit is sometimes referred to as the metabit.

ASCII terminal

A text-based terminal. Contrast with *graphical display* (page 973).

ASP

Application Service Provider.   A company that provides applications over the Internet.

asynchronous event

An event that does not occur regularly or synchronously with another event. Linux system signals are asynchronous; they can occur at any time because they can be initiated by any number of nonregular events.

attachment

A file that is attached to, but is not part of, a piece of email. Attachments are frequently opened by programs (including your Internet browser) that are called by your mail program so you may not be aware that they are not an integral part of an email message.

authentication

The verification of the identity of a person or process. In a communication system, authentication verifies that a message comes from its stated source. Some of the methods of authentication on a Linux system include the **/etc/passwd** and **/etc/shadow** files, LDAP, Kerberos 5, and SMB authentication.[FOLDOC]

automatic mounting

A way of demand mounting directories from remote hosts without having them hard configured into **/etc/fstab**. Also called *automounting*.

avoided

An object, such as a panel, that should not normally be covered by another object, such as a window.

back door

A security hole deliberately left in place by designers or maintainers of a system. The motivation for such holes is not always sinister; some operating systems, for example, come out of the box with privileged accounts intended for use by field service technicians or the vendor's maintenance programmers.

Ken Thompson's 1983 Turing Award lecture to the ACM revealed the existence, in early UNIX versions, of a back door that may be the most fiendishly clever security hack of all time. The C compiler contained code that would recognize when the **login** command was being recompiled and would insert some code recognizing a password chosen by Thompson, giving him entry to the system whether or not an account had been created for him.

Normally, such a back door could be removed by removing it from the source code for the compiler and recompiling the compiler. But to recompile the compiler, you have to *use* the compiler, so Thompson also arranged that the compiler would *recognize when it was compiling a version of itself*. It would insert into the recompiled compiler the code to insert into the recompiled **login** the code to allow Thompson entry, and, of course, the code to recognize itself and do the whole thing again the next time around. Having done this once, he was then able to recompile the compiler from the original sources; the hack perpetuated itself invisibly, leaving the back door in place and active but with no trace in the sources. Sometimes called a wormhole. Also *trap door*.ᶠᴼᴸᴰᴼᶜ

background process

A process that is not run in the foreground. Also called a *detached process*, a background process is initiated by a command line that ends with an ampersand (&). You do not have to wait for a background process to run to completion before giving the shell additional commands. If you have job control, you can move background processes to the foreground, and vice versa.

basename

The name of a file that, in contrast with a pathname, does not mention any of the directories containing the file (and therefore does not contain any slashes [/]). For example, **hosts** is the basename of **/etc/hosts**.ᶠᴼᴸᴰᴼᶜ

baud

The maximum information-carrying capacity of a communication channel in symbols (state transitions or level transitions) per second. This coincides with bits per second only for two-level modulation with no framing or stop bits. A symbol is a unique state of the communication channel, distinguishable by the receiver from all other possible states. For example, it may be one of two voltage levels on a wire for a direct digital connection, or it might be the phase or frequency of a carrier.ᶠᴼᴸᴰᴼᶜ

Baud is often mistakenly used as a synonym for bits per second.

baud rate	Transmission speed. Usually used to measure terminal or modem speed. Common baud rates range from 110 to 19,200 baud. See *baud*.
Berkeley UNIX	One of the two major versions of the UNIX operating system. Berkeley UNIX was developed at the University of California at Berkeley by the Computer Systems Research Group and is often referred to as *BSD* (Berkeley Software Distribution).
BIND	Berkeley Internet Name Domain. An implementation of a *DNS* (page 968) server developed and distributed by the University of California at Berkeley
BIOS	Basic Input/Output System. On PCs, *EEPROM*-based (page 969) system software that provides the lowest-level interface to peripheral devices and controls the first stage of the *bootstrap* (page 960) process, which loads the operating system. The BIOS can be stored in different types of memory. The memory must be nonvolatile so that it remembers the systems settings even when the system is turned off. Also BIOS ROM. Refer to page 25 for instructions on how to open the BIOS screens for maintenance.
bit	The smallest piece of information a computer can handle. A *bit* is a binary digit: either 1 or 0 (*on* or *off*).
bit depth	Same as *color depth* (page 963).
bit-mapped display	A graphical display device in which each pixel on the screen is controlled by an underlying representation of zeros and ones.
blank character	Either a SPACE or a TAB character, also called *whitespace* (page 1005). In some contexts, NEWLINEs are also considered blank characters.
block	A section of a disk or tape (usually 1,024 bytes long but shorter or longer on some systems) that is written at one time.
block device	A disk or tape drive. A block device stores information in blocks of characters. A block device is represented by a block device (block special) file. Contrast with *character device* (page 962).
block number	Disk and tape *blocks* are numbered so that Linux can keep track of the data on the device.
blocking factor	The number of logical blocks that make up a physical block on a tape or disk. When you write 1K logical blocks to a tape with a physical block size of 30K, the blocking factor is 30.
boot	See *bootstrap*.

boot loader	A very small program that takes its place in the *bootstrap* process that brings a computer from off or reset to a fully functional state. See *Boot Loader* on page 514.
bootstrap	Derived from "Pull oneself up by one's own bootstraps," the incremental process of loading an operating system kernel into memory and starting it running without any outside assistance. Frequently shortened to *boot*.
Bourne Again Shell	bash. GNU's command interpreter for UNIX, bash is a POSIX-compliant shell with full Bourne Shell syntax and some C Shell commands built in. The Bourne Again Shell supports emacs-style command line editing, job control, functions, and online help.^{FOLDOC}
Bourne Shell	sh. A UNIX command processor. It was developed by Steve Bourne at AT&T Bell Laboratories. See *shell* on page 995.
brace	A left brace ({) and a right brace (}). Braces have special meanings to the shell.
bracket	Either a *square bracket* (page 998) or an *angle bracket* (page 956).
branch	In a tree structure, a branch connects nodes, leaves, and the root. The Linux filesystem hierarchy is often conceptualized as an upside-down tree. The branches connect files and directories. In a source code control system, such as SCCS or RCS, a branch occurs when a revision is made to a file and is not included in other, subsequent revisions to the file.
bridge	Typically a two-port device originally used for extending networks at layer 2 (data link) of the Internet Protocol model.
broadcast	A transmission to multiple, unspecified recipients. On Ethernet a broadcast packet is a special type of multicast packet that has a special address indicating that all devices that receive it should process it. Broadcast traffic exists at several layers of the network stack, including Ethernet and IP. Broadcast traffic has one source but indeterminate destinations (all hosts on the local network).
broadcast address	The last address on a subnet (usually 255), reserved as shorthand to mean all hosts.
broadcast network	A type of network, such as Ethernet, in which any system can transmit information at any time, and all systems receive every message.
BSD	See *Berkeley UNIX* on page 959.
buffer	An area of memory that stores data until it can be used. When you write information to a file on a disk, Linux stores the information in a disk buffer until there is enough to write to the disk or until the disk is ready to receive the information.

bug An unwanted and unintended program property, especially one that causes the program to malfunction.FOLDOC

builtin (command) A command that is built into a shell. Each of the three major shells—the Bourne Again, TC, and Z Shells—has its own set of builtins. Refer to "Builtins" on page 211.

byte A component in the machine data hierarchy, usually larger than a bit and smaller than a word; now most often eight bits and the smallest addressable unit of storage. A byte typically holds one character.FOLDOC

C programming language A modern systems language that has high-level features for efficient, modular programming, as well as lower-level features that make it suitable as a systems programming language. It is machine independent so that carefully written C programs can be easily transported to run on different machines. Most of the Linux operating system is written in C, and Linux provides an ideal environment for programming in C.

C Shell csh.   The C Shell is a UNIX command processor. Developed by Bill Joy for BSD UNIX. It was named for the C programming language because its programming constructs are similar to those of C. See *shell* on page 995.

cable modem A type of modem that allows you to access the Internet by using your cable television connection.

cache Holding recently accessed data, a small, fast memory designed to speed up subsequent access to the same data. Most often applied to processor-memory access but also used for a local copy of data accessible over a network, from a hard disk, and so on.FOLDOC

calling environment A list of variables and their values that is made available to a called program. Refer to "Executing a Command" on page 270.

cascading stylesheet See *CSS* on page 966.

cascading windows An arrangement of windows such that they overlap, generally with at least part of the title bar visible. Opposite of *tiled windows* (page 1001).

case sensitive Able to distinguish between upper- and lowercase characters. Unless you set the **ignorecase** parameter, vi performs case-sensitive searches. The grep utility performs case-sensitive searches unless you use the **–i** option.

catenate To join sequentially, or end to end. The Linux cat utility catenates files: It displays them one after the other. Also *concatenate*.

chain loading   The technique used by a boot loader to load unsupported operating systems. Used for loading such operating systems as DOS or Windows, it works by loading another boot loader.

character class   In a regular expression, a group of characters that defines which characters can occupy a single character position. A character class definition is usually surrounded by square brackets. The character class defined by [abcr] represents a character position that can be occupied by a, b, c, or r. Also *list operator*.

character device   A terminal, printer, or modem. A character device stores or displays characters one at a time. A character device is represented by a character device (character special) file. Contrast with *block device* (page 959).

character-based   A program, utility, or interface that works only with *ASCII* (page 957) characters. This set of characters includes some simple graphics, such as lines and corners, and can display colored characters but cannot display true graphics. Contrast with *GUI* (page 973).

character-based terminal   A terminal that displays only characters and very limited graphics. See *character-based*.

checksum   A computed value that depends on the contents of a block of data and is transmitted or stored along with the data in order to detect corruption of the data. The receiving system recomputes the checksum based on the received data and compares this value with the one sent with the data. If the two values are the same, the receiver has some confidence that the data was received correctly.

The checksum may be 8 bits (modulo 256 sum), 16, 32, or some other size. It is computed by summing the bytes or words of the data block ignoring overflow. The checksum may be negated so that the total of the data words plus the checksum is zero.

Internet packets use a 32-bit checksum.ᶠᴼᴸᴰᴼᶜ

child process   A process that was created by another process, the parent process. Every process is a child process except for the first process, which is started when Linux begins execution. When you run a command from the shell, the shell spawns a child process to run the command. See *process* on page 990.

CIDR   Classless Inter-Domain Routing.   A scheme that allocates blocks of Internet addresses in a way that allows summarization into a smaller number of routing table entries. A CIDR block is a block of Internet addresses assigned to an ISP by the Internic (page 334).ᶠᴼᴸᴰᴼᶜ Refer to "CIDR: Classless Inter-Domain Routing" on page 337.

CIFS	Common Internet File System. An Internet filesystem protocol based on *SMB* (page 996). CIFS runs on top of TCP/IP, uses DNS, and is optimized to support slower dialup Internet connections. SMB and CIFS are used interchangeably.^{FOLDOC}
CIPE	Crypto IP *Encapsulation* (page 969). This *protocol* (page 990) *tunnels* (page 1002) IP packets within encrypted *UDP* (page 1003) packets, is lightweight and simple, and works over dynamic addresses, *NAT* (page 984), and *SOCKS* (page 997) *proxies* (page 990).
cipher (cypher)	A cryptographic system that uses a key to transpose/substitute characters within a message, the key itself, or the message.
ciphertext	Text that is encrypted. Contrast with *plaintext* (page 988). See also "Encryption" on page 922.
Classless Inter-Domain Routing	See *CIDR* on page 962.
cleartext	Text that is not encrypted; also *plaintext*. Contrast with *ciphertext*.
CLI	Command Line Interface. See also *character-based* (page 962).
client	A computer or program that requests one or more services from a server.
CODEC	Coder/decoder or compressor/decompressor. A hardware and/or software technology that codes and decodes data. MPEG is a popular CODEC for computer video.
color depth	The number of bits used to generate a pixel. Usually 8, 16, 24, or 32. The color depth is directly related to the number of colors that can be generated. The number of colors that can be generated is 2 raised to the color-depth power so that a 24-bit video adapter can generate about 16.7 million colors.
color quality	See *color depth*.
combo box	A combination of a list and text entry box. A user can either select an option from a provided list or enter his own option.
command	What you give the shell in response to a prompt. When you give the shell a command, it executes a utility, another program, a builtin command, or a shell script. Utilities are often referred to as commands. When you are using an interactive utility, such as vi or mail, you use commands that are appropriate to that utility.

command line   A line of instructions and arguments that executes a command. This term usually refers to a line that you enter in response to a shell prompt on a character-based terminal or terminal emulator (page 86).

command substitution   Replacing a command with its output. The shells perform command substitution when you enclose a command between $(and) or between a pair of backtics (` `), also called grave accent marks.

component architecture   A notion in object-oriented programming where "components" of a program are completely generic. Instead of having a specialized set of methods and fields, they have generic methods through which the component can advertise the functionality it supports to the system into which it is loaded. This enables completely dynamic loading of objects. JavaBeans is an example of a component architecture.FOLDOC

concatenate   See *catenate* on page 961.

condition code   See *exit status* on page 970.

connectionless protocol   The data communication method in which communication occurs between hosts with no previous setup. Packets sent between two hosts may take different routes. There is no guarantee that packets will arrive as transmitted or that they will arrive at the destination at all. *UDP* (page 1003) is a connectionless protocol. Also called packet switching. Contrast circuit switching and *connection-oriented protocol*. FOLDOC

connection-oriented protocol   A type of transport layer data communication service that allows a host to send data in a continuous stream to another host. The transport service guarantees that all data will be delivered to the other end in the same order as sent and without duplication. Communication proceeds through three well-defined phases: connection establishment, data transfer, connection release. The most common example is *TCP* (page 1000).

Also called connection-based protocol and stream-oriented protocol. Contrast *connectionless protocol* and *datagram* (page 966).FOLDOC

console   See *system console* on page 1000.

console terminal   See *system console* on page 1000.

control character   A character that is not a graphic character, such as a letter, number, or punctuation mark. Such characters are called control characters because they frequently act to control a peripheral device. RETURN and FORMFEED are control characters that control a terminal or printer.

control character (continued)
The word CONTROL is shown in this book in THIS FONT because it is a key that appears on most terminal keyboards. Control characters are represented by ASCII codes less than 32 (decimal). See also *nonprinting character* on page 986.

control structure
A statement used to change the order of execution of commands in a shell script or other program. Each one of the shells provides control structures, such as **If** and **While**, as well as other commands that alter the order of execution (for example, exec). Also *control flow commands*.

cookie
Data stored on a client system by a server. The client system browser sends the cookie back to the server each time it accesses that server. For example, a catalog shopping service may store a cookie on your system when you place your first order. When you return to the site, it knows who you are and can supply your name and address for subsequent orders. You may consider cookies an invasion of privacy.

CPU
Central Processing Unit. The part of a computer that controls all the other parts. The CPU includes the control unit and the arithmetic and logic unit (ALU). The control unit fetches instructions from memory and decodes them to produce signals that control the other parts of the computer. These signals can cause data to be transferred between memory and ALU or peripherals to perform input or output. A CPU that is housed on a single chip is called a microprocessor. Also *processor* and *central processor*.

cracker
An individual who attempts to gain unauthorized access to a computer system. These individuals are often malicious and have many means at their disposal for breaking into a system. Contrast with *hacker* (page 973). FOLDOC

crash
The system suddenly stops/fails when you do not intend it to. Derived from the action of the hard disk heads on the surface of the disk when the air gap between the two collapses.

cryptography
The practice and study of encryption and decryption—encoding data so that only a specific individual/machine can decode it. A system for encrypting and decrypting data is a cryptosystem. These usually involve an algorithm for combining the original data (plaintext) with one or more keys—numbers or strings of characters known only to the sender and/or recipient. The resulting output is called *ciphertext* (page 963).

The security of a cryptosystem usually depends on the secrecy of keys rather than on the supposed secrecy of an algorithm. Because a strong cryptosystem has a large range of keys, it is not possible to try all of them. Ciphertext appears random to standard statistical tests and resists known methods for breaking codes. FOLDOC

.cshrc file   In your home directory, a file that the TC Shell executes each time you invoke a new TC Shell. You can use this file to establish variables and aliases.

CSS   Cascading stylesheet.   Describes how documents are presented on screen and in print. Attaching a stylesheet to a structured document can affect the way it looks without adding new HTML (or other) tags and without giving up device independence. Also *stylesheet*.

current (process, line, character, directory, event, and so on)   The item that is immediately available, working, or being used. The current process controls the program you are running, the current line or character is the one the cursor is on, and the current directory is the working directory.

cursor   A small lighted rectangle, underscore, or vertical bar that appears on the terminal screen and indicates where the next character is going to appear. Differs from the *mouse pointer* (page 984).

daemon   A program that is not invoked explicitly but lies dormant, waiting for some condition(s) to occur. The idea is that the perpetrator of the condition need not be aware that a daemon is lurking (although often a program will commit an action only because it knows that it will implicitly invoke a daemon). From the mythological meaning, later rationalized as the acronym Disk And Execution MONitor.FOLDOC See Table 10-4 on page 355 for a list of daemons.

data structure   A particular format for storing, organizing, working with, and retrieving data. Frequently, data structures are designed to work with specific algorithms that facilitate these tasks. Common data structures include trees, files, records, tables, arrays, and so on.

datagram   A self-contained, independent entity of data carrying sufficient information to be routed from the source to the destination computer without reliance on earlier exchanges between this source and destination computer and the transporting network. *UDP* (page 1003) uses datagrams; *IP* (page 977) uses *packets* (page 987). Packets are indivisible at the network layer; datagrams are not.FOLDOC See also *frame* (page 972).

dataless   A computer, usually a workstation, that uses a local disk to boot a copy of the operating system and access system files but does not use a local disk to store user files.

dbm   A standard, simple database manager. Implemented as **gdbm** (GNU database manager), it uses hashes to speed searching. The most common versions of the **dbm** database are **dbm**, **ndbm**, and **gdbm**.

DDoS attack   Distributed Denial of Service attack.   A *DoS attack* (page 968) from many systems that do not belong to the perpetrator of the attack.

debug To correct a program by removing its bugs (that is, errors).

default Something that is selected without being explicitly specified. For example, when used without an argument, ls displays a list of the files in the working directory by default.

delta A set of changes made to a file that has been encoded by the Source Code Control System (SCCS).

denial of service *See DoS attack* on page 968.

dereference When speaking of symbolic links, follow the link rather than working with the reference to the link. For example, the −L or −−dereference option causes ls to list the entry that a symbolic link points to rather than the symbolic link (the reference) itself.

desktop A collection of windows, toolbars, and icons/buttons, some or all of which appear on your display. A desktop comprises one or more *workspaces* (page 1006). Refer to "Getting the Most from the Desktop" on page 78.

desktop manager An icon- and menu-based user interface to system services that allows you to run applications and use the filesystem without using the system's command line interface.

detached process See *background process* on page 958.

device A disk drive, printer, terminal, plotter, or other input/output unit that can be attached to the computer.

device driver Part of the Linux kernel that controls a device, such as a terminal, disk drive, or printer.

device file A file that represents a device. Also *special file*.

device filename The pathname of a device file. All Linux systems have two kinds of device files: block and character device files. Linux also has FIFOs (named pipes) and sockets. Device files are traditionally located in the **/dev** directory.

device number See *major device number* (page 982) and *minor device number* (page 983).

DHCP Dynamic Host Configuration Protocol. A protocol that dynamically allocates IP addresses to computers on a LAN.ᶠᵒᴸᴰᴼᶜ Refer to "DHCP" on page 408.

directory Short for *directory file*. A file that contains a list of other files.

directory hierarchy A directory, called the root of the directory hierarchy, and all the directory and ordinary files below it (its children).

directory service   A structured repository of information on people and resources within an organization, facilitating management and communication.FOLDOC

disk partition   See *partition* on page 988.

diskless   A computer, usually a workstation, that has no disk and must contact another computer (a server) to boot a copy of the operating system and access the necessary system files.

distributed computing   A style of computing in which tasks or services are performed by a network of cooperating systems, some of which may be specialized.

DMZ   Demilitarized zone.   A host or small network that is a neutral zone between a LAN and the Internet. It can serve Web pages and other data to the Internet and allow local systems access to the Internet while preventing LAN access to unauthorized Internet users. Even if a DMZ is compromised, it holds no data that is private and none that cannot be easily reproduced.

DNS   Domain Name Service.   A distributed service that manages the correspondence of full hostnames (those that include a domain name) to IP addresses and other system characteristics.

DNS domain name   See *domain name*.

document object model   See *DOM*.

DOM   Document Object Model.   A platform-/language-independent interface that enables a program to update the content, structure, and style of a document dynamically. The changes can then be made part of the displayed document. Go to www.w3.org/DOM for more information.

domain name   A name associated with an organization, or part of an organization, to help identify systems uniquely. Technically, the part of the *FQDN* (page 972) to the right of the leftmost period. Domain names are assigned hierarchically; the domain berkeley.edu refers to the University of California at Berkeley, for example (part of the top-level edu [education] domain). Also DNS domain name. Different than *NIS domain name* (page 986).

Domain Name Service   See *DNS*.

door   An evolving filesystem-based *RPC* (page 994) mechanism.

DoS attack   Denial of Service attack.   An attack that attempts to make the target host or network unusable by flooding it with useless traffic.

DPMS   Display Power Management Signaling. A standard that can extend the life of CRT monitors and conserve energy. DPMS supports four modes for a monitor: Normal, Standby (power supply on, monitor ready to come to display images almost instantly), Suspend (power supply off, monitor takes up to ten seconds to display an image), and Off.

drag   To move an icon from one position or application to another, usually in the context of a window manager. The motion part of drag-and-drop.

druid   In role-playing games, a character that represents a magical user. Red Hat uses the term *druid* at the ends of names of programs that guide you through a task-driven chain of steps. Other operating systems call these types of programs *wizards*.

DSA   Digital Signature Algorithm. A public key cipher used to generate digital signatures.

DSL   Digital Subscriber Line/Loop. Provides high-speed digital communication over a specialized, conditioned telephone line. See also *xDSL* (page 1006).

Dynamic Host Configuration Protocol   See *DHCP* on page 967.

editor   A utility, such as vim or emacs, that creates and modifies text files.

EEPROM   Electrically Erasable, Programmable, Read-Only Memory. A *PROM* (page 990) that can be written to.

effective user ID   The user ID that a process appears to have; usually the same as the user ID. For example, while you are running a setuid program, the effective user ID of the process running the program is that of the owner of the program.

element   One thing, usually a basic part of a group of things. An element of a numeric array is one of the numbers stored in the array.

emoticon   See *smiley* on page 996.

encapsulation   See *tunneling* on page 1002.

environment   See *calling environment* on page 961.

EOF   End of file.

EPROM   Erasable Programmable Read-Only Memory. A *PROM* (page 990) that can be written to by applying a higher than normal voltage.

escape	See *quote* on page 991.
Ethernet	A type of *LAN* (page 979) capable of transfer rates up to 1,000 megabits per second. Refer to "Ethernet" on page 327.
event	An occurrence, or happening, of significance to a task or program, such as the completion of an asynchronous input/output operation, such as a keypress or mouse click.FOLDOC
exabyte	2^{60} bytes or about 10^{18} bytes. See also *large number* (page 980).
exit status	The status returned by a process; either successful (usually 0) or unsuccessful (usually 1).
exploit	A security hole or an instance of taking advantage of a security hole.FOLDOC
expression	See *logical expression* (page 981) and *arithmetic expression* (page 957).
extranet	A network extension for a subset of users (such as students at a particular school or engineers working for the same company), an extranet limits access to private information even though it travels on the public Internet.
failsafe session	A session that allows you to log in on a minimal desktop in case your standard login does not work well enough to allow you to log in to fix a login problem.
FDDI	Fiber Distributed Data Interface. A type of *LAN* (page 979) designed to transport data at the rate of 100 million bits per second over fiberoptic cable.
file	A collection of related information referred to with a *filename* and frequently stored on a disk. Text files typically contain memos, reports, messages, program source code, lists, or manuscripts. Binary or executable files contain utilities or programs that you can run. Refer to "Directory and Ordinary Files" on page 158.
filename	The name of a file. A filename refers to a file.
filename completion	Automatic completion of a filename after you specify a unique prefix.
filename extension	The part of a filename following a period.
filename generation	What occurs when the shell expands ambiguous file references. See *ambiguous file reference* on page 956.

filesystem   A *data structure* (page 966) that usually resides on part of a disk. All Linux systems have a root filesystem, and most have at least a few other filesystems. Each filesystem is composed of some number of blocks, depending on the size of the disk partition that has been assigned to the filesystem. Each filesystem has a control block, named the superblock, that contains information about the filesystem. The other blocks in a filesystem are inodes, which contain control information about individual files, and data blocks, which contain the information in the files.

filling   A variant of maximizing in which window edges are pushed out as far as they can go without overlapping another window.

filter   A command that can take its input from standard input and send its output to standard output. A filter transforms the input stream of data and sends it to standard output. A pipe usually connects a filter's input to standard output of one command, and a second pipe connects the filter's output to standard input of another command. The grep and sort utilities are commonly used as filters.

firewall   A device for policy-based traffic management used to keep a network secure. A firewall can be implemented in a single router that filters out unwanted packets, or it can use a combination of routers, proxy servers, and other devices. Firewalls are widely used to give users access to the Internet in a secure fashion and to separate a company's public WWW server from its internal network. Firewalls are also used to keep internal network segments more secure.

Recently, the term has come to be defined more loosely to include a simple packet filter running on an endpoint machine.

See also *proxy server* on page 991.

focus, desktop   On a desktop the window that is active. The window with the desktop focus receives the characters you type on the keyboard. Same as *active window* (page 956).

footer   The part of a format that goes at the bottom (or foot) of a page. Contrast with *header* (page 974).

foreground process   When you run a command in the foreground, the shell waits for the command to finish before giving you another prompt. You must wait for a foreground process to run to completion before you can give the shell another command. If you have job control, you can move background processes to the foreground, and vice versa. See *job control* on page 978. Contrast with *background process* (page 958).

fork   To create a process. When one process creates another process, it forks a process. Also *spawn*.

FQDN   Fully Qualified Domain Name.   The full name of a system, consisting of its hostname and its domain name, including the top-level domain. Technically, the name that **gethostbyname**(2) returns for the host named by **gethostname**(2). For example, **speedy** is a hostname and **speedy.example.com** is an FQDN. An FQDN is sufficient to determine a unique Internet address for a machine on the Internet.ᶠᴼᴸᴰᴼᶜ

frame   A data link layer packet that contains, in addition to data, the header and trailer information required by the physical medium. Network layer packets are encapsulated to become frames.ᶠᴼᴸᴰᴼᶜ See also *datagram* (page 966) and *packet* (page 987).

free list   In a filesystem, the list of blocks that are available for use. Information about the free list is kept in the superblock of the filesystem.

free software   Refer to Appendix D, "The Free Software Definition" (page 943).

free space   The portion of a hard disk that is not within a partition. A new hard disk has no partitions and contains all free space.

full duplex   The ability to receive and transmit data simultaneously. A *network switch* (page 985) is typically a full-duplex device. Contrast with *half duplex* (page 973).

fully qualified domain name   See *FQDN* on page 972.

function   See *shell function* on page 996.

gateway   A generic term for a computer or a special device connected to more than one dissimilar type of network to pass data between them. Unlike a router, a gateway often must convert the information into a different format before passing it on. The historical usage of gateway to designate a router is deprecated.

GCOS   See *GECOS*.

GECOS   General Electric Comprehensive Operating System.   For historical reasons, the user information field in the **/etc/passwd** file is called the GECOS field. Also GCOS.

giga-   In the binary system, the prefix giga- multiplies by 2^{30}, or 1,073,741,824. Gigabit and gigabyte are common uses of this prefix. Abbreviated as G. See also *large number* on page 980.

glyph   A symbol that communicates a specific piece of information nonverbally. A *smiley* (page 996) is a glyph.

GMT   Greenwich Mean Time. See *UTC* on page 1004.

graphical display   A bitmapped monitor that can display graphical images. Contrast with *ASCII terminal* (page 957).

graphical user   See *GUI* on page 973.
interface

group (of users)   A collection of users. Groups are used as a basis for determining file access permissions. If you are not the owner of a file and you belong to the group the file is assigned to, you are subject to the group access permissions for the file. A user can simultaneously belong to several groups.

group (of   A way to identify similar windows so they can be displayed and acted on similarly. Typically, windows started by a given application belong to the same group.
windows)

group ID   A unique number that identifies a set of users. It is stored in the password and group databases (**/etc/passwd** and **/etc/group** files or their NIS equivalents). The group database associates group IDs with group names.

GUI   Graphical User Interface. A GUI provides a way to interact with a computer system by choosing items from menus or manipulating pictures drawn on a display screen instead of by typing command lines. Under Linux, the X Window System provides a graphical display and mouse/keyboard input. GNOME and KDE are two popular desktop managers that run under X. Contrast with *character-based* (page 962).

hacker   A person who enjoys exploring the details of programmable systems and how to stretch their capabilities, as opposed to users, who prefer to learn only the minimum necessary. One who programs enthusiastically (even obsessively) or who enjoys programming rather than just theorizing about programming.[FOLDOC] Contrast with *cracker* (page 965).

half duplex   A half-duplex device can only receive or transmit at a given moment; it cannot do both. A *hub* (page 975) is typically a half-duplex device. Contrast with *full duplex* (page 972).

hard link   A directory entry that contains the filename and inode number for a file. The inode number identifies the location of control information for the file on the disk, which in turn identifies the location of the file's contents on the disk. Every file has at least one hard link, which locates the file in a directory. When you remove the last hard link to a file, you can no longer access the file. See *link* (page 980) and *symbolic link* (page 1000).

hash
A string that is generated from another string. See *one-way hash function* on page 986. When used for security, a hash can prove, almost to a certainty, that a message has not been tampered with during transmission: The sender generates a hash of a message; encrypts the message and hash; sends the encrypted message and hash to the recipient, who decrypts the message and hash; generates a second hash from the message; and compares the hash that the sender generated to the new hash. When they are the same, the message has probably not been tampered with. A hash can also be used to create an index called a *hash table*. Also *hash value*.

hash table
An index created from hashes of the items to be indexed. The hash function makes it highly unlikely that two items will create the same hash. To look up an item in the index, create a hash of the item and search for the hash. Because the hash is typically shorter than the item, the search is more efficient.

header
When you are formatting a document, the header goes at the top, or head, of a page. In electronic mail the header identifies who sent the message, when it was sent, the subject of the message, and so forth.

here document
A shell script that takes its input from the file that contains the script.

hesiod
The nameserver of project Athena. Hesiod is a name service library that is derived from *BIND* (page 959) and leverages a DNS infrastructure.

heterogeneous
Consisting of different parts. A heterogeneous network includes systems produced by different manufacturers and/or running different operating systems.

hexadecimal number
A base 16 number. Hexadecimal (or *hex*) numbers are composed of the hexadecimal digits 0–9 and A–F. See Table G-1.

hidden file
See *invisible file* on page 977.

hierarchy
An organization with a few things, or thing—one at the top—and with several things below each other thing. An inverted tree structure. Examples in computing include a file tree where each directory may contain files or other directories, a hierarchical network, and a class hierarchy in object-oriented programming.FOLDOC Refer to "The Hierarchical Filesystem" on page 157.

history
A shell mechanism that enables you to modify and reexecute recent commands.

home directory
The directory that is your working directory when you first log in. The pathname of this directory is stored in the **HOME** shell variable.

hover
To leave the mouse pointer stationary for a moment over an object. In many cases, this displays a *tooltip* (page 1002).

table G-1 ‖   **Decimal, Octal, and Hexadecimal Numbers**

Decimal	Octal	Hex	Decimal	Octal	Hex
1	1	1	17	21	11
2	2	2	18	22	12
3	3	3	19	23	13
4	4	4	20	24	14
5	5	5	21	25	15
6	6	6	31	37	1F
7	7	7	32	40	20
8	10	8	33	41	21
9	11	9	64	100	40
10	12	A	96	140	60
11	13	B	100	144	64
12	14	C	128	200	80
13	15	D	254	376	FE
14	16	E	255	377	FF
15	17	F	256	400	100
16	20	10	257	401	101

HTML Hypertext Markup Language.   A *hypertext* (page 976) document format used on the World Wide Web. Tags, which are embedded in the text, consist of a less than sign (<), a directive, zero or more parameters, and a greater than sign (>). Matched pairs of directives, such as <TITLE> and </TITLE>, delimit text that is to appear in a special place or style.FOLDOC For more information on HTML, go to www.htmlhelp.com/faq/html/all.html.

HTTP Hypertext Transfer Protocol.   The client/server TCP/IP protocol used on the World Wide Web for the exchange of *HTML* documents.

hub A multiport repeater. A hub rebroadcasts all packets it receives on all ports. This term is frequently used to refer to small hubs and switches, regardless of device intelligence. A generic term for a layer -2 shared-media networking device. Today the term *hub* is sometimes used to refer to small intelligent devices, although that was not its original meaning. Contrast with *network switch* (page 985).

hypertext	A collection of documents/nodes containing (usually highlighted or underlined) cross-references or links, which, with the aid of an interactive browser program, allow the reader to move easily from one document to another.FOLDOC
Hypertext Markup Language	See *HTML* on page 975.
Hypertext Transfer Protocol	See *HTTP* on page 975.
i/o device	Input/output device. See *device* on page 967.
IANA	Internet Assigned Numbers Authority. A group that maintains a database of all permanent, registered system services (www.iana.org).
ICMP	Internet Control Message Protocol. A type of network packet that carries only messages, no data.
icon	In a GUI, a small picture representing a file, directory, action, program, and so on. When you click an icon, an action, such as opening a window and starting a program or displaying a directory or Web site, takes place. From miniature religious statues.FOLDOC
iconify	The process of changing a window into an *icon*. Contrast with *restore* (page 993).
ignored window	A state in which a window has no decoration and therefore no buttons or titlebar to control it with.
indentation	See *indention*.
indention	The blank space between the margin and the beginning of a line that is set in from the margin.
inode	A *data structure* (page 966) that contains information about a file. An inode for a file contains the file's length, the times the file was last accessed and modified, the time the inode was last modified, owner and group IDs, access privileges, number of links, and pointers to the data blocks that contain the file itself. Each directory entry associates a filename with an inode. Although a single file may have several filenames (one for each link), it has only one inode.
input	Information that is fed to a program from a terminal or other file. See *standard input* on page 998.
installation	A computer at a specific location. Some aspects of the Linux system are installation dependent. Also *site*.

interactive	A program that allows ongoing dialog with the user. When you give commands in response to shell prompts, you are using the shell interactively. Also, when you give commands to utilities, such as vi and mail, you are using the utilities interactively.
interface	The meeting point of two subsystems. When two programs work together, their interface includes every aspect of either program that the other deals with. The *user interface* (page 1003) of a program includes every program aspect the user comes into contact with: the syntax and semantics involved in invoking the program, the input and output of the program, and its error and informational messages. The shell and each of the utilities and built-in commands have a user interface.
International Organization for Standardization	See *ISO* on page 978.
internet	A large network that encompasses other, smaller networks.
Internet	The largest internet in the world. The Internet (capital I) is a multilevel hierarchy composed of backbone networks (ARPAnet, NSFNet, MILNET, and others), midlevel networks, and stub networks. These include commercial (**.com** or **.co**), university (**.ac** or **.edu**), research (**.org** or **.net**), and military (**.mil**) networks and span many different physical networks around the world with various protocols, including the Internet Protocol (IP). Outside the United States, country code domains are popular (**.us**, **.es**, **.mx**, **.de**, and so forth), although you will see them used within the United States too.
Internet Protocol	See *IP*.
Internet Service Provider	See *ISP* on page 978.
intranet	An inhouse network designed to serve a group of people such as a corporation or school. The general public on the Internet does not have access to the intranet. See page 324.
invisible file	A file whose filename starts with a period. These files are called invisible because the ls utility does not normally list them. Use the –a option of ls to list all files, including invisible ones. Also, the shell does not expand a leading asterisk (٭) in an ambiguous file reference to match the filename of an invisible file. Also *hidden file*.
IP	Internet Protocol. The network layer for TCP/IP. IP is a best-effort, packet-switching, *connectionless protocol* (page 964) that provides packet routing, fragmentation, and reassembly through the data link layer. Version IPv4 is slowly giving way to version *IPv6* (page 978).FOLDOC

IP address	Internet Protocol address. A four-part address associated with a particular network connection for a system using the Internet Protocol (IP). A system that is attached to multiple networks that use the IP will have a different IP address for each network interface.
IP multicast	See *multicast* on page 984.
IP spoofing	A technique used to gain unauthorized access to a computer. The would-be intruder sends messages to the target machine. These messages contain an IP address indicating that the messages are coming from a trusted host (page 343). The target machine responds to the messages, giving the intruder (privileged) access to the target.
IPC	Inter-Process Communication. A method to communicate specific information between programs.
IPv4	See *IP* and *IPv6*.
IPv6	*IP* version 6. The next generation of Internet Protocol, which provides a much larger address space (2^{128} bits versus 2^{32} for IPv4) that is designed to accommodate the rapidly growing number of Internet addressable devices. IPv6 also has built-in autoconfiguration, enhanced security, better multicast support, and many other features.
ISDN	Integrated Services Digital Network. A set of communications standards that allows a single pair of digital or standard telephone wires to carry voice, data, and video at a rate of 64 kilobits per second.
ISO	International Organization for Standardization. A voluntary, nontreaty organization founded in 1946. It is responsible for creating international standards in many areas, including computers and communications. Its members are the national standards organizations of 89 countries, including the American National Standards Institute.ᶠᴼᴸᴰᴼᶜ
ISO9660	The *ISO* standard defining a filesystem for CD-ROMs.
ISP	Internet Service Provider. Provides Internet access to its customers.
job control	A facility that enables you to move commands from the foreground to the background and vice versa. Job control enables you to stop commands temporarily.
journaling filesystem	A filesystem that maintains a noncached log file, or journal, which records all transactions involving the filesystem. When a transaction is complete, it is marked as complete in the log file.

The log file results in greatly reduced time spent recovering a filesystem after a crash, making it particularly valuable in systems where high availability is an issue. |

JPEG Joint Photographic Experts Group. The name of the committee that designed the standard image-compression algorithm. JPEG is designed for compressing either full-color or gray-scale digital images of natural, real-world scenes and does not work as well on nonrealistic images, such as cartoons or line drawings. Filename extensions: **.jpg**, **.jpeg**.FOLDOC

justify To expand a line of type to the right margin in the process of formatting text. A line is justified by increasing the space between words and sometimes between letters on the line.

Kerberos An MIT-developed security system that authenticates users and machines. It does not provide authorization to services or databases; it establishes identity at logon, which is used throughout the session. Once you are authenticated, you can open as many terminals, windows, services, or other network accesses until your session expires.

kernel The part of the operating system that allocates machine resources, including memory, disk space, and *CPU* (page 965) cycles, to all the other programs that run on a computer. The kernel includes the low-level hardware interfaces (drivers) and manages *processes* (page 990), the means by which Linux executes programs. The kernel is the part of the Linux system that Linus Torvalds originally wrote (see the beginning of Chapter 1).

kernelspace The part of memory (RAM) where the kernel resides. Code running in kernelspace has full access to hardware and all other processes in memory. See the *KernelAnalysis-HOWTO*.

key binding A *keyboard* key is said to be bound to the action that results from pressing it. Typically, keys are bound to the letters that appear on the keycaps: When you press **A**, an **A** appears on the screen. Key binding usually refers to what happens when you press a combination of keys, one of which is CONTROL, ALT, META, or SHIFT, or when you press a series of keys, the first of which is typically ESCAPE.

keyboard A hardware input device consisting of a number of mechanical buttons (keys) that the user presses to input characters to a computer. By default a keyboard is connected to standard input of a shell.FOLDOC

kilo- In the binary system, the prefix kilo- multiplies by 2^{10}, or 1,024. Kilobit and kilobyte are common uses of this prefix. Abbreviated as k.

Korn Shell ksh. A command processor, developed by David Korn at AT&T Bell Laboratories, that is compatible with the Bourne Shell but includes many extensions. See also *shell* on page 995.

LAN Local area network. A network that connects computers within a localized area (such as a single site, building, or department).

large number	Go to mathworld.wolfram.com/LargeNumber.html for a comprehensive list.
LDAP	Lightweight Directory Access Protocol. A simple protocol for accessing online directory services. Traditionally, LDAP is used to access information such as email directories; in some cases, it can be used as an alternative for services such as NIS. Given a name, many mail clients can use LDAP to discover the corresponding email address. See *directory service* on page 968.
leaf	In a tree structure, the end of a branch that cannot support other branches. When the Linux filesystem hierarchy is conceptualized as a tree, files that are not directories are leaves. See *node* on page 986.
least privilege, concept of	Mistakes that Superuser makes can be much more devastating than those made by an ordinary user. When you are working on the computer, especially when you are working as the system administrator, always perform any task using the least privilege possible. If you can perform a task logged in as an ordinary user, do so. If you must be logged in as Superuser, do as much as you can as an ordinary user, log in or su so you are Superuser, do as much of the task that has to be done as Superuser, and revert to being an ordinary user as soon as you can.

Because you are more likely to make a mistake when you are rushing, this concept becomes more important when you have less time to apply it. |
Lightweight Directory Access Protocol	See *LDAP*.
link	A pointer to a file. There are two kinds of links: hard links and symbolic (soft) links. A hard link associates a filename with a place on the disk where the contents of the file is located. A symbolic link associates a filename with the pathname of a hard link to a file. See *hard link* (page 973) and *symbolic link* (page 1000).
Linux-PAM	See *PAM* on page 987.
Linux-Pluggable Authentication Modules	See *PAM* on page 987.
loadable kernel module	See *loadable module*.
loadable module	A portion of the operating system that controls a special device and that can be loaded automatically into a running kernel as needed to access that device. See "Using Loadable Kernel Modules" on page 512.

local area network	See *LAN* on page 979.
locale	The language; date, time, and currency formats; character sets; and so forth that pertain to a geopolitical place or area. For example, en_US specifies English as spoken in the United States and dollars; en_UK specifies English as spoken in the United Kingdom and pounds. See the **locale** (5) man page for more information.
log in	To gain access to a computer system by responding correctly to the **login:** and **Password:** prompts. Also, *log on, login*.
log out	To end your session by exiting from your login shell. Also *log off*.
logical expression	A collection of strings separated by logical operators (>, >=, =, !=, <=, and <) that can be evaluated as *true* or *false*. Also *Boolean expression*.
.login file	A file that the TC Shell executes when you log in. You can use this file to set environment variables and to run commands that you want executed at the beginning of each session.
login name	The name you enter in response to the **login:** prompt. Other users use your login name when they send you mail or write to you. Each login name has a corresponding user ID, which is the numeric identifier for the user. Both the login name and the user ID are stored in the **passwd** database (**/etc/passwd** or the NIS equivalent).
login shell	The shell that you are using when you log in. The login shell can fork other processes that can run other shells, utilities, and programs.
.logout file	A file that the TC Shell executes when you log out, assuming that the TC Shell is your login shell. You can put in the **.logout** file commands that you want run each time you log out.
MAC address	Media access control address. The unique hardware address of a device connected to a shared network medium. Each Ethernet adaptor has a globally unique MAC address in ROM. MAC addresses are 6 bytes long, enabling 256^6 (about three hundred trillion) possible addresses or 65, 536 addresses for each possible IPv4 address. A MAC address performs the same role for Ethernet that an IP addresses performs for TCP/IP: It provides a unique way to identify a host.
machine collating sequence	The sequence in which the computer orders characters. The machine collating sequence affects the outcome of sorts and other procedures that put lists in alphabetical order. Many computers use ASCII codes so their machine collating sequences correspond to the ordering of the ASCII codes for characters.

macro   A single instruction that a program replaces by several (usually more complex) instructions. The C compiler recognizes macros, which are defined using a **#define** instruction to the preprocessor.

magic number   A magic number, which occurs in the first 512 bytes of a binary file, is a 1-, 2-, or 4-byte numeric value or character string that uniquely identifies the type of file (much like a DOS 3-character filename extension). See **/usr/share/magic** and the **magic** man page (5) for more information.

main memory   Random access memory (RAM), an integral part of the computer; contrasted with disk storage. Although disk storage is sometimes referred to as memory, it is never referred to as main memory.

major device number   A number assigned to a class of devices, such as terminals, printers, or disk drives. Using the **ls** utility with the **–l** option to list the contents of the **/dev** directory displays the major and minor device numbers of many devices (as major, minor).

MAN   Metropolitan area network.   A network that connects computers and *LANs* (page 979) at multiple sites in a small regional area, such as a city.

masquerade   To appear to come from one domain or IP address when actually coming from another. Said of a packet (**iptables**) or message (**sendmail**).

MD5   Message Digest 5.   A *one-way hash function* (page 986).

MDA   Mail Delivery Agent.   One of the three components of a mail system; the other two are MTA and MUA. An MDA accepts inbound mail from an MTA and delivers it to a local user.

mega-   In the binary system the prefix mega- multiplies by 2^{20}, or 1,048,576. Megabit and megabyte are common uses of this prefix. Abbreviated as M.

menu   A list from which the user may select an operation to be performed. This is often done with a mouse or other pointing device under a GUI but may also be controlled from the keyboard. Very convenient for beginners, menus show what commands are available and make experimenting with a new program easy, often reducing the need for user documentation. Experienced users, however, usually prefer keyboard commands, especially for frequently used operations, because they are faster to use.FOLDOC

merge   To combine two ordered lists so that the resulting list is still in order. The **sort** utility can merge files.

META key   On the keyboard, a key that is labeled META or ALT. Use this key as you would the SHIFT key. While holding it down, press another key. The **emacs** editor makes extensive use of the META key.

metacharacter A character that has a special meaning to the shell or another program in a particular context. Metacharacters are used in the ambiguous file references recognized by the shell and in the regular expressions recognized by several utilities. You must quote a metacharacter if you want to use it without invoking its special meaning. See *regular character* (page 992) and *special character* (page 997).

metadata Data about data. In data processing, metadata is definitional data that provides information about, or documentation of, other data managed within an application or environment.

For example, metadata can document data about data elements or attributes (name, size, data type, and so on), records or *data structures* (page 966) (length, fields, columns, and so on), and data itself (where it is located, how it is associated, who owns it, and so on). Metadata can include descriptive information about the context, quality and condition, or characteristics of the data.[FOLDOC]

metropolitan area network See *MAN* on page 982.

MIME Multipurpose Internet Mail Extension. Originally used to describe how specific types of files that were attached to email were to be handled. Today MIME types describe how a file is to be opened or worked with, based on its filename extension.

minimize See *iconify* on page 976.

minor device number A number assigned to a specific device within a class of devices. See *major device number* on page 982.

modem Modulate/demodulate. A peripheral device that modulates digital data into analog data for transmission over a voice-grade telephone line. Another modem demodulates the data at the other end.

module See *loadable module* on page 980.

mount To make a filesystem accessible to system users. When a filesystem is not mounted, you cannot read from or write to files it contains.

mount point A directory that you mount a local or remote filesystem on (page 442).

mouse A device you use to point to a particular location on a display screen, typically so you can choose a menu item, draw a line, or highlight some text. You control a pointer on the screen by sliding a mouse around on a flat surface; the position of the pointer moves relative to the movement of the mouse. You select items by pressing one or more buttons on the mouse.

mouse pointer   In a GUI, a marker that moves in correspondence with the mouse. It is usually a small black **X** with a white border or an arrow. Differs from the *cursor* (page 966).

mouseover   The action of passing the mouse pointer over an icon or other object on the screen.

MTA   Mail Transfer Agent.   One of the three components of a mail system; the other two are MDA and MUA. An MTA accepts mail from users and MTAs.

MUA   Mail User Agent.   One of the three components of a mail system; the other two are MDA and MTA. An MUA is an end user mail program such as Kmail, mutt, and Outlook.

multiboot
specification   Specifies an interface between a boot loader and an operating system. With compliant boot loaders and operating systems, any boot loader should be able to load any operating system. The object of this specification is to get different operating systems to work on a single machine. For more information, go to odin-os.sourceforge.net/guides/multiboot.html.

multicast   A multicast packet has one source and multiple destinations. In multicast, source hosts register at a special address to transmit data. Destination hosts register at the same address to receive data. In contrast with *broadcast* (page 960), which is LAN based, multicast traffic is designed to work across routed networks on a subscription basis. Multicast reduces network traffic by transmitting a packet one time, with the router at the end of the path breaking it apart as needed for multiple recipients.

multitasking   A computer system that allows a user to run more than one job at a time. One trait of a multitasking system, such as Linux, is that it allows you to run a job in the background while running a job in the foreground.

multiuser system   A computer system that can be used by more than one person at a time. Linux is a multiuser operating system. Contrast with *single-user system* (page 996).

NAT   Network Address Translation.   A scheme that enables a LAN to use one set of IP addresses internally and a different set externally. The internal set is for LAN (private) use. The external set is typically used on the Internet and is Internet unique. NAT provides some privacy by hiding internal IP addresses and allows multiple internal addresses to connect to the Internet through a single external IP address.

NBT   NetBIOS over TCP/IP.   A protocol that supports NetBIOS services in a TCP/IP environment. Also *NetBT*.

NetBIOS   Network Basic Input/Output System.   An *API* (page 956) for writing network-aware applications.

netboot	To boot a computer over the network as opposed to booting from a local disk.
netiquette	The conventions of politeness recognized on Usenet and in mailing lists, such as not (cross-)posting to inappropriate groups and refraining from commercial advertising outside the business groups.
	The most important rule of netiquette is "Think before you post." If what you intend to post will not make a positive contribution to the newsgroup and be of interest to several readers, do not post it. Personal messages to one or two individuals should not be posted to newsgroups; use private email instead.^{FOLDOC}
netmask	A 32-bit mask (for IPv4), which shows how an Internet address is to be divided into network, subnet, and host parts. The netmask has 1s in the bit positions in the 32-bit address that are to be used for the network and subnet parts; 0s, for the host part. The mask should contain at least the standard network portion (as determined by the address class), and the subnet field should be contiguous with the network portion.^{FOLDOC}
network address	The network portion (**netid**) of an IP address. For a class A network, this is the first byte, or segment, of the IP address; for class B, it is the first two bytes; and for class C, it is the first three bytes. In each case, the balance of the IP address is the host address (**hostid**). Assigned network addresses are globally unique within the Internet. Also *network number*. See also "Host Address" on page 334.
Network Filesystem	See *NFS* on page 986.
Network Information Service	See *NIS* on page 986.
network number	See *network address*.
network segment	A part of an Ethernet or other network on which all message traffic is common to all nodes; that is, it is broadcast from one node on the segment and received by all others. This is normally because the segment is a single continuous conductor. Communication between nodes on different segments is via one or more routers.^{FOLDOC}
network switch	A connecting device in networks. Switches are increasingly replacing shared media hubs in order to increase bandwidth. For example, a 16-port 10BaseT hub shares the total 10 megabits per second bandwidth with all 16 attached nodes. By replacing the hub with a switch, each sender and receiver has the full 10 megabits per second capacity. Each port on the switch can give full bandwidth to a single server or client station or to a hub with several stations. Network switch refers to a device with intelligence. Contrast with *hub* (page 975).

Network Time Protocol	See *NTP* on page 986.
NFS	Network Filesystem. A remote filesystem designed by Sun Microsystems, available on computers from most UNIX system vendors.
NIC	Network Interface Card (or Controller). An adapter circuit board installed in a computer to provide a physical connection to a network.FOLDOC
NIS	Network Information Service. A distributed service built on a shared database to manage system-independent information (such as login names and passwords).
NIS domain name	A name that describes a group of systems that share a set of NIS files. Different than *domain name* (page 968).
NNTP	Network News Transfer Protocol. Refer to "Usenet" on page 359.
node	In a tree structure, the end of a branch that can support other branches. When the Linux filesystem hierarchy is conceptualized as a tree, directories are nodes. See *leaf* on page 980.
nonprinting character	See *control character* on page 964. Also *nonprintable character*.
nonvolatile storage	A storage device whose contents are preserved when its power is off. Also NVS and persistent storage. Some examples are CD-ROM, paper punch tape, hard disk, *ROM* (page 993), *PROM* (page 990), *EPROM* (page 969), and *EEPROM* (page 969). Contrast with *RAM* (page 991).
NTP	Network Time Protocol. Built on top of TCP/IP, NTP maintains accurate local time by referring to known accurate clocks on the Internet.
null string	A string that could contain characters but does not. A string of zero length.
octal number	A base 8 number. Octal numbers are composed of the digits 0–7, inclusive. Refer to Table G-1 on page 975.
one-way hash function	A one-way function that takes a variable-length message and produces a fixed-length hash. Given the hash, it is computationally infeasible to find a message with that hash; in fact, you cannot determine any usable information about a message with that hash. Also *message digest function*. See also *hash* (page 974).
OpenSSH	A free version of the SSH (secure shell) protocol suite that replaces TELNET, rlogin, and more with secure programs that encrypt all communication, even passwords, over a network. Refer to "OpenSSH: Secure Network Communication" on page 563.

operating system A control program for a computer that allocates computer resources, schedules tasks, and provides the user with a way to access resources.

option A command line argument that modifies the effects of a command. Options are usually preceded by hyphens on the command line and traditionally have single-character names (such as **–h**, **–n**). Some commands allow you to group options following a single hyphen (for example, **–hn**). GNU utilities frequently have two arguments that do the same thing: a single-character argument and a longer, more descriptive argument that is preceded by two hyphens (such as **––show-all**, **––invert-match**).

ordinary file A file that is used to store a program, text, or other user data. See *directory* (page 967) and *device file* (page 967).

output Information that a program sends to the terminal or another file. See *standard output* on page 998.

P2P Peer-to-Peer. A network that does not divide nodes into clients and servers. Each computer on a P2P network can fulfil the roles of client and server. In the context of a file sharing network, this ability means that once a node has downloaded (part of) a file, it can act as a server. BitTorrent implements a P2P network.

packet A unit of data sent across a network. *Packet* is a generic term used to describe a unit of data at any layer of the OSI protocol stack, but it is most correctly used to describe network- or application-layer (page 332) data units ("application protocol data unit," APDU).ᶠᵒˡᵈᵒᶜ See also *frame* (page 972) and *datagram* (page 966).

packet filtering A technique used to block network traffic based on specified criteria, such as the origin, destination, or type of each packet. See also *firewall* (page 971).

packet sniffer A program or device that monitors packets on a network. See *sniff* on page 997.

pager A utility that allows you to view a file one screen at a time (for example, less and more).

paging The process by which virtual memory is maintained by the operating system. The contents of process memory is moved (paged out) to the *swap space* (page 1000) as needed to make room for other processes.

PAM Linux-PAM or Linux Pluggable Authentication Modules. These modules allow a system administrator to determine how various applications authenticate users. Refer to "PAM" on page 416.

parent process A process that forks other processes. See *process* (page 990) and *child process* (page 962).

partition	A section of a (hard) disk that has a name so you can address it separately from other sections. A disk partition can hold a filesystem or another structure, such as the swap area. Under DOS/Windows, partitions (and sometimes whole disks) are labeled **C:**, **D:**, and so on. Also, *disk partition* and *slice*.
passive FTP	Allows FTP to work through a firewall by allowing the flow of data to be initiated and controlled by the client FTP program instead of the server. Also called PASV FTP because it uses the FTP PASV command.
passphrase	A string of words and characters that you type in to authenticate yourself. A passphrase differs from *password* only in length. A password is usually short— 6 to 10 characters. A passphrase is usually much longer—up to 100 characters or more. The greater length makes a passphrase harder to guess or reproduce than a password and therefore more secure.<small>FOLDOC</small>
password	In order to prevent unauthorized access to a user's account, an arbitrary string of characters chosen by the user or system administrator and used to authenticate the user when attempting to log in.<small>FOLDOC</small> See also *passphrase*.
PASV FTP	See *passive FTP*.
pathname	A list of directories separated by slashes (/) and ending with the name of a file, which can be a directory. A pathname is used to trace a path through the file structure to locate or identify a file.
pathname element	One of the filenames that forms a pathname.
pathname, last element of a	The part of a pathname following the final /, or the whole filename if there is no /. A simple filename. Also *basename*.
peripheral device	See *device* on page 967.
persistent	Data that is stored on nonvolatile media, such as a hard disk.
physical device	A tangible device, such as a disk drive, that is physically separate from other, similar devices.
PID	Process identification, usually followed by the word *number*. Linux assigns a unique PID number as each process is initiated.
pipe	A connection between programs such that standard output of one is connected to standard input of the next. Also *pipeline*.
pixel	The smallest element of a picture, typically a single dot on a display screen.
plaintext	Text that is not encrypted. Contrast with *ciphertext* (page 963). See also "Encryption" on page 922.

Pluggable Authentication Modules	See *PAM* on page 987.
point-to-point link	A connection limited to two endpoints, such as the connection between a pair of modems.
port	A logical channel or channel endpoint in a communications system. The *TCP* (page 1000) and *UDP* (page 1003) transport layer protocols used on Ethernet use port numbers to distinguish between different logical channels on the same network interface on the same computer.
	The **/etc/services** file (see the beginning of this file for more information) or the *NIS* (page 986) **services** database specifies a unique port number for each application program. The number links incoming data to the correct service (program). Standard, well-known ports are used by everyone: Port 80 is used for HTTP (Web) traffic. Some protocols, such as TELNET and HTTP (which is a special form of TELNET), have default ports specified as mentioned earlier but can use other ports as well.ᶠᵒˡᵈᵒᶜ
port forwarding	The process by which a network *port* on one computer is transparently connected to a port on another computer. If port X is forwarded from system A to system B, any data sent to port X on system A is sent to system B automatically. The connection can be between different ports on the two systems.
portmapper	A server that converts TCP/IP port numbers into *RPC* (page 994) program numbers. See "RPC Network Services" on page 358.
printable character	One of the graphic characters: a letter, number, or punctuation mark; contrasted with a nonprintable, or CONTROL, character. Also *printing character*.
private address space	*IANA* (page 976) has reserved three blocks of IP addresses for private internets or LANs. The blocks are

```
10.0.0.0   - 10.255.255.255
172.16.0.0 - 172.31.255.255
192.168.0.0 - 192.168.255.255
```

You can use these addresses without coordinating with anyone outside of your LAN (you do not have to register the system name or address). Systems using these IP addresses cannot communicate directly with hosts using the global address space but must go through a gateway. Because private addresses have no global meaning, routing information is not stored by DNSs, and most ISPs reject privately addressed packets. Make sure that your router is set up not to forward these packets onto the Internet.

privileged port   A *port* (page 989) with a number less than 1024. On Linux and other UNIX-like systems, only **root** can bind to a privileged port. Any user on Windows 98 and earlier Windows systems can bind to any port.

procedure   A sequence of instructions for performing a particular task. Most programming languages, including machine languages, enable a programmer to define procedures that allow the procedure code to be called from multiple places. Also *sub-routine.*FOLDOC

process   The execution of a command by Linux. See "Processes" on page 267.

.profile file   A startup file that a Bourne Again or Z login shell executes when you log in. The TC Shell executes **.login** instead. You can use the **.profile** file to run commands, set variables, and define functions.

program   A sequence of executable computer instructions contained in a file. Linux utilities, applications, and shell scripts are all programs. Whenever you run a command that is not built into a shell, you are executing a program.

PROM   Programmable read-only memory. A kind of nonvolatile storage. *ROM* (page 993) that can be written to using a PROM programmer.

prompt   A cue from a program, usually displayed on the screen, indicating that it is waiting for input. The shell displays a prompt, as do some of the interactive utilities, such as mail. By default, the Bourne Again and Z Shells use a dollar sign (**$**) as a prompt, and the TC Shell uses a percent sign (**%**).

protocol   A set of formal rules describing how to transmit data, especially across a network. Low-level protocols define the electrical and physical standards, bit and byte ordering, and transmission, error detection, and correction of the bit stream. High-level protocols deal with the data formatting, including message syntax, terminal-to-computer dialog, character sets, sequencing of messages, and so forth.FOLDOC

proxy   A service that is authorized to act for a system while not being part of that system. See also *proxy gateway* and *proxy server.*

proxy gateway   A computer that separates clients (such as browsers) from the Internet, working as a trusted agent that accesses the Internet on their behalf. A proxy gateway passes a request for data from an Internet service, such as HTTP from a browser/client, to a remote server. The data that the server returns goes back through the proxy gateway to the requesting service. A proxy gateway should be transparent to the user.

A proxy gateway often runs on a *firewall* (page 971) machine as a barrier to malicious users. A proxy gateway hides the IP addresses of the local computers inside the firewall from Internet users outside the firewall.

proxy gateway (continued)   You can configure browsers, such as Mozilla and Netscape, to use a different proxy gateway or use no proxy for each URL access method including FTP, netnews, SNMP, HTTPS, and HTTP. See also *proxy*.

proxy server   A *proxy gateway* that usually includes a *cache* (page 961) that holds frequently used Web pages so that the next request for that page is available locally (and therefore more quickly). See also *proxy*. The terms proxy server and proxy gateway are frequently interchanged so that the use of cache does not rest exclusively with the proxy server.

Python   A simple, high-level, interpreted, object-oriented, interactive language that bridges the gap between C and shell programming. Suitable for rapid prototyping or as an extension language for C applications, Python supports packages, modules, classes, user-defined exceptions, a good C interface, and dynamic loading of C modules. It has no arbitrary restrictions. For more information, see www.python.org FOLDOC

quote   When you quote a character, you take away any special meaning that it has in the current context. You can quote a character by preceding it with a backslash. When you are interacting with the shell, you can also quote a character by surrounding it with single quotation marks. For example, the command **echo *** or **echo '*'** displays *. The command **echo *** displays a list of the files in the working directory. See also *escape* on page 970. See *ambiguous file reference* (page 956), *metacharacter* (page 983), *regular character* (page 992), *regular expression* (page 992), and *special character* (page 997).

radio button   A group of buttons similar to those used to select the station on a radio. Only one button can be selected at a time.

RAID   Redundant Array of Inexpensive/Independent Disks. Two or more (hard) disk drives used in combination to improve fault tolerance and performance. RAID can be implemented in hardware or software.

RAM   Random Access Memory. A kind of volatile storage. A data storage device for which the order of access to different locations does not affect the speed of access. Contrast with a hard disk or tape drive, which provides quicker access to sequential data because accessing a nonsequential location requires physical movement of the storage medium and/or read-write head rather than just electronic switching. Contrast with *nonvolatile storage* (page 986). FOLDOC

RAM disk   *RAM* that is made to look like a floppy diskette or hard disk. RAM disk is frequently used as part of the *boot* (page 959) process.

RAS Remote Access Server.   In a network, a computer that provides access to remote users via analog modem or ISDN connections. RAS includes the dial-up protocols and access control (authentication) and may be a regular file server with remote access software or a proprietary system, such as Shiva's LAN-Rover. The modems may be internal or external to the device.

RDF Resource Description Framework.   Being developed by W3C (the main standards body for the World Wide Web), a standard that specifies a mechanism for encoding and transferring *metadata* (page 983). RDF does not specify what the metadata should or can be. RDF can integrate many kinds of applications and data, using XML as an interchange syntax. Some examples of the kinds of data that can be integrated are library catalogs and worldwide directories, syndication and aggregation of news, software, and content, and collections of music and photographs. Go to www.w3.org/RDF for more information.

redirection The process of directing standard input for a program to come from a file rather than from the keyboard. Also, directing standard output or standard error to go to a file rather than to the screen.

reentrant Code that can have multiple simultaneous, interleaved, or nested invocations that do not interfere with one another. Noninterference is important for parallel processing, recursive programming, and interrupt handling.

It is usually easy to arrange for multiple invocations (that is, calls to a subroutine) to share one copy of the code and any readonly data. But for the code to be reentrant, each invocation must use its own copy of any modifiable data (or synchronized access to shared data). This is most often achieved by using a stack and allocating local variables in a new stack frame for each invocation. Alternatively, the caller may pass in a pointer to a block of memory that that invocation can use (usually for output), or the code may allocate some memory on a heap, especially if the data must survive after the routine returns.

Reentrant code is often found in system software, such as operating systems and teleprocessing monitors. It is also a crucial component of multithreaded programs, where the term *thread-safe* is often used instead of reentrant.FOLDOC

regular character A character that always represents itself in an ambiguous file reference or another type of regular expression. Contrast with *special character*.

regular expression A string—composed of letters, numbers, and special symbols—that defines one or more strings. See Appendix A.

relative pathname A pathname that starts from the working directory. Contrast with *absolute pathname* (page 955).

remote access server See *RAS* on page 992.

remote filesystem   A filesystem on a remote computer that has been set up so that you can access (usually over a network) its files as though they were stored on your local computer's disks. An example of a remote filesystem is NFS.

Remote procedure call   See *RPC* on page 994.

resolver   The TCP/IP library software that formats requests to be sent to the *DNS* (page 968) for hostname-to-Internet address conversion.^{FOLDOC}

Resource Description Framework   See *RDF* on page 992.

restore   The process of turning an icon into a window. Contrast with *iconify* (page 976)

return code   See *exit status* on page 970.

RFC   Request for Comments.   Begun in 1969, one of a series of numbered Internet informational documents and standards widely followed by commercial software and freeware in the Internet and UNIX/Linux communities. Few RFCs are standards, but all Internet standards are recorded in RFCs. Perhaps the single most influential RFC has been RFC 822, the Internet electronic mail format standard.

The RFCs are unusual in that they are floated by technical experts acting on their own initiative and reviewed by the Internet at large rather than formally promulgated through an institution such as ANSI. For this reason, they remain known as RFCs, even once they are adopted as standards. The RFC tradition of pragmatic, experience-driven, after-the-fact standard writing done by individuals or small working groups has important advantages over the more formal, committee-driven process typical of ANSI or ISO. For a complete list of RFCs, go to www.rfc-editor.org.^{FOLDOC}

roam   To move a computer between *wireless access points* (page 1005) on a wireless network without the user or applications being aware of the transition. Moving between access points typically results in some packet loss, although this is transparent to programs that use TCP.

ROM   Read-Only Memory.   A kind of nonvolatile storage. A data storage device that is manufactured with fixed contents. In general, ROM describes any storage system whose contents cannot be altered, such as a gramophone record or printed book. When used in reference to electronics and computers, ROM describes semiconductor integrated circuit memories, of which there are several types, and CD-ROM.

ROM (continued)   ROM is nonvolatile storage—it retains its contents even after power has been removed; contrast with *RAM* (page 991). ROM is often used to hold programs for embedded systems, as these usually have a fixed purpose. ROM is also used for storage of the *BIOS* (page 959) in a computer.ᶠᴼᴸᴰᴼᶜ

root directory   The ancestor of all directories and the start of all absolute pathnames. The name of the root directory is /.

root filesystem   The filesystem that is available when the system is brought up in single-user mode. The name of this filesystem is always /. You cannot unmount or mount the root filesystem. You can remount root to change its mount options (page 387).

root login   Usually the login name of *Superuser* (page 999).

rotate   When a file, such as a log file, gets indefinitely larger, you must keep it from taking up too much space on the disk. Because you may need to refer to the information in the log files in the near future, it is generally not a good idea to delete the contents of the file until it has aged. Toward this end, you can periodically save the current log file under a new name and create a new, empty file as the current log file. You can keep a series of these files, renaming each as a new one is saved. You will then *rotate* the files. For example, you might remove xyzlog.4, xyzlog.3→xyzlog.4, xyzlog.2→xyzlog.3, xyzlog.1→xyzlog.2, xyzlog→xyzlog.1, and create a new xyzlog file. By the time you remove xyzlog.4, it will not contain any information more recent than you want to remove.

router   A device, often a computer, that is connected to more than one similar type of network to pass data between them. See *gateway* on page 972.

RPC   Remote Procedure Call.   A call to a *procedure* (page 990) that acts transparently across a network. The procedure itself is responsible for accessing and using the network. The RPC libraries make sure that network access is transparent to the application. RPC runs on top of TCP/IP or UDP/IP.

RSA   A public key encryption (page 923) technology that is based on the lack of an efficient way to factor very large numbers. Because of this lack, it takes an extraordinary amount of computer processing time and power to deduce an RSA key. The RSA algorithm is the de facto standard for data sent over the Internet.

run   To execute a program.

Samba   A free suite of programs that implement the Server Message Block (SMB) protocol. See *SMB* (page 996).

schema   Within a GUI, a pattern that helps you see and interpret the information that is presented in a window, making it easier to understand new information that is presented using the same schema.

scroll   To move lines on a terminal or window up and down or left and right.

scrollbar   A widget found in graphical user interfaces that controls (scrolls) which part of a document is visible in the window. A window can have a horizontal scroll bar, a vertical scroll bar (more common), or both.FOLDOC

server   A powerful centralized computer (or program) designed to provide information to clients (smaller computers or programs) on request.

session   The lifetime of a process. For a desktop, it is the desktop session manager. For a character-based terminal, it is the user's login shell process. In KDE, it is launched by kdeinit. Or the sequence of events between when you start using a program, such as an editor, and when you finish.

setgid   When you execute a file that has setgid (set group ID) permission, the process executing the file takes on the privileges of the group the file belongs to. The ls utility shows setgid permission as an **s** in the group's executable position. See also *setuid*.

setuid   When you execute a file that has setuid (set user ID) permission, the process executing the file takes on the privileges of the owner of the file. As an example, if you run a setuid program that removes all the files in a directory, you can remove files in any of the file owner's directories, even if you do not normally have permission to do so. When the program is owned by **root**, you can remove files in any directory that **root** can remove files from. The ls utility shows setuid permission as an **s** in the owner's executable position. See also *setgid*.

sexillion   In the British system, 10^{36}. In the American system this number is named *undecillion*. See also *large number* (page 980).

share   A directory and the filesystem hierarchy below it that are shared with another system using *SMB* (page 996). Also *Windows share* (page 1005).

shared network topology   A network, such as Ethernet, in which each packet may be seen by systems other than its destination system. *Shared* means that the network bandwidth is shared by all users.

shell   A Linux system command processor. The three major shells are the *Bourne Again Shell* (page 960), the *TC Shell* (page 1000), and the *Z Shell* (page 1007).

shell function   A series of commands that the shell stores for execution at a later time. Shell functions are like shell scripts but run more quickly because they are stored in the computer's main memory rather than in files. Also, a shell function is run in the environment of the shell that calls it (unlike a shell script, which is typically run in a subshell).

shell script   An ASCII file containing shell commands. Also *shell program.*

signal   A very brief message that the UNIX system can send to a process, apart from the process's standard input. Refer to "**trap:** Catches a Signal" on page 889.

simple filename   A single filename containing no slashes (*/*). A simple filename is the simplest form of pathname. Also the last element of a pathname. Also *basename* (page 958).

single-user system   A computer system that only one person can use at a time. Contrast with *multi-user system* (page 984).

SMB   Server Message Block.   Developed in the early 1980s by Intel, Microsoft, and IBM, SMB is a client/server protocol that is the native method of file and printer sharing for Windows. In addition, SMB can share serial ports and communications abstractions, such as named pipes and mail slots. SMB is similar to remote procedure call, *RPC* (page 994), specialized for filesystem access. Also *Microsoft Networking.*FOLDOC

smiley   A character-based *glyph* (page 972), typically used in email, that conveys an emotion. The characters :-) in a message portray a smiley face (look at it sideways). Because it can be difficult to tell when the writer of an electronic message is saying something in jest or in seriousness, email users often use :-) to indicate humor. The two original smileys, designed by Scott Fahlman, were :-) and :-(. Also *emoticon, smileys,* and *smilies.* For more information search on **smiley** on the Internet.

smilies   See *smiley.*

SMTP   Simple Mail Transfer Protocol.   A protocol used to transfer electronic mail between computers. It is a server-to-server protocol, so other protocols are used to access the messages. The SMTP dialog usually happens in the background under the control of a message transport system such as **sendmail.**FOLDOC

snap (windows)   As you drag a window toward another window or edge of the workspace, it can move suddenly so that it is adjacent to the other window/edge. Thus the window *snaps* into position.

sneakernet   Using hand-carried magnetic media to transfer files between machines.

sniff
To monitor packets on a network. A system administrator can legitimately sniff packets and a malicious user can sniff packets to obtain information such as usernames and passwords. See also *packet sniffer* (page 987).

SOCKS
A networking proxy protocol embodied in a SOCKS server, which performs the same functions as a *proxy gateway* (page 990) or *proxy server* (page 991). The difference is that SOCKS works at the application level, requiring that an application be modified to work with the SOCKS protocol, whereas a *proxy* (page 990) makes no demands on the application.

SOCKSv4 does not support authentication or UDP proxy. SOCKSv5 supports a variety of authentication methods and UDP proxy.

sort
To put in a specified order, usually alphabetic or numeric.

SPACE character
A character that appears as the absence of a visible character. Even though you cannot see it, a SPACE is a printable character. It is represented by the ASCII code 32 (decimal). A SPACE character is considered a *blank,* or *whitespace* (page 1005).

spam
Posting irrelevant or inappropriate messages to one or more Usenet newsgroups or mailing lists in deliberate or accidental violation of *netiquette* (page 985). Also, sending large amounts of unsolicited email indiscriminately. This email usually promotes a product or service. Spam is the electronic equivalent of junk mail. From the Monty Python "Spam" song.^{FOLDOC}

sparse file
A file that is large but takes up little disk space. The data in a sparse file is not dense (thus its name). Examples of sparse files are core files, dbm files, and /etc/utmp (→/var/adm/utmp).

spawn
See *fork* on page 971.

special character
A character that has a special meaning when it occurs in an ambiguous file reference or another type of regular expression, unless it is quoted. The special characters most commonly used with the shell are ✳ and ?. Also *metacharacter* (page 983) and *wildcard*.

special file
See *device file* on page 967.

spinner
In a GUI, a type of *text box* (page 1001) that holds a number you can change by typing over it or using the up and down arrows at the end of the box.

spoofing
See *IP spoofing* on page 978.

spool
To place items in a queue, each waiting its turn for some action. Often used when speaking about the printers. Also used to describe the queue.

SQL   Structured Query Language.   A language that provides a user interface to relational database management systems (RDBMS). SQL, the de facto standard, is also an ISO and ANSI standard and is often embedded in other programming languages.FOLDOC

square bracket   There are a left square bracket ([) and a right square bracket (]). They are special characters that define character classes in ambiguous file references and other regular expressions.

SSH Communications Security   The company that created the original SSH (secure shell) protocol suite (www.ssh.com). Linux uses openSSH. See *OpenSSH* on page 986.

standard error   A file to which a program can send output. Usually only error messages are sent to this file. Unless you instruct the shell otherwise, it directs this output to the screen (that is, to the device file that represents the screen).

standard input   A file from which a program can receive input. Unless you instruct the shell otherwise, it directs this input so that it comes from the keyboard (that is, from the device file that represents the keyboard).

standard output   A file to which a program can send output. Unless you instruct the shell otherwise, it directs this output to the screen (that is, to the device file that represents the screen).

startup file   A file that the login shell runs when you log in. The Bourne Again and Z Shells run **.profile**, and the TC Shell runs **.login**. The TC Shell also runs **.cshrc** whenever a new TC Shell or a subshell is invoked. The Z Shell runs an analogous file whose name is identified by the **ENV** variable.

status line   The bottom (usually the twenty-fourth) line of the terminal. The vi editor uses the status line to display information about what is happening during an editing session.

sticky bit   An access permission bit that causes an executable program to remain on the swap area of the disk. It takes less time to load a program that has its sticky bit set than one that does not. Only Superuser can set the sticky bit. If the sticky bit is set on a directory that is publicly writable, only the owner of a file in that directory can remove the file.

streaming tape   A tape that moves at a constant speed past the read/write heads rather than speeding up and slowing down, which can slow the process of writing to or reading from the tape. A proper blocking factor helps ensure that the tape device will be kept streaming.

streams   See *connection-oriented protocol* on page 964.

string   A sequence of characters.

stylesheet   *See CSS on page 966.*

subdirectory   A directory that is located within another directory. Every directory except the root directory is a subdirectory.

subnet   Subnetwork. A portion of a network, which may be a physically independent network segment, that shares a network address with other portions of the network and is distinguished by a subnet number. A subnet is to a network what a network is to an internet.^{FOLDOC}

subnet address   The subnet portion of an IP address. In a subnetted network, the host portion of an IP address is split into a subnet portion and a host portion using a subnet mask (also address mask). See also *subnet number*.

subnet mask   A bit mask used to identify which bits in an IP address correspond to the network address and subnet portions of the address. Called a subnet mask because the network portion of the address is determined by the number of bits that are set in the mask. The subnet mask has ones in positions corresponding to the network and subnet numbers and zeros in the host number positions. Also *address mask*.

subnet number   The subnet portion of an IP address. In a subnetted network, the host portion of an IP address is split into a subnet portion and a host portion using a *subnet mask* (also address mask). See also *subnet address*.

subpixel hinting   Similar to *antialiasing* (page 956) but takes advantage of colors to do the antialiasing. Particularly useful on LCD screens.

subroutine   See *procedure* on page 990.

subshell   A shell that is forked as a duplicate of its parent shell. When you run an executable file that contains a shell script by using its filename on the command line, the shell forks a subshell to run the script. Also, commands surrounded with parentheses are run in a subshell.

superblock   A block that contains control information for a filesystem. The superblock contains housekeeping information, such as the number of inodes in the filesystem and free list information.

superserver   The extended Internet services daemon. Refer to xinetd on page 357.

Superuser   A privileged user having access to anything any other system user has access to and more. The system administrator must be able to become Superuser in order to establish new accounts, change passwords, and perform other administrative tasks. The login name of Superuser is typically **root**.

swap

The operating system moving a process from main memory to a disk, or vice versa. Swapping a process to the disk allows another process to begin or continue execution. Refer to "swap" on page 435.

swap space

An area of a disk (that is, a swap file) used to store the portion of a process's memory that has been paged out. Under a virtual memory system, it is the amount of swap space rather than the amount of physical memory that determines the maximum size of a single process and the maximum total size of all active processes. Also, *swap area* or *swapping area*.FOLDOC

switch

See *network switch* on page 985.

symbolic link

A directory entry that points to the pathname of another file. In most cases, a symbolic link to a file can be used in the same ways a hard link can be used. Unlike a hard link, a symbolic link can span filesystems and can connect to a directory.

system administrator

The person responsible for the upkeep of the system. The system administrator has the ability to log in as Superuser. See *Superuser*.

system console

The main system terminal, usually directly connected to the computer and the one that receives system error messages. Also *console, console terminal*.

system mode

The designation for the state of the system while it is doing system work. Some examples are making system calls, running NFS and autofs, processing network traffic, and performing kernel operations on behalf of system. Contrast with *user mode* (page 1003).

System V

One of the two major versions of the UNIX system.

TC Shell

tcsh. An enhanced but completely compatible version of the BSD UNIX C shell, csh.

TCP

Transmission Control Protocol. The most common transport layer protocol used on the Internet. It is the connection-oriented protocol built on top of *IP* (page 977) and is nearly always seen in the combination TCP/IP (TCP over *IP*). TCP adds reliable communication, sequencing, and flow-control and provides full-duplex, process-to-process connections. *UDP* (page 1003), although connectionless, is the other protocol that runs on top of *IP*.FOLDOC

tera-

In the binary system the prefix tera- multiplies by 2^{40}, or 1,099,511,627,776. Terabyte is a common use of this prefix. Abbreviated as T. See also *large number* on page 980.

termcap	Terminal capability. The **/etc/termcap** file contains a list of various types of terminals and their characteristics. *System V* (page 1000) replaced the function of this file with the *terminfo* system.
terminal	Differentiated from a *workstation* (page 1006) by its lack of intelligence, a terminal connects to a computer that runs Linux. A workstation runs Linux on itself.
terminfo	Terminal information. The **/usr/lib/terminfo** directory contains many subdirectories, each containing several files, each of which is named for and contains a summary of the functional characteristics of a particular terminal. Visually oriented text-based programs, such as vi, use these files. An alternative to the ***termcap*** file.
text box	In a GUI, a box you can type in.
theme	Defined as an implicit or recurrent idea, *theme* is used in a GUI to describe a look that is consistent for all elements of a desktop. Go to themes.freshmeat.net for examples.
thicknet	A type of coaxial cable (thick) used for an Ethernet network. Devices are attached to thicknet by tapping the cable at fixed points.
thinnet	A type of coaxial cable (thin) used for an Ethernet network. Thinnet cable is smaller in diameter and more flexible than *thicknet* cable. Each device is typically attached to two separate cable segments by using a T-shaped connector; one segment leads to the device ahead of it on the network and one to the device that follows it.
thread-safe	See *reentrant* on page 992.
thumb	The moveable button in the scrollbar that positions the image in the window. The size of the thumb reflects the amount of information in buffer. Also *bubble*.
tiff	Tagged Image File Format. A file format used for still-image bitmaps, stored in tagged fields. Application programs can use the tags to accept or ignore fields, depending on their capabilities.^{FOLDOC}
tiled windows	An arrangement of windows such that no window overlaps another. Opposite of *cascading windows* (page 961).
time to live	See *TTL* on page 1002.
toggle	To switch between one of two positions. For example, the ftp **glob** command toggles the **glob** feature: Give the command once, and it turns the feature on or off; give the command again, and it sets the feature back to its original state.

token	A basic, grammatically indivisible unit of a language, such as a keyword, operator, or identifier.^{FOLDOC}
token ring	A type of *LAN* (page 979) in which computers are attached to a ring of cable. A token packet circulates continuously around the ring; a computer can transmit information only when it holds the token.
tooltip	A minicontext help system that you activate by allowing your mouse pointer to *hover* (page 974) over a button, icon, or applet (such as those on a panel).
transient window	A dialog or other window that is displayed for only a short time.
Transmission Control Protocol	See *TCP* on page 1000.
Trojan horse	A program that does something destructive or disruptive to your system. Its action is not documented, and the system administrator would not approve of it if he were aware of it. See "Avoiding a Trojan Horse" (page 378).
	The term *Trojan horse* was coined by MIT-hacker-turned-NSA-spook Dan Edwards. A malicious security-breaking program that is disguised as something benign, such as a directory lister, archive utility, game, or (in one notorious 1990 case on the Mac) a program to find and destroy viruses. Similar to *back door* (page 958).^{FOLDOC}
TTL	Time to live.
	1. All DNS records specify how long they are good for, usually up to a week at most. This time is called the record's *time to live*. When a DNS server or an application stores this record in *cache* (page 961), it decrements the TTL value and removes the record from cache when the value reaches zero. A DNS server passes a cached record to another server with the current (decremented) TTL guaranteeing the proper TTL, no matter how many servers the record passes through.
	2. In the IP header, a field that indicates how many more hops the packet should be allowed to make before being discarded or returned.
TTY	Teletypewriter. The terminal device that UNIX was first run from. Today TTY refers to the screen (or window, in the case of a terminal emulator), keyboard, and mouse that are connected to a computer. This term appears in UNIX, and Linux has kept the term for the sake of consistency and tradition.
tunneling	Encapsulation of protocol A within packets carried by protocol B, such that A treats B as though it were a data link layer. Tunneling is used to get data between administrative domains that use a protocol not supported by the internet connecting those domains. It can also be used to encrypt data sent over a public internet, as when you use ssh to tunnel a protocol over the Internet.^{FOLDOC} See also *VPN* (page 1004).

UDP

User Datagram Protocol.   The Internet standard transport layer protocol that provides simple but unreliable datagram services. UDP is a *connectionless protocol* (page 964) that, like *TCP* (page 1000), is layered on top of *IP* (page 977).

Unlike *TCP*, UDP neither guarantees delivery nor requires a connection. As a result, it is lightweight and efficient, but all error processing and retransmission must be taken care of by the application program. UDP is often used for sending time-sensitive data that is not particularly sensitive to minor loss, such as audio and video data.FOLDOC

UID

User ID.   A number that the **passwd** database associates with a login name.

undecillion

In the American system, 10^{36}. In the British system, this number is named *sexillion*. See also *large number* (page 980).

Unicast

A packet sent from one host to another host. Unicast means one source and one destination.

unmanaged window

See *ignored window* on page 976.

URI

Universal Resource Identifier.   The generic set of all names and addresses that are short strings referring to objects (typically on the Internet). The most common kinds of URIs are *URLs*.FOLDOC

URL

Uniform (was Universal) Resource Locator.   A standard way of specifying the location of an object, typically a Web page, on the Internet. URLs are a subset of *URIs*.

usage message

A message displayed by a command when you call the command using incorrect command line arguments.

User Datagram Protocol

See *UDP*.

User ID

See *UID*.

user interface

See *interface* on page 977.

user mode

The designation for the state of the system while it is doing user work, such as running a user program (but not the system calls made by the program). Contrast with *system mode* (page 1000).

userspace

The part of memory (RAM) where applications reside. Code running in userspace cannot access hardware directly and cannot access memory allocated to other applications. Also *userland*. See the *KernelAnalysis-HOWTO*.

UTC	Coordinated Universal Time. UTC is the equivalent to the mean solar time at the prime meridian (0 degrees longitude). Also called Zulu time (Z stands for longitude zero) and GMT (Greenwich Mean Time).
utility	A program included as a standard part of Linux. You typically invoke a utility either by giving a command in response to a shell prompt or by calling it from within a shell script. Utilities are often referred to as commands. Contrast with *builtin (command)* (page 961).
variable	A name and an associated value. The shell allows you to create variables and use them in shell scripts. Also, the shell inherits several variables when it is invoked, and it maintains those and other variables while it is running. Some shell variables establish characteristics of the shell environment, whereas others have values that reflect different aspects of your ongoing interaction with the shell.
viewport	Same as *workspace* (page 1006).
virtual console	Additional consoles, or displays, that you can view on the system, or physical, console. See page 103 for more information.
virus	A *cracker* (page 965) program that searches out other programs and "infects" them by embedding a copy of itself in them, so that they become *Trojan horses* (page 1002). When these programs are executed, the embedded virus is executed too, propagating the "infection," usually without the user's knowledge. By analogy with biological viruses.FOLDOC
VLAN	Virtual LAN. A logical grouping of two or more nodes that are not necessarily on the same physical network segment but that share the same network number. A VLAN is often associated with switched Ethernet.FOLDOC
VPN	Virtual Private Network. A private network that exists on a public network, such as the Internet. A VPN is a less expensive substitute for company-owned/leased lines and uses encryption (page 922) to ensure privacy. A nice side effect is that you can send non-Internet protocols, such as Appletalk, IPX, or Netbios, over the VPN connection by *tunneling* (page 1002) them through the VPN IP stream.
W2K	Windows 2000 Professional or Server.
W3C	World Wide Web Consortium (www.w3.org).
WAN	Wide Area Network. A network that interconnects *LANs* (page 979) and *MANs* (page 982), spanning a large geographic area (typically states or countries).
WAP	See *wireless access point* on page 1005.

Web ring   A collection of Web sites that provide information on a single topic or group of related topics. Each home page that is part of the Web ring has a series of links that let you go from site to site.

whitespace   A collective name for SPACEs and/or TABs and occasionally NEWLINEs. Also, *white space*.

wide area network   See *WAN*.

widget   The basic objects of a graphical user interface. Buttons, text fields, and scrollbars are examples of widgets.

wild card   See *metacharacter* on page 983.

Wi-Fi   Wireless Fidelity.   A generic term that refers to any type of *802.11* (page 955) wireless network.

window   On a display screen, a region that runs or is controlled by a particular program.

window manager   A program that controls how windows appear on a display screen and how you manipulate them.

Windows share   See *share* on page 995.

WINS   Windows Internet Naming Service.   The service responsible for mapping NetBIOS names to IP addresses. WINS has the same relationship to NetBIOS names that DNS has to Internet domain names.

WINS server   The program responsible for handling WINS requests. This program caches name information about hosts on a local network and resolves them to IP addresses.

wireless access point   A bridge or router between wired and wireless networks. Wireless access points typically support some form of access control to prevent unauthorized clients from connecting to the network. Also *WAP*.

word   A sequence of one or more nonblank characters separated from other words by TABs, SPACEs, or NEWLINEs. Used to refer to individual command line arguments. In vi, a word is similar to a word in the English language—a string of one or more characters bounded by a punctuation mark, a numeral, a TAB, a SPACE, or a NEWLINE.

work buffer   A location where vi stores text while it is being edited. The information in the Work buffer is not written to the file on the disk until you give the editor a command to write it.

working directory   The directory that you are associated with at any given time. The relative pathnames you use are *relative to* the working directory. Also *current directory*.

workspace   A subdivision of a *desktop* (page 967) that occupies the entire display. Refer to "Getting the Most from the Desktop" on page 78.

workstation   A small computer, typically designed to fit in an office and be used by one person and usually equipped with a bit-mapped graphical display, keyboard, and mouse. Differentiated from a *terminal* (page 1001) by its intelligence. A workstation runs Linux on itself while a terminal connects to a computer that runs Linux.

worm   A program that propagates itself over a network, reproducing itself as it goes. Today the term has negative connotations, as it is assumed that only *crackers* (page 965) write worms. Compare to *virus* (page 1004) and *Trojan horse* (page 1002). From **Tapeworm** in John Brunner's novel, *The Shockwave Rider*, Ballantine Books, 1990. (via XEROX PARC)ᶠᵒˡᵈᵒᶜ

wysiwyg   What You See Is What You Get. A graphical application, such as a word processor, whose display is similar to its printed output.

X terminal   A graphics terminal designed to run the X Window System.

X Window System   A design and set of tools for writing flexible, portable windowing applications, created jointly by researchers at MIT and several leading computer manufacturers.

XDMCP   X Display Manager Control Protocol. XDMCP allows the login server to accept requests from network displays. XDMCP is built into many X terminals.

xDSL   Different types of *DSL* (page 969) are identified by a prefix, for example, ADSL, HDSL, SDSL, and VDSL.

Xinerama   An extension to XFree86 Release 6 Version 4.0 (X4.0). Xinerama allows window managers and applications to use the two or more physical displays as one large virtual display. Refer to the Xinerama-HOWTO.

XML   Extensible Markup Language. A universal format for structured documents and data on the Web. Developed by *W3C* (page 1004), XML is a pared-down version of SGML. See www.w3.org/XML and www.w3.org/XML/1999/XML-in-10-points.

XSM   X Session Manager. This program allows you to create a session that includes certain applications. While the session is running, you can perform a *checkpoint* (saves the application state) or a *shutdown* (saves the state and exits from the session). When you log back in, you can load your session so that everything in your session is running just as it was when you logged off.

Z Shell   zsh.   A *shell* (page 995) that incorporates many of the features of the *Bourne Again Shell* (page 960), *Korn Shell* (page 979), and *TC Shell* (page 1000), as well as many original features.

Zulu time   See *UTC* on page 1004.

Index